CRITICAL SURVEY OF
Poetry
Fourth Edition

American Poets

CRITICAL SURVEY OF

Poetry

Fourth Edition

American Poets

Volume 4
William Jay Smith—Louis Zukofsky
Resources
Indexes

Editor, Fourth Edition
Rosemary M. Canfield Reisman
Charleston Southern University

SALEM PRESS
Pasadena, California
Hackensack, New Jersey

Editor in Chief: Dawn P. Dawson

Editorial Director: Christina J. Moose   *Research Supervisor:* Jeffry Jensen

Development Editor: Tracy Irons-Georges   *Research Assistant:* Keli Trousdale

Project Editor: Rowena Wildin   *Production Editor:* Andrea E. Miller

Manuscript Editor: Desiree Dreeuws   *Page Desion:* James Hutson

Acquisitions Editor: Mark Rehn   *Layout:* Mary Overell

Editorial Assistant: Brett S. Weisberg   *Photo Editor:* Cynthia Breslin Beres

Cover photo: Lawrence Ferlinghetti (Getty Images)

Some of the essays in this work, which have been updated, originally appeared in the following Salem Press publications, *Critical Survey of Poetry, English Language Series* (1983), *Critical Survey of Poetry: Foreign Language Series* (1984), *Critical Survey of Poetry, Supplement* (1987), *Critical Survey of Poetry, English Language Series, Revised Edition*, (1992; preceding volumes edited by Frank N. Magill), *Critical Survey of Poetry, Second Revised Edition* (2003; edited by Philip K. Jason).

∞ The paper used in these volumes conforms to the American National Standard for Permanence of Paper for Printed Library Materials, X39.48-1992 (R1997).

Library of Congress Cataloging-in-Publication Data

Critical survey of poetry. — 4th ed. / editor, Rosemary M. Canfield Reisman.

    v. cm.

Includes bibliographical references and index.

  ISBN 978-1-58765-582-1 (set : alk. paper) — ISBN 978-1-58765-583-8 (set : American poets : alk. paper) — ISBN 978-1-58765-584-5 (v. 1 : American poets : alk. paper) — ISBN 978-1-58765-585-2 (v. 2 : American poets : alk. paper) — ISBN 978-1-58765-586-9 (v. 3 : American poets : alk. paper) — ISBN 978-1-58765-587-6 (v. 4 : American poets : alk. paper)

1. Poetry—History and criticism—Dictionaries. 2. Poetry—Bio-bibliography. 3. Poets—Biography—Dictionaries. I. Reisman, Rosemary M. Canfield.

  PN1021.C7 2011

  809.1'003--dc22

                                  2010045095

First Printing

PRINTED IN THE UNITED STATES OF AMERICA

CONTENTS

COMPLETE LIST OF CONTENTS

VOLUME 1

VOLUME 2

VOLUME 3

VOLUME 4

Contents lxi
Pronunciation Key lxix

RESOURCES

INDEXES

PRONUNCIATION KEY

To help users of the *Critical Survey of Poetry* pronounce unfamiliar names of profiled poets correctly, phonetic spellings using the character symbols listed below appear in parentheses immediately after the first mention of the poet's name in the narrative text. Stressed syllables are indicated in capital letters, and syllables are separated by hyphens.

VOWEL SOUNDS

Symbol	*Spelled (Pronounced)*
a	answer (AN-suhr), laugh (laf), sample (SAM-puhl), that (that)
ah	father (FAH-thur), hospital (HAHS-pih-tuhl)
aw	awful (AW-fuhl), caught (kawt)
ay	blaze (blayz), fade (fayd), waiter (WAYT-ur), weigh (way)
eh	bed (behd), head (hehd), said (sehd)
ee	believe (bee-LEEV), cedar (SEE-dur), leader (LEED-ur), liter (LEE-tur)
ew	boot (bewt), lose (lewz)
i	buy (bi), height (hit), lie (li), surprise (sur-PRIZ)
ih	bitter (BIH-tur), pill (pihl)
o	cotton (KO-tuhn), hot (hot)
oh	below (bee-LOH), coat (koht), note (noht), wholesome (HOHL-suhm)
oo	good (good), look (look)
ow	couch (kowch), how (how)
oy	boy (boy), coin (koyn)
uh	about (uh-BOWT), butter (BUH-tuhr), enough (ee-NUHF), other (UH-thur)

CONSONANT SOUNDS

Symbol	*Spelled (Pronounced)*
ch	beach (beech), chimp (chihmp)
g	beg (behg), disguise (dihs-GIZ), get (geht)
j	digit (DIH-juht), edge (ehj), jet (jeht)
k	cat (kat), kitten (KIH-tuhn), hex (hehks)
s	cellar (SEHL-ur), save (sayv), scent (sehnt)
sh	champagne (sham-PAYN), issue (IH-shew), shop (shop)
ur	birth (burth), disturb (dihs-TURB), earth (urth), letter (LEH-tur)
y	useful (YEWS-fuhl), young (yuhng)
z	business (BIHZ-nehs), zest (zehst)
zh	vision (VIH-zhuhn)

CRITICAL SURVEY OF
Poetry
Fourth Edition

American Poets

WILLIAM JAY SMITH

Born: Winnfield, Louisiana; April 22, 1918

PRINCIPAL POETRY

Poems, 1947
Celebration at Dark, 1950
Laughing Time, 1956
Boy Blue's Book of Beasts, 1957 (juvenile)
Poems, 1947-1957, 1957
Puptents and Pebbles, 1959 (juvenile)
Typewriter Town, 1960 (juvenile)
What Did I See?, 1962
The Tin Can, and Other Poems, 1966
Mr. Smith and Other Nonsense, 1968
New and Selected Poems, 1970
The Traveler's Tree: New and Selected Poems,
    1980
Plain Talk, 1988
The World Below the Window: Poems, 1937-1997,
    1998
Here Is My Heart: Love Poems, 1999
The Cherokee Lottery, 2000
The Girl in Glass: Love Poems, 2002
Words by the Water, 2008

OTHER LITERARY FORMS

Although William Jay Smith published mainly original poetry for adults and children, he also compiled a number of volumes of poetry, including *The Golden Journey: Poems for Young People* (1965) with Louise Bogan and *Poems From France* (1967). He edited numerous books of poetry and adapted the Swedish poetry of Elsa Beskow as *Children of the Forest* (1970). His publication of Valéry Larbaud's *Poems of a Multimillionaire* (1955) and *The Selected Writings of Jules Laforgue* (1956) established him as an important translator. He translated *Two Plays by Charles Bertin* in 1970.

In addition to poetry, Smith wrote essays and a study of well-known literary hoaxes and lampoons, *The Spectra Hoax* (1961). *The Streaks of the Tulip*, a collection of literary criticism, appeared in 1972. He published *Children and Poetry: A Selective Annotated Bibliography* in 1969. He has contributed to a vast number of poetry anthologies and has presented television programs on poetry for children.

ACHIEVEMENTS

Probably the most impressive accomplishment of William Jay Smith is his poetry's great diversity in form and content. Although he demonstrates a conviction that poetic feeling can best be developed through submission to discipline and form, he expresses more expansive feelings in his free-verse experiments later in his career. Despite the judgment of some critics that he sacrifices rhyme for wordiness, he apparently reached a point in his career that evoked a deepening range. His later complexity is evident in *New and Selected Poems*, a somewhat slender volume that indicates evolving sensibilities and a shift in his philosophy of composition.

As diversified as his experience, his poetry has many voices. Sometimes delicate and aesthetic, and at others intense and compelling, his range of subject and tone can extend from rich, courtly, precise phrases to witty, nonsense verses for children. Smith has the power to rejuvenate his readers. Serious statements are frequently disguised as children's whimsy to gain distance from reality and thereby create a more complex imaginative realm.

In his long, distinguished career, Smith has received numerous awards, including *Poetry* magazine's Young Poet's Prize (1945), the Union League Civic and Arts Poetry Prize from *Poetry* magazine (1963), a Ford Foundation Grant in drama (1964), three National Endowment for the Arts Grants (1972, 1975, 1989), the Russell Loines Award (1972), an Ingram Merrill Foundation Grant (1982), a California Children's Book and Video Awards recognition for excellence (1990), the French Academy's medal for Service to French Language (1991), and the Louisiana Writer Award (2002). He served as consultant in poetry (poet laureate) to the Library of Congress from 1968 to 1970.

BIOGRAPHY

William Jay Smith was born in Winnfield, Louisiana, in 1918, the older of two sons, to Jay Smith and Georgia Ella (Campster) Smith. His *Army Brat, a*

Memoir (1980), describes his early life at Jefferson Barracks, a U.S. Army post near St. Louis, Missouri, where his father was an enlisted clarinetist in the Sixth Infantry Band. Smith recounts his generally happy life on the base with his family, enlivened by his father's experiment with making and selling an illegal, alcoholic beverage, "home brew." It was there that Smith learned his mother was part Choctaw, a revelation that answered some questions about his and his mother's striking physical characteristics and generated a lifelong interest in his heritage.

Because his father continued to reenlist in the Army, Smith lived at Jefferson Barracks until he graduated from Cleveland High School. He attended Washington University in St. Louis on a scholarship. There he developed a friendship with a shy, quiet student named Thomas Lanier Williams, who later became better known as the playwright Tennessee Williams. Together, they reveled in the works of T. S. Eliot, William Butler Yeats, and other younger English poets, as well as those of Robert Frost and Wallace Stevens.

Smith earned his B.A. in 1939, and on the day in

William Jay Smith (©Lawrence B. Fink)

1941 on which he was awarded his master's degree in French, he received his draft notice. He was reassigned from naval reserve to regular duty in the U.S. Navy and was soon ordered to report to Pearl Harbor. While completing his training, he sent two recently written poems to *Poetry*, the Chicago magazine of verse, and learned shortly before he left that one of them had been accepted for publication.

After the war, Smith pursued graduate study at Columbia University from 1946 to 1947, attended Oxford University as a Rhodes scholar from 1947 to 1948, and was at the University of Florence from 1948 to 1950. He became a lecturer in English at Williams College, Williamstown, Massachusetts, in 1951. He accepted the post of writer-in-residence at Arena Stage, Washington, D.C. (1964-1965) and later became writer-in-residence at Hollins College (1965-1966). He served as professor of English literature at Hollins College from 1970 through 1980, when he became professor emeritus.

Smith's impressive literary career spans various positions, including editorial consultant for Grove Press (1952-1953), poetry reviewer of *Harper's* (1961-1964), Boy Scouts of America committeeman (1962-1963), Fulbright Lecturer at Moscow State University (1981), and poet-in-residence, Cathedral of St. John the Divine (1985-1988). He served a term in the Vermont House of Representatives from 1960 to 1962. In addition to numerous lectures at colleges, clubs, and book fairs, Smith presented the award-winning television program for children *Mr. Smith and Other Nonsense* on National Educational Television in 1970.

Smith married Barbara Howes, a poet, on October 1, 1947; the couple had two sons, David Emerson and Gregory Jay. Following their divorce in June, 1964, Smith married Sonja Haussmann. He has visited and resided in England, Italy, Haiti, and France, and has traveled on cultural exchange visits for the Department of State to Japan and East Asia in 1969 and to the Soviet Union, Eastern Europe, and the Middle East in 1970. An avid traveler and painter, he established homes in Cummington, Massachusetts, and Paris.

Analysis

As a lyric poet, William Jay Smith celebrates the things of this world with a sensuous delight. However, underlying his poems is a sadness and a helplessness in the face of ruin, decay, and death. Loving harmony and measure and hating sloppiness in any form, Smith restrains his emotional response to loss in somewhat muted and reflective statements. Distrusting emotional extravagance, he turns his attention to seasons, places, times of day, and creatures of the natural world with detailed precision. He seems obsessed with time, change, and ultimate deprivation, approaching these themes in his early poetry in conventional forms with polished, disciplined language.

Later in his career, his creative vision shifted from Romantic to the prophetic, from a concern (similar to John Keats's) with truth and beauty to a more prophetic tone suggestive of T. S. Eliot. His free-verse mode acquired black subject matter, darker imagery, and a more pessimistic view of individuals and society facing imminent death and destruction. Surrealistic images depict Smith's preoccupation with the darker side of experience that experimentation with open forms allows him to express.

POEMS, 1947-1957

Poems, 1947-1957, an early collection, contains a sampling of everything he had attempted to that time and demonstrates his range. Many poems echo the vivid imagery employed by Wallace Stevens, whom Smith admired, combined with Smith's own austere verses.

"American Primitive," one of his best-known poems, describes a man who commits suicide for some reason concerning money. Reminiscent of Edwin Arlington Robinson's poem "Richard Cory," the poem comments on the inability of money to supply happiness: "There he is in a shower of gold;/ His pockets are stuffed with folding money,/ His lips are blue, and his hands feel cold." The poem's events are recounted in a singsong voice of a child who observes the chilling sight of the man hanging in the hall:

> Look at him there in his stovepipe hat,
> His high-top shoes, and his handsome collar;
> Only my Daddy could look like that,
> And I love my Daddy like he loves his Dollar.

The same flat declaration is seen in "Plain Talk," a twelve-line poem that concerns the poet's recollection of his father's assessment of people "so dumb" that "they don't know beans from an old bedstead."

LAUGHING TIME

At a time when few collections of poetry were being published, Smith wrote *Laughing Time* with his son David in mind. Anxious to capture the way a four-year-old sees the world, Smith observed his son carefully, hoping to see things the way David saw them. Smith insists that children generally think in images and in rapid shifts and accordingly writes in a lively, playful manner. He maintains that, most important, children's poetry requires the skill, virtuosity, and technical expertise of poetry for adults; it should not just adapt writing and ideas to the needs of the young but should do more toward bringing children within reach of adult perception and thought.

Smith carries children's poems forward with nouns and verbs, not adjectives, and attempts leaps and connections similar to those characteristic of young children. Included are limericks, alphabets, and recipes, with fantastic description. A toaster is a "silver-scaled Dragon with jaws flaming red"; "Old Mrs. Caribou lives by a lake/ In the heart of darkest Make-Believe." Directions for reaching "The Land of Ho-Ho-Hum" are, "When you want to go where you please,/ Just sit down in an old valise,/ And fly off over the apple trees."

FOR CHILDREN

Smith finds children's poetry, with its wide use of strange forms and the range of its nonsense, a liberating device. Dedicated to his two sons, *Boy Blue's Book of Beasts*, illustrated by Juliet Kepes, describes animals humorously and imaginatively and plays games, as in "Tapir."

> How odd it would be if ever a Tapir,
> Wrapped in gold and silver paper
> And tied with a bow in the shape of a T,
> Sat there in the corner beside the tree
> When I tiptoed down at six in the morning—
> A Christmas present from you to me!

Puptents and Pebbles, for Smith's son Gregory, and also illustrated by Kepes, contains delightful excursions into nonsense rhymes for letters of the alphabet: "M is for mask/ It changes a lot/ To add a new face/ To the face you have got;/ Then the person you are/ Is the person you're not."

One section of *Typewriter Town*, dedicated to Smith's two sons and for "all other aficionados of the typewriter," contains limericks about "Typewriter People," accompanied by humorous sketches of them done by typewriter keys:

> There was an Old Lady named Crockett
> Who went to put a plug in a socket;
> But her hands were so wet
> She flew up like a jet
> And came roaring back down like a rocket!

THE TIN CAN, AND OTHER POEMS

Smith maintains that the poet should always venture into new things. In *The Tin Can, and Other Poems*, his open form of poetry achieves depths unknown in his earlier work. The long, rambling lines of "The Tin Can" echo Walt Whitman's "Song of Myself": "O bodies my body has known! Bodies my body has touched and/ remembered—in beds, in baths, in streams, on fields and/ streets—will you remember?" The more personal subject matter of this poem perhaps lends itself better to free verse. The title refers to the Japanese custom of personal seclusion for meditation, called going into the "tin can." Through a series of surrealistic images, the poet takes the reader from a New England winter landscape to a descent into his subconscious in his effort "to confront the horrible, black underside of the world." Beginning with quiet, muted feelings, the poet builds to whirls of extravagant and convoluted self-recognitions and searches out his creative anxieties as he faces an "unseen immensity that will never be contained."

NEW AND SELECTED POEMS

Four poems in *New and Selected Poems* are new and reflect Smith's more extensive use of free verse. "Fishing for Albacore" describes a fishing trip the poet took with his ten-year-old son, which serves as an initiation into manhood, as he began to understand the "beauty and terror of nature."

The darker themes of Smith's later poetry continue in "What Train Will Come?" The poem's title is taken from an inscription on a subway wall—"What train will come to bear me back across so wide a town?"—and is used as a refrain throughout the poem to suggests that the tracks foretell an individual and societal path to destruction. Intensification is achieved through the association of the underground train with death and dissolution.

THE CHEROKEE LOTTERY

In *The Cherokee Lottery*, Smith relates the sad and disturbing story of the forced removal of Cherokee, Choctaw, Chickasaw, Creek, and Seminole Indians to the Oklahoma Territory. More than four thousand of the eighteen thousand individuals forcibly removed died in the harrowing ordeal remembered as the Trail of Tears. Smith fashions imaginative and historical episodes. The title poem describes the lottery that determined the disposition of Native American lands. Other poems describe the first day of the move as the Indians mournfully begin their tragic journey. Other poems detail Sequoyah's creation of the Cherokee alphabet, the death of Seminole chief Osceola, and unforgettable images of starving Native Americans devouring pumpkins in a field. Vividly, Smith depicts a buffalo hunt, a Choctaw stick-ball game, and the theft of unattended baggage of a traveling Shakespeare troupe by Coachooche, who reappeared wearing Prince Hamlet's attire.

THE GIRL IN GLASS

In *The Girl in Glass*, dedicated to his wife, Smith collected his most famous love poems, including "A Pavane for the Nursery," a poem that has been set to music by various composers and has become quite popular for weddings. "Song for a Country Wedding" conveys the poet's hopes for enduring love, and "Wedding Song," written for his son Gregory and his bride, wishes them well on their wedding day.

"Night Music," a strangely musical sonnet, charts in its first eight lines (octet) a thunderstorm's crescendo as it provides background for the lovers' passion that is detailed in the six-line (sestet) resolution. Numerous other poems for lovers are also contained in the collection. The title poem, "The Girl in Glass," limns the plight of a lover who is weary of waiting for his love to cease combing her hair; variations of "Roses Are Red" become personalized love notes; "Venice in the Fog" describes three days of fog that lifted during an erotic afternoon; and "Lovebirds" depicts lovebirds in a cage that are distracted by an amorous couple nearby.

Many of the poems in *The Girl in Glass*, including the wedding songs and "Night Music," employ formal patterns and rhyme, which combined with lyricism, represent formal, classic beauty. Other poems reflect experiments by Smith to free himself from his formal orientation and to use free verse. Following the first six lines of "The Descent of Orpheus," a model of formal style, the narrative becomes a chaotic mixture of styles that suggests Smith's effort to find a less constrictive poetic style. Toward the end of the poem, Smith reverts to rhyme, suggesting his unwillingness to break free from formal patterns. "Venice in the Fog" employs long, open verses that evoke the seemingly interminable and pervasive fog that finally evaporates into joy.

No volume of Smith's poetry would be complete without the satiric or witty poems he wrote throughout his career. "Don Giovanni in Campagna," in strict rhyme and meter, tells of a lumberjack whose delight in woodcutting was supreme until a locomotive's shriek and fire convinced him he was in Hell. "The Ten," written on learning of a woman who was one of the ten best-dressed women, playfully investigates the fates of the other nine; while "The Wooing Lady" narrates a lady's deception practiced on her knight, and "Valentine Verses" proclaim undying love.

Along with other poems of lovers playing or frolicking like children are sensuous appreciations of flowers. In "Roses," Smith acknowledges having heard roses speak with great feeling; he rejoices in a green field of blue cornflowers; and "Chrysanthemums" regales readers with delight in the four glorious chrysanthemums that watch over the lovers. "Butterfly" concerns Smith's most prized living creature—the butterfly that reflects its perfect harmony with the universe and projects the physical-spiritual basis of his Choctaw heritage. However, Smith never ignores the darker aspects of life, specifically the decay of all life; in "Martha's Vineyard," he insists that love is greater than life.

WORDS BY THE WATER

To celebrate turning ninety in 2008, Smith issued *Words by the Water*, containing both new and previously published poems. The book begins with three poems written in 1942 on the Palmyra atoll, where Smith was stationed while in the U.S. Navy, and ends with poems that represent farewells of various kinds. The careful arrangement of poems and songs in this volume reflects the progression of the types of poetry Smith wrote, as well as his growth and mastery of poetic form.

In "Of Islands," "On His Dark Bed," and "Reflection," from the coral atoll where he first began to sense his life's commitment to poetry, Smith describes his perception of life at the farthest end of the earth. Rendered in precise verses with attention to form and discipline, the poems are followed by others written much later in free verse that add more depth of experience. "The Garden" provides a detailed description of Palmyra as a garden, and "The Flight" recounts Smith's fearful flight with his captain in a monoplane. The book's second section, "The Hunt," contains poems that concern war and its aftermath: "Willow Wood" refers to artificial legs for soldiers, which were traditionally made of willow wood; "Invitation to Ground Zero" imagines the reality of the attack on the World Trade Center in 2001; and one poem depicts imaginary demons conspiring to destroy the human spirit.

The third section explores Smith's satiric and light verse as it continues to chart the development of his poetry over the years. Included are "Dachshunds," a tribute to the elongated dogs in their celestial travel; "On the Banks of the Mississippi," Smith's paean to his childhood in Missouri; and, "Oxford Doggerel," a previously unpublished humorous poem about being a Rhodes scholar in 1947. Following these are numerous translations from French, Japanese, Swedish, and Hungarian by Smith, who revels in the beauties of the natural world and how they are subject to time, change, and decay. A comic poem entertains with a picture of the status of hens in a henhouse, and another, "On the Growth of Hair in Middle Age," deplores the proliferation of nose hairs.

The inclusion of epithalamia, or wedding songs, expands a genre of poems of which Smith seems very fond because of his use of rich, beautiful imagery therein, although the poems are occasionally fitted into a somewhat narrower shell of traditional form and rhyme. Immediately following these poems, in the final section of *Words by the Water*, Smith depicts various people preparing to depart, possibly, to leave this earth.

The first poem concerns a Cherokee woman, who, having been removed from her land and her home, prepares to die. The second, "Song of the Dispossessed," bitterly recounts how white men, while vowing to be brothers with the Indians, instead took their land and animals and pushed them farther west into the desert. "Woman at the Piano" sharply observes the void left by the loss of an artist; and the final personal poem, "Words by the Water," peacefully anticipates the poet's final sleep.

OTHER MAJOR WORKS

PLAYS: *The Straw Market*, pr. 1965; *Army Brat*, pr. 1980.

NONFICTION: *The Spectra Hoax*, 1961; *Children and Poetry: A Selective Annotated Bibliography*, 1969; *The Streaks of the Tulip*, 1972; *Army Brat, a Memoir*, 1980; *Green*, 1980; *Dancing in the Garden: A Bittersweet Love Affair with France—A Memoir*, 2008.

TRANSLATIONS: *Poems of a Multimillionaire*, 1955 (of Valéry Larbaud); *The Selected Writings of Jules Laforgue*, 1956; *Children of the Forest*, 1970 (of Elsa Beskow); *Two Plays by Charles Bertin*, 1970; *The Pirate Book*, 1972 (of Lennart Hellsing); *The Telephone*, 1977 (of Kornei Chukovsky); *Agadir*, 1979 (of Artur Lundkvist); *The Pact: My Friendship with Isak Dinesen*, 1983 (of Thorkild Bjoernvig); *Collected Translations: Italian, French, Spanish, Portugese*, 1985; *Moral Tales*, 1985 (of Jules Laforgue); *Wild Bouquet*, 1985 (of Henry Martinson); *Eternal Moment*, 1988 (of Sandor Weoeres); *The Madman and the Medusa*, 1989 (with Sonja Haussmann Smith).

CHILDREN'S LITERATURE: *My Little Book of Big and Little*, 1963 (3 volumes; illustrated by Don Bolognese); *Ho for a Hat!*, 1964 (illustrated by Ivan Chermayeff); *If I Had a Boat*, 1966 (illustrated by Bolognese); *Around My Room, and Other Poems*, 1969 (illustrated by Don Madden); *Grandmother Ostrich, and Other Poems*, 1969 (illustrated by Madden); *The Key*, 1982; *Birds and Beasts*, 1990 (illustrated by Jacques Hnizdovsky).

EDITED TEXTS: *Herrick*, 1962; *The Golden Journey: Poems for Young People*, 1965 (with Louise Bogan); *Poems from France*, 1967; *Poems from Italy*, 1973; *Light Verse and Satires of Witter Bynner*, 1976; *Brazilian Poetry*, 1984 (with Emanuel Brasil); *Behind the*

King's Kitchen, 1992 (with Carol Ra); *The Sun Is Up*, 1996 (with Ra); *Up the Hill and Down: Poems for the Very Young*, 2003.

BIBLIOGRAPHY

Dickey, James. *Babel to Byzantium: Poets and Poetry Now*. New York: Farrar, Straus and Giroux, 1968. Poet Dickey offers a brief but enthusiastic evaluation of Smith's place in American poetry.

Frank, Elizabeth. "The Pleasures of Formal Poetry." Review of *The World Below the Window*. *The Atlantic Monthly* 282, no. 3 (September, 1998): 134-137. Evaluation of Smith's poetry—its various voices and forms—and of his place among modernist contemporary poets who continue to write in traditional rhyme and form.

Meyers, J. "William Jay Smith: *Dancing in the Garden* and *Words by the Water*." Review of *Dancing in the Garden* and *Words by the Water*. *The New Criterion* 27, no. 5 (2009): 65-67. This review looks at both the poetry collection and memoir and notes how Smith's life influenced his writing.

Slavitt, David R. "William Jay Smith." In *American Writers: A Collection of Literary Biographies—Supplement 13, Edward Abbey to William Jay Smith*, edited by Jay Parini. New York: Scribner's, 2003. A brief biography that looks at Smith's life and works.

Smith, William Jay. *Army Brat, a Memoir*. New York: Persea Books, 1980. Smith details his early life as a military child. This coming-of-age book contains insight into Smith's discoveries of language and his poetic talent.

_____. "A Frame for Poetry." In *Poets on Poetry*, edited by Howard Nemerov. New York: Basic Books, 1966. Smith explores several of his poems, commenting extensively on their genesis, his writing process, and creativity.

"William Jay Smith." In *Contemporary Authors, New Revision Series*, edited by Susan M. Trosky. Vol. 44. Detroit: Gale Research, 1994. This article provides an excellent overview of Smith's life and career, focusing on critical attention to his later work, specifically *Army Brat, a Memoir*.

Mary Hurd
Updated by Hurd

W. D. SNODGRASS

Born: Wilkinsburg, Pennsylvania; January 5, 1926
Died: Erieville, New York; January 13, 2009
Also known as: S. S. Gardons

PRINCIPAL POETRY

Heart's Needle, 1959
After Experience: Poems and Translations, 1968
Remains, 1970 (as S. S. Gardons), revised 1985 (as Snodgrass)
The Führer Bunker: A Cycle of Poems in Progress, 1977
If Birds Build with Your Hair, 1979
The Boy Made of Meat, 1983
Magda Goebbels, 1983
D. D. Byrde Callyng Jennie Wrenn, 1984
The Kinder Capers, 1986
A Locked House, 1986
Selected Poems, 1957-1987, 1987
W. D.'s Midnight Carnival, 1988 (paintings by DeLoss McGraw)
The Death of Cock Robin, 1989 (paintings by McGraw)
Each in His Season, 1993
The Fuehrer Bunker: The Complete Cycle, 1995
Not for Specialists: New and Selected Poems, 2006

OTHER LITERARY FORMS

Although W. D. Snodgrass is known primarily as a poet, he also published criticism and translations. *In Radical Pursuit: Critical Essays and Lectures* (1975) offers original perspectives on the works of Homer, Dante, William Shakespeare, Fyodor Dostoevski, and others, but its greatest interest lies in several essays in which Snodgrass follows Edgar Allan Poe in giving his own "philosophy of composition." His translations are diverse and interesting. *Gallows Songs* (1967) and the translations included in *After Experience*, *Miorita* (1975), and *Six Troubadour Songs* (1977), offer a diverse selection of poetry that includes the Romanian folk poem "Miorita" and works by Christian Morgenstern, Gérard de Nerval, Arthur Rimbaud, Rainer Maria Rilke, and Victor Hugo. They are effective English poems that remain faithful to the originals. Snodgrass also became interested in autobiographical sketches, a number of which appeared in magazines.

ACHIEVEMENTS

W. D. Snodgrass's first book, *Heart's Needle*, won the Pulitzer Prize in 1960. He was the recipient of numerous fellowships and grants, from *The Hudson Review* (1958), the National Institute of Arts and Letters (1960), the Ford Foundation (1963), the National Endowment for the Arts (1966), the Guggenheim Foundation (1972), and the Academy of American Poets (1972). His output, though not as prolific as that of others, nevertheless won numerous accolades and honors in addition to the prestigious Pulitzer: the Ingram Merrill Foundation Award in 1958; the Longview Foundation Literary Award in 1959; the Poetry Society of America citation in 1960; the British Guinness Award in 1961, for *Heart's Needle*; the Yaddo Resident Award in 1960, 1961, 1965, 1976, 1977; the Miles Poetry Award in 1966; the Bicentennial Medal from the College of William and Mary in 1976; the Centennial Medal from the government of Romania in 1977; the first prize for translations of Romanian letters from the Colloquium of Translators and Editors, Siaia, Romania in 1995; and the Harold Morton Landon Translation Award in 1999.

BIOGRAPHY

William DeWitt Snodgrass was born in Wilkinsburg, Pennsylvania, on January 5, 1926. After a normal boyhood, he enrolled at nearby Geneva College in 1944. Two years later, he was drafted into the Navy and sent to the Pacific. For the first time, he was truly on his own, away from home and familiar surroundings. World War II and its aftermath carved itself into his memory, and he would draw material from this experience for his poetry.

Following his discharge, two events occurred that were very important in his development as a poet: his marriage and his transfer to the University of Iowa to join the writers' workshop. At the workshop, he found a group of talented students and skilled teachers who encouraged him to perfect his technique. Although he eventually broke with his teachers, who preferred highly intellectual poems following the traditions of the French Symbolists and the English Metaphysical poets, he would later tell an interviewer that he would never have written poetry if he had not gone there. He remained at Iowa for seven years, completing work for an undergraduate degree, an M.A., and an M.F.A. While his years there might have made him into a poet, they had a disastrous effect on his marriage, which ended in a divorce and separation from his young daughter in 1953. Snodgrass tried to adjust to this experience through his writing and through psychoanalysis; the result was the long poem "Heart's Needle," a two-and-a-half-year chronicle written while the events were taking place. The immediacy of the experience and the intensity of his feeling of loss help to give the poem its power.

After leaving the University of Iowa, Snodgrass was a college professor and writer-in-residence at several universities, including Cornell, Wayne State, and Syracuse, as well as a frequent participant in writing conferences. In 1979, he became distinguished visiting professor of English at the University of Delaware in

W. D. Snodgrass

Newark, and he remained at that institution, retiring as distinguished professor emeritus in 1994. After retiring, he taught and lectured at writers' workshops and conferences across the United States. He died of inoperable lung cancer in 2009.

ANALYSIS

W. D. Snodgrass once remarked that few American poets ever have a true "mature" period, and perhaps to ensure such maturity, he did not rush into print until he was thoroughly satisfied with what he had written. The result is that he wrote comparatively little, although his work shows continued growth and variety. After the purely "confessional" poems of *Heart's Needle*, he developed distance and objectivity in *After Experience*, but without losing the human voice of the earlier volume. In *The Führer Bunker* (1977), he made a radical departure in an ambitious effort to draw believable portraits of Adolf Hitler and his principal associates during their final days. In *Selected Poems, 1957-1987*, he collected the best poems from the three earlier volumes and added a number of new poems, which had mostly appeared in hard-to-find, limited editions. For his achievements, he received a number of poetry awards, and his poems are frequently included in anthologies.

Snodgrass's style was equally innovative. Breaking from his teachers and from the prevailing trends of contemporary poetry, he chose a simple, lyrical style rather than the obscure, intellectual style that his models provided. His language was plain, colloquial, and candid, and his images and symbols were drawn from nature or ordinary life and experience. In prosody, he was a traditionalist, employing complex stanza forms and intricate rhyme schemes. In most of his poems, the form is wedded to the content so that they work together to reveal the meaning. In addition, the poems are dramatic. They are concerned with real problems of this world—problems of identity, marriage, academia, art, and war—and the persona is faced with a choice. What he decides is usually either the effect or the cause of the action. Snodgrass's reputation is secure because he spoke so directly about these universal problems.

Henry David Thoreau's words in *Walden* (1854), "I should not talk so much about myself if there were anybody else whom I knew as well," could easily be applied to most of Snodgrass's early poetry. It has been called confessional poetry because of the intense focus on the poet's private life and concerns. Snodgrass, often labeled one of the founders of the confessional movement during the 1950's, used himself as the subject of his first volume of poetry; but while his poems are an examination of his own experience, he did not fall into the role of the moralist, making generalizations about what he learned and suggesting how others can find happiness through his example. One might think that such poetry would be of little interest to anyone other than the poet. Why should the reader be interested in his problems of adjustment, which are not really extraordinary experiences? Other confessional poets have written about insanity, homosexuality, and suicide, but Snodgrass was concerned with mundane affairs, many having to do with the family—leaving home for the first time, the loss of innocence, illusions, and love. It is this quality of familiarity, however, which accounts for the appeal of Snodgrass's first volume.

The persona developed in the poems is honest, candid, and sincere. Snodgrass says in his essay "Finding a Poem":

> I am left with a very old-fashioned measure of a poem's worth—the depth of its sincerity. . . . Our only hope as artists is to continually ask ourselves, "Am I writing what I *really* think? Not what is acceptable; not what my favorite intellectual would think in this situation; not what I wish I felt. Only what I cannot help thinking."

Most important, the persona is human with a voice that one might expect to hear in the world. At times he is pompous, absurd, and silly, but the poetry reveals that he is aware of this weakness. He speaks in this world, about this world, and the reader is better able to understand his own problems of adjustment by living through them with the poet.

HEART'S NEEDLE

Several of the poems in *Heart's Needle* are concerned with identity, with discovering one's own name. Far from being a mere label or external description, a name expresses the profound reality of the being who carries it. In the Old Testament, creation is not completed until all things brought into existence have a name. Further, a name carries with it the possibility of knowledge. By reason of its nature, a name imparts knowledge, and by one's name, one can reveal to others who one is.

In "MHTIS . . . OU TIS," which is dedicated to R. M. Powell, Snodgrass's psychotherapist, the poet uses the story of Odysseus escaping from the Cyclops by a trick, identifying himself as no man (*ou tis*): "I had escaped, by trickery, as no man." This surrender of his identity, he realizes, is a much worse fate, and he implores his psychotherapist to restore him. He calls him his "dead blind guide" because Powell's strategy with him was to remain out of sight at all times, forcing Snodgrass to speak and clarify his problems in his own way and in his own words. The poem closes with these lines: "My dear blind guide, you lead me here to claim/ Still waters that will never wash my hand,/ To kneel by my old face and know my name."

The problem of a name occurs again in "A Cardinal." It is about a poet who goes into the woods for inspiration but finds that he cannot complete his verses because he cannot escape the crass, materialistic world even there. In the underbrush are "beer cans and lover's trash." He hears the squeal of the mill whistles, the whine of the freight cars, the trucks on the super-turnpike, and the chant of the air cadets marching. When he sees a cardinal above him with a green insect in his beak, he recognizes it as a confirmation of the evil that is in all things. Nature is "red in tooth and claw," or, as Snodgrass says it, "celebrate(s) this ordinal/ of the red beak and claw." In the bird-eat-insect, man-eat-man world in which he lives, he is foolish to think that he can write poetry, but then comes the turning point in the poem. He realizes his absurdity in blaming his lack of energy and creativity on something outside himself. When he hears the cardinal sing, he hears it as a song of natural self-assertion: "The world's not done to me;/ it is what I do." In asserting himself, the bird sings his name, confident in his identity, announcing it to the world: "I music out my name/ and what I tell is who/ in all the world I am."

Snodgrass announces his own name in "These Trees Stand. . . ." The line "Snodgrass is walking through the universe" is the natural final step in the process of a very personal poet naming his own name. It is his announcement that he has found his identity and will proclaim it to the whole universe. Snodgrass admits that it is "one of the most absurd and pompous things" he has ever heard, but pomposity has its place in poetry too, as long as one is aware that he is being pompous. He may not be able to reconcile estranged lovers or alter civilization's downward course, but he can wipe his glasses on his shirt to see himself and the world around him more clearly.

Being able to name one's own name is an important concern of a confessional poet such as Snodgrass; acceptance of loss is another. A number of his early poems are about loss. "Ten Days Leave" has a young soldier return to his home to find that his childhood is gone forever. In "Orpheus," he assumes a literary mask in a futile but necessary attempt at rescuing Eurydice, whose only crime was to love, which is impossible in a world ruled "by graft and debt." His most sustained and profound treatment of loss, however, is in the ten-poem sequence, "Heart's Needle."

The title of the poem comes from an old Irish story of a man who, when told of his daughter's death, says, "And an only daughter is the needle of the heart." For Snodgrass, the "Heart's Needle" is the loss of his daughter Cynthia through divorce. The poem in ten parts chronicles a two-and-a-half year period that he spent trying to adjust to this loss. The poem records the two battles that the poet has to wage. The first is external, the fight with his former wife that led to the divorce and continued afterward: "Our states have stood so long at war." The other is the internal one of love and guilt. He loves his child and does not want to give her up, but in the succeeding years, he marries again and has another child. His attempts to maintain a close relationship with Cynthia are only causing her further emotional harm. He is left with the dilemma: "I cannot fight/ or let her go."

Images of war, trapped animals, blasted lives, newly planted seeds, and withered flowers are interspersed with the passing of the seasons, which show the breakup of the marriage and the growing distance between him and his daughter. It is the imagery rather than any overt statement that shows the reader that the poet was able to maintain his identity and establish a workable relationship with his daughter. The poem be-

gins in the winter but ends in the spring. The first poem is set within the context of the "cold war," with soldiers falling and freezing in the snows of Korea, but the final poem is set in the park, where Snodgrass and his daughter roast hot dogs and feed the swans. Earlier, there is an image of a fox with his paw in a trap, but in the final poem, the red fox is trotting around bachelor pens. Together, Snodgrass and his daughter look at the bears imprisoned behind bars, but he has found a way to liberate himself through the knowledge that even though they are separated, "You are still my daughter."

Each part of the poem is carefully crafted; the third section is a good example. It is still early in the separation, but the unrest and pain are apparent. The poem begins with the image of two parents holding the hands of a child and together swinging the child over a puddle; but as soon as the hurdle is successfully cleared, they "stiffen and pull apart." He recalls that they were reading in the newspapers about the Korean War, about the cold and pain, about the land that was won and lost, and about the prisoners that were taken. The outcome of the battles, paralleling those of his own marriage, was satisfactory to no one. Then he returns to the child's hands and remembers that once in a playful game, he tugged too hard, dislocating her wrist. The resolution of the poem recalls the decision that Solomon once had to make in a dispute over a child between two women, each claiming to be its true mother. Like the real mother in that story, Snodgrass offers to give his daughter up for her own good. The three episodes and the conclusion are closely tied together and reflect the inner struggle of the poet. Even the rhyme scheme (*aabccb*) reflects it. Each stanza begins with a couplet, but the second rhyme is delayed in each to emphasize the separation and loss recorded in the last line of each stanza. To reinforce this, the sixth line of each stanza is shortened from four feet to three.

The seasons mark the passing of time and the changing relationships of a man and his daughter. It is not a sentimental recital of events but rather an honest treatment of hurt, shared blame, and a growing awareness of their separateness. Snodgrass said that a poet must write what he really thinks and feels, and in "Heart's Needle," he apparently was successful.

Much of Snodgrass's life was in the world of academe, and he wrote about it in a number of his poems. "The Campus on the Hill" is based on his life while teaching at Cornell, but it could represent many colleges during the 1950's, marked by the complacency of the students in a world that seemed to be falling apart. "The Men's Room in the College Chapel" suggests an inversion of the traditional view of man's spiritual nature triumphing over his animal nature. Whereas earlier cultures retired to caves to carve totemic drawings to their "dark gods" or to the catacombs to write "pious mottos of resistance," the subversive humans of today go into the four gray walls to "scribble of sex and excrement,/ draw bestial pictures and sign their name."

In "April Inventory," the poet turns to himself as a teacher to list his own weaknesses and strengths. Spring is an appropriate season to watch the catalpa tree and the cherry blossom; but then, so quickly, the blossoms fall. The poet realizes that his own period of productivity will be similarly brief, and so far he has not accomplished much that can be measured. The recognition goes to "the solid scholars" who "get the degrees, the jobs, the dollars," but they also get ulcers. He cannot bring himself to read secondary sources, plot summaries, or memorize dates. He prefers to teach "Whitehead's notions" or a song of Gustav Mahler, or to show a child the colors of a luna moth. He prefers to learn "to name my own name," to give enjoyment to the woman he loves, and to ease an old man's dying. At the end of the poem, he seems content that gentleness and loveliness are also important, and that these will survive where other accomplishments will fail.

Snodgrass did not often write satire, but he did in "The Examination." At first reading, the poem appears to be a sinister fantasy of black-robed figures with single eyes and ragged nails performing a lobotomy on a bird man named Garuda. It seems to have happened long ago and far away because they mark on the brain "with a crow's quill dipped into India ink" and use silver saws to cut away the dangerous areas, but they have an anesthetic, which enables them to remove the brain from the skull and stitch up the incision so that there is no seam. It is only in the last few stanzas that one realizes just who these black-robed figures are, who Garuda is, and what are some of the greatest failings in educational institutions. Snodgrass's professors are those who fear any challenge to their own established systems and thus clip Garuda's wings so that he can "fly no higher than his superiors fly." The irony is that even after being stripped of his powers of creative thought, of his reproductive powers, and his sensitivity, their "candidate" will return to thank them and become a black-robed professor himself. Snodgrass's experience taught him that too often it is the academic conformist who receives the high grades and is encouraged to go on to graduate school, where he is again dutifully rewarded for recalling his professor's opinions and returning them to him in an examination.

ART INTERPRETATION

A number of poems on specific paintings are also related to Snodgrass's teaching, since the idea for them grew out of his substituting, for one night, in an adult education course on art. He acknowledged that he knew very little about art, but that did not stop him from teaching that night or from writing poems about the paintings that interested him most. Snodgrass's poems on paintings raise questions that the viewer might have when first looking at a painting, and he offers a guide to understanding what the artist intended to say, a short course in art appreciation through the eyes of a novice art critic. Nevertheless, he was writing poetry, not interpretive notes for a catalog of an art exhibition.

The five paintings he selected were carefully chosen and share a common theme. In the essay "Poems About Paintings," Snodgrass says that this theme was "the transformation of matter into energy." In "Matisse: 'The Red Studio,'" the paintings on the walls draw all the energy of the artist so that he disappears completely, leaving only a blank space at the center of the canvas: "His own room drank him." As his art objects become real, he becomes unreal and is transformed or absorbed into them. In "Vuillard: 'The Mother and Sister of the Artist,'" Snodgrass sees a devouring relationship between the mother and her daughter. All things in the room belong to her and even the child is being transformed into one of her mother's objects. The color of the daughter's dress is the same as the wallpaper behind her, and she appears to be vanishing into the wall. "Monet: 'Les Nympheas'" seems to absorb the viewer in the same way that it does the clouds, which appear to be beneath the lilies in the water.

The last two poems in the series are longer and add a wider significance to the theme. In "Manet: 'The Execution of the Emperor Maximilian,'" Snodgrass is concerned with the public's reaction to the work. Based on a historical event that deeply disturbed all Europe, Édouard Manet's painting treated the execution with cold detachment. It is even comic in comparison to Francisco de Goya's *The Third of May, 1808* on which it is based, and the public almost rioted when Manet's painting was first shown. Snodgrass's poem is a variation of the theme of "transformation of matter into energy" because its focus is on the energy aroused in the viewer.

To include the reaction to the painting in his poem, Snodgrass uses two voices. One, interspersed throughout the poem, gives a poetical prose account of the historical events of Maximilian's life and death. The major part of the poem is the voice of a viewer asking questions and making observations concerning the meaning of the painting in a colloquial, prosy sort of verse. He notes the strangeness of the three portrait groups. The dapper Mexican soldiers in the firing squad, "like ballet girls," are dressed in "natty" European uniforms. One of the soldiers, given a prominent place in the painting, looks "less like a penguin" than the others, but he seems totally unconcerned with what is happening as he inspects his gun. The second group, the peasants watching from the wall, are totally unconcerned with what is happening before their eyes. The viewer says, "Surely someone must come/ Declare significance, solve how these things relate/ To freedom, to their life's course, to eternity." The third group, Maximilian and the two men being shot with him, is the most perplexing because of their total insignificance in the painting. One cannot even be sure which one is the emperor: "Which IS the man? No doubt he should stand at the center,/ Yet who gets shot in a frock coat and sombrero?"

Snodgrass's interpretation of the painting emphasizes the complete breakdown of the order in the state as the Mexican soldiers are given European uniforms and the "Emperor of all the Firmament" is clad in a Mexican sombrero. The indifference of all the principals signals the rise of individualism and relativism where technology (the soldier inspecting his gun) is more important than a human life. By implication, Manet shows in his depiction of Maximilian's death the complete insignificance of any individual life. This bleak view of the world, perhaps more than anything else, caused the furor which first greeted the painting, and Snodgrass has captured it in his poem.

The last painting in the group, "Van Gogh: 'The Starry Night,'" is the clearest representation of pure energy engulfing matter, and Snodgrass emphasizes this in his poem with his contrast between the solidly built town and the swirling, rushing, violet sky overhead. The ordered rows of houses enclose the ordered lives within, while the sky is "a spume of ancient/ vacuum shuddering to reclaim/ its child." To capture the energy of the painting and to show its contrast between order and disorder, Snodgrass uses a form with two alternating styles: Simple, orderly blocks of words describe the town, and wild, disorganized arrangements of words depict the sky. In addition, he has interspersed throughout the poem quotations from Vincent van Gogh's letters, as if to remind the reader that behind the colors and shapes there was an energetic mind fervently at work. In this last poem on paintings, Snodgrass effectively combines form and content to create a remarkable poetic equivalent for the charged energy of the painting.

COMMENTARY ON INHUMANITY

One theme that is pervasive in Snodgrass's poetry is man's inhumanity to man, especially as it is revealed in war. What is human nature when it is sorely tested? "After Experience Taught Me . . ." asks whether the most basic law is that of self-preservation. It is a poem using alternating voices, that of the philosopher Spinoza and that of a military drill officer. Contrasted as they are in language and approach, they nevertheless agree that humans' ultimate wish is "to be, to act, to live." In the last stanza, the poet's voice speaks for the first time to challenge them both: "What evil, what unspeakable crime/ Have you made your life worth?"

Snodgrass raises a similar question in "A Visitation," in which he allows the ghost of Adolf Eichmann to return and confront the speaker with the charge that had he been living in Eichmann's time and in his place, he would have done the same things, for "You've chained men to a steel beam on command." Snodgrass is attempting to say that Eichmann was a human being who went terribly wrong, but he was a human being.

One must remember that humans do have this possibility for evil, even great evil. To deny this possibility is to ignore a vital part of human nature, and so Eichmann's ghost returns to issue a warning.

THE FÜHRER BUNKER

Snodgrass's fullest treatment of the evil brought out by war is in *The Führer Bunker* (originally published in 1977 and reissued in 1995 as *The Fuehrer Bunker: The Complete Cycle*). The book is an ambitious attempt to portray the last month of Adolf Hitler's life as he and his faithful followers huddle in the bunker preparing for their deaths. In twenty poems, Snodgrass allows them, through soliloquies and dramatic monologues, to reveal their true selves, which they have hidden from others and even from themselves. Moreover, for each speaker, the poet selects a different verse form.

Contradictions, character flaws, and irrational acts are vividly portrayed. Magda Goebbels reveals her plan to kill herself and her six children "to preserve them from disloyalty." The contradiction inherent in killing someone to preserve him escapes her, and this is underscored by the modified villanelle form she uses. The complex but artificial verse form suits her character. Four of the poems are spoken by Albert Speer. He appears to be always in control; even his stanzas show the mind of the architect as each line becomes progressively longer to form a one-sided pyramid. However, he is like his friend the cancer specialist who is unknowingly dying of cancer: "He neglects his knowing." Hermann Fegelein, Eva Braun's brother-in-law, deserves death for many reasons, but he is sentenced to die for the wrong reason, being accused of complicity in Himmler's treason. He says, "I wish/ to sweet shit Id of known." Eva considers her death as the reason for her living.

Adolf Hitler, quite predictably, is the most complex of the nine characters who are allowed to speak. He reveals his childhood fantasies, his sexual perversions, and his misplaced affections. He shows his concern for his dog Blondi, but he is oblivious to the torture and death of his own supporters, cursing them as being "Too gutless/ Even to get killed." On his last day, he is reckoning his place in history by the millions whose death he has caused. Hitler reveals himself as almost pure evil. He reveals almost nothing about himself that

would explain the devotion his last followers give to him, unless it is the purity of his evil and his power to accomplish it.

The Führer Bunker is a remarkable work. It was first published with the subtitle "A Cycle of Poems in Progress," and Snodgrass added fifty new poems to the twenty original ones. One of the later poems is "Magda Goebbels 30 April 1945," in which he creates a different, but nevertheless appropriate, verse form to fit her character. Based on the nursery rhyme, the mother speaks to her six children to the tune of "Here we go round the mulberry bush," preparing them for the spoonful of cyanide that she is offering them: "This is the spoon we use to feed/ Men trapped in trouble or in need,/ When weakness or bad luck might lead/ Them to the hands of strangers."

Heinrich Himmler, head of the SS, is a new character added to the cast. Since he based his extermination policies on pseudoscientific experiments and theories, his three poems are written on graph paper in twenty-five-line acrostics. The first line begins with the letter A, and each subsequent line begins with the next letter of the alphabet, omitting only the X. The form shows a methodical but simplistic mind, one interested in logic and order but that fails to see the paradox of slaughtering millions to "benefit humanity." His poems are a defense of "the fully rational mind." Most of the poems, in fact, could be called rational defenses of each character's participation in this inhuman drama.

IF BIRDS BUILD WITH YOUR HAIR

If Birds Build with Your Hair contains a series of realistic poems on nature in which Snodgrass celebrates elm trees, cheery saplings, owls, barns, and other things. "Old Apple Trees" is about the life and individuality shown in these old trees, which have deep roots and twisted but distinct characters. They are different from the pruned, identical nursery trees of his neighbor. The trees are like the battered lives of workmen "bent too long over desks, engines, benches," but they are still full of life. This life is shown by the poet's visit to the Greek bar with the belly dancers and the blessing by the trees when he returns. The trees stand as white-haired elders of Thebes swaying in a dance ritual to remind readers of the poem that they must cherish life and their own uniqueness.

A LOCKED HOUSE

A Locked House returns to the confessional poetry of *Heart's Needle*, with several poems describing the breakup of a marriage. "Mutability" is a villanelle that demonstrates that in human relationships the only certainty is that of change: "It was all different; that, at least, seemed sure." "One Last Time" reveals one last act of gentleness, when the one he had loved caressed him publicly, but that was three years earlier, and it was not repeated. One of the most beautiful and poignant poems in the series is "Old Jewelry." Bracelets, rings, and pins were bought as "emblems of what lasts." They were precious things with long histories, but now they are "Laid out for buyers in a glass showcase," another symbol of love that dies. The title poem, "A Locked House," shows that one can lock a house to keep it safe, but there is no such security for those who live within it. People care for and protect their possessions, but the love of man and wife is lost or stolen before either realizes it. Now, when he returns, the house still stands locked and untouched, because those who wished to protect it have abandoned it.

COCK ROBIN POEMS

Snodgrass's poems on Cock Robin, in collaboration with painter DeLoss McGraw, seem to be a radical departure from his earlier work. The partnership began in 1982, when McGraw wrote to ask permission to use "W. D. Snodgrass" as a character in some color lithographs he was painting. These then led to a series of poems on Cock Robin in which "W. D." plays a key role. Normally, McGraw would first do the painting and Snodgrass would write a poem to accompany it. Since the project involved two of the poet's primary interests, poems on paintings and children's verse, the result was more a continuation rather than a break from his earlier poems. In college, he had written many children's poems, and in 1962, he wrote "The Boy Made of Meat," which answers the question, "Why do they make boys always eat meat?" by listing a number of other foods that are more tasty and just as nutritious.

The Cock Robin poems are difficult to analyze because some are written in nonsense verse, as in "W. D., Don't Fear That Animal": "My hat leaps up when I behold/ A rhino in the sky;/ When crocodiles upon the wing/ Perch on my windowsill to sing." Such verse sounds like William Wordsworth recorded by Lewis Carroll. The more serious problem, however, is access to the paintings that prompted the poems, since they appeared in limited, hard-to-find editions. The book jacket of *Selected Poems, 1957-1987* has a color photograph, *W. D. Creates a Device for Escaping*, which helps explain the references in the poem to the green foot and the red foot, the blood-red hands, and the arm and leg through the spokes of a wheel. W. D.'s burden in carrying the dead Cock Robin is reinforced by the references to Ixion's wheel and "Sisyface" (in reference to the mythical figure Sisyphus) rolling a stone. The paintings do not present a unified narrative, according to McGraw, but Snodgrass has attempted to give it some coherent structure. He calls Cock Robin a comic version of Orpheus, the god of song, and he is, at times, the alter ego of W. D. Based on the nursery rhyme, Snodgrass universalizes the symbol to represent the poet's life, death, and resurrection.

One poem, "The Charges Against Cock Robin," lists his crimes: the content and range of his songs, his dress, and his nonconformity. In other poems, his friends either desert him or practice character assassination. W. D. warns him of his enemies: "The Brutish are coming; the Brutish;/ The Rude-Coats with snares and bum-drumming!" When Cock Robin is killed, unlike the original poem, no one will accept the blame, not even the sparrow. W. D. does escape, however, disguised as Cock Robin, and near the end of the sequence, phoenixlike, he rises from the ashes.

Although the series of poems deals with serious issues, Snodgrass never loses the light touch of nursery rhyme. One of the poems in *The Kinder Capers*, "A Darkling Alphabet," appears to be a children's alphabet rhyme, but it helps the reader to understand Snodgrass's poetic credo. For the letter *Y* he writes: "*Y* is for Yes and that's/ the poet's word. He must affirm/ What makes ideacrats/ and joiners itchy. He can't squirm." The common thread in all of Snodgrass's poetry is an affirmation: the celebration of life, wholeness, and humanity. His achievements entitle him to a secure place in the literature of the twentieth century.

DE/COMPOSITIONS

In a move that redefines poetry criticism, Snodgrass illustrates how celebrated poems by famed poets could have been written differently—or worse, badly—in *De/Compositions: 101 Good Poems Gone Wrong* (2001). Snodgrass actually rewrites poems by authors ranging from Elizabeth Bishop to William Shakespeare, and he displays the reworked version side by side with the original, so readers can appreciate the subtle shifts that occur—word by word, line by line, stanza by stanza—and gain a better understanding of the astonishing merits of the original work. The "de/compositions" are divided into five categories: "Abstract and General vs. Concrete and Specific," "Undercurrents," "The Singular Voice;" "Metrics and Music," and "Structure and Climax."

He changes the specific words and syntax but retains the sense, meter, and length of various poems and asks students to compare the two versions. For example, Shakespeare's Sonnet 129 begins:

> The expense of spirit in a waste of shame
> Is lust in action; and til action, lust
> Is perjured, murderous, bloody, full of blame

In Snodgrass's version, it reads:

> Vigor and spunk drain out to barren guilt
> In casual sex. To bring it off, we lie,
> Accuse, cheat, kill; first tears are split,
> Then blood; we slash, stab, gouge out groin or eye.

E. E. Cummings's "anyone lived in a pretty how town" (here "A certain man lived in a very nice town"), Robert Lowell's "Skunk Hour" ("Raccoon Time"), and Emily Dickinson's "I Never Lost As Much but Twice" (simply "I've Lost So Much")—each possesses a "particular excellence" that Snodgrass attempts to "dissolve or drive out," thereby laying bare the elements that make a poem great. The poems are humorous and instructive and serve well as a teaching tool for students of poetry.

OTHER MAJOR WORKS

PLAY: *The Führer Bunker*, pr. 1980.

NONFICTION: *In Radical Pursuit: Critical Essays and Lectures*, 1975; *W. D. Snodgrass in Conversation with Philip Hoy*, 1998; *After-Images: Autobiographical Sketches*, 1999; *De/Compositions: 101 Good Po-*

ems Gone Wrong, 2001; *To Sound Like Yourself: Essays on Poetry*, 2002.

TRANSLATIONS: *Gallows Songs*, 1967 (with Lore Segal; of Christian Morgenstern); *Miorita*, 1975 (of Romanian ballads); *Six Troubadour Songs*, 1977; *Traditional Hungarian Songs*, 1978; *Six Minnesinger Songs*, 1983 (of high middle German poems); *The Four Seasons*, 1984 (of sonnets including Antonio Vivaldi's music score).

BIBLIOGRAPHY

Gatson, Paul L. *W. D. Snodgrass*. Boston: Twayne, 1978. The first book-length study of Snodgrass, this volume remains a good introduction to his life and works. It offers insightful studies of the major poems in Snodgrass's first three volumes. The text is supplemented by a chronology, notes, a select bibliography, and an index.

Goldstein, Laurence. "*The Führer Bunker* and the New Discourse About Nazism." *Southern Review* 24 (Winter, 1988): 100-114. This article raises a concern that poems about Hitler might elevate him to the stature of a charismatic figure because of the absoluteness of his power. A review of the form and content of the most important poems, however, shows how completely Snodgrass has revealed the twisted nature of Hitler and his supporters.

Haven, Stephen, ed. *The Poetry of W. D. Snodgrass: Everything Human*. Ann Arbor: University of Michigan Press, 1993. Gathers reviews and criticism on Snodgrass and his major collections, by poets and critics such as John Hollander, Hayden Carruth, J. D. McClatchy, Harold Bloom, Hugh Kenner, and Dana Gioia. Haven includes a chronology of the poet's life and work, as well as a bibliography.

McClatchy, J. D. *White Paper on Contemporary American Poetry*. New York: Columbia University Press, 1989. A fellow poet writes a long chapter about the lyricism in Snodgrass's poetry. He sees the confessional mode as dominant in his early poems and then modified in the later works, but never abandoned.

McDonald, William. "W. D. Snodgrass, Eighty-three, a Poet of Intensely Autobiographical Themes." *The New York Times*, January 10, 2009, p. A32. This obituary of Snodgrass describes him as forging a "bold, self-analytical poetic style in postwar America." Describes his life and his influence on the confessional style of poetry, although Snodgrass himself disliked the confessional label.

Phillips, Robert. *The Confessional Poets*. Carbondale: Southern Illinois University Press, 1973. Phillips defines the confessional mode in modern American poetry and discusses the six major poets in the movement. Snodgrass's central role is shown through a close study of the poems in *Heart's Needle* and *Remains*. His success results from his sincerity and his ability to communicate personal loss while avoiding sentimentality.

Raisor, Philip, ed. *Tuned and Under Tension: The Recent Poetry of W. D. Snodgrass*. Newark: University of Delaware Press, 1998. Essays examine Snodgrass's "poetic musics," his use of history, and his standing along with Walt Whitman as a constructor of the American consciousness. Index.

Snodgrass, W. D. "W. D. Snodgrass: An Interview." Interview by Elizabeth Spires. *American Poetry Review* 19 (July/August, 1990): 38-46. The interview covers a wide range of topics, from the origin of Snodgrass's confessional poetry to his intentions in writing *The Death of Cock Robin*. Snodgrass mentions a number of other poets who have influenced him in his development.

_____. "W. D. Snodgrass in Conversation with Philip Hoy." Interview by Philip Hoy. In *Seven American Poets in Conversation: John Ashbery, Donald Hall, Anthony Hecht, Donald Justice, Charles Simic, W. D. Snodgrass, Richard Wilbur*, edited by Peter Dale, Philip Hoy, and J. D. McClatchy. London: Between the Lines, 2008. Snodgrass speaks with poet Hoy on his life and works in this 1998 interview.

Edwin W. Williams
Updated by Sarah Hilbert

GARY SNYDER

Born: San Francisco, California; May 8, 1930

PRINCIPAL POETRY

Riprap, 1959
Myths and Texts, 1960
The Firing, 1964
Hop, Skip, and Jump, 1964
Nanao Knows, 1964
Riprap, and Cold Mountain Poems, 1965
Six Sections from Mountains and Rivers Without End, 1965
A Range of Poems, 1966
Three Worlds, Three Realms, Six Roads, 1966
The Back Country, 1967
The Blue Sky, 1969
Sours of the Hills, 1969
Regarding Wave, 1969, enlarged 1970
Manzanita, 1972
The Fudo Trilogy: Spel Against Demons, Smokey the Bear Sutra, The California Water Plan, 1973
Turtle Island, 1974
All in the Family, 1975
Axe Handles, 1983
Left Out in the Rain: New Poems, 1947-1986, 1986
No Nature: New and Selected Poems, 1992
Mountains and Rivers Without End, 1996
Danger on Peaks, 2004

OTHER LITERARY FORMS

Gary Snyder's pioneering journal of personal environmental discovery, *Earth House Hold: Technical Notes and Queries to Fellow Dharma Revolutionaries* (1969), was an invitation to examine the treasures of the planet and to consider how it might be employed for the benefit of all living species. It represents the culmination of the work Snyder began nearly two decades before when he conceived of a major in literature and anthropology at Reed College, and its somewhat tentative, propositional format expresses the spirit of a movement that recognized the destructive aspects of modern industrial society and sought alternative approaches to the questions of planetary survival. Although Snyder was sometimes referred to disparagingly as "a kind of patron saint of ecology" by critics trapped in more conventional social arrangements, his interest in the environment has proved to be as perceptive and enduring as his best poetry, and the publication of *The Practice of the Wild* (1990) has deepened the context of his interests, offering the wisdom and experience of a lifetime spent living in and thinking about the natural world. The book is a linked series of reflective essays, and its amiable, reasonable tone—similar to Snyder's conversational voice in his interviews, most notably those collected in *The Real Work: Interviews and Talks, 1964-1979* (1980)—permits the power of his intellectual insights, his scholarly investigations, and his political theories to reach an audience beyond the experts he hopes to equal in his argument. Combining energetic conviction and poetic eloquence, Snyder's essays are intended to be a "genuine teaching text" and "a mediation on what it means to be human." They demonstrate his philosophy of composition as it reveals a poetics of existence and have been written to stimulate "a broad range of people and provide them with historical, ecological and personal vision." *A Place in Space: Ethics, Aesthetics, and Watersheds* (1995) continues his exploration of these concerns, which are summarized and extended in *Back on the Fire: Essays* (2007).

ACHIEVEMENTS

Before "ecology" had become a password of political correctness, Gary Snyder was devising a program of study designed to create a language of environmental advocacy; after many trendy Westerners had long since recoiled from the rigors of Eastern thought, Snyder completed a curriculum of apprenticeship in Japan and went on to develop an American version of Zen applicable to his locality. As Native American life and lore gradually seeped into the area of academic interest, Snyder continued his examinations of the primal tribal communities that lived in harmony with the North American land mass for pre-Columbian millennia and worked to apply their successes to contemporary life. While hippies and dropouts returned to the button-down corporate culture after a brief dalliance with a counterculture, Snyder built his own home at the center of a small community that endures as an example of a philosophical position in action. Most of all, while some of the other voices that arose during the post-"Howl" renaissance of the new American poetry have become stale or quaint, Snyder's use of a clear, direct, colloquial but literature-responsive language made it possible for his concerns to reach, touch, and move a substantial audience through his poetry.

Snyder's varied interests have given him extensive material for his poems, but the appeal of his work does not depend on a program calculated to educate or persuade. Much more than argument, the poetry is an outgrowth of the processes of Snyder's life—his work, his family, his intellectual and athletic interests, his cultural convictions, and his rapport with the landscape. He has been able to illustrate effectively how art and life can be intertwined in a reciprocal interchange that does not depend on academic procedures or traditional schools (while not denying their usefulness), an interchange that enriches and expands both realms, and in this he joins Herman Melville (the sailor), Henry David Thoreau (the naturalist), Ralph Waldo Emerson (the philosopher and teacher), and Walt Whitman (the celebrator) in a line of American artists whose work was, in a profound sense, the spiritual and aesthetic expression of their life's focus.

Snyder won the Pulitzer Prize in 1975 for *Turtle Island*. He has received numerous other awards, including the Bess Hokin Prize (1964), an Academy Award from the National Institute of Arts and Letters (1966), the Levinson Prize (1968), the Shelley Memorial Award (1986), the American Book Award from the Before Columbus Foundation (1984), Silver Medals from the Commonwealth Club of California (1986, 2002), the Fred Cody Award for lifetime achievement (1989), the Robert Kirsch Award from the *Los Angeles Times* (1996), the Bollingen Prize (1997), the John Hay Award for Nature Writing (1997), the Lila Wallace-*Reader's Digest* Writers' Award (1998), the Masaoka Shiki International Haiku Grand Prize (2004), and the Ruth Lilly Poetry Prize (2008). He served as chancellor for the Academy of American Poets from 2003 to 2009.

Gary Snyder (©Allen Ginsberg/CORBIS)

BIOGRAPHY

Gary Sherman Snyder was born in San Francisco in 1930, the son of Harold Alton Snyder and Lois Wilkie Snyder. His parents moved back to their native Pacific Northwest in 1932, where they settled on a dairy farm near Puget Sound in Washington. Snyder's mother moved to Portland, Oregon, to work as a newspaperwoman when Snyder was twelve, and she reared Snyder and his younger sister Anthea as a single parent, insisting that Snyder commute downtown to attend Lincoln High, the most intellectually demanding school in the Portland system.

In 1947, he received a scholarship to Reed College, where he devised a unique major in anthropology and literature. Early in his college years, he joined the Mazamas and the Wilderness Society, both outdoors groups, and took up backcountry hiking and skiing and snow-peak mountaineering. His first poems were published in the Reed College literary magazine. He lived in an old house shared by a dozen other students similarly interested in art and politics, including the poets Philip Whalen and Lew Welch, who became his close friends. Snyder wrote for *The Oregonian* newspaper at night and spent the summer of 1950 on an archaeological dig at old Fort Vancouver in Washington. At about that time, he was briefly married to Allison Gass, a fellow student.

Upon graduation from Reed, Snyder completed one semester of graduate studies in linguistics at Indiana University before transferring to the University of California, Berkeley, to study Asian languages. During the summers of the years he pursued graduate work, he took a job first as a fire-watcher in the Cascade mountains and later, after he was fired in the McCarthy-era hysteria of 1954, as a choker-setter for the Warm Springs Lumber Company. Utilizing skills in woodcutting he had learned from his family and neighbors, Snyder "was often supporting himself" in his student years, and his first accomplished poems were related to these experiences as well as to his work on a trail crew in Yosemite in 1955.

That fall, Snyder met Allen Ginsberg and Jack Kerouac and became involved in the exploding art scene in San Francisco, where he took part in the historic Six Gallery reading where Ginsberg read "Howl" in public for the first time. Snyder followed this extraordinary performance with his own poetry in a very different vein and was also successful in capturing the attention of the audience. He and Kerouac shared a cabin in Mill Valley, California, through that winter and spring, and then Snyder traveled to Kyoto, Japan, to take up residence in a Zen temple, beginning a twelve-year sojourn in Japan that was broken by a nine-month hitch as a crewman on the tanker *Sappa Creek* and a brief return to San Francisco in 1958. His translations from the Chinese poet Han-shan, who lived in the seventh century, were published in the *Evergreen Review* in 1958 as "Cold Mountain Poems," and his first collection, *Riprap*, was published by Cid Corman's Origin Press in Japan in 1959.

Working as a part-time translator and researcher of Buddhist texts, Snyder eventually became a student of Rinzai Zen under Oda Sesso, Roshi (master), and established contacts with activist groups concerned with ecology, women's issues, and world peace. His next collection, *Myths and Texts*, was published in 1960, the same year he married the poet Joanne Kyger. In 1962, he traveled to India with Ginsberg, Peter Orlovsky, and Kyger, and his association with the poet Nanao Sakaki drew him into artistic circles in Tokyo in 1964. He returned to the United States to teach at Berkeley in 1965, won a Bollingen grant, and returned to Japan. His marriage with Kyger was over when he met Masa Uehara, a graduate student in English, and they were married in 1967.

With his wife and his son, Kai, who was born in Kyoto, Snyder returned to the Western Hemisphere, settling in the northern Sierra Nevada mountains, where he built a home (called "Kitkitdizze," meaning "mountain misery" in a local dialect) in 1970 with a crew of friends. His first book of poems reflecting his commitment to his native country, *Turtle Island* (from an old Native American name for the continent), was published in 1974 and won the Pulitzer Prize. During this time, Snyder was traveling to universities three or four months a year to read poetry, working on the needs of his immediate mountain community, and serving the state of California as the chairman of its Arts Council. At the end of the decade, he published a collection called *The Real Work*, and in 1983, he published *Axe Handles*, poems written during the previous ten years. In 1985, he joined the English department at the University of California, Davis, where he taught literature and ecological matters until his retirement in 2002. He began to travel widely, visiting Hawaii, Alaska, China, and parts of Europe to speak "on the specifics of Buddhist meditation, ecological practice, language and poetics, and bioregional politics." The poems he had written but left uncollected were published in *Left Out in the Rain: New Poems, 1947-1986*. In 1988, he was divorced from Masa Uehara and married Carole Koda, and in 1990, he completed a book that presented a program for personal renewal and planetary conservation called *The Practice of the Wild*. That same year, a compilation of comments, reminiscences, poems, and assorted other statements was published by the Sierra Club under the title *Gary Snyder: Dimensions of a Life* in celebration of the poet's sixtieth birthday. Snyder completed his epic "poem of process" *Mountains and Rivers Without End* in 1996 and continued to train students at Davis to deal with environmental crises. In the

first decade of the twenty-first century, Snyder traveled extensively, sharing his ideas about environmental advocacy to a worldwide audience that recognized him as one of the visionary founders of an increasingly widespread "deep ecology" movement. His good-natured, inspiring and enlightening comments about the ecosystems of the planet were gathered in the essays of *Back on the Fire*, while his first collection of poems in twenty years, *Danger on Peaks*, was both a recapitulation and reaffirmation of the themes and subjects of his life's work and a mature reflection and reassessment of his most personal concerns. The hero-figure Kerouac patterned after Snyder in *The Dharma Bums* (1958), "Japhy Ryder," has become the source of wisdom, as the poet Snyder has grown into an elder of the tribe.

ANALYSIS

Among many evocative statements about his life and work, a particularly crucial one is Gary Snyder's claim that

> As a poet, I hold the most archaic values on earth. They go back to the late Paleolithic; the fertility of the soil, the magic of animals; the power-vision in solitude, the terrifying initiation and rebirth; the love and ecstasy of the dance, the common work of the tribe.

The social and philosophical principles he has expressed are the fundamental credo of his convictions as a man and an artist. He uses the word "archaic" to suggest "primal" or "original"—the archetype or first pattern from which others may evolve. His citation of the late Paleolithic era as source-ground stems from his belief that essential lessons concerning human consciousness have been learned and then lost. Thus Snyder devotes much time to the study of ancient (and primitive) cultures. The values he holds stand behind and direct his poetry, as it is drawn from his studies and experiences. His values include a respect for land as the source of life and the means of sustaining it; a respect for all sentient creatures and for the animalistic instincts of humans; a recognition of the necessity for the artist to resist social pressure in order to discover and develop power from within; an acknowledgment of the necessity for participation in both communal ritual and individual exploration of the depths of the subconscious to transcend the mundane and risk the extraordinary; an acceptance of the body and the senses—the physical capabilities, pleasures, and demands of the skin; and a feeling for the shared labor of the community, another version of "the real work" that unites the individual with a larger sense and source of meaning. Neither the poet as solitary singer nor as enlightened visionary is sufficient without the complex of relationships that joins the local, the bioregional, and ultimately the planetary in an interdependent chain of reliance, support, and enlightened use of resources. It is with these values in mind that Snyder defines an ethical life as one that "is mindful, mannerly and has style," an attitude that is crucial to the accomplishment of "the real work."

Each of these precepts has an important analogue in the technical execution of the poems themselves. As Jerome Rothenberg has observed, "where I continue to see him best is as he emerges from his poems." Poetically, then, "the fertility of the soil" is worthless without the labor that brings it to fruition, and as Snyder has commented, "the rhythms of my poems follow the rhythms of the physical work I'm doing and life I'm leading at any given time—which makes the music in my head which creates the line." The linkage between the rhythmic movement of the body, the larger rhythmic cycles of the natural world, and the structure of words in a particular poem follows the precepts that Charles Olson prescribed in the landmark essay "Projective Verse" (1950), and Snyder, like Ginsberg, Robert Creeley, and others, has always favored the creation of a particular shape or form to suit the purpose of the poem under attentive development. The rhythms of a particular poem are derived from an "energy-mind-field-dance" that, in turn, often results from labor designed to capitalize on the life of the earth.

Similarly, when Snyder speaks of "the magic of animals," he is identifying one of his central subjects, and the images of many of his poems are based on his observations of animals in the wild. The importance of wilderness and the manner in which animals seem to interact instinctively with their natural surroundings are, for Snyder, keys to his conception of freedom. The magic of their existence is part of a mystery that humans need to penetrate. Thus, as image and subject, animals and their ways are an important part of the "etiquette of freedom" that Snyder's work serves.

The concept of the "power vision in solitude" is derived from both the shamanistic practices that Snyder has studied in primitive societies and the varieties of meditation he has explored in his research into and expressions of Buddhist thought. Its immediate consequence in poetry is the necessity for developing a singular, distinct voice, a language with which one is comfortable, and a style that is true to the artist's entire life. For Snyder, this has meant learning to control the mood of a poem through tonal modulation, matching mood to subject and arranging sequences of poems that can sustain visionary power as well as intimate personal reflection. "The terrifying initiation and rebirth" is a corollary of the power vision. It implies that once a singular voice has been established, it must be followed according to the patterns of its impulsive organization—in other words, to its points of origin in the subconscious. Snyder speaks of the unconscious as "our inner wilderness areas," and sees in the "depths of the mind" the ultimate source of the imagination. The exploration of the wilderness within is vital to the image-making function of poetry.

The "love and ecstasy" Snyder speaks of stems from the revolt that Snyder and his colleagues led against the stiff, formal, distant academic poetry favored by critics in the 1950's, and its application has been to influence the colloquial nature of his language, to encourage the use of primitive techniques such as chant to alter perceptive states, to permit the inclusion of casual data from ordinary existence to inform the poem, and, most of all, to confront the most personal of subjects with honesty and self-awareness. There is a discernible narrative consciousness present in Snyder's poetry even when he avoids—as he generally does—personal pronouns and definite articles. However, his resistance to cultural authority is balanced by his praise for the "common work of the tribe," the artistic accomplishment that he treasures. As he has said, "I feel very strongly that poetry also exists as part of a tradition, and is not simply a matter of only private and personal vision." Explaining his interests in Ezra Pound, William Carlos Williams, Wallace Stevens, John Milton, and others, Snyder says he wants "to know *what* has been done, and to see *how* it has been done. That in a sense is true craft." Almost paradoxically, considering his emphasis on originality, he advocates (and practices) extensive examination of multidisciplinary learning, explaining that knowledge of the past saves one "the trouble of having to repeat things that others have done that need not be done again. And then also he knows when he writes a poem that has never been written before."

Riprap

Snyder's first collection, *Riprap*, is evidence of the writing and thinking that Snyder had been doing through the mid-1950's. *Riprap* took shape while Snyder was working on a backcountry trail crew in 1955, and its title is at first a description of "stone laid on steep, slick rock to make a trail for horses in the mountains," then a symbol of the interlinkage of objects in a region and a figure for the placement of words in a poetic structure. It serves to connect language and action, reflective thought and the work that generates it. The poems in the collection are dedicated to the men Snyder worked with, the "community" of cohesion and effort he joined, men who knew the requirements of the land and who transmitted their skills through demonstration. *Riprap* includes elements of the oral tradition Snyder intersected, and the title "celebrates the work of the hands" while some of the poems "run the risk of invisibility" since they tried "for surface simplicity set with unsettling depths." Poems such as "Above Pate Valley" and "Piute Creek" begin with direct description of landscape and move toward an almost cosmic perspective concerning the passage of time across the land over geological epochs. The specific and the eternal coalesce:

> Hill beyond hill, folded and twisted
> Tough trees crammed
> In thin stone fractures
> A huge moon on it all, is too much.
> The mind wanders. A million
> Summers, night air still and the rocks
> Warm. Sky over endless mountains.
> All the junk that goes with being human
> Drops away, hard rock wavers.

Poetry, as Snyder put it in "Burning: No. 13" from *Myths and Texts*, is "a riprap on the slick road of metaphysics," helping one find meaning and explaining why one reads "Milton by Firelight" (the title of another poem) and finds new versions of hell and "the wheeling sky" in the Sierras.

Myths and Texts

Myths and Texts is Snyder's first attempt to organize his ideas into an evolving, complex structural framework. In it, Snyder's wilderness experience is amplified by the use of Pacific Coast Indian texts, which are set as a kind of corrective for the exploitation and destruction of the environment that Snyder sees as the result of misguided American-European approaches to nature. The crux of the matter is the failure of Judeo-Christian culture to recognize the inherent sacredness of the land, and Snyder uses what he feels is a kind of Buddhist compassion and a Native American empathy as a corrective thrust. The three books of the collection are called "Logging," which uses the lumber industry as an example of "technological drivenness" that destroys resources and shows no respect for the symbolic or ritualistic aspect of the living wilderness; "Hunting," which explores the intricate relationship between the hunter and the quarry (and between mind and body) in primitive societies; and "Burning," which is somewhat less accessible in its intriguing attempt to find or chart a symbolic synthesis that integrates the mythic material Snyder has been presenting into a universal vision of timeless cycles of destruction and rebirth.

As Snyder defines the terms, in a preliminary fashion, the myths and texts are the "two sources of human knowledge—symbols and sense-impressions." The larger context at which he aims—the "one whole thing"—is built on the power of individual poems, and among the best are ones such as "Logging: No. 8," in which the logged ground is likened to a battlefield after a massacre; "Logging: No. 3," in which the lodgepole pine is treated as an emblem of nature's enduring vitality; "Logging: No. 13," in which a fire-watcher reports a fire ("T36N R16E S25/ Is burning. Far to the west") and seems more interested in the abstract beauty of the landscape than in any specific situation; and among several hunting songs, the exceptional

"No. 6," which carries the dedication, "*this poem is for bear*."

Snyder read the original version of "The Woman Who Married a Bear" in an anthropology text in Reed College and was fascinated by the interaction of the human and animal cultures. He devotes a chapter to the story in *The Practice of the Wild*, lamenting that "the bears are being killed, the humans are everywhere, and the green world is being unraveled and shredded and burned by the spreading of a gray world that seems to have no end." His poem is placed at the convergence of several cultures and is structured by the different speaking "voices"—not specifically identified but clear from tone and context. First, in a quote from the anthropological text, the bear speaks: "As for me I am a child of the god of the mountains." Then, a field scientist, observing the data:

> You can see
> Huckleberries in bearshit if you
> Look, this time of year
> If I sneak up on the bear
> It will grunt and run.

This relatively matter-of-fact, outside position is replaced by a tale of the girl who married a bear: "In a house under the mountain/ She gave birth to slick dark children/ With sharp teeth, and lived in the hollow/ Mountain many years." A shift has been made to the Native American culture, and what follows is the burden of the legend, as the girl's tribe goes to reclaim her. The next voice is the hunter addressing the bear:

> honey-eater
> forest apple
> light-foot
> Old man in the fur coat, Bear! come out!
> Die of your own choice!

Now the poet enters, turning the tale (text) into poetry (myth): "Twelve species north of Mexico/ Sucking their paws in the long winter/ Tearing the high-strung caches down/ Whining, crying, jacking off." Then the tale continues, as the girl's brothers "cornered him in the rocks," and finally the "voice" of the bear-spirit speaks, as through a shaman perhaps, in the "Song of the snared bear":

> "Give me my belt.
> "I am near death.
> "I came from the mountain caves
> "At the headwaters,
> "The small streams there
> "Are all dried up.

In a deft conclusion, Snyder reduces the dramatic tension by the interposition of the disarmingly personal. As if inspired by the story, he begins to imagine himself a part of the Paleolithic hunter culture: "I think I'll go hunt bears." However, he is too solidly grounded in reality to go beyond a reading of the text: "Why s— Snyder,/ You couldn't hit a bear in the ass/ with a handful of rice." Although, of course, in the poem, he has hit the target squarely by assimilating the different voices (as different strands of culture) into his own modern version of the myth.

COLD MOUNTAIN POEMS

The *Cold Mountain Poems*, published together with *Riprap* as *Riprap and the Cold Mountain Poems*, are "translations" (in the Poundian sense) from Han-shan, a hermit and poet of the Tang dynasty, and they represent Snyder's identification with a kind of nature prophet at home in the wild as well as his inclination to isolate himself from those aspects of American (or Western) society he found abhorrent until he could fashion a program to combat the social ills he identified. As in most effective translations, there is a correspondence in sensibility between the two artists, and Snyder's comfort with the backcountry, as well as his growing sense of a cross-cultural and transepochal perspective, may be seen in lines like

> Thin grass does for a mattress,
> The blue sky makes a good quilt.
> Happy with a stone underhead
> Let heaven and earth go about their changes.

Calling Han-shan a "mountain madman" or "ragged hermit," Snyder expresses through the translations his admiration for a kind of independence, self-possession, and mindful alertness that he saw as a necessity for psychic survival in the Cold War era, a husbanding of strength to prepare for a return to the social struggle. "Mind solid and sharp," he says, he is gaining the vision to "honor this priceless natural treasure"—the world around him ("the whole clear cloudless sky")—and the insight ("sunk deep in the flesh") to understand the complementary wonder within.

REGARDING WAVE

With *Regarding Wave*, Snyder's work turned from the mythic and philosophical toward the intimate and immediately personal. He had begun a family (his son Kai was born in 1968) and returned to the United States, and the poems recall his last days in the Far East and his sense of how he had to proceed after returning to his native land at a time of strife and turmoil. The family poems are celebratory, written in wonder, open and exuberant in the first flush of parenthood, expressing his delight with his wife Masa and their infant son. There are poems that are like meditations on the sensual: "Song of the View," "Song of the Tangle," or "Song of the Taste," and poems that are drawn from the experience of rearing a child, like "The Bed in the Sky" or "Kai, Today," which is an awestruck reflection on the act of birth, or the supra-mundane "Not Leaving the House," in which Snyder admits "When Kai is born/ I quit going out," and justifies his inward angle of view by concluding "From dawn til late at night/ making a new world of ourselves/ around this life."

After returning to the United States, Snyder found that the political situation was troubling ("Off the coast of Oregon/ The radio is full of hate and anger"), and he was warned that "beards don't make money," so he began to plan a life as a poet and activist in the United States. The effects of his action become clearer in his next collection, but the cast of his mind is apparent in the transitional "What You Should Know to Be a Poet," which calls together what he had learned from his life to that point:

all you can about animals as persons
the names of trees and flowers and weeds
names of stars, and the movements of the planets
                    and the moon.

your own six senses, with a watchful and elegant mind

and then blends it with a kind of resolution to confront the bestial nature of humans to prepare to engage the evil at large in the world, as expressed in the crucial central stanza beginning, "kiss the ass of the devil."

From that point, the poem alternates positive aspects of existence ("& then love the human: wives husbands and friends") with an acceptance of the trials and burdens of life ("long dry hours of dull work swallowed and accepted/ and livd with and finally lovd") until it concludes with an unsettling sense of the future, "real danger. gambles. and the edge of death."

THE FUDO TRILOGY

Snyder's ambivalent feelings about living in the United States are again expressed in the hilarious "Smokey the Bear Sutra," in which the familiar symbol of the forest service is depicted as a kind of Asiatic avenging demon protecting the environment and resisting polluters. Published in 1973 as a part of *The Fudo Trilogy*—a pamphlet that included "The California Water Plan" (a section of *Mountains and Rivers Without End*) and "Spel Against Demons"—it combines Snyder's serious concerns about the environment and his continuing pursuit of Asiatic culture with his characteristically engaging high good humor. The chant, "Drown their butts; soak their butts" is presented in mock seriousness as a mantra of righteousness, while Smokey is depicted more as a lovable child's pet than the fierce scourge of evil that the archetype suggests. The comic conception works to keep Snyder's considerable anger under control, so that he does not turn his poetry into polemic.

TURTLE ISLAND

By the early 1970's, Snyder had become fully involved in the bioregional movement and committed to the local community of San Juan Ridge, where he had built a home. He began to follow a dual course in his poetry. The overarching theme of his work was to protect and preserve "Turtle Island—the old/new name for the continent, based on many creation myths," and it was expressed in poems that "speak of place, and the energy-pathways that sustain life" and in poems that decry the forces of destruction unleashed by the stupidity of "demonic killers" who perpetrate "aimless executions and slaughterings."

The poems were published under the title *Turtle Island*, sold more than 100,000 copies, and won the Pulitzer Prize. Among the most memorable poems Snyder has written, the ones that explore the "energy pathways" sustaining life include "The Bath"—a Whitmanesque rapture in appreciation of the body that challenges the latent Puritanism and fear of the skin in American society by describing in loving detail the physical wonder of his son, his wife, and himself in a bath. The sheer glory of the body glowing with health and the radiant reflection of the natural world around them build toward a feeling of immense physical satisfaction and then toward a complementary feeling of metaphysical well-being. The frankness of the language may be difficult for some readers, but Snyder's tasteful, delicate, and comfortable handling of it makes his declaration "this is our body," an echoing chorus, an assertion of religious appreciation. In an even more directly thankful mode, the translation of a Mohawk "Prayer for the Great Family" unites the basic elements of the cosmos in a linked series of gemlike depictions, concluding with one of Snyder's essential ideas: that there is an infinite space "beyond all powers and thoughts/ and yet is within us—/ Grandfather Space/ The Mind is his Wife." Other expressions of "eternal delight" include "By Frazier Creek Falls," "Source," and "The Dazzle," as well as many poems in the book's last section, a kind of basic history primer called "For the Children," that convey considerable emotion without lapsing into obvious emotional tugging.

The more overtly political poems and sketches tend to be somber, frequently employing a litany of statistics to convey grim information that needs little additional comment, but in "The Call of the Wild," Snyder's anger is projected in language purposefully charged with judgmental fervor. Avoiding easy partisanship, Snyder condemns, first, "ex acid-heads" who have opted for "forever blissful sexless highs" and hidden in fear from what is interesting about life. His image of people missing the point of everything by living in trendy "Geodesic domes, that/ Were stuck like warts/ In the woods" is as devastating as his cartoon conception of advanced technology declaring "a war against earth" waged by pilots with "their women beside them/ in bouffant hairdos/ putting nail-polish on the/ gunship cannon-buttons."

AXE HANDLES

The poems in *Axe Handles* have a reflective tone, moving inward toward the life Snyder has been leading in his local community, to which he dedicated the collection. His concerns do not change, but in a return to

the more spare, lyrical poems of *Riprap*, Snyder condenses and focuses his ideas into "firm, clean lines of verse reminiscent of Ezra Pound's *Rock-Drill* cantos," according to critic Andrew Angyal. The title has a typically dual meaning, referring to language as an instrument for shaping meaning and to the entire meaning of tools in human life. The theme of "cultural continuity" is presented in terms of Snyder's passing his knowledge on to his family, friends, and readers and is explicitly explained in the parable of the title poem. The book evokes an ethos of harmony in cycles of renewal and restoration, rebirth and reconsideration. Snyder moves beyond his specific criticism of human social organizations in the late twentieth century and toward, in Angyal's words, his "own alternative set of values in communal cooperation, conservation, and a nonexploitative way of life that shows respect for the land." The compression and density of Snyder's thinking are evident in the poem "Removing the Plate of the Pump on the Hydraulic System of the Backhoe," which reads in entirety

> Through mud, fouled nuts, black grime
> it opens, a gleam of spotless steel
> machined-fit perfect
> swirl of intake and output
> relentless clarity
> at the heart
> of work.

The pursuit of "relentless clarity" in everything characterizes Snyder's life and art, but the pressures of the search are alleviated by his congenial nature and sense of humor. While emphasizing the importance of Zen "mindfulness," Snyder has also stressed that "a big part of life is just being playful." In accordance with this approach, Snyder has kept dogmatic or simplistic solutions out of his work and has cherished the wild and free nature of humankind. In "Off the Trail," which he wrote for his wife, Koda, he envisions a life in which "all paths are possible" and maintains that "the trial's not the way" to find wisdom or happiness. "We're off the trail,/ You and I," he declares, "and we chose it!" That choice—the decision to go against the grain "to be in line with the big flow"—has led to a poetry of "deeply human richness," as Charles Molesworth puts it in his perceptive study of Snyder's work, in which "a vision of plenitude" leads to a "liminal utopia, poised between fullness and yet more growth."

MOUNTAINS AND RIVERS WITHOUT END

On April 8, 1956, Snyder began to work on a "poem of process" somewhat akin to Pound's *Cantos* (1970) or Williams's *Paterson* (5 volumes, 1946-1956) that he called *Mountains and Rivers Without End*. Initially inspired by East Asian brush painting (*sumi*) on a series of screens and by his own experiences with what he viewed as "a chaotic universe where everything is in place," Snyder brought in elements of Native American styles of narration, his continuing study of Zen Buddhism, Asian art and drama, and the varied landscapes that he traversed on several continents during the next four decades as the primary features of the poem. "It all got more complicated than I predicted and the poems were evasive," Snyder remarked in retrospect about the project. A particular problem involved the central narrative consciousness, since the traditional idea of an epic hero as a focal perspective seemed outmoded. As an alternate center of coherence, Snyder devised an elaborate structural arrangement built on ways in which "walking the landscape can be both ritual and meditation" so that the evolving perceptual matrix of the artist provided a fundamental frame for the materials of the poem.

Drawing on the "yogic implications" of mountains as representations of "a tough spirit of willed self-discipline" and rivers as a projection of "generous and loving spirit of concern for all beings" (as Snyder explained in "The Making of *Mountains and Rivers Without End*," an afterword to the poem), the epic is energized by the interplay between these elemental forces. The essential things of the poet's life—his practice of Zen meditation and action, his abiding concern for the "ark of biodiversity," his love and care for friends and family, his investigative interest in the previous inhabitants of the North American continent, and his sense of himself as an artist whose poetry is an extension of the patterns of his working world—provide the distinct subjects and incidents for the separately composed poems that constitute individual sections, written (as he notes in his signatory final line) from "Marin-an 1956" to "Kitkitdizze 1996."

Like Pound, whom Snyder calls "my direct teacher in these matters," Snyder wanted to include what he considered the most important intellectual, mythological, and cultural aspects of his times, but he noted that "big sections of the *Cantos* aren't interesting." To avoid the kind of obscurity that requires endless emendations, Snyder provided several pages of explanation in endnotes and included a record of publication of the individual parts, which functions as an accompanying chronology. Nevertheless, the technical strategies Snyder employs to "sustain the reader through it" are fairly intricate and designed to maintain a discernible structure that contributes to the cohesion of the poem. The guiding principle behind the entire enterprise depends on Snyder's conviction that, as he stated in an afterword to a 1999 reprint of *Riprap*, the whole universe can be seen as "interconnected, interpenetrating, mutually reflecting and mutually embracing." Therefore, while some individual parts may contain names, ideas, and references that appear esoteric or strictly personal, "there will be enough reverberations and echoes from various sections so that it will be self-informing." Since the poem's progress is not chronological, arranged according to place rather than period, there is no ultimate sense of completion. For Snyder, the poem is not "closed up" but ideally should continue to maintain a "sense of usefulness and relevance" as it offers "stimulation and excitement and imagination" for the reader.

In addition to the widest patterns of intersection, Snyder uses several prominent technical devices to tie things together. Initially, he expected to have twenty-five sections, each centering on a key phrase. While this plan was not maintained for every part of the poem, there are some especially important key phrases, as in the seventh poem ("Bubbs Creek Haircut"), in which the third line from the last, "double mirror waver," is described by Snyder as a "structure point" conveying infinite reflection. Similarly, in "Night Highway 99," the third poem, the image of a "network womb" is described by Snyder as a reference to the Buddhist concept of "the great womb of time and space which intersects itself." The poem "The Blue Sky," which concludes part 1, contains what Snyder describes as a "healing" word, "sky/tent/curve," an image of an arc that connects the disparate horizons of isolated nations. This sense of joining is a crucial philosophical precept in the poem, since the original idea of landscape paintings on screens or scrolls is exemplified by Snyder's remark that he "would like to have the poem close in on itself but on some other level keep going."

The final form of the poem is clarified by the publication record, which indicates an unleashing of energy in the 1960's followed by an ingathering of strength during the mid-1970's to mid-1980's, when Snyder's travels took him to "most of the major collections of Chinese paintings in the United States." His sense of the poem was also "enlarged by walking/working visits to major urban centers," which became important social complements to the portrayals of the natural world. In the 1990's, Snyder says, "the entire cycle clicked for me" and he wrote sixteen of the poem's sections while revising the typography of some earlier parts and reorganizing the placement of the poems in the final version. While each individual poem can function as an independent entity, the completed poem has, as poet Robert Hass has commented, "the force and concentration of a very shaped work of art."

An overview of the poem reveals Snyder's shaping strategies. The first of the four parts deals with the origins of a voyage, the inner and outer landscapes to be traveled, and the ways in which the features of the terrain can be gathered into a personal vision. "Night Highway 99," for instance, is Snyder's *On the Road*, embracing the Pacific Coast route where Snyder hitchhiked south from his home ground and met people like Ginsberg ("A. G."), a road brother. The second part extends the journey to the concrete bleakness and compulsive energy of giant urban complexes. "Walking the New York Bedrock" revels in the sheer magnitude of a great city, which still recalls the "many-footed Manhatta" of Whitman's paean. The parallels Snyder draws here between geologic strata, canyons, and skyscrapers imply a commonality in disparate forms. The third part moves toward a reconciliation of forces and forms, while the fourth, containing poems written more recently, conveys the now mature poet's reflective estimate of enduring values. The poem for Snyder's wife,

Koda, "Cross-Legg'd," is a kind of prayer of appreciation for the rewards of the journey, an expression of serenity and alertness. As a demonstration of the qualities he esteems, its conclusion, "we two be here what comes," celebrates the condition of mindful awareness Snyder sought when he began his study of Buddhist ways.

Toward the poem's conclusion, "The Mountain Spirit" reframes the conception of mountains and rivers that launched the journey. Its declaration, "Streams and mountains never stay the same," is like a motto for the poet's way of being, while its statement "All art is song/ is sacred to the real" reemphasizes his fundamental credo. His quote "nothingness is shapeliness" is at the core of Zen practice, also echoing Ginsberg's claim, "Mind is shapely/ Art is Shapely." The final poem, "Finding the Space in the Heart," explores the infinity of space, which Snyder sees as a symbol of freedom, ending the poem in an ethos of gratitude epitomized by the "quiet heart and distant eye," which he acknowledges as the supreme gift of "the mountain spirit." Even with all of the evocative, vividly descriptive passages illuminating the natural world, Snyder's poetry remains firmly grounded on the human values he sees as the fundamentals of existence. As he has said, "In a visionary way, what we would want poetry to do is guide lovers toward ecstasy, give witness to the dignity of old people, intensify human bonds, elevate the community and improve the public spirit."

DANGER ON PEAKS

Danger on Peaks is both a reflective recollection of important incidents and moments from earlier years and a continuing demonstration of the kinds of energy and insight that have made Snyder's work as a poet and environmental visionary so impressive. The essays in *Back on the Fire*, which acts as a companion volume, explore some of the same subjects that have been Snyder's most enduring concerns and reveal some of the circumstances that shaped the poems. The essays recall and comment on earlier poems, and the poems often illuminate some of the situations that led toward the composition of the essays. Notably, at the close of *Back on the Fire*, Snyder bids farewell to his wife, to whom *Danger on Peaks* is dedicated:

Carole Lynn Koda

OCTOBER 3, 1947-JUNE 29, 2006

gone, gone,   gone beyond
gone beyond beyond

bodhi

svāhā

This deeply emotional statement, cast in direct, clear language imbued with the kind of personal philosophical perspective that has informed Snyder's work, exemplifies the tone and attitude that make the poems in *Danger on Peaks* so appealing for readers familiar with his work and an appropriate introduction for those reading him for the first time. The book is divided into six thematic sections, each one focused on a particular part of Snyder's life recalled and reconsidered for the pleasure of the memory and the revivified moment.

The first section, "Mount St. Helens," evokes the spirit of the landscape that drew Snyder into the wild when he was thirteen. Spirit Lake, when he first saw it, "was clear and still, faint wisps of fog on the smooth silvery surface," but the lake was obliterated when the volcano erupted, and the changes in the small span (in geologic terms) of time since then leads to a meditation on transformation and the value of what endures. The next section, "Yet Older Matters," is a gathering of short lyrics of appreciation for the infinite range and fundamental features of the natural world, followed by versions of haiku expressing the poet's psychological moods at a moment of awareness:

Clumsy at first
my legs, feet and eye learn again to leap
skip through the tumbled rocks

The third section, "Daily Life," is a series of short poetic accounts, mostly on one page, on subjects such as "reading the galley pages of [James] Laughlin's *Collected Poems*," "working on hosting Ko Un great Korean poet," visiting "Mariano Vallejo's Library," and in a high-spirited, rollicking song of pleasure and praise, building an addition to his home, "Old Kitkit-

dizze." The good-humored, energy-charged, inclusive communal atmosphere that has made Snyder's company as well as his writing so appealing is evident in his use of rhyming in short stanzas, listing, naming, and celebrating. The fourth section, "Steady, They Say," is a gallery of portraits, Snyder's friends from the recent (Seamus Heaney) and distant past ("To All the Girls Whose Ears I Pierced Back Then").

The last two sections take a turn toward the contemplative as Snyder offers brief narratives leading toward a poems that is both a commentary on an incident and a kind of concluding thought. The narrations are set as an unfolding present, each poem like a step toward a wider arc of apprehension. In "One Day in Late Summer," Snyder relates how he "had lunch with my old friend Jack Hogan," part of a group who "hung out in North Beach back in the fifties." Then, thinking about a half-century passing, he remarks:

This present moment
that lives on

to become

long ago

The last section, "After Bamiyan" (the valley where the Taliban destroyed colossal statues of Buddha carved in caves in the sixth century) begins as an exchange with "A person who should know better" about the value of art and human life, leading Snyder to insist "Ah yes . . . impermanence. But this is never a reason to let compassion and focus slide, or to pass off the suffering of others." He supports this with Issa's great haiku about the "dew-drop world," in Japanese and then with his own translation, providing poetry and vivid prose in the service of the things Snyder regards as sacred. The volume, appropriately, does not close with a feeling of finality, as the last poem, "Envoy," is succeeded by one of Snyder's own photographs of Mount St. Helens in August, 1945, then two pages of explanatory notes, then "Thanks To" (another list as a poem), a page of acknowledgments, and lastly a photo of Snyder himself, smiling, a benediction and gift for the world to enjoy.

OTHER MAJOR WORKS

NONFICTION: *Earth House Hold: Technical Notes and Queries to Fellow Dharma Revolutionaries*, 1969; *The Old Ways*, 1977; *He Who Hunted Birds in His Father's Village: The Dimensions of a Haida Myth*, 1979; *The Real Work: Interviews and Talks, 1964-1979*, 1980; *Passage Through India*, 1983, expanded 2007; *The Practice of the Wild*, 1990; *A Place in Space: Ethics, Aesthetics, and Watersheds*, 1995; *Gary Snyder Papers*, 1995; *Back on the Fire: Essays*, 2007; *The Selected Letters of Allen Ginsberg and Gary Snyder*, 2009 (Bill Morgan, editor).

MISCELLANEOUS: *The Gary Snyder Reader: Prose, Poetry, and Translations, 1952-1998*, 2000.

BIBLIOGRAPHY

Gray, Timothy. *Gary Snyder and the Pacific Rim*. Iowa City: University of Iowa Press, 2006. An interesting study of the poet, his work, and his countercultural place in literary history.

Hunt, Anthony. *Genesis, Structure, and Meaning in Gary Snyder's "Mountains and Rivers Without End."* Las Vegas: University of Nevada Press, 2004. An intelligent interweaving of Snyder's aesthetic and environmental concerns and the development of his forty-year epic.

Murphy, Patrick. *A Place for Wayfaring: The Poetry and Prose of Gary Snyder*. Corvallis: Oregon State University Press, 2000. After three introductory chapters on themes in Snyder's work, especially mythological themes, Murphy offers close readings of a number of individual poems.

_____. *Understanding Gary Snyder*. Columbia: University of South Carolina Press, 1992. A useful overview, written for students and general readers, of Snyder's work and influences, with detailed explications of his work.

_____, ed. *Critical Essays on Gary Snyder*. Boston: G. K. Hall, 1990. A comprehensive, well-chosen collection of critical essays by one of Snyder's most intelligent critics. This book, which captures the earliest responses to the poet's work as well as the next three decades of criticism, is evidence of the variety of perspectives Snyder's work has brought forth.

Phillips, Rod. *"Forest Beatniks" and "Urban Thoreaus": Gary Snyder, Jack Kerouac, Lew Welch, and Michael McClure*. New York: P. Lang, 2000. Examines the attitudes toward nature, ecology, and conservation in the Beats' poetry, countering the notion that Beat poetry was a purely urban phenomenon.

Schuler, Robert Jordan. *Journeys Toward the Original Mind: The Long Poems of Gary Snyder*. New York: P. Lang, 1994. Close readings of *Myths and Texts* and *Mountains and Rivers Without End*, focusing on Snyder's concept of "original mind," in which the mind is purified of all its cultural baggage in order to comprehend the universe directly.

Scigaj, Leonard M. *Sustainable Poetry: Four American Ecopoets*. Lexington: University Press of Kentucky, 1999. Along with Snyder, discusses and compares A. R. Ammons, Wendell Berry, and W. S. Merwin and their treatment of nature and environmental concerns in their works. Bibliographical references, index.

Smith, Eric Todd. *Reading Gary Snyder's "Mountains and Rivers Without End."* Boise, Idaho: Boise State University Press, 2000. An extended close reading of Snyder's four-decades-long epic of individual environmental exploration and Asian aesthetic expression.

Suiter, John. *Poets on the Peaks: Gary Snyder, Philip Whalen, and Jack Kerouac in the North Cascades*. Washington, D.C.: Counterpoint, 2002. Examines the environmental influences on Snyder, Jack Kerouac, and Philip Whalen that occurred through living in the Pacific Northwest mountains. Includes thirty-five photographs of places where Snyder lived and worked.

Leon Lewis
Updated by Lewis

CATHY SONG

Born: Honolulu, Territory of Hawaii (now in
Hawaii); August 20, 1955

PRINCIPAL POETRY
Picture Bride, 1983
Frameless Windows, Squares of Light, 1988
School Figures, 1994
The Land of Bliss, 2001
Cloud Moving Hands, 2007

OTHER LITERARY FORMS
Cathy Song is primarily a poet. She first wrote short
stories and published one, "Beginnings (For Bok Pil),"
in the Spring, 1976, issue of *Hawaii Review*.

ACHIEVEMENTS
Cathy Song is the first native Hawaiian writer to receive national recognition for her work. She has also
made significant contributions to Asian American literature. Her work is applauded by mainstream critics and
scholars, and she has been included in a variety of important anthologies, including the *Norton Anthology of
American Literature* and the *Heath Anthology of American Literature*. Individual poems have been published
in numerous important journals, including *Michigan
Quarterly Review*, *Poetry*, and *Kenyon Review*.

Song's first book of poetry, *Picture Bride*, was selected for publication in the Yale Series of Younger Poets in 1982 and was nominated for a National Book
Critics Circle Award. In 1986, she received the Frederick Bock Prize from *Poetry* magazine. She also received the Shelley Memorial Award from the Poetry
Society of America and the Hawaii Award for Literature, both in 1994. In 1997, the National Endowment
for the Arts made Song a creative writing fellow. She
was awarded the Pushcart Prize in 1999, and her poetry
earned the Best American Poetry Award in 2000.

BIOGRAPHY
Cathy Song was born in Honolulu in 1955; her
mother, Ella Yee Lan Song, was Chinese American,
and her father, Andrew Sung Mahn Song, was Korean

American and an airline pilot. She grew up in Wahiawa,
a small plantation town in a rural section of Oahu, then
moved to Honolulu with her family when she was
seven years old. She began writing as a high school student and spent two years at the University of Hawaii at
Manoa, mentored by John Unterecker, a poet and critic.
She then moved to New England, completing a bachelor's degree in English literature at Wellesley College in
1977 and a master's degree in creative writing at Boston University in 1981. She and her family lived on the
mainland, in Boston and Colorado, for several years.

Song returned to Hawaii in 1987 with her husband,
Douglas Davenport, a physician. They had three children: one daughter, Rachel, and two sons, Joshua and
Samuel. Song has taught creative writing at various
universities, including the University of Hawaii, and
for the Poets in the Schools program, which she enthusiastically supports.

Song became a member of the Bamboo Ridge study
group, a group of local Hawaiian poets and fiction writers. She has also worked for the Bamboo Ridge Press.
In 1991, Song and Juliet S. Kono edited *Sister Stew:*

Cathy Song (A. Michele Turner/
Courtesy, University of Pittsburgh Press)

Fiction and Poetry by Women, a collection of writing by a variety of Hawaiian women that was published by the press.

ANALYSIS

Cathy Song's poetry is rooted in her own experience and that of her family. She explores especially the role of women, often focusing on her mother and grandmother as well as on her own relationships with her children. Many of her poems focus on the female body—warm poems about pregnancy and sensuality such as "The White Porch" (from *Picture Bride*); troubled poems about aging such as "The Youngest Daughter" (from *Picture Bride*); poems about eating and eating disorders such as "Sunworshippers" and "Eat" (both from *School Figures*). Her love of music and the visual arts is clear in her images and striking use of color. She examines her relationships and her emotions honestly and clearly.

In his introduction to *Picture Bride*, Richard Hugo notes the last line of this book: "Someone very quiet once lived here." Hugo links this to the poet: "In Cathy Song's quietude lies her strength. . . . In her receptivity, passive as it seems, lies passion that is expressed in deceptive quiet and an even tone." There is also strength in the "quietude" and plain language, the images of household objects and lush nature. It is the strength of a careful observer, unafraid to examine who she is, where she comes from, and how the present moment of her life and her poetry connect to her past and her roots.

After Song experienced the loss of her cherished mother, her poetry turned darker. As she focused her poetic powers on analysis of the effects of that loss, the themes of suffering and redemption figured prominently in her work. Song has also experimented with aspectual poetry, looking at loss and suffering from a variety of aspects, and created poetic personae and figures without a direct autobiographic link. After experimenting with dense, mystical long poems in her collection *The Land of Bliss*, Song's *Cloud Moving Hands* featured the poet's return to succinct, shorter poems with accessible meaning.

PICTURE BRIDE

Song's first book, *Picture Bride*, explores the relationships in her family, beginning with the title poem,

which sees in the poet's imagination the arrival of her grandmother, a Korean picture bride, thirteen years younger than the "stranger/ who was her husband." Song makes her emotional connection to her grandmother clear in the first lines of the poem:

> She was a year younger
> than I,
> twenty-three when she left Korea.

Allusions to plantation control of her new environment and of the man who "waited/ turning her photograph/ to the light when the lanterns/ in the camp outside/ Waialua Sugar Mill were lit" cast doubt on the fate of the bride, whose dress, Song imagines, fills with dry wind from the fields where men like her grandfather were burning sugarcane.

"Easter: Wahiawa, 1959" revisits the grandparents and their Americanized family in the year that Hawaii gains statehood. The ambivalence that Song feels about the lives of her grandparents is clear in her paralleling of the grandfather's "long walks" in Korea with those through the sugarcane fields of Hawaii. His eighteen years cutting sugarcane have left their mark:

> His right arm
> grew disproportionately large
> to the rest of his body.
> He could hold three
> grandchildren in that arm.
> I want to think
> that each stalk that fell
> brought him closer
> to a clearing.

In addition to the numerous poems that relate to her family and their immigrant experience, Song devotes significant time to two visual artists to whom she feels a special connection: the nineteenth century Japanese printmaker Utamaro and the modern American painter O'Keeffe. The five sections of this book are named for flowers that are also paintings by O'Keeffe, and two poems address the connection Song feels to O'Keeffe: "Blue and White Lines After O'Keeffe," a poem in five sections, related from O'Keeffe's point of view, and "From the White Place," focused on O'Keeffe's reaction to her lover, photographer Alfred Stieglitz, whose "lens felt like a warm skull," and to the American Southwest.

The "Orchids" section contains three poems referring to Utamaro prints. In "Beauty and Sadness," Song describes some of the "hundreds of women/ in studies unfolding/ like flowers from a fan," women of "pleasure," including actresses, geishas, and courtesans:

> They resembled beautiful iridescent insects,
> creatures from a floating world.
> Utamaro absorbed these women of Edo
> in their moments of melancholy
> as well as of beauty.

Song relates to Utamaro and his "inconsolable eye"; his view of the "melancholy and beauty" in the lives of these women is reminiscent of her own sadness as she examines the lives of her grandmother and other women.

FRAMELESS WINDOWS, SQUARES OF LIGHT

Song's second book, *Frameless Windows, Squares of Light*, expands on her examination of her own experience and family. Critics have noted that it is more generalized and abstract than *Picture Bride*. In writing about this book, Song notes that these poems are about the "timeline that spans the length of your room. The window you occupy day after day. What frames the view is the mind in the diamond pinpoint of light of concentration, tunneling into memory, released by imagination."

The collection begins with "The Day You Are Born," which chronicles the sense of loss in the birth of a last child:

> There was an emptiness
>   waiting for you. The night
>   your mother knew you existed,
> she felt a flicker of sadness
>   for the life, no bigger than her thumbnail,
>   burrowing itself within her body.
> She knew you would be
>   her last child, the last flowering
>   before the pod, like a crippled hand,
> withered shut; . . .

"Humble Jar," a poem that has attracted wide critical attention, focuses on a mayonnaise jar filled with buttons kept by Song's mother. Some of the buttons are useful, ready for "every emergency," but

> Others were less practical,
> the buttons that had been lost
> and then retrieved,
> only to reenter the orphanage,
> the original setting (a cashmere coat,
> a bottle-green evening gown) long gone,
> shipped off to Goodwill
> with the other ousted heirlooms:
> the denture-pink Melmac plates and cups.

Although Song's mother displays other collections, her buttons were "oddly private"—the jar a place where Song's mother "retrieved a moment/ out of a cluttered life—/ before I was born,/ before any of us had made our claims." Another frame from her mother's life is captured both in this poem and in a photograph from the "summer she wore that scalloped dress" and smiled "for life that was certain to be glorious."

SCHOOL FIGURES

As the title poem of *School Figures* makes clear, the reference is to the figures that ice-skaters must practice repeatedly, a measure of discipline and "obedience traced into the crystalline structured,/ unadorned and essential as numbers." In her continued examination of complex family relationships, Song explores the world of her own past and the experience of her mother and other family members.

"The Grammar of Silk" recalls the Saturdays when her mother sent her to Mrs. Umemoto's sewing school and the trip to Kaimuki Dry Goods, where her mother bought her sewing supplies and where "Seamstresses waited at counters/ like librarians to be consulted." Song sees this as a "sanctuary" where mothers and daughters "consulted the oracle,/ the stone tablets of the latest pattern books." She realizes why her mother has sent her:

> She was determined that I should sew
> as if she knew what she herself was missing,
> a moment when she could have come up for air—
> the children asleep,
> the dishes drying on the rack—
> and turned on the lamp
> and pulled back the curtain of sleep.

THE LAND OF BLISS

Song divided her fourth collection of poetry, *The Land of Bliss*, into four parts, each part taking its title from its last poem. The first part focuses on the experience of the persona as a young girl. "Pokanini Girl" features a speaker using Hawaiian pidgin English to encourage a shy skinny girl to be brave: "No be scared, Pokanini girl./ Nobody going hurt you." In "The Pineapple Fields," the persona reflects on the mixed blessings when "Father rescued us from the pineapple fields," moving the family into a "haole neighborhood of swimming pools" (*haole* being a pejorative Hawaiian term for European Americans). Now the persona has to adapt and must speak the "proper English" in which the poem is written. At first, this silences her as she feels the new language to be as "restrictive as the new shoes Father brought home." The issue of bullying is confronted in "Stink Eye," which the poet dedicated to her daughter, Rachel. The persona also addresses issues of her Asian American heritage. Her traditional Chinese aunt is touchingly portrayed in "Pa-ke," and her mother's warming to her European American boyfriend occurs at the conclusion of "Ghost." "My Mother's Name" tells how her mother gave the persona a European first name ". . . that linked for her/ bright bits of charm—" experienced in America.

Song's poems of the second part of *The Land of Bliss* address her mother's slow descent into dementia, which would end with her death three years after publication of the book. In "The Valley Boat," the persona and her family rejoice at her mother's apparent recovery, which is darkly followed by a relapse. In "Stone Soup," Song writes how "the child grieves for the mother." Even the experience of an expensive spa cannot relax the ill mother in "The Expense of Mildew." The husband's love for his wife is celebrated in "Peacefully, on the Wings of Forgiveness." As a side effect of her illness makes her feet swell painfully, the husband "takes her foot as tenderly as once he took her hand." Song's poems here speak to all who have experienced the loss of a dear one through inexplicable illness, and they do so in a language both compassionate and concise.

The third and fourth parts of the book offer poems that look at various forms of suffering endured by other families. The poems also explore inspiration and dangers lying in store for a young woman poet. "Blue-roses" personifies the muse of the nine-year-old persona who exclaims that "we flourished" together. In "Honored Guest," the persona reminds herself to "use the muse that threatens to devour," who represents a "disruptive power" for the young girl. The idea of danger brought on by jealousy of others is explored in "The Bodhisattva Muses," where the outcome is fatal. In contrast, a fellowship of sympathetic women, including the persona's mother, saves her in "Angels on the Way to the Dalai Lama." Finally, in "The Land of Bliss," the persona prefers the promise "that there would be/ that poem waiting" (which she left unfinished the night before) over the promise of Nirvana.

CLOUD MOVING HANDS

The 2004 death of Song's mother, to whom the poet dedicated *Cloud Moving Hands*, is the central topic of many poems in the volume. The other poems in the work also generally focus on human suffering and are embedded in Buddhist belief. However, Song's poems are far from somber. They have life-affirming warmth, and tender irony is discernible in the beautifully crafted lines of her work.

The poems are organized in four sections, each titled after its opening poem. Together they resemble a four-station Buddhist pilgrimage from experience of suffering to acceptance, then awareness and joyful transcendence. The first poem, "Lady Mappo Enters the City of Samsara," is somewhat uncharacteristically whimsical. It is a lighthearted, fairy-tale-style poem about a spoiled noblewoman and her son who lived during Japan's feudal era and are reborn in suburban America. The lady's name alludes to the Buddhist term for the present age of decay, and the city of her destination is named for the Buddhist word for the cycle of life and rebirth that is full of suffering. The poem's ironic tone opens Song's book with light laughter.

Song's sense of soft irony continues as her poems become darker. In "My Mother Stares at the Picture," the persona's mother is firmly in the grip of dementia (Song's mother had vascular dementia). However, as the mother vacantly looks at the picture of a long-haired and blue-eyed Jesus that her husband and daughters have pinned to the wall to soothe her, even though they are not Christian, the persona wonders if her mother may remember that "her daughters brought home/ boyfriends who bore shaggy resemblances" to the man in the picture.

In the second section, "The Burning House," the title poem alludes to the Buddhist teaching that life is a burning house full of suffering. In "Long Before I Enter the Gate," the persona drives home during the "enchanted hour" of late evening only to realize that "Surrounded by beauty, my mother is dying." Accepting this grim fact, Song dedicates the next poem, "Near the End, the Man," to her father. Here, the speaker gently tells a loving husband that he has to let go of his beloved wife with whom he has been "traveling// in the right direction after all" so that she can embark on her "smooth passage" into the next world.

In "The Temple of Our Dilemma," opening the third section, Song envisions the love mothers have for children who die before or shortly after birth, who according to Buddhist belief wait to be born into another life. In this poem, set on the grounds of an imaginary temple, the mothers' love for these children leads to their own redemption.

The poems of the last section, "The Body Remembers Itself in Wholeness," turn to a celebration of life despite suffering. In the title poem, the persona remembers making passionate love in a wild land of a mythical dimension. "Cloud Moving Hands" appears as the second-to-last poem. Alluding to the lines of classical Chinese poetry by Du Fu, the persona envisions that swimming places her ". . . between earth and sky, suspended in a blue globe." Although it appears as if the cloud reflected on the surface of the water moves her hands while swimming, the persona feels that her mother's exit from this earth is a peaceful one. Finally "everything is as it should be" for the persona.

OTHER MAJOR WORK

EDITED TEXT: *Sister Stew: Fiction and Poetry by Women*, 1991 (with Juliet S. Kono).

BIBLIOGRAPHY

Bloyd, Rebekah. "Cultural Convergences in Cathy Song's Poetry." *Peace Review* 10 (September, 1998): 393-400. Looks at the way Song's poetry expresses the tensions felt by women living simultaneously in contemporary and traditional cultures.

Chang, Leslie. Review of *Cloud Moving Hands*. *Southern Review* 44, no. 2 (Spring, 2008): 384-385. Positive review of Song's book includes perceptive analyses of individual poems, their themes and structure. Outlines the Buddhist influence on Song's poems. Excellent introduction to this collection of Song's poetry.

Chen, Fu-Jen. "Body and Female Subjectivity in Cathy Song's *Picture Bride*." *Women's Studies* 33, no. 5 (July/August, 2004): 577-612. Scholarly analysis of Song's poetry, especially in *Picture Bride*, that focuses on the poet's use of images of the body, particularly the female body. Praises Song for her outstanding contribution to Hawaiian and Asian American poetry.

Fujita-Sato, Gayle K. "'Third World' as Place and Paradigm in Cathy Song's *Picture Bride*." *MELUS* 15, no. 1 (Spring, 1988): 49-72. Fujita-Sato analyzes *Picture Bride* in terms of its examination of "relationships among ethnicity, culture, and writing."

Kyhan, Lee. "Korean-American Literature: The Next Generation." *Korean Journal* 34, no. 1 (Spring, 1994): 20-35. Kyhan reviews the history of Korean American literature and devotes the third section of his article to Song, the most widely known of those he considers the "next" or third generation of Korean American writers.

Ratner, Rochelle. Review of *The Land of Bliss*. *Library Journal* 126, no. 20 (December, 2001): 130-131. Mixed review of Song's book. Praises poems with autobiographical ties to the poet, particularly poems about her mother's suffering, and Song's long poems, but rejects more abstract poems as too mysterious and shorter ones as trivial.

Song, Cathy. "Cathy Song: Secret Spaces of Childhood Part 2: A Symposium on Secret Spaces." *Michigan Quarterly Review* 39, no. 3 (Summer, 2000): 506-508. In response to an invitation from editors of this special issue to "describe a private realm of your own early life that has left vivid images in your memory," Song reflects on her fascination with singing, which she links to her dedication to her voice, her poetry.

White, Ashanti. Review of *Cloud Moving Hands*. *Library Journal* 132, no. 17 (October 15, 2007): 71. Brief review of Song's fifth collection of poetry, which the reviewer considers an intellectual as well as an artistic achievement. Contains a discussion of two poems focused on suffering and redemption.

Elsie Galbreath Haley
Updated by R. C. Lutz

GILBERT SORRENTINO

Born: Brooklyn, New York; April 27, 1929
Died: New York, New York; May 18, 2006

PRINCIPAL POETRY

The Darkness Surrounds Us, 1960
Black and White, 1964
The Perfect Fiction, 1968
Corrosive Sublimate, 1971
A Dozen Oranges, 1976
White Sail, 1977
The Orangery, 1978
Selected Poems, 1958-1980, 1981
A Beehive Arranged on Humane Principles, 1986
New and Selected Poems, 1958-1998, 2004

OTHER LITERARY FORMS

Although Gilbert Sorrentino (saw-rehn-TEE-noh) started out writing poetry, his first novel, *The Sky Changes*, was published in 1966. *The Sky Changes* ignores time sequences and scrambles the past, present, and future. This was followed by a remarkable output of fiction: *Steelwork* in 1970, *Imaginative Qualities of Actual Things* the following year, *Red the Fiend* in 1995, and *The Abyss of Human Illusion* in 2009, among others.

Sorrentino's fiction was experimental and won praise from critics, but it was only with the 1979 publication of *Mulligan Stew* that Sorrentino earned popular success. The novel is considered Sorrentino's masterpiece and won rave reviews in almost every influential newspaper. *Mulligan Stew* attacked the conventions of traditional novels, with their linear plot lines, "real" characters, and language subordinated to story.

Sorrentino also published a play, *Flawless Play Restored: The Masque of Fungo* (pb. 1974), and a work of nonfiction, *Something Said*, in 1984.

ACHIEVEMENTS

The controversial Vietnam War and the social upheaval of the Civil Rights movement spurred an experimental writing movement that began in the 1950's and 1960's. Gilbert Sorrentino was among the literary avant-garde of the period, along with Thomas Pynchon, Robert Coover, John Barth, William H. Gass, and LeRoi Jones (Amiri Baraka). In 1956, while at Brooklyn College, he founded the magazine *Neon* with college friends. The issues that Sorrentino edited contained contributions from prominent writers, including William Carlos Williams, Jones, Hubert Selby, Jr., and Joel Oppenheimer. From 1961 to 1963, Sorrentino wrote for and edited *Kulchur*, a literary magazine publishing writers from the Black Mountain school, the Beats, and the New School.

In addition to many grants, including Guggenheim Fellowships in 1973 and 1987, Sorrentino won the John Dos Passos Prize for Literature in 1981, an Academy Award in Literature from the American Academy of Arts and Letters in 1985, the Lannan Literary Award for Fiction in 1992, and the Lannan Lifetime Achievement Award in 2005.

BIOGRAPHY

Gilbert Sorrentino was born in Brooklyn in 1929 to a Sicilian-born father and a third-generation Irish mother. He was raised in Roman Catholic milieus and blue-collar neighborhoods, which form the setting for two of his novels. When he was eighteen years old, he moved across the river to investigate the cultural centers of Manhattan and enrolled in Brooklyn College, but a stint in the U.S. Army Medical Corps in 1951 interrupted his education. He decided to become a writer after two years in the Army and started a novel that was eventually aborted. He returned to Brooklyn College in 1955 and founded the magazine *Neon* with, among others, Hubert Selby, Jr., with whom he formed a lifelong friendship based partly on their common background.

The Darkness Surrounds Us, his first book of poetry, appeared in 1960 and was followed by another collection, *Black and White*, in 1964. The following year, Sorrentino started what was to become a long and distinguished teaching career with a course at Columbia University, and he published his first novel, *The Sky Changes*, in 1966. He worked at Grove Press until 1970 as an assistant, then an editor; his first editing assignment was Alex Haley's *The Autobiography of Malcolm X* (1965). This was followed by teaching stints at the Aspen Writers' Workshop, Sarah Lawrence College, and the New School for Social Research. In 1979 he was appointed Edwin S. Quain Professor of Literature at the University of Scranton in Pennsylvania, and in 1982 he joined the faculty of Stanford University, where he taught creative writing until his retirement in 1999.

ANALYSIS

Although Gilbert Sorrentino is not usually identified with the Beat poets, he was contemporaneous with them and published many as the editor of *Kulchur* magazine from 1961 to 1963. Significantly, Sorrentino's first published book of poetry appeared in 1960. The term "Beat poets" is applied to a loosely knit group of American lyric poets identified more by their shared social attitudes, such as apolitical and anti-intellectual orientations and romantic nihilism, than by stylistic, thematic, or formal unity of expression. They were centered in San Francisco and New York. The term "Beat" expressed both exhaustion and beatification. The writers were tired and disgusted with what they saw as a corrupt, crass, commercial world ruled by materialism and believed that by disassociating with that world they would provide a sort of blissful illumination for it, aided by drugs and alcohol. In the best of the Beats, such as Allen Ginsberg, Gregory Corso, and Jack Kerouac, there is a personal statement and power that goes beyond the jargon and "hip" vocabulary many of them used.

Sorrentino's poetry owes much to the Beat movement, although as his poetry continued to develop it became difficult to classify. Sorrentino had faith in the power of the word and its multiple technical possibilities, which may be the subject of all his works. The only rules that he adhered to were a rigorous parsimony for

Gilbert Sorrentino (©Thomas Victor)

his poetic diction and a luxurious inventiveness for his fictional language.

"MIDNIGHT SPECIAL" AND "NIGHTPIECE"

These two poems from Sorrentino's first book of poems, *The Darkness Surrounds Us*, use techniques that would be found again in his work. The title "Midnight Special" is taken from a song of that name and refers to a midnight special train ride, but in the poem it refers to a nightmare the poet has of his son in a snowy garden. In another ironic twist, the last line of the poem, "shine your everloving light on me," uses the last line of the song's chorus to address the child directly. The world of music would play an important part in Sorrentino's later poetry.

"Nightpiece" is a city poem ostensibly about rats that first are seen along a wall. One of the rats enters a house and is eventually trapped in a room and beset by fear and disorientation. The poem ends with a shocking comparison to men, who "have shot themselves// in the head/ for less reason." The poem uses images of bleak despair that are omnipresent in some of Sorrentino's later collections.

THE PERFECT FICTION

In an interview in 1994, Alexander Laurence asked Sorrentino about his interest in formalism. Sorrentino replied that he had always been interested in the formal, which, in his sense, is

> a structure or series of structures that can, if one is lucky enough, generate "content," or, if you please, the wholeness of the work itself. Almost all of my books are written under the influence of some sort of preconceived constraint or set of rules.

In *The Perfect Fiction*, dedicated to his mother, who died in 1960, Sorrentino presents his vision of the city through a series of untitled poems written in three-line verse units called triplets and populated with shadowy, anonymous, vaguely threatening figures. The tone is uniformly dismal, creating a metropolis inhabited by lonely, lost souls, such as this image: "an old woman maybe// was kind to her cats is dying/ of loneliness. Hers is that face/ in the window, how impossibly// remote." Other characters who populate this city are "a huge black man/ riding on a motorcycle," "The stupid painter," and "stinking" people who "know that they/ are garbage and this fact/ somehow consoles them."

The triplet form of the work occasionally admits slight variations, such as "(*pentagram*)," a poem constructed of ten triplets arranged with five down each side of the page. Each stanza is very brief, the lines consisting of only one or two syllables, or only punctuation, until the last stanza, which begins with the word "nostalgia." Another variation is found in the untitled poem that begins with "Such a long walk to get out/ of any pocket, any abstract/ one," in which the third line of each triplet consists of only one word, spaced to the right of the first two lines.

Although the triplet form has never been used as widely as the couplet or the quatrain, it was used in the collection *The Desert Music and Other Poems* (1954) by William Carlos Williams, a poet whom Sorrentino always admired and whom he published in his literary magazine *Neon*.

A DOZEN ORANGES

A slim paper volume, *A Dozen Oranges* contains twelve poems using the word "orange." It typifies the use of color in Sorrentino's poetry, which became in-creasingly important as he continued to write. All the poems published in *A Dozen Oranges* were reprinted in *The Orangery*, to which Sorrentino added another sixty poems.

WHITE SAIL

White Sail is a collection saturated with color. Although many of the poems feature other colors, such as "Drifting Blue Canoe" and "Navy Blue Room," there are also ten "Orange Sonnets" included here, each a fourteen-line poem using the color orange. One "Orange Sonnet" begins with the line "She was all in black" and expands the shade of black as symbol for the darkness of evil: "We know black here in America./ Why, it's a scream." By the third stanza the black becomes both color and metaphor: "Stick a point of orange in it/ just for fun. Just to see what comes of it." Another "Orange Sonnet" describes a town the poet sees or imagines "across the water," a town drenched in "lime-green haze" and filled with "Mothers and children in blue," where "the sky is blue." Yet the poem ends with a playful reference to orange in a direct address to the reader: "I forgot orange. There."

In a third "Orange Sonnet," subtitled "1939 World's Fair," the poet describes the fair with its "fake orange trees" and includes this image: "My mother was beautiful/ in the blue gloom." Yet by the end of the poem "She died ice-grey in Jersey City" after "Depression and loneliness/ dulled her soft bloom." Color is used here to signify emotional states, and the gentle rhyme of "gloom" with "bloom," echoed by "word" in the last line, gives the poem a certain poignancy.

THE ORANGERY

The Orangery is one of Sorrentino's most memorable collections of poetry. Each poem includes the word "orange," the "preconceived constraint" upon which the poet planned this book. Orange appears and reappears as a color, a fruit, a memory, an intrusion, a word seeking a rhyme, or an unexpected presence. On first publication William Bronk wrote, "In *The Orangery* Sorrentino makes things which are hard, gaudy, and sometimes scary. They are stark artifacts of our world. . . . They are made to last."

The poem titled "King Cole" takes two lines from a song that Nat King Cole made popular—"Wham! Bam! Alla Kazam!/ out of an orange colored sky"—and focuses on the nonsense words. In two spare free-verse stanzas the poet brings the reader's attention to the way the words "Wham! Bam! Alla Kazam!" somehow achieve a meaning of their own within the "foolish song," a meaning wedded to the sound of the words even more powerfully than the image of "a sky colored orange." The poem is modern in its self-referential quality; it is basically about itself and the images contained within it. Yet the last word of the poem, "Fruitless," is ambiguous; the reader does not know if it refers to the "foolish song," to the analytic method of the poem itself, or to both. Sorrentino seems to be experimenting in this poem, trying out tricks to see how they work, such as the use of a parenthesis that is not closed.

Many of the poems in *The Orangery* experiment with form as well as meaning. There are sonnet variations, including the poems "Cento," "Fragments of an Old Song," and "One Negative Vote," which keep the fourteen-line sonnet form but ignore the traditional iambic pentameter and rhyme scheme. One of the most charming poems in this collection is "Villanette," a word that does not exist yet and was presumably created by the poet to title this variation on the venerable villanelle, an Old French form derived from Italian folk song. The villanelle is composed of five tercets (rhyming triplets) in the rhyme scheme *aba*, followed by a closing quatrain in the scheme *abaa*.

Sorrentino's "Villanette" contains only four tercets, which maintain the rhyme scheme, and closes with a rhymed couplet. The subject of the poem is certain words denoting a northern winter, compared to the pleasures of winter in Florida. The form lends a certain dignity to the topic, adds importance, and renders it more memorable.

OTHER MAJOR WORKS

LONG FICTION: *The Sky Changes*, 1966; *Steelwork*, 1970; *Imaginative Qualities of Actual Things*, 1971; *Splendide-Hotel*, 1973; *Mulligan Stew*, 1979; *Aberration of Starlight*, 1980; *Crystal Vision*, 1981; *Blue Pas-*

toral, 1983; *Odd Number*, 1985; *Rose Theatre*, 1987; *Misterioso*, 1989; *Under the Shadow*, 1991; *Red the Fiend*, 1995; *Pack of Lies*, 1997; *Gold Fools*, 1999; *Little Casino*, 2002; *A Strange Commonplace*, 2006; *The Abyss of Human Illusion*, 2009.

SHORT FICTION: *The Moon in Its Flight*, 2004.

PLAY: *Flawless Play Restored: The Masque of Fungo*, pb. 1974.

NONFICTION: *Something Said*, 1984; *Lunar Follies*, 2005.

TRANSLATION: *Suspiciae Elegidia/Elegiacs of Sulpicia*, 1977.

BIBLIOGRAPHY

Conte, Joseph. "Gilbert Sorrentino: A Crystal Vision." *Critique* 51 (2010): 140-146. Conte, a friend and colleague of Sorrentino, remembers the poet-novelist in this brief but informative article.

Howard, Gerald. "A View from the Ridge: Back in the Old Neighborhood with Postmodern Prole Gilbert Sorrentino." *Bookforum*, February/March, 2006. A detailed article on the life and work of Sorrentino.

Klinkowitz, Jerome. *The Life of Fiction*. Urbana: University of Illinois Press, 1977. Explores major developments in American fiction, with an emphasis on modernism and its nucleus in New York. Contains a chapter on Sorrentino.

Mottram, Eric. "The Black Polar Night: The Poetry of Gilbert Sorrentino." *Vort*, 1974, 43-59. This is an exhaustive discussion of Sorrentino's poetry, focusing on his color imagery, his humor, and his poetic techniques. Especially strong in documenting the poet's bleak vision.

O'Brien, John, ed. *Gilbert Sorrentino Number*. Elmwood Park, Ill.: Dalkey Archive, 1981. Contains critical writings on Sorrentino's work.

Sorrentino, Gilbert. "Shoveling Coal." Interview by Barry Alpert. *Jacket* 29 (April, 2006). Sorrentino discusses his life and his works.

Sheila Golburgh Johnson

Gary Soto

Born: Fresno, California; April 12, 1952

Principal poetry

The Elements of San Joaquin, 1977
The Tale of Sunlight, 1978
Where Sparrows Work Hard, 1981
Black Hair, 1985
A Fire in My Hands, 1990 (juvenile)
Who Will Know Us?, 1990
Home Course in Religion, 1991
Neighborhood Odes, 1992 (juvenile)
Canto Familiar, 1995 (juvenile)
New and Selected Poems, 1995
Fearless Fernie: Hanging out with Fernie and Me,
   2002 (juvenile; also known as *Body Parts in
   Rebellion*)
A Natural Man, 1999
One Kind of Faith, 2003
Worlds Apart: Traveling with Fernie and Me, 2005
   (juvenile)
A Simple Plan, 2007
Partly Cloudy: Poems of Love and Longing, 2009
   (juvenile)
Human Nature, 2010

Other literary forms

Gary Soto (SOH-toh) wrote autobiographical essays that deal with his growing up in a Chicano community and address issues such as race, class, and religion. They are collected in *Living up the Street: Narrative Recollections* (1985), *Small Faces* (1986), *Lesser Evils: Ten Quartets* (1988), *A Summer Life* (1990), and *The Effect of Knut Hamsun on a Fresno Boy* (2000). His adult fiction includes *Nickel and Dime* (2000), *Poetry Lover* (2001), and *Amnesia in a Republican County* (2003). Soto has become a prolific and influential writer of stories and novels for children and young adults.

Achievements

Gary Soto has received public and critical praise for his poetry and prose memoirs, which explore the pleasures and difficulties of life for working-class Chicanos. Many readers respond to the direct emotional appeal of his writing and his ability to write clearly and imaginatively about his ethnic background. He received an award from *The Nation* magazine for his poem "The Discovery" in 1975 and the United States Award from the International Poetry Forum in 1976 for his first book, *The Elements of San Joaquin*. His second collection of poems, *The Tale of Sunlight*, was nominated for a Pulitzer Prize. His nonfiction writing has also garnered awards, including the American Book Award from the Before Columbus Foundation in 1985 for *Living up the Street*. Individual poems have won the Bess Hokin Prize (1977) and the Levinson Award (1984) from *Poetry* magazine. *New and Selected Poems* was a National Book Award finalist, and *Petty Crimes* (1998) won the PEN Center West Book Award in 1999. Soto's poetry earned such honors as the Literature Award from the Hispanic Heritage Foundation (1999) and the Author-Illustrator Civil Rights Award from the National Education Association (1999). His producing of the film *Pool Party* won him the 1993 Andrew Carnegie Medal for Film Excellence, and his literacy advocacy earned him the title of Person of the Week from the National Broadcasting Company (NBC) in 1997.

Biography

Gary Soto was born into a Chicano family in 1952 in Fresno, where, according to his essay "Being Mean," his father and grandfather worked in blue-collar jobs at Sun-Maid Raisin, and his mother peeled potatoes at Reddi-Spud. Because of the family's poverty, exacerbated by the father's early death in a work-related accident, Soto was forced to earn money as an agricultural laborer in the San Joaquin Valley and at a tire-retread factory in Fresno. Soto's work, especially his early poems, focuses primarily on this personal history. Although he never mentions it in his poems, Soto does have an impressive academic background: He was graduated magna cum laude from California State University at Fresno (1974), received a master of fine arts degree in creative writing from the University of California, Irvine (1976), and has taught at the University of California, Berkeley, in the departments of English and Chicano studies. He has also been a distinguished professor of creative writing at the University of California, Riverside. Soto married Carolyn Oda, a Japanese American, in 1975, and they have one daughter, Mariko.

ANALYSIS

Although Gary Soto was born into a Roman Catholic family and attended parochial schools in Fresno, California, religious issues are discussed only in his late work; primarily, he has been attracted to and obsessed by the issues of race and poverty that dominated his early life and the importance of memory for a poet.

THE ELEMENTS OF SAN JOAQUIN

The Elements of San Joaquin, Soto's first book, is divided into three sections that neatly compartmentalize his early experiences: He moves from urban portraits of Fresno to the agricultural landscape of the San Joaquin Valley and closes with memories of his childhood and adolescence.

The opening poem, "San Fernando Road," describes and is dedicated to Leonard Cruz, a Chicano working in a factory, and it sets the mood for the first section and the book as a whole. An allusion to the four natural elements of the title—earth, air, fire, and water—is made in the poem, but there is nothing invigorating or revitalizing here. The air Leonard breathes contains "the dust/ Of rubber" from the factory, the water sits in the "toilets/ No one flushed," the men's "arms/ Were bracelets/ Of burns," and the earth on which he sleeps (he is homeless) only makes him shiver "Like the machinery/ That went on and on." It is no wonder that Leonard's body is weakening as he works; he has lost contact with the earth that gives life. The only hint of life or vibrancy comes in the hideous image of a woman "Opening/ In her first rape." Soto evokes the hopelessness of the environment by suggesting that this is not the last time the woman will be violated.

"Mission Tire Factory, 1969" is another version of the opening poem of this collection. In "San Fernando Road," Leonard "swept the dust/ Of rubber . . . into his nostrils" and "Went into ovens/ Squint-eyed," and in the later poem, Soto recalls "the wash of rubber in our lungs" and "the oven we would enter, squinting." Clearly there are problems with returning to familiar sights too often: The language becomes predictable and stale. Soto manages to save the poem, however, by focusing the reader's attention on the particularized humanity of the workers without sentimentalizing them. Manny, injured on the job, is carried to the work shed by his fellow workers (including Peter, who pinches "at his crotch"), and all the bleeding man can say is, "Buy some sandwiches. You guys saved my life." Soto comments with candor and compassion that his ignorance was "outdone only by pain."

Section 2 looks at the lives of farmworkers in the San Joaquin Valley, where "nothing will heal/ Under the rain's broken fingers." A typical poem, "Harvest," once again carefully details the importance of the four elements, but in this case, they do affect the growth cycle. The fire of the sun works on "the vineyard that never failed," the wind moves the dust of the earth and Soto's own voice across the crops, and the "ropes of rain" fall on the "thick harvest." Unfortunately, the worker in the field, Soto himself, does not share in the natural production of wealth: "ropes of rain dropped to pull me/ From the thick harvest that was not mine."

Gary Soto (M. L. Martinelle)

Memories of friends in the neighborhood and family members are the focus of section 3. The oppressive mood of the poems about factory workers and agricultural laborers does not lift here. In fact, the deprivations become engraved in the poet, like the bracelets of burns on the factory workers' arms. In "Moving Away," addressed to Soto's brother, he remembers moments when "the one we hated/ Watched us from under a tree." That gaze is still on him; it belongs to the "white stepfather" who replaced Soto's own father. Although what troubled the stepfather "has been forgotten," Soto, speaking for his brother as well, concludes that "what troubled us has settled/ Like dirt/ In the nests of our knuckles/ And cannot be washed away." There are no purifying waters in this very powerful and depressing first book.

The second section contains another tire-factory poem that is both comic and disturbing. In "Mexicans Begin Jogging" (the title itself is flippantly comic), Soto is apparently working with undocumented immigrants; when the border patrol arrives at the factory, he runs from the shop at his boss's orders. Soto, who shouts that he is an American, does not object to the discrimination, because the boss presses "a dollar in my palm." "Since I was on his time, I ran/ And became the wag of a short tail of Mexicans." Soon he breaks into a yuppie jog and "a great silly, grin" because he has outwitted the prejudiced employer; an exploited worker enjoys few things more than getting paid an hourly wage plus a dollar bonus for doing no work at all. Soto later returns to the subject matter of Mexican immigrants in a prose piece, "Black Hair" from his book *Living up the Street*. Except for the metaphor of the wagging tail, the story is very similar to the poem except in one important detail: In "Black Hair" he is able to address the distance he feels from some of his fellow workers, a distance that is lessened somewhat when he runs with the undocumented workers. "Among the Mexicans I had few friends because I was different, a *pocho* who spoke bad Spanish. At lunch they sat in tires and laughed over burritos, looking up at me to laugh even harder." In the poems, this honest recognition of the separation among the workers is absent.

The third section of *The Elements of San Joaquin* contains a poem that suggests the new directions Soto's work will take in subsequent volumes. "Angel" leaves the world of the economically disfranchised and their tales of work woes and arrives in a gentler, more personal area. Here Soto watches his wife as she sleeps, "heavy/ And tilting with child," and he reflects not on his own grim past, but on the child's future. He pictures the tiny fingers, which "bloom like candles," even though it is still weeks before the baby "slides from water/ And blood, his blue hands/ Tightening on air." He does not despair about the child's future, perhaps because Soto has by this time escaped his old working-class life and joined the privileged world of academics; instead, he can only expectantly wait for "that good day/ When this child will kick/ His joints into place." After the arrival of that child, kicking her joints into place, Soto wrote a number of buoyantly hopeful poems about Mariko, his daughter.

THE TALE OF SUNLIGHT AND WHERE SPARROWS WORK HARD

His second book, *The Tale of Sunlight*, is distinctive in that the poet creates two characters, Molina and Manuel Zaragoza, who take the focus off Soto's own life experiences. Molina, a Chicano alter ego of Soto, and Manuel, a cantina owner in Taxco, Mexico, allow him to escape the solipsistic world of poems narrated in the first person. This is the only time in Soto's career when characters other than the poet become the principal focus of the work.

In *Where Sparrows Work Hard*, Soto returns to familiar sights: the neighborhood, the tire factory, the fields, and family. As this book progresses, however, there are some happy, sometimes comic moments that relieve the despair.

BLACK HAIR

Black Hair examines familiar themes. There is the sense of resignation and bitterness that Soto feels when he recalls his early farmworker experiences: "Work in dust, get up in dust. Beer makes it go." There are recollections of childish mischief directed against the "enemy": With a friend, he "started/ Kicking a Republican's fence,/ The pickets working loose." In the title poem, "Black Hair," there is pride in having brown skin and being a Chicano: Soto, at age eight, worships a baseball player and fellow Chicano, Hector Moreno, and assumes "his crouch . . . before an altar/ Of worn baseball cards" in his room. There are wonderfully surprising metaphors throughout the poems: garbage is a "raffle of eggshells and orange peels"; a column of ants on the ground is a "loose thread to an old coat"; crying is like "rope/ Going taut."

The changes that do appear in this book derive from Soto's relationship with his daughter. The childlike quality of many of his earlier poems is redoubled here because of the young girl's presence. At times, this childlike quality becomes too dull and almost puts the poems to sleep. In France, they walk hand in hand, "smiling/ For no reason other than/ Everything is new"; when his daughter asks "What's that? . . . there's no greater/ Pleasure than saying,/ Beats me. Let's go see." This conversational, matter-of-fact diction can disappoint the reader who seeks sparkling or inventive language. However, the presence of the daughter in these poems allows a new side of Soto's character to shine through. Instead of seeing himself as a victim and the enemy as Republicans, he includes himself in a catalog of human transgressions: While watching and admiring ants with his daughter, he waxes philosophical for a moment and admits that "many people, whole countries,/ May go under because we desire TV/ And chilled drinks, clothes/ That hang well on our bodies." Ants are better than humans, and Soto is human. The daughter, however, also permits Soto to write fairly innocent, anger-free poems about simple joys. Instead of concentrating on the exploitation inherent in the economic system, Soto explains to his daughter that "if we buy a goldfish, someone tries on a hat." The exchange of wealth between buyer and seller seems almost like play; gone are the dust from rubber, the hot ovens the factory workers have to enter, and the injustice of substandard wages. Now "If we buy crayons, someone walks home with a broom"; with "a small purchase here and there,/ And things just keep going."

Soto avoids sentimentality in these generally happy poems by admitting the quirks of childhood. When he wants to walk in nature to a special spot with his daughter, she responds in a typically modern, spoiled way, "Daddy please, why/ Don't we get in the car/ And be over there." His amused annoyance is entertaining. The poems generally are admirable for the new range of emotions that Soto permits himself. With this collec-

tion, he is no longer solely the angry young man; now he is the proud father as well.

WHO WILL KNOW US?

"Who Will Know Us?"—the title poem of Soto's fifth volume—asks the difficult question, "Who will know us when we breathe through the grass?" Despite the gravity of the question, which occurs to him while he is "on a train, rocking toward the cemetery/ To visit the dead," the collection as a whole does not dwell on difficult or macabre questions; instead, it celebrates life in typical Soto fashion—by praising the quotidian and remembering the past.

In "Eve," the poet repeats a story that is similar to one in the prose collection *Lesser Evils: Ten Quartets*. In "Starting Young," the adolescent Soto meets a precocious thirteen-year-old, Sue, in a shed belonging to a neighbor, and they pull down their pants and touch each other. He worries needlessly about impregnating her, and the story of early investigative romance ends sweetly. In "Eve" Soto goes all the way with a girl on her father's workbench in the barn; when she unfastens her skirt, her "kinked hair" is "thick as a child's black scribbling." Again he worries, needlessly, that he has impregnated her; the poem ends with no shotgun solutions to problems, but a melancholy dictum: people said that "it should hurt the first time,/ Then stop . . . how they lied." Pain goes hand in hand with love and sex—first time, every time. The comparison between the versions in prose and poetry reveals little more than the obsessive quality of Soto's work: He returns again and again to subjects that he finds worthy of his attention, not concerned that this is country he has already discovered. He wants to mine the mountain until the ore is gone.

One of the concluding poems in the book, "Evening Walk," is pleasantly self-effacing. Soto, while walking with his daughter, tries to tell her "poor stories" about the old days when he "picked/ Grapes like nobody's business" and "lugged oranges and shared plums with Okies." Mariko will have none of it. Soto concludes that he is "a bore to the end," while Mariko runs and skips ahead, dragging a branch that flutters "like a green fire." Her only eagerness is for an evening without him; the parent-poet-storyteller senses the inevitable hostility of the younger generation. In typical fashion, Soto accepts stoically and with humor the march and skip of time.

HOME COURSE IN RELIGION

When it comes to religion, a subject that Soto largely ignored in his early poems, he nostalgically yearns for old-fashioned sanctity. In *Home Course in Religion*, Soto catalogs the items he misses in post-Vatican II Catholicism: pagan babies, holy water in the cupboard, Mass said in Latin, and meatless Fridays. The modernization of the church has even invaded the most primitive forms of worship: "At the altar of Mary, we have electric bulbs,/ Not candles, sitting in votive cups." The altar "lights up like a pinball machine" when one drops a quarter in the slot for each sin. The early radical Soto has become movingly conservative; he wonders, "How do we kneel and pray at such a place?" Many of these poems also recall his adolescent initiation into the sometimes mysterious, sometimes comic rites of the faith.

This collection also focuses considerable attention on Soto's relationship with his stepfather, Jim, but in this case the poet does not reminisce with pleasure. In contrast to the imaginative re-creations of his father, who died before Soto really knew him, the evocations of his stepfather are hauntingly realistic, almost naturalistic. The father is associated with his La-Z-Boy recliner, his Jack Daniels, his racism, and the "pounding of fists that pounded boxes all day." After Soto records on a cheap tape recorder an argument between his mother and Jim, he replays the vicious piece "until the voices slurred to a crawl/ And the tape recorder died." As the batteries fade, Soto notices that the plastic statue of Jesus, "marble white and hollow," captures the afternoon glow from the window, but it offers no consolation for the fear and anger the young boy is feeling. Soto appreciates the rituals of Catholicism, but he seems to suggest that the value of the faith for relieving anguish is minimal.

In the last few poems of the book, Soto escapes from memories of youth and evaluates his adult life, which seems to be packed with distracting facts and activities. He watches television, reads student papers, studies karate, and examines Japanese and Impressionist art. A moving line positioned amid all this clutter is "I want very badly to know how to talk about Christ." How-

ever, faith is absent; instead, Soto finds whatever redemption there is in his daily existence—his daughter's games, his humor, and his marriage.

A NATURAL MAN

Soto's collections through the 1990's, some of which are aimed at children, find him walking the same path he set out on as a young poet. Though he has not stopped looking around him, and though he continues to examine the father-daughter relationship as the daughter matures, much of his work still conjures up memories of his boyhood. His short, staccato lines and gritty colloquialism create an ever-refined vehicle for his accurate eye, and he builds intriguing tensions through voices poised between innocence and experience, even the middle-aged voices of *A Natural Man*.

A SIMPLE PLAN

In *A Simple Plan*, Soto continues the themes of nostalgia, innocence, and experiential growth. In several poems, in the earliest pages of the work, the speaker expresses a nostalgia for objects of the past. These correlatives are animated or wished into animation and are, like the marbles in "Soap Opera," for instance, representative of melancholy, of longing, and simultaneously, they are symbolic of the early need for escape. In this way, *A Simple Plan* continues to develop the trajectory of maturity, the first poems recalling places and events of youth and youth's aching desire to flee, and the later poems reaching a place of retreat and offering old age and a new kind of search—a search for peace, self-knowledge, and a return to home through childhood memories.

From early in his life, as in "Fresno's Westside Blues" and other pieces, the central speaker quietly but desperately wants to escape, run away, "get outta [there]." He strives to define "what is meant by escape." He must escape the town, the politics, and his parents and their punishments. In the book's title poem, a boy tries to get rid of his dog by tricking him to follow him miles from home, where he can abandon him. In rites of passage or through inevitable growth, the boy is "making [his] getaway," and in poems such as "Police State," he thrives by "hoarding poetry in [his] heart" amid the sensory—the objects and creatures of a nostalgic past—that he has made sensual as a poet. By the book's end, the poet has succeeded, with aid from the very objects and items with him from the start—the birds of conscience, the mules and mice, the desert dusts and flies. By "Breakdown on a Small Road," the young man in flight has evolved to a disgruntled driver of a car that fails him, then to a "thirsty apostle" surviving on the trough water that restores him. By the final poem, "The Artist Thinks, 'So This Is Me,'" the speaker has indeed delivered himself to another place, but it is one in which the adult feels bereft, without shore, insurance, or love. However, it is a place where the poet, who has moved by growing into the present, still has access to the objects of reflection—objects that sustain him, his art, and his work.

The subjects that Soto addresses in his later poems are very similar to those in his earlier poems; however, in many ways, the Soto of the twenty-first century is not the same poet who began writing in the 1970's. As *A Simple Plan* exemplifies in metaphor, Soto has matured; he has established a very successful career by looking into his past, but his later work suggests that his main concern has become trying to find spiritual sustenance in a middle-class, comfortable life. He says, "We invent misery for our bodies,/ Then our minds, and then, having nothing else to do/ Look for ways to make it stop." Voicing his life themes, Soto's poems continue to attempt to stop the pain through nostalgia, humor, and intense living in the present.

OTHER MAJOR WORKS

LONG FICTION: *Nickel and Dime*, 2000; *Poetry Lover*, 2001; *Amnesia in a Republican County*, 2003.

NONFICTION: *Living up the Street: Narrative Recollections*, 1985; *Small Faces*, 1986; *Lesser Evils: Ten Quartets*, 1988; *A Summer Life*, 1990; *The Effect of Knut Hamsun on a Fresno Boy*, 2000.

CHILDREN'S LITERATURE: *Baseball in April, and Other Stories*, 1990; *Taking Sides*, 1991; *Pacific Crossing*, 1992; *The Skirt*, 1992; *Local News*, 1993; *Too Many Tamales*, 1993; *Crazy Weekend*, 1994; *Jesse*, 1994; *Boys at Work*, 1995; *The Cat's Meow*, 1995; *Chato's Kitchen*, 1995; *Off and Running*, 1996; *Buried Onions*, 1997; *Novio Boy*, 1997 (play); *Big Bushy Mustache*, 1998; *Petty Crimes*, 1998; *Chato and the Party Animals*, 1999; *Chato Throws a Pachanga*, 1999; *Nerdlania*, 1999 (play); *Jesse De La Cruz: A Profile of a United Farm Worker*, 2000; *My Little Car*,

2000; *If the Shoe Fits*, 2002; *The Afterlife*, 2003; *Chato Goes Cruisin'*, 2004; *Help Wanted*, 2005; *Accidental Love*, 2006; *Mercy on These Teenage Chimps*, 2007; *Facts of Life: Stories*, 2008.

EDITED TEXTS: *California Childhood: Recollections and Stories of the Golden State*, 1988; *Pieces of the Heart: New Chicano Fiction*, 1993.

BIBLIOGRAPHY

Armour-Hileman, Vicki. Review of *Where Sparrows Work Hard*. *Denver Quarterly* 17 (Summer, 1982): 154-155. Armour-Hileman notes what many critics call attention to the similarity between Soto and his teacher Philip Levine in subject matter, "a surrealistic bent," and short, enjambed lines. She finds fault with the "inaccuracy of the images" in many of Soto's poems and "their elliptical movement." She does admire the poems in which Soto "becomes not an ethnic poet, but a poet who writes about human suffering." His writing in the last third of this collection she considers a "great success."

Constantakis, Sara, ed. *Poetry for Students*. Vol. 32. Detroit: Gale, 2010. Contains an analysis, context, and criticism for Soto's "Oranges."

Cooley, Peter. "Two Young Poets." *Parnassus* 7 (Fall/ Winter, 1979): 299-311. In this extremely laudatory examination of Soto's two earliest collections, Cooley calls Soto "the most important voice among the young Chicano poets." He praises Soto's ability to re-create his lost world of San Joaquin with "an imaginative expansiveness." This is a crucial essay for understanding the initial praise given to Soto and how his work seemed to speak for a generation of Chicanos.

De La Fuente, Patricia. "Entropy in the Poetry of Gary Soto: The Dialectics of Violence." *Discurso Literario* 5, no. 1 (Autumn, 1987): 111-120. De La Fuente examines the use of entropy and how it reinforces the structure of Soto's poetry.

Erben, Rudolf, and Ute Erben. "Popular Culture, Mass Media, and Chicano Identity in Gary Soto's *Living up the Street* and *Small Faces*." *MELUS* 17, no. 3 (Fall, 1991/1992): 43-52. The authors explore the conflict of dual consciousness and social problems that Soto examines.

Mason, Michael Tomasek. "Poetry and Masculinity on the Anglo/Christian Border: Gary Soto, Robert Frost, and Robert Hass." In *The Calvinist Roots of the Modern Era*, edited by Aliki Barnstone, Michael Tomasek Manson, and Carol J. Singley. Hanover: University Press of New England, 1997. Manson carefully traces the evolution of notions of masculinity, "machismo," in Soto's work.

Olivares, Julian. "The Streets of Gary Soto." *Latin America Literary Review* 18, no. 35 (January-June, 1990): 32-49. Olivares explores Soto's ability to universalize the situations his characters face.

Paredes, Raymund A. "Recent Chicano Writing." *Rocky Mountain Review* 41, nos. 1/2 (1987): 124-129. Paredes admires Soto's writing because "ethnic and class consciousness constitutes an essential part of his literary sensibility." He faults Soto, however, for his portrayal of women: "As he depicts them, their roles are wholly conventional." He does not find the portrayals of women to be totally offensive, but he chides the poet for "performing unremarkably" on this issue.

Soto, Gary. "The Childhood Worries, or Why I Became a Writer." Interview by Raymund A. Paredes. *Iowa Review* 25, no. 2 (Spring/Summer, 1995): 105-115. Soto recalls the formative influences later treated in his poetry and the initial motivations for expressing his experiences.

_____. "Gary Soto." http://garysoto.com. Soto's own Web site provides a biography, information on what he is doing and thinking, a catalog of works, a photo gallery, and information on the Gary Soto Literary Museum.

West, Michelle. Review of *The Afterlife*. *Magazine of Fantasy and Science Fiction* 106, no. 5 (May, 2004): 32. From a personal vantage point, West reviews the shape of contemplation of death in Soto's 2003 work, *The Afterlife*, and identifies how Soto turns the thematic concept of justice "on its head."

White, Julianne. "Soto's Oranges." *Explicator* 63, no. 2 (Winter, 2005): 121. White offers a close reading of the literary devices that lend to the simple theme of appreciating childhood in Soto's poetry.

Kevin Boyle; Philip K. Jason
Updated by Roxanne McDonald

JACK SPICER

Born: Los Angeles, California; January 30, 1925
Died: San Francisco, California; August 17, 1965

PRINCIPAL POETRY

After Lorca, 1957
Billy the Kid, 1959
The Heads of the Town up to the Aether, 1962
Lament for the Makers, 1962
The Holy Grail, 1964
Language, 1965
Book of Magazine Verse, 1966
A Book of Music, 1969
A Red Wheelbarrow, 1971
Admonitions, 1974
Fifteen False Propositions About God, 1974
An Ode and Arcadia, 1974 (with Robert Duncan)
The Collected Books of Jack Spicer, 1975 (Robin Blaser, editor)
One Night Stand, and Other Poems, 1980
The Tower of Babel, 1994
Golem, 1999
My Vocabulary Did This to Me: The Collected Poetry of Jack Spicer, 2008

OTHER LITERARY FORMS

Although Jack Spicer often employed prose in his works, the results were more poetic than otherwise, yielding short prose poems that he linked together in series. Spicer stretched literary boundaries by giving poems names normally reserved for prose works, as he did in calling one poem series a "novel." Spicer also employed letters, drawn from either imaginary or real correspondence, as a means of literary expression and included them in his first poetry book, *After Lorca*, as well as in other collections. He did publish some nonfiction, such as notes and reviews for the *Boston Public Library Quarterly*.

ACHIEVEMENTS

Jack Spicer exerted a major influence on West Coast Beat poetry in the late 1950's and early 1960's, initially as a teacher and workshop-leader and subsequently as a poet whose books influenced countless others, especially after his death. His interactions with other poets helped galvanize the poetry scene in San Francisco, especially from 1957 to 1964, while his poems reached their greatest audiences in two posthumous collections, *The Collected Books of Jack Spicer* and *My Vocabulary Did This to Me*. In 2009, Spicer was awarded the American Book Award by the Before Columbus Foundation for *My Vocabulary Did This to Me*.

BIOGRAPHY

Jack Spicer was born John Lester Spicer, in Los Angeles, in 1925 to John Lovely Spicer and Dorothy Clause Spicer, who ran a hotel in Hollywood. At the age of three, Spicer was sent to Minnesota to live with his grandparents while his mother was pregnant with his younger brother. This early separation caused Spicer to resent his sibling and to become estranged from his family.

Spicer attended the University of Redlands from 1943 to 1945, then left for the University of California, Berkeley, where he began working seriously on his poetry. During his time in Berkeley, from 1945 to 1955, he became friends with fellow poets Robert Duncan and Robin Blaser, among others. After a few weeks of exploring life in New York City in 1955, Spicer moved to Boston, where Blaser was living, and found work as editor and curator in the Rare Book Room of the Boston Public Library. He soon returned to the West, settling in San Francisco in 1956. Out of dissatisfaction with his own poetry, he began developing new ideas about its composition. Writing poetry, he came to believe, is a form of "dictation." He made his ideas public during his Poetry as Magic Workshop in 1957, held under the auspices of San Francisco State College. The workshop inspired a follow-up workshop directed by Duncan, as well as a long series of poetry events that enlivened San Francisco bars.

A period of intense creativity followed the 1957 publication of his first book, *After Lorca*. Spicer completed *Admonitions*, *A Book of Music*, *Billy the Kid*, and *Fifteen False Propositions Against God* in 1958. However, none of these poem-series, which he often called "books," saw immediate publication. From 1959 through

1961, Spicer continued producing works, including *Helen: A Revision* and *Lament of the Makers*. The latter saw publication in 1962, as did the collection *The Heads of the Town up to the Aether*, which included "A Fake Novel About the Life of Arthur Rimbaud" and "A Textbook of Poetry." In 1962, Spicer also wrote his ambitious *The Holy Grail*, composed of seven series of poems that drew on figures from the Holy Grail story. In 1964, he wrote *Language*.

After Spicer died from alcohol-induced liver failure in 1965, a number of his works were published posthumously. *Fifteen False Propositions Against God* was published as *Fifteen False Propositions About God*. Blaser edited *The Collected Books of Jack Spicer*, which presented Spicer's works in their original order of composition, based on their original texts, and was published by Black Sparrow Press a decade after the poet's death. A later collection, *My Vocabulary Did This to Me*, included some poems that had not been previously published, including *Helen: A Revision*.

ANALYSIS

Jack Spicer wrote a poetry of imagistic and conceptual juxtaposition reminiscent, at times, of Dadaist randomness. He considered true poetry to be "dictated," and thus removed from the conscious control of the poet. Spicer's own poetry never completely lacks sense or meaning, however. Spicer believed that the "dictated" poem of necessity employs the materials present in the poet's mind. Since the poet's understanding of the world is part of that valid source-material, that understanding might be expected to appear in the dictated work. The poet's understanding does not shape that work, however. Spicer argued that personal experience provides the material or vocabulary for poetry even while the conscious mind provides a less than ideal means for transforming that material into poetry.

In a real sense, Spicer embraced the traditional notion of the Muse, without using the term and without arriving at traditional results in his poetry. He felt and expressed the sense of there being an "Other" who dictated his poems, whom he sometimes humorously identified as a Martian. Although Spicer is often viewed as a Surrealist, this attitude toward "dictation" sets his works apart from those of earlier Surrealist poets. To the degree that he was successfully receptive to such dictation, his poems could be regarded as objective but nonanalytical in nature, in common with Surrealists. His poems are also intentional, however, with their intent often arising from a strong impulse to teach.

After Lorca

Spicer wrote the poems in his first book using the ideas he introduced and developed during his 1957 workshop. In addition to dictation, he arrived at the idea of the poem-series, or "book," which is a larger form that incorporates and helps give meaning to the individual, component poems. His first such grouping, *After Lorca*, uses Federico García Lorca's poems as a jumping-off point. The book begins with a fictitious introduction that is presented as having been written by García Lorca himself, twenty years after his own death. Spicer then presents an extravaganza of erratically bold and freewheeling "translations," intermixed with a series of letters Spicer imagined writing to García Lorca.

The pseudo-translations give Spicer an opportunity to salute such varied figures as Paul Verlaine, Walt Whitman, and Buster Keaton, as well as García Lorca. A freshness of invention animates even the briefest of the poems, while the imaginary letters to García Lorca state some of the poet's ambitions: "I would like to make poems out of real objects. . . . The imagination pictures the real. I would like to point to the real, disclose it, to make a poem that has no sound in it but the pointing of a finger." In this "correspondence" with García Lorca, Spicer plays with the meanings of the word "correspond": "Things do not connect; they correspond. That is what makes it possible for a poet to translate real objects, to bring them across language as easily as he can bring them across time." He notes that his own letter, now an object, will inspire an act akin to his own: "some future poet will write something which *corresponds* to them. That is how we dead men write to each other." Spicer's inclination to engage in verbal discovery, often through use of puns, would reappear in many later works.

"A Textbook of Poetry"

"A Textbook of Poetry" was one of several "books" that appeared under a title that suggested a literary form other than what it actually was. Lacking the straightforward "how to" nature of a handbook, "The Textbook of Poetry" instead presents in imaginative terms Spicer's notions about poetry, its composition, and its meaning. The text is presented as prose, in paragraphs that are fully justified, rather than left-justified as is standard for poetry. All the same, the lines themselves have a character indistinguishable from Spicer's other poetry. After stating "Metaphors are not for humans," Spicer writes this short paragraph:

> The wires dance in the winds of the noise our poems make. The noise without an audience. Because the poems were written for ghosts.

In "The Textbook of Poetry," Spicer further develops his notion of the dictation of poems. The other voice that is within the poet, as well as the true poetry that is contained within the dictated poem, are elusive and perhaps are never completely within the grasp of understanding: "The ghosts the poems were written for are the ghosts of the poems. We have it second-hand. They cannot hear the noise they have been making." However, these inner voices, or "ghosts," are acting with purposeful intent, for they are "teaching an audience."

Spicer's lines approach the mystery of Daoist utterance in attempting to express these elusive notions or images: "I can write a poem about him a hundred times but he is not there. . . . I have not words for him." An element of Plato's concept of reality plays into the poem, with the inexpressible that Spicer "cannot proclaim" being akin to Plato's Ideal, in that it "descends to the real." Spicer even uses the Greek word *logos*, both in association with the name God ("I mean the real God") and, simultaneously, divorced from the notion ("I did not mean the real God").

The unreliable-title approach of "The Textbook of Poetry" was anticipated by his early "The Unvert Manifesto and Other Papers Found in the Rare Book Room of the Boston Public Library in the Handwriting of Oliver Charming," which Spicer wrote during his brief Boston period. Although he called it a "manifesto," it resembled poetry in parts, and, in others, fiction, in its use of narrative and dialog.

Language

Spicer had been working on *Language* in the last two years of his life, and it includes several sequences of poems that show his further exploration of themes and approaches that already had characterized his works. Just as earlier poems had used the Orphic and Holy Grail myths for springboards, "Baseball Predictions, April 1, 1964" uses for its central concern the death of President John F. Kennedy, an event that had already taken on mythic dimensions in American culture. Other poems, including the sequences "Love Poems," "Intermissions," "Transformations," "Phonemics," and "Graphemics," intertwine Spicer's idiosyncratic meditations on love and death, including again Kennedy's death, with his continuing exploration of the nature of poetry. In writing *Language*, Spicer was succumbing yet again to the heuristic impulse and talking about poetry as a way of teaching about poetry. He also, more unusually, seems to have given in to the need for self-explanation: Assertions appear among these lines, as if in self-defense, that what he is writing is, indeed, poetry.

After leading the workshop in San Francisco in 1957, Spicer never managed to depart completely from teaching about his chosen subject: what poetry is and is not, and how it is written, or rather dictated. Even the grail in *The Holy Grail* is presented in such a way as to give insight into poetry: "The grail is the opposite of poetry/ Fills us up instead of using us as a cup the dead drink from." Some of Spicer's continuing influence arises from the fact that he is so engaging and thought-provoking as a teacher, even when at his most enigmatic.

OTHER MAJOR WORKS

NONFICTION: *Dear Ferlinghetti: The Spicer/Ferlinghetti Correspondence: Dear Jack*, 1964 (with Lawrence Ferlinghetti); *The House That Jack Built: The Collected Lectures of Jack Spicer*, 1998 (Peter Gizzi, editor).

BIBLIOGRAPHY

Boyd, Nan Alamilla. *Wide-Open Town: A History of Queer San Francisco to 1965*. Berkeley: University of California Press, 2003. A history of the gay culture within which Spicer lived during his most productive years, covering events up through the time of his death.

Ellingham, Lewis, and Kevin Killian. *Poet Be Like God: Jack Spicer and the San Francisco Renaissance*. Hanover, N.H.: Wesleyan University Press, 1998. This biography emphasizes Spicer's position among the Beats, whose development in 1950's San Francisco he helped catalyze, with discussion of his feelings concerning his lack of success relative to other, higher-profile Beat generation writers.

Foster, Edward Halsey. *Jack Spicer*. Boise, Idaho: Boise State University Press, 1991. An early biography that recognizes Spicer's strengths as a poet of the 1950's and offers evidence of his significance beyond the San Francisco scene. Part of the Western Writers series.

Glaser, Robin. "The Practice of Outside." In *The Collected Books of Jack Spicer*, edited by Glaser. Los Angeles: Black Sparrow Press, 1975. This invaluable essay provides perspective on Spicer's work, with emphasis on his unusual understanding of composition, written by a man who was both longtime friend and fellow poet.

Mayhew, Jonathan. *Apocryphal Lorca: Translation, Parody, Kitsch*. Chicago: University of Chicago Press, 2009. An examination of García Lorca's influence in the United States, especially through translation, with discussions of Robert Duncan, Robert Creeley, and Spicer, among others.

Spicer, Jack. *The House That Jack Built: The Collected Lectures of Jack Spicer*. Edited by Peter Gizzi. Hanover, N.H.: Wesleyan University Press, 1998. Gizzi presents his essay "Jack Spicer and the Practice of Reading" along with his transcriptions of Spicer's lectures. An appendix includes previously uncollected prose by Spicer.

Mark Rich

WILLIAM STAFFORD

Born: Hutchinson, Kansas; January 17, 1914
Died: Lake Oswego, Oregon; August 28, 1993

PRINCIPAL POETRY

West of Your City, 1960
Traveling Through the Dark, 1962
The Rescued Year, 1966
Eleven Untitled Poems, 1968
Weather, 1969
Allegiances, 1970
Temporary Facts, 1970
Poems for Tennessee, 1971 (with Robert Bly and William Matthews)
In the Clock of Reason, 1973
Someday, Maybe, 1973
That Other Alone, 1973
Going Places, 1974
North by West, 1975 (with John Haines)
Braided Apart, 1976 (with Kim Robert Stafford)
The Design in the Oriole, 1977
Stories That Could Be True: New and Collected Poems, 1977
All About Light, 1978
Two About Music, 1978
Things That Happen Where There Aren't Any People, 1980
Sometimes Like a Legend, 1981
A Glass Face in the Rain: New Poems, 1982
Roving Across Fields: A Conversation and Uncollected Poems, 1942-1982, 1983
Segues: A Correspondence in Poetry, 1983 (with Marvin Bell)
Smoke's Way: Poems from Limited Editions, 1968-1981, 1983
Listening Deep, 1984
Stories and Storms and Strangers, 1984
Wyoming, 1985
Brother Wind, 1986
An Oregon Message, 1987
Fin, Feather, Fur, 1989
A Scripture of Leaves, 1989
How to Hold Your Arms When It Rains, 1990

Passwords, 1991
My Name Is William Tell, 1992
The Darkness Around Us Is Deep, 1993 (selected by Bly)
Even in Quiet Places, 1996
The Way It Is: New and Selected Poems, 1998
Another World Instead: The Early Poems of William Stafford, 1937-1947, 2008 (Fred Marchant, editor)

OTHER LITERARY FORMS

In addition to poetry, William Stafford published an autobiographical account of his conscientious objector service during World War II, *Down in My Heart* (1947), and edited poetry volumes and authored chapters in collections of critical analysis. Stafford's *Writing the Australian Crawl: Views on the Writer's Vocation* (1978) and *You Must Revise Your Life* (1986) contain essays on writing and the teaching of writing, as well as interviews with Stafford that were originally published in literary magazines.

ACHIEVEMENTS

William Stafford is considered one of the most prolific of contemporary American poets. He received the Union League Civic and Arts Poetry Prize in 1959 from *Poetry* magazine. Although he was forty-six years old when his first collection of poems was published in 1960, he more than made up for this late start. Stafford's second volume, *Traveling Through the Dark*, won the National Book Award in Poetry in 1963. In 1970-1971, Stafford served as consultant in poetry (poet laureate) to the Library of Congress. Throughout his career, he received numerous awards and honors, such as the Shelley Memorial Award (1964), the Theodore Roethke Prize from *Poetry Northwest* (1966), a Yaddo Foundation Fellowship, a National Endowment for the Arts grant, a Guggenheim Fellowship, a Danforth Foundation grant, the Melville Cane Award (1974), the American Academy and Institute of Arts Award in Literature (1981), and the Frost Medal from the Poetry Society of America (1993).

Widely recognized as a spontaneous, natural poet, Stafford greatly influenced the world of literature with his views on the teaching of writing. Equating the act of writing with coming to know the self, Stafford says that writing consists of finding the way as the process unfolds. He can indulge his impulses—knowing that they will bring recurrent patterns and meaning—because in back of his images is the coherence of the self. In his distinguished career as a professor, Stafford put such views into practice in his teaching and made them available to a wider audience through lectures, interviews, and his many published essays on the process of writing.

BIOGRAPHY

On January 17, 1914, William Edgar Stafford was born to Earl Ingersoll Stafford and Ruby Mayher Stafford in Hutchinson, Kansas. With his younger brother and sister, Stafford grew up in a series of small Kansas towns—Wichita, Liberal, Garden City, and El Dorado—as his father moved the family from place to place in search of work. Earl and Ruby Stafford were nonconformists who held strong moral and spiritual beliefs. They instilled in their children a deep sense of individuality, justice, and tolerance. From long hours with his father in the midwestern countryside, Stafford developed his love of nature. He credits his mother and the gossipy stories she loved to tell with helping him perceive the intricacies of language. Although certainly not scholars, both parents loved books, and the whole family raided the local library each week, vying for their favorites.

As an adolescent during the Depression, Stafford was already helping to support his family: raising vegetables, working as an electrician's helper, and delivering newspapers (at one time their only source of income). After high school, Stafford attended junior college and then enrolled in the University of Kansas, waiting on tables to pay his way. During his undergraduate years, Stafford began his habit of writing daily and began to translate his social and political beliefs into action. He participated in a demonstration against segregation in the university cafeteria and, when World War II broke out, registered as a conscientious objector.

Stafford spent the war incarcerated in conscientious objector camps in Arkansas, California, and Illinois, working on soil-conservation projects and fighting forest fires. These were formative years for him, a time of introspection, for Stafford was acutely aware of his un-

William Stafford

orthodox position against a generally popular war. He rigorously examined the tensions between the outer life of daily appearances and the inner life of conviction, developing a deep patience and an abiding sense of integrity. In order to write before the day's labor began, Stafford arose before dawn; this habit continued into later life. While at a camp in California, Stafford met, and soon married, Dorothy Frantz, a minister's daughter. When the war ended, the couple returned to the University of Kansas, and Stafford began work on his M.A. degree. He submitted an account of his conscientious objector experiences as his thesis project, which was subsequently published as his first book, *Down in My Heart*.

After graduation, Stafford taught high school briefly, worked in a church relief agency, and kept writing stories and poems. From 1948 to 1950, he was an instructor in English at Lewis and Clark College in Portland, Oregon. He then moved, with his wife and small children, to the University of Iowa, where he studied under Robert Penn Warren, Randall Jarrell, Reed Whittemore, Karl Shapiro, and others.

Stafford considered these years to be his reference point for how others lived the literary life. His own writing habits and perspective on the world of letters, however, had already been clearly established. When Stafford left Iowa in 1952, he took with him firmly held, idiosyncratic attitudes about writing and how it should be taught. In 1954, when he received his Ph.D. from Iowa, Stafford was already teaching English at Manchester College in Indiana. Next, he taught briefly at San Jose State College and then returned to Lewis and Clark College, beginning a teaching career there that lasted for almost twenty-five years.

After his first book of poems, *West of Your City*, Stafford published many collections with his major publisher, Harper & Row; more than twenty-five other books or chapbooks of poetry with small presses; several collections of prose; short pieces of critical analysis; and interviews. He traveled widely, lecturing and reading his work in the United States and abroad. During the Vietnam War, American university students discovered Stafford's pacifist beliefs, and he was in great demand on college campuses. Precisely because of these beliefs, however, Stafford never became the antiwar poet that the students were seeking. In 1980, Stafford retired from teaching to become professor emeritus at Lewis and Clark College, continuing to publish new collections of poems. He died on August 28, 1993, in Lake Oswego, Oregon.

ANALYSIS

William Stafford was a poet of the personal and the particular. With an optimistic outlook, he wrote personally but not confessionally, and his particulars are sometimes regional but not provincial. Stafford wrote most often in the first person, both singular and plural, and his poems are characteristically quite short. They investigate the processes of everyday life, looking through specific situations and happenings to uncover universal connections between humans and nature. Although Stafford celebrates nature in his work, this is not an end in itself; rather, it is a means to transcend surface manifestation and uncover the underlying unboundedness of life. In this sense, Stafford has been called a wisdom poet, one who uses nature in pursuit of a higher truth. His poems present situations, objects, and people

that entice the reader to go beyond the towns and settlements of life—where what one knows can be readily seen—and search for what lies at their edges, in the wilderness, to listen to the silence one can come to understand, perhaps, as one's own self.

Although much of Stafford's work grows out of personal memories, a strictly biographical reading can be misleading. His work does not lend itself strictly to chronological investigation, either, for Stafford's key themes and metaphorical language in his first published collection are still characteristic of his later volumes. In addition, the order in which Stafford's poems were published does not necessarily reflect the order in which they were written. He did not prepare his collections as thematic, structured volumes; rather, he viewed them as groupings of self-sufficient fragments. It was the incremental progression in individual works, not collections, that interested Stafford, and his focus was on the process of writing rather than on meaning or content. Though criticized for such an internal perspective, Stafford maintained a steadfast unwillingness to analyze his work intellectually. He believed that one should not defend or value what one has written but rather abandon it; others must decide about its significance.

Because Stafford's vision of life remained essentially stable throughout his literary career, themes, images, and even words recur in his poems and take on specific significance, forming almost a shorthand language in themselves. Stafford's major theme is the spiritual search for the self, represented metaphorically as the search for "home." It is a quest for unity with the Absolute, which he associates with the adjectives "deep," "dark," and "silent." Subthemes are his focus on family and small-town living, much of which can be traced to his Kansas boyhood; the sacredness of nature and of wilderness, often in contrast to war, technology, and human alienation; and the exploration of truth as it unfolds through the common activities of daily life.

Stafford has been criticized for his overt simplicity and for his prose style. On the surface, many of his poems do seem to reflect an idyllic midwestern childhood, a longing for the uncomplicated (and perhaps a bit romanticized) past when people lived in greater harmony with nature. Stafford certainly wrote in a conversational style. However, it is this surface accessibility that invites the reader to enter the poems. Once the reader is in, Stafford hints at deeper levels of reality and may ask his readers to do or be or imagine seemingly impossible things. Many poems have a parable-like quality and present rather didactic messages, often in the last line. After the surface message is delivered, however, the silence resounds. Stafford was a poet who roamed far into his own wilderness. He dreamed, and he tested his dreams through the process of telling their stories. Because Stafford's clear vision was firmly rooted, he had the flexibility to follow where imagination and the sounds of language took him.

DOWN IN MY HEART

Published in 1947, Stafford's first book, *Down in My Heart*, is a spiritual autobiography of his four years in conscientious objector work camps during World War II. Within the context of narratives about firefighting, an altercation with a mob in a small town, and a pacifist wedding, he reveals the concerns of a man alienated from the majority of his countrymen by his social and political beliefs. This volume sows seeds that sprout as major themes in his later poetry. Stafford presents his metaphorical "home" as ultimately free from any particular location in his narrative about building yet another work camp. He also touches on other ideas that will unfold as significant poetic themes, such as the power of storytelling, the nature of the hero, sound and silence, and interactions between the individual and society.

WEST OF YOUR CITY

Stafford's first volume of poetry, *West of Your City*, presents a poet of already mature voice, with a strong sense of his material. Running through these poems, arranged in three sections called "Midwest," "Farwest," and "Outside," is the theme of "home." For Stafford, "home" certainly means the security of the Kansas towns of his boyhood, and the persona of many poems in this collection and the poet himself are very similar. Stafford begins "One Home" with the line "Mine was a Midwest home—you keep your world" and moves through references to his personal history. His vision of home also extends, however, beyond the secure Kansas settlements into the adventure of wilderness at their

edges. He concludes, "Kicking cottonwood leaves we ran toward storms./ Wherever we looked the land would hold us up." Running toward adventure, the speaker finds home wherever he looks. Venturing into the wilderness, into what is unknown, the individual has the chance to get a glimpse of what is closest to him, what he can ultimately know best because it is what he is—the self.

The well-known poem "Bi-focal" presents the sense of double vision that pervades virtually all Stafford's work as it unfolds his theme of underlying legends. The poem begins, "Sometimes up out of this land/ a legend begins to move." It locates "the surface, a map of roads/ leading wherever go miles" and "the legend under,/ fixed, inexorable,/ deep as the darkest mine." The poem concludes, "So, the world happens twice—/ Once what we see it as;/ second it legends itself/ deep, the way it is." This poem contrasts what is seen—what seems to be real on the surface of life—with the unseen, what is "deep." "Deep" is clearly defined as the way the world is. The speaker in the poem, like the poet, is able to see both levels, but it is the deeper way of seeing that Stafford emphasizes in his work. He does so not by denigrating the surface details, but rather by penetrating them and revealing their more profound essence and the silence of legends at their source. The poems in *West of Your City*, written mostly in the first person, draw heavily from Stafford's memories. However, the personal details expand to include his reader's life. Even the title of the volume demands the reader's attention: not west of "my"—the poet's—city, but west of the reader's.

TRAVELING THROUGH THE DARK

Stafford's second collection, *Traveling Through the Dark*, established his reputation and won the National Book Award in 1963. Themes from the first collection reoccur, the subject matter is again straightforward, and the tone is gently conversational. Stafford's voice here is less tentative, more sure, but still it asks questions, encouraging the reader to travel past the everyday world of light into the dark wilderness where the real journey takes place. His image of darkness is firmly established here, and it is not a negative one. He associates darkness with depth, silence, and intuition, the edges toward which life always progresses, the edges beyond which greater understanding of the self may be found.

In this volume, Stafford transcends the boundaries of time and space, of past and future, and explores what he finds in the gaps. He moves beyond what he can see, to listen for what language has to tell him. The poem that gives the volume its title is one of Stafford's most famous works and has been frequently anthologized. It is characteristic of Stafford in that its form and narrative are simple, yet underneath lies more complexity. While driving a mountain road at night, the speaker in the poem comes upon a dead deer. He stops and gets out, confident that he should roll the animal over the edge of the cliff to clear the narrow road for cars that will follow his. As he comes closer and touches the deer, however, he finds that there is an unborn fawn waiting, still alive. The man begins to have doubts about what is the right action. Should he do what might seem to be best on the surface—push the doe over the cliff and avoid further accidents on the road? Or is it possible to save the fawn? If so, would it be the right thing to do? Described with characteristic understatement, the moment of decision is swift: He decides to push her off.

"Traveling Through the Dark" has been read as a poem of conflict between nature and society, symbolized by the car. The speaker clearly sympathizes with the fawn, which "lay there waiting,/ alive, still, never to be born." However, he accepts the forces of technology that caused the problem and realizes that the safety of the next passersby—in cars again—depends on his clearing the road. It has been noted that the personified car, which "aimed ahead its lowered parking lights" and under whose hood "purred the steady engine," is actually the most alive thing in this poem. This may be the ironic voice of a pragmatist who sees nature as something for human beings to use as they please. A more expanded reading, however, would bridge the nature-society dichotomy somewhat by allowing nature to include the car and, by extension, society as well. From such a perspective, the car is both a symbol of death (a significant theme of subject-object unity in Stafford's poetry) and a symbol of life, a part of "our group" in the road. The poem uses the word "swerve" twice. Once the meaning is literal, the anticipated phys-

ical movement of further cars coming upon the carcass in the road. The second time, though, it is the speaker who swerves, and his swerving is internal. Having "thought hard for us all—my only swerving," he makes a decision, but what is he swerving toward, or away from?

It may appear that the speaker's dependence on progress is greater than his ability to control it. Even so, for the moment that he considers saving the fawn, he swerves away from society toward nature. However, perhaps the swerve is in the opposite direction. Perhaps he is swerving from a more simplistic view of nature toward an understanding that encompasses the interests of society within its purview. From his upbringing and especially as a result of his years doing conscientious objector service during World War II, Stafford characteristically considers all sides of his questions. Perhaps the speaker in this poem comes to recognize his own part in the process of the narrative. Is he only the man who finds the dead deer, or does he also bear part of the responsibility for the killing? Underlying the obvious choice to be made—what to do with the deer—may be a suggestion that longing to return to the old ways and escape from society is not really much different from embracing progress without a firm connection with the simplicity and order of nature at its base. There is also the suggestion that Stafford himself may still be making his decisions. When asked about this poem, Stafford responded, "Choices are always Hobson's choices. All you have to do is get a little more alert to see that even your best moves are compromises—and complicated."

The poem does, however, end on an optimistic note. There is still time to prevent further disaster, the speaker decides, and he pushes the doe "over the edge into the river." It is interesting that the poem ends on the image of the river, which, in Stafford's linguistic shorthand, is consistently used as a metaphor for the changing nature of life.

Stafford's voice has been criticized as being simply his real-life "I" speaking normally but in a privileged position, and "Traveling Through the Dark" has been cited as a representative example of the poet firmly in control of all meaning. In refuting this attack, Dick Barnes agrees that Stafford does speak normally, but suggests that artists such as Stafford speak out of a solitude that others can barely imagine, "where the self is dead and the soul opens inward upon eternity. What makes [the artist's] act complete is that, speaking that way, he listens at the same time, and in listening joins any others who may be hearing in a kind of causal communion." Barnes uses "self" here in a relative sense: With death of the self, the individuality that keeps one localized to time and space is no longer restricting the soul.

Stafford, in his wilderness quest, may be in search of something even greater than mere removal of restriction. His death metaphor represents a creative force, a unity of subjectivity and objectivity. A reading of Stafford's work from the perspective of growth of consciousness might suggest that the death of the "self" is first found in the transcendental experience of unbounded awareness that is beyond the limitations of the relative states of consciousness—waking, dreaming, and sleeping. Repeated direct experience of this state of pure consciousness is the basis for the individual's growth toward higher states of consciousness. The "self" rises to the value of the "Self," providing the stable foundation for the eventual unity of subject and object that Stafford is seeking in his poetry.

THE RESCUED YEAR

The Rescued Year was Stafford's second collection with Harper & Row, which—over the years—became his major publisher. It shows a stability of vision, and Stafford has said that he considers this to be his most unified volume. Fourteen of the poems had already appeared in *West of Your City*, and some had been included in Stafford's doctoral dissertation, "Winterward." Others were written at the same time as poems in his earlier volumes. The poems reprinted from *West of Your City* reemphasize Stafford's major interests: home, the quest journey, sound and silence, duality of vision, memory and reality, and the power of the story. One of these reprinted works, "Listening," defines the nature of the father image in Stafford's poems, which has been associated with the more intuitive, deep, unseen values of the wilderness. "My father could hear a little animal step,/ or a moth in the dark against the screen,/ and every far sound called the listening out/ into places where the rest of us had never been." Listening goes beyond seeing. The father understands more

from what he hears in the darkness than the rest of the family could learn from what "came to our porch for us on the wind." The son could watch his father's face change when the understanding came, when "the walls of the world flared, widened." With even this secondary experience of silence, the son was changed. "My father heard so much that we still stand/ inviting the quiet by turning the face." From the father, the son learns to want to hear the sounds of the underlying processes of nature. The son learns patience. In "Listening," the speaker sees little, for little comes to him on the porch, within the familiar. Seeing his father listen, however, he and the other children are inspired to wait "for a time when something in the night/ will touch us too from that other place." They are waiting to be able to hear the silence themselves. This sequence of seeing, touching, and listening is reminiscent of "Traveling Through the Dark," as the speaker first sees the doe, then touches her warm side, and then hears the wilderness listening. Learning from his father, as a representative of deeper levels of reality, is a theme in many of Stafford's poems.

Over a third of the poems in *The Rescued Year* deal with Stafford's boyhood and a Kansas setting. "Across Kansas" tells of traveling through the night as his family sleeps. Driving past the town where he was born, the speaker says, "I drove down an aisle of sound," locating his sense of memory and reality within the sense of hearing. Once he has this experience of sound, even what he sees has more meaning. The speaker "owns" his face more, and he sees his self in everything that the light strikes. Again, as in many poems, the last line is telling: "My state still dark, my dream too long to tell." The traveling is through a darkness much deeper than the Kansas night.

Stafford's imagination creates the story of his reality in much of this volume, yet the collection also focuses on more contemporary issues, as in the long poem "Following the Markings of Dag Hammarskjöld: A Gathering of Poems in the Spirit of His Life and Writings." Some critics have objected to this new subject matter. Considering the confusing time in which this collection was published, however, even Stafford's warnings in such poems as "At the Bomb Test Site" seem gentle.

ALLEGIANCES

With publication of *Allegiances*, critics and scholars started to ask for more discrimination, for Stafford to publish only his best work. Then as now, however, Stafford preferred to let the reader decide what was good. In this volume, his allegiances are generally to people, places, and objects from the rural plains. Stafford suggests that truth is inherent in the common things, if one goes deep enough. His real hero is the common man. In "Allegiances," he says, "It is time for all the heroes to go home/ if they have any, time for all of us common ones/ to locate ourselves by the real things/ we live by." He describes the journey to taste "far streams" where one can touch gold and "come back, changed/ but safe, quiet, grateful." Some have criticized this volume for a sort of blurred perspective that reflects less connection between Stafford's inner and outer lives. Some poems in *Allegiances* do deal with the social and political climate at the time—the assassination of Martin Luther King, Jr., bombings, television news, and the like—but the volume is hardly overtly revolutionary. What it does seem to suggest is that, at a precarious time in the world, Stafford had come to expect moral guidance from himself and other serious writers.

SOMEDAY, MAYBE

The first poem in *Someday, Maybe*, "An Introduction to Some Poems," suggests that this volume will take a changed direction. It begins, "Look: no one ever promised for sure/ that we would sing. We have decided/ to moan." The speaker—clearly Stafford—expresses disillusionment. He is trying to turn his dreams into stories to give them strength. He suggests that the reader should do that too, "and hold them close at you, close at the/ edge we share, to be right." Many of the stories are based on Indian legends, or legends that Stafford fashions. These, perhaps, may offer some direction from a time when people were more in touch with nature than they were in the early 1970's. Though Stafford does not use poetry directly as a political vehicle, his concerns are underlying, and he searches into language for a way of dispelling his doubts about the world. In "After That Sound, After That Sight," the speaker says that "after that sound, we weren't people anymore," and "we are afraid to listen." This is not the optimistic Stafford readers had come to expect. However, poetry—language—is reliable. In "Report from a Far Place," Stafford says words are "snowshoes" with which he can still step across the world. They "creak, sag, bend, but/ hold," and "in war or city or camp/ they could save your life." He thus invites others to follow their tracks.

STORIES THAT COULD BE TRUE

Stories That Could Be True: New and Collected Poems lets critics and scholars see Stafford's work to that date as a whole. The new poems, such as "Song Now," tell the story of the speaker who returns from a far place, from both "Before" and "After," to find a home in the present, where "silence puts a paw/ wherever the music rests." The poem concludes, "Guitar string is:/ it can save this place." Despite growing disillusionment over the changes that were occurring in American society, Stafford continued to seek a reintegration in this volume. With a growing acceptance of death—a significant theme—comes an awareness of the primacy of the present and the desire to live it. The stories are put before the readers not so that they can come to know them in themselves, but so that they can, perhaps, come to know their own stories better. The meaning of the story, for Stafford, is in its telling.

A GLASS FACE IN THE RAIN

In *A Glass Face in the Rain*, Stafford brings the process of storytelling, the process of writing, to the forefront. In his dedication poem, he says that the volume is intended for everyone, but especially for those on a "parallel way." These are the people readers do not see often, he says, or even think of often, "but it is precious to us that they are sharing/ the world." This volume was published after *Things That Happen Where There Aren't Any People*, a collection of more impersonal poems that focus on nature without human presence. Here, once again, however, Stafford's poems are grounded in the world of humanity. In "Glimpses," the speaker is definitely in the present, and his presence there matters. "My debt to the world begins again," he says, "that I am part of this permanent dream." Stafford's part of the dream of life is to write poems. This collection continues to develop his acceptance of his own death, considering a future world that he will not be alive to see. Stafford expanded his desire to be part of the process, and in this volume, he wants to communicate. In "Tuned In Late One Night," the speaker begins, "Listen—this is a faint station/ left alive in the vast universe./ I was left here to tell you a message." In "A Message from Space," he is trying to hear a message from the heavens, but when the message comes, it is surprising. "Everything counts," it says. "The message is the world."

AN OREGON MESSAGE

In 1987, Stafford published a seventh volume with Harper & Row, *An Oregon Message*. By this time, the message had become explicit, and Stafford wanted the reader on his side. For the first time, he added a preface to a volume of his poetry, preceding the poems with a brief prose explanation of his writing process, "Some Notes on Writing." In it, he says that "it is my habit to allow language its own freedom and confidence" even though such poems may bewilder readers who "try to control all emergent elements in discourse for the service of predetermined ends." He continues, "I must be willingly fallible in order to deserve a place in the realm where miracles happen." Stafford is, by extension, inviting the reader, too, to deserve a place in the miracle.

People and places from Stafford's past again figure prominently in this volume. He seems to be taking stock of them in a new way, though, seeking deeper integration than before. He blends the past, present, and future, and a sense of playfulness emerges. In "Thinking About Being Called Simple by a Critic," Stafford alludes to William Carlos Williams's plum poem in his first line, "I wanted the plums, but I waited." While he waits, he hears the echo of a critic who said "how stupid I was." As Stafford probes the truth of these words, he starts to enjoy them and decides that the critic must be a friend: "Who but a friend/ could give so sternly what the sky/ feels for everyone but few learn to/ cherish?" Stafford feels rightly put in his place—and delights in it. He goes to the refrigerator, opens it, sees that "sure enough the light was on," and reaches in to get the plums.

There is also a didactic tone in this volume. Stafford is ready to tell what he has been hearing in the silence all these years. In "Lie Detector," he says that the heart proclaims "the truth all the time, hidden but always/ there," because it is "acting the self, helplessly true." He concludes the poem in a celebration of the present: "At night, no one else near, you walk/ . . . your heart marching along/ with you, saying, 'Now,' saying, 'Yes,'/ saying, 'Here.'" The last poem in the collection, "Maybe Alone on My Bike," is representative of Stafford's blending of the serious and the playful. As he rides home ("maybe alone"), he says, "I listen," and reflects back at the distance he has traveled, thinking of the splendor and marvels of life as it reveals itself. He intones, "O citizens of our great amnesty:/ we might have died. We live," but then comes back to concrete narrative with his concluding line: "and I hear in the [bicycle] chain a chuckle I like to hear." Stafford is still listening, he is still finding meaning, and what was quiet bliss is now bubbling up to the surface as delight.

PASSWORDS

Delight extends into Stafford's eighth collection with a major publisher, *Passwords*. These poems from the heart invite the reader to continue to make serendipitous discoveries through language, memory, and feeling.

LEGACY

Stafford wrote in the same voice all his life. Critics generally consider him to be a poet of place or a poet of myths. However, he created his own myths, and he was at home everywhere. He said that the crucial parts of writing have to do with what is shared by human beings rather than their superficial differences. By exploring the great diversity the world has to offer, Stafford glimpsed a unified vision of nature at its depths. Resting on an undercurrent of optimism, he unfolded this field of all possibilities, locating playfulness in the serious, imagination in the practical, profundity in the commonplace. In doing so, he took the chance of being misunderstood, but that is part of the way he viewed the process of writing. Though he seemed to be giving messages to his readers, Stafford was simply inviting them to find their own way. He said that he preferred not to assert his poems, but to have them "climb toward the reader without my proclaiming anything." He hoped that "sometimes for every reader a poem would arrive: it would go out for him, and find his life."

OTHER MAJOR WORKS

NONFICTION: *Down in My Heart*, 1947; *Friends to This Ground: A Statement for Readers, Teachers, and Writers of Literature*, 1967; *Leftovers, A Care Package: Two Lectures*, 1973; *Writing the Australian Crawl: Views on the Writer's Vocation*, 1978; *You Must Revise Your Life*, 1986; *Writing the World*, 1988; *The Answers Are Inside the Mountains: Meditations on the Writing Life*, 2003 (Paul Merchant and Vincent Wixon, editors); *Every War Has Two Losers: William Stafford on Peace and War*, 2003 (Kim Stafford, editor).

EDITED TEXTS: *The Voices of Prose*, 1966 (with Frederick Caudelaria); *The Achievement of Brother Antonius: A Comprehensive Selection of His Poems with a Critical Introduction*, 1967; *Poems and Perspectives*, 1971 (with Robert H. Ross); *Modern Poetry of Western America*, 1975 (with Clinton F. Larson).

BIBLIOGRAPHY

Andrews, Tom, ed. *On William Stafford: The Worth of Local Things*. Ann Arbor: University of Michigan Press, 1993. Presents an assortment of more than fifty mostly (but not wholly) complimentary essays on Stafford's poetry and prose. Overall, they rank Stafford among the best American poets. Important historical analogies are proposed, favorably comparing his subject matter, voice, and vision to those of poets such as Walt Whitman and Robert Frost. There is enough hard criticism, especially regarding the occasional flatness of Stafford's style, to allow the reader to share in the debate.

Holden, Jonathan. *The Mark to Turn*. Lawrence: University Press of Kansas, 1976. This volume, the first book-length study of Stafford's work, is a useful overview of his major themes and technique. Holden focuses his close readings on poems from Stafford's first published collection and the four collections with his major publisher that followed. The ninety-one-page study includes a biography.

Kitchen, Judith. *Writing the World: Understanding William Stafford*. Corvallis: Oregon State University Press, 1999. This comprehensive volume is accessible for the student as well as the good nonacademic reader. In addition to a short biography and overview of Stafford's work, it presents detailed analysis of seven of Stafford's major collections and also considers his chapbooks and distinguished small-press editions. This 175-page work concludes with a detailed bibliography of primary and secondary sources.

Nordstrom, Lars. "A William Stafford Bibliography." *Studia Neophilologica* 59 (1987): 59-63. Although it is difficult to assemble an exhaustive bibliography because Stafford published frequently with small presses, this relatively complete one includes both primary and secondary sources. In addition to prose and poetry collections, it lists critical studies, symposia, interviews, doctoral dissertations, film, and reference materials.

Pinsker, Sanford. "William Stafford: 'The Real Things We Live By.'" In *Three Pacific Northwest Poets*. Boston: Twayne, 1987. This chapter begins with a biographical sketch and then unfolds a book-by-book analysis of six of Stafford's collections, offering close readings of representative poems to support more general conclusions. It includes a selected bibliography.

Stafford, Kim. *Early Morning: Remembering My Father, William Stafford*. St. Paul, Minn.: Graywolf Press, 2002. The title of this memoir by the poet's daughter refers to her father's habit of writing poetry in the early morning. Kim Stafford used her recollections and her father's papers to create a memoir that reveals the man behind the poetry.

Stitt, Peter. "William Stafford's Wilderness Quest." In *The World, Hieroglyphic Beauty: Five American Poets*. Athens: University of Georgia Press, 1985. This excellent chapter develops Stafford as a "wisdom poet" and explores his process-rather-than-substance view of writing. It includes an interview with Stafford originally conducted at his home in 1976 and updated in 1981 at the Bread Loaf Writers' Conference.

Jean C. Fulton

TIMOTHY STEELE

Born: Burlington, Vermont; January 22, 1948

PRINCIPAL POETRY

Uncertainties and Rest, 1979
The Prudent Heart, 1983
Nine Poems, 1984
On Harmony, 1984
Short Subjects, 1985
Sapphics Against Anger, and Other Poems,
    1986
Beatitudes, 1988
The Color Wheel, 1994
Sapphics and Uncertainties: Poems, 1970-1986,
    1995
Toward the Winter Solstice, 2006

OTHER LITERARY FORMS

Although Timothy Steele rarely reviews books, he is one of the leading prosodists of his generation. In *Missing Measures: Modern Poetry and the Revolt Against Meter* (1990), Steele discusses the flawed historical assumptions behind much of the modernist poetry. His knowledge of both classical and romance languages and literature serves him well here. In a quotation for the book, X. J. Kennedy writes that "Steele's arguments strike me as so forceful, so well thought through, that anyone who assails them will find the going difficult." This has proven all too true as the critical establishment has found it in its own best interests to ignore Steele's argument rather than attempt its refutation.

Steele has also published a book of prosody, *All the Fun's in How You Say a Thing* (1999), which not only is a good introduction to poetics but also helps dispel many modernist assumptions. He makes an excellent case that, regardless of T. S. Eliot's contentions, the iambic measure is alive because of variations within the meter rather than those caused by the breaking of the meter. In addition, Steele makes a persuasive argument for the near nonexistence of the Pyrrhus and spondee in English-language poetry.

ACHIEVEMENTS

Timothy Steele is probably the leading poet-scholar of the New Formalist movement, though he is not its best-known exponent. He is a modest man of very little self-promotion, but the learning displayed in *Missing Measures* shows him to be a scholar of the first rank.

Nonetheless, his poetry has gained considerable attention. Steele is the recipient of a Guggenheim Fellowship (1984-1985), the Peter I. B. Lavan Younger Poets Award of the Academy of American Poets (1986), the Commonwealth Club of California Silver Medal (1986), the Los Angeles PEN Center Literary Award for Poetry (1987), the Elizabeth Matchett Stover Award (2002) from *Southwest Review*, and the Robert Fitzgerald Award for Excellence in the Study of Prosody (2004). He has also won a California Arts Council Grant (1993), as well as the California State University, Los Angeles, Outstanding Professor Award in 1992 and the school's President's Distinguished Professor Award in 1998-1999.

BIOGRAPHY

Timothy Reid Steele was born in Burlington, Vermont, in 1948 to Edward William Steele, a teacher, and Ruth Reid Steele, a nurse. His New England upbringing is readily apparent in many of his poems, despite the fact that he has spent most of his writing life far removed from the Northeast, though Southern California, where Steele lived for several years, also plays a prominent role in his writing.

Steele left Vermont to study at Stanford University, earning his B.A. in 1970. It was at Stanford that Steele came under the influence of Yvor Winters, who reinforced his formalist inclinations. Returning to New England for graduate work at Brandeis University, Steele worked with another important Formalist scholar, J. V. Cunningham. Cunningham's concision and love for the epigram show a real influence on Steele's development, though Steele's dissertation at Brandeis was on the history and conventions of detective fiction. He was awarded his M.A. (1972) and Ph.D. (1977) from Brandeis. He offered to take over *Counter/Measures*, a magazine published by X. J. Kennedy and Dorothy Kennedy, which was one of the few periodicals in the country publishing formal verse at the time and was going out of business. Kennedy urged Steele to instead concentrate on his own work.

While working on his dissertation, Steele crossed the country yet again, returning to Stanford as Jones Lecturer in Poetry from 1975 to 1977. Upon completion of his Ph.D., he assumed a lectureship in English at the University of California, Los Angeles (UCLA) until 1983; in 1979, he married Victoria Lee Erpelding, a librarian of rare books at UCLA, and published his first full-length collection, *Uncertainties and Rest* from Louisiana State University Press, which was a strong debut but attracted little attention. In 1986, Steele took a one-year position as lecturer in English at the University of California, Santa Barbara, and published his second major collection, *Sapphics Against Anger, and Other Poems*; this collection received much more attention than the first, partly because it was from a major publisher, Random House. In 1987, he became professor of English at California State University, Los Angeles, eventually becoming one of the school's most distinguished and honored professors.

In 1990, Steele published one of the major critical works of the late twentieth century, *Missing Measures*. Steele examines the critical and historical assumptions of modernism and finds them flawed; classic, medieval, and Renaissance texts were mistakenly conflated, leading to major misunderstandings in scholarship. One particular strand he traces shows how the words "poetry" and "verse" came to be construed as meaning different things; he also traces the dangers inherent in modernism's fascination with poetry as music. Overall, Steele makes a sustained argument that modernism is a failed revolution that has resulted not in new forms but in the formlessness and inwardness plaguing much poetry today, particularly academic poetry. Steele's wide reading and facility in several languages reveal a first-rate critical mind at work.

In 1994, Steele published his next full-length collection, *The Color Wheel*, from The Johns Hopkins University Press; the following year, University of Arkansas Press brought out *Sapphics and Uncertainties: Poems, 1970-1986*, a compilation of Steele's first two major books. In 1997, Steele edited *The Poems of J. V. Cunningham*, an impressive work of scholarship

whose notes and comments threaten to dwarf the rather slender body of poetry. In 1999, Steele published a book of prosody, *All the Fun's in How You Say a Thing*, the title of which was taken from a poem of Robert Frost.

ANALYSIS

Timothy Steele is the most formal of the major poets associated with New Formalism. While rhyme and meter are common to these poets, Steele works in more ornate stanzaic patterns than most of his contemporaries. Many New Formalists prefer the term expansive poetry, because a return to storytelling is emphasized as much as a return to traditional forms. Steele, however, seems strictly a lyric poet, more likely to write an epigram than an epic.

UNCERTAINTIES AND REST

The wonder of Steele's first collection, *Uncertainties and Rest*, is not how little attention it received at its time of publication despite its quality but the fact that it was published at all. It was the first book of formal verse to be published by a national press for anyone of Steele's generation. By the time other New Formalists were publishing their first books in the mid-1980's, Steele was publishing his second.

The tone of *Uncertainties and Rest*, its title a subtle reference to meter, can be uneven at times, but what comes through clearly is a formally trained voice dealing with matters of the moment. The Kansas in "Over the Rainbow" is not the Kansas of Judy Garland: "At the weigh stations,/ The trucks rev up. All roads and cultures end/ In time and space, and all destinations/ In mere convenience." Then there is the country bar in the Everglades where "At ten of eight, two whores in fine array/ Arrive, and the farmhands start closing in," from "Two for the Road." However, such gritty, slightly tawdry realism does not dominate the volume, and it all but disappears from Steele's subsequent poetry. There are several poems of family and youth here, and from the beginning, Steele has displayed a finely tuned eye for the natural world.

There are also some strong love lyrics here, probably representing some of the later work in the collection, an example of which is "Last Night as You Slept":

The clock's dial a luminous two-ten,
Its faint glow on pillow and sheet,
I woke—and the good fatigue and heat
We'd shared were gone.

Steele also includes epigrams, one of which has been widely anthologized: "Here lies Sir Tact, a diplomatic fellow/ Whose silence was not golden, but just yellow."

SAPPHICS AGAINST ANGER, AND OTHER POEMS

The choice of the title poem for *Sapphics Against Anger, and Other Poems* was appropriate for Steele in at least two ways. For one, the mention of a classical form, of which W. H. Auden was a master, announces that this is a book of formal concerns. Second, it speaks for the spirit of the poems, wherein the voice is restrained and often praiseful; indeed, the title poem ends,

> For what is, after all, the good life save that
> Conducted thoughtfully, and what is passion
> If not the holiest of powers, sustaining
> Only if mastered.

Such might be taken as a good synopsis of Steele's aesthetic. In "The Sheets," the speaker ponders the clean laundry on the line, which leads to biographer Giorgio Vasari's tale of Leonardo da Vinci's buying caged birds and setting them free and on to a childhood memory. "Near Olympic" describes an ethnically mixed neighborhood in West Los Angeles in great detail through the use of rhymed couplets. Despite the use of a form most prominent in the eighteenth century, there is nothing artificial in Steele's use of the measure, nor is the poem in any way condescending to its subject matter. The poem is composed in such a loving fashion as to say these nameless people matter.

"Timothy" calls attention to the fact that the poet shares a name with the hay he's mowing: "And I took pleasure in the thought/ The fresh hay's name was mine as well." This close identification reaches a moment of epiphany at the end of the poem. Work done,

> . . . the grass, which seemed a thing
> In which the lonely and concealed
> Had risen from its sorrowing
> And flourished in the open field.

There are also poems from a general history as well as a personal one: among others, "The Wartburg, 1521-22," Wartburg being where Martin Luther hid after the Diet of Worms, which marks the role one man played in the formation of the modern religious consciousness. When Luther at last leaves, "His mount's as humble as the mount of Christ" and "above the Schloss,/ A widening band of chimney smoke is curled/ Vaguely downward, toward the modern world."

More and more in *Sapphics Against Anger, and Other Poems*, the California landscape starts to demand equal time with that of New England; Steele seems more and more transplanted rather than transported. Although still a New Englander, he sees much to praise in the abundance of Southern California.

THE COLOR WHEEL

Although considerable development of the poet is evident between *Uncertainties and Rest* and *Sapphics Against Anger, and Other Poems*, the progression from the latter volume to *The Color Wheel* seems much less pronounced. This is, to some extent, to be expected, a matter of a poet hitting his stride in his maturity. Steele has not taken the next step to greatness in this collection, but it does confirm him as one of the best and most skillful contemporary poets.

Mixed in with New England memories of childhood are poems distinctly displaying lives of Southern Californians, including Steele's eighty-two-year-old neighbor to whom he brings flowers ("Fae"), and a forty-two-year-old punch-drunk failed boxer ("Cory in April"). Civilization as something precious and fragile is a continued theme in Steele's work, notably here in "The Library." The speaker wants a tidy metaphor but rejects its easiness: "I could construct a weighty paradigm,/ The Library as Mind. It's somehow truer/ To recollect details of closing time." After further meditation, the speaker leaves the library and notes how "The squirrel creeps, nosing round, compelled to hoard/ By instinct, habit and necessity." Once again the reader is made aware of the closeness of the human and the natural world in many of Steele's poems.

Few, if any, other poets could write a poem with a title such as "Beatitudes, While Setting Out the Trash" and make it believable. Steele does, partly through the grace of his versification and partly through humor: "A squirrel on the lawn rears and inspects/ A berry in its paws and seems to hold/ The pose of a Tyrannosaurus Rex." The speaker, after putting the trash on the curb, sticks his hands into his sweatshirt pockets and refers to himself as a "mammal cousin of the kangaroo" and closes the poem describing a bird:

> He grooms, by nuzzling, a raised underwing;
> He shakes and sends a shiver through his breast,
> As if, from where he perches, counseling
> That *Blessed are the meek*, for they are blest.

From poems such as this, Timothy Steele has taken his place not only as the craftsperson of his generation of poets but also as its chief envoy of sanity and demeanor.

TOWARD THE WINTER SOLSTICE

Toward the Winter Solstice is the finely nuanced work of a mature poet of sweeping vision who places hope-inspiring emphasis on the relationships among all things. Unlike earlier volumes, though, this one is pervaded by a deeper, quieter questioning.

"*Didelphis Virginiana*" is typical of Steele's sensitivity, wit, and learning. Taking the unlikely subject of a opossum killed in a crosswalk, the speaker contemplates both motorists' and nature's indifference to the loss of this creature. As befitting an epic hero, the opossum, "nemesis of snails," is buried with honor and a prayer for its afterlife: "And if opossums have Elysium,/ May this one's spirit be already there,/ Shyly approaching and conversing with/ Illustrious figures in its species' history."

The poignant extended metaphor and ode "The Sweet Peas" is another wish for a happy afterlife and a reflection on the impressions that lives leave. An elderly neighbor dying of a brain tumor calls to say how beautiful she finds the speaker's sweet peas. Although the sweet pea season has long since passed at the time the neighbor calls, the speaker kindly agrees. That phone call begins an annual rite of planting sweet peas and a "sometimes hope" that the neighbor was able to retain in the afterlife "The urge to complication and ascent/ Which prints such fresh, bright signatures on air/ That they are read when they're no longer there."

In the collection's title poem, "Toward the Winter Solstice," the speaker muses from the rooftop where he is stringing Christmas lights that regardless of their diverse religious beliefs, he and his neighbors share, as did their ancestors, an appreciation for festivals that mitigate the cold and darkness of winter. Extending further the unifying idea of Christmas as a celebration of and toward the winter solstice, the speaker concludes his contemplation on planes of space and time:

> It's comforting to look up from this roof
> And feel that, while all changes, nothing's lost,
> To recollect that in antiquity
> The winter solstice fell in Capricorn
> And that, in the Orion Nebula,
> From swirling gas, new stars are being born

The thought that civilization may have passed the point of no return is most clearly stated in "April 27, 1937." Using satire written in heroic couplets (the literary weaponry of the preindustrial eighteenth century), Steele traces the application of General Erich Ludendorff's idea of "total war" through World War II and the Vietnam War. Having crossed the line separating military from civilian targets, Steele warns, "We'll reap the whirlwind, who have sown the wind."

If the volume conveys sadness, it is not despairing. In "Yellow Birches," Steele's response to Frost's "Birches," the speaker renounces the easy, visible beauty of Frost's tree for the subtler beauties of the tenacious yellow birch, at once acknowledging his New England roots and demonstrating that his own roots have flourished in California soil. Hope lies in the tenacity of life and the honoring of roots and interconnections. Deceptively simple in diction and emotionally intense, this volume is the richest and most far-reaching of Steele's canon.

OTHER MAJOR WORKS

NONFICTION: *Missing Measures: Modern Poetry and the Revolt Against Meter*, 1990; *All the Fun's in How You Say a Thing*, 1999; *Three Poets in Conversation: Dick Davis, Rachel Hadas, Timothy Steele*, 2007 (with Dick Davis and Rachel Hadas).

EDITED TEXTS: *The Music of His History: Poems for Charles Gullens on His Sixtieth Birthday*, 1989; *The Poems of J. V. Cunningham*, 1997.

BIBLIOGRAPHY

Crosscurrents: A Quarterly 8, no. 2. Special issue titled "Expansionist Poetry: The New Formalism and the New Narrative." This groundbreaking issue on the expansive movement includes many essays essential to understanding that movement and Steele. Steele contributes two poems, "Decisions, Decisions" and "Practice," while taking part in the symposium that forms the center of the issue. A good format to sense Steele's interactions with his peers in the movement.

Feirstein, Frederick, ed. *Expansive Poetry: Essays on the New Narrative and the New Formalism.* Ashland, Oreg.: Story Line Press, 1989. Collection includes Steele's essay "Tradition and Revolution: The Modern Movement and Free Verse," which is an excellent telescoping of the larger argument Steele makes in *Missing Measures.* This collection also includes other perspectives on the New Formalist movement, many of which offer insight into poet Dana Gioia's aesthetic.

McPhillips, Robert. "Reading the New Formalists." In *Poetry After Modernism*, edited by Robert McDowell. Ashland, Oreg.: Story Line Press, 1991. McPhillips deals with several New Formalist poets, prominently featuring Steele, and their relationships to one another and to their craft. This volume is also helpful as a general guide to the New Formalist movement, of which Steele is a prominent practitioner.

Steele, Timothy. "Timothy Steele: An Interview." Interview by Kevin Walzer. *Edge City Review* 2, no. 2 (1996). An in-depth interview with Steele covering his career through 1995. Steele comments on his influences, criticisms of *Missing Measures*, and New Formalism in general.

_____. "Timothy Steele Interview." Interview by Cynthia Haven. *Cortland Review*, June 15, 2001. Steele touches on metrical poetry, New Formalism, and Walt Whitman, with an emphasis on his desire to keep the metrical tradition alive and understandable to new readers.

_____. "Welcome to Timothy Steele's Homepage." http://instructional1.calstatela.edu/tsteele/. The poet's official Web site provides an introduction to the poet, career summary, selected bibliography of works about the poet, audio clips, an introduction to meter and form, and a look at *All the Fun's in How You Say a Thing*.

Robert Darling
Updated by Daryl Holmes

GERTRUDE STEIN

Born: Allegheny (now in Pittsburgh), Pennsylvania; February 3, 1874
Died: Neuilly-sur-Seine, France; July 27, 1946

PRINCIPAL POETRY

Tender Buttons: Objects, Food, Rooms, 1914
Before the Flowers of Friendship Faded Friendship Faded, 1931
Two (Hitherto Unpublished) Poems, 1948
Bee Time Vine, and Other Pieces, 1913-1927, 1953
Stanzas in Meditation, and Other Poems, 1929-1933, 1956

OTHER LITERARY FORMS

Most of Gertrude Stein's works did not appear until much later than the dates of their completion. Much of her writing, including novelettes, shorter poems, plays, prayers, novels, and several portraits, appeared posthumously in the Yale Edition of the Unpublished Writings of Gertrude Stein, in eight volumes edited by Carl Van Vechten. A few of her plays have been set to music, the operas have been performed, and the later children's books have been illustrated by various artists.

ACHIEVEMENTS

Gertrude Stein did not win tangible recognition for her literary achievements, though she did earn the Medal of French Recognition from the French government for services during World War II. Nevertheless, her contribution to art, and specifically to writing, is as great as that of Ezra Pound or James Joyce. It is, however, diametrically opposed to that of these figures in style, content, and underlying philosophy of literature.

Gertrude Stein (Library of Congress)

She advanced mimetic representation to its ultimate, doing away progressively with memory, narration, plot, the strictures of formalized language, and the distinction among styles and genres. Her view of life was founded on a sense of the living present that shunned all theorizing about meaning and purpose, making writing a supreme experience unto itself. For the first fifteen years of her artistic life, she worked at her craft with stubborn persistence while carrying on an active social life among the Parisian avant-garde. She became influential as a person of definite taste and idiosyncratic manners rather than as an artist in her own right. Her parlor became legend, and writers as diverse as Ernest Hemingway and Sherwood Anderson profited from her ideas. In the 1920's, she was the matron of the American expatriates, and her work, by then known to most writers, was either ferociously derided or enthusiastically applauded.

It was the poetry of *Tender Buttons* that first brought Gertrude Stein to the attention of the public. After 1926, however, her novels, critical essays, and prose portraits increasingly circulated. She secured a place in American letters with the publication of *The Autobiography of Alice B. Toklas* (1933), which was also a commercial success. She did not receive any official recognition during her lifetime, except as a curiosity in the world of letters.

Literary criticism has traditionally simply skirted the "problem" of Gertrude Stein, limiting itself to broad generalizations. There exists a group of Stein devotees responsible for preserving the texts; this group includes Robert Bartlett Haas, Carl Van Vechten, Donald Gallup, and Leon Katz. Stein's work has been illuminated by two indispensable scholar-critics, Richard Bridgman and Donald Sutherland; and there are useful interpretive suggestions in studies by Rosalind Miller, Allegra Stewart, Norman Weinstein, and Michael J. Hoffman. Stein's major impact has been on writers of later generations, especially in the late 1950's, through the 1960's, and up to the present time; the poetry of Aram Saroyan, Robert Kelly, Clark Coolidge, Jerome Rothenberg, and Lewis Welch is especially indebted to Stein. New insights into this revolutionary writer in the wake of global revisions of the notion of writing and critical thinking have been offered in short pieces by S. C. Neuman, William H. Gass, and Neil Schmitz. Today, a place of eminence is accorded to Stein's fairy tales and children's stories, the theoretical writings, the major works *The Autobiography of Alice B. Toklas* and *The Making of Americans: Being a History of a Family's Progress* (1925, 1934), the shorter works *Three Lives* (1909) and *Ida, a Novel* (1941), and finally *Tender Buttons*, considered by many to be a masterpiece of twentieth century literature.

BIOGRAPHY

Gertrude Stein was born in Allegheny, Pennsylvania, on February 3, 1874. Her grandfather, Michael Stein, came from Austria in 1841, married Hanna Seliger, and settled in Baltimore. One of his sons, Daniel, Gertrude's father, was in the wholesale wool and clothing industry. Daniel was mildly successful and very temperamental. He married Amelia Keyser in 1864 and had five children, Michael (born in 1865), Simon (1867), Bertha (1870), Leo (1872), and Gertrude (1874). In 1875, the family moved to Vienna, and three years later, Daniel returned to the United States, leaving his family for a one-year stay in Paris. In 1879, the family moved back to the United States and spent a year in Baltimore with Amelia Keyser's family. In 1880, Daniel found work in California, and the family relocated again, to Oakland. Memories of these early moves would dot Gertrude's mature works. Leo and Gertrude found that they had much in common, took drawing and music lessons together, frequented the Oakland and San Francisco public libraries, and had time to devote to their intellectual and aesthetic interests. When their mother died of cancer in 1888, Leo and Gertrude found themselves more and more detached from the rest of the family. In 1892, Daniel Stein died, and the eldest son, Michael, took the family back to Baltimore, but the Steins began to scatter. In 1892, Leo entered Harvard, while Gertrude and Bertha stayed with their aunt, Fannie Bachrach. Michael, always patriarchal and the image of stability, married Sarah Samuels and later moved to Paris, where he became a respected member of the intellectual elite, maintaining a Saturday night open house at their apartment in rue Madame. Matisse's portrait of Michael is now in San Francisco.

Gertrude was a coddled and protected child. At sixteen, she weighed 135 pounds, and later in college she hired a boy to box with her every day to help her lose weight. Her niece, Gertrude Stein Raffel, recalls that her heaviness "was not unbecoming. She was round, roly-poly, and angelic looking." During her adolescent years, she became very introspective and critical, and was often depressed and concerned with death. Already emotionally independent, owing to her mother's protracted invalidism and her father's neglect and false representation of authority, Gertrude saw in her brother Leo her only friend. Their bond would not be broken for another twenty years, and she would follow him everywhere, the two delving into matters of mutual interest.

In 1893, Gertrude Stein entered the Harvard Annex, renamed Radcliffe College the following year. She gravitated toward philosophy and psychology, and took courses with such luminaries as George Santayana, Josiah Royce, Herbert Palmer, and William James. In 1894, she worked in the Harvard Psychological Laboratory with Hugo Münsterberg. Her interest in psychol-

ogy expanded, and in 1896, she published, together with Leon Solomons, a paper on "Normal Motor Automatism," which appeared in the *Psychological Review*. A second article, "Cultivated Motor Automatism," appeared two years later. In 1897, Stein followed her brother to The Johns Hopkins University and began the study of medicine. She specialized in brain research and was encouraged to continue, even though by 1901 her dedication had waned. She attempted four examinations, failed them, and withdrew without a degree.

In 1902, Stein began her travels, first to Italy and then to London, where she met philosopher Bertrand Russell. She spent much time in the British Museum Library studying the Elizabethans, especially William Shakespeare. In the meantime, Leo also abandoned his studies, reverting to an earlier passion for history. A specialist in Renaissance costume, he was drawn to contemporary art, and when, in 1904, he and his sister saw a Paul Cézanne exhibit in Florence, they started buying paintings; Leo would became a major collector of Henri Matisse. The two settled in the now-famous apartment at 27 rue de Fleurus, where Gertrude's literary career began, though her first sustained effort, *Q.E.D.*, written in 1903, remained unpublished until 1950 (as *Things as They Are*). In 1905, while working on a translation of Gustave Flaubert's *Trois contes*, she wrote *Three Lives*. During that period, she met Pablo Picasso, who would be very influential in her thinking about art and with whom she would remain friends for decades. The following year, he painted the famous portrait now at the Metropolitan Museum. These days of intense work and thinking saw Stein fast at work on her first major long novel, *The Making of Americans*, which she completed in 1910.

Gertrude's trips abroad and throughout France from her home base in Paris became an essential part of her existence. In 1907, her brother Michael introduced her to Alice B. Toklas, who soon became her secretary, going to work on the proofs of *Three Lives*. Toklas learned to use a typewriter, and the following year, in Fiesole, Italy, she began to copy parts of the manuscript of *The Making of Americans*. Leo, intellectually independent, was moving toward his own aesthetic, though he was still busy promoting new American and French talents. As a painter, Leo was not successful, and he came eventually to dislike all contemporary painters except the cubists. In 1913, he moved from the rue de Fleurus apartment, and with him went all the Renoirs and most of the Matisses and Cézannes, while Gertrude kept the Picassos. Leo's place had been taken by Toklas, who stayed with Gertrude until her death in 1946.

The writer first began to be noticed as a result of Alfred Stieglitz's publication of her "portraits" of Matisse and Picasso in *Camera Work* in 1912. She spent the summer of that year in Spain, capturing the sense of her idea of the relationship between object and space, with which she had been struggling. Here she began the prose poem *Tender Buttons*, which brought her to the attention of most of her contemporaries, eliciting varying reactions. She continued to write "portraits" while visiting Mabel Dodge in Florence, at the Villa Curonia. At the Armory Show in New York in 1913, Stein was responsible for the presentation of the Pablo Picasso exhibit. When the war broke out, she was in London, where she met the philosopher Alfred North Whitehead. She continued to work intensely, mostly on poetry and plays, and visited Barcelona and Palma de Majorca. In 1916, Stein and Toklas returned to France and the next year did voluntary war relief work in the south. In 1922, Stein was awarded a Medaille de la Reconnaissance Française.

With the appearance of her first collected volume, *Geography and Plays*, in 1922, Stein's fame among the cognoscenti was assured, together with a lively controversy over her truly original style. She was invariably visited by the younger expatriate artists from the United States, and her parlor became a focal point for the exchange of ideas. Sherwood Anderson introduced her to Hemingway in 1922, and the younger writer learned much from her about the craft of writing. Hemingway was influential in securing publication of parts of *The Making of Americans* in Ford Madox Ford's magazine, *Transatlantic Review*. (The nine-hundred-page work was later abridged to half its size by her translator into French, and the shorter version was published in 1925 by Contact Editions, Paris.) Her relationship with Hemingway, however, because of conflicting temperaments, was short-lived; their friendship soon degenerated into bickering.

Stein entered another phase of her life when she was asked to lecture in Oxford and Cambridge in 1926. The text of the conference, "Composition as Explanation," constituted her first critical statement on the art of writing; she subsequently returned to a personal exposition of her ideas in *How to Write* (1931), breaking new ground at the stylistic level. This period of major intellectual and thematic upheaval witnessed several transformations in her art. She began to devote more time to the theater and eventually tackled the difficult task of writing about ideas in the little known *Stanzas in Meditation, and Other Poems, 1929-1933* (not published until 1956). In 1929, she left Paris and moved to Bilignin. Her *Lucy Church Amiably* (1930) had not pleased her, but *Four Saints in Three Acts* (pr., pb. 1934), with music by Virgil Thomson, was successfully produced in New York. After publication of the well-received *The Autobiography of Alice B. Toklas* in 1933, she traveled to the United States for a lecture tour. Her *Lectures in America* (1935) dealt with her philosophy of composition.

Compelled to close her apartment at rue de Fleurus shortly after her return to France, Stein moved with Toklas to rue Christine; with the onset of the war in 1939, however, they returned to Bilignin. During the war, the two women lived for a time in Culoz, where they first witnessed the German occupation and then the arrival of the Americans, which would be recounted in *Wars I Have Seen* (1945). In December, 1944, she returned to Paris, only to leave soon afterward to entertain U.S. troops stationed in occupied Germany. Her views on the U.S. soldier and the society that produced him changed considerably during these two years. In October, 1945, she traveled to Brussels to lecture. Weary and tired, she decided to visit her friend Bernard Fay in the country. Her trip was abruptly interrupted by her illness, and she entered the American Hospital in Neuilly-sur-Seine, where, after an unsuccessful cancer operation, she died on July 27, 1946.

ANALYSIS

It is customary to refer to Gertrude Stein's poetry—and her work in general—with the qualifiers "abstract," "repetitive," and "nonsensical," terms that do little if any justice to a most remarkable literary achievement. The proper evaluation of Stein's work requires a willingness to rethink certain basic notions concerning art, discourse, and life, a task that is perhaps as difficult as the reading of Stein's voluminous production itself. Her work, however, is really not excessively abstract, especially when one considers that her poetic rests on the fundamental axiom of "immediate existing." Nothing could be more concrete than that. Whatever she may be describing, each unit is sure to be a complete, separate assertion, a reality immediately given—in the present, the only time there is.

Repetition is insistence: A rose is a rose is a rose is a rose. Each time it is new, different, unique, because the experience of the word is unique each time it is uttered. Stylistically, this entails the predominance of parataxis and asyndeton, words being "so nextily" in their unfolding. Repetition of the same is often supplanted by repetition of the different, where the juxtaposition is in kind and quality. An example of the latter is the following passage from *A Long Gay Book* (1932):

> All the pudding has the same flow and the sauce is painful, the tunes are played, the crinkling paper is burning, the pot has cover and the standard is excellence.

Whether operating at the syntagmatic or at the paradigmatic level, as above, the repetition serves the purpose of emphasizing and isolating a thing, not simply anything. The break with all previous associations forces one to consider this pudding and this sauce, allowing a concretization of the experience in this particular frame of the present. If the content appears to have no "logical" coherence, it is because it is not meant to, since the experience of the immediate does not warrant ratiocination or understanding of any sort. Art in Stein is perception of the immediate, a capturing of the instantaneity of the word as event, sense, or object. The notion is clearly nonreferential in that art does not need a world to know that it exists. Although it occasionally refers to it, it does not have to—in fact, the less it does, the better. What is of paramount importance is that this self-contained entity comes alive in the continuous present of one's experience of it, and only then. The influence of Stein's painter friends was unequivocal. Not all discourse that links the work of art to history and other realms of life is, properly speaking, a preoccupa-

tion of the artist: It does not constitute an aesthetic experience, remaining just that—criticism, sociology, and philosophy. Meaning is something that comes after the experience, thanks to reflection, the mediation of reason, and the standardization of logic and grammar; it is never given in the immediacy of the poetic expression. Stein's writings attempt to produce the feeling of something happening or being lived—in short, to give things (objects, emotions, ideas, words) a sense that is new and unique and momentary, independent and defiant of what an afterthought may claim to be the "true" meaning or sense of an experience or artistic event. From this perspective, can it still be honestly said that Stein's work is "nonsense," with all the negative implications usually associated with the epithet?

THINGS AS THEY ARE

Stein had from very early in her career a keen sense of the distance that naturally exists between objects and feelings as perceived, and their transposition into conventional formalized speech. Her first novel, *Q.E.D.* (for the Latin *quod erat demonstrandum*, meaning "which was to be proved"), written in 1903 and known after 1950 as *Things as They Are*, dealt with the then taboo topic of lesbianism in a ménage à trois of three women. However, the work is already shorn of such typical narrative features as symbolism, character development, climax, and descriptions of setting, though it is cast in an intelligible variation of standard prose. At the limits of the (Henry) Jamesian novel, what happens among the characters and the space of emotional relatedness is more important than the characters as characters. The focal point is the introspection of these human natures, and all elaborations and complications of feelings remain internal, intimate, within the consciousness of the individual being described or, most often, within the dialectic of the relationship. Doing away with all contingent background material meant zooming in on the poetic process itself; but for all practical purposes the author is still struggling within the precincts of the most sophisticated naturalism: She is still representing, in the tradition of Henry James and Gustave Flaubert, two authors whom she admired greatly. The characters are at odds with the author: They are white American college women constantly preoccupied with the propriety of their relationship and therefore demand of the author a polite, cultivated, and literary realization.

THREE LIVES

The problem of the language to employ in writing is dealt with in the next work, *Three Lives*, where the progressive abandonment of inherited expressive forms is much stronger and can be said to constitute a first milestone in Gertrude Stein's stylistic development, especially in "Melanchta," the last of the three stories. Here Stein describes a love story set among lower-class blacks, where she can explore the intensity of "uneducated" speech and where, as Donald Sutherland quite aptly points out, there exists "a direct relationship between feeling and word." Typical of her entire literary career, at the time of publication the printer inquired whether the author really knew English. In *Three Lives*, Stein was "groping for a continuous present and for using everything again and again." This continuous present is immediate and partakes of the human mind as it exists at any given moment when confronted with the object of writing. It is different from the prolonged present of duration, as in Henri Bergson, where aspects of human nature may enter. At the stylistic level, punctuation is rare and the present participle is employed as a substantive for its value in retaining the sense of process, of continuity in a present mode that knows no before and no after. This "subjective time" of writing is paralleled by similar developments in the visual and plastic arts, from which Stein drew copiously. Her admiration and appreciation of what Cézanne had done for painting was matched by the unrelenting support that she bestowed on the upcoming younger generation of artists, such as Picasso, Matisse, Juan Gris, and Francis Picabia. Cézanne had taught her that there are no less important areas on a canvas vis-à-vis the theme or figure that traditionally dominated representational painting, and he returned to "basics," such as color, tone, distribution, and the underlying abstractions, reaching out for those essentials in the welter of external detail to capture a sense without which there would be no painting. Picasso went even further, forsaking three-dimensional composition for the surface purity of plane geometry, ushering in cubism. For Stein, perception takes place against the tabula rasa of immediate consciousness, and cubism offered the flatness

of an interior time that could be brought to absolute elementalism, simplicity, and finality.

TENDER BUTTONS

Things as They Are and *Three Lives*, for all their stylistic experimentation, are clearly works of prose. In *Tender Buttons*, however, Stein blurs the distinction between prose and poetry. She works with "meaningless" babble, puns, games, rhymes, and repetitions. Much as in Lewis Carroll and Tristam Tzara, the word itself is seen as magic. In a world of pure existence, dialogue disappears, replaced by word lists and one-word utterances. Interactions of characters are no longer tenable, and people give way to objects. The portrait is supplanted by the still life, and the technique of composition is reminiscent of Picasso's collages, not of automatic writing. The intention seems to be to give the work its autonomy independent of both writer and reader: One sees and reads what one sees and reads, the rest being reconstruction from memory or projections of the viewer's intellect. The effort is ambitious: to see language being born. Disparate critical ideas have been invoked to "interpret" *Tender Buttons*, and it is likely that Norman Weinstein (*Gertrude Stein and the Literature of Modern Consciousness*, 1970) comes closest when he summons the studies of Jean Piaget, the Sapir-Whorf language hypothesis, R. D. Laing, and the dimension of schizophrenia. On the opposite bank, Allegra Stewart (*Gertrude Stein and the Present*, 1967) reads the work as a Jungian mandala and relates the alchemical correspondences to all the literary movements of the epoch, such as Dada, Futurism, and so on.

"A jack in kill her, a jack in, makes a meadowed king, makes a to let." The plastic use of language permits the bypassing of the rule where, for example, a substantive is the object of a preposition. The infinitive "to let" appears as the object of a verb and is modified by the indefinite article "a." If analysis emphasizes the dislocation, the derangement, of standard usage, suggesting that alternative modes of expression are possible and even revealing, no matter how unwieldy, it should also note the foregrounding of "events" in an atemporal framework, where even nouns are objects that do not need the passing of ages to be what they are. Sense, if not altogether certain meanings, can be obtained only in the suspended perception of the reading, especially aloud.

This effort to see and write in the "continuous present" requires, Stein said, a passionate identification with the thing to be described: A steady, trance-like concentration on the object will first of all divest it of all its customary appellations and then permit the issuing forth of words and structures that alone can speak as *that* thing in front of the observer.

"POETRY AND GRAMMAR"

In "Poetry and Grammar" (1935), Stein says, "Poetry is concerned with using with abusing, with losing with wanting, with denying with avoiding with adoring with replacing the noun. . . . Poetry is doing nothing but using losing refusing and pleasing and betraying and caressing nouns." In this spirit of reevaluation of the nature and process of naming things she will then go all out in making sure that the things she looks at will by themselves elicit the way they are to be called, never being for a moment worried that such a process may be at odds with the limited range of possibilities offered by conventional reality; she wanted not only to rename things but also to "find out how to know that they were there by their names or by replacing their names." As Shakespeare had done in Arden, the goal was to create "a forest without mentioning the things that make a forest."

With this new discovery, for the ensuing twenty years Stein kept busy revisiting timeworn forms and models of poetic expression, charging them with fresh blood and impetus. The underlying magic would be constant: "looking at anything until something that was not the name of that thing but was in a way that actual thing would come to be written." This process was possible because Stein had arrived at a particular conception of the essence of language: It is not "imitation either of sounds or colors or emotions," but fundamentally an "intellectual recreation." The problem of mimesis and representation was forever behind her, and the idea of play became fundamental in her work.

1920'S AND 1930'S

The third stage of Stein's poetry came in the late 1920's and early 1930's, when she was both very happy at receiving some recognition and much depressed about some new problems of her craft. Of the three materials that she felt art had to deal with—sight, sound, and sense, corresponding to the spatial, the temporal, and the conceptual dimensions of the mind—she had up to then worked intensely on the first two, relegating the third to the background by ignoring it or by simply rejecting it as a response to conventional grammatical and logical sense. At times, she handled the problem of sense by mediating it through her theoretical writings, especially after 1925.

With the ending of the Roaring Twenties, however, much of the spatiality in literature also disappeared. Painting became intellectual, poets became religious or political, and the newer waves did not seem to hold much promise. Stein had also reached a conclusion concerning works of art: that there are no masterpieces containing ideas; in philosophy, there are no masterpieces. Ideas and philosophy require almost by definition a mediated, sequential array of items over time and in history, ideas being about something or other. For a poetic of the unique, concrete thing—again, against all claims that Stein's is a poetic of the abstract—the task of dealing with ideas, which are by nature abstract, posed no small problem. Still, owing also to her attention to religious thought and the artistic implications of meditation, communion, trance, and revelation, she felt the need to come to terms with this hitherto untrodden ground.

STANZAS IN MEDITATION

Stein set about writing a poem of ideas without all the historical and philosophical underpinnings and referents that accompany works such as Ezra Pound's *The Cantos* (1925-1972) and T. S. Eliot's *The Waste Land* (1922). True to the credo that art is immanent and immediate, she wrote *Stanzas in Meditation*, a long poem made up of five parts and running to 163 stanzas, some a line long, others extending over several pages.

Remarkably little has been written about this forgotten but truly major composition, for the difficulty once again is the unpreparedness of criticism to deal with another of Stein's innovations: Instead of writing about ideas, she writes the ideas themselves: Thinking, in other words, does not occur in the mind after reading the words on the page, but the words themselves are the ideas, making ideas partake of the human mind instead of human nature. The old reliable technique of stopping the momentous thoughts on the page as consciousness becomes aware of them creates once again the typical situation with Stein's art: One experiences ideas as one reads; one cannot lean back and expect to put together a "coherent" whole. There are in fact no philosophical terms in the traditional sense and no organization as such. Norman Weinstein writes that "The poem is not *about* philosophy, but *is* philosophy set into motion by verbal action." The disembodied, fragmentary, and discontinuous vision of the cubists is here interwoven with the process-philosophy of William James and Whitehead.

Stylistically, each line tends to be objective and stable and corresponds to what in prose is the sentence. As the lines build up into a stanza, they swell with tension, and, like the paragraph, constitute a specific unit of attention. The poem will occasionally evidence images and allow symbols, but these are accidental, perhaps because the idea itself can best or only be expressed in that particular fashion. According to Sutherland, the poem can be entered in a tradition that lists Plato, Pindar, the English Metaphysicals, and Gerard Manley Hopkins. The poem can be read by simply beginning at random, which is perhaps the best way for the uninitiated to get a "sense" of it and familiarize themselves with the tone, lyricism, and surprisingly deceiving content. The technique of repetition is still present, revealing new contexts for given words, and Stein coins new expressions for ancient truisms. The text is a gold mine of brilliant aphorisms: "There is no hope or use in all," or "That which they like they knew."

THE AUTOBIOGRAPHY OF ALICE B. TOKLAS

Between the time of the appearance of *The Autobiography of Alice B. Toklas* and the publication, shortly before her death, of *The Gertrude Stein First Reader and Three Plays* (1946), thirteen other books came out, among which were the highly successful and important *The Geographical History of America* (1936) and *Everybody's Autobiography* (1937). During these years, Stein's major efforts were directed to the problem of self-presentation and the formal structure of autobiography. She put the writer on the same ground as the reader, ending the privileged position of both biographer and autobiographer. She continued to elaborate the poetic of impersonal, timeless, and spaceless writing, ensuring that experience, flow, and place remain within the confines of the continuous present of perception. Her poetry during this period was chiefly written for children, rhymed and chanted and playful, with no pretense at being anything more than a momentary flash in the continuum of life, a diversion, a game. Many of these works were published either as limited editions or posthumously in the Yale edition of her uncollected writings, where they can now be read in chronological sequence.

OTHER MAJOR WORKS

LONG FICTION: *Three Lives*, 1909; *The Making of Americans: Being a History of a Family's Progress*, 1925 (abridged, 1934); *Lucy Church Amiably*, 1930; *A Long Gay Book*, 1932; *Ida, a Novel*, 1941; *Brewsie and Willie*, 1946; *Blood on the Dining-Room Floor*, 1948; *Things as They Are*, 1950 (originally known as *Q.E.D.*); *Mrs. Reynolds and Five Earlier Novelettes, 1931-1942*, 1952; *A Novel of Thank You*, 1958.

SHORT FICTION: *As Fine as Melanctha*, 1954; *Painted Lace, and Other Pieces, 1914-1937*, 1955; *Alphabets and Birthdays*, 1957.

PLAYS: *Geography and Plays*, pb. 1922; *Operas and Plays*, pb. 1932; *Four Saints in Three Acts*, pr., pb. 1934; *In Savoy: Or, Yes Is for a Very Young Man (A Play of the Resistance in France)*, pr., pb. 1946; *The Mother of Us All*, pr. 1947; *Last Operas and Plays*, pb. 1949; *In a Garden: An Opera in One Act*, pb. 1951; *Lucretia Borgia*, pb. 1968; *Selected Operas and Plays*, 1970.

NONFICTION: *Composition as Explanation*, 1926; *How to Write*, 1931; *Matisse, Picasso, and Gertrude Stein, with Two Shorter Stories*, 1933; *The Autobiography of Alice B. Toklas*, 1933; *Portraits and Prayers*, 1934; *Lectures in America*, 1935; *Narration: Four Lectures*, 1935; *The Geographical History of America*, 1936; *Everybody's Autobiography*, 1937; *Picasso*, 1938; *Paris, France*, 1940; *What Are Masterpieces?*, 1940; *Wars I Have Seen*, 1945; *Four in America*, 1947; *Reflections on the Atomic Bomb*, 1973; *How Writing Is Written*, 1974; *The Letters of Gertrude Stein and Thornton Wilder*, 1996 (Edward Burns and Ulla E. Dydo, editors); *Baby Precious Always Shines: Selected Love Notes Between Gertrude Stein and Alice B. Toklas*, 1999 (Kay Turner, editor).

CHILDREN'S LITERATURE: *The World Is Round*, 1939.

MISCELLANEOUS: *The Gertrude Stein First Reader and Three Plays*, 1946; *The Yale Edition of the Unpublished Writings of Gertrude Stein*, 1951-1958 (8 volumes; Carl Van Vechten, editor); *Selected Writings of Gertrude Stein*, 1962; *The Yale Gertrude Stein*, 1980.

BIBLIOGRAPHY

Curnutt, Kirk, ed. *The Critical Response to Gertrude Stein*. Westport, Conn.: Greenwood Press, 2000. This guide includes quintessential pieces on Stein by Carl Van Vechten, William Carlos Williams, and Katherine Anne Porter, as well as previously obscure estimations from contemporaries such as H. L. Mencken, Mina Loy, and Conrad Aiken.

Dydo, Ulla E., with William Rice. *Gertrude Stein: The Language That Rises, 1923-1934*. Evanston, Ill.: Northwestern University Press, 2003. Dydo, a renowned Stein scholar, provides a comprehensive analysis of the letters, manuscripts, and notebooks Stein generated in a twenty-year period.

Kellner, Bruce, ed. *A Gertrude Stein Companion*. New York: Greenwood Press, 1988. Kellner supplies a helpful introduction on how to read Stein. The volume includes a study of Stein and literary tradition, her manuscripts, and her various styles; and biographical sketches of her friends and "enemies." Includes an annotated bibliography of criticism.

Knapp, Bettina. *Gertrude Stein*. New York: Continuum, 1990. A general introduction to Stein's life and art. Discusses her stylistic breakthrough in the stories in *Three Lives*, focusing on repetition and the use of the continuous present. Devotes a long chapter to *Tender Buttons* as one of Stein's most innovative and esoteric works; discusses the nonreferential nature of language in the fragments.

Malcolm, Janet. *Two Lives: Gertrude and Alice*. New Haven, Conn.: Yale University Press, 2007. Malcolm examines the good and the bad in the life shared by Stein and Alice B. Toklas.

Mitrano, G. F. *Gertrude Stein: Woman Without Qualities*. Burlington, Vt.: Ashgate, 2005. A study of Stein's writing and a look at why it remains relevant to twenty-first century readers.

Murphy, Marguerite S. *A Tradition of Subversion: The Prose Poem in English from Wilde to Ashbery*. Amherst: University of Massachusetts Press, 1992. Devotes a chapter to *Tender Buttons*. Argues that Stein borrowed her genre from painting. Discusses the experimental nature of Stein's prose poems in the collections.

Pierpont, Claudia Roth. *Passionate Minds: Women Rewriting the World*. New York: Alfred A. Knopf, 2000. Evocative, interpretive essays on the life paths and works of twelve women, including Stein, connecting the circumstances of their lives with the shapes, styles, subjects, and situations of their art.

Simon, Linda. *Gertrude Stein Remembered*. Lincoln: University of Nebraska Press, 1994. Consists of short memoirs of the modernist writer by her colleagues and contemporaries. Selections include pieces by Daniel-Henri Kahnweiler, Sylvia Beach, Sherwood Anderson, Cecil Beaton, and Eric Sevareid, each of whom offer intimate and often informal views of Stein.

Wineapple, Brenda. *Sister Brother: Gertrude and Leo Stein*. Lincoln: University of Nebraska Press, 2008. Wineapple looks at the long and close relationship between Stein and her brother, Leo, and the emergence of her writing voice, which may been in part responsible for the rift between the two siblings.

Peter Carravetta

GERALD STERN

Born: Pittsburgh, Pennsylvania; February 22, 1925

PRINCIPAL POETRY

The Pineys, 1969
The Naming of Beasts, and Other Poems, 1973
Rejoicings, 1973
Lucky Life, 1977
The Red Coal, 1981
Father Guzman, 1982
Paradise Poems, 1984
Lovesick, 1987

Learning Another Kingdom: Selected Poems,
   1990
Two Long Poems, 1990
Bread Without Sugar, 1992
Odd Mercy, 1995
This Time: New and Selected Poems, 1998
Last Blue, 2001
American Sonnets, 2002
Everything Is Burning, 2005
The Preacher, 2007
Save the Last Dance, 2008
Early Collected Poems, 1965-1992, 2010

OTHER LITERARY FORMS

Although Gerald Stern is known primarily as a poet, he has also written a number of perceptive essays.

ACHIEVEMENTS

Gerald Stern's poetic achievements have been recognized through many awards and honors. He has received four National Endowment for the Arts grants and fellowships from the Guggenheim Foundation and the Academy of American Poets (1993). His *Lucky Life* was named the Lamont Poetry Selection (1977) and was a finalist for a National Book Critics Circle Award. He received the Bess Hokin Award (1980), the Bernard F. Conners Prize for Poetry from *The Paris Review* (1982), the Melville Cane Award (1982) for *The Red Coal*, the Jerome J. Shestack Poetry Prize (1984) from the *American Poetry Review*, the P.E.N. Award, the Paterson Prize (1992) for *Bread Without Sugar*, the Ruth Lilly Poetry Prize (1996), the National Book Award (1998) for *This Time*, the Wallace Stevens Award (2005), the National Jewish Book Award (2005), and the Paterson Award for Sustained Literary Achievement (2006) for *Everything Is Burning*. *American Sonnets* was shortlisted for the Griffin Poetry Prize in 2003. In 2006, he was elected a chancellor of the Academy of American Poets.

BIOGRAPHY

Born in 1925 into a second-generation Jewish family, Gerald Stern grew up in Pittsburgh. He earned a B.A. from the University of Pittsburgh and an M.A. from Columbia University, and did additional graduate work at the University of Paris. Stern began his working career as an English teacher and a principal. After spending a number of years in Europe, mainly Paris and London, during the 1950's (though with a stint as an English teacher in Glasgow, Scotland), he returned to the United States and began teaching at Temple University in 1957. He also taught at the University of Pennsylvania, Indiana University of Pennsylvania, Somerset County College in New Jersey, and, beginning in 1982, at the University of Iowa. Until his retirement, Stern would divide his time between his home in eastern Pennsylvania and the Writers' Workshop of the University of Iowa, where he was a professor of English. After retirement, he maintained a hectic schedule of readings and workshops while living in both Easton, Penn-

Gerald Stern

sylvania, and New York City. Relocating to Lambert-ville, New Jersey, Stern served as poet laureate of New Jersey from 2000 to 2002, and later was named distinguished poet-in-residence at Drew University in its master of fine arts in poetry program.

ANALYSIS

Unlike the poems of many of his contemporaries, those of Gerald Stern explode upon the reader's attention with high and impassioned rhetoric. The poems seem to tumble forward like trees in a flood, snaring, collecting, and finally sweeping subject matter one would have thought only peripherally connected to the main thrust. By using an engaging conversational tone, combined with the frequent use of repetition to sweep together myriad details, Stern's poems display a direct link to the poetics of Walt Whitman. Moreover, a psalmist's zest for parallelism and anaphora discloses a debt to biblical poetry and reinforces the pervasively spiritual, specifically Jewish, sensibility of Stern's work. His frequent use of surrealistic images, meanwhile, reveals a debt to twentieth century Spanish poets, and his love of humble specifics shows him to be a descendant of Ezra Pound and William Carlos Williams. The poems are, among other things, evidence of an immense curiosity about life set against the depersonalizing matrix of twentieth century history.

Eschewing the drift toward, on one hand, hermeticism, and, on the other, the poetry of confession, Stern's poems, by capitalizing on many of the features of "open" poetry (in various of its historical incarnations), have shown a way for poetry to become equal to the task of transforming both memory and modern history into art. Stern's poetic is both stimulating and eminently suitable for representing and interpreting the variety of American life in a way that encompasses both the tragic and the humorous in its fabric.

REJOICINGS

Rejoicings announces most of the themes and much of the style of Stern's subsequent, better-known work. Already present are the tutelary spirits who people his later poems and the tension between his love of "high" culture as represented by various philosophers and poets, all heroes of the intellect and art, and his yearn-ing for spontaneity and the "natural," represented by home-grown resources, as in "Immanuel Kant and the Hopi":

> I am going to write twenty poems about my ruined
>   country,
>   Please forgive me, my old friends,
> I am walking in the direction of the Hopi!
> I am walking in the direction of Immanuel Kant!
> I am learning to save my thoughts—like
> one of the Dravidians—so that nothing will
> be lost, nothing I tramp upon, nothing I
> chew, nothing I remember.

While holding most of the Western intellectual tradition in high respect, Stern equally holds its neglect of emotion, intuition, and experience to be responsible for much of the misery to which human beings are taught to accommodate themselves. Thus, many of the poems in the collection have an aspect of unlearning about them, even as they continue to extol the finer mentors of Western tradition. Others look for a "third" way somehow to be negotiated between the mind/body dichotomy, as in "By Coming to New Jersey":

> By coming to New Jersey I have discovered the third
>   world
> that hangs between Woodbridge Avenue and Victory
>   Bridge.
> It is a temporary world,
> full of construction and water holes,
> full of barriers and isolated hydrants . . .

The "third world" of experience is one to which he will return again and again, finding it populated with all the things that are of little consequence to the heave of civilization: birds, flowers, weeds, bugs, and the like, as well as human detritus—the junkyards of America, superseded and yet everywhere visible as testimonials to other dimensions of life.

LUCKY LIFE

Although Stern had been publishing steadily for many years, the publication in 1977 of *Lucky Life* proved to be a watershed in his career. Expansive and ebullient, slyly melodramatic and hyperbolic (whether depicting the tragic, the nostalgic, or the mundane) but always wonderfully readable, the poems appeared during a period when the loose aesthetic of the 1960's had been exhausted, and the predictable return to formalism was just getting under way. The book seemed in some ways to partake of neither, though this is only a partial truth, for the poems are certainly more informed by the openness of the 1960's than by the subsequent swing the other way. By reaching back, through Whitman, to the psalmists, and imbuing the various techniques of poetic repetition with a dizzying parade of disjunctive images, emotional outbursts, jeremiads, and tender soliloquies, *Lucky Life* seemed to point the way to a new kind of democratic poetry, a kind of Whitman modernized and extended: "I am going to carry my bed into New York City tonight/ complete with dangling sheets and ripped blankets;/ I am going to push it across three dark highways/ or coast along under 600,000 faint stars."

Just as Whitman found American possibility teeming in New York, Stern, a century and a half later, locates it in the moral imperative to preserve its authentic and unrepeatable artifacts (as well as the national character that went into making them), as in "Straus Park":

> if you yourself go crazy when you walk through
> the old shell
> on Stout's Valley Road,
> then you must know how I felt when I saw Stanley's
> Cafeteria
> boarded up and the sale sign out

To this he opposes "California," that state of mind "with its big rotting sun": "—Don't go to California yet!/ Come with me to Stanley's and spend your life/ weeping in the small park on 106th Street." California is not a state of mind but a fact of life—to some, an ideal (to the poet, the wrong one). Still, it is possible to carry some of Stanley's memories even to California: "Take the iron fence with you/ when you go into the desert./ . . . / Do not burn again for nothing./ Do not cry out again in clumsiness and shame."

The feeling for nostalgic way stations, for what, in a more somber locution, is sometimes called tradition, informs the poet's subject matter in a personal but dynamic way that is nevertheless always under threat by the rise of anonymity, conformity, and the pervasiveness of substitutes. These poems, then, are atavistic expressions of grief and longing for the return of the authentic: "What would you give for your dream/ to be as clear and simple as it was then/ in the dark afternoons, at the old scarred tables?" (from "Stepping Out of Poetry"). Characteristically, the poet often identifies this longing and grief with his Jewishness, as when he stops to examine road kill in "Behaving Like a Jew": "I am going to be unappeased at the opossum's death./ I am going to behave like a Jew/ and touch his face, and stare into his eyes,/ and pull him off the road." Led by a detour to a dilapidated coffeehouse called (the poem's title) "This Is It" ("the first condemned building in the United States"), the poet talks to its owner, a "coughing lady," and commiserates with her over the collapse of the neighborhood. He listens to the stories of her youth, about her dog "and its monotonous existence," and proclaims, "Everyone is into my myth! The whole countryside/ is studying weeds, collecting sadness, dreaming/ of odd connections."

Sometimes, Stern begins his nostalgia on an ironic note before devolving into seriousness, as in "If You Forget the Germans":

> If you forget the Germans climbing up and down
> the Acropolis,
> then I will forget the poet falling through his rotten
> floor in New Brunswick;
> and if you stop telling me about your civilization in
> 1400 B.C.,
> then I will stop telling you about mine in 1750 and
> 1820 and 1935.

After such playful give-and-take, the poet shifts key: "Here are the thoughts I have had;/ here are the people I have talked to and worn out;/ here are the stops in my throat." The real theme—the search for happiness amid the ubiquity of details and through the murderous lurch of time—is discovered in a journey into the poet's own typically broken past, narrated in a mock travelogue ("If you go by bus . . ."). However, after a series of perplexing directions, he admonishes, "Do not bury yourself outright in the litter." Instead, he says, in an ending that finds echoes in Christian liturgy:

Sing and cry and kiss in the ruined dining room
in front of the mirror, in the plush car seat,
a 1949 or '50, still clean and perfect
under the black dust and the newspapers,
     as it was when we cruised back and forth all night
          looking for happiness;
     as it was when we lay down and loved in the old
          darkness.

Happiness is the subject of the title poem: "Lucky life isn't one long string of horrors/ and there are moments of peace, and pleasure, as I lie in between the blows." With age and the accretions of scars and memories, happiness becomes more problematic: "Each year I go down to the island I add/ one more year to the darkness;/ and though I sit up with my dear friends . . ./ after a while they all get lumped together." Announcing that "This year was a crisis," the poet lumbers through memories of past vacations, through dreams of getting lost on South Main Street in a town in New Jersey, of looking for a particular statue of Christopher Columbus, of sitting at a bar listening to World War II veterans, then dreams of himself sitting on a porch "with a whole new set of friends, mostly old and humorless." There follows a burst of apostrophes: "Dear Waves, what will you do for me this year?/ Will you drown out my scream?/ Will you let me rise through the fog?" The poem ends:

Lucky life is like this. Lucky there is an ocean to
     come to.
Lucky you can judge yourself in this water.
Lucky the waves are cold enough to wash out the
     meanness.
Lucky you can be purified over and over again.

THE RED COAL

With the publication of *The Red Coal* in 1981, some critics believed that Stern had fallen into self-imitation and saw the poems as mannered in their style and sometimes bombastic in their treatment of subject matter. For example, the critic for *The New York Times Book Review* asserted, "In poem after poem he sets up for himself some temptation over which he wins a lyrical triumph. The invariability with which he clears those hurdles makes one suspect that the fences have been lowered." A dissenting view, however, would simply note that, in a poem, all triumphs are "lyrical," for in what sense could they be "actual"? Perhaps the insinuation of repetition is the more damaging. Although it is true that Stern's poems offer little in the way of stylistic variation, their range is impressive.

Simply to list the place-names and people who gather to Stern's poems like flocking birds is to suggest the presence of a poet with wide cultural affinities and concerns. Although all the figures and places could, with skepticism, be seen as a form of name-dropping, it is more likely that they play a totemic role, suggesting whole ranges of other experience anterior to the specific subject matter. Nicolaus Copernicus, Isaac Stern, Jascha Heifetz, Emma Goldman, Eugene V. Debs, Pablo Picasso, Vincent van Gogh, Casimir Pulaski, Galileo, Albert Einstein, Fyodor Dostoevski, Guillaume Apollinaire, Hart Crane, Ezra Pound, Thomas Jefferson, Gustave Flaubert, Wyndham Lewis, Maurice Ravel, Aleksandr Nikolayevich Scriabin, Antonio Vivaldi, Eugene O'Neill, Johann Wolfgang von Goethe—all these and many more haunt the poems like figures in a pantheon.

As for the kind of mind necessary for the poet's—and, by extrapolation, modern humanity's—survival, Stern compares a model of Galileo's to one of his own in a poem intriguingly titled "I Remember Galileo": "I remember Galileo describing the mind/ as a piece of paper blown around by the wind,/ and I loved the sight of it sticking to a tree/ or jumping into the back seat of a car." At first, he says he watched paper "for years," as if to test the adequacy of the metaphor, but "yesterday I saw the mind was a squirrel caught crossing/ Route 60 between the wheels of a giant truck." The squirrel escapes, but not before "his life [was] shortened by all that terror." The poet decides that "Paper will do in theory," but the alert, capable squirrel, "his whole soul quivering," finishes his mad scramble across the highway and escapes up his "green ungoverned hillside."

Such seizures and terror, often encountered in retrospect, are usually made over to the poet's advantage, as in "The Red Coal," the title poem, whose central image (most likely derived from the biblical story of the infant Moses, who chose Pharaoh's tray of burning embers over a tray of rubies) presides like a second sun over the poet's difficult but intellectually and spiritually formative years traveling with his friend, the poet Jack Gilbert:

> I didn't live in Paris for nothing and walk
> with Jack Gilbert down the wide sidewalks
> thinking of Hart Crane and Apollinaire
>
> and I didn't save the picture of the two of us
> moving through a crowd of stiff Frenchmen
> and put it beside the one of Pound and Williams
>
> unless I wanted to see what coals had done
> to their lives too . . .

The incandescent coal represents the yearning for knowledge, "as if knowledge is what we needed and now/ we have that knowledge." On the other hand, the coal almost certainly guarantees pain for those who would be its avatars: "The tears are . . . what, all along, the red coal had/ in store for us." However, the tears are not the result of futility or disappointment; they are the liquid registers of experience as it imposes itself on time, the baffling sea change of the body and mind that puts even the most familiar past at a strange remove: "Sometimes I sit in my blue chair trying to remember/ what it was like in the spring of 1950/ before the burning coal entered my life."

Many of the poems in *The Red Coal* cast a backward look over the poet's life, coming to terms with the effects of his commitment, "getting rid of baggage,/ . . . finding a way to change, or salvage, my clumsy life" (from "Here I Am Waiting"). That clumsiness, that self-estrangement, appropriately finds an equivalence, and hence an inward dialogue, with the lowly and dishonored things of the world, from weeds and animals (including insects and spiders) to Emma Goldman inveighing against the tyranny of property and the injustice toward winos whose lives the bright and aggressive world has cast aside. Such pity and commiseration are particularly strong in Stern and at times take on a marked spiritual coloring. In "The Poem of Liberation," the poet observes a large "vegetable garden planted in the rubble/ of a wrecked apartment house, as if to claim/ the spirit back before it could be buried/ in another investment of glass and cement." In "Dear Mole," the title animal is compared to John Ruskin, "always cram-

ming and ramming, spluttering in disgust/ . . . always starting over,/ his head down, his poor soul warbling and wailing." A monkey appears in "For Night to Come":

> All morning we lie
> on our backs, holding hands, listening to birds,
> and making little ant hills in the sand.
> He shakes a little, maybe from the cold,
> maybe a little from memory,
> maybe from dread.

As the day passes, they "watch the stars together/ like the good souls we are,/ a hairy man and a beast/ hugging each other in the white grass."

FATHER GUZMAN

Between his 1981 collection *The Red Coal* and the 1984 *Paradise Poems*, Stern published a book-length dramatic poem, *Father Guzman*. Cast in the form of a half-demented conversation between a savvy fifteen-year-old street urchin and a Maryknoll priest—both prisoners in a South American jail—the poem is an energetic, if at times prosy, political dialogue that touches on the likes of Christopher Columbus, Simón Bolívar, and Abraham Lincoln, by way of Plato, Ovid, Tommaso Campanella, Johann Wolfgang von Goethe, and Dante. Father Guzman, whose head has just been cracked by rifle-butts of the National Guard, sits in his cell and confronts the taunts of the Boy, a native; from the initial exchange extends an impassioned conversation of forty pages. Foulmouthed and in-the-know, the Boy begins the poem by extolling his hero (Bolívar) and his affiliation (anarchist). Father Guzman replies that in the room where he was beaten were two American police officers carrying looseleaf notebooks. He compares them with flies and suggests that their incarceration is the result of the same oppression:

> You know the common fly
> has 33 million microorganisms
> flourishing in its gut and a half billion more
> swarming over its body and legs? You know
> that Bolivar left to his vice-presidents
> the tasks of pity?

Father Guzman concludes that Bolívar was "a Caesar" and "that the Mellons plan to betray the universe/ that Nelson Rockefeller was an ichneumon and/ David Rockefeller is a house fly." This makes the Boy sit up, and, weakly suggesting that his admiration of Bolívar results from the fact that both were orphans, changes the subject to "Venus, Bolívar's favorite goddess." Father Guzman understands how the mythology of heroes is such that even tyrants and demagogues can appeal to the masses through the lens of "love," a lens capable of distorting everyone equally:

> but I have seen enough,
> of what you call love to last me a lifetime;
> and I have read de Rougement and Goethe,
> but I prefer to talk about this slum
> and the nature of oil capitalism . . .

The Boy, buoyed on the crest of his own puberty, continues unconcerned, by listing his "favorites": Plato, the Ovid of *Amores*, the author of the *Kama Sutra* ("The section on plural intercourse/ really turns me on"), and other *maestros* of love. Father Guzman responds that he would like the Boy to experience the pornographic trenches of New York ("you would love New York City"). He admits that he, too, "wanted to burn [his] seed . . . to die!": "What Raleigh fought for, what the insane Spaniards/ dreamed of for a lifetime. I saw the/ issue of their violent quest." The Boy shifts again ("There is true love in the universe, you know that!/ Think of Dante! Think of the Duke of Windsor") but demurs and admits, "you I love more than my own flesh and blood."

In the second section, Father Guzman asks the Boy, "Why is life/ a joke to you?" The Boy replies that he would simply like to go for a swim and forget about history. Father Guzman interjects: "Listen to me! Without a dream you'd die!/ This slime of ours would fill/ the whole world!" The Boy says that his dream is to live "without misery and sickness and hunger." Father Guzman turns the talk to utopias and Campanella's *La cittá del sole* (1602; *The City of the Sun*, 1637), saying that he "worship[s] his spirit," but concedes that he does not like "the Caesar Complex . . ./ and all that control, in industry, education, and art,/ control of the mind, even of the heart." The Boy characteristically focuses on the control of the heart and exclaims, "I hate policemen! I can't stand them/ looking at you as if they

knew/ what you already had in your pockets." Father Guzman wonders why, "in the whole history of the world/ there have never been two months of kindness?" and steers the talk to his admiration of Charles Fourier, "one of the true madmen of love/ and one of the great enemies of repression." The Boy asks Father Guzman what he believes in, and Guzman replies, "my heart is still old-fashioned and I want/ people to be happy in a world I recognize . . ./ . . . where souls can manage a little . . ./ without shaming themselves in front of the rats and weasels."

In section 3, the Boy puts on a dress and convincingly impersonates Father Guzman's former lover, who explains that she left him "when I saw your sadness and confusion." Dramatizing the ritual in painful detail, the Boy concludes, "There's nothing sadder than talking to the dress." They then act out an exchange between the American ambassador (Guzman) and the president (the Boy). The talk then turns to El Dorado. "Gomez" admits that there is no El Dorado but asserts that the dream is nevertheless a good one because it is idealistic, a kind of Holy Grail. The "Ambassador" explains that in North America there is no such dream and consequently the jails are "like hotels": ". . . They sit there,/ all those priests and rabbis, weeping/ in the hallways, lecturing the police."

"Gomez" shows his machismo by describing tortures that he has invented and tries to justify the graft and nepotism he has installed in his country when the Boy breaks through: "I can't do it! I quit!" Guzman concurs, "I don't know how we started in the first place." The pair play one more charade, with Father Guzman playing the part of Columbus: "I challenge anyone on horseback or foot/ to deny my rights to take this place by force." "Columbus" tells the Boy that he can bring him more than he has ever dreamed. The Boy claims not to understand the meaning of Columbus and wonders if in his cynicism he has been too hard on his country: "After all,/ we've changed, haven't we?" Exhausted by the heat of their encounter, the Boy begins to think of exile, and Father Guzman recommends New York: "Brooklyn's the place for you! I understand/ Flatbush is having a comeback. You could go/ either to Brooklyn College or N.Y.U." The poem ends with both prisoners looking at a star, and Father Guzman makes the comment, "Campanella is probably washing him-self/ in the flames. Dante is probably/ explaining the sweetness to Virgil." The Boy replies, "It is a beautiful night. Life is still good./ And full of pleasure—and hope—"

Despite the unconvincing precocity of the Boy and Father Guzman's pervasive profanity, both in thought and in speech, the poem manages to dramatize most of Stern's previous themes: love of pleasure and explora-tion (as symbolized by poets and philosophers), the striving for justice, sympathy for the downtrodden, and hatred of exploitation and greed, especially that which is institutionalized by politics. It is a bold essay into his-tory, poetry, and psychology, and though one can hear the poet's private voice coming through at times, it marks a welcome change from the Whitman-like first-person poems that so markedly characterize his earlier work.

PARADISE POEMS

In *Paradise Poems*, Stern works to bring his poems to a higher rhetorical pitch and, frequently, a longer for-mat. A deeper, more elegiac strain runs through the po-ems, and the most notable poems are formal elegies for poets W. H. Auden ("In Memory of W. H. Auden") and Gil Orlovitz ("At Jane's"), the Yiddish actor Luther Adler ("Adler"), the photographer Alfred Stieglitz ("Kissing Stieglitz Goodbye"), and the poet's father ("The Expulsion"). In the elegy for Auden, the younger Stern plays Caliban to Auden's Prospero, as he waits outside for Auden's "carved face to let me in," hoping, like all young poets, to get the master's nod but realiz-ing "that I would have to wait for ten more years/ or maybe twenty more years for the first riches/ to come my way, and knowing that the stick/ of that old Prospero would never rest/ on my poor head. . . ." Though Auden is "dear . . . with his robes/ and his books of magic," Stern understands that "I had to find my own way back, I had to/ free myself, I had to find my own pleasure/ in my own sweet cave, with my own sweet music."

By contrast, "At Jane's" sets the death of the impov-erished and neglected poet Orlovitz against Stern's ris-ing success. Orlovitz's death in a New York City street is portrayed as a stylish exit, adding a note of poignancy to his loss: "He fell in the street/ in front of a doorman;

oh his death was superb,/ the doorman blew his whistle, Orlovitz climbed/ into a yellow cab, he'd never disap-point/ a doorman."

Stern, meanwhile, finds himself "brooding a little . . ./ saying inside/ one of Orlovitz's poems/ going back again/ into the cave." Later, in a contrapuntal image of American-style safety and success, Stern finds himself among the tea-and-chatter of inconsequential, provin-cial literary life: "I wore my black suit for the reading, I roared/ and whispered through forty poems, I sat like a lamb/ in a mayor's living room, I sat like a dove/ eating cheese and smiling, talking and smiling. . . ."

"The Expulsion" alludes to the expulsion from the Garden into history and memory. The paradise here is the "paradise of two," father and son. The expulsion also means coming to terms with the fact and signifi-cance of mortality. Stern's father has lived the exile of countless immigrants: memories of the old country, the myriad adjustments and new fittings needed for life in America, the striving for success, and then death—almost a cliché—in Florida. It is, in many ways, a typi-cal life, yet it is horrifyingly disjunctive, with so many losses trailing after it, that death itself is somewhat anti-climactic: "He had/ fifty-eight suits, and a bronze cof-fin; he lay/ with his upper body showing, a foot of car-pet." However, this life partakes of a paradise that is revealed only with the father's passing: "My father/ and I are leaving Paradise, an angel/ is shouting, my hand is on my mouth." That paradise will now become a fixture of memory and art, a fertile and yet minatory place:

> Our lives are merging, our shoes
> are not that different. The angel is rushing by,
> her lips are curled, there is a coldness, even
> a madness to her, Adam and Eve are roaring,
> the whole thing takes a minute, a few seconds,
> and we are left on somebody's doorstep . . .

Already this paradise is becoming "the secret rooms, the long and brutal corridor/ down which we sometimes shuffle, and sometimes run."

The universality of exile is the theme of "The Same Moon Above Us," perhaps the most interesting poem in the collection. Here, the figure of Ovid, whose exile from Rome began a literary tradition that modern poets as different as Osip Mandelstam and Derek Walcott have found resonant with significance, is superimposed on the figure of a bum, "a man sleeping over the grilles" of New York. The point is to transform the exile into something triumphant, which these poets, to the greater glory of art, were able to do and which the bum, in his way, must also do: "The truth is he has become his own sad poem." When Stern writes "I think in his fifties he learned a new language/ to go with the freezing rain," one does not know whether this refers to the bum or to Ovid. There is no confusion, however, for the harder one looks at the bum struggling among the garbage, the more Ovid comes into view, and vice versa. The poem is a haunting meditation on displacement and survival by transformation, no doubt the chief theme of this century's most valued poetry.

LOVESICK

Although Stern has never been bashful about either his ecstasies or his laments, *Lovesick* explicitly sustains both categories, as the triple pun in the title suggests: that love brings to people's attention the priority of life (that is, prior to all, including poetry); that the full acknowledgment of that life by means of people's love of it can become a burden—although a blessed one; and that the poet is not afraid to reiterate the "luck" attendant on these seeming truisms. Stern's poems frequently hint that the difference between truisms and the truth is often a matter of perspective, with the twentieth century unfortunately specializing in conversions of the latter into the former. This attention to perspective further suggests the pervasive nostalgia for an Old World sensibility, through which the thought of his poems often loops on its way to the subject.

The volume, indeed, begins with a revisionist point of view toward a familiar subject, a dead dog ("The Dog"). The "speaker" is the dog—a persona unattempted by most contemporary poets, though Philip Levine and Thom Gunn come to mind—who moreover negotiates its soliloquy posthumously. Thus, Stern has set forth a potentially bathetic situation that he neatly escapes by turning the tables on the curiosity seeker, who is both the reader (and, by allusion, the speaker in "Behaving Like a Jew") by exposing anthropomor-

phism for what it is: an attempted escape from people's obligation to love the world by coopting it in their own (linguistic) image. Thus, the dog is both knowing and superior, for it can rely on no such escape:

> I hope the dog's way
> doesn't overtake him, one quick push
> barely that, and the mind freed, something else,
> some other thing, to take its place.

The dog's ploy is to ask for a mutual recognition: "great loving stranger, remember/ the death of dogs . . . give me your pity./ How could there be enough?" In doing so, it questions the sophisticated reader's learned disposition to exclude whole categories of emotion by grossly and obtusely dismissing them as "sentimental." This is not to say that Stern wishes to give sentimentality, as it were, a second chance. Rather, his poems serve as ironic reminders that the objects of rationality have taken more than their share of an intensity originally meant for emotion. This is the "pity" that people "naturally" assign to objects of rationality.

By "pity," with its moral overtones, the reader is also meant to understand *sympathy*—or, in Keatsian terms, "negative capability." As with John Keats, Stern's sympathy extends to the nonhuman kingdoms of plant and animal. In fact, Stern may be said to start there, since it is all the more a matter of sympathy to transcend human limitations to celebrate the virtues of the truly "other." In "Bob Summers' Body," Stern conveys this same feeling toward another kind of otherness, as he watches the corpse of a friend being cremated:

> He turned over twice
> and seemed to hang with one hand to the railing
> as if he had to sit up once and scream
> before he reached the flames.

Seeing death in terms of life has the advantage of emboldening people so that thoughts of it do not "make cowards of us all," as Hamlet imagined. In Stern's revision, "there is such horror/ standing before Persephone with a suit on,/ the name of the manufacturer in the lining." Such horror has its humor, too, for humor often follows from a rearrangement of perspective. In the end, though, the death is a "plush darkness," not only naturalized but humanized as well—one might even argue, "accessorized," thanks to the cozy adjective "plush." A similar fellow-feeling arises in "This Was a Wonderful Night," in which the poet appears to indulge in innocent, fanciful conversations and matter-of-fact pastimes, until it is clear that all the principal figures with whom the poet interacts are dead:

> This was a wonderful night. I heard the Brahms
> piano quintet, I read a poem by [Freidrich] Schiller,
> I read a story, I listened to Gloomy Sunday.
> No one called me, I studied the birthday poem
> of Alvaros de Campos.

Nevertheless, the poet is happy to be "singing/ one or two songs . . . going east and west/ in the new country, my heart forever pounding."

The motion of *Lovesick*, in spite of the trademark forays into the past and into the dimension of the other, is an ascending one, culminating in one of Stern's best poems, "Steps." This poem serves, as well, as the final entry in *Leaving Another Kingdom*, a volume that brings together substantial portions of each of Stern's first five books. Here the poet remembers, and cites his body as testimony to ("I gasp and pant as if I were pulling a mule"), the fact of steps (as well as actual steps) whose climbing took their toll ("The thing about climbing/ is how you give up") in order to return the fact of elevation:

> I gave up on twenty landings,
> I gave up in Paris once, it was impossible,
> you reach a certain point, it is precise,
> you can't go further; sometimes it's shameful, you're in
> the middle of a pair of stairs, you bow
> your head. . . .

Remembering steps in Pittsburgh, in Greece, in West Virginia, and elsewhere, the poet knows that the climb, in spite of its real and allegorical exactions, is the only path to the empyreal:

> Imagine Zeus
> in West Virginia, imagine the temple to Hera
> in Vandergrift, P. A. My heart is resting,
> my back feels good, my breathing is easy. I think
> of all my apartments, all that climbing; I reach
> for a goldenrod, I reach for a poppy. . . .

The image of the poppy (which the poet chews in the poem's final line) confers a feeling of restfulness, and serves as a kind of general benediction for the lovesickness, for "the hands/ that held the books, and the face that froze, and the shoulders/ that fought the wind, and the mouth that struggled for air" ("All I Have Are the Tracks").

BREAD WITHOUT SUGAR

Bread Without Sugar justifiably raised Stern's reputation a few more notches. He assured his place as a great poet of sentiment and of a qualified nostalgia. Not traditionally religious, his poems continue to express a schmaltzy humanism even while the central persona remains a devout sensualist. He is a great elaborator who finds a language and cadence for the rhythms of imagination and memory. He is a constant questioner and yet a thinker, too. Grieving and arguing are two sides of the Stern dialectic. In "Brain of My Heart," two voices talk to each other and talk through him: "one is tormented/ one is full of sappy wisdom." This kind of cheerful self-deflation is part of the continuing Stern charm.

The volume's title poem is a formal elegy, a remembrance of the poet's father that is reminiscent of Allen Ginsberg's "Kaddish," though it is neither as excessively elaborated nor as self-consciously monumental. It opens out, grandly, from the occasion of the graveyard thoughts to offer personal, familial, and cultural ruminations. Unexpected juxtapositions give the poem energy, tension, and wonder.

EVERYTHING IS BURNING

Although Stern's earlier poems often drew their energy from mysterious conjunctions of the present moment and the remembered past, the power of remembrance gains in power in the poet's volumes issued after his years at the Writers' Workshop. *Everything Is Burning*, published a decade after his retirement, appears to take stock of a life full of sensory absorption and the literary transformation of experience. The sense of full engagement with life, which he sometimes expresses with profane exuberance, remains a vital part of his poetry in this important collection. This becomes especially apparent when Stern allows his politics to come to the fore, as for example in "The Trent Lott, The MacNamara Blues," a short poem in which the poet's anger leads him to conjure up acts of contrition he wishes the world might witness from erring politicians.

This sense of direct involvement also fills poems such as "The Tie," in which Stern's life within the writing community preoccupies his reflective spirit. The opening lines suggest the poem has been snipped out of a longer conversation: "The other time I wore a tie my friend Mark/ had called me that Berrigan had died. . . ." The idea of wearing a tie conjures up memories of attending the funeral, and of the writers, friends, and acquaintances in attendance—and of how the tie changed him: "the tie alone gave such a look of dignity/ and even stiffened my neck when it came to lowlife/ poets and painters, dozens of whom were there/ filling up the pews. . . ." Stern's poem, which on the surface seems to do no more than express a random memory brought to mind by a piece of clothing, provides one of those rare moments in which the poet allows the reader to see into the mind of the writer self-conscious of his status. At the same time, it offers evidence of the tribute he was making to poet Ted Berrigan: for Stern ". . . stopped in/ a Goodwill to buy the tie and a jacket . . . ," an effort that separates him from the "lowlife."

Also full of appraisal, criticism, and self-awareness are the three short poems "E. P. I," "E. P. II," and "E. P. III," in which he deals directly with the effects of Pound on his life and thoughts. He begins with a blanket statement that manages to convey, insofar as these are poems referring to one of the most controversial figures of twentieth century literature, a sense of benevolent judgment: "Nothing matters but the quality of the affection." Stern asserts that his admiration for Pound is far from slavish, however, by stating, "But I never trusted his/ paradise, it as too literary, nor his/ final confession, nor what he said to Ginsberg—," and by calling Pound a "lying master." That Pound's influence was pivotal in Stern's life is suggested in "E. P. II," describing the memorial event Stern organized at a community college after Pound's death. In "E. P. III," Stern returns to his comment about Pound's paradise and seems sympathetic to the older poet's dreams and ideas, to the point of invoking his spirit: "beauty was/ not only difficult, it was impossible, meester/ Pound, for Europe was poisoned. How you like Europe/ now? How you like Dubya? Wyoming hath need of thee."

SAVE THE LAST DANCE

In *Save the Last Dance*, Stern's increasing tendency to veer toward reflective meditation on the past comes to the fore. Although the lyricism, humor, and sense of emotional immediacy remain, the focus on loss and absence give these poems a distinct piquancy. Much of Stern's attention remains on his literary past, his literary friends, and his literary influences. Among the most effective new poems is "Rukeyser," which recalls "a visit with Muriel in her New York apartment,/ helping her into the kitchen, making her tea." The poet Muriel Rukeyser is under the care of a nurse, and their meeting is brief. Stern's visit is inspired by his devotion not only to the frail Rukeyser, as a person, but also to the practice of poetry itself. What he acquires during the visit, however, is a sharpened sense of fleeting time and a pronounced sense of loss that is directed both outwardly to Rukeyser and inwardly to himself. Stern's other poems inspired by memories of poets include "Wordsworth" and "Lorca," inspired by literary rather than personal memory. Of particular note is "One Poet," a poem written in tribute to an unnamed poet, which seems to have been written out of the sense of frustration at gazing backward on a lost opportunity that cannot be forgotten. "I wanted to tell him that I read his book," he writes, "but I couldn't tell him that/ nor did I ever write, since I lost his/ letter. . . ." Although several of Stern's most effective works express his responses to the poets who came before him, "One Poet" is exceptional in its recognition of the emotional need to express what could not be said at the time. The failure may have not mattered to the "One Poet" but had enduring importance to the one who failed to speak.

In contrast, the title poem, "Save the Last Dance for Me," combines the senses of recovery and loss. The poet recalls a moment of small triumph when, at age twelve, he rescued a chihuahua that had fallen into a sewer. In this and other poems, Stern's recollections of failure or triumph do not render him helpless, as a merely passive viewer of the past. He makes decisions and is aware even of the possibilities for invention, as is made clear in "Traveling Backwards." In this short poem, Stern states that to go backward in time offers him no difficulties. The means by which he goes backward, however, creates the tempting opportunity to change matters: "for here is the brain and with it I have relived/ one thing after another but I am wavering/ at *only* reliving. . . ."

"The Preacher," a longer work that ends the volume, combines similar reflections with a dialogue between Stern and Peter Richards. The two poets dwell on "holes" of all kinds and also on the biblical figure of "the Preacher," the speaker in the book of Ecclesiastes. Although interesting in its conversational wanderings and insights, "The Preacher" captures little of the lucid brightness of Stern's other works. The heart of the book is contained in his short, lyrical meditations on absence and memory.

Stern's has been one of the more refreshing voices to emerge in American poetry since the 1960's, a voice neither too refined to proclaim its ecstasies nor too decorous to lament its sorrows. Sorrow and ecstasy are, after all, the two horizons of emotional exchange, but they are all too frequently bred or shouldered out of existence by the daily grind, and Stern, a historian of emotions, has clearly sought, throughout his career, to restore them. Because his poems are impatient with limitation, it is perhaps tempting to regard them as the enemies of restraint—restraint by which many believe the gears of civilized life are oiled. One must consider, however, that the battle between freedom and restraint is an ancient contest, and the struggle will doubtless persist as long as human beings exist. Stern's importance will not be decided on the basis of his beliefs but on the strength of his art. The literary son of Whitman yet his own man, Stern has produced an instrument capable of intimating, as perhaps no other contemporary American has, the sheer fullness of life in modern times. That he has not substantially modulated this instrument may be a valid criticism. However, the persistence with which he repeats his enormous embrace of the world in poem after poem suggests a loyalty to his means that is equal to his loyalty to his vision.

OTHER MAJOR WORK

NONFICTION: *What I Can't Bear Losing: Notes from a Life*, 2003.

BIBLIOGRAPHY

Herschthal, Eric. "Late-Blooming Poet." *The New York Jewish Week* 221, no. 51 (May 15, 2009): 49-51. This profile of the poet at age eighty-four examines how he came to write poetry and the Jewish influence on his work.

Hillringhouse, Mark. "The New York School Poets." *Literary Review* 48, no. 4 (Summer, 2005): 146-179. In a series of informal reminiscences, Hillringhouse discusses Stern and other poets of his circle, including mention of an incident that appears in one of Stern's poems.

Hirsch, Edward. "A Tribute to Gerald Stern." *Antioch Review* 67, no. 1 (Winter, 2009): 88-89. A short, perceptive sketch and evaluation of Stern by a fellow poet.

Lewis, Larry. "Eden and My Generation." In *Conversant Essays: Contemporary Poets on Poetry*, edited by James McCorkle. Detroit: Wayne State University Press, 1990. Lewis discusses English poetry's preoccupation with the loss of Eden in his essay. He lists Stern's *Lucky Life* as one of the works he says does *not* reflect a fall from Eden. Instead, he sees Stern's *Lucky Life* as rooted in a sense of home and place.

Somerville, Jane. *Making the Light Come: The Poetry of Gerald Stern*. Detroit: Wayne State University Press, 1990. This full-length study of Stern's poetry pays particular attention to the function of the "eccentric" speaker of the poems—the controlling principle in a "poetry of performance." While acknowledging the role of biography, artistic predecessors, and philosophical sources, Somerville focuses on the function of biblical materials as central to an understanding of Stern's work. The book follows a thematic organization, beginning with Stern's poetic modes, then turns to his treatment of "nostalgia" and, in successive chapters, three elemental roles enacted by the speaker: gardener, rabbi, and angel. The text is supplemented by a bibliography and an index.

Stern, Gerald. "Number Your Answers: An Interview with Gerald Stern." Interview by Lia Purpura. *Writer's Chronicle* 39, no. 5 (March-April, 2007): 8-17. Provides an in-depth discussion of Stern's poetry, techniques, and inspirations, with focus on his sonnets.

_____. "On Politics and Poetry: A Conversation with Gerald Stern." Interview by Kate Beles. *Bellingham Review* 29, no. 2 (Fall, 2006): 36-42. Provides useful insight into Stern's politics in relation to his own writing and that of other poets, and presents his ideas concerning the possible political effectiveness of poetry.

_____. "What Is This Poet?" In *What Is a Poet?*, edited by Hank Lazer. Tuscaloosa: University of Alabama Press, 1987. This document, the product of a symposium on contemporary American poetry held at the University of Alabama in 1984, comes close to being a "testament" of the poet's beliefs and is therefore a valuable document for any serious study of Stern's poetry. The poet addresses a wide spectrum of concerns but emphasizes his education as a poet, including his reading of the Romantics (John Keats and Percy Bysshe Shelley) and their American counterparts (Ralph Waldo Emerson and especially Walt Whitman), and the modernists (T. S. Eliot, Hart Crane, and Ezra Pound).

_____. "You Must Ruin Your Life: An Interview with Gerald Stern." Interview by Even Grubin. *Lyric* no. 4 (Summer/Fall, 2003): 64-80. Presents reminiscences of Stern's personal and literary life, including a remembrance of his interaction with W. H. Auden.

Stitt, Peter. *Uncertainty and Plenitude: Five Contemporary American Poets.* Iowa City: University of Iowa Press, 1997. In a chapter on Stern, Stitt finds little thematic progress in Stern's career or in the ordering of poems in his books, but rather a body of work that gains its strength and coherence from the force of Stern's personality. Exploring the poet's Whitmanesque techniques, Stitt argues that Stern is less a prosodist than an orchestrator of images and subjects. Stern's buoyant vision discovers holiness in his world, but also much that is cruel and chaotic.

David Rigsbee; Philip K. Jason
Updated by Mark Rich

WALLACE STEVENS

Born: Reading, Pennsylvania; October 2, 1879
Died: Hartford, Connecticut; August 2, 1955

PRINCIPAL POETRY

Harmonium, 1923, expanded 1931 (with 14 additional poems)
Ideas of Order, 1935
Owl's Clover, 1936
The Man with the Blue Guitar, and Other Poems, 1937
Notes Toward a Supreme Fiction, 1942
Parts of a World, 1942
Esthétique du Mal, 1945
Transport to Summer, 1947
The Auroras of Autumn, 1950
Selected Poems, 1953
The Collected Poems of Wallace Stevens, 1954

OTHER LITERARY FORMS

Wallace Stevens's significant achievement is in his poetry, but he did write several experimental one-act verse plays, a number of essays on poetry, and numerous letters and journal notes that contain perceptive comments on his work. In 1916, he published in the magazine *Poetry* his first one-act verse play, *Three Travelers Watch a Sunrise*, for which he received a special prize from *Poetry*; in 1920, the play was performed at the Provincetown Playhouse in New York. A second verse play, *Carlos Among the Candles*, was staged in New York in 1917 and later published, again in *Poetry*. A third play, *Bowl, Cat, and Broomstick*, was produced at the Neighborhood Playhouse in New York in the same year but was never published during the poet's life. Between 1942 and 1951, he gave a series of lectures on poetry at Princeton and other universities, and these were collected in *The Necessary Angel: Essays on Reality and the Imagination* (1951). Later essays, as well as a number of uncollected poems and plays, appeared in *Opus Posthumous* (1957). The poet wrote excellent letters, and his daughter, Holly Stevens, collected and edited the best of them in *Letters of Wallace Stevens* (1966). In *Souvenirs and Prophecies: The*

Young Wallace Stevens (1977), she presented important entries from the poet's journal (1898-1914). Focusing on the relationship between the imagination and reality, Stevens's canon is highly unified; the prose and the plays help illuminate the difficult poetry.

ACHIEVEMENTS

Although Wallace Stevens never has had as large an audience as that enjoyed by Robert Frost and did not receive substantial recognition until several years before his death, he is usually considered to be one of the best five or six English-language poets of the twentieth century. *Harmonium* reveals a remarkable style—or, to be more precise, a number of remarkable styles. While critics praised, or more often condemned, the early poetry for its gaudiness, colorful imagery, flamboyant rhetoric, whimsicality, and odd points of view, one also finds in this volume spare Imagist poems as well as ab-

Wallace Stevens (Time & Life Pictures/Getty Images)

stract philosophical poems that anticipate his later work. The purpose of his rhetorical virtuosity in *Harmonium* and in subsequent volumes was not merely to dazzle the reader but to convey the depth of emotion, the subtle complexity of thought, and the associative processes of the mind.

Strongly influenced by early nineteenth century English poets, Stevens became a modern Romantic who transformed and extended the English Romantic tradition as he accommodated it to the twentieth century world. *Harmonium* and subsequent volumes reveal his assimilation of the innovations of avant-garde painting, music, poetry, and philosophy. One finds in his canon, for example, intimations of Pablo Picasso, Henri Matisse, and Henri Bergson, and of cubism, Impressionism, Imagism, and Symbolism. Such influences were always subordinated to the poet's romantic sensibility, however, which struggled with the central Romantic problem—the need to overcome the gulf between the inner, human reality and outer, objective reality. A secular humanist who rejected traditional Christianity, arcane mysticism, and the pessimism of T. S. Eliot's *The Waste Land* (1922) and Ezra Pound's *Cantos* (1925-1972), he succeeded as a Romantic poet in the modern world. His contribution to poetry was recognized with the Levinson Prize from *Poetry* magazine in 1920, the award of the Bollingen Prize in 1950, the Frost Medal from the Poetry Society of America in 1951, and a National Book Award in 1951 for *The Auroras of Autumn*. In 1955, *The Collected Poems of Wallace Stevens* won both a second National Book Award and the Pulitzer Prize. His reputation has continued to grow since his death in 1955.

BIOGRAPHY

On October 2, 1879, in Reading, Pennsylvania, Wallace Stevens was born to Garrett Barcalow Stevens and the former Margaretha Catherine Zeller. Wallace Stevens's father was a successful attorney who occasionally published poetry and prose in the local papers.

In 1897, Stevens graduated from Reading Boys High School and enrolled at Harvard as a special student with the ambition to become a writer. He published stories and poetry in the *Harvard Advocate* and the *Harvard Monthly* and became acquainted with the poet and philosopher George Santayana, whose books provided support for his belief that, in an agnostic age, poetry must assume the role of traditional religion. After completing his special three-year course in English at Harvard, he joined the staff of the *New York Tribune* but failed as a reporter.

In the fall of 1901, he entered the New York Law School and, after passing the bar three years later, began legal practice. He was not successful as a practicing attorney, however, and in 1908, he joined the New York office of the American Bonding Company. The next year, he married Elsie Moll.

In 1916, Stevens joined the Hartford Accident and Indemnity Company and moved to Hartford, Connecticut, which was to be his permanent residence. He now led a double life. During the day, he was a successful businessman, while at night and on weekends, he was a poet. Few of his associates in the insurance world knew of his second career. Beginning in 1914, his work had begun to be published in *Poetry* and the other little magazines. At this time, he became acquainted with an avant-garde group of writers and artists, including William Carlos Williams, Alfred Kreymborg, and Marcel Duchamp. His involvement in the business world, however, permitted only occasional participation in the activities of literary groups.

In 1923, at the age of forty-four, Stevens published his first volume of poetry. *Harmonium* was largely ignored by the critics, however, and he wrote only a few poems in the next five or six years. In 1924, his only child, Holly, was born, and subsequently, he devoted his time to his family and to his business career. In 1931, Alfred A. Knopf reissued *Harmonium*, and in 1934, Stevens was promoted to vice president of his insurance company. With his business career secure and with *Harmonium* receiving some recognition, he began to write and publish again. By the time *The Auroras of Autumn* appeared in 1950, his reputation had been firmly established. Even after the mandatory retirement age of seventy, he continued to work at his insurance company and rejected an offer to be the Charles Eliot Norton lecturer at Harvard for the 1955-1956 aca-

demic year because he felt that he might be forced to retire if he accepted. He died in 1955, two months before his seventy-sixth birthday.

ANALYSIS

Wallace Stevens frequently alludes to or quotes from the English Romantics in his letters and in his essays, and there is little doubt that this twentieth century poet is working within the Romantic tradition. The best evidence for the contention that he is a twentieth century Romantic, however, is his poetry. Repeatedly, one finds in his work the "reality-imagination complex," as he calls it. While one can see the central beliefs of William Wordsworth and John Keats in Stevens's poetry (celebration of nature, acceptance of mutability, rejection of supernatural realms, and belief in the brotherhood of man), the foundation of his Romanticism is his Wordsworthian imagination. The function of this imagination in Stevens's poetry is to make sordid reality, what Wordsworth calls "the dreary intercourse of daily life," palatable without resorting to mysticism. It is a difficult task; failure results in a profound alienation ("dejection" in the language of the Romantics).

Stevens does not merely repeat what Wordsworth and Keats have accomplished in their work but extends the Romantic tradition. He differs from his predecessors in his radical nontranscendentalism. In a May 30, 1910, letter to his wife he quotes from Keats's "Epistle to John Hamilton Reynolds": "It is a flaw/ In happiness, to see beyond our bourn,—/ It forces us in summer skies to mourn,/ It spoils the singing of the Nightingale." This idea is the premise of all Stevens's work. He takes the secular Romanticism of Wordsworth and Keats to its logical conclusion.

"OF MODERN POETRY"

Stevens's poem "Of Modern Poetry" provides a good introduction to both his theory and his method. The modern poem whose origin goes back to the discursive odes of Wordsworth and Keats is "the poem of the mind in the act of finding/ What will suffice." This modern meditation shows the process of the mind confronting reality, searching for a secular solution to the individual person's feeling of meaninglessness. Before the Romantic period (1789-1832), this was not a major problem, and thus there was no need for this type of meditation. Or, as Stevens says: "It has not always had/ To find: the scene was set; it repeated what/ Was in the script." Now the poet ("the actor") is "a metaphysician in the dark," the man of vital imagination who seeks to redeem ugly reality and overcome his alienation by secular meditation. It is a meditation that will not descend to negation or ascend to supernaturalism ("below which it cannot descend,/ Beyond which it has no will to rise").

The meditation uses conversational speech, "the real language of men," as Wordsworth says in the preface to the *Lyrical Ballads* (1798), or the "speech of the place," as Stevens states here, and seeks its affirmation in everyday reality. However, this "poem of the act of the mind" may create heightened moments in everyday reality, "spots of time," as Wordsworth calls them in *The Prelude: Or, The Growth of a Poet's Mind* (1850). It is these "spots of time" that often allow the imagination to redeem reality by ordering it, enchanting it, transforming it, or creating a feeling of stasis, of permanence beyond time. By these heightened moments and by the process of the meditation itself, the imagination strives to rectify the individual's sense of loss.

In short, Stevens expands the Wordsworthian-Keatsian discursive act of the mind in a radical fashion. In a number of his acts of the mind, the only unifying element is the solitary mind searching for what will suffice to ease its alienation. In these acts of the mind, the imagination can create moments of illumination which help regenerate the poet—and regeneration is the central goal of modern meditations, those "poems of our climate."

"POEMS OF OUR CLIMATE"

"Poems of Our Climate" reveals the function and limitation of a spot of time in a secular Romantic meditation. In the first six lines of the poem, the mind seizes a specific, seemingly ordinary moment and freezes it into a timeless moment, reminiscent of the stasis in the beginning of "Ode on a Grecian Urn." Unlike Keats, however, Stevens does not linger over this moment that the imagination has endowed with meaning. He does not wait until the fourth stanza to grow disenchanted but instinctively feels that this cannot be a permanent state—"one desires/ So much more than that." The evanescent and heightened quality of the frozen moment ("The light/ In the room more like a snowy air,/ Reflecting snow") immediately becomes the monotony of "Cold, a cold porcelain, low and round,/ With nothing more than the carnations there."

Stevens must reject this "cold pastoral" because one needs more than purity ("this complete simplicity"). One does not want to be stripped of all his "torments." The vital individual (the "vital I") is "evilly compounded"—an identity forged out of a world of pains and troubles, of good and evil experience.

The spot of time is a temporary relief from the banality or ugliness of reality, but it cannot be a permanent state. The "never-resting mind" always feels the compulsion to return to reality to remeditate and recompose it. "The imperfect is our paradise" might be Stevens's twentieth century reformulation of Keats's essential feeling in "Ode on Melancholy." Like Keats, he is ambivalent—both bitter and delighted over humankind's existence. Instinctively, he desires to escape to an ideal state, but intellectually, he realizes the impossibility of doing so. Humankind finds meaning only in human reality, which is by definition imperfect. Strip life of its torments, and it becomes banality; conceal the dark side of existence or the "evil" aspects of one's nature, and vitality is erased. Pure stasis untainted by life would be meaningless, and an art that mirrored this would be meaningless too. Stevens believes that art should express pain, struggle, and conflict, and thus he prefers the modern poets of "flawed words and stubborn sounds" to the "bawds of euphony." Stevens's poetry is a continual search; it is a continual oscillation between the depths of depression and heightened moments of affirmation. The mind "can never be satisfied, the mind, never" concludes Stevens in "The Well Dressed Man with a Beard."

"LARGE RED MAN READING" AND "DISILLUSIONMENT OF TEN O'CLOCK"

Stevens sees external reality as the Other outside the self. In his poetry, reading and study symbolize meditation, or the life of the imagination. "Large Red Man Reading" is a poem that reveals the crucial importance of the regenerative capacity of the imagination and the need to embrace the everyday world and reject the supernatural. As he seeks to reconcile himself to an earthly reality devoid of supernatural inclinations, Stevens contrasts the vital man of imagination (the large red man reading) with those who are "dead" to the imagination, "the ghosts." Ghosts as symbolic of those dead to the imaginative life occur elsewhere in his work. In "Disillusionment of Ten O'Clock," for example, Stevens complains that "the houses are haunted/ By white night-gowns" who do not "dream" (that is, imagine) of catching tigers "in red weather," as an old sailor does. In the ghostly realms of the modern world, life is colorless—a dreary intercourse of daily life without imagination. In "Large Red Man Reading," the ghosts seem to recognize that a life without the imaginative interaction between the mind and reality is worthless. After leading a dull life on earth, they had hoped to find their paradise in heaven, but they have become dissatisfied with heaven ("the wilderness of stars") and returned to earth. They returned to hear the "large red man reading," for he is the vital individual of the imagination, a true giant in a paltry age.

In the course of the meditation, it becomes clear why the ghosts have returned to Earth. Heaven lacked the reality of earthly existence, its joys and its torments. The ghosts want to hear the large red man read from the "poem of life" in all its prosaic beauty and banality— "the pans above the stove, the pots on the table, the tulips among them." In contrast to the mythic abstraction of heaven, the ghosts would eagerly reach out for any sensory knowledge ("They were those that would have wept to step barefoot into reality"), even though this knowledge might mean pain ("run fingers over leaves/ And against the most coiled thorn") as well as pleasure. Stevens has mocked, with good-natured humor, the traditional belief that people desire to go to a paradisiacal heaven after dissatisfaction with the sinful, painful life on earth. The ghosts return to Earth for the true paradise of an ever-changing sensuous reality ("being") heightened by the imagination ("reading").

THE IMAGINATION

The imagination's attempt to redeem reality, however, is not always completely successful—stalemate or even defeat are possibilities. Stevens is a darker poet than the critics have made him out to be—despite the fact that modern criticism has largely overcome the once popular cliché of the insouciant hedonist of impressionistic, pictorial poems. Often his poems of natu-

ralistic celebration end on a tentative note of affirmation, for the ugly side of reality is an able match for the imagination; the mind can never completely transform reality into something purely positive. Furthermore, in a significant number of his acts of the mind, a sense of loss threatens to dominate. It is in these poems of "the whole of Harmonium," as he would have preferred to call his canon, that one finds a profound sense of loss ("the burden of the mystery," as both Wordsworth and Keats called it) as the very genesis of the work. In these works, the imagination must grapple with "dejection," ascertain its causes or roots, and seek to resolve it as far as possible. These meditations of Stevens are different from his others only in degree. Here, however, the imagination does not appear as potent as in his other acts, and spots of time do not seem to have the intensity, or the frequency, that one finds in his other meditations.

Stevens does not have only one attitude toward this sense of loss—and certainly not one type of "dejection" poem. His imagination takes a variety of forms and attitudes. It is probably a mistake to stress a chronological development in his attitude toward the burden of the mystery, although a case might be made for some lessening of humor and flamboyance and a gradual movement toward an autumnal tone during his career. Instead, one should stress the variety and complexity of his responses. To show that his attitude toward the problem is much more complex than is usually thought, one must examine several of his poems, from his earliest to those written just before his death. Finally, it will also become clear that despite the sophistication of his responses to the problem, he was always a secular romantic who rejected the leap into transcendence and refused to submit to existential despair.

"SUNDAY MORNING"

At the heart of "Sunday Morning" (1915) is a profound sense of loss, evoked by abandonment of traditional religious belief. Modern human beings can no longer justify suffering and death with Christian certitudes. This complicated meditative poem struggles with the problem at length, pondering questions that are central to Stevens's work. How does one dispel one's anxiety when one realizes that all past mythologies are irrelevant? If there is no afterlife, how does one come to terms with death? Even as Keats did, Stevens overcomes his desire for the supernatural and puts his faith in humanist values.

"In the very Temple of Delight/ Veiled Melancholy has her sovran shrine," Keats had proclaimed in "Ode on Melancholy," and Stevens more vehemently reiterates this idea that life is process and there can be no separation of opposites, no separation of pleasure and pain. "Death is the mother of beauty," Stevens's speaker twice asserts in the course of the meditation. The very transiency of things makes them valuable; paradoxically, it is death that makes things beautiful. Stanza 6, reminiscent of Keats's "Ode on a Grecian Urn," shows that a heaven without mortality is a false paradise devoid of life. "Does ripe fruit never fall?" asks the frustrated speaker. The boughs will always hang heavy with fruit in "that perfect sky," and we can only "pick the strings of our insipid lutes" in this monotonous heaven, just as Keats's boughs will never shed their leaves and his bold lovers will always remain in the frustrating position of being poised over each other in the first stage of their lovemaking, a lovemaking of perpetual anticipation, not consummation.

Stevens believes that death is necessary for a true paradise because life can be enjoyed only when there are cycles of desire and fulfillment or disappointment. Death also has some positive value because it makes people aware of their common humanity, what Stevens significantly calls "heavenly fellowship." Wordsworth, in "Lines Composed a Few Miles Above Tintern Abbey" and "Ode: Intimations of Immortality from Recollections of Early Childhood," had expressed similar sentiments, but Stevens's attitude is more extreme. He supposes that the rejection of God results in a world that is intrinsically meaningless, whereupon one realizes that one must return to people as the only source of value.

"Sunday Morning" presents, in short, a radical humanism that Wordsworth and Keats had anticipated a century earlier. Instead of religion ("the thought of heaven"), Stevens offers naturalistic reality, the "beauty of the earth." A person's emotional contact with nature is a substitute for rituals performed before an invisible deity. The only immortality that has any meaning for modern human beings, the poet argues, is the permanence of nature as felt in the seasonal cycle—

nothing endures as "April's green endures." Depression and disillusionment are as natural as joy and hope, and memory of these opposite feelings helps form one's "soul" or identity. Echoing Keats, Stevens suggests that "all pleasures and all pains" are involved in one's responses to nature. In short, one's intense responses to external reality are "measures destined" for the "soul."

"A Postcard from the Volcano"

"A Postcard from the Volcano" (1936) is a meditation with a profound sense of loss at its foundation; about the precise nature of this loss, however, there is no critical agreement. The poem is as perplexing and intriguing as its bizarre title; to understand it, one must account for the sense of loss and explain the shift of tone at the end of the work.

"A Postcard from the Volcano" is divided into two parts by an ellipsis. The first part presents the problem: The poet feels dejected because he realizes that after his death, the imaginative expression of his life in poetry will seem foreign to the new generation. The poet will have become an irrelevant ghost, such as Stevens has elsewhere mocked as the antithesis of the vital life of the imagination. The world of the past, especially that world interpreted by the poet's imagination, will become meaningless to the children of the present.

They will "pick up our bones" but will never be able to comprehend that these once had vitality and a keen sense of participation in the moment ("that these were once/ As quick as foxes on the hill"). They will not be able to perceive the impact of the past on the present, or realize how one can change one's world through the manipulations of language. "We knew for long the mansion's look/ And what we said of it became/ A part of what it is."

Stevens pauses in his meditation. The pause seems to give birth to a new feeling—a change finally occurs when the mind swerves away from its dejection to a reconciling thought in the last two lines. Admittedly, the children ("still weaving budded aureoles") will have an innocent view of reality in which everything is viewed one-dimensionally. They will reiterate the poet's meditations and never comprehend his vision. They will say of his world that it seems "As if he that lived there left behind/ A spirit storming in blank walls,/ A dirty house in a gutted world"—they will see the poet as a mere ghost ranting without an audience. However, Stevens's meditation shifts in the last two lines to a partial reconciliation. While the poet's vision will seem irrelevant and "run down" to the children, it will also be one with "A tatter of shadows peaked to white,/ Smeared with the gold of the opulent sun." That is, they will feel intuitively some of the vitality of the dead poet's vision. They will not intellectually understand the world of the past (it will be a "shadow" to them), but some of the remnants of the past will seem "smeared with the gold of the opulent sun" and consequently reveal the vitalistic imagination of the dead poet.

"THE COURSE OF A PARTICULAR"

In "The Course of a Particular" (1951), Stevens presents a bleak winter landscape. The speaker in this matter-of-fact meditation does not appear to be much concerned with the "nothingness of winter." In fact, the speaker seems to be intellectually aware of the sense of loss but to remain emotionally tranquil, as if he had become accustomed to it. While the nothingness of the winter landscape becomes a "little less" because the poet can accept it more each day, he still feels he should try to humanize the sense of loss. He tries and then pauses. The attempt is halfhearted—"there is a resistance involved."

The humanizing metaphor of the crying leaves does not make the scene more human or more real to him. He tries to imagine harshness and the human responses to it, but the attempt does not work. Stevens discovers here that he cannot rewrite Percy Bysshe Shelley's "Ode to the West Wind" in the 1950's. All he feels is a dull monotonous winter scene; he cannot despair over a cold, inanimate universe. In "Sunday Morning," the separation of the self from nature was the cause for alienation, but now Stevens simply takes the separation for granted. He cannot pretend to be part of nature, even for a moment; if he says he is part of nature, he immediately feels "resistance." He can no longer make the effort. Instead of attempting ennobling interchange of the imagination and reality, he concentrates on the particulars of reality before him. Winter is merely winter, wind-blown trees, snow, and ice.

In the final two stanzas, the poet tries to transform the scene, but the cry of the leaves has no supernatural ("di-vine") significance, nor mythic ("puffed out heroes") significance, nor human significance. The "crying" leaves are simply leaves being blown by the wind; they do not transcend their phenomenological meaning. To imagine them crying is unsatisfactory. Finally, the poet asserts that the cry is simply the shrill winter wind and concerns no one at all. The poet has accepted the nothingness of modern life; the cry of the leaves does not symbolize a sense of loss but is simply another detail of reality.

"FAREWELL WITHOUT A GUITAR"

The sense of loss in "Farewell Without a Guitar" (1954) is subdued. In lesser hands, this poem would have quickly degenerated into sentimental melancholy or nostalgia. However, Stevens, with his few spare images, evokes a genuine feeling; like Ernest Hemingway, he expresses the most elemental emotions by cutting language to the bone. To do otherwise would be to luxuriate in an excess of emotion.

In "Farewell Without a Guitar," he suggests that things have come to their natural finale. While there is a sense of loss, there is also a sense of completion and fulfillment implicit in the meditation. The poem is so titled because Stevens's farewell is not accompanied by the music of lush poetry. Loss (and acceptance of it) is evoked without gaudy imaginative embellishment.

The paradise of spring yields to the autumnal terminal—youth to death, gaudy exuberance to spare imagism, celebration to farewell. Autumn is described as "The thousand leaved red," suggesting its beauty and naturalness, not the desolation of bare trees and cold, lifeless days. "Thunder of light" in the second stanza presages the storm of the third stanza and suggests that this storm is a virile one, one of power, not enervation. The oxymoronic metaphor might also suggest a heightened consciousness of reality, a consciousness that occurs when one comes to the end of life. The riderless horse is an apt image for the symbolic death of the man of imagination, the end of the poet's career. Stevens had previously symbolized the romantic poet, or the man of imagination, as "a youth, a lover with phosphorescent hair,/ Dressed poorly, arrogant of his streaming forces," who on his horse madly passes by the literal-minded Mrs. Alfred Uruguay ("Her no and no made yes impossible") on her slow donkey.

There will be no more imaginative excursions now. Only memories and past acts of the mind remain. However, this activity of the mind and the memory of the past sensory contact with reality ("The blows and buffets of fresh senses/ Of the rider that was") now seem to form "a final construction"—a kind of spot of time that serves as the only immortality one can know. Sensuous reality in the present is heightened by this "construction"—a construction created out of the interchange of past sensuous reality ("male reality"), the imagination ("that other"), and the instinct for affirmation of the romantic poet ("her desire").

The autumnal sense of loss, rooted in Stevens's realization that he has come to the end of his career, is really transformed into an acceptance of loss, the celebration of his own farewell; it is reminiscent of Keats's "To Autumn." Reality is viewed in its most sensuous aspects and affirmed. Reality had also been accepted in "The Course of a Particular," but it hardly appeared positive there. In contrast, in Stevens's final poems, mere existence ("mere being" or a life of process) is accepted and found affirmative.

Stevens differs from most twentieth century poets in his romantic faith in the power of the imagination to affirm mundane reality, or at least to make it palatable. He sees the imagination as the source of humanity's salvation in a godless world. Tough-minded and skeptical, he is not the kind of Romantic abhorred by T. E. Hulme, Ezra Pound, and the Imagists. He is not a visionary Romantic in pursuit of transcendent realms; he believes that the modern poet can reside only in the everyday world.

In his book of essays *The Necessary Angel*, Stevens states that the poet must avoid "the hieratic" and must "move in the direction of the credible." Without completely immersing him- or herself in a sordid everyday world or escaping to an ideal world, the twentieth century romantic strives for the necessary balance between the imagination and reality. In his preface to William Carlos Williams's *Collected Poems, 1921-1931* (1934), reprinted in *Opus Posthumous*, Stevens gives the best description of the "romantic poet nowadays": "he is the hermit who dwells alone with the sun and moon, but insists on taking a rotten newspaper."

OTHER MAJOR WORKS

PLAYS: *Three Travelers Watch a Sunrise*, pb. 1916; *Bowl, Cat, and Broomstick*, pr. 1917; *Carlos Among the Candles*, pr. 1917.

NONFICTION: *Three Academic Pieces*, 1947; *The Necessary Angel: Essays on Reality and the Imagination*, 1951; *Letters of Wallace Stevens*, 1966; *Souvenirs and Prophecies: The Young Wallace Stevens*, 1977; *The Contemplated Spouse: The Letters of Wallace Stevens to Elsie*, 2006.

MISCELLANEOUS: *Opus Posthumous*, 1957 (Samuel French Morse, editor).

BIBLIOGRAPHY

Cook, Eleanor. *A Reader's Guide to Wallace Stevens*. Princeton, N.J.: Princeton University Press, 2007. This work elucidates several of Stevens's poems and discusses some of the difficulties that students often encounter when reading his poetry. Includes a thorough appendix and a guide for reading modern poetry.

Eeckhout, Bart, and Edward Ragg, eds. *Wallace Stevens Across the Atlantic*. New York: Palgrave Macmillan, 2008. This collection of essays examines the influence of Stevens on American and European poetry.

Filreis, Alan. *Modernism from Right to Left: Wallace Stevens, the Thirties, and Literary Radicalism*. New York: Cambridge University Press, 2005. Filreis, using documents from political poets active in the 1930's, argues that the political left played a role in forming the poetry of Stevens.

Ford, Sara J. *Gertrude Stein and Wallace Stevens: The Performance of Modern Consciousness*. New York: Routledge, 2002. Compares the conceptions of consciousness revealed in the poetry of Stein and Stevens.

Holander, Stefan. *Wallace Stevens and the Realities of Poetic Language*. New York: Routledge, 2008. This study concentrates on Stevens's poetic language in the 1930's, when the poet's work reflected some level of social consciousness.

Morris, Tim. *Wallace Stevens: Poetry and Criticism*. Cambridge, England: Salt, 2006. Morris uses various methods of critical analysis and studies of annotations Stevens made in his own books to examine the major long poems.

Santilli, Kristine S. *Poetic Gesture: Myth, Wallace Stevens, and the Motions of Poetic Language*. New York: Routledge, 2002. A study of the role of myth in Stevens's poetry.

Serio, John N., ed. *The Cambridge Companion to Wallace Stevens*. New York: Cambridge University Press, 2007. This work presents a complete picture of Stevens's poetic talents. It examines his life and influences and explains his poetic style and voice. Chronology included.

Sharpe, Tony. *Wallace Stevens: A Literary Life*. New York: St. Martin's Press, 2000. Sharpe explores the symbiotic and antagonistic relations between Stevens's literary life and his working life as a senior executive, outlining the personal, historical, and publishing contexts that shaped his writing career and suggesting how awareness of these contexts throws new light on the poems.

Surette, Leon. *A Modern Dilemma: Wallace Stevens, T. S. Eliot, and Humanism*. Ithaca, N.Y.: McGill-Queen's University Press, 2008. Compares and contrasts the poetry of Stevens and T. S. Eliot, examining how humanism played a role in their writings.

Allan Chavkin

JAMES STILL

Born: Double Creek, Alabama; July 16, 1906
Died: Hindman, Kentucky; April 28, 2001

PRINCIPAL POETRY

Hounds on the Mountain, 1937
River of Earth, 1983
The Wolfpen Poems, 1986
From the Mountain, from the Valley: New and Collected Poems, 2001 (Ted Olson, editor)

OTHER LITERARY FORMS

James Still's highly acclaimed novel *River of Earth* first appeared in 1940. *Sporty Creek* (1977) continues the story of the family introduced in *River of Earth*. Still's short stories are collected in *On Troublesome Creek* (1941), *Pattern of a Man* (1976), and *The Run for the Elbertas* (1983). Like his novels, Still's short stories are admired for their deceptively simple narrative technique, skillful character delineation, and psychological insight. They have been compared to the stories of Anton Chekhov, Katherine Anne Porter, and Bernard Malamud.

The exact, colorful language of Still's novels, short stories, and poems is often achieved through the artful use of folk speech, examples of which are found in two collections of Appalachian riddles and rusties (playful, formulaic uses of language): *Way Down Yonder on Troublesome Creek* (1974) and *The Wolfpen Rusties: Appalachian Riddles and Gee-Haw Whimmy-Diddles* (1975). *Jack and the Wonder Beans* (1977) is a delightful retelling of "Jack and the Beanstalk" in the local idiom. Still also prepared his version of the Mother Goose rhymes as *An Appalachian Mother Goose* (1998).

In *The Wolfpen Notebooks: A Record of Appalachian Life* (1991), Still drew from the notebooks that he kept for more than fifty years, recording the distinctive expressions and customs of the Appalachian region.

Critical attention has been more often directed to Still's novels and short stories than to his poems. Still was rightly admired for his prose, however, because he was first of all a poet. After reading his novel *River of Earth* and the poems in *Hounds on the Mountain*, Katherine Anne Porter said in a letter that the two books should be read together. The novel was "an extension of the poems," while the poems were "further comment on the experience that made the novel." Still's poems, then, are doubly deserving of critical attention. Rewarding in themselves, they also belong to any assessment of his total achievement.

ACHIEVEMENTS

James Still's poems, short stories, and novels consistently received high critical acclaim. *Hounds on the Mountain* was reviewed favorably in *Poetry*, *The Atlantic Monthly*, *The New York Times Book Review*, and other newspapers and journals, while *The Wolfpen Po-*

ems was praised by James Dickey in the *Los Angeles Times Book Review*. Still was the recipient of a number of awards, honors, and prizes. These include two Guggenheim Fellowships, the Southern Authors Award, the O. Henry Memorial Prize, and the Marjorie Peabody Waite Award of the American Academy and Institute of Arts and Letters for the "continuing achievement and integrity of his art." He received a number of honorary doctorates as well. Scholarships and fellowships have been established in his name, including fellowships funded by the Andrew W. Mellon Foundation for Advanced Study in the Humanities and Social Science and in Appalachian studies at the University of Kentucky. The James Still Room at Johnson-Camden Library, Morehead State University, was dedicated in 1961. In 1981, Still received the Milner Award, given by the Kentucky Arts Council, in recognition of outstanding leadership in the arts. In 1987, he was awarded a Book of the Year citation from the Appalachian Writers Association. He served as Kentucky's poet laureate in 1995-1996.

BIOGRAPHY

James Still was born in Double Creek, Alabama, in 1906. He attended Lincoln Memorial University and Vanderbilt University in Tennessee, and the University of Illinois, earning B.A. degrees in both arts and sciences, and the M.A. degree in English. Beginning in the early 1930's, he lived in Knott County, Kentucky (except for time spent in travel and in military service in Africa and the Middle East in World War II). His home on Dead Mare Branch was a two-story log house built before 1840, given to him for life by a farmer and dulcimer maker named Jethro Amburgey. Still served as librarian for the Hindman Settlement School and taught at Morehead State University and a number of other institutions.

Still kept his private life and his life as a writer separate—in order to remain "intact." Those who knew him as a teacher and writer knew little about his day-to-day life among neighbors, for the most part farmers and coal miners, who knew next to nothing about him as a writer. To them he was a farmer, a gardener, and the librarian at the Hindman Settlement School. Still's success in keeping separate his private life and his life as a writer resulted in misunderstandings about both his life and his writing.

Because he lived an apparently isolated life and made no effort to advertise himself or promote his writing, or even to accept awards and honors, and because he published infrequently, Still was perceived as a hermit writer. His failure to accept either the award of the American Academy of Arts and Letters or an invitation to be Phi Beta Kappa poet at Columbia University in the 1940's contributed to his reputation as a recluse. This is a misperception. According to Still, he declined in both instances because he lacked bus fare and suitable clothing for the occasions.

While he appeared to be living an isolated life at the Hindman Settlement School, Still was a constant reader of *The Nation*, *The New Republic*, and *The New York Times*. He was publishing in *The Atlantic Monthly*, *Yale Review*, *Poetry*, and many other magazines and journals. At this time, he numbered among his friends Marjorie Kinnan Rawlings, Katherine Anne Porter, Elizabeth Madox Roberts, and Robert Frost. Still considered himself fortunate to have lived in Knott County, Kentucky, lucky to have been assigned post office box 13 at Hindman. "Hindman was surely the only place you could cash a check at four A.M. and call for your mail at midnight. The cashier was an early riser, the postmaster an insomniac."

The notion that Still was a recluse in flight from modernity is mistaken. Cosmopolitan in his tastes and habits, he read several hours per day for more than seventy years. His favorite writers were the Scandinavians and the Russians, especially Anton Chekhov, Nikolai Gogol, and Ivan Turgenev. He often traveled, spending ten winters in Mexico, Guatemala, Honduras, and El Salvador studying Mayan civilization. His advice to anyone wishing to write was to learn to type. When reminded that William Shakespeare did not type, his response was: "What might Shakespeare not have additionally accomplished with a Coronamatic 2000 [typewriter] with a pop-out ribbon!"

Because Appalachia has been the object of numerous sociological studies concerned with poverty and economic exploitation, there have been efforts to interpret Still's writing from both sociological and political perspectives. Still resisted these efforts, although he was not politically unaware. He helped distribute food and clothing to beleaguered strikers in Wilder, Tennessee, in 1930. He lived in eastern Kentucky during the time of the mine wars. He worked, as a temporary replacement, for the Emergency Relief Administration in the mid-1930's. "To live in that time and place . . . was to be politically aware," Still said. He cited the poems in *Hounds on the Mountain* as evidence of his awareness "that at least in my area something was there that would not last much longer. . . . We were living in the nineteenth century, so to speak, and the twentieth would not long be denied."

Instead of a political consciousness, Still brought the temperament, habits, and, to some extent, the methods of the scientist to bear on his writing. In his notebooks, he recorded every facet of the community in which he lived. He considered himself "something of a botanist" and conducted experiments involving the development by natural selection of the wild strawberry and wild violet. The grounds around his house on Dead Mare Branch he described as a "cross between a botanical garden and an experiment station." Where writing is concerned, however, he had no theories regarding artistic creation and recommended no methods or techniques. He could not imagine having been influenced by other writers, and he was not interested in grooming a protégé. When his advice was solicited, he stressed preparation and familiarity with tools of the trade. "A writer gets ready to enter the profession, just as a truck driver learns to operate a truck. I'm fairly certain Chopin didn't compose his works on the piano with one finger, or even two. The preparation is the point." Still advised against looking too closely "into the springs of creativity." The creative process—if it is a process—remained a mystery to him, and he was content with that. When he talked about how he wrote, however, his imagery suggested the scientific approach. The writing does not begin until he touches the "quick" of the material, as with a scalpel.

In the last two decades of his life, he served as a member of the board of directors of the Kentucky Humanities Council, beginning in 1980; as a speaker at the Lilyan Cohen lecture series, Clinch Valley College, in 1987; and as a commentator for National Public Radio's *All Things Considered* in the 1990's.

ANALYSIS

"I have gone softly," James Still wrote in *Hounds on the Mountain*. He compared himself to a child walking on "a ridge/ Of sleep . . . a slope hung on a night-jar's speech." He was a child "with hands like leaves" and eyes "like swifts that search the darkness in a perilous land" ("With Hands Like Leaves"). The similes define Still's unobtrusive approach to his material—the way that he blended in, to become invisible as a speaker in the poems, insisting on objectivity and exactness of detail. In "Eyes in the Grass," the eyes are those of a speaker unnoticed by either bird or insect. The speaker is "lost to any wandering view"; he is "hill uncharted"; his breathing is the wind; he is "horizon . . . earth's far end."

SOUTHERN APPALACHIA

This approach to a people and a place, and Still's achievement as a poet, can be appreciated only in comparison with the way in which the southern Appalachian region of the United States has been typically depicted. The French critic Roland Barthes maintained (*Mythologies*, 1972) that there is an inherent difficulty in writing about mountains and mountain people, the result of a bourgeois alpine myth that causes writers and readers to take leave of their senses "anytime the ground is uneven."

Whatever the cause or causes, southern Appalachia appears in American writing as a veritable funhouse of distorted and contradictory images that have, since the mid-nineteenth century, suited the needs, motives, and perspectives of abolitionists, social workers, Protestant missionaries, industrialists, and entrepreneurs. Southern Appalachia was known through literature either as a place of problems, poverty, and peculiar people, or as a preserve of fundamentally American virtues and values, sterling Anglo-Saxon and Anglo-Celtic qualities. The region entered the popular American mind during the 1880's by way of local colorists (chief among them Mary N. Murfree, who wrote under the pseudonym Charles Egbert Craddock), who noted the quaint and sensational aspects of an old-fashioned way of life. By the 1920's, a careful student of southern Appalachia remarked that more was known about the region that was not true than about any other part of the country.

At a time when it was fashionable, indeed almost

obligatory, for poetry about southern Appalachia to be either a witless romanticizing of mountains and mountain people, or proletarian verse, Still walked softly. He presented no diagnosis of economic ills, preached no social gospel, and offered no program. He declined to participate in the either/or literature, ambitious to do no more—and no less—than to show people in their place and tell how it was with these people at a particular time.

As a consequence, Still's poems discover neither merely a landscape of beauty and wild freedom nor only visual blight, exploitation, and hard, unrelenting conditions. All these things are caught in a vision that is both local and universal. Still's poems embodied certain universal themes implicit in the experience of people in a particular place and time—the themes of endurance, perseverance, and self-preservation under harsh and perilous circumstances.

Details and images created an impression of a difficult life at subsistence level. In "Court Day," the hill folk rise and set out toward the county seat before dawn, when the day is still "dark as plowed earth." The road into town is a stony creekbed. The waters of Troublesome Creek are a "cold thin flowing." The fields of the county poor farm are "hungry" ("On Double Creek"). Descriptions of coal camps suggest unyielding, inhospitable conditions. Coal camp houses are "hung upon the hills" ("Mountain Coal Town"). Underground, the miners are "Breaking the hard, slow-yielding seams" of coal ("Earth-Bread"). Life is not only difficult and meagerly provided for, but is also somehow blighted. Chestnut trees are "cankered to the heart" ("On Red Bird Creek"). The ridges in "Journey Beyond the Hills" are "stricken and unforested." Early morning hours are "gaunt," the mist "leprous," the day "lean" ("The Hill-Born").

Danger and death are ever-present. Death sits "quiet upon a nest" in "Year of the Pigeons." The furrows of the county poor farm are "crooked as an adder's track" ("On Double Creek"). Stars in the night sky over a mountain coal camp are "cool as the copperhead's eyes." The underground shift of the miners is an "eight-hour death," a "daily burial" ("Earth-Bread"). The quarry in "Fox Hunt" is "gaunt and anxious," his life imperiled by the hounds. In the title poem, the fox turns

at the head of a cove to confront the hounds. The fox's blood laves "the violent shadows" of that place, and even the dry roots "questing beneath the earth."

STARK CONTRASTS

Life under such conditions is characterized by stark contrasts—between the bitterness and sweetness of experience and between toughness and tenderness. Beauty and blight, untrammeled freedom and imprisonment coexist. The "starveling trees" in "The Hill-Born" bear sweet fruit. In "Horse Swapping on Troublesome Creek," the mare is spavined, while the foals have "untamed hearts" and "toss unbound heads/ With flash of hock and unsheared flowing manes." The stark contrasts of this life are implicit in the details of "Infare." The groom is "sunbronzed, resolute and free." His bride is "sweet apples from high green orchards." The old who have gathered for this wedding party have "ashy" faces and "rheumy" eyes. The wildness and freedom found in this place exist, paradoxically, in a setting that imprisons. Still refers to the "prisoned waters" of Troublesome Creek ("The Hill-Born") and to "men within their prisoning hills" ("Journey Beyond the Hills").

From birth to death, the circumscribed life of man and beast is difficult, uncertain, constantly endangered. A foal is dropped "under the hard bead/ Of the crow's eyes" ("On Buckhorn Creek"). Life is vulnerable to powerful natural forces, as suggested by "Spring-tides surging to the naked root" ("The Hill-Born"). The forces of nature continue to work on people, plants, and animals even after death. In "Rain on the Cumberlands," the speaker passes "broken horns within the nettled grass/ . . . hoofs relinquished on the breathing stones/ Eaten with rain-strokes." Rain sweeps down the nests of pigeons that have succumbed to the depredations of men and animals, until "not a slate-blue feather blows on any hill" ("Year of the Pigeons"). The dead are not spared the unrelenting harshness of conditions; they lie "under the hard eyes of hill and tree" ("Graveyard"). The dead are "quartered with the roots/ That split firm stone and suck the marrow out,/ And finger yellowing bones" ("Death on the Mountain").

PERSEVERANCE

The characteristic response to these adverse and unrelenting conditions is to endure, to carry on, as suggested by "Horseback in the Rain." The speaker is wet, hungry, and lonely. His horse's hooves clatter on stone. Nevertheless, he has little choice but to "Halt not. Stay not./ Ride the storm with no ending/ On a road unarriving." The poem "Heritage" expresses a determination to stay on in the "prisoning hills" even though "they topple their barren heads to level earth/ And the forests slide uprooted out of the sky."

The response is not only to persevere, but also to preserve something of one's self and one's experiences. "Child in the Hills" emphasizes the perseverance of the child in a man who has "drifted into years of growth and strange enmeshment." The music of the "Mountain Dulcimer" preserves not only the sounds of mountain life—the ringing anvil, the creak of saddlebags and oxen yokes—but also the stillness, "Bitter as salt drenching the tongue of pain."

The characteristic qualities of his style blend with Still's ever-present themes in the representative "Spring on Troublesome Creek." The restraint and understatement of the opening line is gently insisted on by repetition that suggests conversation, or a ballad: "Not all of us were warm, not all of us." Subsequent lines illustrate Still's simple diction and objective reporting of concrete details: "We are winter-lean, our faces are sharp with cold/ And there is a smell of woodsmoke in our clothes;/ Not all of us were warm, though we hugged the fire/ Through the long chilled nights." The poem concentrates Still's themes of endurance, perseverance, and self-preservation: "We have come out/ Into the sun again, we have untied our knot/ Of flesh." Here too is Still's tendency to see people and place as parts of one subtly interdependent whole. In this poem, the condition of the people resembles that of the animals and plants that have also endured the winter. "We are no thinner than a hound or mare,/ Or an unleaved poplar. We have come through/ To grass, to the cows calving in the lot."

SHARED IDENTITY OF PEOPLE AND PLACE

In a poem titled "Anecdote of Men by the Thousand," Wallace Stevens writes, "There are men of a province/ who are that province." Still's poems suggested a similar identity between people and place. People are like the hills; their physical features, characteristics, and qualities mirror their environment. In the poem "On Troublesome Creek," men wait "as mountains long have waited." Hills are like the people. In "Court Day," the hills are so near they seem like people crowding close at the open courthouse window. The ridges in "Journey Beyond the Hills" are "heavy-hipped." Still's human being is himself land walking, weathered by seasons, loving, aging, dying, and coming back in spring, and the land bears not only the spiritual but also the physical imprint of the person who has lived a life on it, in it, and with it. In the life-landscape, even the wounds are duplicated; the land takes them on:

> Uncle Ambrose, your hands are heavy with years,
> Seamy with the ax's heft, the plow's hewn stock,
> The thorn wound and the stump-dark bruise of time.
> Your face is a map of Knott County
> With hard ridges of flesh, the wrinkled creekbeds,
> The traces and forks carved like wagon tracks on stone;
> And there is Troublesome's valley struck violently
> By a barlow's blade.

Like the dress of Stevens's woman of Lhassa, Still's poems were "an invisible element" of a place "made visible." Making himself almost invisible as a speaker in the poems, concentrating not on sensibility, or on social and economic views, Still allowed an elusive element of a place and people to come into sharp focus. This elusive element, the theme of endurance, perseverance, and self-preservation implicit in the life he wrote about, is rendered visible not only in the content of the poems but also through style and structure. The economy and concreteness of expression as well as the spareness of style reflect not only the laconic quality of folk speech but also the conditions of the life from which the language comes. Structure and content, style and theme are blended in a genuine expression of a people and a place.

PORTRAYAL OF A SHARED EXPERIENCE

Fresh in his expression and point of view, Still avoided the superficiality and sensationalism of local colorists and propagandists. Local colorists give the impression of having looked at mountain people and noted the quainter aspects of their traditional life. Reformers emphasize the deplorable circumstances resulting from the inadequacies of that traditional life, or from its destruction through the incursion of mercantile interests. Still gave the impression not merely of having looked at a place and a people but of having lived with them. While the local colorists and proponents of social and economic points of view say "they," Still says "we."

At its best, according to the novelist Wilma Dykeman, the literature of the Appalachian region is "as unique as churning butter, as universal as getting born." Such a combination of uniqueness and universality, found in the best literature of any time and place, is present in Still's poems. They are poems in which abstractions consist of what particulars ultimately mean. Like all genuine poems, they are, as William Carlos Williams puts it, "a vision of the facts."

OTHER MAJOR WORKS

LONG FICTION: *River of Earth*, 1940, 1968, 1978; *Sporty Creek*, 1977.

SHORT FICTION: *On Troublesome Creek*, 1941; *The Wolfpen Rusties: Appalachian Riddles and Gee-Haw Whimmy-Diddles*, 1975; *Pattern of a Man*, 1976; *The Run for the Elbertas*, 1983.

NONFICTION: *The Man in the Bushes: The Notebooks of James Still, 1935-1987*, 1988; *The Wolfpen Notebooks: A Record of Appalachian Life*, 1991.

CHILDREN'S LITERATURE: *Way Down Yonder on Troublesome Creek*, 1974; *Jack and the Wonder Beans*, 1977; *An Appalachian Mother Goose*, 1998.

BIBLIOGRAPHY

Berry, Wendell. "A Master Language." *Sewanee Review* 105, no. 3 (Summer, 1997): 419-422. Berry discusses the works of Still and the poet's masterful use of dialect and language.

Cadle, Dean. "Pattern of a Writer: Attitudes of James Still." *Appalachian Journal* 15 (Winter, 1988): 104-143. Cadle presents notes from conversations he had with Still in 1958-1959. Includes Still's views on writing; also has photographs of Still, his house, and neighbors and friends.

Dickey, James. Review of *The Wolfpen Poems*. *Los Angeles Times Book Review* 1 (December 7, 1986): 19. Dickey states that these poems establish Still as the "truest and most remarkable poet of mountain culture." Notes his sincerity and modesty and com-

mends him for the feel of the country in his poems. Sees the strength of *The Wolfpen Poems* collection in that it underscores the necessity of Appalachian culture and its values.

Foxfire 22 (Fall, 1988). This special issue on Still concentrates on *The Wolfpen Notebooks*; it contains an interview and selections from the book (not yet published at the time of the issue).

Iron Mountain Review 2 (Summer, 1984). This issue devoted to Still contains an interview with Still, essays on his poetry ("James Still's Poetry: 'The Journey of a Worldly Wonder'" by Jeff Daniel Marion), short fiction, and a Still bibliography.

Olson, Ted, and Kathy H. Olson, eds. *James Still: Critical Essays on the Dean of Appalachian Literature*. Jefferson, N.C.: McFarland, 2007. This first book-length collection of scholarly essays on Still provides valuable information on his works.

Still, James. *James Still in Interviews, Oral Histories, and Memoirs*. Edited by Ted Olson. Jefferson, N.C.: McFarland, 2009. This volume collects numerous interviews with the poet and reminiscences by writers who knew him.

Turner, Martha Billips. "A Vision of Change: Appalachia in James Still's *River of Earth*." *Southern Literary Journal* 24, no. 2 (Spring, 1992): 11. Still's writings have established his reputation as a serious, talented writer of the Appalachian region. Discusses his portrayal of Appalachia in *River of Earth*.

Jim Wayne Miller

MARK STRAND

Born: Summerside, Prince Edward Island, Canada; April 11, 1934

PRINCIPAL POETRY

Sleeping with One Eye Open, 1964
Reasons for Moving, 1968
Darker, 1970
Elegy for My Father, 1973
The Sargeantville Notebook, 1973

The Story of Our Lives, 1973
The Late Hour, 1978
Selected Poems, 1980
Prose: Four Poems, 1987
The Continuous Life, 1990
Dark Harbor, 1993
Blizzard of One, 1998
Chicken, Shadow, Moon, and More, 1999
Man and Camel, 2006
New Selected Poems, 2007

OTHER LITERARY FORMS

In addition to poetry, Mark Strand has written *Mr. and Mrs. Baby, and Other Stories* (1985), a collection of short stories with a bent for fantasy, and *The Monument* (1978), primarily a novel, but which contains a few dozen poems integral to the discourse. Strand has translated poetry into English, the most noteworthy volumes of which are *Eighteen Poems from the Quechua* (1971) and *The Owl's Insomnia: Poems by Rafael Alberti* (1973). He has edited or coedited several anthologies of poetry, the most important of which are *The Contemporary American Poets: American Poetry Since 1940* (1969) and *The Making of a Poem: A Norton Anthology of Poetic Forms* (2000), with Eavan Boland. His books on art include *Hopper* (1994, 2001) and *William Bailey* (1987). In *The Weather of Words: Poetic Invention* (2000), Strand collects many of his magazine essays on poetry. His most successful book for children is *The Planet of Lost Things* (1982).

ACHIEVEMENTS

From early in his career, Mark Strand has been received with respect by critics. His poetry, while grounded in a reality that borders on the surreal, manages to evoke sensations and sensitivity, flavored with a taste for the abstract and bizarre, which convey the haunting, factual nature of the human psyche. Although his poetry is clearly unusual in this ability, and while he has been given a series of awards and other recognitions, his work has not received the final honor—that is, his poems have not been commonly anthologized. Strand's *Blizzard of One* received the Pulitzer Prize in 1999. He also won the Edgar Allan Poe Award for *The Story of Our Lives* from the Academy of

American Poets (1974), an Academy Award in Literature (1975) and a Gold Medal (2009) from the American Academy of Arts and Letters, the Bobbitt National Prize (1992), the Bollingen Prize (1993), the Bingham Poetry Prize (1999), and the Wallace Stevens Award (2004). Strand has been awarded fellowships from the Fulbright Foundation (1960 and 1965), the Guggenheim Foundation (1974), the Academy of American Poets (1979), and the MacArthur Foundation (1987), as well as grants from the Ingram Merrill Foundation (1966), the National Endowment for the Arts (1967), and the Rockefeller Foundation (1968). He served as poet laureate consultant in poetry to the Library of Congress from 1990 to 1991 and as chancellor for the Academy of American Poets from 1995 to 2000.

BIOGRAPHY

Although a Canadian by birth, Mark Strand moved to the United States in 1938, when he was four years old, and has remained there for most of his life. He has consistently described his parents, Robert Joseph Strand and Sonia Apter Strand, as "bookish," intellec-

Mark Strand (©Lilo Raymond)

tual types who emphasized education and the humanities in his childhood. The youth at first fought his parents' influence in this regard and sought to become an athlete, although he was interested in art from an early age. He grew up in the country, spending much time without the companionship of other children. In 1954, he entered Antioch College in northern Ohio, where he immediately came under the influence of Nolan Miller, his freshman English teacher and a respected critic, editor, and writer. In his college years, his attraction to and involvement with poetry became undeniable; he discovered that he liked reading it as well as writing it, and, whether consciously or unconsciously, he set upon a career course that would eventually lead to the announcement that he had been appointed poet laureate of the United States by the Library of Congress.

He earned a bachelor's degree in fine arts from Yale University in 1959, where he also received the Cook Prize and the Bergin Prize. Upon graduation, he was appointed a Fulbright Fellow and spent a year at the University of Florence. In 1961, he was married to Antonia Ratensky, from whom he was divorced in 1973; the marriage saw the birth of one daughter, Jessica. While teaching at the University of Iowa, he earned his third degree, a master of arts, in 1962. He has taught at the University of Brazil, Mount Holyoke College, the University of Washington, Yale, Brooklyn College, Princeton University, Brandeis University, the University of Virginia, Wesleyan University, and Harvard University. From 1981 to 1993, he taught at the University of Utah. Later he taught at The Johns Hopkins University and at the University of Chicago, where he was Andrew MacLeish Distinguished Service Professor of Social Thought until 2005, when he became professor of English and comparative literature at Columbia University.

In the early 1960's, Strand's first poems were accepted for publication by East Coast literary establishment magazines, particularly *The New Yorker*. He consistently published thereafter, with his works (including translations) appearing in more than a dozen volumes. In 1976, he was married to Julia Rumsey Garretson, and with her he had a son, Thomas Summerfield. Ostensibly, Strand's children's books were written in part for his own children, after the fashion of Charles Dickens.

Analysis

Mark Strand's poetry is entirely characteristic of the age in which he writes. Solipsism, alienation, and self-definition are the principal concerns. His work manifests a certain self-involvement that sometimes goes over the line into narcissism. Many of his poems are an inner dialogue that reaches into the realm of clinical schizophrenia. He is unable to define himself, finally, except as a sensitive soul searching for definition. He does not sound a Whitmanesque "barbaric yawp" over the rooftops of the world so much as he makes a distinguishable Eliotian "whimper" from the closet of his bedroom. Overall, Strand's poetry fits clearly, quickly, and neatly into the packaged, near-formulaic modes of poetry manufactured in the second half of the twentieth century. Nevertheless, he has a voice, experience, and expression all quite his own, and certain identifiable attributes of his work do serve not only to separate it from the works of others but also to make it deserving of the attention it has received.

Strand's work depicts, to use his own word, the sourceless "darkness" that pervades human existence. In this depiction, fear is present, to be sure, as are oversensitivity, bifurcation of identity in the voice of the poet(s), spiritual nakedness, a strange combination of fantasy and the almost-surreal, and an elusive peace that never exists in the conscious and remains undiscoverable in both the subconscious and the unconscious. Strand's poetry, then, is not distinctive so much in its subject matter or the ideas it expresses as in the techniques it employs: He thus has a far different domain from those of other poets writing in this subgenre of late modernism and postexistentialism.

The poetry of Strand is distinctive not so much in content as in approach. His contribution to twentieth century American poetry is the singularity in method and mode of expressing ideas common to other poets of his time. He stands apart from others, however, specifically through his estranged—though assuredly successful—mixture of the haunting darkness of reality with the fantastic and sexual, with self-alienation whose form is self-involvement, and with a recognition of the bifurcated personality, neither side of which can be subject functionally to the other. The mark of the superior quality of his works is that somehow he convinces the reader that life truly is this way and that the experiences he describes, however bizarre, are experiences that they share.

SLEEPING WITH ONE EYE OPEN

Two poems from Strand's first published collection, *Sleeping with One Eye Open*, demonstrate most of these qualities. In "The Tunnel," the speaker of the poem is aware of a second self lurking, perpetually lurking, in the front yard of his house, itself a metaphor for his body. The primary persona of the poem experiences angst in both his ability and his inability to confront the other persona of his own self. He shines a flashlight at it, opens the door for a direct confrontation (which turns out to be more of a peek), makes obscene gestures at the other, leaves it suicide notes, tears up his (their) living-room furniture, and, finally, decides to dig a tunnel to escape to a neighbor's yard. The attempt fails; there can be no communication or contact with another until he has first set his own house in order. The poet finishes digging the tunnel to find himself immobilized. He does not enter this escape route, although it is fully prepared; the poem ends with him aware that he is still being watched by the other self, now not in immediate physical visibility, and knowing that he will not leave the other after all. The self will remain fractured, and the fear will not go away. Escape is not possible, because it would be at least a partial enactment of suicide, which is unacceptable, accomplishing nothing.

In "Poem," the primary persona is again visited by the secondary self, who sneaks into his house (again a metaphor for the poet's body), climbs the stairs to the bedroom, where the poet is not sleeping but waiting, and announces that he is going to kill him. In this companion poem to "The Tunnel," the situation is reversed and enhanced. In the first poem, the primary consciousness of the poet's existence tries only to escape the second consciousness and chooses not to do so. In "Poem," the second self succeeds in confronting the first one to announce not escape, but murder. Both halves meet with failure. The would-be murder of self is to be carried out by mutilation: The second self starts cutting away at the body, beginning with the toenails and proceeding upward, to stop only when "nothing is left," at least emotionally. The mutilating

self stops when he reaches the neck; that is, he leaves the head to go on thinking, and he departs. Predictably, the poem ends just as the first one did. Both selves are left only to go on in a dual existence of irresolution and terror.

REASONS FOR MOVING

Strand revisits the same motifs and existence in many of the poems that were collected in *Reasons for Moving*. These are particularly evident in "The Man in the Mirror," a longer poem of thirty quatrains in which the poet reveals his innermost thoughts while routinely confronting himself in a mirror. The reflection becomes first an image, then an embodiment with a personality of its own, as the poet tries to define himself and find meaning in his life. The voyeuristic narcissism and the fact of the fractured self struggling for union and self-comprehension provide the framework, context, and message of the poem. The poet views himself in the mirror on his living-room wall, contemplating the meaning of what he sees—his other self. The emergence of identities is evident early in the poem: "I remember how we used to stand/ wishing the glass/ would dissolve between us." However, this wistful attempt at merging the two parts is incomplete, therefore unsuccessful. "But that was another life./ One day you turned away/ and left me here/ to founder in the stillness of your wake." The body of the poem is then a matter of recording a list of ways in which he had tried to cope with this wake. He watches and studies the other self; he tries to forget him; he is driven to walking around the house, performing strange actions. The other continues to be present, but pointlessly so. Finally, as in the case of the two poems already discussed, the poet gives up; he knows that "it will always be this way./ I stand here scared/ that you will disappear, scared that you will stay."

Strand published "The Dirty Hand" in the same collection. This poem is, for both the poet and the reader, an experience in the self-involvement of narcissism and masturbation. The poet bemoans the fact that his hand is dirty and cannot be cleaned, ostensibly for the reason that he will simply get it dirty again: The stain of the flesh cannot be removed, because the flesh itself is dirt. He is aware of no guilt, only uncleanness. Repeatedly, he washes his hand (notice that the poet never refers to the hand in the plural; only one hand is problematic), scrubbing and polishing yet unable to remove the stain. He tries to hide the hand from others, an endeavor that meets with little success, and he cannot hide the hand from himself either. The intensity of the problem increases, until finally he recognizes that he cannot live with it and proclaims that he will cut it off, chop it into pieces, and throw it into the ocean. This desire to rid himself of his nature, however, is not the main thrust of the poem, which ends with the wish for "another hand" to come to take its place, not at the end of his arm but by fastening itself to his arm. The poet wants someone else to assume the role of self-involvement, which leaves him unclean.

DARKER

Darker, published in 1970, remains Strand's best collection of poetry. These poems focus on the fear and dread of the human consciousness that occur because of the immobility he had recognized and written of in earlier poems. Aware that it is not enough to maintain that individuals are trapped in fear, the poet turns to the "darker" realization that there is no change, no hope, and no progress. In his earlier poems, he had recognized as much, but he now turns to dealing with the consequences of such a realization. Previously, he had expressed himself as entrapped; in *Darker*, the poems worry with the meaning of that permanent and irreversible entrapment.

The third poem in *Darker* is called "Giving Myself Up." In this poem, the poet lists a series of some dozen items that he "gives up," parts of his body as well as his "smell" and his "clothes." The poet gives up every matter of importance to his self-involvement, even the "ghost" that lives in his clothes. The poem concludes, "And you will have none of it because already I am beginning/ again without anything." His surrender to fear, the hopelessness of isolation, and the immobility caused by having two identities accomplishes nothing. He has finished without anything and will start again without anything. He knows that he is hopelessly trapped in a cycle from which there is no escape—only a minimal comprehension of the process. Along with the other side of his schizophrenic self, he will begin again, only to reach the same purposeless point later. Giving up to the other self will not let him out of his

present state. Thus one answer is given to the problem of existing in permanent entrapment: Self-abnegation will not work.

A second meaning of this fixated condition is similarly expressed in several other poems in *Darker*, particularly "Black Maps." Here, the poet maps out his existential life against a background of blackness. He begins the poem by recognizing that his birth (here called "arrival") is unacknowledged either by the "attendance of stones," an image representing the kinds of mental torture and persecution the poet later experiences, or an "applauding wind"; thus he asserts that nature takes no joy from the appearance of the individual. "Nothing will tell you/ where you are" either at the time of birth or later in life. Individuals struggle and cope alone in a present that "is always dark." In this life all "maps are black," and life is a voyage only into the surrounding emptiness. By attempting to study these maps of the dark night of the soul, the poet learns only that "what you thought/ were concerns of yours/ do not exist." The cares and worries of this life are unimportant, because they have no physical or mental reality. In fact, the poet concludes, "Only you are there." Once again, the poet addresses his other self, the recognition of which entirely prevents him from any spiritual mobility. Only a dual loneliness pervades.

Also in *Darker* is a short poem that is in many ways Strand's bleakest expression of his condition. He writes "My Death" from the perspective of the other side of the grave. He asserts that sadness, confusion, and waste are commonplace, expected elements of the event, of which he is consciously aware. The poet seemingly enjoys the chaos he precipitates among his friends and relatives by telling them that he had tried to commit suicide several times. He shocks them into leaving: "Soon I was alone." The poet is now returned, by his own will and force and intention, to his original state: Nothing is gained from death, not even momentary relief from the condition he has had in life.

THE STORY OF OUR LIVES

In *The Story of Our Lives*, Strand presents a new way of looking at his state. On one hand, he is given to the usual self-involvement; on the other, there is a rather complete self-detachment. The title poem, the best in the collection, can be rightfully interpreted in a straightforward manner. The narrator of the poem is addressing someone, presumably a woman whom he loves and to whom he is probably married. He tells her that they have been reading "the story of our lives;" that is, the frame of this long poem is to explore the possibilities of what it would mean to be able to read their lives as though they were recorded in a book, here ostensibly a novel. They jointly read on, learning of themselves as their plots and plights unfold.

The poem, which is one of his better and more readable pieces, is written in seven stanzas of some twenty lines each. In the first one, Strand reports to readers (and undoubtedly to himself) that the "*we*" of the poem are trying to find meaning and direction in their "lives" by reading in a book where, at least, what happens is known. The "*we*" here garners two legitimate interpretations. First, it is clearly the poet himself and the lover whom he is addressing. At the same time, Strand has constructed the poem so as to legitimize it as another fractured-self conversation typical in his works. In either case, the personas of the poem are sitting together on a couch in their living room, knowing that "the book of our lives is empty"; the furniture is never changed; even the rugs become "darker" through the years as "our shadows pass over them." The second stanza opens with "We are reading the story of our lives/ as though we were in it/ as though we had written it." Life is just as vacuous in the novel as in their other, daily existence. The poet recognizes early that if such a book did exist, it would be unable to reveal meaning for him; that, perhaps, would be somebody else's life (or lives). In all stanzas except the first one, a few random passages from the imagined book are interwoven into the poet's own lines so as to make evident the futility of the endeavor. Because the book offers nothing new, the poet records that "it wants to divide us."

In the third and fourth stanzas, the other self becomes both bored and tired and falls asleep, as it is written in the book. The primary narrator-self reads on to see what will happen; of course, he learns that the answer is, more or less, nothing. People fall asleep and people wake up—their lives remain empty whether or not they are well rested. By the fifth stanza, the poet has given up on finding something in the book that would

foretell purpose in his (their) existence; he wishes only for a "perfect moment," one in which he could have momentary relief from the dark. Were there such a moment, so he ponders, he could then perpetually live and relive it by always starting at the beginning of the book and reading to that point. Such a moment is not to be found; it does not exist in their lives and cannot be found in a record of their lives. The concluding stanzas of the poem reinforce such a stance. The poet and his companion are left with loneliness and despair. They grow tired of reading the book, of studying the "tired phantoms" that occupy the "copy" as well as inhabit their own bodies. Thus they determine to accept this truth, realizing that "they are the book and they are/ nothing else."

SELECTED POEMS

Selected Poems contains Strand's best poems, and the volume serves well to represent Strand's life's work to 1980. Five new poems appeared in this publication, the most important of which is the unusual "Shooting Whales." The poet recalls an event from his childhood in which he, his father, and other family members get in a boat to watch fishermen who have gone out to shoot whales in St. Margaret's Bay. They are out all day, and as they are returning, after dark, their boat engine dies. The speaker's father takes the oars and rows all the way home, speechlessly. That night, the young speaker lies in bed envisioning the whales moving in the ocean beneath him: "they were luring me/ downward and downward/ into the murmurous/ water of sleep." His existence, then, is made akin to that of the whales; they are like singing mermaids who would lure him into the depths of his later darkness, self-involvement, and loneliness.

THE CONTINUOUS LIFE

Strand did not publish another major volume of poetry for ten years. The poems in *The Continuous Life* vary in form and content. Many of the poems are ostensibly prose but qualify as poems because each of their meanings is conveyed poetically, through a series of images. More noticeably, there is less focus on split personality and psychosis. Though the poet never gets out of himself to the extent that his subject matter is actually another person, he does focus on external people and conditions in some poems in this volume. A few of these poems are not even written in first person; some are recordings of conversations, almost in dramatic form; two or three of them are called "letters."

The majority of the thirty poems in *The Continuous Life* are composed in the same vein as those already discussed here, with little tampering with previous themes. In "The Continuous Life," Strand gives advice about what parents should tell their children. First, he instructs, "confess/ To your little ones the night is a long way off"—that is, tell them of death but explain that it is far in the distant future. His second advice is to inform them of how "mundane" life is, and he then offers a list of household chores and implements. Parents should also explain that life is a period "between two great darks," birth and death. In the meantime, individuals conduct a great "search" for "something . . . , a piece of the dark that might have been yours." Finally, the poet recognizes the existence and reality of "small tremors of love through your brief,/ Undeniable selves, into your days, and beyond." It is unusual for Strand to acknowledge the existence of love, or even of "small tremors of love," which here arguably counter the darkness on which the bulk of his work focuses. The poet sees love, possibly, as an experience that can give partial and momentary relief in the present.

"The End," the short poem that concludes *The Continuous Life*, serves as a final comment about Strand's life, and therefore his poetry, "Not every man knows what he shall sing at the end," writes the poet in such a way as to suggest that he does. He then gives a short list of typical activities of life that come to an end when a man becomes eternally "motionless" and it is "clear that he'll never go back." The poem concludes, "Not every man knows what is waiting for him, or what he shall sing/ When the ship he is on slips into darkness, there at the end." The poet knows what awaits him at his end and what song he will then sing. Strand has explored his death sufficiently, he foresees, to know that he will comprehend and experience the darkness at that time just as he has lived his life. It will truly change nothing.

DARK HARBOR

In *Dark Harbor*, this darkness is made all the more visible. Strand has fashioned a book-length poetic sequence consisting of forty-five numbered parts intro-

duced by a "Proem." All but one of the individual units fit on a single page, and they are cast in loose, three-line stanzas, occasionally ending in couplets. Strand employs this muffled echo of Dante's terza rima to thread a graceful, somber meditation on loss, dislocation, and the general unease of a mind and spirit strangely alienated from all that they attend to and even accept. Either too decorous or too numb to celebrate or rebel, Strand's persona charts a quiet, restrained course in which a mood of seeming passivity or resignation manages to establish and build tension.

BLIZZARD OF ONE

Blizzard of One will strike many as a rather slight volume for a Pulitzer Prize winner. As ever, Strand's realm is a place caught in the oscillation of the ordinary and the extraordinary. Time's erasure of the many selves one puts on is mourned in various inventive ways. Strand's rich melancholic intonations carry a greater edge of wit here, perhaps the gift of the even greater distancing from tragedy that comes with age. Many of the poems, such as "A Suite of Appearances" and "Five Dogs," are multipart sequences. Most striking is "The Delirium Waltz," a poem that marks a celebratory occasion of some kind without ever pinning down its true nature or meaning. Alternating heavily patterned, pantoum-like quatrains with stretches of prose, the poem seems a gathering of the damned, old friends locked in repetitive patterns of social interaction, the motion everything as they lose whatever recognition they ever had of who they are and why they came. The hours of the waltz become years and then a season. The dancers, many of whom wish to stop, cannot.

MAN AND CAMEL

Strand has not exactly mellowed through the years, but in *Man and Camel*, he seems to have come to terms with life being transitory. In "2032," once dreaded death has become an old man sitting in the backseat of a limousine, waiting for his chauffeur. He has on a lap robe to ward off a chill, his face is pale, his eyes are smaller than before, and he has the same gray hair as the speaker. While the two will meet face to face one day, for now, death poses little threat, having put aside his scythe and hourglass. He no longer lurks in front yards. This is quite a change from Strand's earlier dark, brooding poems in which he is haunted by thoughts of dying.

Man and Camel is divided into three parts, the first written by the fabulist in Strand. In part 1, Strand makes a case for accepting fantasy, presenting in "The King" a tiny monarch hiding in the corner because he would rather sleep than rule. That harmless image is followed by "I Had Been a Polar Explorer," in which the narrator first tells of his adventure-filled youth, then describes a fallow period of adulthood, which is followed by a spurt of great creativity in which he fills page after page with tales of the exotic, before espying that familiar man in the front yard. The writer waves in recognition, but the image fades.

In "2002," Strand says that while he is attempting to ease up on thoughts of death, Death is not only thinking of him but also identifying him by name. Death appears to be looking forward to Strand's company.

In the title poem, "Man and Camel," a man is smoking a cigarette on his front porch when he observes a man and a camel passing by. He takes the event casually until the two begin singing and he wants to know the origin of the tune. The man and camel run back to him, saying he has ruined everything by examining, by breaking the fantasy with thought.

In "Elevator," Strand is either having fun or being dead serious. He takes an elevator to the basement, presumably the end of the line. A man waiting there asks if he is going up, as if going down were an option. The second stanza repeats the first, the last line of each being: "'I'm going down,' I said. 'I won't be going up.'" The question arises if Strand is mocking the man's stupidity or if he has crossed over into the realm of the metaphysical. Is he going to Hell (down) as opposed to Heaven (up)?

Part 2 returns full force to the contemplative, often grim Strand. In "Mother and Son," a man goes to his mother's hospital room, hoping that before dying, she will at last tell him that he is her boy and always will be, but her lips are cold, the "burial of feelings hav[ing] begun." There is more rejection in "The Mirror," when a man sees a woman across the room looking in his direction. Assuming that he has attracted her, he realizes sadly that she is checking the mirror behind him, to see perhaps if the one she awaits is approaching. He says he can never forget that moment without a pang, without feeling that he himself is emerging "breathless and eager" from the mirror into a room full of partying people "only to discover too late that she is not there."

Part 3 is a retelling of Christ's last words as he hangs from the cross: Christ asks forgiveness for the perpetrators; reassures a thief on the next cross that if he is a believer, they will meet in paradise; asks disciple John to look after his mother, Mary; asks God why he has forsaken him; asks for water and is given sour wine; and finally says that his trials are finished and he is giving himself fully to his Father. "Poem After the Seven Last Words" was commissioned by the Brentano String Quartet to be read between movements of Franz Joseph Haydn's Opus 51, in performances at various locations in the United States.

NEW SELECTED POEMS

New Selected Poems is an update of the *Selected Poems* that appeared in 1980. As before, "the worst" is always waiting in the shadows. Strand is clearly under the influence of the great thinkers—Martin Heidegger, Jean-Paul Sartre, Friedrich Nietzsche, and Albert Camus—and the existentialists, with all their apprehension, foreboding, and sense of alienation.

In "Keeping Things Whole," the poet says he has to keep moving so that things can be whole. "In a field/ I am the absence/ of field./ . . ./ Wherever I am/ I am what is missing.// When I walk/ I part the air/ and always/ the air moves in/ to fill the spaces/ where my body's been." This is Strand's take on the transience of life. One can be in a place, but when one dies nothing has changed.

In a new, fifty-two-part poem, "The Monument," Strand has constructed a monument to himself. He then has angry poets come with hammers and little buckets to knock off pieces of the monument to study and use in the making of their own small tombs. He wishes he could inscribe something meaningful that would be remembered. He can only use words lent to him by some literary giants, such as Octavio Paz, William Shakespeare, Anton Chekhov, Walt Whitman, Jorge Luis Borges, and William Wordsworth.

One wistful poem that has been widely anthologized is "Pot Roast," in which the speaker is eating a pot roast dinner and thinking of the first time his mother made this meal for him, leaning over his plate to replenish the potatoes, carrots, onions, and gravy. He inhales the steam and, for a moment, does not "regret the passage of time." He remembers his mother's gravy, "its odor of garlic and celery," and recalls "sopping it up with pieces of bread." He says: "And now/ I taste it again./ The meat of memory./ The meat of no change./ I raise my fork/ and I eat."

Although Strand uses plain language in simple, short sentences, his words have the impact of a power drill. He uses precise language and surreal imagery and deals with absence and negation, loneliness and alienation. He can be hard to understand, but the sounds and arrangements of the words can evoke a mood. Some critics have called him a documentarian, relating what he sees. He says of himself that he shows, but does not explain. He does not proselytize. He does not attempt to answer questions or provide solutions or rail against injustice. His words turn readers inward, force them to consider their own alter egos, their own mortality, and their own way of embracing life before it ends. He sees life as an in-between state starting at birth and heading, always, toward death.

He fears death, or more precisely, the unknown. He knows that writers can create what they think of as the present, but no one can discuss the state of death, the lack of being, because no one has been there. He has, however, come to see that there are moments of great joy and that he must embrace them.

OTHER MAJOR WORKS

LONG FICTION: *The Monument*, 1978.

SHORT FICTION: *Mr. and Mrs. Baby, and Other Stories*, 1985.

NONFICTION: *William Bailey*, 1987; *Hopper*, 1994, 2001; *The Weather of Words: Poetic Invention*, 2000.

TRANSLATIONS: *Eighteen Poems from the Quechua*, 1971; *The Owl's Insomnia: Poems by Rafael Alberti*, 1973; *Souvenir of the Ancient World*, 1976 (of Carlos Drummond de Andrade).

CHILDREN'S LITERATURE: *The Planet of Lost Things*, 1982; *The Night Book*, 1985; *Rembrandt Takes a Walk*, 1986.

EDITED TEXTS: *The Contemporary American Poets:*

American Poetry Since 1940, 1969; *New Poetry of Mexico*, 1970; *Another Republic: Seventeen European and South American Writers*, 1976 (with Charles Simic); *Art of the Real: Nine American Figurative Painters*, 1983; *Travelling in the Family: Poems by Carlos Drummond de Andrade*, 1986 (with Thomas Colchie); *The Best American Poetry: 1991*, 1991; *Stories and Poems*, 1995 (with Tim O'Brien); *The Making of a Poem: A Norton Anthology of Poetic Forms*, 2000 (with Eavan Boland); *One Hundred Great Poems of the Twentieth Century*, 2005.

BIBLIOGRAPHY

Aaron, Jonathan. "About Mark Strand: A Profile." *Ploughshares* 21, no. 4 (Winter, 1995/1996): 202-205. This is an excellent short overview of Strand's career, accomplishments, and sense of himself as a writer. Strand is the guest editor of this issue of the magazine.

Bloom, Harold. "Dark and Radiant Peripheries: Mark Strand and A. R. Ammons." *Southern Review* 8 (Winter, 1972): 133-141. This article is formally divided into four main sections: The introduction and conclusion briefly compare the poetry of Strand and Ammons, while the second section is given to Strand and the third to Ammons. Critical commentary is provided for the title poems of Strand's first three volumes: *Sleeping with One Eye Open*, *Reasons for Moving*, and *Darker*. Bloom focuses on the "dark" elements of Strand's work.

_____, ed. *Mark Strand*. Philadelphia: Chelsea House, 2003. A collection of essays examining four poems: "The Story of Our Lives," "The Way It Is," "Elegy for My Father," and "Dark Harbor."

Gregorson, Linda. "Negative Capability." *Parnassus: Poetry in Review* 9 (1981): 90-114. Gregorson discusses poems from Strand's *Selected Poems*. She focuses on the rhymes and meters of the poetry, as well as the imagery. Also included are some critical analyses of the poet's use of prosody. Her overall effort is to trace the developing forms and formats of the recognizably better poems.

Howard, Richard. "Mark Strand." In *Alone with America: Essays on the Art of Poetry in the United States Since 1950*. New York: Atheneum, 1980. Howard writes critically of Strand's first two collections of poems, *Sleeping with One Eye Open* and *Reasons for Moving*. He sees the second volume as an outgrowth and continuation of the first one. Howard focuses on the duality of Strand's nature and his inability to reconcile the different aspects of his personality.

Kirby, David. *Mark Strand and the Poet's Place in Contemporary American Culture*. Columbia: University of Missouri Press, 1990. A fascinating exploration of the public roles and stances of the poet, with Strand as the central case in point. More a study in the sociology of literature than a work of literary criticism, yet important because Strand's public persona and his writing have a strange symbiotic relationship.

Nicosia, James F. *Reading Mark Strand: His Collected Works, Career, and the Poetics of the Privative*. New York: Palgrave Macmillan, 2007. This work provides detailed analysis of more than seventy poems by Strand. Studying the works chronologically, Nicosia makes enlightening connections between Strand's life and his poetry.

Olsen, Lance. "Entry to the Unaccounted For: Mark Strand's Fantastic Autism." In *The Poetic Fantastic: Studies in an Evolving Genre*, edited by Patrick D. Murphy and Vernon Hyles. New York: Greenwood Press, 1989. In this short article of some ten pages, Olsen interprets much of Strand's work in terms of fantasy. He deals specifically with poems taken from *Sleeping with One Eye Open* and *Reasons for Moving*. The critic sees many elements of science fiction in Strand's poems, as well as metafiction.

Strand, Mark. "Mark Strand: The Art of Poetry LXXVII." Interview by Wallace Shawn. *Paris Review* 40, no. 148 (Fall, 1998): 146-179. Strand discusses his poetic themes and writing style.

Carl Singleton; Philip K. Jason
Updated by Gay Pitman Zieger

LUCIEN STRYK

Born: Kolo, Poland; April 7, 1924

PRINCIPAL POETRY

Taproot, 1953
The Trespasser, 1956
Notes for a Guidebook, 1965
The Pit, and Other Poems, 1969
Awakening, 1973
Selected Poems, 1976
Collected Poems, 1953-1983, 1984
Bells of Lombardy, 1986
Of Pen and Ink and Paper Scraps, 1989
Where We Are: Selected Poems and Zen Translations, 1997
And Still Birds Sing: New and Collected Poems, 1998

OTHER LITERARY FORMS

Although Lucien Stryk (strihk) is known for his significant work as a poet—A. Poulin, Jr., included Stryk's work in several editions of the influential anthology *Contemporary American Poetry*—Stryk has also made innumerable contributions in his work as a translator, editor, and commentator on the importance of Zen philosophy and the art created by those who follow such a philosophy. As a translator, Stryk worked diligently, along with his frequent collaborator Takashi Ikemoto, to shed light on the work of important Zen masters such as Shinkichi Takahashi, Issa, and Matsuo Bashō. Some of his most significant work as a translator is found in *Zen: Poems, Prayers, Sermons, Anecdotes, Interviews* (1965); *Afterimages: Zen Poems of Shinkichi Takahashi* (1970); *Zen Poetry: Let the Spring Breeze Enter* (1977); *Traveler, My Name: Haiku of Basho* (1985); *Triumph of the Sparrow: Zen Poems of Shinkichi Takahashi* (1986); and *The Dumpling Field: Haiku of Issa* (1991). As a Zen Buddhist commentator and practitioner as well as cultural historian, Stryk has created work that has proved to be vitally important in opening up a space first for the study of Zen and later for its celebration. Work relating to Zen Buddhist thought and art may be found in such volumes as *World of*

Buddha: An Introduction to Buddhist Literature (1968) and *Encounter with Zen: Writings on Poetry and Zen* (1981). In his role as editor, Stryk is best known for his celebration of place, specifically the Midwest, in two collections that highlighted the work of emerging and established poets. *Heartland: Poets of the Midwest* (1967) and *Heartland II: Poets of the Midwest* (1975) continue to define the study of poetry in this region. Stryk also edited *The Gift of Great Poetry* (1992), demonstrating his range both as a poet and as a teacher.

ACHIEVEMENTS

Although Lucien Stryk has not won many major awards, he has received numerous grants, including a National Endowment for the Arts Poetry Fellowship, a Rockefeller Foundation Fellowship, a Ford Foundation Fellowship, a Fulbright grant and lectureship, and a National Institute of Arts and Letters award. For his work as a translator, Stryk received the Islands and Continents Translation Award for *The Penguin Book of Zen Poetry* (1977).

BIOGRAPHY

Lucien Stryk was born in Kolo, Poland, to Emil Stryk and Celia (Meinstein) Stryk in early April of 1924. His family moved to the United States in 1928, settling in Chicago and narrowly escaping the horrors that would ravage Poland during the 1930's and 1940's. Although Stryk and his family were spared what undoubtedly would have been an appalling and inevitable march toward death, they still felt the aftermath of the events as members of their extended family remained in Poland, only to meet their untimely deaths at the hands of Nazis.

During the turbulence of the Depression and World War II, Stryk came of age on the South Side of Chicago. Many poems, including "A Sheaf for Chicago" (from *Notes for a Guidebook*) and "White City" (from *Awakening*), chronicle Stryk's everyday life as a boy growing up in an urban landscape that was teeming with immigrants and the sons and daughters of immigrants. Although many reviewers of Stryk's poetry note the influence of his study of Zen thought—a clear and strong force throughout his poems and translations—too few

mention the impact of Stryk's early years as the son of outsiders. As is common with young children and teenagers, the idea that one might be different from a given peer group presents a dilemma that at the time seems staggering, yet that may later offer a better vantage for the creation of art. In "White City," Stryk describes the act of climbing on an abandoned roller-coaster track as other children hurl stones at him. "This was no/ King-of-the-Mountain game," he tells us. Indeed, such a gauntlet presented the very pressures of life and death, of acceptance or rejection based on the foolish dares of those who are members of groups we wish to join. Having to stand at the margins of his community, however, established a perspective for Stryk that leads to many of the quiet, modest, yet profoundly truthful insights that he reaches in the writing of poems later in his career. This sense of difference—a sense of belonging to more than just an American community—manifests itself in Stryk's work in a variety of ways: in his connection to Zen teachings and his translations of Zen texts and poems, in his Polish heritage and the many cities in Europe and Asia that he has lived in or visited, in his understanding of place—moving from the particular to the universal, and in his celebration of the many years he lived in a small, rural midwestern town.

Soon after graduation from high school, Stryk served with the U.S. Army artillery in the South Pacific from 1943 to 1945. At the end of World War II, Stryk returned to the United States and enrolled in the English program at Indiana University, where he received his B.A. in 1948. While studying at Indiana University, Stryk wrote an essay, "The American Scene Versus the International Scene," that establishes a part of the philosophical framework that would continue to support the more universal vision of his poetry throughout his career. In this essay—first published in *Folio*, the Indiana University undergraduate review, in 1947—Stryk explains that the isolationist thought he sees in so much American literature, with the exception of that of Ernest Hemingway, "who identifies himself with the universal man," is harmful and ill advised. Stryk asserts, "The nationalism and regionalism—devotion to regional interests—that so obviously manifest themselves in our literature, art, and science can, with the social implications which follow, prove to be a detriment to international progress." What Stryk calls for is an embrace of the variegated and multifaceted collage that comprises the landscape of the United States. "Men of all creeds, national origins, and races—white, black, brown, yellow, and many intermediate hues—speaking in thousands of languages, strange dialects, esoteric idioms, and fantastic variations of American English," he contends, "are the mighty laboring forces that create the tremendous wealth, power, and grandeur that is the United States of America."

Following his own call for a more cosmopolitan embrace of the world and its riches, in 1948, Stryk studied literature and philosophy at the Sorbonne in Paris, France, under the auspices of the University of Maryland program. During his stay in Paris, Stryk engaged with philosophy under Gaston Bachelard and was particularly attracted to phenomenology. In Paris, he also encountered other artists and intellectuals such as James Baldwin, Roger Blin, and the French Resistance fighter Jean-Paul Baudot, who appears in Stryk's poem "Letter to Jean-Paul Baudot, at Christmas" (from *Awakening*). In 1950, he received a Master of Foreign Study degree from the University of Maryland and then traveled to England to study comparative literature at Queen Mary College, University of London. In 1951, he met and married Helen Esterman, a native Londoner, and in that year, the couple bore their first child, a son named Dan. The young family continued to reside in London from 1952 to 1954. In 1953, Stryk's first book of poems, *Taproot*, was published by Fantasy Press. In January of 1955, he returned to the United States with his family to study writing at the University of Iowa. In 1956, Stryk graduated with the Master of Fine Arts from Iowa and had his second collection of poetry, *The Trespasser*, published by Fantasy Press.

Stryk again left the United States from 1956 to 1958 to journey to Niigata University in Japan, where he held a lectureship. It was during this time that he became involved with the study of Zen Buddhism after a meeting with a Zen priest who happened to be a potter. In *Encounter with Zen*, Stryk explains that his visit with the priest "left an extraordinary impression. Home again, sipping tea from the superb bowl he made for me . . . I began making plans. Soon I was inquiring seriously into Zen. . . . I visited temples and monasteries, meeting masters and priests throughout the country and, most important of all, began to meditate."

This initial encounter with Zen thought and practice has continued to color and inform not only Stryk's poems but also his way of life. Following this revelatory two-year period, in 1958, Stryk accepted an appointment at Northern Illinois University in DeKalb as an assistant professor of English, teaching poetry, poetry writing, and Asian literature. His daughter Lydia was born the same year. He retired in 1991, and he and his wife moved to a suburb of Chicago in 2000.

ANALYSIS

Lucien Stryk's devotion to place grows naturally out of his dedication to Zen principles, and as he suggests in the introduction to his second edited collection of midwestern poetry, *Heartland II*, if one is to find peace as a poet or philosopher or human, then one must, as the Zen master Qingyuan explains, see "mountains as mountains, waters as waters." For Stryk then, there can be no richer place on earth than the Midwest for the creation of poetry. There, he finds the vast sprawl of cities connected by rail and commerce; the dark, furrowed fields undulating with growth to the farthest horizon; and towns rising up out of nowhere, their quiet streets offering passage into what is most human and telling about the human condition. As an editor of two landmark collections of midwestern poetry—*Heartland* and *Heartland II*—and as the author of such poems as "Farmer" and "Scarecrow" (both from *Taproot*), "Return to DeKalb" (from *The Pit, and Other Poems*), and "Fishing with My Daughter in Miller's Meadow" (from *Awakening*), Stryk searches the midwestern landscape, not for spectacle but for daily life. It is in daily living that Stryk moves, capturing in minimalist lines the wonder of a father holding his daughter's hand, walking through a meadow filled with fresh manure and grazing horses, or, in "Farmer," magnifying the farmer's eyes that are "bound tight as wheat, packed/ hard as dirt." Stryk, in an essay titled "Making Poems," which is collected in *Encounter with Zen*, explains that the writing of poetry demands that one engage in "pure seeing," and from such seeing, he creates a poetry of simple midwestern images that illustrate clearly the beauty, diversity, and breadth of life in the heartland.

AND STILL BIRDS SING

Although all the works included in *And Still Birds Sing* are not set exclusively in the Midwest, the vision of life found in this collection is shaped by Stryk's long life as a resident of the Midwest. He explains in the introduction to *Heartland II*:

As one who has worked for a number of years, in Asia and the United States on the translation and interpretation of Zen poetry, I am sometimes asked why in the face of such "exotic" pursuits I have an interest in the poetry of my region—or, worse, why my own poetry is set for the most part in small-town Illinois. To one involved in the study of a philosophy like Zen, the answer to such questions is not difficult: one writes of one's place because it is in every sense as wonderful as any other, whatever its topography and weathers, and because one cannot hope to discover oneself elsewhere.

The discovery of self is at the root of Stryk's poetry. Time and again the poet enters a moment, seemingly mundane in nature, and discovers how he is connected to all life. The search for self—an act of enlightenment—should not be misconstrued as indulgent or selfish in Stryk's poems, however. Far from indulging himself, Stryk's poetry exudes a humility born out of a desire to understand how people are all connected to one another, how any suffering or any joy people encounter must be seen as a shared suffering or joy—not as something that can be hoarded or cloistered away from the rest of the world. A fine example of such a moment occurs in "What Is Moving" (from *Afterimages*). Here the poet watches the sky above the water, but finds no birds flying there. As he munches a sweet potato, he asks, "Do I still live?" The recognition that he does indeed still live comes to him in his understanding of how he relates to others: "The same thing/ Runs through both of us," he declares. "My thought moves the world:/ I move, it moves." Similarly, in "Words" (from *Afterimages*), the poet explains that he does not "take" the words of another, that he cannot possess the other as he or she speaks. Instead, he acknowledges how such words connect the speaker and the listener: "I listen/ To what makes you talk—/ Whatever that is—/ And me listen." People's shared humanity compels them, Stryk suggests, to listen and to speak of the space they all must share as they live in this place and in this time.

AWAKENING

In an interview, Stryk speaks about the "curiosity and hunger . . . that will take a man very far across the earth looking for things." He contends that "This excitement about reality is part and parcel of the making of poems." Such an attitude about discovery—the act of coming into contact with places and people and animals and plants never before encountered—is the other powerful force, the other theme that drives Stryk's work. The path to such encounters, for Stryk, can be found only if one is aware or awake, however. In the title poem of *Awakening*, the poet discovers and celebrates the act of wakefulness—the key to enlightenment within Zen thought. As he gathers shells with his daughter, he considers how perception shapes the universe: "I take them from her,/ make, at her command,/ the universe. Hands clasped,/ making the limits of/ a world, we watch till sundown/ planets whirling in the sand." Unlike some of his contemporaries, Stryk does not struggle with the idea of "limits"—nor does he fear the darkness of people's finite existence. Rather, he concludes "Awakening" with the image of the darkness that "takes" the trees outside his home one by one into the night and proclaims that "At this hour I am always happy,/ ready to be taken myself,/ fully aware." Perhaps this is what distinguishes Stryk's vision and the poems that are created out of that vision: an acceptance of self and world that finds its root in a person who has made peace with the human condition.

OTHER MAJOR WORKS

NONFICTION: *Encounter with Zen: Writings on Poetry and Zen*, 1981.

TRANSLATIONS: *Zen: Poems, Prayers, Sermons, Anecdotes, Interviews*, 1965 (with Takashi Ikemoto); *Afterimages: Zen Poems of Shinkichi Takahashi*, 1970 (with Ikemoto); *The Crane's Bill: Zen Poems of China and Japan*, 1973; *The Penguin Book of Zen Poetry*, 1977 (with Ikemoto); *Zen Poetry: Let the Spring Breeze Enter*, 1977 (with Ikemoto); *On Love and Barley: Haiku of Basho*, 1985; *Traveler, My Name: Haiku of Basho*, 1985; *Triumph of the Sparrow: Zen Poems of*

Shinkichi Takahashi, 1986 (with Ikemoto); *The Dumpling Field: Haiku of Issa*, 1991; *Cage of Fireflies: Modern Japanese Haiku*, 1993.

EDITED TEXTS: *Heartland: Poets of the Midwest*, 1967; *World of Buddha: An Introduction to Buddhist Literature*, 1968; *Heartland II: Poets of the Midwest*, 1975; *The Gift of Great Poetry*, 1992; *The Acorn Book of Contemporary Haiku*, 2000 (with Kevin Bailey).

BIBLIOGRAPHY

Abbot, Craig S., ed. "Lucien Stryk: A Bibliography." *Analytical and Enumerative Bibliography* 5, nos. 3/4 (1991). A comprehensive bibliography. Abbot includes sections that chronicle Stryk's career as a poet, reviewer, and critic.

Krapf, Norbert. "Discovering Lucien Stryk's *Heartland*." *Eclectic Literary Forum* 5, no. 4 (Winter, 1995): 50-52. A close look at Stryk as an editor, particularly of *Heartland*, and his relevance to the Midwest.

Porterfield, Susan. "Portrait of a Poet as a Young Man: Lucien Stryk." *Midwestern Miscellany* 22 (1994): 36-45. An examination of Stryk as a young adult, with emphasis on his Midwest upbringing.

_____, ed. *Zen, Poetry, the Art of Lucien Stryk*. Athens, Ga.: Swallow Press and Ohio University Press, 1993. An extensive collection of essays by Stryk on the making of poems and the study of poetry, Zen Buddhist thought, and the act of translation. It also includes two interviews with Stryk and four critical essays originally published in academic journals. The volume concludes with a selection of Stryk's poetry.

Stryk, Lucien. "'Wherever I Am': An Interview with Lucien Stryk." Interview by T. F. Davis. *Interdisciplinary Literary Studies* 6, no. 5 (2005): 102-116. Stryk discusses Zen Buddhism and its influence on his writings in this interview.

Todd F. Davis

COLE SWENSEN

Born: Kentfield, California; 1955

PRINCIPAL POETRY

It's Alive She Says, 1984
New Math, 1987
Park, 1991
Numen, 1995
Parc, 1995
Noon, 1997
Try, 1999
And Hand, 2000
Oh, 2000
Such Rich Hour, 2001
Goest, 2004
The Book of a Hundred Hands, 2005
Nef, 2005
The Glass Age, 2007
Ours, 2008

OTHER LITERARY FORMS

Cole Swensen is primarily known for her poetry and her translations of contemporary French poets. She has written critical articles and reviews for periodicals and essays for collections. Her critical work has been included in *Boston Review*, *Bloomsbury Review*, *Civil Disobediences: Poetics and Politics in Action* (2004), and *Moving Borders: Three Decades of Innovative Writing by Women* (1998). She coedited *American Hybrid: A Norton Anthology of New Poetry* (2009) with David St. John.

ACHIEVEMENTS

Cole Swensen's *New Math* was selected for the National Poetry Series in 1987. *Numen* was named an International Book of the Year by the *Times Literary Supplement* and was a finalist for the PEN West Award in Poetry in 1996. *Nef* won the New American Writing Award in 1997, and *Oh* was a finalist for the National Poetry Series in 1998. *Try* won the Iowa Poetry Prize in 1998 and the Poetry Center Book Award from San Francisco State University in 1999. *Goest* was a finalist for the National Book Award in 2004. *Island of the*

Dead (2003), Swensen's translation of *L'Île des mortes* (1994) by Jean Frémon, won the 2004 PEN USA Award for Literary Translation. She has also been awarded a Guggenheim Fellowship (2006) and two Pushcart Prizes (2004, 2006).

BIOGRAPHY

Cole Swensen was born near San Francisco in the town of Kentfield, California, in 1955. She became interested in art and writing at a young age; her mother was a painter, and she began writing poetry when she was eleven or twelve years old. Swensen designed her own bachelor's degree at San Francisco State University to include a mix of creative writing, literature, bookbinding, and calligraphy classes. Though she continued to practice the art of bookmaking through her twenties, she decided to stay on at San Francisco State for a master's degree in creative writing. Swensen received a Ph.D. in comparative literature from the University of California, Santa Cruz.

While completing her studies, she began to visit France regularly. Since 1987, she has spent part of each year in France, working on French-to-English translations as well as her own poetry projects. She began translating in earnest around 1992 and prefers to translate living poets' work because she believes doing so ultimately contributes to an ever-evolving, ongoing international conversation about poetics. She also enjoys translating more than one book by a single author in order to better understand the writer's oeuvre. She believes "books are never isolated gestures, but are always interlaced with all the other books by a given author."

Swensen spent six years as a professor at the University of Denver before joining the faculty at the Iowa Writers' Workshop at the University of Iowa. She divides her time between Iowa City; Washington, D.C., where her husband lives and works; and Paris, where she spends her summers and part of her winters. She is the founder and editor of La Presse, a small press that publishes contemporary French poetry translated by English-speaking poets.

ANALYSIS

Cole Swensen's books of poetry can be considered intellectual investigations of art, culture, history, and language. Swensen's use of ekphrasis, or the poetic interpretation or exploration of the plastic arts, has dominated her work. Her own interest in ekphrasis is part of a larger push in contemporary poetry to engage other forms of art because, she says, "there's been a reduction of actual intersection between the arts, or at least between poetry and the visual arts during the last half-century." However, Swensen is not content merely to describe art; she wants, rather, to write with art, to write in collaboration with other arts. Swensen's work is often characterized as postmodern, influenced by Language poetry in its regard for the material nature of language. However, Swensen's poetry maintains a strong lyrical quality by emphasizing the musicality of the line and a visual artist's eye for detail. Angela Ball, in her review of Swensen's *The Glass Age*, describes Swensen's work as "neo-modernist" because of its interest in "high culture." Swensen's poetry is decidedly intellectual, often employing associative linkages to build her poetic sequences, while managing, however, to stay accessible by virtue of her simultaneous commitment to physical realities and sensuality.

Swensen, as a teacher and writer, emphasizes "writing as thinking," and in interviews, she stresses that her poetry writing often occupies for her the same space as her academic essay writing. In fact, she often synthesizes others' texts with her own, using quotations and passages as one would in an academic essay. More often than not, her projects are concerned with historical and critical research, and the resulting books of poems serve not only as a works of art but also as works of intellectual inquiry. For example, *Ours* explores the life and times of André Le Nôtre, head gardener to Louis XIV and designer of the parks and gardens of Versailles. *Such Rich Hour* uses the calendar illuminations of *Les Très Riches Heures du Duc de Berry* (c. 1410), commissioned by Jean, duc de Berry, to investigate Europe's transition from the Middle Ages to the Renaissance. *The Book of a Hundred Hands* is similarly organized. Here, the human hand serves as a concrete example of humanity's unique expression.

In other words, Swensen tackles events, persons, and places of historical significance by zeroing in on the given period's culture, in particular, its artistic life. By building layer upon layer of inquisitive meditation, she plays on and with certain words, phrases, and images of significance to the overall project, while simultaneously musing on the impact of these concepts in the present-day world. In this way, Swensen creates a kind of double vision. She is able to comment both on the past and on the present by working to maintain a point of view that is in flux. This voice or point of view is sometimes collective, sometimes singular, but always universal and accessible, able to span time and space. Swensen often incorporates lyric essays as introductions, afterwords, and bibliographies in order to better frame her projects. Swensen, despite the intellectual intensity of her work, is quick to give her readers the tools they need to help them fully experience and engage with the poetry.

OURS

Ours centers on seventeenth century French gardener and landscape designer André Le Nôtre. This collection meditates not only on the historical figure but also on public versus private land and public versus private pleasures. Le Nôtre was most notably head gardener to King Louis XIV and designer of the gardens at Versailles. While Swensen interprets and explores the history of these rarefied spaces, accessible only to the nobility, she simultaneously sees the gardens as contemporary spaces for middle-class reflection and connection. In fact, she dramatizes the imaginary meeting of historical figures and contemporary tourists in her sections "The Medicis" and "Versailles." In the longer sequence, "The Ghost of Much Later," for example, Swensen describes a scenario in which two nineteenth century women touring Versailles suddenly find themselves back in time. They encounter Marie-Antoinette "sitting in the sun, reading in the backyard of the Petit Trianon." The poem is framed as a kind of cautionary tale, in which landscapes carry the possibility of encounter. History's fluidity, its constant presence, permeates the collection.

Ours is divided into nine separate sections that explore Le Nôtre's life, the sensual qualities of his gardening, and his larger scientific and philosophic impact on the seventeenth century. Swensen begins with a lyric-essay introduction that delineates some important biographical information. By giving the reader context, she shows her desire to communicate and to teach. The separate sections move from Le Nôtre's gardens' conceptual beginnings to a general conversation about gardens as historical, cultural, and artistic phenomena.

In "Paradise," Swensen takes on the "original" garden, writing, "Certain traditions claim that man and garden cannot be separated,/ or if and when they are, will neither still be visible. . . ." Here Swensen suggests that gardens are an ineffable part of what it means to be human; she argues that the desire to shape and tame nature is something that unifies human experience, no matter the era. In the second section, Swensen delves into the "principles" of gardening and the kind of impact gardeners such as Le Nôtre were hoping to have on the viewer. The next several sections deal with other important players in Le Nôtre's coterie and the gardens that influenced and were influenced by Versailles. The last few sections focus on Versailles itself: its design, its construction, and its preeminence as a privileged space. In a later section of "The Ghost of Much Later," Swensen continues to imagine Marie-Antoinette confronted by an open, inclusive Versailles: "She refused to raise her eyes and watch two middle class women have a right to these rooms. . . ." Formally, the poems fluctuate between sections of prose and a fluid blend of long and short lines organized according to the poet's movement of thought. Swensen strikes a delicate balance between essay and poetry, discovering along the way a new and exciting format for art and cultural history.

SUCH RICH HOUR

Such Rich Hour uses *Les Très Riches Heures du Duc de Berry*, a well-known book of hours, as an organizing principle. In the introduction, Swensen describes the fifteenth century work as a "personal devotional text designed to allow individuals to observe religious ritual outside the strict format of the mass" and explains the cultural significance of the text and its illuminations while simultaneously emphasizing its possible significance to her twenty-first century readers. *Such Rich Hour* moves sequentially according to the calendar year, taking the opportunity to comment, along the way, on feast days, festivals, and historical events pertinent to the end of the fourteenth and the beginning of the fifteenth centuries. The poems are most often titled after specific dates. They share many of the hallmarks of Swensen's poetics in general, namely multiple points of view, and voices and quotations from a variety of sources, culminating in a compelling synthesis between her own text and historical texts. For example, the poem "January 17: St. Antony's Day: Les Flammes" begins, "'There's a disease that eats up the limbs that feels like ants are eating them' (*St./ Antoine! St. Antoine...*) and/ there was a disease that dried up the heart from the inside out, and another that/ began as spots of light on the skin that grew and grew and then enormously died." Swensen, by combining quotations with the speaker's subjective reality, provides the reader with a full, rich depiction of fifteenth century life during the Black Plague.

Throughout *Such Rich Hour*, Swensen reimagines the past from a decidedly twenty-first century perspective. By deconstructing the language of religion, art, and even the passage of time, Swensen invigorates and electrifies the reader's connection to history. Throughout *Such Rich Hour*, Swensen also attempts to investigate a single event or concept via multiple points of view. In "August 17, 1427: The First Record of Gypsies in Europe," Swensen employs a collective voice to describe one of Europe's vital changes during this period: ". . . the word for ugly is the same as the word for dark." A line like this is charged with not only historical but also twenty-first century significance. Swensen has perfected a poetics that enables her to make the past vital, pertinent, and engaging. In "April in the Garden," Swensen writes, "Beauty is no less unlikely for having been invented." This kind of penetrating insight gives her projects such depth and breadth.

OTHER MAJOR WORKS

TRANSLATIONS: *Interrmittances II*, 1994 (of Jean Tortel); *Past Travels*, 1994 (of Olivier Cadiot); *Natural Gaits*, 1995 (of Pierre Alferi); *Bayart*, 2002 (of Pascalle Monnier); *Future, Former, Fugitive*, 2003 (of Cadiot); *Island of the Dead*, 2003 (of Jean Frémon's *L'Île des mortes*); *Oxo*, 2004 (of Alferi); *Physis*, 2007 (of Nicholas Pesqués); *The Real Life of Shadows*, 2009 (of Frémon's *Vraie nature des ombres*).

EDITED TEXT: *American Hybrid: A Norton Anthology of New Poetry*, 2009 (with David St. John).

BIBLIOGRAPHY

Ball, Angela. "The History of Sight." Review of *The Glass Age. American Book Review* 29, no. 4 (May/June, 2008): 19-20. Ball describes Swensen's work as "neo-modernist" for its commitment to the importance and seriousness of art.

Fischer, Barbara K. *Museum Mediations: Reframing Ekphrasis in Contemporary American Poetry*. New York: Routledge, 2006. Examines the relationship between poetry and the visual arts. Contains analysis of some of Swensen's poems.

Keller, Lynn. "Poems Living with Paintings: Cole Swensen's Ekphrastic *Try*." In *Thinking Poetry: Readings in Contemporary Women's Exploratory Poetics*. Iowa City: University of Iowa Press, 2010. Keller discusses Swensen's *Try* and its unique approach to ekphrastic poetry. Her introduction to this volume also sheds light on Swensen's poetry.

_____. "Singing Spaces: Fractal Geometries in Cole Swensen's *Oh*." *Journal of Modern Literature* 31, no. 1 (Fall, 2007): 136-160. Keller discusses Swensen's book *Oh* in respect to its innovative use of space on the page.

Logan, William. "Shock and Awe." Review of *Ours. New Criterion* 27, no. 4 (December, 2008): 36-43. Logan discusses Swensen's *Ours* in respect to environmental poetry and poetry of landscape.

Lesley Jenike

MAY SWENSON

Born: Logan, Utah; May 28, 1919
Died: Ocean View, Delaware; December 4, 1989

PRINCIPAL POETRY

Another Animal, 1954
A Cage of Spines, 1958
To Mix with Time: New and Selected Poems, 1963
Half Sun Half Sleep, 1967
Iconographs, 1970
New and Selected Things Taking Place, 1978
In Other Words, 1987

The Love Poems of May Swenson, 1991
Nature: Poems Old and New, 1994
May Out West: Poems of May Swenson, 1996
The Complete Love Poems of May Swenson,
    2003

OTHER LITERARY FORMS

May Swenson's forays away from poetry included short fiction, drama, and criticism. A number of her short stories have appeared in magazines and anthologies. A play, *The Floor*, was produced in New York in 1966 and published a year later. Her best-known critical essay, "The Experience of Poetry in a Scientific Age," appeared in *Poets on Poetry* (1966). She also wrote the introduction to the 1962 Collier edition of Edgar Lee Masters's *Spoon River Anthology*.

Several books for young people have expanded the audience for Swenson's poetry. *Poems to Solve* (1966), *More Poems to Solve* (1971), and *The Complete Poems to Solve* (1993) are selections of her riddle poems. For still younger children, there is *The Guess and Spell Coloring Book* (1976). Many poets owe a heavy debt to their childhoods, and few have discharged that debt more gratefully or delightfully. As a child, Swenson learned from her immigrant parents the language that she would later render into English in *Windows and Stones: Selected Poems by Tomas Tranströmer* (1972), a translation (with Leif Sjöberg) for which she won the International Poetry Forum Translation Medal. She recorded her own poems on both the Folkways and the Caedmon labels.

ACHIEVEMENTS

As traditional as she was inventive, as alliteratively Anglo-Saxon as she was typographically contemporary, May Swenson was well respected among twentieth century American poets. Her thirty-five-year career was an ongoing celebration of language wed to life-as-it-is. Her sharp-eyed curiosity led her to address a broader and more diverse range of subjects than did many of her contemporaries: She was rural and urban, scientific and mythic, innocent and worldly, and, sometimes, even literary, and she could be any number of these within the same poem. Once she fixed her attention on something, she had a remarkable gift for let-

May Swenson (©Henry Carlisle)

ting that object of her curiosity find its voice and for allowing the poem to determine its own form. No poet wrote more perceptively or persuasively about birds—or about astronauts.

Swenson was a member of the American Academy of Arts and Letters (1970-1989) and a chancellor of the Academy of American Poets from 1980 to her death. She was awarded grants and fellowships by a number of agencies and organizations, including the Ford, Rockefeller, and Guggenheim Foundations, and the National Endowment for the Arts. She received a National Institute of Arts and Letters Award in 1960, the Shelley Memorial Award in 1968, and the Academy of American Poets Fellowship in 1979. In 1981, she shared with fellow poet Howard Nemerov the prestigious Bollingen Prize in Poetry, in recognition of her collection *New and Selected Things Taking Place*. She also served as a judge for the Lamont Poetry Selection of the Academy of American Poets and for the National Book Awards. Her frequent readings and visiting professorships at a number of colleges and universities enhanced her contribution to American letters.

BIOGRAPHY

The daughter of Swedish immigrants, Anne Thilda May Swenson grew up in Logan, Utah, a small college town. Her parents had left behind both their native land and their Lutheran faith to follow the teachings of the Mormon Church, which Swenson came to reject in spite of (or perhaps because of) her strict upbringing among the Latter-day Saints. As the oldest daughter in a large family, she learned early to value solitude, and at the age of thirteen, alone with her father's typewriter, she pecked out with two fingers a short piece she had written. When she looked at the resultant shape of the words on the page, she said, "This is a poem"; her life's work had begun.

Swenson's father taught woodworking and carpentry at Utah State University, which at the time was known as Utah State Agricultural College. Swenson studied English and art there and received her B.A. degree in 1939. She then worked as a reporter for a Salt Lake City newspaper, but after about a year, she made her break with home and family and moved to New York's Greenwich Village. Before gaining recognition as a poet, she worked at a variety of office jobs and, after a few years, began publishing in various magazines, including *Poetry* and *The New Yorker*. In 1954, a selection of her poems was chosen to appear with the work of two other poets (Harry Duncan and Murray Noss) in the first volume of Scribner's *Poets of Today* series. Within the next few years, she began the round of fellowships, residencies, and visiting professorships that sustained her for the rest of her career. Among her more notable positions and appointments were the editorship of New Directions Press, 1959-1966; positions as poet-in-residence at Purdue University, 1966-1967, at the University of North Carolina at Greensboro, 1968-1969 and 1975, at Lethbridge University in the Canadian province of Alberta, 1970, and at the University of California, Riverside, 1973; she also held a position on the staff of the Bread Loaf Writers' Conference, 1976. In addition, she spent time at the Yaddo and MacDowell colonies, sojourned in Europe, and traveled widely in the United States, giving readings and teaching. From 1970 until her death in 1989, Swenson and her longtime friend and companion, Rozanne Knudson, made their home in what Swenson called an "Adirondack shack" in Sea Cliff, New York, on Long Island Sound.

ANALYSIS

In his introduction to the first volume of the *Poets of Today* series, John Hall Wheelock assessed the task of the contemporary poet as one of rediscovery and revelation, in which a world gone stale must be renewed: "A poem gives the world back to the maker of the poem, in all its original strangeness, the shock of its first surprise. It is capable of doing the same for the rest of us." That volume included May Swenson's first book-length collection of poems, *Another Animal*. In the thirty-five years to follow, no voice in contemporary poetry showed more commitment to that task of poetic revelation and renewal. Although she was often spoken of as a nature poet, Swenson was as adept at celebrating the skyline of Brooklyn as a quiet wood. She was equally at home with astronauts and angels, with swans and subways. If she could bring her senses to bear upon a subject, it was the stuff of poetry.

ANOTHER ANIMAL

Swenson's verse can be classified as poetry of the senses—especially of and for the eye. A good starting point for a consideration of her work is "Horses in Central Park," a celebration of light, color, and texture: "Colors of horses like leaves or stones/ or wealthy textures/ liquors of light." A horse is not, at first glance, very much like a leaf or a stone, but Swenson always looks past that first glance to something more. The alliteration in the third line is only a mild example of her wordplay, which ranges from pure Anglo-Saxon to latter-day E. E. Cummings. Everything works together; the poem introduces a liquid tone, the sense suggests intoxication. What follows is no mere catalog of horses, but the play of light and words put through their paces. There is an autumnal truth, a lean horse the color of "sere October," fall cantering through fall. The procession continues, as "mole-gray back" and a "dappled haunch" pass by, along with "fox-red bay/ and buckskin blond as wheat." The reader takes in all the richness of the harvest and of October's light, distilled into the colors and liquid movements of horses. One need only witness the "Sober chestnut burnished/ by his sweat/ to veined and glowing oak" to let one's eyes at last convince the mind of what it may have shied away from at the poem's opening. Not only does this comparison of horse to oak leaf work but also could not be better. This effortless rhetoric of the senses distinguishes Swenson's verse. One cannot believe everything one sees or hears, she seems to say, but one had better believe in it.

ICONOGRAPHS

Swenson's verse is variously described as fierce, fresh, inquisitive, innovative, and sensuous. Her frequent experimentation with the physical appearance of her poems, however, has caused such adjectives to alight in the wrong places. Though she had dealt from the start in unorthodox punctuation, spacing, and typographic arrangements, Swenson's experiments in this direction culminated in *Iconographs*. This collection of shaped poems—"image-writing," as she described them—is mistakenly referred to by some as concrete poetry. Swenson makes it clear in an afterword that the poems were all finished down to the last word before being arranged into shapes that would enhance the words. In visual terms, the poems are the paintings, the shapes only frames. Thus, a poem on a José de Rivera mobile twists and turns on the page. In a poem called "The Blue Bottle," the words outline the shape of a bottle; in "How Everything Happens," a poem written after close observation of how ocean waves gather, break, and recede, the lines of the poem gather, break, and recede in a visual variation on the poem's message. Such devices are certainly consistent with Swenson's belief that words are, among other things, objects, and that a poem is itself an object, to be encountered by the eye and its companion senses, not merely by the intellect. These shaped poems are innovative enough in their appearance before they are even read, but it is not in their shapes that they succeed as poetry. When these or any of Swenson's poems succeed, it is because of an absolute sureness of touch and rightness of language.

Her images are at times startling, but they work upon the senses and emotions in such a way that readers cannot help giving in to their aptness and inevitability. In "The Garden at St. John's," a mother caresses her baby, whose hair is "as soft as soft/ as down as the down in the wingpits of angels." Any momentary hesitation over "wingpits" is lulled by the enchanting repetition of "soft" and "down," and the image rings, or rather, whispers, true. "Water Picture," the upside-down world reflected in the surface of a pond, would seem to be a conventional enough idea for a poem, but Swenson is not so interested in ideas as in things, and it is, indeed, the thing that finds expression here. Everyone has gazed into still water and watched the reflections, but when, in this poem, "A flag/ wags like a fishhook/ down there in the sky," when a swan bends to the surface to "kiss herself," and the "tree-limbs tangle, the bridge/ folds like a fan," one is there with a powerful immediacy.

RIDDLING POEMS

Again and again Swenson affirmed that the wonders of the world are too good merely to be described or talked about. They must be shared as directly as possible. Her mode of sharing experience was to involve herself completely in an experience, to "live into" the experience in order to express it. Thus, there is much more to poetry than the mere recording or labeling of experience. Some of Swenson's most successful poems came out of the avoidance of simply giving a name to an object. Many of these are her "riddling" poems, in which the object shared is never named, but only hinted at. As one might expect, the images are heavily sensory, most often visual. One of her best known riddle poems is "By Morning":

> Some for everyone
> plenty
> and more coming
> Fresh   dainty   airily arriving
> everywhere at once.

As in most of Swenson's riddles, the clues reveal rather than obscure their answer. One need not read far into this particular poem to realize that it is about snow, but the real charm of the poem lies much deeper than the simple solution of the riddle. Systems of imagery are at work as "a gracious fleece" that spreads "like youth like wheat/ over the city." "Fleece" is picked up several lines down in the prediction that "Streets will be fields/ cars be fumbling sheep." "Youth" and "wheat" resolve themselves together at the poem's conclusion: "A deep bright harvest will be seeded/ in a night/ By morning we'll be children/ feeding on manna/ a new loaf on every doorsill." The avoidance of any explicit reference to snow is part of the poem's success, but the real strength of the piece is in the same rightness of expression that Swenson's work so consistently displays, right down to the use of extra space between certain words to vary the tempo, and, at times, the sense of a line.

THE SCIENCE POEMS

In her work of "living into" the world, Swenson explored one territory that many poets have avoided— science. She wrote poems on electronic sound patterns and on the deoxyribonucleic acid (DNA) molecule, as well as a number of poems on the U.S. space program. To one who can derive so much wonder from the ordinary and familiar, the astronaut is a wonderful figure, though not solemnly so. In "August 19, Pad 19," the astronaut waits in his cramped capsule, "Positioned for either breech birth/ or urn burial," anticipating the lift-off that will drag him "backward through 121 sunsets." Just before the mission is aborted on account of weather, he puts himself into an unheroic perspective:

> Never so impotent, so important.
> So naked, wrapped, equipped, and immobile,
> cared for by 5000 nurses.
> Let them siphon my urine to the nearest star.

The treatment is more playful than disrespectful. The fun is not at the astronaut's expense; on the contrary, he knows to what extent he is to be admired, to what extent to be pitied, yet asks for neither admiration nor pity. He is no longer so distant from humanity as he might have seemed in space, umbilicaled, "belted and bolted in" ten stories above the pad. As he gazes through the capsule's tiny window seeing "innocent drops of rain" and "Lightning's golden sneer," the reader can sneer right back with him; the same things that ruin simple Sunday picnics ruin his splendid plans as well.

NEW AND SELECTED THINGS TAKING PLACE

To say Swenson strove for variety in her work would not be quite accurate. Her variety came naturally; more often than not it came from within a poem. Once a poem had found its form, discovered its voice, and appeared in print, she rarely revised it. An apparent exception to this rule is the selection of formerly shaped poems that appear in *New and Selected Things Taking Place*, minus their iconographic frames. Probably this

indicates that, having done as much as she cared to do with the iconographic poem, she chose to second-guess herself and present some of these in more conventional configurations.

A thorough study of this comprehensive collection reveals something else. Beginning with her early work, Swenson moved toward more conventional form in her poems; certainly her punctuation grew less experimental. Behind her later verses is a mature poet, more aware than ever of her considerable strengths and less willing to divert the reader's attention in any way from what she does best. One of the finest poems of her later years is "October." It speaks in hard, clear images of growing older gracefully. In one of the poem's seven sections:

> I sit with braided fingers
> and closed eyes
> in a span of late sunlight.
> The spokes are closing.
> It is fall: warm milk of light,
> though from an aging breast.

Here, many years after the dappled light of "Horses in Central Park," light keeps its liquid quality but is less intoxicating, a more nourishing, comforting distillate. In this "warm milk" of a later, mellower light, the watcher is moved to something like prayer, in spite of herself.

Swenson was not an intensely literary poet, conscious of working in a particular tradition. Certainly any poet who addressed herself so fully to "the thing" could be expected to feel a special kinship with such writers as Marianne Moore and Elizabeth Bishop. Swenson acknowledged that kinship, as well as a special feeling for another master of wordplay, Cummings. There are, as well, poets whom she considered "healthy to read," and they are rather a mixed bag— Theodore Roethke, Gerard Manley Hopkins, Emily Dickinson, Walt Whitman, and among Swenson's contemporaries, Richard Wilbur, Anthony Hecht, Anne Sexton, and James Merrill, but this is no matter of influence or imitation. Swenson acknowledged as much affinity with such visual artists as Georgia O'Keeffe and Marcel Duchamp as with any literary artist.

The poetry of others rarely moved her to song, and "literary" poems are rare among her works. Typically, a poem on Robert Frost, "R. F. at Bread Loaf His Hand Against a Tree," avoids the temptation to indulge in literary assessment and instead addresses Frost as part of the literal scene: "Companions he and the cross/ grained bark. . . ." What might have been, in other hands, literary history in verse is rendered instead into an exuberant portrait in wordplay. For purposes of inspiration, Swenson was less likely to look to literature than to the newspaper, the zoo, *Scientific American*, a walk in the woods, or a ride on the subway.

IN OTHER WORDS

In this regard, Swenson's last volume of poems, *In Other Words*, is of a piece with her earlier work. Here are plenty of examples of Swenson's gift for discovering poetry taking place in unexpected places—a hospital blood test; the consignment of Charlie McCarthy, perhaps history's most famous ventriloquist's dummy, to the Smithsonian after the death of Edgar Bergen; and a magazine ad for a digital watch. In Swenson's hands, all are the stuff of poetry.

A package received in the mail prompts "A Thank-You Letter." For the package? No, for "the wonderful cord 174″ long" that bound the package. The poem ends with the narrator's cat entangled in the string, "having a wonderful puzzle-playtime." The narrator admits,

> . . . I haven't yet

> taken the sturdy paper off your package.
> I hardly feel I want to. The gift has been
> given! For which, thank you ever so much.

The process in this poem in many ways encapsulates Swenson's approach to poetry as a whole: Swenson's approach is eclectic in the very best sense, for "eclectic" means, at its root, not "to throw together" but "to pick out."

Because she picked and chose so well, because she was so much a part of the experiences that she made into poetry, and because her poems are so resistant to paraphrase and explication, her works are their own best commentary. "A Navajo Blanket" is a sort of guided tour of one of the "Eye-dazzlers the Indians weave." Having worked in from the edges over paths of brilliant colors,

> You can sleep at the center,
> attended by Sun that never fades, by Moon
> that cools. Then, slipping free of zigzag and
> hypnotic diamond, find your way out
> by the spirit trail, a faint Green thread that
> secretly crosses the border, where your mind
> is rinsed and returned to you like a white cup.

No matter what colors she worked in, what patterns she wove, Swenson was always careful to include that "faint Green thread" that was her perpetual wonder at things as they are. By following that thread, the reader can embrace the world, a world clean and new, good to look upon and good to hold.

OTHER MAJOR WORKS

PLAY: *The Floor*, pr. 1966.

NONFICTION: *The Contemporary Poet as Artist and Critic*, 1964; "The Experience of Poetry in a Scientific Age," 1966; *Made with Words*, 1998 (Gardner McFall, editor).

TRANSLATION: *Windows and Stones: Selected Poems by Tomas Tranströmer*, 1972 (with Leif Sjöberg; of Tomas Tranströmer).

CHILDREN'S LITERATURE: *Poems to Solve*, 1966; *More Poems to Solve*, 1971; *The Guess and Spell Coloring Book*, 1976; *The Complete Poems to Solve*, 1993.

MISCELLANEOUS: *Dear Elizabeth: Five Poems and Three Letters to Elizabeth Bishop*, 2000.

BIBLIOGRAPHY

Crumbley, Paul, and Patricia M. Gantt, eds. *Body My House: May Swenson's Work and Life*. Logan: Utah State University Press, 2006. A collection of critical essays that discuss many aspects of Swenson's life and work, including her nature poems, her explorations of sexuality, and her friendships with other writers.

Doty, Mark. "Queen Sweet Thrills: Reading May Swenson." *Yale Review* 88, no. 1 (January, 2000): 86-110. Doty discusses Swenson's work, describing how, over the course of her eleven books of poetry, the poet developed a dramatic dialogue between revelation and concealment.

Gould, Jean. *Modern American Women Poets*. New York: Dodd, Mead, 1984. Account of Swenson's life includes details of her childhood, the influence—or lack of influence—of her parents' Mormon faith, and her associations with other writers, especially Robert Frost and Elizabeth Bishop. Gould also explores Swenson's longtime relationship with teacher and children's author Rozanne Knudson.

Howard, Richard. *Alone with America*. New York: Atheneum, 1969. This book-length study of modern American poets includes a chapter on Swenson, "Turned Back to the Wild by Love." Howard provides a fine, detailed study of Swenson's poetics and technique, illustrated by dozens of examples from her early poems.

Salter, Mary Jo. "No Other Words." Review of *In Other Words*. *The New Republic* 201 (March 7, 1988): 40-41. This review of Swenson's last volume of poems offers a brief but perceptive discussion of her poetic strengths and limitations. Salter compares her work to that of poets as diverse as Elizabeth Bishop, Gerard Manley Hopkins, and George Herbert.

Stanford, Ann. "May Swenson: The Art of Perceiving." *Southern Review* 5 (Winter, 1969): 58-75. This essay treats Swenson as a master of observation and perception. Through numerous examples—drawn mostly from the poet's nature poems—Stanford explores Swenson's ability to surprise and delight the reader by observing the world from unexpected angles or by simply noticing and recording the easily overlooked detail.

Swenson, May. "An Interview with May Swenson: July 14, 1978." Interview by Karla Hammond. *Parnassus: Poetry in Review* 7 (Fall/Winter, 1978): 60-75. In this piece, Swenson talks in some detail on a range of subjects, from her childhood and education to her writing habits, her approach to poetry, and her admiration for such poets as Elizabeth Bishop and E. E. Cummings. Throughout, she illustrates the discussion with examples from her work.

Zona, Kirstin Hotelling. "A 'Dangerous Game of Change': Images of Desire in the Love Poems of May Swenson." *Twentieth Century Literature* 44, no. 2 (Summer, 1998): 219-241. Zona argues that Swenson's strategy of employing blatantly heterosexual or stereotypically gendered tropes is central to the relationship between sexuality and subjectivity that shapes her larger poetic.

Richard A. Eichwald

T

ALLEN TATE

Born: Winchester, Kentucky; November 19, 1899
Died: Nashville, Tennessee; February 9, 1979

PRINCIPAL POETRY

The Golden Mean, and Other Poems, 1923 (with Ridley Wills)
Mr. Pope, and Other Poems, 1928
Poems, 1928-1931, 1932
The Mediterranean, and Other Poems, 1936
Selected Poems, 1937
The Winter Sea, 1944
Poems, 1920-1945, 1947
Poems, 1922-1947, 1948
Poems, 1960
The Swimmers, and Other Selected Poems, 1971
Collected Poems, 1919-1976, 1977

OTHER LITERARY FORMS

Although Allen Tate earned his literary reputation as a poet, the majority of his published works are prose. He is well known as an essayist, having published nine books of essays and contributed essays to a number of anthologies, including the Agrarian manifesto *I'll Take My Stand* (1930). His other nonfiction works include two biographies, *Stonewall Jackson: The Good Soldier* (1928) and *Jefferson Davis: His Rise and Fall* (1929). He also published a critically acclaimed novel, *The Fathers* (1938), set during the Civil War. Tate also worked as an editor and a translator, editing poetry anthologies and other literary works and translating some of the works of Charles Baudelaire and various classical poets. Each of these works demonstrates at least one of Tate's three major concerns: poetry, history, and the state of modern culture.

ACHIEVEMENTS

Much of Allen Tate's popular reputation as a poet rests on a single poem, "Ode to the Confederate Dead," written before he was twenty-six years old. It brought its author considerable fame both in the United States and abroad, but unfortunately it "typecast" him. Tate later wrote poems that were perhaps better and certainly ideologically different, but he was and still is so strongly identified with that work that his later poetry was for the most part neglected.

If the public saw him as a one-poem poet, however, he fared better at the hands of critics. He received a number of honors, including many honorary degrees; perhaps his most outstanding award was the National Medal for Literature in 1976. He also received an Academy Award in Literature from the American Academy of Arts and Letters in 1948, the Bollingen Prize for Poetry in 1957, the Brandeis University Medal for Poetry in 1961, the Gold Medal of the Dante Society of Florence in 1962, the Academy of American Poets Fellowship in 1963, and the Lenore Marshall Prize for Poetry in 1978 for *Collected Poems, 1919-1976*. He was elected to the American Academy of Arts and Letters in 1949 and the American Academy of Arts and Sciences in 1965. He served as consultant in poetry to the Library of Congress (poet laureate) from 1943 to 1944. He became a member of the American Academy of Arts and Letters in 1949 and served as chancellor for the Academy of American Poets from 1966 to 1979.

Tate was one of the most widely known of the Agrarian/Fugitive poets. While some of his themes, techniques, and concerns were similar to those of his southern colleagues, unlike some of them, he was not labeled (and subsequently dismissed as) a "regional" poet. Tate was as popular and as comfortable in the literary circles of New York and Europe as he was in that of his Vanderbilt associates, and his poetry demonstrates that southern concerns are universal concerns as well.

BIOGRAPHY

John Orley Allen Tate was born in Winchester, Kentucky, the third son of John Orley and Eleanor Varnell Tate. His early life foreshadowed the gypsy-like wanderings of his later years; because of his father's various business interests, the family moved frequently. These moves resulted in Tate's rather sketchy education. As a teenager, he wrote a few poems, but his real love was music. He studied the violin under excellent teachers at the Cincinnati Conservatory of Music but left when his teachers concluded that, while he had some talent, he had no exceptional gift for music.

Tate, his musical ambitions thwarted, was accepted at Vanderbilt University and entered in 1918. He had no particular interest in literature when his college career began. He was, however, strongly influenced by some of his teachers, especially Walter Clyde Curry. The medieval and Renaissance scholar lent him books, encouraged him to write poetry, and introduced him to John Crowe Ransom, with whom he later studied. Under the influence of these two gifted teachers, Tate joined Vanderbilt's Calumet Club, a literary society whose membership also included Donald Davidson. Davidson invited Tate to participate in a discussion group that evolved into the Fugitives. Tate was an eager participant in this group of teachers and students and contributed many poems to its literary journal, *The Fugitive*. He graduated from Vanderbilt in 1923 after having taken a year off from his studies because of poor health; his diploma was dated 1922, so that technically he graduated "with his class." In his last year at Vanderbilt, he met Robert Penn Warren, a sixteen-year-old sophomore, who became his lifelong friend.

Tate had envisioned New York as the literary mecca of the United States, and he visited the city in 1924. He met Hart Crane, whose work he admired, as well as other authors. Upon his return, he visited the Warrens, and there he met Caroline Gordon, the first of his three wives. After their marriage, they moved to New York, where Tate worked as an editor and continued to contribute to *The Fugitive* until it ceased publication in 1925. The Tates remained in New York until 1930, except for two years spent abroad on a Guggenheim Fellowship; then they moved back to Tennessee.

In Tennessee, Tate was able to enjoy the company of almost all his old friends again. From this "reunion" arose the Agrarian movement. In 1934, Tate, seriously in debt, turned to college teaching. He taught at a number of colleges, but not until 1951 was he offered a tenured position, at the University of Minnesota, where he

taught until his retirement in 1968. After his retirement, he returned to Sewanee, Tennessee.

Tate was a southern poet in every sense of the term, but he was not limited to regional issues and popularity. His circle of literary friends included T. S. Eliot, Ford Madox Ford, and John Peale Bishop; his fame was international.

ANALYSIS

Allen Tate's poetry has often been described as obscure, but although it is difficult and frequently misunderstood, it is not obscure. The difficulties in reading Tate's poems arise mainly from his allusions, many of which are classical.

A facet of Tate's poetry that is frequently misunderstood is his use of history as a theme. To Tate, a sense of history is no mere nostalgic longing for bygone glory. It is rather an understanding of those qualities of earlier cultures which made them human. In several poems, Tate expresses the belief that modern people have discarded too many of these qualities and thus have become less human. Tate does not suggest that people turn their backs on modern culture and attempt to return to a more classical and simpler way of life, but he does seem to believe that modern technology and humanism are mutually exclusive. He is in favor of the creation of a new culture rather than the re-creation of an older one.

Tate's techniques as well as his themes are worthy of study. He rejected at first, but later acknowledged, the truism that form and content should be inextricably related, and he described free verse as a failure. His poems show experimentation with many different forms. Also typical of Tate's poems is the use of unusual adjectives. "Ambitious November" and "brute curiosity of an angel's stare" (both from "Ode to the Confederate Dead") may be cited. These adjectives have the effect of capturing the attention of readers and forcing them to explore the images in order to understand them. A similar technique is his play of word on word, frequently by exact repetition. Tate's poetry is also characterized by the use of concrete details to modify highly abstract language. Such details, sometimes consisting of single words only, are somewhat jarring to the reader, as they are no doubt meant to be. Finally, Tate can move easily from a formal, "scholarly" style to the use of highly sensuous diction, often within the same poem. He seems to be acutely aware of the tension that is produced by the contrast between Latinate and Anglo-Saxon vocabulary. He chooses the diction suited to his subject, with the language illustrating changes in imagery or tone.

Much attention has been focused on the effect other poets have had on Tate's poetic techniques and themes. His early poetry has been compared with that of his teacher and friend John Crowe Ransom, while his later work is often compared to that of T. S. Eliot, whom Tate greatly admired. Tate was, however, writing such poetry before he had even read Eliot. In any case, the issue of anyone's "influence" on Tate is nebulous; certainly his work is not derivative, whatever the generalized debt he may owe Ransom, Eliot, and other writers with whose work he was familiar.

Throughout his poetry, Tate's major concern is the state of modern culture and modern humankind. He is a sort of prophet, warning people of the consequences of their way of life. In some of his works, he offers remedies for human dilemmas, although he does not hesitate to blame people for being the cause of their own problems. Tate's poems will no doubt be read in the future as a fairly accurate record of the concerns of twentieth century humanity. Read in the chronological order in which they appear in *Collected Poems, 1919-1976*, they further serve as a record of the spiritual development of Tate himself, a poet of considerable talent and vision.

"THE MEDITERRANEAN"

A good introduction to Tate's poetry is "The Mediterranean," a poem which displays many of his techniques and concerns. In fact, this poem appears as the first item in each of his collections (except *Collected Poems, 1919-1976*, which is arranged in order of first publication); it is considered to be one of the best of his shorter pieces. The poem begins with a Latin motto, which, as usual, Tate neither identifies nor translates. The motto comes from the first book of the *Aeneid* (c. 29-19 B.C.E.; English translation, 1553) and in the original reads "Quem das finem, rex magne, laborum?" ("What limit, great king, do you place on their labors?") Tate changes "laborum" to "dolorum" (pain, either physical or mental, but here probably mental).

This motto should indicate to the reader that a knowledge of the *Aeneid* is necessary to an understanding of the poem. Indeed, a reader without a great deal of knowledge of the *Aeneid* would probably overlook or not understand many of Tate's allusions to it. The poem is, first of all, dramatic; it can be read simply as a description of the dramatic setting. Beneath this surface, however, is the reference, maintained throughout the poem, to the events in the *Aeneid*, as well as a commentary on the modern human condition by contrast with the past.

The dramatic situation of the poem is simple: a group of people is on a boat trip, a sort of party. The speaker is a member of that group. The voyage of Aeneas is recalled by the speaker, setting up what seems to be an unlikely parallel, although many a weekend sailor may imagine himself to be a Columbus, a Magellan—or even an Aeneas.

In the first stanza, the setting is described. It is a long bay surrounded by a cliff, similar to the bay on which Aeneas landed in Italy. The cliff, called the "peaked margin of antiquity's delay," serves as a symbol of the border between the past and present. Time is an important element here, and the first image illustrates Tate's belief that a difficult barrier exists between the past and present. This idea is developed throughout the poem by means of a contrast between the mythical past, represented by the heroic Aeneas, and the monotonous present, represented by the modern sailors who are attempting to retreat into antiquity. They themselves, however, as symbols of modern humanity, have made that return impossible.

The third stanza contains an important allusion to the *Aeneid* which continues to develop the contrast between the past and present. The speaker says that the party "made feast and in our secret need/ Devoured the very plates Aeneas bore." The reference is to the third book of the *Aeneid*, in which the harpies place a curse on Aeneas and his men: Aeneas will not find the land he is searching for until he and his men have become desperate enough to eat the plates they are carrying. The terms of the curse are fulfilled when the men eat wheat cakes on which they have placed food, thus signaling that they have arrived at their destination. The modern sailors parody this fulfillment of the curse on Aeneas;

they too are "cursed" and are seeking another land. The image is repeated in the fourth and fifth stanzas, emphasizing the idea of the removal of a curse.

The curse is explored in the last four stanzas; a question indicates what the curse is: "What prophecy of eaten plates could landless/ Wanderers fulfill by the ancient sea?" By sailing on the "ancient sea" and recalling Aeneas, the wanderers have established some contact with the past, but the contact is incomplete and ephemeral. Tate tells the reader why this is so in stanza 6: It is modern people's "lust for power" that has been their undoing. His final, strong image is that of a land of plenty in which what should be a bountiful harvest is left to "rot on the vine." This is the land, he reminds the reader, where he was born; one needs not seek a foreign land to regain the qualities of a great culture.

"ODE TO THE CONFEDERATE DEAD"

A somewhat similar theme is treated in Tate's best-known poem, "Ode to the Confederate Dead." The title of the poem is somewhat misleading, since the poem is not an ode, or public celebration, to the dead Confederate soldiers. The speaker is a modern man who must face the fact of his isolation, which becomes evident to him through his reflection on the various symbols in the poem, most significant of which is the cemetery where he stands. The speaker is not characterized; in fact, his lack of individuality is an important element in the poem.

Like many of Tate's other poems, "Ode to the Confederate Dead" contains striking diction. He makes use of unusual adjectives, oxymorons, and other techniques and figures, letting the reader know immediately that the poem is not a conventional glorification of the men who fought and died for the Confederacy. Tate's vision is broader than that, and his theme is more universal.

The first section contains a great deal of nature imagery, the speaker personifying nature in an almost Romantic fashion. It is interesting to note, however, that he describes the wind as whirring, a sound associated with machinery rather than nature. This section also contains an extended image of piles of fallen leaves; the month is, as is made explicit in the next section, November. The deadness of the leaves is emphasized, drawing a parallel between the leaves and the soldiers.

In the second section, the speaker focuses his attention on the graves. The graves, like the men who lie in them, have been unable to withstand the effects of time. The stone angels on the graves have been stained, chipped, and even broken. This section also reveals that the speaker sees the dead soldiers as having lost their individual identities; they have become merely the "Confederate dead," a group of people from whom time has removed all sense of individuality. The speaker sympathizes with such a loss, for he feels that he has been similarly imposed on by modern culture.

The third and fourth sections emphasize this sense of loss. The speaker feels that modern humanity is ineffectual; people have "waited for the angry resolution/ Of those desires that should be yours tomorrow." Modern people have praise for the dead Confederate soldiers, he says, but does not see that the dead soldiers were "hurried beyond decision" to their deaths.

The last sections of the poem contain a question. How, the speaker asks, should people commemorate the dead soldiers? He refers again to their anonymity and uses the word "chivalry," an idea he has merely suggested before. "Chivalry" connotes high ideals and historical tradition, but the tradition died because its followers failed to put its ideals into practice. The speaker has no desire to recapture the past of the dead soldiers; it seems to him no better than the present, which, by the end of the poem, he has come to accept.

The speaker in "Ode to the Confederate Dead" is a philosopher, but he is also a solipsist, believing that the self is the only reality. This flaw, the belief only in self, is a failing that Tate seems to feel is typical of modern humanity. Thus the theme is similar to that of "The Mediterranean," as well as others of Tate's poems. The concerns of modern humanity, he suggests, are petty, somehow not human. There is, however, no resolution to the problem; the tone is despairing. Several critics have pointed out that "Ode to the Confederate Dead" is "dark," containing none of the images of light of which Tate was so fond. The speaker seems truly doomed by his inability to see beyond himself.

"SEASONS OF THE SOUL"

The problems and failings of modern humanity also dominate "Seasons of the Soul," considered by many critics to be the best of Tate's later poetry. The poem is dedicated to John Peale Bishop, Tate's friend and a poet for whom he had great respect. The two men occasionally wrote companion poems and frequently criticized each other's work. Following the dedication in the poem, there is an epigraph, which, like the motto in "The Mediterranean," is neither identified nor translated (it is from Dante's *Inferno*, in *La divina commedia*, c. 1320; *The Divine Comedy*, 1802). In the lines quoted, the speaker says that he reached up and broke a branch from a thorn tree, which cried out asking, "Why have you torn me apart?" Imprisoned inside the tree is the soul of a man, presumably a man who has died by suicide. The punishment fits the crime; the soul which denied its human form has been given a nonhuman exterior in which to spend eternity. The epigraph is significant in three ways. First, Dante in this part (canto 13) of the *Inferno* is describing the punishment of the violent, and Tate feels that violence is another of modern humanity's great flaws. Second, there is the suggestion that modern people, in denying their humanity, have damned themselves to a fate similar to that of suicide. Finally, the epigraph alerts the reader to the presence of allusions to Dante in the poem.

"Seasons of the Soul" is divided into four sections named for each of the seasons, and critics disagree on their significance in the poem. Some have seen a correspondence between the seasons and the elements, while others argue that the seasons represent the recurring obsessions of humankind. The idea of the unending rotation of the seasons is emphasized in several places. Three of the sections, "Summer," "Winter," and "Spring," begin similarly with an invocation, a technique associated with the epic tradition. The epic poets asked in their invocations for help in treating their subjects adequately, for they wrote of great deeds far beyond their own capabilities. They sought to go beyond their own limitations through the aid of the muse, who represented the epic tradition. In "Seasons of the Soul," Tate's use of the invocation is ironic, since a major element in the poem is humankind's search for salvation through some source outside itself, a search that is futile. The one section without an invocation is "Autumn." The most likely explanation for this omission, according to George Hemphill in *Allen Tate* (1964), is

that this section is devoted to the obsessions of humankind as solipsist. Since solipsistic humans are unable to accept anything but themselves as reality (and, by extension, as significant), they would not feel the need to invoke the aid of any muse or god.

The seasons are presented in sequence, beginning with summer. By choosing thus to begin the poem, Tate indicates that he is not using the four seasons in the traditional manner to represent the four ages of humanity; using the seasons in that manner would necessitate beginning with spring. In fact, most critics have noticed a logical progression in the poem from season to season and have pointed out that much of its meaning is lost if the reader attempts to begin reading the sequence at some section other than "Summer." The sequence is representative of humankind's development; to return to Hemphill's interpretation of the poem's sections, "Summer" concerns humans as activists or politicians, "Autumn" concerns them as solipsists, "Winter" concerns them as sexual beings, and "Spring" concerns them as religious beings. These concerns are similar to the seasons in their unrelenting reoccurrence.

In "Summer," Tate is concerned with the effects of political activity, especially war, on people's humanity, and he once again denounces whatever leads to dehumanization. The poem refers to World War II and the occupation of "Green France," a basically agrarian culture, by the "caterpillar feet" of Germany's technical culture. Here Tate's view of war is that of a true conscientious objector; he seems to feel that no war is justified, since the effect of violence on people's souls is so devastating as to render every victory Pyrrhic.

The season of the second part of the poem is autumn, the season of "Ode to the Confederate Dead." The speaker, often identified as the poet, relates a dream he had of falling down a well into a house. He tries to leave the house, but what appears to be the front door is a false door. His parents are in the house, but they do not recognize him. The speaker seems to have wandered (or, more accurately, fallen) into a hell especially designed for him since it fulfills his worst fear, that of the loss of his own identity. In losing his identity, the solipsist loses all. He has been damned by his inability to transcend himself, like the speaker in "Ode to the Confederate Dead." Once again Tate warns of the dangers of modern humanity's egocentricity.

While a logical link exists between the first and second sections of the poem, some critics have been unable to see such a transition between the second and third sections. Since the third is about sex, apparently that is the retreat of the speaker from his personal hell. He looks for comfort and perhaps even salvation in sex, for he begins with an invocation to Venus, goddess of love. He asks her to return to the sea, from which she came; this impossible act, the speaker feels, is preferable to modern religion in which God is seen as dried up, no longer bearing the wounds of Christ, which represent humanity's salvation. God is as dead to modern humans as the sea gods such as Neptune are. Unlike these gods, Venus is still alive as far as modern humans are concerned. Tate, however, uses images of coldness and violence to describe modern humans' sexual feelings. The shark is a symbol of sexual "perversion." This section ends with a return to the section of the *Inferno* from which the epigraph comes. The speaker breaks a branch from a tree and hears the blood of a suicide speak to him as it drips on him from the tree. The blood tells him that it is the blood of men who have killed themselves because of love's deceit. The reference to blood is reminiscent of all the water imagery used throughout this section. The blood imagery further reminds the reader that this section deals with the heart, whereas the previous section deals with the mind and the first section with the tension between the mind and heart. There clearly is no salvation through sex for modern humans.

The final section deals with religion; humans, having found no help elsewhere, turn to Christianity. The invocation is to spring, described as "irritable"—reminiscent of T. S. Eliot's description of April as "the cruelest month" in *The Waste Land* (1922). Spring is irritable because it is unable to stay and settle down. In the second stanza, the speaker recalls his childhood innocence, which refused to acknowledge the reality of death but was amused, rather, by the "ancient pun" that equated death and orgasm.

In the fourth stanza, Tate suggests that humans can find peace only when they accept the idea of death. Although this concept is Christian, the imagery is pagan, with references to Plato's cave and Sisyphus's rock. Tate moves from this thought into the specific mother imagery of the last two stanzas. The first mother has been identified as Saint Monica, mother of Saint Augustine of Hippo. According to legend, Saint Monica was a difficult mother, insisting that her son become a Christian. The early images of death as a gentle, loving "mother of silences" are continued through the reference to Saint Monica, a stern mother who led her son to the salvation of Christianity, and the nameless mother of the last stanza. In this final stanza, Tate raises a question that he does not answer: Is death a "kindness"? Certainly the orthodox view of Christianity insists that humans turn their eyes toward heaven where a "better life" awaits them. Tate, however, is a rather unorthodox Christian and in this poem is still trying to come to terms with religious questions.

OTHER MAJOR WORKS

LONG FICTION: *The Fathers*, 1938.

NONFICTION: *Stonewall Jackson: The Good Soldier*, 1928; *Jefferson Davis: His Rise and Fall*, 1929; *Reactionary Essays on Poetry and Ideas*, 1936; *Reason in Madness, Critical Essays*, 1941; *On the Limits of Poetry, Selected Essays, 1928-1948*, 1948; *The Hovering Fly, and Other Essays*, 1949; *The Forlorn Demon: Didactic and Critical Essays*, 1953; *The Man of Letters in the Modern World: Selected Essays, 1928-1955*, 1955; *Collected Essays*, 1959; *Essays of Four Decades*, 1968; *The Poetry Reviews of Allen Tate, 1924-1944*, 1983; *Cleanth Brooks and Allen Tate: Collected Letters, 1933-1976*, 1998 (Alphonse Vinh, editor).

BIBLIOGRAPHY

Bishop, Ferman. *Allen Tate*. New York: Twayne, 1967. Though composed while Tate was still writing, Bishop's book offers a good survey of his life and work up to that point; Tate's final years did not change much. Includes chronology, detailed notes and references, and select bibliography.

Bloom, Harold, ed. *Allen Tate*. Philadelphia: Chelsea House, 2004. This collection of essays contains a brief biography as well as critical analysis of "Ode to the Confederate Dead," "The Mediterranean," "The Swimmers," and "Aeneas at Washington."

Brooks, Cleanth, and Allen Tate. *Cleanth Brooks and Allen Tate: Collected Letters, 1933-1976*. Edited by Alphonse Vinh. Columbia: University of Missouri Press, 1998. A selection of letters that constitute a feisty and enjoyable account of the history of two leading participants in the literary critical wars during an era when the way to read and to teach poetry in the English language was being profoundly recast.

Dupree, Robert S. *Allen Tate and the Augustinian Imagination: A Study of the Poetry*. Baton Rouge: Louisiana State University Press, 1983. Dupree has accomplished here a thorough traversal of Tate's poetry, but he does confine his attention to the poetry. His approach is methodical and comprehensive, disclosing ingenious insights. Includes an index, a bibliography, and notes.

Hammer, Langdon. *Hart Crane and Allen Tate*. Princeton, N.J.: Princeton University Press, 1993. Three chapters are devoted to Tate, the focus of the study being on the two poets' relationship within the framing context of literary modernism. Includes bibliography, index.

Huff, Peter A. *Allen Tate and the Catholic Revival: Trace of the Fugitive Gods*. New York: Paulist Press, 1996. Examines Tate in the context of the Catholic Revival following the lost generation's post-World War I years. Tate incorporated the revival's Christian humanism into his critique of secular industrial society.

Malvasi, Mark G. *The Unregenerate South: The Agrarian Thought of John Crowe Ransom, Allen Tate, and Donald Davidson*. Baton Rouge: Louisiana State University Press, 1997. Addresses these poets' approaches to social issues including rural poverty, religion, race relations, and the effects of the New Deal on the twentieth century South, tracing the influence that their literary views had on their social and political thought. Two chapters are devoted to Tate. Index.

Montgomery, Marion. *John Crowe Ransom and Allen Tate: At Odds About the Ends of History and the Mystery of Nature*. Jefferson, N.C.: McFarland, 2003. Examines the relationships among the two poets, the Fugitives, and the Agrarians.

Squires, Radcliffe. *Allen Tate: A Literary Biography*. New York: Bobbs-Merrill, 1971. Written before Tate's death, this book is primarily a writing biography—that is, it considers the life of the writer with reference to his writings. Benefits from the personal acquaintance of Squires with Tate. Contains much anecdotal material, bibliography, indexes, and notes.

_____, ed. *Allen Tate and His Work: Critical Evaluations*. Minneapolis: University of Minnesota Press, 1972. Squires here assembles essays on all phases of Tate's writing, editing, teaching, and life. Contains a bibliography.

Underwood, Thomas A. *Allen Tate: Orphan of the South*. Princeton, N.J.: Princeton University Press, 2000. A biographical study of Tate and his part in the Agrarian and Fugitive movements. Includes bibliographical references and index.

Claire Clements Morton

JAMES TATE

Born: Kansas City, Missouri; December 8, 1943

PRINCIPAL POETRY
The Lost Pilot, 1967
The Oblivion Ha-Ha, 1970
Hints to Pilgrims, 1971, 1982
Absences: New Poems, 1972
Viper Jazz, 1976
Riven Doggeries, 1979
Constant Defender, 1983
Reckoner, 1986
Distance from Loved Ones, 1990
Selected Poems, 1991
Worshipful Company of Fletchers, 1994
Shroud of the Gnome, 1997
Police Story, 1999
Memoir of the Hawk, 2001
Lost River, 2003
Return to the City of White Donkeys, 2004
The Ghost Soldiers, 2008

OTHER LITERARY FORMS

James Tate is known primarily as a poet, although he has produced some fiction and nonfiction.

ACHIEVEMENTS

James Tate came onto the literary scene at the age of twenty-three, when his first full-length manuscript of poems, *The Lost Pilot*, was selected for publication in the prestigious Yale Younger Poets Series by Yale University Press. Other works, long and short, followed, and Tate became editor of the *Dickinson Review* in 1967. He has also served as an associate editor at Pym-Randall Press and Barn Dream Press (small presses located in Cambridge, Massachusetts) and as a consultant to the Coordinating Council of Literary Magazines. For two years running, in 1968 and 1969, and again in 1980, he received writing fellowships from the National Endowment for the Arts. In 1972, he was the Phi Beta Kappa poet at Brown University. He won a National Institute of Arts and Letters Award in 1974, followed two years later by a Guggenheim Fellowship. He was awarded the Pulitzer Prize in poetry in 1992 for *Se-*

James Tate (©Jill Krementz)

lected Poems. In 1994, he was honored with a National Book Award for *Worshipful Company of Fletchers*, and in 1995 with a Wallace Stevens Award from the American Academy of Poets. He edited *The Best American Poetry, 1997* (1997), and his poems have been included in many editions of the anthology. He became a member of the American Academy of Arts and Letters in 2004 and served as chancellor for the Academy of American Poets from 2001 to 2007.

Tate has established himself as a formidable exponent of literary surrealism of a peculiarly American kind. His work has garnered the praise of many academic critics and journal reviewers; his poetry has appeared across the gamut of magazines in North America and England and has influenced the style of many young writers.

BIOGRAPHY

James Vincent Tate was born in Kansas City, Missouri, in 1943. He began college study at the University of Missouri in Columbia and finished his B.A. at Kansas State College in Pittsburg, Kansas, in 1965. He entered the Writers' Workshop at the University of Iowa and received an M.F.A. in poetry in 1967. In 1966, Tate began teaching creative writing and literature courses at the University of Iowa (1966-1967), the University of California, Berkeley (1967-1968), Columbia University (1969-1971), and Emerson College in Boston (poet-in-residence, 1970-1971). He joined the regular teaching faculty at the University of Massachusetts at Amherst in 1971, where he would remain except for short periods of residence in such places as Sweden, Ireland, and Spain.

ANALYSIS

There are two kinds of poets in the world: those who grow with age and alter style, outlook, and argument over the years, and those who burst onto the scene fully fledged and polish what is in essence an unchanging perception of life throughout their careers. James Tate is of the second sort; his stunning appearance in his first major book, *The Lost Pilot*, set the pattern for all he would write over the succeeding decades. The poetry of *Distance from Loved Ones* is a richer, denser, more masterful execution of the style and themes he set for himself as a young man.

Variation for Tate is a subtle thing; beneath the variances of style and diction lies a core of subjects and emotions that are constant in his poetry: loss of relations, the quixotic world of appearances, and a violent underworld of emotion waiting to erupt through the crevices of the mundane. The central theme running throughout Tate's canon is the desire to shatter superficial experience, to break through the sterility of suburban life and drown it in erotic passion. His characters languish from unfulfilled longings; the objects he contemplates are all prisoners of definition and stereotype; life is a desert of routine expectation waiting to blow up from the forces of liberated imagination, whimsy, outrage, and humor.

Tate joins a long line of midwestern writers who fought in their writing against the domestic tedium of their region. Theodore Dreiser set the pattern of the rebellious midwestern writer in his novels about youths trapped in the social coils of work, poverty, and loveless marriages; Sherwood Anderson paved the way of modernist writers through his depictions of the sterile sanity of small-town life in his novel *Winesburg, Ohio: A Group of Tales of Ohio Small Town Life* (1919). F. Scott Fitzgerald and Ernest Hemingway explored the unrealizable dreams of their characters, who had escaped only partway from their families and bleak pasts. Poets of the Midwest, including T. S. Eliot, Ezra Pound, and Carl Sandburg, emphasized realistic detail in their unflinching reports of what had gone wrong in American society in their time.

THE LOST PILOT

The Lost Pilot joins this tradition of harsh assessments of midwestern life; the argument itself is a rather somber account of a young man's loneliness, despair, and feelings of isolation. "The End of the Line," from the middle section of the book, is emblematic of the themes treated in the poems. "We plan our love's rejuvenation/ one last time," the speaker comments, but the jaunty tone of the piece breaks down as he admits that the relationship has gone sour for good. The poems acutely examine the meaning of relationships, the risk of loving someone, and the desolation at losing a father or lover through unexplained accident or fatal whim. This instability lying at the heart of emotion makes everything else around him equally shimmering and unreal.

Tate's use of surrealist language, the dreamy, irrational figures and images that define his view of things, is derived from European and South American writing of the twentieth century. The original motives of Surrealism sprang from the devastations of war and the corruption of the state. For Tate, though, the corruption lies somewhere else: in the incapacity of human beings to face their dilemmas honestly, to admit that the heart is wild, immoral, anarchic, or that life is essentially a reality beyond the grasp of moral principles. For Tate, the American situation is the opposite of war-torn Europe or politically corrupt South America. The American scene is too stable, too ordered and domesticated; underneath the neat appearances of reality lies a universe of chaotic energies waiting to spring back. To that degree, one may casually link Tate's vision to the horrific suspense of Stephen King's novels or to the wounded idealism of Tom Wolfe and Hunter Thompson. In each of these writers lives a certain purity of taste for the natural world and for the lost values of a pastoral and Edenic past that modernity has outraged and insulted.

To love in Tate's poetry is to tap into this hidden volcano of irrationality, to tease its powers awake. Most often, his lovers quake at the first sign of wilderness in their emotions and drift back to the safety of their homely, selfish worlds. To fall in love is to touch nature directly and to break through to the other side of reality. This sentiment is expressed at the close of *The Lost Pilot* when Tate writes, "I am falling, falling/ falling in love, and desire to leave this place." The place he desires to leave is that parched desert of convention where all of his characters languish.

The poetry of this first collection generates a kind of philosophical earthquake in its brief descriptions, debunking the moral fictions of an ordered life through the riotous outpouring of illogical imagery. This is a poetry of emotional purgings, of discreet, Janovian primal screams into the bedroom mirror.

The Lost Pilot is grounded by its title poem, an elegy combining a son's wit, fantasy, and tears over the death of his father in World War II. The phrase itself is instructive; a pilot is one who finds his way through dark skies. The father as lost pilot compounds the son's forlornness; here is a father who has disappeared, a guide without compass who leaves his son behind in a dull, seemingly trackless void. The reader learns in the poem that the son keeps an annual vigil and looks up to see his father orbiting overhead—a curious, droll, and yet appropriate image for the son's grief. Another poem, written to the boy's mother, commemorates Father's Day in an ironic reference to the missing father. A careful look at all the poems reveals the image of the missing father in each of them: He haunts the world as a peculiar absence of love, as when lovers leave the poet, or emotion goes rank and sour.

In the closing poem, "Today I Am Falling," even the title suggests something of Tate's humor in poetry: The falling has no object, but in the text, the reader finds that the falling is toward love, which in turn leads only to the desire to escape. The place the speaker is trying to reach is a "sodium pentothal landscape," a place of lost memories aroused by the intravenous intake of a "truth serum" once used in psychotherapy. That landscape lies behind repression and emotional stagnation, its "bud about to break open." The trembling surface of Tate's language here and elsewhere is that effort to break through the false appearance of things, the dull veneer of human convention concealing passion and the energy of nature.

However, for a poet trying to break through, the early poems are terse, carefully worked miniatures that technically belie their purpose. Tate prefers a short, three-line stanza as his measure, with a varying line of between five and six syllables, usually end-stopped—that is, punctuated with a comma-length pause or ended with a period. The flow of speech often requires enjambment, the running through of one line to the next, but not in the free-verse fashion of breaking lines arbitrarily at prepositions, adjectives, and nouns after the manner of prose. Instead, Tate makes sure his phrases are well-defined rhythmically before cutting to the next line. If he carries the rhythm through to the next line, or allows it to leap over a stanza break, usually he has found some emphatic word to terminate the line before he does so.

The poems on the page look slightly cramped and compressed, as if the thinking were squeezed down to an essence of protest. The poetry written by Tate's con-temporaries is expansive, even sprawling by comparison. Few poets took the medium to these limits of compression, and when they did, they were freer with the pattern of line and accent. One may speculate that Tate's statements are intended as whispers in tight places—quick, emergency pleas to the reader or to himself. However they are intended, the language is uniformly limpid, purified, the hesitation revised out of each smoothly cresting phrase. There is high finish in the wording and phrasing, which may at times work against the sense of emotional torment Tate wants to convey.

Thumbing through the pages of *The Lost Pilot*, one is struck by the contradiction between polished execution and troubled content. The move in poetry after 1945 was to incorporate into the linguistic and prosodic structure of the poem the movement of emotion tracked by the meaning of words. The poem should come apart in sympathy with, or in representation of, the emotional disarray of the speaker, and the language of the poem should involve the detritus of spent or erupting emotion in its configuration. Distillation of language down to an essence was in some ways a Christian aesthetic carried over into "closed" or traditional poetics—a sense of language as having a spiritual inner text that the poet pared down to achieve communication with the soul. The throwing up of verbal dross and trivia into the language stream of lyric after 1945 was an effort to join "soul music" with the blunt, earthy matter of nature; hence the languorous and wayward course of much lyric energy in the postmodern era. In Tate, however, and in a contingent of southern male poets who came of age with him, one finds uniformly tidy and balanced typographical structures that avoid technical deformation.

Tate's aesthetic tradition, which includes Wallace Stevens, Robert Frost, the European Symbolists, and the Deep Image movement of Robert Bly and James Wright, rejected a projective aesthetic that would incorporate the turmoil of mind into the finished artwork. That distinction between content and execution may have proved over the years to be confining to the range of Tate's subject matter and stylistic virtuosity. There is the hint of a technical repression of feeling in this mode of terse lyric, of funneling into sparse and smoothly patterned verses the chaos of longing and rage intended by the poems. The risk one takes in keeping to this method of writing is that emotional diversity may be diluted by the repetition of lyric forms.

Through the succession of Tate's later books, the poem does not change its technical strategy except to grow in size: Stanza and line are fleshed out, articulation is fuller and more sonorous, and rhythm has greater sweep, but the poet set his stylistic signature in *The Lost Pilot*, and the rules he gave himself were essentially unalterable thereafter. The burden on readers is to pay keen attention to content against a background of similar, even uniform measures, to make out with sympathetic attention the varying inner world that has been systematized in repetitive lyrical patterns. The burden on Tate is to risk everything on the line itself, to dazzle, compel, and sweep away the reader on the force of an image, a powerful phrase, the stunning resolution of a whole poem on a single word.

THE OBLIVION HA-HA

In *The Oblivion Ha-Ha*, a three-stanza poem, "The Pet Deer," works on the principle of the single line holding the poem aloft. Stanza 1 is purely functional exposition, given in limpid phrases; stanza 2 sets up the conflict implied in the deer's realizing that it is a kind of centaur in love with a human girl; and stanza 3 builds slowly toward the closing line, revealing that the girl is unaware of "what/ the deer dreams or desires." Here repression is located in an animal, a deft reversal of Tate's usual argument. The girl is placid, lovely, unaffected in her sexual allure; the deer is the captive soul unable to break out and satisfy desire.

The poem hangs by the thread of its final line along with the touches in several other phrases, but in sum, it works on the plainness of its exposition, its setup of an incident, which it transforms by a single lyric thrust of insight. This is Symbolist methodology given an American stamp by Tate's withholding the intellectual and ideological motives of the lyric act. In Symbolist poetry, almost any incident will reveal the poet's own psyche, which he will have expressed referentially through an object, animal, or character.

The deer is, by the twists of psychic projection in this poem, the poet himself, the girl a combination of lovers longed for and lost. The art of the poem is to raise the ordinary theme of repression and longing to a degree of generality that turns experience into fable, myth, or even allegory. Too broad a stroke, and the delicate suggestibility of language collapses; too little said, and the poem remains a mere fragment of thought without affect.

"Here is my heart,/ I don't know what to do with it," Tate writes in "Plea Based on a Sentence from a Letter Received by the Indiana State Welfare Department." The line expresses succinctly the theme of *The Oblivion Ha-Ha*. The title has confused critics; it is usually taken to mean a kind of maniacal laughter in the face of a bitter world. However, a secondary definition of "ha-ha" is a garden enclosure, usually of hedge or earthwork, separating one small planting bed from surrounding ground. In early Roman gardens, a raised inner court often supported a small statue of Adonis, a chthonic god of fertility; in modern times, gazebos and small terraces take the same role as the Adonis mound. Curiously, the garden meaning of the word, derived from French, bears the same hyphen as the first meaning. Tate's conceit may be that one laughs helplessly at sight of the enclosed Eden, thus doubling the meanings into one trope.

That inner garden reserve, perhaps, is the point of the title, an inner garden that is shut in or inaccessibly remote and psychological, but rooted in the familiar world of human senses. The oblivion ha-ha is the soul, the secret inner self in its own mound of earth, which the poems try to capture.

In "The Salute," a man dreams about a black widow spider whom he loves; yet he "completely misunderstood" her "little language." The secret soul is located on one side or another of broken relationships; lovers who try to reach across the distance confront either the sorrows of the deer or the suicidal love of this dreamer, willing to mate with a spider who kills her lovers. "Nobody gets what he wants," Tate writes in "Consumed," which closes on this characteristic remark about a lover: "You are the stranger/ who gets stranger by the hour." Another poem on parents, "Leaving Mother Waiting for Father," returns to the theme of loss, with the speaker leaving his doll-like, decrepit mother leaning against a hotel, as he goes off into the world an adult orphan.

ABSENCES

In every case, Tate creates a portrait of an isolated heart longing for relation and failing to achieve it. The world that denies love to his characters is superficially intact, but beneath appearance it festers with neurotic passion and chaos. It is no wonder, therefore, that he would write a book called *Absences*. In it, Tate experiments with a looser style; prose poems appear in section 3, while long poems occupy section 2. The title poem and "Cycle of Dust" are sequential works that have more diffuse imagery and lack the point of surprise perfected in the short lyric.

The interesting turn in *Absences* is in the image-making itself; it focuses on characters who dismantle themselves, or try to disappear, in their blind effort to cross over to the "other" side of reality. These figures do not quite make it; they practice escaping from the blind literalism of things but end up dismantling only their defined selves. They do not reach Paradise. The shift to decomposing this part of reality marks Tate's decision to alter the lyric path he was on. From here onward, Tate drops the Edenic or pastoral ideal altogether and concentrates instead on exploding the empirical world of sense and definition. Experience itself will be his target.

Put another way, in *Absences* and beyond, one-half of the metaphoric principle of his poetry drops away, the ideal and hidden dimension of vision. What remains is the imploding and decaying half of reality, the objects metaphor dwells on to hint at possibilities in the dream world. There are only the objects themselves now, deformed, fragmentary, increasingly meaningless as the stuff of lyric. More and more, Tate will imply the end of such language: There is still the need to escape, to break out of reality into the other world, but references to the other world by image or suggestion are rare. His poems dwell on the disappearance of reality itself, its decomposition into fantasy and paradox. In "Harm Alarm," the second poem of *Absences*, a man fearfully examines his street, decides that all harm lies "in a cradle/ across the ocean," and resumes his walk after observing that his "other" self should "just about awake now" as the source of that harm. The divided self splits evenly between dream and waking, serene emptiness and conflicted, wounded

life. Pain abounds as the defining attribute of consciousness; the pin functions as a motif in a number of these poems.

There is little or no plot, and no organization to narrate the flow of language. The poems accumulate around the thematic abstraction of reality's own breakup. That means that individual lines and sentences have the burden of forming the book. Reading Tate, one looks for lines, images, and stunning metaphors as the point of poetry. There is no structural principle embodying language or visionary argument. Tate's assumption is that reality is dead, and the surreal lyric depicts that through its own formlessness and its occasional glimpses into magic through a phrase or word. Another position would hold that the poem itself is an object of nature, an expression of creative principles. Tate's metaphysic, however, is still linked with the Christian view that meaning derives from a spiritual source outside nature. These poems, strange and irrational as they are, are secularized forms of prayer, beseeching an "outside" for grace and succor.

These matters are summed up in "Wait for Me," when he writes, "A dream of life a dream of birth/ a dream of moving/ from one world into another// All night dismantling the synapses/ unplugging the veins and arteries." The rest of the poem is about the dissolving self, the fading consciousness, as the reader continues to watch, in this world, with him. The tone is not far removed from the self-abnegating fervor of the medieval martyr, whose longing to purify life and join God is merely the extreme of Tate's lyrics of self-abandonment. "I hear a laugh swim up/ from the part of myself/ I've killed," he writes in "Delicate Riders," in which the reader sees that it is the spiritual self that has died out in the contemporary desert of materialism. "I who have no home have no destination either," he writes in "The Boy." "One bone against another,/ I carve what I carve/ to be rid of myself by morning/ by deep dreams disintegrated."

Tate's feud with reality is that it has no soul; it is the broken world of modern, spiritless philosophy. What remains is the memory of soul in magical lyricism, which surveys the fallen world and discovers fading glimmers of spirit in paradox, accidental juxtaposition, chaotic series, and the like.

VIPER JAZZ

This mordant perspective on the world is the subject of his next major book, *Viper Jazz*, published in the Wesleyan Poetry Program series (Wesleyan University Press) in 1976. In it, Tate reins in the experimentalism of *Absences* and writes in short, stanzaic lyrics and prose poems on the theme of "worlds refused by worlds." A man goes crazy with his obsessions in "Many Problems," his suffering soul dying on "the boneyard of vegetables/ the whole world is built on." In "Read the Great Poets," the couch allows "the spirit to leave/ the broken body and wander at will" through "this great dull life."

In "Blank-Stare Encounter," the speaker blurts out a new imperative, "I want to start a new religion," but the dead world's "blank stare drags me along." The point is, however, that no "new religion" is forthcoming from Tate. Midway through *Viper Jazz*, one begins to feel a withdrawal from that premise and the setting in of a reductive new attitude that is partly resignation and partly a return to the chattier, amusing voice of early lyrics. There is a quality here of stand-up comedian, the one-liner gag writer who keeps his audience off balance by surrealist turns.

RIVEN DOGGERIES

From *Viper Jazz* to the following book, *Riven Doggeries*, one notes with misgivings a certain carelessness in the work; the language is flimsy, form is lazily sketched in, and poems turn on anecdote and coincidence, sometimes without the clinching phrase to energize them. The theme for much of *Riven Doggeries* is travel, both actual and in the mind, the feverish transport into and out of reality as the locus of mere existence. By now it is obvious that there is no Paradise opening through the mist; instead, Tate's style hardens into a parody of the real world, a burlesque of the poet's daily life to which the shreds of a previous idealism still cling. "We are all members/ of Nature's alphabet. But we wanted more," he writes in "Nature Poem: Demanding Stiff Sentences," a pun-laced and well-crafted lyric tucked into the middle of the book. However, such reminders of his romantic principles do not make up for his lax writing.

As a sign that the verse poem may be wearing out here, Tate turns increasingly to the prose poem as miniature short story and frame for the fantasized speech he is using. In "Missionwork," part 3 of *Riven Doggeries*, the language is dense and humorous again, and self-mocking. "It's a sickness, this desire to fly," he notes. Here too the ideal slips away in a dozen forms, from fireflies to dogs—the dog is an essential motif of the absconding spirit throughout the book, the "rivening" of the title.

The prose poem, used here with skill, crept into poetry and has become a standard form in the American repertoire. Beginning with the French poet Charles Baudelaire's *Petits Poèmes en prose* (1869; also known as *Le Spleen de Paris*; *Poems in Prose*, 1905, also known as *Paris Spleen, 1869*, 1947), an early experiment in the mode, poets have discovered its use as a form of fantasizing meditation, but without the rhythmic intimacy or precision required in verse. Prose is borderless, a more "submerged" form of writing in that line breaks and phrasings are no longer functions of intense feeling or ideation. A poet's prose makes the presumption of being literal, often somber self-analysis, just as fantasy and the absurd slowly decompose the argument. The trick is to construct an elaborate ruse of confidentiality that is undone the moment the next improbable detail is sprung on the reader's belief, crushing it. Some writers, including Tate and his friend Charles Simic, compound the irony by going past the point of disbelief to reestablish partial credibility.

CONSTANT DEFENDER

Beginning with *Riven Doggeries*, Tate is trying to find ways to open the poem, to spread out its intricate patterns and create more space for rambling monologue and humorous asides. He directs his efforts at colloquializing his verse speech, which begins to take effect in *Constant Defender*. Here a well-balanced fantasy mixes with verse compression, though the clinching phrase is often muted in the process. The dialectic between spiritual ideals and the morbidity of the real take subtler form, as in "Tall Trees by Still Waters," where "the actual world was pretending again,/ no, not pretending, imagining an episode/ of unbelievable cruelty, involving invalids."

The self of these poems is more harried, beaten down, and Kafkaesque than in previous books. One detects the wearing down of the idealist in such poetry, intimated in the title—the wearying vigilance of the "constant defender" of his beliefs. The theme running throughout is of abandoned houses to which the speaker returns forlornly, disillusioned once more at cruelty and indifference. In "Tell Them Was Here," the "I" intentionally omitted, the poem ends, "Started to leave,// turned, scratched out my name—/ then wrote it back again." A darker look at self occurs in "Lousy in Center Field," a wonderful poem with dazzling imagery that remarks, "I'm frozen once again/ in an attitude of unfortunate/ interior crumbling mouse-holes." He is the ballplayer who has lost all interest in catching the ball, which flies over him in a cobwebbed sky.

The landscape is filling up with the dead souls of the modern city. This theme, though tentative and sketchy in *Constant Defender*, becomes pronounced in *Reckoner* and *Distance from Loved Ones*. Both continue the breezier, conversational style that set in with *Constant Defender*. The poems work as accumulations of one-line observations, some pithy, some empty, with here and there a humorous turn or a startling image to enliven the pace of what are often tedious aggregates of lines. One poem flows into the next in these books, in which a manic speaker seems desperate to keep up his chatter against a growing sense of loss in his life.

RECKONER

Reckoner mixes prose poems and lyric or narrative verse; the tone shifts slightly from one to the other, but Tate has turned his attention away from the formality and finish of individual poems to the sense of words running together across boundaries to create a metatextual whole. The poems no longer hold up as unique, intricately structured maps of thought; their titles and shapes on the page maintain a certain ghost of formality over which the content leaps. The resulting flow of commentary creates the impression of a speaker's feverish avoidance of some impending tragedy. Even the humor is shrill, worn out, the emotions exhausted by frenetic articulation. The jokes and grotesque exaggeration have an almost menacing insistence; the reader has come upon their formulas many times before in Tate.

Many of the poems open on the same frenetic tempo, with fully punctuated sentences lined up as stanzas, as in "The Flithering Ignominy of Baba Ganoosh," which begins,

> He played the bongo drums and dated infant
> actresses.
> His signature still glitters in all the most exhausted
> hotels.
> He has positive contempt for rain, for chattering.
> His sofa was designed by a butcher.

This is the sort of shtick Henny Youngman made famous, the one-liner that waits for guffaws or the drummer's rim shot in the background. A pace of this kind wears out humor and begins arousing other emotions by its drugged repetition. Poem after poem renounces the minutiae of the waking world, as some other, darker voice hints that the underlying hidden world has sealed itself for good. The speaker is someone left behind, unable to imagine the possibility of regaining what he somewhere calls the "parallel world." "I've been feeling so cooped up in this hotel," begins a prose poem, "Magazines," where banter goes on for a page without resolution, without argument, without premise even, but for this dejection that pervades all of *Reckoner*.

DISTANCE FROM LOVED ONES

In *Distance from Loved Ones*, the pace does not slacken, but the theme of universal death gathers emphasis and becomes a central motif, with many references to death, the dying, and the already deceased who are memories of the speakers. There are now "citizens of the deep," as the speaker remarks in the opening poem, "Quabbin Reservoir," while he alone kills time along the shore as the last of the living voices. Other ghosts are portrayed, as in "Peggy in the Twilight," who "spent half of each day trying to wake up, and/ the other half preparing for sleep."

Tate's characters in *Distance from Loved Ones* keep lonely vigils among the dead; their voices have turned to memory. Many of the poems are variations on the elegy, the very form with which *The Lost Pilot* began. The poems' characters, variations on that youthful speaker who awaited his father's orbital return each birthday, live futile, empty lives waiting to join the dead around them. They have no purpose in life; their only defense against remorse is their disjunctive humor, their ability to disconnect the tedious logic of their world and playfully deconstruct their own identities.

In "How Happy We Were," one of these loners notes that his vision of eternity included "a few of the little angels/ whose sole job it is to fake weeping for people like us." Crowds in America practice "dead mall worship," he writes in "Beaucoup Vets," and in "Anatomy," a beautiful girl studies anatomy and continually cries. The others "know she is dying inside." In "Taxidermy," "Everything is dead anyway." In a sense, the death of the father in Tate's first book has spread out over his many books to encompass the world; the memory of the dead father created a glimmering afterlife Tate never could bring into sharp focus or make the basis of a sustaining vision. His poetry began as elegy and has built a vast edifice of language to exhaust the content of that emotion.

WORSHIPFUL COMPANY OF FLETCHERS

The title of National Book Award winner *Worshipful Company of Fletchers* refers to the ancient guild of arrow makers. The tone shifts to the sort of dark humor of Paul Auster's novels, particularly his dystopian fantasy *In the Country of Last Things* (1987). In that book and in Tate's later poetry, one finds a deepening sense of gloom over the future of cities, and something of the mordant tone of the poet Leonard Cohen's lyric, "the future is murder," and of Don DeLillo's wry assessment, "The future is crowds." For Tate, the city is fast becoming a barren landscape of parentless people, those without fathers who accept routine merely because it distracts them from desperate loneliness and a sense of futility.

In the title poem, a small boy, Tate's alter ego, is confronted by the older poet, who notes that he "lives at the edge of the woods" and that it is "still not clear to me where he really lives." The "really" underscores the ironic tone of the story: In Tate's world, no one appears to be living in reality; rather, one escapes from reality by means of fantasy and self-delusion. The speaker goes on to note that "he'd live with animals if they'd take him in," and thus withdraw altogether from an untrustworthy community of adults. The woods are still

poet Frost's place of retreat, where the mind may heal itself from the woes of this world, and William Wordsworth's woods, where innocence may live unviolated by the evils of city life. At the "edge" of the woods, however, one is neither protected by the animals nor free of adult corruptions, and the boy's vaguely orphaned state permits Tate to expand on his identity as the picture of Everyman groping for relationships, loath to accept the meager terms of existence he might find in his suburban neighborhood.

The poems are still page-length lyrical narratives or commentaries, nearly all of which are composed in Tate's wry, drily surreal style, which derives part of its voice from the matter-of-fact tone of Frost, who depicts a life of drudging and narrow-mindedness from which he tries to escape by remembering his childhood and by proposing outrageous questions to his dowdy neighbors. Tate grows out of the same rebellious nature set against uneventful lives, whose language has leapt beyond mere representation of events to fracture common sense by shifting to different subjects without transition or logical connectives.

In this sense, Tate has moved all his strategies from his previous books into a single thrust of reasoning aimed at the disenchanted world of adulthood and its mundane circumstances. He is the confirmed orphan living without benefit of a father's counsel or affection, who finds others laboring without joy and merely using up their mortal span. His defense against this empty materialism is to bend logic by allowing dreams and the anarchy of the unconscious to erupt at will. Tate's definition of the orphan soul is that it is without membranes between a rational self and its fortified ego, on one hand, and the great swampy interiors of one's dream self and the night world of longings and unfulfilled love, on the other.

In page after page of this and succeeding books, the poems report events from a slightly cracked perspective. The company of fletchers who feather arrow shafts take their work seriously, though their product belongs mainly to the fantasy lives of boys who look for their roots in myth and folklore and wilderness landscapes, like the orphan in the title poem. By means of his fractured accounts of daily life, Tate creates a Norman Rockwell painting of ordinary America in which the certainties in the background—small houses and neat little roads—peel away from the surface to reveal some other landscape that the soul longs for and cannot reach. Tate's humor is laced with bitterness and disillusionment that he could not grow up normally after losing a father in the war when he was an infant.

Some other, more difficult motive is at play in this and the books to come: a desire to so muddle the usual progress of lyric argument as to make each word an unpredictable event, thus preventing the reader from feeling as if the language could be anticipated and thus ignored. The poem becomes resistant to being read, to being predicted or interrupted by the reader's own wandering thoughts. Average poems have about them what the poet Charles Bernstein calls "absorptiveness," or a kind of senseless spongy believability in which readers even forget that what they are reading is a poem or that there is any alternative reality to the thing being read. The "anti-absorptive" work of art is so fashioned as to make the reader aware of its every word as if it were a physical object, not a convenient screen of illusion in which to lose one's self. Tate's thinly veiled surrealism is enough to make the reader uncomfortable, slightly puzzled, and on guard against all the rug pulling in the average Tate lyric. In the last poem of this volume, "Happy as the Day Is Long," the fallen world of mere reality is itemized:

I take the long walk up the staircase to my secret room.
Today's big news: they found Amelia Earhart's shoe,
    size 9.
1992: Charlie Christian is bebopping at Minton's in
    1941.
Today, the presidential primaries have failed us once
    again.
We'll look for our excitement elsewhere, in the last
    snow
that is falling, in tomorrow's Gospel Concert in
    Springfield.
It's a good day to be a cat and just sleep.

SHROUD OF THE GNOME

Shroud of the Gnome opens with the poem "Where Do Babies Come From?," the perennial question of growing youngsters to their parents, which receives this jaundiced report about hapless orphans forced into hard labor:

Many are from the Maldives,
    southwest of India, and must begin
collecting shells immediately.
The larger ones may prefer coconuts.
Survivors move from island to island
hopping over one another and never
looking back. After the typhoons
have had their pick, and the birds of prey
have finished with theirs, the remaining few
must build boats.

Other poems move into poet Stevens's tropical landscape of cockatiels and sunny rooms, only to find reality equally dismembered in Tate's world. If reality is Tate's target, he snips at its ligaments with surgical scissors in this volume, keeping up the pretense that his form of chatter has rails under it, when in fact it races off its track from line to line, silently mocking the flimsy laws of grammar and veracity on which most conversation is based. Tate is a metaphysical satirist, a comedian of the laws of verisimilitude, who finds everything floating on illusory foundations. Hence, his poems read like idle chitchat after dinner among half-educated well-meaning suburbanites, whose generalities and clichés allow readers to glimpse the quicksand on which reality has built its world.

Shrouds are winding sheets of the dead, and gnomes are out of fairy tales; the title doubles the references to a world at the edge of consciousness, where gnomes have died but live on in some other dimension to haunt us. Reality has excluded them, but the mere act of juxtaposing items creates a nonsense argument in which things happen in spite of one's attempts to "make sense" of life. This "cut up" method, invented by the novelist William Burroughs, is used here with drier, but more telling, effect. Here is how the method works in the title poem,

And what amazes me is that none of our modern
   inventions
surprise or interest him, even a little. I tell him
it is time he got his booster shots, but then
I realize I have no power over him whatsoever.
He becomes increasingly light footed until I lose sight
of him downtown between the federal building and
the post office. A registered nurse is taking her
coffee break. I myself needed a break, so I sat down
next to her at the counter. "Don't mind me," I said,
"I'm just a hungry little gnostic in need of a sandwich."

The "gnostic" may be a clue to the subversive logic of
Tate's entire canon, for gnostic wisdom is based on intuitive glimpses into mysteries independent of the
senses or the logic of empiricism. The gnostic believes
in other worlds and their power to merge with our own
sensory experience. Tate's speaker is often confronting
those who have no alternative world to draw from,
making his own "gnostic" processes seem disjointed
and absurd, as in the poem, "Same as You":

I put my pants on one day at a time.
Then I hop around in circles hobbledehoy.
A projectile of some sort pokes me,
in the eye—I think it's a bird
or a flying pyramid that resembles a bird.

MEMOIR OF THE HAWK

In *Memoir of the Hawk*, Tate covers a widening
range of subjects that include a young woman's desire
to see a "blue antelope," in the closing poem, and after
removing her clothes in a park she begins to see them
moving "like angels" toward her. The situation is a
page torn from Eugène Ionesco's Surrealist one-act
play *Rhinocéros* (pr., pb. 1959; *Rhinoceros*, 1959), although without the menacing suggestion of fascism's
contagious spirit. This "antelope" is a creature of innocence longed for by a woman and a man who both lie
naked as if to return to childhood and visionary experience. The poem, like so many others before it, is a testament to Tate's enduring ability to find new expressions
for a lifelong antidote to the sorrows of aging and the
burden of the merely material world, made orthodox
long ago as the logical view of things. He has challenged this view by drawing on the literature of rebellion from Romanticism to Surrealism to make the case

that other worlds are sandwiched between the objects
of reality and signify a multitude of possibilities excluded by an official grammar of experience.

LOST RIVER

In *Lost River*, Tate has assembled twenty narrative-
like poems that emphasize a sense of people being disconnected from the human experience. Although Tate
opens the collection with "The Memories of Fish," he
appears to funnel the poems through the title poem
"Lost River." The speaker in "Lost River" details his
journey with his wife to a legendary village, where they
anticipate purchasing a pterodactyl wing from a man.
When they are detoured to a deserted store, the couple
unexpectedly encounters an old man, who coinciden-
tally has a pterodactyl wing and offers it to them, free of
charge. Tate's preference to juxtapose the real with the
surreal resonates in "Lost River" and is particularly effective in illustrating how people lose touch with the
human experience. Moreover, Tate's desire to show
people who are incapable of allowing the human experience to penetrate them is authenticated through the
speaker's detached perspective. The poem concludes
with the couple accepting the generous gift and continuing their journey. Tate's depiction of the couple's being oblivious to any deeper meaning of their encounter
with the old man shows the blind motivation with
which people may attempt to seek fulfilment. While
traditional connoisseurs of poetry may feel disconnected because of the nontraditional themes conveyed
and forms employed in poems such as "Lost River,"
Tate's modern-day style does more to free the reader's
intellect than it does to paralyze it. Because of his use of
free-verse forms that emulate the often satirical characteristics of the novella, Tate's poetry could plausibly be
likened to the fiction of Flannery O'Connor in that both
are unparalleled in their ability to merge the mundane
aspects of life with situations that mirror the mysterious
and absurd aspects of life.

Several other works in the collection involve unusual encounters with animals, which illustrate a sense
of disconnect to nature. For example, "Never Enough
Darts" shows a bear invading a town as if it were in its
natural habitat. Although the townspeople are described as longing to reconnect with nature, their desire
is contingent on maintaining an adequate food supply.

In "It Happens Like This," Tate offers a fantasy-like narrative as he depicts a goat befriending a man. The narrative concludes with an image of the goat and the man walking off into unknown territory. While "Never Enough Darts" implies how a society becomes blind to its self-serving wants, "It Happens Like This" suggests that humankind can function as a partner with nature rather than try to dominate it. The fact that these eclectic works are assembled in a collection with "lost" in its title reinforces Tate's poetic vision, which aims to portray the ways in which a society can lose control of its moral compass.

RETURN TO THE CITY OF WHITE DONKEYS

Return to the City of White Donkeys contains more than one hundred works. As a whole, the collection explores feelings of otherworldliness, and Tate continues to employ his technique of conveying a narrative through free-verse poetry. The title poem, "Return to the City of White Donkeys," may surprise some readers because although the "city of white donkeys" is an underground world populated by albino donkeys and alien-like people, the city is not an uninviting place. Tate's description of these colorless life-forms suggests that this underground world has not been tainted by situations that often mar the human condition. The narrative unfolds through the dialogue between the speaker and his lifelong friend, who claims to be a native of the underground world. The irony of the narrative is that the speaker's friend paints a bleak picture of the lives of the inhabitants of this underground world, who live in mud houses and subsist on indigenous harvests; however, these alien-like people experience the same range of emotions that humans experience—happiness, love, and sadness. That Tate depicts an undesirable underground world as a world to be preferred underscores one of his constant themes—accepting what may be possible versus what is probable.

THE GHOST SOLDIERS

The Ghost Soldiers contains more than ninety poems that embody many of the topics and themes of Tate's previous publications, such as the disillusionment and isolation that people experience when life fails to live up to the ideas longed for by one's heart. Written in Tate's signature narrative-like style, the title poem explores how a society forgets the sacrifices made by those who have lost their lives in battle. The speaker opens the poem by describing his journey to a downtown Memorial Day parade. Tate injects a mournful tone through images of disabled veterans standing along a route crowded with silent townspeople. He portrays the townspeople as feeling insulted by the fact that none of the town's soldiers has returned home alive, and in this way, he underscores the dehumanizing effect on even those people who do not have firsthand experience of deadly combat war zones.

OTHER MAJOR WORKS

LONG FICTION: *Lucky Darryl*, 1977 (with Bill Knott).

SHORT FICTION: *Hottentot's Ossuary*, 1974; *Dreams of a Robot Dancing Bee: Forty-four Stories*, 2002.

NONFICTION: *The Route as Briefed*, 1999.

EDITED TEXT: *The Best American Poetry, 1997*, 1997.

BIBLIOGRAPHY

Harms, James. "Clarity Instead of Order: The Practice of Postmodernism in the Poetry of James Tate." In *A Poetry Criticism Reader*, edited by Jerry Harp and Jan Weissmiller. Iowa City: University of Iowa Press, 2006. Examines Tate's poetry and what characterizes it as postmodern poetry. Says Tate's poems "exist in that nether region which is redolent of dreams but saturated with reality."

Henry, Brian, ed. *On James Tate*. Ann Arbor: University of Michigan Press, 2004. Contains essays on Tate's poetry, including his use of the prose poem, and numerous reviews of his works, from early to late.

McDaniel, Craig. "James Tate's Secret Co-Pilot." *New England Review* 23, no. 2 (Spring, 2002): 55-74. Examines Tate's development as a poet in relationship to Fyodor Dostoevski's prose and how it influenced "The Lost Pilot."

Revell, Donald. "The Lost Pilot." In *Masterplots II: Poetry Series*, edited by Philip K. Jason. Rev. ed. Pasadena, Calif.: Salem Press, 2002. Contains an in-depth analysis of the poem.

Rosen, R. D. "James Tate and Sidney Goldfarb and the Inexhaustible Nature of the Murmur." In *American Poetry Since 1960: Some Critical Perspectives*, edited by Robert B. Shaw. Cheshire, England: Carcanet Press, 1973. Argues that both Tate and Goldfarb belong to a generation that uses poetry to escape from the postwar age; their writing, notes Rosen, is that of moral outlaws.

Tate, James. *The Route as Briefed*. Ann Arbor: University of Michigan Press, 1999. Collects Tate's interviews, essays, and occasional writings; he comments on his composing method and fields questions from various interviewers about the peculiar nature of his lyric arguments, his influences, and the like.

Upton, Lee. *The Muse of Abandonment: Origin, Identity, Mastery in Five American Poets*. London: Associated University Presses, 1998. A critical study of the works of five twentieth century American poets, including Tate, and their points of view on alienation, power, and identity. Includes bibliographical references and index.

Paul Christensen
Updated by Theresa E. Dozier

EDWARD TAYLOR

Born: Near Sketchley, Leicestershire, England; c. 1645

Died: Westfield, Massachusetts; June 24, 1729

PRINCIPAL POETRY

The Poetical Works of Edward Taylor, 1939 (Thomas H. Johnson, editor)

The Poems of Edward Taylor, 1960 (Donald E. Stanford, editor)

A Transcript of Edward Taylor's Metrical History of Christianity, 1962 (Stanford, editor)

Edward Taylor's Minor Poetry, 1981 (volume 3 of *The Unpublished Writings of Edward Taylor*, 1981; Thomas M. Davis and Virginia L. Davis, editors)

OTHER LITERARY FORMS

Edward Taylor is best known today for his poetry. To his congregation at Westfield, Massachusetts, how-

ever, he was far better known for his sermons. He did apparently write the moral sequence of thirty-five poems, "God's Determinations," as a guide for members of his congregation, who were unable to assure themselves that they had achieved the state of grace. Even so, the Westfield minister did not intend that his poems should ever be published. There is some indication, however, that he did plan to publish some of his sermons, particularly those gathered together by Norman S. Grabo as *Edward Taylor's Treatise Concerning the Lord's Supper* (1966); these eight sermons attack Solomon Stoddard's liberal position regarding the admission of persons to the Eucharist who were not always certain they possessed the gift of God's grace.

The fourteen sermons collected, again by Grabo, as Edward Taylor's *Christographia* (1962) deal with two major issues: first, that the "blessed Theanthropie," God's Son united with man in the body of Jesus of Nazareth, was a necessary condition created by God to redeem the elect among humankind; and second, that this God-man constitutes the perfect model after whom each of the saints should construct his life. These fourteen sermons correspond precisely in subject matter to poems 42 through 56 of the "Preparatory Meditations," second series. All these published sermons are necessary reading for serious students of Taylor's poetry; they reveal his public attitudes toward many issues with which he grapples in his private poetry. In 1981, there appeared a three-volume set, *The Unpublished Writings of Edward Taylor* (Thomas M. Davis and Virginia L. Davis, editors), which includes Taylor's church records, minor poems, and additional sermons.

In 1977, an extensive holograph manuscript of thirty-six sermons, dating from 1693 to 1706, was recovered. These as-yet-unpublished sermons treat "types": events, persons, or things in the Old Testament that represent or shadow forth similar events, persons (particularly Jesus of Nazareth), or things in the New Testament. Taylor's *Diary* has been published (1964, F. Murphy, editor); he kept this record during his journey to New England and until he located at Westfield, after graduation from Harvard in 1671. The style of the *Diary* is candid and immediate; one almost shares with Taylor his vividly described seasickness.

ACHIEVEMENTS

For today's readers, Edward Taylor's finest achievement is his poetry. Those of his own time, however, remembered Taylor for his accomplishments as minister and physician to the Westfield, Massachusetts, community. In his edition of Taylor's poems, Thomas H. Johnson lists an inventory of the poet's library that includes the titles of several now arcane books on surgery and alchemy. Appropriately enough, the vocabulary of Taylor's medical practice often makes its way into his poetry.

Perhaps it was this professional versatility that enabled Taylor to construct elaborate metaphysical conceits with such agility. His poems can bear comparison to the work of John Donne, George Herbert, and Andrew Marvell. Indeed, Taylor's best poems are among the finest composed by an American.

BIOGRAPHY

The details of Edward Taylor's life are not abundant. He was born in or near Sketchley, Leicestershire, England, probably in the year 1645. He may have attended the University of Cambridge or one of the dissenting academies, for when he was admitted to Harvard in 1668, he was given advanced standing. It is certain that he early began training for the ministry. He had been brought to New England by the Act of Uniformity of Charles II; passed in 1662, this law required all schoolmasters (Taylor may have served in that capacity at Bagworth, Leicestershire) and ministers to take an oath of allegiance to the Anglican Church. Of course, Taylor's religious orthodoxy in the Puritan mode of worship prevented him, in good conscience, from taking the oath.

Taylor records his voyage across the Atlantic with vivid precision in his *Diary*. Even before his ship could get away from the British Isles, it was beset by a "violent storm" that filled the forecastle of the ship "ankle-deep" with water and so bathed the mate that "the water ran out of the waist of his breeches." Although the young man often found himself subdued by the constant rocking of the vessel, he was particularly taken with the life he discovered in the sea; he describes more than ten different types of fishes and several kinds of "sea fowl." On a few occasions, he and the crew spotted different kinds of driftwood. One such event held a pleasant surprise for them. Upon finding "a piece of white fir-wood full of barnacles, which are things like dew-worm skins about two inches long hanging to the wood," they learned that the other end housed a species of shellfish, so "we had a dish of them." Toward the end of the journey as the vessel approached land, Taylor saw his first fireflies: "About eight I saw a flying creature like a spark of red fire (about the bigness of an bumble bee) fly by the side of the ship; and presently after, there flew another by. The men said they were fireflies." The poet's fascination with nature continued in later years, as poems such as "Upon a Spider Catching a Fly" and "Upon a Wasp Chilled with Cold" attest.

The *Diary* also records his admission to Harvard, some humorous incidents that occurred there, and his calling, after graduation in 1671, to minister to the congregation at Westfield. While he was at Harvard, he roomed with Samuel Sewall, author of the famous *Diary* (1878-1882) and the judge at the Salem witch trials. In later years, Sewall names Taylor some fourteen times in the *Diary* and records in a letter that it was Taylor who induced him to attend Harvard. During his student days, the future minister of Westfield served as college Butler, a position of responsibility that, however, did not prevent him from becoming involved in some youthful acts of relatively innocuous consequence. He took his calling to the ministry of the Westfield congregation, however, very seriously; in his *Diary*, he records his doubts about his suitability as a minister. This sincere examination of his conscience before God establishes for the first time in Taylor's known writings the pattern that prevails in his private, poetic "Meditations," series 1 and 2.

On November 5, 1674, after courting her through letters and verse, Taylor married Elizabeth Fitch of Norwich, Connecticut. Elizabeth died some fifteen years later, having given birth to eight children. Taylor recorded his grief in one of his most moving poems, "A Funerall Poem upon the Death of My Ever Endeared and Tender Wife." In 1692, at the age of about fifty, the Westfield minister was married again, to Ruth Wyllys of Hartford, who bore him six more children and who survived him by about six months. Taylor's ministry of almost sixty years was a fruitful one. While bearing the responsibility of meeting his congregation's medical as well as spiritual needs, Taylor wrote his "Preparatory Meditations," attacked Stoddard's "liberalism" (Stoddard, who attended Taylor's ordination on August 27, 1679, had served as Harvard's first librarian during Taylor's attendance at the college), received an M.A. degree from Harvard in 1720, and visited Sewall, whom he solicited on one occasion (in 1691) to supervise the apprenticeship of one of his sons to a shopkeeper at Ipswich. Taylor died on June 24, 1729, a much-loved and revered divine whose tombstone records that as a "Venerable, Learned, and Pious Pastor" he "had served God and his Generation Faithfully."

ANALYSIS

At the time when English poetry, following the lead of John Dryden, was moving into a century of neoclassicism, Edward Taylor was writing verse in the Metaphysical mode of Donne, characterized by complex syntax, striking conceits, and intimate direct address: Most of Taylor's poems are addressed to God. In addition to his Metaphysical style, of primary interest to today's readers of Taylor's poetry are his propensity to employ the meditative technique, his practice of coordinating private poetic meditation with public sermon, his perhaps unexpected but nevertheless felicitous use of classical allusions, and his attention to the function of the fancy or the imagination in the poetic process.

"HUSWIFERY"

"Huswifery," perhaps Taylor's most famous poem, also displays one of his most eloquent conceits. As did most Puritans of his time, Taylor often found evidence of God's providence in the quotidian. In "Huswifery," he discovers God's purpose for the poet's public ministry in his wife's spinning wheel, perdurable symbol of America's pioneer struggle. The poem begins with this arresting plea, "Make me, O Lord, Thy spinning wheel complete." The poet then develops this conceit in a logical fashion, first according to ingenious analogies drawn between the various components of the spinning wheel and second by focusing on the machine's product, clothing. That which holds the fibers of wool to be spun, the distaff, becomes "Thy holy word"; the flyers that twist the fibers into thread (or yarn) represent the

poet's religious emotions; and the spool that collects the thread embodies his soul. Extending the spinning wheel conceit a bit further, the poet next asserts that the loom on which the threads are woven into cloth serves, like a minister of God's message, as the instrument for delivering his message to those in need (his congregation). The clothes prepared in this fashion should then become the minister's apparel, displaying God's "shine" and revealing that he is "clothed in holy robes for glory."

"MEDITATION 39"

Another poem that employs conceits with equal success is Taylor's "Meditation 39" (first series). This longer poem develops two conceits: sin as poison, and Jesus of Nazareth as "the sinner's advocate" or defense attorney before God. The inspiration for this meditation is I John 2:1 "If any man sin, we have an advocate with the Father, Jesus Christ the righteous." Taylor opens the poem with the exclamation: "My sin! My sin, My God, these cursed dregs,/ Green, yellow, blue streaked poison." These "Bubs [pustules] hatched in nature's nest on serpents' eggs" act in his soul like poisons in his stomach and "set his soul acramp." He alone cannot conquer then, "cannot them destroy." Alone and unassisted without God's help, these "Black imps . . . snap, bite, drag to bring/ And pitch me headlong hell's dread whirlpool in." By delaying the preposition "in" until the end of the line, Taylor startles his readers, thereby focusing attention on his wretched predicament as sinner. To be sure, Taylor's intention, since he wrote these poems as private meditations with God, in preparation for the administration of the Eucharist, was not to appeal to an audience schooled in the Metaphysical style. Such recognition does not, however, lessen the certainty that his intention is most definitely to appeal to an even more critical audience, his God, whose attention he does indeed want to capture and hold.

At this most critical point in his acknowledgment of his fallen state, the poet catches a glimpse of "a twinkling ray of hope," Christ as advocate; for him, then, "a door is ope." With this introduction of an advocate, Taylor begins to build his legal conceit. The sight of the advocate first engenders a promise of release from his pain. Temporary joy is replaced by a renewed sense of guilt, however, as he realizes that all his advocate has to work with is "the state/ The case is in." That is, if the case his advocate pleads before God, the final judge, is short of merit, then judgment may still go against him. As Taylor puts it, if the case is bad: "it's bad in plaint." He continues by observing, "My papers do contain no pleas that do/ Secure me from, but knock me down to, woe." Again the poet wrenches the syntax, but again for the same reason. Despite the "ray of hope," he fears that the gravity of his "Black imps" may yet doom him to hellfire. As before, his purpose is to focus on his apparently hopeless condition. His reason then begins to instruct him. Even though the biblical text causes him to recall his past sins while also promising him a defense attorney before God, he concludes, without benefit of understanding, "I have no plea mine advocate to give." He is forced to cry out, "What now?" His reason teaches him that his advocate is unique; as God's only Son, he has sacrificed his human body to provide the believing and worthy sinner the gift of redemption. These "dear bought arguments" are "good pleas" indeed. Following this grasp of his reason that informs him that the "ray of hope" is constant and true, the poet asks "What shall I do, my Lord?" How can he act or conduct his life so "that I/ May have Thee plead my case?" He exercises his will and decides to "fee" or pay his lawyer "With faith, repentence, and obediently" give the efforts of his ministry to fighting against the commission of "satanic sins" among his parishioners. This unique agreement between lawyer and client obliges the lawyer "My sin [to] make Thine," while at the same time it emboldens the client, the poet, "Thy pleas [to] make mine hereby."

The agreement is struck, then; "Thou wilt me save; I will thee celebrate." Taylor intends, however, not merely to celebrate his advocate through his works "'gainst satanic sins," but he desires intensely that "my rough feet shall Thy smooth praises sing." This intense desire to please God in return for God's love freely given, the eros-*agape* motif, pervades Taylor's meditative poetry. The *ababcc* rhyme scheme, which Taylor adopts for all his meditations, serves a purpose beyond that ordinarily expected; the final words of each line are "I," "advocate" (the noun), "hereby," "celebrate," "within," and "Sing." With slight rearrangement, these words make this fitting statement: I hereby celebrate

[my] advocate within song. Thus, Taylor accomplishes his end both directly and implicitly. In doing so, he well fulfills John Calvin's dictum in *The Institutes of the Christian Religion* (1536) that "We recommend the voice and singing as a support of speech [in the worship service], where accompanying love [that is] pure of spirit."

The process that governs this poem's construction is that of the meditation, an intellectual exercise codified by Saint Ignatius of Loyola in his *Ejercicios espirituales* (1548; *The Spiritual Exercises*, 1736) and passed on to Taylor probably through the widely circulated and immensely popular (among Puritans) *The Saints' Everlasting Rest* (1650), written by one of the seventeenth century's foremost Puritan authorities on meditation, Richard Baxter. While this mental process or guide to philosophical contemplation was implicitly understood from pre-Christian days, Saint Ignatius's *The Spiritual Exercises* did much to make commonplace this process, which uses the mental faculties of memory, understanding, and will. As the poem itself illustrates, the memory of the one engaged in meditation is jogged or aroused, usually by some biblical text; the understanding or reason of the meditator then grapples with the significance of this memory recalled in conjunction with the biblical text; and, finally, the meditator's grasp of the significance of text and memory lead him to pledge to serve God with the new understanding he has acquired. The biblical text, "If any man sin, we have an advocate with the Father, Jesus Christ the righteous," causes the poet to remember his own poisonous sins, and to recall his redeemer, but also to fear that his sins may weigh too heavily against him in the balance of God's justice. His understanding then reassures him that Christ, having bought his sins in his human sacrifice, is a formidable advocate in his behalf and that the strength of his belief will give his advocate all the "surety" he will need. The knowledge of God's gift of his only Son so overwhelms the poet or meditator that he pledges to serve him in both deeds and poetry.

"MEDITATION 8"

Taylor adopts this basic mode of construction in many of his meditations, as a brief examination of "Meditation 8" (first series) affirms. This poem derives its inspiration from another biblical text, John 6:51, part of which is "I am the living bread which came down from heaven." This text moves the poet to conjure up a vision in which he is looking up toward heaven, trying to discover how man can ever have "pecked the fruit forbad" and consequently have "lost . . . the golden days" and fallen into "celestial famine sore." What is man to do now? How can he regain paradise? His reason informs him that, alone and without God's help, this earth "cannot yield thee/ here the smallest crumb" of that living bread. According to the poem, the only way out of this barren mortality is by way of "The purest wheat in heaven, His dear—dear Son." The fallen sinner must "eat thy fill of this, thy God's white loaf." If a person exercises his will and chooses to eat this "soul bread," then "thou shalt never die." Once again Scripture provokes memory, which in turn stimulates the understanding, which finally brings about a resolve of the will.

"MEDITATION 56" AND "SERMON 14"

One can easily see how this meditative process accords well with preparation and resolve to administer God's word with as much intensity and expression as a sincere and gifted pastor can muster. Investigation among those sermons with which scholars are able to align specific meditative poems proves rewarding indeed. All the fourteen sermons of the *Christographia*, for example, correspond exactly to the "Meditations" (second series), 42 through 56. The examination of but one such pair, sermon and poem, serves the present purpose. Both "Meditation 56" and the fourteenth sermon of the *Christographia* collection are based on the same biblical text, John 15:24: "Had I not done amongst them the works, that none other man hath done, they had not had Sin." This final sermon of the series marks the culmination of Taylor's analysis of the "blessed Theanthropie," his explanation for the person of God's divine Son. In this concluding homily, the minister attempts to establish that no works of men or of nature (since God is the author of both) surpass the works of God or his Son; God, therefore, commands the devotion of his believers.

The sermon opens with the observation that the white blossom of the clove tree, when "turned to be green, . . . yields the pleasentest [sic] Smell in the World." The minister uses this clove blossom imagery

as a structural device by means of which, when he returns to it at the sermon's conclusion, he unifies his text, for the flower that exudes the most pleasant odor predicts the closing corollary that the works of Christ are "the Sweetest Roses, and brightest flowers of his own Excellency." This flower imagery does not, however, play a significant structural role in the poem. The poet delays this sensuous appeal to smell until the thirteenth line. Preceding the poem's "White-green'd blossoms" are evocations of other senses, including the sight of his "Damask Web of Velvet Verse" that the poet offers in humility to God, and the taste of "Fruits so sweete that grow/ On the trees of righteousness." This explication of the senses follows rather closely Loyola's recommendation given in some of his *Spiritual Exercises*; Taylor, therefore, here conforms, whether consciously or not, to Loyola's famous codification of the meditative process. The purpose of the sermon, however, is clearly not meditation but utilitarian and effective communication of the doctrine, which the minister articulates as follows: "That Christ's works were so excellent, that never any did the like thereto."

Throughout both sermon and poem, the author expands upon the Tree of Life metaphor, which appears first in Genesis. In the popular *The Figures or Types of the Old Testament* (1683), a copy of which Taylor owned and annotated, Samuel Mather, whose nephew was one of Taylor's classmates at Harvard, explains that "the Tree of Life in Paradise was a Type of Christ." This Old Testament Tree of Life, which was located in the center of Eden, "shadows forth" or prefigures Christ in the New Testament. When Adam and Eve were cast out of Paradise, they were denied the gift of God's grace available to them from the eating of the fruit of this tree; according to Christian understanding of the Adamic myth, it then became necessary for Christ to come into the world of humans in order to restore this "fruit" of God's grace; that is, to redeem fallen humanity. Understandably, Taylor often refers to this myth in his poems and sermons, but he does so with particular intensity in this sermon and this poem. The minister tells his parishioners that "his [Christ's] Works are his rich Ornaments," while the poet extolls Christ as "a Tree of Perfect nature trim" whose branches "doe out/ shine the sun."

This "Tree of Perfect nature" produces, in the poem, fruits of this perfection which Taylor identifies as God's gift of grace. The minister is also, of course, much interested in the question of grace, but he does not regale his congregation with conceits spun about the Tree of Life; rather, with attention to practicality, he emphasizes "Christ's works mediatoriall" [sic] which translate "the Soule from a State of Sin, and a Sinfull life, into a State of holiness." Underscoring this distinction between the poem's richness of imagery and the sermon's concentration on the delivery of practical doctrine are their respective descriptions of Christ. While the sermon calls Christ "the brightness of his Fathers Glory," the poem more extravagantly describes him as one whose "fruits adorne/ Thyselfe, and Works, more shining than the morn" and as one whose "Flowers more sweet than spice/ Bende down to us."

The sweet flowers of Christ's works, says the minister, far exceed "Kingly Performances." Kings and rulers of the temporal world "ofttimes build their Palaces in oppression." The minister does not expand his case to include the naming of specific illustrations. The poet, however, provides rich examples of worldly power. Indeed, he names Psammetichos's huge labyrinth, supposed to have been built by Daedalus; the Roman emperor Titus (40-81 C.E.) and his Colosseum; Nero's Golden Palace; and other symbols of temporal power. Whereas the poet heaps up specific cases of earthly artifice and thereby poignantly contrasts God's works and humanity's most ambitious constructions, the minister, more simply concerned with the transience of earthy mortality, explains how humankind's buildings, no matter how magnificent, "are but of Clayy natures."

The minister is also disposed to contrast the egalitarian nature of the laws of God, which apply to all people equally, with the laws of kings that "are like Copwebs that catch little flies, but are Snapt in pieces by the greater." This web imagery occurs in the poem, but in a quite different context. As noted above, the poet sees his verse as "A Damask Web of Velvet," hardly as an ensnaring "copweb." It is possible, however, that the labyrinthine image of Psammetichos's maze conjured up in the mind of the minister the image of human laws seen as oppressive "copwebs." It should be observed,

nevertheless, that at this point as at others, poems and sermon are not always in exact agreement.

The conclusion of Taylor's sermon is the more interesting precisely because it does not appear to agree fully with the poem. In the poem, Taylor prays that his God will "Adorn my Life well with thy works" and will "make faire/ My Person with apparrell thou prepar'st," for, if he is so clothed, his "Boughs," extending the Tree of Life conceit to himself, "shall loaded bee with fruits that spring/ Up from thy Works." Such a prayer reveals the preparation of a sincere minister about to deliver God's word to his flock. The minister, however, appears to rebuke the poet for his extravagance. In the sermon's conclusion, the minister declares that all the most excellent works of humankind in this world "are but dull drudgeries and lifeless painted cloaths compared to Christs." Of especial significance at this crucial point in the sermon's concluding lines, however, is the comparison that Taylor draws between humankind's works and those of God.

He cites the example of the famous Alexandrian painter, Apelles, who rebuked one of his students for overlaying a painting of Venus with gold; Apelles told the student that he had not created a beautiful representation, but simply a rich one. Taylor the poet has done precisely the same thing in his poem; he has decorated God's word with elaborate images and drawn out conceits, but he has expressed the hope that God will adorn him in a similar fashion. The minister determinedly concludes that human works are "of no worth." "Ours are Worth nothing," the minister says "without he puts . . . the Worthiness of his on them." To be sure, the poet is as devoted to God as the minister is, and has carefully sought God's assistance in the construction of his poem. Nevertheless, the minister, who has written a much less "adorned" sermon, appears to admonish the poet, as well as his congregation, not to forget that the "clothes" he would wear both in the poem and in the sermon are worn with God's benevolence. What appears to be reticence on the part of the poet here was full-blown trepidation at an earlier point in Taylor's poetic career. The twenty-first meditation of the first series (1686) displays this fear in unmistakable candor: "Yet I feare/ To say a Syllable [as poet] lest at thy day [Judgment Day]/ I be presented for my Tattling here."

In his introduction to his edition of *Christographia*, Grabo concludes, as others have, that Taylor's "sermons seem to explicate the poems." This observation is no less true of "Meditation 56" and "Sermon 14." More appears to be at work, however, in this pair. The medium of the poem, with its possibilities for elaborate tropes and figures, together with the poem's condition of privacy, allows Taylor to pursue his personal devotion to God with virtually limitless zeal; indeed, knowing that his heavenly audience, God, will hardly misconstrue his motives but that his earthly audience, the members of his congregation, very well may, Taylor the poet can, his earlier trepidation notwithstanding, express himself with more candor and fervor than Taylor the minister can. As a result, his meditations are always richer and more passionate than his often somber and always sober sermons. Two other factors that characterize his poetry corroborate this assumption: his use of classical allusions and the manner in which he describes the function of the imagination in the poetic process.

USE OF CLASSICAL ALLUSIONS

As is the case of the Apelles allusion, Taylor uses classical allusions in his sermons as exempla or as instructional illustrations for the benefit of his parishioners. In his poems, his application of them is quite predictably more figurative. Wholly unexpected, however, is the fact that Taylor applies references to classical paganism in contexts that are usually positive or favorable. For example, in the long series of thirty-five poems, "Gods Determinations," the poet seems to revel in drawing implied allusions to Greek mythology when describing God's creation of the world in the first poem of the sequence. The poet asks, "Who blew the Bellows of his Furnace Vast?"—doubtless a reference to Hephaestus, Greek god of the hearth and metalworking. Surely Atlas stands beneath the line "Where stand the Pillars upon which it stands?"

This engaging use of classical references usually gives way to a more serious and often more complex application. In the seventy-ninth meditation of the second series, for example, Taylor, contrary to the expected and even prescribed convention, extends the practice of typology to classical mythology. The poet's practice here is of particular significance since it points toward the nineteenth century emphasis on symbolism to be found in the works of such American writers as Herman Melville and Nathaniel Hawthorne. The text for this meditation is Canticles 2:16; "My beloved is mine and I am his." Since the Puritans (and many others) interpreted this entire book, which contains some of the most sensuous and sensual poetry in the Bible, as an allegory of humankind's relation to God, one might conclude that the subject of this poem must be the analogy between sexual love (eros) and God's unconditional, unselfish love for humankind (*agape*).

With that expectation, one may find the first four lines of the poem somewhat puzzling: "Had I Promethius' filching Ferula [fennel]/ Filld with its sacred theft the stoln Fire:/ To animate my Fancy lodg'd in clay,/ Pandora's Box would peps [pelt] the theft with ire." Knowledge of the Greek myth of Prometheus, who stole fire from the gods and gave it to humanity, helps to explain what is happening in these lines. Prometheus was seen by the ancients as a truly heroic champion of humankind, as Aeschylus's tragedy *Prometheus desmōtēs* (date unknown; *Prometheus Bound*, 1777) illustrates. As a consequence of Prometheus's defiance, however, Zeus sent Pandora, whom he forced to bring to humans the infamous box of woes and tribulations. Zeus forbade Pandora to open the box, but knowing her to be inverately curious, he also knew that her opening of the box would merely be a matter of time. Now the typology may be made clear. Taylor has obviously rejected the Prometheus myth as insufficient to animate his "Fancy lodg'd in clay"; that is, to set his imagination into motion so that he can compose a meditation appropriate to his devotion to God. The stanza's final lines, however, do suggest to him the source suitable for the kind and degree of inspiration he requires: "But if thy Love, My Lord, shall animate/ My Clay with holy fire, 'twill flame in State."

The Prometheus myth fails to give him the necessary inspiration, not because it is pagan but because, in Taylor's conception here, it is typological of the Adamic myth (of humanity's fall from grace). Prometheus, like Satan, defies Zeus, or God, and Pandora, a type of Eve, manifests the unfortunate trait of curiosity that causes her to disobey Zeus, just as Eve's curiosity prompts her to disobey God and to yield to Satan's temptation to eat of the Tree of Knowledge (of good and evil). Although Taylor's complex typology here is aesthetically pleasing, it is surprising, since Mather had cautioned against such a practice. In *The Figures or Types of the Old Testament*, which, it will be recalled, the poet owned and annotated, Mather unequivocally states, "It is not safe to make any thing a type meerly upon our own fansies and imaginations; it is *Gods* Perogative to make *Types*." Here Taylor clearly exceeds the limitations that his Puritan compatriots would impose on him. Perhaps Taylor recognized this quality in his poetry and such recognition led to his request that his poems not be published.

THE IMAGINATION

At any rate, as the investigation of the Prometheus myth suggests, the drawing out of typologies that are not God's is not the only practice for which Taylor could have received censure had his poems appeared in print. As Taylor's lines and Mather's dictum suggest, the poet is here "guilty" of indulging himself with the making of inventions of his own imagination. Whereas his attitude toward the use of classical allusions is unguarded, particularly in his poetry—he simply uses such references when he feels moved by the demands of the verse to do so, often creating rich and satisfying lines—such is not the case with his management of the imagination. Toward this essentially aesthetic idea, Taylor sometimes appears to be ambivalent. Certainly Mather's injunction against its use offers a partial explanation of Taylor's ambivalence. Earlier in the seventeenth century, William Perkins, renowned patriarch of English Puritanism, wrote *A Treatise of Mans Imaginations* (1607) in which he calls the imagination a "corrupt fountaine." He arrives at this conclusion from Genesis 8:21, "the imaginacion of mans heart is evil even from his youth" (from the Geneva Bible). In one of his *Christographia* sermons, Taylor himself espouses a similar position when he admonishes his congregation not to be deluded by "Fictitious imaginations" which "indeed are the Efficacy of Errors."

Regarding his attitude toward the imagination, Taylor the poet contradicts Taylor the minister. Unlike the minister who refers to the imagination only twice in his published sermons (both times in a negative context), the poet cites "fancy," "Phansy," or some other form of this word (as verb or adjective) forty-six times in his published poetry. He never uses the synonym "imagination" in his poetry, probably preferring the disyllabic "fancy" to the pentasyllabic synonym for purposes of rhythm. When he cites "fancy" and its various spellings and forms, he does so in a manner that establishes a readily discernible pattern. When the word occurs at the beginning of a poem, always in a meditation, it is invariably used within the positive context of serving the poet as a necessary tool for setting poesies into motion. When "fancy" appears somewhere internally within a poem, however, as it does twice in the perhaps publicly recited "Gods Determinations," the concept usually identifies the imperfect human attempt to construe points of Puritan theology; these imperfect attempts to interpret theological or doctrinal matters without dependence on the truly regenerate heart (informed by the gift of God's grace) always conclude incorrectly.

In the "Second Ranke Accused," from the "Gods Determinations" series, for example, the poet-minister threatens that those captured by God's justice, the so-called regenerate, may not be regenerate if their hearts are not filled with the "sweet perfume" of God's grace; if such is not the case, "Your Faith's a Phancy," and therefore untrue. In those poems that begin with the concept of the fancy, however, the poet applies it to the initiation of his meditative process. It is Taylor's recognition of the necessary role of the imagination in the writing of exalted verse (in his case, his most impassioned "talks" with God) that most interests today's readers. Of great significance, then, is the fact that the poet identifies the essential role of the imagination in the "Prologue" to the "Preparatory Meditations." Here he describes himself as but a "Crumb of Dust which is design'd/ To make my Pen unto thy Praise alone." Immediately following this exercise in self-deprecation, however, he writes: "And my dull Phancy I would gladly grinde/ Unto an Edge of Zion Precious Stone." At one point in the second series meditations, the poet asks God's angels to "Make me a pen thereof that best will write./ Lende me your fancy, and Angellick skill/ To treat this theme, more rich than Rubies bright." Another of the same series opens with this enthusiastic line: "I fain would have a rich, fine Phansy ripe." Finally, the discussion of the Prometheus typology that begins the seventy-ninth meditation of this series establishes that, although the subject of the entire poem is the eros-*agape* theme, the poem's first problem is to discover the difference between human myths, which served ancient poets such as Vergil, Catullus, and Ovid for poetic inspiration, and God's Word, which, finally, can alone animate the poetic process of this believer's "Fancy lodg'd in clay."

There can be little doubt, then, that, despite injunctions against the allegedly "evil" fruits of this mental faculty, Taylor the private poet found it a necessary tool for colloquies with his God. A possible explanation for this contradiction between private poet and public minister (who was also author of "Gods Determinations") may be offered by observing that Loyola had prescribed, in his *Spiritual Exercises*, the use of the imagination as requisite to begin the process of meditation. The exercitant must place himself in the proper frame of mind for meditation by picturing to himself events in the life of Christ or biblical history or occurrences in his own life that prompt him to recognize the need for spiritual colloquy. Later in his own century, Baxter appears somewhat to mollify Perkins's attitude toward this mental faculty when he advises, in *The Saints' Everlasting Rest*, that the person engaged in meditation should focus his mental attention on the joys of heaven by getting "the liveliest Picture of them in thy minde that thou canst." At the same time, nevertheless, it should be observed that, in *A Treatise Concerning Religious Affections* (1746), Jonathan Edwards, some seventeen years after Taylor's death, summarily condemns this faculty as that means by which the devil produces evil thoughts in the soul; as the Great Awakener puts it, "it must be only by the imagination that Satan has access to the soul, to tempt and delude it."

Taylor's consistent acknowledgment of the power of the imagination should make him appealing to contemporary students of American literature. At a time when attitudes toward the imagination were, for the most part, hostile (recall Alexander Pope's line from *An Essay on Man*, 1733-1734, "Imagination plies her dang'rous art," II, 143), Taylor identified the concept as a paramount significance to poesies, anticipating Samuel Taylor Coleridge's analysis of imagination in *Biographia Literaria* (1817).

OTHER MAJOR WORKS

NONFICTION: *Christographia*, 1962 (Norman S. Grabo, editor); *Diary*, 1964 (F. Murphy, editor); *Edward Taylor's Treatise Concerning the Lord's Supper*, 1966 (Grabo, editor).

MISCELLANEOUS: *The Unpublished Writings of Edward Taylor*, 1981 (3 volumes; Thomas M. Davis and Virginia L. Davis, editors).

BIBLIOGRAPHY

Craig, Raymond A. *A Concordance to the Major Poems of Edward Taylor*. Lewiston, N.Y.: Edwin Mellen Press, 2008. An important reference work of significant value to anyone studying the poetry of Taylor.

Gatta, John. *Gracious Laughter: The Meditative Wit of Edward Taylor*. Columbia: University of Missouri Press, 1989. Gatta, an insightful expositor of Taylor's poetry, opened up a new avenue of inquiry into Taylor's acknowledged supremacy as a colonial poet, positing his wit as the bridge between his theology and his poetics. Includes comprehensive bibliography.

Grabo, Norman. *Edward Taylor*. Rev. ed. Boston: Twayne, 1988. Biocritical introduction to Taylor's life and work is an excellent source of explication of Taylor's aesthetic and theological influences.

Guruswamy, Rosemary Fithian. *The Poems of Edward Taylor: A Reference Guide*. Westport, Conn.: Greenwood Press, 2003. A bibliography of Taylor's poems that is part of the Greenwood Guides to Literature series.

Hammond, Jeffrey A. *Edward Taylor: Fifty Years of Scholarship and Criticism*. Columbia, S.C.: Camden House, 1993. Five chapters examine Taylor scholarship in chronological order, from its beginnings to the later decades of the twentieth century. Includes bibliography and index.

Miller, David G. *The Word Made Flesh Made Word: The Failure and Redemption of Metaphor in Edward Taylor's "Christographia."* Selinsgrove, Pa.: Susquehanna University Press, 1995. Provides a reading of Taylor's *Christographia* sermon material and a study of the use of metaphorical language in the sermons.

Rowe, Karen E. *Saint and Sinner: Edward Taylor's Typology and the Poetics of Meditation*. 1986. Reprint. New York: Cambridge University Press, 2009. Rowe notes the relationship between Puritan typology—its use of Old Testament narratives as a guide to the meaning of the mundane devotional life of colonial believers—and its role in Taylor's craftsmanship as a poet. Includes appendixes that examine the relationship between individual Taylor poems and their sources in sermons.

Schuldiner, Michael, ed. *The Tayloring Shop: Essays on the Poetry of Edward Taylor*. Newark: University of Delaware Press, 1997. This collection of critical essays on Taylor's poems provides readers with insights into several traditions of the past that informed Taylor's poetry, from the Puritan concept of nature to Puritan casuistry. Includes bibliographical references and index.

Stanford, Donald. *Edward Taylor*. 1965. Reprint. Minneapolis: University of Minnesota Press, 1998. This early pamphlet in the University of Minnesota series is still an incisive introduction to Taylor's poetics and, in particular, his personal version of Milton's *Paradise Lost*, "God Determinations." Stanford hits his target consistently and elucidates Taylor's opposition to the heretical view of the Lord's Supper propounded by his Colonial adversary, Richard Henry Stoddard.

John C. Shields

HENRY TAYLOR

Born: Loudoun County, Virginia; June 21, 1942

PRINCIPAL POETRY

The Horse Show at Midnight, 1966
Breakings, 1971
An Afternoon of Pocket Billiards, 1975
Desperado, 1979
The Flying Change, 1985
Understanding Fiction: Poems, 1986-1996, 1996
Brief Candles: 101 Clerihews, 2000
Crooked Run, 2006

OTHER LITERARY FORMS

Although Henry Taylor is known primarily for his poetry collections, he has also published a number of significant works in other genres. Competent in several languages, his translations include Euripides' *The Children of Herakles* (1981; with Robert A. Brooks) and Bulgarian poet Vladimir Levchev's *Leaves from the Dry Tree* (1996) and *Black Book of the Endangered Species* (1999). Taylor's translations of international writers' poetry were printed in *Crossing the River: Selected Poems Translated from the Hebrew/Moshe Dor* (1989; Seymour Mayne, editor), *Window on the Black Sea: Bulgarian Poetry in Translation* (1992; Richard Harteis, editor, with William Meredith), and *World Literature Today* (Winter, 1993).

Taylor has also been active as a literary scholar and critic, having published the text *Poetry: Points of Departure* (1974). Taylor's scholarship includes articles in *Masterplots*; *Magill's Literary Annual*, for which he served as a consultant and associate editor in the early 1970's; and *The Pure Clear Word: Essays on the Poetry of James Wright* (1982; Dave Smith, editor). His *Compulsory Figures: Essays on Recent American Poets*, a collection of critical essays on the works of seventeen twentieth century American poets, was published in 1992.

ACHIEVEMENTS

Richard Dillard observed in *Hollins Critic* that Henry Taylor's poems have "all the ring and authority of an American [Thomas] Hardy, intensely aware of the darkness that moves around us and in us." Taylor's pronounced sense of irony, combined with a style that tends decidedly toward the formal, distinguishes his poetry from that of many of his contemporaries. His disciplined, introspective style has garnered recognition and praise from a wide array of sources. Taylor won awards from the Academy of American Poets in 1962 and 1964 while he was a University of Virginia undergraduate. He received prizes for his poetry from the Utah State Institute of Fine Arts in 1969 and 1971. The National Endowment for the Arts presented Taylor a 1978 creative writing fellowship, then continued to fund his work. Taylor received a research grant in 1980 from the National Endowment for the Humanities to examine his native Loudoun Valley's culture. The Virginia Commission for the Arts also granted Taylor a fellowship. In 1984, he was awarded the Witter Bynner Prize for Poetry by the American Academy and Institute of Arts and Letters, which later presented Taylor the Michael Braude Award in 2002. Taylor attained one of poetry's highest honors, the Pulitzer Prize, in 1986 for *The Flying Change*. The American Literary Translators Association's Washington Chapter gave Taylor its 1989 Golden Crane Award. He also received the Aiken Taylor Award in Modern American Poetry in 2004 from *Sewanee Review*. The Louisiana State University Press presented Taylor with its 2006 L. E. Phillabaum Poetry Award for *Crooked Run*.

BIOGRAPHY

Henry Splawn Taylor was born in 1942 in Loudoun County, Virginia. His father, Thomas Edward Taylor, was a high school English teacher and dairy farmer who encouraged his son to recognize literary elements of poetry. Taylor's mother, Mary Marshall (Splawn) Taylor, was an economist and the daughter of Dr. Walter M. W. Splawn, an economics professor, university president, and lawyer who served as the federal Interstate Commerce Commission chairman in the mid-1930's. Taylor and his three sisters grew up near the Lincoln community on farmland owned by his paternal grandparents that had belonged to the Taylor family since the late eighteenth century. Taylor's family and artistic neighbors shaped his appreciation for cultural activities. He attended public schools in Loudoun County for nine grades before enrolling in the George School, a Quaker boarding institution in Pennsylvania, by 1958. At that school, Taylor aspired to become a writer. He competed in track and equestrian sports.

In 1960, Taylor began studies at the University of Virginia. As an undergraduate, he served as editor of the literary magazine *Plume and Sword*, participated in the campus drama club the Virginia Players, and was mentored in poetry by Fred Bornhauser and George Garrett. His erratic academic performance resulted in him withdrawing from classes. He used his time off to write poetry that he published in *New Writing from Virginia* (1963), *Shenandoah*, *The Sixties*, *Georgia Review*, *Encounter*, and other publications. Taylor re-

Henry Taylor (©Sandra Ehrenkranz)

sumed course work, graduating with a B.A. in English in 1965. He secured a book contract from the Louisiana State University Press for his debut poetry collection, which was published as *The Horse Show at Midnight* in 1966. Taylor married Sarah Bean in June, 1965. That year, he enrolled in the graduate creative writing program at Hollins College in Roanoke, Virginia, writing poems for that school's literary magazine, *Cargoes*. Garrett anthologized Taylor's short story, "And Bid a Fond Farewell to Tennessee," written at Hollins, in *The Girl in the Black Raincoat* (1966). Annie Dillard and Lee Smith, who both became acclaimed writers, were students in writing seminars during the time Taylor was at Hollins. In 1966, Taylor received an M.A. in creative writing, writing his thesis "An Afternoon of Pocket Billiards," which the University of Utah later published.

In 1966, Taylor began an impressive career as an academic and teacher of writing. Between 1966 and 1968, he served as an instructor of English at Roanoke College in Salem, Virginia, a community near Hollins. He and James Dickey critiqued poems written by students at Hollins in spring, 1967. After his 1967 divorce, Taylor married Frances "Frannie" Ferguson Carney, a Hollins graduate, the next year. They had two sons, Thomas and Richard. From 1968 through 1971, Taylor was an assistant professor of English at the University of Utah, where he directed the University of Utah Writers' Conference starting in 1969. He later edited a festschrift celebrating that conference's founder, Brewster Ghiselin.

In June, 1970, Taylor participated in the Hollins Conference in Creative Writing and Cinema, where radio host John Graham interviewed him. The transcripts and biographical profile featuring Taylor were printed in *Craft So Hard to Learn: Conversations with Poets and Novelists About the Teaching of Writing* (1972) and *The Writer's Voice: Conversations with Contemporary Writers* (1973), both edited by Garrett. Since 1970, he has served as a contributing editor for *Hollins Critic*, also writing articles for that journal. Taylor accepted a position in 1971 as associate professor of literature at American University in Washington, D.C., where he was promoted to professor in 1976. During 1978, he returned to Hollins as its writer-in-residence. He also served as director of both American University's M.F.A. program in creative writing as of 1982 and its American studies program from 1983 to 1985. He was poetry editor of *New Virginia Review* in 1989.

Taylor continued to publish his poetry in numerous journals and anthologies, including *Contemporary Southern Poetry: An Anthology* (1979; Guy Owen and Mary C. Williams, editors), *The Morrow Anthology of Younger American Poets* (1985; Dave Smith and David Bottoms, editors), *Southern Review*, *Nation*, *Poetry*, *Ploughshares*, *The Chronicle of the Horse*, *Virginia Quarterly Review*, and *Elvis in Oz: New Stories and Poem from the Hollins College Creative Writing Program* (1992; Mary Flinn and Garrett, editors). He often presented his work at poetry readings. His peers noted Taylor's talent for writing parodies and impersonating poets' voices and mannerisms at readings. He wrote poems specifically for Phi Beta Kappa induction ceremonies at the State University of New York at Stony Brook and the College of William and Mary.

Taylor participated in Poetry in the Schools workshops with Loudoun County elementary students. He researched local history and geography, wrote columns printed in *Washingtonian* that described practical aspects of country life, and was the Goose Creek Quaker Meeting clerk, a position his ancestors had also held. Taylor and Frannie divorced, and he reunited with his first wife, whom he wed again circa 1996. In 1998, Taylor received radiation treatment for a cancerous jawbone. He donated his papers, including manuscripts and letters, to Hollins' archives in 2001. That year the Fellowship of Southern Writers selected Taylor for induction. After his second marriage to Sarah ended, Taylor wed a woman named Mooshe on May 23, 2002, and retired from American University in 2003, becoming a literature professor emeritus. During his teaching career, Taylor maintained homes in Maine; Leesburg, Virginia; and near Bethesda, Maryland. In the early twenty-first century, he moved to Gig Harbor, Washington.

ANALYSIS

Two aspects of Henry Taylor's background significantly influence his poetry—his upbringing as a rural farmer and his Quaker faith. Born into a largely Quaker community that had already flourished in Loudoun County for nearly two centuries, Taylor has infused his poetry with its strong reverence for tradition, charity, and sense of place. From his childhood as a southern farmer, Taylor has retained a keen sense of the subtle and delicate workings of the natural world. In addition, his work with horses as a young boy has brought his poetry again and again to that animal, which is a totemic image in his work. Equine imagery permeates Taylor's first major books of poetry, *An Afternoon of Pocket Billiards* and *Desperado*. A horse motif even emblazons the cover of *The Flying Change*, which employs the animal as its central metaphor and has proven to be Taylor's most widely embraced collection, receiving the Pulitzer Prize in poetry in 1986.

Although Taylor's poetry primarily chooses rural settings and themes for its subject matter, it cannot accurately be described as "pastoral." As critic Sharon Hall has observed, Taylor's poems instead expose "the horror and violence of country life as well as its beauty, describing rural life with humor and unflinching realism." This makes them a unique study in contrasts;

while they embrace the redemptive qualities of rural living, they remind the reader at every turn that destruction, fatality, and absurdity are also common in country life, as they are in urban environments. In this way, Taylor seeks to point out that darkness, mystery, and irony inhabit all corners of the human experience, even its most isolated and bucolic.

His later poetry examines how urban development transforms rural places, rendering once familiar landscapes into unrecognizable tracts filled by identical structures and displacing indigenous life: plants, animals, and humans. Modern usages erase evidence of past memories, as highways alter landscapes, humans divert waterways, and buildings are razed for what some people consider progress. The land is a steadfast character that observes changes as each generation of humans appropriates, utilizes, improves, or damages places and resources for specific needs and agendas according to its situations, often affected by historical factors such as war. Taylor notes the irony that this intrusive development is usually equated with progress.

"RIDING A ONE-EYED HORSE"

From Taylor's earliest mature collection, *An Afternoon of Pocket Billiards*, "Riding a One-Eyed Horse" epitomizes two of the poet's seminal traits: equestrian themes and formal structural regularity. Taylor has observed of his own writing, particularly the poems in *An Afternoon of Pocket Billiards*, "I think in terms of analogies to equitation when I'm writing. Nerve and touch, and timing." In "Riding a One-Eyed Horse," the reader comes to know just what he means. A poem of four four-line stanzas, the poem reflects structurally the cadenced rhythm of a well-trained horse's gait, suggesting parallels to Taylor's own belief in the importance of regularity and discipline in poetry.

Thematically, the poem explores an idea common in Taylor's work—the need to impose a sense of order on even the most chaotic situation. A sort of "how to" tutorial on the seemingly absurd act of training a visually impaired animal to function as a fully sighted one would, the poem suggests metaphorically that meaning may be extracted from, if not imposed on, even the most absurd of circumstances. The speaker initially remarks of the horse, "One side of his world is always missing," but through an act of determined faith in human will, he is able to summon from the animal an extraordinary effort:

> Do not forget
> to turn his head and let what comes come seen:
> he will jump the fences he has to if you swing
> toward them from the side that he can see

This "side" the animal "can see" represents that part of humans that continually beckons them to reconsider what they may have overlooked, to revisit what they have deemed lost. "Riding a One-Eyed Horse" expresses Taylor's optimism, albeit tinged with an almost rigid sobriety, in the desire to embrace all the possibilities people are routinely encouraged to dismiss.

"BERNARD AND SARAH"

In "Bernard and Sarah," also from *An Afternoon of Pocket Billiards*, Taylor seeks to come to grips with an ancestral heritage that seems both vague and tangible at the same time. Even those people who have countless photos and artifacts that link them with their ancestors often have problems connecting with their humanness, with bridging the gap between their world and the past. The speaker of "Bernard and Sarah" is no exception. When presented with a photograph of his "great-great-great-grandparents," taken in an era "when photography was young, and they were not," the speaker and his father are at a loss with what to do with it. The father decides to stow the portrait in a closet, taking it out "only on such occasions as the marriage/ of one of his own children," when he tersely instructs each of them, "I think you ought/ to know the stock you're joining with."

Ironically, the speaker's father feels no stronger connection with this "stock" than his children do. However, gazing into the distant but curiously familiar faces of his progenitors, the speaker develops a relentless compulsion to see what the photograph has to show him. This drive leads to the poem's resolute, confident conclusion, in which the speaker finds himself turning repeatedly to the photograph, which reveals to him important insights into the deepest, most enduring mysteries of family. In his mind's eye, the speaker's ancestors "light up the closet of my brain/ to draw me toward the place I started from,/ and when I have come home, they take me in."

"LANDSCAPE WITH TRACTOR"

Perhaps Taylor's most widely discussed poem, "Landscape with Tractor," the opening poem of *The Flying Change*, has all the trappings of the quintessential Taylor lyric—a rural setting, a tightly regular and disciplined structure, and a trained eye for the unexpectedly grotesque. In the poem, a middle-aged male narrator describes the experience of discovering a corpse while mowing a field on a remote part of his farm. Stirred from an otherwise routine, almost meditative chore by this unsettling encounter with mortality, he initially has a difficult time coming to terms with it. From the helm of his oversized "bushhog" mower, he thinks the body is "a clothing-store dummy, for God's sake," and that "People/ will toss all kinds of crap from their cars."

Gradually, however, he realizes that he must "contend with it," by acknowledging that it is the result of some horrifically violent act and notifying the authorities. Later he hears much local gossip and speculation "at the post office" as to how the body got there, but he never learns the real story. This draws the narrator into a round of deep introspection in which he realizes that regardless of how much or little he knows about the actualities of the corpse he has discovered, it has brought to him a more profound, universal message about the inevitability and certitude of his own death. He ominously muses that from this point on he will continue "putting gas in the tractor, keeping down thistles,// and seeing . . ./ . . . the bright yellow skirt,/ black shoes, the thing not quite like a face" and knowing that it will "stay in that field till you die."

"GREEN SPRINGS THE TREE"

Also from *The Flying Change*, "Green Springs the Tree" is one of those rare but poignant Taylor poems that concerns itself more with where family relationships are going rather than where they have been. One of the shortest, but metaphorically rich, poems in the collection, it examines a relationship between a father and his young son. Written from the father's point of view, it describes his fear of the awesome responsibility of ensuring his son's comfort, safety, and survival. The speaker explains that "Most of the time/ I am too far away to break the fall/ that seldom comes," expressing beautifully the exquisite and nearly overwhelming irony that even though humans are pathologically fallible, in many ways parenting demands an almost inhuman perfection. He laments that he prays "for skill in this," a "high wire [his son] will keep/ both of us on" until he one day steps into his own father's shoes.

BRIEF CANDLES

Brief Candles marks an unexpected and whimsical stylistic departure for Taylor. The slender volume attempts to resurrect a long-forgotten poetic form, the clerihew, and explores its playfully sardonic possibilities in a contemporary context. The clerihew, a light verse quatrain written in lines of unspecified length in an *aabb* rhyme scheme, typically concerns the deeds or character of the person named in its opening line. It was invented by British poet Edmund Clerihew Bentley, who popularized it in the early decades of the twentieth century. The clerihew was taken up by some other notable poets, including W. H. Auden and Clifton Fadiman, but was dismissed by the subsequent generation as a limited, even anachronistic form.

However, *Brief Candles* suggests that the clerihew is hardly ready for retirement, particularly considering its possibilities as a vehicle for scathing but good-natured satire. Although never devoid of humor, Taylor's previous poetry was marked by a preoccupation with the ironic, disquieting aspects of human nature; this makes the bulk of his work brooding in tone. However, *Brief Candles* shows a different side to Taylor, suggesting that he too can poke fun at poetry's often overly self-absorbed elitism. Poems like the following show that no figure is too revered, no poetic cliché too sacred, to elude comic scrutiny:

> Jerry Falwell
> may not think at all well
> but has done some sharp dealing
> with organized feeling.

CROOKED RUN

Taylor continues to examine rural themes in *Crooked Run*, which a reviewer described as an elegy. Divided into three sections, this collection's poems explore aspects of Taylor's family and community history, with people and events linked to the Virginia landscape through which the creek named Crooked Run flows. Taylor contemplates the creek's role, metaphorically considering it as kin and neighbor. Taylor's poetry shows how through time the creek has persisted. Time is a recurring theme in Taylor's work. His poems reveal how the land is stationary, but like the creek's water, it is also dynamic, experiencing surface changes as humans and animals modify habitats. In the first poem, "Creek Walk," Taylor refers to ancient beavers and frogs that inhabited Crooked Run, remarking how their descendants follow similar patterns, being prey and predators, often succumbing to disease or hunger.

Taylor attempts to understand how his ancestors interacted with the land and creek by consulting historical records. His imagined scenarios, usually presented with anecdotes and imagery, convey themes of transition as the landscape is transferred to new settlers and adapted to meet different needs in various eras. He emphasizes how people's connections to the land and creek form their sense of identity, purpose, and stability. Taylor features his great-grandfather Henry S. Taylor in "A Straight Stretch on the Far Side of Coolbrook." Referring to his ancestor's nineteenth century daybook, Taylor reconstructs scenes relevant to life on the family's homestead, including when his great-grandfather physically changed a section of Crooked Run, an alteration that still exists, symbolizing how this man's power reached beyond his time.

Loss is a persistent theme. Taylor mourns the boundless creek he experienced in his youth, which has become disjointed as boundaries designate its presence across numerous properties controlled by diverse owners. He recognizes sacrifices his kin and residents endured while associated with the creek's territory. "My Dear Sister Hannah," a narrative poem based on a relative's letter, voices the despair and powerlessness Carrie Taylor felt when federal troops approached her family's farm in 1864, intending to burn the property as they raided the countryside. Although Carrie convinced the soldiers not to set fire to her home, they confiscated livestock and belongings.

Carrie's ordeal parallels urban development threatening the creek's territory in the twenty-first century. Humans transform rural acreage with subdivisions and other urban infrastructure. In "Vision at Wood's Edge," Taylor notes the juxtaposition of the farm laborers of past decades and the carpoolers who now inhabit the pasture his uncle once owned; he also discloses a horrific accident that ended one life and foreshadowed the death of a lifestyle. Asphalt smothers fields sectioned into sixty lots for houses topped with copper in "Aka Fawn Meadow." Taylor comments on how quaint street names using agricultural terms identify locations, but the residents will raise only lawns, not sustenance. His "A Trace of Old Road Work" reveals that nature ultimately prevails, concealing evidence of human interference, as evidenced by the honeysuckle wrapping around an abandoned drill bit. The skeletal remains of a hound that the narrator encounters in "Creek Walk" remind him that nature's consistent rhythms will someday result in him too becoming part of Crooked Run's history.

OTHER MAJOR WORKS

NONFICTION: *Compulsory Figures: Essays on Recent American Poets*, 1992.

EDITED TEXTS: *Poetry: Points of Departure*, 1974; *The Water of Light: A Miscellany in Honor of Brewster Ghiselin*, 1976.

TRANSLATIONS: *The Children of Herakles*, 1981 (with Robert A. Brooks; of Euripides' *Hērakleidai*); *Leaves from the Dry Tree*, 1996 (of Vladimir Levchev); *Black Book of the Endangered Species*, 1999 (of Levchev).

BIBLIOGRAPHY

"Books by Our Editors." *Hollins Critic* 43, no. 5 (December, 2006): 21. Reviews *Crooked Run* and two books by Garrett. This concise evaluation of Taylor's work notes how it recalls a vanishing culture in a rural locale intrinsic to the poet's life and that his memories, local history knowledge, literary depictions of time, and appreciation of absurdity effectively shape his poetry.

Grossberg, Benjamin S. Review of *Crooked Run. Antioch Review* 64, no. 4 (Fall, 2006): 828. Succinct review examines literary techniques that Taylor uses to depict history in his poetry, analyzing how he effectively shows how the past is essential to modern perceptions and comprehension of place and people. Discusses the roles of memory, contemplation, self-preservation, and loss.

Hall, Sharon K., ed. *Contemporary Literary Criticism: Yearbook 1986*. Vol. 44. Detroit: Gale Research, 1987. Provides selections from the major critical responses to Taylor's most widely reviewed book of poetry, *The Flying Change*. Contains the reactions of several critics, including Daniel L. Guillory, Joseph Parisi, and Reed Whittemore.

Parrish, Nancy C. *Lee Smith, Annie Dillard, and the Hollins Group: A Genesis of Writers*. Baton Rouge: Louisiana State University Press, 1998. Although this book focuses on female writers, it depicts the Hollins creative writing community, including faculty and visiting writers, at the time when Taylor was a graduate student. Provides quotations and information concerning Taylor's time on campus and continued affiliation with his alma mater.

Pfefferle, W. T. *Poets on Place: Tales and Interviews from the Road*. Foreword by David St. John. Logan: Utah State University Press, 2005. Describes the author's visit with Taylor, who was his M.F.A. adviser at American University, and his interview, in which they discuss the literary impact of setting and Taylor's incorporation of storytelling elements in poetry. Taylor makes references to *Crooked Run*. Supplemented with Taylor's poem "Harvest" and a photograph of him.

Sharp, Nicholas A. "Taylor's 'One Morning, Shoeing Horses.'" *Explicator* 57, no. 1 (Fall, 1998): 62-65. A close examination of "One Morning, Shoeing Horses," a sonnet from *Understanding Fiction*.

Turner, Daniel Cross. "Restoration, Metanostalgia, and Critical Memory: Forms of Nostalgia in Contemporary Southern Poetry." *Southern Literary Journal* 40, no. 2 (Spring, 2008): 182-206. Studies Taylor's poems, in addition to work by Donald Justice and George Scarbrough, regarding how their poetry conforms to or rejects the expected literary style associated with southern writers, specifically their implementation of sentimental elements.

Gregory D. Horn
Updated by Elizabeth D. Schafer

SARA TEASDALE

Born: St. Louis, Missouri; August 8, 1884
Died: New York, New York; January 29, 1933

PRINCIPAL POETRY

Sonnets to Duse, and Other Poems, 1907
Helen of Troy, and Other Poems, 1911
Rivers to the Sea, 1915
Love Songs, 1917
Flame and Shadow, 1920
Dark of the Moon, 1926
Stars To-Night: Verses New and Old for Boys and Girls, 1930
Strange Victory, 1933
The Collected Poems of Sara Teasdale, 1937
Mirror of the Heart: Poems of Sara Teasdale, 1984

OTHER LITERARY FORMS

Sara Teasdale (TEEZ-dayl) attempted drama in a one-act play, *On the Tower* (pb. 1911), which appeared in *Helen of Troy, and Other Poems*. She began a biography of Christina Rossetti, her favorite woman poet, in 1931, but never completed it. Finally, Teasdale edited two anthologies: *The Answering Voice: One Hundred Love Lyrics by Women* (1917) and *Rainbow Gold: Poems Old and New Selected for Boys and Girls* (1922).

ACHIEVEMENTS

Sara Teasdale is remembered as a lyric poet. She was one of the most widely read poets in the United States in the years before her death in 1933. Her later collections, *Flame and Shadow, Dark of the Moon*, and *Strange Victory*, are considered her best. Her collection *Love Songs* went through five editions in 1917, and she was awarded a five-hundred-dollar prize, the forerunner of the Pulitzer Prize, by Columbia University in 1918.

BIOGRAPHY

A line of Sara Trevor Teasdale's poetry aptly describes her early life: "I was the flower amid a toiling world." Teasdale grew up in a sheltered atmosphere of reading, painting, and music, and literary interests became a large part of her life at an early age. Because of her frail health, she had fewer activities than the average child and was doted on by her middle-aged, wealthy parents. She was the youngest of four children of Mary Elizabeth Willard and John Warren Teasdale.

Teasdale's family, Puritanical and devout, embraced the ideals of a New England education brought to St. Louis, Missouri, by T. S. Eliot's grandfather, the Reverend William Greenleaf Eliot, who founded the Mary Institute for girls. Born in St. Louis, Teasdale attended the Mary Institute and later Hosman Hall, from 1898 to 1903, and the intellectual and social influence of these schools was strong. She did translations of Heinrich Heine, her first poetic influence, and she began writing poetry as a schoolgirl. Her contributions to the *Wheel*, a monthly magazine published by herself and her friends, the "Potters," 1904-1907, just after high school, revealed her early talent for lyrics, songs, and sonnets.

Teasdale had a gift for friendship. She formed strong and lasting friendships with some of the most interesting writers of her generation, many of them living in St. Louis, which in the late nineteenth and early twentieth centuries was an intellectual hub. Her friends among fellow poets included John Myers O'Hara, John Wheelock, Orrick Johns, Amy Lowell, Joyce Kilmer, and Vachel Lindsay. Her friendships with women were strong and she remained close to some of the "Potters," including Grace and Willamina Parish, Caroline Risque, and Vine Colby, as well as having special friendships with Marion Cummings, Marguerite Wilkinson, and Margaret Conklin. The latter was a young woman whom she met at the Connecticut College for Women who was a faithful companion at the end of her life.

Teasdale will be remembered as the woman who rebuffed Lindsay's offer of marriage. To Lindsay, Teasdale was a "jewel-girl," and he immortalized his love for her in his poem "The Chinese Nightingale." Teasdale, though fond of Lindsay and cherishing their friendship, had quite a different "angle" on life. Lindsay was usually penniless, full of vitality and energy, a man of the soil in life and in his poetry; Teasdale was used to a life of luxury, easily sapped of energy, and desirous of seclusion. She married a man of her own class

and background who would take care of her. She and Ernst Filsinger, an expert on international trade, were married on December 14, 1914, and the early years of their marriage were happy. They lived in New York City, which Teasdale captured in several of her poems in *Helen of Troy, and Other Poems* and *Rivers to the Sea*.

In the late 1920's, Teasdale decided to leave her husband because of his constant traveling and preoccupation with business. She took a painful trip to Reno and secured a divorce while Filsinger was in South America. After that, she became more and more reclusive and her health worsened. Like Alice James, she renounced full participation in life, using her ill health as a weapon. She began a biography of Christina Rossetti in 1931 but was not able to complete it. Greatly affected by her friend Marguerite Wilkinson's drowning, her divorce from Filsinger, and Lindsay's suicide in 1931, and suffering from the aftereffects of an attack of pneumonia, Teasdale was found submerged in a bathtub, dead from an overdose of barbiturates, in New York City, in 1933.

Sara Teasdale (Hulton Archive/Getty Images)

ANALYSIS

Sara Teasdale is distinguished as a lyric poet who evokes moods related to romantic love, the beauty of nature, and death. The substance of much of her early poetry is longing and dreams, and the image of the fantasy lover is virtually omnipresent: a lover who is elusive and disembodied, like the male figures in the work of the lonely Emily Brontë.

RESTRAINT AND RENUNCIATION

A major theme, a concomitant of the fantasy lover image in Teasdale's poetry, is delight in restraint and renunciation, "the kiss ungiven and long desired." This delight in restraint has its origins in four strands of Teasdale's life and reading that interweave in her poetry: the Romantic tradition of John Keats, Percy Bysshe Shelley, Algernon Charles Swinburne, and, later, Christina Rossetti; her devout Puritan background; her ill health, which separated her from full participation in life and led her to imagine rather than to participate in experience; and the role of women in the early twentieth century. This delight in the unattainable is evident in her early poems, such as "The Look," one of her most widely reprinted poems: "Strephon's kiss was lost in jest,/ Robins's lost in play/ But the kiss in Colin's eyes/ Haunts me night and day." Though long an admirer of Eleonora Duse, it is said that when she had the opportunity actually to see Duse dance, she chose not to. It was very typical of Teasdale; the idea of Duse's art was enough for her.

This theme of renunciation in her life and poetry is related to her religious background. Though religious sentiment was never overtly expressed in her poetry, she followed a strict moral code all her life. Her official biographer, Margaret Haley Carpenter, notes that Teasdale was never tempted to enter the bohemian lifestyle of some of her contemporaries even though Teasdale herself noted that the Puritan and the pagan warred within her. She remained a sensitive, shy, orderly, restrained woman throughout her life, and this reticence is reflected in her poetry. Except for "kisses," "looks," and "voices," the physical body is not present in her poetry, even though much of it deals with romantic love.

In the experience of nature, unlike the experience of love, there is a sense of Teasdale's presence and participation. Her joy in the beauty of nature, particularly the

sea and the stars, is embodied in many of her most successful poems. Her early poems reveal this delight—not quite the animal "appetite" found in William Wordsworth, but a direct and simple emotion that continues to charm the reader. Her nature poems are like gem-cut lockets holding precious snippets of experience; not surprisingly, they were intriguing to the Japanese, who have translated many of them. She, in turn, loved the idea of Japan and said of Japanese writing, "When I look at those vertical lines, they remind me of wisteria blooms."

LATER POETRY

In her later poetry, *Flame and Shadow*, *Dark of the Moon*, and *Strange Victory*, however, the beauty and simplicity of nature turn into a kind of terror related to death, as in "The Sea Wind":

> In the dead of night when the sky is deep
> The wind comes awaking me out of sleep—
> Why does it always bring to me
> The far-off, terrible call of the sea?

The death of Teasdale's mother and her older brother, George, in 1924, transformed her perspective and a new somberness and awareness of death entered her poetry. Her later verse expresses the attitude, ripened toward the end of her life, of one who is self-sufficient and possesses one's soul in silence, as in "The Solitary":

> My heart has grown rich with the passing of years,
>   I have less need now than when I was young
> To share myself with every comer
>   Or shape my thoughts into words with my tongue.

Teasdale's use of simple, unaffected language, easily accessible to readers, together with her interest in presenting the feminine experience of love, links her with her contemporaries. In her anthology *The Answering Voice: One Hundred Love Lyrics by Women*, she notes that sincere love poems by women are rare in England and the United States in the nineteenth century; in making her selections, she "avoided poems in which the poet dramatized a man's feelings rather than her own." Although the modern reader may feel that Teasdale's fantasy lovers, her denial of the body, and her frail romantic moods do not go far enough in representing the subtleties and complexities of women's re-lationships with men, she must be acknowledged to be a woman who found her voice.

OTHER MAJOR WORKS

PLAY: *On the Tower*, pb. 1911.

EDITED TEXTS: *The Answering Voice: One Hundred Love Lyrics by Women*, 1917; *Rainbow Gold: Poems Old and New Selected for Boys and Girls*, 1922.

BIBLIOGRAPHY

Carpenter, Margaret Haley. *Sara Teasdale: A Biography*. 1960. Reprint. Norfolk, Va.: Pentelic Press, 1977. This early biography is particularly good in its treatment of Teasdale's early life, especially the Potter period. Its extensive use of letters to Teasdale also gives a vivid picture of her relationship with Vachel Lindsay.

Drake, William. *Sara Teasdale: Woman and Poet*. 1979. Reprint. Knoxville: University of Tennessee Press, 1989. This psychologically oriented biography attempts to place Teasdale in the context of the transitional period between Victorianism and modernism. Although its conclusions about her motivations are speculative, this book's attention to Teasdale as a product of her time and its conflicts offers a reading of her character that is less idealized than that of the Carpenter book.

Gould, Jean. *American Woman Poets: Pioneers of Modern Poetry*. New York: Dodd, Mead, 1980. This collection of biographical reviews of early twentieth century poets gives a sympathetic overview of Teasdale's life and places her in the first rank of lyric poets.

Larsen, Jeanne. "Lowell, Teasdale, Wylie, Millay, and Bogan." In *The Columbia History of American Poetry*, edited by Jay Parini and Brett C. Millier. New York: Columbia University Press, 1993. A biographical and critical study of Teasdale and her American contemporaries.

Mannino, Mary Ann. "Sara Teasdale: Fitting Tunes to Everything." *Turn-of-the-Century Women* 5 (1990): 37-41. This brief study of Teasdale's metrics places her in the context of turn-of-the-century experimentation and argues that the formal aspects of her work deserve more attention than they have so far received.

Monroe, Harriet. *A Poet's Life*. New York: Macmillan, 1938. A useful survey of Teasdale's life and work by a close friend. It contains many fascinating recollections and is easy to read. Monroe makes frequent perceptive comments on Teasdale's poetic achievements. The work is useful primarily for anecdotal and biographical information. Supplemented by an index and a bibliography.

Schoen, Carol B. *Sara Teasdale*. Boston: Twayne, 1986. This chronologically ordered overview is the first book-length study of Teasdale's work. Essentially sympathetic, it focuses on her use of images and on the development of her ideas about love, solitude, beauty, and death, arguing that the critical neglect of Teasdale's work is unjustified.

Walker, Cheryl. *Masks Outrageous and Austere: Culture, Psyche, and Persona in Modern Women Poets*. Bloomington: Indiana University Press, 1991. Feminist in its focus, this study views Teasdale as representative of one reaction to nineteenth century views of women and women's poetry. It holds that her treatment of the conflict between independence and the desire for love is archetypal.

Patricia Ondek Laurence

HENRY DAVID THOREAU

Born: Concord, Massachusetts; July 12, 1817
Died: Concord, Massachusetts; May 6, 1862

PRINCIPAL POETRY

Poems of Nature, 1895
Collected Poems of Henry Thoreau, 1943 (first critical edition)

OTHER LITERARY FORMS

Henry David Thoreau (thuh-ROH) published two books during his lifetime: *A Week on the Concord and Merrimack Rivers* (1849) and *Walden: Or, Life in the Woods* (1854). Three additional books edited by his sister Sophia and his friend William Ellery Channing were published soon after his death: a collection of his travel essays titled *Excursions* (1863), *The Maine Woods* (1864), and *Cape Cod* (1865). During his lifetime, Thoreau also published essays in various periodicals. They were generally of three kinds: travel essays such as "A Yankee in Canada," nature essays such as "Walking," and social and political essays such as "Life Without Principle" and "Civil Disobedience." Those essays are collected in the standard "Walden" edition of Thoreau's complete writings, and the best of them are generally available today in paperback collections. Thoreau also dabbled in translations and occasionally published in *The Dial* his translations of Greek and Roman poetry. Perhaps Thoreau's greatest literary work, however, is his journal, which he kept throughout most of his adult life and most of which is available in the last fourteen volumes of the "Walden" edition of

his collected writings. A portion of the journal from 1840 to 1841 was omitted from the collected writings but was later edited and published by Perry Miller in *Consciousness in Concord* (1958). Also not included in the collected writings were portions of the journal dealing with Thoreau's first trip to Maine and portions that Thoreau himself cut out for use in his books. The Princeton University Press brought together Thoreau's journals in a more unified way in *Journal*, a seven-volume edition published between 1981 and 2002.

ACHIEVEMENTS

During his own lifetime, Henry David Thoreau met with only modest literary success. His early poems and essays published in *The Dial* were well known and appreciated in Transcendentalist circles but were generally unknown to popular audiences. As a lecturer, his talks were appreciated by the most liberal of his audiences but were generally found to be obscure or even dangerous by more conservative listeners. Thus, he had brief spurts of popularity as a lecturer, particularly in 1859 to 1860, but was not generally popular on the lecture circuit. His first book, *A Week on the Concord and Merrimack Rivers*, was published in 1849 at his own expense in an edition of one thousand copies. It met with very little success; only 294 copies were sold or given away, while the remaining copies were finally shipped four years later to Thoreau himself, who sarcastically remarked in his journal, "I have now a library of nearly nine hundred volumes, over seven hundred of which I wrote myself: Is it not well that the author should behold the fruits of his labor?" Although *A Week on the Concord and Merrimack Rivers* carried an advertisement of the forthcoming publication of *Walden*, the failure of the first book prompted Thoreau to withhold publication of the later one until he could feel more certain of its success. After much revision, Thoreau published *Walden* in 1854. It met with generally favorable reviews and good sales, over seventeen hundred copies of an edition of two thousand being sold in the first year. By 1859, it was out of print, but it was reissued in a second edition shortly after Thoreau's death. *Walden* won Thoreau some fame with general audiences and created a small but devoted number of disciples who would occasionally visit Thoreau in Concord or send

Henry David Thoreau (Library of Congress)

him complimentary copies of books. After the success of *Walden*, Thoreau found it easier to publish his essays in the more popular periodicals, such as *Putnam's Magazine* and *The Atlantic Monthly*. In his last years, he also acquired some notoriety as an abolitionist through his impassioned lectures and essays on John Brown.

Thoreau's literary reputation has risen steadily since his death, his writings appealing primarily to two very different kinds of readers: those who see him as an escapist nature writer and those who see him as a political radical. As Michael Meyer suggests, his advice to people to simplify their lives and return to an appreciation of nature has had especially strong appeal in times of economic difficulty such as the 1920's and 1930's, and it has also served to cushion criticism of Thoreau in times such as the 1940's, when his political views seemed unpatriotic. In the twenty-first century, it is probably still his nature writing that appeals to most readers. His social and political views, particularly his concept of passive resistance expressed in his essay "Civil Disobedience," have periodically made their influence felt in the actions of major social and political reformers such as Mahatma Gandhi and Martin Luther King, Jr. Thoreau's popularity peaked in the 1960's when his nature writing and his political views simultaneously found an audience of young American rebels advocating retreat from urban ugliness and materialism and passive resistance to an unpopular war. Since the 1960's, his popularity has subsided somewhat, but he continues to be widely read, and his place among the great writers of American literature seems secure.

BIOGRAPHY

Henry David Thoreau (christened David Henry Thoreau) was born in Concord, Massachusetts, on July 12, 1817, the third of four children of John Thoreau and Cynthia Thoreau. His father was a quiet man whose seeming lack of ambition had led to a series of unsuccessful attempts to establish himself as a shopkeeper prior to his finally establishing a very successful pencil factory in Concord. His mother was an outgoing, talkative woman who took in boarders to supplement the family's income. Both parents were fond of nature and could often be seen taking the children picnicking in the Concord woods.

Thoreau received a good grammar school education at the Concord Academy and seems to have had an essentially pleasant and typical boyhood. He attended Harvard College from 1833 to 1837, taking time out during his junior year to recuperate from a prolonged illness and to supplement his income by teaching for several months in Canton, Massachusetts. Upon being graduated near the top of his class, he took a teaching job in the Concord public schools, but after a few weeks he resigned in protest over the school board's insistence that he use corporal punishment to discipline his students. Unable to find another position, Thoreau opened a private school of his own and was eventually joined by his older brother John. John's cheerful disposition together with Henry's high academic standards made the school very successful until it was closed in 1841 because of John's prolonged illness.

During these years as a teacher, Thoreau traveled to Maine, took, with his brother, the famous excursion on the Concord and Merrimack rivers that eventually became the subject of his first book, delivered his first lecture, and published his first essay and his first poetry in *The Dial*. Through one of his students, Edmund Sewall (whom he praises in one of his best-known poems, "Lately, Alas, I Knew a Gentle Boy") he met Ellen Sewall, the only woman to whom he seems to have been romantically attracted in any serious way. Ellen seems to have been the subject or recipient of a number of Thoreau's poems of 1839 and 1840, but his brother John was the more forward of the two in courting Ellen, and it was after John's proposal to Ellen had failed that Henry also proposed, only to be rejected as John had been.

After the closing of the school, Thoreau was invited to live with Ralph Waldo Emerson's family as a handyman; he stayed two years, during which time he continued to contribute to and occasionally help Emerson edit *The Dial*. In 1842, his brother John died suddenly of a tetanus infection, leaving Thoreau so devastated that he himself briefly exhibited psychosomatic symptoms of the disease. The following year, a brief stint as a tutor to William Emerson's family on Staten Island confirmed his prejudice against cities, so he returned to Concord, where in 1844, he and a companion accidentally set fire to the Concord Woods, thus earning some rather long-lasting ill will from some of his neighbors and some long-lasting damage to his reputation as a woodsman.

For several years, Thoreau had contemplated buying a house and some land of his own, but in 1845, he settled for permission from Emerson to use some land near Walden Pond to build his own cabin. He built a one-room cabin and moved in on July 4, thus declaring his intention to be free to work on his writing and on a personal experiment in economic self-reliance. He continued to use the cabin as his main residence for two years, during which time he wrote *A Week on the Concord and Merrimack Rivers* and much of *Walden*, raised beans, took a trip to the Maine Woods, and spent his famous night in the Concord jail for nonpayment of taxes. An invitation from Emerson to spend another year as a resident handyman finally prompted him to leave the pond in the fall of 1847, but he left with little regret, because, as he says in *Walden*, "I had several more lives to live, and I could not spare any more time for that one." The fruits of his stay at the pond finally began to appear in 1849, when *A Week on the Concord and Merrimack Rivers* and his essay on "Resistance to Civil Government" (later renamed "Civil Disobedience") were both published.

Throughout the 1840's, Thoreau had become increasingly interested in the natural sciences, and he began to spend much time gathering and measuring specimens, often at the expense of his writing, so that by 1851, he had reason to complain in his journal, "I feel that the character of my knowledge is from year to year becoming more distinct and scientific; that, in exchange for views as wide as heaven's scope, I am being narrowed down to the field of the microscope." His scientific and mechanical abilities had benefits for the family's pencil-making business, however, because in 1843 he had developed a more effective means of securing the graphite in the pencils and was later to improve the quality of pencils still further. Throughout his life he maintained of necessity an interest in the family business, although he seldom enjoyed having to take active part in it. His aversion to the routine of regular employment also applied to his surveying talents, which were called on by his neighbors increasingly after 1850. Although by 1851 Thoreau seems to have felt

that life was passing him by without his having been able to achieve his goals, the publication of *Walden* in 1854 revived his self-esteem when the book sold well and brought a small but devoted group of admirers.

Throughout the 1850's, Thoreau made several excursions to Canada, the Maine Woods, and Cape Cod, which culminated in travel essays in popular periodicals. He also traveled to New Jersey and to Brooklyn, where he met Walt Whitman, with whom he was favorably impressed. Thoreau's admiration for Whitman's raw genius was surpassed only by his admiration for Brown, the abolitionist, whom he first met in 1857 and whose cause he vigorously supported in lectures and published essays.

In 1860, Thoreau caught a bad cold and eventually was diagnosed with tuberculosis. Advised to seek a different climate, Thoreau took a trip to Minnesota in 1861, a trip that provided him with some brief glimpses of "uncivilized" Indians but with no relief from his illness. After returning to Concord, his health continued to deteriorate, and he died at home on May 6, 1862.

ANALYSIS

For Henry David Thoreau, the value of poetry lay not primarily in the poem itself, but in the act of writing the poem and in that act's influence on the poet's life. The importance of poetry to the poet is, as he says in *A Week on the Concord and Merrimack Rivers*, in "what he has become through his work." Since for the Transcendentalists life was superior to art, Thoreau could assert that "My life has been the poem I would have writ,/ But I could not both live and utter it." No art form could surpass God's act of creating nature or a person's act of shaping his or her own life. In his journal for 1840, Thoreau suggests that the best an artist can hope for is to equal nature, not to surpass it. The poet's job is to publish nature's truth accurately, and thus at times, verse seemed to him to be the best vehicle for publicizing nature because of its greater precision. By the mid-1840's, however, he had mostly abandoned verse and concluded that "Great prose, of equal elevation, commands our respect more than great verse, since it implies a more permanent and level height. . . . The poet often only makes an irruption . . . but the prose writer has conquered . . . and settled colonies." In 1851, he found it necessary to warn himself to beware "of youthful poetry, which is impotent." Another problem with poetry was that it was too artificial. One could not capture in words the rhythms of the wind or the birds. He found that "the music now runs before and then behind the sense, but is never coincident with it." One could make music, or one could make sense; Thoreau eventually preferred the latter.

Because of this ambiguous attitude toward the value of verse (he eventually came to speak of both good verse and good prose as "poetry"), Thoreau's poetry is seldom first-rate, and even at its best, it does not rival that of such contemporaries as Emily Dickinson and Whitman. Nevertheless, it is of significance to the modern reader, first, because it demonstrates vividly the problems that American poets faced in freeing themselves artistically from European influences, and second, because it provides some fresh insights, not available as fully in his prose, into some of the deepest problems of Thoreau's life, especially his attempts to cope with the problems of love and friendship and of his own role as an artist.

Thoreau could never quite free himself from imitating the great poets he admired to find a voice of his own. He mined his expert knowledge of Greek and Latin to write epigrams or odes (essentially Horatian in form) such as "Let Such Pure Hate Still Underprop," which is also reminiscent of the seventeenth century Metaphysical poets in its use of paradox. Indeed, it is the Metaphysicals to whom Thoreau seems to have turned most often as muses for his own poetry: the paradoxes, introspection, and elaborate conceits of John Donne or Andrew Marvell. At other times, one can find in Thoreau's verse the loose rhythms of John Skelton's near-doggerel dimeter, as in "The Old Marlborough Road," or the more graceful tetrameter couplets, which are Thoreau's most frequently used form and which, as critic Henry Wells suggests, can also be traced to the Metaphysicals. Finally, Thoreau frequently employs the three-part structure and tight stanza form of George Herbert's meditations. The stanza form of "I Am a Parcel of Vain Strivings Tied," for example, is clearly modeled on Herbert, while a poem such as "The Poet's Delay" has, as H. Grant Sampson suggests, the three-part meditative structure that moves from a particular scene in nature to the poet's awareness of the scene's wider implications, and finally to the poet's recognition of the scene's specific spiritual meaning for him.

THE INFLUENCE OF THE ROMANTIC POETS

Although Thoreau most frequently looked to the past for poetic models, he did admire some of the Romantic poets of his own day, particularly William Wordsworth. Thoreau's "I Knew a Man by Sight," for example, portrays a typical Wordsworthian rustic wanderer, while in Thoreau's unfortunate attempt at rhyme in the lines "Late in a wilderness/ I shared his mess" readers also see the glaring difference in poetic skill between the two poets. In "My Books I'd Fain Cast Off, I Cannot Read," Thoreau expresses a view of the superiority of nature to books, very much like that in Wordsworth's "Expostulation and Reply." In several other poems, he seems to echo Wordsworth's theories of human development. In "Manhood," for example, Thoreau presents the same view of the child as father of the man that Wordsworth presents in "Ode: Intimations of Immortality from Recollections of Early Childhood." In "Music," he also presents a view of a person's loss of youthful faculties and of compensation for that loss with adult wisdom similar to that presented by Wordsworth in "Lines Composed a Few Miles Above Tintern Abbey" and in *The Prelude: Or, The Growth of a Poet's Mind* (1850).

From this unlikely mixture of classical, Metaphysical, and Romantic influences, Thoreau apparently hoped to create a poetry that would express his own love of paradox, introspection, and nature, while creating a style both stately and rugged, at once elevated and natural. The task was, as Thoreau himself came to realize, impossible. It is also interesting to note, however, that Thoreau seems not to have looked to his own countrymen, except perhaps Emerson, for models. His diction and rhythms are most frequently traceable to European influence, and when he attempts to break free of that influence, he usually meets with only modest success or complete failure.

Because Thoreau's prose is generally more effective than his poetry, when he deals with a topic in both genres, the poetry is generally valuable primarily as a gloss on the prose. In "Wait Not Till Slaves Pronounce the Word," for example, Thoreau reminds the reader that slavery is as much a state of mind as an external condition: "Think not the tyrant sits afar/ In your own breasts ye have/ The District of Columbia/ And power to free the Slave." His statement in *Walden*, however, makes the same point more powerfully: "It is hard to have a Southern overseer; it is worse to have a Northern one; but worst of all when you are the slave driver of yourself." Some of Thoreau's nature poems do present some fresh minor insights into Thoreau's view of nature, but those poems that are of most value and interest in their own right are those that shed autobiographical light on some of his personal dilemmas either unexpressed or not expressed as well in his prose, particularly his attempt to find an ideal friendship and his attempt to meet the artistic goals he set for himself.

THE IDEAL OF FRIENDSHIP

Thoreau's ideal of friendship, expressed most fully in the "Wednesday" chapter of *A Week on the Concord and Merrimack Rivers*, is typically Transcendentalist in its insistence on paradox in human relationships. To Thoreau, friends were to be united with one another and yet separate. They were to love one another's strengths while at the same time hating one another's weaknesses, to be committed to one another and yet be free, to express their love and yet remain silent. They were to be equal, and yet he insists that only a friendship contracted with one's superior is worthwhile. Friendship, as he suggests in a manuscript poem titled "Friendship," was to combine truth, beauty, and goodness in a platonic spiritual oneness, symbolized in the poem by two oak trees that barely touch above the ground but are inseparably intertwined in their roots. Although he tends to overintellectualize this concept of friendship, Thoreau was quite in earnest in seeking it in his friends, especially after his college years when he was trying to define his own identity through those he cared about. The person who perhaps came closest to being the soul mate whom Thoreau sought was his brother John. Unfortunately, as is often the case with affection for relatives, Thoreau found that he could seldom express his love for John adequately. When John died, his only outlet was to pour out his affection in his writings by dedicating his first book to him and by writing a gently moving poem, "Brother Where Dost Thou Dwell."

Others who for a time seemed to realize his ideal were Edmund Sewall (one of his students) and Edmund's sister, Ellen. To Edmund, Thoreau wrote one of his best poems, "Lately, Alas, I Knew a Gentle Boy." In this poem, Edmund is described as one who effortlessly wins the love of all around him by his quiet virtue. Mutual respect between the poet and the boy leads them both to keep their love unexpressed, however, and they paradoxically find themselves "less acquainted than when first we met." The friendship thus slips away without being overtly expressed, and the poet is left to cherish only "that virtue which he is." Although this poem certainly has androgynous qualities and is sometimes used to suggest a youthful homosexuality in Thoreau, it seems wiser to take it for what it more obviously is: one of the clearest and most moving of Thoreau's expressions of the joys and frustrations of platonic love. His poems to Edmund's sister, Ellen, are similarly platonic in tone. In one poem ("Love"), for example, he describes himself and Ellen as a "double star" revolving "about one center." In "The Breeze's Invitation," he adds a pastoral touch, describing himself and Ellen as a carefree king and queen of a "peaceful little green." In such poems, the reader sees a Thoreau who, beneath the platonic and pastoral conventions, is a young man earnestly seeking affection— a young man much more vulnerable than the didactic prose philosophizer of *A Week on the Concord and Merrimack Rivers* or the self-confident chanticleer in *Walden*.

ARTISTIC HOPES

That same human vulnerability is also the most striking quality of those poems that deal with Thoreau's artistic goals. Aside from his journals, it is in his poems that Thoreau most fully reveals his artistic hopes and disappointments. Those hopes were a typically romantic mixture of active achievement and passive reception. On one hand, as he suggests in "The Hero," a man must contribute something new to his world; he must, as he says in *Walden*, "affect the quality of the day." On the other hand, he can achieve such results only if he is receptive to the inspiration of God through nature. Such inspiration at its most powerful culminates in the sort of mystical experience described by Thoreau in his poem "The Bluebirds," in which he describes his feelings as if "the heavens were all around,/ And the earth was all below" and as if he were a "waking thought—/ A something I hardly knew."

INSPIRATION

Such mystical experiences were the crucial source of the poet's action, whether in writing or in deeds; thus, as Paul O. Williams has demonstrated, much of Thoreau's poetry deals directly or indirectly with the subject of inspiration. The fullest and clearest treatment of the theme is in "Inspiration," a poem in which he describes having occasionally felt a godlike sensitivity to the world so powerful that he felt thoroughly reborn and ready to "fathom hell or climb to heaven." The poet's predicament, however, was that such pure inspiration could seldom be translated untainted into action, and it is this predicament which is at the heart of several of his best poems. In "Light-Winged Smoke, Icarian Bird," one of the most often reprinted and discussed of his poems, he cryptically describes himself as a flame and his poetry as the smoke that he sends heavenward to God. Unfortunately, as the smoke rises to God, it also blots out the truth of God's sun and negates the poet's purpose of clarifying that truth. Thoreau's point here, as Eberhard Alsen convincingly argues, is that even the "clear flame" of the poet is not pure enough to avoid misrepresenting God's truths. That sense of the human artist's limitations in a world of infinite wonder sometimes led Thoreau to feel that his life was being wasted, as in "The Poet's Delay," in which he expresses his fear that while nature's seasons progress into autumn and bear fruit, his own "spring does not begin." Elsewhere, however, as in "I Am a Parcel of Vain Strivings Tied," he consoles himself with a sacrificial satisfaction that his own failures will allow others to be more fruitful. If he is a parcel of picked flowers unable to produce further beauty, at least the other flowers can bloom more beautifully because his have been thinned out of the garden.

In such poems as these, one realizes that Thoreau sensed early what is quite clear when one surveys the body of his poetry: that verse was not the best vehicle for his thoughts but that it freed him to make his prose more powerful. He would have to wait until the publi-cation of *Walden* to feel that the slow-paced seasons of his artistic life had truly begun to bear fruit. Nevertheless, his poetry served him both as a valuable testing ground for his ideas and as an outlet for some of his deepest private problems. It is also worth the modern reader's time because it provides an occasional peek behind the persona of his prose works and because it helps in understanding the dilemma of the Romantic artist, attempting to convey the ideal while being hindered by the very real limitations of human language—a problem that confronts many modern poets as well.

OTHER MAJOR WORKS

NONFICTION: "Civil Disobedience," 1849 (also known as "Resistance to Civil Government"); *A Week on the Concord and Merrimack Rivers*, 1849; *Walden: Or, Life in the Woods*, 1854; *Excursions*, 1863; *The Maine Woods*, 1864; *Cape Cod*, 1865; *Letters to Various Persons*, 1865 (Ralph Waldo Emerson, editor); *A Yankee in Canada, with Anti-Slavery and Reform Papers*, 1866; *Early Spring in Massachusetts*, 1881; *Summer*, 1884; *Winter*, 1888; *Autumn*, 1892; *Familiar Letters of Henry David Thoreau*, 1894 (F. B. Sanborn, editor); *Journal*, 1981-2002 (7 volumes); *Letters to a Spiritual Seeker*, 2004 (Bradley P. Dean, editor).

MISCELLANEOUS: *The Writings of Henry David Thoreau*, 1906 (20 volumes); *Collected Essays and Poems*, 2001.

BIBLIOGRAPHY

Cain, William E. *A Historical Guide to Henry David Thoreau*. New York: Oxford University Press, 2000. Historical and biographical context and treatment of Thoreau.

Hahn, Stephen. *On Thoreau*. Belmont, Calif.: Wadsworth, 2000. A concise study intended to assist a beginning student in understanding Thoreau's philosophy and thinking. Includes bibliographical references.

Kerting, Verena. *Henry David Thoreau's Aesthetics: A Modern Approach to the World*. New York: Peter Lang, 2006. Examines Thoreau's writings for his worldview and aesthetics.

McSweeney, Kerry. *The Language of the Senses: Sen-

sory-Perceptual Dynamics in Wordsworth, Cole-ridge, Thoreau, Whitman, and Dickinson. Montreal: McGill-Queen's University Press, 1998. Compares and contrasts the senses in the poetry of Thoreau, William Wordsworth, Samuel Taylor Coleridge, Walt Whitman, and Emily Dickinson.

Myerson, Joel, ed. *The Cambridge Companion to Henry David Thoreau.* 1995. Reprint. New York: Cambridge University Press, 2006. A guide to the works and to the biographical, historical, and literary contexts. Includes a chronology and further readings.

Richardson, Robert D. *Henry Thoreau: A Life of the Mind.* Berkeley: University of California Press, 1986. This study focuses primarily on the development of Thoreau's leading themes and the formulation of his working philosophy. Richardson offers clear accounts of some of the writer's complex theories. Provides notes, a bibliography, and an index.

Smith, Larry. *Thoreau's Lost Journal: Poems.* Toledo, Ohio: Westron Press, 2001. Smith concentrates on Thoreau's poetry as found in his journal.

Sullivan, Robert. *The Thoreau You Don't Know: What the Prophet of Environmentalism Really Meant.* New York: Collins, 2009. Although this work examines *Walden* more than the poetry, it presents a different perspective on Thoreau, one that suggests that the work was meant to be a communal work, an inspiration, rather than a reclusive work.

Tauber, Alfred I. *Henry David Thoreau and the Moral Agency of Knowing.* Berkeley: University of California Press, 2001. Tauber shows how Thoreau's metaphysics of self-knowing informed all that this multifaceted writer, thinker, and scientist did. A clear presentation of the man in the context of social and intellectual history.

Thoreau, Henry David. *I to Myself: An Annotated Selection from the Journal of Henry D. Thoreau.* Edited by Jeffrey S. Cramer. New Haven, Conn.: Yale University Press, 2007. This work offers selections from Thoreau's journals from 1837-1861. Includes comprehensive annotations that uncover allusions, provide biographical information, and offer word definitions.

Richard J. Schneider

MELVIN B. TOLSON

Born: Moberly, Missouri; February 6, 1898
Died: Dallas, Texas; August 29, 1966

PRINCIPAL POETRY

Rendezvous with America, 1944
Libretto for the Republic of Liberia, 1953
Harlem Gallery: Book I, The Curator, 1965
A Gallery of Harlem Portraits, pb. 1979
    (wr. 1932)
"Harlem Gallery," and Other Poems of Melvin B. Tolson, 1999

OTHER LITERARY FORMS

Melvin B. Tolson wrote three unpublished novels, "Beyond the Zaretto" (written in late 1920's), "The Lion and the Jackal" (written in late 1930's), and "All Aboard" (written in 1950's). In addition, he composed a number of full-length and one-act plays, including "The Moses of Beale Street," "Southern Front," "Bivouac on the Santa Fe," and "The House by the Side of the Tracks," all of which were unpublished. From 1937 to 1944, Tolson wrote a column titled "Caviar and Cabbage" for the *Washington Tribune*.

ACHIEVEMENTS

While Melvin B. Tolson earned little critical attention throughout most of his life, his work was not without recognition. In 1939, he won first place in the National Poetry Contest award sponsored by the American Negro Exposition in Chicago for "Dark Symphony." In 1945, he won the Omega Psi Phi Award for creative writing, and in 1951, he earned *Poetry* magazine's Bess Hokin Prize for "E. & O. E." He served as poet laureate of Liberia, Africa, in 1947, and was appointed permanent Bread Loaf Fellow in Poetry and Drama, 1954. The 1960's brought two additional distinctions, the District of Columbia Citation and Award for Cultural Achievement in Fine Arts in 1965 and the National Institute and American Academy of Arts and Letters Award in Literature in 1966. Tolson also earned fellowships from the Rockefeller Foundation and Omega Psi Phi and served as mayor of Langston,

Oklahoma, from 1952 to 1958. Posthumously, Tolson won the Ralph Ellison Award from the Oklahoma Center for the Book in 1998.

BIOGRAPHY

Melvin Beaunorus Tolson was born on February 6, 1898, to the Reverend Alonzo Tolson and Lera Tolson. Tolson's father was, as his grandfather had been, a minister in the Methodist Episcopal Church. His father, who was fond of discussing Western philosophy during fishing trips, expected Tolson to follow him into the ministry and was disappointed when his son chose a different vocation. Tolson's mother was part Cherokee Indian by heritage and her father had been killed for resisting enslavement. Thanks to a family friend, Mrs. George Markwell, a white woman who made her library available to the precocious youth, Tolson had the early benefit of knowledge and learning in his immediate surroundings. The family moved from Missouri to Oklahoma, and then to Iowa, but wherever he went, Tolson was a popular classmate. In high school, he captained the football team, participated in debating contests, and directed plays for the school's theater.

In 1919, Tolson entered Fisk University in Nashville, Tennessee. He later transferred to Lincoln University, the nation's oldest historically black college, in Oxford, Pennsylvania. In 1923, his senior year, he met the woman he would marry, Ruth Southall. After his graduation, they wed and moved to Marshall, Texas, where Tolson had secured his first teaching post, at Wiley College.

Although he continued writing plays, fiction, and poetry at Wiley, it was as the debating team coach that Tolson's name became well known throughout the Southwest. Putting his students through relentless drills, Tolson led his debate teams to nationwide championships for ten consecutive years. All the while, Tolson was still writing poetry, producing a manuscript more than three hundred pages long, *A Gallery of Harlem Portraits*, in 1932, shortly after completing the course work for his master's degree at Columbia University. Though Tolson had modeled his poems on Edgar Lee Masters's popular *Spoon River Anthology* (1915), he could not find a publisher who believed in

the marketability of the manuscript. These early poems would not be published in book form until 1979, thirteen years after Tolson's death.

In 1947, Tolson left Wiley College for Langston University, Langston, Oklahoma (just north of Oklahoma City), where he would remain until his retirement in 1964. Tolson was named poet laureate of Liberia and commissioned to write a poem celebrating the centennial of the country's birth. That led to *Libretto for the Republic of Liberia*, published as a book in 1953. This work showcases Tolson's shift from the free-verse directness of *Rendezvous with America* to a more modernist, nonlinear style, characterized by obscure allusions, dramatic monologues, puns, and semischolarly footnotes.

Tolson had intended to revise his early manuscript, *A Gallery of Harlem Portraits*, but felt dissatisfied with its populist lyricism. He had been studying the modernists—in particular, Ezra Pound, T. S. Eliot, and Hart Crane—and decided to revamp the project entirely. He planned to produce an epic, five-book history of the black man's journey in America that would, even more so than *Rendezvous with America*, demonstrate how well he had digested—and superseded—the modern poets. However, he managed to complete only the first volume, *Harlem Gallery*, before his death in 1966.

ANALYSIS

The precise meaning of the life and career of Melvin B. Tolson has vexed the literary establishment ever since his shift from the populist poetry of his first two books to the difficult, allusion-ridden poetry of his last work, *Harlem Gallery: Book I, The Curator*, published just before his death. Was Tolson so enthralled by the call to "make it new," articulated and demonstrated in the essays and poetry of Ezra Pound and T. S. Eliot, that he "sold out" the populist poetics of the Harlem Renaissance? Or did Tolson try to find a new poetics, navigating his poetic enterprise between the Scylla and Charybdis of Anglo-American modernism and African American populism?

Insofar as the debate around Tolson's work still rages, there is still no consensus within the African American literary community, much less the literary community at large, about the value of his poetry. Still, excepting Joy Flasch's book-length appreciation, *Melvin B. Tolson* (1972), it was not until the 1990's that critical commentators—Michael Bérubé, Hermine Dolerez, Craig Werner, and Aldon Nielsen among them—started to reread and argue for the revolutionary, if incomplete, modernism of Tolson's poetic output.

In their introductory remarks to Tolson's second and third published books, *Libretto for the Republic of Liberia* and *Harlem Gallery*, both Allen Tate and Karl Shapiro focus on the extent to which Tolson's convoluted, experimental poems constitute black poetry. Both answer in the affirmative but for different reasons. For Tate, writing about *Libretto for the Republic of Liberia*, Tolson is "more" black than, for example, the Harlem Renaissance poets because, unlike them, he focuses on poetry as an art first and as an opportunity for the dissemination of political ideas second. Shapiro dismisses the issue of Tolson's relationship to high modernism. For him, Tolson "writes and thinks in Negro, which is to say, a possible American language." Both critics were taken to task by black and white commentators, Tate for his self-serving racism (Tolson is a poet because he writes like Eliot and Crane), Shapiro for his ignorance (Tolson's poetry could not be any less black). Tolson's work is, in toto, a contribution to this "debate," one that embraces the complications of what it means to be an artist in America even as it undermines presumptions about what it means to be a black artist in America.

A GALLERY OF HARLEM PORTRAITS

Although it was published posthumously in 1979, *A Gallery of Harlem Portraits* represents Tolson's earliest poetic style, largely influenced by the populism of Carl Sandburg and Langston Hughes. Simplicity of language and characterization is the prevailing attribute of this kind of poetry. The concept of the "portrait" was taken from Masters's *Spoon River Anthology*, itself a pedestrian version of Amy Lowell's—as opposed to Ezra Pound's—"Imagism," a poetics that deemphasizes duration and narrative in favor of the moment (a "snapshot" or "still life"). Like the politics of Sandburg and Hughes, Tolson's leftist politics influenced his poetic technique, which he viewed as another version of social realism.

RENDEZVOUS WITH AMERICA

If the structure of *A Gallery of Harlem Portraits* is, in part, the formal model for Tolson's last book, *Harlem Gallery*, then *Rendezvous with America* is its thematic link. Just as Tolson will claim all world culture and learning as part of what it means to be a black artist in his last book, so in this book he claims all America for all Americans:

> America is the Black Man's country,
> The Red Man's, the Yellow Man's,
> The Brown Man's, the White Man's.

The poems in this book, including "Dark Symphony," work to undermine the prevailing assumption of the early twentieth century that America could do without the contributions of "minorities." Here Tolson's revisionist history of America is meant to demystify and enlighten.

LIBRETTO FOR THE REPUBLIC OF LIBERIA

Commissioned by the cultural attache of Liberia, Tolson's third volume of poetry (the second to be published during his lifetime) is perhaps most significant because of its stylistic break from the traditional verse of *A Gallery of Harlem Portraits* and *Rendezvous with America* (1944). Although enjambment still dominates the poetic line, the poem is self-consciously organized by Tolson on the basis of the diatonic scale. Each section "represents" a musical note of the octave, from do, re, mi, and fa, to so, la, ti, and do. For Tolson, the rising musical scale becomes, as narrative structure, the evolutionary story of Liberia, as it grew from a haven from slavery into a utopian model for all Africa. This developmental schema is reinforced at the linguistic level by repetition, dialectical opposition, and the use of free verse and metrical verse stanza forms.

HARLEM GALLERY

As the title of *Harlem Gallery* suggests, Tolson's last published book of poetry is structurally modeled on his first one, *A Gallery of Harlem Portraits*. Here, Tolson perfects the oblique invocations of classical learning and pedestrian colloquialisms that first appeared in the *Libretto for the Republic of Liberia*. Just as the *Libretto for the Republic of Liberia* is organized according to the Western diatonic musical scale, so

Harlem Gallery is organized according to the Greek alphabet, proceeding from "Alpha" to "Omega."

Unlike the first book, which remained true to the spirit of Masters's *Spoon River Anthology*, *Harlem Gallery* philosophizes on the nature of African American art and African American artists in relationship to their culture in general. Not surprisingly, Tolson endorses unqualified freedom for artists. Still, he does not ignore the complex issue of artists' responsibility to their community.

Situated as primarily a three-way debate between the curator, Dr. Okomo, and Hideho Heights, *Harlem Gallery* presents a broad spectrum of opinions on social, class, and racial issues. The issue, for his characters as for Tolson, revolves around the very nature of the black person. Is he or she primarily African or primarily American? What is "black culture"? Is the artist obligated to please a contemporary audience or to risk oblivion by creating art for an audience that may never exist?

Finally, one of the major unresolved tensions in the work is the way it savages the black middle class for copying white middle-class culture—the relevant text, cited several times, is sociologist E. F. Franklin Frazier's controversial *The Black Bourgeoisie* (1957)—while it also extols the black artist who mixes African and European artistic traditions in order to raise the level of black art. The difference in value Tolson assigns to black economic success and black artistic success is based on his cosmopolitanism and his belief in inclusion and in egalitarianism. For Tolson, a parochial art would be the cultural equivalent of capitalist self-interest. In a context where black urban populations found themselves trying to keep pace with their white counterparts, Tolson's rejection of individualistic self-interest on the economic front—and endorsement of apparent self-interest on the artistic front—placed him at odds with both the black bourgeoisie and black proletarian artists, such as Langston Hughes, Haki R. Madhubuti, and Amiri Baraka.

OTHER MAJOR WORKS

NONFICTION: *Caviar and Cabbage: Selected Columns by Melvin B. Tolson from the "Washington Tribune," 1937-1944*, 1982; *The Harlem Group of Negro Writers*, 2001.

BIBLIOGRAPHY

Bérubé, Michael. "Masks, Margins, and African American Modernism: Melvin Tolson's *Harlem Gallery.*" *Publications of the Modern Language Association of America* 105, no. 1 (January, 1990): 57-69. This article argues that Hideho Heights's infamous parable of the "sea-turtle and shark" in the "Phi" section of *Harlem Gallery* offers insight into Tolson's views on the African American artist's relationship to modernism in particular and African American culture's relationship to Anglo-American culture in general. Just as the sea-turtle, swallowed by a shark, can chew its way out safely through the stomach (as opposed to trying to escape through the mouth and risk being bitten), so too African Americans must "exit" Anglo-American culture from "within."

Bloom, Harold, ed. *African-American Poets: Phillis Wheatley Through Melvin B. Tolson*. Philadelphia: Chelsea House, 2003. Essays in this work examine the style of poetry in Tolson's work as well as his sonnets.

Farnsworth, Robert M. *Melvin B. Tolson, 1898-1966: Plain Talk and Poetic Prophecy*. Columbia: University of Missouri Press, 1984. A complete biography.

Flasch, Joy. *Melvin B. Tolson*. New York: Twayne, 1972. This is the first extended consideration of Tolson's life and works, produced by the company that published his last two books of poetry.

Hart, Matthew. *Nations of Nothing but Poetry: Modernism, Transnationalism, and Synthetic Vernacular Writing*. New York: Oxford University Press, 2010. This work on poetry contains a chapter discussing Tolson and Harryette Mullen and the politics of Afro-modernism.

Lenhart, Gary. "Caviar and Cabbage." *American Poetry Review* (March/April, 2000): 35-39. This article argues that Tolson's shift to a modernist poetics with the publication of *Libretto for the Republic of Liberia* was primarily influenced by Tolson's reading of Hart Crane's *The Bridge* (1930) rather than T. S. Eliot's *The Waste Land* (1922), that it was a way for Tolson to engage in—not escape—social and cultural issues. Thus, Tolson's modernism was never at odds with his commitment to political activism.

Neilsen, Aldon L. "Melvin B. Tolson and the Deterritorialization of Modernism." *African American Review* 26, no. 2 (1992): 241-255. Argues that Tolson's adaptation of modernist procedures in his later poetry was not a form of assimilation but, instead, an assertion of ownership. Insofar as modernism's roots are largely African and Asian, Tolson's later poetry reclaims modernism as an authentic, non-Western phenomenon.

Nelson, Raymond. "*Harlem Gallery*: An Advertisement and User's Manual." *Virginia Quarterly Review* 75, no. 3 (Summer, 1999): 528-543. A thoughtful, urbane, jargon-free introduction to *Harlem Gallery* and to the rest of Tolson's work.

Shevin, David. "The Poetry of Melvin B. Tolson." In *Masterplots II: African American Literature*, edited by Tyrone Williams. Rev. ed. Pasadena, Calif.: Salem Press, 2009. Provides an in-depth analysis of this work and background on Tolson's life.

Tolson, Melvin B., Jr. "The Poetry of Melvin B. Tolson (1898-1966)." *World Literature Today* 64, no. 3 (Summer, 1990): 395-400. Tolson's son, a professor of French at the University of Oklahoma, provides personal insight into his father's ideas and methods.

Woodson, Jon. "Melvin B. Tolson and the Art of Being Difficult." In *Black American Poets Between Worlds, 1940-1960*, edited by R. Baxter. Knoxville: University of Tennessee Press, 1986. Woodson argues that the footnotes Tolson later added to *Libretto for the Republic of Liberia*, suggested by poet Karl Shapiro, were not only meant to align his work with that of the high modernists (in particular, T. S. Eliot and Hart Crane) but also to blur the line between documentation and creation. Woodson argues that the footnotes became an additional stage of creativity for Tolson, insofar as they not only document sources but also recover modes of knowledge (African and Asian in particular) suppressed by Western history.

Tyrone Williams

JEAN TOOMER

Born: Washington, D.C.; December 26, 1894
Died: Doylestown, Pennsylvania; March 30, 1967

PRINCIPAL POETRY
"Banking Coal," 1922
"Blue Meridian," 1936
The Collected Poems of Jean Toomer, 1988

OTHER LITERARY FORMS

Most of the work of Jean Toomer (TEW-muhr) was in genres other than poetry. His one published volume of creative writing, *Cane* (1923), contains only fifteen poems, mostly short, and fourteen pieces that appear to be in prose. However, they are all informed with the poet's rather than the novelist's sensibility, and some of them are poems in all but line breaks, while all of them use assorted poetic devices either throughout or sporadically.

Toomer published several pieces of fiction after *Cane*, generally quite experimental inasmuch as they lacked plot, often included philosophical meditations, and indeed often worked more like poetry, with impressionistic scenes and descriptions and an emphasis on developing a theme through juxtaposition of sections rather than an overall sequence of action. Among these are "Winter on Earth" (*The Second American Caravan*, 1929), "Mr. Costyve Duditch" (*The Dial*, 1928), and "York Beach" (*New American Caravan*, 1929). The first two were collected in the posthumous volume *The Wayward and the Seeking* (1980), edited by Darwin T. Turner, along with a previously unpublished story from 1930, "Withered Skin of Berries," which is more in the style of *Cane*, though much longer than most of the pieces in that book.

Toomer published one short, fragmentary play during his lifetime, "Balo," in Alain Locke's collection *Plays of Negro Life* (1927), and two of several other plays which he wrote in *The Wayward and the Seeking*.

Nonfiction predominates in Toomer's work, indicating his concerns with philosophical and spiritual goals, as in "Race Problems and Modern Society"

(1929), "The Flavor of Man" (1949), and *Essentials: Definitions and Aphorisms* (privately printed in 1931, some of its aphorisms having been printed earlier in *The Dial* and *Crisis*, with many appearing much later in *The Wayward and the Seeking*). These aphorisms are occasionally poetic and certainly worthy of contemplation, but they might be stronger if incorporated into actual poems. Portions of several versions of Toomer's autobiography appear in *The Wayward and the Seeking*. The rest of his many unpublished works, including many poems, remain in the Toomer Collection of the Fisk University Library.

ACHIEVEMENTS

Jean Toomer's *Cane* is one of the most memorable and appealing books in African American literature, conveying a vivid sense of the life of southern blacks around 1920 (though little changed since the time of slavery) and showing clearly the conflicts between the feelings of black people and the desensitizing and spirit-diminishing urban life they found in the North. However, *Cane* is significant not only for its content but also for its innovative form and style. Its combination of prose and verse, stories and poems, produces a unified impression, with poems foreshadowing or commenting on adjacent stories and the stories and sketches exploring a multitude of perspectives on black life, rural and urban.

Toomer's impressionistic style, his seductive but not mechanical rhythms, his brilliant imagery and figurative language, and his manipulation of language to produce a wide range of emotional and literary effects were refreshing to many black writers during and after the Harlem Renaissance of the 1920's. Instead of adhering strictly to traditional European models of form and meter (like that of his major black contemporaries Claude McKay and Countée Cullen) or the literary realism and straightforward narrative style of black fiction to that date, he joined the progression of revolutionary poets and fiction writers who were creating literary modernism, from Walt Whitman on through James Joyce, D. H. Lawrence, Gertrude Stein, Sherwood Anderson, and T. S. Eliot, up to Toomer's friend and contemporary Hart Crane.

Very few of Toomer's other works come even close

Jean Toomer (Beinecke Rare Book and Manuscript Library, Yale University)

to the towering achievement of *Cane*, but its poems and poetic prose provided later writers a successful means of evoking the feel of the black experience. A reader can still sense echoes of its style in the evocative prose of novelist Toni Morrison.

BIOGRAPHY

Jean Toomer (born Nathan Eugene Toomer) spent most of his life resisting a specific racial label for himself. His childhood and youth were spent in white or racially mixed middle-class neighborhoods in Washington, and his parents were both light skinned. Jean's father left shortly after his birth and his mother died after remarrying, so that the most potent adult influences on his life were his maternal grandparents, with whom he lived until his twenties. His grandfather, P. B. S. Pinchback, had been elected lieutenant-governor in Reconstruction Louisiana and served as acting governor in 1873. Toomer believed that his victory was helped by his announcement that he had black blood, although Toomer denied knowing whether it was true.

One thing is clear: Pinchback had indeed served the Union cause in the "Corps d'Afrique."

Later in life, Toomer denied that he was a Negro—an acceptable statement if one understands his definition of "Negro" as one who identifies solely with the black race, for he, with certainly a great deal of non-black ancestry, saw himself as not white, either, but "American," a member of a new race which would unify the heretofore conflicting racial groups through a mixture of racial strains. The attainment of such an "American" race remained his goal throughout most of his life after *Cane*.

Toomer's education after high school was varied, from agriculture at the University of Wisconsin to the American College of Physical Training in Chicago. Rather than completing courses toward a formal degree, however, he pursued his own reading in literature and social issues while working at assorted jobs until he decided to devote all his efforts to writing.

The real nudge came in the form of a three-month stint as substitute principal of a school in a small Georgia town in the fall of 1921. He returned to Washington in November with material for a whole book. He published several poems and stories in assorted periodicals the following year and then gathered most of them and many new ones into a carefully structured book called *Cane*, published in 1923 by Boni and Liveright. The book caused a considerable stir among the influential white literati with whom he associated (such as Waldo Frank, Sherwood Anderson, and Hart Crane) and among black writers and intellectuals as well. However, in its two printings (the second in 1927), it sold fewer than a thousand copies.

That same year, Toomer met the Russian mystic George Gurdjieff and embraced his philosophy of higher consciousness. After studying with him in France, Toomer returned to spread his teachings in the United States. A ten-month marriage to a white poet, Margery Latimer, ended with her death in childbirth in 1932. Two years later, he married another white woman, Marjorie Content, and spent the rest of his life with her. This period in Toomer's life was largely devoted to self-improvement for himself and others, as he lectured and continued to write primarily philosophical and spiritually oriented work. He continued to publish

some literary works until 1936, when his career came virtually to an end, despite attempts to have other works published. He became a Quaker and maintained no further identity with the black race, dying in 1967 largely forgotten.

ANALYSIS

Jean Toomer was the writer of one book; no matter how often the phrase is used to disparage him, it cannot be denied. Beyond *Cane*, his only other works of value are the long poem "Blue Meridian," a small amount of short fiction, and his autobiographical writings. His plays, most of his other poetry, and his nonfiction are negligible, yet even if he had written only *Cane*, he would always be remembered as a major African American author—and primarily as a poet.

CANE

Cane is an eccentric book, experimental and unclassifiable in its combination of poems and what is technically prose—pieces which are generally developed as short stories (somewhat like those of Anderson or Joyce) but are occasionally "mere" sketches, sometimes prose poems without plot, encompassing no more than a few pages and conveying impressionistically the sense of a person's spirit. Some of the pieces approach drama, with conversation printed like dialogue, setting described as meticulously as for a stage designer, and action presented in the present tense.

Whether prose, drama, or verse, all are imbued with a poet's sensibility: precise depiction of details using all the senses vividly, a rhythmic quality without slavish adherence to metrics, a sensitivity to words, phrasing, variations of theme, a fine ear for sound, and a polished sense of organic structure. Few books, whether prose or verse, have less of the prosaic than this one, which can put readers in an almost unabated state of intensity and exaltation, drawing them in by language, sound, rhythm, and form.

Toomer's purpose in this work is to embody what he sees as the dying folk spirit of the South by depicting the lives of its people and re-creating their feelings through language and rhythm. *Cane* achieves a vivid sense of the sensuality of its women, the alternating anguish and joy of life in the South, the toughness and beauty of the land of Georgia. These themes appear primarily in the first third of the book; the second third moves into the city in the North, where blacks from the South have difficulty fitting into the white-dominated social patterns while retaining roots in the South; in the final third, Ralph Kabnis, a northern black man, comes South and the focus is on his conflict with the South, looking ahead to William Faulkner's *Absalom, Absalom!* (1936) and Quentin Compson's climatic cry "I don't hate the South!" Throughout the book, Toomer shows both attraction to the South and a sense of holding back from it—on the part of a narrator in the first third, of Kabnis in the last third, and of assorted northern-based characters in the middle third, who are losing touch with their black roots. The book, however, is hardly a glorification of the way of life of southern blacks: Kabnis notes that things are not so bad as the North thinks; yet the South still hosts an occasional lynching, as Toomer several times reminds his readers. Still, Toomer appreciates a vitality in southern blacks that disappears when they are removed from the land, a process that Toomer views as unfortunately inevitable in the modern world.

To create this sense of vitality and closeness to the land and the natural world, Toomer uses a vast array of references to nature—the pines, the cane fields, the sky at dusk, the red soil—as images themselves, as similes or metaphors in connection with his characters, or as recurring leitmotifs in the operatic development of his sketches. He uses rhythm and repetition to engage the reader in the immediacy of these sensory experiences. A close analysis of one of his pieces—"Karintha," the opening sketch in *Cane*—will illustrate Toomer's typical methods.

"KARINTHA"

Like other pieces in the book, "Karintha" opens with an epigraph, a songlike refrain of four lines that recurs throughout the sketch as a unifying device. The first of four paragraphs of varying lengths then introduces Karintha as a child, summing her up in the first sentence, which is poetically accretive rather than prosaically structured; the final adjective cluster echoes words from the epigraph's refrain. Two sentences in parallel construction follow, dealing with the actions the old men and the young men take with her, followed by two sentences in response to these, describing their respective feelings about her. The final sentence sums up the paragraph and "this interest of the male," with a metaphoric interpretation of it and a note of foreboding.

The second paragraph re-creates her girlhood in terms of concrete actions and images: visual (color, shape, light), auditory (sounds of feet, voice, silence), kinetic (running, wind), and tactile (stoning the cows, touching the earth). It sums up her sexual nature as well and ends with two sentences referring to the wishes of the old and young men from the first paragraph, regarding Karintha as she matures. Before Karintha is shown as a woman, the refrain of the epigraph is repeated, the first three lines each being cut by a few words. The new rhythm creates a pace appropriately faster than the wondering, more meditative earlier version.

The third paragraph makes assorted references to the subject matter and phrasing of earlier paragraphs. Repetitions of actual sentences and phrases and of sentence structure (in a series of short sentences showing what young men do for Karintha) evoke the sense of poetry, as does the second half of the paragraph, which, through indirection, reveals Karintha's murder of her infant. The birth is presented as a kind of emotionless miracle unconnected with Karintha herself, while the scene is given sensory richness. Juxtaposed, after ellipses, is the description of a nearby sawmill, its smoldering sawdust pile, and the heaviness of the smoke after Karintha's return. Ending this paragraph is a short song that someone makes up about smoke rising to "take my soul to Jesus," an unconsciously appropriate elegy for the unwanted baby.

The final paragraph begins as the third did, "Karintha is a woman," and then echoes the last sentence of the first paragraph: "Men do not know that the soul of her was a growing thing ripened too soon." Toomer then suggests her unbreachable remoteness from men; the last sentence recalls the first in this sketch, describing her at twenty in the phrases used to describe her as a child. After a last repetition of her name, followed by ellipses, comes a repetition of the epigraph, followed by an ominous repetition of its last two words, "Goes down," and then more ellipses, hinting at the inevitable descent and defeat of this beautiful, vital creature, brought to maturity too soon through misuse by men.

Though printed as prose, this piece is essentially poetic; the outer details of Karintha's life are merely hinted, but Toomer's poetic prose gives a full sense of Karintha's person and appeal through the precise sensory details of the second paragraph, the recurring patterns of the old and young men's responses to her, and the use of songs as commentary. The echoes and repetitions of images and phrases act as leitmotifs, and Toomer's careful arrangement of them gives the piece a satisfying structure and a strong sense of Karintha's doom, trapped in an unchanging pattern.

FORM, STYLE, AND TONE

Such leitmotifs, along with vivid imagery and sentence patterns that are short, repeated, and often fragmentary, are used throughout the prose pieces of *Cane* in place of rhyme and meter and line division to produce the quality of poetry. Indeed, many of these pieces (including "Rhobert," "Calling Jesus," "Seventh Street") must be read, like "Karintha," more as poetry than as fiction.

In the pieces clearly printed as poetry, Toomer is less experimental. Many of his poems use orthodox rhyme schemes and meters that a Henry Wadsworth Longfellow or James Russell Lowell would approve. However, scarce as the poems in *Cane* are, they cover a variety of forms that few single books of poetry display. "Song of the Son," for example, is skillfully rhymed, beautifully evoking in five stanzas of flowing iambic pentameter the southern music that the poet is trying to capture in literature—as he says in this poem, before it vanishes. There are poems of rhymed couplets and brief pieces such as the Imagists might produce. There is a "Cotton Song," such as the work songs that slaves or free but poor farmhands might sing. There is much free verse, notably in "Harvest Song." Toomer's choices are not arbitrary; they suit the moods and subjects of their respective poems, conveying the spectrum of feelings that the writer wishes to present, from joy and exaltation to bitterness and despair.

Toomer also varies style and tone, as well as form, to suit theme and mood. Grim and laconic irony flavors "Conversion," as the African succumbs to "a white-faced sardonic god." "Georgia Dusk" offers lush images both of southern life and of the African past (a recurring motif throughout the book). "Portrait in Georgia," with its short free-verse lines, reads like a catalog of bodily parts, such as an auctioneer would have prepared. Each is described through images of southern white violence: "lyncher's rope," "fagots," "scars," "blisters," "the ash of black flesh after flame." This poem makes no explicit statement, but the juxtaposition of human parts with these images, presented so simply and concisely, evokes a subtle sense of horror and sets up an appropriately ominous mood for the following story, "Blood-Burning Moon," which ends with an actual lynching. However attractive may be the Georgia of pines, red soil, sweet-smelling cane, and beauteous dusks, Toomer insists on reminding his reader of the dangers there as well, even without explicit condemnation of the bigoted whites or the oppressive social system. Toomer works by indirection, but without diminished effect.

"HARVEST SONG"

A similarly strong but quite different effect is achieved in "Harvest Song," which presents a field worker suffering at the end of a long day from chill, hunger, thirst, and fatigue. Each poetic "line" is made up of one or more sentences and takes up between one and five lines of print on the page. These sentences are generally short, simple statements that the speaker can barely utter, and they are often repeated, emphasizing his basic human needs, which remain unsatisfied. Toomer's words may not be those that the worker would actually use, but they mirror his thoughts closely, just as the prose pieces of *Cane* give a clear sense of their characters' minds and lives without using their actual language. The simple sentences and their repetition give an accurate sense of the worker's numbness. The poem's last long line (five sentences) is a more exalted outburst, though still despairing: The harvester beats his soft palms against the stubble in his field, causing himself pain that takes away his awareness of hunger, as the last sentence makes shockingly clear. "Harvest Song" indeed! The speaker hardly feels like singing with his throat parched from thirst; and what he harvests for himself means only more pain. Through the use of first-person narration and a simple style, Toomer evokes not pity for the poor worker, not an external look as in Edwin Markham's "The Man with the Hoe," but rather an empathy from within, allowing the reader to participate fully in the experience.

SPIRITUAL AND PHILOSOPHICAL BELIEFS

Too often, unfortunately, Toomer's later poetry drops the effective devices used in *Cane* and becomes didactic, explicitly philosophical, lacking *Cane*'s brilliantly realized images of concrete reality or its sharp, often startling metaphors. Toomer was mightily inspired by his few months in Georgia, and his sojourn even affected his interpretations of his own more familiar Washington and New York life; but after he had said what he had to say about the South, and the North in relation to the South, he seems to have exhausted his inspiration, except for his more "universal" themes, with only a little sense of poetry left, to be used in "Blue Meridian" and his stories "Winter on Earth" and "Withered Skin of Berries." The latter story returned Toomer to the lyrical style and poetic sense of structure of the *Cane* stories, but for the most part, Toomer preferred to ignore stylistic and literary matters and chose to express his spiritual and philosophical beliefs, largely influenced by Gurdjieff's teachings, urging a regeneration of humanity that would eliminate the differences imposed by racial and other categories and bring people closer to God, one another, and the natural world.

"BLUE MERIDIAN"

This is the point that Toomer makes explicitly in his last major work, the long poem "Blue Meridian," first published in full in *New American Caravan* (1936) after a selection from an earlier version had appeared in *Adelphi* and *Pagany*. A further revised version is printed in Langston Hughes and Arna Bontemps's anthology *The Poetry of the Negro, 1746-1949* (1949), which places more emphasis on God and more clearly reveals Toomer's notion of the transformed America. A few of the more minor revisions are for the better. This is the version published in *The Wayward and the Seeking*, with some incidental changes.

"Blue Meridian" follows a structure much like that of Walt Whitman's longer poems, such as "Passage to India" or "Crossing Brooklyn Ferry," with recurring phrases or stanzas, often significantly altered. While it is not divided into individual sections, as T. S. Eliot's *The Waste Land* (1922) and Hart Crane's *The Bridge* (1930) are—nor does it use the range of poetic forms of which Eliot and Crane availed themselves—it nevertheless follows those poems in being an examination

and criticism of the twentieth century world, achieving a multifaceted view by varying tone and form.

Written largely in a hortatory, exalted style in an effort to invoke Toomer's higher spiritual goals for a better world and unified humankind, "Blue Meridian" explores the past and current conditions of America. The European, African, and "red" races are presented in appropriate images—even stereotypes—each being shown as incomplete. Toomer's goal, as in much of his prose, is to achieve a new race beyond individual racial identities, a "universal human being" to be called the "blue meridian," the highest stage of development beyond white and black, beyond divisions of East and West, of religion, race, class, sex, and occupational classification, and transcending the materialism of a commercial culture and the private concerns of individuals. The message is not so different from Whitman's, except for greater criticism of modern business and the insistence on the mingling of the races.

DETRACTIONS OF LATER WORK

Racial themes and the black experience are missing from Toomer's later poems—and even some of his earlier ones, such as "Banking Coal" (*Crisis*, 1922). He was living with a white wife, quite isolated from the African American literary world, or from any literary world at all. Certainly one should not say that a black writer (even one with so little black ancestry as Toomer) should write only on black themes, but any writer should write out of direct experience; too much of Toomer's poetry aside from *Cane* is vague and didactic, too intentionally "universal," too generally spiritualized, and essentially prosaic, like his aphorisms, which lack the bite of Ralph Waldo Emerson's.

Unfortunately, Toomer's vocabulary in this later poetry—including "Blue Meridian"—too often emulates that of Whitman at his most inflated moments, even when Toomer has a true poetic idea, as in "The Lost Dancer," which opens: "Spatial depths of being survive/ The birth to death recurrences. . . ." It is not so much the Latinate vocabulary, which Toomer's great contemporaries Crane and Wallace Stevens also used, but rather that, while they made much of the orotund, sensual sounds and suggestiveness of Latinate words, Toomer's word choices are flat and vague, words made familiar through bombastic social-science jargon.

Whereas the *Cane* poems stand out particularly for the vitality of their imagery, the apt metaphors and similes in "Face" and "Portrait in Georgia," the richness of language and sensory detail in "Song of the Son" and "Georgia Dusk," and the harshness of the concrete nouns, verbs, and adjectives in "Harvest Song," images in the later poetry are greatly minimized. Here Toomer abandons the exalted Romantic eloquence of "Song of the Son" and the verbal and emotional starkness of "Harvest Song" in favor of making philosophical statements.

At his best, Toomer was a brilliant artist in words, a sensitive portrayer of the life he lived and observed, as well as a sincere and concerned member of the human race. *Cane* will forever keep his name alive and arouse an interest in his other work, however inferior most of it has turned out to be. The musical quality of his best poetry and prose will be admired, not for its mere beauty but for its aptness to its subjects: the beauty and appeal as well as the tragedy of the life of the South.

OTHER MAJOR WORKS

SHORT FICTION: "Mr. Costyve Duditch," 1928; "York Beach," 1929.

PLAY: *Balo*, pb. 1927.

NONFICTION: "Race Problems and Modern Society," 1929; "Winter on Earth," 1929; *Essentials: Definitions and Aphorisms*, 1931; "The Flavor of Man," 1949; *Jean Toomer: Selected Essays and Literary Criticism*, 1996 (Robert B. Jones, editor); *The Letters of Jean Toomer, 1919-1924*, 2006 (Mark Whalan, editor).

MISCELLANEOUS: *Cane*, 1923 (prose and poetry); *The Wayward and the Seeking*, 1980 (prose and poetry; Darwin T. Turner, editor); *A Jean Toomer Reader: Selected Unpublished Writings*, 1993 (Frederik L. Rusch, editor).

BIBLIOGRAPHY

Byrd, Rudolph. *Jean Toomer's Years with Gurdjieff: Portrait of an Artist, 1923-1936*. Athens: University of Georgia Press, 1990. A good introduction to Toomer's years of studying Orientalism and the mystical philosophy of George Gurdjieff. It indicates that, although Toomer was an African American writer, his concerns were primarily spiritual and philosophical rather than social and ethnic. It is a fascinating account of one part of Toomer's life.

Fabre, Geneviève, and Michel Feith, eds. *Jean Toomer and the Harlem Renaissance*. New Brunswick, N.J.: Rutgers University Press, 2001. A collection of essays that reexamine Toomer, placing the novelist among his contemporaries in America and in Europe.

Ford, Karen Jackson. *Split-Gut Song: Jean Toomer and the Poetics of Modernity*. Tuscaloosa: University of Alabama Press, 2005. A study of Toomer's poetics, concentrating on *Cane* but also describing the poet's later life.

Grant, Nathan. *Masculinist Impulses: Toomer, Hurston, Black Writing, and Modernity*. Columbia: University of Missouri Press, 2004. Grant compares and contrasts the works of Toomer and Zora Neale Hurston, looking at the ideas of masculinity and modernism.

Griffin, John Chandler. *Biography of American Author Jean Toomer, 1894-1967*. Lewiston, N.Y.: Edwin Mellen Press, 2002. The author traces Toomer's life from its beginnings to his work on *Cane*, to his meeting with Gurdjieff, and to the decline in his later years.

Kerman, Cynthia. *The Lives of Jean Toomer: A Hunger for Wholeness*. Baton Rouge: Louisiana State University Press, 1988. This book gives an account of the various stages of Toomer's life and his attempts to find spiritual guidance and revelation throughout his lifetime. An interesting account of a fascinating life.

Scruggs, Charles, and Lee VanDemarr. *Jean Toomer and the Terrors of American History*. Philadelphia: University of Pennsylvania Press, 1998. Provides critical evaluation of *Cane* and other Toomer works. Includes bibliographical references and an index.

Taylor, Paul Beekman. *Shadows of Heaven*. York Beach, Maine: S. Weiser, 1998. Examines the lives and works of Toomer, George Gurdjieff, and A. R. Orage.

Vetter, Lara. *Modernist Writings and Religio-scientific Discourse: H. D., Loy, and Toomer*. New York: Palgrave Macmillan, 2010. Vetter examines Toomer, H. D., and Mina Loy in terms of how their writings reflect modernism, science, and spirituality.

Scott Giantvalley

NATASHA TRETHEWEY

Born: Gulfport, Mississippi; April 26, 1966

PRINCIPAL POETRY

Domestic Work, 2000
Bellocq's Ophelia, 2002
Native Guard, 2006

OTHER LITERARY FORMS

Natasha Trethewey (TREHTH-eh-way) is known primarily for her poetry.

ACHIEVEMENTS

Natasha Trethewey was awarded the Pulitzer Prize in poetry in 2007 for *Native Guard*. *Domestic Work*, *Bellocq's Ophelia*, and *Native Guard* all won Mississippi Institute of Arts and Letters Book Prizes (2001, 2003, and 2007, respectively). *Domestic Work* was selected by Rita Dove, former poet laureate of the United States, as winner of the 1999 Cave Canem Poetry Prize. Trethewey twice received the Lillian Smith Book Award for Poetry (2001, 2007). She has been awarded fellowships from the Guggenheim Foundation, the Radcliffe Institute for Advanced Study at Harvard (the Bunting Fellowship), the National Endowment for the Arts, and the Rockefeller Foundation. In 2008, she received the Mississippi Governor's Award for Literary Excellence and was also named Georgia Woman of the Year. She has also been inducted into the Fellowship of Southern Writers. Trethewey has been recognized for her blending of autobiography and history. She is also noted for examining the complexity of biracial identity.

BIOGRAPHY

Natasha Trethewey is the daughter of Eric Trethewey, a white Canadian immigrant and poet, and his wife, Gwendolyn Ann Turnbough, a black social worker. Her parents met as students in Kentucky, but because interracial marriage was illegal in the state at that time, her parents had to go to Ohio to marry. Trethewey spent her early years in Mississippi, but when her parents divorced when she was six, she moved with her mother to Atlanta. She then spent summers with her mother's family in Mississippi and visited with her father, who was at Tulane University in New Orleans. With her father's encouragement, she began to write both poetry and fiction.

While Trethewey was a student at the University of Georgia in 1985, her mother was murdered by her former second husband whom she had divorced a year earlier. Trethewey persevered at the university and earned her bachelor's degree in English in 1989. She spent several months as a social worker in Augusta, Georgia, before entering Hollins College (now University), where her father was teaching English. She studied En-

Natasha Trethewey (AP/Wide World Photos)

glish and creative writing and was awarded an M.A. in 1991. She then enrolled at the University of Massachusetts at Amherst, where she earned an M.F.A. in poetry in 1995.

Around this time, Trethewey became associated with the Dark Room Collective, a group of young African American writers founded by Thomas Sayers Ellis and Sharan Strange. Their purpose was to bring together established and young black writers. Trethewey's work started to appear in literary journals, and her poems began to be selected for anthologies. Her first book of poetry, *Domestic Work*, was published in 2000.

In 1998, she married Brett Gadsden, a professor of African American studies. Trethewey began her teaching career at Auburn University in Alabama in 1997. In 2001, she became a member of the faculty at Emory University in Atlanta, Georgia, where she became professor of English and the Phillis Wheatley Distinguished Chair in Poetry.

ANALYSIS

Natasha Trethewey often writes of the intersection of her personal and family history with public history. Her themes include the exploration of dichotomies such as that of insider and outsider, physical rootedness and psychological estrangement, memory and forgetting. Because of her background, she often examines the significance of racial identity with a focus on the personal and social questions that arise from racial categorization. She is also interested in recovering the stories of those who have been overlooked in history. Conscious of form, she skillfully uses stanza patterns and rhyme as well as free verse.

DOMESTIC WORK

The title of *Domestic Work*, which also serves as the title of part 2 of the collection, indicates the overall theme. In general, it refers to the many ordinary jobs or duties that help a society or a family run smoothly but that are often overlooked. Most of the poems feature strong imagery. In part 2, dedicated to Trethewey's maternal grandmother, poems explore the various jobs open to an African American woman of the mid-twentieth century: housekeeper, elevator operator, hair stylist, factory seamstress, and self-employed seamstress.

Some poems describe the personal work of maintaining a marriage and raising a child. In an interview in *Five Points: A Journal of Literature and Art* (September, 2007), Trethewey says that in this early work, she "was already, by using dates or other historical events within the poems, working to blend personal or family stories with collective history." This subject, she realizes, is a "long term obsession" of hers.

Parts 3 and 4 relate to Trethewey's childhood and her parents. "White Lies," "Microscope," and "Saturday Matinee" consider Trethewey's feelings about her biracial identity. In "White Lies," the speaker allows a white classmate to assume that she too is white. When her mother discovers this lie, she washes out her mouth with, ironically, Ivory soap, telling her that this will clean her and her lying tongue. The daughter swallows the soap, believing that it will make her "ivory" from the inside out.

The final poem of the volume, "Limen," was selected for *The Best American Poetry 2000*. The word "limen" comes from the Latin word meaning "threshold." In the poem, the insistent knocking of a woodpecker on a catalpa tree becomes for Trethewey "... a door knocker/ to the cluttered house of memory ...," and she imagines she sees her mother again, hanging sheets on a clothesline. This experience sums up the theme of several poems in the collection: the sense of being on the boundary of two worlds. In "Limen," the boundary could be the line between the present world and memory or between reality and imagination.

BELLOCQ'S OPHELIA

Bellocq's Ophelia, named a notable book by the American Library Association in 2003, centers on the life of Ophelia, a New Orleans prostitute of the early twentieth century. Ophelia tells her story in verse letters to a former teacher and in diary entries, which are a free-verse sonnet sequence. She traces her growth from someone who is an object for others to one who asserts control in her own life. Trethewey's character was inspired by the historical photographs of E. J. Bellocq, who photographed New Orleans prostitutes in the early twentieth century.

The child of a white man and a black woman, Ophelia is pale enough to pass for white. Intrigued by photography when Bellocq takes her picture, Ophelia buys herself a Kodak camera and begins framing her world herself ("Letters from Storyville. September 1911"). The last poem in the book, "Vignette," completes the photography metaphor. In it, Bellocq carefully arranges the objects in the camera's frame, including Ophelia, but after the flash, she steps out of the frame to live her life, free of the constricting frames imposed by others. Her last note to her friend reveals that she is leaving New Orleans and heading west.

NATIVE GUARD

In *Native Guard*, dedicated to her mother, Trethewey memorializes those who have no monument (on a personal level, her mother, and in history, the Louisiana Native Guard). When asked about the significance of the title beyond its literal meaning, Trethewey responded, in the *Five Points* interview, that she thinks that a "native guardian" takes care of "not only personal memory but also of collective memory—and that is certainly what poets are often charged with doing, representing the collective memory of a people." She continues, "And as a native daughter, a native guardian, that is my charge. To my mother and her memory, preservation." In this volume, she also claims her own place in southern literature.

The poems of part 1 contain memories of Trethewey's mother and emotions about her loss. "Graveyard Blues" is a haunting blues sonnet that describes the day her mother was buried. The sonnet uses four triplets following the blues format, rather than three quatrains, with a final couplet. "After Your Death," selected for *The Best American Poetry 2003*, meditates on the emptiness in the speaker's life after her mother's death. When she thinks of tomorrow, she imagines it as an empty bowl that must somehow be filled.

Focusing on Mississippi, part 2 contains some freestanding poems, a section of poems inspired by old photographs ("Scenes from a Documentary History of Mississippi"), and the sonnet sequence "Native Guard." The subject of "Native Guard" is the Louisiana Native Guard, an African American regiment of the Union Army assigned to guard Confederate prisoners at Fort Massachusetts on Ship Island in Louisiana during the Civil War. Trethewey's family often went to Ship Island for vacations when she was younger, and she ob-

served the plaque placed to honor Confederate prisoners who were held there, but there was no monument to commemorate the guards. Not until she was an adult did she learn that the guards there were members of one of the first black units in the Union Army. She was inspired to investigate their story.

The persona of the sonnets is a former slave who was taught to read and write by his former master. Irony abounds in the poems. For example, the former slaves guard those who would enslave them, and the literate black narrator writes letters for the illiterate white prisoners. Another irony is found in the colonel's words after the Guard are fired on by their own side in an engagement. The colonel coldly comforts the troops with the idea that their names will be remembered. The narrator, more realistically and accurately, thinks, "Some names shall deck the page of history/ as it is written on stone. Some will not." The sonnet sequence begins with "Truth be told" as the first words, and these are also the last words of the last sonnet, reminding the reader to seek the truth in history. The form of "Native Guard" is an adaptation of the sonnet sequence known as a crown of sonnets, or corona sonnet, a series of sonnets with repeating lines. In Trethewey's sequence, the last line of the previous sonnet becomes the first line of the next sonnet, and "Truth be told," the last three words of the last sonnet, repeats the first three words of the first sonnet to complete the sequence.

In part 3, poems allude to poet Walt Whitman, specific southern writers (Robert Penn Warren, William Faulkner, Allen Tate, and the Vanderbilt University-associated Fugitive poets), and *Gone with the Wind* (1939), as Trethewey asserts her place in southern literature as an African American female poet. In "Pastoral," a free-verse sonnet, she imagines herself being photographed with the Fugitive poets (all dead now), who championed southern traditionalism and regionalism, as though taking her place as a modern representative of the southern literary tradition. The poem also acknowledges her mixed emotions about the South. "My Mother Dreams Another Country" describes her mother's dream of a country where no hurtful words will be addressed to her biracial child. The poem ends with a television image of the American flag waving as the national anthem plays, an ironic but hopeful symbol of what the country could be. The final poem in this section, "South," weaves together many of the themes from throughout the book. The repeated phrase "I returned" emphasizes Trethewey's connection to the South, claimed as her "native land" in the final line, despite her continuing ambivalence about it.

BIBLIOGRAPHY

Debo, Annette. "Ophelia Speaks: Resurrecting Lives in Natasha Trethewey's *Bellocq's Ophelia*." *African American Review* 42, no. 2 (Summer, 2008): 201-215. Analyzes the poetry in *Bellocq's Ophelia* and discusses the social and cultural milieu of early twentieth century New Orleans.

McFarland, Ron. "*Native Guard*." In *Masterplots II: African American Literature*, edited by Tyrone Williams. Rev. ed. Pasadena, Calif: Salem Press, 2009. Provides an in-depth analysis of *Native Guard*, looking at themes and critical analysis.

Milne, Ira Mark, ed. *Poetry for Students*. Vol. 27. Detroit: Thomson/Gale Group, 2008. Contains an analysis of "Native Guard."

Mlinko, Ange. "More than Meets the I." Review of *Native Guard*. *Poetry* 191, no. 1 (October, 2007): 56-59. Comments on the theme of synthesis in reviewing *Native Guard*.

Shipers, Carrie. Review of *Native Guard*. *Prairie Schooner* 80, no. 4 (Winter, 2006): 199-201. Praises Trethewey's control of emotion and of form in the poems.

Solomon, Deborah. "Native Daughter." *The New York Times Magazine*, May 13, 2007, 15. Covers some biographical information and generally discusses *Native Guard*.

Trethewey, Natasha. "An Interview with Natasha Trethewey." Interview by Pearl Amelia McHaney. *Five Points: A Journal of Literature and Art* 11, no. 3 (September, 2007): 96-116. Contains a lengthy discussion of *Native Guard*, including comments on the specific poetic forms that Trethewey used. Briefly covers the two previous books and includes information on her life.

_____. "Q&A/Natasha Trethewey, Pulitzer Prize-Winning Poet and Emory Professor: 'Poems Captivate Me in a Way that Nothing Else Does.'"

Interview by Teresa Weaver. *The Atlanta Journal-Constitution*, April 29, 2007, pp. 1B, B4. Contains comments on Trethewey's life, her winning the Pulitzer, the South, her writing process, and the role of poetry.

Wojahn, David. "History Shaping Selves: Four Poets." *Southern Review* 43, no. 1 (Winter, 2007): 218-231. Discusses *Native Guard* as revealing growth in Trethewey's technical skill and as further developing themes she treated in her two previous volumes.

Young, Kevin. Review of *Domestic Work*. *Ploughshares* 26, no. 4 (Winter, 2000): 205. Refers to motifs of hands at work, of photography, and of absence. Observes Trethewey's attention to poetic form.

Carol J. Luther

FREDERICK GODDARD TUCKERMAN

Born: Boston, Massachusetts; February 4, 1821
Died: Greenfield, Massachusetts; May 9, 1873

PRINCIPAL POETRY

Poems, 1860
The Sonnets of Frederick Goddard Tuckerman, 1931 (Witter Bynner, editor)
The Complete Poems of Frederick Goddard Tuckerman, 1965 (N. Scott Momaday, editor)

OTHER LITERARY FORMS

Frederick Goddard Tuckerman is recognized primarily for his poety. Like Henry David Thoreau, he was an accomplished naturalist who kept a journal, and during his lifetime, he published observations of astronomical and meteorological phenomena.

ACHIEVEMENTS

Following almost complete obscurity during the late 1800's, Frederick Goddard Tuckerman has received considerable acclaim from modern critics and writers. In 1931, Witter Bynner ranked his sonnets "with the noblest in the language." Yvor Winters, in 1965, placed him with Emily Dickinson and Jones Very as "the three most remarkable American poets of the nineteenth century." Galway Kinnell, at a 1981 reading in Kansas City, Missouri, called Tuckerman the equal of Walt Whitman, Stephen Crane, and Dickinson. These judgments have, to some extent, been validated by the inclusion of Tuckerman's verse in recent anthologies. Although Tuckerman published only one book of poems, in 1860, his current critical recognition—particularly for his sonnets—is high. Not only is he praised for the quality of his verse, but also he is seen as an important figure opposing the mainstream of nineteenth century American Romanticism.

BIOGRAPHY

Frederick Goddard Tuckerman was born on February 4, 1821, in Boston, the youngest son of Edward and Sophia (May) Tuckerman. The poet's father was a partner in the Boston firm of Tuckerman, Rogers and Cushing, Wholesalers and Importers; he died in 1842, leaving an ample inheritance. Frederick—named for F. W. Goddard (a kinsman whose accidental death in 1820 while crossing the Lake of Zurich was the subject of an elegy by his traveling companion, William Wordsworth)—prepared for college at the private school of Bishop John Henry Hopkins and at the Boston Latin School. He entered Harvard with the class of 1841, but eye trouble forced him to leave college for a time. Later, he entered the law school, graduated in 1842, and, after reading law in the office of Edward D. Schier, was admitted to the Suffolk bar in 1844. In 1847, he moved from Boston to Greenfield, in western Massachusetts. On June 17, 1847, he married Hannah Lucinda Jones, daughter of David S. Jones of Greenfield. They had three children: Edward, Anna, and Frederick. At Greenfield, Tuckerman abandoned the practice of law and lived a life of relative seclusion and retirement. He studied botany and astronomy, and he wrote poetry. Twice he traveled abroad. On the first of these excursions, in 1851, he met Alfred, Lord Tennyson. During the second visit, in 1855, he was Tennyson's guest at Farringford, the Isle of Wight. The friendship between the two men appears to have been cordial.

Tuckerman wrote to his brother Edward, "At parting Mr. Tennyson gave me the original ms. of 'Locksley Hall,' a favour of which I may be justly proud, as he says he has never done such a thing in his life before, for anybody."

Several of Tuckerman's poems first appeared in *The Living Age*, *Putnam's*, and *The Atlantic Monthly*. In 1854, he had prepared a manuscript version of a book of poems. It is possible that he carried this manuscript with him when he visited Tennyson in 1855. In 1857, within a week after the birth of their third child, Hannah Tuckerman died. His wife's death caused Tuckerman to become even more withdrawn from the public. It was not until 1860 that the poems in the 1854 manuscript were printed, privately, by Ticknor and Fields of Boston. The volume was reprinted twice in the United States, in 1864 and 1869; there was also an English edition in 1863. Tuckerman sent complimentary copies of the 1860 *Poems* to an impressive list of his contemporaries: In addition to William Gladstone, the list included Ralph Waldo Emerson, Nathaniel Hawthorne, Henry Wadsworth Longfellow, William Cullen Bryant, and Jones Very (who had been his tutor, briefly, at Harvard). Thereafter, although he continued to write (his last sonnet sequence was written in 1872), he apparently made no further effort to gain public recognition. Tuckerman died Friday, May 9, 1873, at his boarding place, the American House, in Greenfield, Massachusetts.

ANALYSIS

Frederick Goddard Tuckerman's career as a poet illustrates a typical pattern in American letters: Honored by some recognition during his lifetime, he received virtually no critical attention until 1931, when his poetry was rediscovered, reexamined, and placed back on the reading lists of American scholars. This critical revival—like that of the Metaphysical school of poetry or that of the poetry of Robert Browning—has been sustained primarily in the academic world. With this pattern in mind, it is difficult to arrive at an objective evaluation of Tuckerman's work. Contemporaries such as Emerson, Hawthorne, and Longfellow gave his poetry careful praise. Emerson was most enthusiastic, commenting favorably on Tuckerman's "love of native flowers, the skill to name them and delight in words that are melodies. . . ." Hawthorne judged the 1860 volume of poems to be "A remarkable one," but he cautioned:

> I question whether the poems will obtain a very early or wide acceptance from the public . . . because their merit does not lie upon the surface, but must be looked for with faith and sympathy, and a kind of insight as when you look into a carbuncle to discover its hidden fire.

Longfellow assured Tuckerman that he had a "very favorable" opinion of the poems, but, like Hawthorne, he warned that "external success with the world" might be something quite different from "internal success."

"RHOTRUDA"

Tuckerman's "Rhotruda," which Emerson singled out for praise, is a good example of the kind of narrative poetry that won Tuckerman the cautious approval of his contemporaries. The poem, set in the time of Charlemagne, is about two lovers, Rhotruda and Eginardus. Visiting Rhotruda after curfew one night, Eginardus is trapped by a snowstorm; he cannot return to his room across the courtyard because the snow would reveal his footsteps. Rhotruda carries him on her shoulders so that only her footsteps mark the snow. Charlemagne, however, has seen the act. The next morning, he confronts the lovers with the truth. Instead of sentencing Eginardus to death, however, he orders the two lovers to marry. The final image of the poem is vividly expressed:

> like a picture framed in battle-pikes
> And bristling swords, it hangs before our view—
> The palace court white with the fallen snow,
> The good king leaning out into the night,
> And Rhotruda bearing Eginard on her back.

It is Tuckerman's unconventional sonnets, however, rather than his more traditional Tennysonian narratives, that have won for him his current recognition. Witter Bynner, in his appreciative introduction to the sonnets, sounded the keynote in Tuckerman's revival by recognizing in his work a style "as modern as any twentieth century sonneteer." He defended Tuckerman's liberties with metrics and rhyme schemes, asserting: "He was as tenderly conscious of his form as

was ever any maker of the sonnet. Instead of bungling or staling the sonnet-form, he renewed it and, moulding it to his emotion, made it inevitable." Bynner also praised the intellectual honesty that Tuckerman brought to his work: "Never did a man write poetry more straightly to himself—with nothing fictitious. He is isolated in an intense integrity toward nature, toward his own mind, and toward the unknown God."

SONNET X

Sonnet X, in the fourth series of sonnets (*The Complete Poems of Frederick Goddard Tuckerman*), dated 1860-1872, illustrates the qualities of Tuckerman's poetry that Bynner most admired. The first eight lines are marked by uneven metrics; one line has thirteen syllables. The rhyme scheme begins as a traditional Italian sonnet but skews itself into a curiously distorted figure: *abba, cdeedc, fggf*. In substance, the sonnet seems to follow the traditional Italian form: question, followed by answer. The question, however, is multiple: The listener is asked whether he has seen "reversed the prophet's miracle" (the worm that takes on the appearance of a twig), or whether he has wondered at the "craft that makes/ The twirling spider at once invisible," or "heard the singing sand," or "ever plucked the little chick-wintergreen star/ And tasted the sour of its leaf?" The answer is both mysterious and promising:

> Then come
> With me betimes, and I will show thee more
> Than these, of nature's secrecies the least:
> In the first morning, overcast and chill,
> And in the day's young sunshine, seeking still
> For earliest flowers and gathering to the east.

"REFRIGERIUM"

N. Scott Momaday, in his introduction to *The Complete Poems of Frederick Goddard Tuckerman*, continued in the direction initiated by Bynner. Momaday called Tuckerman's view of nature "noticeably different than that which predominates in the literature of his time and place," noting, "Where Emerson found realized in nature the transcendent spirit of the universe, Tuckerman saw only a various and inscrutable mask." Momaday characterized Tuckerman as a poet who kept "the stage properties of contemporary Romantic literature" but defined the Romantic sense of isolation "in terms of intellectual honesty rather than self-reliance"; who celebrated "fact" rather than "sentiment"; who trained his attention "upon the surfaces rather than the symbols of his world." "Tuckerman," Momaday wrote, "was a man who made herbariums. . . . His poems are remarkable, point-blank descriptions of nature; they are filled with small, precise, and whole things: purring bees and vervain spikes, shives and amaryllis, wind flowers and stramony."

Even in the sentimental "Refrigerium," this gift for description is evident. The poem, in three stanzas of seven lines each, is a lament for a lost love, "lying/ In a slumber sweet and cold." The specific details—the natural objects and furnishings of earth's vast "refrigerium"—are, however, presented with a naturalist's objectivity and accuracy: "Let the slow rain come and bring/ Brake and stargrass, speedwell, harebell,/ All the fulness of the spring. . . ." In many ways, the specificity of details contributes to the sentiment. The speaker notes, for example, how graves have run together in "the blending earth," the stones even being linked together by spider webs.

"THE CRICKET"

Winters, in the foreword to *The Complete Poems of Frederick Goddard Tuckerman*, sees in Tuckerman a modern sensibility that rivals that of the French Symbolists with its structure of "controlled association." "The Cricket," not published until 1950, illustrates what Winters most admires about Tuckerman's verse: imagery, combined with abstract statement sufficient to support a theme "of some intellectual scope." The poem, in five sections, is an ode (in the tradition of the "great odes" of John Dryden, Thomas Gray, John Keats, and William Wordsworth). In the first section, the poet invokes as his muse "a little cooing cricket." In section 2, the speaker describes, with concrete, vivid detail, the sleepy afternoon; by the end of the day, the cricket muse has multiplied: "From tingling tassle, blade, and sheath,/ Rising from nets of river vines,/ Winrows and ricks . . ./ Rising and falling like the sea,/ Acres of cricks!" In section 3, the significance of the poet's choice of muse is made clear: The cricket is both celebrant of sunshine and "bringer of all things dark." In section 4, the speaker recalls the classical role of the

cricket as a singer of grief. In section 5, the speaker brings together the themes of the preceding sections: praise, change, life, death. The poem concludes with a stoical celebration of the limited possibilities that life offers: "Rejoice! rejoice! whilst yet the hours exist—/ Rejoice or mourn, and let the world swing on/ Unmoved by cricket song of thee or me."

CRITICAL RECEPTION

Tuckerman's present reputation seems to be based on two characteristics: the close observation of nature—of facts rather than symbols—that placed him in opposition to his contemporaries and a concern with the metaphysical enigma of life that gives his poetry a peculiarly modern tension and pessimism. Some critics have seen this latter quality as "a kind of chronic melancholy which for the most part appears to be indulgence." Others, however—particularly Momaday—value Tuckerman's poetry for both its artistic and its intellectual opposition to the mainstream of American Romanticism.

BIBLIOGRAPHY

Donoghue, Denis. *Connoisseurs of Chaos: Ideas of Order in Modern American Poetry.* 2d ed. New York: Columbia University Press, 1984. This wide-ranging study devotes a chapter to recurrent oppositional themes in Tuckerman's poetry: public and private, human and natural, physical and metaphysical, and truth and ambiguity. Also offers brief comparisons of Tuckerman to other modern poets such as Emily Dickinson, T. S. Eliot, William Empson, Wallace Stevens, and Walt Whitman.

England, Eugene. *Beyond Romanticism: Tuckerman's Life and Poetry.* Albany: State University of New York Press, 1991. A combined biography and critical study, and the best source for information about Tuckerman. Written by the foremost expert on the poet, the book examines how Tuckerman was molded by, and yet reacted against, Romanticism. Includes extensive readings of individual poems, an index, and an exhaustive bibliography.

_____. "Tuckerman and Tennyson: 'Two Friends . . . on Either Side of the Atlantic.'" *New England Quarterly* 57 (June, 1984): 225-239. Essay explores how Tuckerman's poetry was strongly influenced by his friendship with Alfred, Lord Tennyson. The first half examines letters between the two men; the second half demonstrates how, through his close study of the English poet, Tuckerman moved beyond him as a model and established his own unique poetic identity.

Golden, Samuel. *Frederick Goddard Tuckerman*. New York: Twayne, 1966. Provides basic information about Tuckerman's life and several readings of his poems. Some of Golden's biographical reconstructions, however, are based too fully on Tuckerman's sonnets and not fully enough on other kinds of historical materials.

Hudgins, Andrew. "'A Monument of Labor Lost': The Sonnets of Frederick Goddard Tuckerman." *Chicago Review* 37, no. 1 (Winter, 1990): 64-79. A critical study of Tuckerman's sonnets.

Seed, David. "Alone with God and Nature: The Poetry of Jones Very and Frederick Goddard Tuckerman." In *Nineteenth Century American Poetry*, edited by A. Robert Lee. Totowa, N.J.: Barnes and Noble, 1985. A comparative study of the poetry of Tuckerman and Jones Very.

Robert C. Jones

CHASE TWICHELL

Born: New Haven, Connecticut; August 20, 1950

PRINCIPAL POETRY

Northern Spy: Poems, 1981
The Odds, 1986
Perdido, 1991
The Ghost of Eden, 1995
The Snow Watcher, 1998
Dog Language, 2005
Horses Where the Answers Should Have Been: New and Selected Poems, 2010

OTHER LITERARY FORMS

Along with Robin Behn, Chase Twichell (TWIH-chehl) is editor of *The Practice of Poetry: Writing Ex-*

ercises from *Poets Who Teach* (1992), a popular collection of poets' exercises collected from a wide variety of practicing poets who also teach creative writing. She is also editor of *An Ausable Reader: A Decade of Poetry Against the Current, 1999-2008* (2008), and she translated, with Tony K. Stewart, *The Lover of God* (2003) by Rabindranath Tagore.

ACHIEVEMENTS

Twichell received fellowships from the National Endowment for the Arts in 1987 and 1993, and from the Artists Foundation in Boston, the New Jersey State Council on the Arts, and the John Simon Guggenheim Memorial Foundation in 1990. In 1994, she won the Literature Award of the American Academy of Arts and Letters. She won, in 1997, the Alice Fay Di Castagnola Award from the Poetry Society of America for *The Snow Watcher*, and she received a Smart Family Foundation Award in 2004 for her poems published in the *Yale Review*.

BIOGRAPHY

Chase Twichell grew up in the midst of the stresses of her parents' disintegrating marriage. Her father taught Latin at a prestigious boys' school; her mother raised Twichell and her two sisters while working in a bookstore. The family spent the summers in the Adirondacks, providing Twichell with a sense of connection to the wilderness that has been important to her life both personally and as a writer.

After elementary school in New Haven, Twichell attended an extremely strict boarding school in Maryland. She suffered from attention deficit disorder and consequently did poorly in school, but she managed to discover her calling to poetry while she was there.

Twichell received a bachelor of arts degree from Trinity College in Hartford, Connecticut, in 1973 after studying at a number of other schools, including Wesleyan, where she studied with poet Richard Wilbur and began to publish her own poems and investigate Buddhism. After graduation from Trinity, she attended the Writers' Workshop at the University of Iowa, receiving her master of fine arts degree from that institution in 1976. Also while she was at Iowa, Twichell studied graphic design and printing, thus gaining the skills that enabled her to fulfill a childhood ambition to work in printing. After graduation from Iowa, she worked for Pennyroyal Press in Massachusetts, perfecting her ability in the printer's craft. Her first two books of poems were published during these years.

In 1985, Twichell joined the faculty of the master of fine arts program at the University of Alabama, where she taught for three years, spending her summers in the Adirondacks. It was at Alabama that she met novelist Russell Banks, whom she married in 1989.

Twichell and Banks lived for a time in Princeton, New Jersey, where they taught during the academic year, continuing to summer in the Adirondacks. During this time she published *The Practice of Poetry* and *The Ghost of Eden*, the latter a collection of poems recording her commitment to the importance and preservation of wilderness. In a 1993 essay for *Ploughshares*, she said that this commitment informs her main critical judgments, and she also indicated that she had come to believe that all good poetry was of necessity political and that poetry that makes no reference to the larger world outside the poet is merely self-absorbed. Similarly, she rejected decoration in poetry, calling it "prettification" and thus gratuitous.

In 1998, Twichell and Banks left Princeton to live in the Adirondacks full time. There, Twichell began to teach in Goddard College's master of fine arts program, continued to study Zen Buddhism, and founded the Ausable Press.

ANALYSIS

Chase Twichell's announcement of her poetics in *Ploughshares* is her effort to reconcile her belief that the relationship between human beings and nature has undergone a deep and fatal change in the last decades, a change that heralds the death of nature in any traditional sense, along with her desire to express that belief in poetry. Clearly, if such poetry is to have impact, it must address the crisis directly, and so in *The Ghost of Eden* the poems repeat her concern directly and often: Human beings are killing the planet. Typically, the message is tied to a narrative that exemplifies the issue in Twichell's own clear, direct language, her short lines and brief stanzas.

Chase Twichell (©Miriam Berkley)

THE GHOST OF EDEN

In *The Ghost of Eden*, the pictures of the animal world are sharp and vivid; often they are pictures of animals suffering because of the actions of human beings. "Animal Graves" provides a good example. It begins when the speaker has hit a baby garter snake with the lawn mower. The snake is badly wounded but still alive, so she must hit it again and again with the mower. As she does, she recalls the graves she made for animals when she was a child. She buried house pets and wild animals alike and marked the animal graveyard with the skull of a deer she found in the forest.

Now the dying snake coils itself upward to hiss at the mower, an instinctive gesture, which Twichell calls "dancing in the roar/ and shadow of its death." She imagines its grave in the same childhood pet cemetery where the deer skull was finally carried off by neighborhood dogs "to bury/ in the larger graveyard of the world." In that world everything will finally be buried; nevertheless, she implies, fortunate creatures will meet a worthier death than the little snake sacrificed to a tidy lawn.

In "The Devil I Don't Know" the vegetarian speaker pushes her cart through the grocery store, looking with revulsion at the contents of the meat case, where the packages "look like body parts to me/ since I stopped eating them." The slaughtered animals, the animals stuffed with steroids, the package of chops that looks "like a litter of stillborn puppies"—all this evidence of human beings' unnatural treatment of animals make the speaker desire to make an elegy, a prayer in their honor. She cannot do so, however, because the death of these creatures seems to her like the death of God; what has died is "the holy thing itself." She must turn away from the devil she knows, the devil that eats these animals. Popular wisdom says this devil is safer than the one that is unknown, but Twichell disagrees. She longs for a new object of worship, a devil she does not know, but she fears that with the death of nature all worship is dead, too. The poem ends with the image of a swordfish, "gutted, garnished, laid out on ice."

Much of the imagery of "The Aisle of Dogs" recalls that of "The Devil I Don't Know." In this poem the speaker has gone to an animal shelter for kittens; as she walks the aisles, she sees dozens of dogs that have been brutalized by human beings. The worst is a pit bull that still lives, although someone has skinned it. It is being kept alive as evidence for the courts; when the case is finished the dog will be put down. Twichell's sympathies often lie with predatory animals, as here, where she seems drawn to the pit bull and "its incurable hatred/ of my species."

Some critics have considered Twichell's tone of *The Ghost of Eden* to be unnecessarily shrill in poems like "The Aisle of Dogs" or "The Devil I Don't Know." "The Smell of Snow" demonstrates Twichell's strongest voice in addressing her themes of the holiness of nature without relying on human brutality as a backdrop.

The poem begins with a night hike through an early winter forest, a dangerous time because the hunting season is open. The speaker and her companion hike without flashlights, since "only in the dark does the spectral magic/ survive"; she names the fox, raccoon, bear, and deer they see.

Suddenly a fisher, a larger cousin of mink and ermine, appears before her, powerful and utterly wild. It smells like snow, a smell that, as a child, she associated with the smell of God because it seemed so foreign to all human smells, just as the eyes of the fisher seem to see only wilderness. As she gazes after it, she feels "a sudden carnal ache," a longing to be the fisher's victim, "the one he would tear open/ drag off in pieces to devour." Devoured by the fisher, and it in turn devoured by coyotes or other animals, she would live united with the god of the planet, "become/ the words the wind says/ to the birch tatters"; she would survive as "spirit free of any human/ vision of the afterlife," the innocent devoured by the innocent.

THE SNOW WATCHER

In *The Snow Watcher*, the reader can see how Twichell has grown in new directions without compromising the old ones. These poems often appear like those of the earlier volume, but these join Twichell's concern for the planet with her interest in Zen Buddhism and its practice—a practice that urges the practitioner to view herself as one being in the multitude of beings in the universe. The result is that these poems are shorter, sparer, more oblique and often less didactic than those of the earlier volume.

Many are based on the Japanese form called the tanka, a five-line poem of five, seven, five, seven, and five syllables. The first three lines are supposed to make a complete statement on which the last two lines comment. Two poems about horses seem to exemplify this form. In "Wild Mare," the mare staring at the speaker seems to suggest the implacable otherness of nature. "Horse" proposes something similar—that horse and rider might be like soul and body. The human being is the rider, Twichell says "but everyone looks at the horse."

Twichell's spiritual growth in Buddhism is the central subject of these poems, which make up a sort of journal of her experience in the exercise. Some describe her childhood, a source for her desire to experience the emptying of self that Buddhism offers. A number of the poems describe the seated meditation called zazen; in it the practitioner learns to still the mind's running voice. Other poems are designated *Dokusan*, the term for the student's private interview with a teacher; during it the student is to demonstrate his or her spiritual growth. These "Imaginary Dokusan" allow the reader into the interview while they pretend to address the teacher. Almost all of the poems draw on nature, an intimate part of the Zen poet's view of the world.

The poems depicting the poet's childhood portray the effects of the parents' discord on the child. In "The Black Triangle," for example, the parents' quarrel at dinner sends the child's mind far away: "It stands behind itself and looks out," somewhat in the way meditation trains the mind to detach from the physical world. In "The Wars," Twichell pictures a child who waits for the voices of the adults to grow dull so that she can slip unnoticed in to dinner. This training in detachment seems good preparation for the discipline of Buddhism, but still more is demanded of the student.

In "Zazen, Wired & Tired," Twichell talks of her impatience with the exercise: "Sitting zazen is like trying to be a tree," but gradually she progresses. In "A Last Look Back," she notes how change can occur behind one's back or while one is not looking. She thinks of the snow-filled forest and of a deer's tracks there, empty in the snow. "Each change in me" she says, "is a stone step/ beneath the blur of snow." The step's edges will appear in the spring, when she will look back to see her "former selves,/ numerous as the trees."

Students of Zen Buddhism often note its playful quality; that quality seems to have freed Twichell to use quiet humor in this volume. In "Imaginary Dokusan: Rat," Twichell calls herself "Ms. Zen, taking secret notes for a poem,/ about to slouch back into all her bad habits." In "Walking Meditation," she begins by calling herself "the first tall animal/ to walk the trail today. Apologies to the spiders."

The end of Buddhist meditation—the release of the student from the demands of all desire—is necessarily at odds with the poet's urge to share the right words with a reader. The result is a paradox, which Twichell notes several times near the end of this volume, most directly in "To the Reader: If You Asked Me." Here she laments that having the reader with her ends her privacy, filling her silent rooms with talk even though she

wants that reader's visit. At the same time she knows that language is not all; her discipline has taken her far beyond it. She concludes that her role in this volume has been that of a broom sweeping an empty factory, feeling neither hostility nor nostalgia—just doing the job that must be done.

DOG LANGUAGE

The poems in *Dog Language* are blunt as studies, in part, of aging and death and impermanence, and they are personal. Twichell, in the words of the poem "How Zen Ruins Poets," asks

> What language does the mind
> speak before thinking, before
> thinking gives birth to words?
> I tried to write without embellishment,
> to tell no lies while keeping death in mind.
> To write what was still unthought-about.

Twichell is a poet of simplicity, truth, and the memory of death.

In another poem, Twichell laments the passing of her father, who spent some time in a nursing home: "Let's talk about his death,/ right now in progress." She also celebrates her longtime companions, her dogs: "Stay with me, dogs/ black-and-white spirits/ asleep by the door."

OTHER MAJOR WORKS

TRANSLATION: *The Lover of God*, 2003 (of Rabindranath Tagore; with Tony K. Stewart).

EDITED TEXTS: *The Practice of Poetry: Writing Exercises from Poets Who Teach*, 1992 (with Robin Behn); *An Ausable Reader: A Decade of Poetry Against the Current, 1999-2008*, 2008.

BIBLIOGRAPHY

Burt, Stephen. Review of *The Ghost of Eden. Times Literary Supplement* (July 7, 1995): 14. Praises the stark meditations of the book, though noting the shrillness of some poems. Compares the best favorably with Louise Glück.

Daniel, David. "About Chase Twichell." *Ploughshares* 19 (Winter, 1993/1994): 214-217. Daniel includes some biographical material and describes Twichell's poetics at that stage of her career, emphasizing her commitment to the importance of preserving nature.

Hirshfield, Jane. "Editors' Shelf." *Ploughshares* 25 (Spring, 1999): 195. As part of a series of brief reviews, poet Hirshfield recommends *The Snow Watcher* for its use of Zen practice blended with American language.

Olsen, William. "Lyric Detachment: Two New Books of Poetry." *Chicago Review* 38 (Summer, 1991): 76-89. Olsen reviews *Perdido* (along with a volume by Jorie Graham) in detail, praising Twichell's concrete imagery, which creates a sort of journey into a psychic underworld.

Twichell, Chase. "Psychopharmacology and Its Discontents." In *Poets on Prozac: Mental Illness, Treatment, and the Creative Process*, edited by Richard M. Berlin. Baltimore: The Johns Hopkins University Press, 2008. Twichell discusses the creative process of the poet in this collection of essays on poets and mental illness.

Ann D. Garbett

U

LOUIS UNTERMEYER

Born: New York, New York; October 1, 1885
Died: Newtown, Connecticut; December 18, 1977

PRINCIPAL POETRY

The Younger Quire, 1910
First Love, 1911
Challenge, 1914
. . . and Other Poets, 1916
These Times, 1917
Including Horace, 1919
The New Adam, 1920
Heavens, 1922
Roast Leviathan, 1923
Collected Parodies, 1926
Poems, 1927 (with Richard Untermeyer)
Burning Bush, 1928
Adirondack Cycle, 1929
Food and Drink, 1932
First Words Before Spring, 1933
Selected Poems and Parodies, 1935
Long Feud: Selected Poems, 1962

OTHER LITERARY FORMS

The poetry of Louis Untermeyer (UHN-tuhr-mi-uhr) represents only a fraction of his total work. He put his name on well over a hundred books, ranging from *The Kitten Who Barked* (1962, a children's story) to *A Treasury of Ribaldry* (1956), and from his historical novel *Moses* (1928) to *A Century of Candymaking, 1837-1947* (1947). Most of his effort, however, went into four areas: anthologies of poetry, criticism, biography, and children's literature. Some of the most important works that he edited were *Modern American Poetry* (1919), *Modern British Poetry* (1920), and *A Treasury of Great Poems* (1942, 1955). He broke new ground in criticism with *The New Era in American Poetry* (1919, 1971) and provided a useful literary reappraisal in *American Poetry from the Beginning to Whitman* (1931), which he edited. His early textbook *Poetry: Its Understanding and Enjoyment* (1934, with Carter Davidson) paved the way for *Understanding Poetry: An Anthology for College Students* (1938), edited by Cleanth Brooks and Robert Penn Warren, and a host of other works. Although Untermeyer published one massive analytical biography, *Heinrich Heine: Paradox and Poet* (1937), he was better known for the biographical essays in *Makers of the Modern World* (1955) and *Lives of the Poets* (1959). Untermeyer's contributions to children's literature include collections of poetry such as *This Singing World* (1923-1926) and *Stars to Steer By* (1941), as well as many stories and collections of stories—among them, *Chip: My Life and Times* (1933), *The Donkey of God* (1932; winner of the 1932 Italian Enit Award for a book on Italy by a non-Italian), *The Last Pirate: Tales from the Gilbert and Sullivan Operas* (1934), and *The Golden Treasury of Children's Literature* (1959, with Byrna Untermeyer).

ACHIEVEMENTS

Louis Untermeyer exerted a shaping influence on modern American poetry. That influence, however, did not derive from his own voluminous verse. Indeed, Untermeyer has not been greatly honored as a poet. His verse has escaped the scrutiny of modern scholars, and his work was never awarded a Pulitzer Prize, although he did serve as consultant in poetry (poet laureate) to the Library of Congress from 1961 to 1963. Moreover, Untermeyer seemed to regret his poetic profligacy and lamented that "too many facile lines of praise and protest" had filled his volumes. In *Long Feud*, he trimmed the canon of poems he cared to preserve to a spartan 118 pages.

If Untermeyer's impact as a poet was limited, his impact as a critic, critical biographer, and anthologist was almost limitless. He has been described as Robert Frost's Boswell, but he really ought to be seen as a twentieth century version of James Boswell and Samuel Johnson combined. Through appreciative reviews, loving editorial labors, and reverent selections in his anthologies, Untermeyer was able to do more for Frost than Boswell ever did for Johnson. Moreover, Untermeyer's engaging *Lives of the Poets* is a worthy sequel to Johnson's biographical sketches and is massively supplemented by the scientific, political, and literary biographies in his *Makers of the Modern World*.

Although Untermeyer modestly understated his contribution to Frost's success, Frost himself was quick to acknowledge it, saying publicly, "Sometimes I think I am a figment of Louis' imagination." Indeed, in an article for the Chicago *Evening Post* on April 23, 1915, Untermeyer became the first reviewer in the United States to praise Frost's *North of Boston* (1914). He was the second scholar to praise Frost's poetry in a book, *The New Era in American Poetry*, and he was among the first to include Frost in an anthology.

As the friendship between the two poets strengthened, Untermeyer's advocacy continued. Every new edition of *Modern American Poetry* included more poems by Frost, who wrote appreciatively to his friend in 1941, "I look on [the anthology] as having done more to spread my poetry than any one other thing." Unter-

Louis Untermeyer (Hulton Archive/Getty Images)

meyer continued to write warm reviews of Frost's poetry. He became Frost's earliest biographer and published the first volume of Frost's letters and conversations. In 1943, Untermeyer made himself "somewhat unpleasant" with his fellow judges on the Pulitzer poetry jury by insisting in a minority report that the year's prize should be awarded to *A Witness Tree*, making Frost the only author ever to win four Pulitzer Prizes.

What Untermeyer did massively for Frost, he did less passionately but just as selflessly for many other poets. *The New Era in American Poetry* devoted whole chapters to Vachel Lindsay, Carl Sandburg, Edwin Arlington Robinson, Amy Lowell, Edgar Lee Masters, and Ezra Pound, while also giving prominence to Sara Teasdale, H. D., Stephen Vincent Benét, and William Rose Benét. His ten editions of *Modern American Poetry* and nine editions of *Modern British Poetry* helped to win recognition and popularity for three generations of young poets. His service for nearly a quarter century as chairman of the Pulitzer poetry jury allowed him to assist the careers of Mark Van Doren, both Benéts, Karl Shapiro, Robert Lowell, W. H. Auden, Peter Viereck, Gwendolyn Brooks, Carl Sandburg, Marianne Moore, Archibald MacLeish, Theodore Roethke, Wallace Stevens, Elizabeth Bishop, Richard Wilbur, Robert Penn Warren, Stanley Kunitz, W. D. Snodgrass, Phyllis McGinley, and William Carlos Williams. He served as Merrill Moore's literary adviser during Moore's life, and he was a faithful literary executor after Moore's death.

In brief, through poems, lectures, reviews, anthologies, and personal services, Untermeyer did more than any of his contemporaries to win a popular audience for modern poetry.

BIOGRAPHY

Louis Untermeyer was born in 1885 into a well-to-do family of German-Jewish jewelers. His formal education ended at fifteen when he refused to return to high school and discovered that Columbia University would not admit him without passing marks in algebra and geometry. He then worked in the family jewelry business while establishing his career as a poet and literary jack-of-all-trades. His literary successes allowed him to devote less and less time to the jewelry business until he formally resigned at the age of thirty-seven.

Untermeyer eventually moved away from New York City and bought Stony Water, a 160-acre farm in the Adirondacks that became the setting for some of his finest lyrics. Although he continued to earn his living through writing and lecturing, he made a brief stab at commercial farming, raising Hampshire pigs and Jersey cows, tapping maples, harvesting apples, and marketing Stony Water preserves. In his autobiography *Bygones: The Recollections of Louis Untermeyer* (1965), Untermeyer compared his situation with that of the gentleman farmer who celebrated the first anniversary of his venture into dairy farming by proposing a toast: "Friends," he said, "you will notice that there are two shaped bottles on the table. One shape contains champagne; the other contains milk. Help yourself to them carefully; they cost the same per quart."

The outbreak of World War II brought Untermeyer back to the city. He joined the Office of War Information, where he worked with Howard Fast, Santha Rama Rau, and the film director John Houseman. Later, as editor of the Armed Services Editions, Untermeyer oversaw the republication of forty works of literature a month. By the end of the war, he had helped to deliver some 122 million books into the hands of American servicemen.

When the war ended, Untermeyer wished to remain in a salaried position for a variety of reasons, not the least of which was the expense associated with his growing contingent of former wives. He accepted a position with Decca Records directing its efforts to sell recordings of plays and poetry. In 1950, he became a celebrity as one of the original panelists on CBS-TV's *What's My Line?* McCarthyism was, however, frothing and unfettered in the early 1950's, and Untermeyer became its victim, not because of communist sympathies on his part, but because nearly forty years earlier he had published a book titled *Challenge* (criticized at the time for too lavish praise of democracy) and worked on a liberal magazine called *The Masses*. The baseless hostility of the self-appointed censors was sufficiently rabid that Untermeyer was forced from the show and even from public life.

He retreated to the Connecticut countryside, where

he soon became intimate with Arthur Miller, Van Wyck Brooks, Robert Penn Warren, Malcolm Cowley, and actress Margaret Sullavan. Untermeyer's complete repatriation did not come until 1961, when he was honored by being chosen consultant in poetry to the Library of Congress. During the next two years, he was twice asked by the State Department to serve as a literary ambassador, giving lectures in India and Japan. In 1963, Untermeyer returned to his home in Connecticut, where he wrote his memoirs, published books for children, and continued to update his anthologies until his death on December 18, 1977.

The love of poetry demonstrated in Untermeyer's anthologies was in large part a love of passion, and for him a life of emotion was not a vicarious ideal only. In life, particularly in married life, Untermeyer experienced every variation of happiness, heartache, and humorous complexity. In all, he was married six times and divorced five times by a total of four women. In 1907, he married his first wife, the respected poet Jean Starr; he divorced her sixteen years later in Mexico and remarried her shortly thereafter in New Jersey (*not* New York, since state law there held that he had always remained married to Jean). These complications led Louis to wonder "which state was the state of matrimony" and whether he "might be committing bigamy by illegally marrying the same wife twice." Virginia, his second wife, married Louis in Mexico in 1923, became pregnant in Switzerland, delivered a baby in London, and divorced Louis (who had returned to Jean) in Missouri—all within a period of two years. Esther, the third wife and a lawyer, helped Louis obtain a second Mexican divorce from Jean—this time by mail. Esther then married Louis in 1933 in a ceremony performed, appropriately, by a professional comedian. Louis and Esther lived together in contentment for a number of years before they gradually drifted apart. At the age of sixty-two, Untermeyer divorced Esther in Mexico to marry his fourth wife, Byrna. When Esther learned of the divorce, she sued, alleging that Louis's Mexican divorce from Jean had been valid, while his Mexican divorce from her was not. The somewhat bemused judge ruled that Untermeyer had never been married to Esther or Virginia, was not married to Byrna, and remained legally tied to Jean from whom he had been separated for more than twenty years. Untermeyer subsequently persuaded Jean to divorce him in Nevada (their third divorce) so that he could marry Byrna a second time and live legally with the woman he loved.

Despite his fondness for children, Untermeyer was generally too busy to take much part in rearing his own sons. Richard, his son by his first wife, hanged himself at the age of nineteen. His second son, John, was reared by Virginia, who rarely allowed Louis to see the child. His adopted sons, Lawrence and Joseph, were reared less by Untermeyer than by his caretakers at Stony Water.

ANALYSIS

The qualities of mind and temperament that made Louis Untermeyer such a superb anthologist kept him from attaining the same level of excellence in his poetry. He was too appreciative of the moods, approaches, and words of others—too prone to imitation and parody. He was rarely able to find his own voice; or rather, his own voice was often the mockingbird's, wryly reproducing the songs of others. Moreover, the virtues of his impressionistic criticism—directness and clarity—were poetic vices in a period of Empsonian ambiguity.

Untermeyer's poems fall into five broad categories: parodies; modern re-creations of religious or mythological events; adaptations of another poet's spirit, tone, or verse form; idealistic exhortations concerning social consciousness; and a few entirely new creations. Thus, Untermeyer's poems range from the overtly imitative to the mildly innovative. They vary widely in subject and style but are unified by romanticism undercut with irony. This romanticism was a fundamental part of Untermeyer's personality. It guided him as he exuberantly collected belongings, friends, experiences, passions, and poems.

The instincts of a romantic collector were evident throughout Untermeyer's life. His earliest memories were of the "colorful mélange" of assorted portraits, porcelains, and petit-point cushions that littered his parent's home. During reveries before a Dutch landscape or a jeweled bird, Untermeyer's mind turned to fantasy, while his taste was tutored by delight in the diversity of the family's collections. His love of fantasy

led him to read, as he put it, "a hodge-podge of everything I could lay my mind on": *Alf laya wa-laya* (fifteenth century; *The Arabian Nights' Entertainments*, 1706-1708), books from Edward Stratemeyers's Rover Boys series, Alexandre Dumas, père's *Les Trois Mousquetaires* (1844; *The Three Musketeers*, 1846), Samuel Taylor Coleridge's *The Rime of the Ancient Mariner* (1798), Jean de La Fontaine's *Fables choisies, mises en vers* (1668-1694; *Fables Written in Verse*, 1735), Alfred, Lord Tennyson's *Idylls of the King* (1859-1885), Dante's *Inferno* (in *La divina commedia*, c. 1320; *The Divine Comedy*, 1802), and so on. This eclectic but diverting reading in bed by night naturally reduced Untermeyer to mediocrity in school by day. He found the classroom too limiting and controlled in its approach to life and learning.

Thus, at the age of seventeen, Untermeyer entered the family jewelry business—the first in what was to become the startlingly diverse collection of his occupations. Yet, even the jewelry business was too mundane for Louis. He devoted long afternoons to the unfinished verses he kept concealed in his desk beneath production reports and packets of gemstones. In the evenings, he wrote poems and reviews, for which he found a ready market. His first collection of poems, *First Love*, was a vanity press edition subsidized by his father, but its sales quickly offset the cost of publication. His next volume, *Challenge*, was picked up by the Century Company, and Untermeyer's poetic career was launched.

The dual careers of poet and businessman were insufficient to quench Untermeyer's romantic thirst for experience. He used his contacts in the literary world to help him to his third career as a magazine editor. He first obtained a position as a contributing editor to *The Masses*, where he made friends of such prominent left-wing personalities as Max Eastman and John Reed. He then became one of the founding editors of *The Seven Arts*, a short-lived (1916-1917) literary magazine that published pieces by Sherwood Anderson, D. H. Lawrence, Carl Sandburg, Robert Frost, Eugene O'Neill, Vachel Lindsay, and John Dewey. From 1918 to 1924, he was a contributing editor to the *Liberator*; from 1934 to 1937, he was poetry editor of the *American Mercury*; and for many years, he wrote a weekly column for the *Saturday Review* (known as *Saturday Review of Literature* until 1952).

In 1919, Untermeyer collected and revised a number of his impressionistic reviews and published them in *The New Era in American Poetry*. When Alfred Harcourt decided to bring out an anthology of modern American poetry, Untermeyer was the logical editor. *Modern American Poetry* was followed in the next year by *Modern British Poetry*. Thus, Untermeyer, who had already been a success as a jeweler, poet, and magazine editor, now assumed the role of anthologist. It was the right task for a man who, by his own confession, had "the mind of a magpie" and who collected stamps, flowers, pictures of actresses in cigarette packs, cats (both living and artificial), careers, and wives. This multiplicity of interests continued to shape Untermeyer's life. In subsequent years, he became a gentleman farmer, publisher, record producer, and television celebrity. Despite these varied careers, Untermeyer always felt most at home at his desk. There, he wrote, "I am doing what I am supposed to do: fulfilling my function whether I write in the role of biographer, storyteller, editor of anthologies, impressionistic critic, or, occasionally, poet." The order of those activities says much about Untermeyer's own priorities and poetic self-image.

WORKS OF PARODY

For a collector who wished to be a poet, parody was the natural literary mode. Indeed, Untermeyer's first booklet, *The Younger Quire*, was a parody of *The Younger Choir*, an anthology of youthful poets (including Untermeyer) that was introduced and lavishly praised by Edwin Markham. Untermeyer's parody came to exactly twenty-four pages (one quire) and included a series of "back-of-the-hand tributes" combining "simulated innocence and real malice." He continued to write burlesques throughout his long career, publishing them in *. . . and Other Poets, Including Horace*, *Collected Parodies*, and *Selected Poems and Parodies*.

RELIGIOUS THEMES

Parody is, however, parasitic, and Untermeyer was too thoughtful and creative to remain locked into such a limited style. In another large group of poems, the penchant for parody is reined in as Untermeyer re-creates a religious, mythological, or literary event from a modern perspective. In "Eve Speaks," for example, Eve asks God to pause before judging her. She argues that Eden was a place for child's play and angelic calm but not a place for Adam who, being neither child nor angel, was formed to struggle and create. Untermeyer implies that eating the fruit of the tree of knowledge was essential to human fulfillment and that God had been wrong to forbid it. Thus, the poem is a typical statement of Untermeyer's philosophy of life. He implies that the Judeo-Christian religions have distorted the old myths in an effort to impose order and morality. For Untermeyer, the romantic collector, life is truly lived only through struggle, passion, sexuality, creation, and experience. All these were to be gained only through knowledge, the forbidden fruit.

Untermeyer's romantic sensuality led him to fill his poems with descriptions of almost Keatsian opulence and vividness. The terrors of Judgment Day, for example, are suggested by phenomena: "trampling winds," "stark and cowering skies," "the red flame" of God's anger licking up worlds, the stars falling "in a golden rain." Here, the pathetic fallacy, which often mars other descriptions by Untermeyer, becomes an effective indication of God's fearful power; before his wrath, the elements, too, cringe and flee. By standing unterrified amid such fury, Eve immediately wins the reader's respect, just as her boldness in questioning God's judgment had piqued the reader's interest. As she begins to explain herself, her description of Paradise is traditional except for the contemptuousness of the occasional reference to its "drowsy luxury" and "glittering hours." Such descriptive phrases prepare the reader to see Eden as Eve saw it, a place where Man and Woman are treated like children, "swaddled with ease" and "lulled with . . . softest dreams." The circling night-bird "out beyond the wood," the "broadening stream," and the distant hills become symbols of freedom, symbols of the unknown. Eve learns that individuality can be obtained only through rebellion, that knowledge must be reached through uncertainty, and that creation grows out of struggle. She eats of the fruit of sensual knowledge, as Untermeyer would have all men and women do.

Untermeyer makes other particularly interesting attempts to modernize religious mythology in "Sic Semper," "God's Youth," and "Burning Bush." The first of these looks at the myth of the Fall from another perspective. In "Eve Speaks," Untermeyer had made no mention of Satan; Eve's revolt grew out of her understanding of Adam's human needs. In "Sic Semper," Untermeyer brilliantly and economically overturns the traditional view of Satan. The fallen angel becomes "the Light-Bringer, Fire-Scatterer"—humankind's benefactor and not its foe. Lucifer and Prometheus become one, bringing light to minds in darkness. Then, in a horrifying betrayal, man—knowing too well the future costs of truth, wisdom, and love—puts Lucifer in hell.

Similarly, "God's Youth" is a delightful reconception of deity. The God of the Old Testament is himself old—bored by the unchanging march of years and the "yawning seasons." During the Creation, Untermeyer insists, "God was young and blithe and whimsical," letting loose his desires and filling the earth with "fancies, wild and frank." During the Creation, then, the child-god lived as Untermeyer would have the man-child continue to live.

"Burning Bush" is by far the most sacrilegious of Untermeyer's biblical re-creations. The poem's title is an allusion to Exodus 3:2 in which the angel of the Lord appears to Moses in the form of a burning bush. Through imagery that is intentionally indirect and metaphoric, Untermeyer transforms the burning bush into a sexual symbol. In the still of the night "runners of the flame" fill the "narrowest veins," and in "an agony of Love" bodies burn but are not consumed. The biblical voice of God becomes the ecstatic cries of the lovers that later give way to "the still, small voice" of contentment in the postcoital quiet. The sexual act, which is itself "knowledge," passion, creation, and experience, becomes a metaphor for the presence of God, who still speaks to humankind through the burning bush. Through this metaphor, the poem becomes a twelve-line exposition of Untermeyer's temperament and philosophy of life.

EMULATION OF ROMANTIC THEMES

The poems in the third category of Untermeyer's verse all involve emulation. Many of them reflect the spirit and sometimes the words of the favorite poets of Untermeyer's youth: Robert Herrick, Heinrich Heine, A. E. Housman, Thomas Hardy, and Horace. They tend to be witty, ironic, and sensuous. They frequently deal with the traditional subject matter of romantic poetry—love, spring, snow, dawn, sunset, birdsongs, the moon, and the stars—but Untermeyer is well aware that these poetic topics can often become substitutes for real passions. The romanticism of many of these poems is, therefore, undercut by irony; in others—"Georgian Anthology" and "Portrait of a Poet," for example—Untermeyer is openly scornful of formalized, passionless romanticism. For this reason, Untermeyer classified himself (along with John Crowe Ransom, Robert Lowell, and Richard Wilbur) as a romantic ironist, but given his devotion to passion, struggle, and creativity, one can question the sincerity of much of the irony. One feels that Untermeyer's scorn of the romantic posturing of others is itself a form of romantic posturing.

On the whole, these are Untermeyer's least successful poems. Untermeyer was a romantic and therefore became a romantic ironist only with difficulty. Moreover, most of the poems give one the impression of having been written before and better by others. A typical example is "Fairmount Cemetery," a poem in Housman's style. The speaker looks back on the cemetery, his first trysting spot, and remembers his extravagant claims that "love is all that saves"; meanwhile, the dead men lie "Chuckling in their graves." The cemetery setting is too obviously a contrivance, the claims of the lover are overblown and unrealistic, and the concluding commentary of the dead injects a crude blatancy. The only part of Untermeyer's personality that shows up in "Fairmount Cemetery" is the collector's love of varied poetic styles.

INFLUENCE OF ROBERT FROST

A smaller, but far better, group of poems was written in imitation of Frost's understated style. As in Frost's best lyrics, an understanding of life's tragic possibilities emerges through the speaker's recollection of an occurrence in nature. "Nightmare by Day," for example, begins with a setting and even a verse form that are nearly identical to Frost's in "Dust of Snow." In search of peace, the speaker has walked alone far into the woods until there are no more tracks in the snow. Something in front of him, glimpsed but not yet recognized, makes his "pulses freeze," and, as he watches, a trail of blood begins to grow, spreading as it melts the snow. The mystery of this image of death in a place of peaceful isolation disturbs the speaker so that ever after he himself awaits the sudden blow and the red droplets on the snow.

The impact of this terrifying incident is augmented by the plain diction and the stark imagery. In the poem, 98 of the 110 words are monosyllables; the average sentence contains only 9 words; the only colors are white, black, and red; and the only objects are the snow, the speaker, the trees, the trail of blood, and one "chuckling crow." However, upon reflection, the incident itself is both mysterious and premonitory, just as the simple, unforced verse reveals, upon reflection, the technical difficulty of densely rhymed iambic dimeter.

If the poem has a weakness, it is in the improbability of the events described. At its best, Frost's lyric poetry grows out of an ordinary occurrence. That is not the case in "Nightmare by Day." Here, the ultimate situation is extraordinary. The blood is very fresh, but there has been no sign of a bleeding animal or of a hunter, and no sound of gunfire. These are not insuperable difficulties, of course; hawks and owls, for example, hunt silently and leave no trail. Untermeyer is, however, less interested in the incident as a natural phenomenon than as a symbol of sudden, unpredictable violence and impending death. Hence, he makes no effort to explain the ominous scene. Nevertheless, the odd congruence of events, the dreamlike improbability, demands recognition, and Untermeyer does recognize it, calling the entire incident a "dream" in the final stanza. The poem's title, however, "Nightmare by Day," emphasizes that the events have been real, and the nightmarish reality of this waking dream contributes largely to its impact.

An equally good imitation of Frost's style is found in "The Scraping of the Scythe." The poem grows out of the contrasts between two sounds: the song of the bluebird and the screech of the sharpening scythe. The one is a song of leisure, the other a sound of labor; the one pleasurable, the other painful; the one the call of summer, the other the call of fall. As the speaker notes, when the two fill the air at once, one need not hear the words, "To know what had transpired." The sharpening of the scythe is an omen of colder weather to come

and a symbol of inevitable death. Thus, in order not to hear that sound, the speaker never allows his own fields to be cut, but the reader knows that nothing can postpone the fall—and the speaker does, too.

The success of these poems arises at least in part from the fact that they are compatible with Untermeyer's outlook on life. If death is unavoidable and unpredictable, then it makes all the more sense to live fully, freely, and passionately. As much as Untermeyer admired Frost and Frost's poetry, he could not wholly endorse the somber pessimism embodied in Frost's style or the conservatism of Frost's personality. For a more compatible political and emotional outlook, Untermeyer occasionally turned to William Blake, whose radical politics and unconventional piety were much closer to his own views. Hence, Untermeyer's religious re-creations make many of the same points that Blake did in his poems objecting to those who would bind "with briars [his] joys and desires."

INFLUENCE OF WILLIAM BLAKE

Sometimes Blake's influence on Untermeyer gives rise to weak imitation, as in "Envy," a poem in the manner of Blake's "The Clod and the Pebble," which pits the rooted willow against the meandering brook in a debate about lifestyles; a poem such as "Glad Day (After a Color Print by Blake)," however, grows out of inspiration more than out of imitation. This paean to daylight is pure Untermeyer—lover of generosity, confidence, sensuality, clarity, and joy. Like "Eve Speaks," this poem excels in its descriptions, particularly in the personification of day, which becomes a naked body, free, outgiving, and rejoicing. Hence, as before, the pathetic fallacy is made tolerable because it is a "given," a part of Blake's drawing that Untermeyer must accept and explain.

Thus, Untermeyer's parodies, re-creations, and imitations derive from, and play upon, his strengths as a collector and a romantic, appreciative reader. The two final groupings are more original. One group of poems is largely hortatory. They include some of Untermeyer's most widely known pieces—"Caliban in the Coal Mines," "Prayer," and "On the Birth of a Child." They are light verse suitable for communicating their overt moral and political messages, but too blatantly propagandizing to qualify as significant poems. The best that can be said is that in them Untermeyer remains true to himself. Particularly in "Prayer," he speaks from the heart as he asks to remain "ever insurgent," "more daring than devout," "filled with a buoyant doubt," and wide-eyed and sensual while cognizant of others' misery. His final prayer, that of a thoroughgoing romantic, is to remain at the end of life "still unsatisfied."

INFLUENCE OF WALT WHITMAN

If the last group of Untermeyer's poems is derivative at all, it owes its inspiration to Walt Whitman. In a style all his own, Untermeyer attempts to describe common aspects of the contemporary world, often striving to see mundane things with a childlike wonder and a romantic imagination. The poems' titles identify their unconventional subjects: "In the Subway," "To a Vine-Clad Telegraph Pole," "A Side Street," "Boy and Tadpoles," "Food and Drink," "Hairdressing," "Hands," "Portrait of a Child," "Portrait of a Dead Horse," "Portrait of a Machine," and so on. In these poems, Untermeyer eschews both the subject matter of romantic poetry and the introspective approach of most modern verse. The poem "Still Life" is both an example of Untermeyer's approach and an explanation of it. Like Untermeyer's poems, a still-life painting portrays things, "A bowl of fruit upon a piece of silk," but it also conveys emotions through the choice of color and form. The still life contains no direct autobiography, but the artist's "voice so full of vehement life" can still be "heard." In the same way, Untermeyer's poems about modern life convey his perspective without descending into private symbolism, autobiographical digressions, or Freudian associations.

"Coal Fire" is a good example of what can be achieved through such verse. The poem explains to a child why fire comes out of coal. In doing so, it uses poetic devices that particularly appeal to children, yet it uses those devices with a mastery that should delight adults. The actual content of the poem is, however, entirely mundane; coal is the remnant of ancient trees. To interest the child, Untermeyer personifies parts of these trees, putting them in situations with which a child could empathize. Like children, each leaf must be "taught the right/ Way to drink light." Each twig must "learn/ How to catch flame and yet not burn." Each branch must grow strong on this "diet of heat." Simul-

taneously, Untermeyer develops a series of delightful paradoxes. The dead black coal was once a living green net. Before there was any running thing to ensnare, this net snared the sun. Paradoxically, the leaves "drink light," catch flame without burning, and eat heat. Finally, the poem's heavy alliteration and frequent rhyme heighten the delight, especially since the alliteration and the rhyme so frequently emphasize key words: "these . . . were trees," "to learn . . . not burn," "branch and . . . bough began," "to eat . . . of heat," and so on. More important, however, this lucid examination of coal fire subtly describes the burning coal as though the light within it were passion imprisoned. The intensity of the verse increases as the fire fingers the air, grows bolder, twists free, consumes the imprisoning coal, "leaps, is done,/ And goes back to the sun." There is nothing allegorical in the poem, but a reader would have to be curiously insensitive not to recognize in it Untermeyer's love of freedom, light, and passion.

"A DISPLACED ORPHEUS"

In 1955, when Untermeyer had already lived his biblically allotted three score years and ten, he was selected Phi Beta Kappa poet by Harvard University. For a man who had virtually ceased composing poetry twenty years earlier, it was a rare opportunity to pronounce dispassionate judgment upon his long and extraordinarily varied career. The poem he wrote, "A Displaced Orpheus," did just that. In it, Orpheus awakens after a long silence to discover that he has lost the knack of moving mountains and assuaging lions. He attends a series of universities to relearn the lost art and produces sterile stanzas in the manner of W. H. Auden, T. S. Eliot, and William Empson. Although Untermeyer intended these parodies to illustrate the deficiencies of much modern poetry, they also illustrate the limitations of his own imitative approach to composition. Thus, Orpheus's situation becomes Untermeyer's. Time has stripped him of his reputation, and his failures have cost him the woman he loves. All that remains is the desire to struggle, the urge to create. Only when he retrieves his "still unbroken lute" and sings for "that last listener, himself" does he rediscover his power. The birds and beasts gather about him, the trees bow down, and his woman looks upon him with "rediscovering eyes."

One could wish that Untermeyer had taken Orpheus's lesson more truly to heart and that he had sung for himself more often, but perhaps then the passionate collector would only have delighted himself with more parodies. Songs coming out of the soul often have a hard and bitter birth. All but a few are stillborn. In "Eve Speaks," "Nightmare by Day," "Coal Fire," "A Displaced Orpheus," and a handful of others, Untermeyer produced more healthy offspring than most poets do. Posterity should be grateful.

OTHER MAJOR WORKS

LONG FICTION: *Moses*, 1928; *The Wonderful Adventures of Paul Bunyan*, 1945.

NONFICTION: *The New Era in American Poetry*, 1919, 1971; *Poetry: Its Understanding and Enjoyment*, 1934 (with Carter Davidson); *Heinrich Heine: Paradox and Poet*, 1937; *From Another World*, 1939; *A Century of Candymaking, 1837-1947*, 1947; *Makers of the Modern World*, 1955; *Lives of the Poets*, 1959; *The Letters of Robert Frost and Louis Untermeyer*, 1963; *Bygones: The Recollections of Louis Untermeyer*, 1965.

CHILDREN'S LITERATURE: *This Singing World*, 1923-1926 (3 volumes); *The Donkey of God*, 1932; *Chip: My Life and Times*, 1933; *The Last Pirate: Tales from the Gilbert and Sullivan Operas*, 1934; *Stars to Steer By*, 1941; *The Golden Treasury of Children's Literature*, 1959 (with Byrna Untermeyer); *The Kitten Who Barked*, 1962.

EDITED TEXTS: *Modern American Poetry*, 1919; *Modern British Poetry*, 1920; *American Poetry from the Beginning to Whitman*, 1931; *A Treasury of Great Poems*, 1942, 1955.

MISCELLANEOUS: *A Treasury of Ribaldry*, 1956.

BIBLIOGRAPHY

Frost, Robert, and Louis Untermeyer. *The Letters of Robert Frost to Louis Untermeyer*. New York: Holt, Rinehart and Winston, 1963. The most valuable collection of Frost's letters to Untermeyer in a correspondence that lasted almost fifty years. The letters are remarkably edited.

Harcourt, Brace. *Sixteen Authors: Brief Histories, Together with Lists of Their Respective Works*. New York: Author, 1926. Offers short histories of sixteen authors and their works, including Sinclair Lewis, Carl Sandburg, Virginia Woolf, and Untermeyer. The entry on Untermeyer provides a fine assessment of his poetry and poetic development. Contains illustrations and a bibliography.

Lowell, Amy. "A Poet of the Present." Review of *These Times. Poetry* 11 (December, 1917): 157-164. This review of Untermeyer's early verse volume, *These Times*, turns out to be a lovely appreciation of the young poet.

Pound, Ezra. *EP to LU: Nine Letters Written to Louis Untermeyer by Ezra Pound*. Edited by J. A. Robbins. Bloomington: Indiana University Press, 1963. A fine collection of letters written by Pound to Untermeyer. Useful as a source of information on Pound's perception of Untermeyer.

Untermeyer, Louis. *From Another World: The Autobiography of Louis Untermeyer*. New York: Harcourt, Brace, 1939. Untermeyer's first attempt at autobiography is devoted to anecdotes and comments on the author's friends and acquaintances among the literary community. Untermeyer passes judgments, comments on works and relationships, and tells stories and jokes. In general he deals only with the surfaces of events and encounters and does not explore any issue in great depth. His style and energy are as vivid as the range of his acquaintances is impressive.

_____. *Bygones: The Recollections of Louis Untermeyer*. New York: Harcourt, Brace & World, 1965. The second of Untermeyer's reminiscences, in which the eighty-year-old looks back on his life. Where the earlier (1939) "autobiography" was about other people, this one is primarily, and self-consciously so, about the author. It is a very personal volume focusing on the highlights of Untermeyer's career, including excellent chapters on the McCarthy years, his tenure at the Library of Congress, and his travels.

Jeffrey D. Hoeper

JOHN UPDIKE

Born: Reading, Pennsylvania; March 18, 1932
Died: Danvers, Massachusetts; January 27, 2009

PRINCIPAL POETRY

The Carpentered Hen, and Other Tame Creatures,
    1958
Telephone Poles, and Other Poems, 1963
Dog's Death, 1965
Verse, 1965
The Angels, 1968
Bath After Sailing, 1968
Midpoint, and Other Poems, 1969
Seventy Poems, 1972
Six Poems, 1973
Cunts (Upon Receiving the Swingers Life Club
    Membership Solicitation), 1974
Query, 1974
Tossing and Turning, 1977
Sixteen Sonnets, 1979
Five Poems, 1980
Jester's Dozen, 1984
Facing Nature, 1985
Mites, and Other Poems in Miniature, 1990
Collected Poems, 1953-1993, 1993
A Helpful Alphabet of Friendly Objects, 1995
Americana, and Other Poems, 2001
Endpoint, and Other Poems, 2009

OTHER LITERARY FORMS

A prolific writer in all genres, John Updike was known chiefly as a novelist. His major works were best sellers and won significant critical acclaim both from reviewers for highbrow publications and from academics. Among his most noted novels are *The Centaur* (1963), *Couples* (1968), and the four novels depicting the life of Harry "Rabbit" Angstrom: *Rabbit, Run* (1960), *Rabbit Redux* (1971), *Rabbit Is Rich* (1981), and *Rabbit at Rest* (1990). He was also an accomplished and respected writer of short stories, of which he published numerous volumes, and a first-rate critic and essayist, as well as an accomplished poet.

ACHIEVEMENTS

John Updike was the recipient of numerous honors during his illustrious career. He received Pulitzer Prizes for *Rabbit Is Rich* and *Rabbit at Rest,* in 1982 and 1991, respectively. Other awards include a Guggenheim Fellowship (1959), a Rosenthal Award (1960), National Book Awards (1964, 1982), O. Henry Awards (1966, 1991), France's Foreign Book Prize (1966), a New England Poetry Club Golden Rose (1979), a MacDowell Medal (1981), National Book Critics Circle Awards for both fiction (1981, 1990) and criticism (1983), the Union League Club's Abraham Lincoln Award (1982), a National Arts Club Medal of Honor (1984), a National Medal of the Arts (1989), a William Dean Howells Award (1995), the Campion Award (1997), a Harvard Arts Medal (1998), a Medal for Distinguished Contribution to American Letters from the National Book Foundation (1998), a National Medal for the Humanities (2003), a PEN/Faulkner Award (2004), a Rea Award for the Short Story (2006), and a Gold Medal for Fiction (2007) from the American Academy of Arts and Letters.

Updike achieved his fame largely through his novels. These works, and his growing collection of prose essays and reviews, earned for him a reputation as one of America's leading literary voices. His poetry, on the other hand, brought only modest acclaim. Many critics considered him only a dilettante in this genre, a show-off who was clearly skilled in handling poetic forms both traditional and modern. Since much of his work is gentle satire and light verse, he was often accused of lacking substance. Updike's record of publication for individual poems, however, belies that judgment to some degree. His poems appeared in such journals as *The New Yorker* and *The Atlantic,* and even in *Scientific American.* As with much of his prose, Updike showed an ability to deal in verse with a wide variety of experiences, making both the commonplace and the abstruse immediately accessible to his readers.

BIOGRAPHY

Born March 18, 1932, John Hoyer Updike grew up during the Depression in Shillington, Pennsylvania, and in the farming country outside this northeastern town. His father was a mathematics teacher, his mother an intelligent, well-read woman and aspiring fiction writer who encouraged her son's reading. The Updikes lived with John's grandparents during the novelist's earliest years; many of the boy's memories of life in that household have found their way into his fiction and poetry. An excellent student in high school, Updike went to Harvard in 1950 on a full scholarship. There, while majoring in English, he edited the *Lampoon* and entertained visions of becoming a commercial cartoonist. While still a student at Harvard in 1953, Updike married Mary Pennington, an art student at Radcliffe. The following year, he was graduated summa cum laude.

Updike's own artistic talent was further fostered by a year's study at the Ruskin School of Drawing and Fine Art in Oxford, England, immediately following graduation. There, his first child, Elizabeth, was born. She was to be followed in the next six years by three others: David (1957), Michael (1959), and Miranda (1960).

Updike's desire to achieve fame through the visual arts was put aside in 1955, when he received an offer to join the staff of *The New Yorker*, to which he had sold his first story the year before. His full-time association with the magazine ended in 1957, however, when he took the daring step of becoming an independent writer, moving his family to Ipswich, Massachusetts, and establishing an office there. His first book, a collection of poems entitled *The Carpentered Hen, and Other Tame Creatures*, appeared in 1958.

The publication of two novels, *The Poorhouse Fair* (1959) and *Rabbit, Run*, brought Updike both critical and popular acclaim. For *The Centaur*, he received the National Book Award in 1964 and in the same year was elected to the National Institute of Arts and Letters. These were but the first of many honors.

Though a resident of New England continuously after 1957, Updike frequently traveled abroad. His first important trip was in 1964-1965, when he visited the Soviet Union, Romania, Bulgaria, and Czechoslovakia as a member of the U.S.S.R.-United States Cultural Exchange Program. In 1973, he served as a Fulbright lec-

turer in Africa. From his experiences in these countries, Updike brought back a wealth of materials that allowed him to expand his repertoire of characters beyond New England and Pennsylvania to include two of his most memorable creations: the middle-aged Jewish novelist Henry Bech and the African ruler Hakim Ellelou.

Updike and his family remained residents of Ipswich until 1974, when he and his wife were divorced. Shortly after the breakup of his marriage, Updike moved to Boston, then to Georgetown, Massachusetts. In 1977, he married Martha Bernhard, a divorcée whom he had known when both lived in Ipswich. Even during this period of personal difficulty, Updike's stream of writings poured forth unabated, and he went on to display both skill and versatility in a variety of literary genres.

Updike continued his prolific output through the 1980's, 1990's, and into the new millennium, winning his second Pulitzer Prize in 1991 for *Rabbit at Rest* and producing new novels, criticism, and children's poetry such as *A Helpful Alphabet of Friendly Objects*. Updike

John Updike (©Davis Freeman)

died of cancer in 2009 at the age of seventy-six, the same year that *My Father's Tears, and Other Stories* and *Endpoint, and Other Poems* were published.

ANALYSIS

An appropriate starting point for an analysis of John Updike's poetry is Charles T. Samuels's summary remark in his brief study of the writer: "In verse," Samuels notes, Updike "frequently exploits the familiar," often simply "as an occasion to display his talent for comic rhyme." What strikes the reader immediately about Updike's poems is his heavy reliance on everyday experience, whether autobiographical or generic, and the way he manipulates language to achieve distinctive, often unusual and amusing, rhyming and rhythmical patterns. Reviewers of individual volumes of Updike's work have not always been convinced, however, that this kind of rhetorical gamesmanship has offered sufficient compensation for a body of works that are, in fact, intellectually lightweight when compared with the serious fiction that Updike has produced during the past two decades. As a result, the serious student of Updike's poetry is faced with examining the work in a critical vacuum or in the constant context of his fiction.

One can see, though, that Updike's poetry demonstrates his ability to work deftly within a variety of forms, turning them to his own purposes. His published poems include sonnets, free verse modeled on that of Walt Whitman and contemporary figures, Spenserian stanzas, elegiac quatrains, extended commentary in heroic couplets, and works that follow (at times almost slavishly) other poetic conventions. More often than not, the forms are used in parody, as are the manifold rhyme schemes that remind one of the cantos of Lord Byron's *Don Juan* (1819-1824) in their variety and in their reliance on sight rhyme or colloquial pronunciation for effect. For example, in "Agatha Christie and Beatrix Potter," Updike closes his short, humorous comparison of these authors (whose works he sees as essentially similar) with a couplet of praise for having given readers "cozy scares and chases/ That end with innocence acquitted—/ Except for Cotton-tail, who did it." Similarly, in a light limerick poking fun at young Swedish scholars, he opens with the couplet: "There

was a young student of Lund/ Whose -erstanding was not always und."

Updike's art, especially his poetry, is thus intentionally enigmatic, because it contains a discoverable but not self-evident truth. The surface finish, whether comic, ironic, or sexually explicit, is often simply the bait to lure readers into the world of the poem. Once there, Updike asks his readers to look closely at their own lives, often challenging them to be as introspective about themselves as he is about his own experiences. In that way, he hopes to help others make sense of a world that he believes is essentially good and in which good people can prosper.

Like many contemporary poets, Updike also relies on the appearance of the poem on the page for effect. In poems such as "Typical Optical" (from *Facing Nature*), he prints various lines in different type styles and sizes to make his point: As one gets older, one's vision (literally) changes, and what one could see at close range as a child becomes blurred to more mature eyes. As a result, when Updike says that the novels of Marcel Proust and the poetry of John Donne "Recede from my ken in/ Their eight-point Granjon," he emphasizes the problem by printing the phrase "eight-point Granjon" in the type face and size to which it refers. Then, in his closing remark that his "old eyeballs" can now "enfold/ No print any finer/ Than sans-serif bold," he prints the final phrase in sans-serif type and has the final word in bold print. Similarly, the lines of the poem "Pendulum" (from *The Carpentered Hen, and Other Tame Creatures*) are printed beneath the title at angles resembling the swinging of a pendulum on a clock, and individual words in the poem "Letter Slot" (from the same volume) are arranged on the page to suggest letters falling through a mail slot onto the floor.

The reader often laughs at Updike's tricks, but the poetry cannot be judged first-rate simply for the author's ability to manipulate both the language and the conventions of the tradition in which he works. As a consequence, Updike is too often dismissed as a dilettante in this field. A close examination of his published volumes, however, reveals that the author himself is careful to distinguish between "poetry" and "light verse." Much of what Updike calls "light verse" is simply poetic exercise, intended to highlight the wonderful ability of language to evoke amusement and thought in both reader and writer. Often the impetus for such poetry comes from the world around Updike: newspaper accounts, books that are popular best sellers, visits he has made to various places where the benign incongruities of life manifest themselves to him. Poems such as "V. B. Nimble, V. B. Quick" (from *The Carpentered Hen, and Other Tame Creatures*) may not offer substantial food for thought: The genesis of the poem—an entry in the British Broadcasting Corporation's *Radio Times* that "V. B. Wigglesworth, F.R.S., Quick Professor of Biology" will speak on an upcoming program— triggers in Updike's mind a humorous comparison with the hero of the nursery rhyme "Jack Be Nimble, Jack Be Quick," and the resultant verse about a frenetic scientist dashing off experiments and hurrying off to talk about them provides momentary pleasure to readers without trying to make a serious observation about the world of science. This poem, and many others like it in the Updike canon, are simply offered as tidbits to evoke humor and sympathy in an otherwise somber world.

Because Updike is so facile at handling the many demands facing the poet, it is easy to overlook the serious nature of much of his output. A substantial number of his poems are attempts to examine the significance of his own life's experiences and to explore questions of importance to contemporary society. As in his fiction, Updike is especially concerned with the place of religion in the modern world, and often, beneath the surface playfulness, one can see the poet grappling with complex moral and philosophical issues. He is also a careful student of the literary tradition he has inherited, and his attempts to examine the place of literature as an interpreter of experience often find their way into his poems.

"LOVE SONNET"

The way in which Updike combines the comic and the serious is illustrated quite well in his poem "Love Sonnet" (from *Midpoint, and Other Poems*). Its title suggests its subject, but the content is at first glance enigmatic. The opening line, "In Love's rubber armor I come to you," is followed by a string of letters printed down the page, as if they were the endings of lines which have been omitted: "b/ oo/ b./ c,/ d/ c/ d:/ e/ f—/ e/ f./ g/ g." The form of the sonnet has thus been pre-

served (the "oo" sound of the third line rhyming with the "you" at the end of the first line), but the content is absent. Adding simultaneously to the confusion and to the humor is the overt sexual implication of the only full line: One cannot mistake the literal meaning of the proposition. Nevertheless, a closer look at the poem, especially in the light of the literary tradition that it seems to parody, suggests that there may in fact be serious purpose here. Traditionally, sonnets have been poems about love. Although their content has varied, the form itself has usually suggested to readers the kind of interpretation the poet expects. One looks for the words in a sonnet to be metaphors describing the way in which a speaker feels about his beloved. In this poem, however, the process is reversed. The overt reference to physical lovemaking is the metaphor: "Love's rubber armor" is the sonnet form itself, an elastic medium in which the lover, working within conventions—and protected by them—is able to "come to" his beloved and display both his wit and his devotion. In this way, then, Updike is making a comment on the literary tradition: The sonnet form has both strengths and weaknesses; its conventions provide a way to ensure that meaning is conveyed but limit the extent to which the writer may put the form to use without risking misinterpretation. Appearing at first to be a risqué comic piece about a subject much talked of and trivialized in Updike's own society, "Love Sonnet" emerges as a serious statement about the nature of poetry itself.

The special strengths and weaknesses of Updike as a poet can be seen in those poems that he presented to the world as "poems" rather than verses. In these, he is often franker in discussions of sex, and the explicit language may offend some readers. No subject seems sacred, yet it is precisely the concern Updike had for sacred things in human life that led him to write graphically about human relationships. From his study of everyday occurrences, Updike tried to isolate that which is important for humans, to show how people construct meaning from the disparate events of their own lives.

"MIDPOINT"

The most extended example of Updike's use of individual events to make statements about universals occurs in his long autobiographical poem "Midpoint."

Published as the centerpiece of the 1969 collection *Midpoint, and Other Poems*, "Midpoint" is a collage of text, drawings, and photographs that traces the poet's life from infancy to its midpoint, as Updike reaches age thirty-six. Though the poem has been dismissed by some critics as "quirky," Updike himself insists that in it he demonstrates what is for him an artistic credo, a search for "the reality behind the immediately apparent." In "Midpoint," Updike reveals himself to be a believer in "pointillism" as both technique and philosophy: "Praise Pointillism, Calculus and all/ That turn the world infinitesimal." Like Whitman in *Leaves of Grass* (1855), Updike takes his own life as an example of the human condition, finding in it something of value to share with others.

"Midpoint" consists of five cantos, four of which are modeled closely on writers of the past. Each is preceded by a short "argument" reminiscent of that provided by John Milton in *Paradise Lost* (1667, 1674), in which Updike provides the reader with clues to the action of the canto. In the first, in stanzas reminiscent of those in Dante's *La divina commedia* (c. 1320; *The Divine Comedy*, 1802), Updike reviews his childhood and his growing awareness of himself as a discrete entity in the universe. An only child, he comes to see himself as the center of that universe, a point around which the world revolves. Though to sing of himself (an allusion to Whitman) is "all wrong," he has no choice since he has no other subject so appropriate or about which he knows so much. The second canto consists exclusively of photographs: Updike as baby and young child, his parents, himself as a teenager, himself and his wife, their first child. These are printed with varying degrees of sharpness: Some appear crisply defined, some are little more than a blur of dots on the page. This intentional shifting of focus carries out graphically the theme Updike expresses in the "argument" that he prints at the beginning of the canto: "Distance improves vision." In a sense, the action in this canto repeats that of the first, but from another perspective: The reader sees what he has just read about.

The third canto, composed in Spenserian stanzas, is titled "The Dance of the Solids." Based on Updike's readings in *Scientific American*, it presents in verse a view of the way the universe is constructed. The bonding of atomic particles into larger and larger structures eventually "yield[s],/ In Units growing visible, the World we wield!" It would be easy to lose sight of the poet's purpose in these most ingenious iambic pentameter lines. Updike uses the language of science, and even mathematical formulas, with exceptional precision to present his argument. For example, in explaining what happens when a solid is heated, he writes: "$T = 3Nk$ is much too neat." The stanzas are not simply virtuoso performances; in them, Updike provides an analogy for examining the human condition. Just as the visible world is composed of subatomic particles combined in meaningful ways, so are people's lives simply the ordered and meaningful arrangements of individual incidents. To understand the meaning, one must first isolate and describe the incident.

The fourth canto, "The Play of Memory," contains text, line drawings, and close-ups from the photographs that appear in canto 2. The text is modeled on Whitman's poetic technique of free verse. In this section of the poem, Updike explores his marriage and the role sex plays in shaping human lives. The final canto, written in couplets that suggest the method of Alexander Pope in *An Essay on Man* (1733-1734), is a review of the modern scene in which Updike the poet finds himself. In it, he offers advice, alternately serious and satiric, for living. In the fashion of Arthur Hugh Clough in "The Last Decalogue," a parody of the Ten Commandments, Updike admonishes his readers: "Don't kill; or if you must, while killing grieve"; "Doubt not; that is, until you can't believe"; "Don't covet Mrs. X; or if you do,/ Make sure, before you leap, she covets you." As in the third canto, readers may become so enraptured with the wise witticisms and the deft handling of poetic form that they lose the sense of the canto's place within the poem. In fact, the poem has prompted more than one reader to wonder, as did the reviewer for *Library Journal* in 1970, what Updike was "up to" in "Midpoint."

If, however, one accepts what Updike himself has said about "Midpoint," that in it he attempts to explain his own attitudes about his life and art, one can see the poem as a kind of poetic credo, a systematic statement about the poet's acceptance of his role as poet. The many references to other artists and the conscious use of recognizable forms associated with specific poets and poems suggest that Updike is using his own life to make a statement about the way art is created. In fact, in the closing lines of the fifth canto, he observes, "The time is gone, when *Pope* could ladle Wit/ In couplet droplets, and decanter it." No longer can "*Wordsworth's* sweet brooding" or "*Tennyson's* unease" be effective as vehicles for explaining the human condition. The world is now a sad and perhaps an absurd place, and art has followed suit by offering those who come to it only "blank explosions and a hostile smile." Updike, who has accepted the notion of the absurd from modern theologians who have pointed out that faith cannot be rational even if it is essential, offers this poem as an ironic, sometimes comic, and sometimes highly personal and hence prejudicial view of the world. For Updike, autobiography has become metaphor, because only by viewing the world through others' eyes can individuals hope to understand something of the significance of their own predicament. Similarly, as he has used the events of his own life to make a statement about life itself, Updike uses the forms of his predecessors to make a statement about the efficacy of art in the modern world.

AMERICANA, AND OTHER POEMS

In *Americana, and Other Poems*, Updike continues to use his own life experiences to draw readers' interest and then to lead to important realizations about human life in general, and with the same dazzlingly skillful and ironically humorous techniques. The title poem interweaves creative descriptions of people and places in urban and suburban America with philosophic commentary derived therefrom, to the effect that "the American way" leaves beauty to survive on its own, without the guidance of kings or cultural leaders. Updike humorously illustrates this point by admitting to losing the unfinished poem in travel and finding and completing it later, at another location, and then only to lose it again by virtue of transfer to the readers, who will of course fail to completely comprehend or appreciate it. Such mixture of creative technique, lightly humorous tone, and philosophic insight make this title poem among the best in this collection.

Updike's humorously satiric insight is also obvious in "Phoenix," in which he describes this converted desert area as an artificial universe of fast-food restaurants and high-rise buildings, a world of make-believe created by wealth, with golf courses, fake gardens, and jogging paths that, ironically, trap rather than liberate the swarm of retired persons struggling to defeat death. The shift from artificial human creations to minimalized humans as a metaphoric swarm of insects effectively undercuts the egotism of the wealthy gathered in Phoenix. Updike makes the same point just as creatively in "Slum Lords," in which he criticizes the super-rich as bad neighbors because they are almost never home, given they have so many homes they feel compelled to visit, or because they constantly tear down homes and rebuild bigger ones, then leave again. Thus, the neighborhoods of the super-rich are ghost towns like Tombstone after the silver rush, so Updike avows excluding them because, oxymoronically, their wealth is a form of poverty.

There are also several instances in *Americana, and Other Poems* of Updike's creative use of the sonnet form, probably most effectively in "To a Skylark." Obviously a deliberate use of the title of Percy Bysshe Shelley's famous Romantic poem, Updike reverses the normal expectation of ironic use of the title and instead writes absolutely consistently with Shelley's longer poem. He presents the skylark as lifting him out of his earthbound struggles—in the specific circumstance, his problems with golf—and through empathy making him one with the bird's "sheer blithe being." Such conscious, skillful use of Shelley's poem in a different form, sonnet rather than ode, is a testament both to Updike's admiration of Shelley and to Updike's own poetic skill.

Probably most consistent with the entire volume, though, in its preoccupation with aging and death, obvious concerns of Updike late in life, when these poems were written, is the long poem "Song of Myself," a title borrowed from Whitman. Updike does write somewhat ironically in this poem. Rather than the optimistic inclusiveness of Whitman's poem, this poem is focused on Updike's decline in health and is a bemoaning of death rather than a celebration of life. Updike considers his slowness to heal, his sun-damaged skin, his difficulty praying and sleeping, his painful dental implants, the scars from a dog's bite in childhood, and other maladies as he declines toward death, and yet, ultimately, he finds affirmation in the very power of the methodical forces that destroy him. He realizes that this same "shame of time" also controls everything else, leading him to the realization that he and his skin have shared experiences with a larger force, which "rides and sees," meaning a deity of some type in which he can, finally, believe and to whom he is reconciled. Thus, even this seeming reversal of Whitman's optimism is only a semireversal, in its creative presentation of a life in decline that is still somehow affirmed.

ENDPOINT, AND OTHER POEMS

Endpoint, and Other Poems collects poems written in the last seven years of Updike's life and brought together weeks before his death. It is more serious than many of his collections, as its main theme is the poet's aging and death. The title poem, "Endpoint," is a series of poems, a number of which were written on his birthdays. In these poems, he remembers incidents from his childhood, his career as writer, and his personal life, and reflects on his aged body and his terminal illness. In "Birthday Shopping, 2007," he is startled by his reflection in the mirror of a movie theater, wondering "Where was the freckled boy who used to peek/ into the front-hall mirror, off to school?" In "Hospital 11/23-27/08," he writes of dying: "God save us from ever ending, though billions have./ The world is blanket by foregone deaths,/ small beads of ego, bright with appetite,/ whose pin-sized price of light winked out." The other sections in this volume contain light verse and sonnets.

OTHER MAJOR WORKS

LONG FICTION: *The Poorhouse Fair*, 1959; *Rabbit, Run*, 1960; *The Centaur*, 1963; *Of the Farm*, 1965; *Couples*, 1968; *Bech: A Book*, 1970; *Rabbit Redux*, 1971; *A Month of Sundays*, 1975; *Marry Me: A Romance*, 1976; *The Coup*, 1978; *Rabbit Is Rich*, 1981; *The Witches of Eastwick*, 1984; *Roger's Version*, 1986; *S.*, 1988; *Rabbit at Rest*, 1990; *Memories of the Ford Administration*, 1992; *Brazil*, 1994; *In the Beauty of the Lilies*, 1996; *Toward the End of Time*, 1997; *Bech at Bay: A Quasi-Novel*, 1998; *Gertrude and Claudius*, 2000; *Seek My Face*, 2002; *Villages*, 2004; *Terrorist*, 2006; *The Widows of Eastwick*, 2008.

SHORT FICTION: *The Same Door*, 1959; *Pigeon Feathers, and Other Stories*, 1962; *Olinger Stories: A Selection*, 1964; *The Music School*, 1966; *Museums and Women, and Other Stories*, 1972; *Problems, and Other Stories*, 1979; *Three Illuminations in the Life of an American Author*, 1979; *Too Far to Go: The Maples Stories*, 1979; *The Chaste Planet*, 1980; *Bech Is Back*, 1982; *The Beloved*, 1982; *Trust Me*, 1987; *Brother Grasshopper*, 1990 (limited edition); *The Afterlife, and Other Stories*, 1994; *Licks of Love: Short Stories and a Sequel, "Rabbit Remembered,"* 2000; *The Complete Henry Bech: Twenty Stories*, 2001; *The Early Stories, 1953-1975*, 2003; *The Maples Stories*, 2009; *My Father's Tears, and Other Stories*, 2009.

PLAYS: *Three Texts from Early Ipswich: A Pageant*, pb. 1968; *Buchanan Dying*, pb. 1974.

NONFICTION: *Assorted Prose*, 1965; *Picked-Up Pieces*, 1975; *Hugging the Shore: Essays and Criticism*, 1983; *Just Looking: Essays on Art*, 1989; *Self-Consciousness: Memoirs*, 1989; *Odd Jobs: Essays and Criticism*, 1991; *Golf Dreams: Writings on Golf*, 1996; *More Matter: Essays and Criticism*, 1999; *Still Looking: Essays on American Art*, 2005; *Due Considerations: Essays and Criticism*, 2007; *Updike in Cincinnati: A Literary Performance*, 2007.

EDITED TEXT: *The Best American Short Stories of the Century*, 2000.

BIBLIOGRAPHY

Boswell, Marshall. *John Updike's Rabbit Tetralogy: Mastered Irony in Motion*. Columbia: University of Missouri Press, 2001. A study of Harry Angstrom's literary journey through life.

Campbell, James. *Syncopations: Beats, New Yorkers, and Writers in the Dark*. Berkeley: University of California Press, 2008. Broad-ranging study of contemporary American fiction writers and poets, with two chapters on Updike, including some discussion of *Americana, and Other Poems*.

DeBellis, Jack, and Michael Broomfield, eds. *John Updike: A Bibliography of Primary and Secondary Materials, 1948-2006*. New Castle, Del.: Oak Knoll Press, 2007. A comprehensive bibliography covering Updike's works through 2006.

Detweiler, Robert. *John Updike*. Rev. ed. Boston: Twayne, 1984. An excellent introductory survey of

Updike's work through 1983. Contains a chronology, a biographical sketch, analysis of the fiction and its sources, a select bibliography, and an index.

Greiner, Donald J. *The Other John Updike: Poems, Short Stories, Prose, Play*. Athens: Ohio University Press, 1981. While devoting a considerable amount of space to other critics, Greiner, who has written three books about Updike, here traces Updike's artistic development in his writing that both parallels and extends the themes of the novels.

James, Clive. "Final Act." Review of *Endpoint, and Other Poems*. *The New York Times*, May 3, 2009, p. BR15. James finds the tone in Updike's final poetry collection to be darker and praises the consistency of theme. He feels Updike's poetry deserves more acclaim.

Lehmann-Haupt, Christopher. "John Updike, a Lyrical Writer of the Middle-Class Man, Dies at Seventy-six." *The New York Times*, January 28, 2009, p. A28. A lengthy obituary describes the life and writings of Updike, providing some discussion of his primary novels and short stories.

Miller, D. Quentin. *John Updike and the Cold War: Drawing the Iron Curtain*. Columbia: University of Missouri Press, 2001. Studies the influence of Cold War society and politics in forming Updike's worldview.

Olster, Stacey, ed. *The Cambridge Companion to John Updike*. New York: Cambridge University Press, 2006. Comprehensive, detailed treatment of the full range of Updike's writing, with some discussion of *Americana, and Other Poems*.

Pritchard, William H. *Updike: America's Man of Letters*. South Royalton, Vt.: Steerforth Press, 2000. A biography of the novelist, who Pritchard sees as the heir to such American storytellers as William Dean Howells and Henry James, alone in a sea of metafiction.

Laurence W. Mazzeno
Updated by John L. Grigsby

V

Jean Valentine

Born: Chicago, Illinois; April 27, 1934

Principal poetry

Dream Barker, and Other Poems, 1965
Pilgrims, 1969
Ordinary Things, 1974
The Messenger, 1979
Home Deep Blue: New and Selected Poems, 1989
The River at Wolf, 1992
The Under Voice: Selected Poems, 1995
Growing Darkness, Growing Light, 1997
The Cradle of the Real Life, 2000
*Door in the Mountain: New and Collected Poems,
    1965-2003*, 2004
Little Boat, 2007
Break the Glass, 2010

Other literary forms

Although Jean Valentine is principally known as a poet, she edited *The Lighthouse Keeper: Essays on the Poetry of Eleanor Ross Taylor* (2001) in an effort to expand poetry readers' exposure to the North Carolinian poet. Valentine also served as a visiting editor for the winter, 2008-2009, issue of *Ploughshares*.

Achievements

Jean Valentine's creative efforts have been acknowledged with the Shelley Memorial Award from the Poetry Society of America (1999) and the Maurice English Poetry Award (2000). *Home Deep Blue* garnered her the Beatrice Hawley Award. The poet's visibility was raised to new levels when Valentine received the 2004 National Book Award in Poetry for *Door in the Mountain*. This award was followed by the Morton Dauwen Zabel Award in 2006 and the Wallace Stevens Award in 2009. She served as New York's state poet from 2008 to 2010.

Valentine has received a Guggenheim Fellowship, a National Endowment for the Arts Literature Fellowship in Poetry, and grants from the New York State Council for the Arts, the New York Foundation for the Arts, the National Endowment for the Arts, the Rockefeller Foundation, and the Bunting Institute.

Biography

On April 27, 1934, Jean Valentine was born to John W. Valentine and Jean Purcell Valentine in Chicago, Illinois. When she was three, her family moved to New York State. Seven years later, her father returned from serving in the U.S. Navy during World War II, but he had what would later be known as post-traumatic stress syndrome. The ramifications for the Valentine family were psychological instability, frequent moves, and emotional uncertainty. The only consistent stability in the young Valentine's life was a summer retreat, referred to as "the farm." It provided a sanctuary of calm and solace for the young poet, for it was there she found aunts and uncles who treated her as though she were a beloved grandchild. The family moved to Massachusetts, where Valentine attended Milton Academy for Girls' School. She entered Radcliffe College in 1952 and majored in English. In 1956, while she was still a student, her composition "Poem" was published in *The Harvard Advocate*. She graduated cum laude.

In 1957, Valentine married a man three years her senior, James Clark Chace, a leading foreign-policy historian and author. The couple had two daughters, Sarah (born 1958) and Rebecca (born 1960), before being divorced in 1968.

In her late thirties, Valentine faced a watershed moment. A fear of the darker elements of poetry seeped into her consciousness, and she worried that it was the darkness that historically had driven poets to commit suicide. She sought professional guidance to help her deal with the fear and her alcoholism. She did not write from 1982 to 1987.

In 1989, Valentine went to Ireland to live with abstract painter Barrie Cook. They married in 1991. Following their divorce in 1996, Valentine returned to her longtime home, New York City. A respected teacher, Valentine has instructed students at Sarah Lawrence College; held workshops at Swarthmore College, Yale

University, and the Ninety-Second Street Y in New York City; and led graduate writing programs for New York University and Columbia University.

ANALYSIS

Jean Valentine's poetic recognition came much later than for most poets, yet the postponement of her success serves to underline her determination and steadfastness in writing in a genre that receives limited recognition from the general public and publishers.

Nearly ten years after her first poem appeared in *The Harvard Advocate*, she published her first collection, *Dream Barker, and Other Poems*. She had almost given up on poetry and was working on a novel when her collection was chosen from more than three hundred entries to be published in the Yale Series of Younger Poets.

Valentine's style is unique. Minimalism and brevity are the words used to describe much of her work. At times the sparse, taunting words almost attain the level of exclusion. However, readers can make a connection if they let go of the need for control and enter a dream-like consciousness without boundaries. Valentine has frequently said her poetry is strongly driven and shaped by dreams. It is in that state of existence between waking and sleeping that connections to distant memories fill the mind. Her language works to catch the buried filaments of the readers' experiences, to awaken their personal memories, and to allow them to shade in the white spaces she leaves behind. The links between the words on the page and readers' memories are like gossamer tendrils reaching out and fastening on to feelings kept hidden, except during sleep.

DOOR IN THE MOUNTAIN

Door in the Mountain received the 2004 National Book Award in Poetry; this award created a larger audience for Valentine's restrained and provocative style. In the title poem, Valentine thrusts the reader into the elusive world of dreams: "Never ran this hard through the valley/ never ate so many stars." She is running while carrying a dead deer slung over her neck and shoulders, its legs in front of her. She ends the poem with "People are not wanting/ to let me in// Door in the mountain/ let me in." The reader is left to interpret what the mountain is—sanctuary or rejection, success or

Jean Valentine (AP/Wide World Photos)

failure. Just what the door is and whether it shuts people out or welcomes them in is not certain. Therefore, readers will view the door, the deer, and the mountain through their individual filters of experiences, making the poem's impact personal and magical.

Mists of dreamy detachment, swirling with reason and imagination, are characteristic of Valentine's lyrics. An abstract, ethereal voice urges readers to follow as the poet seeks to reveal the tangible world through language. Valentine's evocative words pull readers deeper into a realm of exquisite mysteries. The words provide elusive clues that slide out of reach when readers try to grasp the meaning. Sometimes readers feel cheated and sense that Valentine is withholding information, as if she does not want to reveal what she sees. The compression created by Valentine's style leaves open spaces, silences to be completed by readers' personal histories. Thus, understanding comes only when readers listen to her poems with their inner voices. The meaning lies underneath the silence, as in "We cut the new day," which begins: "We cut the new day/ like a key:/ betrayal."

THE RIVER AT WOLF

The inner life of dreams and transcendence is strongly woven into *The River at Wolf*. The words are starkly laid down on the page, like silhouettes against a sheer curtain, yet their tone of intimacy shimmers beneath the surface, as in "The Under Voice," which ends "Everyone else may leave you, I will never leave you, fugitive."

"Seeing You," which contains autobiographical details, was written when Valentine was coping with the death of her mother and, at the same time, falling in love with the man who would be her husband. The poem is in two parts. The first section paints images of how the poet saw her mother, first as a parent ("I was born under the mudbank/ and you gave me your boat"), then as a woman ("I could see your fear and your love,/ I could see you, brilliance magnified"). The second part reveals how the intense mother-daughter relationship parallels a deep relationship with a lover: "I could see you,/ Brilliance, at the bottom. Trust you// stillness in the last red inside place./ Then past the middle of the earth it got light again." "Seeing You" is a highly visual poem that uses the imagery of water and includes layers of symbolism and psychological nuances. The visceral quality of water permeates the poem's tone, from the mother giving her daughter a boat to the lake of trust. Within the water images are the universal topics of life, fear, and love: "I dove down my mental lake fear and love:/ first fear then under it love."

LITTLE BOAT

Little Boat is a slender collection of poetry that requires the reader to listen and become involved in the poems' intention. The words are spare, but the subtext vibrates with dichotomies and spaces waiting to be filled in by the reader. Valentine explores subjects such as life and death, life of an artist in prison, fairy tales, love, and Jesus in all their complexities as she focuses on the soul's journey. Her tools are suggestive words that are restrained and complex. The meaning inside the coiled language is elusive, but the words hint at possibilities. The poems ask a reader to probe beneath the camou-

flage of reality and journey to the world of the spiritual and unknown. One section deals with contacting Jesus, and with its spiritual and religious tones, it moves Valentine deeper into a numinous style. In hope of reaching Jesus, the speaker in "This Side" carries an antenna with him, ever hopeful he will receive a message.

In "The Eleventh Hour," based on the Hans Christian Andersen fairy tale "The Wild Swans," a princess must mutely weave eleven coats out of nettles to transform her brothers from swans back into princes. The poet's voice patiently seeks insight, yet leaves the conclusion unclear: "your sister had finished weaving your other arm/ she dove down to give it to you// through the gray water. You couldn't/ take it. You wouldn't."

The lingering feel to the collection is that of a writer looking back at a life through time-shaped eyes, trying to see below and above where existence has brought her. This collection invites readers to reach inside, as Valentine often does, to view their own private book of memories.

OTHER MAJOR WORK

EDITED TEXT: *The Lighthouse Keeper: Essays on the Poetry of Eleanor Ross Taylor*, 2001.

BIBLIOGRAPHY

Bland, Celia. "The World as Her Own: A Profile of Jean Valentine." *Poets and Writers* (November/ December, 2004): 48-53. The article provides a penetrating profile of the poet and her personal challenges. Valentine's responses help place the poet in the world of contemporary poetry. It yields more of the woman behind the poetry, while using her publications as guides.

Hacht, Anne Marie, and Ira Mark Milne, eds. *Poetry for Students*. Vol. 24. Detroit: Gale, 2006. This clearly written discussion of "Seeing You" offers points of reference that remove the mystery for a novice poetry reader and provides a starting point from which to understand Valentine's stark style.

Rivard, David. Review of *The River at Wolf. Plough-shares* 19, no. 2 (Fall, 1993): 246. Helps place Valentine in the contemporary poetry movement. Rivard clearly shows the book's strengths and weaknesses. Rivard discusses Valentine's tendency to expose feelings too long hidden, which serves to generate an intimacy in her poetry that unsettles and comforts.

Upton, Lee. "'Dream Barker': Preoedepal Fusion and Radiant Boundaries in Jean Valentine." In *The Muse of Abandonment: Origin, Identity, Mastery in Five American Poets*. London: Associated University Presses, 1998. Discussion of Valentine's use of dreams and their imagery in her poetry, starting with *Dream Barker, and Other Poems* and later volumes as well. Includes bibliographical references and index.

Valentine, Jean. "A Conversation with Jean Valentine." Interview by Eve Grubin. *Crossroads* 59 (2002). Valentine discusses some of the topics she explores in her poems—war, politics, and feminism—and the impact of dreams and the unseen on her poems. She also mentions poets who influenced her poetry.

_____. Interview by Michael Klein. *American Poetry Review* 20, no. 4 (July/August, 1991): 39-44. Klein's interview of Valentine provides insight into how she approaches the writing process. The poet's description of her life allows deeper understanding of her restrained lyrics and how dreams are critical to her writing.

_____. "Jean Valentine." http://www.jeanvalentine .com. Valentine's official Web site offers a biography, list of books, and information on readings.

Modrea Mitchell-Reichert

MARK VAN DOREN

Born: Hope, Illinois; June 13, 1894
Died: Torrington, Connecticut; December 10, 1972

PRINCIPAL POETRY

Spring Thunder, and Other Poems, 1924
7 P.M., and Other Poems, 1926
Now the Sky, and Other Poems, 1928
Jonathan Gentry, 1931
A Winter Diary, and Other Poems, 1935
The Last Look, and Other Poems, 1937
Collected Poems, 1922-1938, 1939

The Mayfield Deer, 1941
Our Lady Peace, and Other War Poems, 1942
The Seven Sleepers, and Other Poems, 1944
The Country Year, 1946
The Careless Clock: Poems About Children in the Family, 1947
New Poems, 1948
Humanity Unlimited: Twelve Sonnets, 1950
In That Far Land, 1951
Mortal Summer, 1953
Spring Birth, and Other Poems, 1953
Selected Poems, 1954
Morning Worship, and Other Poems, 1960
Collected and New Poems, 1924-1963, 1963
The Narrative Poems, 1964
That Shining Place: New Poems, 1969
Good Morning: Last Poems, 1973

OTHER LITERARY FORMS

In addition to poetry, Mark Van Doren also wrote drama, fiction, and various nonfiction works. Two of his plays, *The Last Days of Lincoln* (1959) and *Never, Never Ask His Name* (pr. 1965), werc produced in 1961 and 1965, respectively. The latter was published in *Three Plays* (1966), together with two unproduced plays, *A Little Night Music* and *The Weekend That Was*. His works of fiction include the novels *The Transients* (1935), *Windless Cabins* (1940), *Tilda* (1943), and *Home with Hazel* (1957), as well as several books of short stories that were eventually published in three volumes as *Collected Stories* (1962-1968). Van Doren also wrote three books of children's fiction.

Van Doren's nonfiction works include *The Autobiography of Mark Van Doren* (1958) and critical and biographical works on various authors. He also did a great deal of editorial work, including anthologies and critical editions of works of fiction and nonfiction. The authors with whom he dealt critically include John Dryden, Henry David Thoreau, William Shakespeare, and Nathaniel Hawthorne.

ACHIEVEMENTS

One of Mark Van Doren's most impressive achievements is the sheer volume of his work; he was the author of fifty-six books and the editor of twenty-three books. He was honored with the Pulitzer Prize in 1940 for his *Collected Poems, 1922-1938*. His other awards include Columbia University's Alexander Hamilton Medal in 1959, the Hale Award in 1960, the Huntington Hartford Creative Award in 1962, the Emerson-Thoreau Award in 1963, and the Academy of American Poets Fellowship in 1967. He also received many honorary degrees. In addition to formal awards, Van Doren's poetry won praise for its craftsmanship from other better-known poets, including Robert Frost, Allen Tate, and T. S. Eliot. Van Doren became a member of the American Academy of Arts and Letters in 1940 and served as chancellor for the Academy of American Poets from 1949 to 1952.

BIOGRAPHY

Mark Albert Van Doren, the son of physician Charles Lucius Van Doren and Dora Ann Butz, was

Mark Van Doren (Time & Life Pictures/Getty Images)

born on his parents' farm near Hope, Illinois, and lived there for the first six years of his life. Then Van Doren's parents moved with him and his four brothers to the university town of Urbana, Illinois, where Van Doren's father had planned to retire but instead continued to practice medicine.

Van Doren attended the University of Illinois at Urbana, as his well-known older brother Carl had done. Both men were strongly influenced by Stuart Sherman, an English professor, and Mark was also taught by Leonard Bloomfield, the linguist, then a young instructor of German. Van Doren received his bachelor's degree in 1914 and entered the university's graduate program in English. A course with Sherman in nineteenth century prose writers introduced Van Doren to the writings of Thoreau, the subject of his master's thesis, which was published in 1916. He received his master's degree in 1915.

Mark Van Doren again followed his brother Carl's footsteps, going in 1915 to study at Columbia University, where Carl had studied and where, at the time, he was teaching English. Carl helped to guide his brother's doctoral studies and even suggested the topic of Mark's dissertation, Dryden's poetry. Van Doren's academic career was interrupted in 1917 by World War I. His Army career, during which he never left the United States, consisted mainly of paperwork and ended with the armistice in 1918.

At the beginning of 1919, Van Doren returned to New York to continue work on his dissertation. He was awarded a fellowship to study abroad in 1920 and spent the year in London and Paris, finishing his dissertation in London and receiving his degree upon his return home. His dissertation, like his master's thesis, was published. He spent the summer of 1920 serving as literary editor of *The Nation*, replacing Carl, who wanted some free time to devote to other literary projects. He began teaching at Columbia in the fall of 1920. Although he had planned to teach for only a short time, he remained at Columbia until his retirement in 1959. He also lectured regularly at St. John's College in Annapolis, Maryland, from 1937 to 1957, and in 1963, he came out of retirement to accept a visiting professorship at Harvard University.

In 1922, Van Doren married Dorothy Graffe, with

whom he had worked on *The Nation*. They had two sons, Charles and John, and lived in New York and on a farm in Cornwall, Connecticut.

In addition to his teaching and writing, Van Doren also resumed work on *The Nation*. He served as literary editor from 1924 to 1928 and as film critic from 1935 to 1938, as well as being a frequent contributor in the period between those two positions. As literary editor, he published the works of then unknown poets such as Robert Graves, Hart Crane, and Allen Tate. *The Nation* was virtually a Van Doren family publication, with Carl, his first wife, Irita, and Mark and his wife all serving in various editorial positions.

Another of Van Doren's professional activities was his participation in a radio program called *Invitation to Learning* from 1940 to 1942. This weekly CBS program consisted of the discussion each week of a great literary work. For a year, the panel members were Van Doren, his friend Allen Tate, and Huntington Cairns. Van Doren also spent seven weeks reading Nathaniel Hawthorne's *The Scarlet Letter* (1850), fifteen minutes a day, for a CBS radio broadcast.

In 1953, Van Doren was semiretired from Columbia. He spent most of his time writing and traveling with his wife, the author of numerous books, including a biography of her husband. Six years later, at the age of sixty-five, Van Doren retired completely from college teaching. He continued to write until his death in 1972.

ANALYSIS

Although Mark Van Doren wrote more than one thousand poems, critics have not responded commensurately. Very few critics have seriously treated Van Doren's poetry, although other poets have praised it and almost no one has made unfavorable comments about it. More than one critic has suggested that the volume of the work has discouraged criticism. Since Van Doren wrote many good poems but none which have been singled out for special merit, a comprehensive study of his work would be a lengthy task. Van Doren's subject matter and style also vary so widely that choosing "representative" poems for study is virtually impossible. Finally, and most significantly, his poems can generally be grasped at first reading by any reader; unlike some of his contemporaries, Van Doren did not write poems requiring extensive annotation to be understood by the average reader. His poetry is therefore much more accessible than the work of many other modern poets, making the critic's work as interpreter for the most part unnecessary.

Despite the variety of Van Doren's poetry, some common themes do emerge. He frequently wrote about family and friends, love, death, animals, and nature—familiar poetic topics treated in a traditional manner. His imagery may be effective but is not startling or brilliant; his diction is precise but not unusual. His love for New England in general and his Connecticut farm in particular has caused critics to compare him to Robert Frost. Van Doren has also been compared to various other poets, from John Dryden to Edwin Arlington Robinson, but as Allen Tate observed, any traces of other poets are blended to create a unique body of poetry. Taken as a whole, Van Doren's poetry is like no one else's. It is highly personal in that it is centered around the events, people, concerns, and literature he knew well.

A complete study of Van Doren's poetry reveals no poetic innovations or surprises; it is the work of a competent poet and careful craftsman. Several critics have accurately applied the term "lucidity" to his work. Even his most complex poems are not obscure, although they were written at a time in which obscurity in poetry often seemed to be considered more of a virtue than a flaw.

The most admirable quality of Van Doren's poetry, says Richard Howard in his foreword to *Good Morning*, is his insistence that each poem be the first poem, as he says in "The First Poem." This insistence probably accounts for the breadth of his poetry, for he approached each new poem as if it possessed not only newness but also primacy, and he regarded the poetry of others in the same manner as he regarded his own. At the same time, he acknowledged his debt to the many English lyric poets who preceded him and whose tradition he helped to continue.

"A WINTER DIARY"

Some of Van Doren's poetry deals with typically American subjects. "A Winter Diary," one of his longest poems, is a fictitious verse diary of a winter spent on his Connecticut farm. The poem is written in heroic couplets, the form which Dryden popularized in his poetic dramas. At the beginning of the poem, the speaker explains the reason for its being written: After a "certain winter" had ended, he wanted to record his many memories of it because he felt they were already beginning to fade.

Those memories begin with the end of the summer, when the speaker and his family see their neighbors, who have spent the summer in the country, returning to town. In previous years, the speaker has joined in this exodus, but this time he is staying in the country and looking forward to the solitude that fall will bring. The poem records the memories and thoughts of the speaker through the winter to the beginning of spring. The events described in the poem are commonplace—a snowfall, family meals, games—but they are magnified by the joy and the sense of newness that the speaker feels. The winter, with its country solitude, has brought peace to him, and for once the spring represents an unwelcome intrusion. The poem, with its personal, "homey" tone, had much popular appeal and was admired by critics as well.

"THE SAGE IN THE SIERRA"

Another of Van Doren's poems, "The Sage in the Sierra," is also rather typically American. Its subtitle is "Emerson: 1871" and the speaker in the poem is Ralph Waldo Emerson himself. By 1871, Emerson had already written everything he was to write; speaking in the poem, he says that "they," a pronoun that in this poem is neither given nor requires an antecedent, are disappointed; they pity him because he is no longer writing. They want him to write, and they assume that he would if he could. Emerson, however, does not want to be seen or to see himself merely as the hand that holds the pen. From the Sierra and a Concord brook, he has learned the power and importance of silence and is for the time being content, like them, simply to exist. In his youth, he says, his mind was a forest and he felt the need to capture every bird in words. Now that he is older, his mind is still a forest, but he is content with only watching the birds. Even storms, emotional as well as actual, pass over him with little effect.

Emerson compares the "pure fire" of his present life to the "smoke" of his writing, which has obscured his experiences rather than making them clearer to him. In his writing, he says, he attempted to give the world truth and knowledge. He suggests that his youthful arrogance was greater than his own knowledge at the time and that having since then experienced what he had previously written about, he no longer feels the need to serve as the world's teacher. The poem ends with the statement that he wishes to be left alone to live his life quietly, for he refuses to help others experience life at the expense of his own. The poem is sensitive in its portrayal of Emerson and imaginative in its argument: Emerson stopped writing by choice, not because of the decline of his abilities. Van Doren uses Emerson as a representative of all creative artists, whom he sees here as sacrificing their own lives for their art and for humankind.

"NOW THE SKY"

Van Doren uses a more traditional theme in "Now the Sky." This poem is echoed in a section of "A Winter Diary" that uses the same astronomical imagery. The speaker, gazing at the stars on a calm night, asks himself a rather trite question: For how many years have men done what I am doing now? The stars are often seen as a symbol of eternity, since they existed before humanity and have outlasted centuries of people who have looked at them. The speaker sees the constellations first in these historical terms, but he says that modern people have knowledge that the earlier stargazers did not possess. People once saw the constellations, he says, as pictures drawn on the sky, but modern people know that this view is incorrect. People looked on the stars as a sort of nightly drama, with the characters interacting and heralding the arrival of each new season. The speaker says that the sky was like a room to ancient humans, which people entered and left in predictable fashion.

To modern people, however, the constellations hold neither drama nor mystery. People have tamed the animals and forsaken the heroes of the constellations through their scientific knowledge. They still have a "game" to play, however—the game of pretending that "the board was never lost," that people have kept the civilizing influence of earlier, less scientific ages. In its theme, the poem is more "modern" than much of Van Doren's poetry.

SONNETS

Van Doren's thirty-two sonnets are traditional and Shakespearean in form and similar to Renaissance sonnet sequences in subject matter, particularly to Edmund Spenser's *Amoretti* (1595). The thoughts expressed in the sonnets are neither original nor remarkable, but Van Doren's diction, in its clarity and simplicity, never descends to triteness. Like "A Winter's Diary," these sonnets show Van Doren's interest in traditional poetic forms that other modern poets had largely abandoned.

OTHER MAJOR WORKS

LONG FICTION: *The Transients*, 1935; *Windless Cabins*, 1940; *Tilda*, 1943; *Home with Hazel*, 1957.

SHORT FICTION: *Nobody Say a Word, and Other Stories*, 1953; *Collected Stories*, 1962-1968.

PLAYS: *The Last Days of Lincoln*, pb. 1959; *Three Plays*, 1966 (includes *Never, Never Ask His Name*, pr. 1965).

NONFICTION: *Henry David Thoreau*, 1916 (master's thesis); *The Poetry of John Dryden*, 1920 (dissertation); *Shakespeare*, 1939; *Liberal Education*, 1942; *Private Reader*, 1942; *Noble Voice*, 1946; *Nathaniel Hawthorne*, 1949; *The Autobiography of Mark Van Doren*, 1958; *The Professor and I*, 1958; *The Happy Critic, and Other Essays*, 1961; *The Essays of Mark Van Doren*, 1980.

CHILDREN'S LITERATURE: *Dick and Tom: Tales of Two Ponies*, 1931; *Dick and Tom in Town*, 1932; *The Transparent Tree*, 1940.

EDITED TEXTS: *An Anthology of World Poetry*, 1928; *The Oxford Book of American Prose*, 1932; *Walt Whitman*, 1945; *The Portable Emerson*, 1946.

BIBLIOGRAPHY

Bradbury, Eric, et al., eds. *The Penguin Companion to American Literature*. New York: McGraw-Hill, 1971. This source gives a few biographical details and lists many of Van Doren's major works.

Claire, William, ed. *The Essays of Mark Van Doren, 1942-1972*. Westport, Conn.: Greenwood Press, 1980. Although the emphasis here is on Van Doren's work as a critic, the introduction by Claire provides useful information on Van Doren's poetry and prose, discussing his early influences and development as a writer. Notes that Van Doren's critical approach was consistent with his position as a poet, namely that a poet "made statements and gave opinions as a professional on the theory that a civilized audience existed to hear them."

Curley, Maurice Kramer, et al., eds. *Modern American Literature*. Vol. 3. New York: Frederick Ungar, 1969. This source provides critical commentary on Van Doren's works. Several different critics and sources are represented.

Hart, James D., ed. *The Oxford Companion to American Literature*. New York: Oxford University Press, 1995. This source gives a listing of Van Doren's major works.

Hendrick, George, ed. *The Selected Letters of Mark Van Doren*. Baton Rouge: Louisiana State University Press, 1987. These letters, arranged chronologically, give insight into the literary and cultural world in which Van Doren lived. The introduction, although brief, provides some useful details about his poetry, such as his early influences and what other writers and critics thought of him.

Ledbetter, J. T. *Mark Van Doren*. New York: Peter Lang, 1996. A study of Van Doren's literary life and an examination of the major themes found in his work, focusing particularly on his poetry. Includes bibliographical references and index.

Perkins, George, et al., eds. *Benét's Reader's Encyclopedia of American Literature*. New York: HarperCollins, 1991. Includes a biography with emphasis on Van Doren's major works.

Rood, Karen L., ed. *American Literary Almanac from 1608 to the Present*. New York: Bruccoli Clark Layman, 1988. This source includes details about Van Doren and discussions about other literary figures with whom he associated.

Wakefield, Dan. "Lion: A Memoir of Mark Van Doren." *Ploughshares* 17, nos. 2/3 (Fall, 1991): 100. A former student recalls Van Doren in several anecdotes. Van Doren's most lasting lesson was that one must be true to one's deepest instincts, one's "noble voice," and never pander to the marketplace.

Claire Clements Morton

MONA VAN DUYN

Born: Waterloo, Iowa; May 9, 1921
Died: University City, Missouri; December 2, 2004

PRINCIPAL POETRY

Valentines to the Wide World, 1959
A Time of Bees, 1964
To See, to Take, 1970
Bedtime Stories, 1972
Merciful Disguises, 1973
Letters from a Father, and Other Poems, 1982
Near Changes, 1990
Firefall, 1993
If It Be Not I: Collected Poems, 1959-1982, 1993
Selected Poems, 2002

OTHER LITERARY FORMS

Two short stories by Mona Van Duyn (van DINE) were published in *Kenyon Review* in the 1940's. She also published reviews and criticism in *College English*, *American Prefaces*, and many literary magazines.

ACHIEVEMENTS

One of the few modern poets who succeeded in incorporating a contemporary sensibility within tight and traditional forms, Mona Van Duyn did not receive appropriate recognition until 1971, when she won the Bollingen Prize for Poetry and *To See, To Take* received the National Book Award. She had, however, won several prizes previous to those—the Eunice Tietjens Award, the Harriet Monroe Award from *Poetry*, the Helen Bullis Award from *Poetry Northwest*, the Hart Crane Memorial Award from American Weave Press, and first prize in the Borestone Mountain Awards Volume of 1968. She was one of the first five American poets to be awarded a grant from the National Endowment for the Arts. In 1972-1973, she held a Guggenheim Fellowship. She received the Russell Loines Award from the American Academy and Institute of Arts and Letters in 1976, the Academy of American Poets Fellowship in 1980, the Shelley Memorial Award in 1987, the Ruth Lilly Poetry Prize in 1989, and

the Pulitzer Prize in 1991 for *Near Changes*. She became a member of the American Academy of Arts and Letters in 1983 and served as chancellor for the Academy of American Poets from 1985 to 1998. She received honorary doctorates from Washington University, Cornell College, the University of Northern Iowa, the University of the South, George Washington University, and Georgetown University. She was named poet laureate consultant in poetry to the Library of Congress for 1992-1993.

Van Duyn published steadily after the appearance of her first collection, *Valentines to the Wide World*, in 1959. Her work has been praised by fellow poets as diverse as Carolyn Kizer, Richard Howard, Maxine Kumin, James Dickey, Alfred Corn, and Howard Nemerov. Critic David Kalstone spoke of her work as manifesting "a whole life *grasped*, in the most urgent and rewarding sense of the word." She achieved her effects by hard work, revising each poem extensively. "What I try to do," she stated, "is move readers' minds and feelings simultaneously with a structure which is intense and formal. If beauty means integrity, then a poem should be beautiful."

BIOGRAPHY

Born in Waterloo, Iowa, in 1921, Mona Jane Van Duyn began her career by being class poet in the first grade in Eldora, Iowa, where her father ran a service station, a cigar store, and a soda fountain. She wrote poems throughout childhood and adolescence, then studied writing at Iowa State Teachers College (University of Northern Iowa) and the University of Iowa. She met her husband, Jarvis Thurston, later professor of English at Washington University, while they were students. They were married on August 31, 1943.

In 1947, Van Duyn and her husband founded and became coeditors of the magazine *Perspective, a Quarterly of Literature*, in whose pages they introduced such poets as W. S. Merwin and W. D. Snodgrass and other writers of stature. Van Duyn was instructor in English at the University of Iowa in 1945 and at the University of Louisville from 1946 to 1950. From 1950 to 1967, she was lecturer in English at Washington University, St. Louis, and later taught at the Salzburg Seminar in American Studies, at Bread Loaf, and at various other writers' workshops throughout the United States. Her first collection, *Valentines to the Wide World*, came out in 1959 in a fine art edition from Cummington Press, illustrated with prints by Fred Becker. Her next collection, *A Time of Bees*, was published by the University of North Carolina in its paperback series in 1964. Her poems were collected in *If It Be Not I* and *Selected Poems*. Van Duyn and her husband lived in St. Louis, where they were the center of a literary community that included such poets and novelists as Donald Finkel, Constance Urdang, Nemerov, William H. Gass, and Stanley Elkin. Van Duyn died of bone cancer at her home in Missouri on December 2, 2004.

ANALYSIS

In an epigraph to one of her poems, Mona Van Duyn cited Norman O. Brown: "Freud says that ideas are libidinal cathexes, that is to say, acts of love." For Van Duyn also, ideas were acts of love. Hers is a poetry shaped around the impact of ideas on one who is in love with them. To write poetry was, for her, to engage in an act of love. To write poetry was to make real the world, which, although it exists externally, becomes known only when the mind's projections play over it. The life from which she wrote was the life of the mind; there are few overtly dramatic events in her poetry. Her mind was excited by language—hence the frequent literary references in her poems—but it was also excited by what is not-mind, everyday accidental happenings, intense emotions, whatever is irrational, recalcitrant, and unyielding to intellectual analysis or explanation. Her poems burst out of the tension between these polarities, the poem itself—often self-reflexive—being the only method she could find to maintain truth and sanity.

"VALENTINES TO THE WIDE WORLD"

A kind of poetic manifesto appears in an early poem, the second "Valentines to the Wide World" in the volume of that title, in which Van Duyn describes her dislike of panoramic scenes because they are too abstract; the vast view of nature provides only a useless exhilaration. She finds "the poem" more useful because its pressure breaks through the surface of experience and because it is specific. "It starts with the creature/ and stays there." This "pressure of speech," even if it is painful or akin to madness, is still what makes her

appreciate her life, feeling that to spend it "on such old premises is a privilege." In the third "valentine," she sees the beauty of the world as "merciless and intemperate," as a "rage" that one must temper with "love and art, which are compassionate."

Compassion is an outstanding characteristic of Van Duyn's poetry, both as motive and expression, and yet it is manifested through a wrestling with intellectual questions and an urge to apply her knowledge. Van Duyn's long lines are particularly suitable for expressing discursive thought. Love and beauty are traditional themes of Romantic poets, but in Van Duyn, they are united with an affinity for the forms and emphases of literary classicism reminiscent of the eighteenth century, with its bent toward philosophizing in poetry and its allegiance to strict and rhyming forms, especially the heroic couplet.

"FROM YELLOW LAKE"

A classic philosophical problem therefore arose for Van Duyn in her early poems—the split between mind and body. In "From Yellow Lake: An Interval" (from *Valentines to the Wide World*), she expresses discon-

Mona Van Duyn (AP/Wide World Photos)

tent with her body as an impediment to overcoming the separateness she feels. The language of the poem has theological undertones: The beetles are "black as our disgrace," a reference to human sin and evil. Crows flying overhead become her dark thoughts, feeding upon "my mind, dear carrion." The poet sees each creature as an analogue of something human—the turtle is "flat as our fate" and the pike's "fierce faith" hooks him fatally on the fisherman's lure. Having a modern mind, the poet cannot find any theological answer to her questioning of the meaning of the creation that painfully yet beautifully surrounds her. The poem supplies the only resolution: Summer has warmed her but she must go back to "the wintry work of living," that is, the life of the mind of an ordinary human being, and "conspire in the nailing, brutal and indoors,/ that pounds to the poem's shape a summer's metaphors." The notion of Original Sin has here been given a new twist: The animal body is "innocent," a parable or metaphor, a natural "given," and the summer is the warmth of love, whereas the mind is that which creates separation, which construes evil and perversely invents the forms of pain. The mind, even if separated from the natural world, is still the only thing she has to work with. Only the poem—actually the process of making a work of art—can heal the split between mind and body, winter and summer, pain and love, by creating reality through metaphor.

"To My Godson, on His Christening"

In part 1 of "To My Godson, on His Christening" (from *If It Be Not I*), Van Duyn continues in a mildly theological context to ponder her awareness of human imperfection (the classical definition of Original Sin), which not even the poet's artistic effort can completely escape. Here "metaphors" are in effect charitable deeds, "beautiful doors" out of the walled-up room of existence that is everyone's fated life. In part 2, a lexicon is the poet's gift to the baby, to help him learn words, since his world will not come into existence until he can name it—that is, use language, the way God made the world by speaking the Word, the Logos. This remnant of Christian thought fades into the background as, in part 3, the poet's mind concentrates on the uniqueness and transitoriness of each individual and of the species. This recognition nevertheless provides a

"feast of awareness" and pleasure in the new life that is the positive aspect of the transitory; the reader is reminded that both dying and being born continue constantly. Being born means coming into a world of pain, but also into a circle of other people, who, like the poet, will oversee the child and care for him. This caring, whether religiously motivated or not, reveals the charity and generosity that is Van Duyn's most characteristic and attractive attitude throughout her work.

A Time of Bees

Charity, of course, is a synonym for compassionate love, and love in Van Duyn's poetry is a reiterated word and theme. The word "love" appears in all but three of the poems in *A Time of Bees*, the collection that followed *Valentines to the Wide World*. Van Duyn does not abandon the theme of poetry, but here unites it with the theme of love in the long poem "An Essay on Criticism," a tour de force in couplets that echoes Alexander Pope's eighteenth century poem of the same title and also explores the aesthetics of its day, leavening this subject matter with contemporary sensibility, idiom, and wit.

In the frame of this poem, the poet, about to open and cook a package of dehydrated onion soup, is interrupted by the arrival of a friend, a young girl who has fallen in love and has discovered "how love is like a poem." In the dialogue that follows, many famous critical theories of poetry are cited and explored. The girl in love speaks first. She clutches the poet's arm "like the Mariner," an allusion to Samuel Taylor Coleridge's *The Rime of the Ancient Mariner* (1798), which the poet employs to join an intense, even obsessed, Romantic view of poetry in one embrace with the classic love of intellect and rationality.

After the girl leaves, the poet continues to talk to herself as if gripping "a theoretical Wedding Guest"— a reference to Coleridge again—and to grapple inwardly and intellectually with various aspects of the interaction between life and art. She takes the side of the poem, "for I believe in art's process of working through otherness to recognition/ and in its power that comes from acceptance, and not imposition." At this point, she finds tears falling into her onion soup, but onions did not cause them; the thought of love did. The poem has to be completed in a human reader's heart. In the complex punning of the last line—tears as "essay" (attempt)—life is asserted to be victorious over art, but poem making is plainly what maintains their intricate and fruitful balance.

TO SEE, TO TAKE

In *To See, To Take*, Van Duyn endeavored to step away from autobiographical reference and to elucidate her concerns by adopting the technique of the persona. In "Eros to Howard Nemerov," for example, she speaks through the traditional personification of love, the Greek god, who is addressing the representative modern American poet with a humorous eye turned on the posturings and vagaries of hippie love in the 1960's. Van Duyn's observant eye and sense of humor led her directly to satire in "Billings and Cooings from 'The Berkeley Barb,'" a satire still apropos now that "personal" want ads have become institutionalized. Many Van Duyn poems begin with newspaper quotations as epigraphs, a method she used to initiate subtle and accurate political and social commentary; by this device she avoided the obvious or propagandistic rhetoric that often mars overtly "political" poetry.

Van Duyn cannot be said to have been entirely apolitical, but her focus was always personal. Personal love, individual consciousness of passing time was what she stressed. The theme of the passage of time emerges particularly in this volume in two memorial poems, "The Creation" and "A Day in Late October." In "The Creation," Van Duyn mourns a friend's death; as art is a metaphor for life, she sees the friend's life as having been taken away as a pencil drawing is erased. "A Day in Late October," written after the death of Randall Jarrell, asserts the primacy of death, life's inseparable companion, over art—the art of poetry—by means of an extraordinary divagation for this poet: She breaks out of the poetic form altogether and falls back on prose, which is a kind of death of poetry, to express "what cannot be imagined: your death, my death." Death and the passing of time cannot fail to reinvoke a sense of the preciousness of love; the word "love" is repeated as often in this collection as in the previous one.

Despite her adoption of the persona to avoid excessive "personality," two fine poems in this volume spring from autobiography, a mode in which she has both sharpened her technical skills and widened her attitude of appreciation. "Postcards from Cape Split" show her gift for straightforward description of the natural world. The facts of the place where she is vacationing in Maine carry their own intrinsic symbolic weight, so simply stating them is enough. The central motif of "Postcards from Cape Split" is abundance—unearned richness exemplified by hillsides covered with heliotrope, the sea surrounding the house whose interior mirrors the sea, a plethora of villages and shops, generous neighbors, flourishing vegetable gardens. The poet is dazzled and appreciative: "The world blooms and we all bend and bring/ from ground and sea and mind its handsome harvests." The mind remains a primary locus, but the emphasis here is on contentment and gratitude; the world's unasked for generosity is indispensable.

The second autobiographical poem, "Remedies, Maladies, Reasons" strikes quite a different note, although its power also stems from a straightforward statement of facts—the facts of Van Duyn's childhood. It is a record of her mother's acts and speeches that imposed on the child a view of herself as weak, ill, and in danger of dying. The record is brutal and nauseating; it continues in the mother's letters describing her own symptoms simply quoted in her own words, so overwhelming a body hatred and self-hatred that it is miraculous that the poet survived it. The word "remedies" in the title has a heavily ironic ring, but by the time the poem ends, it has taken another turn of meaning: Implicitly the act of making a poem from these horrors relieves them. It provides a remedy by evoking the sight of her mother as an attractive woman and as the mother the child wanted, who came in the night when called and defended the child against her felt enemy, sickness. The poem's last line—"Do you think I don't know how love hallucinates?"—constructs a complex balance, reasserting that love still exists but has maintained itself internally by a costly distortion of external fact. Without overtly referring to poetry as an aid, this poem is a remarkable testimony to the capacity of shaped language to restore a sane perspective and to enable one's mind to open to revision of memory, an act of love that is analogous to revision of the language of a poem.

If vision and revision are the loving acts that give rise to the making of a poem, the poem itself is the "merciful disguise of metaphor" that masks the horror and brutality of the world, making it possible for humans to live with its limitations. The most stringent and widespread personal limitation that love undertakes culturally is marriage. Marriage is to love what the heroic couplet is to poetry. Van Duyn has chosen—or has found herself unable to escape from—both rigors. In *Valentines to the Wide World*, she explores marriage as "the politics of love" in the wryly witty, rather lighthearted "Toward a Definition of Marriage." At the end of *To See, to Take* appears the tough-minded, occasionally viciously clear-eyed poem "Marriage, with Beasts" in which one feels that the imagery of animals in a zoo, Swiftian in its satiric accuracy, hardly qualifies as "merciful disguise." It is pitiless exposé.

Marital combat is elevated to a cosmic, mythic vision of antagonistic masculine and feminine principles in the previously unpublished poem "A View" in the last section of *Merciful Disguises*. The "you" and the "I" of the poem are driving through Colorado. The mountain with its "evergreen masculinity" is obliviously and continuously ascendant over the depleted "mined-out" female earth. The ending is covertly linked with marriage: The "you," the car's driver, male by cultural definition as well as presumably in fact, asks the "I" how she is, and she says that she is "admiring the scenery, and am O.K." The "view" of the title is a pun indicating "opinion" as well as landscape; it is the closest that Van Duyn's poetry—always centered on a woman's consciousness—comes to embodying a feminist perspective as it presents a seemingly unbridgeable gap between the man's state of well-being and the woman's unending state of struggle and exhaustion.

LETTERS FROM A FATHER, AND OTHER POEMS

By the time of the publication of *Letters from a Father, and Other Poems* in 1982, the poet is far better than merely self-deprecatingly "O.K." The complexity of her relationship with her parents resolved itself in the gentleness and forgiveness that came with their deaths in 1980, within three months of each other. The title poem, "Letters from a Father," is a foreshadowing of those deaths as well as a revival and revision of the poet's childhood memories. This poem's power comes from its almost verbatim quotation of her father's

words, a technique that verifies the poet's loving ability to give herself and her art wholly to someone else. She thereby redeems both the sad intractable fact of death and also the self-entangled contemporary language of poetry, which badly needs a reminder that it must have reference to something outside itself.

In "The Stream," about the death of her mother, the poet returns to her original and perennial concern, love, and, in an extended metaphor, sees love as a narrow stream running below ground, held down, unseen, but finally finding its way up until it is visible. This vision of the stream of love also suggests the stream of time flowing toward death, a flow echoed by the long flowing line whose form—the couplet with slant end-rhyme, Van Duyn's favorite—seems to constitute the same sort of facilitating obstacle that the rock and earth present to the underground stream of water. That water rises higher in a narrow tube is a physical fact; thus love rises under "the dense pressure of thwarted needs, the replay/ of old misreadings." Her mother's death has brought the stream of love to light, revealing to her "the welling water—to which I add these tears."

The tears and the poem, as in the earlier but different context of "An Essay on Criticism," join in felicitous confluence. The stringent form, when one gives in to it, is what produces genuine depth and maturation in life as well as in art. Van Duyn's development as a poet has been steady and straightforward, even relentlessly undeviating, without sudden switches of style or experimental or uncertain phases. She has never gone back on her commitment to work with tight forms, to deal with the world's pain, and to remain in love with the world despite its worst. "Since You Asked Me . . ." answers the question which must have been put to her a number of times: Why do you use rhyme and measure, since these are so old-fashioned and out of date? She says that she uses rhyme "to say I love you to language" and to combat the current linguistic sloppiness of "y'know?" and "Wow!" She uses measure because it is "not just style but lifestyle."

NEAR CHANGES

In *Near Changes*, for which she won the Pulitzer Prize in poetry, Van Duyn continues an exploration of her own situation as survivor. The death of both parents, chronicled in *Letters from a Father, and Other*

Poems, is part of a series of losses. In "The Block," the large house she and her husband bought in 1950 "just in case" they might still have children gradually becomes part of a "middle-aged block" and then an elderly one, where widows now reside where once there were couples, and where Mr. and Mrs. Thurston watch other people's grandchildren. This—like other long poems in this volume, especially "Glad Heart at the Supermarket" and "Falling in Love at Sixty-five"—demonstrates the absurdity of pigeonholing Van Duyn as a "domestic" poet. While her matter may include Coleman lanterns, lawn care, snow shoveling, bean curd, and complex carbohydrates, her meanings are as profound as those of any other poet drawn to the connections between life and death, constancy and change. The collection provides new evidence of her technical virtuosity as well: "Memoir, for Harry Ford" is a sestina; "Condemned Site," a distinguished villanelle recounting the loss of five good friends, some of whose first names many readers will recognize as major twentieth century American poets.

FIREFALL

Firefall (along with *If It Be Not I*) was published on the occasion of Van Duyn's appointment as U.S. poet laureate. In this volume, she continues to develop major themes of her lifework, among them love and marriage, friendship, work, travel, stewardship, and the luminous quality of the ordinary. Many of the poems are about the work of other poets and poetry itself. The volume includes a number of what she calls "minimalist sonnets," poems that preserve the fourteen-line count and the conventional rhyme patterns of Italian and English sonnets, but reduce the number of syllables and otherwise "deconstruct" the venerable form. "Summer Virus" is an attractive example of what she can do with such minimalism, as her rising temperature brings both mind and body to a state of "incandescence."

The book takes its title from a phenomenon she describes in "Falls," a memoir in free verse that begins in the flatness of her native Iowa and then takes her to the mysterious "firefall" of Yosemite (which she explains in one of her rare notes) and the "thunderous boasts" of Niagara, to college, to books, and to a lifetime of writing poems—a waterfall of words. "Falls" ends in a formal quatrain, in which a poet toward the end of her ca-

reer invokes the "kernel hints" of her that the future reader may find among the "husks," returning to the Iowa cornfields among which the memoir begins.

SELECTED POEMS

In 2002, Alfred Knopf released a collection of Van Duyn's poems, *Selected Poems*. The poems in this work originally appeared in Van Duyn's earlier collections, including *Valentines to the Wide World*, *A Time of Bees*, *To See, To Take*, *Bedtime Stories*, *Merciful Disguises*, *Letters from a Father, and Other Poems*, *Near Changes*, and *Firefall*. *Selected Poems* showcases nearly one hundred of Van Duyn's poems, providing readers with a sampling of her most celebrated and beloved pieces, including "Three Valentines to the Wide World," "Notes from a Suburban Heart," "Remedies, Maladies, Reasons," "Bedtime Stories," "Midas and Wife," "Photographs," "The Insight Lady of St. Louis on Zoos," and "Falls."

In "Notes from a Suburban Heart" (originally appearing in *A Time of Bees*), Van Duyn furthers her themes of love and life in the domestic sphere by ruminating on tasks such as buying and using lawn fertilizer in the summer, feeding the birds during winter, and the flowers' tentative blooms in the spring. The narrator loves her life, which Van Duyn chronicles by moving through the seasons, thus emphasizing that while the seasons change, the narrator's life and her fondness for it remain the same.

"Midas and Wife" (originally appearing in *Merciful Disguises*), re-envisions the myth of King Midas, the ruler who turned whatever he touched to gold. Van Duyn gives both life and voice to Midas's wife. She opens the poem with mentioning how King Midas loved—and somewhat envied—his wife for her ability to touch objects freely, especially living objects such as the grass and birds. In the poem, the queen tells Midas she cannot bear not being touched by him, and he goes from room to room and touches whatever his wife has touched in an effort to feel connected and close to her. The queen implores Midas to touch her; he does, and she turns into a statue. Then Dionysus releases Midas from his curse (just as the god does in the myth). Many versions of the Midas myth do not focus on or even mention the queen, or the love between Midas and his wife. Van Duyn's modification of the myth emphasizes the theme of love and the role of woman as wife, both important elements in Van Duyn's canon.

Van Duyn had not published a new collection of poems since *Firefall*, and some readers wondered about the release of *Selected Poems* since the book was an assemblage of previously published pieces. Some critics felt Alfred Knopf's releasing Van Duyn's *Selected Poems* without including any new work was a means to honor and highlight Van Duyn's former status as poet laureate. One reviewer, Henry Brian of *The New York Times*, suggested that while *Selected Poems* does not provide readers with any new material by Van Duyn, the book proves informative to her fans for another reason: The collection shows which poems were Van Duyn's favorites.

A POET OF IDEAS

In a lecture delivered at the Library of Congress in 1993, Van Duyn discussed the difficulty women poets have had in getting published and understood. As successful as she was, she noted that,

Blinded by the assumption that women do not have thoughts, do not write about ideas, reviewers who are incredibly talented at understanding the most difficult and private poetry of their own sex announce blithely that a poem of mine about the need for form in life and art is about walking a dog, or an analysis of friendship is about shopping for groceries.

She wondered in fact whether such reviewers even consider the possibility of metaphor. As light as her touch and as familiar as her subject matter could be, all but the most casual reader must recognize that Van Duyn is indeed a poet of ideas, one of the most accomplished and distinguished poets of her time.

BIBLIOGRAPHY

Boyle, Kevin. "Remedies, Maladies, Reasons." In *Masterplots II: Poetry Series*, edited by Philip K. Jason. Rev. ed. Pasadena, Calif.: Salem Press, 2002. Contains an in-depth analysis of the poem.

Burns, Michael, ed. *Discovery and Reminiscence: Essays on the Poetry of Mona Van Duyn*. Fayetteville: University of Arkansas Press, 1998. Contains tributes by fellow poets, critical and interpretative essays, biographical notes, and "Matters of Poetry," the revised text of Van Duyn's 1993 lecture at the Library of Congress.

Hacht, Anne Marie, ed. *Poetry for Students*. Vol. 20. Detroit: Thomson/Gale, 2004. Contains an in-depth analysis of Van Duyn's "Memoir," as well as context and criticism.

Henry, Brian. "Poetry in the Suburbs." Review of *Selected Poems*. *The New York Times*, September 15, 2002. Henry observes that the collection—though it contains no new work—acknowledges Van Duyn's status as a member of the American poetry canon.

Logan, William. "Old Faithfuls: W. S. Merwin, Mona Van Duyn, John Ashbery." In *Desperate Measures*. Gainesville: University Press of Florida, 2002. Logan examines Van Duyn's work in contrast to that of Merwin and Ashbery.

Prunty, Wyatt. "Making and Taking." *Kenyon Review* 31, no. 1 (Winter 2009): 194-206. Van Duyn wrote a poem for the dying Howard Nemerov, to which he wrote a poem in response. Prunty explores who owns the "turf," as he calls it, of these poems: Van Duyn, for starting the poetical exchange, or Nemerov, whose impending death started the exchange.

_____. "Pattern of Similitude." In *"Fallen from the Symboled World": Precedents for the New Formalism*. New York: Oxford University Press, 1990. Prunty discusses Van Duyn and places her within twentieth century poets and notes her relation to New Formalism.

Spiegelman, William. "The Nineties Revisited." *Contemporary Literature* 42, no. 2 (Summer, 2001): 206-237. Spiegelman explores Van Duyn's work in the context of popular poetic forms and practices of the 1990's.

Jane Augustine; William T. Hamilton
Updated by Karley K. Adney

JONES VERY

Born: Salem, Massachusetts; August 28, 1813
Died: Salem, Massachusetts; May 8, 1880

PRINCIPAL POETRY

Essays and Poems, 1839
Poems by Jones Very with an Introductory Memoir by William P. Andrews, 1883
Poems and Essays by Jones Very: Complete and Revised Edition, 1886
Poems and Essays by Jones Very: James Freeman Clarke's Enlarged Collection of 1886 Re-edited with a Thematic and Topical Index, 1965
Jones Very: Selected Poems, 1966
Jones Very: The Complete Poems, 1993

OTHER LITERARY FORMS

Jones Very (VEH-ree) wrote a few critical essays, the best of which were originally collected, along with a selection of his poetry, in *Essays and Poems*. Such essays as "Epic Poetry," "Hamlet," and "Shakespeare" have been particularly rich resources for biographers and literary critics interested in understanding Very's poetic goals and practices. Also, about 117 sermons survive in manuscript form, the results of his service as a supply minister for nearly four decades.

ACHIEVEMENTS

Both during his life and after, Jones Very's significance as a poet has generally been understood in relationship to the American Transcendentalist movement. Of particular importance to biographers and critics has been Very's connection to Ralph Waldo Emerson, Transcendentalism's chief spokesperson and writer. Certainly, Emerson's sponsorship of Very resulted in the only book-length publication of Very's poems during Very's lifetime, in 1839, a volume which Emerson edited and for which he made the necessary contacts with a publisher. For a very short period, during the years 1838 and 1839, Very seemed to Emerson and his associates to be the epitome of the American Transcendentalist poet linked to divinity, expressing intuitive insights and truths about the universe in pure and beautiful language.

Later biographers and literary critics have been able to observe that Very's connection to the Transcendentalists and Emerson was at best a mixed blessing. Although it resulted in early publication of his efforts, it also made it difficult to perceive that Very, at least for a short time, was a unique and powerfully mystical poet in his own right. Interestingly, many of the poems that Emerson chose not to include in his selection of poetry for Very's first publication are the ones that now seem most central and original. Since the majority of Very's poems are sonnets, he also has assumed importance as one of the most successful of America's writers of poetry in the sonnet form.

BIOGRAPHY

Jones Very was born in Salem, Massachusetts, in 1813 to a sea captain father and a strong-minded, highly independent, and somewhat atheistic mother. Very sailed with his father for nearly two years, beginning at age nine, but after his father's untimely death in 1824, Very attended school in Salem for three years, excelling as a scholar, until at age fourteen he left for employment in an auction room. He refused to give up his goal of enrolling at Harvard, however, and continued his self-education through extensive reading, eventually obtaining the help of a special tutor as well as securing employment as an assistant in a Latin school, preparing younger boys for entrance into college. During this time, his earliest, rather imitative poems began appearing in a local newspaper, the Salem *Observer*.

So advanced was Very in his scholarly ability that he was able to enter Harvard in February, 1834, as a second-term sophomore. His years at Harvard were crucial in Very's progress as a scholar, poet, and religious thinker. He distinguished himself as a student, eventually graduating second in his class in 1836 with particular expertise in Latin and Greek. He continued to write poetry, including the class songs for his sophomore and senior years, as well as poems imitative of William Wordsworth and William Cullen Bryant.

Most important, however, under the influence of some of his Unitarian teachers and classmates, he began to turn to religion in a serious way for the first time in his life, thus deviating radically from his mother's skepticism. Particularly in his senior year, he experienced what he called "a change of heart," becoming convinced "that all we have belongs to God and that we ought to have no *will* of our own." During the next two years, while staying on at Harvard as a tutor in Greek and a student at the Divinity School, he gave himself to the struggle of ridding himself of his own will and becoming perfectly conformed to the will of God working within him. His poetry writing more and more partook of this spiritual battle, centering on intense religious feelings and intuitions within the framework of the traditional Shakespearean sonnet form.

Very delivered a lyceum lecture on the subject of epic poetry in Salem in December of 1837. Elizabeth Palmer Peabody, a prominent Transcendentalist and reformer, attended this lecture and immediately recognized the uncommon promise of Very as a thinker. Knowing nothing of his poetry writing, she immediately set up a connection between Very and Ralph Waldo Emerson, which resulted in Very's lecturing at Concord in April of 1838. Very also began attending some of the so-called Transcendental Club meetings during the spring and summer of 1838. Emerson was much taken with Very's depth of thought and his insights into William Shakespeare and encouraged him to continue his writing about poetry, but Emerson, like Peabody, seems to have been unaware of Very's own poetic productions during these months.

Very's spiritual journey reached some sort of a high point in the fall of 1838, when he evidently experienced what he thought was the total replacement of his own will by the will of God. This perhaps mystical experience immediately resulted in his proclaiming to students and friends that the end of the world and Christ's Second Coming were occurring, as evidenced in Very's own new relationship with divinity. He claimed that the Holy Spirit was speaking through him, and he urged those who listened to experience this Second Coming through a similar banishing of their own wills. Such statements were upsetting to some students and brought the displeasure of the Harvard authorities. Very was sent home to Salem, where his similar proclamations to ministers and leaders regarding their need of repentance and reformation led to his being removed to the McLean Asylum in Charlestown as one who was perhaps insane.

Although Very was released from the hospital after a month, his newfound spiritual intensity continued to challenge his new Transcendentalist friends and Salem society. It was during this period of heightened spiritual feeling that Very's poetry began to flow rapidly from his pen, with more than three hundred sonnets produced during just over one year of religious exaltation from September, 1838, to the latter part of 1839. Emerson became aware of Very's poetry during this time and undertook the job of selecting and editing the poems that were collected in the small volume *Essays and Poems*.

Interestingly, the publication of the poems seemed to coincide with the decline of Very's religious intensity and with his return to a more mundane, albeit dedicated, religious life. For the next forty years, he lived in Salem with his siblings, never marrying but serving as a supply minister to Unitarian churches in the New England area, presenting sermons in the absence of the regular ministers. He continued to produce poetry, but not at the rate nor with the intensity and originality of the poems authored in 1838 and 1839. He died in 1880 in relative obscurity.

ANALYSIS

During the course of his long poetic career, Jones Very wrote some 870 separate poems, many of them published in newspapers and magazines of his day, but only 65 appearing in the thin volume edited by Emerson in 1839. It is common for biographers and literary critics to separate the poems written by Very during his period of growing religious excitement in the late 1830's from the largely imitative poems written before that period and the competent but not strikingly intense poems written in the four decades after that period. It is the poetry of the so-called ecstatic period that most interested and challenged the Transcendentalists and has continued to impress readers in the various generations since. Although repetitious in themes and format, the sonnets from the religiously intense phase of Very's experience carry a certain power and originality markedly lacking in the poetry written before and after this period.

POEMS OF SPIRITUAL INTENSITY

During the late 1830's, poems poured from Very's pen, sometimes, according to Peabody, at the rate of one or two a day. Very, convinced that his will had been totally replaced by the will of divinity, believed that these sonnets were in essence not authored by him but rather were the words of God or the Holy Spirit. Written rapidly, seemingly without revision (how could one revise the words of God?), with little attention to formalities such as spelling and punctuation, the poems of this phase have presented serious editorial issues to editors from Emerson to the present. Yet, the lack of formality and polish helps to bring immediacy to the poems, the best of which seem particularly forceful in their expression of religious passion.

"The New Birth," a sonnet that seemingly recalls Very's intense feelings of change as a result of the key mystical experience in the fall of 1838 when he became convinced of the subjugation of his own will, nicely illustrates the power of Very's poetry during this period. The poem begins with the announcement that "'Tis a new life," followed by a vivid figure of how "thoughts" no longer "move" as before, "With slow uncertain steps," but now "In thronging haste" like "the viewless wind" (a traditional biblical image for the Holy Spirit) enter "fast pressing" through "The portals." Such a change has resulted because human "pride" (the will) has been "laid" in the "dust." The thoughts demand "utterance strong" (perhaps the writing of poetry as well as the face-to-face confrontation with teachers and friends), imaged as the sound of "Storm-lifted waves swift rushing to the shore" whose "thunders roar" "through the cave-worn rocks." The poem ends with the speaker in the poem ecstatically announcing as "a child of God" his new freedom, his awakening from "death's slumbers to eternity."

Most of the other sonnets written during this period of high religious feeling center on the traditional Christian themes of death, rebirth, the Second Coming, resurrection, and hope, often with figures and allusions highly dependent on biblical sources. Not all of them are successful, often being little more than paraphrases of Scripture.

However, some of them are very striking, perhaps the most interesting to modern readers being those poems in which the poet or the speaker in the poem assumes the voice of God or Christ, poems so stunningly transcendental in their linkage of humanity to divinity that they were not for the most part included by Emerson in the little volume published in 1839, perhaps because he feared the probable attacks of conservative Christians. For example, Christ seems to be the speaker in "I Am the Bread of Life," while God seems the central voice in "The Message." Even more complicated is a poem such as "Terror," which centers on the end of the world. The poem begins with the speaker as a seemingly human witness to end-time events: "Within the streets I hear no voices loud,/ They pass along with low, continuous cry." Yet by the end of the poem, the speaker has become God, who calls loudly to humans: "Repent! why do ye still uncertain stand,/ The kingdom of my son is nigh at hand!" Although this seemingly audacious commandeering of a divine voice is perfectly understandable, given Very's belief that his poems during this period were indeed the products of divine authorship, for the uninitiated reader such a mixture of the human and the divine is at minimum attention getting as well as a challenge to ordinary religious thinking.

EARLIER AND LATER POEMS

The largely imitative poems written before the late 1830's show a poet progressing in competence and often center on themes and didactic approaches typical of the early Romantic movement in England and the United States. Very's poems about nature, for example, usually focus first on some observable aspect of his surroundings, followed by overt linkage, often somewhat sentimentally, to an appropriate lesson. "The Wind-Flower" begins with the personification of this early spring blossom as one that "lookest up with meek, confiding eye/ Upon the clouded smile of April's face" and then praises the "faith" of this frail flower, willing to bloom with the threat of winter still around, as being "More glorious" than that of "Israel's wisest king" (Solomon). Such innocent "trust" is, the poem suggests, something humans can learn from, as the last line of the poem underscores, "A lesson taught by Him, who loved all human kind." Other nature poems of the early period which illustrate this tying of the observation of natural phenomena to religious and moral lessons include "The Robin" and "The Columbine."

Throughout the last four decades of his life, Very continued to write moralizing poems on nature as well as poems centering on the biblical themes characteristic of the sonnets composed during his ecstatic period of the late 1830's. He also turned to writing poems with links to the social and historical events of his time. Such poems show his poetic competence and his interest in current events but usually do not achieve anything like lasting artistic merit. His abolitionist stance is mirrored in the poem "The Fugitive Slaves," for example, while his reaction to the Civil War and Reconstruction can be seen in such poems as "Faith in the Time of War" and "National Unity." Very also penned the lyrics to numerous hymns during this final phase of his poetic career, including such relatively well-known examples as "Father, Thy Wonders Do Not Singly Stand" and "We Go Not on a Pilgrimage."

BIBLIOGRAPHY

Barlett, William Irving. *Jones Very: Emerson's "Brave Saint."* Durham, N.C.: Duke University Press, 1942. This first "modern" biographical and critical study of Very presents a balanced analysis of his life and poetry, and perhaps most important, publishes numerous poems heretofore uncollected, thus bringing to light some of the best poetry of Very written during his ecstatic period.

Clayton, Sarah Turner. *The Angelic Sins of Jones Very.* New York: Peter Lang, 1999. This full-length study of Very centers on a New Historicist approach to how readers in various decades have received and understood Very's poetry, from the time of the Transcendentalists to the present age. The book is particularly effective at bringing together an abundance of scholarly and critical responses to Very's poetry while illuminating how certain lasting qualities of Very's writing continue to fascinate readers.

Gittleman, Edwin. *Jones Very: The Effective Years, 1833-1840.* New York: Columbia University Press, 1967. This work presents an exhaustive treatment of Very's life and writing during the years of his religious awakening. Gittleman approaches Very's biography from a psychological perspective and asserts that Very's religious mania had its roots in family relationships.

Very, Jones. *Jones Very: Selected Poems.* Edited by Nathan Lyons. New Brunswick, N.J.: Rutgers University Press, 1966. Perhaps more important than the poems selected by Lyons are his considerations of Very's religious stance and his interpretations of key Very poems in the introduction to this work.

_____. *Jones Very: The Complete Poems.* Edited by Helen R. Deese. Athens: University of Georgia Press, 1993. Deese has provided an inestimable service for readers interested in Very's poetry by bringing together all the poems and editing them with an appropriate scholarly approach and apparatus. Of immense value, also, is her introduction to the volume, which covers Very as a person, thinker, and poet, perhaps the most concise and insightful review of the research on Very.

Delmer Davis

PETER VIERECK

Born: New York, New York; August 5, 1916
Died: South Hadley, Massachusetts; May 13, 2006

PRINCIPAL POETRY

Terror and Decorum: Poems, 1940-1948, 1948
Strike Through the Mask!, 1950
The First Morning, 1952
The Persimmon Tree, 1956
The Tree Witch: A Poem and a Play (First of All a Poem), 1961
New and Selected Poems, 1967
Archer in the Marrow, 1987
Tide and Continuities: Last and First Poems, 1995-1938, 1995
Door, 2005

OTHER LITERARY FORMS

Metapolitics: From the Romantics to Hitler (1941) is a criticism of nineteenth century Romanticism, which Peter Viereck (VIHR-ehk) argued lies at the base of Nazism. Viereck also wrote several volumes defending his variety of political conservatism, including *Conservatism Revisited: The Revolt Against Revolt, 1815-1949* (1949), *Shame and Glory of the Intellectuals* (1953), and *The Unadjusted Man* (1956).

ACHIEVEMENTS

Beginning in the 1940's, Peter Viereck won wide recognition for his poetry, which follows the style he called Manhattan classicism. His poetry emphasizes form and rhyme and displays remarkably effective wordplay. He placed great stress on morality and used his verse to defend the humanist values he professed. Critics sometimes accused him of being overly didactic, but many consider him a major American poet. Viereck received a Guggenheim Fellowship for his poetry and won the Pulitzer Prize in poetry in 1949, the New England Poetry Club Prize in 1998, and the Anne Sexton Poetry Prize, awarded by *Agni* magazine, in 1999.

BIOGRAPHY

Peter Robert Edwin Viereck was born in New York City on August 5, 1916. He achieved remarkable scholastic success in his college years and graduated from Harvard University summa cum laude in 1937. After attending the University of Oxford on a fellowship, he returned to Harvard, where he received his M.A. and Ph.D. in European history.

Parallel with Viereck's rise in the academic world, a more dramatic story was taking place. Viereck's father, George Sylvester Viereck, was a noted journalist and author whose circle of friends included Sigmund Freud, H. L. Mencken, and Kaiser Wilhelm II. He had temporarily lost popularity during World War I, since his sympathy for Germany put him at odds with the policy of the United States. The 1920's, however, was characterized by disillusionment with American participation in the war, and Viereck was to a large extent restored to favor. Adolf Hitler's rise to power in January, 1933, changed the picture once more. It soon became evident that Viereck was not prepared to abandon his sympathy for Germany. He became an apologist for Hitler (indeed a paid agent of the Reich), and almost all of his friends deserted him. During World War II, he was arrested and tried for sedition.

Peter Viereck broke with his father and rarely mentioned him in his writing. Perhaps as a reaction against the senior Viereck, much of his activity as a historian concentrated on analyzing the rise of the Nazis to power.

During World War II, Viereck wrote intelligence reports in Africa and Italy. In 1945, Viereck married Anya De Markov, a Russian resistance fighter. The couple had two children before divorcing in 1970. In 1972, Viereck married Betty Falkenberg. He taught at several universities and soon settled permanently at Mount Holyoke College in Massachusetts. To Viereck, academic life was not a detached pursuit of knowledge but rather a way of coming to grips with current problems. He developed an unusual variety of conservatism and wrote several books explaining and defending it. Although his books were widely reviewed, few American conservatives count themselves as his followers.

Viereck's reputation rests principally on his work as a poet; collections of his poetry won for him considerable attention and admiration. Although respected by most critics as a presence in American poetry, he did not have much influence on other poets. In 1987, Viereck retired as professor emeritus of Russian and Eurasian history from Mount Holyoke College, where he had been a scholar and teacher throughout most of his writing and teaching career. He continued to teach until 1997.

In 2005, journalist Tom Reiss profiled Viereck in the *New Yorker*, noting that he had started the conservative movement but later attacked the conservatives in a 1962 essay in *The New Republic*, "The New Conservatism: One of Its Founders Asks What Went Wrong," and was abandoned by the conservatives. The Reiss article revived interest in Viereck, and some of his early works were republished. In 2005, Vireck published his last volume of poems, *Door*. He died the following year in South Hadley, Massachusetts.

ANALYSIS

Peter Viereck was remarkably consistent in adhering to certain principles throughout his career as a poet. Together, these principles make up the "Manhattan classicism" mentioned earlier; understanding them is crucial for anyone who wishes to read him.

Deeply affected by the rise of Nazism and Communism in the twentieth century, Viereck asked one fundamental question throughout his career: How did these nefarious systems arise and maintain themselves? In part, the answer lies in the particular historical circumstances of each case. In Viereck's opinion, a deeper and more general cause underlay the events that preoccupy most historians. Romanticism is the culprit;

it was Viereck's principal aim in both his poetry and his prose to expose and combat this artistic movement.

His conclusion at once raises a further question: What did Viereck mean by Romanticism? He had chiefly in mind the uncontrolled display of emotion. Romantic artists such as Richard Wagner thought that their superiority to the ordinary run of men entitled them to disregard moral restraint in their work. What counted was that artists express themselves fully, and they need answer to no one but themselves. This approach has had disastrous consequences when extended from art to politics. Viereck rejected the notion that what is true in art can be false in politics and held that since the ignoring of moral restraint has been disastrous in politics, it must be halted at its artistic source.

Rather than be the expression of the artist's unbridled feelings, a poem should illustrate "humanist values," Viereck said. He did not intend anything controversial by this phrase; he had in mind the ordinary moral virtues. Although interested in religion, he did not require poets to adhere to Christianity or any other creed; he himself was not a believer.

It may appear so far that much fuss was made over very little. After all, few poets see themselves as Nietzschean immoralists. However, Viereck did not think it sufficient for poets to accept morality in their lives or even to avoid contradicting its rules in their poetry. He maintained that poets have the duty to defend and explain moral principles in their work. His didactic notion of proper poetry was rejected by most of his contemporaries, though some poets, most notably Yvor Winters, profess a similar view.

Viereck carried the point one step further. A writer should not only defend correct morality but also must assail those writers who set themselves against its unyielding requirements. To Viereck, the main twentieth century example of the betrayal of artistic responsibility was Ezra Pound. Pound's devotion to the fascist regime of Benito Mussolini was in Viereck's opinion the logical outcome of his poetic principles. Pound's main work, the voluminous *The Cantos* (1970), advocates a repellent political and ethical position—and this suffices to discredit it as outstanding poetry. So great was Viereck's distaste for Pound that some mention of him surfaced in nearly everything Viereck wrote.

The requirements of humanist values extend beyond content. Many twentieth century poets have curtailed or abandoned altogether the use of meter and rhyme. To Viereck, this represented the lack of discipline that is the core of Romanticism. His own poetry was almost always written in standard metrical form and displays to the full his talent for rhyme.

TERROR AND DECORUM

These principles were fully evident in Viereck's first published verse collection, *Terror and Decorum*. The opening verse, "Poet," exemplifies Viereck's artistic credo. In part influenced by Charles Baudelaire and T. S. Eliot, Viereck views the poet as the guardian of language, with the responsibility to maintain a tight control over it; if this task is not attended to, "lush adverbs" and other uncontrolled parts of speech may get out of hand. True to his own principles, Viereck wrote "Poet" in strict iambic pentameter, his favorite poetic form.

"Poet" displays the tensions and paradoxes of Viereck's position. Although Romanticism is anathema, the exalted view of the poet he professes here is a key doctrine of the great Romantics. Like Percy Bysshe Shelley, to whom poets are the unacknowledged legislators of humankind, Viereck considers the poet to be a monarch. Through poets' control of language, they can dominate the politics of their time. Further, although "Poet" calls for restraint, it itself is characterized by elaborate metaphor and personification.

The reader might so far have the impression that Viereck is a grim Savonarola, incapable of humor. This is decidedly not the case; indeed, one of Viereck's chief weapons in his struggle against disorder is satire. He also indulges in ordinary wit; in one notable instance, he constructs a long poem from the World War II slogan "Kilroy was here."

Although "Kilroy" treats the slogan humorously, it soon becomes apparent that Viereck has a serious message to expound. The anonymous soldier who writes "Kilroy was here" wherever he goes symbolizes the adventurer, and Viereck compares him to Ulysses, Orestes, and, in the poem's climax, God. Kilroy displays the spirit of free individualism that Viereck holds to be the proper human attitude. Unsure of what, if anything, is the ultimate basis of the world and of values, the individual must make his or her own way.

"Kilroy," like "Poet," shows Viereck's love-hate relation with Romanticism. The adventurer is a stock figure of Romanticism, but the supposed anti-Romantic Viereck devotes the poem to praise and advocacy of him. The tension in Viereck's position extends to the poem's style. Viereck defends strict adherence to form, but "Kilroy" is an unusual mix of genres. It begins as a humorous poem but shifts to a serious expression of Viereck's ethics and metaphysics. It does not follow from the presence of dissonances in his work that Viereck was a bad poet. His efforts to maintain a system of belief against certain contrary tendencies in his personality add to his poems' interest.

THE FIRST MORNING

Like that of any other good poet, Viereck's work is not all of a piece. As his career developed, his verse tended to become more lyrical. A good example of his lyrical style is "Arethusa, the First Morning," which appeared in *The First Morning*. Arethusa was a sea nymph changed by Artemis into a spring. The poem pictures the former nymph wondering what has happened to her. Viereck uses her perplexity to introduce a meditation about the stages of life and the nature of consciousness. What, if anything, can one really know?

Viereck has no answer to this question. Rather, his response is that human beings cannot have any knowledge of what lies behind the world that appears to them. Specifically, there is no reason to think that life has any meaning beyond what individuals can give it. There is no life beyond death, and human beings do not fit into a cosmic scheme of things.

The annihilation of death fills Viereck with dread. This reaction is present in other works besides "Arethusa." What ought one's response to be? When a doe steps into the spring, Arethusa feels a kinship with her and a sympathy for all nature. Viereck suggests that the experience of the unity of the world can help humankind deal with the fear of death, to the extent that anything can do so. The attitudes displayed in "Arethusa" are of great importance to Viereck; perhaps anxious that readers not forget them, he included another version of the poem, titled "River," in *New and Selected Poems*. The new version drops the mythological references but retains the message of the original.

As always, Viereck finds enemies of correct doctrine to combat; in *The First Morning*, it is New Criticism that is the target of his wrath. He assails this style of criticism in a section of the book called "Irreverences," which consists of a series of short rhyming verses, written in a mocking style; "1912-1952, Full Cycle" is probably the poem in this group that most effectively conveys his thought.

Viereck's mockery was motivated by much more than personal rivalry or the fact that the New Critics did not care for his verse and rarely if ever discussed it. He thought that their views were inimical to sound art. They contended that a poem was an artifact that ought to be studied apart from the intentions of the author, which at best were a matter of conjecture. The historical background of the poem was also irrelevant: History and criticism were separate disciplines that ought not to be mixed.

To Viereck, these views were merely a variant of the Romantic artist's betrayal of moral responsibility. Adherence to them would prevent poets and critics from teaching the very lessons Viereck thought it most urgent to convey. If a poem was a self-contained entity, it could not at the same time be an instrument for teaching virtue. Small wonder that Viereck believed himself justified in using every literary weapon at his command against New Critics such as Allen Tate. Satire was his chosen instrument in "Irreverences," but to a large extent, his project backfired. Many of the volume's reviewers failed to see the serious purpose behind his work, and the book was not very favorably received.

THE PERSIMMON TREE

"Nostalgia," a poem included in *The Persimmon Tree*, enables the reader to come to a fuller understanding of Viereck's ideas. The poem depicts God, who has absented himself from the world for eight thousand years, deciding to return to Earth for a surprise visit. Instead of receiving a warm welcome from his creation, he is recognized by no one; he is no longer worshiped. The poem makes evident that for Viereck, God, if he exists at all, has no benevolent intentions or even much interest in human beings. He is an arbitrary and capricious power, and people must make their way without him.

"Nostalgia" illustrates another tension in Viereck's position. Many people who lack religious belief think that morality can be built on nonreligious foundations. The questions "Does God exist?" and "What are the foundations of morality?" are to philosophers such as David Hume and John Stuart Mill distinct and independent. Viereck is not entirely in their camp. The reader senses that Viereck's absence of faith makes him doubt the basis of morals as well. When he insists on upholding the virtues and condemns poets who fail to do so, he is in part suppressing his fear that morality is in fact without basis.

THE TREE WITCH

Another part of Viereck's philosophy comes to expression in *The Tree Witch*. This is both a poem and a play, but only the former will be discussed here. The work has an unusual theme. An old tree has been cut down to make room for an eight-lane highway, and some "fifty-year old children" separate a dryad from the tree and chain it in a garage (a dryad is a tree spirit; talking trees are featured in *Terror and Decorum* and are a trademark of Viereck's poetry). The poem features alternating lines by the human beings and the dryad. Viereck's sympathies are clearly on the dryad's side. The men who imprison her claim to be acting for her welfare, but they are enemies of nature. By taking her away from the tree, they (along with those who have cut down the tree) kill her.

Viereck uses this bizarre account to symbolize the struggle between nature and technology that he thinks characteristic of the twentieth century. Machines, once built, have a dynamic of their own that leads people to fall victim to these supposed tools. People increasingly subordinate themselves to machines; labor has become monotonous and overly rapid.

True value lies in harmony with nature, which must be respected for its own sake rather than viewed as raw material for the creation of tools. Technology out of control returns Viereck to a theme prominent early in his career. He views it as a central element of the rise of Nazism and Communism. The correct attitude toward nature is an essential part of the humanist values Viereck defends.

Here once more Viereck is led into paradox. The defense of nature against all-powerful machines is a mainstay of Romanticism. Many of the people Viereck is most concerned to attack for their political follies are fervent proponents of this view. The philosopher Martin Heidegger, whom Viereck attacks as a Nazi in *Metapolitics*, made warnings about the imminent takeover of the world by technology a key theme of his teaching. For a professed anti-Romantic, Viereck adopts a large number of Romantic positions.

ARCHER IN THE MARROW

Viereck issued his longest continuous work, *Archer in the Marrow*, in 1987. This is an epic poem composed in "cycles" on which Viereck worked for twenty years. The work depicts a three-way conversation between God, the man he has created, and contemporary humankind. The theme of the epic is whether human beings are "things" determined by outside forces or, on the contrary, have the power to control their own fate and surpass themselves.

Viereck presents God as eager to keep human beings under his thumb. Human beings cannot withstand the divine power, but they have an ally who gives them a fighting chance in the struggle for autonomy. God is afraid of Eve or Aphrodite, whose feminine nature symbolizes attunement with nature. Eve rarely appears directly in the poem, and her views and characteristics must be pieced together from the lines of the other characters. In spite of her elusiveness, she is humankind's best chance for salvation. Viereck, apparently worried that readers might not get the message, included in the book a commentary explaining his poem.

Throughout his career, Viereck defended a clearly expressed set of values. He braved the perils of nonconformity, since didactic poetry was out of fashion. Much more than a preacher in verse, Viereck was a gifted literary artist who devoted his poetic talents to conveying a message he thought of vital concern. The tensions in his views show that he had to struggle against himself to keep his poetry under the firm control he thought proper.

TIDE AND CONTINUITIES

In 1995, Viereck, at age seventy-nine and in deteriorating health, published what he expected to be his last collection of poetry (although it was followed by *Door*, in 2005). He told a reporter for the *Daily Hampshire Gazette* that he was retiring from writing life and that he intended to dedicate the proceeds from his last book to the Clio-Melpomene Prize, an award he had established for maverick students at Mount Holyoke College who were doing creative, original work in poetry or history. *Tide and Continuities* is by far the best collection of Viereck's poetry because it contains, in addition to his latest poetic works, poems he personally selected from past publications to represent him after his death. The poems in part 1, titled "Mostly Hospital and Old Age," were, as Viereck states in his preface, "mostly begun in hospitals in my seventies." Their theme is "old age and its coming to terms with the archetypal trio: Persephone, Dionysus, Pluto (here the farmer's daughter, the traveling salesman, the basement janitor)."

Part 6 of *Tide and Continuities* is titled "Tide and Completions." This section consists of three long poems composed between 1992 and 1995 and intended to unify the poems of the past and the present. As Viereck says with characteristic humor, "The occasional repetition of certain leitmotif phrases is serving this unifying function. Often the 'I' in the newer poems is not me but a goofy dying Everyman, trying to ululate [i.e., howl, wail, lament] past doc and nurse." Viereck may have lost his health but not his quirky sense of humor or his zest for life. What is most impressive about his later poems is his courage in the face of pain and death. He uses his personal plight as an occasion for discussing the Promethean plight of humankind as a whole. He remained remarkably consistent in his philosophic views throughout his long career and remarkably consistent in his rationale of poetic technique. He discussed technical aspects of poetry in the preface to this work.

Tide and Continuities received deplorably scant notice by literary critics. An exception was the long review in *Humanitas* by Professor Michael A. Weinstein, who obviously considered Viereck one of the most important American poets of modern times.

DOOR

Viereck published a last volume of poetry, *Door*, the year before his death. This collection of new poetry covered familiar themes such as freedom, knowledge, death, and time. It also used rhyme and syntax in much the way his other books had. He included a selection of German and Russian poems from poets whom he admired.

OTHER MAJOR WORKS

NONFICTION: *Metapolitics: From the Romantics to Hitler*, 1941; *Conservatism Revisited: The Revolt Against Revolt, 1815-1949*, 1949; *Shame and Glory of the Intellectuals*, 1953; *Conservatism: From John Adams to Churchill*, 1956; *The Unadjusted Man*, 1956; *Strict Wildness: Discoveries in Poetry and History*, 2008; *Transplantings: Essays on Great German Poets with Translations*, 2008.

BIBLIOGRAPHY

Brodsky, Joseph. Foreword to *Tide and Continuities: Last and First Poems, 1995-1938*, by Peter Viereck. Fayetteville: University of Arkansas Press, 1995. Prominent Russian-born poet Brodsky contributed a rhymed foreword to Viereck's book. This amusing but sincere tribute contains an edifying overview of Viereck's life and personality as well as a shrewd analysis of his contribution to literature.

Fox, Margalit. "Peter Viereck, Poet and Conservative Theorist, Dies at Eighty-nine." *The New York Times*, May 19, 2006, p. A26. This obituary discusses Viereck's life and how he made conservatism an intellectual movement. In his poetry, Fox says Viereck "combined lyrical and pastoral preoccupations with a parodic wit" that produced complex poetry that met with mixed reviews. Notes that his serious verse was better received.

Hacht, Anne Marie, ed. *Poetry for Students*. Vol. 14. Detroit: Gale, 2002. Analyzes Viereck's "Kilroy." Contains the poem, summary, themes, style, historical context, critical overview, and criticism. Includes bibliography and index.

Hénault, Marie. *Peter Viereck*. New York: Twayne, 1969. A rare book-length study of Viereck's work. It gives a relatively comprehensive account of Viereck's poetry and prose to the date of publication, although some of the poetry is not discussed. Hénault is very favorable to Viereck and defends him against negative reviewers.

Kirby, David. "Lasting Words." Review of *Tide and Continuities*. *Parnassus: Poetry in Review* 21 (1996): 113-130. Kirby uses his review as a springboard to analyze the aging poet's life's work. He compares Viereck with another distinguished elderly poet,

Theodore Weiss. Kirby irreverently remarks that "each is the kind of old-boy writer your average performance poet or radical feminist would shove cheerfully into the wood chipper."

Reiss, Tom. "The First Conservative: Life and Letters." *The New Yorker* 81, no. 33 (October 24, 2005): 42. This profile of Viereck describes how his 1941 essay in *The Atlantic Monthly* on conservatism inspired a movement that subsequently abandoned him. Describes Viereck's life and philosophy.

Ryn, Claes G. "Peter Viereck and Conservativism." In *Conservatism Revisited: The Revolt Against Ideology*, by Peter Viereck. New Brunswick, N.J.: Transaction, 2005. Rym provides an essay on Viereck that serves to introduce a reprint of one of Viereck's early works, originally published in 1949 as *Conservatism Revisited: The Revolt Against Revolt, 1815-1949*. He examines Viereck as a conservative and poet, and notes his legacy.

Weinstein, Michael A. "Dignity in Old Age: The Poetical Meditations of Peter Viereck." Review of *Tide and Continuities*. *Humanitas* 8, no. 2 (1995): 53-67. In this lengthy review, Weinstein lauds Viereck as a formidable philosophical poet, a civilized humanist, and a civilized existentialist. Weinstein focuses his discussion on four poems that illuminate Viereck's mature vision of human existence: "Crass Times Redeemed by Dignity of Souls," "Rogue," "At My Hospital Window," and "Persephone and the Old Poet."

Bill Delaney
Updated by Delaney

JOSÉ GARCÍA VILLA

Born: Manila, Philippines; August 5, 1914
Died: New York, New York; February 7, 1997

PRINCIPAL POETRY

Many Voices, 1939
Poems by Doveglion, 1941
Have Come, Am Here, 1942
Volume Two, 1949

Selected Poems and New, 1958
Poems 55, 1962
Poems in Praise of Love, 1962
Appassionata: Poems in Praise of Love, 1979

OTHER LITERARY FORMS

In 1929, José García Villa (VEE-yah) edited the first comprehensive anthology of Filipino short stories in English, for the *Philippines Free Press*. The earliest published volume of his own work was also a collection of stories, *Footnote to Youth: Tales of the Philippines and Others*, released by Scribner's in 1933. Many of these tales had appeared earlier in *Clay*, the mimeographed literary magazine which he founded at the University of New Mexico and which first drew the attention of Edward O'Brien. *The Best American Short Stories of 1932*, in fact, was dedicated to Villa by O'Brien, whose introduction included Villa "among the half-dozen short story writers in America who count" and compared him with one of O'Brien's earlier discoveries, Sherwood Anderson. Even as O'Brien was prophesying a career for Villa as novelist, however, the young writer had already turned his attention exclusively to poetry. The stories, therefore, retain their interest chiefly as preliminaries to attitudes and techniques associated with Villa's poems.

A third of the twenty-one stories in *Footnote to Youth* are semiautobiographical portraits of a hermit protagonist suffering self-imposed isolation in the Philippines, New Mexico, and New York City. There is a repetitive pattern of rejected illegitimate children, either unwanted or inadequately cared for; of antagonism between fathers and grown sons; of the protagonist's alienation from those with whom he is, only temporarily, most intimate; of a love-hate identification with José Rizal, martyred hero of the 1896 Revolution, as a father-image whose own paternity is clouded; of rejection in courtship and marriage; and of self-importance recovered through sentimentalized identification with the suffering Christ, the god mocked and misunderstood.

This sense of recoil from hurt was conveyed in Villa's stories principally through antinarrative devices. In some cases, the paragraphs are numbered and condensed, so that typographically they resemble stanzas in a poem. Also, incident is not allowed to flow into incident. O'Brien wrote of Villa's combining "a native sensuousness of perception and impression" with the "traditionally Spanish expression of passionate feeling in classical reticence of form." More likely, however, the compartmentalization of the narrative indicates the aftermath of a series of unhappy encounters between a sensitive personality and an insensitive world unprepared to give him the recognition he deserves. The stories dazzle with color, their principal emotion being intensely lyrical.

ACHIEVEMENTS

As a self-exile from the Philippines for decades, José García Villa earned awards and a reputation in both the Western and Asian worlds. In the United States, he was the recipient of a Guggenheim Fellowship, an Academy Award for literature from the American Academy of Arts and Letters in 1946, a Bollingen Fellowship, and a Rockefeller grant. In Greenwich Village during the 1940's and 1950's, he was considered a "regular," as a member of the New Directions avant-garde. In Great Britain, his reputation also flourished, as a result of Edith Sitwell's high praise of his "great and perfectly original work." Gradually such distinction, coming from overseas, influenced his countrymen at home. Although there were complaints that he did not write about subjects identifiably Filipino, and that he did not write with the folk simplicity of Carlos Bulosan's *New Yorker* tales of sweet-sour satire, an entire generation of college-educated Filipinos began not only to envy his success but also to emulate his sophistication and inventiveness. The prominence given him by this growing cult assisted in securing for him a Pro Patria Award, in 1961, and a Cultural Heritage Award in 1962. In 1973, he became the first Filipino writer in English to be declared a National Artist, with a government pension for life.

BIOGRAPHY

José García Villa once insisted that "Biography I have none and shall have none. All my Pure shall beggar and defy biography." He was requiring that his identity be sought exclusively in his poems, his purer self. For most of his life, he maintained just such distances, shunning intimacies.

Whenever he boasted that his physician-father was

José García Villa (Library of Congress)

chief of staff for General Emilio Aguinaldo during the Revolution of 1896, he identified himself less with the healer, in that figure, than with the power of the prototypical rebel. In fact, he strenuously resisted his father's attempt to make a doctor of him. At the University of the Philippines, he turned instead to the study of law, whose logic and case-history specifics he also soon found too constraining. He was temporarily suspended from college in June, 1929, for having written "Man Songs," a poem too sexually explicit for the times and the authorities. In that same year, for his story "Mir-i-Nisa," a fable of native courtship, he became the first recipient of an award in what was to become a distinguished annual contest in the *Philippines Free Press*. Because he felt unappreciated by his father and inadequately recognized by his fellow Filipinos, he spent the prize money taking himself into exile in the United States. He was determined to be answerable only to himself.

In 1932, he received a B.A. from the University of New Mexico, where his literary magazine *Clay* published the first work (a poem) by William Saroyan, the early writing of William March, David Cornel de Jong, and others, as well as many of his own short stories. These attracted the attention of O'Brien, who dedicated *The Best American Short Stories of 1932* to Villa and placed eleven of his tales on that year's list of distinctive stories. Elated, Villa went to New York City, taking *Clay* with him, the magazine that O'Brien declared to be the prospective rival of Whit and Hallie Burnett's *Story* magazine. Although Villa had difficulty finding salaried work during the Great Depression and claimed that he was discriminated against because of his nationality, in 1933, Scribner's published his collection of stories, *Footnote to Youth*, dedicated to O'Brien, who wrote an introduction to the volume. In 1939, his first book of poems, *Many Voices*, appeared in Manila; in 1940, it won honorable mention in the Commonwealth Literary Contest. The following year, *Poems by Doveglion* was published in Manila and *Have Come, Am Here* in the United States in 1942. The latter was in close contention for the Pulitzer Prize. Befriended by Mark Van Doren, Villa pursued graduate studies at Columbia on a partial scholarship from that university and another from the Commonwealth of the Philippines. As an avocation, he painted geometric portraits in the cubist mode and hung them in his apartment next to several by E. E. Cummings.

By 1942, he was working for the Philippine embassy in Washington, D.C., clipping newspaper stories of the battles on Bataan and Corregidor. His mind, however, was less on his clerical duties than on his own writing. When he was refused a raise because he typed so slowly, Villa exclaimed, "What do you take me for, a mechanic?" He returned to New York at once and married Rosemarie Lamb, by whom he later had two sons. In 1949, he published *Volume Two*, the book that introduced his experimental "comma poems." He became an associate editor with New Directions, as well as with the Harvard *Wake* for special issues on Marianne Moore and Cummings. His poems have consistently appeared in American and world anthologies since the 1940's. In 1958, a largely retrospective work, *Selected Poems and New*, was released. He taught poetry workshops at both the City College of New York and, from 1964 to 1973, the New School for Social Research. In various ways, he was also attached to the Philippine Mission to the United Nations until he was declared a National Artist in 1973. In the 1980's, he served as editor of *Bravo: The Poet's Magazine*. Near the end of his life in 1997, his work had been out of the public eye for more than thirty years, and out of print for more than fifteen. Despite his withdrawal from the public literary scene, he continued to devote his critical powers to formulating a philosophy of poetics and teaching at New York colleges. He also conducted poetry workshops at his apartment. As a former student remembered, "Along with strong, extremely dry martinis, Villa served critiques of his students' poems. He tore apart narrative pieces, arguing that real poetry was lyrical, 'written with words, not ideas.' He even told pupils not to read fiction, to purge their work of any narrative element."

ANALYSIS

Both José García Villa's admirers and his detractors agree on the essential inwardness of his poetry. For the latter, this is a symptom of narcissism hardly useful to the urgent needs of a newly independent nation. For the former, it is a sign of a transcendent mysticism whose universality should be given priority over nationalism. The poet himself declared that he was not at all interested in externals, "nor in the contemporary scene, but in *essence*." His dominant concern was not description but metaphysics, a penetration of the inner maze of humankind's identity within the entire "mystery of creation."

The poems themselves, however, often suggest something less than such perfection and therefore something more exciting: purification-in-process, the sensual nature in humans struggling to survive transfiguration. The body strains to avoid emasculation even as the spirit ascends. Consequently, the flesh seems glorified, although not in any ordinary spiritual manner that would diminish the splendor of the sense. Sitwell, in her preface to *The American Genius* (1951), refers to this paradox as an expression of "absolute sensation," mingling a "strange luminosity" with a "strange darkness." Villa himself best epitomized the blinding heat of this attempted fusion by repeatedly adopting the persona/pseudonym Doveglion: a composite Dove-eagle-lion.

MANY VOICES AND POEMS BY DOVEGLION

Even the ordinary early poems, replete with piety and puppy love and first gathered in *Many Voices*, then in *Poems by Doveglion*, occasionally manage to move the imagination toward the outermost limits of language, a crafted inarticulateness conveying the inexpressible. When he was seventeen, Villa could compare the "nipple" on the coconut with a maiden's breast, and drink from each; but later lyrics match God and genius, both suffering "The ache of the unfound love" and, in their lonely perfection, left contending for primacy with each other. For Villa, these maturer poems were also the first attempts to create by wordplay, combining "brilliance and/ consecration." A romantic vocabulary emerges, repeated like a code or incantation: star, wind, birds, roses, tigers, dark parts, the sun, doves, the divine. More experimentally, he inverted phrases and therefore logic, in expectation of profound meaning beyond the rational. He wrote, "Tomorrow is very past/ As yesterday is so future" and "Your profundity is very light./ My lightness is very profound." Above all, he is trying to "announce me": "I am most of all, most." The defiant rebel who was his own cause begins to be apparent in these poems published in the Philippines.

HAVE COME, AM HERE

Even as *Many Voices* and *Poems by Doveglion* were going to press, however, his experiments had taken a quantum leap forward. When Sylvia Townsend Warner came to New York in 1939 as Britain's delegate to the Third Congress of American Writers, she was astounded by the verses being prepared for *Have Come, Am Here*, which included the best of Villa's previous work and much more. It was two years later that the book reached the hands of Sitwell, whose eyes fell on the poem "My most. My most. O my lost!," a brief litany of the protagonist's "terrible Accost" with God; she was moved by its "ineffable beauty." The volume is a mixture of adoring love lyrics and joyous, combative rivalry with God. To convey their "strange luminosity," she felt compelled to make comparisons with the religious ecstasies of William Blake and Jakob Boehme, as well as with such other mystics as Saint Catherine of Genoa and Meister Eckhart.

It was a matter of special pride for Villa to note that in six of his poems, he introduced a wholly new method of rhyming which he called "reversed consonance." As he explained it, "a rhyme for *near* would be *run, green, reign*," with the initial *n-r* combination reversed in each instance. Such a rhyme, of course, is visible if the reader has been forewarned, but even then the ear can hardly notice the event. Still, the device is one more variation among Villa's many attempts, through decreation and reassemblage, to penetrate the energy fields of convention and release explosive forces from the very "depths of Being," as Sitwell puts it. Much more interesting, however, and more successful than reversed consonance in satisfying this quest for fire is the inexorable forward force of both his love lyrics and his "divine poems." Occasionally these poems are indistinguishable from one another because the protagonist addresses both his beloved and his God with the same possessive, mastering rhetoric: "Between God's eyelashes I look at you,/ Contend with the Lord to love you. . . ." At times in compulsive narcissism, the protagonist even treats them as mirrors for himself, then briefly relents, guiltily considering himself to be Lucifer or Judas. Such interplays of ambiguity are made inevitable by the poems' brevity and density, the constant ellipses and startling juxtapositions: oranges and giraffes, pigeons and watermelons, yellow strawberries, "pink monks eating blue raisins," the crucified Christ as peacock, the wind shining and sun blowing.

Sometimes in these poems, one can recognize the synesthesia of the French Symbolists, Cummings's curtailments of standard grammar, Blakean nature as divine emblems, or the equivalent of cubist/Surrealist transformations of reality. Mostly, however, Villa was an original. One senses in him a compelling inner necessity to prove that purity proceeds from the proper combination of what are normally considered impurities. His was the rebel's revenge against mediocrity, a Promethean ascent-in-force to regain godhead. Fellow poet Rolando Tinio, in *Brown Heritage* (1967), says that Villa "speaks of God becoming Man and concludes that Man has become God." Villa's countrymen grudgingly accepted his preeminence abroad. Villa, however, always thought of himself as too exceptional to be a representative Filipino. He would not live in the shadow of his wealthy father in the Philippines; at best he could make a desperate living in New York during the Depression and World War II. Emotionally homeless, he fortified his exile by offering in his poetry a protagonist both essential and universal. For Villa, that meant a rejection of common codes and orders, a rising above all local circumstances. *Have Come, Am Here* reflects this profound need for self-justification.

Resounding critical acclaim for the poems of *Have Come, Am Here* came instantly, from Sitwell, Richard Eberhart, Horace Gregory, Moore, and well over a dozen world anthologists. For them, Villa's poetry was as cryptic as a Zen koan and therefore as rewarding as any other religious meditation, the very dislocation of syntax soliciting a revelation. Still others, entranced by their initial experience of *Have Come, Am Here*, have reported that later readings showed a tendency in Villa toward formula that was too facile, as if, were any poem shaken hard enough, its words would finally form another, by the laws of chance and permutation. The poetic vocabulary is not only too romantic for pragmatic readers, but it is also rather impoverished because it is more repetitive than resonant. Similarly, these poems, whether sacred or profane, ultimately manifest the same basic love for a self more praised than explored. Readers accustomed to tangible substance and foreseeable consequences are troubled by an incandescence that, for them, blinds more than it illuminates.

VOLUME TWO

The same polarity of reaction occurred with the appearance of the "comma poems" in *Volume Two*. Between each word in these poems Villa placed an unspaced comma, "regulating the poem's density and time movement." His intent was to control the pace of each poem's progress with measured dignity. The effect resembles musical notation, although Villa preferred to compare the technique with Georges Seurat's pointillism. Unlike reversed consonance, this innovative device does indeed add "visual distinction." It cannot, however, rescue such verses as Villa's "Caprices" or most of his aphorisms; it can only make them seem pretentious. Some of the new "divine poems," nevertheless, were among the author's best, their dynamics

rising from the mystery of things seen in mid-metamorphosis: for example, "The, bright, Centipede" beginning its stampede from "What, celestial, province!" Villa's quarrels with his co-Creator ("My dark hero") also managed a magnificence that can pass beyond self-celebration. There is as much visionary quickening in the image of "God, dancing, on, phosphorescent, toes,/ Among, the, strawberries" as in the inscrutable Lion carrying "God, the, Dark, Corpse!" down Jacob's ladder. In poems as powerful as these, the commas seem like sacerdotal vestments woven from metallic mesh. In lesser poems, however, the commas serve merely as a façade to conceal or decorate an inner vacuousness. A few poems, in fact, were rescued from his earliest volumes and have merely been rehabilitated through use of this fresh overlay.

More serious questions than those raised by *Volume Two*'s unevenness have been directed toward Villa's perpetual reliance on a small cluster of romantic terms whose effect was reduced as their possible combinations approach exhaustion. Furthermore, the prolonged role of rebel led Villa to virtual self-imitation in the steady use of reversals, negatives, and reductives. The "not-face" and "un-ears" of his earlier lyrics became an established pattern later: "In, my, undream, of, death,/ I, unspoke, the, Word"; "the, Holy,/ Unghost—"; "Unnight,/ Me"; "In, not, getting, there, is, perfect, Arrival"; "The, clock, was, not, a, clock"; "May, spring, from, *Un*—,/ Light. . . ." By substitution, strange, suggestive equations can emerge ("Myself, as, Absence, discoverer,/ Myself, as, Presence, searcher"), but so can codes so manneristic that others can imitate them successfully ("Yesterday, I, awoke, today"; gold blackbirds; blue-eyed trees). Two different kinds of innocence are offered: that of the true visionary breaking through the barriers of ordinary reality to a tranquillity beyond words and worry; and that of the mindless child playing at anagrams with alphabet blocks (as the poet himself much earlier playfully signed himself "O. Sevilla").

Much mirroring is bound to occur in a poet who is less God-driven, as Eberhart claims Villa was, than obsessed with the trinity of his own godhead (Poet, Word, and Poem), as Tinio suggests. Within those confinements, intensity has to compensate for lack of variety;

and critics of all persuasions admit that, at his best, Villa did brilliantly manage that irresistible tenacity, that sense of seizure, even if at the expense of the subject's being its sole object. Dismissing nakedness for the sake of translucent nudity, he came to sacrifice more and more the sensate body of other persons to exclamations on his own exultant sensibility. That habit limits the plausibility of comparisons that Villa offered between his own work and the paintings of Seurat or Pablo Picasso. Seurat, understanding the optics of his day, provides in each canvas the subjective process of atomized vision and the objective configurations of person, place, and thing which that process projects. Picasso, similarly, even in a hundred portraits of the same model, admits and conveys the realization of plenitude, of multiple perspectives, as both perceiver and perceived undergo subtle alterations in time, angle of vision, psychological attitude, degree of rapport, and the like.

SELECTED POEMS AND NEW

That no such plenitude, no such endless surprise was available to Villa became clear with the publication of *Selected Poems and New*. There are several noteworthy new comma poems in this collection, though no startling innovations within that general usage. "Xalome," "And, if, Theseus—then, Minotaur," "Death and Dylan Thomas," and "The Anchored Angel" at least offer ponderous objects for contemplation that, unlike his aphorisms, his lighthearted cries over the blue-eyed bird in a tree, and "A Valentine for Edith Sitwell," appropriate with ease the pace provided by the commas. Such objects also warrant the invitation to meditation that Villa's associational techniques offered in the best of his poems.

By far the larger part of the previously unpublished section of this volume is devoted to forty-eight "adaptations," conversions of other people's prose into poems. His sources were Rainer Maria Rilke's letters, Simone Weil's notebooks, André Gide's journals, and book reviews and letters to the editors of *Time* and *Life*. No word of his own is interjected into the originals, although "to achieve the tightness of verse" he omitted occasional "connectives and extra adjectives." In several cases, borrowing from the visual arts, Villa offered what he calls collages: the original lines of a *Life* magazine caption, for example, rearranged in their sequence;

or portions from two different sections of a book brought together. Many of these adaptations received critical praise, particularly as they showed a masterful control of musical phrasing, in a variety of tempos and turns that indicate once more the limitations of the comma as a single musical measure. The value of the adaptations naturally depends so heavily on the intrinsic merit of the originals—Franz Kafka, Henry Miller, William Carlos Williams—that one might have expected the application of this kind of craft to others' work as an early stage of apprenticeship. The adaptations lack, for example, the degree of participation-beyond-translation visible in Robert Lowell's volume of "collaborations," *Imitations* (1961); nor have they generated any insights or techniques, as did Ezra Pound's experience with free translations from Provençal poetry that allowed him, in his *The Cantos* (1979), to adapt documents from American history as well as selected phrases and ideograms from the Italian and the Chinese.

CULTURAL REIDENTIFICATION

After *Selected Poems and New*, Villa's effort was devoted less to improving his reputation than to maintaining it, particularly in the Philippines. A number of chapbooks appeared in Manila, in 1962, reprinting portions of his earlier writing, to reestablish himself in his native land. This latter-day identification with a culture that finds no specific presence in his poems and from which he remains geographically remote seemed rather anomalous, but there are Filipinos who think he performed better ambassadorial service than many foreign affairs officers. Villa's egocentric poetry is at the opposite extreme from the Filipinos' sense of togetherness (*bayanihan*) or the family extended through ritual kinship. His role as rebel was not incongruous, however, if viewed from his people's long history of oppression as a Spanish colony; the Philippine Revolution of 1896, which briefly established a republic whose rejection by the United States caused the Philippine-American War, 1899 to 1902; the Commonwealth years, during which Filipinos had to prove their superiority in order to be considered equals; the guerrilla years of World War II; and the strains of political but not quite economic independence thereafter.

Whether he intended it or not, Villa reinforced the feeling of those Filipinos who demand that they be defined by their own mores and folkways; his "unson-ment" poems can be taken as collective resentment of paternalism, however benevolent, proffered by former colonial powers. Even the seeming blasphemy of certain "divine poems" resembles the hybrid religious observances among Asia's only Christian people, once resentful of Spanish religious orders that served as arms of overseas administrations. The nationalists can understand in Villa their defiance and aspiration, the right to self-determination, the refusal to be humiliated by anyone. For these various reasons, Villa continued to be ranked highest among an increasing number of distinguished Filipino poets.

OTHER MAJOR WORKS

SHORT FICTION: *Footnote to Youth: Tales of the Philippines and Others*, 1933; *Selected Stories*, 1962.

NONFICTION: *The Critical Villa: Essays in Literary Criticism*, 2002 (Jonathan Chua, editor).

EDITED TEXTS: *Philippine Short Stories*, 1929; *A Celebration for Edith Sitwell*, 1946; *The New Dove-glion Book of Philippines Poetry*, 1993.

MISCELLANEOUS: *The Portable Villa*, 1962 (stories and poems); *The Essential Villa*, 1965; *The Anchored Angel*, 1999.

BIBLIOGRAPHY

Abad, Gemimo. "One Hundred Years of Filipino Poetry: An Overview." *World Literature Today* 74, no. 2 (2000): 327-331. Identifies the various periods of Filipino poetry in the twentieth century, placing Villa as a Romantic.

Cowen, John Edwin. "Doveglion: The E. E. Cummings and José García Villa Connection." *Knight Ridder Tribune Business News*, December 3, 2006, p. 1. A book of poetry by E. E. Cummings inspired Villa to write poetry. Villa would write to Cummings and they developed a relationship.

Cullum, Linda E. *Contemporary American Ethnic Poets: Lives, Works, Sources*. Westport, Conn.: Greenwood Press, 2004. Contains a short biography of Villa.

Espiritu, Augusto Fauni. *Five Faces of Exile: The Nation and Filipino American Intellectuals*. Stanford, Calif.: Stanford University Press, 2007. A chapter on Villa discusses the difficulty of placing the Filipino writer whose poetry bore little mention of the Philippines.

Francia, Luis H. Introduction to *Doveglion: Collected Poems*, edited by John Cowan. New York: Penguin Books, 2008. Provides a perspective on the life and works of Villa. The collection draws from poems throughout the poet's career.

Grow, L. M. "José García Villa: The Poetry of Calibration." *World Literature Written in English* 27 (Autumn, 1987): 326-344. This article contends that Villa is usually revered for the wrong reasons. He is hampered by moral earnestness and thus does not make the fullest use of his lyric gifts, which are visible in spectacular opening lines.

Tabios, Eileen, ed. *Anchored Angel: Selected Writings of José García Villa*. New York: Kaya, 1999. Brings together a collection of Villa's writings with critical essays by a number of leading Filipino and Filipino American scholars. Among the contributors of critical essays are E. San Juan, Jr., Luis Francia, Nick Carbo, Nick Joaquin, and Alfred Yuson.

Yu, Timothy. "'The Hand of a Chinese Master': José García Villa and Modernist Orientalism." *MELUS* 29, no. 1 (Spring, 2004): 41-60. This lengthy examination of Villa's poetry looks at his place as a Filipino poet and as an American poet.

Leonard R. Casper

ELLEN BRYANT VOIGT

Born: Danville, Virginia; May 9, 1943

PRINCIPAL POETRY
Claiming Kin, 1976
The Forces of Plenty, 1983
The Lotus Flowers, 1987
Two Trees, 1992
Kyrie, 1995
Shadow of Heaven, 2002
Messenger: New and Selected Poems, 1976-2006, 2007

OTHER LITERARY FORMS

Ellen Bryant Voigt (voyt) is also known for her critical essays on poetry, collected in *The Flexible Lyric* (1999). She explores and defines lyric, narrative, style, structure, form, and other concepts of genre and versification: tone, image, diction, gender, tension, and voice. The central concern is testing differentiation between the modes and impulses of lyric and narrative.

The lengthy title essay develops definitions of lyric and narrative, form and structure, texture and voice that reveal how the elements of each pair are set in tension in the best poetry. Quoting from Randall Jarrell, who regarded tension as "a struggle between opposites," Voigt considers unity in a poem to emerge from tension, and this emergence is a poem's necessary function. Lyric is "a moment lifted out of time but not static, movement that is centripetal and centrifugal rather than linear; an examination of self which discovers universal predicament; insight embodied in individuated particulars and at the same time overriding them." Voigt illustrates her point by briefly tracing the evolution of lyric poetry from the Renaissance through the present to show that form does not limit the poet's freedom but rather impels the evolution of lyric poetry.

ACHIEVEMENTS

Ellen Bryant Voigt's awards include the Alice Fay di Castagnola Award (1983), the Emily Clark Balch Award (1987), the Hanes Award for Poetry (1993), the Lila Wallace-*Reader's Digest* Writers' Award (1998), an Academy Award in Literature from the American Academy of Arts and Letters (2000), the O. B. Hardison, Jr., Poetry Prize (2002), and Pushcart Prizes (2003, 2006). She has received grants and fellowships from the National Endowment for the Arts, the Guggenheim Foundation, the Vermont Council on the Arts, and the Academy of American Poets (2001). *Kyrie* was a finalist for a National Book Critics Circle Award, and *Messenger* was a finalist for the National Book Award and the Pulitzer Prize in poetry. From 1999 to 2003, Voigt was poet laureate of Vermont. In 2002, she was inducted into the Fellowship of Southern Writers, and she served as a chancellor of the Academy of American Poets from 2003 to 2009. In 2009, she received the Poets' Prize for *Messenger*.

BIOGRAPHY

Ellen Bryant was brought up in Chatham, Virginia, by Lloyd Gilmore Bryant, a farmer, and Missouri Yeats Bryant, an elementary school teacher. Experiences of family, along with will and destiny, hard work and choice, natural order and persistence in the face of the unpredictable afforded by farm life, are at the heart of her concerns.

She credits her early and long training in music as her central artistic influence. Not only was it formative in her "impulse for order," but also it contributed to her love of "solitude." Surrounded by many relatives, Voigt found her life "exceedingly claustrophobic." Playing piano was her time to herself:

> I can look back and see poem after poem that takes up the friction between that solitary individual and whatever that social unit is, be it small or large.

Music resounds in the body, eliciting sensory feeling. At the same time, it provides a sense of control through form, both constraining and fluid. Relating this to her writing, Voigt has said, "I make a musical decision before I make any other kind of decision. . . . If I can't hear it, it just never gets written."

Voigt's music education began with piano lessons at age four and continued through a degree in 1964 at Converse College in Spartanburg, South Carolina, where she discovered her dislike of performance, her love for music theory, and her passion for literature. While she was working a summer job playing lounge music at a resort, a friend introduced her to the poetry of Rainer Maria Rilke, E. E. Cummings, and William Butler Yeats.

Voigt earned a master of fine arts degree from the University of Iowa in 1966, studying principally with Donald Justice. She married Francis Voigt, a college dean, in 1965, and they had two children. Major concerns of her art are the family relationship, its disorders and orders, choice and fate, and opportunities for truth and moral reflection. She taught at Goddard College and the Massachusetts Institute of Technology before accepting a position at Warren Wilson College in 1981.

Each of her books explores the nature of lyric and narrative and their interaction as she strives to keep narrative in the background while plumbing the depths of lyric. Her 1995 collection, *Kyrie*, disperses narrative through a long sequence of sonnets.

ANALYSIS

Ellen Bryant Voigt is known for finely wrought, compressed forms delivered with a passionate moral sensibility. Profoundly influenced by her extensive early musical training and formalism, her poems push the limits of lyric and narrative as she sets emotionally heightened moments out of time—singing—against the storied linear past and tries to unite them.

"SONG AND STORY"

"Song and Story," the concluding poem of *Two Trees*, Voigt's fourth volume of poems, distills the chief concern of her artistic life. She gathers and articulates the two impulses that have driven her, that she sees driving human life. Music reaches from the nontemporal realm into story with its softening, easing rhythms; the singer has emerged from pain and reaches back to another who is immersed in pain. The impulse of lyric is thus hope, promise, choice to continue, and praise of the nontemporal or cyclical against story's inevitable onward movement toward death of the individual. As Stephen Cramer has written, "Voigt's work as a whole recites the tale of one artist's 'will to change.'" Her own story encapsulates the story of human choice.

CLAIMING KIN

Voigt's vision matured over two decades from discovery of the body's music, its breathings and varied motions in the midst of life. The rhythms of family are set harmonically and then oppositionally, as in the title poem, "Claiming Kin." Writing of her mother, the poet begins:

> Insistent as a whistle, her voice up
> the stairs pried open the blanket's
> tight lid and piped me
> down to the pressure cooker's steam and rattle.

Other household objects the mother wields make their insistent noises, while the poet as a small child is a "pale lump blinking at the light" of her mother's "shiny kingdom" of noisy "razzle-dazzle." The mother has another, a night rhythm apposite to the poet's self, a "Soft ghost, plush as a pillow," who "wove and fruited against the black hours."

In "The Feast of the Assumption of the Virgin," the Madonna "Mourns . . . as if reaching for fruit," and a priest's blessing of young girls joins music and fruit, joy and hurt:

> when the bells release
> a shower of pollen,
> each mouth opens to rapture
> like a wound.

Pain is the price of joy. Composed of loose iambics and snatches of ballad rhythms, these poems' rhythms function to advance and constrain extremity let loose by often shocking images: the beheading of a hen, a jealous child wishing her older sister dead, a dream life of murdering, "stones/ with their mouths sewn shut." Music reaches into silence to seed it, but each person remains isolated; song is not much help to any but the poet herself.

THE FORCES OF PLENTY

In her second collection, *The Forces of Plenty*, Voigt shifted toward narrative. Less concerned with capturing the intense emotion in a moment of time through lyric's music, she renders small vignettes with people now listening to the sounds the world offers. The music is quieter, calmed by interludes of stopping the daily round to listen. In "The Spire," a poem about the function of lyric and reminiscent of Marianne Moore's "The Steeple-Jack," a church on a mountain provides connection to townspeople. Forms made by human hands and thought "can extend the flawed earth/ and embody us," giving lives the continuity of story. However, the bells of the church ring over "the village/ houses . . . allied in a formal shape/ beside a stream, the streets concluding/ at the monument. Again the ravishing moment/ of the bell," at which the townspeople are pictured stopping each of their various businesses, each having its own ongoing rhythm, as the bell inserts sound into their time to call them momentarily out of linear time to lyric ecstasy.

In Voigt's estimation, "Taking the Fire Out," was a "watershed" pointing toward *The Lotus Flowers*. Each of the poem's six sections presents a small narrative scene rendered with lyric intensity and questioning. The repeated line "Nothing is learned by turning away" bespeaks the poet's honest effort to choose to know what is true.

THE LOTUS FLOWERS

Composed in the wake of her parents' deaths, *The Lotus Flowers* revisits the poet's southern childhood and revises its terms and story, moving sharply and clearly in short narratives toward lyric conclusions. Writing in "Short Story" of her grandfather killing a mule, she is not sure what the truth is, "The story varied/ in the telling." Each person has a version, each according to his experience, highlighting the difficulty of reaching across a gulf separating each. "A Song" portrays an alienated singer who can find no comfort, no way out of pain.

In "The Lotus Flowers," a group of adolescent girls camping in the wilderness is connected like spokes in a wheel, each small self necessary to the bright whole as the lesser stars in the constellations they view overhead are essential to constellations and the stories told about them. In this poem, narrative delivers a clear vision that resolves on the timeless intensity that is lyric's signature.

TWO TREES

In *Two Trees*, Voigt arrives at her matured vision: The singer, who has emerged from grief, now reaches back to those still suffering. The poems move on classical and biblical myths of innocence and experience. The rhythms too are more classical, more certainly iambic, weaving in and out of pentameter. The rhythmic strategy holds tradition in its bosom as the men and women Voigt writes about hold the story of birth, life, death, and begetting in wisdom and sorrow. Lines move in and out of tradition, in desire of reaching "over the wall" of the line, as the "first man and woman" do in "Two Trees," desiring both Edenic trees—of knowledge and of life—that are "over the wall." The formal problem is recognized as one of balance between story and song, but it is song that the poet aligns with hope, with the human will to strive for the beauty and felt fulfillment of oneness and connection, the theme that marks this volume.

KYRIE

Kyrie threads a narrative line across fifty-eight sonnets, each a moment of lyric expression in the voice of one of several recurring character-speakers from a small New England town during the winter of 1917-1918, as World War I was concluding and a deadly influenza epidemic raged. By giving voice to individuals immersed in loss, fear, and grief, Voigt reaches into the heart of lyric's capacity to express common bonds in the depths of shared feeling. The rhythmic strategy of moving from the sonnet's conventional iambic pentameter base reaffirms lyric's tradition of reaffirming social contact. The volume recalls Edgar Lee Masters's *Spoon River Anthology* (1915), but instead of speaking honestly finally only from death as his characters do, Voigt's speak from life, drawing forth emotional energies to cope with the threat of death surrounding them on two fronts. The power of the combined voices singing rises over and against epidemic and war, "The sun still up everywhere in the kingdom." Unlike the constricted, mostly failed lives of Masters's characters, Voigt's continue to look forward with hope. Singing celebrates life, exceeds the time of destruction and its effects.

SHADOW OF HEAVEN

Voigt's sixth book, *Shadow of Heaven*, presents a sustained vision of nature's double largess, providential and violent. From the opening section ("The Winter Field"), the sounds of the outdoors clatter and bang, the dead will not "shut up," but the poet recognizes that whole life is made from the "one stubborn root," which gives rise to "this one life." In a sequence of fifteen twelve-line lyrics, moments of attention bring things into being: a flower, a construction machine, a squirrel, a hawk, emerge in a "swivel" of the head. They transform: A hawk becomes the poet's daughter, who has flown and "salted" the mother's garden; grief revolves with plenty, but humans are exiles who do best "to keep a little distance from what we are."

MESSENGER

Messenger, a selection of poems from Voigt's previous six books plus ten new poems, condenses the power of her craft and vision. The new poems drive home color and sound, wildly reverberating nature's largesse in the figures of trees, small birds, a thistle, and a chunk of fat laid out to lure beings into sight. The poet stands apart, still the exile, but now one who has returned "To do something with it: to make something of it" through language ("The Hive"). The messenger, unlike the angel of the Annunciation, does not bear comfort, but a sword announcing death. The poet who had started out in lyric as a way of stopping time writes here of the inability to stop time, counterweighted—eased—by the *in potentia* of artworks hidden from their birth in material wood, voice, and language.

OTHER MAJOR WORKS

NONFICTION: *The Flexible Lyric*, 1999; *The Art of Syntax: Rhythm of Thought, Rhythm of Song*, 2009.

EDITED TEXT: *Hammer and Blaze: A Gathering of Contemporary American Poets*, 2002 (with Heather McHugh).

BIBLIOGRAPHY

Birkerts, Sven. "From the Farm." Review of *Messenger*. *The New York Times Book Review*, February 25, 2007, p. 26. Birkerts notes how Voigt's poems look at the world from a rural perspective. He calls her a "seasoned poet in full confident stride."

Chappell, Fred. "Ellen Bryant Voigt and 'The Art of Distance.'" *Sewanee Review* 113, no. 3 (Summer, 2005): 422-441. Poet Chappell examines a seven-poet sequence called "The Art of Distance" in *Shadow of Heaven*. He finds her poetry "arresting" and "affecting."

Hacht, Anne Marie, and David Kelly, eds. *Poetry for Students*. Vol. 23. Detroit: Thomson/Gale, 2006. Contains an analysis of Voigt's poem "Practice."

Holden, Jonathan. "The Free Verse Line." In *The Line in Postmodern Poetry*, edited by Robert Joseph Frank and Henry M. Sayre. Urbana: University of Illinois Press, 1988. Holden uses Voigt's poetry to show how good free-verse poetry is made of rhythmic phrases that match the poet's attention.

Voigt, Ellen Bryant. "A Conversation with Ellen Bryant Voigt." Interview by Candice Baxter and Wendy Sumner Winter. *Missouri Review* 32, no. 1 (Spring, 2009): 70-83. Voigt talks about being a poet and her poetry.

_____. "Ellen Bryant Voight." Interview by Ernest Suarez. In *Southbound: Interviews with Southern Poets*, edited by Suarez, T. W. Stanford, and Amy Verner. Columbia: University of Missouri Press, 1999. Voigt talks about her poetry and life, including how she got started writing poetry.

Rosemary Winslow
Updated by Winslow

W

DAVID WAGONER

Born: Massillon, Ohio; June 5, 1926

PRINCIPAL POETRY

Dry Sun, Dry Wind, 1953
A Place to Stand, 1958
Poems, 1959
The Nesting Ground, 1963
Staying Alive, 1966
New and Selected Poems, 1969
Working Against Time, 1970
Riverbed, 1972
Sleeping in the Woods, 1974
A Guide to Dungeness Spit, 1975
Collected Poems, 1956-1976, 1976
Travelling Light, 1976
Who Shall Be the Sun?, 1978
In Broken Country, 1979
Landfall, 1981
First Light, 1983
Through the Forest: New and Selected Poems,
1977-1987, 1987
Walt Whitman Bathing, 1996
Traveling Light: Collected and New Poems, 1999
The House of Song, 2002
Good Morning and Good Night, 2005
A Map of the Night, 2008

OTHER LITERARY FORMS

Best known as a poet and novelist, David Wagoner (WAG-uh-nuhr) has also written plays—*An Eye for an Eye for an Eye* was produced in Seattle in 1973—as well as short fiction and essays. He edited and wrote the introduction to *Straw for the Fire: From the Notebooks of Theodore Roethke, 1943-1963* (1972).

ACHIEVEMENTS

It is possible that David Wagoner will be best remembered as one of the finest "nature" and "regional" poets of twentieth century America, and as one who has been instrumental in generating renewed interest in Native American lore. To categorize him so narrowly, however, does disservice to his versatility, and to the breadth of his talent and interests. Publishing steadily since the early 1950's, Wagoner has created a body of work that impresses not only for the number of volumes produced, but also for their quality. His novels have been praised for their energy and humor and in many cases for the immediacy of their Old West atmosphere. He received a Ford Fellowship for drama (1964), but it is as a poet that he has been most often honored: with a Guggenheim Fellowship (1956), a National Institute of Arts and Letters Grant (1967), and a National Endowment for the Arts Grant (1969). *Poetry* has awarded him its Morton Dauwen Zabel Prize (1967), its Oscar Blumenthal Prize (1974), its Eunice Tietjens Memorial Prize (1971), its Levinson Prize (1994), and its Union League Civic and Arts Poetry Prize (1997). *Sleeping in the Woods*, *Collected Poems, 1956-1976*, and *In Broken Country* were nominated for National Book Awards. He won Pushcart Prizes in 1979 and 1983. Wagoner served as a chancellor of the Academy of American Poets from 1978 to 1999, succeeding Robert Lowell. He received an Academy Award in literature (1987) from the American Academy of Arts and Letters. He was awarded the Ruth Lilly Poetry Prize (1991), the Ohioana Book Award (1997) for *Walt Whitman Bathing*, and two Washington State Book Awards in Poetry (2000, 2009).

BIOGRAPHY

David Russell Wagoner was born on June 5, 1926, in Massillon, Ohio, and was reared in Whiting, Indiana, the son of a steelworker. After receiving his B.A. degree from Pennsylvania State University in 1947 and his M.A. from Indiana University two years later, Wagoner began his teaching career at DePauw University, returning after a year to Pennsylvania State University. During this time, he was deeply influenced by Theodore Roethke, with whom he had studied as an undergraduate. In 1954, Roethke was instrumental in Wagoner's move to the University of Washington, where he taught until his retirement in 2002. X. J. Kennedy has speculated that perhaps "the most valuable service

David Wagoner (©Paul V. Thomas)

Roethke ever performed for Wagoner was to bring him to the Pacific Northwest and expose him to rain forests"—and to the culture of the Northwest Coast and Plateau Indians, one might add. Not only has Wagoner made use in his own poems of specific Native American myths and legends, but he has also absorbed the Indians' animistic spiritualism into his own philosophy. In the author's note to *Who Shall Be the Sun?*, he explains that Indians "did not place themselves above their organic and inorganic companions on earth but recognized with awe that they shared the planet as equals." Wagoner finds this equality "admirable and worthy of imitation," as much of his poetry indicates.

When not teaching, Wagoner has worked as a railroad section hand, a park police officer, and a short-order cook. He is a member of the Society of American Magicians. He served as editor of *Poetry Northwest* from 1966 until it ceased publication in 2002, and he has contributed poetry and commentary to a range of literary journals, including *Antioch Review*, *The Atlantic*, *Harvard Review*, *New England Review*, *Poetry*, and *Prairie Schooner*.

ANALYSIS

Despite David Wagoner's accomplishments and honors, and despite the fact that his poems appear regularly in mass-circulation magazines such as *The New Yorker* and *The Atlantic*, as well as the literary quarterlies, he is generally regarded as one of the most underappreciated of American poets. His works, with the exception of "Staying Alive," had not been included in major poetry anthologies until the early twenty-first century, when his poems began appearing in collections such as *The Best American Poetry* (2003, 2004, 2005, 2006). There are several possible explanations for this. First, he lives in Seattle and has chosen as his primary subject matter the land and people of the Pacific Northwest—thus giving rise to the dismissive "regional" label. It is also possible that some of his own best qualities may work against him. His subject matter is anything but trendy; the reader searches his poems in vain for the issues of the day. The only explicit social comment one is likely to find is contained in a half dozen or so poems addressing the Weyerhaeuser Company, a logging firm, and its practice of clear-cutting three-mile swaths of virgin forest.

Perhaps the major problem, as X. J. Kennedy suggests, is Wagoner's very "readability." Much of his poetry seems, at least on first encounter, curiously unpoetic, even prosy. His unpretentious language and casual, conversational tone frequently combine with his sense of humor to create a deceptively simple surface for his complex and serious ideas. This simplicity does make the work accessible; on the other hand, it may actually encourage the casual or first-time reader to dismiss Wagoner's work as lightweight.

Even in his most alienated and melancholy early poems, Wagoner's wit continually asserts itself. He is fond of puns, palindromes, and other forms of wordplay, and makes frequent use of colloquialisms, folk sayings, clichés, non sequiturs, and other lunacies of ordinary speech, often twisting words or phrases in such a way that they take on startling new meanings. Still, it is not as a semantic magician that Wagoner should be remembered; there are not a great many "quotable" lines—in the sense of the exquisite image of dazzling insight to be isolated for admiration out of context—in his work. Wagoner is at least as much philosopher as poet, and his poems, effective as they are when looked at individually, together take on cumulative power and meaning. Outwardly dissimilar poems are often interrelated below the surface to a marked degree. The result is a coherent, explicitly delineated philosophy, a "way" of life based on acceptance, self-reliance, and a profound reverence for the natural world.

Those who insist on calling Wagoner a regional or nature poet are certainly correct, to a point. From his earliest collection on, his work has amply indicated a sensitivity to the landscape around him. Later poems, in particular, have been praised for their descriptive qualities. The same can be said of many writers, but the use to which Wagoner has put his rain forests, mountains, rivers, and coastlines is uniquely his own. His wilderness, with its unsentimental, uncompromising beauty, serves on one level as a conventional metaphor: the landscape, physical and spiritual, through which one travels on one's life journey. Rather than seeing rocks, trees, and animals, however, as separate entities to be reacted to—climbed over, caught and eaten, run from—Wagoner views the natural world as the medium through which humans can best learn to know themselves. Put another way, if one can accept one's place as a part of the ongoing natural processes of life, death, decay, and rebirth, one begins to "see things whole." It is this sense of wholeness, this appreciation for the interrelatedness of all the "organic and inorganic companions on earth" to which Wagoner invites his reader, as if to a feast.

The way to this ideal state involves an apparent paradox: To find oneself, one must first lose oneself, shedding the subject/object, mind/body, spirit/intellect dualities typical of "rational" Western thought. In "Staying Alive," a traveler lost in the woods is faced not only with problems of physical survival but also with "the problem of recognition," by anyone or anything external that might be looking for him, as well as recognition of his own true nature. Unable to make contact with others, the traveler is advised that "You should have a mirror/ With a tiny hole in the back . . ." that will reflect the sun and flash messages, that will reflect one's familiar physical image and that, because of the aperture, will also allow one to see through one's phys-

ical self to the wholeness of the surrounding natural world.

It is clear that, in Wagoner's view, modern industrial society has created too many wastelands and polluted waterways, and more than enough fragmented citizens such as "The Man from the Top of the Mind," with "the light bulb screwed into his head,/ The vacuum tube of his sex, the electric eye." This gleaming creature of pure intellect can "Bump through our mazes like a genius rat" but is incapable of any human emotion except destructive rage. On every level, it would appear, one has become estranged—from oneself, from others and from one's environment.

HANDBOOK POEMS

In place of this fragmentation and alienation, Wagoner offers synthesis: the ability to see and experience things whole. In a remarkable series of poems, he not only extends the offer but also provides an explicit, step-by-step guide—a Scouts' handbook or survival manual for the reader to follow.

Although these handbook poems span several volumes (from *Staying Alive* through *In Broken Country*), they are best read as a single group. All are similar in language and tone; all address an unnamed "you," offering advice for coping with problems that might arise on a wilderness trip. Should one find oneself lost, one need only remember that "Staying alive . . . is a matter of calming down." Further poems instruct one on what to do when "Breaking Camp," or "Meeting a Bear" ("try your meekest behavior,/ . . . eyes downcast"), even after "Being Shot" ("if you haven't fallen involuntarily, you may/ Volunteer now . . ."). In each case, "you," the reader, are put in touch—in most cases both literally and figuratively—with something that has previously seemed foreign or outside the realm of ordinary human experience. In other words, lack of sensitivity to natural processes results in estrangement and isolation. By becoming more receptive, and perhaps less "top of the mind" rational, one allows for the possibility of "rescue" in the form of new understanding.

Frequently, since they typically involve a stripping away of the ego, these new insights prove to be humbling. Traveling "From Here to There," one can see the destination easily, while the distance deceives and one is confused by mirages: "Water put out like fire, . . . flying islands,/ The unbalancing act of mountains upside down." The problem of recognition resurfaces; nothing is what it seems. There is nothing to do but keep slogging: "One Damn Thing After Another," until finally, having "shrugged off most illusions" you "find yourself" in a place "where nothing is the matter/ . . . asking one more lesson." Still harder to accept are the lessons that teach acquiescence in mortality; lessons that teach that even a violent death is as much a part of the life process as birth. In "Being Shot," one finds oneself helpless on the forest floor, "study[ing]/ At first hand . . . the symptoms of shock." With Wagoner's open and accepting life view, death is as natural and therefore as necessary as birth, and "To burrow deep, for a deep winter," as "Staying Alive" advises, will result, come spring, in a renewal of some kind, if only because—should one not survive—one's decaying body will provide nutrients with which to feed other forms of life.

A series of poems in the final section of *In Broken Country* provide a guide to survival in the desert rather than the forest. Similar in tone and intent to the earlier handbook poems, these divert from "The Right Direction" past "The Point of No Return," where ". . . from here on/ It will take more courage to turn than to keep going." The process is what matters.

The "you" in these poems is never identified. There is a strong sense that the reader is being addressed directly, as if he or she has enrolled in an Outward Bound course and is receiving a curious mix of practical and cryptic last-minute advice before setting out on a solo adventure. There is also a sense of the poet talking to himself, working his own way both from the industrialized northern Indiana of his youth to the rain forests of Washington, and, in a parallel journey, from a sense of alienation to one of harmony.

DRY SUN, DRY WIND

In *Dry Sun, Dry Wind*, Wagoner's first collection, his affinity with nature is already apparent, but no real contact seems possible. The poet remains isolated, seeing about him images of destruction ("sun carries death to leaves"), decay, and uncertainty ("last year's gully is this year's hill"). Time flies; memory is unable to delay it. The natural environment, blighted though it is, is "Too much to breathe, think, see" ("Warning"). In the early poems, the relationship between humans and na-

ture—or humans and anything or anyone else—was generally one of conflict, an ongoing struggle for control resulting in disillusionment: a war, rather than a reconciliation, of opposites. "Progress" was often best achieved through violence to the land, and the stillness that in later works will open the way to enlightenment has precisely the opposite effect in early poems such as "Lull." Recognition, and, by extension, synthesis, are possible only when "the wind hums or wheels," creating movement, a kind of artificial life.

It is perhaps significant that none of the poems from this first volume has been included in any subsequent collection. The suggestion is that Wagoner quickly moved beyond these early efforts, struggling with his own problem of recognition as he searched for a true voice of his own. The major themes are there, often apparent only in their negative aspects, as, for example, the fragmentation and conflict that will yield in later poems to synthesis. In addition, there is at least one poem that deserves reading on its own merit.

"Sam the Aerialist" is "sick of walking." He wants to fly. Like the poet, like the trickster of Native American myth, like dreamers everywhere, he hungers for the impossible and yearns to exceed his natural bounds. In this, Sam is like most of the human race. His crime is not so much his desire to fly as it is his attitude, which is aggressive, self-serving, exploitative: Sam has a "lust for air" that is anything but properly reverent. The birds, therefore, instead of sharing their secrets with him, "have kept/ Far from his mind." "Birds are evil," Sam concludes,

> they fly
> Against the wind. How many have I pulled
> Apart . . .
> To learn the secret?

Sam learns by destroying. He lacks the empathy that could move him toward true understanding, and he remains isolated, cut off from his own nature as well as that around him.

Although he is never again referred to by name, there is a sense in which Sam the Aerialist's presence is felt throughout Wagoner's later poetry. He represents a kind of high-technology Everyman; his failings are the failings of society at large. He makes a stubborn but useful pupil. If such a one can absorb the early wisdom of "The Nesting Ground," that sometimes standing still will gain one more than flight; if he can follow where the handbook poems lead and lose himself in the discovery that there is a bottom as well as a top to his mind, then perhaps all is not lost. Certainly, there is an aspect of Sam in the "you" to whom the handbook poems speak.

"SEVEN SONGS FOR AN OLD VOICE"

Another step beyond specific survival lore in Wagoner's progress from alienation to harmony is represented by several groups of poems based on the mythology of the Northwest Coast and the Plateau Indians. Wagoner's interest in Native American culture is longstanding. "Talking to the Forest," included in *Staying Alive*, responds to a Skagit tribesman's statement: "When we can understand animals, we will know the change is halfway. When we can talk to the forest, we will know the change has come." In *Riverbed*, "Old Man, Old Man" teaches that "Every secret is as near as your fingers."

It was in the 1974 collection *Sleeping in the Woods*, however, that the pivotal group, "Seven Songs for an Old Voice," first appeared. This Voice, still singing the ancient animistic wisdom as reverently as it did in the days before the Iron People (whites) arrived, offers hymns equally to Fire, which keeps enemies away, and to the Maker of Nightmares, who "eat[s] my sleep for . . . food." Other songs address death, the soul leaving the body and returning to it, and the First People, nonhumans who became rocks, animals, plants, and water when they learned of the coming of humankind. No matter what the subject, the tone is one of acceptance and awe. Death is part of life. Terrifying as they are, nightmares are not to be denied. The Voice promises to "drink what you bring me in my broken skull,/ The bitter water which once was sweet as morning."

WHO SHALL BE THE SUN?

These "Seven Songs for an Old Voice" are included in *Who Shall Be the Sun?* along with other previously collected poems, new groups of "Songs for the Dream-Catchers," "Songs of Only-One," "Songs of He-Catches-Nothing," and two groups of myths and legends—one each from the Plateau and Northwest Coast

Indian tribes. Wagoner explains in his author's note that the myths and legends are retellings of existing stories. The songs are original works, but Wagoner stresses his debt to the Indians' spirit if not their words.

As Robert K. Cording points out, these Indian-lore poems allow Wagoner to blend several hitherto separate themes. For the Native American, the interrelationship of humans and nature has traditionally been a given, as has a belief in the power of various religious and quasi-religious rituals and practices that non-Indians might call magic. Magic, as a motif, appears fairly frequently in Wagoner's earlier work; in this collection, human beings "magically" converse with the spirits of the First People in the trees above them and the dust beneath their feet. It is not only the First People who are capable of such transformations. Animals also can take on human shapes; humans can put on different skins. In certain situations, the dead can return to earth and the living can cross in safety to the land of the dead. Magic here is more than sleight-of-hand and an Indian's dreams are tools more powerful than the technology of Sam the Aerialist, as the title poem shows. "Who Shall Be the Sun?" the People ask, and despite his apparent lack of suitability for the job, Snake's ability to dream, coupled with his seemly modesty, allows him to succeed where the assertive, egocentric Raven, Hawk, and Coyote (who can merely think) have failed.

"Who Shall Be the Sun?" and other poems in the myth and legend sections are written in a language that closely echoes the cadences of English prose translations of Indian legends with which the reader may be familiar. The song groups are distinct from one another, the tone and rhythm consistent with each singer's personality and the subject addressed. It should be noted that although the pervading attitude is one of reverence and peace, not all of these poems present such a harmonious picture. Coyote and Raven, classic tricksters, are as likely to cause harm with their pranks as they are to improve the lot of those they purport to help, as the Indian culture, like any other, has always had its share of misfits, liars, and thieves. There is disease, madness, and death, of course, as well as someone called Only-One, who, half-blinded by the beak of an injured heron he had attempted to heal, sees only halves of things. Scarred by smallpox, neither truly dead nor truly alive, Only-One is an isolated soul. He dances with Dead Man, and the half-girl he takes for his bride turns out to be the bird that blinded him.

IN BROKEN COUNTRY AND LANDFALL

Following *Who Shall Be the Sun?*, Wagoner returned to a more characteristic range of subjects. *In Broken Country* mixes poems about love, childhood memories, parents, poets (including a lovely elegy to Roethke), bums, and prisoners (Wagoner himself included). A dozen desert handbook poems are preceded by a series of self-parodying mock-handbook entries.

Landfall also covers a broad range, although a particularly strong unifying cord runs throughout. A number of the most moving poems are about making contact with one's past, not merely in the sense of looking back and remembering, but in trying for reconciliation with aspects of one's life that may have caused one pain. Over the years, Wagoner has written poems about his father—puttering around the house, building a wall—a pleasant-seeming man, drained by his job in the steel mill. A certain edgy ambivalence of tone in these poems has kept the elder Wagoner an insubstantial figure. "My Father's Garden" changes this, introducing the reader to a man who picked "flowers" for his family: "small gears and cogwheels/ With teeth like petals," found in the scrapheap he passed on his way to work, work which "melted" his mind to the point that all he retained of an education in the classics was enough Latin and Greek for crossword puzzles. Paired with this is "My Father's Ghost," an extraordinary piece based on a Midwestern folk saying and reminiscent in tone of the Indian songs. Having performed the proper rituals, the poet should be able to see his father's spirit; but the charms do not work. The room stays empty. It is necessary to "imagine him," then; "and dream him/ Returning unarmed, unharmed. Words, words. I hold/ My father's ghost in my arms in his dark doorway."

The final section, "A Sea Change," describes a journey with no destination, in which the poet and his wife leave forest, desert, and marsh behind and head out to sea. This sea voyage is more explicitly psychological than the handbook poems, but here, too, reconciliations

take place. The travelers must come to terms with the unfamiliar element to which they have entrusted their lives; in doing so, they will discover that it is not so foreign as they thought. They must overcome their dread of the dimly seen monsters coiling in the depths. In doing so, they discover that the monsters never break through the "mirror" of the water's surface—suggesting, perhaps, that to accept one's demons as the Old Voice singer accepted nightmares and death is to rob them of much of their power. In contrast to Wagoner's explicitly instructive poems, the Sea Change group does not explain precisely by what means these primal fears are to be overcome or how other changes are to be brought about. At journey's end, "Landfall," the two travelers simply come "wallowing" ashore like their "hesitant helpless curious ancestors," having somehow been in touch with a past too dim for memory or rational understanding. On feet that "keep believing/ In the sea," they regain firm ground, asking, "Have we come home? Is this where we were born? . . . this place/ Where, again, we must learn to walk?"

Wagoner's own answer to this would be yes, over and over again, on all ground and in all weather, backward, on our hands, on water, and on air. Getting there means starting over; starting over means rebirth, renewal, a second chance to see things whole. In many ways, this is just what Wagoner has been doing throughout his career.

WALT WHITMAN BATHING

In *Walt Whitman Bathing*, Wagoner finds inspiration in American experience and landscape, translating it into stacked, searching clauses: "Above the river, over the broad hillside/ and down the slope in clusters and strewn throngs,/ cross-tangled and intermingled,/ wildflowers are blooming, seemingly all at once." Story and lyric take alternating turns at center stage, and his lines consistently find their breath—long and short, substantial and supple—as in "Mapmaking," from the compelling sequence on landscapes: "You fix your eyes on [landmarks], one at a time,/ And learn the hard way/ How hard it is to fabricate broken country."

The first half of the book consists of poems of nostalgic, personal reminiscence and public eulogies. He advises, in "In the Woods," that as "you" find "yourself" contemplating the trees,

Now you may make yourself at home by doing without
The pointless heroics of moving, by remaining
Quiet, by holding still
To take your place as they have taken theirs: by right
Of discovery in this immanent domain,
Simply by growing
Accustomed to being here instead of nowhere.

The book's second half revisits many of Wagoner's familiar settings, themes, and stylistics: there is nature without trivial transcendence, flora and fauna, and verses heavy with pronouns, addressed to his ever-present and insistent "you." His insights run deep and are expressed with a soft-spoken directness intimately linked to his skepticism about humankind's role in the cosmos. Wagoner talks quietly with the reader—when not penned in the second-person singular, his poetry beckons the reader near—about the relativity of the self and about "Searching for more than you at the end of you."

Wagoner also presents moving poems about human affection, often set during his midwestern boyhood. "My Father Laughing in the Chicago Theater" memorably portrays "Two hundred and twenty horizontal pounds/ Of defensive lineman, of open-hearth melter" doubling over at the quips of vaudeville comics. Several poems also center on American Gothic-era memories (red-nosed cops, trained bears, boys who wear "nightgowns"), images kept from cliché by Wagoner's sure touch. Never folksy, the poems are plainspoken and display a formal virtuosity that allows Wagoner to penetrate beneath the surface, as when sketching his parents in three-stress lines: "They stand by the empty car,/ By the open driver's door,/ Waiting. The evening sun/ is glowing like pig-iron." The sum effect of the book is authoritative but detached, descriptive yet minimalistic.

TRAVELING LIGHT

Culling poems from forty-five years of published work, *Traveling Light*, a generous retrospective, calls on Wagoner's experiences of hiking and camping in mountain wilderness, comments on angst and paranoia based on his everyday urban existence, and provides a glimpse into his personal experience with literature, love, and death. His plain midwestern diction and even tone prevent him from moving into portentousness à la

Carl Sandburg, whom he meets and raises stakes on in such poems as "A Day in the City" and "The Apotheosis of the Garbageman." With a nod to Robert Penn Warren, he masters the poetic sequence ("Landscapes" or "Traveling Light"), and in a series on his late father, a steel-mill worker, he colloquially recalls his own sympathetic gestures:

I shook the dying and dead
Ashes down through the grate
And, with firetongs, hauled out clinkers
Like the vertebrae of monsters.

THE HOUSE OF SONG

Poems in *The House of Song*, *Good Morning and Good Night*, and *A Map of the Night* carry forward Wagoner's extraordinary variety of poetic voices; his eye for significant concrete details; his ear for easy rhythms, deceptively prose-like but subtle in their placement of pauses and emphasis; his wit, manifested in puns, irony, and metaphor; and his themes of the integration of the self with nature, family, tradition, and the world.

In the title poem of *The House of Song*, a Gilbert Islander made a song out of his environment each year, taught his song to his community, and then sat silent "As the people became that song,/ As the whole village around him and around them/ Became the house of that song." Wagoner, like the Gilbert Island singer makes the world around him—around the reader—into poetry.

In "Arranging a Book of Poems" (from *Good Morning and Good Night*), Wagoner describes his care in ordering his poems, and in the first section of *The House of Song*, he moves from the house of song to the greater, mysterious, but enlightening world beyond song. "The Book of Moonlight" begins with a quotation from Wallace Stevens: "The Book of Moonlight is not written yet." Wagoner asks, "Why should we ever write it?" Our "illiterate fingers" cannot make sense of the mystery of its overflowing brightness.

"Elegy on the First Day of Spring" describes the flowers' struggle against the poor soil and the hard climate of Wagoner's mother's garden, paralleling her own later struggles with dementia, which erased even her recognition of her family, but let her still play and sing songs about flowers. Wagoner himself moved on to a place where flowers grow abundantly, where "The earth wants to make music," and where the sun can be ". . . as astonished as we are/ At everything we can still remember."

The last words of the last poem of *The House of Song*, written from a Native American point of view, bring the reader full circle from the collection's title poem: "We must become more than what is left of our bodies/ And will see and become what is always/ Rushing toward us and around us."

GOOD MORNING AND GOOD NIGHT

Good Morning and Good Night begins with Federico García Lorca dreaming a beautiful poem and awakening to hear it actually sung—as he discovers—by an illiterate street sweeper. Possessing the gift of literacy, García Lorca returns to his bed "To lie there stark awake as sleeplessly/ As a poet who'd been told he was immortal." The collection ends with a series of poems on the night and the morning, some of them ironic. The final poem, "At the Foot of the Mountain," set in the early morning, seems to have nothing to do with the night—actual or metaphoric—until the unexpected last word: at the end of the poem "you"—one of Wagoner's common subjects, here a reluctant climber—finally join other climbers in "their uninterrupted *chanting*" [emphasis added]. Perhaps, then, this too is not only a good morning but a good night poem and the climb a metaphor for mortality, seen as challenge, duty, and ritual.

This collection also contains several handbook poems, a set of which are military instructions, and a section of poems about poetry. In "Trying to Make Music," the poet confronts not only unsympathetic listeners but also his own self-doubts. In "Poetry in Motion," he questions whether poetry can ". . . move itself and more/ Than itself and not be here, flat on the page." In "A Date with the Muse," the poet finds the muse repeatedly unresponsive to his offers. However, in the metaphorical "On Being Asked to Discuss Poetic Theory," the poet describes finding snow falling in the mountains and following the snowmelt as it courses down to the ocean. Even if the white tops of the mountains disappear behind clouds, he knows that snow is falling again. Clouded in mystery, the sources of the poet's inspiration do not fail.

A MAP OF THE NIGHT

Many of the poems in *A Map of the Night* are companion pieces to poems previously published. For instance, "My Father's Dance" is a counterpart to "Elegy to the First Day of Spring" in *The House of Song*, "Thoreau and the Mud Turtle" and "Thoreau and the Quagmire" add to the set of Thoreau poems also in *The House of Song*, and several military "Handbook" poems extend those in *Good Morning and Good Night*.

Wagoner's wit is displayed in several poems: In "Trying to Write a Poem While the Couple in the Apartment Overhead Make Love," the rhythms of Wagoner's poem neatly match the rhythms of the subject. In "Attention" (a military "Handbook" poem), the typography of the short two-stress lines makes the poem stand at attention on the page. Wagoner's focus on decorum in this, as in all of his "Handbook" poems, tends to put readers in their places. In "On First Looking Through the Wrong End of the Telescope," a series of puns puts all humankind in its place.

This collection also includes "On a Glass of Ale Under a Reading Lamp," in which small flies, like the drinker, risk ". . . a desire/ . . . to drink without drowning// to touch the good bitterness/ again, not knowing why." Another memorable poem is "On an Island," the protagonist of which, once again "you," is on a beach, with the sea on one side and a "dense interior" on the other. Here "you" must ". . . reconsider the unromantic agony/ of change without progress . . . ," finding ". . . yourself/ beginning where you were and seeing/ what you tried your best to remember/ or dismiss and forget."

Wagoner's poetry is readily accessible, not overly formal, expressive, even emphatic, sometimes witty, sometimes metaphorical, and solidly based in concrete images. Wagoner continues to advance his worldview of humankind in harmony with the familial, social, and, above all, natural orders.

OTHER MAJOR WORKS

LONG FICTION: *The Man in the Middle*, 1954, 1955; *Money, Money, Money*, 1955; *Rock*, 1958; *The Escape Artist*, 1965; *Baby, Come On Inside*, 1968; *Where Is My Wandering Boy Tonight?*, 1970; *The Road to Many a Wonder*, 1974; *Tracker*, 1975; *Whole Hog*, 1976; *The Hanging Garden*, 1980.

PLAY: *An Eye for an Eye for an Eye*, pr. 1973.

EDITED TEXTS: *Straw for the Fire: From the Notebooks of Theodore Roethke, 1943-1963*, 1972; *The Best American Poetry 2009*, 2009 (with David Lehman).

BIBLIOGRAPHY

Boyers, Robert. "The Poetry of David Wagoner." Review of *Staying Alive. Kenyon Review* 32 (Spring, 1970): 176-181. An appreciative review noting that *Staying Alive* marks a turning point in Wagoner's development. Boyers states that from this point forward, Wagoner could claim to be a major figure in contemporary American poetry.

Durczak, Joanna. "David Wagoner: Instructor Against Instructors." *Treading Softly, Speaking Low: Contemporary American Poetry in the Didactic Mode.* Lublin, Poland: Wydawnictwo Uniwersytetu, 1994. Uniquely useful as an extended analysis of Wagoner's "Handbook" poems.

Lieberman, Laurence. "David Wagoner: The Cold Speech of the Earth." In *Unassigned Frequencies: American Poetry in Review, 1964-1977*. Urbana: University of Illinois Press, 1977. Looks at how this poet maps out a topography through his choice of words and images. Compares the later poems with the earlier ones and cites the same imagination but with greater depth of vision. Offers strong, in-depth criticism of *Collected Poems, 1956-1976* and places Wagoner in the company of Walt Whitman, Robert Frost, Edgar Lee Masters, and William Stafford.

McFarland, Ronald E. *The World of David Wagoner.* Moscow: University of Idaho Press, 1997. Presents literary criticism and interpretation of Wagoner's writings and looks at the role of the American Midwest and Northwest in literature.

Peters, Robert. "Thirteen Ways of Looking at David Wagoner's New Poems." Review of *Landfall. Western Humanities Review* 35, no. 3 (Autumn, 1981): 267-272. A provocative review, unusual among commentaries on Wagoner's poetry in its stress on what Peters takes to be Wagoner's lack of imagination and risk-taking.

Waggoner, Hyatt H. *American Visionary Poetry.* Baton Rouge: Louisiana State University Press, 1982. Chapter 7, "Traveling Light," explores Wagoner's identity as a visionary poet through his nature poems. Examines Wagoner's portrayal of the wilderness and how he guards himself in his poems. A sympathetic critique that praises Wagoner's volume *The Nesting Ground*.

Wagoner, David. "David Wagoner." Interview by Nicholas O'Connell. In *At the Field's End: Interviews with Twenty Pacific Northwest Writers*, edited by O'Connell. Seattle: Madrona, 1987. The interviewer explores with Wagoner the subjects of his poems and how he has re-created the Northwest landscape on paper. Examines the structure and sense of rhythm in his poems. Of particular note is a discussion of *Who Shall Be the Sun?*, a collection of poems that Wagoner read aloud to the Blackfeet tribe and for which he received much praise.

_____. "David Wagoner." Interview by Sanford Pinsker. In *Three Pacific Northwest Poets: William Stafford, Richard Hugo, and David Wagoner.* Boston: Twayne, 1987. A useful and insightful introduction to Wagoner's poems, analyzing his choice of themes and techniques. Contains critical commentary on all of his major poems. Notes that among Wagoner's strengths is his "sense of the dramatic."

_____. "David Wagoner—Slightly Different Ways of Thinking: An Interview." Interview by Kate Gray. In *Page to Page: Retrospectives of Writers from the "Seattle Review,"* edited by Colleen J. McElroy. Seattle: University of Washington Press, 2006. An account of a wide-ranging interview, accompanied by photographs, a bibliography, and three poems by Wagoner.

Sara McAulay; Sarah Hilbert
Updated by David W. Cole

DIANE WAKOSKI

Born: Whittier, California; August 3, 1937

PRINCIPAL POETRY

Coins and Coffins, 1962
Discrepancies and Apparitions, 1966
The George Washington Poems, 1967
Inside the Blood Factory, 1968
The Moon Has a Complicated Geography,
  1969
The Magellanic Clouds, 1970
The Motorcycle Betrayal Poems, 1971
Smudging, 1972
Dancing on the Grave of a Son of a Bitch, 1973
Looking for the King of Spain, 1974
Virtuoso Literature for Two and Four Hands,
  1975
Waiting for the King of Spain, 1976
The Man Who Shook Hands, 1978
Cap of Darkness, 1980
The Magician's Feastletters, 1982
The Collected Greed, Parts 1-13, 1984 (part 1 pb.
  in 1968)
The Rings of Saturn, 1986
Emerald Ice: Selected Poems, 1962-1987,
  1988
Medea the Sorceress, 1991
Jason the Sailor, 1993
The Emerald City of Las Vegas, 1995
Argonaut Rose, 1998
*The Butcher's Apron: New and Selected Poems,
  Including "Greed: Part 14,"* 2000

OTHER LITERARY FORMS

Diane Wakoski (wah-KAH-skee) wrote three critical essays that were published by Black Sparrow Press: *Form Is an Extension of Content* (1972), *Creating a Personal Mythology* (1975), and *Variations on a Theme* (1976). These essays, with other essays that had originally appeared in *American Poetry Review*, where she was a regular columnist between 1972 and 1974, and in her books of poetry, were reprinted in *Toward a New Poetry* (1980).

ACHIEVEMENTS

More popular with poetry readers than with poetry critics, Diane Wakoski has nevertheless carved a niche for herself in American poetry. A prolific writer (she has published some fifty books of poetry) and indefatigable reader of her own poetry, she has gained a following of readers who appreciate her intensely personal subject matter, her personal mythology, her structural use of digression and repetition, and her long narrative forms. Throughout her work, the subject is herself, and the themes of loss, betrayal, and identity recur as she probes her relationships with others, most often father figures and lovers. Though her poems are read sympathetically by feminists, she is herself not political and rejects the notion that she can be identified with a particular ideology or school of poetry. Her work has brought her several awards, among them the Bread Loaf Robert Frost Fellowship and the Cassandra Foundation Award, as well as grants from such sources as the Guggenheim Foundation and the National Endowment for the Arts. *Emerald Ice* won the Poetry Society of America's William Carlos Williams Award in 1989.

Her work, sometimes criticized for its perceived self-pity, actually uses loss or betrayal as the impetus for the speaker to work through different self-images and gender reversals to celebrate—usually with a trace of ironic self-awareness—beauty or the self and, in effect, to solve the problem posed at the beginning of the poem.

BIOGRAPHY

Diane Wakoski was born in Whittier, California, in 1937 to parents who shaped not only her life but also her poetry. Shortly after her birth, her father, John Joseph Wakoski, reenlisted in the U.S. Navy and made it his career. Her contact with the "Prince Charming" figure, as she describes him in an autobiographical account, was infrequent and unfulfilling, leaving her with a sense of loss she later explored in her poetry. Her relations with her mother were equally unsatisfying and stressful; by the time she left high school, Wakoski says, she found her mother, whom her father had divorced, a "burden." Speaking of her childhood, Wakoski claims that she was born into a "world of silence," that she was "surrounded by silent people." She was poor, emotionally isolated (she also had few friends), and—from her own point of view—physically unattractive. These factors surely relate to the fixation with male figures and subsequent betrayal in her poems and explain, to some extent, the compulsive need to analyze, to dissect, and to communicate at length in a prolific body of work.

The only positive reinforcement she received in high school was from sympathetic teachers who encouraged the development of her academic talents. She also discovered that she enjoyed performing for an audience. (This "exhibitionistic" tendency, as she has described it, is reflected in her poetry readings, which are very much "performances.") After graduation from high school, she passed up a scholarship to the University of California, Berkeley, and attended Fullerton Junior College because she expected her high school sweetheart to enroll there as well. When he attended a different college and responded dutifully, not supportively, to the news of her pregnancy, she experienced a "betrayal," rejected his marriage proposal, and subsequently gave up her baby for adoption.

In the fall of 1956, after attending a poetry class at Whittier College, she enrolled at Berkeley, where she began writing poetry in earnest, publishing some of it in *Occident*, the campus literary magazine. Wakoski believes that her career was launched when her student poetry reading at the San Francisco Poetry Center resulted in another reading there, this time as a "real" poet. Before she left Berkeley, she was pregnant again, this time by a fellow artist-musician with whom she later moved to New York; since marriage did not seem appropriate and both were career-minded, she again gave up her baby for adoption.

In New York, Wakoski continued to write poetry and give poetry readings, while she became acquainted with several established writers, one of whom, LeRoi Jones (later Amiri Baraka), published some of her poems in *Four Young Lady Poets* in 1962. *Coins and Coffins*, her first book of poems, was also published in 1962, but it was not until 1966, with the publication of *Discrepancies and Apparitions* by a major publishing house, Doubleday, that she became an established poet. In rapid succession, she published two of her most important books, *The George Washington Poems* and *In-*

side the Blood Factory, as well as the first four parts of *Greed*. During the late 1960's, she also experienced a failed first marriage and a few failed romantic relationships, one of which produced the raw material for *The Motorcycle Betrayal Poems*, her most publicized collection of verse.

The 1970's were a productive decade for Wakoski, who published regularly, maintained an almost frenetic pace with poetry readings, and gained at the University of Virginia the first of many academic posts as writer-in-residence. She also began a long-standing association with Black Sparrow Press, which has published many of her books. Of particular interest in this decade is the appearance of two collections of poetry concerning yet another mythological figure, the King of Spain. During this period, she turned her attention to criticism, writing a regular column for *American Poetry Review* and publishing a collection of her criticism in *Toward a New Poetry*.

Wakoski's personal life continued to provide content for her verse: Her second marriage ended in divorce in 1975. The following year, she began teaching

Diane Wakoski (©Thomas Victor)

at Michigan State University, where she would remain. In 1977, she renewed her friendship with poet Robert Turney and was married to him in 1982. The 1980's also saw the completion of *Greed*, which she had begun in 1968, and other books of poetry, though her productivity decreased. Other significant publications included *The Rings of Saturn* and *Medea the Sorceress*, two volumes that rework old themes and myths but also extend Wakoski's "universe," which is at once personal and all-inclusive. *Medea the Sorceress* became the first of four books that make up her series *The Archaeology of Movies and Books*, her major endeavor of the 1990's.

ANALYSIS

Since Diane Wakoski believes that "the poems in her published books give all the important information about her life," her life and her art are inextricably related. She states that the poem "must organically come out of the writer's life," that "all poems are letters," so personal in fact that she has been considered, though she rejects the term, a confessional poet. While most readers have been taught to distinguish between the author and the "speaker" of the poem, Wakoski is, and is not, author and speaker. She refers to real people and to real events in her life in detail that some critics find too personal as she works through a problem: "A poem is a way of solving a problem." For Wakoski, writing a poem is almost therapeutic; it is talking the problem out, not to a counselor or even to the reader, but to herself. She has said, "The purpose of the poem is to complete an act that can't be completed in real life"—a statement that does suggest that there are both reality and the poem, which is then the "completed" dream. As a pragmatist, she has learned to live with these two worlds.

Wakoski believes that once a poet has something to say, he or she finds the appropriate form in which to express this content. In her case, the narrative, rather than the lyric, mode is appropriate; free verse, digression, repetition, and oral music are other aspects of that form. She carves out a territory narrowly confined to self and then uses the universe (the moon, the rings of Saturn, Magellanic clouds), history (George Washington, the King of Spain), personal experience (the motorcycle betrayal poems), and literary feuds to create, in the manner of William Butler Yeats, her personal mythology. The mythology is, in turn, used to develop her themes: loss and acceptance, ugliness and beauty, loss of identity and the development of self. Her themes are dualistic and, significantly, susceptible to the resolution she achieves in the poem. For her, poetry is healing, not fragmenting.

COINS AND COFFINS

Coins and Coffins, Wakoski's first book of poetry, is dedicated to La Monte Young, the father of her second child and another in a series of lost loves. In this volume, she introduces the image of the lost lover, thereby creating her own personal mythology. "Justice Is Reason Enough" is a poem indebted to Yeats: "the great form and its beating wings" suggests "Leda and the Swan." The "form" in this poem, however, is that of her apocryphal twin brother, David, with whom she commits incest. She mourns her brother, "dead by his own hand," because of the justice that "balances the beauty in the world." Since beauty is mentioned in the last line of the poem, the final mood is one of acceptance and affirmation.

DISCREPANCIES AND APPARITIONS

The missing lover is also the central figure of *Discrepancies and Apparitions*, which contains "Follow That Stagecoach," a poem that Wakoski regards as one of her best and most representative. Though the setting is ostensibly the West, with the archetypal sheriff and Dry Gulch Hollow, the hollow quickly becomes a river; the speaker, a swimmer in a black rubber skin-diving suit; and the tough Western sheriff, a gay authority figure. The opening lines of the poem, "The sense of disguise is a/ rattlesnake," suggest the poses and masks, even the genders, she and the lover-sheriff put on and discard as he fails her: "oh yes you are putting on your skin-diving suit very fast running to the/ ocean and slipping away from this girl who carries a loaded gun." The roles are reversed as she assigns herself the potency he lacks: His gun "wanders into/ hand," while her phallic gun is constantly with her. The poem ends with characteristic confidence: "So I'll write you a love poem if I want to. I'm a Westerner and/ not afraid/ of my shadow." The cliché cleverly alludes to the "shadow" as the alter ego, her second, masculine self; the lover, it is implied, rejects his own wholeness.

THE GEORGE WASHINGTON POEMS

In *The George Washington Poems*, dedicated to her father and her husband, Wakoski continues to debunk the American hero, this time taking on "the father of my country" (a title that is given to one of the poems), the patriarchal political and militaristic establishment. In the twenty-three poems in the volume, "George Washington" appears in his historical roles as surveyor, tree chopper, general politician, and slave owner; however, he also anachronistically appears as the speaker's confidant, absentee father, and (sometimes absentee) lover. When the first poem, "George Washington and the Loss of His Teeth," begins with the image of "George's" (Wakoski refers irreverently to "George" throughout the poems) false teeth, Wakoski wittily and facetiously undercuts the historical image of male leadership in the United States.

In "The Father of My Country," Wakoski demonstrates both the extraordinary versatility of the "George Washington" figure and the way repetition, music, and digression provide structure. The first verse-paragraph develops the idea that "all fathers in Western civilization must have/ a military origin," that all authority figures have been the "general at one time or other," and concludes with Washington, "the rough military man," winning the hearts of his country. Often equating militancy and fatherhood and suggesting that it is the military that elicits American admiration, the speaker abruptly begins a digression about her father; yet the lengthy digression actually develops the father motif of the first verse-paragraph and examines the influence he has had on her life. Although his is a name she does not cherish because he early abandoned her, he has provided her with "military,/ militant" origins, made her a "maverick," and caused her failed relationships. Having thought her father handsome and having wondered why he left her, she is left with the idea of a Prince Charming at once desirable and unattainable. When she speaks of "Father who makes me know all men will leave me/ if I love them," she implies that all her relationships are fated reenactments of childhood love betrayed.

At the end of the poem she declares that "George" has become her "father,/ in his 20th. century naval uniform" and concludes with a chant, with repetitions and parallels, that expresses both her happiness and her uncertainty: "And I say the name to chant it. To sing it. To lace it around/ me like weaving cloth. Like a happy child on that shining afternoon/ in the palmtree sunset her mother's trunk yielding treasures,/ I cry and/ cry,/ Father,/ Father,/ Father,/ have you really come home?"

INSIDE THE BLOOD FACTORY

Inside the Blood Factory, Wakoski's next major poetic work, also concerns George Washington and her absentee father, but in this volume, her range of subject matter is much wider. There is Ludwig van Beethoven, who appears in later poems; a sequence concerning the Tarot deck; a man in a silver Ferrari; and images of Egypt—but pervading all is the sense of loss. In this volume, the focus, as the title implies, is on physiological responses as these are expressed in visceral imagery. The speaker wants to think with the body, to accept and work with the dualities she finds in life and within herself.

Inside the Blood Factory also introduces another of Wakoski's recurring images, the moon, developed more extensively later in *The Moon Has a Complicated Geography* and *The Magellanic Clouds*. For Wakoski, the moon is the stereotypical image of the unfaithful woman, but it is also concrete woman breast-feeding her children, bathing, communicating with lovers, and menstruating. Wakoski insists on the physicality of the moon-woman who is related to the sun-lover, but who is also fiercely independent. She loves her lover but wants to be alone, desires intimacy ("wants to be in your wrist, a pulse") but does not want to be "in your house," a possession. (Possession becomes the focus for the ongoing thirteen parts of *Greed*.) When the question of infidelity arises, the speaker is more concerned with being faithful to herself than to her lover(s). In this poem ("3 of Swords—for dark men under the white moon" in the Tarot sequence) the moon-woman can be both submissive and independent, while the sun-lover both gives her love and indulges in his militaristic-phallic "sword play."

As is often the case in Wakoski's poetry, an image appears in one volume and then is developed in later volumes. Isis, a central figure in *The Magellanic Clouds*, is introduced in "The Ice Eagle" of *Inside the Blood Factory*. The Egyptian goddess-creator, who is simultaneously mother and virgin, appears as the symbolic object of male fear: "the veiled woman, Isis mother, whom they fear to be greater than all else." Men prefer the surface, whether it be a woman's body or the eagle ice sculpture that melts in the punch bowl at a cocktail party; men fear what lies beneath the surface—the woman, the anima—in their nature.

THE MAGELLANIC CLOUDS

The Magellanic Clouds looks back at earlier volumes in its reworking of George Washington and the moon figures, but it also looks ahead to the motorcycle betrayal figure and the King of Spain. Of Wakoski's many volumes of poetry, *The Magellanic Clouds* is perhaps the most violent as the speaker plumbs the depth of her pain. Nowhere is the imaging more violent than in the "Poems from the Impossible," a series of prose poems that contain references to gouged-out eyes, bleeding hands, and cut lips.

Isis, the Queen of the Night speaker, figures prominently in *The Magellanic Clouds*. In "Reaching Out with the Hands of the Sun," the speaker first describes the creative power of the masculine sun, cataloging a cornucopia of sweetmeats that ironically create "fat thighs" and a "puffy face" in a woman. The catalog then switches to the speaker's physical liabilities, ones that render her unbeautiful and unloved; with the "mask of a falcon," she has roamed the earth and observed the universal effect that beauty has on men. At the end of the poem, the speaker reaches out to touch the "men/ with fire/ direct from the solar disk," but they betray their gifts by "brooding" and rejecting the hands proffered them.

In "The Queen of Night Walks Her Thin Dog," the speaker uses poetry, the "singing" that recurs in Whitmanesque lines, to penetrate the various veils that would separate her from "houses," perhaps bodies, in the night. The poem itself may be the key in the locked door that is either an entrance or an exit—at the end of the poem, "Entrance./ Exit./ The lips" suggests a sexual and poetic act. In the third poem, "The Prince of Darkness Passing Through This House," the speaker refers to the "Queen of Night's running barking dog" and to "this house," but the Prince of Darkness and the Queen of Night are merged like elemental fire and water. Like a Metaphysical poet, Wakoski suggests that the universe can be coalesced into their bodies ("our earlobes and eyelids") as they hold "live coals/ of commitment,/ of purpose,/ of love." This positive image, however, is undercut by the final image, "the power of fish/ living in strange waters," which implies that such a union may be possible only in a different world.

The last poem in the volume, "A Poem for My Thirty-second Birthday," provides a capsule summary of the speaker's images, themes, and relationships. In the course of the poem, she associates a mechanic with a Doberman that bites, and then she becomes, in her anger, the Doberman as she seeks revenge on a lover who makes her happy while he destroys her with possessive eyes that penetrate the "fences" she has erected. After mentioning her father and her relatives, who have achieved "sound measure/ of love" ("sound measure" suggests substance but also a prosaic doling out of love), she turns to her mother, who threatens her with a long rifle that becomes a fishing pole with hooks that ensnare her. The speaker reverts to her "doberman" behavior, and, though she persists in maintaining "distance," she uses her poems and songs to achieve acceptance: "I felt alive./ I was glad for my jade memories."

THE MOTORCYCLE BETRAYAL POEMS

In *The Motorcycle Betrayal Poems*, betrayal, always a theme in Wakoski's poetry, becomes the central focus; the motorcycle mechanic represents all the men who have betrayed her. The tone is at times humorous, so much so that the poems may not be taken seriously enough, but there is also a sense of desperation. These poems explore the different roles and images available to define identity, and the roles are not gender-bound. The speaker, who expresses her condition in images of isolation and entrapment, is fascinated with aggressive male roles, embodied in the motorcyclist. While she wryly admits that she is the "pink dress," she at times would like to reverse the roles; she is also aware, however, that the male roles do not satisfy her needs, do not mesh with her sexual identity. In this collection her identity is again developed in terms of lunar imagery, this time with reference to Diana, associated with the moon and the huntress, here of the sexual variety, and with the desert: both are lifeless, and both reflect the sterility of her life. The speaker does suggest, through the water imagery that pervades her poems, that this condition is not permanent, that her life can be sustained, but only through a man's love. Ultimately, the speaker is plagued with another duality: She desires what has persistently destroyed her.

SMUDGING

The same contradictory feelings about men are reflected in the title poem of *Smudging*, a collection of verse that includes King of Spain poems, prose poems, two parts of *Greed*, and miscellaneous poems touching on recurrent themes, motifs, and myths. "Smudging," another of Wakoski's favorite poems, encapsulates many of the themes as it probes the divided self. There are two "parts" of the speaker, the part that searches "for the warmth of the smudge pot" and the "part of me that takes your hand confidently." That is, the speaker both believes that she has the warmth and fears that she lacks it. Like her mother, she must fear the "husband who left her alone for the salty ocean" (with associations of sterility and isolation); yet she, like the orange she metaphorically becomes, transcends this fear through "visions" and the roles she plays in her head—these make her "the golden orange every prince will fight/ to own."

With Wakoski, transcendence seems always transitory; each poem must solve a problem, often the same one, so that the speaker is often on a tightrope, performing a balancing act between fear and fulfillment. As the poem moves to its solution, the speaker continues to waver, as is the case in "Smudging." At the beginning of the poem, the speaker revels in warmth and luxuriance; she refers to amber, honey, music, and gold as she equates gold with "your house," perhaps also her lover's body, and affirms her love for him. Even before the change signaled by "but" occurs in the next line, she tempers the image: "the honeysuckle of an island" is not their world but "in my head," and the repetition of "your" rather than "our" suggests the nagging doubts that lead to memories of her childhood in Orange County, California. The fear of the laborers outside the house, the memory of the absentee father—she has left these behind as she finds love and warmth with her mechanic lover, whose warmth is suspect, however, because he "threw me out once/ for a whole year." Mechanically expert, he does not understand or appreciate her "running parts" and remains, despite their reunion, "the voices in those dark nights" of her childhood. She,

on the other hand, has become the "hot metal," "the golden orange" that exists independently of him.

DANCING ON THE GRAVE OF A SON OF A BITCH

Dancing on the Grave of a Son of a Bitch is a bit of a departure from Wakoski's earlier poetry, although it is consistent in mythology and themes with the rest of her work. The title poem, dedicated to her motorcycle betrayer, the mechanic of "Smudging," reiterates past injustices and betrayals, but the speaker is more assured than vengeful. Despite the opening curse, "God damn it," and her acknowledgment that his leaving made her "as miserable/ as an earthworm with no earth," she not only has "crawled out of the ground," resurrecting herself, but also has learned to "sing new songs," to write new poems. She denies that hers is an angry statement, affirming instead that it is joyful, and her tone at the end of the poem is playful as she evokes the country singer's "for every time/ you done me wrong."

There is similar progression in the "Astronomer Poems" of the volume. As in earlier poems, she uses the moon/sun dichotomy, but there is more acceptance, assurance, and assertiveness as she explores these myths. In "Sun Gods Have Sun Spots," she not only suggests male-sun blemishes but also affirms her own divinity in a clever role reversal: "I am/ also a ruler of the sun." While "the sun has an angry face," the speaker in "The Mirror of a Day Chiming Marigold" still yearns for the poet or astronomer to study "my moon." Wakoski thus at least tentatively resolves two earlier themes, but she continues to develop the King of Spain figure, to refer to the "rings of Saturn," to include some Buddha poems and some prose fables, and to use chants as a means of conveying meaning and music. In her introduction to the book, she explains that she wishes readers to read the poems aloud, being "cognizant" of the chanted parts. Since Wakoski is a performing poet, the notion of chants, developed by Jerome Rothenberg, was almost inevitable, considering her interest in the piano (another theme for future development) and music. In fact, Wakoski uses chants, as in "Chants/Chance," to allow for different speakers within the poem.

VIRTUOSO LITERATURE FOR TWO AND FOUR HANDS

Virtuoso Literature for Two and Four Hands, a relatively slender volume of poetry, not only alludes to

Wakoski's fifteen years of piano study but also plays upon the keyboard-typewriter analogy to explore past relationships and her visionary life. Two of Wakoski's favorite poems, "The Story of Richard Maxfield" and "Driving Gloves," which are included in this volume, involve people she resembles, one a dead composer and artist and one a Greek scholar with a failed father, but the poems conclude with affirmations about the future. It is not Maxfield's suicide that disturbs the speaker; she is concerned with his "falling apart," the antithesis of his "well-organized" composing. The poem, despite the repetition of "fall apart," ends with her certainty "that just as I would never fall apart,/ I would also never jump out of a window." In the other poem, the speaker begins with familiar lamentations about her sad childhood and turns to genes and the idea of repeating a parent's failures. Noting that she, like her mother, wears driving gloves, she is terrified that she will be like her boring, unimaginative mother; Anne, like her unpublished novelist/father, is a bad driver. Despite Anne's belief that "we're all like some parent/ or ancestor," the speaker tells Anne that "you learned to drive because you are not your father" and states that she wears gloves "because I like to wear them." Asserting that their lives are their own, she dismisses the past as "only something/ we have all lived/ through." This attitude seems a marked departure from earlier poems in which her life and behavior are attributed to her father's influence.

WAITING FOR THE KING OF SPAIN

While *Waiting for the King of Spain* features staple Wakoski figures (George Washington, the motorcycle mechanic, the King of Spain), lunar imagery (one section consists of fifteen poems about an unseen lunar eclipse, and one is titled "Daughter Moon"), and the use of chants and prose poems, it also includes a number of short poems—a startling departure for Wakoski, who has often stated a preference for long narrative poems. As a whole, the poems continue the affirmative mood of *Virtuoso Literature for Two and Four Hands*. The King of Spain, the idealized lover who loves her "as you do not./ And as no man ever has," appears and reappears, the wearer of the "cap of darkness" (the title of a later collection), in stark contrast to the betrayers and the George Washington persona. Here, too, there is less

emphasis on the masculine sun imagery, though it appears, and more of a celebration of the moon imagery.

The two poems in the collection that Wakoski considers most illustrative of her critical principles are warm, accepting, flippant, and amusing. In "Ode to a Lebanese Crock of Olives" the speaker again refers to the body she regards as physically unattractive, but she accepts her "failed beach girl" status and stacks the deck metaphorically in favor of abundance ("the richness of burgundy,/ dark brown gravies") over the bland ("their tan fashionable body"). In fact, the "fashionable" (always a negative word for Wakoski) body provides the point of contrast to affirm Wakoski's own beauty: "Beauty is everywhere/ in contrasts and unities." This condemnation of thinness is extended to art and poetry in "To the Thin and Elegant Woman Who Resides Inside of Alix Nelson." For Wakoski, fullness is all: "Now is the time to love flesh." Renouncing the Weight Watchers and *Vogue* models of life and poetry, she argues for the unfettered fullness of "American drama" and the "substantial narrative." Wakoski declares, "My body is full of the juice of poetry," and concludes the poem with an amusing parody of the Lord's Prayer, ending with "Ah, men" (surely the source of the false doctrine of beauty).

THE MAN WHO SHOOK HANDS

The Man Who Shook Hands represents a point of departure for Wakoski, who seems in this volume to return to the anger, hostility, and bitterness of her earlier poems. The feelings of betrayal, here embodied in the figure of a man who merely shakes hands the morning after a one-night relationship, resurface as the speaker's quest for love is again unsuccessful. The speaker in "Running Men" is left with the "lesson" the departing lover "so gently taught in your kind final gesture,/ that stiff embrace." The sarcasm in "gently" and "kind" is not redeemed by her concluding statement that she lives "in her head" and that the only perfect bodies are in museums and in art. This realization prepares the reader for the last line of the volume: "How I hate my destiny."

GREED

Although the temporally complete *Greed*, all thirteen parts, was published in 1984, parts of it were printed as early as 1968, and Wakoski has often included the parts in other collections of her poetry. It is bound by a single theme, even if greed is defined in such general terms that it can encompass almost everything. It is the failure to choose, the unwillingness to "give up one thing/ for another." Because the early parts were often published with other poems, they tend to reflect the same themes—concerns with parents, lovers, poetry—and to be written in a similar style. Of particular interest, however, given Wakoski's preference for narrative, is part 12, "The Greed to Be Fulfilled," which tends to be dramatic in form. What begins as a conversation between the speaker and George becomes a masque, "The Moon Loses Her Shoes," in which the actors are the stock figures of Wakoski mythology. The resolution of the poem for the speaker is the movement from emotional concerns to intellectual ones, a movement reflected in the poetry-music analogy developed in part 13.

LATER POETRY

Wakoski's other later poetry suggests that she is reworking older themes while she incorporates new ones, which also relate to her own life. In *Cap of Darkness* and *The Magician's Feastletters* she explores the problem of aging in a culture that worships youth and consumption; this concern is consistent with the themes of *Virtuoso Literature for Two and Four Hands*.

The Rings of Saturn, with the symbolic piano and ring, and *Medea the Sorceress*, with its focus on mythology and woman as poet-visionary, reflect earlier poetry but also reflect the changing emphasis, the movement from emotion to intellect, while retaining the subjectivity, as well as the desire for fulfillment, beauty, and truth, that characterize the entire body of her work. The latter volume became the first part of a major Wakowski endeavor with the collective title *The Archaeology of Movies and Books*. *Jason the Sailor*, *The Emerald City of Las Vegas*, and *Argonaut Rose* are the other three parts.

The best introduction to Wakoski's art—her themes and methods—is *The Butcher's Apron: New and Selected Poems, Including "Greed: Part 14,"* published in 2000. In fashioning this collection, Wakoski decided to cut across a wide body of work by selecting those poems that concern food and drink. Moreover, as she writes in the introduction, "All of the poems in this col-

lection . . . focus on the on-going process of discovering beauty and claiming it for myself." At the same time, she has built a structure that outlines her personal mythology as it is revealed by or rooted in geographical and cultural landscapes. Part 1, "A California Girl," concerns her self-projection "as a daughter of the Golden State," while later parts elaborate and complicate Wakoski's shifting personae. Thus, her arrangement of older and newer poems is made in the service of a mythic map of her inner terrain.

Though often compared to Sylvia Plath, a comparison she destroys in part 9 of *Greed*, and often seen as squarely in the feminist mainstream, Wakoski remains a unique and intensely personal voice in American poetry. She is constantly inventive, rarely predictable, and, in a way that somehow seems healthy and unthreatening, enormously ambitious.

OTHER MAJOR WORKS

NONFICTION: *Form Is an Extension of Content*, 1972; *Creating a Personal Mythology*, 1975; *Variations on a Theme*, 1976; *Toward a New Poetry*, 1980.

BIBLIOGRAPHY

Brown, David M. "Wakoski's 'The Fear of Fat Children.'" *Explicator* 48, no. 4 (Summer, 1990): 292-294. Brown observes how the poem's common diction and grotesque imagery work to create a successful postmodern confessional in which the speaker expresses not only guilt but also the urge for self-reformation.

Gannon, Catherine, and Clayton Lein. "Diane Wakoski and the Language of Self." *San Jose Studies* 5 (Spring, 1979): 84-98. Focusing on *The Motorcycle Betrayal Poems*, Gannon and Lein discuss the betrayal motif in terms of the speaker's struggle for identity. The poems' speaker uses the moon image to consider possible alternative images for herself, and in the last poem of the book she achieves a "richer comprehension of her being."

Hughes, Gertrude Reif. "Readers Digest." *Women's Review of Books* 18, no. 7 (April, 2001): 14-16. Treats *The Butcher's Apron* along with collected works by Carolyn Kizer and Kathleen Raine. Gives high praise to "Greed, Part 14," which is granted the status of a major long poem that redeems much else in the collection.

Lauter, Estella. *Women as Mythmakers: Poetry and Visual Art by Twentieth-Century Women*. Bloomington: Indiana University Press, 1984. Lauter devotes one chapter to Wakoski's handling of moon imagery in several of the poet's books. There is also a related discussion of Isis and Diana as aspects of the speaker's personality.

Martin, Taffy Wynne. "Diane Wakoski's Personal Mythology: Dionysian Music, Created Presence." *Boundary 2: A Journal of Postmodern Literature* 10 (Fall, 1982): 155-172. According to Martin, Wakoski's sense of absence and lost love prompts desire, which in turn animates the poetry, giving it life. Martin also discusses Wakoski's mythmaking, her use of digression as a structural device, and her use of musical repetition.

Newton, Robert. *Diane Wakoski: A Descriptive Bibliography*. Jefferson, N.C.: McFarland, 1987. Newton unravels Wakoski's career in print through its first quarter century.

Ostriker, Alicia Luskin. *Stealing the Language: The Emergence of Women's Poetry in America*. Boston: Beacon Press, 1986. An outstanding history of women's poetry, Ostriker's book includes extended readings of some of Wakoski's works, especially *The George Washington Poems*. For the most part, Ostriker focuses on the divided self (the all-nothing and the strong-weak) in Wakoski's poetry and discusses the ways in which the poet's masks and disguises become flesh. There is an extensive bibliography concerning women's poetry.

Wakoski, Diane. "An Interview with Diane Wakoski." Interview by Deborah Gillespie. *South Carolina Review* 38, no. 1 (Fall, 2005): 14-21. Wakoski discusses her childhood and her life as a writer. She describes what and who influenced her.

_____. *Toward a New Poetry*. Ann Arbor: University of Michigan Press, 1980. The book includes not only Wakoski's criticism, much of which is commentary to her own poetry, but also five revealing interviews, only two of which had previously been published in major journals. In the introduction, Wakoski lists her "best" poems, the ones she be-lieves illustrate her personal mythology, her use of image and digression, and the kind of music she thinks is important to contemporary poetry.

Thomas L. Erskine
Updated by Philip K. Jason

ANNE WALDMAN

Born: Millville, New Jersey; April 2, 1945

PRINCIPAL POETRY

On the Wing, 1968
Giant Night: Selected Poems, 1970
Baby Breakdown, 1970
Memorial Day, 1971 (with Ted Berrigan)
No Hassles, 1971
Life Notes, 1973
Fast Speaking Woman and Other Chants, 1975 (revised as *Fast Speaking Woman: Chants and Essays*, 1996)
Shaman/Shamane, 1977
Four Travels, 1979 (with Reed Bye)
First Baby Poems, 1983
Makeup on Empty Space, 1983
Invention, 1985
Skin Meat Bones, 1985
Helping the Dreamer: New and Selected Poems, 1966-1988, 1989
Iovis: All Is Full of Jove, 1993, 1997
Troubairitz, 1993
Polemics, 1998 (with Anselm Hollo and Jack Collom)
Marriage: A Sentence, 2000
In the Room of Never Grieve: New and Selected Poems, 1985-2003, 2003
Zombie Dawn, 2003 (with Tom Clark)
Fleuve Flâneur, 2004 (with Mary Kite)
Structure of the World Compared to a Bubble, 2004
Manatee/Humanity, 2009

OTHER LITERARY FORMS

Anne Waldman is known primarily for her poetry.

ACHIEVEMENTS

Anne Waldman has written more than thirty books of poetry and has edited numerous anthologies. She was assistant director, and later director, of the St. Mark's Poetry Project from 1968 to 1978. She co-founded the Jack Kerouac School of Disembodied Poetics at Naropa Institute in Boulder, Colorado. Waldman has received numerous grants and awards, including the Dylan Thomas Memorial Award (1967), a Poets Foundation Award (1969), a National Endowment for the Arts Grant (1979-1980), the Poetry Society of America's Shelley Memorial Award (1996), an Atlantic Center for the Arts Residency (2002), and a fellowship from the Emily Harvey Foundation, Venice (Winter, 2007). In 2001, she received a grant from the Foundation for Contemporary Arts; the same year, she was a resident at the Vermont Studio School.

In March, 2002, the University of Michigan officially opened an archive of Waldman's works and mementoes, calling her "one of the most vibrant writers of the post-Beat generation, . . . a performance poet of electric intensity."

BIOGRAPHY

Anne Waldman was born in Millville, New Jersey, in 1945. Before her fifth birthday, her parents, John Waldman and Frances Waldman, moved to Greenwich Village. Her father encouraged her to read omnivorously, but she learned a special love of poetry from her mother, who translated the work of a Greek poet. Waldman graduated from the Friends Seminary High School, where she first read the work of the Beat poets, which, along with her parental influence, was instrumental in her decision to devote her life to poetry. Her studies at Bennington College further reinforced this dedication.

In 1965, while still enrolled in college, she traveled to California to participate in the Berkeley Poetry Conference. There, she met Allen Ginsberg, with whom she was to form a close literary alliance. After graduating from Bennington in 1966, Waldman became assistant director, and later director, of the Poetry Project at St. Mark's Church-in-the-Bowery in New York. In that capacity, between 1968 and 1978, she met many more of the Beat poets in person.

Also at the St. Mark's Poetry Project, Waldman began to give high-energy public readings of her own work and became known as a pioneering performance poet. She published her first book, *On the Wing*, in 1968, and in 1975, her performance poem *Fast-Speaking Woman* was published by Lawrence Ferlinghetti's City Lights.

In the same period, Waldman, whose interest in Eastern religion dates from high school, began to study with Chögyam Trungpa Rinpoche, a meditation master of Tibetan Buddhism. In 1974, Waldman participated with Ginsberg, Trungpa, and others in founding the Jack Kerouac School of Disembodied Poetics at Naropa Institute in Boulder, Colorado. She later came to serve as a distinguished professor of poetics and director of Naropa's Summer Writing Program. Her son Ambrose Bye is a musician with whom she frequently collaborates in poetry performances.

Overall, Waldman's influence has served to extend the boundaries of poetry well beyond the printed page. As a performance poet, she combines in her work an intense political activism, strong feminism, a critique of all gender identity, extreme departure from conventional poetic forms, and ambitiously long poems embracing large subjects.

ANALYSIS

Despite her connection with two generations of Beat poets, Anne Waldman has never considered herself to be one. In fact, her poetic inspiration has virtually worldwide sources; moreover, unlike the largely apolitical Beats, she has been deeply involved in protest politics. Her work is an intense expression of her advocacy for feminist, environmental, and human-rights concerns. She has also written powerful love lyrics and spiritual meditations.

While describing herself as an "outrider" or as part of "a hybrid outsider tradition," Waldman is an avowed formalist, although the tremendous range, vitality and unconventionality of her work, especially her performance poetry, often belies its own structural underpinnings. For political and aesthetic reasons, her poetic practice has been highly inclusive, assimilating the forms of Asia, the ancient Mediterranean, Western Europe, and contemporary America. With the incantatory work of poet Charles Olson as one of her chief in-spirations, she delivers her performance pieces in the "vatic" style of a crazed prophet, attempting to embrace the whole of human social experience and even that of other species. Overall, Waldman's influence has served to revivify the oral tradition of poetry and to extend the boundaries of poetry far beyond the printed page.

GIANT NIGHT

Giant Night displays Waldman's exuberant, expansive consciousness of the world and people around her. Her use of meter, a rapid alternation among spondees, anapests, and iambs, reinforces the impression of constant change. Underlying the mutable surface, however, is a profound and paradoxical sense of timelessness. In the title poem, she declares:

> Awake in a giant night
> is where I am
>   There is a river where my soul,
> hungry as a horse drinks beside me
>
> An hour of immense possibility flies by
> and I do nothing but sit in the present
> which keeps changing moment to moment

"What's New" conveys her deep sense of connection with other beings:

> when you sit down and write
> at a big desk
> think of everyone everywhere writing

FAST SPEAKING WOMAN

Fast Speaking Woman was first published in 1975; in 1996, a twentieth anniversary edition was published, augmenting the original text with essays based on her teachings about chant and performance poetry. The title poem is a long "list chant" listing the attributes of a phrase repeated at the beginning of each line. Waldman presents the list as descriptive of both herself and "everywoman:" "I'm an abalone woman/ I'm the abandoned woman/ I'm the woman abashed, the gibberish woman/ the aborigine woman, the woman absconding."

While the "list chant" form was originated by the Indians of Mexico, Waldman's use of it also contains echoes of the Greek poetess Sappho and William Butler Yeats; in addition, she makes reference to Tibetan Buddhism and ancient magical doctrines. *Fast Speaking Woman* is considered an outstanding contemporary example of performance poetry, with the spoken word lending itself to a more complete experience of the poems than that created by the printed page alone.

IOVIS

Iovis, a monumentally ambitious work, was published in two books, in 1993 and 1997. (A third installment was added in 2003 when it was incorporated into *In the Room of Never Grieve*.) Combined, the books exceed six hundred pages in length. The first two books address the themes of male and female energy, history, mythology, mystical and Eastern religion, and politics. Critics were not cordial to the first book, calling it self-indulgent, overlong, "patched together," and obscure. The second part fared better critically, though even appreciative reviewers noted that the work would be best heard aloud.

Waldman's introduction to book 2 announces that the work is not to be judged by conventional, hierarchical standards: "I feel myself always an open system (woman) available to any words or sounds I'm informed by." The poem defies attempts to summarize its prosody or its formal structure; perhaps this indefinable nature can be taken as a feminist statement. Waldman avoids exclusionary feminist rhetoric, however. Indeed, she asserts that both women and men harbor multiple identities. For example: "What is this identification with young men? Are they playful tricksters inside the hag?" In this and many other ways, Waldman attempts to assimilate all of modern experience, from the ineffable to the quotidian.

MARRIAGE

The energetic and lyrical poems in *Marriage* embody the playful contemplation of marriage as a social institution. The work is not a feminist diatribe against that institution, as Waldman enumerates both the happy and the unhappy aspects of marriage. Moreover, she recognizes marriage in all of its contemporary forms, including traditional, same-sex, and nuclear couples at the center of an extended family. Waldman bases her work on the traditional *haibun* form originated by the Japanese poet Matsuo Bashō, which pairs prose poems with similarly themed lyric poems. With her characteristic inclusiveness, she has said that her goal was spiritual revivification of marriage in its diverse contemporary forms. Critics praised *Marriage* as being accessible to the average reader.

IN THE ROOM OF NEVER GRIEVE

In her introduction to *In the Room of Never Grieve*, a collection of new and old poems from 1985 to 2003, Waldman explains the title: "It's the little girl biting the bullet: *I will stay in this room forever, I will be strong, I will never grieve.*" She describes her goal in poetry as being "To reclaim the imagination, to free our language from the stench of manipulation, . . . [to] examine how the mind moves in language that seeks to create alternative ways to live, to survive, and to sing. These are the tasks, the disciplines." She speaks of her books, this collection in particular, as having "efficacious possibility." In a possible reference to deconstruction—one of the many disciplines she has sought to assimilate—she declares her intention to "question the role of language as it plays with its own markers." Collectively, the poems in this collection fulfill this agenda, displaying the evolution of Waldman's thought regarding the major spiritual, aesthetic, and political themes of her work. The collection was sold with a compact disc containing a selection of the live poetry performances for which she is noted.

The new poems in this collection include statements on current events such as the September 11, 2001, terrorist attacks on the United States and the war in Iraq, as well as the third installment of Waldman's epic *Iovis*. Waldman is convinced that poetry can make a defining difference at this critical juncture of history only by escaping its traditional boundaries. She challenges the reader to think: "If the very future of the world is at stake, is it enough to deconstruct, to mystify, to obviate? Would beauty still be the call? Or love?"

MANATEE/HUMANITY

Manatee/Humanity is a contribution to the genre of ecopoetry, the title playing on the similarity of sound between the words "humanity" and "manatee," the name of the animal popularly known as sea cows. The book exemplifies Waldman's interest in Kalachakra, an Eastern spiritual practice promoting empathy with nonhuman species. In incantatory style, she explores the profound subtleties of interspecies communication and meditates on evolution, neuroscience, endangered species, and the varieties of consciousness.

The title poem begins with a line evocative of the motion it describes: "the manatee is found in shallow slow moving rivers." Among other things, the poem is a kind of primer on a less-familiar animal:

> a manatee calf is born every 2-5 years
> a manatee gestates for a year in the manatee womb
> 8,400 miles of tidal waters could be for the manatee

OTHER MAJOR WORKS

TRANSLATION: *Songs of the Sons and Daughters of Buddha*, 1996 (with Andrew Schelling).

EDITED TEXTS: *The World Anthology: Poems from the St. Mark's Poetry Project*, 1969; *Talking Poetics from Naropa Institute: Annals of the Jack Kerouac School of Disembodied Poetics*, 1978 (with Marilyn Webb); *Nice to See You: Homage to Ted Berrigan*, 1991; *Disembodied Poetics: Annals of the Jack Kerouac School*, 1994 (with Andrew Schelling); *Civil Disobediences: Poetics and Politics in Action*, 2004 (with Lisa Birman); *The Beat Book: Poems and Fiction of the Beat Generation*, 1996; *Beats at Naropa: An Anthology*, 2009 (with Laura E. Wright).

MISCELLANEOUS: *Vow to Poetry: Essays, Interviews, and Manifestos*, 2001; *Outrider: Poems, Essays, Interviews*, 2006.

BIBLIOGRAPHY

Notley, Alice. "Iovis Omnia Plena." Review of *Iovis*. *Chicago Review* 44, no. 1 (1998): 117-130. This review from a feminist critical perspective suggests that Waldman's choice of a male mythical god for her title was deliberately ironic given her feminism and shows how Waldman begins by celebrating Jove but then brings in female myths from Najavo and Gaelic culture, which, along with her own story, come to dominate the poem.

Osman, Jena. "Tracking a Poem in Time: The Shifting States of Anne Waldman's 'Makeup on Empty Space.'" *Jacket* 27 (April, 2005). Examines Waldman's concept of the "wakeful state, through language that stays alive." Focuses on Waldman's poem "Makeup on Empty Space," showing how this concept is realized through an "organic" method of collaborative change, with the poem leading outside itself to other ideas and works of art—a poem, a dance, a book, a day.

Sadoff, Ira. "On the Margins: Part Two." *American Poetry Review* 35, no. 2 (March/April, 2006): 51-55. This article discusses several experimental poets' work and literary style, including themes of Waldman's prose poems. Focuses on her dramatic poem "Stereo." Also touches on the stylistic techniques of women poets Lyn Hejinian and Claudia Rankine.

Smith, Larry. "Embracing the Wild Mind." Review of *Outrider*. *American Book Review* 28, no. 3 (March/April, 2007): 19. Explains Waldman's intuitive discovery of structure in action, rather than prescribed poetic form with its "structured coherence." Describes how Waldman's beliefs as a Buddhist and rebel poet, as well as the influence of Charles Olson's "open poetics," led her toward creation by association, intuition, accumulation of imagery, and leaps of the imagination.

Waldman Anne, and Lisa Birman, eds. *Civil Disobediences: Poetics and Politics in Action*. Minneapolis, Minn.: Coffee House Books, 2004. In her introduction, Waldman denounces a "disturbing disjunct or rip in our culture that calls for an articulate active response to the current repressive agenda" and sets her own agenda for poetry to reverse this trend. Supporting this agenda in the volume are essays, interviews, and lectures from poets of many schools and all ages. Waldman herself contributes "Femanifestos" as a handbook for women poet-activists of the future.

_____. *Vow to Poetry: Essays, Interviews, and Manifestos*. Minneapolis, Minn.: Coffee House Press, 2001. Besides the dedication to poetry indicated by the title, Waldman, in this collection of autobiography, interviews, and essays, reports on her life as a poet and political dissenter. Contending that "Language . . . arrives, it manifests, it is a relationship," she details her own poetic practice and offers a how-to guide for young writers.

Thomas Rankin

ALICE WALKER

Born: Eatonton, Georgia; February 9, 1944

PRINCIPAL POETRY

Once, 1968
Five Poems, 1972
Revolutionary Petunias, and Other Poems, 1973
Good Night, Willie Lee, I'll See You in the Morning, 1979
Horses Make a Landscape Look More Beautiful, 1984
Her Blue Body Everything We Know: Earthling Poems, 1965-1990 Complete, 1991
Absolute Trust in the Goodness of the Earth: New Poems, 2003
A Poem Traveled Down My Arm: Poems and Drawings, 2003

OTHER LITERARY FORMS

Although Alice Walker's poetry is cherished by her admirers, she is primarily known as a fiction writer. The novel *The Color Purple* (1982), generally regarded as her masterpiece, achieved both popular and critical success, winning the Pulitzer Prize and the National Book Award. The Steven Spielberg film of the same name, for which Walker acted as consultant, reached an immense international audience.

Other Walker fiction has received less attention. Her first novel, *The Third Life of Grange Copeland* (1970), depicts violence and family dysfunction among people psychologically maimed by racism. *Meridian* (1976) mirrors the Civil Rights movement, of which the youthful Walker was actively a part. Later novels, *The Temple of My Familiar* (1989), *Possessing the Secret of Joy* (1992), and *By the Light of My Father's Smile* (1998) have employed narrative as little more than a vehicle for ideas on racial and sexual exploitation, abuse of animals and the earth, and New Age spirituality. *In Love and Trouble: Stories of Black Women* (1973) and *You Can't Keep a Good Woman Down* (1981) revealed Walker to be one of the finest of late twentieth century American short-story writers. She also has written an occasional children's book (*To Hell with Dying*, 1988, is particularly notable) and several collections of essays (*In Search of Our Mothers' Gardens: Womanist Prose*, 1983, is the most lyrical) that present impassioned pleas for the causes Walker espouses.

ACHIEVEMENTS

At numerous colleges, as a teacher and writer-in-residence, Alice Walker established herself as a mentor, particularly to young African American women. Her crusades became international. To alert the world to the problem of female circumcision in Africa, she collaborated with an Anglo-Indian filmmaker on a book and film. She has been a voice for artistic freedom, defending her own controversial writings and those of others, such as Salman Rushdie. In her writings and later open lifestyle, she affirmed lesbian and bisexual experience. However, the accomplishment in which she took the most pride was her resurrection of the reputation of Zora Neale Hurston, a germinal African American anthropologist and novelist, whose books had gone out of print.

Walker won the Rosenthal Award of the National Institute of Arts and Letters for *In Love and Trouble* and received a Charles Merrill writing fellowship, a National Endowment for the Arts award, and a Guggenheim Fellowship. Her second book of poetry, *Revolutionary Petunias, and Other Poems*, received the Lillian Smith Award and was nominated for a National Book Award. Her highest acclaim came with the novel *The Color Purple*, for which she won the National Book Award and the 1983 Pulitzer Prize. She received the Fred Cody Award for lifetime achievement in 1990. Walker was inducted into the California Hall of Fame in 2006.

BIOGRAPHY

Alice Malsenior Walker was the youngest of eight children born to a Georgia sharecropper and his wife. Her father earned about three hundred dollars per year, while her mother, the stronger figure, supplemented the family income by working as a maid. Walker herself was a bright, confident child until an accident at age eight blinded her in one eye and temporarily marred her beauty. At this time, she established what was to be-

come a lifelong pattern of savoring solitude and making the most of adversity. She started reading and writing poetry.

Because of her partial blindness and her outstanding high school record, Walker qualified for a special scholarship offered to disabled students by Spelman College, the prestigious black women's college in Atlanta. When she matriculated there in 1961, her neighbors raised the bus fare of seventy-five dollars to get her to Atlanta.

As a Spelman student, Walker was "moved to wakefulness" by the emerging Civil Rights movement. She took part in demonstrations downtown, which brought her into conflict with the conservative administration of the school. Finding the rules generally too restrictive and refreshed with her new consciousness, she secured a scholarship at Sarah Lawrence College in Bronxville, New York. She then felt closer to the real

Alice Walker (AP/Wide World Photos)

action that was changing the country. At Sarah Lawrence College, she came under the influence of the poet Muriel Rukeyser, who recognized her talent and arranged for her first publications. She also took a summer off for a trip to her "spiritual home," Africa. She returned depressed and pregnant, contemplated suicide for a time, but instead underwent an abortion and poured her emotions into poetry.

After graduation, Walker worked for a time in the New York City Welfare Department before returning to the South to write, teach, and promote voter registration. She married Melvyn Leventhal, a white Jew, and worked with him on desegregation legal cases and Head Start programs. Their child, Rebecca, was born during this highly productive period. By the time the marriage ended in 1976, Walker was already becoming recognized as a writer, though she did not become internationally famous until after the publication of *The Color Purple*.

Walker continued to write during the 1980's and 1990's, though never again achieving the acclaim or the notoriety that *The Color Purple* brought her. Critics complained of her stridency, the factual inaccuracies in her writings, and her tendency to turn her works of fiction into polemics. Many African Americans felt that her writings cast black society in a grim light. Walker moved to California and lived for several years with Robert Allen, the editor of *Black Scholar*. Times had changed; the motto was no longer "black and white together": marriages between Jews and African Americans were out, and black-black relationships were in.

Walker also became more alert to the problems women of color faced throughout the world. Taking a female partner, she decided to devote her time and talents to celebrating women and rectifying wrongs committed against them. In March of 2003, Walker was arrested for protesting the Iraq War. In 2009, Walker visited Gaza to promote peace and friendlier relations between Egypt and Israel. Walker has always encouraged awareness of important issues in her writing, but she has attracted attention to issues such as problems in the black culture, violence against women, and the ravages of war by personally participating in or protesting events about which she feels passionately.

ANALYSIS

Alice Walker writes free verse, employing concrete images. She resorts to few of the conceits, the extended metaphors, the Latinate language, and other common conventions of poetry. Readers frequently say that her verses hardly seem like poetry at all; they resemble the conversation of a highly articulate, observant woman. Although her poetry often seems like prose, her fiction is highly poetic. The thoughts of Miss Celie, the first-person narrator of *The Color Purple*, would not have been out of place in a book of poetry. Boundaries between prose and poetry are minimal in the work of Walker. Her verse, like her prose, is always rhythmic; if she rhymes or alliterates, it seems to be by accident. The poetry appears so effortless that its precision, its choice of exact image or word to convey the nuance the poet wishes, is not immediately evident. Only close scrutiny reveals the skill with which this highly lettered poet has assimilated her influences, chiefly E. E. Cummings, Emily Dickinson, Robert Graves, Japanese haiku, Li Bo, Ovid, Zen epigrams, and William Carlos Williams.

Walker's poetry is personal and generally didactic, generated by events in her life, causes she has advocated, and injustices over which she has agonized. The reader feels that it is the message that counts, before realizing that the medium is part of the message. Several of her poems echo traumatic events in her own life, such as her abortion. She remembers the words her mother uttered over the casket of her father, and she makes a poem of them. Other poems recall ambivalent emotions of childhood: Sunday school lessons which, even then, were filled with discrepancies. Some poems deal with the creative process itself: She calls herself a medium through whom the Old Ones, formerly mute, find their voice at last.

Some readers are surprised to discover that Walker's poems are both mystical and socially revolutionary, one moment exuberant and the next reeking with despair. Her mysticism is tied to reverence for the earth, a sense of unity with all living creatures, a bond of sisterhood with women throughout the world, and a joyous celebration of the female principle in the divine. On the other hand, she may lament that injustice reigns in society: Poor black people toil so that white men may savor the jewels that adorn heads of state.

ONCE

Walker's first collection of poetry, *Once*, communicates her youthful impressions of Africa and her state of mind during her early travels there and the melancholy and thoughts of death and suicide she felt on her return to United States, where racism persisted. Perhaps the epigram from French philosopher Albert Camus, which prefaces the book, expresses its mood best: "Misery kept me from believing that all was well under the sun, and the sun taught me that history wasn't everything."

The title poem of the collection contains several loosely connected scenes of injustice in the American South, small black children run down by vans because "they were in the way," Jewish Civil Rights workers who cannot be cremated because their remains cannot be found, and finally a black child waving an American flag, but from "the very/ tips/ of her/ fingers," an image perhaps of irony or perhaps of hope. There are meditations on white lovers—blond, Teutonic, golden—who dare kiss this poet who is "brown-er/ Than a jew." There are memories of black churches, where her mother shouts, her father snores, and she feels uncomfortable.

The most striking poem is certainly "African Images," an assortment of vignettes from the ancestral homeland: shy gazelles, the bluish peaks of Mount Kenya, the sound of elephants trumpeting, and rain forests with red orchids. However, even when viewed in the idealism of youth, Africa is not total paradise. The leg of a slain elephant is fashioned into an umbrella holder in a shop; a rhinoceros is killed so that its horn may be made into an aphrodisiac.

REVOLUTIONARY PETUNIAS, AND OTHER POEMS

Revolutionary Petunias, and Other Poems is divided into two parts. The first is titled "In These Dissenting Times . . . Surrounding Ground and Autobiography." She proposes to write "of the old men I knew/ And the young men/ I loved/ And of the gold toothed women/ Mighty of arm/ Who dragged us all/ To church." She writes also "To acknowledge our ancestors" with the awareness that "we did not make/ ourselves, that the line stretches/ all the way back, perhaps, to God; or/ to Gods." She recalls her baptism

"dunked . . . in the creek," with "gooey . . . rotting leaves,/ a greenish mold floating." She was a slight figure, "All in white./ With God's mud ruining my snowy/ socks and his bullfrog spoors/ gluing up my face."

The last half of the collection, "Revolutionary Petunias . . . the Living Through," begins with yet another epigram from Camus, reminding the reader that there will come a time when revolutions, though not made by beauty, will discover the need for beauty. The poems, especially those referred to as "Crucifixions," become more anguished, more angered. Walker becomes skeptical of the doctrine of nonviolence, hinting that the time for more direct action may have come. The tone of the last poems in the collection may be expressed best by the opening lines to the verse Walker called "Rage." "In me, " she wrote, "there is a rage to defy/ the order of the stars/ despite their pretty patterns."

GOOD NIGHT, WILLIE LEE, I'LL SEE YOU IN THE MORNING

Good Night, Willie Lee, I'll See You in the Morning expands on earlier themes and further exploits personal and family experiences for lessons in living. The title poem is perhaps the most moving and characteristic of the collection. Walker shared it again on May 22, 1995, in a commencement day speech delivered at Spelman College. As a lesson in forgiveness, she recalled the words her mother, who had much to endure and much to forgive, uttered above her father's casket. Her last words to the man with whom she had lived for so many years, beside whom she had labored in the fields, and with whom she had raised so many children were, "Good night, Willie Lee, I'll see you in the morning." This gentle instinctive act of her mother taught Walker the enduring lesson that "the healing of all our wounds is forgiveness/ that permits a promise/ of our return/ at the end."

HORSES MAKE A LANDSCAPE LOOK MORE BEAUTIFUL

Horses Make a Landscape Look More Beautiful took its title from words of Lame Deer, an Indian seer who contemplated the gifts of the white man—chiefly whiskey and horses—and found the beauty of horses almost made her forget the whiskey. This thought establishes the tone of the collection. These are movement poems, but as always, they remain intensely personal and frequently elegiac. The poet seems herself to speak:

> I am the woman
> with the blessed
> dark skin
> I am the woman
> with teeth repaired
> I am the woman
> with the healing eye
> the ear that hears.

There is also lamentation for lost love:

> When I no longer have your heart
> I will not request your body
> your presence
> or even your polite conversation.
> I will go away to a far country
> separated from you by the sea
> —on which I cannot walk—
> and refrain even from sending
> letters
> describing my pain.

HER BLUE BODY EVERYTHING WE KNOW

Her Blue Body Everything We Know contains a selection of poems written between 1965 and 1990, along with a few new verses and revealing commentary. This collection includes poems from *Once*; *Revolutionary Petunias, and Other Poems*; *Good Night, Willie Lee, I'll See You in the Morning*; and *Horses Make a Landscape Look More Beautiful*. Walker provides readers with insights on the art of poetry (in poems such as "How Poems Are Made: A Discredited View" and "I Said to Poetry"). In her introduction to the final section of the collection, Walker relates how she once felt jealous of how musicians connect with their work and seem to be one with it, but that during career as a writer, she has learned that poets share a similar relationship with their poetry. Walker, a woman of passion, shows how her personal beliefs about Africa (in the first section of this collection, "African Images: Glimpses from a Tiger's Back"), multiracial relationships (in the poem "Johann"), and the pangs of love (in poems such as "Did This Happen to Your Mother? Did Your Sister Throw Up a Lot?") are intricately intertwined and evident in her poetic creations.

Walker calls the final section "We Have a Beautiful Mother: Previously Uncollected Poems." The poems in this section, including "Some Things I Like About My Triple Bloods," "If There Was Any Justice," "We Have a Map of the World," and "Telling," are deeply personal and challenge readers to think about boundaries between cultures, countries, and hearts.

ABSOLUTE TRUST IN THE GOODNESS OF THE EARTH

In the preface to *Absolute Trust in the Goodness of the Earth*, Walker confides that she thought that she had reached the end of her career as a poet and was at peace with this, but after the terrorist attacks of September, 11, 2001, on the United States, Walker found herself writing poems regularly. After the attacks, Walker feared imminent war, and her poems in this book reflect that anxiety, including pieces such as "Thousands of Feet Below You," "Not Children," and "Why War Is Never a Good Idea." The narrator of "Thousands of Feet Below You" mentions a boy, running away from the bombs of war, who eventually is shredded to pieces in a violent explosion. Walker shares similar feelings about the concept of war in "Not Children," in which she refers to war as a cowardly act and an event that the world can do without. The title of "Why War Is Never a Good Idea" is self-explanatory, the subtitle of which ("A Picture Poem for Children Blinded by War") emphasizes Walker's stance on the issue.

Walker also continuously challenges readers to think about race relations in the United States, and how they might be improved. For example, "Patriot" encourages readers to respect all Americans, no matter what their country of origin is (she mentions Middle Eastern men, American Indian men, and African women, in particular), because these people all combine to make and define the United States. "Projection" encourages readers to look beyond the stereotypes associated with certain ethnicities (such as Indians, Germans, and Arabs) and remember that, inside each person, exists an innocent child.

In the preface to *Absolute Trust in the Goodness of the Earth*, Walker also shares her interest in and admiration for the environment and plants in particular. These feelings about the natural world are represented clearly in the title of this collection, which praises the earth for its beauty and righteousness. Walker, like many writers, associates nature with an inherent sense of peace. Natural imagery abounds in this collection, appearing in poems such as "Even When I Walked Away," "Red Petals Sticking Out," "Inside My Rooms," and "The Tree." Walker's plant and flower images remind readers of her belief that humankind is deeply rooted in and connected to the earth.

A POEM TRAVELED DOWN MY ARM

In the introduction to *A Poem Traveled Down My Arm*, Walker explains that her publisher sent her blank pages to autograph; these pages would later be bound into copies of *Absolute Trust in the Goodness of the Earth* to save Walker time at forthcoming book signings. Tired of signing her own name so many times, Walker says that she suddenly started drawing little sketches on the pieces of paper. Soon, she was scrambling to keep up with writing down poems that sprang to mind, inspired by the images she had drawn. Walker feels this collection is strange when compared with her others, especially because she thought she was done writing poetry a few years earlier. Instead, she published two collections of poetry in a single year.

The poems in *A Poem Traveled Down My Arm* typically hover around ten words each. These succinct poetic creations address topics prevalent in the rest of Walker's canon, including love, peace, nature, and war. The untitled poems function almost like a series of proverbs, offering her readers advice about living a healthy spiritual life while respecting Earth and all of humanity.

OTHER MAJOR WORKS

LONG FICTION: *The Third Life of Grange Copeland*, 1970; *Meridian*, 1976; *The Color Purple*, 1982; *The Temple of My Familiar*, 1989; *Possessing the Secret of Joy*, 1992; *By the Light of My Father's Smile*, 1998; *Now Is the Time to Open Your Heart*, 2004.

SHORT FICTION: *In Love and Trouble: Stories of Black Women*, 1973; *You Can't Keep a Good Woman Down*, 1981; *The Complete Stories*, 1994; *Alice Walker Banned*, 1996 (stories and commentary).

NONFICTION: *In Search of Our Mothers' Gardens: Womanist Prose*, 1983; *Living by the Word: Selected Writings, 1973-1987*, 1988; *Warrior Marks: Female Genital Mutilation and the Sexual Blinding of Women*, 1993 (with Pratibha Parmar); *The Same River Twice: Honoring the Difficult*, 1996; *Anything We Love Can Be Saved: A Writer's Activism*, 1997; *The Way Forward Is with a Broken Heart*, 2000; *Sent by Earth: A Message from the Grandmother Spirit After the Attacks on the World Trade Center and Pentagon*, 2001; *We Are the Ones We Have Been Waiting For: Light in a Time of Darkness*, 2006; *The World Has Changed: Conversations with Alice Walker*, 2010 (Rudolph P. Byrd, editor).

CHILDREN'S LITERATURE: *Langston Hughes: American Poet*, 1974; *To Hell with Dying*, 1988; *Finding the Green Stone*, 1991; *There Is a Flower at the Tip of My Nose Smelling Me*, 2006; *Why War Is Never a Good Idea*, 2007.

EDITED TEXT: *I Love Myself When I Am Laughing . . . and Then Again When I Am Looking Mean and Impressive: A Zora Neale Hurston Reader*, 1979.

BIBLIOGRAPHY

Bates, Gerri. *Alice Walker: A Critical Companion*. Westport, Conn.: Greenwood Press, 2005. A well-crafted biography that discusses Walker's major works, tracing the themes of her novels to her life.

Bloom, Harold, ed. *Alice Walker*. New York: Chelsea House, 1989. An important collection of critical essays examining the fiction, poetry, and essays of Walker from a variety of perspectives. The fourteen essays, including Bloom's brief introduction, are arranged chronologically. Contains useful discussions of her first three novels, brief analyses of individual short stories, poems, and essays, and assessments of Walker's social and political views in connection with her works and other African American female authors. Chronology and bibliography.

Bloxham, Laura J. "Alice (Malsenior) Walker." In *Contemporary Fiction Writers of the South*, edited by Joseph M. Flora and Robert Bain. Westport, Conn.: Greenwood Press, 1993. A general introduction to Walker's "womanist" themes of oppression of black women and change through affirmation of self. Provides a brief summary and critique of previous criticism of Walker's work.

Gates, Henry Louis, Jr., and K. A. Appiah, eds. *Alice*

Walker: Critical Perspectives Past and Present. New York: Amistad, 1993. Contains reviews of Walker's first five novels and critical analyses of several of her works of short and long fiction. Also includes two interviews with Walker, a chronology of her works, and an extensive bibliography of essays and texts.

Gentry, Tony. *Alice Walker.* New York: Chelsea House, 1993. Examines the life and work of Walker. Includes bibliographical references and index.

Lauret, Maria. *Alice Walker.* New York: St. Martin's Press, 2000. Provocative discussions of Walker's ideas on politics, race, feminism, and literary theory. Of special interest is the exploration of Walker's literary debt to Zora Neale Hurston, Virginia Woolf, and even Bessie Smith.

Simcikova, Karla. *To Live Fully, Here and Now: The Healing Vision in the Works of Alice Walker.* Lanham, Md.: Lexington Books, 2007. Simcikova focuses on Walker's spirituality, her relationship with nature, and how these beliefs and connections present themselves in her oeuvre of work.

Smith, Lindsey Claire. "Alice Walker's Eco-'Warriors.'" In *Indians, Environment, and Identity on the Borders of American Literature: From Faulkner and Morrison to Walker and Silko.* New York: Palgrave Macmillan, 2008. Smith analyzes boundaries delineating cultural, geographical, and racial differences in Walker's canon.

Walker, Rebecca. *Black, White, and Jewish: Autobiography of a Shifting Self.* New York: Riverhead, 2001. A self-indulgent but nevertheless insightful memoir by Alice Walker's daughter, Rebecca Walker. She describes herself as "a movement child," growing up torn between two families, two races, and two traditions, always in the shadow of an increasingly famous and absorbed mother.

White, Evelyn C. *Alice Walker: A Life.* New York: Norton, 2004. The life and accomplishments of Walker are chronicled in this biography through interviews with Walker, her family, and friends.

Allene Phy-Olsen
Updated by Karley K. Adney

MARGARET WALKER

Born: Birmingham, Alabama; July 7, 1915
Died: Chicago, Illinois; November 30, 1998
Also known as: Margaret Walker Alexander

PRINCIPAL POETRY

For My People, 1942
The Ballad of the Free, 1966
Prophets for a New Day, 1970
October Journey, 1973
For Farish Street Green, 1986
This Is My Century: New and Collected Poems,
   1989

OTHER LITERARY FORMS

Margaret Walker's nonfiction publications included a biography of Richard Wright (1908-1960), several volumes of critical essays, and a collection of her talks with the poet and activist Nikki Giovanni. The posthumous work *Conversations with Margaret Walker* (2002) contains much of the material that would have been in a projected autobiography. Walker's literary reputation, however, rests primarily on her poetry and on her novel *Jubilee* (1966).

ACHIEVEMENTS

When *For My People* was selected for the Yale Series of Younger Poets in 1942, Margaret Walker became the first African American woman to be awarded a national prize for a poetry collection. In 1966, Walker received a Houghton Mifflin literary award for *Jubilee,* which became a best seller and served as a model for later historical fiction by black writers. Walker's novel was especially influential in drawing attention to the strength and heroism of African American women. In her later years, Walker was honored for her many achievements as a writer, a teacher, and an activist. Among the awards presented to her were a Langston Hughes Award (1983), Senior Fellowship from the National Endowment for the Humanities for Lifetime Achievement and Contributions to American Literature (1991), a Lifetime Achievement Award from the College Language Association (1992), and a Lifetime

Achievement Award from the Before Columbus Foundation (1993). In 1995, the Margaret Walker Alexander National Research Center for the Study of Twentieth Century African Americans, which Walker had established in 1968 at Jackson State University, held a weeklong celebration in her honor, and in October, 1998, Walker was inducted into the African American Literary Hall of Fame at the Gwendolyn Brooks Writers' Conference.

BIOGRAPHY

Margaret Abigail Walker was born in Birmingham, Alabama, on July 7, 1915. She was the first of four children of the Reverend Sigismund Constantine Walker, a Methodist minister originally from Jamaica, and Marion Dozier Walker, a musician and teacher. From her scholarly father, Margaret acquired her love of reading, while her mother helped her to develop a sensitivity to the rhythms of music and of poetry. After Margaret's birth, Marion's mother, Elvira Ware Dozier, moved in with the family; it was from her that Margaret heard the family stories that she later incorporated into *Jubilee.*

In 1920, the Walkers moved to Meridian, Mississippi, and enrolled Margaret in first grade. Five years later, the family moved to New Orleans. After graduating from Gilbert Academy in 1930, Margaret enrolled in New Orleans University (now Dillard University), but two years later, she transferred to Northwestern University. In 1934, she published her first poem in W. E. B. Du Bois's magazine *The Crisis.* In a creative writing class her senior year, Margaret wrote the first draft of *Jubilee.* In August, 1935, she received a B.A. in English, and the following March, she began working for the Federal Writers Project of the Works Progress Administration. Soon afterward, she joined the (Chicago) South Side Writers Group. During this period, Walker met many writers who would become famous, among them Richard Wright, whom she befriended. In 1937, Walker's poem "For My People" was published in *Poetry.*

In 1939, Walker enrolled in the University of Iowa Writers' Workshop, where she completed her collection *For My People.* She received an M.A. in 1940, then taught briefly at Livingstone College in Salisbury,

Margaret Walker (Courtesy, Chicago Public Library)

North Carolina, and at West Virginia State College. On June 13, 1943, she married Firnist James Alexander. They had four children.

In 1949, Walker joined the English department at Jackson State College (now Jackson State University) in Mississippi. She would remain on the faculty until her retirement in 1979. In 1962, however, she took a two-year leave so that she could enter a doctoral program at the University of Iowa. After submitting the completed manuscript of *Jubilee* as her dissertation, in June, 1965, she was awarded a Ph.D.

Throughout her life, Walker was plagued by ill health, and her later years were further darkened by the failure of a lawsuit charging Alex Haley with plagiarism; by the death of her husband in 1980; and by a long conflict with the widow of Wright, which was finally resolved in 1988. However, Walker continued to publish significant works, but also was honored by groups all over the United States. Her happiest times, however, were those spent with her children and her grandchildren. In June, 1998, she was diagnosed with cancer, and she moved to Chicago so that her oldest daughter could care for her. Walker died there on November 30. On December 4, she was buried in Jackson, Mississippi.

ANALYSIS

As the title *For My People* suggests, Margaret Walker always thought of herself as the voice of those who did not have a voice of their own. In *Jubilee*, she told the stories of her own forebears; in her poetry, however, Walker spoke for all African Americans, the real heroes and the legendary ones, winners and losers, men and women, adults and children. As a poet, Walker cast herself as a prophet or an oracle, connecting with her audience not by logic but through their emotions. She often relied on the techniques used so effectively by African American preachers, including ritualistic repetition or the call-and-response format. Sometimes she used the kind of elevated language one would expect to hear in a sermon; at other times, however, she adopted the slangy, succinct vernacular. Walker exhibited the same versatility in her use of poetic forms. Often she wrote in verse paragraphs or in free verse loosely tied together by rhythm or repetition. For a folk story or folk characters, however, she would select a ballad form, and for formal expressions of sentiment, Walker turned to the traditional sonnet.

Though as a member of her generation, it was inevitable that much of her poetry would be cast as a protest against racism, Walker also crusaded against two other kinds of evil. One of them was fascism, the political impulse that she believed leads to war and economic ruin, and the other was sexism, the contempt for women that results in their being denied freedom and fulfillment. However, like the biblical prophets to whom she often refers, Walker had faith in the power of good to overcome evil. In the beauty of nature, especially as represented in the landscape of her native South, she saw the possibility of a new Eden, cleansed of evil, where people would live in peace and freedom.

FOR MY PEOPLE

In her first book-length collection of poems, *For My People*, Walker displayed the command of language and of poetic forms that would make her one of the most admired poets of her time. Her versatility is evi-

dent in the marked differences between the three sections of the book. The book begins with the title poem, written in verse paragraphs that roll along majestically, in a manner reminiscent of the nineteenth century American poet Walt Whitman. Like Whitman, Walker is both a realist and an optimist. Though in "For My People" she catalogues the miseries of her race, she concludes the poem by calling for her people to rise up and fight for freedom. In the five poems that follow, Walker uses the same poetic form and the same high level of language. In "We Have Been Believers," she lashes out against the gods on whom her people have too long depended, and again she calls for an uprising. "Dark Blood," "Southern Song," "Sorrow Home," and "Delta" share a theme to which Walker would return throughout her life: her love for the South and her longing for it to be redeemed. After three short free-verse poems, all written in formal language, Walker concludes the section with "Today," which is meant as a wake-up call for white northerners, unaware of the struggles of her people.

The second section of *For My People* is different from the first in almost every respect. It consists of ten ballads, all written with the economy of language one expects from that form, and all loaded with colloquialisms, dialectical misspellings, and sly, folk humor. Each of the poems is a character sketch. Big John Henry and Bad-Man Stagolee are both legendary characters. However, Big John Henry was admired as the Delta equivalent of Samson, while Stagolee was a fabled cop-killer whose claim to fame was that he never got caught. There is abundant vigor but not much virtue in most of Walker's other characters. Molly Means is a witch, Poppa Chicken, a pimp, and though Walker explains sympathetically why Kissie Lee turned bad, she is still a girl that everyone fears. Three of the characters, Yalluh Hammuh, Two-Gun Buster, and Teacher, get just what they deserve, and so does Long John, for after her death, Long John regrets being unfaithful to his Sweetie Pie. Though Gus, the lineman, broke no laws, folk wisdom always points out that it is dangerous to boast about being immune to death.

The final section of the book consists of six fourteen-line poems that are sonnetlike in structure, though they veer away from a conventional rhyme scheme and sometimes avoid rhyme altogether. As in the first section, the language is formal, but the tone of the poems is contemplative.

PROPHETS FOR A NEW DAY

When *For My People* was written, the battle for civil rights was still in its infancy. By the time *Prophets for a New Day* appeared twenty-eight years later, victory was in sight. Therefore this slim volume can be read as a history of the Civil Rights movement; in fact, only two poems, "Ballad of the Hoppy-Toad" and "Elegy" do not deal with that subject. Most of the poems are written in free verse. Though they do not have the sweeping rhythms of the poems in the first section of "For My People," they are just as powerful. One reason they are so effective is that they deal with real events and real heroes and heroines. Some of them are nameless, for example, the young girl so eager to participate in "Street Demonstration" and the one in "Girl Held Without Bail," who is so proud of being imprisoned for her convictions. Many of the poems, however, pay tribute to real heroes, such as the three civil rights workers who were murdered in Mississippi, memorialized in the poem "For Andy Goodman—Michael Schwerner—and James Chaney." The fact that over the years Walker abandoned her Marxist loathing of religion and became committed to Christianity is evident in her equating civil rights leaders with biblical prophets, for example, casting Benjamin Mays as Jeremiah, Martin Luther King, Jr., as Amos, Whitney Young as Isaiah, and Medgar Evers as Micah. Though Walker herself would continue to voice her convictions with prophetic fury, she now could draw strength from her belief that God favored the cause of freedom.

OTHER MAJOR WORKS

LONG FICTION: *Jubilee*, 1966.

NONFICTION: *How I Wrote "Jubilee,"* 1972; *A Poetic Equation: Conversations Between Nikki Giovanni and Margaret Walker*, 1974; *Richard Wright: Daemonic Genius*, 1988; *How I Wrote "Jubilee," and Other Essays on Life and Literature*, 1990; *God Touched My Life: The Inspiring Autobiography of the Nun Who Brought Song, Celebration, and Soul to the World*, 1992; *On Being Female, Black, and Free: Essays by Margaret Walker, 1932-1992*, 1997 (Mary-

emma Graham, editor); *Conversations with Margaret Walker*, 2002 (Graham, editor).

MISCELLANEOUS: *Margaret Walker's "For My People": A Tribute*, 1992.

BIBLIOGRAPHY

Baraka, Amiri. "Margaret Walker Alexander." *The Nation* 26, no. 1 (January 4, 1999): 32-33. A tribute to Walker, delivered at New York University after her death, in which she is lauded for using the rhythms of African American sermons in prose and poetry that reflect her faith in the future.

Barksdale, Richard K. "Margaret Walker: Folk Orature and Historical Prophecy." In *Black American Poets Between Worlds, 1940-1960*, edited by R. Baxter Miller. Knoxville: University of Tennessee Press, 1986. Shows how Walker's language and her subject matter reflect both the influence of African American folk traditions and of biblical prophecy.

Berke, Nancy. *Women Poets on the Left: Lola Ridge, Genevieve Taggard, Margaret Walker*. Gainesville: University Press of Florida, 2001. Places three radical women writers of the first half of the twentieth century within a historical and social context. In Walker's case, focuses on the experiences in Chicago that inspired her to write *For My People*. Bibliography and index.

Graham, Maryemma, ed. *Fields Watered with Blood: Critical Essays on Margaret Walker*. Athens: University of Georgia Press, 2001. Scholarly essays are divided into three sections, one emphasizing Walker's life and her intellectual development, another focusing on her poetry, and the final one devoted to her novel *Jubilee*. Includes an insightful introduction, chronology, bibliography, and index.

Walker, Margaret. *Conversations with Margaret Walker*. Edited by Maryemma Graham. Jackson: University Press of Mississippi, 2002. A collection of interviews, in which Walker discusses topics ranging from her experiences as a mother and her own family history to race relations and African American culture. Includes the 1972 dialogue between Walker and her fellow poet Nikki Giovanni. Bibliographical references and index.

_____. *On Being Female, Black, and Free: Essays by*

Margaret Walker, 1932-1992. Edited by Maryemma Graham. Knoxville: University of Tennessee Press, 1997. Essays range from reflections on her experiences as a black feminist and a political activist to her relationships with other writers, among them, Zora Neale Hurston, Eudora Welty, and Richard Wright.

Rosemary M. Canfield Reisman

RONALD WALLACE

Born: Cedar Rapids, Iowa; February 18, 1945

PRINCIPAL POETRY

Plums, Stones, Kisses, and Hooks, 1981
Tunes for Bears to Dance To, 1983
People and Dog in the Sun, 1987
The Makings of Happiness, 1991
Time's Fancy, 1994
The Uses of Adversity, 1998
Long for This World: New and Selected Poems,
   2003
For a Limited Time Only, 2008

OTHER LITERARY FORMS

Ronald Wallace has published short fiction, books of literary criticism, and scholarly articles and reviews in a number of journals. In 1989, he edited a poetry anthology, *Vital Signs: Contemporary American Poetry from the University Presses*.

ACHIEVEMENTS

Ronald Wallace's writing has garnered many honors, including several poetry awards from the Council for Wisconsin Writers. A book of short stories won the Mid-List Press First Fiction Award. He has received a creative writing fellowship and three creative writing grants from the Wisconsin Arts Board. He also won a Distinguished Teaching Award from the University of Wisconsin, Madison. His *For a Limited Time Only* won the 2008 Posner Book-Length Poetry Award and the 2009 Wisconsin Library Association Outstanding Achievement in Poetry Award.

BIOGRAPHY

Ronald William Wallace grew up in St. Louis, Missouri. A voracious reader in grade school, his interest in writing began in fifth grade, when he started to keep a diary. He became interested in poetry in ninth grade when a weary teacher attempted to entertain her class by giving students poems to read. Reading Emily Dickinson, Wallace says he was moved though he did not understand the poems, nor did he think his friends would appreciate his newfound interest. After reading Dickinson, he said, "I wrote poetry in secret, I read poetry in secret, and I dreamed of one day being a real poet and writer."

At the College of Wooster, Wallace enrolled in premedicine studies but found he liked only the English courses. After a breakup with a girlfriend, Wallace dealt with the pain by writing poetry and ultimately decided that he would become a poet.

After earning his Ph.D. but feeling uncommitted to teaching, Wallace and his wife spent a year in Europe, where he wrote poems, some of which appeared in his first book, *Plums, Stones, Kisses, and Hooks*, a work rejected by ninety-nine publishers before being accepted. He then published additional books of poetry, a number of chapbooks, works of literary criticism, and short stories. He once said that he was most interested in poets "who embrace the personal, the simple, the clear, the straightforward, the accessible. Many of these poets are exploring traditional forms and humor as a way of renewing poetry and possibly reaching a larger audience." The statement aptly describes Wallace's poetry as well.

Hired at the University of Wisconsin, Madison, for a one-year position, Wallace established himself there, founding *Madison Review* and building the creative writing program to six staff members and six fellows teaching in one of the few postgraduate fine arts programs in the United States. He became director of creative writing at Madison, director of the Wisconsin Institute for Creative Writing, and poetry editor for the University of Wisconsin Press.

ANALYSIS

Ronald Wallace writes with great clarity about common, everyday subjects: relationships with his family, including his memories of an ambivalent relationship with his father, who suffered from multiple sclerosis; nature and things bucolic, especially life on his farm and his observations of animals; food; and people he has known. The poems have a confessional quality to them. Reviewers have used the word "honest" to refer to his voice and "moving" to describe the effect of the poems, which are characterized by an openness and willingness to reflect on aspects of life that are not always pleasant. Linda Falkenstein points out that every one of Wallace's collections has contained a poem about worry; it is also the title of one of his chapbooks of fiction.

Contrasting himself with the Language poets, Wallace admires "clear accessible language, the sense that you're hearing what the poet really does think and believe and has done or seen or experienced." Two additional characteristics of Wallace's work that reflect trends in contemporary American poetry are an interest in traditional forms and the use of humor.

Besides his books of poetry, Wallace has published more than five hundred poems in magazines and anthologies. His later work uses closed forms extensively. Having grown up believing free verse to be "the only form of poetry worth writing," Wallace says he never expected to be considered a New Formalist. Although closed-form poems appear in some of his earlier collections, *Time's Fancy* includes many more.

PLUMS, STONES, KISSES, AND HOOKS

Wallace's first book introduces the topics of family and nature, which are the mainstay for much of his work. Several poems focus on his father and children, and in some of the poems, Wallace writes from others' points of view, such as his father, his daughter, a bullhead, a cat, a hippopotamus, and a medicine man.

"Oranges" is characteristic of how Wallace develops metaphor. The poem begins with the eating of an orange. Then,

> I walk across the lake.
> Ice fishermen twitch their poles until
> perch flicker the surface, quick
> and bright as orange slices.
> The sun ripens in the sky.
> The wind turns thin and citrus,
> the day precise, fragile.

The orange in the poem acts as both tenor and vehicle. For the reader, the poem creates the impression of unified experience, with the various characteristics of an orange becoming a means of apprehending other things. Such description represents experience in a fresh way and "makes it new," in the words of Ezra Pound and the style of the Imagist poets.

In "Oranges" and in other poems, Wallace uses nature not so much as an end in itself but rather as a means to reflect on the human. In "Prayer for Flowers," the qualities that help plants thrive become goals for successful human life: "Show me the disguises of coral root/ that I may go unnoticed among enemies,/ the tenacity of columbine/ that I might thrive in the unlikely place."

While there is little rhyme or formal verse, the sound of the language, through assonance, consonance, and alliteration, sometimes rises to music, as in these lines from "Cleaning House": "You feel this September enter your head/ to sweep up the clutter of summer:/ its tractors and grackles, its harvests and roots,/ its skies stuffed with sunshine and pollen."

TUNES FOR BEARS TO DANCE TO

In terms of his personal relationships, the poems are revealing and not always complimentary to Wallace himself. In "Picture of Two Bugs, Hugging," he describes the situation of a daughter believed to be disabled: "At six months, white, unlovely as a slug,/ the doctors clucking their tongues: *Microcephalic*." Later in the poem he describes his feelings: "How I wanted/ to swat you away, smash those cries/ against wall or ceiling, take you by your/ furry legs, and pin you, sprawling, down."

The passage above includes the characteristic extended-type metaphor. "Wild Strawberries" too uses nature metaphorically to examine relationships, as Wallace writes about picking strawberries with his wife. The poem reflects on the challenge of marriage and, along with others, points out the fragility of human relationships.

The poems are not all solemn, however; Wallace shows his sense of humor in a number of them, sometimes mocking himself. In "The Assistant Professor's Nightmare," Wallace the professor is impressed with his lecturing ability ("all the pencils nodding their heads/ in astonishment") until the shaking head of a teaching assistant rattles him: "Suddenly confidence/ slips out of my voice, sits down/ in the front row, snoring." "In a Pig's Eye" satirizes political correctness. "You Can't Write a Poem About McDonald's" proves the statement is not true. "The Facts of Life" describes parents explaining sex to their six-year-old. Like his earlier book, *Tunes for Bears to Dance To* uses much free verse, though it also contains sestinas and sonnets.

PEOPLE AND DOG IN THE SUN

Falkenstein writes, "Wallace sees the upside constantly balanced by the downside." Her statement describes well the poems in this book, which again are a mixture of open and closed forms and which include the familiar topics of Wallace's father and the farm. The poems about the farm celebrate nature and the simple grandeur of living things, but that tone is in contrast to the poems about Wallace's father. The opening poem refers to the American ideal of changing one's life by moving to the country, but clearly Wallace's old farm is no utopian world, "the pastures gone to boulders and weeds,/ a fury of dandelions and wild mustard." Indeed, in "The Cinematics of Loss," written in third person, the farm becomes an imagined place of loneliness and isolation.

In the background of many of these poems is an awareness of the passage of time and of loss. In "Assembling," Wallace struggles to assemble a piece of equipment, thinking, "And now, here at the flanged end/ of late middle age, I find myself/ rattled by the simplest instructions."

In the sestina "The Poet, Graveside," Wallace reminds himself "Soon enough, we'll all be nothing more/ than figures in some unforgotten poem/ (if we're lucky). *God, don't let us be/ cut off, incomplete, like a sestina, ending here.*" In "Poppies," a poem that combines the painting of Georgia O'Keeffe and the loss of his father, Wallace writes about the dissolution of the intensity of grief itself as a kind of loss. However, the awareness of time passed does not preclude a happier tone. "Matheny" and "Thirteen" portray affectionate memories of adolescence. "Softball," another sestina, shows Wallace wondering if he is too old to play the game but ends with him hitting the ball "over the field-

ers' heads and the field,/ smaller and smaller until it's nothing like a ball." In the title poem, he muses on the situation of old couples, aware they are close to death, "their names written on water," but as in "The Poet, Graveside" there is hope that perhaps art may somehow mitigate life's losses.

THE MAKINGS OF HAPPINESS

The tension between hope and pessimism continues in Wallace's fourth book, published in 1991. It is most evident in the contrast between the second and third sections of the collection, titled "Breakdown" and "The Makings of Happiness," respectively. The first section of this book of mostly open forms includes poems about family and Wallace's memories of his youth: basketball, sexual experience, smoking, and summer Bible camp.

"Breakdown" focuses on personal and social struggle: parental fears, awareness of impending death, violence, and war. In "Headlines," a car accident raises a question about the possibility of keeping children "safe inside the formal garden you've prepared/ for them." Two poems reflect on being forty years old. In "At Forty," death looms in consciousness. In "Turning Forty," the theme of memory, important in the first part of the book, also emerges. Time "spirals, silent, circling/ back on itself, an old dog, settling/ on the same tired spot again." The poem's suggestion that time is not progression so much as cycle anticipates a theme in Wallace's subsequent book, *Time's Fancy*. "The Hell Mural" (panels 1 and 2, the first a sestina, the second a villanelle) reflects on Hiroshima, Japan, and artists' portrayals of human suffering.

The third section offers a hopeful perspective. "Building an Outhouse" creates an analogy between the builder and the poet, humorously overturning the notion of time-as-ravager: "let the nub of your plain-spoken pencil prevail/ and it's up! Functional. Tight as a sonnet./ It will last forever (or at least for awhile)/ though the critics come sit on it, and sit on it." Hope is not always easy, however, but sometimes hard won through tribulation. In "Apple Cider," the harvest is carried out against a backdrop of remembered deaths: "Memory squeezes us dry/ beyond sweetness, beyond weeping." However, the poem ends by affirming life even as one is aware of the world's hostility. While the ties created by family bring with them pain or frustration, they also seem to provide the best solace, and Wallace celebrates kinship in "The Fat of the Land," about a family reunion.

TIME'S FANCY

This is a darker, more philosophical, and more abstract book than Wallace's others, and it uses more closed forms than the others as well, including Petrarchan and Shakespearean sonnets, canzones, ballades, and a pantoum. The title, from a passage by W. H. Auden, suggests time will have its way with humans. "Quick Bright Things" is a somewhat-Keatsian reflection on the change of seasons and, ultimately, on change itself. Wallace describes the "tenuous" beauty of late summer and reflects on the relationship between ephemeral beauty and the desire to prevent change: "Against the permanence/ of darkness and silence, we'll spin out/ a tenuous deliquescence. We'll sing."

Paradoxically, there is affirmation in the knowledge of death itself, since it involves an appreciation of beauty. In fact, many other poems in this volume imply an interdependence between opposites, or at minimum an attempt to understand the world as a cyclical interplay of dichotomies.

The theme receives humorous treatment in "Why I Am Not a Nudist," which explains how romantic love is nurtured by a glimpse rather than an open vista: "the still small pleasure/ of the withheld sweet familiar/ stays mysterious after all." Here pleasure, conventionally associated with possession, instead emerges from what is "withheld." In "Why God Permits Evil," Wallace states that without it, "who/ could know or choose the good?" While the poem is philosophical, it is not ponderous, because it is grounded in the humorous dilemma of a sixth-grader embarrassed by his lack of pubic hair.

Often, the poems' forms reinforce their themes and contain a "turn" or shift in tone or thought. This is a natural tendency in a form such as the sonnet but is used effectively in other poems as well.

THE USES OF ADVERSITY

Wallace explained the impetus for this collection of one hundred sonnets: "On May 31, 1994, it came to me that I should write a sonnet a day for a year." Writing in such a form allows him to "tap" into the "great energy"

of the tradition, and it also serves the more practical function of encouraging composition. He stated, "formal verse helps *generate* poems. Technique is discovery." The poems, covering topics from childhood to adulthood, are variations on the sonnet, sometimes with a strict rhyme scheme, sometimes without, sometimes following the Petrarchan, sometimes the Shakespearean form, sometimes combining both. Jay Rogoff observes that the poems in the book reveal a deliberate progression to "a moving ritual defense against darkness."

FOR A LIMITED TIME ONLY

Wallace has described *For a Limited Time Only* as his most meditative work, a collection of poems that focuses, mostly, on illness, aging, and mortality, and that is told through a character called Mr. Grim. Mr. Grim is, according to Wallace, "angry, self-pitying, gruff, comic, self-deprecating, nostalgic, and defeated," yet "hopeful" about "the human condition." This collection does evoke human misery, but it also thrives on the wonder of human experience.

OTHER MAJOR WORKS

SHORT FICTION: *Quick Bright Things: Stories*, 2000.

NONFICTION: *Henry James and the Comic Form*, 1975; *The Last Laugh: Form and Affirmation in the Contemporary American Comic Novel*, 1979; *God Be with the Clown: Humor in American Poetry*, 1984.

EDITED TEXT: *Vital Signs: Contemporary American Poetry from the University Presses*, 1989.

BIBLIOGRAPHY

Falkenstein, Linda. "The Hero of Ron Wallace's New Fiction Looks a Lot Like the Author Himself: Or Does He?" *Isthmus* (February 25, 1995). This article focuses mainly on the short-story collection *Quick Bright Things* but includes biographical information and Wallace's thoughts about writing in general.

Wallace, Ronald. "'He Is Mad Which Makes Two': A Sonnet Project." *AWP Chronicle* 30, no. 1 (1997). This article details the writing of *The Uses of Adversity*. In it, Wallace explains how he came to write the book, as well as his ideas about poetic form.

_____. "'To Tell One's Name': The Audience for

Poetry." *Wisconsin Academy Review* (Summer, 1996): 9-13. This essay contains biographical information and an overview of trends in contemporary American poetry.

Steven R. Luebke

ROBERT PENN WARREN

Born: Guthrie, Kentucky; April 24, 1905
Died: West Wardsboro, near Stratton, Vermont;
  September 15, 1989

PRINCIPAL POETRY

Thirty-six Poems, 1935
Eleven Poems on the Same Theme, 1942
Selected Poems, 1923-1943, 1944
Brother to Dragons: A Tale in Verse and Voices,
  1953
Promises: Poems, 1954-1956, 1957
You, Emperors, and Others: Poems, 1957-1960,
  1960
Selected Poems: New and Old, 1923-1966, 1966
Incarnations: Poems, 1966-1968, 1968
Audubon: A Vision, 1969
Or Else—Poem/Poems, 1968-1974, 1974
Selected Poems: 1923-1975, 1976
Now and Then: Poems, 1976-1978, 1978
Brother to Dragons: A New Version, 1979
Ballad of a Sweet Dream of Peace, 1980 (with Bill
  Komodore)
Being Here: Poetry 1977-1980, 1980
Rumor Verified: Poems, 1979-1980, 1981
Chief Joseph of the Nez Percé, 1983
New and Selected Poems, 1923-1985, 1985
The Collected Poems of Robert Penn Warren, 1998
  (John Burt, editor)

OTHER LITERARY FORMS

In an era when poets were often as renowned and influential as critics, Robert Penn Warren nevertheless stands out inasmuch as he achieved success on two creative fronts, having as great a critical reputation as a novelist as he had as a poet. This accomplishment is not limited to the production of one singular work or of a sporadic body of work; rather it is a sustained record of development and achievement spanning more than three decades. His fiction includes the novels *Night Rider* (1939), *At Heaven's Gate* (1943), *All the King's Men* (1946), *World Enough and Time: A Romantic Novel* (1950), *Band of Angels* (1955), *The Cave* (1959), *Wilderness: A Tale of the Civil War* (1961), and *Flood: A Romance of Our Time* (1964), and there is also a short-story collection, *The Circus in the Attic, and Other Stories* (1947). There can be no doubt that *All the King's Men*, a highly fictionalized and richly wrought retelling of the rise and fall, by assassination, of the demagogic Louisiana governor Huey Long, has justifiably attained the status of an American classic; it is not only Warren's best novel but also his best-known work. The story of Willie Stark, the country-boy idealist who becomes far worse an exploiter of the public trust than the corrupt professional politicians he at first sets his heart and soul against, embodies many of Warren's most persistent themes, in particular the fumbling process self-definition becomes in a universe awry with irony and a world alive with betrayal and mendacity. Made into an Oscar-winning film, the novel was also very successfully adapted as a play by Warren in the 1950's.

Warren's considerable influence on the life of letters in twentieth century America was also exercised in a series of textbooks that he edited jointly with the noted critic Cleanth Brooks. The first, *An Approach to Literature* (1936), coedited as well by John Thibault Purser, was followed by *Understanding Poetry: An Anthology for College Students*, edited by Warren and Brooks, in 1938, and *Understanding Fiction*, also edited by Warren and Brooks, in 1943. These texts utilized the practices (just then being formulated) of New Criticism, which encouraged a close attention to the literary text as a self-contained, self-referring statement. It is certain that several generations of readers have had their entire attitude toward literature and literary interpretation determined by Warren and Brooks's effort, either directly or through the influence of teachers and critics whose values were shaped by these landmark works.

ACHIEVEMENTS

Robert Penn Warren was undoubtedly one of the most honored men of letters in American history. Among his numerous awards and honors were a Houghton-Mifflin Literary Fellowship (1936) for his first novel, *Night Rider*, the Levinson Prize from *Poetry* magazine (1936), Guggenheim Fellowships (1939-1940, 1947-1948), the Shelley Memorial Award (1943), the Pulitzer Prize in fiction (1947) for his novel *All the King's Men*, and Pulitzer Prizes in poetry for *Promises* and *Now and Then* (1958 and 1979, respectively). He also won a Union League Civic and Arts Poetry Prize (1953), the National Book Award in Poetry (1958) for *Promises*, the Bollingen Prize for Poetry (1967), the National Medal for Literature (1970), the Theodore Roethke Memorial Poetry Prize (1971) for *Incarnations*, the Copernicus Award (1976), the Presidential Medal of Freedom (1980), the Gold Medal from the American Academy of Arts and Letters (1985), the Frost Medal from the Poetry Society of America (1985), and the Ambassador Book Award (1999) for *The Collected Poems of Robert Penn Warren*. He was one of the first recipients of a genius grant, a Prize Fellowship from the MacArthur Foundation, in 1981. He served as consultant in poetry (poet laureate) to the Library of Congress from 1944 to 1945 and as poet laureate consultant in poetry from 1986 to 1987, when he resigned because of age and ill health. He became a member of the American Academy of Arts and Letters in 1950 and served as chancellor for the Academy of American Poets from 1972 to 1988.

BIOGRAPHY

Robert Penn Warren was born on April 24, 1905, amid the rolling hills of the tobacco country of southwestern Kentucky, in the town of Guthrie; he was the son of Robert Franklin Warren, a businessman, and Anna Ruth (Penn) Warren. He spent his boyhood there, and summers on his grandparents' farm in nearby Trigg County. Both grandfathers were Confederate veterans of the Civil War, and he was often regaled with firsthand accounts of battles and skirmishes with Union forces. The young Warren grew up wanting to be a sea captain, and after completing his secondary education in neighboring Clarksville, Tennessee, he did obtain an

appointment to the United States Naval Academy at Annapolis.

A serious eye injury prevented his attending, however, and in 1920, Warren matriculated instead at Vanderbilt University in Nashville, set on becoming an electrical engineer. In his freshman English class, Warren's interest took a fateful turn as the young professor John Crowe Ransom and an advanced student, Allen Tate, introduced him to the world of poetry. The two were at the center of a campus literary group called the Fugitives, and Warren began attending their meetings and soon was contributing to their bimonthly magazine, *The Fugitive*, which he edited in his senior year. Under the tutelage of Tate and Ransom, he became an intense student not only of earlier English poets, particularly the Elizabethans and such seventeenth century Metaphysical poets as John Donne and Andrew Marvell, but also of the contemporary schools that were emerging from the writings of older poets such as A. E.

Robert Penn Warren (©Washington Post/
Courtesy, D.C. Public Library)

Housman and Thomas Hardy, as well as from the work of William Butler Yeats and T. S. Eliot.

Warren graduated summa cum laude from Vanderbilt in 1925, taking a B.A. degree, and he continued his graduate studies at the University of California, Berkeley, from which he obtained an M.A. in 1927. He then enrolled in another year of graduate courses at Yale University and went on to spend two years as a Rhodes Scholar at the University of Oxford in England, which awarded him a B.Litt. degree in 1931.

While at Oxford, Warren completed his first published book, *John Brown: The Making of a Martyr* (1929), which took a rather callow, Southerner's view of the legendary hero of the abolitionist cause. When Paul Rosenberg, one of the editors of the *American Caravan* annual, invited him to submit a story, Warren "stumbled on" fiction writing, as he later recounted the incident. The result, "Prime Leaf," a story about labor troubles among tobacco growers back in his native Kentucky, would later find fuller expression in his first published novel, *Night Rider*.

Back in the United States, Warren joined the Agrarian movement, an informal confederation of many of his old Fugitive colleagues who were now espousing a return to agrarian, regional ideals in a Depression-ravaged America that was rapidly becoming more and more industrialized, urbanized, and, at least inasmuch as the images generated by popular culture were concerned, homogenized.

After teaching for a year as an assistant professor of English at Southwestern College in Memphis, he became, in 1931, an acting assistant professor of English at Vanderbilt. He remained there until 1934, when he moved on to accept a position at Louisiana State University in Baton Rouge. After promotion to associate professor in 1936, Warren took a full professorship at the University of Minnesota in 1942.

In 1935, while at Louisiana State, Warren had cofounded *Southern Review*, an influential journal with which he would remain until it folded in 1942. From 1938 to 1961, meanwhile, Warren served on the advisory board of another prestigious quarterly, *Kenyon Review*.

In 1930, Warren had married Emma Brescia, whom he divorced in 1951, shortly after accepting a position

as professor of playwriting at the School of Drama of Yale University. On December 7, 1952, Warren married the writer Eleanor Clark, with whom he would have two children, Rosanna, born in 1953, and Gabriel, born in 1955. Warren left his position with the drama school in 1956, but in 1961, he returned to New Haven, Connecticut, to rejoin the Yale faculty as a professor of English. From that time onward, he made his home in nearby Fairfield and summered in Stratton, Vermont.

Warren continued his distinguished career as a teacher, poet, novelist, critic, editor, and lecturer virtually to the end of his long life. In February, 1986, the Library of Congress named him the first official poet laureate consultant in poetry of the United States, a position he held until 1987. On September 15, 1989, the poet died at his summer home in West Wardsboro, near Stratton. He was eighty-four years old.

ANALYSIS

Robert Penn Warren was blessed twice over. He was a son of and grew up in a region of the country renowned for its love of the land and devotion to earthy folk wisdom and the art of storytelling. There was also a love of language, particularly the fustian spirit of the orator and the preacher, based on a deep, dark respect for the Word, orotund and oracular.

Added to that, however, Warren spent his formative years in a world that was making the transition from the comparative bucolic and optimistic sensibilities of the late nineteenth century to the frenzied, fearful, frenetic pace of the post-World War I 1920's. Poetry was being called into service by young people everywhere to try to explain what had happened, or at least give it manageable shape. T. S. Eliot's *The Waste Land* (1922) set the tone. At Vanderbilt among his fellow Fugitives, Warren was quickly put in touch with the new poetry that was emerging.

It is this combination of effects and influences that made Warren's poetry and gave it its vision. From the first, he hovered between the old and new—the mannered style, the modern flip; the natural scene, the symbolic backdrop; the open gesture, the hidden motive; Original Sin, the religion of humankind. This peculiar vantage point scored his vision, for it allowed him to know at first hand what his age was surrendering at the same time that it allowed him to question the motives for the surrender and the terms of the victory, the name of the enemy—or, better yet, his face.

Warren can bring the personal into the most profound metaphysical musings without blinking an eye or losing a beat, because finally the source of all vision, at least for Warren, is the darkest of selves at the heart of one's being, the unknown brother who shares not only one's bed but also one's body and makes, or so it seems, one's decisions. Self-discovery is Warren's trail, and the reader who follows it discovers that while it begins in coming to grips with the painful processes of caring in an uncaring world, it concludes in accepting caring as a moral obligation rather than merely a state of mind or soul. Like most twentieth century poets, Warren was really trying to reinvigorate the heroic ideal.

EARLY POEMS

The early poem "To a Face in a Crowd" echoes the world-weary angst typical of the period, the 1920's, by rendering an urban apocalypse in the bleak, stark terms of lonely souls lost in vacant vistas, finding their meager consolations in passing strangers who may—or may not—be spiritual kindred with similar dreams and like despairs. It is night, and adjectives and nouns collide in a litany of pessimism and negativism: "lascivious," "lust," "bitter," "woe," "dolorous," "dim," "shroud." This vision is mitigated, however, by the markedly poetic tone of the language: "Brother, my brother, whither do you pass?/ Unto what hill at dawn, unto what glen. . . . ?" While there is hope, the speaker seems to be saying that the idyllic interlude is no longer a viable option; instead, "we must meet/ As weary nomads in this desert at last,/ Borne in the lost procession of these feet."

Among these early poems, "The Return: An Elegy" is by far the most successful effort, for in it, Warren eschewed the derivative and imitative tone, mood, and theme of poems such as "To a Face in the Crowd" and found what time would prove to be the beginnings of his own voice and vision.

The setting is simple, though not at first easily discerned: in a Pullman as the train carries the speaker back home to the hills to attend his mother's funeral.

Sentiment is kept at bay, almost with a vengeance, it might seem: "give me the nickels off your eyes/ . . ./ then I could buy a pack of cigarettes." Only an occasional, italicized lapse into poeticized feeling—"*does my mother wake*"—among the details of the rugged mountain-country landscape that the speaker intersperses with his thoughts gives the sense that a profound emotional turmoil is seething beneath the modernist "flip": "Pines drip without motion/ The hairy boughs no longer shake/ Shaggy mist, crookbacked, ascends."

As the poem continues, however, the reader is gradually forced to realize that it is the tension between the speaker's grief and his desire not to sentimentalize his loss that gives the poetry its incredible and peculiarly modern motive power: "*the old fox is dead*/ what have I said." Thus, the speaker earns the right to lapse into the unabashed sentiment, at poem's end, of "this dark and swollen orchid of my sorrow."

This rare ability to combine the most enduring verbal expressions of human feelings with the most fleeting of contemporary realities and attitudes in a poetry that magically maintains its precarious balance between traditional poetic tone and style and the most ragged-edged and flippant of modern sensibilities continued to give Warren's work its own shape and direction as he expanded his range in the 1930's and 1940's. In "Pursuit," for example, his vision of the urban landscape has hardly improved, but it is peopled with three-dimensional emblems of a faltering, seeking humanity—"the hunchback on the corner," "that girl the other guests shun," "the little old lady in black." "Original Sin: A Short Story," meanwhile, places the reader in Omaha and the Harvard Yard and speaks of as cosmopolitan an image as "the abstract Jew," yet it ends its commentary on humanity's fated failings with country images of "the backyard and . . . an old horse cold in pasture."

So much is in keeping, of course, with the social and literary ideals that the original Fugitives formulated when they coalesced into the Agrarian movement. Their notion was that American democracy was not an urban but a rural phenomenon, forged by a link between the people and the land. In this regard, regionalism—the countryman's sense of place and of a devotion to his people—was not a pernicious thing but involved the very health of the nation, a health that the increasing pressures toward homogeneity of people and culture in sprawling urban centers could not only threaten but perhaps even destroy. Poets such as Warren became spokespersons both for that lost agrarian ideal and for the simple country folk forced by economic necessity into the anonymity of large cities, where they lived at the edge of squalor and struggled to maintain their small-town dignities.

Warren combines all these themes and concerns in "The Ballad of Billie Potts." As the speaker recounts the story of Big Billie, his wife, and their son, Little Billie, he mixes in long, parenthetical sections in which he seems to be addressing himself rather than the readers, urging himself to return—as if he could—to the lifestyles of those hillbillies "in the section between the rivers," where they were poor by urban standards but rich in spirit, in faith in themselves, and in the power of familial love. In the lost idyll mode reminiscent of William Wordsworth's "The Ruined Cottage" and "Michael," the story of Little Billie's travails and his parents' despair when circumstances force the boy to leave "his Pappy in Old Kaintuck/ And [head]Warren, Robert Penn West to try his luck" is really a twentieth century throwback's yearnings for what were simpler and certainly more communal times. For him now, there is only the endless urban tedium, the vacant, lonely sameness, maddeningly monotonous and vaguely threatening: "And the clock ticked all night long in the furnished room/ And would not stop/ And the *El*-train passed on the quarters with a whish like a terrible broom/ And would not stop."

Warren never ceased to contrast the earthiness of country values and country life with the mind-forged manacles that constrain the individual within the modern industrial landscape. At the heart of his vision, however, is a sense of the sad wasting of time and of love that mortality forces one constantly to consider. Clearly the problem is not "out there"; it is within us. The increasing urbanization of the United States is not the enemy, then, it is simply the latest battlefield—not the disease, but the symptom. The disease is life, and the ageless enemy is our insatiable need to try to make it make sense, to try to make it hurt less.

For Warren, then, one can hope only to keep oneself spiritually and emotionally—and painfully—alive in a world that tends undeniably toward death and decay. His villains become those who deny that life is hardship, as much as those who visit hardships on others. Behind the indictment, though, there is always the lance of forgiveness, aimed as much at the heart of the speaker who dreads the pain of his feelings as at the iniquities that arouse it.

As the poet himself became a father and middle-aged, children rather than the lonely crowd figured more and more as the best emblems of the tragic core of the human condition, as well as of the human capacity to endure and transcend. The poetry consequently finds its locus more and more in personal experience, the day to day providing sufficient grist for the poet's thinking and feeling mill.

PROMISES

"The Child Next Door," from the prizewinning volume *Promises*, focuses not on the child "who is defective because the mother," burdened with seven already, "took a pill," but on an older sister, who is twelve and "beautiful like a saint," and who takes care of "the monster all day":

I come, and her joy and triptych beauty and joy stir hate
—Is it hate?—in my heart. Fool, doesn't she know that the process
Is not that joyous or simple, to bless, or unbless,
The malfeasance of nature or the filth of fate?

Warren's unstinting, almost embarrassing honesty as he records his feelings and attitudes, an honesty exercised in his poetry from as early as "The Return," gains him an edge of intimate moral ambiguity in this more mature poetry. The present poem concludes: "I think of your goldness, of joy, how empires grind, stars are hurled,/ I smile stiff, saying *ciao*, saying *ciao*, and think: this is the world." Whether that is the expression of a bitter resignation or a casual dismissal or a measure of joyful acceptance, the speaker will give no clue: "this is the world." Readers are left to measure the sizes of their own hearts and thereby experience both the pain of observing life too closely and, if they wish, the expiation of letting it go.

By now a cosmopolitan himself, a Yale professor

with an Oxford degree and summer home in Vermont, the boy who is father to the man did not forget the Kentucky hill country source of his vision. In reminiscences such as "Country Burying (1919)," the autobiographical rather than symbolical and metaphysical seems to prevail, but there is still a telling tale. The poem is a requiem for all those lost "boy's afternoon[s]" when life was so present, even there amid tokens of death, and the mind more receptive, but the spirit would be somewhere else: "Why doesn't that fly stop buzzing—stop buzzing up there!" Apologies to Emily Dickinson aside, those were a boy's thoughts in 1919: In the poem, they are some measure of the adult's remorse as he reached mid-century. Now there is not only the pain of the present to endure, but there is the pain of the past, its loss, as well.

BROTHER TO DRAGONS

This sense of remorse was never absent from Warren's poetry, but now it is outspoken and unremitting, and it becomes a major motivating factor in the later poetry. *Brother to Dragons*, a historical novel in verse written in the form of a play that the author calls a poem, is the apex of all Warren's previous pessimism, displaying little of his often-whimsical capacity to turn heel but not turn coat on caring too much for the human condition. In the largest sense, the poem is a severe indictment of the human animal. With some liberties but no real distortion of the facts, it recounts the tale of Lilburn Clarke, a Kentuckian who in the early nineteenth century brutally murdered a black slave over a trifling offense. Beyond the tragic scope of those facts, there was an even more tragic rub in Warren's view: Clarke was the nephew of Thomas Jefferson, himself a paradoxical figure who could pen the Declaration of Independence and still be a slaveholder and who believed in the perfectibility of humankind.

Warren, who appears himself as a character in the poem by carrying on a pointed philosophical debate with Jefferson, used the bare bones of the story to call into question the worth, let alone the authenticity, of all human ideals. Still, in the lengthy monologue with which the poem concludes, he insists that despite this sorry record of human endeavor in the name of ideals that are always betrayed, "we must argue the necessity of virtue."

YOU, EMPERORS, AND OTHERS

By the time the 1950's ended, Warren had established a new métier as a social commentator with an equally self-accusatory eye. In *You, Emperors, and Others*, the public and the private, the man and the child, the father and the son all find expression. "Man in the Street," with its singsong rhythms and nursery-rhyme, chorus-like echoes, hits the gray flannel suits with their black knit ties and Brooks Brothers shirts not where they live but where they work, where each of them somehow makes accommodations with the vacuities of the corporate world. If it is a vision that virtually lends an air of nostalgic romance to an early poem such as "To a Face in the Crowd," "Mortmain" harks back to "The Return." It is the speaker's father who is dying now, but the irreverent flippancy of the earlier poem is not even there to be turned away from: "All things . . .// Were snatched from me, and I could not move,/ Naked in that black blast of his love." It is a poem in five parts, and in the last of those, "A Vision: Circa 1880," he imagines his father as a boy, "in patched britches and that idleness of boyhood/ Which asks nothing and is its own fulfillment." The poem ends with a turn to pure lyricism, without any reaching out to metaphysical solutions or conceits, merely the wholly verbal bounty of language giving life to dead time in images of a present, natural splendor.

POETRY THEMES

Warren published seven additional volumes of poetry from 1960 to 1980, and the lyrical mode itself intensified into the speculative tone that he apparently could not abandon. Still, as he reminds the reader in the 1968 volume, *Incarnations*, "You think I am speaking in riddles./ But I am not, for// The world means only itself" ("Riddle in the Garden"). In *Audubon*, meanwhile, he asks, "What is love," and reminds the reader that "one name for it is knowledge," as if attempting to justify his lifelong preoccupation with trying to understand human beings and their place on Earth and in the universe.

As the poet grew older, mortality became even more of an obsessive theme, and the issues of time past and time present, the poet now having a wealth of experience to draw upon, found even more expression in this new admixture of a metaphysical lyricism. In "Paradox," for example, from the "Can I See Arcturus from Where I Stand?" section of *Selected Poems: 1923-1975*, stargazer man is brought down to Earth, or at least to a sense of his limits, when he confronts a retelling of Zeno's paradox of the arrow and its unreachable goal. The natural simplicity and personal quality of the setting—a run on a beach that causes the speaker to recollect an earlier spirited chase—remove from the poem the bane of a *de profundis* that often intruded into Warren's most youthful metaphysical flights; the information is presented not as insight but as the sort of everyday truth any feeling, thinking person might draw from experience, should he or she care to. Indeed, the poem is finally a tender love lyric worthy, in its formal rhapsodic effect, of A. E. Housman:

> I saw, when your foot fulfilled its stride,
> How the sand, compressed, burst to silver light,
> But when I had reached that aureoled spot
> There was only another in further stride.

This bringing all vision down to earth is best exemplified in a late poem such as "Last Meeting." It is another hill-country recollection; the poet, now by all accounts elderly, recalls being back home once and meeting an elderly woman who had known him as a boy. Now she too is dead. "All's changed. The faces on the street/ Are changed. I'm rarely back. But once/ I tried to find her grave." He failed, he explains, but promises that he will yet succeed. Still, "It's nigh half a lifetime I haven't managed,/ But there must be enough time left for that." People's failures are little things, he seems to be saying toward the end of his creative life, and because Warren has done such an incredible job of exploring them in every other permutation throughout his long career, the reader should pay heed to the conclusions he reaches. People's failures, no matter how great, are little things; it is the burden of remorse they carry for them that is great.

Like Thomas Hart Benton, who painted the great vistas of Western deserts in his later years, Warren turns to the overlooked and the insignificant to find beauty as well as significance that he may have missed. In "Arizona Midnight," "dimly I do see/ Against that darkness, lifting in blunt agony,/ The single great cactus." He strains to see the cactus; "it has/ its own neces-

sary beauty." One must see through the apparent agony into the heart of the thing and seek out the beauty there, rather than pausing too long to reflect only on the tragic surface—which one can see only dimly, in any event.

CHIEF JOSEPH OF THE NEZ PERCÉ

It is no wonder, then, that one of Warren's last completed volumes was *Chief Joseph of the Nez Percé*. Here he returns to the tragic record that is the past, to betrayal and injustice and the bitter agony of exile despite one's having "done the right thing." However, this time, in Joseph's enduring the arrogance of office and the proud man's contumely, Warren finds an emblem of triumph despite apparent defeat. Now he can see history not as irony, filled with the tragic remorse that looking back can bring, but as process and "sometimes, under/ The scrutinizing prism of Time,/ Triumphant." It seems to be the declaration of a total peace, and one cannot help but hear, as Warren surely must have hoped one would, echoing behind those words Chief Joseph's own: "I will fight no more forever."

A victory that is won against no odds is a sham. A victory that is won against life's own bitter truths is poetry. It certainly is Warren's.

OTHER MAJOR WORKS

LONG FICTION: *Night Rider*, 1939; *At Heaven's Gate*, 1943; *All the King's Men*, 1946; *World Enough and Time: A Romantic Novel*, 1950; *Band of Angels*, 1955; *The Cave*, 1959; *Wilderness: A Tale of the Civil War*, 1961; *Flood: A Romance of Our Time*, 1964; *Meet Me in the Green Glen*, 1971; *A Place to Come To*, 1977.

SHORT FICTION: *Blackberry Winter*, 1946; *The Circus in the Attic, and Other Stories*, 1947.

PLAYS: *Proud Flesh*, pr. 1947; *All the King's Men*, pr. 1958 (adaptation of his novel).

NONFICTION: *John Brown: The Making of a Martyr*, 1929; *Modern Rhetoric*, 1949 (with Cleanth Brooks); *Segregation: The Inner Conflict in the South*, 1956; *Selected Essays*, 1958; *The Legacy of the Civil War: Meditations on the Centennial*, 1961; *Who Speaks for the Negro?*, 1965; *Democracy and Poetry*, 1975; *Portrait of a Father*, 1988; *New and Selected Essays*, 1989; *Cleanth Brooks and Robert Penn Warren: A Literary Correspondence*, 1998 (James A. Grimshaw, Jr., editor); *Selected Lettes of Robert Penn Warren*, 2000-2006 (4 volumes; William Bedford Clark, editor).

EDITED TEXTS: *An Approach to Literature*, 1936 (with Cleanth Brooks and John Thibault Purser); *Understanding Poetry: An Anthology for College Students*, 1938 (with Brooks); *Understanding Fiction*, 1943 (with Brooks); *Faulkner: A Collection of Critical Essays*, 1966; *Randall Jarrell, 1914-1965*, 1967 (with Robert Lowell and Peter Taylor); *American Literature: The Makers and the Making*, 1973 (with R. W. B. Lewis).

BIBLIOGRAPHY

Blotner, Joseph. *Robert Penn Warren: A Biography.* New York: Random House, 1997. Blotner began work on his biography while Warren was still alive and had the good fortune to have the cooperation not only of his subject but also of the larger Warren family. Blotner's book is straightforward and chronological.

Burt, John. *Robert Penn Warren and American Idealism.* New Haven, Conn.: Yale University Press, 1988. Burt describes his work as traversing "regions" of Warren's work: the elegies, the narrative poems, and three major novels—*Night Rider*, *All the King's Men*, and *World Enough and Time*. What unifies these works, Burt maintains, is Warren's ambivalence about experience, an ambivalence endemic to American idealism.

Grimshaw, James A. *Understanding Robert Penn Warren.* Columbia: University of South Carolina Press, 2001. An introduction to Warren's novels, poems, and plays.

Madden, David, ed. *The Legacy of Robert Penn Warren.* Baton Rouge: Louisiana State University Press, 2000. A collection of critical and biographical essays on Warren's life and work. Includes bibliographical references and an index.

Millichap, Joseph R. *Robert Penn Warren After "Audubon": The Work of Aging and the Quest for Transcendence in His Later Poetry.* Baton Rouge: Louisiana State University Press, 2010. This work examines the later poetry and the themes and ideas it contained.

Runyon, Randolph Paul. *Ghostly Parallels: Robert Penn Warren and the Lyric Poetic Sequence.* Knoxville: University of Tennessee Press, 2006. An examination of Warren's poetry that traces the Perseus myth. Discusses poems from collections such as *Thirty-six Poems, You, Emperors, and Others, Tale of Time,* and *Incarnations*.

Ruppersburg, Hugh. *Robert Penn Warren and the American Imagination.* Athens: University of Georgia Press, 1990. Ruppersburg considers the Warren opus an attempt to define a national identity. He focuses, in particular, on *Brother to Dragons, Audubon,* and *Chief Joseph of the Nez Percé.* Subscribing to Warren's notion that he was not a historical writer, Ruppersburg also attempts to place Warren in a contemporary context, emphasizing such modern American concerns as civil rights and nuclear warfare.

Szczesiul, Anthony. *Racial Politics and Robert Penn Warren's Poetry.* Gainesville: University Press of Florida, 2002. Addresses Warren's poetry in terms of his political views, especially those relating to race and civil rights. Includes bibliographical references and index.

Walker, Marshall. *Robert Penn Warren: A Vision Earned.* 2d ed. Glasgow: Humming Earth, 2008. A biography of Warren that examines his role as a southern writer.

Warren, Robert Penn. *Conversations with Robert Penn Warren.* Edited by Gloria L. Cronin and Ben Siegel. Jackson: University Press of Mississippi, 2005. A collection of interviews with Warren, revealing aspects of his life and career.

Russell Elliott Murphy

BRUCE WEIGL

Born: Lorain, Ohio; January 27, 1949

PRINCIPAL POETRY

Executioner, 1976
A Sack Full of Old Quarrels, 1976
A Romance, 1979
The Monkey Wars, 1985
Song of Napalm, 1988
What Saves Us, 1992
Lies, Grace, and Redemption, 1995 (Harry Humes, editor)
Not on the Map, 1996 (with Kevin Bowen; John Deane, editor)
Sweet Lorain, 1996
After the Others, 1999
Archeology of the Circle: New and Selected Poems, 1999
The Unraveling Strangeness: Poems, 2002
Declension in the Village of Chung Luong: New Poems, 2006

OTHER LITERARY FORMS

Although Bruce Weigl (WI-gehl) has published primarily poetry, he also translated poetry from the Vietnamese—*Poems from Captured Documents* (1994; with Thanh Nguyen) and *Mountain River: Vietnamese Poetry from the Wars, 1945-1995* (1998; with Nguyen Ba Chung and Kevin Bowen)—and Romanian, Liliana Ursu's *Angel Riding a Beast* (1998; with the author). Weigl's translations make available poems that are not readily accessible to the common reader. Weigl has spoken of how pervasive poetry is in Southeast Asia; reading the Vietnamese perspective provides a fuller picture of the impact of the war. In addition, Weigl has written several volumes of criticism, including *The Giver of Morning: On Dave Smith* (1982), *The Imagination as Glory: The Poetry of James Dickey* (1984; with T. R. Hummer), and *Charles Simic: Essays on the Poetry* (1996), as well as a memoir, *The Circle of Hahn: A Memoir* (2000).

ACHIEVEMENTS

Published internationally, Bruce Weigl's poetry has been translated into Vietnamese, Czech, Dutch, German, Spanish, Chinese, Slovenian, Bulgarian, and Romanian. He has received many national awards, including a Paterson Poetry Prize, two Pushcart Prizes, a Cleveland Arts Prize, and the Poet's Prize from the Academy of American Poets, as well as fellowships from the Bread Loaf Writers' Conference, the Yaddo Foundation, and the National Endowment for the Arts. In 1988, he was nominated for a Pulitzer Prize for *Song of Napalm*. He served as a poetry panel chair for the National Book Award in 2003 and won the Lannan Literary Award for Poetry in 2006 and the Ohioana Book Award for Poetry in 2007. His poems have appeared in *The Nation*, *American Poetry Review*, *Ploughshares*, *The New Yorker*, and *Paris Review*, as well as many other magazines and journals.

BIOGRAPHY

Bruce Weigl was born in Lorain, Ohio, on January 27, 1949, to Albert Louis Weigl and Zora Grasa Weigl. Weigl served in the U.S. Army in Vietnam from 1967 until 1970, earning the Bronze Star. He earned a B.A. in English from Oberlin College in 1974 and an M.A. from the University of New Hampshire in 1975. In 1979, he received a Ph.D. from the University of Utah, where he was mentored by poet Dave Smith. He has two children (a son and a daughter) with his wife, artist Jean Kondo.

Weigl has had an extensive teaching career. He was an instructor at Lorain County Community College from 1975 to 1976 and assistant professor of English at the University of Arkansas, Little Rock. At Old Dominion University in Norfolk, Virginia, he was assistant professor of English and director of the associated writing program. He then taught in the writing program at Pennsylvania State University for fourteen years and in the M.F.A. in writing program at Vermont College. In 2000, he became a visiting distinguished professor at Lorain County Community College.

ANALYSIS

In the poetry of Bruce Weigl, two themes emerge, seemingly at cross purposes. First is the horror of war, especially its effect on the psyches of young men who were ill prepared for what would come. The second is the primacy of love that at once underscores that horror and attempts to atone for it. The love poems undercut the rules of the society that would control the course of love, as war situations do.

Weigl describes the impetus for his work by saying that a writer must come to terms with his or her background, as it is the major source of the writer's subject matter. Weigl grew up in and around industry, amid steel mills and the working class. Weigel was born in industrial and agricultural Middle America, and his working-class background informs his poetry and shapes the way he perceives the Vietnam War. The speaker of these poems is often a young, fairly naïve man who gets caught up in an unpopular cause and who must find a way to transcend the limitations of mere survival. The poet, therefore, finds himself trying to bring his imaginative sensibilities to a hostile environment in an attempt to transform it and make it livable, with as little cost to his psyche as he can manage. Weigl's poetry clearly demonstrates the care that the poet takes to render a full account of the situations in which he finds himself and to do so with a high degree of craft. The artistic development of his style does not take a backseat to his important message, however.

INFLUENCE OF THE VIETNAM WAR

Except for the American Civil War, no war in American history has been as controversial or as divisive as the Vietnam War. Soldiers did not come home to the welcoming crowds that filled World War II newsreels. Called "baby killers" and generally reviled, soldiers had few official support systems to help them return to a society that disowned them. Sometimes, families themselves embodied national divisions, with members for and against the war living under the same roof. Thus, Weigl's poetry reflects a common reality of personal and familial rupture.

Poems speaking about familial life stateside seem to present a conclusion to the struggle to relate. In some poems, when Weigl speaks with great tenderness about his wife and child, about chance encounters in a supermarket, or about memories of work, a pervasive sadness still informs the poems. However, an emotional

salvation occurs for the poet when he is able to ground himself in those relationships that are stronger than his nightmares about the war. "The Happiness of Others," the poet says in the poem of that name, "is not like the music I hear/ after sex/ with my wife of the decades." He refers to her as "my wife my rope my bread." His wife is the rope that holds him firmly tethered to the present, the bread that nourishes his existence. Without her, the horrible trauma of his war memories could overtake his soul.

Although his private world is forever marked by his war experiences, it is beauty (found in his familial attachments, the natural world, and language itself) that provides the safe haven necessary to access those memories without being overwhelmed by them. The great body of work results from the poet's willingness to go into a darkened landscape and emerge wholly creative.

Weigl's poetry serves to give voice to thousands of soldiers who saw action in the Vietnam War during the late 1960's and early 1970's. If Tim O'Brien may be considered the prose writer of the horror, trauma, and

Bruce Weigl (Courtesy, Grove Press)

regret of the Vietnam War, Weigl could be rightly called the poet. War casts a deep shadow over Weigl's writings, and the disillusionment generated from his experiences in Vietnam seep into even his more hopeful lines. Although he is often considered a Vietnam War poet by literary critics, Weigl's extensive use of irony and craft with blank verse elevate his poetry beyond such a label. While the sincerity of these poems provides a forum of discourse so that these experiences may benefit from national attention, their high literary quality merits the esteem in which they are held as literature.

"Song of Napalm"

"Song of Napalm," from *The Monkey Wars*, begins with a bucolic description of horses that the speaker and his wife watch. The initial description of the poet and his wife lifts them beyond the concerns of this world into a holy realm. However, this domestic scene foreshadows a frightening darkness that the poet experiences: "Trees scraped their voices in the wind, branches/ Crisscrossed the sky like barbed wire/ But you said they were only branches."

The speaker pauses as if to catch his breath and take stock of himself, believing that the "old curses" have gone. However, visions from his war experiences intrude once again:

> Still I close my eyes and see the girl
> Running from her village, napalm
> Stuck to her dress like jelly,
> Her hands reaching for the no one
> Who waits in waves of heat before her.

These lines evoke the famous photograph of a young Vietnamese girl burned by napalm, running naked along a road toward the camera that immortalized her. The poet is alienated from both the domestic tranquility that his wife represents and the haunting visions that his memory brings; however, he forces a door to open between these two worlds.

The girl runs with wings of escape beating inside her, using a freedom that she does not possess. In fact, she is able to run only a few feet before her burns and wounds bring her down, as she dies in a fetal position: "Nothing/ Can change that, she is burned behind my eyes." The poet is forced to accept the world as something that his words alone cannot change. Not even the redemptive, healing love of his wife fades this vision. A persistent theme in Weigl's other poems is the poet's struggle to find solace in the love of family and friends to dispel the power that his war experience exerts.

"On the Anniversary of Her Grace"

In "On the Anniversary of Her Grace," from *Song of Napalm*, the poet evokes his power to show how the war scarred his ability to love. The opening description of weather conditions foreshadows the desperate state of the poet's mind. Images of darkness, floods, and destruction presage the devastation that the war wreaks on the poet's spirit. Although the poet dreams of his beloved, these dreams are restive in spite of his recalling a kiss, because "Inside me the war had eaten a hole./ I could not touch anyone." The war robs the poet of his openness to love, central to his self-image.

Often the use of repetition induces a meditative, trancelike state. The poet uses that device, repeating "I could . . . I could," until finally he says, "I could not." The effect mesmerizes. Images of the war erode his sensibilities, ensuring that the poet cannot accept the forgiveness and healing which the woman offers. He fears his "body would catch fire," recalling the image of the napalm-burned children, joining them in their unwilling sacrifice.

Intense feelings of love remind the poet that he is a stranger in two worlds, with one foot planted firmly in each. Even when the poet is not ostensibly narrating his experiences of the war, even when the love poem focuses on the beloved, the war intrudes as if he cannot manage two disparate worlds.

"First Letter to Calumpang"

In "First Letter to Calumpang," from *Sweet Lorain*, the poet expresses love to his wife by using images that reflect the war: "There is a blood from touching, and a fire;/ I've had them in my mouth." The poet's use of blood echoes both the blood rush of sexual excitement and the blood certainly present in war. Fire carries the dual connotation of sexual desire and the fire of war and napalm. With these images that are at once tender and fierce, the war is never far away.

Archeology of the Circle

The poems in *Archeology of the Circle* represent both new works and selections from Weigl's previous volumes. In them, he continues to struggle with his feelings of love for others as well as self-acceptance. The war has taken its toll. In "Anniversary of Myself," the poet says:

> The fingers of my gloves had holes.
> I don't know what I was doing.
> There had been a war
> and my people
> had grown disenchanted.

Disillusionment comes from the poet's growing awareness of his numbness to his inner being, the core of himself, the part of himself that nurtures love relationships.

Consequently, the poet comes to relive the advice that he was given during the war, in "Our Independence Day," saying, "Let it go, boy,// let the green/ untangle from your body." These poems represent a letting go that empowers the speaker. These are not poems of surrender to a greater power; instead, the poet releases these poems into the community of discourse wherein they can become change agents in the lives of other men and women who know war.

THE UNRAVELING STRANGENESS

Weigl's common themes of guilt, regret, and loss receive a more nuanced and sedate treatment in *The Unraveling Strangeness* than in some of his previous collections. There is a haunting weight to the lines that belies the mixture of nostalgia and regret that characterizes many of the poems here. Weigl's rearview gaze provides ample fodder for introspection and the comingling of past events with the present in poems such as "Oh, Atonement," "I Waited for the Spirit Soldiers" (both initially published in *American Poetry Review*), and the lengthy "Incident at Eagle's Peak," all of which showcase the regret that constantly looking back to the past often engenders.

However, Weigl asserts an obligation in the midst of memory in "Nixon." Referring to the fallen soldiers of the Vietnam War, the speaker remarks, ". . . Anymore/ the anniversaries of the deaths/ are so many/ that there is little time/ for anything else." Weigl reminds his reader that the act of remembering can be its own sacred duty. Having little time for anything besides observing the death of fallen comrades implies surviving carries with it an obligation to those who did not live. In

this way, the specter of war again haunts many of the lines in this collection, unifying them around a common desire for healing.

Many of the poems in this volume, like the others, speak of a longing for redemption that the speaker seems skeptical of ever obtaining. In "For A, At Fourteen," the speaker observes that, "We need at last a life without the grief/ we've brought into the house. A life that would/ allow us both our tenderness, our pain released." Here, the house serves as a metaphor for a common place of interaction between human beings. However, the grief that all human beings carry with them seems to keep both the adult speaker and the teenage subject from the desired communion. The poet suggests a similar longing for wholeness in "Baby Crying, 3 A.M.," in which he writes, ". . . Our eyes/ won't close as easily, our nights arranged/ around the hungry cry that comes in waves." Here, a baby's hungry cry becomes a symbol of the desperate longing for completion that Weigl offers as a universal characteristic of the human condition.

As in previous collections, Weigl does seem to find respite and solace within the natural world. Poems such as "My Autumn Leaves" and "Incident at Eagle's Peak" depict natural beauty as a salve for the human spirit. Weigl often uses natural objects and landscapes as metaphors for the emotional states of his speakers in ways that help these characters access and interpret traumatic events. The predominance of natural imagery unites his body of work and links Weigl to great American poets such as Emily Dickinson and Robert Frost.

DECLENSION IN THE VILLAGE OF CHUNG LUONG

Declension in the Village of Chung Luong contains many of the same stylistic patterns as *The Unraveling Strangeness* and earlier volumes. Both books are divided into three sections, which mirror one another thematically. Both rely on blank verse and terse line breaks to convey irony and emotion. The language in these volumes is stripped down and sparse, as if cognizant of the inability of language to convey emotional associations with any certainty (or suspicious of its ability to convey anything at all). Instead, Weigl conjures up phrases, glimpses of meaning floating by, as if waiting for his reader to seize the words, arrest their dissipation, and extract some level of meaning from them. Although some view Weigl as a confessional poet (in the sense of one who writes of their own experiences using a first-person speaker), this volume applies its themes of regret, trauma, and loss to the experiences of modern life more generally than his previous collections, especially in its discussion of war.

Declension in the Village of Chung Luong provides a window into the trauma of modern life through its discussion of the modern American military engagements of the early twenty-first century. "Home of the Brave" (originally published in the *American Poetry Review*) discusses the aftermath of the terrorist attacks on the World Trade Center on September 11, 2001, lamenting that, "so much was taken from them, and a hole/ had been torn into their world,/ that one man hung a thousand flags from his house." "Portal" (first published in *Irish Pages*) shifts that window onto the effects of war on the children inside the countries against which America retaliated, who, "sleep the sleep of weary warriors/ beaten down and left for nothing in their lonely deaths/ that come so slowly you would wish/ your own heart empty of blood." War functions as an important site for individual reflection in these poems, but unlike in earlier collections, Weigl evokes the conflicts in Iraq and Afghanistan instead of his personal experience in Vietnam. As a result, the emotions stirred up by these poems are intimately familiar to a new generation of readers whose lives may not have been directly touched by the Vietnam War.

However, it would be overly simplistic to assert that all of Weigl's poetry is of war. Weigl shifts between deeply introspective musings on his own subjective experiences to more general observations of the current state of American society. For example, Weigl's "Elegy for Biggie Smalls" could apply to many superstars transfixed within the modern media's incessant spotlight. Weigl's lines, "no one stays at the edge too long there's no song/ that can keep you or defeat you no one to beseech you/ to step back from the edge when you're Big," aptly capture the power and freedom of fame, while simultaneously proffering a cautionary observation of the inevitable loneliness of the human condition. In fact, these lines illustrate one of the primary attrac-

tions of this modern poet, who deftly holds up his own feelings of regret and loss to events within the popular society more generally, suggesting that his own experiences, although unique and personal, mirror those of an entire culture.

OTHER MAJOR WORKS

NONFICTION: *The Giver of Morning: On Dave Smith*, 1982; *The Imagination as Glory: The Poetry of James Dickey*, 1984 (with T. R. Hummer); *Charles Simic: Essays on the Poetry*, 1996; *The Circle of Hahn: A Memoir*, 2000.

TRANSLATIONS: *Poems from Captured Documents*, 1994 (with Thanh Nguyen); *Angel Riding a Beast*, 1998 (of Liliana Ursu; with the author); *Mountain River: Vietnamese Poetry from the Wars, 1945-1995*, 1998 (with Nguyen Ba Chung and Kevin Bowen).

EDITED TEXT: *Writing Between the Lines: An Anthology on War and Its Social Consequences*, 1997 (with Kevin Bowen).

BIBLIOGRAPHY

Beidler, Philip. *Re-writing America: Vietnam Authors in Their Generation*. Athens: University of Georgia Press, 1991. Beidler notes the development of Weigl's career as a direct emergence from the evolution of his mythic consciousness as a result of the war. The book presents an examination of *A Romance* and *The Monkey Wars* within the tradition of a visionary quest.

Christopher, Renny. *The Viet Nam War: The American War*. Amherst: University of Massachusetts Press, 1995. This book discusses how Weigl's poetry moves beyond reportage into a realm of introspection, an internal dialogue in the context of external events. Uses "Him, on the Bicycle" to illustrate Weigl's use of perceived and experienced distance from self and other as an attempt to bridge cultures.

Gotera, Vincente F. "Bringing Vietnam Home: Bruce Weigl's *The Monkey Wars*." In *Search and Clear*, edited by William J. Searle. Bowling Green, Ohio: Bowling Green State University Popular Press, 1988. The author notes how Weigl never allows the reader to dismiss the inextricable link to American violence and pathos. War is an exaggeration of common forms of violence. Weigl's work breaks apart the myth that the United States regained national innocence by admitting that its involvement in Vietnam was a mistake.

Humes, Harry. "Death, Beauty, and Redemption." *Southern Review* 36, no. 4 (Autumn, 2000): 870-873. Offers an excellent close reading of *After the Others* and explicates common themes found in Weigl's poetry according to the poet's own life. His discussion of the search for meaning and redemption amidst the trauma of war are especially cogent.

Jason, Philip K. *Acts and Shadows: The Vietnam War in American Culture*. Lanham, Md.: Rowman and Littlefield, 2000. Presents an examination of *Song of Napalm*. The author questions the source of love and cruelty and notes that the poems speak of the poet's awareness of violence deep within all people. A further examination of those images that confront, then upset, reader expectations.

Keplinger, David. "On Bruce Weigl: Finding a Shape for the Litany of Terror." *War, Literature, and the Arts* 12, no. 2 (Fall/Winter, 2000): 141-158. Written by a former student of Weigl's, this article explains why Weigl is more than a mere poet of the Vietnam War. The author examines Weigl's poetic style and influences in the first part of this piece; the second contains an interview between the former student and poet.

Parini, Jay, ed. *American Writers: A Collection of Literary Biographies—David Budbill to Bruce Weigl*. Supplement 19. Farmington Hills, Mich.: Thomson Gale, 2010. Contains an entry on Weigl.

Rielly, Edward J. "Bruce Weigl: Out of the Landscape of His Past." *Journal of American Culture* 16, no. 3 (1993): 47-52. Explains the function of memory in Weigl's body of work by exploring the ways past experiences are "superimposed" on the present. He illustrates war's influence over poems that do not deal explicitly with that experience.

Weigl, Bruce. "Poetry Grabbed Me by the Throat." Interview by Eric James Schroeder. In *Vietnam: We've All Been There*, edited by Schroeder. Westport, Conn.: Praeger, 1992. Weigl emphatically rejects the notion that writing was a form of therapy for him. He suggests, paradoxically, that the war

both ruined his life and made him a writer. He speaks of his emergence as a poet and his affinity to Wilfred Owen's work. Weigl states that writing is the greatest act of affirmation life can accomplish.

Martha Modena Vertreace-Doody
Updated by Ryan D. Stryffeler

JAMES WELCH

Born: Browning, Montana; November 18, 1940
Died: Missoula, Montana; August 24, 2003

PRINCIPAL POETRY

Riding the Earthboy Forty, 1971, 1975

OTHER LITERARY FORMS

Although his first book was a poetry collection, James Welch is known primarily as a novelist. His five novels, beginning with *Winter in the Blood* (1974), have garnered considerable praise and critical commentary, and they are frequently taught in Native American literature classes at the college level. His volume of nonfiction, *Killing Custer: The Battle of the Little Bighorn and the Fate of the Plains Indians* (1994) has also drawn attention as a text on the famous battle written from an American Indian point of view.

ACHIEVEMENTS

James Welch's single collection of poems has remained in print for decades; a revised edition won the Pacific Northwest Booksellers Award in 1976, and in 2004, Penguin published a reprint with an introduction by poet James Tate. In 1978, a special issue of *American Indian Quarterly* was devoted to essays concerning Welch's first novel, *Winter in the Blood*. In 1981, Welch received the Indian Council Fire National Achievement Award and the Montana Governor's Award. His novel *Fools Crow* (1986), which recounts events that led up to the Marias River Massacre in 1870, won the American Book Award from the Before Columbus Foundation in 1987. In 1994, following the publication of *Killing Custer*, Welch won the Western

James Welch (©Marc Hefty)

Literature Association's Distinguished Achievement Award and the John Dos Passos Prize for Literature. The next year, he was named a Chevalier of the Ordres des Artes et des Lettres by the French cultural ministry. In 1997, he won a Lifetime Achievement Award from the Native Writers Circle of the Americas.

BIOGRAPHY

Although James Welch's father was Blackfeet (Welch preferred that to Blackfoot) and his mother, Gros Ventres, was connected with the Arapaho, Welch claimed to be as much Irish as he was Indian. He grew up and attended schools on the Blackfeet reservation in Browning and the Gros Ventre reservation at Fort Belknap, both in northern Montana. His family moved to Minneapolis, where he graduated from high school in 1958. He has described himself as a "mediocre student" who preferred athletics to reading and who scribbled bad poems during study hall. He briefly attended the University of Minnesota before leaving school to work on a natural gas pipeline and as a groundskeeper in a cemetery.

He attended Northern Montana College in Havre before moving to the University of Montana in Missoula, where he completed his bachelor's degree in 1965 and began work on his M.F.A. in poetry under Madeline DeFrees and the charismatic and very influential Richard Hugo, a former student of Theodore Roethke at the University of Washington, who became a close friend.

He never completed his graduate degree, but by 1967, some of his poems were being published in literary magazines, and with the assistance of a grant from the National Endowment for the Arts, Welch was able to complete the poems of *Riding the Earthboy Forty*, published in 1971 and in 1975 in a revised and expanded version. In 1968, he married Lois Monk, who was then teaching comparative literature at the University of Montana. The writing community in Missoula has long been recognized as one of the most vibrant in the country, with writers such as William Kittredge and Hugo then at the center of a world of trout fishing, city league softball, hoop shooting, smoking, and drinking. Welch also worked with Kittredge and Annick Smith on the ambitious Montana anthology, *The Last Best Place*, published in 1988.

Kittredge helped Welch construct his first novel, *Winter in the Blood*, which has been praised, as have his other novels, for its often lyrical prose. Each of the five novels has taken a different direction, from the picaresque and sometimes surreal prose of *Winter in the Blood*, a very short novel like the dark, even tragic, *The Death of Jim Loney* (1979), which followed it, to the more lengthy historical novels, *Fools Crow* and *The Heartsong of Charging Elk* (2000). In between these came *The Indian Lawyer* (1990), which might be described as a novel of intrigue.

Welch's poems have been noted for their regional imagery that sometimes shows evidence of surreal qualities and for characters and episodes drawn from reservation and small-town Montana life. Welch died of lung cancer in 2003.

ANALYSIS

"I have benefitted materially from being an Indian poet," James Welch wrote in a brief piece for the *South Dakota Review* in 1973, "but I just hope that in twenty or thirty years people will take me seriously as a poet." Most students of Native American writing would agree that Welch's hopes have been realized. In his observations, Welch noted that while he likes "to use the legends, the traditions, and the myths" of his people, he also likes "to write contemporary poetry" about "what's going on in the reservations" today. He suggested that he did not intend for his poems to be "bitter or angry," but that they do end up being "very intense."

The fifty-nine poems in *Riding the Earthboy Forty*—the title refers to the forty acres leased by a family named Earthboy that lived next to Welch's parents in northern Montana—range from eight to thirty-five lines; nearly half of the poems run under twenty lines. The influence of the poems, however, has little to do with their bulk or critical mass. Appearing as they did just two years after the occupation of Alcatraz by the Indians of All Tribes in 1969 and two years before the siege at Wounded Knee on the Pine Ridge Reservation in South Dakota in 1973, involving members of the American Indian movement, *Riding the Earthboy Forty* might be regarded as propitiously timed: It was the right book of poems at the right moment. Just three years earlier, in 1968, N. Scott Momaday had made a notable impression on the literary establishment when his novel, *House Made of Dawn*, was awarded a Pulitzer Prize.

Various critics, including Alan R. Velie in *Four American Indian Literary Masters: N. Scott Momaday, James Welch, Leslie Marmon Silko, and Gerald Vizenor* (1982), have traced the surreal or deep imagery that dominates some of Welch's poems in the techniques of Peruvian poet Cesar Vallejo. In *Understanding James Welch* (2000), Ron McFarland traces the apparent influences of Welch's mentor and friend Richard Hugo on several of the poems. The poems vary considerably in voice and accessibility. Some of the shortest and sparest poems, like the opening poem, "Magic Fox," which runs just eighteen clipped lines (the longest come to just six words), will mystify with their dreamlike images that appear to have neither a narrative nor a cause-effect organization. Other poems, such as "Grandma's Man," which is composed in thirty relatively long lines, tend toward narrative, and still others, such as "In My First Hard Spring," depict char-

acters from the reservation, described usually from a first-person point of view.

"When asked why he did not write poetry anymore," Kathryn W. Shanley writes in her introduction to a special memorial issue of *Studies in American Indian Literatures* (fall, 2006) devoted to James Welch, "Jim often commented that he would like to believe poetry resides within his prose." Most readers of Welch's novels would likely assent. However, this is not to devalue the achievement of his single volume of poems. Philip H. Round describes *Riding the Earthboy Forty* as "a watershed in American poetry" that has made a significant "intercultural impact."

"Knives"

The first of the four sections that make up *Riding the Earthboy Forty*, "Knives" consists of fifteen poems, most of which are cast in the surreal mode. One might describe the poems generally as windswept and elegiac. Poems such as "Verifying the Dead," "Dreaming Winter," "Blue Like Death," and "Life Support System" suggest something of their substance in their very titles, but even in a poem with the promising title "Picnic Weather," the reader finds only "the drab blue of spring" and "Winter now: here your image dies." The poem concludes with the first-person speaker killing "you," apparently a bull snake, but unable to imitate "the music in your bones." Several of the poems, including "Directions to the Nomad," "Gesture Down to Guatemala," and "Arizona Highways," feature lone individuals in transit. "Fools by chance, we traveled/ cavalier toward death. . . ." opens the poem "Trestles by the Blackfoot," and at least half of the poems in this section touch on death in some way. The poems also frequently involve dreams, as if to imply that the only way out of the winter blue distance of people's lives must be through dreaming.

"The Renegade Wants Words"

The play on words in "The Renegade Wants Words" ("wants" meaning both "desires" and "lacks" or "needs"), which is also the title of one poem among the sixteen in this section, suggests that the poet is something of a renegade. Although Welch tends to move away from the predominantly surreal mode of the opening section here, most of the poems retain their surreal moments. In the opening poem, "In My First

Hard Springtime," Welch appears to open the door to more overt social comment on the harsh lives of the Indians: "Those red men you offended were my brothers." His drinking friends, like Albert Heavy Runner, are "never civic." The "you" in the poem appears to be the speaker's white ("fed and fair") lover, and at the end of the poem, he claims he is "starved to visions," but instead of denying them, he elects to ". . . ride you down with/ hunger." The poems in this section include the longest in the book, "Harlem, Montana: Just Off the Reservation," and some of Welch's most frequently anthologized and critiqued pieces, from the title poem of the book to "Christmas Comes to Moccasin Flat," "The Only Bar in Dixon," and "Going to Remake This World," which ends playfully, "Sometimes,/ you know, the snow never falls forever." The reader encounters increasing examples of Welch's understated humor as the book advances. "The wages of sin" in "The Last Priest Didn't Even Say Goodbye," is not death, but ". . . to live where/ the mountains give down to the Indian town."

"Day After Chasing Porcupines"

Wind, which might be regarded as the recurring or master symbol of "Day After Chasing Porcupines," clearly dominates the ten spare, perhaps even minimalist poems of the third section, which range in length from just eight to nineteen lines. In the title poem of the section, rain, wind, and dream combine to set the atmosphere of the poems that follow (six of the ten directly mention dreams). Surviving, as a poem by that title demonstrates, is not easy; it requires stories and dreams, in effect, these poems. In "Getting Things Straight," the longest poem of this section, the speaker attempts to adopt the hawk as his totem, as his spirit or vision animal, but significantly the poem is composed almost entirely of questions (only three of the thirteen sentences are declarative). Four of the questions strategically scattered throughout the poem effectually represent the speaker's existential uncertainty (the last two constitute the final lines of the poem): "It means nothing?"; "What does it mean?"; "Am I strangling in his grip?/ Is he my vision?"

"The Day the Children Took Over"

In the final dozen poems of "The Day the Children Took Over," an emotional uplift of sorts occurs, beginning with the title poem, in which snow falls on lovers and priests who leave their pulpits for "fine new" wives, and children "create life" by building snowmen "in their own image." Or consider the concluding lines of "Grandma's Man": ". . . LIFE seldom came/ the shade he wanted. Well, and yes, he died well,/ but you should have seen how well his friends/ took it." The last poem in the book draws from a W. C. Fields movie, *Never Give a Sucker an Even Break* (1941), in which Welch substitutes the word "bum" for "sucker." The humor tends toward the absurd or "dark," but the poem leaves the reader on a somewhat surprisingly upbeat note, as "we" crawl out from under an old bridge ready ". . . to settle/ old scores or create new roles, our masks/ glittering in a comic rain."

Other major works

long fiction: *Winter in the Blood*, 1974; *The Death of Jim Loney*, 1979; *Fools Crow*, 1986; *The Indian Lawyer*, 1990; *The Heartsong of Charging Elk*, 2000.

nonfiction: *Killing Custer: The Battle of the Little Bighorn and the Fate of the Plains Indians*, 1994.

Bibliography

McFarland. Ron. *Understanding James Welch*. Columbia: University of South Carolina, 2000. Devotes a chapter of nearly thirty pages to the poems, surveys the critical response, and provides close readings of several poems.

_____, ed. *James Welch*. Lewiston, Idaho: Confluence, 1986. Includes ten poems from *Riding the Earthboy Forty*, a substantial essay on the poetry by Kenneth Lincoln, a shorter essay by Peter Wild, and Kim Stafford's comments on "The Only Bar in Dixon."

Studies in American Indian Literatures (Fall, 2006). This special issue, edited by Kathryn W. Shanley, is devoted to James Welch. Among the essays included are various tributes to Welch as a poet, including the editor's introductory piece, Phillip H. Round's close reading of "There Is a Right Way," and Gail Tremblay's commentary on "Getting Things Straight."

Wild, Peter. *James Welch*. Boise, Idaho: Boise State

University Press, 1983. Part of the Western Writers series. In this booklet, Arizona poet Wild devotes more than a dozen pages to the poetry, but although he finds several of the poems to be "exemplary pieces for a young writer," he finds that "more often than not his poems fail" and that "sometimes the surrealism is overdone and gratuitous."

Ron McFarland

PHILIP WHALEN

Born: Portland, Oregon; October 20, 1923
Died: San Francisco, California; June 26, 2002

PRINCIPAL POETRY

Three Satires, 1951 (privately printed)
Self Portrait from Another Direction, 1959
Like I Say, 1960
Memoirs of an Interglacial Age, 1960
Monday in the Evening, 1964 (privately printed)
Three Mornings, 1964
Every Day, 1965
The Invention of the Letter: A Beastly Morality, 1967
T/O, 1967
On Bear's Head, 1969
Scenes of Life at the Capital, 1970
Severance Pay, 1970
The Kindness of Strangers: Poems, 1969-1974, 1976
Prolegomena to a Study of the Universe, 1976
Zenshinji, 1977
Decompressions: Selected Poems, 1978
Enough Said: Fluctuat Nec Mergitur—Poems, 1974-1979, 1980
Tara, 1981
Heavy Breathing: Poems, 1967-1980, 1983
Two Variations: All About Love, 1983
A Vision of the Bodhisattvas, 1984
For C., 1984
The Elizabethan Phrase, 1985
Window Peak, 1986

Driving Immediately Past, 1989
Canoeing Up Cabarga Creek: Buddhist Poems, 1955-1986, 1996
Mark Other Place, 1997
Overtime: Selected Poems, 1999
Some of These Days, 1999
The Collected Poems of Philp Whalen, 2007
    (Michael Rothenberg, editor)

OTHER LITERARY FORMS

Although he gave priority to his poetry, Philip Whalen (WAY-lehn) enjoyed success as a novelist. His first novel, *You Didn't Even Try* (1967), drew upon his experiences in San Francisco in the years 1959-1964. In the year it was published, he began work on his second novel, *Imaginary Speeches for a Brazen Head* (1972), while in Kyoto, Japan. His third, *The Diamond Noodle* (1980), likewise had its origins in the 1960's. Whalen also wrote nonfiction and journals, and he produced short volumes of calligraphic and "doodle" works, including *Highgrade: Doodles, Poems*, published in 1966.

ACHIEVEMENTS

Numerous literary organizations have recognized Philip Whalen's importance in the American poetry scene. His awards include the Poets Foundation Award (1962) and V. K. Ratcliff Award (1964). A grant-in-aid award from the American Academy of Arts and Letters assisted Whalen in his move to Japan. In 1968, 1970, and 1971, he received grants from the Committee on Poetry. The American Academy of Arts and Letters further honored him with the 1985 Morton Dauwen Zabel Award, and in 2001, he received a Lifetime Achievement Award from the Before Columbus Foundation.

BIOGRAPHY

Philip Whalen grew up in the small town of The Dalles on the Columbia River, where he attended public school. In his high school years, he contributed to his high school literary magazine and commenced his readings in Asian literature and philosophy. Since his family was unable to send him to college, after his graduation in 1941, Whalen took minor jobs before being drafted into the U.S. Army Air Corps. He received training in radio operation and maintenance and was given stateside military posting during the war. His military service left him adequate free time to continue pursuing his writing.

Receiving his military discharge in 1946, Whalen returned to Oregon, where he enrolled at Reed College on the G.I. Bill. He pursued a course in creative writing and developed several important friendships, including with fellow students Lew Welch and Gary Snyder. The trio shared lodgings in a rooming house in 1950, the year they also met and received encouragement from William Carlos Williams, who spent a week at Reed on a reading tour. The encounter marked the point when Whalen began taking himself seriously as a writer. After leaving Reed, Whalen supported himself with a string of odd jobs along the West Coast that ended with summer employment as a fire spotter in Mount Baker National Forest, in 1955. This experience is reflected in his poem "Sourdough Mountain Lookout." That fall, he moved to San Francisco, and at Snyder's invitation took part in the historic Six Gallery reading of October 13 at which Allen Ginsberg presented his groundbreaking "Howl" for the first time. The event was pivotal, marking the beginning of the West Coast Beat movement. Whalen's circle of literary friends expanded rapidly, growing to include Ginsberg, Jack Kerouac, and Gregory Corso, among others. Ginsberg and Kerouac were expecially influential in freeing Whalen's poetic sensibility from earlier conventions.

The maturing of Whalen's poetic voice during the mid-1950's saw fruition in 1960, when two major Whalen collections, *Like I Say* and *Memoirs of an Interglacial Age*, were published. In the same year, he was included in Donald Allen's influential anthology, *The New American Poetry, 1945-1960*. In the mid-1960's, he joined Snyder in Kyoto, Japan. Kyoto would serve as his primary residence until the early 1970's, although he spent time in the United States in 1969 overseeing the publication of his first major volume of collected poems, *On Boar's Head*. After his final return to the United States, he moved to the San Francisco Zen Center, where he was ordained as a Zen monk in 1973. Several volumes of Whalen's poetry appeared in the 1970's, subsequently collected in *Heavy Breathing*. In 1991, he was made abbot of San Francisco's Hartford Street Zen Center. At the end of the decade, in 1999, his

major collection *Overtime* was published. He died in 2002, after a long illness.

ANALYSIS

Although often considered experimental and sometimes obscure, the poetry of Philip Whalen is marked by a directness of expression that matches his concern with directness of experience. The seemingly oblique or broken sentences reflect the movements of mind, in its perceptions and thoughts.

"FOR C."

The poem "For C.," written in 1957, presents one of the clearest expressions of a mode characteristic of Whalen's work. Perhaps tellingly for a man who became ordained as a Zen monk, a note of retrospective longing comes to the fore in many poems, with the object of longing often being, or being represented by, a woman in his life. "For C." begins with a moment of vulnerability: "I wanted to bring you this Jap iris/ Orchid-white with yellow blazons/ But I couldn't face carrying it down the street/ Afraid everyone would laugh/ And now they're dying of my cowardice." His embarrassment arises from the idea of the "yellow blazons" announcing to the world his sexual desire, which ironically he displays to the world in the poem itself. His awkward yearning for bodily satisfaction finds its counterpoint in his other embarrassments, including the recurring worry over being overweight. The poem itself is expression of frustration: "After all this fuss about flowers I walked out/ Just to walk, not going to see you (I had nothing to bring—/ This poem wasn't finished, didn't say/ What was on my mind; I'd given up)."

The directness of "For C." recalls the 1956 poem "Invocation and Dark Sayings in the Tibetan Style," another expression of sexual longing and loneliness, which identifies "the biggest problem in the world" as the question, "Where are you?" The young poet presents his sexual feelings for his absent lover unabashedly, while offering a parallel presentation of his feelings, in lines he is "not saying." What he is not saying, Whalen tells the reader, are lines such as, "This is a picture of a man./ The man is hiding something./ Try to guess what it is." Although Whalen rarely points directly to the fact that in his poems he is passing along direct experience of the moment, by offering the reader what he might have written, had he been trying to transform the moment poetically, he effectively does so.

"SMALL TANTRIC SERMON"

Similarly another 1956 poem, "Small Tantric Sermon," treats the sexual act itself as seriously as poets of a previous century might have treated the purely emotional quality of romantic love. In this poem, he finds that the effort to talk directly about sex ". . . breaks down,/ Here, on paper," although the effort to do so has its own rewards, as he notes by continuing, "although I am free/ To spread these words, putting them/ Where I want them (something of a release/ In itself)."

"DELIGHTS OF WINTER AT THE SHORE"

Other frustrations provide Whalen with the galvanizing impulse toward poetic expression, including problems relating to simple existence. In one poem that vacillates between emotional distress and objective acceptance of his situation in the world, 1958's "Delights of Winter at the Shore," Whalen engages in a series of self-searching reflections as he recalls an editor asking him "Why don't you just sit down & write a novel?" The question is voiced at a time when the poet's mortgage is nearly foreclosed and his power is threatened with being shut off. Downturns of fortune likewise affect the worldly achievements others have expected of him—"It goes like that, all the 'talent,' the 'promise'"—which provokes him to a moment of personal crisis: "How loyal have I been to myself?/ How far do I trust . . . anything?/ I wonder 'self-confidence' *vs.* years of self-indulgence/ (am I feeling guilty?)/ How would anything get done if I quit? Stopped/ whatever it is you choose to call it?" The crisis forces him to look both inward and outward, as he assesses the achievement of being one who has spent his life working at "whatever it is."

HIGHGRADE

Made up of quite short poems, or individual pages of calligraphy and pen drawings that may be regarded as poems, *Highgrade* gives insight into Whalen's compositional process. Whalen had used calligraphy in his work since his Reed College days and had grown used to using the India-ink pen for writing drafts of his poem. *Highgrade* provides examples of how Whalen "sees" his poems. In the printed versions of his poems,

for example, words often appear in all capitals, which some readers might take as "shouting" or overemphasis. In these poems the upper-case words appear with naturalness on the page, where they can be seen as elements of graphic design.

Whalen's calligraphic work aims not for the elegant perfection of typical calligraphy, but rather for the emulation of font types, in a variety of styles and sizes. The impulsive and sometimes whimsically humorous character of Whalen's writing becomes more pronounced in this format. The posthumously published calligraphic work, *The Unidentified Accomplice: Or, The Transmissions of C. W. Moss* (2005), is revealing for the same reason.

"THE GARDEN"

"The Garden" brings Whalen's talent for expressing the immediate into the foreground. His tendency to focus on minutiae overlooked by others finds itself mirrored in scenes around his Japanese lodgings, as he observes the landlady. While she is sweeping leaves off the moss, she is joined in her sweeping by her husband. Whalen intermixes direct observation with commentary on Japanese life, then arrives at a moment of deep concentration: "They sweep the shrubs and bushes, too,/ Old man has an elegant whiskbroom, a giant shaving brush/ Gets rid of dust and spiders, leaf by leaf." This 1966 poem represents Whalen's achievement of what he attributed to an ancient Greek poet, in 1952's "Homage to Lucretius": for he is presenting to the reader "A world not entirely new/ but realized."

Similarly, in his 1957 poem written in Berkeley, "The Same Old Jazz," Whalen points to the direct relation between inner and outer worlds: "And it all snaps into focus/ The world inside my head & the cat outside the window/ A one-to-one relationship." Although the lines address perception, both inner and outer, the breakthrough they describe also has to do with poetry, since the two lines immediately beforehand are these: "She wants to sleep & I get up naked at the table/ Writing."

Simultaneous reflections on the self and on the outer world animate many of the writings of Whalen. As in "Delights of Winter at the Shore," the question of self-indulgence may arise, just as they arise with the work of most poets associated with the Beat movement. In Whalen's case, the self-awareness is not self-absorption, and the "one-to-one relationship" between inner and outer worlds in Whalen's poetry makes it perhaps the most balanced of Beat-influenced work, even when his poetry is at its most intimately revealing.

OTHER MAJOR WORKS

LONG FICTION: *You Didn't Even Try*, 1967; *Imaginary Speeches for a Brazen Head*, 1972; *The Diamond Noodle*, 1980; *Two Novels* (*You Didn't Even Try* and *Imaginary Speeches for a Brazen Head*), 1985.

NONFICTION: *Intransit: The Education Continues Along Including Voyages, a TransPacific Journal*, 1967; *Prose [Out]Takes*, 2002.

MISCELLANEOUS: *Highgrade: Doodles, Poems*, 1966; *The Unidentified Accomplice: Or, The Transmissions of C. W. Moss*, 2005.

BIBLIOGRAPHY

Kherdian, David. *Six Poets of the San Francisco Renaissance: Portraits and Checklists.* Fresno, Calif.: Giligia Press, 1965. Provides valuable source material on the San Francisco Beat movement and Whalen.

Rothenberg, Michael, and Suzi, Winson, eds. *Continuous Flame: A Tribute to Philip Whalen.* New York: Fish Drum, 2005. A collection of tributes to Whalen, demonstrating the degree to which he served as an example and inspiration to other writers.

Snyder, Gary, Lew Welch, and Philip Whalen. *On Bread and Poetry: A Panel Discussion with Gary Snyder, Lew Welch, and Philip Whalen.* Edited by Donald Allen. Berkeley, Calif.: Grey Fox Press, 1973. A wide-ranging reunion discussion between three poet friends.

Suiter, John. *Poets on the Peaks: Gary Snyder, Philip Whalen, and Jack Kerouac in the Cascades.* Berkeley, Calif.: Counterpoint, 2002. An illustrated exploration of the years the three Beat writers spent as fire spotters in the Cascades, including an interview with Whalen covering topics including his ordination as a Zen monk.

Whalen, Philip. Interview by Donald Allen. In *Off the Wall: Interviews with Philip Whalen.* Edited by Allen. Bolinas, Calif.: Grey Fox Press, 1978. An exploration of the attitudes and ideas of the poet in his early years of being a Zen monk.

_____. "Philip Whalen." Interview by David Meltzer. In *San Francisco Beat: Talking with the Poets*, edited by Meltzer. San Francisco: City Lights, 2001. Whalen discusses his involvement in the San Francisco scene, his interest in Japan, and his training in Buddhism, along with his poetry.

Mark Rich

_____

PHILLIS WHEATLEY

Born: West Coast of Africa (possibly the Senegal-Gambia region); 1753(?)
Died: Boston, Massachusetts; December 5, 1784

PRINCIPAL POETRY

Poems on Various Subjects, Religious and Moral, 1773
The Poems of Phillis Wheatley, 1966, 1989 (Julian D. Mason, Jr., editor)

OTHER LITERARY FORMS

Phillis Wheatley's cultivation of the letter as a literary form is attested by her inclusion of the titles of several letters in each of her proposals for future volumes subsequent to the publication of her *Poems on Various Subjects, Religious and Moral* (1773). Regrettably, none of these proposals provoked enough response to secure publication of any new volumes. Scholars continue to discover both poems and letters that Wheatley names in these proposals. The letters mentioned in them are addressed to such noted persons as William Legge, second earl of Dartmouth; Selina Hastings, countess of Huntingdon; Benjamin Rush; and George Washington. They display a graceful style and articulate some of Wheatley's strongest protestations in support of the cause of American independence and in condemnation of Christian hypocrisy regarding slavery.

ACHIEVEMENTS

From the time of Phillis Wheatley's first published piece to the present day, controversy has surrounded the life and work of America's first black poet and only its second published woman poet, after Anne Bradstreet. Few poets of any age have been so scornfully maligned, so passionately defended, so fervently celebrated, and so patronizingly tolerated. However, during the years of her young adulthood, Wheatley was the toast of England and the colonies. For years before she attempted to find a Boston publisher for her poems, she had published numerous elegies commemorating the deaths of many of the city's most prominent citizens. In 1770, she wrote her most famous and most often-reprinted elegy, on the death of "the voice of the Great Awakening," George Whitefield, chaplain to the countess of Huntingdon, who was one of the leading benefactors of the Methodist evangelical movement in England and the colonies.

Not finding Boston to be in sympathy with her 1772 proposal for a volume, Wheatley found substantial support the following year in the countess of Huntingdon, whose interest had been stirred by the young poet's noble tribute to her chaplain. Subsequently, Wheatley was sent to London, ostensibly for her health; this trip curiously accords, however, with the very weeks that her book was being printed. It is likely that she proofread the galleys herself. At any rate, she was much sought after among the intellectual, literary set of London, and Sir Brook Watson, who was to become Lord Mayor of London within a year, presented her with a copy of John Milton's *Paradise Lost* (1667, 1674) in folio. The earl of Dartmouth, who was at the time secretary of state for the colonies and president of the board of Trade and Foreign Plantations, gave her a copy of Tobias Smollett's *Don Quixote* (1755), a translation of Miguel de Cervantes's *El ingenioso hidalgo don Quixote de la Mancha* (1605, 1615; *The History of the Valorous and Wittie Knight-Errant, Don Quixote of the Mancha*, 1612-1620; better known as *Don Quixote de la Mancha*). Benjamin Franklin, to whom she would later inscribe her second book of poetry (never published), has even recorded that, while in London briefly, he called on Wheatley to see whether "there were any service I could do her."

In the opening pages of her 1773 volume appears a letter of authentication of Wheatley's authorship, which is signed by still another of the signatories of the Declaration of Independence, John Hancock. Added to

Phillis Wheatley (Library of Congress)

the list of attesters are other outstanding Bostonians, including Thomas Hutchinson, then governor of Massachusetts, and James Bowdoin, one of the founders of Bowdoin College. Later, during the early months of the American Revolution, Wheatley wrote a poem in praise of General Washington, "To His Excellency General Washington." As a result, she received an invitation to visit the general at his headquarters, and her poem was published by Tom Paine in *The Pennsylvania Magazine*. John Paul Jones, who also appreciated Wheatley's celebration of freedom, even asked one of his officers to secure him a copy of her *Poems on Various Subjects, Religious and Moral*.

Nevertheless, she did not continue to enjoy such fame. A country ravaged by war has little time, finally, for poetry, and Wheatley regrettably, perhaps tragically, faced the rejection of two more proposals for a volume of new poems. Thwarted by the vicissitudes of war and poverty, Wheatley died from complications resulting from childbirth. Even so, her poetry has survived and is now considered to be among the best of its period produced in America or in England. It is just beginning to be recognized that, contrary to the opinion of those who would dispose of Wheatley as a mere imitator, she produced sophisticated, original poems whose creative theories of the imagination and the sublime anticipate the Romantic movement.

BIOGRAPHY

The known details of Phillis Wheatley's life are few. According to her master, John Wheatley of Boston, she "was brought from Africa to America in the Year 1761, between Seven and Eight Years of Age [sic]." Her parents were apparently sun-worshipers, for she is supposed to have recalled to her white captors that she remembered seeing her mother pouring out water to the sun every morning. If such be the case, it would help to explain why the sun is predominant as an image in her poetry.

Her life with the Wheatleys, John and Susanna and their two children, the twins Mary and Nathaniel, was probably not too demanding for one whose disposition toward asthma (brought on or no doubt exacerbated by the horrible "middle passage") greatly weakened her. The Wheatleys' son attended Harvard, so it is likely that Nathaniel served as the eager young girl's Latin tutor. At any rate, it is certain that Wheatley knew Latin well; her translation of the Niobe episode from Ovid's *Metamorphoses* (c. 8 C.E.; English translation, 1567), book 6, displays a learned knowledge and appreciation of the Latin original. Wheatley's classical learning is evident throughout her poetry, which is thick with allusions to ancient historical and mythological figures.

The turning point of Wheatley's career, not only as an author but also as a human being, came when her *Poems on Various Subjects, Religious and Moral* was published in London in 1773. After she returned from England, having been recalled because of Susanna Wheatley's worsening illness, she was manumitted sometime during September, 1773. It is probable that Wheatley was freed because of the severe censure that some English reviewers of her *Poems on Various Subjects, Religious and Moral* had directed at the owners of a learned author who "still remained a slave." At this very point, however, the poet's fortunes began a slow decline. In 1778, at the height of the war and after the deaths of both John and Susanna Wheatley, she mar-

ried John Peters, a black man of some learning who failed to rescue the poet from poverty.

Wheatley died alone and unattended in a hovel somewhere in the back streets of the Boston slums in 1784, truly an ignominious end for one who had enjoyed such favor. She was preceded in death by two of her children, as well as by the third, to whom she had just given birth. She was at most only thirty-one years old. Given Wheatley's vision of the world "Oppress'd with woes, a painful endless train," it should not be surprising that her most frequently adopted poetic form is the elegy, in which she always celebrates death as the achievement of ultimate freedom—suggesting the thanatos-eros (desire for death) motif of Romanticism.

ANALYSIS

Beginning in the 1970's, Phillis Wheatley began to receive the attention she deserves. George McMichael and others, editors of the influential two-volume *Anthology of American Literature* (1974, 1980), observe that she and Philip Freneau were "the most important poets" of America's Revolutionary War era. To be sure, one of the major subjects of her poetry is the American struggle for independence. Temporal freedom is not her only subject, however; she is also much concerned with the quest for spiritual freedom. Consequently, the elegy, in which she celebrates the Christian rewards of eternal life and absolute freedom after death, is her favorite poetic form. In addition, she delights in describing God's creation of nature's splendors and sometimes appears to enjoy the beauties of nature for their own sake and not simply as acts of God's providence. It is in "On Imagination," however, that Wheatley waxes most eloquent; in this poem, perhaps her most important single work, she articulates a theory of the imagination that strikingly anticipates that of Samuel Taylor Coleridge. Indeed, Wheatley's affinities with Romanticism, which run throughout her poetry, may come to be seen as her surest claim to a place in literary history.

Such an approach to this early American poet contradicts the widespread critical view that Wheatley was a highly derivative poet, inextricably mired in the neoclassical tradition. Her preference for the heroic couplet, one of the hallmarks of neoclassicism, has deceived many into immediately classifying her as neoclassical. One must recall, however, that Lord Byron also had a passion for the couplet. Surely, then, one must not be satisfied with a cursory glance at Wheatley's adoption of the heroic couplet; one must go on to explore the content of her poetry.

POLITICAL POEMS

Her political poems document major incidents of the American struggle for independence. In 1768, she wrote "To the King's Most Excellent Majesty on His Repealing the American Stamp Act." When it appeared, much revised, in *Poems on Various Subjects, Religious and Moral*, the poet diplomatically deleted the last two lines of the original, which read, "When wars came on [against George] the proudest rebel fled/ God thunder'd fury on their guilty head." By that time, the threat of the King's retaliation did not seem so forbidding nor the injustice of rebellion against him so grave.

"America," a poem probably written about the same time but published more than two hundred years later, admonishes Britain to treat "americus," the British child, with more deference. According to the poem, the child, now a growing seat of "Liberty," is no mere adorer of an overwhelming "Majesty," but has acquired strength of his own: "Fearing his strength which she [Britain] undoubted knew/ She laid some taxes on her darling son." Recognizing her mistake, "great Britannia" promised to lift the burden, but the promise proved only "seeming Sympathy and Love." Now the Child "weeps afresh to feel this Iron chain." The urge to draw an analogy here between the poem's "Iron chain" and Wheatley's own predicament is irresistible; while America longs for its own independence, Wheatley no doubt yearns for hers.

The year 1770 marked the beginning of armed resistance against Britain. Wheatley chronicles such resistance in two poems, the second of which is now lost. The first, "On the Death of Mr. Snider Murder'd by Richardson," appeared initially along with "America." The poem tells how Ebenezer Richardson, an informer on American traders involved in circumventing British taxation, found his home surrounded on the evening of February 22, 1770, by an angry mob of colonial sympathizers. Much alarmed, Richardson emerged from his house armed with a musket and fired indiscriminately into the mob, killing the eleven- or twelve-year-old son of Snider, a poor German colonist. Wheatley calls young Christopher Snider, of whose death Richardson was later found guilty in a trial by jury, "the first martyr for the common good," rather than those men killed less than two weeks later in the Boston Massacre. The poem's fine closing couplet suggests that even those not in sympathy with the quest for freedom can grasp the nobility of that quest and are made indignant by its sacrifice: "With Secret rage fair freedom's foes beneath/ See in thy corse ev'n Majesty in Death."

Wheatley does not, however, ignore the Boston Massacre. In a proposal for a volume which was to have been published in Boston in 1772, she lists, among twenty-seven titles of poems (the 1773 volume had thirty-nine), "On the Affray in King Street, on the Evening of the 5th of March." This title, naming the time and place of the massacre, suggests that the poet probably celebrated the martyrdom of Crispus Attucks, the first black to lose his life in the American struggle, along with the deaths of two whites. Regrettably, the poem has not yet been recovered. Even so, the title alone confirms Wheatley's continued recording of America's struggle for freedom. This concern shifted in tone from obedient praise for the British regime to supplicatory admonition and then to guarded defiance. Since she finally found a publisher not in Boston but in London, she prudently omitted "America" and the poems about Snider and the Boston Massacre from her 1773 volume.

She chose to include, however, a poem dedicated to the earl of Dartmouth, who was appointed secretary of state for the colonies in August, 1772. In this poem, "To the Right Honourable William, Earl of Dartmouth, His Majesty's Principal Secretary of State for North America," she gives the earl extravagant praise as one who will lay to rest "hatred faction." She knew of the earl's reputation as a humanitarian through the London contacts of her mistress, Susanna. When the earl proved to support oppressive British policies, the poet's expectations were not realized; within four years of the poem's date, America had declared its independence. Since her optimism was undaunted by foreknowledge, Wheatley wrote a poem that was even more laudatory than "To

The King's Most Excellent Majesty on His Repealing the American Stamp Act." Perhaps she was not totally convinced, however; the poem contains some unusually bold passages for a colonist who is also both a woman and a slave.

For example, she remarks that, with Dartmouth's secretaryship, America need no longer "dread the iron chain,/ Which wanton *Tyranny* with lawless hand/ Had made, and with it meant t'enslave the land." Once again Wheatley uses the slave metaphor of the iron chain. Quite clearly she also accuses the Crown of "wanton *Tyranny*," which it had wielded illegally and with the basest of motives—to reduce the colonies to the inhuman condition of slave states. Here rebellious defiance, no longer guarded, is unmistakable; the tone matches that of the Declaration of Independence. It is a mystery how these lines could have gone unnoticed in the London reviews, all of them positive, of her 1773 volume. Perhaps the reviewers were too bedazzled by the "improbability" that a black woman could produce such a volume to take the content of her poetry seriously.

In this poem, Wheatley also presents a rare autobiographical portrait describing the manner in which she was taken from her native Africa. The manuscript version of this passage is more spontaneous and direct than the more formally correct one printed in the 1773 volume and thus is closer to the poet's true feelings. It was "Seeming cruel fate" that snatched her "from Afric's fancy'd happy seat." Fate here is only apparently cruel, since her capture has enabled her to become a Christian; the young poet's piety resounds throughout her poetry and letters. Her days in her native land were, nevertheless, happy ones, and her abduction at the hands of ruthless slavers doubtless left behind inconsolable parents. Such a bitter memory of the circumstances of her abduction fully qualifies her to "deplore the day/ When Britons weep beneath Tyrannic sway"; the later version reads: "And can I then but pray/ Others may never feel tyranic sway?" Besides toning down the diction, this passage alters her statement to a question and replaces "Britons" with the neutral "others." The question might suggest uncertainty, but it more probably reflects the author's polite deportment toward a London audience. Since, in the earlier version, she believed Dartmouth to be sympathetic with her cause, she

had no reason to exercise deference toward him; she thought she could be frank. The shift from "Britons" to "others" provokes a more compelling explanation. In the fall of 1772, Wheatley could still think of herself as a British subject. Later, however, after rejoicing that the earl's administration had given way to restive disillusionment, perhaps the poet was less certain about her citizenship.

Three years after the publication of her 1773 volume, Wheatley unabashedly celebrated the opposition to the "tyrannic sway" of Britain in "To His Excellency General Washington," newly appointed commander in chief of the Continental Army; the war of ideas had become one of arms. In this piece, which is more a paean to freedom than a eulogy to Washington, she describes freedom as "divinely fair,/ Olive and laurel bind her golden hair"; yet "She flashes dreadful in refulgent arms." The poet accents this image of martial glory with an epic simile, comparing the American forces to the power of the fierce king of the winds:

> As when Eolus heaven's fair face deforms,
> Enwrapp'd in tempest and a night of storms;
> Astonish'd ocean feels the wild uproar,
> The refluent surges beat the sounding shore.

For the young poet, America is now "The land of freedom's heaven-defended race!" While the eyes of the world's nations are fixed "on the scales,/ For in their hopes Columbia's arm prevails," the poet records Britain's regret over her loss: "Ah! cruel blindness to Columbia's state!/ Lament thy thirst of boundless power too late." The temper of this couplet is in keeping with Wheatley's earlier attitudes toward oppression. The piece closes as the poet urges Washington to pursue his objective with the knowledge that virtue is on his side. If he allows the fair goddess Freedom to be his guide, Washington will surely emerge not only as the leader of a victorious army but also as the head of the newly established state.

In Wheatley's last political poem, "freedom's heaven-defended race" has won its battle. Written in 1784 within a year after the Treaty of Paris, "Liberty and Peace" is a demonstrative celebration of American independence. British tyranny, the agent of American oppression, has now been taught to fear "americus" her child, "And new-born *Rome* shall give *Britannia* Law." Wheatley concludes this piece with two pleasing couplets in praise of America, whose future is assured by heaven's approval:

> Auspicious Heaven shall fill with favoring Gales,
> Where e'er *Columbia* spreads her swelling Sails:
> To every Realm shall *Peace* her Charms display,
> And Heavenly *Freedom* spread her golden Ray.

Personified as Peace and Freedom, Columbia (America) will act as a world emissary, an emanating force like the rays of the sun. In this last couplet, Wheatley has captured, perhaps for the first time in poetry, America's ideal mission to the rest of the world.

The fact that Wheatley so energetically proclaims America's success in the political arena certainly attests her sympathies—not with the neoclassic obsession never to challenge the established order nor to breach the rules of political and social decorum—but with the Romantic notion that a people who find themselves unable to accept a present, unsatisfactory government have the right to change that government, even if such a change can be accomplished only through armed revolt. The American Revolution against Britain was the first successful such revolt and was one of the sparks of the French Revolution. Wheatley's steadfast literary participation in the American Revolution clearly aligns her with such politically active English Romantic poets as Percy Bysshe Shelley and Lord Byron.

THE ELEGIES

In her elegies, on the other hand, Wheatley displays her devotion to spiritual freedom. As do her political poems, her elegies exalt specific occasions, the deaths of people usually known to her within the social and religious community of the poet's Old South Congregational Church of Boston. As do her poems on political events, however, her elegies exceed the boundaries of occasional verse. The early, but most famous of her elegies, "On the Death of the Rev. Mr. George Whitefield, 1770," both illustrates the general structure in which she cast all seventeen of her extant elegies and indicates her recurring ideological concerns.

Wheatley's elegies conform for the most part to the Puritan funeral elegy. They include two major divi-

sions: First comes the portrait, in which the poet pictures the life of the subject; then follows the exhortation, encouraging the reader to seek the heavenly rewards gained by the subject in death. The portrait usually comprises three biographical steps: vocation or conversion; sanctification, or evidence of good works; and glorification, or joyous treatment of the deceased's reception into heaven. Wheatley's elegy on Whitefield surprisingly opens with the glorification of the Great Awakener, already in heaven and occupying his "immortal throne." She celebrates the minister's conversion or vocation in an alliterative line as "The greatest gift that ev'n a God can give." Of course, she writes many lines describing the good works of a man wholly devoted to the winning of souls during the seven visits he made to America during and after the period of the Great Awakening.

Whitefield died in Newburyport, Massachusetts, on September 30, 1770, having left Boston only a week or so before, where he had apparently lodged with the Wheatley family. Indeed, the young poet of sixteen or seventeen appears to recollect from personal experience when she observes that the minister "long'd to see *America* excel" and "charg'd its youth that ev'ry grace divine/ Should with full lustre in their conduct shine." She also seizes this opportunity to proclaim to the world Whitefield's assertion that even Africans would find Jesus of Nazareth an "*Impartial Saviour.*" The poem closes with a ten-line exhortation to the living to aspire toward Whitefield's example: "Let ev'ry heart to this bright vision rise."

As one can see, Wheatley's elegies are not sad affairs; quite to the contrary, they enact joyful occasions after which deceased believers may hope to unite, as she states in "On the Death of the Rev. Dr. Sewell, 1769," with "Great God, incomprehensible, unknown/ By sense." Although people's senses may limit their firsthand acquaintance with God, these same senses do enable them to learn about God, especially about God's works in nature. The poem in the extant Wheatley canon that most pointedly addresses God's works in nature is "Thoughts on the Works of Providence." This poem of 131 lines opens with a 10-line invocation to the "Celestial muse," resembling Milton's heavenly muse of *Paradise Lost.*

Identifying God as the force behind planetary movement, she writes, "Ador'd [is] the God that whirls surrounding spheres" which rotate ceaselessly about "the monarch of the earth and skies." From this sublime image she moves to yet another: "'Let there be light,' he said: from his profound/ Old chaos heard and trembled at the sound." It should not go unremarked that Wheatley could, indeed, find much in nature to foster her belief, but little in the mundane world of ordinary humans to sustain her spiritually. The frequency of nature imagery but the relative lack of scenes drawn from human society (with the exception of her political poems, and even these are occasions for abstract departures into the investigation of political ideologies) probably reflects the poet's insecurity and uncertainty about a world which first made her a slave and then gave her, at best, only second-class citizenship.

In "An Hymn to the Morning," one of her most lyrical poems, Wheatley interprets the morn (recall her mother's morning ritual of pouring out water to the rising sun) as the source of poetic afflatus or inspiration. The speaker of the poem, Wheatley herself, first perceives the light of the rising sun as a reflection in the eye of one of the "feather'd race." After she hears the song of the bird that welcomes the day, she turns to find the source of melody and sees the bird "Dart the bright eye, and shake the painted plume." Here the poet captures with great precision the bird's rapid eye movement. The bird, archetypal symbol of poetic song, has received the dawn's warm rays that stimulate him to sing. When the poet turns to discover the source of melody, however, what she sees first is not Aurora, the dawning sun, but Aurora the stimulus of song reflected within the "bright eye" of the bird.

In the next stanza, the poet identifies the dawn as the ultimate source of poetic inspiration when she remarks that the sun has awakened Calliope, here the personification of inspiration, while her sisters, the other Muses, "fan the pleasing fire" of the stimulus to create. Hence both the song of the bird and the light reflected in its eye have instructed her to acknowledge the source of the bird's melody; for she aspires to sing with the same pleasing fire that animates the song of the bird. Like many of the Romantics who followed her, Wheatley perceives nature both as a means to know ultimate freedom and as an inspiration to create, to make art.

It is in her superlative poem, "On Imagination," however, that Wheatley most forcefully brings both aspirations, to know God and to create fine poetry, into clear focus. To the young black poet, the imagination was sufficiently important to demand from her pen a fifty-three-line poem. The piece opens with this four-line apostrophe:

Thy various works, imperial queen, we see,
How bright their forms! how deck'd with pomp by thee!
Thy wond'rous acts in beauteous order stand,
And all attest how potent is thine hand.

Clearly, Wheatley's imagination is a regal presence in full control of her poetic world, a world in which her "wond'rous acts" of creation stand in harmony, capturing a "beauteous order." These acts themselves testify to the queen's creative power. Following a four-line invocation to the Muse, however, the poet distinguishes the imagination from its subordinate fancy:

Now, here, now there, the roving Fancy flies;
Till some lov'd object strikes her wand'ring eyes,
Whose silken fetters all the senses bind,
And soft captivity involves the mind.

Unlike the controlled, harmonious imagination, the subordinate fancy flies about here and there, searching for some appropriate and desired object worthy of setting into motion the creative powers of her superior.

FANCY AND MEMORY

In "Thoughts on the Works of Providence," the poet describes the psychology of sleep in similar fashion. Having entered the world of dreams, the mind discovers a realm where "ideas range/ Licentious and unbounded o'er the plains/ Where Fancy's queen in giddy triumph reigns." Wheatley maintains that in sleep the imagination, once again "Fancy's queen," creates worlds that lack the "beauteous order" of the poet sitting before a writing desk; nevertheless, these dreamworlds provoke memorable images. In "On Recollection," Wheatley describes the memory as the repository on which the mind draws to create its dreams. What may be "long-forgotten," the memory "calls from night" and "plays before the fancy's sight." By analogy, Wheatley maintains, the memory provides the poet "ample treasure" from her "secret stores" to create poetry: "in her pomp of images display'd,/ To the high-raptur'd poet gives her aid." "On Recollection" asserts a strong affinity between the poet's memory, analogous to the world of dreams, and the fancy, the associative faculty subordinate to the imagination. Recollection for Wheatley functions as the poet's storehouse of images, while the fancy channels the force of the imagination through its associative powers. Both the memory and the fancy, then, serve the imagination.

Wheatley's description of fancy and memory departs markedly from what eighteenth century aestheticians, including John Locke and Joseph Addison, generally understood as the imagination. The faculty of mind that they termed "imagination" Wheatley relegates to recollection (memory) and fancy. Her description of recollection and fancy closely parallels Coleridge's in the famous thirteenth chapter of *Biographia Literaria* (1817), where he states that fancy "is indeed no other than a mode of Memory emancipated from the order of time and space." Wheatley's identification of the fancy as roving "Now here, now there" whose movement is analogous to the dream state, where "ideas range/ Licentious and unbounded," certainly frees it from the limits of time and space. Coleridge further limits the fancy to the capacity of choice. "But equally with the ordinary memory," he insists, "the Fancy must receive all its materials ready made from the law of association." Like Coleridge's, Wheatley's fancy exercises choice by association as it finally settles on "some lov'd object."

If fancy and memory are the imagination's subordinates, then how does the imagination function in the poet's creative process? Following her description of fancy in "On Imagination," Wheatley details the role the imagination plays in her poetry. According to her, the power of the imagination enables her to soar "through air to find the bright abode,/ Th' empyreal palace of the thund'ring God." The central focus of her poetry remains contemplation of God. Foreshadowing William Wordsworth's "winds that will be howling at all hours," Wheatley exclaims that on the wings of the imagination she "can surpass the wind/ And leave the rolling universe behind." In the realm of the imagina-

tion, the poet can "with new worlds amaze th' unbounded soul."

Immediately following this arresting line, Wheatley illustrates in a ten-line stanza the power of the imagination to create new worlds. Even though winter and the "frozen deeps" prevail in the real world, the imagination can take one out of unpleasant reality and build a pleasant, mythic world of fragrant flowers and verdant groves where "Fair Flora" spreads "her fragrant reign," where Sylvanus crowns the forest with leaves, and where "Show'rs may descend, and dews their gems disclose,/ And nectar sparkle on the blooming rose." Such is the power of imagination to promote poetic creation and to release one from an unsatisfactory world. Unfortunately, like reality's painful intrusion on the delicate, unsustainable song of John Keats's immortal bird, gelid winter and its severe "northern tempests damp the rising fire," cut short the indulgence of her poetic world, and lamentably force Wheatley to end her short-lived lyric: "Cease then, my song, cease the unequal lay." Her lyric must end because no poet can indefinitely sustain a mythic world.

In her use of the imagination to create "new worlds," Wheatley's departure from eighteenth century theories of this faculty is radical and once again points toward Coleridge. Although she does not distinguish between "primary" and "secondary" imagination as he does, Wheatley nevertheless constructs a theory which approaches his "secondary" imagination. According to Coleridge, the secondary imagination, which attends the creative faculty, intensifies the primary imagination common to all people. Coleridge describes how the secondary imagination operates in this well-known passage: "It dissolves, diffuses, dissipates, in order to recreate;/ or where this process is rendered impossible, yet still at all/ events it struggles to idealize and to unify." In spite of the fact that Wheatley's attempt to dissolve, diffuse, and dissipate is assuredly more modest than Coleridge's "swift half-intermitted burst" in "Kubla Khan," she does, nevertheless, like the apocalyptic Romantics, idealize, unify, and shape a mythopoeic world. Proceeding in a systematic fashion, she first constructs a theory of mental faculty that, when assisted by the associative fancy, builds, out of an act of the mind, a new world that does indeed stand in "beauteous order." This faculty, which she identifies as the imagination, she uses as a tool to achieve freedom, however momentary.

Wheatley was, then, an innovator who used the imagination as a means to transcend an unacceptable present and even to construct "new worlds [to] amaze the unbounded soul"; this practice, along with her celebration of death, her loyalty to the American struggle for political independence, and her consistent praise of nature, places her firmly in that flow of thought that culminated in nineteenth century Romanticism. Her diction may strike a modern audience as occasionally "got up" and stiff, and her reliance on the heroic couplet may appear outdated and worn, but the content of her poetry is innovative, refreshing, and even, for her times, revolutionary. She wrote during the pre-Revolutionary and Revolutionary War eras in America, when little poetry of great merit was produced. Wheatley, laboring under the disadvantages of being not only a black slave but also a woman, nevertheless did find the time to depict that political struggle for freedom and to trace her personal battle for release. If one looks beyond the limitations of her sincere if dogmatic piety and her frequent dependence on what Wordsworth called poetic diction, one is sure to discover in her works a fine mind engaged in creating some of the best early American poetry.

OTHER MAJOR WORKS

MISCELLANEOUS: *Memoir and Poems of Phillis Wheatley: A Native African and a Slave*, 1833; *The Collected Works of Phillis Wheatley*, 1988 (John Shields, editor).

BIBLIOGRAPHY

Cook, William W., and James Tatum. *African American Writers and Classical Tradition*. Chicago: University of Chicago Press, 2010. Examines the relationship of African American writers, beginning with Wheatley, to Greek and Roman classics.

Engberg, Kathrynn Seidler. *The Right to Write: The Literary Politics of Anne Bradstreet and Phillis Wheatley*. Lanham, Md.: University Press of America, 2010. Examines the first two published women poets of the United States and the problems and challenges they faced.

Gates, Henry Louis, Jr. *The Trials of Phillis Wheatley: America's First Black Poet and Her Encounters with the Founding Fathers*. 2003. Reprint. New York: Basic Civitas Books, 2010. A biography of Wheatley that examines her life and works, including Thomas Jefferson's harsh critique of her work and her lack of popularity among African Americans.

Hayden, Lucy K. "*Poems on Various Subjects, Religious and Moral*." In *Masterplots II: African American Literature*, edited by Tyrone Williams. Rev. ed. Pasadena, Calif.: Salem Press, 2009. Examines this work in detail, looking at themes and meanings and the critical context.

Morton, Gerald W. *Phillis Wheatley: Slave and Poet*. Baltimore: PublishAmerica, 2008. A biography that looks at Wheatley's life and writings.

Robinson, William H. *Phillis Wheatley and Her Writings*. New York: Garland, 1984. A fine introduction to Wheatley, by an eminent Wheatley scholar. Presents a brief biography, the text of all the poems and surviving letters (several in facsimile) with an analysis, nine appendixes providing background information, bibliography, and index.

Shields, John C. *Phillis Wheatley and the Romantics*. Knoxville: University of Tennessee Press, 2010. Looks at the poetry of Wheatley and how it influenced the Romantics who followed her.

_____. *Phillis Wheatley's Poetics of Liberation: Backgrounds and Contexts*. Knoxville: University of Tennessee Press, 2008. Examines how evaluation of Wheatley's poetry has changed over the years.

John C. Shields

JOHN HALL WHEELOCK

Born: Far Rockaway, Long Island, New York;
September 9, 1886
Died: New York, New York; March 22, 1978

PRINCIPAL POETRY

Verses by Two Undergraduates, 1905 (with Van
Wyck Brooks)
The Human Fantasy, 1911
The Beloved Adventure, 1912
Dust and Light, 1919
The Black Panther: A Book of Poems, 1922
The Bright Doom: A Book of Poems, 1927
Poems, 1911-1936, 1936
Poems Old and New, 1956
The Gardener, and Other Poems, 1961
Dear Men and Women: New Poems, 1966
*By Daylight and in Dream: New and Collected
Poems, 1904-1970*, 1970
In Love and Song: Poems, 1971
*This Blessed Earth: New and Selected Poems,
1927-1977*, 1978

OTHER LITERARY FORMS

Although John Hall Wheelock employed a prose section in his first volume of poetry, he remained largely devoted to poetic expression throughout his writing life. His *What Is Poetry?* (1963) was also dedicated to his preferred art.

Wheelock engaged in important work as editor, however. Of significance was *Editor to Author: The Letters of Maxwell E. Perkins*, to which he supplied an introduction. He also edited the influential anthology series *Poets of Today*, issued in eight volumes from 1954 to 1961. Among the previously unpublished poets he introduced in these volumes were May Swenson, James Dickey, and Louis Simpson.

ACHIEVEMENTS

John Hall Wheelock's collected *Poems, 1911-1936*, won the 1937 Golden Rose Award of the New England Poetry Society. Nearly twenty years later, *Poems Old and New* was honored with the Ridgely Torrence Me-

morial Award in 1956 and the Borestone Mountain Poetry Award in 1957. In 1962, Wheelock received the Bollingen Prize for Poetry and, three years later, the Signet Society Medal of Harvard University, for distinguished achievement in the arts. In 1974, the Poetry Society of America presented him with its Frost Medal.

Wheelock's status in American letters was reflected by the number of positions in the arts he held beginning in the 1940's, including the vice presidencies of the Poetry Society of America and the National Institute of Arts and Letters. In 1947, he became a chancellor of the Academy of American Poets, a position he held until he was named an honorary fellow in 1971. Wheelock was also member of the American Academy of Arts and Letters (1948-1978), and honorary consultant in American letters of the Library of Congress.

BIOGRAPHY

John Hall Wheelock was born in Far Rockaway, New York, to William Efner Wheelock and Emily Charlotte Hall Wheelock. He grew up spending summers on the shore at East Hampton, Long Island, where he developed a deep affection for the sea. His verse writing began at a young age. By the time he enrolled at Harvard University, Wheelock was firmly set on the course that would lead him to a career in writing and publishing poetry that would extend over a span of more than sixty years.

At Harvard, Wheelock had the good fortune, in September, 1904, to begin a friendship with the surprisingly widely read Van Wyck Brooks. Wheelock and Brooks shared a deeply seated enthusiasm for Walt Whitman's *Leaves of Grass* (1855); and in 1905, the two collaborated in anonymously publishing a small collection entitled *Verses by Two Undergraduates*. After leaving Harvard, where his honors had included serving as class poet, Wheelock pursued studies at the Universities of Göttingen and Berlin.

In 1910, after two years abroad, Wheelock returned to find Brooks working for the Funk and Wagnall's *Standard Dictionary*. Wheelock undertook the same work for a time, although he proved less successful than his friend at what amounted to literary hackwork and was let go. During this period his preferred literary efforts, however, were beginning to meet with success, with his verses appearing in *Scribner's* and *The American Magazine*.

In 1911, Wheelock's first volume, *The Human Fantasy*, was published by the Boston firm of Sherman, French. Unusually ambitious for a first book, it consisted mainly of the title poem, which followed the course of a doomed love affair from beginning to end. In the same year, Wheelock joined the editorial house of Charles Scribner's Sons, beginning what would be a lifelong association. He became a close associate of Maxwell Perkins, a youthful friend of Brooks whom Wheelock had met at Harvard.

Wheelock's career as a published poet was beginning to flourish, with continued appearances in *Scribner's* and *The American Magazine* as well as *The Century*, *The Smart Set*, and *Harper's Monthly*. His second and third volumes of poetry followed in quick succession in 1912 and 1913, both again from his Boston publisher. Although critics including Louis Untermeyer had lauded Wheelock's earlier efforts, his third book won less glowing reviews, leading to a hiatus of five years before Wheelock's fourth book appeared. *Dust and Light* was published by the firm that also employed him. Wheelock's collections of poems would continue appearing from Scribner's for the remainder of his long career.

Wheelock thrived at Scribner's, in 1932 becoming a director of the corporation. Although only two collections of his poems had appeared in the 1920's, and none at all in the early 1930's, the collection *Poems, 1911-1936*, proved an important publication that solidified his position in American letters. In 1940, he married Phyllis E. de Kay, daughter of poet and art critic Charles de Kay. In 1942, he became treasurer at Scribner's, and in 1947, upon the death of Perkins, senior editor. Nine years later, in 1956, his first collection in two decades appeared. His retirement from Scribner's the following year sparked a revitalization of his writing career, resulting in the appearance of three new volumes before his death in 1978. *This Blessed Earth* was published posthumously.

ANALYSIS

Although John Hall Wheelock's early verse has lively, romantic exuberance of expression, the more measured poems of his maturity became the ones to win him the most attention and critical approval. Quieter of tone and conscientiously structured, they gained him a reputation as a traditionalist. His frequent subjects were ones he shared with other lyric poets of the earlier century, including expressions of romantic love and lost love, meditations on the place of humankind in the universe, and reflections inspired by the sea. Despite his reputation for formal accomplishment and traditionalism, Wheelock's works were not dry exercises in versification but rather poems that were as diverse in their approaches as they were in their subject matter. Many were quietly exploratory, in terms of rhythm and form, rather than experimental; and despite his thematic emphasis on love, his works remained robust and never mawkish. All were emotionally honest.

THE HUMAN FANTASY

"The Human Fantasy," the title poem that takes up most of the pages of Wheelock's first collection, is an expansive, adventuresome work based around a simple story of a romance. The story is sketched out in its entirety in a prose piece set early among the diverse, short offerings that make up the whole. Unlike many of Wheelock's later poems, the verses making up "The Human Fantasy" employ recurring images evoking the vastness of the astronomical universe and contrast that vision with depictions of a vibrantly alive, modern city. The city proves to be as important a character in the long poem as are the two lovers.

Wheelock's debut collection concludes with a miscellany of short poems, including "Sunday Evening in the Common," a meditation on "The infinite stars that brood above us here,/ And the gray city in the soft June weather," which seems directed toward Brooks, to whom it is dedicated in later reprintings. Others include the longer poems "The Mad-Man" and "Irma," which offer darkly depressive counterpoint to the vision of the bustling and brilliant city presented in "The Human Fantasy."

DUST AND LIGHT

Wheelock's fourth collection, *Dust and Light*, contains numerous noteworty works, especially "Earth," one of his most frequently reprinted works. "Earth" is, in a sense, a poem about poetry, although the subject might equally well be any of the arts. It begins with a quatrain that exhibits the clarity and the music of which Wheelock was proving to be increasingly capable: "Grasshopper, your fairy song/ And my poem alike belong/ To the dark and silent earth/ From which all poetry has birth." This poem established, for many readers, the quiet, intelligent tone they came to expect from him. The collection also includes "April Lightning," a narrative of love made up of numbered verses. Among them is the fourteenth, which describes a dream in which the poet, or the viewpoint character of the narrative, arrives at a house of death, and learns that the one who has died is his sole kindred soul, the fated lover whom he has never met and never will meet, and who has died. The verse's riveting imagery is presented with the simple clarity of a fable.

DEAR MEN AND WOMEN

The title poem of *Dear Men and Women* is one of Wheelock's most powerful works. Dedicated to the memory of Brooks, "Dear Men and Women" contains some of the poet's most musical language, as in its opening lines: "In the quiet before cockcrow when the cricket's/ Mandolin falters, when the light of the past/ Falling from the high stars yet haunts the earth." It also contains a compelling development of the theme of acceptance of the "heartbreak at the heart of things," telling of the joy to be found in the vanished past. "Dear Men and Women" is an unusual poem of age, memory, and friendship, unembittered and radiant in its approach to joy.

The phrase "dear men and women" reappears in the longer, less strictly structured poem "Amagansett Beach Revisited," which also approaches the subjects of aging, memory and regret. In this case, the thoughts are inspired by a walk beside the sea. Although they are tinged with sadness and bitterness, the lines are also alive with a love for life and for what life has brought to the poet through the decades. It achieves an effect similar to that of "Dear Men and Women," by entirely different means.

THIS BLESSED EARTH

This Blessed Earth, published posthumously, combines reprints of some of Wheelock's finest shorter poems with thirteen poems written in the poet's last years. Although all are of exceptional quality, among them are outstanding gems of verbal grace and lucid insight.

The opening lyric "To You, Perhaps Yet Unborn," only eight lines long, addresses Wheelock's own future reader: "It is night, and we are alone together; your head/ Bends over the open book, your feeding eyes devour/ The substance of my dream. . . ." The surprisingly sensuous "Aphrodite, 1906" recalls a moment apparently from the poet's youth. The poem's language is richly descriptive and melodious, with an impact at first sensuous and, in the end, poignant: "And the world was young. O love and song and fame/ Were part of youth's still ever believed-in story,/ And hope crowned all, when in dear and in queenly glory,/ Out of the snow-cold sea to me you came."

OTHER MAJOR WORKS

NONFICTION: *A Bibliography of Theodore Roosevelt*, 1920; *What Is Poetry?*, 1963.

EDITED TEXTS: *Editor to Author: The Letters of Maxwell E. Perkins*, 1950; *Poets Today*, 1954-1961 (8 volumes).

BIBLIOGRAPHY

Berg, A. Scott. *Max Perkins: Editor of Genius*. New York: Riverhead Trade, 1997. A striking portrait of Wheelock's colleague and friend that describes the professional world in which the two were working and their relation with some of the most important early to mid-twentieth century American writers.

Brooks, Van Wyck. *Days of the Phoenix: The Nineteen-Twenties I Remember*. New York: E. P. Dutton, 1957. Brooks recalls a turbulent decade in his life, during which his friend Wheelock played an important role in confronting severe mental difficulties.

Wheelock, John Hall. "Literary Sketches." *Paris Review* 163 (Fall, 2002): 220-237. An illuminating series of sketches of literary personalities and celebrities Wheelock had known, including Sara Teasdale, Vachel Lindsay, Robert Frost, and Marianne Moore. Includes photographs.

Wheelock, John Hall, with Matthew Joseph Bruccoli, and Judith S. Baughman, eds. *The Last Romantic: A Poet Among Publishers—The Oral Autobiography of John Hall Wheelock*. Columbia: University of

South Carolina Press, 2002. This account, drawn from dictated memoirs, covers the poet and editor's full life and explores the world of publishing in detail.

Mark Rich

JOHN WHEELWRIGHT

Born: Milton, Massachusetts; September 9, 1897

Died: Boston, Massachusetts; September 15, 1940

PRINCIPAL POETRY

North Atlantic Passage, 1925
Rock and Shell: Poems, 1923-1933, 1933
Footsteps, 1934
Masque with Clowns, 1936
Mirrors of Venus: A Novel in Sonnets, 1914-1938, 1938
Political Self-Portrait, 1919-1939, 1940
John Wheelwright: Selected Poems, 1941
Collected Poems of John Wheelwright, 1972

OTHER LITERARY FORMS

Upon his death in 1940, an obituary in *Time* magazine described John Wheelwright as "one of the most famous unheard-of poets in the U.S." As well as being a poet, however, Wheelwright was a militant in the realm of socialist theory and practice who wrote numerous essays for periodicals such as the *Partisan Review* and *The New Republic*. He was also the author of speeches on contemporary political events and issues, which he delivered from soapboxes in public settings in and around Boston.

The themes Wheelwright explored in his prose writing included his views on poetry, architecture, and developments in socialist politics in the United States. The highly literate and cultured writer also saw the possibilities of radio as a powerful vehicle for poetry and made extensive use of the medium in broadcasts in the Boston area.

ACHIEVEMENTS

John Wheelwright is an uncommon case of a poet whose political activities, commitments, and ideals find coherent, organic, and fresh expression in verse. Wheelwright's complex, rich background combined a rebellious, iconoclastic streak inherited from his ancestor John Wheelwright (1592-1679), an antinomian who founded settlements in New England, and a classicist education based on the Bible and Latin and Greek philosophy and literature. This background, together with vigorous reading and a committed practice of socialist principles, makes for a poet whose work is often didactic. "The main point," wrote Wheelwright "is not what noise poetry makes, but how it makes you think and act—not what you make of it, but what it makes of you."

Wheelwright wrote "revolutionary poetry" that was a sophisticated expression of the spirit of euphoric optimism of the 1920's and the social upheaval that marked the 1930's. As a public figure, Wheelwright had an important impact on intellectuals and workers of his time and extended the New England freethinking tradition of such figures as Thomas Paine, Ralph Waldo Emerson, and Henry David Thoreau.

BIOGRAPHY

John Taylor Wheelwright was born in Milton, Massachusetts, on September 9, 1897, into a socially prominent family. His father, Edmund March (Ned) Wheelwright, a descendant of the eighteenth century minister and political figure John Wheelwright, was a creative architect and freethinker who designed some of Boston's most remarkable public buildings. John's mother, Elizabeth (Bessie) Boott Brooks, was a descendant of Peter Chardon Brooks (1767-1849), a prosperous merchant who at one time was called the richest man in New England. As Alan Wald remarked in his book *The Revolutionary Imagination* (1983), a "blended heritage of saints, traders, political and military leaders, pioneers, and Brahmins profoundly shaped the mind and the art of the poet John Wheelwright."

From his father's side, Wheelwright acquired intellectual curiosity and a penchant for rebellion. His father's suicide, two years after a mental and emotional breakdown, created a spiritual crisis for the teenage John, who was provided guidance by his teachers at St. George's preparatory school in Rhode Island. Seeking solace in religious thought, Wheelwright at one point considered entering the priesthood and believed the role of the poet to be similar to that of the priest.

Wheelwright remained profoundly religious throughout his short life, rejecting his parents' Unitarianism for the Anglican Church. In the 1930's, he adopted a socialism whose idealism paralleled, if it did not replace, his religious fervor. Socialism allowed the poet, a man of the word in every sense, to channel a deeply ingrained sense of justice into community action and become a man of word and deed.

From his mother, he acquired a sense of pride and authority. Her public manner and awareness of social place and responsibility shaped Wheelwright's uncompromising bearing in the public sphere, to which he chose to devote his energies.

After a privileged childhood of private schools, during which he nurtured interests in poetry, drama, and ideas, Wheelwright, like his father, attended Harvard University. He was eventually expelled because of poor grades, which resulted not from lack of talent but from a lack of application; he frequently skipped classes and missed examinations. This did not prevent Wheelwright from participating fully in the activities and publications of the Harvard Poetry Society. He published poems in *Eight More Harvard Poets* in 1923.

During a stay with his mother in Florence, Italy, Wheelwright published his first important collection, *North Atlantic Passage*. This, like much of his other work, was privately printed. Wheelwright followed his father's example and sought training in architecture in the late 1920's at the Massachusetts Institute of Technology. Without obtaining a degree, he briefly set up a practice. At the time of his death, among the books he had in preparation was a history of Romantic architecture.

Although the early phase of Wheelwright's poetic career combined self-examination with an unorthodox interest in the Bible, the 1930's brought public involvement. He was a member of the New England

John Wheelwright

Poetry Club, an organization that he discussed in his *A History of the New England Poetry Club, 1915-1931* (1932). He became a member of the Socialist Party of Massachusetts in 1932. He taught, edited publications, and prepared and delivered speeches for public assemblies. The poetry from this period incorporated and developed themes addressed in his public life. These were collected in *Political Self-Portrait, 1919-1939*, published in the last year of his life, which was suddenly ended when he was hit by a drunken driver while crossing the street. Wheelwright was forty-three.

ANALYSIS

John Wheelwright's poetic work remains outside the canon of great literature, despite a quiet revival of interest in Wheelwright after the 1960's, and his work is still undergoing assessment. Public ignorance of Wheelwright's literary achievement has at times been attributed to an alleged obscurity in his work, but the political nature of his didacticism may also have played a part in his marginalization. Nonetheless, Wheelwright's oeuvre can be richly rewarding to explore. From the precociously individual work of his youth to the "more dissonant and more complex" statements of his maturity, noted Matthew Josephson in *Southern Review* in 1971, emerges the voice of a man who "was forthright and had the strength and courage for life on his own terms."

ROCK AND SHELL

Wheelwright's first major collection, *Rock and Shell*, contained two remarkable long poems. The first, "North Atlantic Passage," originally published in pamphlet form in Florence, Italy, in 1923, makes use of the then-emerging Surrealist technique of associative logic and imagery, and the modernist feature of polyphonic voices to explore the theme of "the One and the Many." The second, "Forty Days," is a revision of the story of the apostle Thomas, which the poet based on a reading of the apocryphal Gospels. It presents Wheelwright's unorthodox ideas on religious material, exploring, as it does, the poet's own confrontation with doubt and faith. Wheelwright's budding social conscience resulted in such poems as "Come Over and Help Us," based on the 1920's murder case of Nicola Sacco and Bartolomeo Vanzetti. Notable among the shorter poems are elegies on his friend Harry Crosby and renowned poet Hart Crane.

MAGAZINES AND RADIO

Wheelwright's evolving political convictions, deeply ingrained sense of justice, and desire for involvement in public life found some satisfaction in his work on radio, in his correspondence course on rebel poetry for workers, and in his setting up a small magazine called *Poems for a Dime*. A notable contribution to the popular publication was Wheelwright's own *Footsteps*, a verse drama in the tradition of English poets Percy Bysshe Shelley and Lord Byron, which deals with labor issues. It was also at this time that Wheelwright wrote poetry and criticism for *Arise!*, a monthly publication of the Socialist Party, and presented his weekly poetry readings and commentary on Boston radio stations WORL and WIXAL.

In "Verse + Radio = Poetry," a brief, unpublished commentary on the possibilities of radio, Wheelwright offered insights into his poetics, stressing orality and voice:

How poetry looks is as the smell of turpentine to a painter's pigment. Radio compels poetry to sound. . . . [A] printed poem is not a poem. Only a spoken poem is a poem. A poem must speak. . . . Inflection even more than vocabulary conveys thought. . . . If people speak out, they think out straight. If they think out straight, they take chances to better life about them.

MIRRORS OF VENUS

In *Mirrors of Venus*, a sonnet sequence that critic Austin Warren called "a modern *In Memoriam*" (referring to Alfred, Lord Tennyson's elegy), Wheelwright's experimentations with form move into the foreground. The poet's classicist education and reading make for poetry that is filled with allusions to Greek mythology, biblical archetypes, and other tropes derived from the history of Western civilization, but Wheelwright's phrasing and handling of form are strikingly unconventional.

One poem, "Spider," even recalls the brevity, tone, and phrase quality of Japanese verse:

> While the spider Sun drops down her web of sky
> viol phrases of the bridges are resounding . . .
> Their staccato street lamp notes are pitched too high
> to reach our ears with their crescendent sounding . . .
>
> Why do we labor to make metaphors
> Debussy, Whistler, and both of us are bores . . .
> In your hair, also is a Hokusai!

The sonnet sequence is given the structure of a novel, with five chapters, through which a development of the themes of love, death, guilt, and redemption are developed. The speaker comes to terms with the experience of loss (of his father and his friend Ned Couch). In these poems, Wheelwright progresses from self-examination and self-disgust to a renewed faith.

POLITICAL SELF-PORTRAIT, 1919-1939

The "renewed faith" involved what Wheelwright termed "social hope" and "eternal solidarity," which he found possible in his commitment to working for the betterment of the common lot with the Socialist Party. This marks the last and most productive phase of Wheelwright's life. The fusion of poetic talent, religious questioning, and social good deeds allowed the poet to attain his poetic ideals. The poetry in *Political*

Self-Portrait, 1919-1939 is evidence of the "word made into deed," a central issue in Wheelwright's thinking. He addresses it explicitly in at least two poems: "The Word Is Deed" opens the collection with

> John begins like *Genesis:*
> *In the Beginning was the Word;*
> Engles misread: *Was the Deed.*
> But, before ever any Deed came
> the sound of the last of the Deed, coming
> came with the coming Word
> (which answers everything with dancing).

In "Bread-Word Giver," a poem that invokes Wheelwright's like-minded ancestor and namesake, Wheelwright calls to "John, founder of towns,—dweller in none;/ Wheelwright, schismatic,—schismatic from schismatics" to "keep us alive with your ghostly disputation." Although the connecting thread is the split between word and deed, there is a broad range of thematic nuance in *Political Self-Portrait, 1919-1939*, expressed in lyrics and two dramatic poems that explore theory and practice, thought and action.

"DUSK TO DUSK"

At the time of his death, Wheelwright had several writing projects either completed or near completion. Among these was a group of poems titled "Dusk to Dusk," which were included in *Collected Poems of John Wheelwright*, edited by Alvin H. Rosenfeld and Austin Warren and published in 1972. Although "Dusk to Dusk" contains numerous lyrics of a personal nature, the dramatic poems are particularly powerful. "Masque with Clowns," which originally appeared in *Poems for a Dime*, describes a national election campaign and circumscribes the issues faced by farmers and workers during the 1930's. "Evening Mystery in Three Episodes" addresses class power struggles and the issue of race, making use, all the while, of allegorical figures such as Loyalty and Nihilism. "Morning: A Paraphrase" returns to the apostle Thomas's theme found in the earlier "Forty Days." Again, polyphonic voices are interwoven as the dramatic poems splice together language of poetic romanticism, classical allusions, billboards, slogans, and common speech. These late poems, like his first, reveal the truth in editor Warren's observation that Wheelwright was "constitutionally in-

capable of imitating or being schooled, and he sounds like no one else."

OTHER MAJOR WORK

NONFICTION: *A History of the New England Poetry Club, 1915-1931*, 1932.

BIBLIOGRAPHY

Ashbery, John. *Other Traditions*. Cambridge, Mass.: Harvard University Press, 2000. Wheelwright is considered alongside fellow writers John Clare, Thomas Lovell Beddoes, Raymond Roussel, Laura Riding, and David Schubert in this publication of a Charles Eliot Norton Lecture delivered by Ashbery at Harvard in 1989. Ashbery shares many similarities with Wheelwright, and he celebrates the poet's eccentricities and the richness of possible interpretations of his work.

Damon, S. Foster, and Alvin H. Rosenfeld. "John Wheelwright: New England's Colloquy with the World." *Southern Review* 7 (April, 1972): 311-348. "Wheelwright's writing remains largely ignored. Both the man and his work clearly stand in need of being reintroduced," write the authors, who go on to show how Wheelwright is a poet of "intense imagination and strong critical intelligence." This essay provides an excellent critical overview of Wheelwright's activities as a writer, editor, and social activist and provides some glimpses into the family history and personal psychology of the poet.

Gregory, Horace, and Marya Zaturensak. *A History of American Poetry, 1900-1940*. New York: Harcourt, Brace, 1946. Written shortly after Wheelwright's death, this book contains a chapter on the 1920's, in the context of which Wheelwright's poetry is considered. Close attention is given to select quoted passages, and the authors place the poet in the context of both his historical antecedents and the issues of the poet's contemporaries, providing anecdotes and bits of biography along the way.

Josephson, Matthew. "Improper Bostonian: John Wheelwright and His Poetry." *Southern Review* 7 (Spring, 1971): 509-541. Josephson provides a personal but well-informed and responsibly researched account of Wheelwright's activities and his place in the history of American letters. Passages of poetry and prose are examined and discussed with the goal of providing insights into Wheelwright's personal and professional evolution.

Wald, Alan M. *The Revolutionary Imagination: The Poetry and Politics of John Wheelwright and Sherry Mangan*. Chapel Hill: University of North Carolina Press, 1983. An excellent, detailed study of Wheelwright and contemporary Sherry Mangan, both of whom were active in the political left in the 1930's United States. A highly defined picture of the poet emerges, with as much attention given to family history, psychological portrait sketching, outlining of the currents of thought, and public events of the period, while bringing in the poetry to show how the life and work meshed.

Warren, Austin. *New England Saints*. Ann Arbor: University of Michigan Press, 1956. Warren identifies two strains in the New England character—the "Yankee trader" and the "Yankee saint"—and devotes his book to a study of the latter. Wheelwright's family, of course, contained both, but the poet himself was devoted in word and deed to the betterment of himself and others and earns, in Warren's estimation, the designation of "saint." The chapter on Wheelwright served as introduction to the *Collected Poems of John Wheelwright*, published in 1972.

Paul Serralheiro

WALT WHITMAN

Born: West Hills, New York; May 31, 1819
Died: Camden, New Jersey; March 26, 1892

PRINCIPAL POETRY

"Song of Myself," 1855
Leaves of Grass, 1855, 1856, 1860, 1867, 1871, 1876, 1881-1882, 1889, 1891-1892
Drum-Taps, 1865
Sequel to Drum-Taps, 1865-1866
After All, Not to Create Only, 1871

Passage to India, 1871
As a Strong Bird on Pinions Free, 1872
Two Rivulets, 1876
November Boughs, 1888
Good-bye My Fancy, 1891
Complete Poetry and Selected Prose, 1959 (James E. Miller, editor)

OTHER LITERARY FORMS

Walt Whitman published several important essays and studies during his lifetime. *Democratic Vistas* (1871), *Memoranda During the War* (1875-1876), *Specimen Days and Collect* (1882-1883, autobiographical sketches), and the *Complete Prose Works* (1892) are the most significant. He also tried his hand at short fiction, collected in *The Half-Breed, and Other Stories* (1927), and a novel, *Franklin Evans* (1842). Many of his letters and journals have appeared either in early editions or as parts of the New York University Press edition of *The Collected Writings of Walt Whitman* (1961-1984; 22 volumes).

ACHIEVEMENTS

Walt Whitman's stature rests largely on two major contributions to the literature of the United States. First, although detractors are numerous and the poet's organizing principle is sometimes blurred, *Leaves of Grass* stands as the most fully realized American epic poem. Written in the midst of natural grandeur and burgeoning materialism, Whitman's book traces the geographical, social, and spiritual contours of an expanding nation. It embraces the science and commercialism of industrial America while trying to direct these practical energies toward the "higher mind" of literature, culture, and the soul. In his preface to the first edition of *Leaves of Grass*, Whitman referred to the United States itself as "essentially the greatest poem." He saw the self-esteem, sympathy, candor, and deathless attachment to freedom of the common people as "unrhymed poetry," which awaited the "gigantic and generous treatment worthy of it." *Leaves of Grass* was to be that treatment.

The poet's second achievement was in language and poetic technique. Readers take for granted the modern American poet's emphasis on free verse and ordinary diction, forgetting Whitman's revolutionary impact. His free-verse form departed from stanzaic patterns and regular lines, taking its power instead from individual, rolling, oratorical lines of cadenced speech. He subordinated traditional poetic techniques, such as alliteration, repetition, inversion, and conventional meter, to this expansive form. He also violated popular rules of poetic diction by extracting a rich vocabulary from foreign languages, science, opera, various trades, and the ordinary language of town and country. Finally, Whitman broke taboos with his extensive use of sexual imagery, incorporated not to titillate or shock, but to portray life in its wholeness. He determined to be the poet of procreation, to celebrate the elemental and primal life force that permeates humans and nature. Thus, "forbidden voices" are unveiled, clarified, and transfigured by the poet's vision of their place in an organic universe.

Whitman himself said he wrote but "one or two indicative words for the future." He expected the "main things" from poets, orators, singers, and musicians to come. They would prove and define a national culture, thus justifying his faith in American democracy. These apologetic words, along with the early tendency to read Whitman as "untranslatable," or barbaric and undisciplined, long delayed his acceptance as one of America's greatest poets. In fact, if judged by the poet's own test of greatness, he is a failure, for he said the "proof of a poet is that his country absorbs him as affectionately as he has absorbed it." Whitman has not been absorbed by the common people to whom he paid tribute in his poetry. However, with recognition from both the academic community and such poets as Hart Crane, William Carlos Williams, Karl Shapiro, and Randall Jarrell, his *Leaves of Grass* has taken its place among the great masterworks of American literature.

BIOGRAPHY

Walter Whitman, Jr., was born in West Hills, Long Island on May 31, 1819. His mother, Louisa Van Velsor, was descended from a long line of New York Dutch farmers, and his father,

Walter Whitman, was a Long Island farmer and carpenter. In 1823, the father moved his family to Brooklyn in search of work. One of nine children in an undistinguished family, Whitman received only a meager formal education between 1825 and 1830, when he turned to the printing trade for the next five years. At the age of seventeen, he began teaching at various Long Island schools and continued to teach until he went to New York City to be a printer for the *New World* and a reporter for the *Democratic Review* in 1841. From then on, Whitman generally made a living at journalism. Besides reporting and freelance writing, he edited several Brooklyn newspapers, including the *Daily Eagle* (1846-1848), the *Freeman* (1848-1849), and the *Times* (1857-1859). Some of Whitman's experiences during this period influenced the poetry that seemed to burst into print in 1855. While in New York, Whitman frequented the opera and the public library, both of which furnished him with a sense of heritage and of connec-

Walt Whitman (Library of Congress)

tion with the bards and singers of the past. In 1848, Whitman met and was hired by a representative of the New Orleans *Crescent*. Although the job lasted only a few months, the journey by train, stagecoach, and steamboat through what Whitman always referred to as "inland America" certainly helped to stimulate his vision of the country's democratic future. Perhaps most obviously influential was Whitman's trade itself. His flair for action and vignette, as well as descriptive detail, surely was sharpened by his journalistic writing. The reporter's keen eye for the daily scene is everywhere evident in *Leaves of Grass*.

When the first edition of his poems appeared, Whitman received little money but some attention from reviewers. Included among the responses was a famous letter from Ralph Waldo Emerson, who praised Whitman for his brave thought and greeted him at the beginning of a great career. Whitman continued to write and edit, but was unemployed during the winter of 1859-1860, when he began to frequent Pfaff's bohemian restaurant. There he may have established the "manly love" relationships that inspired the "Calamus" poems of the 1860 edition of *Leaves of Grass*. Again, this third edition created a stir with readers, but the outbreak of the Civil War soon turned everyone's attention to more pressing matters. Whitman himself was too old for military service, but he did experience the war by caring for wounded soldiers in Washington, D.C., hospitals. While in Washington as a government clerk, Whitman witnessed Abraham Lincoln's second inauguration, mourned over the president's assassination in April, printed *Drum-Taps* in May, and later added to these Civil War lyrics a sequel, which contained "When Lilacs Last in the Dooryard Bloom'd."

The postwar years saw Whitman's reputation steadily increasing in England, thanks to William Rossetti's *Selections* in 1868, Algernon Swinburne's praise, and a long, admiring review of his work by Anne Gilchrist in 1870. In fact, Gilchrist fell in love with the poet after reading *Leaves of Grass* and even moved to Philadelphia in 1876 to be near him, but her hopes of marrying Whitman died with her in 1885. Because of books by William D. O'Connor and John Burroughs, Whitman also became better known in the United States, but any satisfaction he may have derived from this recognition

was tempered by two severe blows in 1873. He suffered a paralytic stroke in January, and his mother, to whom he was very devoted, died in May. Unable to work, Whitman returned to stay with his brother George at Camden, New Jersey, spending summers on a farm at Timber Creek.

Although Whitman recuperated sufficiently to take trips to New York or Boston, and even to Colorado and Canada in 1879-1880, he was never again to be the robust man he had so proudly described in early editions of *Leaves of Grass*. His declining years, however, gave him time to revise and establish the structure of his book. When the seventh edition of *Leaves of Grass* was published in Philadelphia in 1881-1882, Whitman had achieved a total vision of his work. With the money from a centennial edition (1876) and an occasional lecture on Lincoln, Whitman was able by 1884 to purchase a small house on Mickle Street in Camden. Although he was determined not to be "house-bound," a sunstroke in 1885 and a second paralytic stroke in 1888 made him increasingly dependent on friends. He found especially gratifying the friendship of his secretary and companion, Horace Traubel, who recorded the poet's life and opinions during these last years. Despite the care of Traubel and several doctors and nurses, Whitman died of complications from a stroke on March 26, 1892.

ANALYSIS

An approach to Walt Whitman's poetry profitably begins with the "Inscriptions" to *Leaves of Grass*, for these short, individual pieces introduce the main ideas and methods of Whitman's book. In general, they stake out the ground of what Miller has called the prototypical New World personality, a merging of the individual with the national and cosmic, or universal, selves. That democratic principles are at the root of Whitman's views becomes immediately clear in "One's-Self I Sing," the first poem in *Leaves of Grass*. Here, Whitman refers to the self as a "simple separate person," yet utters the "word Democratic, the word En-Masse." Citizens of America alternately assert their individuality—obey little, resist often—and yet see themselves as a brotherhood of the future, inextricably bound by the vision of a great new society of and for the masses. This encompassing vision requires a sense of "the Form complete," rejecting neither body nor soul, singing equally of the Female and Male, embracing both realistic, scientific, modern humanity and the infinite, eternal life of the spirit.

LEAVES OF GRASS

Whitman takes on various roles to lead his readers to a fuller understanding of this democratic universal. In "Me Imperturbe," he is at ease as an element of nature, able to confront the accidents and rebuffs of life with the implacability of trees and animals. As he suggests in *Democratic Vistas*, the true idea of nature in all its power and glory must become fully restored and must furnish the "pervading atmosphere" to poems of American democracy. Whitman must also empathize with rational things—with humanity at large and in particular—so he constructs what sometimes seem to be endless catalogs of Americans at work and play. This technique appears in "I Hear America Singing," which essentially lists the varied carols of carpenter, boatman, shoemaker, woodcutter, mother, and so on, all "singing what belongs to him or her and to none else" as they ply their trades. In longer poems, such as "Starting from Paumanok," Whitman extends his catalog to all the states of the Union. He intends to acknowledge contemporary lands, salute employments and cities large and small, and report heroism on land and sea from an American point of view. He marks down all of what constitutes unified life, including the body, sexual love, and comradeship, or "manly love." Finally, the poet must join the greatness of love and democracy to the greatness of religion. These programs expand to take up large parts of even longer poems, such as "Song of Myself" or to claim space of their own in sections of *Leaves of Grass*.

Whitman uses another technique to underscore the democratic principle of his art: He makes the reader a fellow poet, a "camerado" who joins hands with him to traverse the poetic landscape. In "To You," he sees the poet and reader as passing strangers who desire to speak to one another and urges that they do so. In "Song of the Open Road," Whitman travels the highways with his "delicious burdens" of men and women, calling them all to come forth and move forever forward, well armed to take their places in "the procession of souls along the grand roads of the universe." His view of the reader as fellow traveler and seer is especially clear in the closing lines of the poem:

> Camerado, I give you my hand!
> I give you my love more precious than money,
> I give you myself before preaching or law;
> Will you give me yourself? will you come travel
>   with me?
> Shall we stick by each other as long as we live?

Finally, this comradeship means willingness to set out on one's own, for Whitman says in "Song of Myself" that the reader most honors his style "who learns under it to destroy the teacher." The questions one asks are one's own to puzzle out. The poet's role is to lead his reader up on a knoll, wash the gum from his eyes, and then let him become habituated to the "dazzle of light" that is the natural world. In other words, Whitman intends to help his reader become a "poet" of insight and perception and then release him to travel the public roads of a democratic nation.

This democratic unification of multiplicity, empathic identification, and comradeship exists in most of Whitman's poems. They do not depend on his growth as poet or thinker. However, in preparing to analyze representative poems from *Leaves of Grass*, it is helpful to establish a general plan for the various sections of the book. Whitman revised and reordered his poems until the 1881 edition, which established a form that was to remain essentially unchanged through succeeding editions. He merely annexed materials to the 1881 order until just before his death in 1892, then authorized the 1891-1892 version for all future printings. Works originally published apart from *Leaves of Grass*, such as *Drum-Taps* or *Passage to India*, were eventually incorporated in the parent volume. Thus, an analysis of the best poems in five important sections of this final *Leaves of Grass* will help delineate Whitman's movement toward integration of self and nation, within his prescribed portals of birth and death.

"SONG OF MYSELF"

"Song of Myself," Whitman's great lyric poem, exemplifies his democratic "programs" without diminishing the intense feeling that so startled his first readers. It successfully combines paeans to the individual, the nation, and life at large, including nature, sexuality, and death. Above all, "Song of Myself" is a poem of incessant motion, as though Whitman's energy is spontaneously bursting into lines. Even in the contemplative sections of the poem, when Whitman leans and loafs at his ease observing a spear of summer grass, his senses of hearing, taste, and sight are working at fever pitch. In the opening section, he calls himself "nature without check with original energy." Having once begun to speak, he hopes "to cease not till death." Whitman says that although others may talk of the beginning and the end, he finds his subject in the now—in the "urge and urge and urge" of the procreant world.

One method by which Whitman's energy escapes boundaries is the poet's ability to "become" other people and things. He will not be measured by time and space, nor by physical form. Rather, he effuses his flesh in eddies and drifts it in lacy jags, taking on new identities with every line. His opening lines show that he is speaking not of himself alone but of all selves. What he assumes, the reader shall assume; every atom of him, and therefore of the world, belongs to the reader as well. In section 24, he represents himself as a "Kosmos," which contains multitudes and reconciles apparent opposites. He speaks the password and sign of democracy and accepts nothing that all cannot share. To stress this egalitarian vision, Whitman employs the catalog with skill and variety. Many parts of "Song of Myself" list or name characters, places, occupations, or experiences, but section 33 most clearly shows the two major techniques that give these lists vitality. First, Whitman composes long single-sentence movements of action and description, which attempt to unify nature and civilization. The poet is alternately weeding his onion patch, hoeing, prospecting, hauling his boat down a shallow river, scaling mountains, walking paths, and speeding through space. He then follows each set of actions with a series of place lines, beginning with "where," "over," "at," or "upon," which unite farmhouses, hearth furnaces, hot-air balloons, or steamships with plants and animals of land and sea. Second, Whitman interrupts these long listings with more detailed vignettes, which show the "large hearts of heroes"—a sea captain, a hounded slave, a fireman trapped and broken under debris, an artillerist. Sections 34-36 then extend the narrative to tales of the Alamo and an old-time sea fight, vividly brought forth with sounds and dialogue. In each case, the poet becomes the hero and is actually in the scene to suffer or succeed.

This unchecked energy and empathy carry over into Whitman's ebullient imagery to help capture the physical power of human bodies in procreant motion. At one point Whitman calls himself "hankering, gross, mystical, nude." He finds no sweeter flesh than that which sticks to his own bones, or to the bones of others. Sexual imagery, including vividly suggestive descriptions of the male and female body, is central to the poem. Although the soul must take its equal place with the body, neither abasing itself before the other, Whitman's mystical union of soul and body is a sexual experience as well. He loves the hum of the soul's "valved voice" and remembers how, on a transparent summer morning, the soul settled its head athwart his hips and turned over on him. It parted the shirt from the poet's "bosom-bone," plunged its tongue to his "bare-stript heart," and reached until it felt his beard and held his feet. From this experience came peace and the knowledge that love is fundamental to a unified, continuous creation. Poetic metaphor, which identifies and binds hidden likenesses in nature, is therefore emblematic of the organic world. For example, in answering a child's question, "What is the grass?" the poet offers a series of metaphors that join human, natural, and spiritual impulses:

> I guess it must be the flag of my disposition, out of
>   hopeful green stuff woven.
> Or I guess it is the handkerchief of the Lord,
> A scented gift and remembrancer designedly dropt,
> Bearing the owner's name someway in the corners,
>   that we may see and remark, and say *Whose*?

The grass becomes hair from the breasts of young men, from the heads and beards of old people, or from offspring, and it "speaks" from under the faint red roofs of mouths. The smallest sprout shows that there is no death, for "nothing collapses," and to die is "luckier" than anyone had supposed. This excerpt from the well-known sixth section of "Song of Myself" illustrates how image making signifies for Whitman a kind of triumph over death itself.

Because of its position near the beginning of *Leaves of Grass* and its encompassing of Whitman's major themes, "Song of Myself" is a foundation for the volume. The "self" in this poem is a replica of the nation as self, and its delineation in the cosmos is akin to the growth of the United States in the world. Without putting undue stress on this nationalistic interpretation, however, the reader can find many reasons to admire "Song of Myself." Its dynamic form, beauty of language, and psychological insights are sufficient to make Whitman a first-rate poet, even if he had written nothing else.

CELEBRATION OF SELF AND SEXUALITY

The passionate celebration of the self and of sexuality is Whitman's great revolutionary theme. In "Children of Adam," he is the procreative father of multitudes, a champion of heterosexual love and the "body electric." In "From Pent-Up Aching Rivers," he sings of the need for superb children, brought forth by the "muscular urge" of "stalwart loins." In "I Sing the Body Electric," he celebrates the perfection of well-made male and female bodies. Sections 5 and 9 are explicit descriptions of sexual intercourse and physical "apparatus," respectively. Whitman does not shy away from the fierce attraction of the female form or the ebb and flow of "limitless limpid jets of love hot and enormous" that undulate into the willing and yielding "gates of the body." Because he sees the body as sacred, as imbued with divine power, he considers these enumerations to be poems of the soul as much as of the body.

Indeed, "A Woman Waits for Me" specifically states that sex contains all—bodies and souls. Thus, the poet seeks warm-blooded and sufficient women to receive the pent-up rivers of himself, to start new sons and daughters fit for the great nation that will be these United States. The procreative urge operates on more than one level in "Children of Adam"—it is physical sex and birthing, the union of body and soul, and the metaphorical insemination of the poet's words and spirit into national life. In several ways, then, words are to become flesh. Try as some early Whitman apologists might to explain them away, raw sexual impulses are the driving force of these poems.

"CALAMUS" POEMS

Whitman's contemporaries were shocked by the explicit sexual content of "Children of Adam," but modern readers and critics have been much more intrigued by the apparent homoeroticism of the poems in the "Calamus" section of the 1860 edition of *Leaves of Grass*. Although it is ultimately impossible to say whether these poems reflect Whitman's gay associations in New York, it is obvious that comradeship extends here to both spiritual and physical contact between men. "In Paths Untrodden" states the poet's intention to sing of "manly attachment" or types of "athletic love," to celebrate the need of comrades. "Whoever You Are Holding Me Now in Hand" deepens the physical nature of this love, including the stealthy meeting of male friends in a wood, behind some rock in the open air, or on the beach of some quiet island. There the poet would permit the comrade's long-dwelling kiss on the lips and a touch that would carry him eternally forth over land and sea. "These I Singing in Spring" refers to "him that tenderly loves me" and pledges the hardiest spears of grass, the calamus-root, to those who love as the poet himself is capable of loving.

Finally, two of Whitman's best lyrics concern this robust but clandestine relationship. "I Saw in Louisiana a Live-Oak Growing" is a poignant contrast between the live oak's ability to "utter joyous leaves" while it stands in solitude, without companions, and the poet's inability to live without a friend or lover near. There is no mistaking the equally personal tone of "When I Heard at the Close of the Day," probably Whitman's finest "Calamus" poem. The plaudits of others are meaningless and unsatisfying, says Whitman, until he thinks of how his dear friend and lover is on his way to see him. When his friend arrives one evening, the hissing rustle of rolling waves becomes congratulatory and joyful. Once the person he loves most lies sleeping by him under the same cover, face inclined toward him in the autumn moonbeams and arm lightly lying around his breast, he is happy.

Other short poems in "Calamus," such as "For You O Democracy," "The Prairie Grass Dividing," or "A Promise to California," are less obviously personal. Rather, they extend passionate friendship between men to the larger ideal of democratic brotherhood. Just as procreative love has its metaphorical implications for the nation, so too does Whitman promise to make the continent indissoluble and cities inseparable, arms about each other's necks, with companionship and the "manly love of comrades." Still other poems move this comradeship into wider spans of space and time. "The Moment Yearning and Thoughtful" joins the poet with men of Europe and Asia in happy brotherhood, thus transcending national and continental boundaries. "The Base of All Metaphysics" extends this principle through historical time, for the Greek, Germanic, and Christian systems all suggest that the attraction of friend to friend is the basis of civilization. The last poem in the "Calamus" section, "Full of Life Now," completes Whitman's panoramic view by carrying friendship into the future. His words communicate the compact, visible to readers of a century or any number of centuries hence. Each seeking the other past time's invisible boundaries, poet and reader are united physically through Whitman's poetry.

"CROSSING BROOKLYN FERRY"

"Crossing Brooklyn Ferry" is the natural product of Whitman's idea that love and companionship will bind the world's peoples to one another. In a sense it gives the poet immortality through creation of a living artifact: the poem itself. Whitman stands motionless on a moving ferry, immersed in the stream of life and yet suspended in time through the existence of his words on the page. Consequently, he can say that neither time nor place nor distance matters, because he is with each reader and each fellow traveler in the future. He points out that hundreds of years hence others will enter the gates of the ferry and cross from shore to shore, will see the sun half an hour high and watch the seagulls floating in circles with motionless wings. Others will also watch the endless scallop-edged waves cresting and falling, as though they are experiencing the same moment as the poet, with the same mixture of joy and sorrow. Thus, Whitman confidently calls upon the "dumb ministers" of nature to keep up their ceaseless motion—to flow, fly, and frolic on—because they furnish their parts toward eternity and toward the soul.

Techniques match perfectly with these themes in "Crossing Brooklyn Ferry." Whitman's frequent repetition of the main images—sunrise and sunset, ebb and flow of the sea and river, seagulls oscillating in the sky—reinforces the belief in timeless, recurring human experience. Descriptions of schooners and steamers at work along the shore are among his most powerful evocations of color and sound. Finally, Whitman's employment of pronouns to mark a shift in the sharing of experiences also shows the poem's careful design. Whitman begins the poem with an "I" who looks at the scenes or crowds of people and calls to "you" who are among the crowds and readers of present and future. In section 8, however, he reaches across generations to fuse himself and pour his meaning into the "you." At the end of this section, he and others have become "we," who understand and receive experience with free senses and love, united in the organic continuity of nature.

"SEA-DRIFT" POEMS

The short section of *Leaves of Grass* entitled "Sea-Drift" contains the first real signs of a more somber Whitman, who must come to terms with hardship, sorrow, and death. In one way, this resignation and accommodation follow the natural progression of the self from active, perhaps callow, youth to contemplative old age. They are also an outgrowth of Whitman's belief that life and death are a continuum, that life is a symphony of both sonatas and dirges, which the true poet of nature must capture fully on the page. Whereas in other poems the ocean often signifies birth and creation, with fish-shaped Paumanok (Manhattan) rising from the sea, in "Tears," it is the repository of sorrow. Its white shore lies in solitude, dark and desolate, holding a ghost or "shapeless lump" that cries streaming, sobbing tears. In "As I Ebb'd with the Ocean of Life," Whitman is distressed with himself for daring to "blab" so much without having the least idea who or what he really is. Nature darts on the poet and stings him, because he has not understood anything and because no man ever can. He calls himself but a "trail of drift and debris," who has left his poems like "little wrecks" on Paumanok's shores. However, he must continue to throw himself on the ocean of life, clinging to the breast of the land that is his father, and gathering from the moaning sea the "sobbing dirge of Nature." He believes the flow will return, but meanwhile he must wait and lie in drifts at his readers' feet.

"OUT OF THE CRADLE ENDLESSLY ROCKING"

"Out of the Cradle Endlessly Rocking" is a fuller, finally more optimistic, treatment of the poet's confrontation with loss. Commonly acknowledged as one of Whitman's finest works, this poem uses lyrical language and operatic structure to trace the origin of his poetic powers in the experience of death. Two "songs" unite with the whispering cry of the sea to communicate this experience to him. Central to the poem is Whitman's seaside reminiscence of a bird and his mate, who build and tend a nest of eggs. When the female fails to return one evening, never to appear again, the male becomes a solitary singer of his sorrows, whose notes are "translated" by the listening boy-poet. The bird's song is an aria of lonesome love, an outpouring carol of yearning, hope, and finally, death. As the boy absorbs the bird's song, his soul awakens in sympathy. From this moment forward, his destiny will be to perpetuate the bird's "cries of unsatisfied love." More important, though, Whitman must learn the truth that this phrase masks, must conquer "the word" that has caused the bird's cries:

> Whereto answering, the sea,
> Delaying not, hurrying not,
> Whisper'd me through the night, and very plainly before daybreak,
> Lisp'd to me the low and delicious word death,
> And again death, death, death, death.

Whitman then fuses the bird's song and his own with death, which the sea, "like some old crone rocking the cradle," has whispered to him. This final image of the sea as an old crone soothing an infant underscores the central point of "Out of the Cradle Endlessly Rocking": Old age and death are part of a natural flux. Against the threat of darkness, one must live and sing.

DRUM-TAPS

Like the tone of the "Sea-Drift" section, darker hues permeate Whitman's Civil War lyrics. His experiences as a hospital worker in Washington, D.C., are clearly behind the sometimes wrenching imagery of *Drum-Taps*. As a wound dresser, he saw the destruction of healthy young bodies and minds at first hand. These spectacles were in part a test of Whitman's own courage and comradeship, but they were also a test of the nation's ability to survive and grow. As Whitman says in "Long, Too Long America," the country had long traveled roads "all even and peaceful," learning only

from joys and prosperity, but now it must face "crises of anguish" without recoiling and show the world what its "children enmasse really are." Many of the *Drum-Taps* lyrics show Whitman facing this reality, but "The Wound Dresser" is representative. The poet's persona is an old man who is called on years after the Civil War to "paint the mightiest armies of earth," to tell what experience of the war stays with him latest and deepest. Although he mentions the long marches, rushing charges, and toils of battle, he does not dwell on soldiers' perils or soldiers' joys. Rather, he vividly describes the wounded and dying at battlegrounds, hospital tents, or roofed hospitals, as he goes with "hinged knees and steady hand to dress wounds." He does not recoil or give out at the sight of crushed heads, shattered throats, amputated stumps of hands and arms, the gnawing and putrid gangrenous foot or shoulder. Nevertheless, within him rests a burning flame, the memory of youths suffering or dead.

Confronted with these horrors, Whitman had to find a way to surmount them, and that way was love. If there could be a positive quality in war, Whitman found it in the comradeship of common soldiers, who risked all for their fellows. In "As Toilsome I Wander'd Virginia's Woods," for example, Whitman discovers the grave of a soldier buried beneath a tree. Hastily dug on a retreat from battle, the grave is nevertheless marked by a sign: "Bold, cautious, true, and my loving comrade." That inscription remains with the poet through many changeful seasons and scenes to follow, as evidence of this brotherly love. Similarly, "Vigil Strange I Kept on the Field One Night" tells of a soldier who sees his comrade struck down in battle and returns to find him cold with death. He watches by him through "immortal and mystic hours" until, just as dawn is breaking, he folds the young man in a blanket and buries him in a rude-dug grave where he fell. This tale of tearless mourning perfectly evokes the loss caused by war.

Eventually, Whitman finds some ritual significance in these deaths, as though they are atonement for those yet living. In "A Sight in Camp in the Daybreak Gray and Dim," he marks three covered forms on stretchers near a hospital tent. One by one he uncovers their faces. The first is an elderly man, gaunt and grim, but a comrade nevertheless. The second is a sweet boy "with cheeks yet blooming." When he exposes the third face, however, he finds it calm, of yellow-white ivory, and of indeterminable age. He sees in it the face of Christ himself, "dead and divine and brother of all." "Over the Carnage Rose Prophetic a Voice" suggests that these Christian sacrifices will finally lead to a united Columbia. Even though a thousand may have to "sternly immolate themselves for one," those who love one another shall become invincible, and "affection shall solve the problems of freedom." As in other sections of *Leaves of Grass*, Whitman believes the United States will be held together not by lawyers, paper agreements, or force of arms, but by the cohesive power of love and fellowship.

"WHEN LILACS LAST IN THE DOORYARD BLOOM'D"

"When Lilacs Last in the Dooryard Bloom'd," another of Whitman's acknowledged masterpieces, repeats the process underlying *Drum-Taps*. The poet must come to terms with the loss of one he loves—in this case, the slain President Lincoln. Death and mourning must eventually give way to consolation and hope for the future. Cast in the form of a traditional elegy, the poem traces the processional of Lincoln's coffin across country, past the poet himself, to the president's final resting place.

To objectify his emotional struggle between grief, on one hand, and spiritual reconciliation with death on the other, Whitman employs several vivid symbols. The lilac blooming perennially, with its heart-shaped leaves, represents the poet's perpetual mourning and love. The "powerful fallen star," which now lies in a "harsh surrounding could" of black night, is Lincoln, fallen and shrouded in his coffin. The solitary hermit thrush that warbles "death's outlet song of life" from a secluded swamp is the soul or spiritual world. Initially, Whitman is held powerless by the death of his departing comrade. Although he can hear the bashful notes of the thrush and will come to understand them, he thinks only of showering the coffin with sprigs of lilac to commemorate his love for Lincoln. He must also warble his own song before he can absorb the bird's message of consolation. Eventually, as he sits amidst the teeming daily activities described in section 14, he is struck by the "sacred knowledge of death," and the bird's carol

thus becomes intelligible to him. Death is lovely, soothing, and delicate. It is a "strong deliveress" who comes to nestle the grateful body in her flood of bliss. Rapt with the charm of the bird's song, Whitman sees myriad battle corpses in a vision—the debris of all the slain soldiers of the war—yet realizes that they are fully at rest and no longer suffering. The power of this realization gives him strength to let go of the hand of his comrade. An ever-blooming lilac now signifies renewal, just as death takes its rightful place as the harbinger of new life, the life of the eternal soul.

MATTERS OF SPIRIT

Whitman's deepening concern with matters of the spirit permeates the last sections of *Leaves of Grass*. Having passed the test of the Civil War and having done his part to reunite the United States, Whitman turned his attention to America's place in the world and his own place in God's design. As he points out in "A Clear Midnight," he gives his last poems to the soul and its "free flight into the wordless," to ponder the themes he loves best: "Night, sleep, death and the stars." Such poems as "Chanting the Square Deific" and "A Noiseless Patient Spider" invoke either the general soul, the "Santa Spirita" that pervades all created life, or the toils of individual souls, flinging out gossamer threads to connect themselves with this holy spirit.

"PASSAGE TO INDIA"

Whitman was still able to produce fine lyrics in his old age. One of these successful poems, "Passage to India," announces Whitman's intention to join modern science to fables and dreams of old, to weld past and future, and to show that the United States is but a "bridge" in the "vast rondure" of the world. Just as the Suez Canal connected Europe and Asia, Whitman says, America's transcontinental railroad ties the eastern to the western sea, thus verifying Christopher Columbus's dream. Beyond these material thoughts of exploration, however, lies the poet's realm of love and spirit. The poet is a "true son of God," who will soothe the hearts of restlessly exploring, never-happy humanity. He will link all human affections, justify the "cold, impassive, voiceless earth," and absolutely fuse nature and humanity. This fusion takes place not in the material world but in the swelling of the soul toward God, who is a mighty "centre of the true, the good, the loving." Passage to these superior universes transcends time and space and death. It is a "passage to more than India," through the deep waters that no mariner has traveled, and for which the poet must "risk the ship, ourselves and all."

"PRAYER OF COLUMBUS"

Whitman also uses a seagoing metaphor for spiritual passage in "Prayer of Columbus," which is almost a continuation of "Passage to India." In the latter, Whitman aggressively flings himself into the active voyage toward God, but in "Prayer of Columbus" he is a "batter'd, wreck'd old man," willing to yield his ships to God and wait for the unknown end of all. He recounts his heroic deeds of exploration and attributes their inspiration to a message from the heavens that sped him on. Like Columbus, Whitman is "old, poor, and paralyzed," yet capable of one more effort to speak of the steady interior light that God has granted him. Finally, the works of the past fall away from him, and some divine hand reveals a scene of countless ships sailing on distant seas, from which "anthems in new tongues" salute and comfort him. This implied divine sanction for his life's work was consolation to an old poet, who, at his death in 1892, remained largely unaccepted and unrecognized by contemporary critics and historians.

LEGACY

The grand design of *Leaves of Grass* appears to trace self and nation neatly through sensuous youth, crises of maturity, and soul-searching old age. Although this philosophical or psychological reading of Whitman's work is certainly encouraged by the poet's tinkering with its structure, many fine lyrics do not fit into neat patterns, or even under topical headings. Whitman's reputation rests more on the startling freshness of his language, images, and democratic treatment of the common American citizen than on his success as epic bard. Common to all his poetry, however, are certain major themes: reconciliation of body and soul, purity and unity of physical nature, death as the "mother of beauty," and above all, comradeship or love, which binds and transcends all else. In fact, Whitman encouraged a complex comradeship with his readers to bind his work to future generations. He expected reading to be a gymnastic struggle and the reader to be a re-creator of the poem through imaginative interaction with the poet. Perhaps that is why he said in "So Long" that *Leaves of Grass* was no book, for whoever touches his poetry "touches a man."

OTHER MAJOR WORKS

LONG FICTION: *Franklin Evans*, 1842.

SHORT FICTION: *The Half-Breed, and Other Stories*, 1927.

NONFICTION: *Democratic Vistas*, 1871; *Memoranda During the War*, 1875-1876; *Specimen Days and Collect*, 1882-1883; *Complete Prose Works*, 1892; *Calamus*, 1897 (letters; Richard M. Bucke, editor); *The Wound Dresser*, 1898 (Bucke, editor); *Letters Written by Walt Whitman to His Mother, 1866-1872*, 1902 (Thomas B. Harned, editor); *An American Primer*, 1904; *Walt Whitman's Diary in Canada*, 1904 (William S. Kennedy, editor); *The Letters of Anne Gilchrist and Walt Whitman*, 1918 (Harned, editor).

MISCELLANEOUS: *The Collected Writings of Walt Whitman*, 1961-1984 (22 volumes).

BIBLIOGRAPHY

Canning, Richard. *Whitman*. London: Hesperus, 2010. Part of the Poetic Lives series, this is a basic biography that examines Whitman's life and poetry.

Folsom, Ed. *Re-scripting Walt Whitman: An Introduction to His Life and Work*. Malden, Mass.: Blackwell, 2005. A good starting point for readers of Whitman, delving into his life and literary works.

Genoways, Ted. *Walt Whitman and the Civil War: America's Poet During the Lost Years of 1860/1862*. Berkeley: University of California Press, 2009. Uses unpublished letters and manuscripts to explore Whitman's involvement in the war, debunking his supposed indifference.

Herrero-Brassas, Juan A., ed. *Walt Whitman's Mystical Ethics of Comradeship: Homosexuality and the Marginality of Friendship at the Crossroads of Modernity*. Albany: State University of New York Press, 2010. This collection of essays examines Whitman's mystical religious beliefs, his concept of comradeship, and his homosexuality.

Killlingsworth, M. Jimmie, ed. *The Cambridge Introduction to Walt Whitman*. New York: Cambridge University Press, 2007. A comprehensive work that covers Whitman's life and presents extensive analysis of his poetry, including his prewar poetry, *Leaves of Grass*, "Calamus," "Children of Adam," earth and body poems, and elegies. Also looks at critical reception of his works and the image that was created around him.

Kummings, Donald D., ed. *A Companion to Walt Whitman*. Malden, Mass.: Blackwell, 2006. These thirty-five essays by prominent scholars delve into the life and writing of Whitman. The essays are classified under four sections, concentrating on the author's life, the cultural and literary contexts of his writing, and the texts themselves. Topics such as nature, the city, gender, civil war, and pop culture are discussed at length in relation to Whitman and his writing. Readers will also find this book valuable for the publication history it provides, as well as the thorough bibliography of criticism of Whitman's prose.

Reynolds, David S. *Walt Whitman*. New York: Knopf, 2005. Part of the Lives and Legacies series, this work examines the life and work of Whitman. Reynolds calls Whitman the founder of free verse and the first poet to treat sex candidly.

Robertson, Michael. *Worshipping Walt: The Whitman Disciples*. Princeton, N.J.: Princeton University Press, 2008. In his later years, Whitman developed "disciples," people who admired and supported him. This work examines his disciples, including Anne Gilchrist, John Burroughs, John Addington Symonds, and Horace Traubel.

Stacey, Jason. *Walt Whitman's Multitudes: Labor Reform and Persona in Whitman's Journalism and the First "Leaves of Grass," 1840-1855*. New York: Peter Lang, 2008. Focuses on the political views of Whitman as expressed in his journalism and in the first edition of *Leaves of Grass*. Whitman wrote on artisans who had lost their economic status, blaming them in part for becoming involved in consumerism and affectation.

Williams, C. K. *On Whitman*. Princeton, N.J.: Princeton University Press, 2010. Part of the Writers on Writers series, this work looks at Whitman from the standpoint of another poet and delves into Whitman's influence.

Perry D. Luckett

REED WHITTEMORE

Born: New Haven, Connecticut; September 11, 1919

PRINCIPAL POETRY

Heroes and Heroines, 1946
An American Takes a Walk, 1956
The Self-Made Man, and Other Poems, 1959
Poems, New and Selected, 1967
Fifty Poems Fifty, 1970
The Mother's Breast and the Father's House, 1974
The Feel of Rock: Poems of Three Decades, 1982
The Past, the Future, the Present: Poems Selected and New, 1990

OTHER LITERARY FORMS

Reed Whittemore has published many essays and reviews in magazines, most of them of a literary nature, but also essays on education, science, and television. *From Zero to Absolute* (1968) consists mainly of a series of lectures he gave on poetry at Beloit College in 1966. *The Poet as Journalist: Life at The New Republic* (1976) is made up of the short pieces he wrote for *The New Republic* when he was the literary editor for that magazine. In his literary essays, he often praises, with some qualifications, the early modern poets such as Ezra Pound and T. S. Eliot but is rather critical of most of his contemporaries, particularly the Beat poets, whom he has mocked in his satirical verse.

The publication of Whittemore's *William Carlos Williams: Poet from Jersey* (1975) was a surprising departure for this writer of short personal essays. The biography was criticized by some reviewers for being too casually written and for taking, at times, an irreverent attitude toward its subject, yet the book does give a clear and sympathetic portrait of Williams and, at the same time, punctures some of the more pretentious opinions of Williams and his disciples about free verse and other poetic matters.

Whittemore's biography of Williams has led him to write books about the nature of biography: *Pure Lives: The Early Biographers* (1988) and *Whole Lives: Shapers of Modern Biography* (1990). These wide-ranging, erudite, and lively works trace biographical art from its beginnings (Plutarch, Aelfric) all the way to late twentieth century literary biographers (Richard Ellmann and Leon Edel). As in the Williams biography, Whittemore manages to combine his scholarly matter with a casual manner in interesting ways.

ACHIEVEMENTS

The most striking characteristic of Reed Whittemore's verse is its comedy. As Howard Nemerov pointed out many years ago, Whittemore is not only witty (an admirable trait) but also funny (a suspect one). His most distinctive poems are those about serious subjects—the failure of belief, the difficulties of heroism, the search for the true self—that make intelligent statements while at the same time being very clever and humorous. Whittemore's emphasis on intelligence, moderation, and comedy makes him a rather unfashionable writer today, but these very qualities account for the success of his best poems. He served as consultant in poetry (poet laureate) to the Library of Congress from 1964 to 1965 and from 1984 to 1985. He received an Award of Merit from the American Academy of Arts and Letters in 1970.

BIOGRAPHY

Reed Whittemore was born in New Haven in 1919 as Edward Reed Whittemore II, named after his physician father. He graduated from Yale in 1941, and he served in the Army Air Force during World War II and was discharged as a captain. He continued his education at Princeton after the war, although he never received an advanced degree. He married Helen Lundeen in 1952, and they had four children. He often depicts himself in his poetry as a middle-class figure, with middle-class burdens of family and job. Although his poetry is not of a confessional nature, a picture of Whittemore as an affectionate and concerned family man does emerge from his poetry.

Whittemore taught in the English department at Carleton College in Minnesota for nearly twenty years beginning in 1947 and was for a part of that time chairman of the department. In 1964, he was consultant in poetry at the Library of Congress. In 1968, he moved to the University of Maryland, eventually becoming professor emeritus.

Whittemore is rightly well known and admired as a magazine editor. From 1939 to 1953, he was the editor of *Furioso*, one of the liveliest literary publications of the period. What distinguished this magazine from all its competitors was its fondness for comic parody and satire. This tradition was carried on with nearly equal distinction when Whittemore edited *The Carleton Miscellany* from 1960 to 1964. His work as the literary editor of *The New Republic* from 1969 to 1974 added some zest to the pages of that venerable publication.

ANALYSIS

Reed Whittemore has published fewer poems than many of his contemporaries have done, and most of them have been written in an ironic vein. His targets are the pretentious—both romantic and bureaucratic, both individual and institutional—against which he sets his own balanced, moderate point of view. The poems imply that the realism at their center is all the modern world has to offer in the way of belief.

At times, Whittemore runs the risk of being merely a writer of light verse, a maker of clever rhymed jokes, but in his best work he combines the sensible note of comedy with a seriousness of theme. This combination, along with his subtle command of form and sound in verse, make him a poet of consequence.

HEROES AND HEROINES

Whittemore's first book, *Heroes and Heroines*, consists primarily of poems about literature and literary figures. It is an amusing book that explores, through a series of comic poems, the idea of heroism in portraits of Don Quixote, Lord Jim, Hester Prynne, Lady Ashley, Gulliver, and many other characters from books. The poems display Whittemore's fondness for traditional verse forms—particularly the sonnet—his wit, and his interest in the theme of heroism; yet it is a book of very limited range that only hints at his potential as a poet.

AN AMERICAN TAKES A WALK

In Whittemore's second book, *An American Takes a Walk*, that potential is clearly displayed as he develops the comic tone that becomes the trademark of his work. That tone can be seen in his often reprinted poem "Lines (Composed upon Reading an Announcement by Civil Defense Authorities Recommending that I

Build a Bombshelter in My Backyard)." The poem begins with a description of the dugout that the speaker and his friends had built as children and that he identifies with some vague notion of heroic fantasy, "some brave kind of decay." Now he is being asked to dig another hole "under the new and terrible rules of romance." "But I'll not, no, not do it, not go back," the poem proclaims; he knows that this time, if he conforms to the government's wishes, he will not be able to return to "the grown-up's house" as he had done as a child. This time the seeming child's play is play in earnest, a deadly absurdity. As Nemerov has pointed out, Whittemore's poetry is filled with images of entrapment and burial, and this poem can be read as more than a satirical thrust at Civil Defense. It contains the poet's rejection of safety and security as a kind of living death and seems to long for some world where daring and risk have meaning.

The problem, however, Whittemore's work implies, is that a heroism that risks all often leads to nothing. One of his funniest poems, "A Day with the Foreign Legion," makes a number of tough statements about the failure of heroic action, or its meaninglessness. The poem is based on a beau geste version of the Foreign Legion as it appears in motion pictures, where, when everything seems darkest, the characters make speeches that "serve as the turning point":

> After which the Arabs seem doped and perfectly
>   helpless,
> Water springs up from the ground, the horses come
>   back,
> Plenty of food is discovered in some old cave,
> And reinforcements arrive led by the girl
> From Canada.

That is what usually happens, but in this instance it is too hot; there is no magical ending and the audience is bitterly disappointed. The poem asks who is to blame—the film, the projector, "the man in the booth, who hastened away, as soon as the feature was over"? The poem answers, in a series of purposely confusing repetitions, that none of them is to blame, or all of them are, or possibly the culture is to blame. "It was the time, the time and the place, and how could one blame them?" The poem seems to be saying that in this time (modern) and this place (the United States) the world of romance and happy endings is finished.

The title poem, "An American Takes a Walk," mocks the idea of a tragic or sacred vision existing in the United States or American literature. When the American of the poem comes across a wood reminiscent of Dante's world of hell, it is a pleasant wood, hell in a "motherly habit."

> How in that Arden could human
> Frailty be but glossed?
> How in that Eden could Adam
> Be really, wholly lost?

The emphasis on innocence and on success in the United States, according to Whittemore, leads the American writer to adopt the demands of his culture. In "The Line of an American Poet," the poet writes for the market, following the supply-and-demand economy. He produces works, "Uniform, safe and pure," becoming another American success story.

Whittemore once described poetry "as a thing of the mind," saying that he "tends to judge it . . . by the qualities of the mind it displays" (*Poets on Poetry*, Nemerov, editor). This emphasis on the mind, on intelligence, is an unusual one for a contemporary American poet. In recent years, the instinctual and the irrational have usually been seen as the sources of poetry. Whittemore's attitude is what leads him to reject the theatrical and fantastic, to be a realist and ironist. At the same time, however, it can be argued that this dominating intelligence in his work limits Whittemore, giving his poetry a kind of self-consciousness, a too-ready irony. He has written many poems about writing poems ("A Week of Doodle," "After Some Day of Decision," and "Preface to an Unwritten Text," for example, in *An American Takes a Walk*), about the difficulties of writing poems, about the fact that he has not written any poems. These pieces are often funny, but still they seem to point to some problem with his very notion of being a poet, a kind of debilitating self-awareness. At times he seems burdened with the idea of being a poet, as if it were a pompous occupation, apologizing for not offering a worldview of proper scope for one who would call himself a poet.

"THE SELF AND THE WEATHER"

In his next few volumes, Whittemore continues the style developed in *An American Takes a Walk*. His poems give an amusing picture of suburbia and the academic life, worlds where trivial things matter. Even the weather—as in "The Self and the Weather"—can depress one's mood. The poem begins by declaring that it is tiresome to talk about the weather and goes on to talk about it—very amusingly—at considerable length. The poet finds he cannot write on a rainy day, staring out the window "at wet leaves, wet grass, wet laundry and so on," but he feels that a better man, "any man of resolve, any man with a mission," would rise above the weather, rise to where it always was sunny, and write. Such a person, however, would write treatises, not poems, "for treatises seldom/ Traffic in weather as poems do." These treatises would be written in underground rooms where the outside world will be represented by "a picture by some gay cubist of what could not possibly/ Be wet leaves, wet grass, wet laundry, and so on."

SATIRIC POEMS

The only new element in Whittemore's work at this time in his career is found in a number of long, satiric poems written in rhyming, loosely metrical couplets. The purposely forced comic rhymes seem to imitate both Ogden Nash and Lord Byron. The targets range from the Beat poets to rocket scientists, and although almost all the poems have amusing passages, they go on at entirely too great a length for their satiric purposes.

POEMS, NEW AND SELECTED

Although there is no revolutionary change in Whittemore's poetry after *An American Takes a Walk*, his poems do wear a somewhat more experimental guise, opening up in language and form, in the new poems that appeared in *Poems, New and Selected* in 1967. In the six poems labeled "shaggy" ("Flint Shaggy," "Geneva Shaggy," and so on), Whittemore slips into a black-faced comedian's voice reminiscent of the comic language of John Berryman's *The Dream Songs* (1969). In other poems from this collection, such as "The Bad Daddy," and poems from later volumes, such as "Death," "The Mother's Breast and the Father's House," and "Marriage," he moves toward an irrational side of his psyche that his earlier work explicitly rejected. Whittemore presents marriage as pigs eating each other

and death as the lord that lives in the marrow: "Holy illiterate . . . spider of bone." A kind of fierce bitterness overwhelms these poems at times, in a manner not seen in his previous poetry.

"CLAMMING"

In "Clamming," Whittemore writes one of his most successful antiromantic poems in his more familiar, amusing style. The poem begins with the poet telling of how he often repeats a story about the time he was trapped on a sandbar while clamming as a little boy and faced the Long Island Sound as his possible fate. There is not much to the story, but he keeps telling it because "it serves my small lust/ To be thought of as someone who's lived." He cannot get away from his ego: "The self, what a brute it is. It wants, wants./ It will not let go of its even most fictional grandeur." Now he has a son, small and sickly, and he would like to protect him from the sea and other dangers, but a greater danger might be too much self-regard, as represented by the oft-told tale of clamming, and that he does not want to pass on to his son. Finally, his advice to his son is to be careful but not too careful: "Lest you care too much and brag of the caring/ And bore your best friends and inhibit your children and sicken/ At last into opera on somebody's sandbar. Son, when you clam,/ Clam." The plea for realism and modesty in the ending of "Clamming" sums up very nicely the attitudes and strengths of Whittemore's poetry.

THE FEEL OF ROCK AND THE PAST, THE FUTURE, THE PRESENT

In 1982, in *The Feel of Rock*, and more extensively in 1990, in *The Past, the Future, the Present*, Whittemore again created volumes selected from his previous poetry, adding a few new poems on both occasions. The small number of new poems added seems to show that Whittemore was concentrating on the writing of prose in the 1980's rather than the writing of poetry.

A number of the new poems continue Whittemore's satiric expressions of dissatisfaction with modern American culture: "It's a terrible thing to come to despise one's country," he states in one of his poems, but he obviously thinks that the ideals of the United States have been lost in the modern political and social scene. In "The Destruction of Washington," he imagines some future archaeologists exploring the destroyed capital. Whatever they discover, he hopes that at least their ignorance will be less than that of people in the twentieth century.

Whittemore also began exploring his childhood and the lives of his parents in a few poems in these two volumes. "Mother's Past" is about the inability of his mother to take good photos, as she is always moving or putting her finger in front of the lens. The photos are often of young people going off on automobile excursions, while the photographer—the mother—remains behind. The speaker is dissatisfied with the record of a life represented by the photos: "Ask how many were missed that it takes to make a good/ Past for a life or a book./ The answer is always more pictures than poor mother took.

In "The Feel of Rock," the early life of the speaker's home is portrayed in the ironies of the opening stanza:

My father went broke on a shaded street.
My mother drank there.
My brothers removed themselves; they were complete.
I kept to my room and slicked down my hair.

As the poem continues, the speaker realizes that he resembles his father in his loneliness and unhappiness. Then he goes on to think about his father's burial (the mother already dead); the feel of rocks becomes the gravestones of his family. On a later return to the cemetery, he loses himself amid the maze of stones and wonders where his father has gone and whether life is only the world of rocks.

In "The Feel of Rock" and "Mother's Past," Whittemore is risking a personal tone rarely seen before in his work. Although the poems have at times a tentative quality, they add a new element to the work of this always interesting writer.

OTHER MAJOR WORKS

NONFICTION: *From Zero to Absolute*, 1968; *William Carlos Williams: Poet from Jersey*, 1975; *The Poet as Journalist: Life at The New Republic*, 1976; *Pure Lives: The Early Biographers*, 1988; *Whole Lives: Shapers of Modern Biography*, 1989; *Six Literary Lives: The Shared Impiety of Adams, London, Sinclair, Williams, Dos Passos, and Tate*, 1993; *Against the Grain: The Literary Life of a Poet*, 2007.

MISCELLANEOUS: *The Boy from Iowa*, 1961 (poetry and essays); *The Fascination of the Abomination*, 1963 (poetry, stories, and essays).

BIBLIOGRAPHY

Bloom, Harold, ed. *Twentieth-Century American Literature*. Vol. 7. New York: Chelsea House, 1988. Contains a short biographical essay on Whittemore that also offers literary criticism.

Dickey, James. *Babel to Byzantium: Poets and Poetry Now*. 1968. Reprint. New York: Ecco Press, 1981. Dickey classifies Whittemore as essentially a satirist, but he modifies his praise of his work because of Whittemore's tendency not to go deeply and personally into his subjects.

Whittemore, Reed. *Against the Grain: The Literary Life of a Poet*. Washington, D.C.: Dryad Press/University of Alaska Press, 2007. Whittemore relates his memoirs through his alter ego "R," from his days at *Furioso*, to his experiences during World War II, and his years at Carleton College and *The New Republic*. Contains a foreword by Garrison Keillor, a former student of Whittemore.

Michael Paul Novak

JOHN GREENLEAF WHITTIER

Born: Haverhill, Massachusetts; December 17, 1807
Died: Hampton Falls, New Hampshire; September 7, 1892

PRINCIPAL POETRY

Legends of New-England, 1831
Moll Pitcher, 1832
Mogg Megone, 1836
Poems Written During the Progress of the Abolition Question in the United States, 1837
Poems, 1838
Lays of My Home, and Other Poems, 1843
Hymns, 1846 (pb. in Samuel Longfellow and Samuel Johnson's *A Book of Hymns*)
Voices of Freedom, 1846

Poems, 1849

Songs of Labor, and Other Poems, 1850

The Chapel of the Hermits, and Other Poems, 1853

The Panorama, and Other Poems, 1856

The Sycamores, 1857

The Poetical Works of John Greenleaf Whittier,
     1857, 1869, 1880, 1894

Home Ballads and Poems, 1860

In War Time, 1863

Snow-Bound: A Winter Idyl, 1866

The Tent on the Beach, and Other Poems, 1867

Among the Hills, and Other Poems, 1869

Ballads of New England, 1869

Maud Muller, 1869

Miriam, and Other Poems, 1871

The Pennsylvania Pilgrim, and Other Poems, 1872

Hazel-Blossoms, 1875

Mabel Martin, 1876

Favorite Poems, 1877

The Vision of Echard, and Other Poems, 1878

The King's Missive, and Other Poems, 1881

The Bay of Seven Islands, and Other Poems, 1883

Saint Gregory's Guest and Recent Poems, 1886

At Sundown, 1890

OTHER LITERARY FORMS

Besides his extensive poetry, John Greenleaf Whittier (WIH-tee-uhr) wrote numerous antislavery tracts, compiled editions of New England legends, edited various newspapers, and was active in abolitionist politics. Whittier's *Legends of New-England*, his earliest collection, was followed by the antislavery arguments in *Justice and Expediency: Or, Slavery Considered with a View to Its Rightful and Effectual Remedy, Abolition* (1833), and *The Supernaturalism of New England* (1847). Whittier's finest prose work is perhaps *Leaves from Margaret Smith's Journal* (1849), a Quaker novel in journal form. *Old Portraits and Modern Sketches* (1850) and *Literary Recreations and Miscellanies* (1854) followed, and the *Prose Works of John Greenleaf Whittier* were collected in two volumes in 1866.

Whittier also edited *Child Life* (1872) and *Child Life in Prose* (1874), as well as *Songs of Three Centuries* (1876). He wrote a masterful introduction to his edition

of *The Journal of John Woolman* (1871), another notable American Quaker writer. A full collection of Whittier's prose can be found in *The Writings of John Greenleaf Whittier* (1888-1889).

ACHIEVEMENTS

John Greenleaf Whittier was a remarkably prolific writer and reformer. As poet, editor, abolitionist, and religious humanist, Whittier managed to produce more than forty volumes of poetry and prose during his lifetime, not counting his uncollected journalistic work. Through his antislavery poems, he spoke for the conscience of New England, and he later celebrated the virtues of village life for an age that looked back on them with nostalgia. Although honored and venerated as a poet during his later years, he was curiously guarded about his literary reputation, remarking to his first biographer, "I am a *man*, not a mere verse-maker." His belief that morality was the basis of all literature may have made him finally more of a moralist than a poet; his Quaker conscience would not permit him to produce art for art's sake.

Early in life, he patterned his verse after Robert Burns, writing dialect imitations of the Scottish poet to the extent of being called the American Burns. He further corrupted his muse by imitating the worst of the popular, sentimental, and genteel verse of his age and did not achieve a distinctive poetic voice until midcareer. Like many a self-educated poet, Whittier lacked a clear sense of critical taste and judgment, especially in regard to his own work. He wrote too much too quickly and could not distinguish between his best poems and his inferior work. Even his later work is often tainted by melodrama, moralizing, and sentimentality; yet when the worst has been said, the abiding strength of his work transcends its weaknesses.

His most obvious poetic strength is accessibility. Whittier wrote popular poetry that did not make great intellectual demands on his readers. Unlike the modernists, who wrote for a select, highly educated audience, Whittier tried to reach the ordinary reader. Instead of composing dense, ironic, highly allusive verse requiring careful explication, Whittier's narratives and ballads were written in a common idiom that could be readily understood. His poetical materials were regional legend and folklore, topical events, and the personal resources of his Quaker faith. Their moral perspective is clear and forthright, at times didactic or moralistic, and it lacks the ambiguity or tentativeness favored by the New Critics. George Arms argues persuasively that Whittier and the other schoolroom poets (also known as the Fireside poets) simply cannot be appreciated according to current standards of taste and, therefore, have been too often simply dismissed instead of being understood. Their strengths are seen as liabilities and they are faulted for lacking qualities foreign to their age.

The purview of Whittier's work was "common, natural things"—the realm of ordinary life. He rarely dealt with the extremes of human experience, except in some of his abolitionist poems. He shared the optimism and piety of his age and held to a romantic view of nature and a belief in the moral progress of humanity. His sense of moral order and probity may seem merely

John Greenleaf Whittier (Library of Congress)

quaint or old-fashioned to the modern reader, but his poems reflect moral convictions sincerely held. He devoted thirty years to the struggle against slavery and committed the better part of his talents and energy to that issue. If he lost his sense of social justice later in life and failed to comprehend the problems of an industrial society, that might well be excused by his age. Few people are capable of devoting themselves to more than one cause in a lifetime.

The alleged deficiencies in Whittier's poetics should also be judged in terms of his commitment to a popular rather than an academic style. Whittier favored a light, relaxed approach to his verse. Perhaps he overused mechanical rhymes, ballad meter, apostrophe, and hyperbole, but in his "Proem," he is frank to confess his limitations. His muse was not given to exalted flights but spoke plainly for freedom and democracy. Whittier's readership steadily grew during his later years so that his reputation once seemed secure, but like those of the other Fireside poets, it has suffered a sharp decline since his death. He is now read, if at all, as the author of "Snow-Bound: A Winter Idyl" and other nostalgic portraits of New England village life rather than as one of the leading poets of his age. Though his reputation may now be eclipsed by those of Walt Whitman, Emily Dickinson, and Herman Melville, no American poet of the nineteenth century better deserves the title of "poet of the common man" than Whittier.

BIOGRAPHY

John Greenleaf Whittier was born in Haverhill, Massachusetts, on December 17, 1807, in an old family homestead built by a Quaker ancestor. He was the second of four children in the family of John Whittier and Abigail Whittier, of old Quaker stock. Besides John Greenleaf, the Whittier children included an older sister Mary, a younger brother Matthew Franklin, and a younger sister Elizabeth Hussey. Several other relatives lived with the family, including a paternal grandmother, a bachelor uncle, and a maiden aunt. The poet's father was an honest, industrious farmer who tilled his hard, rocky land in the Merrimack Valley with only marginal success. Whittier's mother was a model of quiet strength and deep refinement. She was noted in the community for her domestic industry and "exquisite Quaker neatness." The entire family attended Friends' services at Amesbury, nine miles away, even in poor weather.

Whittier's childhood was one of hard farmwork (that eventually weakened his health) and the occasional freedom of the outdoors—a life of frugality, harmony, and affection later idealized in "Snow-Bound" and "The Barefoot Boy." There were few books in the Whittier household besides the Bible and John Bunyan's *The Pilgrim's Progress* (1678, 1684), and the family depended for entertainment on the tales of his uncle Moses and the stories brought by itinerant Yankee peddlers and gypsies. Whittier's education was meager, consisting of sporadic attendance at the district school and several terms at Haverhill Academy. One of the local teachers, Joshua Coffin, introduced him to the poetry of Burns, and made such a lasting impression on young Whittier that he was later commemorated in "To My Old School Master." As a boy, Whittier showed a natural gift for rhymes and verse, and wrote simple ballads in imitation of Burns and Sir Walter Scott. His sister Mary sent one of these to the local newspaper, the Newburyport *Free Press*. The editor there, William Lloyd Garrison, was so impressed that he paid a personal visit to the Whittiers to urge further education for their son. Whittier's father was said to have replied to Garrison, "Sir, poetry will not get him bread."

His father finally relented, and Whittier was allowed to enter Haverhill Academy at the age of nineteen. To pay his expenses, he learned the craft of shoemaking, a common winter vocation among New England country folk. Meanwhile, his poems continued to appear in the Haverhill *Gazette* and other publications. At Garrison's behest, Whittier entered the world of Boston journalism and at twenty-two became editor of the *American Manufacturer*, a Whig trade weekly. In the summer of 1829, he was called home by the illness and death of his father, which required him to manage the farm and provide for his family. Still unhappy with the drudgery of farm life, Whittier gladly accepted an invitation from Hartford, Connecticut, in July, 1830, to edit the *Weekly Review*. Unfortunately, his health failed, and Whittier was forced to resign from this attractive position within eighteen months and return to Haverhill in 1832. He was now twenty-five

years old, ambitious, but without purpose or direction. A letter from Garrison in the spring of 1833 restored Whittier's spirits when he was invited to apply his talents to the abolitionist movement. From 1833 to the end of the Civil War, the abolition of slavery became the abiding goal of Whittier's life.

Immersion in abolitionist politics made him a master of satire and invective but at the expense of his literary gifts. Out of his new commitment came *Justice and Expediency*, and that same year he was elected to the National Anti-Slavery Convention in Philadelphia. Thus began a thirty-year career of antislavery advocacy and agitation. Several times he was exposed to the threat of mob violence and barely escaped personal injury. He later said that he was prouder of his abolitionist work than of all his authorship, but this comment must be taken in the perspective of his career.

As a young man, Whittier had struggled to reconcile his worldly literary ambitions with his Quaker reticence and piety. As a poor country boy, he had aspired to Boston gentility but lacked the education or means to move in Brahmin circles. One-third of his poetry was written before he was twenty-five, though much of it was sentimental and imitative. When he shrewdly realized that poetry would not bring him the fame he sought, he turned to politics and reformism instead. The abolitionist movement gave him a focus for his talents and energies. He became involved in Essex County politics and by 1835 was elected to the Massachusetts legislature. The following year he sold the Haverhill farm and moved to a small house in Amesbury, where he briefly edited the Amesbury *Village Transcript*. The next twenty years saw him editing various antislavery newspapers and writing numerous abolitionist poems and articles. Much of this was obviously hackwork, but occasionally he would write a notable poem in the heat of indignation, such as "Massachusetts to Virginia," "Barbara Frietchie," or "Laus Deo." His reform efforts interfered with his lyric gifts as a poet, however, and his best work came later in life, in his fifties and sixties, especially after the Civil War. The War Between the States presented a particular dilemma to Whittier in pitting his antislavery sentiments against his Quaker commitment to nonviolence. He saw the need for emancipation but did not approve of secession or the drift toward armed conflict. However, he remained a loyal unionist and wrote poems and broadsides in favor of the Union cause. Titles such as "Our Countrymen in Chains" and "The Sabbath Scene" are little more than propaganda, but Whittier was writing to appeal to the emotions and feelings of ordinary people, and these antislavery verses enjoyed great popular success. Next to Harriet Beecher Stowe, he was perhaps the most effective propagandist for the abolitionist cause.

In his personal life, Whittier remained a resolute bachelor, despite several romantic attractions to Quaker admirers. He lived with his mother, two sisters, and a brother in Amesbury and cherished the company of his family. Their successive deaths in the 1850's and 1860's, however, particularly the loss of his beloved sister Elizabeth in 1864, left him increasingly isolated. The idyllic poem "Snow-Bound" was written partially in memory of his tight-knit family, and with its publication in 1866, Whittier enjoyed his first large commercial success and thereafter was able to live comfortably on his literary earnings. Henceforth his volumes of poetry came out regularly and sold well, but he was plagued with persistently poor health and never felt fully comfortable with his new fame or with the many visitors to his Amesbury cottage. Occasionally he would venture into Boston to join Ralph Waldo Emerson, Henry Wadsworth Longfellow, and Oliver Wendell Holmes at the Saturday Club, but more often he preferred to enjoy the simple company of his niece and her family at their country estate in Danvers.

After the war, Whittier had gradually become institutionalized as one of the Fireside poets, and with this increased popularity came other honors. He served as a Harvard overseer from 1858 onward and as a trustee of Brown University from 1869 to 1892. Harvard also awarded him an honorary LL.D., in 1886, although Whittier was prevented by illness from attending the ceremony in person. On his seventieth birthday, his friends held a formal dinner in his honor, on which occasion Mark Twain embarrassed the guests when his humor misfired, his intended tribute being taken by some as parody.

In his later years, Whittier increasingly assumed the role of New England patriarch, invoking in his poems a sentimental and nostalgic view of village life. He felt out of touch with the changes in the postwar America of the Gilded Age, and increasingly withdrew to the quiet meditation of his Quaker faith. On September 3, 1892, he suffered a paralytic stroke, which led to his death four days later, on September 7, at the age of eighty-four. Holmes spoke at his funeral, after which Whittier was buried in the Friends' section of the Union Cemetery in Haverhill, next to his parents and sister.

Analysis

In the collected edition of his work, John Greenleaf Whittier decided to arrange his poems by topic, in ten categories, rather than present them in chronological order. He also suppressed many of the early verses that had proved embarrassing to him so that the supposedly complete 1894 edition of *The Poetical Works of John Greenleaf Whittier* is not really definitive, though it reflects the poet's final intentions. This arrangement obscures Whittier's development as a poet, but it does tell something about his major concerns and about the poetic forms in which he felt most comfortable. These include antislavery poems, songs of labor and reform, ballads, narratives and legends, nature poems, personal poems, historical poems, occasional verses, hymns and religious lyrics, and genre poems and country idylls.

From Whittier's collected verse, perhaps a dozen or so titles are distinctive. These include "Ichabod," "Massachusetts to Virginia," "Barbara Frietchie," "Telling the Bees," "Laus Deo," "The Trailing Arbutus," "Skipper Ireson's Ride," "First-Day Thoughts," and of course "Snow-Bound." A few other selections should be mentioned—"In School-Days," "The Barefoot Boy," and "Dear Lord and Father of Mankind"—simply because they are part of America's popular culture.

Abolitionist poems

Many of Whittier's abolitionist poems are little more than crude propaganda, but with "Ichabod," he produced a masterpiece of political satire and invective. Cast in terms of a prophetic rebuke, the poem is directed at Daniel Webster, whose "Seventh of March" speech in favor of the Fugitive Slave Law aroused the wrath and enmity of many Northern abolitionists, who accused him of selling out to slave interests. Whittier portrays Webster, in terms of bitter denunciation, as a leader who has betrayed his countrymen and extinguished the life of his soul. His audience would certainly have caught the disparaging reference to I Samuel 4:21, "And she named the child Ichabod, saying the glory is departed from Israel!" Webster, a contemporary "Ichabod" in his fall from glory, becomes the object of scorn and pity for his betrayal of the antislavery cause.

This same contentious tone is also evident in another antislavery poem, "Massachusetts to Virginia," which contrasts the free strength of the North with the moral decadence brought about by slavery in the South. The poem recalls that both Commonwealth States had stood united in the War for Independence, and appeals to that sense of common fellowship in freedom. Though some passages are marred by stock declamatory phrases and excessive use of formal diction and hyperbole, the poem ably makes its point and ends with a ringing slogan, "No fetters in the Bay State,—No slaves upon our Land!"

To a staunch abolitionist, the ratification of the Thirteenth Amendment on December 18, 1865, was reason enough for an occasional poem, but Whittier's "Laus Deo" (literally "praise God") expresses his personal jubilation at seeing a lifetime's work brought to completion. The poem describes the ringing of bells and firing of guns in Amesbury that accompanied the announcement that slavery had officially been abolished throughout the Union. The ten stanzas of trochaic tetrameter create a hymn of celebration and gratitude in which the Lord sanctions the righteousness of the Union cause.

On a more personal note, Whittier wrote many memorable verses in tribute to his Quaker faith, the finest of these perhaps being "First-Day Thoughts," in which he evoked the quiet grace and deep spirituality of the Friends' service. He captures the essence of Christian worship in the soul's contemplation of its creator through "the still small voice" of silent meditation. This same note of profound spiritual depth and reverence for the inner life appears in his famous hymn, "Dear Lord and Father of Mankind," which was adapted from the last six stanzas of "The Brewing of Soma." This inner faith grew with age and led Rufus M. Jones to comment later that Whittier "grasped more steadily, felt more

profoundly, and interpreted more adequately the essential aspects of the Quaker life and faith" than any other of his age.

COUNTRY IDYLLS AND GENRE POEMS

Whittier's most lasting accomplishment, however, rests with his country idylls and genre poems, those set pieces and descriptive verses in which he evokes a memory of his childhood or presents an idealized view of the pleasures of rural life. In "The Trailing Arbutus," for example, a glimpse of this early spring flower on an otherwise cold and bitter day becomes the occasion for a moment of natural rapture. A better poem, "Telling the Bees," uses the New England custom of draping bee hives after a family death as a way of foreshadowing the narrator's sorrow at the loss of his beloved Mary. This particular poem, occasioned by the death of the poet's mother, contains some of his finest descriptive passages. Another genre poem, "In School-Days," treats of bashful love and childhood regrets nostalgically remembered, while "The Barefoot Boy" presents a stilted and somewhat generalized picture of rural childhood: Only in the middle stanzas does the poem rise above platitudes to a realistic glimpse of the poet's actual boyhood. With "Skipper Ireson's Ride," Whittier turned a New England legend into the material for a memorable folk ballad, although at the expense of historical veracity. The poem's mock-heroic tone does not mask the cruelty of the incident, in which Old Floyd Ireson was "tarred and feathered and carried in a cart" by the women of Marblehead for allegedly failing to rescue the survivors of another sinking fishing vessel. However factually inaccurate, Whittier's version of the legend captures the essential qualities of mob behavior in what one critic has called the most effective nineteenth century American ballad.

"SNOW-BOUND"

"Snow-Bound," subtitled "A Winter Idyl," is probably Whittier's most lasting achievement. The founding of *The Atlantic Monthly* in 1857 had given him a steady market for his verse, and when the editor, James Russell Lowell, wrote to him in 1865 requesting a "Yankee pastoral," Whittier responded with "Snow-Bound," which was published in the February, 1866, issue. The epigrams from Agrippa von Nettesheim's *Occult Philosophy* (1533) and Emerson's "The Snow

Storm" establish the parameters of the poem in what John B. Pickard has called the protective circle of the family and hearth against the ominous power of the winter storm. Through an extended narrative in four-beat rhymed couplets, Whittier recalls the self-sufficiency of his family and recounts their close-knit circle of domestic affection as seen through a week of enforced winter isolation. This theme is enhanced through a series of contrasts between light and dark, warmth and cold, indoors and outdoors, fire and snow. After taking the reader through the round of barnyard chores, the poet shifts his perspective indoors to describe the sitting room of the Whittier homestead. Part 2 of the poem begins with Whittier's recollections of the tales and stories the family shared during their long evenings before the fire, with father, mother, uncle, aunt, schoolteacher, and another female guest each taking turns with the storytelling. The evening's entertainment finally ends as the fire burns low in the hearth and each family member retires from the pleasant circle of light and warmth. Part 3 of the poem gradually shifts from the past back to the present, as the poet's memories of "these Flemish pictures of old days" gradually fade; just as the fireplace logs had earlier faded to glowing embers covered with gray ash, so the poet will now gradually relinquish these recollections that have warmed "the hads of memory." His concluding lines express the hope that these memories will touch other readers and uplift their hearts, like the fresh odors of newly cut meadows, or pond lilies' fragrance on a summer breeze. The shift in season enforces the contrast between past and present, distancing Whittier from his family, most of whom had since died.

LEGACY

While he was not a major poet, Whittier learned early from Burns the value of the commonplace, and his best poetry reflects an affectionate understanding of New England country life. If his muse flew no higher than popular and occasional verse, at least he wrote well of what he knew best—the customs and folkways of Yankee farming; the spiritual resources of his Quaker faith, which taught him to place spiritual concerns over material needs; and the history and legends of Essex County. His most accomplished poems look ahead to Edwin Arlington Robinson and Robert Frost,

who would further probe the diminished world of the New England farm and village. Whittier stands directly in this tradition. His reputation has held better than those of the other Fireside poets, and he will continue to be read for his grasp of several essential truths: the value of family affections, the importance of firm moral character, and the simple attractions of country life.

OTHER MAJOR WORKS

LONG FICTION: *Narrative of James Williams: An American Slave*, 1838; *Leaves from Margaret Smith's Journal*, 1849.

EDITED TEXTS: *The Journal of John Woolman*, 1871; *Child Life*, 1872; *Child Life in Prose*, 1874; *Songs of Three Centuries*, 1876.

NONFICTION: *Justice and Expediency: Or, Slavery Considered with a View to Its Rightful and Effectual Remedy, Abolition*, 1833; *The Supernaturalism of New England*, 1847; *Old Portraits and Modern Sketches*, 1850; *Literary Recreations and Miscellanies*, 1854; *Whittier on Writers and Writing: The Uncollected Critical Writings of John Greenleaf Whittier*, 1950 (Edwin H. Cady and Harry Hayden Clark, editors); *The Letters of John Greenleaf Whittier*, 1975 (John B. Pickard, editor).

MISCELLANEOUS: *Prose Works of John Greenleaf Whittier*, 1866; *The Writings of John Greenleaf Whittier*, 1888-1889.

BIBLIOGRAPHY

Fenner, Pamela, ed. and comp. *Celebrating Whittier: New England's Quaker Poet and Abolitionist—America's 1907 Centennial*. Foreword by John B. Pickard. Amesbury, Mass.: Michaelmas Press, 2010. Republication of documents relating to the one-hundredth anniversary of Whittier's birth.

Grant, David. "'The Unequal Sovereigns of a Slaveholding Land': The North as Subject in Whittier's 'The Panorama.'" *Criticism* 38, no. 4 (Fall, 1996): 521-549. Whittier's "The Panorama" discusses the interdependence of the two ideals exploited by the Republicans and Democrats: sovereignty and Union. The poem places the slave system at the root of the threats to the North.

Kribbs, Jayne K., comp. *Critical Essays on John Green-*

leaf Whittier. Boston: G. K. Hall, 1980. Kribbs's extended introduction locates four periods of the poet's writing career and suggests in conclusion that the central question about Whittier is not how great, but how minor a figure he is in American literature. All the essays are written by respected scholars. Contains a bibliography and an index.

Leonard, Angela M. "The Topography of Violence in John Greenleaf Whittier's 'Antislavery Poems.'" In *Political Poetry as Discourse: Rereading John Greenleaf Whittier, Ebenezer Elliot, Hip-hop-ology*. Lanham, Md.: Lexington Books, 2010. Examines Whittier's antislavery poems and the violence contained within.

Pickard, Samuel Thomas. *Life and Letters of John Greenleaf Whittier*. Vol. 1. Honolulu, Hawaii: University Press of the Pacific, 2005. The first volume in a biography of Whittier that covers his life and works.

Rogal, Samuel J. *Congregational Hymns from the Poetry of John Greenleaf Whittier: A Comparative Study of the Sources and Final Works, with a Bibliographic Catalog of the Hymns*. Jefferson, N.C.: McFarland, 2010. Compares Whittier's original poems with the hymns, showing how they were adapted and, in the process, providing extensive explication of the poetry.

Wagenknecht, Edward. *John Greenleaf Whittier: A Portrait in Paradox*. New York: Oxford University Press, 1967. Wagenknecht arranges his facts and anecdotes topically rather than chronologically. The result is a vibrant and energetic portrait of Whittier that displays the richness of his inner and outer life. The thesis of this book is that many facets of Whittier's life seem paradoxical to one another. Includes bibliography.

Warren, Robert Penn. *John Greenleaf Whittier's Poetry: An Appraisal and a Selection*. 1971. Reprint. Minneapolis: University of Minnesota Press, 1992. Warren discusses "Snow-Bound," "Telling the Bees," "Ichabod," "To My Old Schoolmaster," and other poems addressing themes of childhood and nostalgia, as well as a controversial Freudian view of the poet's development. Includes thirty-six poems by Whittier.

Woodwell, R. H. *John Greenleaf Whittier: A Biography*. Haverhill, Mass.: Trustees of the John Greenleaf Whittier Homestead, 1985. This biography, based on years of research, is encyclopedic but has a very good index. Includes a useful review of Whittier's criticism.

Andrew J. Angyal

RICHARD WILBUR

Born: New York, New York; March 1, 1921

PRINCIPAL POETRY

The Beautiful Changes, and Other Poems, 1947
Ceremony, and Other Poems, 1950
Things of This World, 1956
Poems, 1943-1956, 1957
Advice to a Prophet, and Other Poems, 1961
Loudmouse, 1963 (juvenile)
The Poems of Richard Wilbur, 1963
Walking to Sleep: New Poems and Translations, 1969
Digging for China, 1970
Opposites, 1973 (juvenile)
The Mind-Reader: New Poems, 1976
Seven Poems, 1981
New and Collected Poems, 1988
More Opposites, 1991 (juvenile)
Runaway Opposites, 1995 (juvenile)
The Disappearing Alphabet, 1998 (juvenile)
Mayflies: New Poems and Translations, 2000
Collected Poems, 1943-2004, 2004
Anterooms: New Poems and Translations, 2010

OTHER LITERARY FORMS

In addition to his success as a poet, Richard Wilbur has won acclaim as a translator. Interspersed among his own poems are translations of Charles Baudelaire, Jorge Guillén, François Villon, and many others. His interest in drama is most notably shown in his translations of four Molière plays: *The Misanthrope* (1955), *Tartuffe* (1963), *The School for Wives* (1971), and *The*

Learned Ladies (1978). In 1957, Random House published *Candide: A Comic Operetta* with lyrics by Wilbur, book by Lillian Hellman, and score by Leonard Bernstein. Wilbur admits that he attempted to write a play in 1952, but he found its characters unconvincing and "all very wooden." He turned to translating Molière, thinking he "might learn something about poetic theater by translating *the master*."

Wilbur has edited several books, including *A Bestiary*, with Alexander Calder (1955), *Poe: Complete Poems* (1959), and *Shakespeare: Poems*, with coeditor Alfred Harbage (1966). In 1976, Wilbur published *Responses, Prose Pieces: 1953-1976*, a collection of essays which he describes as containing "some prose by-products of a poet's life." His essays and other prose pieces are collected in *The Catbird's Song: Prose Pieces, 1963-1995* (1997). Most of his manuscripts are in the Robert Frost Library at Amherst College. His

Richard Wilbur (Stathis Orphanos)

early work is housed in the Lockwood Memorial Library at the State University of New York at Buffalo.

ACHIEVEMENTS

Richard Wilbur has been the recipient of many awards and honors, including honorary degrees from colleges and universities. He received two Guggenheim Fellowships (1952-1953, 1963), the Prix de Rome (1954), a Ford Fellowship (1960-1961), and a Camargo Foundation Fellowship (1985). In 1957, *Things of This World* brought him a Pulitzer Prize, the National Book Award, and the Edna St. Vincent Millay Memorial Award, and he became a member of the American Academy of Arts and Letters. He received the Bollingen Prize (with Mona Van Duyn) in 1971, the Shelley Memorial Award in 1973, and the Aiken Taylor Award in Modern American Poetry in 1988. He served as chancellor for the Academy of American Poets (1961-1995) and as poet laureate consultant in poetry to the Library of Congress (1987-1988). *New and Collected Poems* won a second Pulitzer Prize in 1989 and a Los Angeles Times Book Prize in 1988. In 1991, he was awarded a Gold Medal from the American Academy of Arts and Letters. President Bill Clinton bestowed the National Medal of the Arts on Wilbur in 1994. In 1996, he received the Frost Medal from the Poetry Society of America and the Ingersoll Foundation's T. S. Eliot Award for Creative Writing. He received the Corrington Award for Literary Excellence from Centenary College of Louisiana (1998-1999), the Wallace Stevens Award (2003), and the Ruth Lilly Poetry Prize (2006).

BIOGRAPHY

Born to Lawrence Wilbur and Helen Purdy Wilbur, Richard Purdy Wilbur was reared in a family that was moderately interested in art and language. His father was an artist, and his mother was a daughter of an editor with the *Baltimore Sun*. His maternal great-grandfather was also an editor and a publisher who established newspapers supporting the Democratic platform. In 1923, the family moved to a farm in North Caldwell, New Jersey, and Wilbur and his brother enjoyed their childhoods investigating nature, an activity that remains a strong focal point in his poems. His father's painting and his mother's link with newspapers led him at times to think of becoming a cartoonist, an artist, or a journalist. His love of cartooning continues, for he illustrated *Opposites* with bold line drawings. His interests were many, however, and he was encouraged by his family to explore any talents he wished. After graduating from Montclair High School in 1938, he entered Amherst College, where he edited the newspaper and contributed to *Touchstone*, the campus humor magazine. He spent summers hoboing around the country.

After graduation in 1942, Wilbur married Charlotte Hayes Ward (with whom he had four children), joined the Enlisted Reserve Corps, and saw active duty in Europe with the Thirty-sixth Infantry Division. At Cassino, Anzio, and the Siegfried line, he began writing poetry seriously, embarking on what he calls creation of "an experience" through a poem. He sent his work home, where it remained until he returned from the war to pursue a master's degree in English at Harvard. The French poet André du Bouchet read the poems, pronounced Wilbur a poet, and sent the works to be published. They were released as *The Beautiful Changes, and Other Poems* in 1947; in 1952, the same year Wilbur received his master of arts degree from Harvard, he was elected to the Society of Fellows.

His status as a poet established, Wilbur began his teaching career. From 1950 to 1954, he was an assistant professor of English at Harvard. Then, from 1954 to 1957, he served as an associate professor at Wellesley College; during that time his award-winning *Things of This World* was published. In 1957, he went to Wesleyan University as a professor of English. He stayed there until 1977, when he accepted the position of writer-in-residence at Smith College, where he remained until 1986. In 2008, he returned to Amherst College to teach.

ANALYSIS

Eschewing any obvious poetic version or formal, personal set of guidelines, Richard Wilbur has come to be regarded as a master craftsman of modern poetry. Although he sees himself as an inheritor of the vast wealth of language and form used by poets before him, Wilbur has consistently striven to create and maintain his own artistic signature and control over his own

work. Having begun his career immediately after World War II and having been exposed to what has been called the Beat generation, Wilbur creates his poetry from an intriguing blend of imaginative insights and strict adherence to the niceties of conventional poetics. His is not the poetry of confession or hatred readily exemplified by Sylvia Plath, nor is it hallucinatory or mystical, as is much of Allen Ginsberg's work.

Wilbur began to write poetry because the war prompted him to confront the fear and the physical and spiritual detachment brought about by a world in upheaval. He says that he "wrote poems to calm [his] nerves." It is this sense of imposed order on a disorderly world that has caused some readers to think of Wilbur's poetry as a distant investigation into human life addressed to a small, educated audience and delivered by a seemingly aloof but omniscient observer. Nearly all Wilbur's poems are metrical, and many of them employ rhyme. Perhaps if a feeling of detachment exists, it comes not from Wilbur the poet but from the very standards of poetic expression. Every persona established by a poet is, in Wilbur's words, "a contrived self." This voice is the intelligent recorder of experience and emotion. It is Wilbur's voice in the sense that, like the poet, the persona discovers relationships between ideas and events that are grounded in concrete reality but that lead to abstracted views of nature, love, endurance, and place. He uses concrete images—a fountain, a tree, a hole in the floor—to explore imagination. His flights into imagery are not sojourns into fantasy; they are deliberate attempts to be a witness to the disordered and altogether varied life around him.

Wilbur achieves brilliantly what he sees poetry doing best: compacting experience into language that excites the intellect and vivifies the imagination. His voice and the cautious pace at which he works are not to be taken as self-conscious gestures. They are, to use his word, matters demanding "carefulness." He finds "gaudiness annoying, richness not." Wilbur's poetry is rich; it is wealthy in imagery and plot and rhythmic movement. He seems to believe that language cannot be guarded unless it is used to carry as much meaning as it can possibly bear. This freedom with language is not prodigal but controlled. Betraying poetry's ancestry would be anarchy for Wilbur. At the heart of his canon is the verbal liberty he finds in formalism. Consequently, in each line he hopes that at least one word will disturb the reader, providing a freedom found only within the architectonics of poetry's conventions. His poems enjoy humor and quiet meditation, and they lend themselves easily to being read aloud. Because of the freedom the rules of poetry give to them, Wilbur's poems are energetic, and his persona, peripatetic.

A SENSE OF DECORUM

If readers were to limit their interest in Wilbur's poetry to a discussion of imagery, they would be misunderstanding and distorting some of the basic premises on which he builds his poetry. Just as he sees each of his poems as an independent unit free of any entanglement with other poems in a collection or with a superimposed, unifying theme, so he views the creation of a poem as an individual response to something noticed or deeply felt. Because all worthwhile poetry is a personal vision of the world, Wilbur heightens the tension and irony found in his poems by establishing a voice enchanted by what is happening in the poem but controlled so that the persona is nearly always a reasonable voice recording details and events in an entirely believable way. His sense of decorum, then, plays a major role in creating the relationship between reader and poet.

Readers often react to Wilbur's decorum in one of two ways: Either they laud the fictive persona as a trustworthy human being, lacking deceit, or they hear him speaking from a plateau that is at best inaccessible to the reader because it is too distant from the mundane. Wilbur's decorum actually creates a median between these two extremes. Like Robert Frost, Wilbur believes that poetry must present shared experiences in extraordinary ways. His persona is not directed toward readers solely as readers of poetry. Rather, the voice is aimed sharply at defining the experiences that both readers and poet hold in common. Wilbur never talks at the reader, but rather, he addresses himself to the human condition. Often his voice is much more vulnerable and humorous than readers admit. Many of his poems are reminiscent of soliloquies. A reader may come to the poems the way a person may discover a man talking out loud to himself about personal experiences, all the while using the most imaginative, sonorous language

to describe them. At his best, Wilbur provides moments when readers can recognize the deep humanity that runs through his work.

Although he looks for no overriding idea or central metaphor when he organizes a collection, Wilbur does return to themes that are at the heart of human life: nature, love, a sense of goodness and contentment, the search for direction, the need to feel a part of a larger unknown, a wider life. All of these topics are spiritual concerns. Unlike Edgar Allan Poe, whom he considers a writer who ignores reality to construct a world colored by the fantastic, Wilbur grounds his spiritual wanderings in the world that readers know. In this respect, he is capturing what is abstract in the mesh of concrete imagery, a feat also successfully accomplished by Frost and Emily Dickinson.

"LAMARCK ELABORATED"

Perhaps nowhere else do Wilbur's major themes so intelligently and ironically coalesce as in "Lamarck Elaborated" (from *Things of This World*), a poem dealing not only with nature and love but also with the inner and outer worlds that humans inhabit. Humankind's place in these two worlds and the ability to balance them provide a common experience for both poet and reader. The inner world of humans, represented by the senses and the intellect, perceives the outer world framed by nature, which, in turn, has the power to shape people's ability to interpret what they sense to be the physical world. Chevalier de Lamarck, a French naturalist whose life straddles the seventeenth and eighteenth centuries, believed that the environment causes structural changes that can be passed on genetically. Although humans may assign names to the animals, plants, and objects that surround them, they are unable to control the changes that may occur in nature and that may, in turn, change them. Humans have adapted to nature. Paradoxically, humankind's attempts at analyzing the natural state of things leads them to "whirling worlds we could not know," and what people think is love is simply an overwhelming desire causing dizziness. The poem's voice records people's obsession with their place in a scheme they wish to dominate but cannot. Literally and figuratively, the balance between the inner and outer worlds "rolls in seas of thought."

The balance implied in "Lamarck Elaborated" is

also investigated in "Another Voice" (from *Advice to a Prophet, and Other Poems*). Here Wilbur probes the soul's ability to do good when humans' nature is often to do bad. How can the soul feel sympathy when evil has been committed? How can it transform violence into "dear concerns"? Can the "giddy ghost" do battle with malevolence? Wilbur seems to suggest that the soul's response should be one of endurance as it acknowledges evil without becoming evil. The soul may not be able to rid itself of its "anxiety and hate," two powerful forces, but neither will it relinquish its quiet sympathy that serves as a witness for compassion.

"RUNNING"

Although "Another Voice" may conjure up a spirit of resignation as the poet ponders the weaknesses of the human soul, Wilbur's poetry contains many examples of contentment, complete happiness, and mature acknowledgment of human limitations. Wilbur reminds his readers that human beings cannot be or do all that they might wish to become or accomplish. "1933," "Patriot's Day," and "Dodwells Road" form a thematic triptych, "Running" (from *Walking to Sleep*), in which Wilbur muses about the stages of life and the reactions human beings have to these stages. The first poem is an account of the persona's memories of his boyhood and the abandonment that running provided. In the second, the persona is an observer of the Boston Marathon and of "Our champion Kelley who would win again,/ Rocked in his will, at rest within his run." The third poem presents the persona as both participant and observer. Having taken up the sport of jogging, as if to reaffirm his physical well-being, the speaker runs out of the forest and is brought to a halt by "A good ache in my ribcage." He feels comfortable in the natural setting surrounding him, a "part of that great going." The shouts of two boys (possibly the persona's sons) and the barking of a dog break the quiet, and the speaker finds delight in their running and leaping. In a gesture as inevitable as it is moving, the speaker gives the "clean gift" of his own childhood, his own vigor, to the boys.

"A HOLE IN THE FLOOR"

The voice that Wilbur assumes in his poems is often that of a person discovering or attempting to discover something unknown or removed. Usually the epiphany that the persona undergoes is centered around ordinary conditions or experiences. Sometimes the enlightenment produces extraordinary insights into human nature, the fragility of life, or the inexorable passage of time. A poem that manages to evoke poignancy, humor, and fear is "A Hole in the Floor" (from *Advice to a Prophet, and Other Poems*), in which the speaker stands directly above an opening a carpenter has made "In the parlor floor." The use of the word "parlor" brings to mind turn-of-the-century home-life, a certain quaintness and security. Now that this sanctum sanctorum has been defiled, the speaker stares into the hole to view an unexpected scene. He is poised on the brink of a discovery and compares himself with Heinrich Schliemann, the excavator of Troy and Mycenae. He sees in the hole the vestiges of the house's origins: sawdust, wood shavings "From the time when the floor was laid."

Wilbur heightens the mythological tone of the poem by comparing the shavings to the pared skins of the golden apples guarded by the Hesperides in the garden on the Isles of the Blest. Although in the dim light the curly lengths of shaved wood may seem "silvery-gold," they remain concrete reminders of the carpenter's trade and of the creation of the structure in which the speaker now stands. If he senses that something primordial has been uncovered, he cannot quite convey his feelings. The speaker, of course, has given in to his own curiosity and wishes to be the explorer of unknown territories, the uncoverer of what had been private and hidden, but, at the same time, close by. Reveling in his investigation of the joists and pipes, he finally wonders what it is he thought he would see. He brings his consciousness back to the steady, mundane world of the parlor and upbraids himself for his curiosity and romanticism. He asks himself if he expected to find a treasure or even the hidden gardens of the Hesperides. Perhaps, he ponders, he has come face-to-face with "The house's very soul."

Unlike Frost's figure who is content to kneel by a well, see his own reflection, and then catch a glimmer of something at the bottom, Wilbur's speaker understands that what he discovers or believes he has discovered is something beyond the orderly, formal restrictions imposed upon him by the parlor. Somehow, the hidden realm on which the house stands adds an importance to what can in fact be known. Paradoxically, what the persona knows is his inability to fathom the unknowable, that "buried strangeness/ which nourishes the known." The parlor suddenly becomes "dangerous" because its serenity rests on uncertainty, darkness, and private beginnings. The "buried strangeness" not only resides at the foundation of the house, but it is also found in any human construction, a building, a passion, a theory, or a poem.

BALANCING OPPOSITES

"A Hole in the Floor" is further representative of Wilbur's poetry because it balances two opposites, and these contraries work on several levels: curiosity and expectation, the known and the unknown, and reality and imagination. It is a complex and beautifully crafted poem. Other poems, also from *Advice to a Prophet, and Other Poems*, that also investigate the balance between opposites include "Another Voice," "Advice to a Prophet," "Gemini," and "Someone Talking to Himself." Wilbur's obvious pleasure in riddles is another example of this taut balance between the unknown and the known, the question and the answer, the pause and the reply. In addition, *Opposites*, charming and witty as it is, has this same tense equilibrium built into it.

The contrast between opposing ideas is probably most evident in what could be called Wilbur's "two-voice" poems, those in which he presents "two voices going against each other. One is a kind of lofty and angelic voice, the other is a slob voice, and these are two parts of myself quarreling in public." The poem "Two Voices in a Meadow," which begins *Advice to a Prophet, and Other Poems*, juxtaposes a milkweed's flexibility with a stone's tenacity. The milkweed yields to the wind's power to carry its cherubic seeds to the soil, and the stone attributes the solid foundation of heaven to its immovable nature. In "The Aspen and the Stream" (from the same volume), the tree and the brook carry on a dialogue in which the aspen's metaphysics are countered by the stream's no-nonsense, literal approach to its place in the universal scheme of life.

Sometimes Wilbur's interest in opposites takes the form of a study of reconciliation through religion. Such poems as "Water Walker" (from *The Beautiful Changes, and Other Poems*) and "A Christmas Hymn"

(from *Advice to a Prophet, and Other Poems*) suggest his concern with religious doctrine and its influence on private action and public thought. At other times, the balance is jarred because the persona is duped into believing something false or is misled because of naïveté. A more gullible person than the one in "A Hole in the Floor," the character in "Digging for China" (from *Things of This World*) burrows into the earth thinking that he can reach China. The speaker digs and digs to no avail, of course, and becomes obsessed and then delirious, "blinking and staggering while the earth went round." Admitting his folly, he confesses that "Until I got my balance back again/ All that I saw was China, China, China." He returns to whatever balance he may have known before his futile attempt to reach China, but he enjoys no enlightenment of the spirit.

The tense balance between knowledge and ignorance may appear in Wilbur's poems when the persona is confronted with an abstraction so amorphous and foreign that it cannot adequately be defined, as in "A Hole in the Floor." At other times, Wilbur allows his characters to confront ideas, events, or feelings that are much more readily and vividly recognized. In such cases, the emotions, although private, have a larger, perhaps a more cosmic significance added to them; these are shared emotions, easily identifiable because nearly all human beings have experienced them. Even if a person stands on the edge or the margins of experience, he or she is from time to time thrust squarely into life's demands and responsibilities. Wilbur elucidates this idea in poems such as "Marginalia" (from *Things of This World*), in which "Things concentrate at the edges," and "Our riches are centrifugal."

"BOY AT THE WINDOW"

Two poems that combine both the experience of living life fully and the experience of participating at its edges are "Boy at the Window" (from *Things of This World*) and "The Pardon" (from *Ceremony, and Other Poems*). Both have titles which would befit paintings, and indeed, Wilbur presents concrete stories colored and framed by his language and the structure of the poems themselves. Each has as its main character a boy who is both witness and participant. "Boy at the Window" is reminiscent of a classic Italian sonnet in its form and meter, although Wilbur divides the two sections into equal parts of eight lines each. Looking out from a window toward a snowman he has built, the boy is confronted by the "god-forsaken stare" of the figure "with bitumen eyes." The structure of the poem reinforces the balanced stares given by the boy and the snowman. Safe and warm, the boy intuitively knows that the snowman is an "outcast" from the world that the boy, himself, enjoys. The boy, however, does not mourn for the snowman; rather, the snowman "melts enough to drop from one soft eye/ A trickle of the purest rain, a tear." Surrounded as he is by "light" and "love," the boy understands, perhaps for the first time, fear and dread. The poem provides a quiet moment when the boy in his silence recognizes something about sin and futility and innocence and contentment. With its blending of childhood trust and energy with a maturer reflection on humankind's fall from grace, it evokes much the same mood as Dylan Thomas's "Fern Hill."

"THE PARDON"

"The Pardon" has as its plot a boy's confrontation with the death of his dog. At first he refuses to accept the event and tries to mask the experience just as "the heavy honeysuckle-smell" masks the odor of the decaying body. Admitting fear and the inability to "forgive the sad or strange/ In beast or man," the child cannot bring himself to bury the dog he loved "while he kept alive." After the boy's father buries the dog, the child sleeps and dreams of the dog's coming toward him. The boy wants to "call his name" to ask "forgiveness of his tongueless head." His attempts are checked, however, and he feels betrayed by his horror and his guilt. The poem is told from the perspective of a grown man who is remembering his childhood. Knowing the gesture may be ludicrous or ineffective, he "begs death's pardon now." Whether redemption occurs or the guilt is lifted is not told, but the very act of confronting this long-ago event is in itself a mature gesture of reconciliation and remorse, covered, perhaps, with shame and embarrassment. The rhyme scheme of the poem also suggests the persona's growing control over the incident, a control made possible by the passing of years and the accumulation of experience. The boy lacked a perspective; the man he has become provides it. Like his father before him, the speaker hopes to have the strength and the will to bury the dog, if not literally,

then at least symbolically. As the persona moves toward this strength, the rhyme scheme, chaotic at the poem's beginning, settles into an obvious, harmonious pattern that parallels the speaker's growing dominance over his sorrow.

"WALKING TO SLEEP"

Wilbur is known and admired for his short poems, whose imagery and subjects are compacted by his mastery of language and poetic convention. As if to reaffirm his commitment to the richness of these standards, his later collections have included long, dramatic monologues that remind readers of the oral tradition in poetry. "Walking to Sleep" (from *Walking to Sleep*) and "The Mind-Reader" (from *The Mind-Reader*) are poems that invite Wilbur's audience to explore the frontier, the wilderness of conscious thought and subconscious ruminating. The poems are both accessible and cryptic. Nowhere else has Wilbur created such sustained narrations, such talkative, complex tellers of his tales. In fact, he has noted that "Walking to Sleep" requires eight minutes to read aloud. The narrators are both conjurers and straightforward friends. Readers wish to believe them, but, at the same time, their manipulative language and their careful choice of details and information suggest an artifice. Both poems deal with the equilibrium between what is private, sleep and thought, and what is public, consciousness and action. Readers are led through the poems by the narrators, who help the audience balance its way as if on a tightrope. In addition, the poems seem to be inviting readers to lose themselves in their own minds, an activity calling for leisure, courage, and an eagerness to embrace the unknown and the uncontrollable.

On its surface, "Walking to Sleep" is a sensuous account of sleep, sweeping from scene to scene, mirroring the act of dreaming. It begins in medias res, and readers are asked to have the poise of a queen or a general as they give themselves over to sleep and, more important, to the devices of the poem itself. Wilbur explores in ways that are whimsical, horrifying, and provocative the images that appear to a sleeper and to a poet as well. The poem may well be an exploration into the origins of poetry, and the narrator-poet may be speaking to himself as much as he is to an audience. His only direct warning to himself and his readers is the speaker's suggestion that the imagination never be allowed to become too comfortable; it must remain "numb" with a "grudging circumspection." Readers can feel the rhythms of sleep and love, creativity, and balance in the poem just as vividly as they sense the rhythms of meter, imagery, humor, and resignation. The poem is a masterful work controlled by the limitless power of man's imagination.

"THE MIND-READER"

"The Mind-Reader" deals with a man who thinks other people's thoughts. The narrator describes himself as a person condemned to finding what is lost, remembering what is forgotten, or foreseeing what is unknown. He is able to manipulate his listeners and his followers because of their superstitious awe of his ability, which they are afraid to disprove. He confesses that he "sometimes cheats a little," admitting that he has no clear, easy answers to give to questions about love, careers, or doubts. He sees his duties as being those of a listener rather than those of a man capable of prescience, and he wonders if "selfish hopes/ And small anxieties" have replaced the "reputed rarities of the soul." The irony in the poem is underscored when the speaker turns to his readers and asks them a question of huge, religious proportions. Like his audience, he now longs for guidance, "some . . . affection" capable of discovering "in the worst rancor a deflected sweetness." Ironically, he dulls his mind with drink and satiates himself with "concupiscence." To the great question of whether a gentle, proper, and completely honest, cosmic mind-reader exists, he has no answer.

"THIS PLEASING ANXIOUS BEING"

In "This Pleasing Anxious Being," one of twenty-five new poems included in *Mayflies*, Wilbur looks back on a childhood scene, a somewhat formal dinner, presumably a holiday feast such as Thanksgiving. The family is gathered around the table. The servant, Roberta, brings yams and succotash after the mother has rung the little bell to summon her. The father carves at the sideboard. Wilbur refers to this scene as the one where safety was. He speaks of the lambent table and of the family whose faces drink the candlelight, using language in singular ways. Then, dwelling as he often does on opposites, he remembers that this recollected past was once a hurried present that was fretful and unsure.

As the poem ends, the recollection is of a small boy, feet kicking beneath the table, eager to be off to his play. Again, Wilbur employs opposites effectively, as he juxtaposes the formality of the dining room scene to the freedom and informality of child's play. The poem also juxtaposes real time and events and recollected time and events, becoming imbued with a sense of how nostalgia colors perceptions.

"A BARRED OWL"

In the celebrated "A Barred Owl" (from *Mayflies*), Wilbur again uses opposites to demonstrate how a single event can have different meanings, depending on how it is presented and how it is perceived by those who are exposed to it. In this case, what Wilbur, in the first six-line rhyming stanza, calls the "boom/ Of an owl's voice" frightens a child awakened in a dark room. Those who rush to comfort her, presumably her parents, explain to her that what she has heard is merely a question posed by a forest bird that asks twice, "Who cooks for you?"

In the second six-line stanza, Wilbur philosophizes about how language can soften such realities as the frightening call of an owl that captures small rodents in its claw and eats them raw, a brutal act from which words protect the child. Pacified by the explanation she receives, the child is calmed and now can go back to sleeping peacefully.

In twelve rhyming lines, Wilbur creates two worlds, one of fear and terror, the other of peace and security. He possesses a rare sense of when to use the exact word, as in the second stanza, where he writes that words can "domesticate a fear." The four-syllable word "domesticate" is surrounded by simple one-syllable words, making it stand out and evoking the reader's attention in precisely the manner that Wilbur wishes. This—the only unusual word in the entire poem, with its preponderance of one- and two-syllable words—fixes attention on the line as little else could.

"A SHORT HISTORY"

In this two-line poem, "A Short History" (from *Mayflies*), Wilbur achieves a prodigious act of compression. In essence, he reduces the history of humankind to fifteen words: "Corn planted us; tamed cattle made us tame;/ Thence hut and citadel and kingdom came." In these few words, the poet traces life as people know it back to humankind's progress from a nomadic society to an agrarian society, one that required permanent structures and governments. In this poem, the leap from hut (a humble dwelling) to citadel (a fortification) to kingdom (a governmental construct) speaks much more than the simple nouns that express this complex social progression. The first three words immediately demand attention. Wilbur might have written, "We planted corn," but to have done so would have been to rob the line of the very vitality that draws readers into it. Just as Dickinson used brief, clipped lines and unique grammatical constructions to give her lines the vitality that good poems require, so does Wilbur capture succinctly the precise constructions that vivify his lines.

COLLECTED POEMS

In *Collected Poems*, Wilbur makes no major changes in style or subject matter. In a sense, in using rhyme and meter, he is holding that the past of literature is not only alive but also valuable. The introductory poem, "The Reader," in a supple blank verse, is about the multiplicity of experience in particular. It is about the effects on and the meanings of great literature to the reader, about why people can go back again and again to what they have read and still have a rich experience. The reader, a woman, no longer young, rereads the stories that charmed her youth, but now, in the rereading she is aware not only of what has happened but also what will happen to the characters. However, though she is more aware, seeing things more clearly, she still shares "being" with the characters, "The blind delight of being, ready still/ To enter life on life and see them through."

"Man Running," in its subject, seems an entirely different poem, but it picks up almost the same theme as "The Reader." A fugitive, perhaps a criminal, running from pursuit, still draws sympathy from the poem's speaker, since in a sense the fugitive shares people's human past, people's animal and historical experience, their fright and weariness, "when we descended from the trees," not "lords of nature yet, but naked prey." However, the threat to order suggested here is the first in a group of poems in which that threat becomes the subject.

"Sir David Brewster's Toy," a poem on the inventor of the kaleidoscope, returns the reader to the theme of creativity, of how a "toy" can create remarkable and unrepeated, perhaps unrepeatable beauty. However, the poem's ending suggests that its meaning is a religious thought, that the kaleidoscope, in its beauty and variety, gives people an image of the beauty and eternal differences of heavenly beauty.

"Security Lights, Key West," patterned in quatrains, gives the reader the images of suburban houses lit up and protected by halogen lights. However, the eerie glow of those lights arouses, in the speaker, images from past literature and history, most from tragic stories, for that light makes the modern world, these houses, strange, and so the speaker sees that even here, in this apparent security and peace, there is the possibility of terrible drama. Those quatrains are a sign of, and a means of, giving order to possible disorder.

"In Trackless Woods" (a title that suggests the theme of the poem) is about escape from the human world: The speaker finds, in the woods, four trees, rock maples, standing in a perfect line, as if planted so. There is no sign of human habitation; nature has made its own order, beautiful and purposeless. The speaker will go farther into these woods, finding pattern after pattern, "not subject to our stiff geometries." In short, the poem is about order but not human order—an order more free and therefore, perhaps, more lovely.

In contrast, "The Sleepwalker" conjures up a different, much more threatening world. The sleeper's head is deep in his pillow "like an axe-head sunk in a stump," a simile of violence. A window shade, blown by the wind, crashes back against the screen, setting off the sleeper's subtly threatening dream or nightmare. However, in the day, it no longer haunts him except when his "mood" momentarily changes and he feels, "mortally/ Beset and in need of ransom." The poem, then, is about the human condition, and, one could argue, about the Christian answer to that condition, although this is almost hidden.

The last two poems in this first section return to the natural world for their imagery, using it to suggest both loss and richness. "Green" paradoxically celebrates the leaf color that, "with no apparent role," (beyond the visual) fades in autumn, leaving "only reds and blues," but the green is a sign of "largesse," a gift of nature rather than simply a use. "Blackberries for Amelia" is also about largesse in the face of endings. It is June, the blackberries are leafing out and flowering like stars, but the speaker speaks of the actual stars, receding from us, "that ever faster do they bolt away," until at last they have disappeared and there will be only blackness. However, this realization of endings leads the speaker to celebrate the moment and intensity of life, the time in August when the blackberries ripen and he and his grandchild can pick them.

The second section is more mixed. The first poem is a translation of riddles by the Latin poet Symphosius (the answers to the riddles are given at the end of the section). These are interesting in that they are concerned with language and its meanings, that permanent concern of Wilbur.

The second entry, "To a Comedian," is a more directly moral statement from Wilbur, for it is a satire of the comedian himself (as well as of his audience); the comedian demeans himself by satisfying his audience's desire for the slightly or more than slightly dirty joke, but without real wit.

The final poem is a deeply felt but also an almost light tribute, "An Eightieth Birthday Ballade for Anthony Hecht." The ballade form is an old French pattern, addressed to a "prince." The formality of the poem is an element of its underlying seriousness. The poet Hecht is praised for his daring to "Describe man's inhumanities" but who, in his "darkest verse" shows how "style and . . . intellect/Can both instruct and greatly please!" However, Hecht could also be witty, "many-sided," a gifted translator, a "true Parnassian."

THEMES

In the past, Wilbur's craft has been narrowly defined as the poetry of a mind-set apart from the everyday world that human beings inhabit. Although his interest in balance is evident, his keen insight into contraries and the inner and outer lives of his characters is equally important to an understanding of what he is attempting in his poems. His work focuses on the enlightenment of the human spirit, but it never denies the darker impulses or fears that are brought to bear when doubt, resignation, or apathy appear as challenges to the harmony that civilized man strives to achieve. His poems are not so much reaffirmations of the beauty of life as they are records of an attempt at order, an order

certainly suggested by the conventions of poetry. These conventions govern a poetic talent whose use of subject, meter, rhyme, and imagery provokes the senses and provides an ordinary understanding of life in an extraordinary and uncompromising way.

OTHER MAJOR WORKS

PLAY: *Candide: A Comic Operetta*, pr. 1956 (lyrics; book by Lillian Hellman, music by Leonard Bernstein).

NONFICTION: *Responses, Prose Pieces: 1953-1976*, 1976, expanded 2000; *On My Own Work*, 1983; *Conversations with Richard Wilbur*, 1990 (William Butts, editor); *The Catbird's Song: Prose Pieces, 1963-1995*, 1997.

TRANSLATIONS: *The Misanthrope*, 1955 (of Molière); *Tartuffe*, 1963 (of Molière); *The School for Wives*, 1971 (of Molière); *The Learned Ladies*, 1978 (of Molière); *Andromache*, 1982 (of Jean Racine); *Four Comedies*, 1982 (of Molière); *Phaedra*, 1986 (of Racine); *The School for Husbands*, 1991 (of Molière); *The Imaginary Cuckold: Or, Sgarnarelle*, 1993 (of Molière); *Amphitryon*, 1995 (of Molière); *The Bungler*, 2000 (of Molière); *Don Juan*, 2001 (of Molière); *The Suitors*, 2001 (of Racine).

EDITED TEXTS: *A Bestiary*, 1955; *Modern America and Modern British Poetry*, 1955 (with Louis Untermeyer and Karl Shapiro); *Poe: Complete Poems*, 1959; *Shakespeare: Poems*, 1966 (with Alfred Harbage); *The Narrative Poems and Poems of Doubtful Authenticity*, 1974; *Poems and Poetics*, 2003 (by Edgar Allan Poe).

BIBLIOGRAPHY

Bixler, Frances. *Richard Wilbur: A Reference Guide.* Boston: G. K. Hall, 1991. A useful bibliographical guide to Wilbur's work and its criticism.

Cummins, Paul F. *Richard Wilbur: A Critical Essay.* Grand Rapids, Mich.: Wm. B. Eerdmans, 1971. Defends Wilbur's poetry against the charge of passionless elegance; argues that the poet uses rhyme and meter skillfully to enhance tone and meaning. A largely thematic study.

Edgecombe, Rodney Stenning. *A Reader's Guide to the Poetry of Richard Wilbur.* Tuscaloosa: University of Alabama Press, 1995. Edgecombe provides some worthwhile insights into Wilbur's poems up to those included in *New and Collected Poems*. He provides a brief but penetrating introduction, as well as an extensive bibliography and a serviceable index.

Field, John P. *Richard Wilbur: A Bibliographical Checklist*. Kent, Ohio: Kent State University Press, 1971. For the student wishing to make further forays into Wilbur's poetry and thinking, this volume provides a valuable detailed listing of the poetry collections and their contents, articles, stories, edited works, book reviews, interviews, and manuscripts. A list of secondary sources is also supplied.

Hill, Donald L. *Richard Wilbur*. New York: Twayne, 1967. The biographical chronology extends only through 1964. Devotes a chapter each to *The Beautiful Changes, and Other Poems*, *Ceremony, and Other Poems*, *Things of This World*, and *Advice to a Prophet, and Other Poems*, with both thematic and technical discussions. A final chapter looks at Wilbur's prose writings and evaluates his place among twentieth century poets. Notes, a bibliography, and an index are included.

Hougen, John B. *Ecstasy Within Discipline: The Poetry of Richard Wilbur*. Atlanta: Scholar's Press, 1995. The author's chief concerns are theological. Hougen provides some useful insights into the formal aspects of Wilbur's writing.

Michelson, Bruce. *Wilbur's Poetry: Music in a Scattering Time*. Amherst: University of Massachusetts Press, 1991. In this first comprehensive study of Wilbur's poetry since the late 1960's, Michelson attempts to counter the widespread opinion that Wilbur is a bland poet. Michelson's close readings of the major poems contradict and dispel much that has been written critically about the poet.

Milne, Ira Mark, ed. *Poetry for Students*. Vol. 27. Detroit: Thomson/Gale Group, 2008. Contains an analysis of "Love Calls Us to the Things of This World."

Salinger, Wendy, ed. *Richard Wilbur's Creation*. Ann Arbor: University of Michigan Press, 1983. A rich collection featuring, in part 1, many previously published reviews of Wilbur's chief works through 1976; contributors include such luminaries as Louise Bogan, Randall Jarrell, Donald Hall, and John Ciardi. The second half presents more comprehensive critical essays on various aspects of the poet's themes and craft. Valuable for its scope and for the quality of its writing.

Wilbur, Richard. "Richard Wilbur in Conversation with Peter Dale." Interview by Peter Dale. In *Seven American Poets in Conversation: John Ashbery, Donald Hall, Anthony Hecht, Donald Justice, Charles Simic, W. D. Snodgrass, Richard Wilbur*, edited by Peter Dale, Philip Hoy, and J. D. McClatchy. London: Between the Lines, 2008. Wilbur talks about his life, poetry, and influences.

Walter B. Freed, Jr.; R. Baird Shuman
Updated by L. L. Lee

C. K. WILLIAMS

Born: Newark, New Jersey; November 4, 1936

PRINCIPAL POETRY

A Day for Anne Frank, 1968
Lies, 1969
I Am the Bitter Name, 1972
The Sensuous President, 1972
With Ignorance, 1977
Tar, 1983
Flesh and Blood, 1987
Poems, 1963-1983, 1988
A Dream of Mind, 1992
Selected Poems, 1994
New and Selected Poems, 1995
The Vigil, 1997
Repair, 1999
Love About Love, 2001
The Singing, 2003
Collected Poems, 2006
Wait, 2010

OTHER LITERARY FORMS

In collaboration with classical scholars, C. K. Williams has written verse translations of two Greek tragedies: one, in 1978, of Sophocles' *Trachinai* (435-429

B.C.E.; *The Women of Trachis*, 1729), and the other, in 1985, of Euripides' *Bakchai* (405 B.C.E.; *The Bacchae*, 1781). The translations, as their notes indicate, are for the modern stage as well as for modern readers. Williams hopes for a flowering of the "kernel" of Sophocles' tragedy within the translator's historical moment, "a clearing away of some of the accumulations of reverence that confuse the work and the genius who made them." The translations are thus not staid or literal but do aim for thematic accuracy and life. Williams also translated poems from Issa under the title *The Lark, the Thrush, the Starling* (1983). He has also translated *Selected Poems* (1994) of Francis Ponge (with John Montague and Margaret Guiton) and *Canvas* (1991) of poetry by Adam Zagajewski (with Renata Gorczynski and Benjamin Ivry). Williams published personal and critical essays in *Poetry and Consciousness* (1998); an award-winning memoir, *Misgivings: My Mother, My Father, Myself* (2000); and *On Whitman* (2010), an intimate rediscovery of America's first great poet, Walt Whitman. Williams has also written and cowritten children's books, such as *How the Nobble Was Finally Found* (2009; with Stephen Gammell) and *A Not Scary Story About Big Scary Things* (2010).

ACHIEVEMENTS

C. K. Williams has received many and various recognitions. *Repair* won both the Pulitzer Prize (2000) and the Los Angeles Times Book Prize for poetry (1999). Other honors and awards include a Guggenheim Fellowship, the Bernard F. Conners Prize for Poetry from *Paris Review* (1983), the Morton Dauwen Zabel Award (1989), the Lila Wallace-*Reader's Digest* Writers' Award (1992), the PEN/Voelcker Award (1998), an Academy Award in Literature from the American Academy of Arts and Letters (1999), the Berlin Prize, the Corrington Award for Literary Excellence from Centenary College of Louisiana (2001-2002), and the Pushcart Prize. *Flesh and Blood* won the National Book Critics Circle Award (1987), and *The Singing* won the National Book Award (2003). His memoir, *Misgivings*, won the PEN America Center 2001 Literary Award. In 2005, Williams received the Ruth Lilly Poetry Prize, an honor given to acknowledge lifetime achievement.

BIOGRAPHY

Born November 4, 1936, in Newark, New Jersey, the son of Paul B. Williams and Dossie (Kasdin) Williams, Charles Kenneth Williams was educated at Bucknell University and at the University of Pennsylvania, from which he received a B.A. in 1959. In 1965, he married Sarah Jones, and they had one daughter, Jessica Anne, who figures in Williams's personal poems. At the Pennsylvania Hospital in Philadelphia, he founded a program of poetry therapy and was a group therapist for disturbed adolescents.

A Day for Anne Frank led to the publication of two volumes of poetry, *Lies* in 1969 and *I Am the Bitter Name* in 1972, that established Williams as a protest poet of the Nixon era. In 1975, Williams married Catherine Mauger, a jeweler, and with her had one son. He was a visiting professor at Franklin and Marshall College in 1977 and at the University of California, Irvine, in 1978 before becoming professor of English at George Mason University. After spending many years at George Mason, he joined the creative writing faculty at Princeton in 1996. He has taught creative writing at various workshops and colleges, including Boston University and Columbia University. He became a member of the American Academy of Arts and Letters in 2003 and a chancellor of the American Academy of Poets in 2005. He has been dividing his time between teaching at Princeton and living in France.

ANALYSIS

C. K. Williams achieved early success in the era of cynicism and protest surrounding the Vietnam War. His early work sketches in a tough, cryptic style the nightmare visions of a godforsaken world. *I Am the Bitter Name* is a howl of protest against the various corruptions of the world, lacking even the tonal variety and scant hope of his earlier work. Though powerful, Williams's protest poetry was seen by critics as an artistic dead end.

During the five-year interim between the publication of *I Am the Bitter Name* and *With Ignorance*, Williams remade his style, writing in long lines that fold back from the margin of the page and tell stories with proselike lucidity. The sense of human suffering and isolation common in the earlier poems remains, but the long-line poems narrate dramatic tales set in American cities: scenes of family life, recollections of childhood, and views from the windows of urban apartments. Exact description and conventional punctuation replace the blurred grammar and dreamlike flow of the earlier verse. The later Williams poses in his poems as a survivor who, seeing clearly the complexities and disillusionment of contemporary life, shares astonishing personal associations with the reader.

Stylistic originality distinguished C. K. Williams's earliest work, and he has continued to evolve as a poet. Consistent in all periods of his work has been a "metaphysical" roughness and avoidance of merely literary polish. Meanwhile, he has treated frightening realities that are not conventionally subjects of poetry. His experimental style began with dreamlike lyrics with short run-on lines, sporadic punctuation, and startling leaps of image and diction. Strident in tone, sometimes shocking, the early poems found quick acceptance in the Nixon years.

LIES

Lies includes the long poem *A Day for Anne Frank*, which was published in a limited edition the previous year. In *Lies*, Williams anatomizes the horrors of modern history and existential despair. The absence of divine order grounds a series of nightmare visions with titles such as "Don't," "The Long Naked Walk of the Dead," "Loss," "Trash," "Downward," "Our Grey," and "It Is This Way with Men," which allegorizes men as spikes driven into the ground, pounded each time they attempt to rise. Williams's universe is the indifferent or hostile one of classic American naturalism, but it takes much of its apocalyptic substance from the Holocaust and from the Vietnam War. In spite of the negativity of his lyric outcries against suffering and waste, Williams's early poems burn not only with terror but also with a passion that things should be better. Optimism, authority, and poetic form are smashed like atoms. Williams's complaint is that of the child-man against the parent universe in which he finds himself an unloved stepson.

There is monotony, even callowness, in this stance, in improbable metaphors and scatological language flaunted for shock value—a gnostic rejection of his prison-body in the inhospitable universe. Nevertheless,

C. K. Williams (©Jim Kallet)

Lies was critically acclaimed for its fusion of moral seriousness and verbal ingenuity. It concludes with the long poem about Anne Frank, the quintessential victim of history; to borrow a comparison from one of Williams's poems, she was like a little box turtle run over by a bus. "It's horrible," he says in that lyric. *A Day for Anne Frank* displays the horrible motto "God hates you!"

I AM THE BITTER NAME

I Am the Bitter Name takes the technique of *Lies* one step further toward the abolition of technique—one step too far, most critics have argued. More homogeneous than *Lies*, this collection appears to try for and achieve self-portraits of apocalyptic incoherence. The poet displays, piled like monstrous fish, the products of his vigorous dredging of his nightmare unconscious. Critic Jascha Kessler, in one of the more positive reviews of Williams's work, catalogs his strengths and failings: "the simplicity, clarity of diction, haste and jumbling of his thought by the unremitting stroboscopic, kaleidoscopic pulsing of a voice from thought to speech to image to unvoiced thought." Impressed that the source of Williams's expression is valid, calling the book "real poems," Kessler is nevertheless disoriented by it. Other critics were less positive, charging that Williams's passionate flailings missed their targets or even dismissing the poems as sentimental and blurred.

As the tonal consistency of *I Am the Bitter Name* suggests, and as his later work confirms, Williams is a deliberate experimental stylist. Purged of commas, capitals, and periods, the poems sprout unpredictable question marks, exclamation points, and quotations. The sense spills over the ends of the short, jagged lines, so that it becomes almost a rule in these poems that a line end does *not* signal a break in sense. The effect is one of breathlessness, of a mind that, insofar as it is conscious at all, barely understands what it is saying. The reader seems to be hearing the raw material of poetry at the moment of creation. Williams's vocabulary, too, suggests breathless, regressive speech, almost childishly simple but scatological—especially in the political poems. The voice again suggests a righteous man-child, outraged to surreal protest by the extent to which the real God and the real governments betray his standards.

Sometimes the words in *I Am the Bitter Name* are explicitly political, as in "A Poem for the Governments." This poem offers itself as an onion to make governments cry for the family of the imprisoned Miguel Hernandes, whose family has nothing but onions to eat. Reminding "mr old men" how they have eaten Miguel and "everything good in the world," the poem becomes "one onion/ your history" and concludes self-referentially, "eat this." Such explicit ordering of metaphor, common in *Lies*, is not the rule in *I Am the Bitter Name*, where even poems on political subjects dissolve into cryptic collisions of word and image. "The Admiral Fan," for example, begins with a "lady from the city" removing her girdle and baring her "white backside" in a barnyard and dissolves into a vision of her dismemberment, apparently not only by farm animals but also by a Washington lobbyist in a long car. She is emptied of "dolls." Her breasts become "dawn amity peace exaltation" in a vegetable field identified—as the grammar blurs—with nothingness, and flashing stoplights. Like the poems of André Breton, these let go

even of grammatical structure in submission to the up-rush of image and emotion.

WITH IGNORANCE

Between 1972 and 1977, Williams was divorced, remarried, and received grants and teaching appointments; during this time, he dramatically reinvented his poetic style. Except for its closing title poem, *With Ignorance* withdraws from the nightmare abyss and grounds its associations on human stories expressed in conventionally punctuated long lines with all the clarity of good prose. The change was presumably as much psychological as stylistic. The mature Williams, turned forty, tells his daughter that he has already had the bad dreams: "what comes now is calm and abstract." Later, in "Friends," he stands outside the terrors of his earlier poems to observe that "visions I had then were all death: they were hideous and absurd and had nothing to do with my life." The style of these self-possessed reflections is easy informal prose, the style of a personal letter refined in its very plainness, which sets the stage in the more effective poems for sudden outbreaks of metaphysical anguish or human pathos equal to the best of his earlier verse.

In "The Sanctity," Williams remembers going home with a married coworker from a construction site and seeing homicidal hostility between his friend's mother and wife, and the coworker's rage—a dark side of his character wholly masked by the ironic idyll of the workplace. The construction site is the only place, apparently, where the workmen feel joy, where they feel in power. Printed sources prompt some of the incantatory stories: an SS officer spitting into a rabbi's mouth to help him defile the Torah, until they are kissing like lovers; a girl paralyzed by a stray police bullet. However, Williams usually draws from his experience: a veteran met in a bar, a friend in a mental hospital, an old bum seen after a marital quarrel, a girl he "stabbed" with a piece of "broken-off car antenna" when he was eight. Here, in grotesque anecdotes, Williams again examines the irrational in human life, the inevitable discord and suffering, but with a sympathy for recognizable human faces and characters missing from most of his earlier work. Political concerns are implicit in the presence of veterans and police bullets, but there is no preaching. The one short poem not narrative is "Hog

Heaven," which begins, "It stinks," and develops in biblical repetitions and variations an enveloping nausea for the flesh, a theme and method common in the protest poems but expanded here in limber, Whitmanesque lines.

TAR

Tar demonstrates greater mastery of the anecdotal long-line style, telling longer and more complex stories with more restraint and power and returning at times to openly political themes. The title poem recalls the day of the near-disaster at the Three Mile Island nuclear plant, which was also a day of roofing work on the narrator's apartment building. Without ceasing to be themselves, the workmen become both trolls from the underworld and representatives of vulnerable humanity, their black tar-pots associated with the nuclear threat to the north. Williams's old vision of the apocalypse is here, but the symbols are stronger because they move in a narrative with a persuasive surface of its own. Williams is reclaiming techniques that many contemporary poets have abandoned to fiction. As he masters the long-line narrative style, the lines become less plain—not necessarily more ornate, but more susceptible to ornamentation without losing their naturalness and tone of the grotesque.

Some of the poems in *Tar* begin with nature imagery and are leavened by it, though the suffering face of the city still always shows. "From My Window," for example, begins with the first fragrances of spring, budding sycamore, crocus spikes, a pretty girl jogging—but this is only an overture to the movement outside the narrator's window of two alcoholic veterans, one of whom is in a wheelchair, and their tragicomic accident in the street, which reveals the unlovely, childlike nakedness of the crippled one. Like many of Williams's narratives, this one takes a sudden turn near the end, recalling the able-bodied veteran pacing wildly in a vacant lot in falling snow, struggling to leave his imprint while the buildings stare coldly down.

Tar is almost as much a book of short fiction as of poems; characters include a man falling in love with a black woman who walks her hideously ill dog outside his window, a boy awakening to night terrors in the city, a decaying luxury hotel taken over by drug users, mental patients, and old women. A pornographic tin-type centers a fantasy on immigrant life; a welterweight fighter awakens memories of a German widow, a refugee following her husband's plot against Adolf Hitler, who encouraged her daughter's affair with the narrator—as if his Jewishness could expiate her guilt. Two of the most interesting poems, "Neglect" and "The Regulars," narrate no unusual events but are minimal narrative sketches of a bus layover in a faded coal town and old men in a neighborhood undergoing gentrification—short stories in their use of description and dialogue, but in the cadences of Williams's taut, long lines.

FLESH AND BLOOD

Some of the poems in *Tar* use quatrains, four long lines clustered and endstopped. In *Flesh and Blood*, Williams invents and writes a sequence of lines in a form comparable to the sonnet in length and rhetorical, eight lines of about twenty syllables each, usually shifting direction after the fifth line. Moving away from the extended stories of earlier works, Williams does not lose focus on the pathos and character of the urban world, but, necessarily, his tales shrink into the frame—either to vignettes or to terse summaries like a gossiping conversation. Williams portrays victims of stroke and Alzheimer's disease, a poetry-loving bum, an unhappy wife, a sobbing child, a girlfriend who hates her body, and in one subsequence, readers in a variety of places and poses.

There is always clarity in these portrait poems, usually wisdom and complexity, but little of the frenzy that burned in the earlier work. *Flesh and Blood* includes poems that develop allegorical subjects in abstract language, despite earlier critical disapproval of this method—particularly in "One of the Muses," the only poem in *Tar* that critics judged a failure. It is Williams's way, however, to take chances. His characteristic strength is his restlessness and formal creativity—his refusal to remain confined within a style after he has mastered it.

THE VIGIL

In the 1990's, Williams continued to expand his range, refine his art, and please greater numbers of readers and critics. In *The Vigil*, Williams again employs, with little variety, the long, rolling, syntactically suspenseful line that is not a line at all—at least not a conventionally measured line. Though Williams gives the reader rich stretches of intellectual and philosophical rumination, critic Richard Howard is probably correct in asserting that this technique works best in narrative and descriptive passages, in which Williams excels. It also works well in the poem or passage that is based on inventorying or list making. In this volume, the eight-part sequence titled "Symbols" succeeds as a fine, organic correlation of Williams's aesthetic medium and his subject and theme.

REPAIR

Repair represents the work of a mature poet not only polishing a technique that is comfortable while applying his formula to new subjects, but also an artist for whom new experiences dictate formal departures. Perhaps this combination of factors—a rich and distinctive thirty-year body of work and evidence of new directions—brought this volume the Pulitzer Prize. Many of the poems in *Repair* are only newly finished; Williams had worked on them for many years and they have a familiar feel to those who had learned to read his work. Other poems have a more conventional stanza pattern and shorter lines than much of Williams's earlier work. One poem that deals with his experiences as a grandfather takes the poet and the reader into new territory. Some will feel that the physical smallness and the youth of the grandchild gave rise to the unexpected short line in "Owen: Seven Days." Williams has commented on simply hearing a new, more jagged music that required what for him is an uncharacteristic prosodic result. Many of the poems, like the magnificent "Invisible Mending," have to do with reconciliation and acceptance. These activities of the heart, which are among the key meanings of the book's title, indicate the inner place that Williams has reached in the arc of life reflected in poems, an arc begun in protest and anger.

THE SINGING

The Singing is a title that suggests a lighter tone than the contents reveal, but singing, like poetry, is an art whose business is to carry for people that which they cannot bear alone. The title poem itself conveys how difficult it is to bridge the distance between individuals. On a neighborhood walk, Williams overhears a young man composing angry lines and feels an affinity, but the young man lets him know through his lyrics that there can be no such thing, ". . . both of us knew just

where we were/ in the duet we composed the equation we made the conventions to which we were condemned." As in his earliest, angriest work, Williams makes use of an enjambed, unpunctuated line that carries a flow of emotion and observation, of questions lifted up, unanswered. It is as though the encounter calls up his own youthful self, from a different place and time, but filled with the same anger, the same refusal to be "nice." Williams ends the poem with the feeling that, in spite of the alienation that pervades the world, and even without people's conscious intention, there is something in them that moves people toward connection and repair.

As in *Repair*, though Williams continues to use his typical long line and weighty blocks of text, there are also poems of more brevity. "Scale I" and "Scale II" are gorgeous and touching evocations of his response to his wife's physical presence. Their short lines allow the reader to savor each image and sound.

In many of the poems in *The Singing*, Williams pits his intense awareness of ugliness against his compulsion to find and acknowledge what is beautiful, as in "Doves." He begins, "So much crap in my head,/ so many rubbishy facts," lamenting all he knows that he does not care to know. He wishes he knew instead the names of the trees he passes, could recognize birds by their song. Nevertheless, the morning is lovely, the sounds of the morning lovely, even traffic, "even the idiot doves.// And within me,/ along with the garbage, faces, faces,/ and voices, so many/ lives woven into mine." By entertaining mundane complaints, Williams pushes himself toward what shines.

The Singing is inevitably shaded by the destruction of the World Trade Center on September 11, 2001, and the subsequent U.S. involvement in Afghanistan and Iraq. Oddly, it is in poems about war that Williams retreats into abstraction; "War" and "Low Relief" are curiously distant and artful treatments of what is clearly, for him, a distressing subject. Most of the time, however, his words are as alive as words can be, carrying their meanings with such particularity that no other words could possibly do.

COLLECTED POEMS

One impression a reader might come away with when considering *Collected Poems* is that Williams is always willing to rake himself over the coals for the sake of poetry. There can be no doubt that the poet who wrote *Lies* and *I Am the Bitter Name* meant every tortured word, that with his own body and soul he felt the world's pain. The reader looks over Williams's shoulder as he wrenches the details of his failures from the attics of memory, brushes off petty rationalizations, accepts his human fallibility, and renews his desire to be better, to use his intellect to light his way rather than to obscure his culpability. The form he invents, long lines in massive blocks of text, is the ideal vehicle for the exquisite detail and the many outlying branches of thought Williams employs. He does not limit his fierceness to self-portraits—Williams addresses the world with the same scrutiny. His is an art of unflinching examination of every part of life, every strata of existence.

The U.S. involvement in Iraq and Afghanistan continue to be of concern, and in the new poems that end the book, Williams exposes a darker, more discouraged view than in his earlier volumes. "Shrapnel" begins with a description of exactly what shrapnel is and what it does to "insufficiently resistant materials" such as human flesh. The pain of war is too fresh: All Williams can manage to do is assemble shrapnel-like fragments from films and television news, distance himself with speculations about propaganda, and distract himself with inane facts ("named after its inventor . . . later awarded a generous stipend"). On the screen, a man runs with his "rag-limp" son in his arms, "chest and abdomen speckled with deep, dark gashes and smears of blood." Williams tries to locate his feelings, slides off into facts again, then finds there is no way to escape what he knows. "One war passes into the next. One wound is the next and the next. Something howls. Something cries."

The new works are heavy with all that is hard and painful: aging, decay, death, shame, loss, and destruction. The overall tone is of resignation; the chances that humankind will become more careful and thoughtful, more loving, more just, are slim indeed. However, Williams will not let sorrow be all that he sees. There is joy glimmering in the shadows, a plum tree that, with rotting fruit and lost limbs, nevertheless "waits naked in the naked/ day-glare for branches/ to bring leaves forth again,// and fruit forth, not for us,/ or the flies, but just to

be/ gold again in the moonlight,/ silver in the silvery starlight."

OTHER MAJOR WORKS

NONFICTION: *Poetry and Consciousness*, 1998; *Misgivings: My Mother, My Father, Myself*, 2000; *On Whitman*, 2010.

CHILDREN'S LITERATURE: *How the Nobble Was Finally Found*, 2009 (with Stephen Gammell); *A Not Scary Story About Big Scary Things*, 2010.

TRANSLATIONS: *Women of Trachis*, 1978 (of Sophocles' play *Trachinai*; with Gregory Dickerson); *The Lark, the Thrush, the Starling*, 1983 (of Issa's poetry); *The Bacchae*, 1985 (of Euripides' play *Bakchai*; with H. Golder); *The Bacchae of Euripides: A New Version*, 1990; *Canvas*, 1991 (of Adam Zagajewski's poetry; with Renata Gorczynski and Benjamin Ivry); *Selected Poems*, 1994 (of Francis Ponge; with John Montague and Margaret Guiton).

EDITED TEXTS: *Selected and Last Poems*, 1989 (by Paul Zweig); *The Essential Hopkins*, 1992 (by Gerard Manley Hopkins).

BIBLIOGRAPHY

Chiasson, Dan. "False Consolations." Review of *Collected Poems*. *The New York Times Book Review*, December 24, 2006, p. 15L. Chiasson calls Williams to task for what he sees as Williams's departure from technical and intellectual subtlety and scrupulous clarity to a sort of hazy middle-class discontent.

Eder, Richard. "A Poet Watches Himself As He Watches the World." Review of *Collected Poems*. *The New York Times*, December 25, 2006, p. E22L. Eder's review is a balanced assessment of the poet's body of work, acknowledging the pitfalls of Williams's tendency to focus so intently on his own experience that it eclipses all else, yet praising Williams's intelligence and sensitivity, his skill, and the freight of treasure his poems carry.

Hedges, Chris. "Poet Marshals His Moral Passion Against the War." *The New York Times*, January 13, 2005, p. B4. Hedges marks Williams's return to the more overt antiwar stance of his early poetry.

Howard, Richard. Review of *The Vigil*. *Boston Review*

(Summer, 1997). Although Howard has serious and well-expressed reservations about the formal imposition of an extremely long line, he allows himself to admire those poems and passages in which Williams's technique works effectively. Howard praises Williams's successes in rendering "immediacy of sensation."

Jarman, Mark. "The Pragmatic Imagination and the Secret of Poetry." In *The Secret of Poetry*. Ashland, Oreg.: Story Line Press, 2001. Compares Williams with Charles Wright and Philip Levine.

Phillips, Brian. "Plainly, but with Flair." *The New Republic*, September 18, 2000, 42-45. Phillips reviews both *Repair* and the memoir *Misgivings*. He objects to Williams's habit of glossing the beginning of a poem at the end. Williams forces the reader away from direct experience toward a preferred comprehension. This habit undermines his great descriptive powers. Phillips also notes the tension between Williams's colloquial diction and his erudite range of references.

Riding, Alan. "American Bard in Paris Stokes Poetic Home Fires." *The New York Times*, October 4, 2000, p. E4. This flavorful piece of biographical journalism treats Williams's relationship with Paris as well as the patterns of his writing and teaching careers.

Sadoff, Ira. "Dreaming Creatures." *American Poetry Review* (January/February, 2005). Sadoff considers Gerald Stern and Williams as Jewish writers, seeing them as embodiments of a tradition of strictly truthful perception of things as they are—shabby, even sordid, yet also mysteriously lovely—which allows them to persist hopefully, to dream of what is possible, if not inevitable.

Santos, Sherod. "A Solving Emptiness: C. K. Williams and Charles Wright." In *A Poetry of Two Minds*. Athens: University of Georgia Press, 2000. In a comparison of midcareer poems by both poets, Santos examines parallel aesthetic experimentation and the determination to overcome despair through art.

Williams, C. K. "C. K. Williams." http://ckwilliams .com. The official Web site for Williams offers a biography and list of publications.

William H. Green; Philip K. Jason
Updated by Donna Munro

MILLER WILLIAMS

Born: Hoxie, Arkansas; April 8, 1930

PRINCIPAL POETRY

A Circle of Stone, 1964
Recital, 1964
So Long at the Fair, 1968
The Only World There Is, 1971
Halfway from Hoxie, 1977
Why God Permits Evil: New Poems, 1977
Distractions, 1981
The Boys on Their Bony Mules, 1983
Imperfect Love, 1986
Living on the Surface: New and Selected Poems, 1989
Adjusting to the Light, 1992
Points of Departure, 1995
The Ways We Touch, 1997
Some Jazz for a While: Collected Poems, 1998
Time and the Tilting Earth, 2008

OTHER LITERARY FORMS

In addition to his works of poetry, Miller Williams's books include literary criticism, translations, works on prosody, and anthologies of poetry and fiction. The list includes a history of American railroads (with James Alan McPherson), translations from the work of Nicanor Parra and Giuiseppe Belli, critical analyses on John Crowe Ransom and John Ciardi, and a standard reference on prosodics titled *Patterns of Poetry: An Encyclopedia of Forms* (1986). He has also edited anthologies of poetry and has published many of his own poems, stories, critical essays, and translations in journals in the United States and abroad.

ACHIEVEMENTS

Miller Williams has been awarded the Henry Bellaman Poetry Prize, the Amy Lowell Award in Poetry from Harvard University, the New York Arts Fund Award for Significant Contribution to American Letters, the Prix de Rome for Literature and the Academy Award for Literature (both from the American Academy of Arts and Letters), the Poets' Prize, the Charity

Randall Citation for Contribution to Poetry as a Spoken Art from the International Poetry Forum, and the John William Corrington Award for Literary Excellence. He has also received honorary doctorates from Lander College and Hendrix College. In 1994, he was named Socio Benemerito dell'Associazione, Centro Romanesco Trilussa, Roma. He was chosen to compose and read a poem for the second inauguration of President Bill Clinton in 1997. In 1999, the multinational editorial board of *Voices International* named him one of the twenty best poets in the world writing in English. He was selected one of the five hundred most important poets of all languages in the twentieth century, for inclusion by Roth Publishing Company on the compact disc *Poetry of Our Time*.

BIOGRAPHY

Miller Williams was born on April 8, 1930, in Hoxie, Arkansas, the son of a Methodist minister. He received a B.S. in zoology from Arkansas State College and completed his M.S. at the University of Arkansas in Fayetteville, after which he became a science teacher. In 1961, he received a Bread Loaf Fellowship, and in 1962, he joined the English department of Louisiana State University.

In 1971, Williams moved to the University of Arkansas and joined the creative writing program, working with the graduate program in creative writing and in translation. His academic career has included serving as visiting professor of U.S. literature at the University of Chile and as Fulbright Professor of American Studies at the National University of Mexico. For seven years, he was a member of the poetry faculty at the Bread Loaf Writers' Conference. In 1976, he was made a fellow of the American Academy in Rome.

He has represented the U.S. State Department on reading and lecturing tours throughout Latin America, Europe, and Asia. His stories, translations, poems, and critical essays have appeared in a variety of journals in English, and his poems have been translated into several languages.

He has served as president of the American Literary Translators Association, founding editor of the *New Orleans Review*, founding director of the University of Arkansas Press, and Latin American editor for the third

edition of *Benet's Reader's Encyclopedia*. He was also named university professor of English and foreign languages at the University of Arkansas. He became professor emeritus in 2003.

ANALYSIS

Miller Williams's poetry offers an insightful look at the preoccupations and concerns of his time, from the mundane to the metaphysical, presented with an emphasis on the ordinary and on conversational language. In addition, he so skillfully uses form, meter, and rhyme that the patterns of his poems do not announce themselves. In conversational, straightforward language, his poems include blank verse, sonnets, sestinas, villanelles, dramatic monologues, and other variations of the simple and the intricate. The greatest strength of Williams as a poet may be how natural he makes the most intricate poetic forms sound on the page. As he says in "For All Our Great-Grandchildren": "If you can listen/ I'll try to make it not sound like a lesson." Williams takes as his task seeing the hidden behind the visible and turning it into art. In "Notes from the Agent on Earth: How to Be Human," he provides a succinct summation of his work: "Life is change that finds a changing pattern;/ art is change we put a pattern to." While characterizing his wide body of poetry in overall terms proves impossible, several themes recur.

HUMOR

One of the first things one notices in Williams's work is the humor that plays out in humans' visions of themselves, in wordplay, and in worldview. Williams has said, "I think of most of my poems as having a touch of dark, hopefully ironic humor about them." Titles of individual poems exemplify this: "After You Die You Don't Give a Piddling Damn," "Why God Permits Evil: For Answer to This Question of Interest to Many Write Bible Answers, Dept. E-7," "Talking to Himself He Gets a Few Things Settled in His Mind," "Note to God Concerning an Earlier Communication," and "In Your Own Words Without Lying Tell Something of Your Background with Particular Attention to Anything Relating to the Position for Which You Are Applying, Press Down."

Along with the humor provided by the narrators'

and characters' views of themselves and their world, and what they misunderstand about it, Williams finds humor in wordplay. In "On a Trailways Bus a Man Who Holds His Head Strangely Speaks to the Seat Beside Him," the speaker tells those around him that "I thanked a woman twice and kissed her hand/ because she said I was a perfect stranger."

"Style" offers a humorous take on the fads of poetry, describing a man who made a series of circles on a page and decided to call it a poem, "Not wanting to waste the paper or the time" and "having a dean impressed with anything." The poem succeeds, is anthologized, and creates numerous requests "for explanations he never gives." The narrator tells the reader that some would call it poetry, "assuming of course that it was done sincerely."

Williams's humor, from the line level to the ironic vision of many poems, extends to himself as well. "My Wife Reads the Paper at Breakfast on the Birthday of the Scottish Poet" reads in its entirety: "Poet Burns to Be Honored, the headline read./ She put it down. 'They found you out,' she said."

WHAT IS LEFT UNSAID

Williams once said, "We live life as if it were what we wanted; we read a poem as if it got to the truth of our lives. It never does, but the poet fails only because we all fail." Within the lines of his poetry, he comments on the inability of words to convey all that people intend and the attempts of poets to do so. In "On Hearing About the Death of Mitzi Mayfair," he says,

> There has never been a poem
> to explain anything.
> For that reason
> many people who would otherwise
> write poems do not.
> Praise such people.

Williams's poetry concerns the precise fact, concrete imagery, and visual detail, yet relies as well on what does not get said. In "For Rebecca, for Whom Nothing Has Been Written Page After Page," Williams writes, "What matters when all the words are written and read/ is what remains not said,/ which is what long silences are for." Williams also comments on how, and why, to write poetry. In "Let Me Tell You," he tells po-

ets to "First notice everything," because "You cannot twist the fact you do not know," even though "Nothing is less important/ than a fact." He emphasizes conversational tone by including the following: "Be suspicious of any word you learned/ and were proud of learning./ It will go bad." The reader is told to "take notes" on the tragedies as well as the trivialities of life to write poetry. The potential power of that poetry becomes clear in "Form and Theory of Poetry," which compares it to the power of a hurricane.

COMMENTING ON HUMAN NATURE

Much of Williams's work deals with individual human beings and the moments of insight, tragedy, triumph, failure, and routine in their lives. In "The Associate Professor Delivers an Exhortation to His Failing Students," what binds humans together is their fears, which the professor asks his students to list, to "Make a catechism" of, for "These are the gravity that holds us together/ toward our common sun." He tells his students that if they are ever asked "the only thing that matters after all," they should say "failing is an act of love/ because/ like sin/ it is the commonality within."

In Williams's poems, the reader sees a man having a moment of great insight, about to be lost on a bus ("One of Those Rare Occurrences on a City Bus"); a man who stopped at an accident but failed to wait for the ambulance to arrive ("Accident: A Short Story"); a senator rationalizing his decisions ("A Senator Explains a Vote"); an actress asking "How would you like it, never being able/ to grow old all together, to have yourself/ from different times of your life running around?" ("The Aging Actress Sees Herself a Starlet on the Late Show"); a truck-stop waitress recounting her life ("Ruby Tells All"); and various interpretations of Judas's act ("Think of Judas That He Did Love Jesus"). All these characters, and many more, illustrate moments of doubt, anxiety, insight, or regret.

Williams said, "I like a poem to be a little short story." Nowhere is that more evident than his character sketches, where ordinary, believable human beings wrangle with love, hate, death, despair, faith, and disappointment. Whether offering an epiphany or an illusion, his characters illuminate human nature in both the abstract and the particular. Many characters also illustrate the subjective nature of living in one's own head, how individual human beings create the meaning around them. In "Believing in Symbols," the narrator ponders the blinking number eight on his broken calculator, "the figure all the figures are made from," and notes the importance of symbols: "Believing in symbols has led us into war,/ if sometimes into bed with interesting people." In "The True Story of What Happened," the narrator sees an airplane fly by and imagines, when it is out of sight, that it has therefore crashed: "Inside my head two hundred seventy people/ including a crew of eleven disappeared/ leaving no trace but only vacancies."

QUESTIONS OF RELIGION

Often, religion plays a part in the characters' caught moments. From the preacher "building the gospel work by believable word/ out of the wooden syllables of the South" ("And When in Scenes of Glory") to the preacher's admission that "What we call acts and scientists call events/ are equally beyond us" ("During the Hymn before the Christmas Sermon the Mind of the Young Preacher Wanders Again"), questions of God and the devil, heaven and hell, faith and doubt recur. On one hand, "What do we know that matters that Aeschylus did not know?" ("After the Revolution for Jesus a Secular Man Prepares His Final Remarks"). On the other hand, what people do not, and cannot, know remains both reassuring and terrifying. In "If Every Person There Is but One," the reader is told to "Think of whatever moves as God/ or if nothing moves/ think how still we stand."

OTHER MAJOR WORKS

SHORT FICTION: *The Lives of Kevin Fletcher: Stories Mostly Short*, 2002.

NONFICTION: *The Poetry of John Crowe Ransom*, 1972; *How Does a Poem Mean?*, 1975 (with John Ciardi); *Patterns of Poetry: An Encyclopedia of Forms*, 1986; *Making a Poem: Some Thoughts About Poetry and the People Who Write It*, 2006.

TRANSLATIONS: *Poems and Antipoems*, 1967 (of Nicanor Parra); *Emergency Poems*, 1972 (of Parra); *Sonnets of Giuiseppe Belli*, 1981.

EDITED TEXTS: *Southern Writing in the Sixties: Fiction and Poetry*, 1966-1967 (2 volumes; with John William Corrington); *Chile: Contemporary Writing in the Longest Land*, 1967; *Chile: An Anthology of New Writing*, 1968; *Contemporary Poetry in America*, 1973; *Railroad: Trains and Train People in American Culture*, 1976 (with James A. McPherson); *A Roman Collection*, 1980; *Ozark*, 1981.

BIBLIOGRAPHY

Baker, David. "To Advantage Dressed: Miller Williams Among the Naked Poets." *Southern Review* 26, no. 4 (Autumn, 1990): 814. Discusses Williams's development of a "verbal style" that draws readers into his work.

Brower, Joel. "Cosmos in a Coffee Cup." Review of *Time and the Tilting Earth*. *The New York Times Book Review*, February 22, 2009, p. 17. Brower calls Williams a "poet of formidable gifts and influence" and praises his latest collection.

Burns, Michael, ed. *Miller Williams and the Poetry of the Particular*. Columbia: University of Missouri Press, 1991. A collection of essays on Williams and his poetry, including entries by Howard Nemerov, Maxine Kumin, and X. J. Kennedy. It also includes an interview with Williams.

Cifelli, Edward M. "The Poems of Miller Williams: Poetry from Illinois." Review of *Some Jazz for a While*. *Art and Letters: A Journal of Contemporary Culture* (Fall, 2000). A review of Williams's collected poems, published by the University of Illinois Press.

Quinn, Judy. "Inauguration Day Will Be Miller Time." *Publishers Weekly* 244, no. 1 (January 6, 1997): 20. Williams discusses his poem for U.S. president Bill Clinton's inauguration and the collection *The Ways We Touch* (1997).

Caroline Carvill

SHERLEY ANNE WILLIAMS

Born: Bakersfield, California; August 25, 1944
Died: San Diego, California: July 6, 1999

PRINCIPAL POETRY

The Peacock Poems, 1975
Some One Sweet Angel Chile, 1982

OTHER LITERARY FORMS

Sherley Anne Williams began her writing career by publishing short stories in periodicals and anthologies. She also wrote literary criticism, which was printed in scholarly journals and collected in her first book, *Give Birth to Brightness: A Thematic Study in Neo-Black Literature* (1972). Williams published a historical novel, *Dessa Rose*, in 1986. Her poetry inspired her to create two picture books for children, *Working Cotton* (1992) and *Girls Together* (1999). Williams contributed introductions for editions of Zora Neale Hurston's *Their Eyes Were Watching God* (1991) and Mark Twain's *The Tragedy of Pudd'nhead Wilson* (1996).

ACHIEVEMENTS

Sherley Anne Williams's poetry collection *The Peacock Poems* was a 1976 National Book Award finalist. In 1984, her literary scholarship secured her an appointment to teach at the University of Ghana as a Fulbright Scholar. The periodical *Parents* chose *Working Cotton* as an outstanding 1992 book for young readers. The American Library Association selected *Working Cotton* as an honor book for both the 1993 Caldecott and Coretta Scott King Medals. In 1998, Williams received the African American Literature and Culture Society's Stephen E. Henderson Award.

BIOGRAPHY

Sherley Anne Williams was born on August 25, 1944, in Bakersfield, California. She lived with her parents, Jesse Winson Williams and Lena-Leila Marie (Siler) Williams, and her three sisters in a housing project in Fresno, California. Her parents were migrant agricultural workers who harvested cotton and fruit in the San Joaquin Valley. Williams was eight when her fa-

ther, who had tuberculosis, died. At age sixteen, she mourned her mother's sudden death.

Williams read constantly as a child. Several teachers recognized her potential and suggested that she take advanced classes. Williams graduated from Edison High School in 1962. At Fresno State College (later California State University, Fresno), she concentrated on history and literature courses, and admired Harlem Renaissance poet Langston Hughes's work. In 1966, Williams received a bachelor of arts degree. She moved to Nashville, Tennessee, to attend Robert Hayden's poetry classes at Fisk University, then to Washington, D.C., to study poetry with Sterling A. Brown at Howard University.

Williams returned to California, giving birth to her son John Malcolm Stewart in September, 1968. She and her son moved to Providence, Rhode Island, where Williams started graduate school at Brown University, pursuing her goal of becoming a college professor. She earned a master of arts degree in American literature in 1972; her thesis "Give Birth to Brightness: A Thematic Study in Neo-Black Literature" was published in book form that year. Williams decided not to seek a doctoral degree so she could focus on her writing.

She accepted an associate professor position at California State University, Fresno, in 1972. The next year, she became an assistant professor at the University of California, San Diego, teaching creative writing and African American literature courses. Wesleyan University Press published Williams's debut poetry collection, *The Peacock Poems*, in 1975. By 1982, Williams had attained the rank of professor, and her second poetry book, *Some One Sweet Angel Chile*, was released. Williams's historical novel, *Dessa Rose*, was published in 1986. She strived to present aspects of history that writers often marginalized or misinterpreted. Reviewers noted that Williams's poetry techniques, especially imagery and figurative language, enhanced her prose style.

Williams contributed writing to *American Poetry Review*, *Black Scholar*, *Essence*, and *Iowa Review*. Anthologies printing her poetry included *Piecework: Nineteen Fresno Poets* (1987); *Highway 99: A Literary Journey Through California's Great Central Valley* (1996); and *How Much Earth: The Fresno Poets*

(2001). Williams served as a consultant to the *Langston Hughes Review* and *Callaloo*. She developed her first children's book, *Working Cotton*, from "the trimming of the feathers" and "conejo" in *The Peacock Poems*.

After being diagnosed with cancer, Williams continued teaching and writing. In May, 1998, the University of California, San Diego, hosted a conference celebrating Williams. She died on July 6, 1999, in San Diego.

ANALYSIS

Sherley Anne Williams endeavored to present truth through authentic portrayals of African Americans in her poems. Her poetry uses realism and honesty to convey strong emotions and intimate revelations through characters, mostly female and including Williams, who express frustration with the social and economic situations in which they find themselves. Williams creates a voice for the despair of vulnerable and misunderstood people. She writes of the resourcefulness, determination, and survival of the speakers of her poems as they are tested by poverty, abandonment, and other problems. Freedom is a consistent theme as her characters strive to become independent of whatever controls them and to get around their limitations. Dignity and optimism resonate in Williams's poems as people attempt to improve, not worsen, their conditions. Williams urges African Americans to recognize the importance of community, both family and neighbors. Her poems expand readers' awareness of their personal and cultural responsibilities.

Williams's poetry is often compared to African American music. She discussed musical influences on literary structure, themes, and language in "The Blues Roots of Contemporary Afro-American Poetry" (*Massachusetts Review*, 1977). Williams uses the blues format to reiterate and rephrase in successive lines of verse the emotional pain people suffer from intolerable circumstances. She addresses concerns tormenting many African Americans, including broken relationships, oppression, and ostracism. Her characters yearn for others to comprehend and respect their actions and feelings without rejecting or punishing them. The creation of blues-inspired poetry enabled Williams to connect modern readers with historic examples of how Af-

rican Americans used music to communicate. The musical nature of Williams's rhythmic lines and her use of vernacular and dialect effectively convey tone, motifs, and imagery.

THE PEACOCK POEMS

In her first poetry collection, *The Peacock Poems*, Williams focuses on her experiences as an African American woman. Williams addresses relationships, a frequent blues theme, in these poems, presenting her interactions with her son as a mother, with her parents as a daughter, and with men as a lover. The peacock of the title refers to people who flaunt themselves or their prized possessions much as peacocks fan their magnificent feathers and preen themselves to demand attention. Williams shows off her pride for her only child in many of the collection's poems. In others, she confesses flaws and failures most people might choose to hide.

Williams acknowledges that her poetry depicts episodes from her life, especially those involving losses, frustrations, and disappointments. She believes her experiences have universal elements that many women will recognize. Her comprehension of blues music enables her to present the conflicting emotions that women often feel and their desperation as they encounter detrimental people and situations they cannot control. Her repetition of wording and lines to emphasize statements and feelings are reminiscent of musical refrains.

In "Any Woman's Blues," the loneliness of an empty bed causes Williams to contemplate solitude. Abandonment is a constant theme, as lovers reject Williams, producing a sadness she equates with silence. She announces her pregnancy in paragraphs, describing the San Joaquin Valley's agricultural abundance as a symbol of her fertility. She depicts her son's life, starting with the poem, "Say Hello to John." Williams adjusts to her new identity as a single mother in "If He Let Us Go Now," as she and her son, John, drive away from his father, wishing that he would ask them to stay. Agitated, she keeps moving because change comforts her. Like Williams, John is a wanderer, traveling with her and asking about his father, wondering why he and Williams have different surnames. In "Time," Williams explores her transient nature and realizes that her son grounds her, gives her life purpose, and motivates her to establish a consistent home environment, both physically and emotionally.

Williams frequently uses bird imagery to reinforce the peacock motif. In "The Killing of the Birds," Williams's mother primps before a mirror, coating her lips with red lipstick and styling her hair before visiting her husband in the hospital. She wears a fancy dress that accentuates her black skin. In "The House of Desire," Williams enjoys gratifying her lover by emphasizing the qualities that he finds attractive, like a peacock displays its beauty. Later in the poem, Williams, spurned by men, compares herself to a bird whose feathers have been plucked. She says her house, devoid of a steady man, is like a bird that has lost its feathers by molting or that is lifeless and filled with stuffing. In "The Peacock Song," Williams relies on plumage to conceal damages.

SOME ONE SWEET ANGEL CHILE

Some One Sweet Angel Chile, Williams's second collection, also incorporates blues elements. In the first section, "Letters from a New England Negro," Williams's poems are presented as correspondence that an African American teacher, Hannah, who has traveled South to instruct former slaves, sends to her northern friends. This section examines the theme of memory, a basic concept in all of Williams's poetry. Overwhelmed by cultural differences and embarrassed by her privileges, Hannah conceals the fact she was born free and was never enslaved. Initially, she identifies more with her white patrons than her black students. The poems show her transformation, revealed in her phrasings, which begin to reflect African American speech when music and dancing awaken her sense of cultural connection to her new community and she can no longer remember details of her past.

Williams devotes the next section, "Regular Reefer," to blues singer Bessie Smith, who is the "sweet angel chile" referred to in this collection's title. Smith provides a figurative sanctuary for Williams because she identifies with the singer. Williams's "Recollections" and "Fragments" rejoice in Smith's existence, showing how Smith epitomized love and hope for Williams. "Bessie on My Wall" and "Fifteen" celebrate the inner beauty and strength that Smith possessed and that Williams recognized in herself. Williams appropriates

Smith's experiences to create poems with biographical elements, conveying themes of loss, betrayal, hardship, and defiance similar to those used in Smith's songs. The rhythmic lines of Williams's poems, such as "them ol young woman Blues," sound like Smith's songs and communicate the singer's and Williams's energetic determination to pursue their aspirations, asserting their independence and confidence. Williams mourns Smith's death in "Down Torrey Pines Road."

Williams dedicates the third section, "The Songs of the Grown," to her son. Many of these poems depict her collegiate experiences as a civil rights activist, repeating slogans such as "black power" and telling how disparate groups united in protest, burning effigies of white men for whom campus buildings were named. In "Witness," she bluntly calls out the racism of academics who misinterpret or ignore truths of African American history. She encounters segregated rural places as she travels by bus in "Middle Passage," finding relief from such restrictions when she reaches her urban destination.

In section four, "The Iconography of Childhood," Williams focuses on her early history. A melancholic tone develops as characters display a lack of security and become fragile because of their burdens. Williams's images and words evoke intense emotions. In the opening untitled stanzas and in "The Wishon Line," Williams speaks of her father's illness and her mother's exhaustion. In "Miss Le'a's Chile," she praises her mother's strength in resisting officials who try to seize the family's children because they have judged her mother to be unfit to raise them. In "You Were Never Miss Brown to Me," Williams contemplates her respect for women who survived despite seemingly insurmountable obstacles, acknowledging how their stories of perseverance reinforced her and recognizing that it is her turn to share her knowledge.

OTHER MAJOR WORKS

LONG FICTION: *Dessa Rose*, 1986.

NONFICTION: *Give Birth to Brightness: A Thematic Study in Neo-Black Literature*, 1972.

CHILDREN'S LITERATURE: *Working Cotton*, 1992 (illustrated by Carole Byard); *Girls Together*, 1999 (illustrated by Synthia Saint James).

BIBLIOGRAPHY

Anderson, Paul Allen. *Deep River: Music and Memory in Harlem Renaissance Thought*. Durham, N.C.: Duke University Press, 2001. Comments on Williams's blues concepts regarding literary structure and tone in an analysis of poetry by Langston Hughes; notes that Williams thought that blues served to convey desired emotions in poems.

Beaulieu, Elizabeth Ann. "'Cause I Can': Race, Gender, and Power in Sherley Anne Williams's *Dessa Rose*." In *Black Women Writers and the American Neo-Slave Narrative: Femininity Unfettered*. Westport, Conn.: Greenwood Press, 1999. Explores the literary techniques Williams used to depict strong women characters.

Chow, Balance. "The Poetry of Sherley Anne Williams." In *Masterplots II: African American Literature*, edited by Tyrone Williams. Rev. ed. Pasadena, Calif.: Salem Press, 2009. This analysis notes that Williams was a poet of the underclass and takes a close look at *The Peacock Poems* and *Some One Sweet Angel Chile*.

Fox-Good, Jacquelyn A. "Singing the Unsayable: Theorizing Music in *Dessa Rose*." In *Black Orpheus: Music in African American Fiction from the Harlem Renaissance to Toni Morrison*, edited by Saadi A. Simawe. New York: Garland, 2000. Places Williams's appropriation of the blues in context with other African American literature, providing scholarly insights regarding her literary style applicable to interpretation of her poetry.

Ryan, Jennifer D. "Finding Her Voice: The Body Politics of Sherley Anne Williams's Blues." In *Post-Jazz Poetics: A Social History*. New York: Palgrave Macmillan, 2010. Examines Williams's poetry in terms of its musicality, particularly how it relates to jazz poetry.

Williams, Sherley Anne. "Conversation." Interview by Deborah McDowell. In *The Furious Flowering of African American Poetry*, edited by Joanne V. Gabbin. Charlottesville: University of Virginia Press, 1999. In this interview conducted by scholar Deborah McDowell at the 1994 Furious Flower Conference, Williams discusses how she writes poetry and racial issues relevant to education, litcrature, gender, and culture. Williams appears on "Volume 3: Seers" of the companion video anthology released in 1998.

_____. "Conversation with Sherley Anne Williams." Interview by Claudia Tate. In *Black Women Writers at Work*, edited by Tate. New York: Continuum, 1989. Williams describes her writing process, reasons for incorporating blues music elements in poetry, and motivations for writing about marginalized African American females.

_____. "Sherley Anne Williams." Interview by Shirley Marie Jordan. In *Broken Silences: Interviews with Black and White Women Writers*, edited by Jordan. New Brunswick, N.J.: Rutgers University Press, 1993. In this November, 1989, interview, Williams examines her perspectives of writing historical literature, how readers influence her writing, and African American literary criticism. Photograph of Williams.

Elizabeth D. Schafer

WILLIAM CARLOS WILLIAMS

Born: Rutherford, New Jersey; September 17, 1883
Died: Rutherford, New Jersey; March 4, 1963

PRINCIPAL POETRY

Poems, 1909
The Tempers, 1913
Al Que Quiere!, 1917
Kora in Hell: Improvisations, 1920
Sour Grapes, 1921
Spring and All, 1923
Collected Poems, 1921-1931, 1934
An Early Martyr, and Other Poems, 1935
Adam and Eve and the City, 1936
The Complete Collected Poems of William Carlos Williams, 1906-1938, 1938
The Broken Span, 1941
The Wedge, 1944
Paterson, 1946-1958
The Clouds, 1948

Selected Poems, 1949

Collected Later Poems, 1950, 1963

Collected Earlier Poems, 1951

The Desert Music, and Other Poems, 1954

Journey to Love, 1955

Pictures from Brueghel, 1962

Selected Poems, 1985

The Collected Poems of William Carlos Williams: Volume I, 1909-1939, 1986

The Collected Poems of William Carlos Williams: Volume II, 1939-1962, 1988

Selected Poems, 2004 (Robert Pinsky, editor)

OTHER LITERARY FORMS

William Carlos Williams is best known for his poetry, but he did not limit himself to that form. His short-story collections include *The Knife of the Times, and Other Stories* (1932), *Life Along the Passaic River* (1938), *Make Light of It: Collected Stories* (1950), and *The Farmers' Daughters: The Collected Stories of William Carlos Williams* (1961). Among his novels are *The Great American Novel* (1923), *A Voyage to Pagany* (1928), and the Stecher trilogy, composed of *White Mule* (1937), *In the Money* (1940), and *The Build-Up* (1952), and his best-known collection of plays is *Many Loves, and Other Plays* (1961). He also wrote criticism and an autobiography. His essay collections include *In the American Grain* (1925) and *Selected Essays of William Carlos Williams* (1954). In addition, he and his mother published two translations, *Last Nights of Paris* (1929) by Philippe Soupault and *A Dog and the Fever* (1954) by Francisco Gómez de Quevedo y Villegas.

ACHIEVEMENTS

William Carlos Williams's recognition was late in coming, although he received the Dial Award for Services to American Literature in 1926 for the "Paterson" poem and the Guarantor's Prize from *Poetry* in 1931; Louis Zukofsky's Objectivist issue of *Poetry* in 1931 featured Williams. The critics, other poets and writers, as well as the public, however, largely ignored his poetry until 1946, when *Paterson*, book 1 appeared. From that time on, his recognition increased steadily. He was made a fellow of the Library of Congress, 1948-1949,

and appointed consultant in poetry (poet laureate) to the Library of Congress in 1952, but he never served because of political opposition to his alleged left-wing principles. In 1948, he received the Russell Loines Award for *Paterson*, book 2, and, in 1950, the National Book Award for *Selected Poems* and *Paterson*, book 3; in 1953, he shared with Archibald MacLeish the Bollingen Prize for excellence in contemporary verse. He received the Levinson Prize from *Poetry* magazine in 1954 and the Academy of American Poets Fellowship in 1956. Finally, in May, 1963, he was posthumously awarded the Pulitzer Prize for *Pictures from Brueghel* and the Gold Medal for poetry from the American Academy of Arts and Letters.

BIOGRAPHY

William Carlos Williams was born in Rutherford, New Jersey, on September 17, 1883. His father (William George Williams) was an Englishman who never gave up his British citizenship, and his mother (Raquel Hélène Rose Hoheb, known as Elena) was a Puerto Rican of Basque, Dutch, Spanish, and Jewish descent. His father was an Episcopalian who turned Unitarian and his mother was Roman Catholic. Williams was educated at schools in New York City and briefly in Europe and graduated with a medical degree from the University of Pennsylvania in 1909. After an internship in New York City and graduate study in pediatrics in Leipzig, he returned to his native Rutherford, where he practiced medicine until he retired. He proposed to Florence "Floss" Herman in 1909 and they were married in 1912. Their first son, William Eric Williams, was born in 1914 and their second, Paul Herman Williams, in 1916.

Williams, a melting pot in himself, had deep roots as a second-generation citizen of the United States. From early in his life he felt that the United States was his only home and that he must possess it in order to know himself. Possessing the America of the past and the present would enable him to renew himself continually and find his own humanity. Unlike many writers of his generation who went to Europe, such as his friend Ezra Pound, Williams committed himself to living in the United States because he believed he had to live in a place to be able to grasp it imaginatively.

Williams met Pound when they were both at the University of Pennsylvania; their friendship was fierce and uneven throughout their lives. While at the university, Williams also met Hilda Doolittle (H. D.) and the painter Charles Demuth. In his early poetry, he imitated Pound and the Imagists, accepting the Imagist credo as presented in *Poetry*. His natural inclination was to treat things directly with brevity of language and without conventional metrics. He was also influenced by his painter friends, particularly by the cubists and the expressionists. Modern painters filled their canvases with mechanisms, and Williams called a poem a "machine made of words." During 1915 and 1916, he attended literary gatherings with the *Others* group and met Alfred Kreymborg, Marianne Moore, and Wallace Stevens.

He began writing poetry in a poetic wasteland that did not want new or experimental poetry. The poets who had been popularly admired were the three-name poets so greatly influenced by the English tradition. Walt Whitman was not regarded highly, and Emily Dickinson was unknown.

Although he devoted much of his time to being a full-time physician in Rutherford, Williams was a prolific writer—a poet, short-story writer, novelist, playwright, essayist, and translator. He was neglected both by the general public and by the literary establishment for most of his career, and often in his frustration, he erupted against his critics and other practicing poets. With the publication of *Paterson*, book 1, in 1946, however, he began to receive the recognition he felt he deserved.

During most of the last fifteen years of his life, he continued to write even though he was not in good health. In 1948, when he was sixty-five years old, he suffered a heart attack, and in 1951, he had his first stroke, which was followed by another serious one a year later. The next year, he was hospitalized because of severe depression. Finally, in 1961, two years before his death, he gave up writing after he suffered a series of strokes. On March 4, 1963, at the age of seventy-nine, he died in Rutherford, where he had been born and had lived all his life.

ANALYSIS

Like Walt Whitman, William Carlos Williams attempted to create an American voice for American poetry. Both Whitman and Williams wanted to record the unique American experience in a distinctively American idiom, a language freed from the constraints of traditional English prosody. Whitman, as Williams says in his autobiography, broke from the traditional iambic pentameter, but he had only begun the necessary revolution. It was then up to Williams to use "the new dialect" to continue Whitman's work by constructing a prosody based on actual American speech.

Williams's search for a new language using the American idiom was intertwined with his search for a new poetic measure. Although he wanted to recover the relationship between poetry and the measured dance from which he believed it derived, his concept of measure is elusive. He believed that Whitman's free verse lacked structure. Williams sought a new foot that

William Carlos Williams (Hulton Archive/Getty Images)

would be fairly stable, yet at the same time was variable, a foot that was not fixed but allowed for variation according to what the language called for. While the traditional poetic foot is based on the number of syllables in a line, Williams based his poetic foot on "a measure of the ear." The proper measure would allow him to present the American idiom as controlled by the rhythm of American speech.

When Williams wrote his early poems, he had not yet developed his own poetical theory; he first wrote conventionally and then according to the Imagist credo. He created some very good pictures of "things," and his poems achieved a reality of their own, but they did not go beyond the particulars to express universal truths—something that involves more than merely recreating data.

In "The Red Wheelbarrow," for example, all the reader is left with is the picture of the red wheelbarrow and the white chickens beside it standing in the rain. In "Poem," the cat climbs over the jamcloset into the empty flower pot; Williams conveys nothing more than this picture. Other examples of Williams's poems of this period include "The Locust Tree in Flower" (the locust tree in flower is sweet and white, and brings May again), "Between Walls" (behind the hospital in the cinders of the courtyard shine the pieces of a broken green bottle), and "This Is Just to Say" (the poet tells his wife he has eaten the plums she was saving in the icebox).

In "To a Poor Old Woman," Williams does not convey any meaning beyond the picture he evokes of an old woman munching on a plum that she has taken from a bag she is holding in her hand. He does, however, experiment with the way he places the words of the line "They taste good to her" on the page. He repeats the line three times. First, he puts all the words on one line without a period at the end of the line; then he writes "They taste good/ to her. They taste/ good to her." He is searching for the correct form to use—the elusive measure needed.

PATERSON

In the epic poem *Paterson*, Williams sought to cover the landscape of contemporary American society and to discover himself as an American poet. His twenty-year journey in *Paterson* is similar to that of Hart Crane in *The Bridge* (1930), Ezra Pound in the *Cantos* (1925-1972), and T. S. Eliot in *The Waste Land* (1922) and *Four Quartets* (1943). Just as Whitman revised the poems of *Leaves of Grass* (1855) continuously and frequently moved them from section to section within the volume, so Williams identified *Paterson* with his own continuing life as a poet.

Paterson consists of five books and a projected sixth; each book is made up of three sections. In "The Delineaments of the Giants" (*Paterson*, book 1, 1946), Mr. Paterson, as he wanders through the city Paterson, describes details of the town and the area around it: the valley, the Passaic Falls, and Garret Mountain. Williams creates a history for the city as he describes past and present inhabitants and events concerning both them and the city. In "Sunday in the Park" (*Paterson*, book 2, 1948), the persona walks through Garret Mountain Park on a Sunday afternoon; there he views the workers of Paterson in their Sunday leisure activities. "The Library" (*Paterson*, book 3, 1949) takes place in the library, where the persona searches to discover how best to express the aspects of the city of Paterson that he has described in the first two books. "The Run to the Sea" (*Paterson*, book 4, 1951) takes place in two locales—New York City and an entrance to the sea. The first section consists mostly of dialogues between Corydon and Phyllis, and Phyllis and Paterson. The section involves Madame Marie Curie's discovery of uranium and a digressive discussion of economics in America. The final section of the fourth book presents accounts of events, mostly violent, concerning the inhabitants of Paterson; it ends with the persona and a dog headed inland after they have emerged from the sea. *Paterson*, book 5, which does not have a title, takes place in the Cloisters, a museum on the Hudson River in New York City. This book is shorter than the others and some critics refer to it as a coda to *Paterson*, books 1-4. Having grown old, the persona contemplates the meaning of a series of unicorn tapestries in the museum.

Paterson can be difficult reading. The persona of the poem does not remain constant; moreover, "Paterson" refers to both the city and the man. There are a number of other personas in *Paterson* who are sometimes ambiguously fused. Paterson the city becomes

Paterson the man, who is also a woman, who becomes the poet writing *Paterson*, who is also William Carlos Williams, a poet and a man.

In addition, Williams shifts from verse to prose without transitional devices, and there are many such shifts within verse passages, from persona to persona, and from subject matter to subject matter. The prose passages, sometimes taken directly from an exterior source, range from newspaper clippings and quotations from various books to letters by Williams's fictional personas.

Paterson is Williams's attempt to delineate his culture and to define himself poetically. The two quests are interrelated. Williams can present details of the America that he sees and describe aspects of its culture. He wants, however, to convey the truths in what he describes and the universals concerning his vision. To be able to do so, he must work out his poetic theory and discover himself as a poet.

In *Paterson*, Williams relied importantly on local particulars. First, he chose a city that actually existed. In *The Autobiography of William Carlos Williams*, he writes of taking the city Paterson and working it up as a case, just as he worked up cases as a doctor. According to Joel Conarroe in *William Carlos Williams' "Paterson"* (1970), Paterson was a city that was similar to Williams's native Rutherford, but one that better possessed the characteristics that Williams needed for his poem. Paterson had existed since the beginning of America and therefore had a history. It was a very American city with a diverse population, about one-third of which was foreign-born. Located on the Passaic River with the Passaic Falls, Paterson was bounded on one side by Garret Mountain. Partially because of these natural resources, it was one of the first industrial cities in America. Furthermore, its industry grew steadily, and it was often the scene of well-known strikes. Fortunately for the action of the poem, Paterson also suffered a major fire, flood, and tornado.

Williams peoples his poem with persons who actually existed and uses events that actually occurred. Often, in the prose passages, he gives the specifics about the inhabitants and events. In *Paterson*, book 1, Williams develops a history for the city of Paterson. He tells the reader the number of inhabitants of each na-

tionality living in Paterson in 1870. He describes some of the inhabitants. David Hower, for example, is a poor shoemaker who in February, 1857, while eating mussels, finds substances that turn out to be pearls. A gentleman in the Revolutionary Army describes a monster in human form, Pieter Van Winkle. His description is followed by the account of a 126-pound monster fish taken by John Winters and other boys. Sarah Cumming, the wife of the Reverend Hopper Cumming for two months, mysteriously disappears into the falls just after her husband turns from the cataract to go home. When the bridge that Timothy B. Crane built is being placed across the falls, Sam Patch jumps to retrieve a rolling pin and thus begins his career as a famous jumper, a career that ends when he attempts to jump the falls of the Genessee River in 1829. The reader learns exactly what Cornelius Doremus owned when he died at eighty-nine years of age and what each item was worth. At one time, the men of Paterson ravage the river and kill almost all its fish. Finally, the reader is told about Leonard Sandford, who discovers a human body near the falls.

In *Paterson*, Books II-V, Williams continues to present details about the geography, inhabitants, and events of Paterson; as the poem progresses, however, he relies less on prose from historical accounts in books and newspapers and more on letters, dialogues, and verse. The particulars also become more personally related to the fictional poet of the poem or to Bill (Dr. Williams). There are passages about the Indians who first lived in the area. Williams includes a tabular account of the specimens found when men were digging an artesian well at the Passaic Rolling Mill, Paterson, and an advertisement concerning borrowing money on the credit of the United States. Phyllis, an uneducated black woman, writes several letters to her father. Throughout the poem, a woman poet (C. or Cress), another poet (A. G.), and Edward or E. D. (Edward Dahlberg) write letters to a person without a name, to Dr. Paterson, to Dr. Williams, and to Bill.

In addition to all these particulars, Williams deals with aspects of American society. A major weakness of contemporary American culture is the inability of people to communicate with others and even with themselves. In *Paterson*, book 1, Williams immediately introduces the problems with language faced by the inhabitants of Paterson. Industrialization is one of the sources of their difficulties; industrialization and materialism separate them from themselves and from each other. The people walk incommunicado; they do not know the words with which to communicate. It is as if they face an equation that cannot be solved, for language fails them. Although there is a torrent in their minds, they cannot unlock that torrent since they do not know themselves.

Sam Patch is an example of a man who dies incommunicado. Before he attempts to dive into the falls of the Genessee River, he makes a short speech. The words, however, are drained of meaning and they fail him. He disappears into the stream and is not seen until the following spring, when he is found frozen in ice, still locked in by his inability to communicate.

In the second part of *Paterson*, book 2, Williams describes Madame Curie's discovery of uranium, a discovery that he relates to the need in America for the discovery of a new credit system. This system would be like "the radiant gist" that Madame Curie discovered and would cure America's economic cancer, a condition contributing to people's inability to communicate. The lust for money and the industrialization of society cut people off from their roots and from other people.

Humanity's problems with language are reflected in the relationships between man and woman. The love of man and woman consummated in marriage should be a means of communication, but in contemporary society "divorce" is the common word: "The language/ is divorced from their minds." In *Paterson*, book 1, Williams tells of Sarah Cumming, who after two months of marriage has everything to look forward to, but who mysteriously disappears into the falls after her husband turns his back on her. Marriage, then, is no answer to the problem of communication. The words locked in the "falls" of the human mind must be released. Immediately after the prose section about Sarah Cumming comes the passage "A false language. A true. A false language pouring—a/ language (misunderstood) pouring (misinterpreted) without/ dignity, without minister, crashing upon a stone ear. At least/ it settled it for her."

In *Paterson*, book 2, as Paterson walks through Garret Mountain Park, the breakdown of language is re-

flected in the religious and sexual life of the Paterson workers as they spend their leisure time on a Sunday afternoon. A sermon by the itinerant evangelist Klaus Ehrens is a meaningless harangue; he does not communicate with those in the park. The relationship between man and woman is reduced to a sexual act of lust without meaning; it is not even an act that will produce children. Language and communication between man and woman is exhausted. Ironically, B. is told in a letter by someone who has been caring for a dog that the dog is going to have puppies; animals, unlike humans, remain fertile.

The first section of *Paterson*, book 4, is primarily a narrative consisting of dialogues between Corydon and Phyllis, and Phyllis and Paterson. In both relationships, the participants fail to communicate successfully. Corydon is an old lesbian who is halfheartedly attempting to seduce Phyllis, a virgin. Paterson is also an unsuccessful lover of the young black nurse. Phyllis writes letters to her Pappy in uneducated English. In the last letter, she tells him of a trip with Corydon to Anticosti—a name that sounds Italian but is French. The two women have a guide who speaks French with Corydon. Phyllis cannot understand what they are saying; she does not care, however, because she can speak her own language. The dialogues reveal relationships in which there is a potential for love and communication, but in which there is a failure to communicate.

Williams describes the predicament of Paterson, but he wants to convey the universals of American society and go beyond the "facts" to the "ideas." Being able to express the general through "things" is part of Williams's quest to define himself as a poet. *Paterson* is a search for the redeeming language needed to enable contemporary humans to communicate; the quest itself, however, is valuable even if the redeeming language is not discovered.

In the preface to *Paterson*, Williams states that the poem is the quest to find the needed language ("beauty") that is locked in his mind. Soon after, in *Paterson*, book 1, Williams indicates that he is attempting to determine "what common language to unravel." Mr. Paterson, the persona, will go away to rest and write. Thus, Williams begins his quest for the redeeming language.

Paterson, book 1, ends with a quotation from *Studies of Greek Poets* (1873) by John Addington Symonds in which Symonds discusses Hipponax's attempt to use a meter appropriate for prose and common speech. Symonds also notes that the Greeks used the "deformed verse" of Hipponax for subjects dealing with humanity's perversions. Thus, the Greek poets devised a prosody suitable to their society, just as Williams seeks a measure to express American society.

Throughout *Paterson*, several letters by the woman poet C., or Cress, interrelate the theme of man's failure to communicate, especially through heterosexual love, and the poet's function to solve this problem of language. The longest of her letters, covering six-and-a-half pages, appears at the end of *Paterson*, book 2. In it she complains about woman's wretched position in society. She is particularly upset about her relationship, or lack of relationship, with Dr. P. She has tried to communicate intimately and has shared thoughts with him that she has not shared with anyone else. He has rejected her. She accuses him of having used her; he has encouraged her first letters only because he could turn them into literature and use them in his poem. As long as her letters were only literature—a literature divorced from life—their relationship was satisfactory, but when she attempted to use her letters to communicate on a personal level, he turned his back on her. When her writings became an expression of herself, their friendship failed. She thus expresses an idea that E. D. had stated earlier in the poem—that the literary work and its author cannot be separated. An artist derives a unity of being and a freedom to be himself when he achieves a successful relationship between the externals, such as the paint, clay, or language that he uses, and his shaping of these externals.

In *Paterson*, book 2, the persona goes to the library to try to learn how, as a poet, to express the details of the city described in the first two books. The library contains many acts of communication, but all of them are from the past and will not serve the poet in his quest for the redeeming language that will free humanity and himself. The poet in the poem, and Williams himself by implication, have failed to communicate, both as poets and as men.

Briefly at the beginning of *Paterson*, book 3, Williams suggests the need for an "invention" without which the old will return with deadly repetitiveness. Only invention will bring the new line that in turn brings the new word, a word that is required now that words have crumbled like chalk. Invention requires the poet to reject old forms and exhausted words in order to find the new-measured language. Throughout this book, there is destruction and violence. The natural disasters that occurred in Paterson (the flood, the fire, and the tornado) and made it necessary for the inhabitants to rebuild sections of the city suggest the poet's search in which he finds it necessary to destroy in order to create. The poet does not find what he is searching for, because both the invention and words are lacking. Nevertheless, he continues his search for "the beautiful thing."

Near the end of *Paterson*, book 3, the poet experiments with form and language. On one page, Williams places the lines almost at random. It is as if someone has taped various typed lines carelessly on the page without making sure that the lines are parallel or that they make sense when read. There are numbers and words in both English and French. The reader is invited to consider the meanings evoked by "funeral *designed*," "plants," and "wedding bouquets." On the following page there are four passages in which the words are abbreviations meant to be a phonological representation of the words of an illiterate person. Immediately after these passages appears the tabular account of the specimens found when a water well is being dug. Water brings life and rebirth. The poet wants to unlock the language of the falls that had filled his head earlier and to create the new-measured language. He concludes that "*American poetry is a very easy subject to discuss for the/ simple reason that it does not exist*."

In *Paterson*, book 4, Williams returns to Madame Curie's "radiant gist"; the poet hopes to make a similar discovery in his poetry so that he can heal those who suffer from an inadequate language. The poet reminds himself that his "virgin" purpose is the language and that he must forget the past. At the end of the book, he emerges from the sea, which has been presented in terms of violence, and heads inland eating a plum and followed by a dog that has also been swimming in the sea. Williams concludes that "This is the blast/ the eternal close/ the spiral/ the final somersault/ the end." Williams suggests process in this end; the end is a spiral similar to a Möbius strip in which the end is always a return to the beginning.

Again Williams interrelates the poet's art and the process of love. Both are a means of communication between man and woman and a way for a person to discover himself; both, he explains in *Paterson*, book 5, involve a paradox. The virgin's maidenhead must be violently destroyed in the sexual act for her to realize her potential to create another human being. The poet must destroy past forms to discover the form appropriate for his time; Williams must reject the language and form of past poetry to create the new-measured language that will express contemporary American society and provide for communication among men.

Paterson, book 5, contains a question-and-answer section in which Williams discusses his theory of poetry. Poetry is made of words that have been organized rhythmically; a poem is a complete entity that has a separate existence. If the poem is any good, it expresses the life of the poet and tells the reader what the poet is. Anything can be the subject of poetry. The poet in America must use the American idiom, but the manner in which the words are presented is of the greatest importance. Sometimes a modern poet ignores the sense of words. In prose, words mean what they say, but in poetry words present two different things: what they actually mean and what their shape means. Williams cites Pieter Brueghel as an artist who saw from two sides. Brueghel painted authentically what he saw, yet at the same time served the imagination. The measured dance, life as it is presented in art by the imagination, is all that humans can know. The answer to the poet's quest is that "We know nothing and can know nothing/ but/ the dance, to dance to a measure/ contrapuntally,/ Satyrically, the tragic foot." The poet presents life in a form appropriate to the time in which he lives; he presents the particulars of life that are a contrast or interplay of elements directed by his sexual desires and need for love, his humanity.

LATER POEMS

It is in the poems that Williams wrote during the last ten years of his life that he achieves greatness—the poems collected in *The Desert Music, and Other Poems*, *Journey to Love*, and *Pictures from Brueghel*. In these, he uses the new-measured language he had sought in *Paterson*, books 1-5, but more important, he goes beyond "things" to "ideas." The poems are more than pretty subjects; in them he discovers "the beautiful thing."

Some of the best poems of this period are "To Daphne and Virginia," "The Sparrow (To My Father)," "A Negro Woman," "Self-Portrait," "The Hunters in the Snow," "The Wedding Dance in the Open Air," "The Parable of the Blind," "Children's Games," "Song" (beginning "beauty is a shell"), "The Wood-thrush," and "Asphodel, That Greeny Flower."

When Williams was asked in 1961 to choose his favorite poem for an anthology called *Poet's Choice*, he selected "The Descent" from *Paterson*, book 2. He said that he had been using "the variable foot" for many years, but "The Descent" was the first in that form that completely satisfied him. "Asphodel, That Greeny Flower," from *Journey to Love*, is another poem in which Williams truly succeeds, and a discussion of that poem provides a good summary to a discussion of Williams's poetry.

"ASPHODEL, THAT GREENY FLOWER"

In "Asphodel, That Greeny Flower," Williams uses his new-measured language, containing "fresh" words (the American idiom) written in a measure appropriate to his times and controlled by the rhythm of American speech ("the variable foot" in the triadic stanza). He is also concerned with creating a poem that has its own existence and is a "thing" in itself. Williams draws from the particulars of American life and his own life to evoke images of the United States and its culture; now that he has discovered the new-measured language, however, he can express universal truths about America and its culture. The poem at the same time expresses Williams's life as a poet and points to what he is and believes.

Williams uses his new-measured language to capture the flow of American speech as well as to reinforce and emphasize the content and meaning of the poem. For example, in one passage, the measure of the lines suggests the urgency of the present, then slows into memory and reminiscence and finally into silence. At another point, Williams's measure gives the sense of the rolling sea. James Breslin in *William Carlos Wil-*

liams: An American Artist (1970) discusses in detail Williams's use of the American idiom presented in "the variable foot" and triadic stanza.

Williams uses natural details such as the asphodel, the honeysuckle, the bee, the lily, the hummingbird, apple blossoms, strawberries, the lily of the valley, and daisies. He uses particulars from his own life: a trip he took with his wife, a time he was separated from her, and their wedding day. He makes references to his own poetry; a young artist likes Williams's poem about the broken green bottle lying in the cinders in the hospital courtyard and says he has heard about, but not read, Williams's poem on gay wallpaper.

The new-measured language enables Williams to draw from the facts and details of the locale to reach the realm of the imagination and convey truths about humanity. He begins the poem by addressing the asphodel, but immediately, his "song" becomes one addressed to his wife of many years, not to the flower. Throughout the poem there is constant shifting between the image of the asphodel and Floss, as well as a fusing of the two particulars. The flower at times becomes a symbol. As Breslin explains, the poem is a continuing process as the "things" expand to the "ideas" beyond them, and the truths expressed contract back into the particular images.

The poem is a realistic love song that conveys the nature of the man who is the poet creating the poem. He asks his wife to forgive him because too often medicine, poetry, and other women have been his prime concerns, not her and their life together. The asphodel becomes a symbol of his renewed love for her in his old age. He can ask for her forgiveness because he has come to realize that love has the power to undo what has been done. Love must often serve a function similar to that of the poet, for the poet also must undo what has been done by destroying past forms in order to create new ones.

In "Asphodel, That Greeny Flower," Williams regrets that he has reached a time when he can no longer put down the words that come to him out of the air and create poems. Through the details of his poetry, he has attempted to express the general truths of the imagination. With his old age, however, he has gained knowledge that makes him optimistic. "Are facts not flowers/ and flowers facts/ or poems flowers/ or all words of the imagination,/ interchangeable?" "Flowers" or "facts," "poems" and "words of the imagination" are interchangeable, for everything is a work of the imagination. What is important is that love is a force of the imagination that rules things, words, and poems; love is life's form for poetry. Through love and poetry, all people will be able to communicate. Both love and works of the imagination, be they artistic endeavors or otherwise, are creative powers that are people's means of escaping death. This is the universal truth, the "idea" that Williams has come to, through the particulars of his poetry and his life.

OTHER MAJOR WORKS

LONG FICTION: *The Great American Novel*, 1923; *A Voyage to Pagany*, 1928; *White Mule*, 1937; *In the Money*, 1940; *The Build-Up*, 1952.

SHORT FICTION: *The Knife of the Times, and Other Stories*, 1932; *Life Along the Passaic River*, 1938; *Make Light of It: Collected Stories*, 1950; *The Farmers' Daughters: The Collected Stories of William Carlos Williams*, 1961; *The Doctor Stories*, 1984; *The Collected Stories of William Carlos Williams*, 1996.

PLAYS: *A Dream of Love*, pb. 1948; *Many Loves, and Other Plays*, 1961.

NONFICTION: *In the American Grain*, 1925; *A Novelette, and Other Prose*, 1932; *The Autobiography of William Carlos Williams*, 1951; *Selected Essays of William Carlos Williams*, 1954; *The Selected Letters of William Carlos Williams*, 1957; *I Wanted to Write a Poem: The Autobiography of the Works of a Poet*, 1958; *The Embodiment of Knowledge*, 1974; *A Recognizable Image*, 1978; *William Carlos Williams, John Sanford: A Correspondence*, 1984; *William Carlos Williams and James Laughlin: Selected Letters*, 1989; *Pound/Williams: Selected Letters of Ezra Pound and William Carlos Williams*, 1996 (Hugh Witemeyer, editor); *The Correspondence of William Carlos Williams and Louis Zukofsky*, 2003 (Barry Ahearn, editor); *The Humane Particulars: The Collected Letters of William Carlos Williams and Kenneth Burke*, 2003 (James H. East, editor); *The Letters of William Carlos Williams to Edgar Irving Williams, 1902-1912*, 2009 (Andrew J. Krivak, editor).

TRANSLATIONS: *Last Nights of Paris*, 1929 (with Raquel Hélène Williams; of Philippe Soupault); *A Dog and the Fever*, 1954 (with Williams; of Francisco Gómez de Quevedo y Villegas).

MISCELLANEOUS: *The Descent of Winter*, 1928 (includes poetry, prose, and anecdotes); *Imaginations*, 1970 (includes poetry, fiction, and nonfiction).

BIBLIOGRAPHY

Axelrod, Steven Gould, and Helen Deese, eds. *Critical Essays on William Carlos Williams*. New York: G. K. Hall, 1995. A solid collection of essays on the life and work of Williams.

Beck, John. *Writing the Radical Center: William Carlos Williams, John Dewey, and American Cultural Politics*. Albany: State University of New York Press, 2001. Analyzes Williams's political convictions as reflected in his writings, and compares them with those of philosopher John Dewey.

Bloom, Harold, ed. *William Carlos Williams: Comprehensive Research and Study Guide*. Broomal, Pa.: Chelsea House, 2002. Bloom's study guide provides a basis for research on Williams's life and works.

Bremen, Brian A. *William Carlos Williams and the Diagnostics of Culture*. New York: Oxford University Press, 1993. An examination of the development of Williams's poetry, focused on his fascination with the effects of poetry and prose, and his friendship with Kenneth Burke. Using the theoretical writings and correspondence of Burke and Williams, and the works of contemporary cultural critics, Bremen looks at how the methodological empiricism in Williams's poetic strategy is tied to his medical practice.

Copestake, Ian, ed. *The Legacy of William Carlos Williams: Points of Contact*. Newcastle, England: Cambridge Scholars, 2007. This collection of essays examines the poet Williams and how he influenced other writers and artists.

Fisher-Wirth, Ann W. *William Carlos Williams and Autobiography: The Woods of His Own Nature*. University Park: Pennsylvania State University Press, 1989. Considers the autobiographical aspects of certain works by Williams. Adds new insight into Williams's conception of the self and its relationship to the world. Supplemented by thorough notes and an index.

Hatlen, Burton, and Demetres Tryphonopoulos, eds. *William Carlos Williams and the Language of Poetry*. Orono: National Poetry Foundation, University of Maine, 2002. A collection of essays that closely examines Williams's poetry, looking at technique, style, and language.

Laughlin, James. *Remembering William Carlos Williams*. New York: New Directions, 1995. The founder of the publishing firm New Directions excerpts his *Byways* verse memoir of the many poets he has published over the years, capturing both humorous and poignant memories of poet-physician Williams.

Lowney, John. *The American Avant-Garde Tradition: William Carlos Williams, Postmodern Poetry, and the Politics of Cultural Memory*. Lewisburg, Pa.: Bucknell University Press, 1997. A good examination of postmodernism and Williams's poetry and literature.

O'Brien, Kevin. *Saying Yes at Lightning: Threat and the Provisional Image in Post-Romantic Poetry*. New York: Peter Lang, 2002. Looks at the theme of threat in works by Williams, H. D., Gerard Manley Hopkins, and Osip Mandelstam. Chapter on Williams is devoted to a discussion of *Paterson*.

Sherry G. Southard

YVOR WINTERS

Born: Chicago, Illinois; October 17, 1900
Died: Palo Alto, California; January 25, 1968

PRINCIPAL POETRY
The Immobile Wind, 1921
The Magpie's Shadow, 1922
The Bare Hills, 1927
The Proof, 1930
The Journey, and Other Poems, 1931
Before Disaster, 1934

Poems, 1940

The Giant Weapon, 1943

To the Holy Spirit, 1947

Collected Poems, 1952, 1960

The Early Poems of Yvor Winters, 1920-1928, 1966

The Collected Poems of Yvor Winters, 1978

The Uncollected Poems of Yvor Winters, 1919-1928, 1997 (R. L. Barth, editor)

The Uncollected Poems of Yvor Winters, 1929-1957, 1997 (Barth, editor)

Selected Poems, 2003 (Thom Gunn, editor)

OTHER LITERARY FORMS

Though Yvor Winters believed his poetry to be his principal work, he was, during his lifetime, better known as a critic. His criticism was virtually coextensive with his poetry, the first published essays appearing in 1922 and the last volume in 1967. Controversial because of its wide-ranging and detailed revaluations of both major and minor writers in American, British, and French literature, the criticism indirectly but indisputably illuminates his own work as poet by suggesting explanations for the changes it underwent, for the main styles he attempted, and even for details in individual poems.

His single short story, "The Brink of Darkness" (1932, 1947), is autobiographical. Its setting (the southwestern United States) and subject matter (hypersensitivity in isolation, the advent of death, psychological obsession to the brink of madness, the recovery of identity) are those of many poems, especially early ones, in the Winters canon.

ACHIEVEMENTS

Among his contemporaries, Yvor Winters was something of an anomaly. Instead of moving from traditional to experimental forms, he seemed to reverse that process. Before 1928, his published work was largely what is loosely called free verse, influenced by such diverse sources as the Imagists and French Symbolists, possibly Emily Dickinson, and certainly translations of Japanese and American Indian poetry. After 1930, Winters's published work used traditional metric and rhyme patterns exclusively.

He appeared to stand against all the main poetic currents of his time.

At no time, however, early or late, did his poetry ignore modern influences. Among the poets he continued most to admire and emulate were Charles Baudelaire, Paul Valéry, Thomas Hardy, Robert Bridges, and Wallace Stevens. His effort consistently was to make use of the most fruitful traditions among all at his disposal, not merely those in fashion. Thus, many of his later poems are written in the great plain style of the Renaissance. In his most distinctive work, Winters tried to combine the sensitivity of perception that the recent associative and experimental methods had made possible with the rational structures characteristic of the older methods. The result was something unique in modern poetry. Even before his death, his influence was beginning to be felt in such poets as Edgar Bowers, J. V. Cunningham, Catherine Davis, Thom Gunn, Janet Lewis, N. Scott Momaday, Alan Stephens, and others.

In his criticism also, Winters went his own way, challenging accepted opinions and making enemies in the process. Not only did he define what he believed were mistaken and possibly dangerous directions in the thinking and methods of many American poets, novelists, and prose writers, but also, in his final volume, *Forms of Discovery: Critical and Historical Essays on the Forms of the Short Poem in English* (1967), he offered new and, for many readers, unpopular perspectives on the history of the short poem, both in Great Britain and in the United States. His criticism, however, is not primarily destructive in bent. For one thing, he revised the reputations of many distinguished poets who had already begun to sink into oblivion, such as George Gascoigne, Fulke Greville, and Charles Churchill from the older periods, and Bridges, T. Sturge Moore, and Frederick Goddard Tuckerman from more recent times. For another, he found forgotten poems and qualities of major writers that deserved attention—such poets as Ben Jonson, George Herbert, Henry Vaughan, Hardy, Stevens, and Edwin Arlington Robinson. Finally, he formulated coherent theories about poems, and in fact all literary forms, as works of art, theories to which his own work as a poet and his evaluations of the work of others consistently subscribe. To ignore or dismiss this copious and wide-ranging body of work is to overlook one of the clearest, most precisely analytical, and most disturbingly persuasive voices in American criticism.

Of all the honors he received during his lifetime, Winters said he was proudest of an issue of the Stanford undergraduate magazine, *Sequoia*, which paid tribute to him in 1961. He received a National Institute of Arts and Letters Award (1952), the Bollingen Prize from Yale University (1961) and the Harriet Monroe Poetry Award from the University of Chicago (1961). Having served on the faculty of Stanford University since 1928, Winters was made full professor in 1949, and in 1962, he became the first holder of the Albert L. Guerard Professorship in English. In 1961-1962, a Guggenheim grant enabled Winters to complete the work on his last volume of criticism. By the end of his life, he was beginning to receive the acclaim that was due him. In 1981, *Southern Review* honored him with an entire issue devoted to studies of his life and work.

BIOGRAPHY

Born in the first year of the twentieth century, Arthur Yvor Winters spent his earliest years in Chicago and in Eagle Rock (a district of Los Angeles), California. The landscape of Southern California near Pasadena provides the setting for two major poems in heroic couplets, "The Slow Pacific Swell" and "On a View of Pasadena from the Hills." Later, he returned to Chicago, graduated from high school, and for one year attended the University of Chicago, where, in 1917, he became a member of the Poetry Club, which, in his own words, "was a very intelligent group, worth more than most courses in literature." By then, he had begun to study his contemporaries—Ezra Pound, William Carlos Williams, Stevens, William Butler Yeats—and the diverse poetic styles appearing in the little magazines.

In 1918, having contracted tuberculosis, he was forced to move to Santa Fe, New Mexico, and confined to a sanatorium for three years. The debilitating fatigue and pain, the resultant hypersensitivity to sound and sight and touch, and the sense of death hovering were experiences indelibly etched in his poetry, then and later. In 1921, Winters began teaching grade school—

English, French, zoology, boxing, basketball—in a coal-mining camp called Madrid, and he taught high school the following year in Cerrillos. These five years in the southwestern United States were a slow period of recovery in isolation, a time when his own study of poetry continued and his correspondence with many contemporary poets was active. It was also the time of his earliest publications. The landscape of New Mexico suffuses the poetry of his first four volumes.

In the summer of 1923, Winters began the academic study that would eventually bring him to Stanford for his doctorate, earning a B.A. and an M.A. in romance languages, with a minor in Latin from the University of Colorado. The skills he acquired enabled him to translate many poems from French and Spanish (including thirteenth century Galician) and, between 1925 and 1927, to teach French and Spanish at the University of Idaho at Moscow. During this period, he married Janet Lewis, later a distinguished novelist and poet, whom he had met in 1921 on a return visit to Chicago; their wedding was in 1926 in Santa Fe, where she, too, had gone to cure tuberculosis. Together now, they moved to Stanford in 1927, when Winters was twenty-six years old; then, under the tutelage of his admired mentor in Renaissance studies, William Dinsmore Briggs, he began the systematic study of poetry in English that occupied him for the rest of his life.

Winters's life in California as a teacher, husband, father, and involved citizen is reflected everywhere in his later poetry. He became a legend at Stanford. Depending on which students were reporting, he was dogmatic, shy, reasonable, surly, kind, hilarious, humorless, a petty tyrant, or an intellectual giant. His disciples and detractors felt intensely about him; few were indifferent. The marriage of Winters and Janet Lewis was a lasting and loving one, and it nurtured their independent careers as writers. Their daughter Joanna was born in 1931 and their son Daniel in 1938. Hardly one to withdraw into an ivory tower, Winters liked to get his hands dirty. The raising and breeding of Airedale terriers was a lifelong activity. He kept goats and a garden. He became deeply involved with the trial of David Lamson, a friend unjustly accused of murdering his wife. During World War II, he served as a Citizens' Defense Corps zone warden for Los Altos. These experiences are the kinds of occasions he wrote about in his later work.

Before his retirement from Stanford in 1966, Winters had already endured the first of two operations for cancer, the disease that killed him in 1968. His final effort as a writer, amid acute pain, was to see his last book, *Forms of Discovery*, through to publication after the death of his publisher and old friend, Alan Swallow.

ANALYSIS

The change in poetic forms from experimental to traditional—from Imagistic free verse to formalist poetry using the traditional plain style or post-Symbolist imagery—which Yvor Winters's poetry exhibits after 1930 is so dramatic that it is easy to overlook the continuity of certain stylistic features and thematic preoccupations throughout his career. From the very beginning of his poetic life, he abhorred an indulgent rhetoric in excess of subject matter; always he attempted an exact adjustment of feeling to intellectual content. He paid strict attention to the value of each word as an amalgam of denotative, connotative, rhythmic, and aural properties; to the integrity of the poetic line and the perfect placing of each word within it; and to the clarity and economy of a style that avoids cliché. A poem was for him a means of contemplating human experience in such a way that the meaning of that experience and the feelings appropriate to the meaning are precisely rendered.

THE IMMOBILE WIND

Thematic continuity exists also. His first volume of poems, *The Immobile Wind*, whatever immaturities of style it may exhibit, contains themes that he worked and reworked in all his poems thereafter. As a collection, it speaks of humans alone in an empty universe; their end is death and their choices are existence or creation. They live and observe. If this is all, life remains an unrealized potential, the experience of which may be beautiful or terror-ridden but will lack the possibility of meaning that artists may be able to create. To do this, artists must choose their reality, must will it; to create their own world, they must give over the things of this one, for this world is merely phenomenal, the raw material of vision, a means at best, not an end: "And all these things would take/ My life from me." The end for

all is death, and in addition for artists, the possibility of awareness. Religion offers no solace. The subject of the book is the poet, his growth and mission and death. The images in *The Immobile Wind* are sharp and self-contained and their meanings elusive; as one reads through these poems, however, the subjects and images repeat themselves, interweaving, and patterns of meaning begin to emerge.

In its continual allusiveness to itself and to its own images and in its occasional obscurities, *The Immobile Wind* is an irritating book, but it is not impenetrable. More accessible is *The Magpie's Shadow*, which consists of a series of six-syllable poems (a few stretch to seven) grouped according to the season of the year. Each is intended to convey a sharp sense impression; each as an evocation of a season is evocative also of the passage of time and hence of change and death. "The Aspen's Song," from the summer section, is characteristic: "The summer holds me here." That is the poem. The aspen tree is celebrating its moment of being alive, a moment that creates an illusion of permanence and immobility, an illusion because the summer is transient and the motion of change is there in the tree at every moment. The motion/stasis paradox of this image—present also in the oxymoronic title *The Immobile Wind*—recurs through Winters's poetry. No doubt inspired by translations of American Indian and Japanese originals, it also may be seen as an early manifestation of what he later came to call the post-Symbolist method: the sharp sensory image of metaphysical import.

THE BARE HILLS

The Bare Hills is Winters's last and most successful book devoted entirely to experimental forms. It is divided into three sections. The first, called "Upper River Country: Rio Grande," consists of twelve poems, each describing a month of the year; together, they are emblematic of the poet's progress through life, the poet growing more sensitive to the beauty and brutality around him and more aware of the meaninglessness of life and the inevitability of death. The second, called "The Bare Hills," consists of seven groups of three, four, or five poems each; it tells of the poet surrounded by death and cruelty but trying to learn, feeling inadequate to his task of creation, lacking an audience: He has but "this cold eye for the fact; that keeps me/ quiet, walking toward a/ stinging end: I am alone. . . ." The third section, called "The Passing Night," consists of two prose poems describing a bleak landscape of endless cold, a minimal level of existence, almost void of hope; the poet waits and remembers and observes, and that is all.

In many of these poems, Winters is continuing to experiment with the evocative image. For example, here is the third of four stanzas from one of the finest poems in this collection, "The Upper Meadows":

> Apricots
> The clustered
> Fur of bees
> Above the gray rocks of the uplands.

Out of context, the images seem vivid, perhaps, but randomly juxtaposed; in context, which has been describing the dying leaves at the advent of autumn, the transience of these living beings—apricots and bees—is felt, reinforced by the final stanza, ending with this line: "But motion, aging." The landscape evoked in the poem is beautiful, vibrantly alive, and dying. In an early review of *The Bare Hills*, Agnes Lee Freer called it "a book inspiring in its absolute originality."

THE PROOF

The Proof exhibits the transition from experimental to traditional forms. The first half of the volume consists of poems in the Imagistic/free-verse manner of his early work; the second half contains several sonnets and a few poems in various traditional stanzaic patterns. Winters himself has said, "It was becoming increasingly obvious to me that the poets whom I most admired were Baudelaire and Valéry, and Hardy, Bridges, and Stevens in a few poems each, and that I could never hope to approach the quality of their work by the method which I was using." He had come to believe that, in poems of firm metrical pattern, more precise and hence more expressive rhythmical and aural effects were possible, the result being the communication of greater complexity of feeling. He adhered to this belief for the rest of his life.

"The Fable," originally a blank-verse sonnet but reduced to ten lines in the *Collected Poems*, is illustrative. After describing the sea, which "Gathers and washes and is gone," he writes:

> But the crossed rock braces the hills and makes
> A steady quiet of the steady music,
> Massive with peace
>   And listen, now:
> The foam receding down the sand silvers
> Between the grains, thin, pure as virgin words,
> Lending a sheen to Nothing, whispering.

The sea is the wilderness surrounding us, emblematic of the empty universe and, in its ceaseless motion and ominous quiet, the process of dying. In the first line of this passage, the reversed feet in the first and third positions are metrical irregularities that, by contrast, emphasize the slow evenness of the next two lines, an evenness that recalls the quiet heaving of the sea itself. The sibilant sounds in the fourth line quoted are also descriptively accurate and metaphysically charged: The sound of the sea washing through the sand is the voice of the emptiness itself, of "Nothing, whispering."

THE JOURNEY, AND OTHER POEMS

His next volume, *The Journey, and Other Poems*, consists of eight poems in heroic couplets. The first, "The Critiad," his longest poem, is an attempt to create satirical portraits in the manner of Alexander Pope; Winters chose to preserve neither it nor the last poem, "December Eclogue," in his collected works. The other six poems, most of them longer than his usual efforts, are among his most original, for they put the heroic couplet to new uses. "The Journey" through Snake River Country, for example, describes in forty-four lines a train trip at night through Wyoming and arrival at a destination in the morning. On a descriptive level, the poem is detailed and exact. On a symbolic level, it depicts a journey through hell, at the end of which the poet emerges intact from his spiritual trial. The following lines describe the poet's sudden awareness of the brutal and meaningless wilderness, the landscape of despair:

> Once when the train paused in an empty place,
> I met the unmoved landscape face to face;
> Smoothing abysses that no stream could slake,
> Deep in its black gulch crept the heavy Snake,
> The sound diffused, and so intently firm,
> It seemed the silence, having change nor term.

The poet has been describing the violence and squalor of life in the towns the train has passed through, and now he contemplates the empty landscape that harbors those towns. Descriptively, the language is very exact: The abysses are "Smoothing"—that is, being smoothed and stretching for endless distances—because of the river's ceaseless motion; the river's sound is diffused but also there, inevitably, forever, having neither change nor termination. One finds again the motion/stasis paradox, which here is also a sound/silence paradox. In this quiet scene, decay is alive and busy; the river is the Snake, evil, eternal, obliterating all "Deep in its black gulch." Iambic pentameter couplets have not been used in this way before.

BEFORE DISASTER

The next volume, *Before Disaster*, is a miscellaneous collection of poems in traditional forms: quatrains of three, four, or five feet; some sonnets; and a few poems in rhymed couplets of varying line lengths. The subject matter is equally various: personal, as in "To My Infant Daughter" and "For My Father's Grave"; mythological, as in "Midas," "Orpheus," and "Chiron"; occasional, as in "Elegy on a Young Airedale Bitch Lost Some Years Since in the Salt-Marsh," "The Anniversary," "On the Death of Senator Thomas J. Walsh," "Dedication for a Book of Criticism," and so on. Here is the final stanza from a poem in the plain style called "To a Young Writer":

> Write little; do it well.
> Your knowledge will be such,
> At last, as to dispel
> What moves you overmuch.

Nothing could be plainer or seem simpler, but what is conveyed is a weighty sense of classical restraint and control, the power of realized truth.

COLLECTED POEMS

All the collections that follow are republications of old work, supplemented with either some new work or old work never before published in a book. The 1960 revision of his *Collected Poems*, however, represents something more than merely a new grouping. Even though it is a selection, hence incomplete, it arranges in chronological order the poetry Winters wished to keep, beginning with four poems from *The Immobile Wind* and ending with his last poems, "At the San Francisco Airport" and "Two Old-Fashioned Songs." Thus,

it is a record of Winters's poetic life. The poems it contains are meditations on a wide variety of subjects: on the greatness of historical heroes, such as Socrates, Herman Melville, John Sutter, and John Day; on the greatness of legendary heroes, such as Theseus, Sir Gawaine, and Hercules; on the evil that people do, as in the poems that deal with World War II; on the vast beauty of the world, in such things as an orchard, a dirigible, California wine, the ancient manzanita, a Renaissance portrait, "summer grasses brown with heat," the "soft voice of the nesting dove," and so on; and on the ever-encroaching wilderness and people's proximity to death: "Ceaseless, the dead leaves gather, mound on mound." The book is a reflection of a great mind, one at every moment intellectually alive as well as hypersensitive to physical reality. To read it is to partake of the richness, the depths of Winters's inner life. Because the poems exhibit the three very different methods Winters perfected—free verse, traditional plain style, and post-Symbolist imagery—to read the book is to understand something of poetry as an art. If Winters's belief in the power of literature to alter one's being is true, it is to change for the better as well.

OTHER MAJOR WORKS

SHORT FICTION: "The Brink of Darkness," 1932, 1947.

NONFICTION: *Primitivism and Decadence: A Study of American Experimental Poetry*, 1937; *Maule's Curse: Seven Studies in the History of American Obscurantism*, 1938; *The Anatomy of Nonsense*, 1943; *Edwin Arlington Robinson*, 1946; *In Defense of Reason*, 1947; *The Function of Criticism: Problems and Exercises*, 1957; *On Modern Poets*, 1957; *The Poetry of W. B. Yeats*, 1960; *Forms of Discovery: Critical and Historical Essays on the Forms of the Short Poem in English*, 1967; *Uncollected Essays and Reviews*, 1973 (Francis Murphy, editor); *Hart Crane and Yvor Winters: Their Literary Correspondence*, 1978; *The Selected Letters of Yvor Winters*, 2000 (R. L. Barth, editor).

EDITED TEXTS: *Twelve Poets of the Pacific*, 1937; *Selected Poems*, 1948 (by Elizabeth Daryush); *Poets of the Pacific*, 1949 (second series).

BIBLIOGRAPHY

Gelpi, Albert. "Yvor Winters and Robinson Jeffers." In *A Coherent Splendor*. New York: Cambridge University Press, 1987. Gelpi notes that Winters's early poems belie his critical precepts. They display the strong influence of Ezra Pound and William Carlos Williams, despite Winters's furious anti-Romantic denigration of both poets in his criticism. Winters strongly identified with the California landscape, as can be seen in *The Magpie's Shadow*.

Gunn, Thom. "On a Drying Hill." In *The Occasions of Poetry*. San Francisco: North Point Press, 1985. Gunn was a student of Winters at Stanford University. He describes Winters's strong personality and his efforts to convert his students to his critical principles. Foremost among these was the rejection of Romantic poetry.

Hoffpauir, Richard. *The Contemplative Poetry of Edwin Arlington Robinson, Robert Frost, and Yvor Winters*. Lewiston, N.Y.: Edwin Mellen Press, 2002. Hoffpauir compares and contrasts the poetry of Winters, Edward Arlington Robinson, and Robert Frost, concentrating on what Winters terms "contemplative poetry."

Kaye, Howard. "The Post-Symbolist Poetry of Yvor Winters." *Southern Review* 7, no. 1 (Winter, 1971): 176-197. Winters's poetry strongly evokes landscape. His ability to portray the external world in a precise manner was remarkable. In Kaye's view, Winters counts as one of the great twentieth century poets. His stress upon rationality and control reflects a fear of being overwhelmed by death and strong emotion. Winters's struggle with his emotions is a leitmotif of his poetry. He attempted to extirpate his own Romantic tendencies.

Rexroth, Kenneth. *American Poetry in the Twentieth Century*. New York: Herder, 1971. Rexroth contends that Winters was the true exile of his generation of writers. Most of his friends went to Paris, but health problems forced Winters to live in a dry climate. His move to Northern California kept him isolated, and his criticism became cranky and cliquish. He was an important poet who created an original variant of neoclassicism.

Wellek, René. "Yvor Winters." In *A History of Modern Criticism: American Criticism, 1900-1950*. Vol. 6. New Haven, Conn.: Yale University Press, 1986. Wellek gives a careful summary of the principles that underlie Winters's poetry and criticism. A poem should express a moral judgment. The judgment, based on absolute moral values, is ideally incapable of being paraphrased. Winters deprecated the expression of emotion not under the strict dominance of reason.

Winters, Yvor. *The Selected Letters of Yvor Winters*. Edited by R. L. Barth. Athens: Ohio University Press, 2000. Selected correspondence offering insights into the life of a brilliant man, erudite writer, and lofty poet. Includes bibliographical references and indexes.

Joseph Maltby

DAVID WOJAHN

Born: St. Paul, Minnesota; August 22, 1953

PRINCIPAL POETRY

Icehouse Lights, 1982
Glassworks, 1987
Mystery Train, 1990
Late Empire, 1994
The Falling Hour, 1997
Spirit Cabinet, 2002
Interrogation Palace: New and Selected Poems, 1982-2004, 2006

OTHER LITERARY FORMS

Although David Wojahn (WOH-jahn) is primarily a poet, he edited *The Pushcart Prize XI: Best of the Small Presses* (1986), along with Bill Henderson and Philip Levine, and with Jack Myers, a comprehensive anthology of contemporary poetry, *A Profile of Twentieth Century American Poetry* (1991). He edited two posthumous collections of poetry by his wife, Lynda Hull, *The Only World* (1995) and *Collected Poems* (2006). He wrote *Strange Good Fortune: Essays on Contemporary Poetry* (2000).

ACHIEVEMENTS

David Wojahn merited success early in his career. Richard Hugo selected Wojahn's first collection, *Icehouse Lights*, for publication in the Yale Series of Younger Poets. Wojahn received the William Carlos Williams Award from the Poetry Society of America for *Icehouse Lights*, the Society of Midland Authors' Award (1987) for *Glassworks*, the Celia B. Wagner Award from the Poetry Society of America, the George Kent Memorial Prize from *Poetry* magazine, the O. B. Hardison, Jr., Poetry Prize from the Folger Shakespeare Library (2007), and the Carole Weinstein Prize in Poetry (2008), a $10,000 annual award that recognizes poets with strong ties to Central Virginia who have contributed significantly to the art of poetry. In 2007, *Interrogation Palace* was a finalist for the Pulitzer Prize in poetry and was the sole finalist in the competition to receive the Lenore Marshall Poetry Prize given by the Academy of American Poets. His poems have appeared in *Georgia Review*, *The New Yorker*, *American Poetry Review*, *Antioch Review*, and many other magazines and journals.

From 1987 to 1988, he was the Amy Lowell Poetry Traveling Scholar. He has earned several major fellowships, including awards from the National Endowment for the Arts, the Fine Arts Work Center in Provincetown, Massachusetts, and the John Simon Guggenheim Foundation. The State Council of Higher Education for Virginia and the Dominion Foundation named Wojahn as one of twelve recipients of the 2009 Outstanding Faculty Award. Wojahn also received Virginia Commonwealth University's Distinguished Scholarship Award in 2009. Wojahn has regularly been invited to judge regional and national poetry competitions. Since 2003, he has served on the advisory board for the literary quarterly *Hunger Mountain* and as contributing editor for the Pushcart Prize series.

BIOGRAPHY

David Charles Wojahn was born and raised in St. Paul, Minnesota. His father, R. C. Wojahn, was employed by the Great Northern Railroad, on the Fargo-Minot-Whitefish run. Virginia Wojahn, his mother, was a bookkeeper for General Tire and Northwest Bank. Wojahn earned his bachelor of arts degree at the University of Minnesota, Twin Cities, in 1977, and his master of fine arts degree at the University of Arizona in 1980. He was married to the poet Lynda Hull from 1984 to 1994, when she died in a car accident.

Wojahn has taught at the University of New Orleans, the University of Arkansas at Little Rock, the University of Houston, and Indiana University, where he became the Lilly Professor of English. In 2003, he became professor of English and director of creative writing at Virginia Commonwealth University. He has also been a member of the faculty of the master in fine arts in writing program of the Vermont College of the Fine Arts.

ANALYSIS

David Wojahn's poetry weaves personal biography with events that extend to the outside world. Consequently, his poetry is not a self-contained body of work that seeks its own reference; rather, each poem finds itself within cultural patterns that confront the speaker. Often, these poems speak of loss and longing. What comfort the poet receives comes from processing his feelings through writing. Several poems illustrate the healing that comes from the artist's search for meaning and closure. His poems question the ultimate meaning of life in light of human tragedies and of war, madness, and death. His struggle to understand the inevitable outcome and ultimately to make peace with himself empowers these poems.

GLASSWORKS

Glassworks features poems about real people—the poet's friends and family—embedded in a gentle narrative line that does not overwhelm the poem; rather, its flow allows each character to come forth, very human, very alive. "Satin Doll" uses a reference to big band music to explore the world of an aunt whose marriage failed. Looking at her sepia photo taken six years before he was born, the poet recalls the events of her life, which seemed to extinguish her passion. He compares her to a drowned woman, her eyes staring back at the crowd. The poet imagines his aunt growing stronger and taking control, a very tender moment. Such moments strengthen Wojahn's poetry, rendered without irony or apology.

The poet uses the stuff of his life as source material.

"Starlings" is a lovely, sad poem about a woman who stays awake worrying about the safe return of her husband, who may be drunk, and her son, who stays awake worrying about her. The form of the poem imitates the movement of the starlings—"Outside, they're waking too"—whose noise keeps his mother awake. The son says:

> I want to be
> the book she reads, before the noise
> begins to deafen us, before
> she wakes and never sleeps again.

Wojahn crafts this final stanza, weaving the poignancy of the situation with the presence of these birds without naïve sentimentality.

"Dark-House Spearing" illustrates the difficulties a father and son experience in relating to each other, finally working out safe ways of communicating. However, the father wants company, not words, because of the death of his brother, who fell into an alcoholic coma ten years earlier. The poet/son tries to re-create memories for them, memories that could potentially heal the rift between them. However, after he tells his father the created version, his father says that the details are wrong. Because the father cannot remember the last words he said to his brother, he begins to distrust words altogether.

In the "Third Language," the poet's grandfather appears as a ghostly presence who fled Germany to escape the kaiser's army. This poem considers the effect that different language systems have on the emotional ties that speakers maintain. His German-speaking grandfather lands in Boston, where he believes that his knowledge of Morse code will be useful. However, Morse code has been made obsolete by the invention of radio, and the fact that he speaks only German makes him an object of suspicion in the eyes of his neighbors.

Other poems illustrate the fragility of life and the permanence of art. "Glassworks at Saratoga" describes the death of James White. Beginning with the bizarre death of a millionaire who cut his throat when shaving aboard a train that lurched at the wrong moment, the poem takes a chilling turn at a glassworks, where the poet purchased White's book. Finding a glass fragment that reminds him of when he deliberately slashed his wrist after a woman left him, the poet recognizes himself as someone who knows loss—whether that loss is permanent (death) or holds the possibility of recovery (the end of a significant relationship)—then affirms his own desire to live. These lines are poetry from the inside.

The pain of loss is central to the next two poems. "Lot's Wife" gives voice to the woman who was turned into a pillar of salt because she looked back at the destruction of Sodom, a biblical rendering of the mythical Orpheus-Eurydice story. The poet allows the wife to discuss her relationship with Lot, who would have saved her. Wondering whom Lot has become, she realizes that she has lost her very self to a husband who can see only what he believes that God has saved. Consequently, both lose. The husband loses his wife; the wife ultimately loses her selfhood.

Likewise, "Steam" examines the nature of loss, but without the protective cover of myth. The poet addresses his lover, expounding on the tension between what he needs from her and what she can give. Dark poignancy of deep pain evolves in these lines, as the reader becomes an intruder listening to the private conversation of two people who have lost the ability to talk to each other. The speaker seeks mutual healing through a renewal of trust but feels helpless when in her sleep she cries out the name of someone else, someone who has hurt her.

The way the poet handles very painful occurrences, whether his or someone else's experiences, brings the reader into that world. These poems do not vampirize pain; instead, they are the poet's attempts to make whatever sense is possible of such experiences.

MYSTERY TRAIN

A thirty-five-section sequence exploring rock and roll highlights, *Mystery Train* presents a cross-cultural experience of contemporary popular music. Wojahn relates the musicians to poetry and to news events, enhancing situations creatively while maintaining an emotional accuracy.

In Jim Elledge's *Sweet Nothings: An Anthology of Rock and Roll in American Poetry* (1994), Wojahn describes his attraction to this material, noting his avid listening and collecting. Most of the poems in this section are sonnets, whose form the poet has artistically explored. One such poem is "W. C. W. Watching Presley's Second Appearance on the 'Ed Sullivan Show': Mercy Hospital, Newark, 1956." While the line breaks and stanzaic pattern are similar to a William Carlos Williams poem, the poem is a sonnet, using couplets:

> The tube,
>   like the sonnet,
>   is a fascist form.
> I read they refused
>   to show this kid's
>   wriggling bum.

Using the sonnet, Wojahn suggests the conservative culture that looked askance at rock and roll, and from which the music liberated itself. Creative tension between that culture and the music itself is embodied in the liberties that Wojahn takes with the sonnet form, as if using a received form constituted an act of aesthetic rebellion as complex and concrete as the music of which he writes. These poems do not glamorize the destructive aspects of the lives of these musicians, nor do they take a one-sided view of the cultural assumptions against which the musicians struggled. While the poems celebrate the music, an air of sadness ultimately prevails within and between the lines.

Other poems return to the familiar topics that Wojahn explores. In "Armageddon: Private Gabriel Calvin Wojahn, 1900-18," the poet addresses a relative killed during World War I, buried in a paper shroud used during the war to conserve cloth and timber. The poet gives his relative ecstatic visions of his own death, raised among "God-mad zealots/ Who . . . kept all books but the Bible from your sight." Illiterate, the man dictated letters home to his commandant, then signed them with his thumbprint. The poem's conclusion disallows for the easy solace found in fanatic visions: "Above the mass grave, a chaplain muttered scripture./ What survives of you? Neither words nor paper." In the end, Wojahn's poems challenge the reader, and the poet himself, to engage fully in life's mystery in such a way that no answers come easy.

LATE EMPIRE

Perhaps the darkest of Wojahn's collections, *Late Empire* contains many ideas and concerns that he continues from earlier volumes. However, there is no at-

tempt to mollify their effects, either on himself or on the reader. No mask protects the reader from the insights of these poems, which are raw in their emotional energy. They speak of the end of the world as the poet knows it, not of the physical world accessible to anyone, but the destruction that comes through psychic turmoil.

The sonnet series "Wartime Photos of My Father" considers the poet's father's need for electroshock treatments, with his subsequent need for Thorazine. The reader profoundly experiences the father's mind. Because of these invasive treatments, the reader is caught between the father's sense of reality and delusion; struggle is very real in these poems. Again, the sonnet emphasizes the regularity of stanzaic demands compared to the mental shattering that the poet's father, and the poet as well, experience:

> Words to describe him: stranger, cipher, father.
> The son invents a cruelty, a hurt
> From years before the son was born—a unit
> For measuring distance, the white noise that shimmers
> Between our stuttering conversations,
> Two men who cannot talk or touch.

At one point, for example, the father tells a story about the tormenting of a German prisoner of war, in order to explain the grisly humor of a photograph, only to say that the event never happened. The sonnet effectively contrasts the disruption of war and its lasting aftermath with the regularity of a form that usually speaks of love.

Several poems concentrate on circumstances external to the poet's family. "Tomis" recounts the disappearance in Latin America of a woman's daughter, who had become active in political demonstrations. Her body was later found, reduced to bones. Other poems recount the destruction of a religious cult, similar to Jonestown, formed around a charismatic but crazy woman. Other poems speak of the impending destruction of Earth through disasters caused by people, such as the 1986 nuclear accident at Chernobyl. Wojahn handles these situations by keeping the reader drawn into the poems, not allowing either his rhetoric or his narration to overcome the general experience.

The Falling Hour

The creative intelligence that informs the poems in *The Falling Hour* is characteristic of Wojahn's style. While continuing to evoke familiar themes, his work explores new territory as well. "Rajah in Babylon" begins with the description of a tiger who, anesthetized, will be a sperm donor. Noelle, the poet's wife, must get a good shot with the tranquilizer gun. Touching the sleeping tiger who is "one four-thousandth of the world's tigers," the poet realizes complexity of the ties between life and death, how easily sundered they are, how varied and strange:

> I touch the ribs, the whorled sleeping flank,
> stutter of heartbeat, . . .
>
> *and there we wailed as we/ remembered Zion.*
> And slowly the liquid pearls in the flask, churn.

With allusions to the book of Psalms, the poet William Blake, and musician Jimmy Cliff, Wojahn continues to mingle different cultural references as commentary.

One of the most beautiful poems in this collection, "God of Journeys and Secret Tidings," is a sonnet that speaks of the death of Wojahn's first wife, Lynda Hull. The restraint that the sonnet as poetic form requires is juxtaposed against the emotional power of the circumstances:

> And how, indeed, could such beauty be borne,
> except by the shoulders of a god? Here on the dome
> of hell it rains, and you are six months' dead.
> The answering machine tonight spins down—
>
> . . . .
> . . . And on them is your voice.

The poet acknowledges the powerful effect that words can have. For Wojahn as poet, words seem possessed of mythic, holy qualities. He writes as if he were a word-shaman, able at will to summon those powers.

Spirit Cabinet

Spirit Cabinet is the name the Shakers give to a portal through which otherworldly voices can speak. The collection is divided into three parts. The first section draws on once-living poets, writers, and musicians for inspiration: French writer Emile Zola ("Zola the Hobbyist, 1895"), Russian figurehead Joseph Stalin ("Stalin's Library Card"), the writer Hart Crane ("For the Centenary of Hart Crane,") and country-folk music singer-songwriter, performer, and poet Townes Van Zandt ("For Townes Van Zandt, 1946-1997). Wojahn admits on Stephen Reichert's online forum to often finding himself "focusing on moments of crisis or traumatic events because," he says, "those events tend to focus and allegorize injustice, bring it into high relief, both in terms of the poems' ideology and of its craft." Poems of this kind include the 1995 massacre at Tasmania's Port Arthur historical site ("To the Memory of Paul Celan") and, to some extent, "Crayola: A Sequence," which is principally autobiographical. In the section of "Crayola" entitled "Recollection Including a Textbook Quotation," he writes:

> Turbaned, bathrobed, she shuffled in, "agitated"
> ◆
> (my mother's term) no more. The operation
>   **prone to temper tantrums**
>   **& willfulness before**
> had seen to that, bruise on her forehead
>   ◆
> tiny as a shaving nick. The visiting room—ceiling fan
>   ◆
>   **the animal seemed to become**
>   **almost cheery after**
> hissing shadows on the mah-jongg tiles. They'd changed
>   ◆
> her mind for good. Cousin Beatrice. . . .

"Dirge with Proofs" has as its orator a single speaker, who, according to Wojahn on Reichert's online forum, is "someone who is more or less me." The poem is influenced by American confessional poet John Berryman, who mastered the technique of veering between formal and colloquial diction:

> Kerosene & cowshit & a rented truck, heavy-laden
>   ◆
> & we have "a low-order explosive device."
>   ◆
> Remote engaged. Radio waves, surfing to detonation.
>   ◆
> Pockmarked sky, the color of a bruise,
>   ◆
> then recoil, the building's trepanned north side.

The symbols punctuating the poem create an ambiguity of voice, making it unclear whether there is a single orator or more than one subject and speaker. The observations themselves emphasize this ambiguity through the language used in various lines. Like many of Wojahn's oratory voices, the voices in this poem are sometimes colloquial and sometimes formal, but always highly evocative.

INTERROGATION PALACE

Interrogation Palace is organized into seven parts, or "books," each representing a chapter in the development of Wojahn's poetic oeuvre spanning twenty-two years. The title poem, "Interrogation Palace," creates an image of the genuine Spanish building where members of the fascist military undertook interrogations. The collection features new poems as well as works found in Wojahn's other collections. The new poems in the section "For the Poltergeists: New Poems" evidence how key figures and personalities have continually influenced and inspired Wojahn's work. "Radnóti in a Trench Coat" has as its inspiration the Hungarian poet and translator Miklós Radnóti, considered one of the most important Hungarian poets of the twentieth century. "Homage to Blind Willie Johnson" pays tribute to American blues singer and guitarist Blind Willie Johnson in a poem blurring the lines between autobiography and an homage to the popular culture of blues:

Past cylinder disk & quarter note, past undulating neon
& a primitive mike in a Dallas hotel, 3 December 1927,
A back-up band of foot stomp & the engineer coughing,

Blind Willie Johnson is flying.
On the Voyager Spacecraft he is flying,
With a Brandenburg concerto & Olivier

Intoning Hamlet, with the symbol for pi
He is flying, message in a bleeping whirring bottle
Hurled skyward for the delectation

Other new poems such as "Board Book and the Costume of a Whooping Crane," and "Dithyramb and Lamentation" highlight Wojahn's frustration at President George W. Bush. In "Board Book and the Costume of a Whooping Crane," Wojahn observes that:

The President's rodent eye pulses out from CNN,
    darting & glazed,
        squinting for the next thing

to lift to the mouth, for he must eat & eat. . . .

Wojahn also evidences his aggravation and dissatisfaction at President Bush in the "Exam Room Six" section of "Dithyramb and Lamentation": "on a Bush campaign ad,/Air Force One soaring down from clouds/Like the opening of *Triumph of the Will*, the ferret face in slow dissolve."

Further, Wojahn prefaces a section of "Dithyramb and Lamentation" entitled "George W. Bush in Hell" with a canto from Dante's *Inferno* (in *La divina commedia*, c. 1320; *The Divine Comedy*, 1802). Dante and Virgil encounter Bush, forever entombed in a ball of fire. It is clear in this poem that juxtaposition functions as an important formal element in Wojahn's poetry.

In an interview with Anna Journey, Wojahn notes that Greek poet and activist Yiannis Ritsos calls poems "meeting places," and argues that spatial metaphors and images from high and popular culture can combine and intermingle in poems. The juxtaposition of apparently unlike images, claims Wojahn, can make for some very fortuitous meetings.

OTHER MAJOR WORKS

NONFICTION: *Strange Good Fortune: Essays on Contemporary Poets*, 2000.

EDITED TEXTS: *The Pushcart Prize XI: Best of the Small Presses*, 1986 (with Bill Henderson and Philip Levine); *A Profile of Twentieth Century American Poetry*, 1991 (with Jack Myers); *The Only World*, 1995 (by Lynda Hull); *Collected Poems*, 2006 (by Hull).

BIBLIOGRAPHY

Elledge, Jim, ed. *Sweet Nothings: An Anthology of Rock and Roll in American Poetry*. Bloomington: Indiana University Press, 1994. This anthology presents a collection of poems that use rock and roll as source material. Elledge includes Wojahn's comments about the poems collected here. Included are "Buddy Holly" (*Icehouse Lights*), "Song of the Burning" (*Glassworks*), and "W. C. W. Watching

Presley's Second Appearance on 'The Ed Sullivan Show'" (*Mystery Train*).

Jauss, David. "To Become Music or Break: Lynda Hull as an Undergraduate." *Crazyhorse* 55 (Winter, 1998). A poignant essay discussing the poetry of Lynda Hull, Wojahn's deceased wife. Written by one of her teachers, the essay discusses Wojahn's influence on her poetry. Both men were her instructors at the University of Arkansas at Little Rock.

Rogoff, Jay. "Better Poetry Through Chemistry." Review of *Interrogation Palace*. *Southern Review* 43, no. 2 (Spring, 2007): 451-462. Refers to an essay by T. S. Eliot in his description of Wojahn's ability to combine disparate narratives in his poetry. Traces the poet's development through his collections, with reference to this technique.

Stein, Kevin. "Manipulating Cultural Assumptions: Transgressions and Obedience in David Wojahn's Rock 'n' Roll Sonnets." In *Private Poets, Worldly Acts*. Athens: Ohio University Press, 1997. Presents a cogent analysis of Wojahn's use of rock and roll, especially how he deals with the cultural assumptions against which the poems work.

Wojahn, David. "How Do You Bottle the Lightning?" Interview by Anna Journey. *Gulf Coast: A Journal of Literature and Fine Arts* 22, no. 1 (Winter/Spring, 2010). An in-depth and very informative interview with Wojahn conducted at Wojahn's home in July, 2008.

_____. "'If You Have to Be Sure Don't Write': Poetry and Self-Doubt." In *Words Overflown by Stars: Creative Writing Instruction and Insight from the Vermont College of Fine Arts M.F.A. Program*, edited by David Jauss. Cincinnati, Ohio: Writers Digest Books, 2009. In an essay designed for writers, Wojahn discusses the composition of poetry and the necessary mind-set.

_____. "An Interview with David Wojahn." Interview by Jonathan Veitch. *Contemporary Literature* 36, no. 3 (Fall, 1995): 393-411. Wojahn comments on the influences that have shaped his poems. He notes his love for poets such as James Wright and Richard Hugo and his interest in family history, especially the way the mind works to remember events and details.

Martha Modena Vertreace-Doody
Updated by Nicole Anae

BARON WORMSER

Born: Baltimore, Maryland; February 4, 1948

PRINCIPAL POETRY

The White Words, 1983
Good Trembling, 1985
Atoms, Soul Music, and Other Poems, 1989
When, 1997
Mulroney and Others: Poems, 2000
Subject Matter: Poems, 2003
Carthage, 2005
Scattered Chapters: New and Selected Poems, 2008

OTHER LITERARY FORMS

Baron Wormser (WURM-sur) has written essays and book reviews for various literary magazines. Two important book reviews, extensive analyses of the works of Polish poets Adam Zagajewski and Czesław Miłosz, reveal Wormser's extraordinary knowledge of Western poetry, history, and culture. He has published essays concerning William Blake, the spirit of poetry in a democracy, and the necessity of religious poetry in our time. In 2000, he melded his vast wisdom about poetry with his love of teaching into a book, written with David Cappella, titled *Teaching the Art of Poetry: The Moves*. His memoir of his years in rural Maine, *The Road Washes Out in Spring: A Poet's Memoir of Living Off The Grid*, appeared in 2006. Wormser published *The Poetry Life: Ten Stories* (2008), a book of ten short fictional narratives about poets from Blake in the eighteenth century to Sylvia Plath and Joe Bolton in the late twentieth century and how their work figured in the lives of imagined characters. The range of poets addressed—from formalists such as Weldon Kees to Beat poets such as Gregory Corso—helps Wormser imagine the significance of poetry in people's personal triumphs and struggles. *The Poetry Life* is vital for understanding Wormser's vision of what poetry is and can be.

ACHIEVEMENTS

Baron Wormser started gaining critical stature in the 1980's and 1990's, as evidenced by the honors he accrued during these decades. In 1982, he won the Frederick Bock Prize from *Poetry* magazine, and in 1996, he won the Kathryn A. Morton Prize in Poetry. In 2000, he was appointed Maine's poet laureate, a position in which he served until 2005. He also received fellowships from the National Endowment for the Arts and the John Guggenheim Memorial Foundation. His poems, reviews, and essays have appeared in literary magazines such as *Paris Review*, *Sewanee Review*, *Harper's*, *The New Republic*, and *Poetry*.

BIOGRAPHY

Born and reared in Baltimore, Baron Wormser grew up enjoying the city's rich ethnic diversity. He attended Baltimore City College, then a citywide public boys' school located near Memorial Stadium. In 1970, he was graduated from The Johns Hopkins University. He was married to Janet Garbose in 1969 in Brookline, Massachusetts. He briefly pursued graduate study at the University of California, Irvine, and the University of Maine. Toward the end of 1970, he and his wife chose rural living, homesteading on a one-hundred-acre parcel at the end of an old logging road in Mercer, Maine. There they reared a daughter, Maisie, and a son, Owen. In 1972, Wormser began work as the librarian of School Administrative District 54 in Madison, Maine, a mill town approximately twenty-five miles from his home. Wormser's living in a house with no electricity and no indoor plumbing reflects not only his deep commitment to the natural world but also his serious endeavor to live as much of a life of the spirit as is possible in contemporary America and his determination to renounce as far as possible the distractions of sophisticated life and the pretensions of the urban elite. Although Wormser left Maine in 1998 to live in Cabot, Vermont, he still remains strongly rooted in a rural and regional identity. However, his poems are not particularly

in a local-color mode and possess a discursive quality that gives them a broad interrelation with poetry in English worldwide and through the centuries. Wormser's public and civic emphasis precludes his being a poet merely of his own region, and he does not write exclusively autobiographical or observational poetry.

While maintaining an active writing life and working as a high school librarian, Wormser began to teach creative writing to high school students and discovered his gift for teaching. From the late 1980's onward, Wormser was busy teaching the writing of poetry at the University of Maine at Farmington, serving in 2000 as a visiting professor at the University of South Dakota, and conducting workshops and seminars at the Frost Place in Franconia, New Hampshire. Wormser continues to lecture frequently in New England and in selected national and international venues. His poetry has gained new exposure through the determined championship of Philip Fried, editor of the *Manhattan Review*, who has been a persistent advocate of Wormser's work

Baron Wormser (©John Suiter)

and has placed it in a world context. From 2000 to 2005, he served as Maine's poet laureate, even though at that point he no longer lived in the state. He has directed the Frost Place Conference on poetry and teaching in Franconia Notch, new Hampshire. He began teaching at the Stonecoast master of fine arts in writing program in 2002 and the Fairfield University master of fine arts program in 2009.

Analysis

Baron Wormser's poetry offers a deeply sympathetic look at what it means to be human. His distinctive voice, intelligent observations of the particulars of existence, and sense of humor blend with superior technical skill to reveal the strange complexities that underlie people's actions. Addressing a broad range of topics in his poetry, Wormser brings a heightened awareness of life's predicaments by tackling its large truths, revealing what humans share as they live.

Wormser's poetry seems to represent a departure for American poetry. His intellectualism clearly reveals a multifaceted vision of the world; however, for him, intellect is not distant and cool, rather it is a passion, a mode of apprehending reality. His technical skill formalizes these glimpses of humanity. Wormser is an American poet with a sensibility that elevates his subject matter into a larger context. His imagination blends an eye for the obvious with intellectual perceptions about culture and civilization to create extraordinary insights into why people are the way they are. In this sense, Wormser's sensibility is quite distinguishable from that of his contemporaries and more akin to that of poets of Central and Eastern Europe such as Zagajewski, Miłosz, or Jaan Kaplinski.

Considered as a whole, Wormser's work epitomizes the idea of poetry as aspiring toward the status of a spiritual gift. It is a poetry of exuberance, alive with the wonder of being, and filled with a deep knowledge of the world. Beauty manifests itself in the daily drama enacted by the individual, replete with obvious experience and natural emotion. This celebration of the commonality of life's rich pageant reveals the essentially religious nature of Wormser's poetry. It is poetry that teaches the reader about human existence by articulating its source—the soul.

The White Words

In *The White Words*, the tension and irony created as the sublime rubs constantly against the everyday demonstrate the supreme beauty of life. It is people that act out this drama. "Passing Significance," taking place in the sitting room of an inn, brings travelers together, each involved in his own interior world. Some read, some write, the innkeeper's wife worries about who is going to pay, a baby cries, a woman quietly sings, and a clerk rustles a newspaper. Even a dog sighs. The chief assessor, however, barges into the room, stamping snow off his boots, and decides immediately that there is "no one of importance here." Such is not the case. The poem informs the reader that each of these people in the sitting room is significant, and that a special state of mind must inhere within an individual for him or her to understand this simple yet complex fact of life. Fittingly, the poem ends with an epigrammatic lesson: "To study other people/ You must be free and easy and remember nothing."

Wormser's poetry is a poetry of nuance; it sees through the obviousness of how people live. This quality is well exemplified in "Of Small Towns." Here the poet describes the mundane lives of the citizens of a small town, elevating them by revealing the nature of their humanity. In doing so, he dignifies not only the purpose of their lives but also the purpose of their town, showing how it ennobles the lives of its people. Ultimately, the town is its people, and vice versa.

What is distinctive about Wormser's poetry is this ability to exalt human experience, employing both the intellect and the imagination. While the heart and soul of New England gently seep into almost every one of Wormser's poems, his insights transcend place. For example, in "Cord of Birch," a typically New England problem becomes a quest. After cutting some birch, the narrator decides to ask around the neighborhood about how well birch burns. After seeking out and listening to various contradictory opinions, he wanders home, pouting and disgruntled about his pile of wood. Eventually, it is winter that frees him of his worries. He burns the birch because he has no choice: Need lends him wisdom. Wormser accomplishes this progression from the exterior to the interior, from summer to winter, through the use of tightly controlled rhyming couplets.

In "Letter from New England," an odd moment during a midwinter funeral and a comment by the narrator's daughter inspire a realization of what an image can conjure, of what it means for an individual even to be aware of an image. "Beech Trees," a meditation on human nature, not only addresses the fact that stingy beech leaves refuse to fall even in the dead of winter but also uses the image of their dangling on a sapling in January to initiate a rumination about the lingering as well as the ending of things—a rumination that concludes with the revelatory notion that people and leaves are not all that different.

Wormser's poetry is more than regional. Throughout *The White Words*, his wide-ranging intellect is brought to bear on political, social, philosophical, historical, and literary themes. Such themes emerge from specific contexts. In "Some Recollections Concerning the Exiled Revolutionary, Leon Trotsky," the poet sees Trotsky and even imagines his voice. Through the man's thinking, he elaborates on the essence of politics, providing a glimpse of what it means to be exiled and to be a revolutionary.

A poem such as "Report on the Victorians" displays Wormser's extensive knowledge of history and social mores. In a sharp narrative flow, anchored by a well-choreographed rhyme scheme, Wormser investigates the sensibility of Victorianism. For him, what is essential is how Victorians saw, felt, and responded to their times. Their manners, their prejudices, and their hopes and dreams interest him. In their customs and intellectual sensibilities, Wormser perceives an inherent archetype within humanity that is composed of a duality, in this case fiendishness and hope, each element of which is found within the other. This archetype is an indelible part of human nature that connects all eras.

Wormser also tackles the philosophical. His formal and intellectual approach to a subject, which is very European, separates him from most of his contemporaries. The finely woven sonnet titled "Hegel and Co." is an example of Wormser's gift for shaping substantive material and filtering it through his imaginative lens so that the reader freshly perceives Georg Wilhelm Friedrich Hegel's awareness of his intellectual climate. Wormser seeks to re-create within the reader's mind the internal workings of the philosopher. Similarly,

"Henry James," which ues a formal stanza, ponders the novelist's milieu.

Wormser is very much a poet of the human environment. Setting and circumstance provide him with particular images that in turn allow him to probe the emotional domain. "Piano Lessons" is the quintessential example of how Wormser uses quotidian human activity to elicit a profound sympathy for and a deep understanding of the human predicament. Here the pathos of a young boy who cannot play the piano and of his teacher who cannot escape her lonely situation manifests itself in the last couplet, when, as the boy recalls, teacher and student "walked into the room where the piano stood/ For all that we wanted to do yet never would."

GOOD TREMBLING

With his second volume, *Good Trembling*, Wormser extends this sympathy for being human by fusing it with a larger cultural relevance. His brief statement "Words to the Reader" implicitly conveys a deepening concern for human conduct. His poems become paradigms of sharing, and they reveal the meaning in people's lives by allowing them to sympathize with one another. Poetry functions to lead its readers to understanding about being human.

The narrow settings of place and time within each poem of this volume widen into the larger realm of history and culture. Wormser uses the concrete in order to contemplate these broad forces that continually sweep over individuals' lives. This type of sensibility, the ability to see the universal in the particular, reveals Wormser's brilliant capacity to capture the essence of human existence. Again, such a sensibility seems more European than American. Thus, "Shards," for example, moves beyond a description of the remnants of an old homestead to become a reflection on what drives people to act the way they do.

Wormser envisions the sweep of history as a landscape shaped by the conduct of individuals. "By-Products," taking place in a stale, eerily lit Legion Hall, exposes the outcome of United States foreign policy through a legless Vietnam veteran's words and behavior. When the veteran Stan vocalizes his feelings, the force of history becomes a personal drama, not an abstraction.

In such poems as "Tutorial on the Metaphysics of

Foreign Policy," "Europe," and "The Fall of the Human Empire," Wormser turns his intellectual and philosophic gaze toward the circumstances of being American. These circumstances are viewed from various perspectives that range from musing on U.S. government policies to delineating how the remnant sensibility of Europe resides in a small New England town to using a run-over dog to symbolize how people, as individuals, fit into the scheme of civilization.

One particular poem in this volume skillfully addresses the abstract nature of history and civilization alongside the concrete nature of life at the moment when they meet head-on. "I Try to Explain to My Children a Newspaper Article Which Says That According to a Computer a Nuclear War Is Likely to Occur in the Next Twenty Years" uses the common, all-too-real situation of a parent explaining the idea of death (with a wonderful use of personification) to his children as a means to stress the higher concern of how humankind has surrendered the natural world to the vastly indifferent world of politics.

ATOMS, SOUL MUSIC, AND OTHER POEMS

Atoms, Soul Music, and Other Poems, Wormser's third collection, represents the poet at his most ambitious and most visionary. As he deftly observes contemporary dilemmas, he explores the large ideas of history and civilization in terms of humankind's spiritual capacity. For him, the quality of being human in the present age can be measured by the depth of one's connection to this spirituality. Merely the titles of a group of poems in the first section of the book—"Kitchen, 1952," "1967," "1968," "1969," "Dropping Acid at Aunt Bea's and Uncle Harry's 40th Wedding Anniversary Celebration," and "Embracing a Cloud: Rural Commune, 1971"—suggest Wormser's sense of history as he contemplates life in twentieth century America. His chronicling of Americans' spiritual state extends across a range of modern experiences, including an Otis Redding and Aretha Franklin concert and an anniversary celebration at which one celebrant has taken a psychedelic drug. Nothing is trivialized in these portraits of modern life. Wormser's explorations probe the heart of Americans' daily rites. A fine example of this process is "Married Sex." Here the poet unmasks the psyche of people's sexual selves through a nimble portrait of passion in marriage—the

web of familiarity that steals spontaneity even while it creates a ritualized joy in a couple's sexual encounters.

The long poem "Atoms" constitutes the second and final section of Wormser's third volume. Using the voices of several characters, Wormser ponders the trajectory of American culture by exploring the darker side of the covenant (an unspoken one) that every culture makes with death. "Atoms" exposes how nations are really at war with themselves and thus with their own people. Through the poem's characters, Wormser demonstrates how foolish it is to think that having a nuclear arsenal has prevented nuclear war. As he discusses politics in a postnuclear age, Wormser delves into the manner in which a culture conceives of evil. According to the poet, American society has colluded with evil and has thus made death an unnatural danger. This collusion conceals itself in the political and social orthodoxy of the present—an orthodoxy that, although couched cunningly in rationalism as well as sincerity, inevitably results in war, death, and subjugation.

The central characters of "Atoms" give flesh to this crisis of modernity. They are pilgrims on a journey, and they contain the fire of atoms. Airman Hawkins wonders about the world he inhabits, a stranger in a strange landscape. John Lennon rocks and rolls for peace, his own messy soul a sad prophecy. The clergyman grounds his protests in a faith smothered by an indifferent, purgatorial world. The bureaucrat Keats, "an underdeputy for Nuclear Security Policy," and his superior, Horace, exemplify the granite officiousness of government policy. Wormser's description and juxtaposition of the characters' inner lives evoke the turbulence of contemporary America's spiritual state.

"Atoms" transcends its political observations to become an examination of spiritual worthiness. Only through a significant repentance of the internal, volitional kind, along with the nurturing of conscience, will Americans rescue themselves, Wormser seems to say. Atonement and humility become the means that allow people to accomplish the noblest of tasks—finding and speaking the truth. Thus, "Atoms" is one of America's few truly religious poems.

The cumulative power of "Atoms," derived from the poet's ability to modulate gnomic utterances, is built up through an incantatory rhythm that gives it the structure of an extended prayer. By using tight lines of uncommon clarity, Wormser keeps this rhythm pulsing through the varied depictions of each pilgrim character. Sharp images of human activity (at times ridiculously trite and indifferent) are continually contrasted with images of the innate, organic energy of life within all people. This multilayered texture of "Atoms" serves to illuminate the general theme of how the salvation of any civilization is, finally, determined by the spiritual actions of its members.

WHEN

In *When*, whether in Las Vegas, Sun City, or driving a Ford in 1978 on "The Nuclear Bullet Tour," Wormser beholds the myth of America: a myth of contradictions, covenants, and prayers for the unruly middle class— but a myth "you'd be a fool to refuse." The collection is a mix of autobiography and storytelling that never forgets a basic writerly tenet: Locality is the only universality. Alice Fulton, who selected this volume for the Kathryn A. Morton Prize in 1996, commented that Wormser does not succumb to "the emotional gush and self-dramatization that characterize much contemporary poetry," a sentiment that testifies to his primary focus on the lives of others. Wormser hones in on specific details of his characters' actions, whether the subject is Beethoven's maid hearing strange sounds, a deli waiter bemoaning his work, or Wormser as a boy walking through Pikesville, Maryland, and imagining it to be Charles Baudelaire's Paris. However, the insights the characters achieve and the emotions they feel are universal: A trucker who "skidded the better part of a quarter-mile/ toward a stopped school bus/ . . . and he said he saw himself as a boy." There are also a handful of extremely sensitive portraits and testimonials that again focus on other lives: a young man dead of acquired immunodeficiency syndrome (AIDS), a Jew imagining that Dachau will be peaceful countryside. Taken together, the poems of *When* present a menagerie of wonderfully familiar strangers.

MULRONEY AND OTHERS

Mulroney and Others revisits Wormser's unique perspective on the world around him and again calls forth a universality of experience. The collection provides glimpses of Wormser's childhood, adolescence, and adulthood, as well as accounts of Vietnam veterans, draft dodgers, socialites, and outcasts. In "Fatality," there is the finality of ending, not just in poetic structure but also with the thought woven into the fabric of the poem: the suddenness of death, followed by the quiet aftermath when life picks up and continues. Wormser's invitation to engage in seeing is irresistible, especially as he models the process with such impassioned interest. His poems tempt the reader to trade the obscurity of facile assumption for the powerful illumination of wonder. In Wormser's words, the universe is irrefutably personal.

SUBJECT MATTER

Subject Matter presents a more inward and perplexed mental state than readers have become accustomed to seeing in Wormser. A sense of change and peril is in the air, and the buff discursiveness present in Wormser's earlier poems is here as a kind of reassuring backbeat determined to see the reader through the storm, not the directly appealing credo it had been in his works of the 1980's and 1990's. "Bankruptcy" lambastes the rich and indolent, tacitly linking them to the policies of then-President George W. Bush in what the poet perceives as their uncaring hedonism. Wormser's mood is angry here, filled with a *saeva indignatio* (righteous indignation) associated with eighteenth century satirists such as Jonathan Swift:

> The *condottieri* of money emblazon
> their glad handed chicanery on frail paper
> monumentalize their visions in acronyms

When these plutocrats go bankrupt, the poet frankly exults. Most likely written in response to the Enron and other corporate scandals of 2002, the poem retained its impact when read in the light of the economic near-collapse of 2008. Wormser's wrath permits him to employ more elevated diction than he usually does, as if he is confident that the purity of his spleen will safeguard him against any sense of pretension or showing off.

"Anecdotes" is the first poem in *Subject Matter*. It is a seemingly slight but ultimately subtle poem, which comes to terms with poetry's ability to marshal ordinary experience into meaning while realizing that this can often be a way to attribute a false unity or facile overall leaning to aspects of experience that are in themselves disparate and autonomous. Wormser, though, in a sense provides the answer to his own dilemma here, as poetry not only can stitch events together but also testify and delight in their radical singularity. It can provide an umbrella philosophy of life, but it can also delight in anarchy and randomness. Unlike faith, poetry both gives and takes away; its innate property is to do both. Comparable to "Poetry and Religion" (1987, by the Australian poet Les Murray) in its rigorous diagnosis of what poetry can and cannot offer, Wormser's poem steals up on the reader, transmogrifying itself from trifle to illumination.

Both sides of this equation continue to be canvassed in two subsequent poems in the volume, "Israel" and "Genius." In "Israel," two dogs fight while two old men quibble about God. A boy notes sophomorically that "dog" is "God" spelled backward. Reverence, irreverence, and animal insensibility are all part of the same experiential field. There is a sense that spirituality lies beyond an affirmation of an explicit credo: The same boy who jokes about God's name assures his mother that he regularly talks with God privately at night. Wormser suggests that if finite things are let be and are allowed to reside in their own place on the continuum, the infinite can somehow be solicited and an impasse of the merely finite can be evaded.

In "Genius," Wormser recalls the definition of "extravagant" as "extra-vagant," wandering beyond appointed limits, going outside boundaries. Modernist art prided itself on extravagance, furled both its rebellion and its latent spirituality in its self-heralding of its own aesthetic innovation. Recalling a visit to the Museum of Modern Art in New York, the poet looks with both appreciation and a layer of irony at the way the museum becomes a temple of art. Wormser is not entirely spoofing the high aspirations of the modernists. Indeed, he greatly honors them, but he realizes that, at times, modernism took itself too seriously and became the sort of absolutism it had earlier opposed.

"Anti-Depressant" has one of the most bracing openings of all of Wormser's poems.

> "What a pig happiness is. Plus
> I'm a body living with an anti-body
> You probably don't know how that goes
> One of my hang-ups is trying to tell you

The sense of inward dissatisfaction and psychological incongruity is unusual in a Wormser poem, as most of his poems' themes customarily address nature or history rather than the experience of the self. However, Wormser's jaunty jocularity, and his ever-overt awareness of even the most private poetry as a public speech act, carries the reader through as if on a conveyor belt:

> The pills tell me to let sincerity lapse
> I used to talk a blue streak but now
> I honor mute science as dryly as
> the next atheist . . .

This poem most likely does not reflect any personal experience taking antidepressants on Wormser's part nor is it a comment on their effect on eloquence—the taking of antidepressants is believed to have enabled the British poet Geoffrey Hill to compose his later work—but rather how the impulse to always be comfortable leads people to give up too much. Another aspect of the poem is that Wormser, often seen as more a poet of equilibrium than of affect, is reminding himself and his readers how important a virtue affect is to poetry; that even the most responsible poetry relinquishes affect at great peril. It may be ridiculous for the poet to cry at "ratty English sparrows" foraging in the hay, but if the poet does not do this nobody will. If people all prevent themselves from feeling because they fear suffering, there will be no poetry.

CARTHAGE AND SCATTERED CHAPTERS

Carthage was a series of satiric poems echoing some of the political themes of *Subject Matter*, but in a much lighter vein in its satire of a George W. Bush-like president. *Scattered Chapters* was largely a compilation of Wormser's previous few volumes, along with new poems that continued Wormser's characteristic mix of pasionate ferocity and discursive responsibility.

The promulgation and furtherance of poetry has been the mission of Wormser's poetic career. As teacher, as prose writer, and pivotally, as wise, confident poet, he has, over three decades, made a forceful and steady dedication of his talent to poetry—its nuances, its dangers, its sense of an earned grace—a remnant saved from the flux of experience.

OTHER MAJOR WORKS

SHORT FICTION: *The Poetry Life: Ten Stories*, 2008.

NONFICTION: *Teaching the Art of Poetry: The Moves*, 2000 (with David Cappella); *A Surge of Language: Teaching Poetry Day by Day*, 2004 (with Cappella); *The Road Washes Out in Spring: A Poet's Memoir of Living Off the Grid*, 2006.

BIBLIOGRAPHY

Birkerts, Sven. *The Electric Life: Essays on Modern Poetry*. New York: William Morrow, 1989. This wide-ranging book includes a condensed discussion of Wormser, connecting the poet's sense of place and occasion with his ability to enlarge on the particular. A solid overview of the poet that hints at his larger, spiritual themes and the complex subtleties of his thinking process.

Boruch, Marianne. "Comment: The Feel of a Century." *American Poetry Review* 19 (July/August, 1990): 18-19. Included in this lengthy review of several poets is a discussion of Wormser's *Atoms, Soul Music, and Other Poems*. Despite the brief treatment of the book, two major points are made about his long poem "Atoms": that it tackles American culture and that it exemplifies the poet's attempt to capture the private and specific in a public manner.

Briggs, Edwin. "Poet Shapes an Image That's Fresh and True." Review of *The White Words*. *The Boston Globe*, May 29, 1983, p. D3. This review gives a succinct account of Wormser's attitude toward language and of his use of tone and images to control the subject matter. It is an insightful glimpse into the poet's stance.

Finch, Robert. "'Living Inside a Poem': A Meditation About Twenty Years in the Maine Woods, Thinking Deliberately, Working Creatively." *Boston Globe*, November 19, 2006, p. R6. Underlines important similarities and differences between Wormser's valuation of the land and the simple life described by earlier American writers, especially Henry David Thoreau.

Johnson, Greg. "Essential Themes: Elegant Variations." *Georgia Review* 67, no. 9 (Summer, 2009): 336-344. Discusses *The Poetry Life*, critiquing what Johnson sees as its overly essayistic quality but also conceding that this was perhaps necessary to bring home Wormser's ideas about how poetry actually mattered to people.

Mesic, Penelope. Review of *The White Words*. *Poetry* 144 (February, 1984): 302-303. In a balanced look at the poet's first book, this terse yet praiseworthy review commends the poet's wit, technical skill, and use of details.

Wormser, Baron. "Populous Worlds of a Quiet Laureate." Interview by Sally Read. *South Dakota Review* 39, no. 2 (Summer, 2001): 121-122. This interview conducted during Wormser's tenure as a visiting professor at the University of South Dakota is a crucial one for understanding issues of voice, tone, and reference in Wormser's oeuvre.

David Cappella; Sarah Hilbert
Updated by Nicholas Birns

————————

C. D. WRIGHT

Born: Mountain Home, Arkansas; January 6, 1949

PRINCIPAL POETRY

Alla Breve Loving, 1976
Room Rented by a Single Woman, 1977
Terrorism, 1979
Translations of the Gospel Back into Tongues, 1982
Further Adventures with You, 1986
String Light, 1991
Just Whistle: A Valentine, 1993 (photography by Deborah Luster)
Tremble, 1996
Deepstep Come Shining, 1998
Steal Away: Selected and New Poems, 2001
One Big Self: Prisoners of Louisiana, 2003, 2007 (photography by Luster)
Cooling Time: An American Poetry Vigil, 2005
Like Something Flying Backwards: New and Selected Poems, 2007
Rising, Falling, Hovering, 2008

OTHER LITERARY FORMS

C. D. Wright is known principally for her poetry, but in recent volumes, her expanding line has led to a sort of prose poem that seems to morph into essay. Wright has also worked with photographer Deborah Luster (who did photography for *Just Whistle*), most notably in their joint project *One Big Self*, in which Luster's prison photographs join with Wright's long poem to create a portrait of the lives of the incarcerated. The work was reprinted without the photographs in 2007. *Cooling Time* is a sort of hybrid joining of essay, epigram, and poem, mostly offering insights into Wright's life and poetics. Wright has also written a collection of short biographies of Arkansas writers, *The Lost Roads Project: A Walk-in Book of Arkansas*, published in 1994.

ACHIEVEMENTS

C. D. Wright's career has been marked by a growing list of honors beginning in 1981 with a National Endowment for the Arts award. She won the Witter Bynner Prize for Poetry of the American Academy and Institute of Arts and Letters (1986), the Whiting Writers' Award (1989), the Rhode Island Governor's Award for the Arts (1990), the Poetry Center Book Award from San Francisco State University (1991) for *String Light*, and the Lila Wallace-*Reader's Digest* Writers' Award (1992). In 1994, she began a five-year appointment as state poet of Rhode Island. With Deborah Luster, she won the Dorothea Langue-Paul Taylor Prize for collaboration from the Center for Documentary Studies in 2000. In 1999, she received the Lannan Literary Award for Poetry. She was shortlisted for the Griffin Poetry Prize in 2003 for *Steal Away*. Wright received a MacArthur Fellowship in 2004 and the Griffin Poetry Prize in 2009 for *Rising, Falling, Hovering*.

BIOGRAPHY

Carolyn D. Wright was born on January 6, 1949, in Mountain Home, Arkansas, a small town in the north Ozarks. Her parents, Ernie Wright, a chancery judge, and Alyce Wright, a court reporter, named her Carolyn Doris. (She has used her initials in her writing to avoid confusion with another poet.) When she was six, her parents moved to Harrison, Arkansas, another small town, where she grew up absorbing Ozarks culture and dialect, both of which permeate her writing without evoking the "hillbilly" stereotype which, like most Ozarks citizens, she disdains. Her writing about her early life pictures her mother as a model of female independence and strength. Wright has also recalled her early love of reading, including her discovery of E. E. Cummings, whose typographical innovations seemed liberating to her. It was only in college, however, that she began to read women writers from the south, especially Flannery O'Connor whose use of southern dialect in her unsentimental pictures of rural people is recalled in Wright's work.

Wright received a B.A. degree in French from Memphis State in 1971. While in Memphis, she met the woman she calls "Mrs. Vititow" in her autobiographical essay in *Cooling Time;* in her Wright saw a self-educated woman who conducted her life as she wished, without regard for others' opinions, and Wright cites her as an important influence on her growth. In 1973, Wright entered the M.F.A. program in creative writing at the University of Arkansas; she received the degree in 1976. Her thesis, *Alla Breve Loving*, became her first published book.

While at the University of Arkansas, Wright came under the influence of poet Frank Stanford, with whom she had an intense love affair. Together they founded Lost Roads Publishers to publish Arkansas writers. Stanford was married, and a quarrel with his wife over the affair led to his suicide, an event that marked Wright deeply. Oblique references to him, his work, and their affair appear throughout Wright's poems.

After Stanford's death, Wright left her position with the Arkansas Arts and Humanities office and moved to San Francisco to work at the Poetry Center. In San Francisco, she encountered Language poetry for the first time and began to experiment with poems that were more interested in language than content. The effects of her interest continue to color her later work, freeing her from a rigid adherence to narrative. She met her future husband, poet Forrest Gander, there. When *Translations of the Gospel Back into Tongues* was published in 1982, she and Gander moved to Dolores Hidalgo, Mexico, for part of a year and then back to Arkansas. In 1983, Wright was hired to teach in the creative writing program at Brown University. She directed the program from 1989 to 2001 when she became the Israel J. Kapstein Professor of English. She and Gander have a son, Brecht.

ANALYSIS

C. D. Wright's work has never been extremely narrative, but her earlier poems are more nearly conventional, headed by titles and often containing some narrative elements that may make them feel accessible to new readers. In later volumes, she has come to rely more and more on repeated images, fragments of dialogue, long lines, and prose poems that may segue from one to another to make an entire volume without discrete poems. The power of image—whether concerned with place or with human relationships—to command one's imagination dominates her work, although other thematic threads such as political and ecological references are also present.

STRING LIGHT

Many of the poems in *String Light* seem explicitly autobiographical, growing from events in Wright's own life or the lives of those around her. "King's Daughters, Home for Unwed Mothers, 1948," for example, imagines the birth of Frank Stanford. His mother comes from rural poverty; his father has disappeared. Although, as the poem claims, his parents will outlive him, his accomplishments will far exceed their imaginations.

"The Night I Met Little Floyd" and "The Next Time I Crossed the Line into Oklahoma" evoke graduate school events, including trips from northwest Arkansas to Tulsa. In the former poem, "Jessie" is taken to Tulsa for an abortion. Back home, the household is filled with visiting poets and other university town characters including "Sonnyman," perhaps a name for Stanford. The same characters appear in the second poem, this time in the narrative of a trip to buy marijuana.

"What No One Could Have Told Them" records details from the first year or so of a child's life—his first words, his baby peccadilloes such as pouring furniture polish on the dog—each stanza made of two or three lines of prose representing things no one could tell a parent before the child's birth. The speaker relates a particularly striking example: "Naked in a splash of

sun, he pees into a paper plate the guest/ set down in the grass as she reached for potato chips." The two poems that follow this demonstrate Wright's interest in Language poetry by taking details such as the sentence about the child peeing into the guest's plate and working a number of variations on its syntax, rearranging subject and verb, moving adverbs, adding or deleting small details.

"The Ozark Odes" are a group of short poems evoking the Ozarks in a variety of voices and modes. "Table Grace," for example, asks a blessing on everything from brown recluse spiders to copperheads, goiters, and cowchips—all of them deserving of praise "for doing their utmost." "Arkansas Towns" is an alphabetical list of small towns, mostly with curious names—Greasy Corner, Marked Tree, Four Sisters, and Self. "Dry County Bar" offers a rural voice: "Bourbon not fit to put on a sore." "Remedy" presents an old charm against sty.

"The box this comes in," the last poem in the book, is a prose description of the contents of a wooden box of keepsakes. At the dressing table on which the box sits, Wright says, she faces herself every morning, "a poet of forty," who has used whatever has come her way to create poetry. The box demonstrates what she does as she writes: "The box this comes in is mine. . . ."

DEEPSTEP COME SHINING

Deepstep Come Shining demonstrates Wright's movement to the long poem that relies on an interweaving of imagery and other fragments to create its own dreamlike logic. It is possible to recognize a level of narrative here, but Wright is not really interested in storytelling.

The poem "Deepstep Come Shining" records a car trip through the deep South which Wright made with photographer Luster. The tiny hamlet of Deepstep, Georgia supplied the title. The poem begins with an epigraph from William Shakespeare's *King Lear* (pr. c. 1605-1606), when Lear asks the blinded Gloucester if he sees "how this world goes" and Gloucester responds "I see it feelingly," a comment that invites the reader also to see the world of the car trip with feelings and a wealth of imagery dealing with eyes, light, and vision.

Segments of the book are marked by brief prose passages. The first of these establishes the car as an important setting and also introduces the image of a white pi-ano which floats dreamily through the rest of the volume. The cities of the south appear as well. In Georgia, the speaker finds Rome and Athens, as well as Poetry. "Wonder who lives there."

The character of the boneman also appears and re-appears, an evocation of the herbal doctor who still works in some rural African American communities. Along with towns and characters come references to southern vegetables, including tomatoes, Vidalia onions, and Silver Queen corn.

Wright lists her sources at the book's end under the heading "*Stimulants, Poultices, Goads*," and includes in the wide-ranging list a work on optics as well as other works involving eyes. She also lists a number of southern writers including O'Connor, whom she references in the section in which she visits O'Connor's home town of Milledgeville, Georgia, with allusions to the writer's pea fowl and quoting her mock-redneck dictum: "When in Rome. Do as they done in Milledgeville."

ONE BIG SELF

Although the poems of *One Big Self* have individual titles, the techniques here resemble those of *Deepstep Come Shining*. Wright has woven together sentences and fragments of sentences from the Louisiana prisoners whom she (along with Luster in the photographic version of the work) interviewed. Lists in the poem record things to be counted (as the prisoners themselves are counted), including numbers of cells, number of days, and number of gunshot wounds. She has also included material from radio preachers and billboards along with regional advertising.

Intermingled with images from the prisons, Wright has included moralistic bits of instruction from a nineteenth-century board game called "The Mansion of Happiness": "Whoever gets into IDLENESS/ Must come to POVERTY." One of the last of these instructions threatens that a player who is reduced to prison or ruin must start the game again from square one.

OTHER MAJOR WORK

EDITED TEXT: *The Lost Roads Project: A Walk-in Book of Arkansas*, 1994 (photography by Deborah Luster).

BIBLIOGRAPHY

Colburn, Nadia Herman. "About C. D. Wright." *Ploughshares* 28 (Winter, 2002): 204-209. Colburn offers a biographical sketch of Wright with attention to Wright's growth away from strict "poetry" and into a hybrid of poetry and prose.

Keller, Lynn. *Thinking Poetry: Readings in Contemporary Women's Exploratory Poetics*. Iowa City: University of Iowa Press, 2010. Contains a chapter on Wright's experimental poetry.

Orr, David. Review of *Steal Away*. *Poetry* 182 (June, 2003): 170-173. A meaty review of Wright's volume of collected work, giving particular attention to her use of southern vernacular.

Parini, Jay, ed. *American Writers: A Collection of Literary Biographies—Woody Allen to C. D. Wright*. Supplement 15. Detroit: Scribners, 2006. Contains an entry on the life and works of Wright.

Wright, C. D. "During the Compositions of *Rising, Falling, Hovering*: A Personal Document of the War, of Mexico, and an American Family's Halting Progress." *Chicago Review* 53 (Summer, 2008): 349-355. Wright discusses her various times spent in Mexico as well as her difficult relationship with her teenaged son while America's war with Iraq raged to illustrate the process by which the poem was composed.

_____. "Provisional Remarks on Being/ a Poet/ of Arkansas." *Southern Review* 30 (Autumn, 1994): 809. Wright states some of her beliefs about how poetry works and cites her allegiance to southern dialect. She also comments on the limits of narrative.

Ann D. Garbett

CHARLES WRIGHT

Born: Pickwick Dam, Hardin County, Tennessee;
    August 25, 1935

PRINCIPAL POETRY

The Voyage, 1963
The Dream Animal, 1968
The Grave of the Right Hand, 1970
The Venice Notebook, 1971
Hard Freight, 1973
Bloodlines, 1975
China Trace, 1977
The Southern Cross, 1981
Country Music: Selected Early Poems, 1982, 1991
The Other Side of the River, 1984
A Journal of the Year of the Ox, 1988
Zone Journals, 1988
*The World of the Ten Thousand Things: Poems,
    1980-1990*, 1990
Xiona, 1990
Chickamauga, 1995
Black Zodiac, 1997
Appalachia, 1998
Negative Blue: Selected Later Poems, 2000
A Short History of the Shadow, 2002
Buffalo Yoga, 2004
The Wrong End of the Rainbow, 2005
Scar Tissue, 2006
Littlefoot, 2007
Sestets, 2009

OTHER LITERARY FORMS

Halflife: Improvisations and Interviews, 1977-1987 (1988) is a collection of writings about poetry, Charles Wright's own and others, in the form of passages from his notebooks, essays, and interviews. *Quarter Notes: Improvisations and Interviews* (1995) is a similar volume. *Uncollected Prose: Six Guys and a Supplement* (2000) gathered other essays. Wright has translated Eugenio Montale's *The Storm, and Other Poems* (1978), Dino Campana's *Orphic Songs* (1984), and Odes 3.8 and 4.12 from Horace in *The Odes: A New Translation by Contemporary Poets* (2002).

ACHIEVEMENTS

A major figure in American poetry, Charles Wright has received extensive critical recognition. Among his many awards are a Guggenheim Fellowship, the Edgar Allan Poe Award of the Academy of American Poets (1976), an Academy Award in Literature from the American Academy and Institute of Arts and Letters (1977), the PEN Translation Prize (1979), and the National Book Award in Poetry (1983). He received the Award of Merit Medal in poetry from the American Academy of Arts and Letters in 1992, the Ruth Lilly Poetry Prize in 1993, and the J. Howard and Barbara M. J. Wood Prize from *Poetry* magazine in 1996. In 1995, Wright was elected to membership in the American Academy of Arts and Letters. *Chickamauga* won the Lenore Marshall Poetry Prize (1996), and *Black Zodiac* was awarded the Pulitzer Prize (1998), the National Book Critics Circle Award (1997), and a *Los Angeles Times* Book Prize (1997). He served as chancellor for the Academy of American Poets from 1999 to 2002. Wright was elected as a fellow of the American Academy of Arts and Sciences in 2002. In 2007, he received the Griffin Poetry Prize for *Scar Tissue* and the Leoncino d'Oro Award for his engagement with Italian literature. In 2008, he won the Premio Internazionale Mario Luzi Award for lifetime achievement and the Bobbitt National Prize for lifetime achievement. In 2009, he was the recipient of the Carole Weinstein Poetry Prize.

BIOGRAPHY

Charles Penzel Wright, Jr., was born in Hardin County, Tennessee, in 1935. After World War II, his family moved to Kingsport, Tennessee, where he was reared. During his final two years of high school, he attended Christ School, an Episcopal preparatory school in Arden, North Carolina. This experience, and his upbringing in the Episcopal church, has contributed profoundly to the religious quality of his poetry, what he has called its "spiritual anxieties." After graduation from Davidson College, Wright served four years (1957-1961) in the United States Army. For three years he was stationed in Italy, an experience of extreme importance; while living in Verona, he acquired a copy of *The Selected Poems of Ezra Pound* (1928), and reading these poems in their Italian settings moved him to begin

Charles Wright (©Nancy Crampton)

writing poetry himself in 1959. Pound has remained among Wright's major poetic influences.

After military service, Wright attended the University of Iowa Writers' Workshop, from 1961 to 1963. He spent the next two years as a Fulbright student at the University of Rome, translating Montale's poetry, and then returned to the Iowa Writers' Workshop in 1965-1966. He taught at the University of California, Irvine, for seventeen years before returning to the South in 1983 as writer-in-residence and professor at the University of Virginia. He and his wife, the photographer Holly Wright, settled in Charlottesville, Virginia, and Wright was appointed the Souter Family Professor of English at the University of Virginia in 1988. While living and working primarily in Charlottesville, Wright has spent considerable time in Europe, serving as a distinguished visiting professor at Universita Degli Studi in Florence in 1992 among other appointments. From 1999 to 2001, he was the poetry editor of *The New Republic* and, in 2005, was honored in Vancouver, B.C., by the program "Charles Wright at Seventy: A Celebration and Retrospective."

ANALYSIS

Charles Wright's poetry, characterized by high ambition and profound seriousness, is suffused with spiritual yearning, seeking to discover a transcendent realm beyond the reality of the everyday physical world. His poems exploit memory and metaphysical speculation, moving easily between his past, his present, and his future death and dispersal. Intensely compressed and allusive, Wright's poetry can often be difficult to access when focused on the philosophical matters that most concern him, but he frequently employs a more casual vernacular style touching on local cultural materials, and the seriousness of intention may be mingled with a gentle type of humor that tends to welcome the reader to his world. Basically lyrical and imagistic, the poems are structured in terms of the gradual accretion of material in layers, imagery, metaphor, and (in the later poems) anecdote, developing by association rather than by narrative.

This disjointed style is a chief innovation, characterized by what Wright has called the "submerged narrative" that runs beneath the poem, only occasionally breaking the surface. His insistence on the primacy of the line, as a discrete unit, rather than the stanza, is partly responsible for the disconnected style. Wright has explained, "I think a line has a specific weight and heft, that it is melodic and tactile. It is as though the lines were each sections of the poem attached by invisible strings to the title." The line, which in books following *China Trace* becomes unusually long and image-filled, is the basic structural unit. In early work, Wright tended to use the iambic line as a foundation, although after *The Grave of the Right Hand* he depended on it less frequently, retaining the iambic ground in his carefully crafted free verse in conjunction with the practice of composing lines formed of an odd number of syllables, which accounts for the engrossing rhythmic effects of many poems.

For Wright, poetry is a conduit to God. He believes that its purest purpose is contemplation of the mysteries of the divine. Wright admits that for him poetry is a substitute for religion. If so, it is a limited religion, one that only concedes the possibility of God and that merely savors the concept of redemption. "All my poems seem to be an ongoing argument with myself about the unlikelihood of salvation," he has said. Wright seeks to penetrate commonplace surfaces to explore ultimate reality, and the image is paramount in this endeavor. Because the tangible world is all the human being can experience directly, through the senses, Wright must seek the infinite through the concrete image. Replacing religious faith with belief in the numinous image, he resigns himself to an acceptance of language and metaphor as a simulacrum of the divine, thus the importance of the landscape in his poems, which are centered geographically in Italy, in eastern Tennessee near North Carolina, and along the Blue Ridge in southwestern Virginia in later work. Wright has said that he sees "that part of Appalachia, as containing heavenly aspects, which I know is not true for most people, but they were for me."

These two continental regions are the most vital for Wright. He associates Italy with the life of the mind, with the wonder of intellectual and artistic awakening, while Tennessee and North Carolina evoke his childhood, and represent a tangible, specific aspect of human existence. Landscape has transcendent qualities in Wright's poetry, particularly the landscape as seen from the region of the Blue Ridge around Charlottesville, Virginia, and the listing of place-names is a kind of incantation. Because memory and his personal past play a central role, Wright's poems tend to have a pervasive autobiographical quality. This autobiography is not explicitly personal, however, since it is subsumed in his main subject, the search for God, although Wright's search does have a distinctly individual quality given Wright's profile of himself as a "God-fearing non-believer."

THE GRAVE OF THE RIGHT HAND

The Grave of the Right Hand collects apprentice work. Most of the poems are in regular stanza patterns, especially tercets, and in basically iambic short lines. They look traditional, unlike the poems in *China Trace*, the pivotal book in Wright's career, and succeeding volumes. Though most of Wright's stylistic innovation came later, *The Grave of the Right Hand* exhibits certain preoccupations that remain constant in his work: the emphasis on the image rather than rhetoric and a native obliqueness. From the start, Wright sought to communicate by suggestion instead of disclosure. He pre-

sents an imagistic gestalt that coheres, for the diligent reader, into transcendent moments that reveal fleeting glimpses of abstract meaning. The characteristic images are already present: light, stars, blood, flowers, fog, clouds. Also evident are the landscape (one section is titled "American Landscape"), the elegiac quality and melancholy atmosphere, and the concern with absence, the negation of death.

"Self-Portrait" is the first of many poems with this title or some variation of it. This poem has a surreal flavor, with images that seem to have been selected from Giorgio De Chirico's paintings: "There is a street which runs/ Slanting into a square/ There is a marble hand." This street is eerily deserted. The poet, whose self-portrait the poem evidently paints, is notably absent. The final image, a pair of gloves nailed to a door, suggests both crucifixion and death, a parody of Christ's death and the poet's dread of his own mortality. There is no promise of salvation in the symbol, merely the intimation of redemption coupled with the certainty of death: The gloves, empty of human hands, remain behind like shed skins. This speculation about death and the dim possibility of transcendence is central to Wright's poetry.

HARD FREIGHT

Hard Freight, *Bloodlines*, and *China Trace* constitute a trilogy. Containing poems about place, childhood, family, adulthood, and spiritual longings, the books make up a sort of sketchy autobiography. The sequence is not chronological, since the first volume, *Hard Freight*, deals with the poet's present, while the second volume, *Bloodlines*, deals with his childhood, and *China Trace* with a speculative spiritual future.

Hard Freight is made up of individual lyrics that tend to be abstract and cryptic. It concerns Wright's adolescence and adulthood, including his life as a poet; thus it begins with several poems in homage to writers who have influenced him or who otherwise have been important to him. "Homage to Ezra Pound" does not absolve Pound, "Awash in the wrong life," for his political stupidity (he broadcast fascist propaganda during World War II and was arrested for treason following the American occupation of Italy) but recognizes Pound's poetic capabilities and acknowledges Wright's debt of influence, characteristically using liturgical diction:

"Here is your garment,/ Coldblooded father of light—/ Rise and be whole again."

Many of the poems ponder death, a constant theme for Wright. "Definitions" begins, typically, as a description of the flora in an unspecified setting. The images are threatening:

> The blades of the dwarf palm,
> Honing themselves in the wind;
> The ice plant, blistering red along
> Its green, immaculate skin.

Wright finds no consolation or hope in nature; instead, the organic world is unsettling, because it foreshadows his eventual death. The palm, ice plant, moon, and dark waters (presumably the Pacific Ocean near his Laguna Beach, California, home) become dreadful omens, "something to listen for—/ A scar, fat worm, which feeds at the lungs;/ A cough, the blood in the handkerchief."

Hard Freight is autobiographical in an abstract way: It chronicles the evolution of a mind. Only a handful of poems narrate specific events or situations in the poet's life, and these generally center on a place from Wright's childhood or youth. He revisits the site as an adult, or via memory, generating from the emotions associated with it new and more complex feelings. So much referential detail has been abstracted from the poems that Wright usually depends on the title to identify the locale and situation. Without the tag *Bible Camp, 1949* at the end of "Northhanger Ridge," the reader would not know the specific setting, which is crucial to the poem's meaning. Wright struggles with his religious upbringing, belittling organized religion, the "Bow-wow and arf" of "Father Dog" (God). Praying children "talk to the nothingness." Finally, Wright rejects the Christian belief in corporeal resurrection: salvation "sleeps like a skull in the hard ground,/ . . . as it's always slept, without/ Shadow, waiting for nothing." Northhanger Ridge is aptly described as "half-bridge over nothingness," for Wright's Christian training has degenerated into disbelief; nevertheless, the yearning for redemption abides, a "half-bridge" jutting into the void of his inevitable demise.

BLOODLINES

This wistful need to believe in an impossible salvation dominates the books from *China Trace* onward.

According to Wright, *Bloodlines* and *Hard Freight* both deal with his childhood conflict with the Episcopal church. Most of the poems in *Bloodlines* depend on memories of Wright's childhood and are thus more clearly autobiographical than those of the previous volume. With *Bloodlines*, he established his practice of writing whole books of poetry rather than collecting disparate poems. The individual poems are linked by subject and form, and the structural heart of the volume is formed of two long complementary sequences, "Tattoos" and "Skins."

The two long poems were conceived as counterparts: "Tattoos" is composed of actual situations, whereas "Skins" is conceptual, its sections pertaining to abstractions such as truth and beauty. The twenty autobiographical sections of "Tattoos" describe momentous incidents in Wright's life, what he has called "psychic tattoos"—hence the title. Setting and narrative frame have been abstracted so that the poet can get to the pith of each experience, making the sequence an impressionistic collage. The lack of reference necessitates the notes that identify the place and situation of each section. Wright put the notes at the end of the sequence, to maintain its structural integrity. Most of the incidents are drawn from his childhood: the death of his father, a snake-handling religious service he witnessed in Tennessee, fainting at the altar as an acolyte, handwriting class.

The first poem begins with the image of fallen camellia blossoms outside his home in Laguna Beach; the red and white petals remind him of the red and white rose symbolism of Mother's Day. The wind of remembrance takes him back thirty years to his days as an acolyte at Saint Paul's Episcopal Church in Kingsport, Tennessee. The disagreeableness of his religious background is suggested by the image of memory as "the wind . . . bad breath/ Of thirty-odd years, and catching up." The roots of the camellia bush represent Wright's childhood, and the metaphorical description of petals as "scales of blood" suggests the pain and loss suffered in life. "Where would you have me return?/ What songs would I sing," asks the poet of the camellia bush, and answers his own questions in the succeeding poems. This initial section clearly introduces the motifs and concerns developed in the sequence, all characteristic of Wright's poetry: memory, death, religious skepticism, visionary longing for Heaven, Italy, and the importance of art to his life.

Wright conceived of "Skins" as a continuation of "Tattoos," but as an abstract, conceptual counterpart to the autobiographical specificity of the first poem. Thus "Skins," despite its corporal title, chronicles his intellectual evolution. Each section is built on a particular abstract reference. The poem is structured as a stepladder, with ten sections ascending and ten descending, ending at the point of departure.

The subjects, as identified by Wright, are lofty: (1) Situation, Point A; (2) Beauty; (3) Truth; (4) Eventual Destruction of the Universe; (5) Organized Religion; (6) Metamorphosis; (7) Water; (8) Water/Earth; (9) Earth/Fire; (10) Aether, the fifth element; (11) Primitive Magic; (12) Necromancy; (13) Black Magic; (14) Alchemy; (15) Allegory; (16) Fire; (17) Air; (18) Water; (19) Earth; (20) Situation, Point A. The purpose is to organize and concretize Wright's attitudes toward elemental things. In effect, he is trying to understand the metaphysical nature of human life and his own position in the universe. The individual poems center on the four elements—earth, air, water, fire—all that human beings can know empirically about creation. These the poet accepts; he rejects false systems of transcendence—magic, necromancy, alchemy, and allegory.

CHINA TRACE

Wright intended "Skins," rather than the last three poems in *Bloodlines*, to be the launching point for *China Trace*, the final volume in the trilogy. Both books are suffused with spiritual yearning. *China Trace*, in fact, is an imaginative exploration of the poet's spiritual future. The book begins with a poem in which the speaker bids farewell to childhood, irrevocably ended by the death of his parents. Growing up entails many losses, especially of people, and their loss presages the poet's own: The poem says good-bye to "the names/ Falling into the darkness, face/ After face, like beads from a broken rosary." The last line fades into a symbol of lost faith.

The spiritual future Wright explores is his eventual death and his wish, in the face of skepticism, that he might be resurrected. Because he finds it impossible to

believe any longer in the Christian Heaven, the closest he can come to salvation is decomposition and admixture with nature. This conviction is evident in many of the poems, particularly "Self-Portrait in 2035," in which the poet envisions himself after death as dirt and wood-rot: "The root becomes him, the road ruts/ That are sift and grain in the powderlight/ Recast him."

Hard Freight and *Bloodlines* both concern Wright's past, while *China Trace* deals with his present. That is, the triggering situations of the poems are grounded in his present, but only to provide a launching point for speculation about his afterimage. "Snow," for example, appears to have begun as a meditation on the physical presence of snow. The evanescence of snow and its cycle of transmogrification from water to snow and back to water elicit the notion of the human body's inevitable reabsorption in nature, and the liturgical echo of "dust to dust": "If we, as we are, are dust, and dust, as it will, rises,/ Then we will rise, and recongregate/ In the wind, in the cloud, and be their issue." The book is paradoxical in that though all the poems express in some way Wright's wish to survive in a realm beyond death they disavow such salvation.

The poems in *China Trace* are short, none longer than twelve lines. Wright decided on this arbitrary limit in an attempt to write the most compressed poetry practicable. This compression contributes to the poems' difficulty and to their gnomic quality, which reveals the influence of Emily Dickinson. Wright remarked that "my impulse remains Dickinsonian," although "my poetry has moved toward larger gestures, more Whitmanian" in later volumes. The condensation, as well as the title, also indicates the influence of Chinese poetry. Wright has said that he has an affinity for Tang Dynasty poets, who focused on the landscape. Whether their interest in landscape kindled Wright's own or merely reflects it, the fact remains that he uses natural imagery in the same way the Tang poets did. Like them, Wright imbues landscape with personal emotion and psychic drama. A preternatural dimension, if it could exist, would be perceptible only through the senses, so the infinite can be glimpsed only as an "undershine" of the finite, imaginary perhaps but still to be desired.

The fifty poems of the book, though discrete, are intended to make a whole. They are unified in one way by the speaker, who remains the same in every poem even though he is referred to in various poems as "I," "you," and "he." This character, whom one must assume to be different aspects of Wright's personality, advances from his parting with childhood in the first poem to a qualified revival as a constellation in the final poem, "Him." The title is a pun on "hymn," and the poem operates as a hymn or prayer, expressing Wright's longing for transcendence. The character's transfiguration into a constellation in the Pacific sky is a metaphor for Wright's curious position—trapped between skepticism and the need to believe. The character's relinquishment of childhood is essentially a liberation from religion, since Wright associates the two. However, this emancipation begets a dilemma, for only through the Christian faith can he gain salvation. His abortive ascension leaves him stranded in what Wright has called "the Heaven of the Fixed Stars (in the Dantescan cosmology)." This literary allusion suggests Wright's poetry. The act of writing a poem is a religious act, but it is ultimately dissatisfying, because while Wright may achieve some sense of transcendence through identifying with nature, he cannot get beyond the finite physical world. Thus his poetry is a heaven of his own making, but a very meager one.

Wright's line in *China Trace*, though tending to lengthen, remains relatively short, and his forms have retained the strictness of those in the earlier books. *China Trace*, however, marks the emergence of Wright's mature voice. In succeeding books, he opens up his forms and lengthens his line. The poems also become more imagistic and anecdotal; the subterranean narrative runs nearer to the surface.

THE SOUTHERN CROSS

The Southern Cross, a spiritual journey, continues the conceptual design of *China Trace*. The dead, a favorite subject of Wright, dominate *The Southern Cross*. The dedication, "For H. W. Wilkinson," actually refers to Wright's past and family history. Wilkinson's name happened to be stenciled on a metal locker Wright bought and in which he stored family relics, old letters, and the like. By dedicating the book to Wilkinson, Wright really was honoring his familial dead, about whom so many of the poems revolve. His unwillingness to ignore his extinct forebears is, perhaps, a reflec-

tion of his dread of oblivion. By writing about his dead, manifold and anonymous though they may be, he is saving them from the void. The ancestral dead in "Homage to Paul Cézanne" echo La Pia in Dante's *Purgatorio* (in *La divina commedia*, c. 1320; *The Divine Comedy*, 1802): "Remember me, speak my name." The title notwithstanding, the poem is not about Cézanne but is intended to acknowledge Wright's long-standing interest in Cézanne's work and that painter's influence on Wright's technique. Wright has said that he tried to adapt Cézanne's painting style to poetry by employing lines and stanzas in a way that approximates the painter's use of color and form. Wright's nonlinear stanzas, which never form an integral narrative, are roughly equivalent to the blocks of color that are not in themselves representational but add up to a coherent whole in Cézanne's paintings.

The second section arranges five self-portraits and four rebirth poems in alternation. The two types complement each other. The self-portraits typically picture Wright's eventual death and dispersal and reunification with the natural world, while the rebirth poems simulate belief in reincarnation, or at least in death as a portal to some other form of existence: "the future we occupied, and will wake to again . . ./ Pushing the cauly hoods back, ready to walk out/ Into the same night and the meadow grass, in step and on time" ("Mount Caribou at Night"). This is a kind of psychic play for Wright, seeming to console him in the manner of the wish-fulfillment dream.

The poems in section 3 resulted from a writer's game that Wright played with himself, setting himself a different challenge for each poem. "California Spring," for example, has a verb in each line, while "Dog Yoga" contains no verbs at all. Among other technical problems posed were to write a pair of poems using images from Dante, to write a verbal watercolor, and to write a poem from a photograph. In "Bar Giamaica, 1959-60," Wright fashioned a photograph he wished he had taken but did not. The poem was inspired by Italian photographer Ugo Mulas's picture of a Verona bar that Wright had frequented while living in Italy. Wright replaces the patrons of Mulas's bar with friends Wright had drunk with six years later. The poem is more than mere technical play; it is an attempt to defy time, to stanch the flow of losses. Such an effort, however, is futile. The congenial warmth of the remembered scene dissipates in an image of loss and emptiness, the outdoor table abandoned to the cold: "the snow falls and no one comes back/ Ever again, all of them gone through the star filter of memory,/ With its small gravel and metal tables and passers-by."

The long, abstract title poem makes up the final section. "The Southern Cross" alludes to Wright's southern roots and the attendant burdens of history and religion. His Christian upbringing compels his constant search for transcendence through language and landscape. Wright has said that memory and transfiguration are the subjects that most interest him. While these inform all of his work, they are the axes around which "The Southern Cross" rotates: "All day I've remembered a lake and a sudsy shoreline,/ Gauze curtains blowing in and out of open windows all over the South."

THE OTHER SIDE OF THE RIVER

Wright sees *The Other Side of the River* as an extension of *The Southern Cross*. Like the previous book, *The Other Side of the River* involves memory and transfiguration, and both are journal-like in their chronological arrangement and attention to quotidian matters. (In this, they anticipate *Zone Journals*.) *The Other Side of the River* is more anecdotal than its predecessor. Although the poems are not narratives, they incorporate fragmentary stories and anecdotes, rather than the autobiographical snippets of earlier poems, into their nonlinear structures. The titles establish the narrative, with the disjunctive anecdotes relating to the title. In the poems of the first section, Wright returns to the Tennessee of his upbringing for the narrative elements, while the poems of the second section are derived from his Italian experience. These are the two most psychically energized landscapes in Wright's world.

Memory works as a means of catharsis and shrift in "Lost Bodies" and "Lost Souls." The first juxtaposes emblems of the sublime to images of the lost world of Wright's childhood, that portion of his life already given over to death. The initial recollection of Torri del Benaco in Italy brings to mind the transcendent image of "almond trees in blossom,/ its cypresses clothed in their dark fire," and his mind instantly leaps to an image

charged with lamentation for the lost faith of his boyhood:

And the words carved on that concrete cross

I passed each day of my life
In Kingsport going to town
    GET RIGHT WITH GOD/ JESUS IS COMING SOON

All that remains of that time is the cross and the absent Christ, whose moral precepts still affect Wright though he is apostate. The poem ends in acceptance of eternal oblivion, the knowledge that "this is as far as it goes," and on a note of sorrow for the lost body of Jesus, whose promise of salvation Wright can no longer believe in: "diesel rigs/ Carry out deaths all night through the endless rain." In the companion piece "Lost Souls," Wright seeks to expiate his survival guilt over the deaths of his parents, the "lost souls" of the title. The poem also emphasizes the importance of memory. After presenting two anecdotes from his young adulthood, Wright declares, "And nobody needs to remember any of that,/ but I do." He needs to remember his past to make sense of his life and, perhaps more important, to enlarge it: the moment is evanescent, and lamentably, the past contains the bulk of his life.

ZONE JOURNALS

Zone Journals, according to the poet, speaks of the interrelationship of landscape and language and the way that landscape communicates metaphysical truths. Wright has treated this theme in all of his work. What he says has not changed, but the way he says it has. He takes his diaristic tendency to its ultimate state, writing poems as journal entries that concern daily matters and an underlying metaphysics, in a form that is looser, more conversational, and more spacious than any before. The inclusiveness of the poems necessitates the expansive form. Composed as irregular journal entries, the poems sprawl all over the page, packed with sensory impressions, reflection, autobiographical details, cultural and literary allusions, biographical facts about writers and artists, didactic intimations, and the like. These journal poems are essentially meditations. By contemplating the material world, Wright seeks to know God. The title suggests the vastness of his reach: "zone" refers to space and "journals" to time. The zones of the poems are sacred places. For Wright, some places possess a numinous force. Foremost among these are eastern Tennessee, the cradle of his spiritual sensibility, and Italy, the source of his creative energies. His enumeration of place-names has an incantatory intention. They are, in his own words, "Zen Koans."

"A Journal of the Year of the Ox" is the central poem of the book. Forty-eight pages long, it chronicles Wright's fiftieth year, running from January to December, 1985. The main hallowed places of the poem are Long Island in the Holston River, near Wright's birthplace of Kingsport, Tennessee, and the Veneto region of northern Italy. Long Island was the sacred ceremonial ground of the Cherokee nation and is thus a doubly significant place. Northern Italy was the site of Wright's intellectual transfiguration, where he discovered the importance of language and culture. His sojourn in Italy altered his worldview and redirected his ambitions. The effect, according to Wright, was that of a religious conversion: The scales dropped from his eyes, revealing the world of poetry, painting, and literature, which he has inhabited ever since.

In "A Journal of the Year of the Ox," Wright sets out on a mental pilgrimage to these two sacred places. One of his intentions apparently is "salvation," to rescue a portion of his past through memory. "Each year I remember less," he writes, and immediately recollects the Long Island of the Holston. Its historical and spiritual significance were unknown to him during his youth but existed despite his ignorance, just as the sublime, despite his inability to perceive it, exists as an "underimage" of the physical world. The unseen world is Wright's real concern; the invisible is more important to him than the visible: "what's outside/ the picture is more important than what's in." In the first journal entry, Wright is troubled and depressed by his current inability to believe this, as he did as a young soldier in Italy: today, he says, "the sky . . . hides no meanings." This is one of his dark moments, but darkness gives way to light, a major symbol in Wright's work. The heart of the poem is a rhapsodic depiction of a room of the Palazzo Schifanoia in Ferrara, and the Renaissance frescoes that cover its walls: "Up there in the third realm, light . . ./ Washes and folds and breaks in small waves." The frescoes' scenes of peasant life, allegory,

and classical divinities portray, Wright has said, "the tripartite levels of existence—everyday life, allegorical life, and ideal life." He finds this layering of worlds fascinating, for it approximates his assumption that a spectral dimension underlies the natural world. The final entry begins with a metaphor that implies Wright's hope of transfiguration: "I am poured out like water."

THE WORLD OF TEN THOUSAND THINGS

The World of Ten Thousand Things, Wright's second volume of selected poems, compiles the preceding three books, *The Southern Cross*, *The Other Side of the River*, and *Zone Journals*, along with a section of new poems titled "Xionia." Like *Country Music*—which collected the trilogy of *Hard Freight*, *Bloodlines*, and *China Trace*—this book is actually an ensemble composed of three book-length sections. Wright seems to conceive of his individual books as units within a tripartite whole. The new poems are labeled journals—for example, "Silent Journal"—but lack the dates and quotidiana of *Zone Journals*. Absent also is the anecdotal material, the ghost-narrative. Short poems alternate with longer ones. In their abstractness and brevity, these poems resemble those of *China Trace*. Wright seems to have circled back to a stylistic position he occupied earlier in his career, when his mature voice first emerged from its chrysalis.

NEGATIVE BLUE

The trilogy structure continues, and perhaps ends, with Wright's work of the 1990's. *Chickamauga*, *Black Zodiac*, and *Appalachia* are recombined into *Negative Blue*, a sequence that traces Wright's journey into middle age. The style remains consistent through these volumes, as does the overall outlook, though each unit has its characteristic tone, mood, and energy. However, in incorporating the parts of his latest trilogy into a single volume, Wright has avoided simply reprinting the individual component titles. Rather, he has dropped a handful of poems and added a new sequence, "North American Bear," consisting of seven new poems. Thus the subtitle, "Selected Later Poems," is in some conflict with the notion of a coherent, planned trilogy. Wright has created something of a publishing paradox.

However, paradox is nothing new to Wright. It is the experiential medium through which his personas swim from decade to decade, at once denying the sufficiency of language and applauding its exclusive territory of truth making. In between the seeing and the contemplating is the stuff of Wright's poetry, a body of utterance that is constantly in the service of contradiction and acceptance. As he tells us in "Broken English," "All speech pulls toward privacy/ and the zones of the infinite," and "Without a syntax, there is no immortality." For Wright, syntax is a structuring device in a fluid linguistic field, and the volumes Wright has published after 2000 utilize syntactical strategies designed to continue his exploration of those "zones" as a way to continue his meditations on "immortality."

SCAR TISSUE

The first poem in *Scar Tissue*, "Appalachian Farewell," balances the vast unknown of the cosmos with the concrete, even the mundane, asking a local muse/ diety, "Goddess of Bad Roads and Inclement Weather" to give him guidance "To hold hard to what was there," and to support his sojourn in "In the country of Narrative" so that he can write poetry "Which spells out our stories in sentences, which gives them an end/and beginning. . . ." The sense of life as a continuing journey is expressed in "Last Supper," which begins "I seem to have come to the end of something, but I don't know what," a confession of accomplishment and bewilderment, and a testament to the value of proceeding without absolute reassurance: "There is no end to the other world,// no matter where it is." As Joel Brower aptly put it, "Wright's poems don't bear toward conclusion, they expand and evanesce," noting that each new collection is "less a book unto itself than the next installment in a continuous poem he's been writing for forty-odd years." Wright himself has described his poetic production as "a quasi-spiritual autobiography."

The poems in *Scar Tissue* continue forms familiar from many previous volumes: somewhat shorter, more lyrical pieces in part 1, which was published as a chapbook, *The Wrong End of the Rainbow;* with the title poem as part 2, an extended meditation on some of the primary philosophic postulates introduced throughout Wright's work. Part 3 takes the generalized philosophic perspective toward its foundations in some of Wright's intellectual areas of inquiry, concluding with the poem "Singing Lessons"—a title recalling William Butler Yeat's "Sailing to Byzantium"—that calls for an

attention to the rhythms of the universe, "the Great Mouth with its two tongues of water and ash." Wright counsels, "Listen to what the words spell, listen and sing the song," which is what he has been doing since the start of his poetic life.

The poems in *Buffalo Yoga* marked a moment of deeper darkness than had been evident in Wright's work to that point, reflections in a "distraught and mournful tone" (as Joe Moffett identifies them). Those in *Scar Tissue* do not suggest any remedy for the trials of human existence, or any kind of resolution to paradoxes and uncertainties, but there is a turn toward the more energized mode of observation and contemplation of earlier volumes. Even as he says in "The Silent Generation II" that "We've told our story. We've told it twice and took our lumps," he concludes, "And so we keep on, stiff lip, slack lip/ Hoping for words that are not impermanent." There is an echo here of F. Scott Fitzgerald's unforgettable exclamation in *The Great Gatsby*, "So we beat on, boats against the current," another assertion of courage in the face of adverse circumstances. This is a way for Wright to address his fear: "Our signatures are scratched in smoke," (echoing Keats's feeling that his "name was writ on water"), and in "The Silent Generation III," he offers some prospect for continuance and connection by instructing, "O you who come after us,/ Read our remains,// study the soundless bones and do otherwise."

LITTLEFOOT

The paradoxical aspect of Wright's work is encapsulated by his pronouncement in the first poem in *Littlefoot*, "What ever it is I've had to say, I've said it," followed by a series of expressions concerning the effects of time's passage, then countered by the self-admonition, "Time to retrench and retool," an expression of his conviction that there are ways to continue the course of a life dedicated to poetry. Wright's insistence that his existence has been defined by language and a striving for form persists even with his acceptance of the mutability of everything. "I am the sign. I am the letter," he declares before also acknowledging "I am silence/ I am what is not found." What gives him the confidence to continue is a recall of some of the strongest images from his life, remembered and recurring—locations in "mountains rehollowed," along rivers and ridges, in towns near and around Kingsport, his home ground. The meditative quality of his comments across an arc of time are personalized by interjections from the local cultural ethos that has always been an important element of his work, lines from the high lonesome songs of the region close to references to Dante, Pound and other important components of his intellectual foundations.

As has long been the case, almost all of the thirty-five closely linked but discrete sections of the poem pivot on a response to the visible world, landscape and skyscape ever engaging, the images wrought with vivid clarity, evocative and sensory. These outward impressions are intricately linked to an inner process of apprehension, the poet's consciousness emerging, as Helen Vendler incisively describes it, as an evolving "almanac of the inner weather of an extended period." Vendler accurately likens the poems to a painter's sketchbook, a mode that Wright has found congenial throughout his work. The effect of lines such as "mountain incisors beginning to bite/ Into the pink flesh of the sundown" is explained by Wright when he says that in traditional Chinese screen painting "plotting in paint, place in poetry,/ Completes composition."

Although not as specifically addressed as in many previous volumes, Wright's sense of the importance of the undefinable spiritual for him remains inherent in the poems. "Master of words, Lord of signs, you've left me, where are you?" he wonders. It has become clear that his quest is eternal, its course itself the reason for the journey, and its way marked by sightings like "these blossoms as white as autumn's frost" among myriad similarly wondrous, infinitely varying phenomena. The spirit of the volume is expressed in the prayer-like aspiration:

> I keep on thinking,
> If I sit here long enough
> A line, one true line,
> Will rise like some miraculous fish to the surface.

Sestet

One of the most impressive and appealing aspects of Wright's poetry is the way in which what has become a distinct, recognizable voice continues to speak in ways that are new enough to seem fresh. Wright has often spoken about the importance of form and structure, while eschewing any regulations that might restrict the poet. In *Sestet*, he has chosen to work with what are fundamentally six-line poems, with Wright's characteristic "drop line" (or, more exactly, "half-line," which Vendler calls "a second wave of second thoughts") acting as an extension that is controlled by a rhythmic pause. The publisher's description of this method as "a masterpiece of formal rigor" is not inaccurate, but detracts from the calm, pleasant conversational voice that Wright employs. The philosophic gravity that the poems project is, if not lightened, made a bit more comfortable by the profusion of items that are local and personal. The casual inquisitiveness of the opening line of "Terrestrial Music," "What's up, grand architect of the universe?" mingles respect with a degree of amusement at the extent of the great mysteries of existence. Part of the query is a recognition of convergence between the poet and the landscape he is always examining, as in the poem beginning, "The older I become, the more the landscape resembles me," which is significant in that the implication is of a way of seeing as much as a literal transformation.

Many of poems in *Sestet* focus on a particular time of the day or night, and there are also seasonal references, explicit and suggested. The effect is of a kind of diary drawn through a year, or a sort of day book recording the poet's impressions and recollections. Vendler notes the ways in which Wright offers a "counter-argument about regeneration and beauty" even as his "images drawn from nature becomes increasingly entropic." Lines like the opening of line 21 in *Littlefoot*, "At seventy, it's always evening," express a mood of diminution that has been apparent in Wright's poetry since *Buffalo Yoga*, but in *Sestet* there is less a feeling of reduction than a renewed ability to respond to landscape (and mindscape) in its largest sense, as well as an enticing kind of dry wit as in lines such as "The past is so dark, you need a flashlight to find your own shoes./ But what shoes! and always half an inch off the floor." The closing lines of the last poem, a fervent hope and belief that "Someone will take our hand,/ some will give us refuge" is at the core of Wright's claim that his poetry has always been written in the service of "Soul-making" (citing Keats), a concept that he has referred to in many interviews and which he intends to be seen as the essential center of his life's work.

OTHER MAJOR WORKS

NONFICTION: *Halflife: Improvisations and Interviews 1977-1987*, 1988; *Quarter Notes: Improvisations and Interviews*, 1995; *Uncollected Prose: Six Guys and a Supplement*, 2000.

TRANSLATIONS: *The Storm, and Other Poems*, 1978 (of Eugenio Montale); *Orphic Songs*, 1984 (of Dino Campana).

EDITED TEXT: *The Best American Poetry, 2008*, 2008 (with David Lehman).

BIBLIOGRAPHY

Denham, Robert D. *Charles Wright: A Companion to the Late Poetry, 1988-2007*. Jefferson, N.C.: McFarland, 2008. A complement to Denham's first volume, continuing the presentation of details about the composition of the poems.

_____. *The Early Poetry of Charles Wright: A Companion, 1960-1990*. Jefferson, N.C.: McFarland, 2009. An informative "reader's guide" designed as an accompaniment to the poems for the "common reader." Wright dedicated *Littlefoot* to Denham, "with gratitude and affection."

Giannelli, Adam, ed. *High Lonesome: On the Poetry of Charles Wright*. Oberlin, Ohio: Oberlin College Press, 2006. A judicious selection of reviews and critical essays presenting the range and response to Wright's work from its inception, revising and updating Tom Andrews's initial gathering of material in 1995.

Moffett, Joe. *Understanding Charles Wright*. Columbia: University of South Carolina Press, 2008. The first book-length study of Wright's work, offering a solid introduction to the poet's central themes and poetic techniques.

Santos, Sherod. "A Solving Emptiness: C. K. Williams and Charles Wright." In *A Poetry of Two Minds*. Athens: University of Georgia Press, 2000. A comparison of midcareer poems by both poets, Santos examines parallel aesthetic experimentation and the shared determination to overcome despair through art.

Upton, Lee. *The Muse of Abandonment: Origin, Identity, Mastery, in Five American Poets*. London: Associated University Presses, 1998. A critical study of five poets, including Wright, dealing with sociological issues in their work. Includes bibliographical references and an index.

Wright, Charles. Interviews. *Charles Wright in Conversation: Interviews, 1979-2006*. Edited by Robert D. Denham. Jefferson, N.C.: McFarland, 2007. An extensive compilation of interviews with Wright, including a selected bibliography.

Rick Lott; Philip K. Jason
Updated by Leon Lewis

FRANZ WRIGHT

Born: Vienna, Austria; March 18, 1953

PRINCIPAL POETRY

Tapping the White Cane of Solitude, 1976
The Earth Without You, 1980
Eight Poems, 1981
The One Whose Eyes Open When You Close Your Eyes, 1982
Going North in Winter, 1986
Entry in an Unknown Hand, 1987
And Still the Hand Will Sleep in Its Glass Ship, 1990
Midnight Postscript, 1990
The Night World and the Word Night, 1993
Rorschach Test, 1995
Ill Lit: Selected and New Poems, 1998
The Beforelife, 2000
God While Creating the Birds Sees Adam in His Thoughts, 2000
Hell, and Other Poems, 2001
Walking to Martha's Vineyard, 2003
God's Silence, 2006
The Catfish, 2007
Earlier Poems, 2007
Wheeling Motel, 2009

OTHER LITERARY FORMS

Franz Wright has translated the poetry of Erica Pedretti, Rainer Maria Rilke, René Char, and, with his wife, Elizabeth Oehlkers Wright, and the author, the poems of Valzhyna Mort. He has published essays in *Field Magazine*.

ACHIEVEMENTS

Franz Wright has received two National Endowment for the Arts grants, a Whiting Writers' Award (1991), and a Guggenheim Fellowship. In 1995, Wright won the Witter Bynner Prize for Poetry from the American Academy of Arts and Letters. In 1998, he received a grant from the Eric Mathieu King Fund. He was awarded the 1996 PEN/Voelcker Award for his book *The Beforelife*, which was also a finalist for the 2002 Pulitzer Prize. In 2004, Wright's collection *Walking to Martha's Vineyard* won the Pulitzer Prize in poetry. His father, the poet James Wright, had been awarded the same prize in 1978 for *Collected Poems*. They are the only father and son in the history of the prize to win for the same category. Franz Wright won the Paterson Poetry Prize in 2008 for *God's Silence*. His poetry and translations have appeared in *Conduit*, *DoubleTake*, *Field*, *The New Republic*, *The New Yorker*, *Salmagundi*, *Slope*, and many other publications. Wright has taught at Emerson College and the University of Arkansas, and in 2009, he finished a three-year appointment as the Jacob Ziskind Visiting Poet-in-Residence at Brandeis University. Wright has also worked with the mentally ill and with grieving children.

BIOGRAPHY

Franz Wright was born in Vienna, Austria, in 1953 to James Wright and Liberty Wright. James, a war veteran and the son of a laborer, would become one of America's most influential poets. When Franz was three months old, the Wrights left Vienna for the United States, where James continued his education at the University of Washington, studying with Theodore Roethke. The family moved again when James got a job teaching at the University of Minnesota. On weekends, they visited the poet Robert Bly on his farm.

When Franz was eight years old, his parents divorced. Franz and his three-year-old brother Marshall moved with their mother to San Francisco. The elder Wright eventually moved to New York to teach at Hunter College.

James Wright's absence was a deep wound for Franz, made worse by the fact that he and his brother were regularly beaten by their new stepfather. Franz describes a mostly solitary existence, exploring San Francisco on foot, reading "the great books" so he could be like his dad, but also enjoying the Green Lantern. Though his loneliness was intense and he longed for his father terribly, he also came to love the solitude of those walks.

The family moved to nearby Walnut Creek, where Franz excelled in school. He had a vague intention to pursue science or music, but that changed in his fifteenth year. Early one morning, while on vacation in northern California, he woke up with a strange feeling. He went for a walk in a nearby orchard, marveling at this wonderful change in himself and the world. Suddenly words arrived, unbidden, and he sat down and wrote a seven-line poem. His joy at this was so powerful that Wright immediately dedicated his life to the pursuit of poetry. It was frightening to shoulder the burden of what seemed like fate. Somehow he knew he would not be able to have a normal life. Still, the intoxication he felt, surprised to be the bearer of something so mysterious and lovely, gave him consolation and hope.

He sent the poem to his father, who famously wrote back, "I'll be damned. You're a poet. Welcome to Hell." They began a correspondence. A few years later, Franz contributed to James Wright's translation of Herman Hesse.

Franz continued to do well at school, taking courses at the University of California, Berkeley. After graduating in 1971, Wright traveled for a few months in Europe, then visited his father in New York. In 1972, he started at Oberlin College in Ohio, not far from where his parents grew up. After graduating in 1977, he attended only a few months of graduate school before deciding it was not for him. There followed a period of wandering, mostly in New York and New England. True to his vision, poetry was Wright's only vocation.

James Wright died in 1980 of cancer. *The Earth Without You*, Franz Wright's first major book, was published later in the year. He was twenty-seven years old.

Wright remained steadfast in his commitment to writing. By his own account Wright couldn't have held a "real" job for long even if he had wanted to. Like his father, he suffered from bipolar disorder and had inherited a vulnerability to alcoholism and addiction. His struggles with mental illness, alcohol, and drugs made him unreliable, at best. This was not the case when it came to poetry, however. When he needed to, Wright could get himself in shape to write. His dedication to poetry, while it presented a challenge, may well have saved his life. His friendship and correspondence with other poets also sustained him. He published many chapbooks and three additional major books during the next twenty-five years, as well as translating books by Rilke and Char.

By the mid-1990's, however, Wright was in extremely poor health, physically and mentally. He had survived other down times, but this one was truly terrifying—for two years, he couldn't write at all. His visits to Catholic churches, where he had always found comfort, now inspired in him the thought that maybe he could become a member—maybe he could be among those who, though they sinned, were still loved. He began his recovery, but it was not by any means a sure thing until Wright reconnected with a former student of his. Their relationship was transformative, and in 1999, Wright and the translator Elizabeth Oehlkers were married.

In 1998, *Ill Lit* was published by Oberlin College Press. It attracted enough attention that his next book, *The Beforelife*, was published by Knopf, which meant that it was widely reviewed not only in literary magazines but also in mainstream periodicals. *Walking to Martha's Vineyard* followed two years later, and in 2004 won the Pulitzer Prize in poetry. *God's Silence* and *Earlier Poems* followed in quick succession. Wright became the Jakob Viskund Visiting Poet-in-Residence at Brandeis University in 2006. *Wheeling Motel* was released in September, 2009.

It would seem that Wright's central aim has been to write poetry that sustains hope in spite of everything that discourages hope. Perhaps that is why he is now one of the most widely read poets in America.

ANALYSIS

Franz Wright is a poet of image and metaphor. His line breaks and spacing change his words into something like musical notation and often result in ambiguous interpretations. Each poem is vast, though most are less than a page long. His diction is a mix of rough vernacular and carefully constructed images of great beauty. The tone is intimate, often dark, though not lacking in humor or pathos. Each of his books forms a coherent whole.

Wright has been able to transform the materials of his own life to create poems that, even at their most despairing, still somehow offer warm companionship and a reassuring presence. Wright is a fellow traveler who has been in some pretty tough places and managed to find what beauty and comfort there was to find. Even a painful truth is bedrock, solid ground to stand on. With the publication of *Walking to Martha's Vineyard*, Wright has found a larger audience, but he is still the same Franz, in love with what words can do.

ILL LIT

Ill Lit is a summation of Wright's work up to that point. It includes selections from four earlier books, *The One Whose Eyes Open When You Close Your Eyes*, *Entry in an Unknown Hand*, *The Night World and the Word Night*, and *Rorschach Test*. Some of the earlier poems have been revised, though most have not. The book also includes Wright's translations of poems by Rilke, Char, and Charles Baudelaire, among others, and ends with twenty-one new poems. For anyone coming to Wright for the first time, this book is a good introduction to his work and its major themes. In the translations, one finds clues to the poet's aspirations and artistic principles. *Ill Lit* is where Wright's work gathers force.

THE BEFORELIFE

The title of *The Beforelife* refers to Wright's transition from addiction to sobriety and all that came with it; he fell in love with and married his wife, he converted to Catholicism. Two very small poems capture something of the movement of this book; first, "The Wedding," a poem of sheer happiness leavened with Wright's deadpan humor; "As in heaven/ all are smiling/ at you/ even/ those/ who know you." Near the end of the book, there is "Request," Wright's nod to the original wound that for so long kept him captive, "Please love me/ and I will play for you/ this poem/ upon the guitar/ I myself made/ out of cardboard and black threads/ when I was ten years old./ Love me or else." In a few lines, with affection and humor, Wright captures the loneliness, rage, love, and longing of his child self.

WALKING TO MARTHA'S VINEYARD

Wright's shift toward a growing sense of redemption and grace does not mean the darkness of the world disappears, drowned out in a blaze of divine light. It does not mean an end to suffering, or even that minor discomforts do not still rankle. Even so, Wright finds reason to give thanks often in the pages of *Walking to Martha's Vineyard*. "One Heart" ends "Thank You for letting me live for a little as one of the/ sane; thank You for letting me know what this is/ like. Thank You for letting me look at your frightening/ blue sky without fear, and your terrible world without/ terror, and your loveless psychotic and hopelessly/ lost/ with this love." Wright's earlier poems to and about his father are aching, angry notes of separation and loss. This too has changed; now he can write, "Since you left me at eight I have always been lonely// star-far from the person right next to me, but// closer to me than my bones you// you are there" ("Flight").

GOD'S SILENCE

At nearly 150 pages, *God's Silence* is an ambitious work, and it is one of Wright's finest books. A few critics were disappointed by the more declarative lyric often in evidence, but there is no lack in these pages of Wright's identification with the lowest of the low, nor does happiness rob him of his ability to write lines of astonishing transcendence. His dark humor is in full force, a sort of loving truthfulness; even as he sees what's wrong, he also sees what's holy; "A sparrow limps past on its little bone crutch saying/ I am Federico García Lorca/ risen from the dead—/ literature will lose, sunlight will win, don't worry" ("Publication Date").

WHEELING MOTEL

In *Wheeling Motel*, Wright considers his own death. In "Hospitalization," he revisits the agony of being desperately ill; "A voice// saying, How are you feeling.// He was so high he was dead.// I feel just like a window with light coming through it, he said." In *God's Silence*,

Wright wrote poems to dead friends, and he has always addressed his dead father. Now he sees his brother as one of the walking dead, irremediably damaged. He is coming to terms with the past, preparing to meet the future, and holding his banner; "Desire/ and the body/ born of desire;/ fame and shame/ unreal./ But this: one/ strange alone/ heart's wish/ to help all/ hearts, this/ was real."

OTHER MAJOR WORKS

TRANSLATIONS: *Jarmila. Flies*, 1976; *The Life of Mary = Das Marien-Leben*, 1981; *The Unknown Rilke*, 1983; *No Seige Is Absolute: Versions of René Char*, 1984; *The Unknown Rilke: Expanded Edition*, 1991; *Factory of Tears*, 2008 (with Elizabeth Oehlkers Wright).

BIBLIOGRAPHY

Kovacs, Liberty. *Liberty's Quest: The Compelling Story of the Wife and Mother of Two Pulitzer Prize Winners, James Wright and Franz Wright*. Bandon, Oreg.: Robert D. Reed, 2008. An account by Wright's mother of her relationship with his father and Wright.

Macklin, Elizabeth. "The Road Home: A Poet Evokes the Trip Back from a Dark Place." Review of *The Beforelife. The New York Times Book Review*, February 4. 2001, p. 22. Macklin, a poet herself, presents an interesting perspective on the book that marks Wright's transition from addiction and despair to sobriety and hope.

Parini, Jay, ed. *American Writers: A Collection of Literary Biographies—Max Apple to Franz Wright*. Supplement 17. Farmington Hills, Mich.: Thomson Gale, 2008. Contains an entry on the life and works of Wright.

Roth, John K., ed. *Masterplots II: Christian Literature*. Pasadena, Calif.: Salem Press, 2008. This comprehensive set contains an analysis of *God's Silence*.

Wright, Franz. "A Conversation with Franz Wright." Interview by Ilya Kaminsky and Katherine Towler. *Image* (Fall, 2006): 57. Lengthy and thorough interview (on the occasion of the publication of *God's Silence*) covers Wright's entire history as poet and human being, including his love of writing, his illness, addictions, and ultimate recovery, his marriage, his conversion to Catholicism, and the effects of success on his work.

_____. "Homages: Emily Dickinson." *Field* 55 (Fall, 1996): 32-38. Wright's fierce and loving homage to the poet Emily Dickinson conveys Wright's own acute awareness of what makes poetry worth reading (and writing).

_____. Introduction to *The Unknown Rilke: Expanded Edition—Selected Poems*. Oberlin, Ohio: Oberlin College Press, 1990. Wright's eleven-page introduction is an outstanding portrait of Rilke, and Rilke is a model for the kind of poet Wright is and aspires to be.

_____. "One Poet's Awakening: An Interview with Franz Wright." Interview by Maureen Abood. *U.S. Catholic* 11 (November, 2004): 26-31. Wright talks at length about religious feeling, poetic inspiration, and intoxication as impulses very close to each other.

Donna Munro

JAMES WRIGHT

Born: Martins Ferry, Ohio; December 13, 1927
Died: New York, New York; March 25, 1980

PRINCIPAL POETRY

The Green Wall, 1957
Saint Judas, 1959
The Branch Will Not Break, 1963
Shall We Gather at the River, 1968
Collected Poems, 1971
Two Citizens, 1973
Moments of the Italian Summer, 1976
To a Blossoming Pear Tree, 1977
This Journey, 1982
Above the River: The Complete Poems, 1990

OTHER LITERARY FORMS

Although his fame rests almost exclusively with his original poetry, James Wright made a valuable contri-

bution in one other area of literary modernism—the translation. Ezra Pound insisted that translation was in itself an art of the highest creative order, and Wright (especially while he was collaborating with Robert Bly) brought the works of many distinguished European and Latin American authors to readers of English. Wright's translations for Bly's Sixties Press included poems by Georg Trakl, César Vallejo, and Pablo Neruda. Wright also translated Hermann Hesse's *Poems* (1970), and, in collaboration with his son Franz Paul Wright, Hesse's *Wandering* (1972). In addition, he translated Theodor Storm's *The Rider on the White Horse, and Selected Stories* (1964), as well as individual poems of several Latin American poets of the twentieth century.

ACHIEVEMENTS

James Wright was widely honored in literary and academic circles, and his *Collected Poems* won the Pulitzer Prize in 1972. Before his graduation from Kenyon College in 1952, Wright was awarded with the Robert Frost Foundation Poetry Prize. He won a National Institute of Arts and Letters Award in 1959, the Ohioana Book Award for Poetry in 1960, and the Academy of American Poets Fellowship in 1971. Wright received a Fulbright scholarship to the University of Vienna, Austria, where he studied the fiction of Theodor Storm. In his experiments with Deep Image poetry, Wright explored alternatives to the strict rhetoric by which Robert Lowell and his followers created one version of the confessional mode of postmodern poetry. His work with this style led James Dickey to call him "one of the few authentic visionary poets writing today."

BIOGRAPHY

As he proclaims in many of his poems, James Arlington Wright was born in Martins Ferry, Ohio. Although he spent much of his adult life in New York City, Wright returned again and again in memory to the Ohio Valley he loved and despised with equal and intense passion for inspiration as well as material for his poems. His imagination was fired by the loneliness and emptiness of the lives of the Ohioans of his youth and by the occasional flashes of kindness, charity, and decency they showed. At the same time, Wright's preoccupation with steel mills and strip mines confirms a profound concern for the beauty of nature that human beings so indifferently trample upon in the name of economic gain.

Wright left Ohio during World War II and served with the American Occupation Forces in Japan. Upon his discharge, he enrolled at Kenyon College, where he studied literature under John Crowe Ransom. Wright has since acknowledged that this association was a turning point for him, and the traditional structures of his first book, *The Green Wall*, reflect Ransom's influence. Wright's second volume, *Saint Judas*, was published in the same year as Robert Lowell's *Life Studies*, the book that more than any other marked the end of literary modernism in poetry. Lowell and Wright were working independently in the same direction, toward freedom from the insistence on objectivity that had characterized such great modern poets as T. S. Eliot, Ezra Pound, and Wallace Stevens. Like Lowell, Wright sought a more direct exploration of the self as poetic subject and embraced the open subjectivity that Lowell had pioneered. He would abandon the ornate rhetoric

James Wright (©Nancy Crampton)

that Lowell was never willing to leave behind and would move well beyond Lowell in his experimentation with organic form.

Wright's chief influence on postmodern poetry may be his exploration of nondiscursive imagery and careful superimposition as a poetic method. His poems aim at a point of discovery, in which the images of the poem combine to produce a sudden realization of the secrets of the inner, unconscious being. Although he repeatedly disavowed any interest in surrealism as an aesthetic credo, critics have regularly associated Wright and Bly with surrealism, and have called their work neo-Imagist or Jungian. The term "emotive imagination" was coined in an effort to define the process by which the poems evoke nondiscursive feelings in the mind of the reader. Perhaps the most appropriate term is Robert Kelly's "deep image," a concept enthusiastically promoted by Bly during the period of his and Wright's closest association. The Deep Image poem describes the effort to discover a specific object that has powerful emotional and prerational associations for the poet and can be controlled through surprise to evoke a similar set of associations in the consciousness of the reader. The effects of Deep Image poetry depend on careful juxtapositions, superimpositions, sudden leaps in tone or logic, timing, and muted shock.

While in Austria on his Fulbright scholarship, Wright became interested in the poems of Georg Trakl and later translated many of Trakl's and Storm's works, as well as those of several European and Latin American poets. These translations were valuable experiences for Wright, for they taught him alternatives to the traditional methods of English prosody, and he incorporated several of these elements into his own art.

Wright continued his education at the University of Washington, from which he took his M.A. degree in 1954 and his Ph.D. in 1959. At Washington, he studied with Theodore Roethke, whose impact on Wright was formative. Wright has acknowledged his personal reverence for Roethke; the extent of Roethke's poetic influence will be debated by scholars in the years to come.

Like many of his contemporaries, Wright pursued the profession of a teacher and the career of a poet. He taught English at the University of Minnesota for seven years, at Macalester College for two, and at Hunter College in New York from 1966 until his death in 1980. Unlike many of his contemporaries, however, Wright chose not to teach creative writing; he preferred to teach literature. He told a class at the University of Illinois in 1973: "I'm a teacher by profession, not a writer. . . . In fact, I don't even teach poetry."

During the final two decades of his life, Wright emerged as one of the foremost voices in postmodern American poetry. Although he did not systematize his artistic views in essays, as many poets of both the modern and postmodern periods have done, Wright exerted a quiet but vigorous influence by his example. His constant experimentation with form offered younger poets an alternative to the studied objectivity and complex rhetoric of the modern period. By the 1970's, Wright had achieved recognition as a superb reader of his own poems and was in regular demand on the lecture circuit. His second marriage, to Anne Runk, brought new inspiration to his art, and the Wrights' travels in Europe, especially Italy, brought a new tenderness to his poems and particularly to his attitude toward Ohio. He died on March 25, 1980 in New York.

ANALYSIS

Readers who come to James Wright's poetry from a traditional or even a modernist orientation are likely to be struck by a distinctive blend of despair, compassion, and self-revelation. Even in a century characterized by anxiety in poetry, a century in which the most influential single poem would be called *The Waste Land* (1922), Wright's vision seems unusually bleak. The pessimism is, however, balanced by a profound compassion for all mortal beings, which is at the heart of Wright's work. Whereas such great modernists as Eliot, Pound, Stevens, and Robert Frost sought objectivity through wit, irony, and rhetorical discontinuity, Wright has written directly of his anguished compassion for his fellow creatures.

"LYING IN A HAMMOCK AT WILLIAM DUFFY'S FARM IN PINE ISLAND, MINNESOTA"

The tone of many of Wright's memorable poems borders on the depressive side. The famous "Lying in a Hammock at William Duffy's Farm in Pine Island, Minnesota" exemplifies the quality and intention of

Wright's poetry of despair. At first, the charming and lengthy title, reminiscent of the chapter titles of the nineteenth century novels Wright loved so much, invites the reader to expect a witty poem celebrating the beauty of nature. Indeed, the poem is carefully built from a series of images that the viewer in such a hammock would be likely to perceive, and all these images initially fulfill the pastoral expectation created by the title. A bronze butterfly gently blows in the wind and the sound of cowbells evokes a rustic placidity. Even horse droppings are invested with elegance, as they "Blaze up into golden stones," and a chicken hawk floats on the air above. The final line is a shocking reversal: "I have wasted my life." Critics are divided on the effect of this line. Some find it too sudden, and the turn to desolation unearned or contrived. Others hold that the line has a periodic effect and that its devastating contrast leads the reader to examine the images again for a principle of structure. To reexamine these contrasts is to discover that there is a carefully crafted intention at work. The images of the poem become progressively ominous, and the attitude they express has that ambiguous quality that Wright appreciated in Frost's poems. Upon this review, one notices that the butterfly is asleep, so its motion is in fact under the control of an outside force, the wind. The pastoral, auditory richness of the cowbells is balanced by a "movement into the distances of the afternoon." The pivotal image, the horse droppings, now carries a new ominous quality, for their transformation into golden stones is after all a matter of individual human perception. The hawk is not merely floating; it is "looking for home." The pessimism of the poem is not, therefore, arbitrary. Things in nature that appear to be or can be perceived as beautiful by humans are in fact part of a process of decay and alienation. Nature speaks to human beings, but the message of nature can be a shocking or a depressing revelation.

LOVE POEMS

Not all of Wright's poems move readers to despair; a few can even be called poems of joy. Several are love poems, and "A Sequence of Love Poems" forms the center of *Saint Judas*. Love poems also are a very important component of *Two Citizens* and *This Journey*. These poems speak of the necessity as well as the rewards of human love, yet they are not simple, for they evoke a sense of separateness that not even love can transcend. In the elegant "Vision Between Waking and Sleeping in the Mountains," Wright's speaker discovers that even lovers must have secrets that cannot be shared. His beloved's secret separates them, as does a memory he cannot share even with his wife. He transforms this unpleasant thought into a genuine celebration of the very separateness of the lovers: "I love your secret. By God I will never violate the wings/ Of snow you found rising in the wind." The compounding of the contemporary curse with the traditional oath ("By God") emphasizes the determination of the poet to respect the secret of the beloved as an expression of the love he feels. All the love poems deal with and ultimately rejoice in the final individuality of lovers. His poems in *Two Citizens* are "an expression of my patriotism, of my love and discovery of my native place. I never knew or loved my America so well, and I began the book as a savage attack upon it. Then I discovered it." The poet did not sentimentalize America, but his critical and judgmental stance came into balance with an appreciation of natural beauty, human kindness, and the blessings of human love. The pessimism of his most influential poetry would be balanced by an awareness of human and natural beauty.

IMAGES OF NATURE

Several of the works other than love poems can be considered celebrations, but the celebration is usually mixed with an awareness of the potential for despair. "Depressed by a Book of Bad Poetry, I Walk Toward an Unused Pasture and Invite the Insects to Join Me" treats the capability of art, or at least of inferior art, to produce depressing effects, but it celebrates the healing power of nature in the manner of William Wordsworth. A cricket's song effectively cancels out the resonance of the bad poems. Wright's deliberate quest for joy and the consolation of nature is most succinctly exemplified by "Today I Was So Happy, So I Made This Poem," a work that should be read in conjunction with "Lying in a Hammock at William Duffy's Farm in Pine Island, Minnesota." In this poem, images from nature combine to grant the poet a temporary release from the pressure of mortality. Observing a plump squirrel and the shining moon leads the poet momentarily beyond his mortality, and he discovers that "Each moment of

time is a mountain." The joy is completed by the vision of an eagle rejoicing in the "oak trees of heaven," and the cry of the eagle becomes the cry of the poet: *"This is what I wanted."* The statement has both ethical and aesthetic implications. The celebration of a momentary escape from mortality and the ability to express that joy are desires of the highest order of artistic aspiration and of a recognition of the possibility of being at peace with the created world.

THE GREEN WALL

In an extraordinarily prophetic introduction to Wright's first volume, *The Green Wall*, W. H. Auden noted a tension that would, in the process of its resolution, lead to the development of Wright's distinctive poetic style. Auden saw in Wright's choice of material a particularly modern sensibility at work and observed that the persons with whom Wright chose to deal included lunatics, murderers, lesbians, and prostitutes. Even at the inception of Wright's poetic career, Auden saw the alienation that would characterize his mature works. Wright's characters "play no part in ruling the City nor is its history made by them, nor, even, are they romantic rebels against its injustices . . . they are the City's passive victims." This interest in the outcast created a dynamic tension, because Wright's early poems have the traditional formal orthodoxy of his acknowledged masters, Frost, Edwin Arlington Robinson, and Ransom. The force of Robinson's and Ransom's influence is especially apparent in the tension created by the use of traditional forms and meters to write about society's misfits and outcasts.

TENSION IN POETRY

In his first two volumes, Wright responded to this tension by aiming at a firm control through traditional prosody. Although he briefly gave up the writing of poems after the publication of *Saint Judas* because he felt he had reached a dead end, some critics have expressed preference for the control in these works over the expressive quality of his mature works. Paul Lacey praises "the power of sensitive spirit disciplined by a firm intellect and a craftsman's skill."

"TO A DEFEATED SAVIOR"

"To a Defeated Savior" handles the subjects of guilt and failure with the formal objectivity that characterizes the early poems. All four stanzas employ the traditional ballad form, alternately rhymed iambic tetrameter with end-stops reserved for the even-numbered lines. The poem addresses the guilt of a youth (Wright has said that an event that happened to his brother Paul inspired this work) who was unable to save a drowning swimmer. The poet's real interest is in the lasting consequences of the failure; the point of the poem is that all men are defeated saviors. Unable in his daily pursuits to forget completely his moment of heroic action, the youth is haunted by the vision of the drowning swimmer. The speaker discovers that the ultimate failure is fear: "You would have raised him, flesh and soul,/ Had you been strong enough to dare. . . ." The guilt derives from an intention on which the savior was unable to act because he could not control his fear.

The critical point is the universality of the savior's failure. This youth had a dramatic chance to reach out, to risk life for the love of his fellow human being. His failure is a synecdoche for the failure of all people at all times to risk enough for others: "The circling tow, the shadowy pool/ Shift underneath us everywhere." The undertow that drowned the swimmer is a synecdoche for the forces that threaten all humanity, so the savior's defeat, the inability to summon courage and strength adequate to the occasion, is universal. The voice of the poem is compassionate toward the savior, for all human beings must share his guilt. Still, the poem does not excuse this failure. It demands that the savior as well as the speaker come to terms with what might have been and by extension with the responsibility all human beings have to one another.

SAINT JUDAS

In *Saint Judas*, Wright continues to explore the tension between form and subject, and it is from this volume that the greatest number of Wright's poems have been anthologized. The influence of Robinson and Frost is still apparent, but the voice of the poems becomes more directly personal, and Wright himself emerges as the subject of most of the lyrics. The author preferred this over any of his other collections, in part because it was a chronicle of his coming to terms with his own pain. By the logic of the synecdoche that informs all of Wright's poems, this coming to terms with personal pain represents the struggle of humanity to come to terms with its existential anguish. "Saint Ju-

das" is a sonnet, the form that has traditionally implied coherence in English poetry. Here the voice, in a book that has struggled toward direct lyrical expression, is that of Judas. Wright has admitted a primarily technical interest as the genesis of the poem. Moved by Robinson's "How Annandale Went Out," he set out to discover whether he too could write a genuine Petrarchan sonnet that would still be a dramatic monologue.

The traditional octave-sestet pattern of the Petrarchan sonnet offers Wright a form he can use for remarkable effects. The octave dramatizes Judas's despair as he goes to take his own life. His chance encounter with the brutal treatment of another man causes Judas to forget for a moment the reprehensible crimes of his own immediate past. A human instinct takes over, and he rescues the victim. The sestet celebrates Judas's sainthood as the instinctive charity of a man who is already damned and on his way to commit the unpardonable sin, yet who automatically comes to the aid of his fellow man. The final lines may be among the most moving in contemporary poetry: "Flayed without hope,/ I held the man for nothing in my arms." Judas has nothing to gain from his act of charity, and for this reason the moment is profoundly moving.

Critics cannot agree on the discursive meaning of the phrase "for nothing." Some, like John Ditsky, associate the term with "bootless action" and therefore see Judas's role as one of whose "personal pointlessness he alone is aware. . . ." Ralph J. Mills, Jr., focusing on the ambiguity of human behavior, believes that the poem means that if a man can be at one moment treacherous and in despair and at another brave and heroic, then people should all be more merciful to their fellow man. Paul Lacey sees Judas not as a study in ethics or philosophy, but as the "supreme riddle, the man who will do evil for pay and good for nothing." The diversity of these views indicates the richness of the poem. Surely Wright wants his readers to reconsider human nature, for even the worst of people in the worst of times is capable of ethical action in and for itself, without an eye for reward in this world or the next.

"AN OFFERING FOR MR. BLUEHART"

"An Offering for Mr. Bluehart," like "To a Defeated Savior," employs the ballad form. It is a retrospective meditation on one of the poet's own childhood pranks, stealing apples from the orchard of a neighborhood grouch. Wright makes ironic use of the Tom Sawyer tone his situation might imply and transforms that tone into an elegy that is at the same time an effort to deal with personal guilt. Each of the three stanzas moves to a periodic reminder of the mutability of all things. In the first, the recollection of the boys' prank contrasts with sparrows that "Denounced us from the broken bough." The mention of the broken bough marks a shift in point of view, and the elegiac tone intensifies as the sparrows "limp along the wind and die./ The apples are all eaten now."

In the second stanza, the contrast between the laughing boys and Bluehart, the "lean satanic owner" who lay in wait for the pranksters, emphasizes the connotations of Eden inherent in the idyllic setting, and that set of contrasts is heightened by the poet's retrospective awareness of both the seriousness of their trespass ("We stole his riches all away") and the brutal futility of the old man's response: "He damned us to the laughing bone,/ And fired his gun across the gray/ Autumn where his life is done." With a sudden twist of his images, Wright moves from a merely crotchety old man to one whose rage provoked an attempt to kill his tormentors, and with a careful superimposition the old man's act of violence blends with his own mortality.

The final stanza is Wright's "offering" for Bluehart, a note of personal mourning such as characterizes many of his poems. The poet now mourns his old adversary by resisting the temptation to pick apples, and he prays, "Now may my abstinence restore/ Peace to the orchard and the dead." This is at best an empty penance, and Wright knows that. His reversion to colloquial diction in the final line, "We shall not nag them anymore," indicates his awareness of the inadequacy of such a gesture. There is at best the effort to make personal retribution for the sins of the past. In its compelling exploration of a trivial human guilt, this poem speaks to the need for all human beings to be aware of the consequences of their actions, for those actions will return in memory.

Identification with society's enemies and the dramatic effects this produces on the structure of the poem form the nucleus of the two most powerful poems of

Saint Judas, "At the Executed Murderer's Grave" and "Saint Judas." The former may appear to express an almost perverse identification with George Doty, murderer, rapist, and thief, who had also been the subject of "A Poem about George Doty in the Death House," in *The Green Wall*.

"AT THE EXECUTED MURDERER'S GRAVE"

In its total impact, "At the Executed Murderer's Grave" is a profound study of the community of human guilt. The real subject of the poem is not Doty, but the killer's inescapable impact on the speaker. This speaker is aggressively Wright himself, for the poem begins with a startling effort at self-definition: "My name is James A. Wright, and I was born/ Twenty-five miles from this infected grave,/ In Martins Ferry, Ohio. . . ." This assertion of the self by name as well as origin launches the poet on a tortured review of his own relationship with Doty.

They share an origin, but one became a murderer and the other a poet. One element in the abiding effect of the poem is Wright's honest questioning of how far apart the two really are. Perhaps, Wright speculates, his own departure from Ohio allowed him to differ from Doty, because "Dying's the best/ Of all the arts men learn in a dead place." Yet the geographical distance between poet and murderer is in important ways an illusion. Doty remains at the center of the poet's consciousness, a ghost to be exorcised at the terrible cost of coming to terms with his own humanity. He declares, in a deliberate echo of the biblical Pharisees, "Doty, if I confess I do not love you,/ Will you let me alone?" To propose such a limit on human compassion is, of course, to evade the issue, for Wright knows that the real challenge is not to escape from or excuse the actions of the killer, but to wrestle with the dread of recognizing that both are part of the human condition, and to discover a viable relationship between the self and the political entity that electrocuted Doty for his crimes. Doty's actions were clearly reprehensible to Wright, yet he ponders the implications of the "eye for an eye" system that condemned the killer: "And yet, nobody had to kill him either."

Even the obvious distinction, the choices the two men made, does not satisfy Wright. It could be argued that the choice to be a murderer and a rapist is to represent the worst in humanity, whereas to be a poet is to represent the best. Such a notion would be consoling, but Wright rejects the cliché of the heroism of artistic commitment. He says, "I croon my tears at fifty cents per line," a cruel indictment of the professionalism of the poet who transforms his grief into words and receives literal as well as metaphorical compensation. The verb "croon" connotes popular music and therefore an evasion of reality. This censure is reinforced when both the drunks and the police "Can do without my widely printed sighing/ Over their pains with paid sincerity." It is not enough, then, to invoke choice as a substantive difference between the self of the poet and the antithetical force, the murderer Doty.

Something about the killer will not let the poet forget their bond as men. He seems to reject uncritical compassion for humanity when he says of the bums and drunks of Ohio, "Christ may restore them whole, for all of me," but ambiguity is at work here. There is an abdication of responsibility to God, yet the modifying clause "for all of me" implies that the poet's own wholeness depends on Christ's restoration of society's outcasts. Doty is, however, not like the drunks. He is censured with Wright's typical ambiguity: "Idiot, he demanded love from girls,/ And murdered one." His action, brutal as it was, perverted an attempt to find love in a loveless world. In this, the worst of men, there is the same aspiration that animates Wright to be a poet, the need to discover an alternative to the passive acceptance of lovelessness.

This shared humanity cannot be escaped: "This grave's gash festers." It is a reminder of the emptiness of a world for which Ohio has become a synecdoche and of the vindictiveness of human justice. The poem speculates on the distinctions among Doty, the poet, and all human beings at the Last Judgment. Like the killer, "we dead stand undefended everywhere" and those transgressions that had been hidden successfully will stand before "God's unpitying stars." This possibility forces Wright to one of the most painful realizations in all his poems: "Staring politely, they will not mark my face/ From any murderer's, buried in this place./ Why should they? We are nothing but a man." At issue here is what in the eyes of God will distinguish those human beings who have not been guilty of crimes from those who have, and the discovery is that one cannot presume to know. Perhaps on the Day of Judgment, all human beings will have to acknowledge their shared humanity before God and affirm the human community in his presence.

Wright is finally able to resign himself to his community with Doty as "killer, imbecile and thief:/ Dirt of my flesh, defeated, underground." Awareness of the evil of Doty's actions blends with recognition of the bonds that unite poet and killer as part of human nature. "At the Executed Murderer's Grave," then, is not simply a poem about compassion for one of society's enemies. Wright never excuses Doty, and he resists, in the dramatic tension created by the poem, the influence of the killer until he must resign himself to it after having considered the Last Judgment. This is a poem of sterner stuff, of coming to terms with the nature all people share with the very worst of their species.

"SAINT JUDAS"

That acceptance takes the form of a very different theme in "Saint Judas." Like Robinson Jeffers thirty years before in "Dear Judas," Wright has the daring to choose as the hero of his poem the archetypal betrayer and the figure associated in the collective mind of a Christian culture with the most contemptible crime in human history. Technically, the poem is the most interesting in *Saint Judas*, for Wright chafed against the limits of traditional form in "At the Executed Murderer's Grave," and broke rather sharply with that orthodoxy in the succeeding books.

"TWO HANGOVERS"

From these poems on, Wright proceeded to discover a voice that was distinctively his own, exploring the implications of selfhood with increasing self-revelation, virtually abandoning traditional rhyme and metrical schemes, and expanding on the potential of the Deep Image poem, which works through surprise to capture a moment in the unconscious life of both reader and poet.

Paul Zweig has proposed that *The Branch Will Not Break* is one of the key books of the 1960's because Wright's articulation of a visionary style has appealed to younger poets as an alternative to the more formal and elaborate rhetoric of Robert Lowell and Richard Wilbur, the pathfinders of the previous decade.

The title of the volume comes from "Two Hangovers," a pair of poems that offer two opposing variations on the traditional motif of the morning hymn. In the first variation, all the images from nature are transformed, as a result of the poet's condition, to disgust. The "old women beyond my window/ Are hunching toward the graveyard," so there is a reminder of mortality. The life-giving sun has a "big stupid face" and offers no consolation as it "staggers in" upon the poet's distorted consciousness. Even a sparrow's song reminds Wright of the Hanna Coal Company, a frequent symbol in the Ohio poems for human rapacity and exploitation of nature. This morning produces disgust: "Ah, turn it off." In the other variation, "I Try to Waken and Greet the World Once Again," a single image leads to joy, just as the several images of the first led to despair. A blue jay moves up and down on a slender branch outside the window, and human and natural delight are fused in an exquisite synthesis: "I laugh, as I see him abandon himself/ To entire delight, for he knows as well as I do/ That the branch will not break." This symbol expresses both an aesthetic and an ethical position. The world is filled with uncertainty, with occasions for delight and despair, all suggested by the vertical motion of the branch. What gives man the courage to continue and the joy to make that continuation worthwhile is the faith that progress through life, though perilous, is sustained by a connection with nature, a branch that will not break. The proper reaction to this faith is joy, and the best human reaction to the perils of life is delight in the process itself. The image has aesthetic implications, for the randomness of the bird's motion is like the freedoms Wright will claim for his art; but there remains that sense of the connectedness of things, the branch with the tree and the poem with a new kind of organic formal control.

Joy is a note that is rare in Wright's mature poems. Although faith in the ultimate harmony of human beings and nature persists, the distinctive poems explore through superimposition of images the inadequacy of individual or institutional reactions to this harmony.

"AUTUMN BEGINS IN MARTINS FERRY, OHIO"

"Autumn Begins in Martins Ferry, Ohio" returns to the detached speaker of the early poems, but the super-imposition of images builds a subtle cause-effect relationship. The poet, in a high school football stadium, thinks about three separate but related character types. He associates, without commentary, "Polacks nursing long beers," the "gray faces of Negroes in the blast furnace" of a steel mill, and the "ruptured night watchman" at yet another mill. Frustration is what the characters have in common, for all of them are "Dreaming of heroes." These specific images are then generalized to represent "All the proud fathers" who, if proud, are also "ashamed to go home." The disparity between the ordinariness of their daily lives and the aspiration of their dreams makes them afraid of their families and even sexually impotent, for their wives are "Dying for love." The element of mortality surfaces again here, but the dominant effect is that the women, and by extension the entire families, are victims of the emptiness the husbands feel.

This extension is fully realized in the causal connection of the final stanza. "Therefore" is reserved to a line by itself to emphasize the causal sequence, and the poem concludes with a devastating indictment of the brutality and beauty of modern institutional life. "Their sons grow suicidally beautiful" because the sons are under pressure to live out the frustrated, proud fathers' dreams of heroism, so each autumn they "gallop terribly against each others' bodies." The pointlessness and disorder of the athletic contest are powerfully felt in this line. Although there is something insane and suicidal about this institutionalization of violence in which the sons are victims of their fathers' aspirations, there is a terrible beauty in the athletic training, and even the sacrifice, of the youths themselves.

"EISENHOWER'S VISIT TO FRANCO, 1959"

The censure of institutions as antithetical to the harmony of human beings and nature becomes overtly political in "Eisenhower's Visit to Franco, 1959," a parallel set of contrasts between light and darkness and between those who rule and those who are ruled. The American president and the Spanish dictator, caught in a ceremonious handshake, are illuminated by the glare of flashbulbs, the searchlights of "Clean new bombers from America," and Franco's polished escort of police. Franco's promise that "all dark things/ Will be hunted down" and the lights of the American airplanes imply cooperation between the two nations to seek out the dark things in Spain.

The contrasting stanza identifies the poet Antonio Machado, a "cave of silent children," and old men as the inhabitants of darkness. The epigraph from Miguel de Unamuno y Jugo, "We die of cold, and not of darkness," becomes critical here, because there is a cold, sterile quality about the scene at the airfield, whereas the darkness features a creative man who walks by moonlight and children, the hope of the future. Wine, with both Dionysian and Eucharistic implications, "darkens in stone jars" and "sleeps in the mouths of old men." As wine darkens, it becomes richer. The political implication is that the life of the community rests with its ordinary citizens and creative outcasts, not in the leaders who conspire against them.

Franco has promised to "hunt down" the dark things, and the United States supplies the technology to implement that promise. The first two lines now become a terrifying thesis: "The American hero must triumph over/ The forces of darkness." The American hero may learn from the dictator how to turn the harsh light of authority on the lifeblood of the community, the private citizens.

"THE MINNEAPOLIS POEM"

The relation between the individual and the institutions that may challenge the integrity of the self is at the center of Wright's most technically remarkable work, "The Minneapolis Poem." In a series of stark images, Wright empathizes with the poor, the outcasts, and the hopeless of the city. Readers are reminded of Auden's prophetic judgment, in the preface to *The Green Wall*, that Wright's characters are "the City's passive victims." Now, however, Wright is no longer an advocate for the victims; he has identified himself completely with them. As the poem moves from one seemingly random portrait of outcasts to another, it becomes clear that Wright's identification with the victims is also a profound questioning of the sociological and institutional ties that bind human beings into a community. The very fragmentary and seemingly random nature of "The Minneapolis Poem" expresses the central theme, the terror, violence, and indifference at the heart of the modern city. Wright laments the name-

less and even numberless old men who committed suicide in the winter and wonders, "How does the city keep lists of its fathers/ Who have no names?" Their anonymity and the indifference of the City leaves them with only the community of death, and Wright, despite his wish to console them, can only "wish my brothers good luck/ And a warm grave" in contrast to the bad luck and cold winters they knew in Minneapolis.

The second section of "The Minneapolis Poem" is a tour de force. Four groups are mentioned, but there is no possibility of their ever getting together to reshape the fragmented city. Even within these groups either fear or some sinister purpose dominates. "The Chippewa young men/ Stab one another shrieking/ Jesus Christ." America's first citizens are outcasts in the heart of America, and they invoke the name of the conqueror's god as a curse. Even their bond is violent; they take out their wrath and frustration on one another. In Wright's depiction of another group with a common purpose, the "Split-lipped homosexuals limp in terror of assault." Their common purpose is to avoid persecution by the heterosexual majority, but their injuries show how unsuccessful their subgroup has been. The middle class is represented when "High school backfields search under benches/ Near the Post Office." For what do they search? The very lack of specificity implies a sinister purpose, and a harsh description reinforces this possibility: "Their faces are the rich/ Raw bacon without eyes." The elite are here, too: "The Walker Art Center crowd stare/ At the Guthrie Theater." Unlike the other groups, this one expresses no purpose, merely anonymous unity. Their response to one of America's cultural landmarks is apathetic and pointless. It is clear that no organization of these groups into a single social unit is possible, and there is no creative force in any of them.

The poem notes other of the city's outcasts and enemies, the "legless beggars" who are gone and the black prostitutes from Chicago who know the police officer who poses as a patron to entrap them. The only things at home in Minneapolis are automobiles, products of modern technology that "consent with a mutter of high good humor/ To take their two naps a day." These autos, described by a felicity that ought to describe human behavior, speak to the impersonality and terror of modern urban life.

The terror turns inward as Wright, not identified with the poor and the nameless, claims that "There are men in this city who labor dawn after dawn/ To sell me my death." Just who these men are is not made explicit, and the uncertain identification fits well with the attitudes of uncertainty, alienation, and dread that the poem has created. Like the beggars, Chippewas, and prostitutes, the dealers in death are nameless. Who they are is less important than what they are: the logical consequences of the human community, the city, gone wrong.

Dread leads Wright logically to a contemplation of death, something close to his mind since the introduction of the suicides in the first stanza. Now death is personal, individual, and related directly to life in the city. He chooses not "To allow my poor brother my body to die/ In Minneapolis" and prays that he not be buried there. At first glance, this may seem to be a morbid sentiment, but Wright intends to dramatize his rejection of the city in the tormented and fragmented form it has taken. He strategically invokes the patron of American poets: "The old man Walt Whitman our countryman/ Is now in America our country/ Dead." This sudden movement is a reminder of the death of the great bard of American democracy, the spokesman of brotherhood who is now one with the suicides and legless beggars of this poem. A closer look at the syntax reveals that the America Whitman knew, loved, and created is also dead.

"The Minneapolis Poem" concludes with Wright's wish not to be buried in the city, but "stored with the secrets of the wheat and the mysterious lives/ Of the unnamed poor." It is a jaded version of the return to nature of the Romantics. A community is asserted, and the image of the wheat suggests vitality in the United States among its citizens. As an alternative to the failed life of the city, the conclusion of "The Minneapolis Poem" is not intellectually satisfying, but as an expression of pain at the failure of a basic human institution to respond to human needs, the ending has a powerful emotional impact.

"Hook"

It is worth noting that "Hook," one of the most memorable poems in *To a Blossoming Pear Tree*, re-

cords a moment of unexpected human warmth in the same city as in "The Minneapolis Poem." A mutilated Sioux Indian gave a despairing Wright cab fare to go home, and the memory leads Wright to one of his understated moments of appreciation for the decency of his fellow man. The money the Sioux gave him symbolizes the capacity of society's outcasts to care for one another.

"A Blessing"

Despite his preoccupation with death, despair, alienation, and anxiety, Wright sought to record moments of joy in his love for people and his reverence for nature. His "A Blessing," a simple account of the delight caused by the greeting of the poet and a nameless friend by two ponies, reaches toward mysticism and shows that this poet, so aware of the pain of modern life, could occasionally articulate moments of rapture.

"A Reply to Matthew Arnold of My Fifth Day in Fano"

In his final volume, *This Journey*, Wright articulates in a prose poem called "A Reply to Matthew Arnold of My Fifth Day in Fano" the artistic and thematic credo to which his poems form a lasting moment: "Briefly in harmony with nature before I die, I welcome the old curse." The curse is the many human failings and moral terrors his poems have documented. The attitude is vigorous welcome for humans and their companion, nature, a defiant celebration of the very fact of mortality.

Other major works

NONFICTION: *Collected Prose*, 1983; *A Wild Perfection: The Selected Letters of James Wright*, 2005 (Anne Wright and Saundra Rose Maley, editors); *The Delicacy and Strength of Lace: Letters Between Leslie Marmon Silko and James Wright*, 2009 (Anne Wright, editor).

TRANSLATIONS: *Twenty Poems of George Trakl*, 1961 (with Robert Bly); *Twenty Poems*, 1962 (with Bly and John Knoepfle; of César Vallejo); *The Rider on the White Horse and Selected Stories*, 1964 (of Theodor Storm); *Twenty Poems of Pablo Neruda*, 1967 (with Bly); *Poems*, 1970 (of Hermann Hesse); *Wandering*, 1972 (with Franz Wright; of Hesse).

BIBLIOGRAPHY

Dougherty, David. *James Wright*. Boston: Twayne, 1987. This essential book provides the reader with a historical study of Wright's development as a craftsman, thereby allowing the individual to judge the poet's historical importance. In addition, the book suggests—and examines—the intended unity in each of Wright's books and provides readers with insightful readings of key Wright texts.

_____. *The Poetry of James Wright*. Tuscaloosa: University of Alabama Press, 1991. Critical interpretation of selected works by Wright. Includes bibliographical references and index.

Kovacs, Liberty. *Liberty's Quest: The Compelling Story of the Wife and Mother of Two Poetry Pulitzer Prize Winners, James Wright and Franz Wright*. Bandon, Oreg.: Robert D. Reed, 2008. Wright's wife, and the mother of Franz, who would become a poet also, describes her life with the elder poet, their divorce, and her subsequent move to San Francisco and remarriage.

Roberson, William. *James Wright: An Annotated Bibliography*. Lanham, Md.: Scarecrow Press, 1995. Good resource for locating articles and other publications by and about Wright.

Smith, Dave. *The Pure Clear Word: Essays on the Poetry of James Wright*. Urbana: University of Illinois Press, 1982. Attempts to determine the degree to which Wright confessed the truth and to which he fabricated reality in his work. The essays include W. H. Auden's foreword to "The Green War," Robert Bly's "The Work of James Wright," and others that cover a variety of topics from Wright's personal life to his poetry. Contains a bibliography.

Stein, Kevin. *James Wright: The Poetry of a Grown Man*. Athens: Ohio University Press, 1989. An academic study that traces the growth of the entire body of Wright's work. The poems are examined to show that his stylistic changes are frequently more apparent than actual, that he experienced an ongoing personal and artistic evolution, and that the transition of his themes from despair to hope is the result of his gradual acceptance of the natural world.

David C. Dougherty

JAY WRIGHT

Born: Albuquerque, New Mexico; May 25, 1935

PRINCIPAL POETRY

Death as History, 1967
The Homecoming Singer, 1971
Dimensions of History, 1976
Soothsayers and Omens, 1976
The Double Invention of Komo, 1980
Explications/Interpretations, 1984
Elaine's Book, 1986
Selected Poems of Jay Wright, 1987
Boleros, 1991
Transfigurations: Collected Poems, 2000
The Guide Signs: Book One and Book Two, 2007
Music's Mask and Measure, 2007
Polynomials and Pollen: Parables, Proverbs, Paradigms, and Praise for Lois, 2008
The Presentable Art of Reading Absence, 2008

OTHER LITERARY FORMS

Jay Wright has published several plays in *Hambone*, *Callaloo*, and *Southern Review*. He has also written essays on African American poetry and poetics, the most important of which is "Desire's Design, Vision's Resonance: Black Poetry's Ritual and Historical Voice," which appeared in *Callaloo* in 1987.

ACHIEVEMENTS

Jay Wright's poetic vision is unique in its cross-cultural approach to African American spiritual and intellectual history. He has been called one of the most original and powerful voices in contemporary American poetry. Though critical acclaim of his work has been slow in coming, he has received a number of prestigious awards: an Ingram Merrill Foundation Award and a Guggenheim Fellowship in 1974; an American Academy of Arts and Letters Award in Literature in 1981; an Oscar Williams and Gene Derwood Writing Award in 1985; a MacArthur Fellowship that spanned the years 1986-1991; and the Academy of American Poets Fellowship in 1996. He received the Lannan Literary Award for Poetry in 2000, Yale University's

Bollingen Prize for Poetry in 2005, and an American Book Award from the Before Columbus Foundation for Lifetime Achievement in 2006.

BIOGRAPHY

Jay Wright was born in 1935 in Albuquerque, New Mexico, to Leona Dailey, a Virginian of black and Native American ancestry. His father, George Murphy, a light-complexioned African American construction worker, jitney driver, and handyman who later adopted the name of Mercer Murphy Wright, claimed both Cherokee and Irish descent. Wright remained with his mother until the age of three, when Leona gave the boy to the cook Frankie Faucett and his wife Daisy, a black Albuquerque couple known for taking in children. Daisy Faucett was as religious as her husband was proud and generous. Wright's early, intense exposure to the African American church was attributable to her. Mercer Wright, in the meantime, had relocated to California. It was not until his son was in his early teens that he went to live with his father, and later his stepmother Billie, in San Pedro. During his high school years in San Pedro, Wright began to play baseball. In the early 1950's, he was a minor-league catcher for the San Diego Padres, the Fresno Cardinals, and the Aguilars of Mexicali. He also learned to play the bass in those days. In 1954 he joined the U.S. Army, and he served in the medical corps until 1957. He was stationed in Germany for most of that time, which gave him the opportunity to travel throughout Europe.

A year after his return to the United States, Wright enrolled at the University of California, Berkeley, under the G.I. Bill. At Berkeley, he devised his own major in comparative literature and graduated after only three years. Before deciding to continue his literary studies, Wright considered studying theology and spent a semester at Union Theological Seminary in New York on a Rockefeller grant. He left Union for Rutgers University in 1962. In 1964, Wright interrupted his graduate studies to spend a year teaching English and medieval history at the Butler Institute in Guadalajara, Mexico. He returned to Rutgers in 1965. During the next three years, Wright completed all the requirements for his doctoral degree except the dissertation. While at Rutgers, Wright lived and worked part-time in Harlem, where he came into contact with a number of other young African American writers, among them Henry Dumas, Larry Neal, and LeRoi Jones (who later changed his name to Amiri Baraka).

In 1968, Wright married Lois Silber, who joined him during his second and longest sojourn in Mexico. The couple lived briefly in Guadalajara and then moved to Jalapa, where they maintained a residence until the autumn of 1971. Many of Wright's poems recall these and other Mexican settings. Wright returned to the United States from time to time, spending brief periods as a writer in residence at Tougaloo and Talladega colleges and at Texas Southern University, as well as several months as a Hodder Fellow at Princeton University. In early 1971, the Wrights departed for Scotland. During Wright's two-year tenure as Joseph Compton Creative Writing Fellow at Dundee University, they lived in Penicuik, outside Edinburgh. Upon their return to the United States in 1973, the Wrights moved first to Warren and then to Piermont, New Hampshire.

Wright has traveled extensively throughout Europe, the United States, Central and South America, and Canada. In 1988, he was part of a group of writers who visited the People's Republic of China under the auspices of the University of California, Los Angeles. Since 1975, he has taught at Yale University; at the universities of Utah, Kentucky, and North Carolina at Chapel Hill; and at Dartmouth College.

ANALYSIS

The most distinctive feature of Jay Wright's poetry is what he himself calls "a passion for what is hidden." This passion for sounding the depths of varied histories and mythologies—Western European, African, Caribbean, North and South American, and Asian—takes the poetic shape of a spiritual quest that is at once intensely personal and compellingly collective. The object of Wright's quest is to restore to African American literature a sense of the breadth, the complexity, and the coherence of its cultural, historical, social, artistic, intellectual, and emotional resources. Writing poetry is his way of uncovering and reinventing eclipsed linkages between cultural traditions often believed to be separate. "For me, multicultural is the fundamental process of human history," he explained in a 1983 interview in *Callaloo*.

Wright's work exemplifies what Guyanese novelist Wilson Harris, whom Wright acknowledges as a major source of inspiration, has termed a "poetics of the cross-cultural imagination." Wright's autobiographical persona embarks on poetic journeys into uncharted territories where familiar temporal, political, and linguistic boundaries blur and dissolve. Fragmented voices from many different historical periods and cultural traditions emerge as the poet's (and the reader's) guides through a veritable maze of historical and mythological references and allusions that ultimately come together in a rather unorthodox vision of African American or black culture. It is unorthodox within a United States context because of Wright's sensitivity to and insistence on continuities across, not just within, cultures. No African American, Wright insists, "can have escaped grounding in other cultures."

Though his poetic vision is firmly grounded in African American historical experience and expressive culture, Wright's sense of what it means to be a black poet is distinctly different from that of most African American poets of his generation. Even if Wright's quest for creativity time and again leads him to specific African religions and folklore, mainly Akan, Nuer, Dogon, and Bambara, that quest is not predicated on a rejection of "Western" traditions. In that respect, Wright's poetics and cultural politics are more akin to those of Robert Hayden and even Melvin Tolson than to the work of Amiri Baraka and others who embraced black cultural nationalism in the late 1960's and early 1970's.

Wright's poetry is remarkable in its erudite and consistently innovative engagement with a wide variety of literary and cultural traditions. The scope of his vision and the depth of his perception can largely be attributed to Wright's extensive research in medieval and Renaissance literatures, music, anthropology, the history of religions, and the history of science. The notes appended to *Explications/Interpretations*, *Dimensions of History*, and especially *The Double Invention of Komo* point to some of the principal holdings of Wright's scholarly archives. The most important texts behind his poems are *The Akan Doctrine of God* (1944), by Ghanaian politician and philosopher J. B. Danquah, and the

Jay Wright (Courtesy, Yale University)

studies of Dogon and Bambara traditional societies conducted in the 1920's and 1930's by a team of French anthropologists under the direction of Marcel Griaule. Most consciously, Wright's poetry takes recourse to Griaule's *Conversations with Ogotemmêli: An Introduction to Dogon Religious Ideas* (1948) and his later collaboration with Germaine Dieterlen, *The Pale Fox* (1965).

Annotations, however, are atypical for Wright, who, though he yielded to the demands of his publishers in these instances, is usually adamant in his refusal to explicate his poetry to those who find it inaccessible. What lies behind this refusal is not arrogance or obscuration, as some critics have assumed, but what Wright sees as an abiding respect for the complexity and difficulty of the social, cultural, and historical processes his poetry tries to represent. An assimilation of a vast body of knowledge, his poetry demands rigorous intellectual and imaginative engagement from each reader.

The formal experiments in which Wright engages

are as extravagant as the texture of his poetry is dense. A mixture of Italian, German, and Spanish interspersed with Dogon and Bambara ideograms, Wright's language is at times so unfamiliar that to describe it as "English" seems inadequate. Musical forms such as blues and jazz, as well as a host of Caribbean and Latin American song and dance forms, are as integral to his poetic endeavors as are attempts at making English verse responsive to the "grammars" and metrics of other languages.

THE HOMECOMING SINGER

Semantic density and formal extravagance are particularly characteristic of the book-length poems that have followed Wright's first collection, *The Homecoming Singer*, which was preceded in 1967 by a chapbook, *Death as History*. These early poems, most of which are reprinted in *Selected Poems of Jay Wright*, tend to be more manageable from both a thematic and a linguistic point of view. *The Homecoming Singer* is important to Wright's canon not only as a record of his early artistic, spiritual, and intellectual development but also because it contains all the seeds of his later writing.

The two opening poems, "Wednesday Night Prayer Meeting" and "The Baptism," inspired by the religious zeal of Daisy Faucett, lament the failure of institutionalized African American religions to provide spiritual resources for what Wright, with Wilson Harris, calls "the redefinition of the person." The tragic lack of "myths to scale your life upon" results in "the senseless, weightless,/ timedenying feeling of not being there" with which the poet is left at the end of "Reflections Before the Charity Hospital." Rather than leading to the despair and violence of LeRoi Jones's "A Poem for Willie Best," a text on which Wright brilliantly meditates in "The Player at the Crossroads" and "Variations on a Theme by LeRoi Jones," this alienation and dispossession heighten the poet's awareness, as in "First Principles," of "the tongues of the exiled dead/ who live in the tongues of the living." In "Destination: Accomplished," this new awareness grows into an abiding emotional and intellectual desire for "something to put in place." It is the death-challenging search for "new categories for the soul/ of those I want to keep" that finally directs Wright toward traditional Af-

rican societies, their rituals and mythologies, in "A Nuer Sacrifice" and "Death As History."

Like all of Wright's poetry, though more explicitly so, *The Homecoming Singer* draws on autobiographical experience as a catalyst for the persona's introspective inquiries into the possible nature of an African American cultural and literary tradition. Memories of his two fathers, in "A Non-Birthday Poem for My Father," "Origins," "First Principles," and "The Hunting-Trip Cook," become occasions for acknowledging and examining the responsibilities the dead confer upon the living. This is what connects these presences from Wright's personal past, which also include his alcoholic stepmother in "Billie's Blues," to "the intense communal daring" of Crispus Attucks and W. E. B. Du Bois.

The Homecoming Singer also acquaints the reader with geographies to which Wright returns throughout his poetic career. In "An Invitation to Madison County," one of the best poems in this collection, the black American South offers unexpected memories and visions of community to the displaced poet, whose journey in this instance follows that of so many other African American writers in search of their cultural origins.

The Southwest, which, along with California, provides the setting for Wright's family remembrances, is another place of origin; its history also connects the persona with the Mexico of "Morning, Leaving Calle Gigantes," "Chapultepec Castle," "Jalapeña Gypsies," and "Bosques de Chapultepec." "A Month in the Country" offers a fleeting glimpse of the "New England reticence" of New Hampshire, to which the persona escapes after "The End of an Ethnic Dream" to soothe his "blistered" brain. In later poems, all these places evolve into full-fledged symbolic geographies. "Sketch for an Aesthetic Project" and "Beginning Again," the two poems that close *The Homecoming Singer*, are the initial attempts of the "aching prodigal" at weaving his memories and his discontent into a poetic design that transcends individual experience. These poems are preludes to *Soothsayers and Omens*, the first volume of a poetic cycle that continues with *Explications/ Interpretations*, *Dimensions of History*, and *The Double Invention of Komo*. Each of these book-length poems is part of a carefully constructed pattern or dramatic movement, and this is the order in which Wright places them.

SOOTHSAYERS AND OMENS

The poem that opens the first of *Soothsayers and Omens*' four parts is significantly titled "The Charge." Reminiscent of Wright's homages to paternal figures in *The Homecoming Singer*, this poem focuses on fathers and sons "gathered in the miracle/ of our own memories." With "The Appearance of a Lost Goddess" and the rise of a female principle to complement and balance the male presences, the poet identifies himself as an initiate who has accepted the charge to reconstruct neglected and severed ties. This reconstruction takes the initial shape of six short poems titled "Sources" with which Wright inaugurates his systematic exploration of African cosmologies. "Sources" draws heavily on West African pre-Columbian mythologies, both of which become part of a collective memory. The two longer poems that follow and change the pace of the first part, "Benjamin Banneker Helps to Build a City" and "Benjamin Banneker Sends His 'Almanac' to Thomas Jefferson," weave elements of Dogon theology around quotations from the letters of the African American astronomer, an "uneasy" stranger in his own land who bemoans "the lost harmony" and the injustices of slavery.

Dogon ritual becomes even more significant in part 4, whose title, "Second Conversations with Ogotemmêl," refers directly to Griaule's anthropological exploits. These are poems of apprenticeship that invoke different components and stages of the creation of the universe, represented by the water spirit Nommo, creator of the First Word (that is, language) and his twin Amma; Lébé, guardian of the dead; and the Pale Fox, agent of chaos. Wright's "Conversations" are characterized by exchanges and relationships very different from those that prevail between anthropologist and informer. For Wright's persona, Ogotemmêli is a spiritual guide or "nani" who "will lead me into the darkness" and whose silences promise the speech of redemption with which to mend "the crack in the universe." The terms and trajectory of Wright's journey into darkness, a sort of Middle Passage in reverse that leads back to Africa, are also indebted to Dante's

search, even if the spiritual map (the "God") Wright's initiate "designs" is different. It is no coincidence, then, that "Homecoming," the poem that announces "a plan of transformations," is laced with quotations from *La divina commedia* (c. 1320, 3 volumes; *The Divine Comedy*, 1802).

At the same time that *Soothsayers and Omens* initiates the reader into African mythologies, it also revisits Mexico and New Mexico, geographies already implicit in the pre-Columbian references of the opening poems. The most remarkable of the transitional poems in parts 2 and 3 is "The Albuquerque Graveyard," a place to which Wright's persona returns to worry the dead, the "small heroes," with a quest for patterns that is as "uneasy" as Benjamin Banneker's. The poet's announcement that "I am going back/ to the Black limbo,/ an unwritten history/ of our own tensions," is a precise summary of his desire and purpose throughout *Soothsayers and Omens*: both to articulate a history that has not been written and to un-write a history that has neglected, even forgotten, the participation of Africans and African Americans in founding what is deceptively called "Western" civilization.

EXPLICATIONS/INTERPRETATIONS

If *Soothsayers and Omens* is the "first design," the first step toward the articulation of a spiritual order, *Explications/Interpretations* marks the next logical stage in what Wright calls his "African-Hellenic-Judaic discourse." Dedicated to poet Robert Hayden and critic Harold Bloom, this volume generates somewhat different patterns and principles of order and also introduces a set of new players on a new stage in "MacIntyre, The Captain, and the Saints." This central dramatic poem enacts Wright's personal and intellectual ties with Scotland. MacIntyre, the Irish-Scottish clan to which the names Murphy and Wright can be traced, is Wright's autobiographical persona who, instead of conversing with Ogotemmêli, now turns to astronomer David Hume, poet Hugh MacDiarmid, and anthropologist Robert Sutherland Rattray. A new element in this poem is the use of ideograms, a strategy indebted to Ezra Pound's works, which Wright explores more fully in *Dimensions of History* and *The Double Invention of Komo*.

Dramatic poetry, a form for which Wright has an undoubted preference, is not the only important formal aspect of this volume. *Explications/Interpretations* is also energized by the vital rhythms of African American music. The poem is divided into three parts, "Polarity's Trio," "Harmony's Trio," and "Love's Dozen," titles that already indicate Wright's concern with music and number. "Tensions and Resolutions" introduces dualism or twinning and balance as concepts that inform the poem's thematic and structural organization: "Each act caresses/ the moment it remembers,/ and the moment it desires." This double "act" is of course the act of writing, which makes Wright's poem a "field of action" along the lines of Charles Olson's "projective verse."

That the rhythms of writing and speaking are formal articulations of the poet's being is crucial to understanding the dynamics of *Explications/Interpretations* and indeed of all of Wright's poems. The arrangement of the poems in groups of three, six, and twelve (plus one) already creates a sense of rhythm, which is rendered most explicit in "The Twenty-Two Tremblings of the Postulant," subtitled "Improvisations Surrounding the Body." This poem is a good example of Wright's kind of blues poetry, in which the compositional principle is derived not from the call-and-response structure of the blues lyrics, as is the case, for instance, in the poetry of Langston Hughes and Sterling Brown, but from the arrangement of the twenty-two short poems across a sequence of chords.

Each poem corresponds not only to a different part of the human body but also to a musical bar that belongs to a specific chord, I, IV, or V. The last two bars, readers are told at the end of the poem, are "tacit," which makes for a total of twenty-four bars, whose musical equivalent is a (doubled) blues line. *Explications/Interpretations* as a whole is a poetic improvisation on this basic blues line, one of the most distinctive rhythms of African American culture. These are the sounds of flesh and bone that constitute the poem's and the poet's "grammar of being." For Wright, who insists on poetry's social and historical responsibilities, these schemes, "the god's elemental bones," are "a launchpad/ into the actual" ("Inscrutability").

Wright's emphasis in *Explications/Interpretations* on the body as a site of knowledge and action is indicative of his rejection of dualisms. The spiritual does not exist in separation from the material any more than male exists without female. They are what Wright conceives of as "twins," and the desired relationship between them is one of balance. This is most clearly articulated in "The Continuing City: Spirit and Body" and "The Body," two poems that lay out aesthetic and philosophical principles indebted to Danquah's *The Akan Doctrine of God*. In his notes, Wright identifies *Explications/Interpretations* as an attempt "to claim this knowledge as part of the continuing creative life of the Americas"; the Americas are what come into full view in *Dimensions of History*.

DIMENSIONS OF HISTORY

Though *Dimensions of History* is dedicated to the late Francis Ferguson, with whom Wright studied at Rutgers, the book owes perhaps its most significant debt to Wilson Harris's notion of "vision as historical dimension." This third volume of Wright's poetic cycle maintains the tripartite structure of *Explications/Interpretations*, a scheme now more explicitly associated with the three stages of an initiation ritual: separation, transition, (re)incorporation.

Part 1, "The Second Eye of the World. The Dimension of Rites and Acts," announces this link not only by being itself divided into three poems but also by offering the reader a Dogon ideogram that, according to Griaule and Dieterlen, represents the separation of the twins, male and female, at the moment of circumcision. The historical dimension of separation within an African American context is (enforced) exile. This historical condition becomes the "special kinship" the poet's persona shares with his other selves, the dead to whose realm he descends and whose claims he seeks to understand in a spiritually barren land from which the god has retreated. Among them are once again Du Bois and Crispus Attucks, who are joined by the voices of and allusions to Frederick Douglass, Saint Augustine, Toussaint L'Ouverture, and many others who congregate in a text brimming with references to Aztec, Mayan, Incaic, Egyptian, Arabic, Christian, Yoruba, Akan, and, of course, Dogon and Bambara mythologies. Ogotemmêli's return in the figure of the blind sage at the beginning of the second poem commences the process of healing: "Anochecí enfermo amanecí bueno" ("I went to bed sick, I woke up well") are the words that open the third poem, at the end of which the persona names himself "a dark and dutiful dyēli,/ searching for the understanding of his deeds."

Part 2, titled "Modulations. The Aesthetic Dimension," consists of an assortment of poetic forms, many of them linked to Caribbean and Latin American musical forms and instruments such as the Cuban *son*, the *areito*, and the *bandola*, a fifteen-string Colombian guitar. The shorter poems in "Rhythms, Charts, and Changes"; "The Body Adorned and Bare," a section reminiscent of the meditations on the body in *Explications/Interpretations*; and "Retablos" (votive paintings) lead up to Wright's "Log Book of Judgments," a series of ethical and aesthetic formulations distilled from the persona's historical and ritualistic experiences. They culminate in the following lines from "Meta-A and the A of Absolutes": "I am good when I know the darkness of all light,/ and accept the darkness, not as sign, but as my body."

Dimensions of History closes with "Landscapes: The Physical Dimension," whose themes and poetic architecture return to the history of the conquest of the Americas and to Náhua (Aztec) mythology and poetry. The most notable formal aspects of this final part are the encyclopedic monoliths, block passages that list the vital statistics of five American nations: Venezuela, Colombia, Panama, Mexico, and the United States. The spaces between these building blocks or "stones" are filled with Wright's own enchanted mortar, a possible translation of the Náhuatl-infused Spanish idiom *cal y canto* (literally, "mortar and song") that joins Wright's compositional principles with his cross-cultural concerns. This syncretic idiom, which also conjures up such Latin American poets as Pablo Neruda and José María Arguedas, is a miniature representation of the rhizomes Wright's poem uncovers. It is one of his "emblems of the ecstatic connection." His poet's Middle Passages temporarily end with an image of the Great Gate of the ancient Mayan city Labná, a sole triumphal arc in a city without fortifications that is both "a gateway to the beautiful" and "the image of our lives among ourselves."

THE DOUBLE INVENTION OF KOMO

The Double Invention of Komo, which is dedicated to the memory of Marcel Griaule, may well be called the most African of Wright's poems. Wright's most sustained and ambitious effort in the genre of dramatic poetry, *The Double Invention of Komo* is a poetic reenactment of the initiation ceremonies performed by the all-male Komo society among the Bambara. The object of these highly formalized ceremonies is to maintain the Bambara's traditional intellectual, religious, and social values. *The Double Invention of Komo* "risks ritual's arrogance" to the extent that the logic and the specifics of this ritualistic process inform the poem's conceptual and formal structures.

Of special importance to Wright are the 266 great signs, a system of ideograms that organizes Bambara cosmology. Each sign inscribes a different "name" or aspect of the god and binds him to the material objects and substances associated with Komo's altars, as in "*Dyibi*—obscurity—gold." As is evident from "The Initiate Takes His First Six Signs, the Design of His Name," such naming is an exceedingly complex process. What Wright is after is the sacred "grammar" of names that, ultimately, evolve into a secular "alphabet" of creation. *The Double Invention of Komo* is quite explicitly and self-consciously a poem about the metaphysics of writing, and this accounts for much of its difficulty.

The central preoccupation of *The Double Invention of Komo* is how to achieve self-knowledge through writing, how to fashion a language that would redress loss and dispossession. Writing, for Wright, is a process of simultaneous dismemberment and reassembly of meaning and community: It is both "scalpel" and "suture," both excision and circumcision. Like the ritual scars on the body of the initiate, poetic writing confers not only knowledge of traditional values but also kinship. It is as if the poet's pen were a ritual knife "cutting" the initiates (and the readers) into kinship, marking them as members of a special community. As the persona's status changes from that of an initiate to that of a "delegate," the statements made in *Dimensions of History*'s "Meta-A and the A of Absolutes" are reformulated: "What is true is the incision./ What is true is the desire for the incision,/ and the signs' flaming in the wound." It is in this sense that the Middle Passage, which all of the persona's journeys reenact, becomes a rite of passage that compensates for the violent psychic dismemberment and the geographical dispersal of the members of Africa's traditional cultures.

Wright's key metaphor, the limbo, refers to Harris, who regards this dance, created on the crowded slave ships, as a form of silent collective resistance. Harris's sense of the limbo as a "structure of freedom" has been an inspiration for Wright since "the Albuquerque Graveyard." It also encapsulates the main concerns that have motivated Wright's explorations of the poetic potential of music and dance.

ELAINE'S BOOK

Given the usually all-male composition of Wright's imaginary communities and especially the emphasis on male initiation rituals in *The Double Invention of Komo*, the foregrounding of female voices in *Elaine's Book* is almost startling. While women are never entirely absent from his poetry, which frequently identifies creativity as a female principle, this is the first book in which they assume historical, rather than exclusively mythological, stature. Women are integral parts of the poetic geographies Wright's persona traverses in his fascinating explorations of female otherness. The female voices in *Elaine's Book* assume many different identities: that of Yemanjá, the Yoruba/Afro-Cuban goddess of the waters; that of Hathor or Aphrodite; that of the Virgin of Guadalupe, whom Wright connects with the Aztec goddess Tonantzin; that of the African American poet Phillis Wheatley; and those of many others who take their places right next to Octavio Paz, Paul Celan, and Friedrich Hölderlin, who now merely provide epigraphs.

Wright's poetic language is as rich as his symbolic geography is varied and extensive. His journey into the night, which begins with the sunset of "Veil, I," not only leads the reader to pre-Columbian Mexico, Spain, Scotland, and back to the United States, but also guides the reader across an ever-changing linguistic surface in which even historical documents, such as letters by Wheatley, by the former slave Judith Cocks, by Louisa Alexander, and by the Harvard astronomer Cecilia Payne Yaposchkin, take on poetic qualities of their own. *Elaine's Book* can be said to achieve resonance as well as consonance: Each fragment sounds new depths as it becomes part of a "nation," which, like the city, is

also a figure for the poem itself. That a poet who lives in uncertain multiplicities, who knows neither his actual birth date nor his real name, should be fascinated by names and dates is hardly surprising.

BOLEROS

In *Boleros*, a book dedicated to his wife, Lois, Wright's preoccupation is with imagining the fictions that, like his own father's stories, lead to names—in this case, names of Greek muses, of saint's days adorned with "graces and the seasons," and of places. "All names," he writes, "are invocations, or curses." Reinventing these stories and histories of origins is the poetic project of *Boleros* and the point of departure for further journeys across far-flung geographies of the spirit. As in *Elaine's Book*, the poet's guides are mostly female—Erato, Calliope, Euterpe, Thalia, Polyhymnia, Clio, Terpsichore, Urania—yet the familiar Greek identities of these muses are complicated by the association of each of their personalities with concepts taken from another of Wright's favorite archives, *The Egyptian Book of the Dead* (first published in English in 1894). The resulting Africanization of the muses recalls Martin Bernal's compelling speculations in *Black Athena: The Afro-Asiatic Roots of Classical Civilization* (1987).

Many of the sites the poet's persona revisits in *Boleros* are familiar ones: Edinburgh, Guadalajara, Jalapa, New Hampshire, and always West Africa. The poet also takes up a number of new residences, however, most significant among them the city of Benares in Uttar Pradesh, one of the intellectual and cultural centers of traditional India. "Black spirits such as mine will always come/ to a crossroads such as this," the persona explains at the shores of the Ganges. As always, these geographic journeys become explorations of poetic form. Most striking in this regard are the six poems in "Sources and Roots" and "Coda," which are the title's most concrete reference points. The relatively brief poems in these final sections, many of which open with lines from popular Latin American songs, are daring in their use of Spanish meter and rhyme in an English-language environment. The results of such unexpected contact are wondrous formal hybrids, whose breaks with English accentuation are infused with Wright's wit and humor:

Esta tierra da de todo.
Oh, perhaps, you will see no sloe
plum, or no white-tailed, ginger doe,
break-dancing at sunset when snow
shows us its blackberry wine skin.

Poems such as this are testimony to the transformations of vision and language at the many crossroads to which Wright's ceaseless poetic journeys lead. These transformations truly are Wright's "gift," for few poets have dared to bridge the troubled waters of cultural difference. Even fewer have succeeded so splendidly.

TRANSFIGURATIONS

Transfigurations collects Wright's work produced over the course of more than twenty-five years of poetic exploration. The volume is hefty, providing more than six hundred pages of densely textured verse, including sixty pages of new poetry. Detailed references to West African, Haitian, Mexican, and European and American Christian religious rituals abound, as well as to the various political and poetic genealogies in which Wright situates himself. Geographic journeys expose the earth itself to the questioning soul of the poet. In a single poem, Wright travels from North Africa to Jamaica to Boston and then on to Spain, dropping historical allusions at every step. The esoteric network of obscure signs and allusions he uses serves to trace his own development in which, for nearly three decades, he has determinedly initiated himself into the mysteries of language, history, and sense.

Transformation and transfiguration act as the axes of this collection. A bulk of the poems in the volume speak to initiation, the human ceremonial act that marks transformation: the Mexican boy to whom a god says, "You must prepare for my eruption/ and the guarded way I have of guarding you," or the West African Dogon boy who undergoes the trials and tribulations of coming into adulthood, "If I were the light's sacred buffoon,/ I could read this meaning and mount/ my own awakening" in the spectacular poem "The Double Invention of Komo."

A transfiguration, similarly, is a change of appearance, one that is accompanied with a sense of revelation. A refinement of vision, put to the service of metamorphosis, is one of Wright's most potent forces. For example, in "The Abstract of Knowledge/the First Test," Wright transfigures the scene of the Dogon boy encountering the first phase of his initiation, in which he must undergo a hallucinatory vision of the universe in the light of the knowledge that he will obtain from his vision. That vision changes knowledge, transfiguring it and transforming it. In these lines, a number of the features of Wright's poetry are apparent: the tightly rhythmical free verse—which lacks enjambment for the most part, the voice of the dramatic persona, the physical details, and a cosmological reach.

OTHER MAJOR WORKS

PLAYS: *Balloons*, pb. 1968; *Love's Equations*, pb. 1983; *The Death and Return of Paul Batuta*, pb. 1984; *Death as History*, pb. 1989.

BIBLIOGRAPHY

Bloom, Harold, ed. *Jay Wright*. Philadelphia: Chelsea House, 2004. Another collection in Bloom's Modern Critical Views series, this book includes an introduction by Bloom and essays examining Wright's life and work from many perspectives.

Callaloo 6 (Fall, 1983). This special issue includes an excellent interview in which Wright outlines the theories behind his poetry. The issue also contains a general introduction to Wright's poetry by Robert B. Stepto, a rather superficial assessment of his early poetry by Gerald Barrax, and detailed commentary by Vera M. Kutzinski on the Benjamin Banneker poems.

Clifford, James. *The Predicament of Culture: Twentieth-Century Ethnography, Literature, and Art*. 1988. Reprint. Cambridge, Mass.: Harvard University Press, 1999. This critical, now-classic look at the rise of modern anthropology and its entwinement with literature is useful background reading for some of Wright's main sources, notably Marcel Griaule and his team. Equally relevant are Clifford's comments on the West's representation of other cultures and the negotiation of cultural differences.

Harris, Wilson. *The Womb of Space: The Cross-Cultural Imagination*. Westport, Conn.: Greenwood Press, 1983. While this study includes a brief discussion of *The Double Invention of Komo*, it is valuable primarily for its conceptualization of the literary dynamics of "the cross-cultural imagination." Though Wright's debt is to Harris's earlier writings, this book summarizes the main concepts and ideas that have guided Harris's thinking.

Kutzinski, Vera M. *Against the American Grain: Myth and History in William Carlos Williams, Jay Wright, and Nicolás Guillén*. Baltimore: The Johns Hopkins University Press, 1987. The second part of this book, "The Black Limbo: Jay Wright's Mythology of Writing," provides full commentary on Wright's poetry. Focusing on *Dimension of History* and its historical and theoretical sources, it places Wright's cross-cultural poetics within the context of the diverse cultural and literary histories of the Americas.

Okpewho, Isidore. "Prodigal's Progress: Jay Wright's Focal Center." *MELUS* 23, no. 3 (Fall, 1998): 187-209. Examines Wright's search for a satisfactory cultural identity through the successive volumes of his poetry. Traces Wright's movement from the autobiographical to the scholarly to a poetic self-creation through ritual and religion.

Stepto, Robert B. "After Modernism, After Hibernation: Michael Harper, Robert Hayden, and Jay Wright." In *Chant of Saints: A Gathering of Afro-American Literature, Art, and Scholarship*, edited by Michael S. Harper and Robert B. Stepto. Urbana: University of Illinois Press, 1979. This chapter concentrates on portions of *Dimensions of History*. It is useful for situating Wright's poetry within the call-and-response structures of an African American literary tradition whose central concern, according to Stepto, is with "freedom and literacy."

Welburn, Ron. "Jay Wright's Poetics: An Appreciation." *MELUS* 18, no. 3 (Fall, 1993): 51. Examines the historical and metaphysical codes that add energy to Wright's poetry. In spite of his relative obscurity, Wright deserves appreciation for his creative intellect.

Vera M. Kutzinski
Updated by Sarah Hilbert

ELINOR WYLIE

Born: Somerville, New Jersey; September 17, 1885
Died: New York, New York; December 16, 1928

PRINCIPAL POETRY

Nets to Catch the Wind, 1921
Black Armour, 1923
Angels and Earthly Creatures, 1928
Trivial Breath, 1928
Collected Poems of Elinor Wylie, 1932
Last Poems, 1943

OTHER LITERARY FORMS

Elinor Wylie (WI-lee) is primarily a poet, but she turned to long fiction to vary her writing days and to add to her income. Both genres received high praise as well as scathing criticism, and both were highly autobiographical. Her heroines were very like her, right down to their taste in clothing, and some of the other characters were easily recognizable. Her last two novels dealt with the long dead Romantic poet Percy Bysshe Shelley, who could be her muse and ideal, her perfect love, because he was not there to disappoint or disillusion her.

ACHIEVEMENTS

Elinor Wylie was honored for her poetry with the June Ellsworth Ford Prize from the Poetry Society (1921) for *Nets to Catch the Wind* and the Levinson Prize from *Poetry* magazine (1928). She served as poetry editor of *Vanity Fair*, 1923-1925; editor of *Literary Guild*, 1926-1928; and contributing editor of *New Republic*, 1926-1928.

BIOGRAPHY

Elinor Morton Hoyt Hichborn Wylie Benét was born Elinor Morton Hoyt into a socially and politically prominent eastern seacoast family on September 17, 1885. Her father, Henry Martyn Hoyt, was a lawyer and future solicitor general of the United States. Her mother, Anna Morton McMichael Hoyt, was the granddaughter of a governor of Pennsylvania and the great-granddaughter of a Philadelphia mayor. Elinor was groomed to be a debutante, marry into a well-established family, and become a society hostess. She went to fine schools and certainly looked the part of a socialite with her exceptional beauty, elegant frame, and delicate and charming manner.

On December 12, 1906, hoping to fulfill her parents' expectations, she married Philip Hichborn, the son of an admiral. President Theodore Roosevelt was a guest at the ceremony. On September 22, 1907, son Philip III was born. By this time, the marriage was not going well, with Philip having frequent outbursts of temper and Elinor not taking to motherhood. She did not fit into this life of conspicuous elegance and proper manners. She felt smothered by convention. Indeed, her own family had hidden behind a facade of respectability: Her father had a long-term mistress, her mother was a chronic hypochondriac, her brother and sister committed suicide, and another brother was unsuccessful in his attempt to end his life. Even her husband proved mentally unstable, and Wylie felt restrained by the ugly world around her.

In 1910, she ran away with Horace Wylie, the father of four children, leaving her own son to be raised by Philip's family. In 1912, with the rumor afloat that his wife might be carrying Wylie's child, Philip killed himself. All these sordid details provided more fodder for the gossip mills, and Elinor and Horace took up residence in France to escape the social isolation. They returned to the states in 1914, but not even their marriage in 1916 stilled the talk and scorn. They attempted to have a family, but Elinor suffered several miscarriages, had a stillborn child and one who died within a week. Horace was seventeen years her senior, and Elinor began to feel cramped in this relationship also. They separated in 1921 and divorced in 1923. In that same year, again on romantic impulse, she married her brother's friend, William Rose Benét, a fellow poet who helped advance her career. This union also resulted in separate living quarters.

Wylie was not easy to live with. She was a narcissist, positioning a large mirror in her living room so that she could frequently catch glimpses of herself. She was mercurial, sometimes giving in to histrionics and ranting in anger, reportedly banging her head against the wall. Her tantrums were attributed to exceedingly high blood pressure and debilitating migraine headaches.

By 1928, she had met a new married man to love, Clifford Woodhouse, but although the feeling may have been returned, Woodhouse was not about to destroy his marriage. With this unconsummated relationship, she may have found the defect-free man she sought. Her final collection of poetry during her lifetime, *Angels and Earthly Creatures*, contained nineteen poems dedicated to this perfect love, based on pure feeling. She was ready to give up the cool detachment evidenced in so much of her poetry. She brought the completed manuscript to Benét's house, not yet having told him of her plans to move to Paris. Sitting in the living room, she called out to Benét in the kitchen to bring her a glass of water. As he came in to hand her the glass, he saw her walking toward him. She stopped abruptly, said, "Is this what it is?" and fell dead to the floor.

The historical circumstances of her life are important for an understanding of her writing in that practically every work is directly related to a life event. Scholars can trace her tragedies, loves, and insecurities by a close reading of both her poetry and novels. Her break from Horace Wylie and turn to Benét, even her belief that she had found her first true love, were reflected in the content, form, and style of her poetry.

ANALYSIS

Elinor Wylie's poetry was sometimes criticized for being derivative, too close in style and form to those writers she loved best, such as William Butler Yeats, John Donne, William Shakespeare, Thomas Gray, T. S. Eliot, William Wordsworth, A. E. Housman, and Shelley. However, even the harshest critics agreed that she enriched the works by giving them her own signature. Her adoration of Shelley, thought unnatural by some, just a little bizarre by others, led her to incorporate some of his poetic structures into her own work, and he certainly affected her worldview. There was some thought that her imaginings might have had her envisioning and talking to him.

Whatever her influences, Wylie was most comfortable with the traditional sonnet form and was meticulous about the sound and look of her words even at the occasional expense of meaning. There were no wasted words. Every word was carefully chosen and used in precisely the correct form. She composed her poetry in her head before committing anything to paper and seldom changed a word.

In writing about her general themes—love, betrayal, and death—she favored certain words and images. She was fascinated with birds, wings, and feathers; with snow and wintry landscapes; with small ceramic figurines; with gemstones, particularly amber and onyx; with balsam and juniper trees; with silver; with sparkling, cold, hard diamonds; with the colors white and gold; with velvet; and with sleep and death.

Wylie's four published collections chronicle four distinct phases of her life and reflect changes in her thinking about the most effective ways of creating works of value. Her first publication met with immediate success.

NETS TO CATCH THE WIND

Nets to Catch the Wind, a collection of thirty-three sonnets, contained a handful of remarkable works alongside some easily forgettable offerings. She used what she liked to refer to as her "small, clean technique" with short lines in short stanzas and great clarity. One often-read poem, "The Eagle and the Mole," advised the reader to "Avoid the reeking herd,/ Shun the polluted flock,/ Live like that stoic bird,/ The eagle of the rock" but suggested that those who needed further removal from horrible reality might "Live like the velvet mole;/ Go burrow underground./ And there hold intercourse/ With roots of trees and stones,/ With rivers at the source,/ And disembodied bones."

The abuse and isolation heaped on Wylie for abandoning her husband and child led her not to question her actions, but to wonder at society's reaction. Certainly the child was a victim, but her husband was seriously unstable, abusive, and not one to allow his wife to grow. She needed to escape and had not expected such a harsh reaction. She craved solitude, as expressed in another popular poem, "Sanctuary," but could not be shut off from the admiration still afforded her by more understanding friends. She says, in building her place of isolation, she can love the "Bare hills, cold silver on a sky of slate/ A thread of water, churned to a milky spate/ Streaming through slanted pastures fenced with stones" but, when "the last brick [is] put in place, not even leaving a chink," she asks, "How can I breathe?" and is answered, "You can't, you fool!!"

In probably her most anthologized poem, "Velvet Shoes," she creates a calm, silent peace with sound muffled by the snow that has covered the land in white. She says "Let us walk in the white snow/ In a soundless space;/ With footsteps quiet and slow,/ At a tranquil pace,/ Under veils of white lace." The speaker is clad in silk shoes and her companion in wool shoes, which later become velvet shoes. "We shall walk through the still town/ In a soundless peace;/ We shall step upon white down,/ Upon silver fleece,/ Upon softer than these."

BLACK ARMOUR

In a way, *Black Armour* explores the inadequacies of Wylie's earlier approach to poetry. She finds a clean style to be insufficient and realizes that she can never reach Shelley's level of skill but tries to accept her limitations. She speaks of being torn between animosity and love for the world, wishing she could go beyond her beauty and womanhood. In keeping with the idea of protective armor, in "Now Let No Charitable Hope," she says: "In masks outrageous and austere/ The years go by in single file;/ But none has merited my fear,/ And none has quite escaped my smile."

TRIVIAL BREATH

Trivial Breath is dedicated to Shelley and expresses Wylie's dismay at being alive while the poet is dead. She also suggests that she feels she is to blame for her failures in love. In "Where, O, Where," she says: "I need not die to go/ So far you cannot know/ You shall see me no more/ Though each night I hide/ In your bed, at your side." There is no solace in love here.

ANGELS AND EARTHLY CREATURES

The nineteen poems in *Angels and Earthly Creatures* detail Wylie's love for Woodhouse. Toward the end, she renounces passion, wanting to return to a life of the mind. This volume is more literary and metaphysical and less clear and concrete. She notes, "I was, being human, born alone;/ I am, being woman, hard beset;/ I live by squeezing from a stone/ The little nourishment I get." She sees herself as having finally experienced the passion that had been lacking throughout her life. However, she also recognizes death as a release. In this last collection, she showed promise of losing the cool detachment of so much of her poetry.

OTHER MAJOR WORKS

LONG FICTION: *Jennifer Lorn: A Sedate Extravaganza*, 1923; *The Venetian Glass Nephew*, 1925; *The Orphan Angel*, 1926; *Mr. Hodge and Mr. Hazard*, 1928.

BIBLIOGRAPHY

Farr, Judith. *The Life and Art of Elinor Wylie*. Baton Rouge: Louisiana State University Press, 1983. This biography reads like a novel but is still true to actual events and supports facts with evidence.

Gray, Thomas A. *Elinor Wylie*. New York: Twayne, 1969. Gray does not color his portrait of Wylie, being at times a little harsh.

Hively, Evelyn Helmick. *A Private Madness: The Genius of Elinor Wylie*. Kent State University Press, 2003. A chronological treatment of Wylie's works that examines all her major publications. Provides biographical background but concentrates on the years in which she was writing.

Miller, Brett C. *Flawed Light: American Women Poets and Alcohol*. Urbana: University of Illinois, 2009. Miller studies how drinking and alcoholism affected prominent American women poets, and how their struggles were reflected in their poetry. Contains an informative chapter on Wylie.

Olson, Stanley. *Eleanor Wylie: A Biography*. New York: The Dial Press, 1979. Good solid discussion, though his weather reports and inclusion of thoughts that might have been going through minds are a little disconcerting.

Gay Pitman Zieger

Y

MITSUYE YAMADA

Born: Fukuoka, Kyushu, Japan; July 5, 1923

PRINCIPAL POETRY

Camp Notes, and Other Poems, 1976

OTHER LITERARY FORMS

Mitsuye Yamada (yah-mah-dah) published two short stories in *Desert Run: Poems and Stories* and, in addition to producing her own work, has collaborated with others in editing poetry collections. Her essays on literature, personal history, and human rights have appeared in anthologies and periodicals, and she compiled a teachers' guide for Amnesty International. In 1981, the Public Broadcasting Service aired a documentary, *Mitsuye and Nellie: Two Asian-American Poets*, featuring Yamada and Chinese American writer Nellie Wong.

ACHIEVEMENTS

Mitsuye Yamada is one of the first writers to publish a personal account of the United States' internment of citizens of Japanese descent. Publication of the "Camp Notes" poems also marked an important event in the resurgence of feminist literature in the 1970's. Yamada has served on the national board of Amnesty International on the organization's Committee on International Development. She has received numerous awards for her writing, teaching, and human rights work.

BIOGRAPHY

Mitsuye May Yamada was born in Fukuoka, Kyushu, Japan, the third child and only daughter of Jack Yasutake and Hide Yasutake. She was brought to the United States at age three. At the age of nine, she went to Japan to live with her father's family for eighteen months. She lived with her parents and three brothers in Seattle until she was nineteen. Her high school educa-

tion was curtailed in 1941 when her father, a translator for the United States Immigration Service, was imprisoned as an enemy alien. Mitsuye, her mother, and her brothers were later removed to internment camps in Puyallup, Washington, and Minidoka, Idaho. She spent eighteen months in the camps, finally leaving to work and study at the University of Cincinnati. She completed her bachelor's degree at New York University and a master of arts degree in English literature at the University of Chicago.

She was able to become a naturalized American citizen following passage of the McCarran-Walter Immigration Act and received citizenship in 1955. In 1950, she married chemist Yoshikazu Yamada (becoming Mitsuye Yasutake Yamada). They lived in New York, where their four children were born, until the early 1960's, when the family moved to Southern California. In 1966, she began teaching in community colleges and was professor of English at Cypress Community College from 1968 until her retirement in 1989. Following publication of *Camp Notes, and Other Poems*, she held many university appointments as visiting professor, artist-in-residence, and consultant.

A lifelong commitment to human rights emerged as Yamada's response to her incarceration, and she has related her sense of urgency on the subject to years of living with a diagnosis of incurable emphysema when her children were very young. She was an early member of Amnesty International and has served on the executive board and national committees in that organization. Her poetry was published by feminist presses; she organized a multicultural women writers group and has participated in numerous projects addressed to the concerns of women, ethnic groups, and environmental awareness.

ANALYSIS

Originally published by Shameless Hussy, a struggling feminist press, Mitsuye Yamada's *Camp Notes, and Other Poems* is a personal volume involving family participation. The cover illustration, by the author's older daughter, Jeni Yamada, is a line drawing of a female figure in three stages: a shy little girl, an older girl walking forward, and a striding woman carrying either a briefcase or suitcase. The ambiguity of the last figure can refer to the camp experience, where internees were able to bring only what they could carry, or to the author's professional life as writer, teacher, and activist. The author's husband contributed the book's calligraphy, and the volume is dedicated to Yamada's parents, husband, two daughters, and two sons. The actual "Camp Notes" poems center the volume and are bracketed by an opening section on the author's parents and a closing series of poems looking to the present and future.

The seven poems in the section "My Issei Parents, Twice Pioneers, Now I Hear Them" were written after the central "camp notes" set, and they look back to parents, grandparents, and great-grandparents. The section opens with a folk saying: "What your Mother tells you now/ in time/ you will come to know." The text appears first in brush-stroke ideograms, then in transliterated Japanese, and finally in the author's translation. The theme permeates the author's work, which engages with the ways that origins—"the mother"—shape a person, through both acceptance and resistance.

The next poem offers a portrait of "Great Grandma" figured in her orderly collection of ordinary objects: "colored stones," "parched persimmons," "powdery green tea." Great Grandma's static world and calm acceptance of fate stand in contrast to the turmoil, pain, and conflict documented in much of Yamada's work.

"Marriage Was a Foreign Country" and "Homecoming" are narrated in the voice of the persona's mother; they tell stories of pain and difficulty of life as a Japanese immigrant woman in a country both alien and hostile. Following these poems are two poems relating to the speaker's father. Contrasting the mother's monologues, these dialogues comment on traditional Japanese wisdom that the father is attempting to impart.

The section titled "Camp Notes" highlights poems composed while Yamada was imprisoned with her mother and brothers in the Minidoka camp. Thirty years later, the poems were culled from their early inscription in a large writing tablet, one of the few possessions the author could take with her to the camp. The section opens with another line drawing by Jeni Yamada, picturing a small child clutching a stuffed animal and seated amid piles of luggage. The first poems tally the upheaval of the removal experience with titles such

as "Evacuation," "Curfew," and "On the Bus." The title of "Harmony at the Fair Grounds" reflects the irony in many of these brief, acrid poems: The "grounds" on which the Japanese Americans were imprisoned were anything but "fair." The last lines offer a stark picture of concentration camp life: "Lines formed for food/ lines for showers/ lines for the john/ lines for shots."

A secondary subheading, "Relocation," designates poems about life in the Minidoka camp. The author continues to document the grim, degrading aspects of prison life, where monotony and uncertainty intensified the physical stresses of primitive, cramped quarters and the denial of amenities such as radios and cameras. Even more demoralizing are the irrationality, stupidity, and lies of the bureaucratic internment system. As the family huddles under bedclothes to survive a "Desert Storm," the speaker observes

> This was not
> im
> prison
> ment.
> This was
> re
> location.

Likewise, the opening of "Block 4 Barrack 4 'Apt' C" demolishes the excuse that relocation benefited the imprisoned, noting that barbed wire protected the inmates from "wildly twisted/ sagebrush." In two poems, the persona notes the paradox of guards locked inside their watchtowers. Hedi Yamada, the author's younger daughter, illustrated "The Watchtower" with a silhouette drawing of an adult holding a child's hand and gazing at such a tower; it is impossible to tell whether they are looking out of or into the prison area. The double bind of Nisei (second-generation Japanese American) citizens emerges in the protest to the "Recruiting Team":

> Why should I volunteer!
> I'm an American
> I have a right to be
> drafted.

As the persona notes in "The Trick Was," notwithstanding propaganda or disinformation, "the mind was not fooled."

Several poems return with poignancy to the theme of family. The author translates two *senryu* poems (three-line unrhymed Japanese poems) written by her father, at that time incarcerated at a camp in New Mexico. "The Night Before Good-Bye" pictures the mother performing the intimately caring task of mending her daughter's clothes. "Cincinnati," written after the actual camp experience, comes to terms with a racist assault, in which the speaker loses a lace handkerchief given her by her mother.

The remaining poems in this volume reflect the author's life from the end of the war through the 1950's and 1960's and introduce themes of personal challenge, illness, raising children, education, and activism. The section opens with another drawing by Jeni Yamada, suggesting a serene Japanese village scene of a cove surrounded by woods and mountains with small boats at anchor and a line of houses on the beach. The past is still important: The author recollects, in the twinned poems "Here" and "There," being taunted as an "outsider" by classmates in both Japan and the United States. "Freedom in Manhattan" opens particularly feminist concerns, depicting police officers' indifference to attempted rape.

DESERT RUN

The professional production of Yamada's second collection, published by Kitchen Table: Women of Color Press, testifies to recognition of the author and establishment of ethnic and women's cultural institutions in the twelve years after the appearance of *Camp Notes, and Other Poems*. The later volume is professionally typeset, pages are numbered, and a single thematic illustration—a calligraphy of the author's name—appears on the cover, section divisions, and end of each poem. The author's husband again contributed the calligraphy, and the book is dedicated to her three brothers.

The poems in *Desert Run* extend themes introduced in *Camp Notes, and Other Poems*, now developed in more discursive, meditative modes. The initial set, headed "Where I Stay," is a sequence completed after a camping trip in the Southern California desert. The experience was unique: Part of an experimental college course co-taught with a biologist to connect creative writing and natural science, it marked for the author a

reexamination of the "desert" experience of internment. The title poem, "Desert Run," meditates on the fragility, power, and beauty of the desert ecology, the author's contrast of her present interest in the desert with the earlier rancor and hatred of the apparently barren landscape and her continuing sense of the irreparable injustice of arbitrary imprisonment. The address of this poem—the author's longest—embodies the speaker's difficult ruminations as she speaks sometimes as a meditative "I" and at other times addresses a "you" that appears in other poems and that implies the "other," the "dominant" or "mainstream" or "official" American perspective. In this section, "Lichens" and "Desert Under Glass" are also notable close observations of nature.

Titles of the three remaining sections—"Returning," "Resisting," and "Connecting"—express the author's continuing project of synthesizing the disparate elements of her life. The poems and short story in "Returning" revisit experience and heritage in Japan. The grandmother's ambivalent pride and resentment over the emigration of the author's father emerges in "American Son," which with "Obon: Festival of the Dead" recollects the months Yamada spent as a child being tutored in Japanese language and culture.

A thread of women's stories and women's plight runs through the "Resisting" section. Two poems are framed in the personas of other women. "Jeni's Complaint," presented as in the voice of the author's daughter, captures the chaos of a multigeneration, multicultural family celebration. "I Learned to Sew" tells, in the Japanese Hawaiian cadence of the author's mother-in-law, a story of immigration, hardship, endurance, and survival; this poem contains a brief retelling of the Japanese folktale of Urashima Taro. The short story "Mrs. Higashi Is Dead" elaborates the anecdote briefly referred to in the poem "Homecoming" in *Camp Notes, and Other Poems*.

The "Connecting" section of *Desert Run* contains half the poems in the volume and recapitulates the major themes: nature, human dignity, family, and roots. Several poems in this section are voiced by "fictional" personas, notably "The Club," a woman's narration of her husband's abuse. "Connecting" also refers to the links between the author's personal experience of injustice with those of others: a Holocaust survivor, a battered wife, even animals sacrificed for fur.

CAMP NOTES, AND OTHER WRITINGS

Camp Notes, and Other Writings (1998) continues a canonization process. The volume reprints both *Camp Notes, and Other Poems* and *Desert Run*. Although it contains no previously unpublished work, the poems and dedication of *Camp Notes, and Other Writings* have been professionally typeset; also, the order of the poems has been substantially altered and the illustrations eliminated. One important addition is the cover illustration. A photograph taken around 1908 of Yamada's mother as a child, it commemorates a grade-school dramatization of the legend of Urashima Taro with Yamada's mother in the title role. (In the legend, Urashima Taro is rewarded for saving a turtle by a visit to the underseas palace of the Dragon King, where he spends a few days in the company of a beautiful princess. The young man returns home to see his parents, but the few days underseas were hundreds of years in his village, and everyone he knew is gone and everything has changed.) A historical and documentary return to the author's origins, complementing anecdotal and personal connections, the photograph also serves as a return and gloss to the translation of the mother's folk saying that opens *Camp Notes, and Other Writings*.

OTHER MAJOR WORKS

EDITED TEXTS: *The Webs We Weave: Orange County Poetry Anthology*, 1986 (with others); *Sowing Ti Leaves: Writings by Multi-Cultural Women*, 1990 (with Sarie Sachie Hylkema).

MISCELLANEOUS: *Desert Run: Poems and Stories*, 1988; *Camp Notes, and Other Writings*, 1998 (includes *Camp Notes, and Other Poems* and *Desert Run*).

BIBLIOGRAPHY

Cheng, Scarlet. "Foreign All Your Life." Review of *Desert Run*, by Mitsuye Yamada, and *Seventeen Syllables*, by Hisaye Yamamoto DeSoto. *Belles Lettres* 4, no. 2 (Winter, 1989). The reviewer finds Yamada's poetry nostalgic and filled with lyricism but notes the way in which poems consistently confront pain and alienation.

Harth, Erika. *Last Witnesses: Reflections on the War-time Internment of Japanese Americans*. New York: Palgrave/St. Martin's Press, 2001. Contains "Legacy of Silence I," by Yamada, which gives *gaman*, the virtue of endurance, as a cultural reason for why the Japanese Americans are not more vocal about their experiences, and "Legacy of Silence II," by Jeni Yamada, in which she explains how her marriage to a Jew exposed her to a group that is not as reluctant to speak about past injustices.

Patterson, Anita Haya. "Resistance to Images of the Internment: Mitsuye Yamada's *Camp Notes*." *MELUS* 23, no. 3 (Fall, 1998): 103-128. Examines poems in *Camp Notes, and Other Writings* in light of the concept of "obligation" and the problematic issue of the seeming nonresistance by Americans of Japanese ancestry to unconstitutional imprisonment in concentration camps. The essay contains photographs from newspapers and other sources to illustrate images of Japanese Americans as visualized in American popular culture during and after World War II.

Schweik, Susan. "A Needle with Mama's Voice: Mitsuye Yamada's *Camp Notes* and the American Canon of War Poetry." In *Arms and the Woman: War, Gender, and Literary Representation*, edited by Helen M. Cooper, Adrienne Auslande Munich, and Susan Merrill Squier. Chapel Hill: University of North Carolina Press, 1989. Examination of Yamada's poems in the context of war poetry by women. The author considers the silencing of Yamada's voice between the writing of the "camp notes" poems and their publication thirty years later and maintains that such silence was brought about by the unique situation of Japanese American women—especially Issei women—who were considered "enemy aliens." The discussion compares mother-daughter and father-daughter expressions in the difference between retelling of transmitted oral tales versus translation of the father's poems.

Srikanth, Rajini, and Esther Y. Inwanaga, eds. *Bold Words: A Century of Asian American Writing*. New Brunswick, N.J.: Rutgers University Press, 2001. This anthology contains several poems by Yamada. The introduction to the poetry section provides context for understanding Yamada.

Woolley, Lisa. "Racial and Ethnic Semiosis in Mitsuye Yamada's 'Mrs. Higashi Is Dead.'" *MELUS* 24, no. 4 (Winter, 1999): 77-92. Using poems from *Camp Notes, and Other Poems*, the author analyzes Yamada's short story "Mrs. Higashi Is Dead" according to a theory called ethnic semiosis. The theory postulates that Americans realize "ethnicity" through performance in instances of contact between individuals from different ethnic backgrounds; these relational moments both define and contest characteristics considered as belonging to particular ethnicities. The analysis of Yamada's story examines how it reflects "ethnic semiosis" in the different ways that a mother and daughter interpret a request from a woman of a different ethnicity.

Yamada, Mitsuye. "A *MELUS* Interview: Mitsuye Yamada." Interview by Helen Jaskoski. *MELUS* 15, no. 1 (Spring, 1988): 97-108. The poet reflects on family influences in her writing (her father founded a society devoted to the Japanese *senryu* poem) and the impact of the concentration camp experience on her life and work. Also mentioned are women's writing, human rights activism, political persecution of poets, and formal aspects of poetry.

Helen Jaskoski

AL YOUNG

Born: Ocean Springs, Mississippi; May 31, 1939

PRINCIPAL POETRY

Dancing, 1969
The Song Turning Back into Itself, 1971
Geography of the Near Past, 1976
The Blues Don't Change: New and Selected Poems, 1982
Heaven: Collected Poems, 1956-1990, 1992
Straight No Chaser, 1994
Conjugal Visits, and Other Poems in Verse and Prose, 1996
The Sound of Dreams Remembered, 1990-2000, 2001

Coastal Nights and Inland Afternoons: Poems, 2001-2006, 2006
Something About the Blues: An Unlikely Collection of Poetry, 2007

OTHER LITERARY FORMS

Al Young is known primarily as a poet and novelist; his novels include *Snakes* (1970), *Who Is Angelina?* (1975), *Sitting Pretty* (1976), *Ask Me Now* (1980), and *Seduction by Light* (1988). He has also published short stories in *Changes*, *Chicago Review*, *Encore*, *Essence*, *Evergreen Review*, *Journal of Black Poetry*, *Massachusetts Review*, *Place*, and *Rolling Stone*. He wrote the introduction to *Yardbird Lives!* (1978), a collection of writings that he and Ishmael Reed compiled from the biennial *Yardbird Reader*. He has written several screenplays, including "Nigger" (unpublished) based on Dick Gregory's autobiography, a film script for his novel *Sitting Pretty*, and the script for *A Piece of the Action* (in collaboration with Bill Cosby and Sidney Poitier).

Young has also written a series of autobiographical anecdotes, in *Bodies and Soul: Musical Memoirs* (1981), each of which is organized around his response to a specific song or musical performance. The title piece, for example, begins with his meditation on Coleman Hawkins's 1939 performance of "Body and Soul." *Bodies and Soul* was followed by other "musical memoirs," including *Kinds of Blue: Musical Memoirs* (1984), *Mingus/Mingus: Two Memoirs* (with Janet Coleman), and *Drowning in a Sea of Love: Musical Memoirs* (1995).

ACHIEVEMENTS

For his first collection, *Dancing*, Al Young won the National Arts Council Award for poetry and the Joseph Henry Jackson Award from the San Francisco Foundation in 1969. In 1968, Young received a National Arts Council Award for editing. In 1970, his first novel, *Snakes*, appeared and was praised for its authentic portrayal of a young man, addicted to jazz, growing up in urban America.

Young received a Guggenheim Fellowship in 1974 and a National Endowment for the Arts Fellowship in 1975. His considerable work on small literary magazines includes founding and editing *Loveletter* (an avant-garde review of the 1960's), editing *Changes* (for the West Coast), and coediting, with Ishmael Reed, *Yardbird Reader*. He cofounded the Yardbird Publishing Cooperative and continues to work actively in small-press publishing.

In the 1980's, Young turned increasingly to writing nonfiction, often on the subjects of music and film. He has received Wallace Stegner, Guggenheim, Fulbright, National Endowment for the Arts, and Arts Council Silicon Valley Fellowships. He earned a PEN-Library of Congress Award for Short Fiction, the PEN-USA Award for Non-Fiction, two *New York Times* Notable Book of the Year citations, two Pushcart Prizes, an American Book Award from the Before Columbus Foundation in 1982 for *Bodies and Soul* and in 2002 for *The Sound of Dreams Remembered*, the Stephen E. Henderson Award in 2006, Radio Pacifica's KPFA Peace Prize, the Glenna Luschei Distinguished Poetry Fellowship, and the Richard Wright Award for Excellence in Literature in 2007. Young served as California's poet laureate from 2005 to 2008. In his last year as poet laureate, he traveled throughout California, visiting small liberal arts colleges under the Woodrow Wilson Visiting Fellows Program. In 2008, he received the Fred Cody Award for lifetime achievement.

BIOGRAPHY

Albert James Young was born in Ocean Springs, Mississippi, near Biloxi, on the Gulf of Mexico. His childhood, which he characterizes as happy, was divided between rural Mississippi and urban Detroit. Though he moved through several communities and schools, he values the flexibility that he gained by adapting to different subcultures. His father was an auto worker (in part, the model for Durwood Knight's father in *Ask Me Now*), and also a professional musician, like his son. For five years, Young sang and played the flute and guitar professionally, at first while attending the University of Michigan, then while working as a disc jockey at radio station KJAZ-FM, in Alameda, California. The character MC in *Snakes* reflects some of Young's aspirations as a young jazz musician, and the poem "A Little More Traveling Music"

Al Young (©Miriam Berkley)

reflects his divided roots in rural and urban music. American blues and jazz and their origins in African music have influenced the themes and the formal structures of Young's fiction and poetry.

Young has credited his interest in writing narratives to his early exposure to the art of southern storytelling, and his fictional and poetic use of regional and ethnic vernacular draws on his memories of southern speech as well as his wide reading in American literature (especially the works of Zora Neale Hurston, Mark Twain, Langston Hughes, and Jesse Stuart) and British and European literature. Young married a freelance artist in 1963 with whom he would have a son. In 1966-1967, Young was a fellow in Advanced Fiction Writing at Stanford University; in 1969, he received his bachelor of arts degree in Spanish at the University of California, Berkeley; from 1969 to 1973, he held a lectureship in creative writing at Stanford. He has worked as a writing instructor for youth groups in San Francisco, Oakland, and Berkeley.

Young also spent many years in the 1970's and 1980's working as a film screenwriter for various Los

Angeles-area studios. He was a writer-in-residence at the University of Washington in Seattle from 1981 to 1982, and served as the vice president of the Yardbird Publishing Cooperative. He became a familiar face on the lecture circuit at universities throughout the United States. In the 1990's, he continued writing, contributing to anthologies and creating "musical memoirs." He has taught at the Berkeley, Santa Cruz, and Davis campuses of the University of California, Bowling Green State University, Foothill College, the Colorado College, Rice University, the University of Washington, the University of Michigan, the University of Arkansas, San Jose State University (where he was appointed the 2002 Lurie Distinguished Professor of Creative Writing), and Charles University in the Czech Republic. He was writer-in-residence at the California College of the Arts in spring, 2010. Though he has traveled widely—in Spain, France, Mexico, and the United States—he has made his home in Northern California. Many of his poems and novels record his sensitive observations on the diverse cultural lives of people in the San Francisco Bay area.

Analysis

Al Young's poetry originates in visual and aural memories and in musical forms that are then developed through suitable language and prosody. The music that inspires his poetry includes rhythm and blues and jazz, and he makes effective use of various American dialects. The metaphor of dancing unites the visual images and musical forms, and suggests both the formality and the spontaneity of design in his poetry.

Young also writes about family relationships and does so with insight, humor, and affection. His fictional characters and poetic personas often center their identities in their family life, which enables them, somehow, to cope with the meanness and injustice of contemporary urban American society. The family relationships are hardly idyllic, and characters habitually annoy and occasionally hurt one another; nevertheless, the love they feel for one another transforms their lives. Although his work offers no simplistic ideological solutions, his poems and novels clearly reflect his belief in the writer's function: to change society by expanding the reader's perception of reality.

Dancing

Dancing, Young's first collection, explores many forms of dance, including "A Dance for Militant Dilettantes," "Dancing Day to Day," "The John Coltrane Dance," "Reading Nijinsky's Diary," "Dancing Pierrot," "A Little More Traveling Music," and "Dancing." Young's rejection of "monocultural values, of whatever hue," is reflected in the diverse cultural backgrounds of the poems in *Dancing*.

At the beginning of his collection, Young places an uncharacteristic poem, perhaps written after the manuscript of *Snakes* had been refused by a series of publishers interested only in black voices that were violently angry and bitter. "A Dance for Militant Dilettantes" implicitly rejects the advice of a friend who urges him to play the stereotypic role of a white-hating African American activist, writing about bloodying "those fabled wine & urine-/ stained hallways." While modifying the Homeric cliché of wine-dark seas, Young's brilliant epithet exposes the contemporary racism of the publisher who wants to market "a furious nigrah" and of the militant dilettantes willing to sell out.

The poet in "Dancing Day to Day" lives in and writes about a multicultural world, in which people are fearful of violence and yet live, fairly contentedly, one day at a time. In the first four lines of this poem, Young echoes T. S. Eliot, in the "come and go" of his monotonous, trivial, habitual Prufrockian world, but, significantly, without Eliot's contempt:

> In my street
> the people mostly go.
> Very few come
> to what I'd call home.

The walking iambic meter of lines 2 and 4 alternates with the emphatic trochees of lines 1 and 3, and his quatrain establishes the dominant metric pattern of the verse paragraphs that follow. This open design, built on no regular line length, perfectly expresses the speaker's relaxed attitude toward his neighbors, as well as the freedom of their daily natural movements.

"The John Coltrane Dance," a tribute to the music of John Coltrane, uses repetition, subtle assonance, and alliteration to suggest the emotional power of Coltrane's musical compositions and performances. The word "sound" occurs seven times, is echoed in "astound" and "surround," and introduces a pattern of sibilants. The line, "Mr Love Trane," occurs only twice (lines 2 and 24), but its distinctive concluding spondee, lengthened by the long vowels, sets a metrical pattern that also occurs in lines 8 ("tree dance"), 14 ("smoothed stones"), 16 ("hurt songs"), and 18 ("sound cures"). Against the implied hesitation of this duple meter, Young syncopates rapidly moving feet of triple meter, such as the dactyl ("hovering," line 6), the anapest ("where that sound," line 14) and the tribrach, or three unaccented syllables ("& cleansed the," line 15, and "on all the," line 23). Traditional prosody offers these terms to describe lines of verse, but readers familiar with open forms in American poetry and listeners familiar with Coltrane's extended and complex rhythmic patterns may not need this abstract analysis to hear the musical phrases of Young's poem. The poem first invokes Coltrane as muse ("Fly on into my poem"), imitating both the sounds and the impact of one of his solo performances, then places his music within the social and political history of black America (the migrations from Alabama, the confrontation over segregated schools in Little Rock, Arkansas, and the urban ghettos in the city of brotherly love, Philadelphia). Citing the function of the blues, expressing pain to soothe and heal it, Young identifies Coltrane's music as creating and keeping alive both collective and individual history. In a temporal metaphor moving from day to night, Young suggests that Coltrane's music also forecasts the future, as the "sunrise" of line 9 is transformed into the "stars" of the final line. It is an optimistic poem, celebrating the growth of the spirit, through a history and an artistic form that recalls dark nights of the soul.

In the playful "Dancing Pierrot," the speaking poet claims to have known the moons of China, Egypt, Mexico, Tokyo, Bahia, San Francisco, Tanzania, and the Moors; further, he claims to have known not merely fat and skinny moons (the lunar phases), but moons that shone "lifetimes ago." Clearly, he claims the international and timeless realm of the poet who speaks to all cultures, to all races, and to all ages. Like Jules Laforgue, whose Pierrot of *L'Imitation de Notre-Dame la lune* (1886; imitation of our lady the moon) appears in the title, Young imagines the poet as a kind of noble lu-

natic, drunk on moonlight. His dancing seems that of the marionette, jerkily bobbing at the end of his strings, an image reinforced by several short two- and three-syllable lines, and by the many one-syllable words; the lyrical fifth stanza, however, echoing "Drink to me only with thine eyes," breaks the confining strings and creates the feeling of freedom. The poet's function appears in the third of the poem's five stanzas, as he observes the effects of moonlight (imagination) on ordinary working people, whose aspirations the poet powerfully images as "armed to the eyes/ with star guns" (lines 28 and 29). The workers, who might seem imprisoned by repetitive movements, have a vision of self-liberating power, which is articulated by the poet.

"Reading Nijinsky's Diary" also considers the madness of the artist, whose dance plays between the extremes of confinement ("bodily concern/ vinetangled nerve") and freedom ("—cut loose, frced/ to know ever for all"). The visual images that Young employs suggest the surviving photographs of Waslaw Nijinsky in costume for his roles as the faun in *Afternoon of a Faun* and as the rose in *Specter of the Rose*. The identification of the dancer with the dance, like that of the poet with the poem, carries the threat of insanity. For Young, unlike Nijinsky, the descent into madness is only temporary, and he is released by the incantation: "'My madness is my love/ for mankind.'"

"A Little More Traveling Music" is the autobiographical sketch of a poet and singer born in Mississippi, reared on the "Colored music, rhythmic & electrifying" broadcast over the radio and on the music of a mother's recited family history. His move "up north" introduced him to the external, daily sounds of urban traffic and the internal music of moonlit dreams, and educated him in the sounds of written poetry. The third stanza narrates the return to "motherly music" and the poet's synthesis of that oral tradition with his formal education. The cycle of personal history culminates in his choice of vocation: "I turned to poetry & to singing." Performing and creating are made possible by listening to his "own background music."

The long poem "Dancing," which gives its title to the collection, responds personally and politically to the crises that Americans endured in the late 1960's. Admonitory rhetoric and judgmental images establish the poet as a cultural historian. The four sections of "Dancing," however, do not trace a chronology, since the work begins and ends in the night before a dawn, with the poet in the dark about his life, but hopeful. There are none of the theological issues that Eliot explores in *The Waste Land* (1922), and yet Young claims the same correlation between personal and cultural crises and records a spiritual descent followed by a mystical elevation. Writing in the oracular tradition of Walt Whitman, Allen Ginsberg, Amiri Baraka, and the Old Testament prophets, Young envisions a decade of personal experience in the context of his jeremiad on contemporary American culture. "Dancing" begins as the writer, struggling with his muse in the early evening, thinks of the world outside and of the roads he might have taken (heroin dealer, drunken bum, drifter).

Sobered by his thought that he "is capable of being assassinated/ at any moment" (as were Martin Luther King, Jr., and Robert Kennedy in 1968), and saddened that people continue to live trivial, habitual lives, that the younger generation seeks violent solutions, and that America's commercialism assigns little value to his grandfather's work on a farm, the poet laments the corruption of "Ahhhhhmerica!/ you old happy whore." Sections 1 and 2 present the poet's confusion and the decline of America, culminating in a descent "to these dark places/ to these waters"—but, significantly, the drowning is only apparent. The moon is associated with the heart pumping blood, "washing the way clear for new origins," and the blood that is ritually spattered is, symbolically, that of fish.

At the end of section 2, the speaker recognizes that attempting to bring "the promiseland" to a chosen few by violent means has only polluted his mind: "the knife doubles back." After this self-inflicted death, section 3 offers a new beginning: "Be the mystic/ & wage ultimate revolution." All stereotypic revolutionary roles are rejected, and the short homily concludes with the admonition to "Be yourself." Section 4 makes the connection between the speaker's own past dreams and his projected life. The steps to this new life he learns from a stranger met in April (in Young's calendar, not the cruellest month, but the time of resurrection). The poem concludes where it began, at the writer's desk in early evening, but with a new optimism. As he works, he en-

visions a people newly energized by the night, he hopes for the dawn, and he pronounces a blessing of peace. The final hortatory line—"Let the revolutions proceed!"—rejects the tyranny of any one ideological movement and advocates the proliferation of individual struggles.

THE SONG TURNING BACK INTO ITSELF

The Song Turning Back into Itself, which takes its name from a long poem in seven parts, includes forty-four poems grouped under the five headings "Loneliness," "The Song Turning Back into Itself," "The Prestidigitator," "Everywhere," and "The Move Continuing." In an interview published in *New Orleans Review*, Young explained that *The Song Turning Back into Itself* has three levels of meaning: that history moves in cycles; that American popular music is returning to its roots in folk, African, and other ethnic music; and that the individual, going through changes, nevertheless returns to an original, unique self.

These three returns are all explored in "The Old Fashioned Cincinnati Blues," which appears in the first group of poems. Dedicated to Jesse "Lone Cat" Fuller, and taking its form and its train-ride setting from the blues, the poem is a nostalgic return to the poet's past— to a trip made by rail from Cincinnati to Meridian, Mississippi, by two young brothers, for a summer visit with grandparents and relatives left behind in the South. Vivid sensual images are fixed in his memory: "RC Cola coolers," "tin tub baths," and "swapping ghost stories." The adult sees himself as essentially the same as the boy he was in 1949. The poet experiences his journey not just as a personal reminiscence, but as part of the American tradition, for the voice of Whitman can be heard in Young's lines: "O Americana!/ United Statesiana!"

The seven numbered poems titled "The Song Turning Back into Itself" are a spiritual autobiography of the poet, from the baby's first breath through the adult shouting joyfully: "SING/ one sweet long song to undo/ all sickness & suffering." This persona draws on many sources for inspiration, including Billie Holiday (who sings "variations on the theme/ of human love &/ its shadow/ loneliness") and Rainer Maria Rilke (whose eighteenth "Sonnet to Orpheus" may be heard in "Feel today/ vibrating/ in the throat"). Singing the blues becomes, in these poems, an exploration of the singer's identity and roots. Images from his personal memories merge with historical events to suggest recurring cycles, as in the speculation: "Consider Nazis & crackers/ on the same stage/ splitting the bill."

GEOGRAPHY OF THE NEAR PAST

Images correlating personal and cultural history are also charted in *Geography of the Near Past*, a volume consisting of five groups of poems: "The Sad Hour of Your Peace," "American Glamour," "Geography of the Near Past," "Some Recent Fiction," and "Boogie with O. O. Gabugah." The first group takes its title from a poem set on a beach at Santa Cruz, California, in which the speaker's sadness at finding a crowded, noisy, banal scene where he had longed for some peace, dissolves in gentle irony as he realizes his nostalgia for a lonely beach where a kid once walked is not a real memory, but "a movie that was never even shot." Most of the poems in this group are occasional, alluding to specific events or observations in an ordinary life: hearing his unborn child move in his wife's womb, eating hot Mexican food with his pregnant wife, a father joyfully recognizing his son's separate life, thoughts while visiting a prison inmate, a meditation while visiting a musician dying of a drug overdose, and the memory of writing in a rented room above a cabaret three nights before the building burned down. The endings and beginnings recorded in these poems intertwine.

The poems of "American Glamour" criticize the self-indulgence and spiritual emptiness found in contemporary culture. "Moss" reflects on the trendiness of The Rolling Stones's drug habit, treated by the media as part of their heroic glamour; in response to that story, the poet cites the suffering and deaths of the heroin addicts Charlie Parker, Holiday, and Bela Lugosi, performers of an earlier era. Drug dependency is only one symptom of an exhausted society; the young couple in "Making Love After Hours" exemplify the emptiness of repeated transgressions. The poet's condemnation of their lifeless, loveless, casual intercourse is given in several correlative images: the motion pictures on television flickering without sound, the "Yawning display in a budget-store window," and the stumbling drunks on the street. In "Ho" (whore), the poet adopts the voice and speech of a young but streetwise boy, who regretfully observes the trap of prostitution, teaching a young

woman that "heaven aint the only H in the dictionary." The success of this poem depends on the voice, which is convincing. The syntax is not standard English, but it conforms perfectly to a different set of rules. "I use to know her family" and "She just a skinny little sister" express his compassion and his sense of being connected with her tragedy.

The eleven poems grouped under the heading "Geography of the Near Past" are a traveling author's impressions of Manhattan, Boston, Providence, New Orleans, Detroit, Denver, Mexico City, any inner city, and an ugly stretch of suburban highway, which, together, compose a spiritual map of America. Here, Young's verses have more regular line lengths, and a loose iambic meter dominates. "Fun City Samba" and "Inner City Blues" conspicuously imitate the musical forms of their titles, and the music of speech heard in the inner city streets mixes easily with the author's more formal language. The final poem of this group is "Geography of the Near Past," and unlike the others, it appears with each line centered on the page, creating an urn-shaped visual image. Written in the Symbolist tradition, "Geography of the Near Past" presents the perceptive individual's movement through life (or, in context, the author's journey across America) in the developing symbol of swimming: in the first stanza, swimming against the current but with the light; in the second stanza, swimming blindly through foam or fog; and, in the final stanza, seeing through the water-filmed eyes of fish surfacing. Rather than the absolute "beauty is truth, truth beauty," Young's poem assumes the relative and mystical truth of "each universe" seen through the imagination and experience of fellow swimmers. Young, in a later poem ("What Is the Blues?" from *The Blues Don't Change*), links this mystical symbol of swimming with a rediscovery of cultural roots, suggesting that the poet, in exploring and charting a personal geography, also unfolds a map of American social history.

"Some Recent Fiction" groups six poems, including a delightfully dry "Teaching," a dramatic prose poem "Cherokees," and a three-part aural dream narrative portraying the black revolutionary lover of a light-skinned woman named Zara, "Some Recent Fiction." The poem reveals the revolutionary's egotistic need to express contempt for others ("gentle reader/ creep who buys my hustle") and to dominate Zara (he speaks to her in imperatives, and she remembers the phrase "'I love you, Hitler'" from her experiences at "Bootlick State"). As in the dramatic monologues of Robert Browning, the speaker in this poem exposes his own shallowness to ridicule.

Young creates another dramatic persona in O. O. Gabugah, for whom he writes a mock literary introduction, giving his place of birth as "125th and Lenox in Harlem" and his real name as "Franklin Delano Watson" (he was born in 1945). Rejecting his parents' choice of a white hero's name, he has adopted the name Our Own Gabugah. "Brother Gabugah" is praised by this fatuous critic as "one of our strongest young Black revolutionary voices," and his character embodies the stereotype first defined in Young's "A Dance for Militant Dilettantes." After listing Gabugah's publications and his "Vanderbilt Fellowship to conduct research on Richard Wright," the editor notes that Gabugah does not write but rather dictates his poems. The four examples that follow are less parodies of actual poems than imitations of the black activist literature that an American public expects: strident, preachy, and meandering expressions of rage. Each of O. O. Gabugah's poems adopts a different form: "The Old O. O. Blues" appears not in any recognizable blues form, but in a western European ballad stanza rhymed *abab*; "Black Queen for More Than a Day" is a delightfully bad free-verse poem, with mixed metaphors and silly similes and relentless alliteration; "What You Seize Is What You Get" approximates the typographic playfulness of E. E. Cummings and painfully spells out each one of its puns; and "A Poem for Players," listing the few occupations open to blacks in America, is written mostly in quatrains of irregular line length and irregular end rhyme, with the refrain "They'll let you play." O. O. Gabugah's simplistic political analysis assumes that an international conspiracy has assassinated blacks involved in political change, but in the final repetition of the refrain, Young's advocacy of individual self-discovery may be heard: "They'll let you play anybody but you." O. O. Gabugah is playing a profitable role, "funky Baaaaaad-ass/ Afro-headed," but it remains as stereotyped as Sambo.

THE BLUES DON'T CHANGE

Young's unique blending of whimsy and social satire also appears in one of the twenty-seven new poems published in *The Blues Don't Change*. It is a poem written in memory of two men who died on the same day in 1973: "W. H. Auden and Mantan Moreland." Not only does Young violate snobbish propriety by considering a poet of high culture, W. H. Auden, in the same text with a popular comic motion-picture actor, Mantan Moreland, but he also overturns his readers' expectations about their speech patterns. The poem consists of a dialogue between these two, in paradise, with Moreland praising Auden's *The Age of Anxiety* (1947) for "doubtless" engaging "our/ innermost emotions & informed imagination," and Auden responding, "No shit!" One can imagine the curiosity of a fellow poet as Young arranges for Moreland to ask Auden why he cut the line "We must all love one another or die" from his poem "September 1, 1939." The line was superfluous, as Auden's reply declares, "We gon die anyway no matter/ how much we love." Having justified Auden's technique, Young also defends Moreland, whose role-playing was harshly judged by militant activists. Auden praises Moreland's technique, "the way you buck them eyes/ & make out like you running sked all the time." That fear, Auden notes, is the essence of "the black/ experience where you be in charge of the scene." Moreland did stop "shufflin'," and Young's poem reclaims with pride this actor's achievements.

Several of the poems in *The Blues Don't Change* are tributes to black American musicians; most notable are "Billie," "The James Cotton Band at Keystone," "My Spanish Heart," and "Lester Leaps In." Each poem recreates the impact of their performances on a rapt listener. Listening to singer Holiday while drinking, he seems to take in her song through his mouth. The sexuality that Holiday projected in her singing is expressed metaphorically in the listener's fantasy of swallowing her delightful body. The song and his drink intoxicate, "whirling/ me through her throaty world and higher." The listener recognizes the seductress that Holiday enacted in his tribute to her "Cleopatric breath." In contrast to the dreamily slow movement of lines in "Billie," "The James Cotton Band at Keystone" plays with a livelier rhythm, demonstrating "Believe me, the blues can be volatile too,/ but the blues don't bruise; they only renew."

The return to cultural roots revitalizes both the individual and society. In "The Blues Don't Change," his apostrophe to the relentless rhythm and brilliant images of the blues, Young again pays tribute to the uniquely American expression of life's pain and sadness, and to the performers whose artistry lifts the spirit. Working within American forms of speech and music, this poet soars, defining his own voice and enriching America's cultural heritage.

THE SOUND OF DREAMS REMEMBERED

More than a decade passed between Young's 1988 collection *Heaven* and his 2001 volume *The Sound of Dreams Remembered. Heaven* filled nearly three hundred pages, displayed an abundant affection for the ordinary world, and showcased several influences (noted in the collection's introduction) that included the poets Baraka, Vladimir Mayakovsky, and Federico García Lorca.

The work of Langston Hughes and Charles Bukowski also makes its mark on *The Sound of Dreams Remembered.* Disjointed thoughts, full of mystique and sentiment, like those of Bukowski, are apparent here. The collection is a readable and topical history of the decade, providing meditations on love, travel, politics, and misbehavior. Casual blank verse gives way to fluid, rhyming iambic pentameter in poems such as "The Old Country":

> What is it want,
> or need to haul or lug like Motorolas
> of the blood? Beep! The mileage we squander
> on these jumps from mayonnaise Minnesotas
> to curry Calcuttas, from Tokyos you could wander.

COASTAL NIGHTS AND INLAND AFTERNOONS

The cover illustration for *Coastal Nights and Inland Afternoons* is *Sunset Jet*, a painting by Lorraine Capparrel, which celebrates the California landscape of seashore and foothills and the lifestyle they symbolize. Also on the cover below the author's name is his title at the time of publication, "California Poet Laureate."

This collection was the first book of poetry Young had published after taking that role. In a humorous and ironic twist, one of the poems in this volume, composed

three years before his appointment, is titled "No California Poet Laureate Blues." At the time he wrote this poem, the position was vacant; although many distinguished poets reside in the state, several had declined to be nominated, preferring to remain part of the loyal opposition. Perhaps this was cause for the blues, but Young wryly observes:

> To seek or look is not to find.
> The wayward miners, 1849 . . .
> Who stands out among the many?
> or would it be savvy to not find any?

Three years later, Young undertook the job with enthusiasm and dedication, continuing his work of "bringing poetry back into the public and popular discourse."

Despite the landscape and lifestyle celebrated in *Coastal Nights and Inland Afternoons*, many of the poems convey a sense of peril, of promises not fulfilled. While chuckling at the difficulty in recruiting a poet laureate, "No California Poet Laureate Blues" also comments:

> . . . Poetic visionaries
> have now displaced missionaries
> in a California dream deferred.

But in keeping with the panorama depicted on the cover, the poems in *Coastal Nights and Inland Afternoons* address a wide range of subjects and of poetic forms, often inspired by musical rhythms. There are several blues poems, which also appear in the later volume *Something About the Blues.* "Dawn at Oakland Airport" in *Coastal Nights and Inland Afternoons* derives its bluesy feel from the experience described: missing a plane after too little sleep and wondering whether things would be any better in another town. Another poem offers a brief eulogy to Rudolph Diesel, inventor of the Diesel engine, who disappeared at sea.

"Alchemy of Destiny" suggests the long natural processes that created an idyllic ambiance (such as California's, though it is not explicitly mentioned) of "Eternal nights . . . under a garden of stars," but warns that they can "melt away" through "quick neglect"— opting for the flashy lifestyle that is also popularly associated with California.

. . . On a planet programmed
for electrifying connections, muted, mutable,
all mood and no work, the alchemy of destiny is prized.

The final poem in *Coastal Nights and Inland Afternoons* is "Notes on the Future of Love," a scathing attack on the use of brutal military tactics—a widespread use, as indicated through the subtle pun "Iraq and another place/ hard hit." It reminds readers that such tactics are not the result of necessity but of deliberate choice:

Meanwhile over in yet another time zone,
somewhere between Iraq and another place
hard hit, the most toxic of gumbos thickens. . . .
In your cozy time zone, sandwiched now somehow
between Iraq and another place hard hit,
where do you come down on the future of love?

SOMETHING ABOUT THE BLUES

Something About the Blues presents more than one hundred poems, new and previously published, about blues music, musicians, fans, and the blues as a mood and as a way of life. Some poems, such as "Blue Monday" or "Blues My Naughty Poetry Taught Me," are inspired directly by blues songs, while others recall encounters with performers, for example "The Elvis I Knew Well Was Spiritual" or "You Catch Yourself on a Train With Yo-Yo Ma."

Although Young believes that the blues are a living musical form that can never be fully defined, he himself has been steeped in the blues over a lifetime, as a performer and as a very young student. In Mississippi during the 1940's, he attended a segregated school where the classroom focus was on black literature such as the works of Hughes and Paul Laurence Dunbar. Hughes was a pioneering blues poet, depicting African American life beginning in the 1920's. His "Weary Blues" (1923) is the first selection in Young's book, and a compact disc that accompanies the book includes a recording of Hughes reading this poignant poem. Young's collection includes tributes to legendary blues performers such as Holiday, Ma Rainey, Lena Horne, and Leadbelly.

Many poems in *Something About the Blues* have other wellsprings than the music, allowing Young to treat a wide range of subjects and moods. One such wellspring is California, where Young settled and has spent several decades. "Watsonville After the Quake" conveys the irony of network television news covering victims of the 1989 Loma Prieta earthquake but ignoring victims of perennial poverty in a California farm town. In "Blues My Naughty Poetry Taught Me," the poet in a bluesy mood surveys California cityscapes from a train window:

Sea-fences, industrial wash-ups, slushy tracks
and rickety light: skies so soulfully watercolored
you'd have to be an arts commissioner not to see it.
Seen across the Bay through trees and the undersides
of freeways San Francisco looks lonely at the end
of one bridge and the beginning of another . . .

Through poems such as this, Young establishes a link between the blues in one's personal life (bad women or men and bad whiskey are not the only causes) and an emotionally depressing landscape. He goes further in this direction with another piece in the volume—not a poem, but a sixteen-page short story "Silent Parrot Blues," about the relatively new concept of environmental racism.

Young is also aware that blues has its cliché side. In "Depression, Blues, Flamenco, Wine, Despair," he pokes fun at the "dark" solemnity of some blues, but also offers positive advice on a more cheerful lifestyle:

Depression, blues, flamenco, wine, despair.
Sunk in, they make you cross your heart and die
for hope. . . .
And so you buy the pain the stress, the restlessness,
the works . . .
Take chances, stretch, jump at the sun.
You just can't spend your whole life acting hip . . .

OTHER MAJOR WORKS

LONG FICTION: *Snakes*, 1970; *Who Is Angelina?*, 1975; *Sitting Pretty*, 1976; *Ask Me Now*, 1980; *Seduction by Light*, 1988.

NONFICTION: *Bodies and Soul: Musical Memoirs*, 1981; *Kinds of Blue: Musical Memoirs*, 1984; *Things Ain't What They Used to Be: Musical Memoirs*, 1987; *Mingus/Mingus: Two Memoirs*, 1989 (with Janet Coleman); *Drowning in the Sea of Love: Musical Memoirs*, 1995.

EDITED TEXTS: *Changing All Those Changes*, 1976 (by James P. Girard); *Zeppelin Coming Down*, 1976 (by William Lawson); *Yardbird Lives!*, 1978 (with Ishmael Reed); *Calafia: An Anthology of California Poets*, 1979 (with Reed and Shawn Hsu Wong); *Quilt*, 1981-1986 (with Reed; 5 volumes); *African American Literature: A Brief Introduction and Anthology*, 1996.

BIBLIOGRAPHY

"Al Young." In *American Ethnic Writers*. Rev. ed. Pasadena, Calif.: Salem Press, 2009. The section on Al Young contains general information as well as analyses of some of his major works, including *Dancing*, *The Blues Don't Change*, and *The Sound of Dreams Remembered*.

Coleman, Janet, and Al Young. *Mingus/Mingus: Two Memoirs*. Berkeley, Calif.: Creative Arts, 1989. Young's memoir is essential for understanding his life and work.

Draper, James P. *Black Literature Criticism: Excerpts from Criticism of the Most Significant Works of Black Authors over the Past Two Hundred Years*. Detroit: Gale Research, 1997. Contains a fifteen-page chapter on Young that includes criticism, interviews from 1976 to 1989, a short biography, and a bibliography.

Koolish, Lynda. *African American Writers: Portraits and Visions*. Jackson: University Press of Mississippi, 2001. Contains a short biography of Young with some critical analysis.

Lee, Don. "About Al Young." *Ploughshares* 19, no. 1 (Spring, 1993): 219. A short profile of Young's life as poet and screenwriter.

Matney, William C., ed. *Who's Who Among Black Americans*. 5th ed. Lake Forest, Ill.: Educational Communications, 1988. A collection of interviews and personal profiles. Contains useful material regarding the manifold interests of the writer.

Nixon, Will. "Better Times for Black Writers?" *Publishers Weekly* 235 (February 17, 1989): 35-40. Young and several other African American writers and editors speak out regarding their reception in the publishing world.

Ross, Michael E. "Hollywood's Civil Servants." *The New York Times Book Review*, February 5, 1989, p. 12. Ross profiles Young and some other African American writers working in Hollywood, a town that is traditionally tough on its artists.

Young, Al. "Al Young." http://alyoung.org. The writer's own Web site contains a biography, schedules, links to resources, photographs, poems and lyrics, and a calendar.

_____. Interview. In *The Writer's Mind: Interviews with American Authors*, edited by Irv Broughton. Vol. 3. Fayetteville: University of Arkansas Press, 1990. In this rare and enlightening interview, Young explains his poetic philosophy.

Judith L. Johnston; Sarah Hilbert
Updated by Thomas Rankin

DEAN YOUNG

Born: Columbia, Pennsylvania; July 18, 1955

PRINCIPAL POETRY

Design with X, 1988
Beloved Infidel, 1992
Strike Anywhere, 1995
First Course in Turbulence, 1999
Skid, 2002
Elegy on a Toy Piano, 2005
Ready-Made Bouquet, 2005
Embryoyo, 2007
Primitive Mentor, 2008
Thirty-one Poems, 1998-2008, 2009

OTHER LITERARY FORMS

Although Dean Young is known primarily for his poetry, he has written a collection of essays on poetics entitled *The Art of Recklessness: Poetry as Assertive Force and Contradiction* (2010), which examines various philosophies and theories in writing and teaching poetry, including sources of inspiration and the relationship between a poem and the reader. He also collaborated with several other poets on the collection *Seven Poets, Four Days, One Book* (2009), and his work has been anthologized in *New American Poets of the Nine-*

ties (1991). Young is the cover artist for several of his collections, including *Skid* and *Primitive Mentor*.

ACHIEVEMENTS

Dean Young's third poetry collection, *Strike Anywhere*, won the Colorado Poetry Prize, and his fifth collection, *Skid*, was a finalist for the Lenore Marshall Poetry Prize. In 2006, *Elegy on a Toy Piano* was selected as a finalist for the Pulitzer Prize in poetry, and in 2009, *Primitive Mentor* was shortlisted for the ninth annual Griffin Poetry Prize.

Young received a Fine Arts Work Center Fellowship in Provincetown, a Stegner Fellowship from Stanford University from 1987 to 1988, National Endowment for the Arts Fellowships in 1988 and 1996, a Guggenheim Fellowship in 2002, and an Academy Award in Literature from the American Academy of Arts and Letters in 2007. Young's poetry has been anthologized in the collection *Best American Poetry* in 1993, 1994, 1997, 2000, 2001, 2006, and 2008. Young is most noted for bringing to modern Surrealist poetry a mixture of humanism, humor, and celebration through his accelerated, disjunctive, and expansive treatment of language and theme. In 2008, he was appointed the William Livingston Chair of Poetry at Austin University.

BIOGRAPHY

Dean Young was born Richard Young in Columbia, Pennsylvania, in 1955. In various interviews, Young comments that he identifies personally and poetically with being misunderstood, which is often an underlying theme of his poems. He spent a year in nursing school, but quickly changed majors, and received his B.A. in English in 1978 and an M.F.A. in 1984, both from Indiana University.

Shortly after finishing his Stegner Fellowship in 1988, Young published his first poetry collection, *Design with X*, which drew heavily from his nursing background. Although this collection shows moments of Young's disjunctive surrealism, the tone of the collection is more solemn than that of his subsequent books. In his third collection, *Strike Anywhere*, Young's poems began to fully exhibit his trademark brand of absurdist humor.

Young divides his time between Austin, Texas, and Berkeley, California, where he lives with his wife, novelist Cornelia Nixon. While Young taught at Loyola University in Chicago, his style grew more expansive, esoteric, and humorous while maintaining a resonant sense of the human condition. By 2005, Young had become a member of the permanent faculty at the Iowa Writers' Workshop. It is at this time that his poems began delving more frequently into themes of family and mortality, as a result of his father's death as well as his own health issues. Young has taught at the low residency M.F.A. program at Warren Wilson College in North Carolina.

ANALYSIS

Dean Young's poetry is noted for its ability to incorporate humor with somber moments, high culture with low, and both Romantic and postmodern sensibilities. Young's poems create a collage of seemingly unrelated images, utterances, and moments by combining, through the use of rapid juxtapositions, the strategies of the Surrealists as well as the standup comedian. In a 2004 *Prairie Schooner* review of *Skid*, Hadara Bar-Nadav suggests that due to Young's shifting poetic strategies, the mixing of literary and popular allusions, and strange lists, it is difficult for the reader to know if Young "is simply observing, critiquing, or making fun of his subjects." Frequently, the answer is all of the above. Young's poetry requires that readers learn the various strategies of its specific, often personal, ordering system. Young's poems work to bring form and order to the subconscious and to illuminate both the expansiveness of people's physical and imaginative world and the role of various relationships in those worlds.

The specific subjects in his work may be politics, literature, popular music, and personal tragedy, sometimes in the same poem. However, recurrent themes in Young's body of work center on the abilities of language and experience to misdirect and confuse, as well as the abilities of the reader to bridge the gaps between his abrupt transitions. Young is often held up as a central figure in contemporary Surrealism, as well as a member of the second generation New York School of poetry.

BELOVED INFIDEL

The poems in Young's second book, *Beloved Infidel*, use a variety of cultural icons—Rastafarian musician Bob Marley, modern artists Mark Rothko and William de Kooning—combined with personal memories. In "The Business of Love Is Cruelty," which is ostensibly about a child telling his mother that he hates her, the poem transitions into a social critique and empathetic understanding of Dr. Frankenstein:

> And Herr Doktor,
> what does he want among the burning villages
> of his proven theories? Well, he wants
> to be a student again

The themes of the poems in *Beloved Infidel* focus on relationships, faith, and alienation, as suggested by the collection's title. The poems in this collection mark evidence of Young's developing style of humor. They derive dramatic tension from his ability to make abrupt shifts in subject matter and strategy, while returning to central themes of alienation, family, and an exploration of the human condition. These surreal examinations of the psyche, through the splicing of culture and personal experience, work to create a common ground between the poet and the reader, while allowing Young to maintain his authorial distance. As a result, the reader is left with a distorted but compassionate reflection of the world.

In the concluding poem of the collection, "The Soul," Young analyzes the philosophy of existence, claiming that Christian religion should not focus on "Christ nailed but brought down," but rather "the tenderness of two summoned women." The poem then ends on another note that draws attention to kind human gestures, what Young suggests is the culmination of human existence, "our momentary gentle attendance as someone calls,/ come look at the moon, come watch the waves." It is this "attendance" to the details and minutia of living and Young's ability to place that minutia in the service of the self that brings cohesion and a Romantic sensibility to this collection.

ELEGY ON A TOY PIANO

In *Elegy on a Toy Piano*, Young continues his critique of modern culture and considers the place of art in that culture, with a strong sense of celebratory playfulness, while simultaneously delving into themes of human relationships and the power of the imagination.

These poems use their sense of the absurd to mediate, and often undercut, subject matters of illness and death. In the title poem, "Elegy on a Toy Piano," the speaker begins with a parable of life and death, "You don't need a pony/ to connect you to the unseeable." This statement requires the reader to work at making meaning out of seeming nonsense by constantly scrambling for connections. After a series of non-sequitur statements, the poem ends with a somber finality as the speaker considers:

> When something becomes ash,
> there's nothing you can do to turn it back.
> About this, even diamonds do not lie.

Elegy on a Toy Piano includes many postmodern moments, which both pronounce Young's aesthetic while simultaneously undercutting it. In "With Hidden Noise," Young strings together several metaphors in a surreal collage of images to help define his relationship to his own writing. In the first line of the poem, Young uses the metaphor "I am a teapot and this is my song." A list of "I am" statements continues until the poem ends with the speaker imploring the reader to attempt writing Surrealist poetry "on your own at home."

Although Young's poems often rely on quick non-sequitur transitions, these strained connections are not arbitrary, but a focused attempt to enact what Danielle Chapman, in her September, 2005, *Poetry* review of *Elegy on a Toy Piano*, called Young's project, to examine "how lonely, how confusing, how ridiculous it is to be an imaginative creature in an ever-streamlining culture."

PRIMITIVE MENTOR

The poems in *Primitive Mentor* show Young being both more serious and more playful than in his previous collections. On the surface, many of these poems pay homage to Young's poetic influences such as William Butler Yeats, Arthur Rimbaud, William Wordsworth, and Walt Whitman. On a broader level, this collection deals more with legacy, mortality, and the speaker's and reader's place in the universe. As a result, the poems in *Primitive Mentor* have an undercurrent of pain that is not as prevalent in his earlier collections. However, Young's poems work more diligently than ever to mediate or soften that pain with his undercutting humor. In the first poem of the first section, "What Form Death," the speaker meditates on death, moving quickly between literary references, memory fragments, punch lines, and wordplay until the speaker imagines addressing a relative who is most likely dead as "Dear mustachioed Aunt Gloria who/ gave me 20 bucks to blow on rubber snakes/ and pinball, what became of you?"

The subjects and themes of *Primitive Mentor* tend more toward the overtly political with poems such as "Enter Fortinbras," which draws parallels between the political climate in William Shakespeare's *Hamlet, Prince of Denmark* (pr. c. 1600-1601) as well as the political and cultural climate prevalent in contemporary America. Young rewrites one of Shakespeare's most famous passages:

> The slings and thongs
> of outrageous fortune, well, no need
> to kill yourself over every bomb and extinction.
>
> To be or not to be, what's the big diff?

This collection's penultimate poem, "Exit Exam," shows Young's speaker contemplating human mortality and the afterlife. In the last lines, Young writes of everyone's inevitable death, and contemplates various institutional beliefs and practices surrounding that death:

> will we be petrified or dashed to even smaller pieces,
> will we be released from the wheelhouse
> or come back as hyena or mouse,
> as a cloud or rock
> or will it be sleep's pure peace of nothingness?

Ending on "nothingness" in this typical Young poem, however, is less a resignation to the inevitability of death as it is the solace of an eventual "pure peace," which reaffirms the importance and vitality of the author's own aesthetic of constant momentum and attentiveness.

OTHER MAJOR WORK

NONFICTION: *The Art of Recklessness: Poetry as Assertive Force and Contradiction*, 2010.

BIBLIOGRAPHY

Harris, Peter. "Difficult and Otherwise: New Work by Ruefle, Young, and Aleshire." *Virginia Quarterly* 73, no. 4 (September, 1997): 680-692. This article works to identify a trend toward Surrealism, the use of condensed language and images in contemporary poetry. In the process, Harris examines Young's collection *Strike Anywhere*, as well as collections by two of Young's peers. Although less than a third of the essay is focused on Young, the sections on Mary Ruefle and Joan Aleshire illuminate principles of Young's aesthetic.

Hoagland, Tony. "The Dean Young Effect." *American Poetry Review* 38, no. 4 (July/August, 2009): 29-33. This article works to place Young into the landscape of contemporary poetry by examining his latest work, his influences, and his influence on younger poets. Hoagland works to clarify some common misconceptions about Young's work and establish him as an important voice in contemporary American poetry.

Logan, William. "The Great American Desert." *The New Criterion* 23 (June, 2005). 66-74. In this essay, Logan reviews several new collections by contemporary authors, including Young's *Elegy on a Toy Piano*. This review takes Young to task for his poetic style and connects that style to that of fellow contemporary American poet John Ashbery.

Young, Dean. "An Interview with Dean Young." Interview by Lee Rossi. *Pedestal Magazine* 53 (May/June, 2009). Rossi and Young discuss poems from *Primitive Mentor*, and Young's various aesthetic concerns, such as his serious use of the joke, his poetic influences, his writing process, and his indebtedness to Latin American Surrealism.

_____. "Surrealism 101." In *Poet's Work, Poet's Play: Essays on the Practice and the Art*, edited by Daniel Tobin and Pimone Triplett. Ann Arbor: University of Michigan Press, 2008. Describes how Surrealism used trauma, confrontation, and destabilization to bring about change. In examining Surrealism and Dadaism, he sheds light on his own poetry.

Roy Seeger

Z

PAUL ZIMMER

Born: Canton, Ohio; September 18, 1934

PRINCIPAL POETRY

A Seed on the Wind, 1960
The Ribs of Death, 1967
The Republic of Many Voices, 1969
The Zimmer Poems, 1976
With Wanda: Town and Country Poems, 1980
The Ancient Wars, 1981
Earthbound Zimmer, 1983
Family Reunion: Selected and New Poems, 1983
The American Zimmer, 1984
Live With Animals, 1987
The Great Bird of Love, 1989
Big Blue Train, 1993
Crossing to Sunlight: Selected Poems, 1996
Crossing to Sunlight Revisited: New and Selected Poems, 2007

OTHER LITERARY FORMS

Paul Zimmer has written a number of other works, including critical essays and personal memoirs, such as "The Importance of Being Zimmer" in *American Poets in 1976* (1976), "In the Palm of My Hand" in *The Atlanta Journal and Constitution Magazine* (1980), *After the Fire: A Writer Finds His Place* (2002), and *Trains in the Distance* (2004). Miscellaneous pieces by Zimmer include "Zimmer's Old-Fashioned Summer Day Mud Cakes," a recipe, in *John Keats's Porridge: Favorite Recipes of American Poets* (1975), and "The Atomic Bomb," "Robert Frost," "Teaching Poetry," and "Strip Mining," radio commentaries written for recitation on *From the Press* between 1977 and 1978.

ACHIEVEMENTS

Although Paul Zimmer has received many major awards such as the Borestone Mountain Award (1971),

the *Yankee* Poetry Prize (1972), the Helen Bullis Award from *Poetry Northwest* (1975), six Pushcart Prizes (1977, 1981, 1993, 2006, 2008, 2010), an Academy Award in Literature from the American Academy and Institute of Arts and Letters Award (1985), two National Endowment for the Arts grants (1975, 1982), a National Poetry Series selection (1988) for *The Great Bird of Love*, two Ohioana Book Award for *Trains in the Distance* and *Crossing to Sunlight Revisited* (2005, 2008, respectively), and the Posner Book-Length Poetry Award from the Council for Wisconsin Writers (2008), he has become equally well known for his refusal of a National Endowment for the Arts Grant (1990) in protest of its revised antiobscenity guidelines.

BIOGRAPHY

Paul Jerome Zimmer was born in Canton, Ohio, on September 18, 1934, to Jerome F. Zimmer and Louise Surmont Zimmer. He enrolled in Kent State University in 1952 but had a tumultuous college career marked by academic ineptitude—he failed freshman English three times. Even his early attempt at a workman's life (he took a job in a steel mill) was tinged by misfortune when the millworkers went on strike ten days later and Zimmer got notice that he had been drafted by the U.S. Army. During Zimmer's time in the military, which provided the young man with much free time and little to do, he discovered that he liked poetry. During those years, he voraciously read and tentatively wrote poetry. After his military service, he returned to college to continue studying poetry with an eye toward writing and publishing. After receiving his bachelor's degree in 1958, Zimmer wrote, "I had this complex that I was not terribly important, so . . . I made poems about other people and spoke through their bodies, their beings." The creator of the archetypical "Zimmer" persona would later find that his creativity abounded in the recollection of his own being.

After college, Zimmer found himself constantly working with books: He was manager of the book department at Macy's department store in San Francisco (1961-1963), manager of the San Francisco News Company (1963-1964), and manager of the University of California, Los Angeles, bookstore (1964-1966). In

1967, he found an outlet for his poetic talents as assistant director of the University of Pittsburgh Press and editor of the Pitt Poetry Series (1967-1978). He directed the University of Georgia Press (1978-1984) and then the University of Iowa Press (1984-1994), after which he reluctantly retired to spend more time on his own poetry and two succeeding volumes of memoirs. The author of "Sonnet: Zimmer Imagines Being Poet-in-Residence," he was twice named a university poet-in-residence, first at Chico State College (now California State University, Chico) in 1970 and then at Hollins University in 2001, where he was named Louis D. Rubin, Jr., Writer-in-Residence. In 2009, he became the Rachel Rivers-Coffey Distinguished Professor of Creative Writing at Appalachian State University.

ANALYSIS

Although Paul Zimmer's poetry frequently features a character named Zimmer (particularly in the later books of verse), to state that Zimmer writes solely autobiographical poems is both misleading and reductive. The poet's works are not simply internal monologues or records of anecdotal experience. Rather, Zimmer depicts in his poems a caricature of himself not only in the persona of "Zimmer," but also through those of Imbellis, Barney, and even Wanda. Zimmer's poems examine the poetic self embodied in its varying characters and spoken in its differing voices. The traditions that shape English-language poetry in general and American verse in particular have weighed heavy on the mind of Zimmer because of his dual careers as poet and publisher. Zimmer's poems, particularly in the context of their literary inheritance from other such American poets as Walt Whitman, both embrace tradition and question its strictures. The self developed in Zimmer's poems, like Whitman, sometimes finds value in American life and experience, but more often speaks doubtfully or angrily about his encounters with American peculiarities.

A SEED ON THE WIND

In many interviews, Zimmer identified his first book of poetry as *The Ribs of Death*. That volume, however, is the first book of his poetry to be published by a major press. His actual first book of verse, privately printed, was *A Seed on the Wind*. This slim vol-

ume, a selection of poems concerning nature, demonstrates the genesis of Zimmer's themes. Nineteen poems laud the beauty and simplicity of the natural world in comparison to the dissolution and complexity of the human world. "A Hunting Song" demonstrates this contrast in fifteen terse, unrhymed lines. The human world, as represented by a foxhunting party, is frantic and murderous, breaking the quiet of the deep wood with the loud barking of its hunting dogs. The natural world, as represented by the foxglove, although to human perceptions a more delicate being than the fox and hunting party, is shown to be more permanent and ever-living:

> Bruised by insect wings and
> Crushed perfumeless by
> Stumbling feet, they will
> Yet survive alone, defying
> The probings of our greenest thumbs.

Nature, as opposed to humanity, is eternal—it preceded and will follow humankind's encroachment, just as the foxglove remains long after the hunting party, having collected its bloody prize, has left the wood.

EARTHBOUND ZIMMER

Earthbound Zimmer, a book-length poem, consists of eleven separate movements, each of which describes a memory and its philosophical consequences. The verses, unrhymed quatrains, expand on and delineate more carefully the preceding prose passages. So the rhythm of the book alternates between expansion and contraction as it moves from prose to verse. The language of verse is such that it explores symbols and archetypes, while the book as a whole develops into a meditation on the greater truths of life.

Even the theme inherent in the volume as a whole is cyclic in its rhythms. As writer Rod Jellerma commented, the poems pursue love through earth, air, fire, and water and also through the four seasons. Initial failure leads inevitably to love, to the birth of two children, and then to a final dissolution of all things in an almost medieval description of the cycle of life. For example, in "Mrs. Scheffley," Zimmer compares images of love and fire in verse, triggered by his memory, in prose, of an old lady in his neighborhood who burned to death in her own backyard trash fire:

Fire was my beginning, begetter
    of the wound I was born in, my parents
broken and smoking, hot darkness, enemies,
    the abrasive tongue of the bear.

Elsewhere, Zimmer describes nature arising to the warmth of spring out of the long, cold sleep of winter. These images of spring have been triggered by his memory of losing a fistfight started by his protest against the killing of baby mice in the spring—another example of his character Zimmer drawn into violence over internal guilt and compassion for living things:

Mountains poke circles in stars,
    fish poke circles in lakes;
I ascend through circumferences
    into the hills of spring,

earth smelling of decisions
    slow division of cells, sudden
boilings of minnows, seeds, cocoons,
    authority of grass once again.

These two verses, like those in the other nine sections of the poem, show Zimmer's careful blending of incidents in his life and stirrings of symbols from the collective unconscious, the deeper level within all humans that inspires myth and fable.

THE GREAT BIRD OF LOVE

The Great Bird of Love, selected by poet William Stafford as one of the five volumes published in 1989 in the National Poetry Series, is, like *Earthbound Zimmer*, a selection of verses crafted by a master poet, celebrating the beauty of language, driven by images of mythological importance. In the title poem, the speaker is transformed into a phenomenal force, signified by a "the" before "Zimmer."

Other poems in the collection also display intense, allegorical imagery. Zimmer's images compel the reader to identify with each situation as the persona of The Zimmer comes of age. The book is a series of verses, each poem an episode of an overall story, filled with the joys and sorrows of life. It celebrates the commonplace in life, such as love and beer, bemoans the aging of one's father, and laments the selling of a childhood home. The poems are full of variety and the humorous voice of an experienced guide to life.

CROSSING TO SUNLIGHT

A collection of more than one hundred poems ranging across thirty-five years, *Crossing to Sunlight* offers both a retrospective and a fresh look at the work of Zimmer. The volume begins with Zimmer's early, more structured and traditional writing, moves through the autobiographical poems of his middle years and the creation of his buoyant persona, Zimmer, and concludes with a generous selection of his mature work with its emphasis on durable basic themes.

A typical poem in this volume describes Zimmer's talent for metaphor and vivid imagery. He reminisces about the emotional impact of what he sees long after the actual occurrence of a triggering incident: "Grouse" describes a bird given as a gift by a neighboring hunter. The flesh of the small corpse is "A ball of delicate meat the size/ Of a small, green apple." He is suffused with compassion for the dead bird at the same time that he is repulsed by its death.

The poems in *Crossing to Sunlight* have varied tone. Some are self-deprecatory, some are clearly parodic, and others are frank love poems. All, however, are touched by Zimmer's sense of humor. "Zimmer Loathing the Gentry" suggests that although people who are wealthy or famous can "sign their names and something happens," Zimmer himself is free of the burden of being significant: "While, Zimmer, I can write, Zimmer,/ All day, and nothing happens."

Crossing to Sunlight shows the Zimmer persona matured in surety and grace from the earliest poems but without having changed his basic function as a speaker of the key truths of life. Although the poet may have flunked freshman English in college and the character (as noted in *Earthbound Zimmer*) "is no native genius," Zimmer's Zimmer has an almost prophetic view of the way the world works. What the Zimmer persona observes and tries to shape into poetic words is often a world riddled with terror and disturbance. However, even such a terror-ridden world is also immensely rewarding. Like the self-portraits of the character Zimmer, the world is a place that gains weight from the sensual enjoyment of beauty.

CROSSING TO SUNLIGHT REVISITED

Eleven years after his seminal poetic work first appeared, Zimmer returned for a second look at the world of his namesake (and alternative persona) "Zimmer." Fifty of the one hundred poems originally published in *Crossing to Sunlight* in 1996 are reprinted in *Crossing to Sunlight Revisited*; twenty-three new verses are included to round out Zimmer's intended purpose of providing readers with one poem for each year he had lived when he composed the revision (seventy-three). Rather than minimizing the impact of his advanced age on his life and work, Zimmer readily acknowledges that he sees himself as an old (not merely aging) poet with his characteristic self-deprecating humor. Zimmer has commented that his most courageous moments have occurred not only because of his desire to uphold the poetic standard of the free and open expression of ideas but also because of his poetry's frank and forward discussion of uncomfortable truths like death, pain, and loss. He has always chosen to face his troubles rather than hide from them. This tendency makes the confessional nature of his work more immediate and less rhetorical than that of other poets. Zimmer can simultaneously show the harshest realities of life and living while highlighting the blackly comic aspects of what he feels are his inadequate responses. The persona of "Zimmer," for example, develops recognizable traits that define his character in verses written across the span of a poetic career. Although driven by his turbulent emotions, "Zimmer" is seen as hopelessly ineffective at changing his circumstances, whether in childhood or in old age.

Crossing to Sunlight Revisited, however, is more than merely an update of a retrospective collection of verse. The selection of reprinted verse, along with the new additions, seems to redefine the overall volume's focus as a meditation on the aging process. Old age can be full of poignant thoughts and memories—in "Because I Am Heir to Many Things," Zimmer considers how the sharp and startled movements of a grouse emerging from the snow is as ridiculous as an aged man's dreams of youth and love. Old age can also be physically hard—"Zimmer Lurches from Chair to Chair" recounts how rarely the titular narrator has a pain-free day and how his perception of his weakness in his old age has made him fearful of confronting strange men crossing his property. Old age can also entail the increasing fear of approaching death. "Three Crows" recounts the appearance of three of the traditional harbingers of death on the author's yard as they, like the three Fates, stand watch over Zimmer during a year of ill-health. All of these concerns, although not solely the concerns of the elderly, take on a somewhat heightened sense of drama when associated with aging. The reader may laugh at the ridiculous aspects of Zimmer's work but must still acknowledge the uncomfortable truth that everything living must grow old and die.

OTHER MAJOR WORKS

NONFICTION: *After the Fire: A Writer Finds His Place*, 2002; *Trains in the Distance*, 2004.

BIBLIOGRAPHY

"After the Fire: A Writer Finds His Place." Review of *After the Fire. Virginia Quarterly Review* 78, no. 4 (Autumn, 2002): 123-124. A review of Zimmer's memoirs that celebrates the volume's open and honest portrayal of a young man's awakening to the complex nature of life.

Aldan, Daisy. "The Words of the Tribe." *Poetry* 118, no. 1 (April, 1971): 35. Aldan suggests that there is a universal language inherent in Zimmer's poetry—that the incidents and emotions Zimmer describes are common to all of humanity. She sees Zimmer as giving a voice and a language to human experience.

Gery, John. "The Atomic Test Poems of Paul Zimmer." *War, Literature, and the Arts* 6, no. 1 (1994): 1-19. Gery is fascinated with Zimmer's descriptions of his stint in the U.S. Army and his involvement with the early nuclear test program. He studies the bleakness of the young soldier's experience of war and deprivation as well as his anxiety about the increasing possibility of nuclear annihilation.

Johnson, Douglas S. "'The Longing Season': Love and Mortality in Paul Zimmer's *Big Blue Train*." *Ohioana Quarterly* 38, no. 3 (1995): 167-70. Johnson observes a common thread behind Zimmer's depictions of love affairs and death—the overriding awareness of loss and the inherent emptiness of desire.

Morgenthaler, Eric. "Buses Prove to Be the Perfect Vehicle for a Poet's Work." *Wall Street Journal*, October 17, 1975. Morgenthaler details the everyday nature of Zimmer's writing. Zimmer's poems are universal in their appeal and accessibility, so it is telling to discover that Zimmer tended to write his poetry, or at least develop his ideas, in the midst of everyday life.

Wallace, Ronald. *God Be with the Clown: Humor in American Poetry.* Columbia: University of Missouri Press, 1984. Wallace's volume, although it deals with humorous verse in American poetry in general, sees Zimmer's poetry as infused with the gentle, self-effacing humor that is common among American poets but at the same time takes the expression of laughter to even more creative heights. Wallace is convincing when he describes humor as the keystone to understanding American poetry.

Zimmer, Paul. "The Holy Words: A Conversation with Paul Zimmer." Interview by Stan Sanvel Rubin. In *The Post-confessionals: Conversations with American Poets of the Eighties,* edited by Earl G. Ingersoll, Judith Kitchen, and Rubin. Cranbury, N.J.: Associated University Presses, 1989. The interviewer calls Zimmer a "postconfessional" poet writing in the tradition of Elizabeth Bishop and Anne Sexton, but also asks the poet to describe where, historically, he sees himself in the context of American verse.

Julia M. Meyers
Updated by Meyers

LOUIS ZUKOFSKY

Born: New York, New York; January 23, 1904
Died: Port Jefferson, New York; May 12, 1978

PRINCIPAL POETRY

Fifty-five Poems, 1941
Anew, 1946
Barely and Widely, 1958
I's (Pronounced "Eyes"), 1963
After I's, 1964
All: The Collected Short Poems, 1923-1958, 1965
All: The Collected Short Poems, 1956-1964, 1965

Little, 1970
All: The Collected Short Poems, 1923-1964, 1971
"A," 1978, 1993
Eighty Flowers, 1978
Complete Short Poetry, 1991

OTHER LITERARY FORMS

Louis Zukofsky (zew-KAHF-skee) was as much respected for his criticism as he was for his poetry. His volumes of criticism include *Le Style Apollinaire* (1934, with René Taupin), *A Test of Poetry* (1948), *Prepositions: The Collected Critical Essays of Louis Zukofsky* (1968, 1981), and *Bottom: On Shakespeare* (1963). In 1932, he edited *An "Objectivists" Anthology.* A play, *Arise, Arise,* was published in 1962; a novel, *Ferdinand, Including "It Was"* in 1968.

ACHIEVEMENTS

Louis Zukofsky was, in many ways, a poet's poet, who won the admiration of such contemporaries as Ezra Pound and William Carlos Williams for his innovative use of language, for his stretching of the boundaries of poetic form, and for his perceptive readings of their works. With George Oppen and Charles Reznikoff, he became known as an Objectivist, a term he chose to distinguish these poets from Amy Lowell's Imagists and the French Symbolists. Objectivists were concerned with the precise use of language, honesty and sincerity in their communication with their audience, and the creation of a poem that in itself would be an object, part of the reader's reality.

Zukofsky's voice was that of an urban American Jew, tied to the Yiddish tradition of his immigrant parents, yet Americanized into twentieth century New York. He was conscious of living in what he called the "age of gears," where machines and technology dominated everyday life, and he was sensitive to social problems and movements—socialism, communism, Marxism, the Depression, urban unrest. His epic *"A"* provides an idiosyncratic autobiography of one poet's life from 1922 to 1976.

Throughout his life, Zukofsky taught at universities and colleges and, with reluctance, read his poetry in public. He was awarded the Lola Ridge Memorial Award of the Poetry Society of America (1949); the

Longview Foundation Award (1961); the Union League Civic and Arts Poetry Prize (1964) and the Oscar Blumenthal/Charles Leviton Prize, both from *Poetry* magazine (1966); the National Endowment for the Arts and American Literary Anthology awards (1967 and 1968); and an Academy Award in Literature from the American Academy and Institute of Arts and Letters (1976). He was nominated for a National Book Award in Poetry in 1968.

BIOGRAPHY

Louis Zukofsky was the son of Russian-Jewish immigrants and was reared on the lower East Side of New York City. His father, a religious and deeply sensitive man, was a presser in a clothing factory; his mother was a gaunt, quiet, introspective woman. Zukofsky's first introduction to literature was through the Yiddish poems and stories read in his home, together with the plays produced at the renowned Thalia theater. In particular, he was attracted to the work of Solomon Bloomgarten, who wrote under the pen name Yehoash (an acronym of the initials of his Hebrew name) and earned much admiration for both his own poetry and for his Yiddish translations of major English and American poems. Zukofsky first read untranslated English literature in the public schools of New York. He began to write poetry in high school, then at Columbia University, where he was encouraged to continue by his professor, Mark Van Doren. Zukofsky received an M.A. degree from Columbia in 1924.

Zukofsky's first submission to *Poetry* was a translation of Yehoash, which was not published. His own work ("Of Dying Beauty") first appeared in the journal in January, 1924, and he published *Poem Beginning "The"* in *Exile*, a journal edited by Ezra Pound, who saw in the young poet a literary heir. Pound dedicated his own *Guide to Kulchur* (1938) to Zukofsky (along with the English poet Basil Bunting), promoted his work in *Exile*, and persuaded Harriet Monroe to turn over an issue of *Poetry* to him as guest editor. It was this issue, appearing in February, 1931, which made Zukofsky's work visible to his contemporaries and established several poets—Oppen, Reznikoff, Bunting, and Zukofsky himself—as Objectivists, a term conceived by Zukofsky but apparently approved by all. The Ob-

jectivists established their own press, To Publishers, a short-lived venture.

Zukofsky found only a small audience for his work, supporting his wife, Celia (a composer, whom he married in 1939), and his son Paul (who became a virtuoso violinist) by teaching technical writing and literature at Brooklyn Polytechnic Institute between 1947 and 1966. He also taught English and comparative literature at the University of Wisconsin, 1930-1931; Shakespeare and Renaissance literature at Colgate University in 1947; creative writing at Queens College, 1947-1948; and in the summer of 1958 was poet-in-residence at San Francisco State College.

Zukofsky preferred to write at night, never going to bed before one or two in the morning, and he revised continually. His epic poem *"A"* was the product of several decades of work, though sections were published at intervals. As his reputation waned, some friends believed he became bitter toward readers who would not take the time and effort to understand him, and the inaccessibility of his later poems seems to reflect his antagonism toward his audience. The 1960's, however, brought renewed interest in the Objectivists, and Zukofsky has been warmly praised by such critics as Hugh Kenner and Guy Davenport.

"A" was going to press and Zukofsky was working on *Eighty Flowers* when, in 1978, he died at the age of seventy-four.

ANALYSIS

Under pressure from Monroe to declare himself part of a new "movement" in poetry, Louis Zukofsky coined the term "Objectivist." Later, he admitted that the term was unfortunate; at the very least, it has been confusing to readers and critics who interpret objectivity as an indication that reality will be rendered undistorted by the poet's personality. Zukofsky did aim at such objective honesty or "care for the detail," as he put it, but he emphasized that being an Objectivist meant that the poet created a poem as an object, in much the same way that a builder constructs a house or a carpenter, a cabinet. These two aims—an objective rendering of reality and the creation of the poem as object—give Zukofsky's poetry its distinction.

The prevailing metaphor throughout Zukofsky's

work is the correspondence between the ego and the sense of sight: "I" equals "eye" in his poetry and the terms are often playfully interchanged, as in the poems "I's (pronounced *eyes*)" or "After I's." Similarly, "see" becomes "sea" or even the letter *c* and "sight" is transformed into "cite." Like Benedictus de Spinoza (who figures in his works along with Ludwig Wittgenstein and Aristotle), Zukofsky was a lens-grinder; but Zukofsky's lenses were organic and his method of sharpening them was an ever closer examination of objects. Just as the objective lens of a microscope is the one in closest proximity to the object being studied, so Zukofsky as Objectivist attempted to apprehend objects directly and report on his findings.

Zukofsky believed that an object must be examined for its "qualities," and once these qualities are recognized, the observer can go no further in his understanding of the object. The object exists in itself and is not dependent on the observer for its existence. It is not the observer's function to postulate theories about the object, to explain, embellish, or comment on it. He merely bears witness to its reality. Only by placing the object in the context of the poem can the poet use the object to communicate something of his own reality. In a poem, juxtapositions imply connections, transitions, and relationships between objects. The poet does not editorialize. "Writing presents the finished matter, *it does not comment*," Zukofsky wrote in *A Test of Poetry*.

In his concern for precise language to express visual perception and to render faithfully the qualities of an object, Zukofsky follows Pound's statements about Imagism: "Direct treatment of the 'thing'" using "no word that does not contribute to the presentation" (*Poetry*, 1912). Zukofsky, however, shared Williams's concern that Imagism, in the years since Pound first promoted the movement, had deteriorated into impressionistic free verse, lacking form. "The Objectivist theory was this," Williams explained in his *The Autobiography of William Carlos Williams* (1951), "We had had 'Imagism' . . . which ran quickly out. That, though it had been useful in ridding the field of verbiage, had no formal necessity implicit in it." The poem, he went on, "is an object, an object that in itself formally presents its case and its meaning by the very form it assumes."

Zukofsky also believed that the poem's form was

one with its meaning. The objects, or elements, of the composition should take their meaning from their placement in the structure. The poet should not intrude his personality into the poem with what Zukofsky called predatory intent: the use of decorative adjectives or adverbs, and especially the use of transitional passages or devices which might explain a poem's interior logic. In *Poem Beginning "The,"* for example, each line is numbered, but the numbers do not imply sequence. "Poetry convinces not by argument," Zukofsky wrote, "but by the *form* it creates to carry its content."

"Hi, Kuh"

Reporting about an object, Zukofsky's initial perception undergoes transformation into poetry. "Hi, Kuh" was Zukofsky's response to the billboard advertisement for Elsie, the Borden dairy company's cow. The advertisement showed "gold'n bees" which appeared to the eyes of the poet as eyes, and then when the astigmatic and myopic Zukofsky removed his glasses, they appeared as the shimmering windows of a skyscraper. "Hi, Kuh" also reminds the reader that the poet's "I" was moved to think of a haiku, with the last unexpected word elevating the meaning of the poem beyond that of a bystander commenting on a billboard. Zukofsky does not explain the thought process that led from Elsie the cow to the towering emblem of the city; he presents, flatly, objects that are assembled to reveal his meaning.

"Mantis"

"Mantis" gives a more elaborate example of Zukofsky's method. The poem begins with a vivid description of a praying mantis encountered in a subway car. Gradually, the incongruity of the object in its surroundings, and its obvious helplessness, leads the poet to thoughts of a similar incongruity: the poor, who are helpless, alone, segregated from society, and as terrified as the mantis of an environment over which they have no control. "Mantis" was written as a sestina, a form Zukofsky rarely used, and one he knew was considered obsolete and archaic by many of his contemporaries. To defend his use of that form, he followed the piece by "'Mantis,' An Interpretation," written, he said, "as an argument against people who are dogmatic" about the use of old metered forms for modern poems.

Zukofsky maintained that both the form and language he used were suited to the experience of finding a mantis lost in the subway, so frightened that it flew against the poet's chest as if to communicate its despair. That experience was "only an incident," Zukofsky said, *"compelling any writing."* The mantis was the object that proved seminal for the poet's analysis of his own reality: "The mantis *can start/* History," Zukofsky wrote; and he was moved to think not only of the urban poor but also of Provençal and Melanesian myths, all alluded to in the poem. He was not interested in explaining how the incident led him to think of other things but tried to build a poem that, in its structure, echoed the experience. The poem's ungainliness reflects the lanky body of the insect; "'the lines' winding around themselves" reflect the contorted emotions of the poet as he experienced the encounter with the mantis; "the repeated end words" show his obsessive return to the same themes.

Zukofsky emphasized in his interpretation that the mantis experience engendered thoughts that were felt immediately, spontaneously, and apparently simultaneously. They were not, as William Wordsworth would have had it, recollected in tranquillity. The poet had no time for analysis or reflection. In the poem, then, Zukofsky tried to create what Gertrude Stein called the "continuous present," an ahistorical interval of time that is not caused by the past and which does not affect the future. By omitting transitions and relying, instead, on juxtaposition, Zukofsky forces the reader to experience an encounter with an object, in this case a mantis, with the same immediacy felt by the poet.

POEM BEGINNING "THE"

Much more complex, but with the same underlying intentions, is Zukofsky's *Poem Beginning "The,"* which he wrote in 1926. The poem begins with a brief preface acknowledging its sources. These include Johann Sebastian Bach, Ludwig van Beethoven, Yehoash, T. S. Eliot, Benito Mussolini, and Pound. Zukofsky had, of course, read Pound's *Hugh Selwyn Mauberley* (1920) and Eliot's *The Waste Land* (1922) which allude to literary sources, and intended, like Pound and Eliot, to challenge the reader to work in order to understand the poem.

The structure is deceptively straightforward: six "movements" (anticipating the sections of *"A,"* the poem which seems to have grown directly from "The") and 330 lines, each numbered to remind the reader to stop before going on to the next line. "The," being a definite article, suggests that the poem might be less amorphous than *"A,"* but it is not easily accessible in its entirety. The first movement, titled "And out of olde bokes, in good feith," asks a series of questions about the meaning of some well-known literary works— among them, James Joyce's *A Portrait of the Artist as a Young Man* (1916) and *Ulysses* (1922), Eliot's *The Waste Land*, E. E. Cummings's *Is Five* (1926), and Virginia Woolf's *Mrs. Dalloway* (1925). Allusions to these works follow one another in a disjointed monologue until, at lines 52 and 53, the poet admits that his "dream" is over and he is awake. After a pause, he decides that men have not lived "by art" or "by letters," though it is never clear why the poet remains unsatisfied by the literary works about which he, apparently, dreamt.

The second movement, "International Episode," deals, for the most part, with a deeply personal incident: the suicide of Richard Chambers, the younger brother of Zukofsky's college friend Whittaker Chambers. This "Ricky" section sensitively portrays the sadness of a young man's death for the poet who grieves. Following the elegy, Zukofsky translates lines from Yehoash that encapsulate the theme of the elegy and transform it to myth. In the Yehoash section, a young Bedouin can only reign in his kingdom at night because he is threatened by the sun, and the "Desert-Night" takes on magical, ethereal qualities; Ricky, in the realm of the dead, also reigns in shadow and darkness "with the stars."

The "Ricky" section is a quiet, reflective core of a movement otherwise raucous and irreverent. The poet is walking on Broadway with an oddly named companion, "Peter Out," whose name suggests sexual puns. While they are trying to decide which show to see, the poet, in a kind of reverie, thinks of Ricky. Suddenly, however, Peter breaks in and the two engage in a vaudevillian dialogue with their exchanges placed in quotation marks as if they were titles of plays.

The fifth movement, "Autobiography," returns to some of the themes already set forth by Zukofsky. There is another translation from Yehoash, a neo-folk song that again, as in the "Ricky" section, lifts the themes of the movement to a mythical level. Here, Zukofsky deals with the immigration of Russian Jews to a place where there are "gastanks, ruts,/ cemetery-tenements" and where their children will be assimilated and will take as their culture Bach, William Shakespeare, Samuel Taylor Coleridge, and John Donne. The poet promises not to forget his heritage, carrying that theme further in "Finale, and After," the final movement, which begins with a Jewish folk song that may well have been sung to him as a child. He ends with a last translation from Yehoash, its inclusion itself a demonstration that his parents' heritage has not been lost; the lines celebrate the ability of the poet to "sing" and endure under any hardship—even that of coming to artistic maturity in a country where few poets are lauded.

In *Poem Beginning "The,"* Zukofsky omits all transitions that would help the reader understand the connection between Ricky and Yehoash, for example, or between Christopher Marlowe and Woolf. Because the poem is relatively short, however, with some accessible sections, it is not as difficult as the poem it most resembles, the epic *"A."*

"A"

"A" begins at a performance of Bach's St. Matthew's Passion in Carnegie Hall on Thursday evening, April 5, 1928, during Passover. As in "Mantis," this incident starts the poet's thoughts spiraling, this time on history, economics, art, Jews, physics, music, his family, Karl Marx, Henry Adams, Mickey Mouse, Hamlet, Walt Whitman, and Wittgenstein. The concert also indicates the poem's form, which consists of long "musical" movements and ideas which develop and interweave as fugues.

"A" is the autobiography of a poet in twentieth century America and may be approached as if it were an archaeological site. From an accumulation of objects, the reader might piece together the reality that existed at the site, but Zukofsky is careful to reveal the objects in precise juxtaposition. The cumulative effect of the objects, then, is more than the sum of the parts. Zukofsky likened a poem to beads on an Egyptian necklace: Each bead might be an interesting artifact, but only when strung in precise order do they form a distinct artistic object.

Each section of *"A"* reveals Zukofsky's care for detail and his effort to structure those details. In "A"-12, for example, the themes of the poet's heritage and his relationship to American culture that were presented in the final sections of *Poem Beginning "The"* are expanded and developed, with Zukofsky's father, Pinchos (anglicized as Paul), and his son, Paul, appearing throughout. The culture that Pinchos brought from Russia is depicted in several vignettes, and Paul's childhood is evoked by the boy's remarks, including even a reproduction of one of his valentines to his father. By interweaving details, Zukofsky reveals the transition from Paul, who fled the czar with his mournful songs, to Paul who has two balloons named Plato and Aristotle and is quickly becoming a prodigy on the violin, playing not his grandfather's Russian melodies but Bach.

"All who achieve constructions apart from themselves, move in effect toward poetry," Zukofsky wrote in *Prepositions*. *"A"* is Zukofsky's most elaborate structure, a report of a witness to modern reality who did not care to comment, only to build.

OTHER MAJOR WORKS

LONG FICTION: *Ferdinand, Including "It Was,"* 1968; *Little, for Careenagers*, 1970; *Collected Fiction,* 1990.

PLAY: *Arise, Arise,* pb. 1962.

NONFICTION: *Le Style Apollinaire,* 1934 (with René Taupin); *A Test of Poetry,* 1948; *Five Statements for Poetry,* 1958; *Bottom: On Shakespeare,* 1963, 1987; *Prepositions: The Collected Critical Essays of Louis Zukofsky,* 1967, 1981 (revised as *Prepositions +: The Collected Critical Essays,* 2000); *Autobiography,* 1970 (text, with poems set to music by Celia Zukofsky); *Pound/Zukofsky: Selected Letters of Ezra Pound and Louis Zukofsky,* 1987 (Barry Ahearn, editor).

TRANSLATION: *Catullus,* 1969 (with Celia Zukofsky; of Gaius Valerius Catullus).

EDITED TEXT: *An "Objectivists" Anthology,* 1932.

BIBLIOGRAPHY

Ahearn, Barry. *Zukofsky's "A": An Introduction.* Berkeley: University of California Press, 1983. Zukofsky once said that a poet writes only one poem for his whole life. He began the eight-hundred-page poem *"A"* in 1928, when he was twenty-four years old, and did not finish it until 1974, when he was seventy. Ahearn gives the student a framework to understand Zukofsky's magnum opus. Includes bibliographical references and indexes.

Leggott, Michele J. *Reading Zukofsky's "Eighty Flowers."* Baltimore: The Johns Hopkins University Press, 1989. Leggott attempts to explain Zukofsky's rare work, written the last four years of his life. Zukofsky wanted to condense the sense of his lifetime of poetry into a last book. Leggott offers a plausible interpretation for *Eighty Flowers* and thus explains the entire philosophy of Zukofsky's writing.

Maerhofer, John W. *Rethinking the Vanguard: Aesthetic and Political Positions in the Modernist Debate, 1917-1962.* Newcastle upon Tyne, England: Cambridge Scholars, 2009. Contains a chapter on Zukofsky that sees him as moving toward a "revolutionary formalism." Looks at his position among the modernists.

Pound, Ezra. *Pound/Zukofsky: Selected Letters of Ezra Pound and Louis Zukofsky.* Edited by Barry Ahearn. New York: New Directions, 1987. Zukofsky considered Pound to be the greatest twentieth century poet writing in English. Therefore, he wrote to Pound more than he wrote to anyone else, in part to glean some words of literary wisdom. The two men met only three times, yet Zukofsky considered Pound to be his literary father.

Quartermain, Peter. *Disjunctive Poetics: From Gertrude Stein and Louis Zukofsky to Susan Howe.* 1992. Reprint. New York: Cambridge University Press, 2009. Examines the poetic style of Zukofsky, Stein, and Howe, who are known for writing less accessible poetry.

Rothenberg, Jerome, and Steven Clay, eds. *Poetics and Polemics, 1980-2005.* Tuscaloosa: University of Alabama Press, 2008. Contains a reminiscence of Zukofsky that looks at his poetics.

Schuster, Joshua. "Looking at Louis Zukofsky's Poetics Through Spinozist Glasses." In *Radical Poetics and Secular Jewish Culture*, edited by Stephen Paul Miller and Daniel Morris. Tuscaloosa: University of Alabama Press, 2010. An analysis of Zukofsky's poetry through the philosophy of Baruch Spinoza.

Scroggins, Mark. *The Poem of a Life: A Biography of Louis Zukofsky.* Emeryville, Calif.: Shoemaker & Hoard, 2007. Biography of Zukofsky examines his life and his long poem *"A."*

Stanley, Sandra Kumamoto. *Louis Zukofsky and the Transformation of a Modern American Poetics.* Berkeley: University of California Press, 1994. Stanley argues that Zukofky's works serve as a crucial link between American modernism and postmodernism. Stanley explains how Zukofsky emphasized the materiality of language and describes his legacy to contemporary poets.

Terrell, Carroll Franklin. *Louis Zukofsky: Man and Poet.* Orono: National Poetry Foundation, University of Maine, 1979. Zukofsky essentially lived the history of twentieth century American poetry. This is the essential Zukofsky biography. It was written shortly after the poet's death in 1978, at the age of seventy-four. Contains a bibliography and an index.

Linda Simon

RESOURCES

EXPLICATING POETRY

Explicating poetry begins with a process of distinguishing the poem's factual and technical elements from the readers' emotional ones. Readers respond to poems in a variety of ways that may initially have little to do with the poetry itself but that result from the events in their own lives, their expectations of art, and their philosophical/theological/psychological complexion.

All serious readers hope to find poems that can blend with the elements of their personal backgrounds in such a way that for a moment or a lifetime their relationship to life and the cosmos becomes more meaningful. This is the ultimate goal of poetry, and when it happens—when meaning, rhythm, and sound fuse with the readers' emotions to create a unified experience—it can only be called the magic of poetry, for something has happened between reader and poet that is inexplicable in rational terms.

When a poem creates such an emotional response in readers, then it is at least a partial success. To be considered excellent, however, a poem must also be able to pass a critical analysis to determine whether it is mechanically superior. Although twenty-first century criticism has tended to judge poetic works solely on their individual content and has treated them as independent of historical influences, such a technique often makes a full explication difficult. The best modern readers realize that good poetry analysis observes all aspects of a poem: its technical success, its historical importance and intellectual force, and its effect on readers' emotions.

Students of poetry will find it useful to begin an explication by analyzing the elements that poets have at their disposal as they create their art: dramatic situation, point of view, imagery, metaphor, symbol, meter, form, and allusion. The outline headed "Checklist for Explicating a Poem" (see page 2274) will help guide the reader through the necessary steps to a detailed explication.

Although explication is not a science, and a variety of observations may be equally valid, these step-by-step procedures can be applied systematically to make the reading of most poems a richer experience for the reader. To illustrate, these steps are applied below to a difficult poem by Edwin Arlington Robinson.

Luke Havergal

Go to the western gate, Luke Havergal,
There where the vines cling crimson on the wall,
And in the twilight wait for what will come.
The leaves will whisper there of her, and some, 4
Like flying words, will strike you as they fall;
But go, and if you listen, she will call.
Go to the western gate, Luke Havergal—
Luke Havergal. 8

No, there is not a dawn in eastern skies
To rift the fiery night that's in your eyes;
But there, where western glooms are gathering,
The dark will end the dark, if anything: 12
God slays Himself with every leaf that flies,
And hell is more than half of paradise.
No, there is not a dawn in eastern skies—
In eastern skies. 16

Out of a grave I come to tell you this,
Out of a grave I come to quench the kiss
That flames upon your forehead with a glow
That blinds you to the way that you must go. 20
Yes, there is yet one way to where she is,
Bitter, but one that faith may never miss.
Out of a grave I come to tell you this—
To tell you this. 24

There is the western gate, Luke Havergal
There are the crimson leaves upon the wall.
Go, for the winds are tearing them away,—
Nor think to riddle the dead words they say, 28
Nor any more to feel them as they fall;
But go, and if you trust her she will call.
There is the western gate, Luke Havergal—
Luke Havergal.

E. A. Robinson, 1897

STEP I-A: *Before reading*

1. "Luke Havergal" is a strophic poem composed of four equally lengthened stanzas. Each stanza is long enough to contain a narrative, an involved description or situation, or a problem and resolution.

2. The title raises several possibilities: Luke Havergal

CHECKLIST FOR EXPLICATING A POEM

I. THE INITIAL READINGS

A. Before reading the poem, the reader should:

1. Notice its form and length.

2. Consider the title, determining, if possible, whether it might function as an allusion, symbol, or poetic image.

3. Notice the date of composition or publication, and identify the general era of the poet.

B. The poem should be read intuitively and emotionally and be allowed to "happen" as much as possible.

C. In order to establish the rhythmic flow, the poem should be re-read. A note should be made as to where the irregular spots (if any) are located.

II. EXPLICATING THE POEM

A. *Dramatic situation.* Studying the poem line by line helps the reader discover the dramatic situation. All elements of the dramatic situation are interrelated and should be viewed as reflecting and affecting one another. The dramatic situation serves a particular function in the poem, adding realism, surrealism, or absurdity; drawing attention to certain parts of the poem; and changing to reinforce other aspects of the poem. All points should be considered. The following questions are particularly helpful to ask in determining dramatic situation:

1. What, if any, is the narrative action in the poem?

2. How many personae appear in the poem? What part do they take in the action?

3. What is the relationship between characters?

4. What is the setting (time and location) of the poem?

B. *Point of view.* An understanding of the poem's point of view is a major step toward comprehending the poet's intended meaning. The reader should ask:

1. Who is the speaker? Is he or she addressing someone else or the reader?

2. Is the narrator able to understand or see everything happening to him or her, or does the reader know things that the narrator does not?

3. Is the narrator reliable?

4. Do point of view and dramatic situation seem consistent? If not, the inconsistencies may provide clues to the poem's meaning.

C. *Images and metaphors.* Images and metaphors are often the most intricately crafted vehicles of the poem for relaying the poet's message. Realizing that the images and metaphors work in harmony with the dramatic situation and point of view will help the reader to see the poem as a whole, rather than as disassociated elements.

1. The reader should identify the concrete images (that is, those that are formed from objects that can be touched, smelled, seen, felt, or tasted). Is the image projected by the poet consistent with the physical object?

2. If the image is abstract, or so different from natural imagery that it cannot be associated with a real object, then what are the properties of the image?

3. To what extent is the reader asked to form his or her own images?

4. Is any image repeated in the poem? If so, how has it been changed? Is there a controlling image?

5. Are any images compared to each other? Do they reinforce one another?

6. Is there any difference between the way the reader perceives the image and the way the narrator sees it?

7. What seems to be the narrator's or persona's attitude toward the image?

D. *Words.* Every substantial word in a poem may have more than one intended meaning, as used by the author. Because of this, the reader should look up many of these words in the dictionary and:

1. Note all definitions that have the slightest connection with the poem.

2. Note any changes in syntactical patterns in the poem.

3. In particular, note those words that could possibly function as symbols or allusions, and refer to any appropriate sources for further information.

E. *Meter, rhyme, structure, and tone.* In scanning the poem, all elements of prosody should be noted by the reader. These elements are often used by a poet to manipulate the reader's emotions, and therefore they should be examined closely to arrive at the poet's specific intention.

1. Does the basic meter follow a traditional pattern such as those found in nursery rhymes or folk songs?

2. Are there any variations in the base meter? Such changes or substitutions are important thematically and should be identified.

3. Are the rhyme schemes traditional or innovative, and what might their form mean to the poem?

4. What devices has the poet used to create sound patterns (such as assonance and alliteration)?

5. Is the stanza form a traditional or innovative one?

6. If the poem is composed of verse paragraphs rather than stanzas, how do they affect the progression of the poem?

7. After examining the above elements, is the resultant tone of the poem casual or formal, pleasant, harsh, emotional, authoritative?

F. *Historical context.* The reader should attempt to place the poem into historical context, checking on events at the time of composition. Archaic language, expressions, images, or symbols should also be looked up.

G. *Themes and motifs.* By seeing the poem as a composite of emotion, intellect, craftsmanship, and tradition, the reader should be able to determine the themes and motifs (smaller recurring ideas) presented in the work. He or she should ask the following questions to help pinpoint these main ideas:

1. Is the poet trying to advocate social, moral, or religious change?

2. Does the poet seem sure of his or her position?

3. Does the poem appeal primarily to the emotions, to the intellect, or to both?

4. Is the poem relying on any particular devices for effect (such as imagery, allusion, paradox, hyperbole, or irony)?

could be a specific person; Luke Havergal could represent a type of person; the name might have symbolic or allusive qualities. Thus, "Luke" may refer to Luke of the Bible or "Luke-warm," meaning indifferent or showing little or no zeal. "Havergal" could be a play on words. "Haver" is a Scotch and Northern English word meaning to talk foolishly. It is clear from the rhyme words that the "gal" of Havergal is pronounced as if it had two "l's," but it is spelled with one "l" for no apparent reason unless it is to play on the word "gal," meaning girl. Because it is pronounced "gall," meaning something bitter or severe, a sore or state of irritation, or an impudent self-assurance, this must also be considered as a possibility. Finally, the "haver" of "Havergal" might be a perversion of "have a."

3. Published in 1897, the poem probably does not contain archaic language unless it is deliberately used. The period of writing is known as the Victorian Age. Historical events that may have influenced the poem may be checked for later.

STEP I-B: *The poem should be read*

STEP I-C: *Rereading the poem*

The frequent use of internal caesuras in stanzas 1 and 2 contrast with the lack of caesuras in stanzas 3 and 4. There are end-stopped lines and much repetition. The poem reads smoothly except for line 28 and the feminine ending on lines 11 and 12.

STEP II-A: *Dramatic situation*

In line 1 of "Luke Havergal," an unidentified speaker is addressing Luke. Because the speaker calls him by his full name, there is a sense that the speaker has assumed a superior (or at least a formal) attitude toward Luke and that the talk that they are having is not a casual conversation.

In addition to knowing something about the relationship in line 1, the reader is led to think, because of the words "go to the western gate," that the personae must be near some sort of enclosed house or city. Perhaps Luke and the speaker are at some "other" gate, since the western gate is specifically pointed out.

Line 2 suggests that the situation at the western gate is different from that elsewhere—there "vines cling crimson on the wall," hinting at some possibilities

about the dramatic situation. (Because flowers and colors are always promising symbols, they must be carefully considered later.)

The vines in line 2 could provide valuable information about the dramatic situation, except that in line 2 the clues are ambiguous. Are the vines perennial? If so, their crimson color suggests that the season is late summer or autumn. Crimson might also be their natural color when in full bloom. Further, are they grape vines (grapes carry numerous connotations and symbolic values), and are the vines desirable? All of this in line 2 is ambiguous. The only certainty is that there is a wall—a barrier that closes something in and something out.

In lines 1-3, the speaker again commands Luke to go and wait. Since Luke is to wait in the twilight, it is probably now daylight. All Luke must do is be passive because whatever is to come will happen without any action on his part.

In line 4, the speaker begins to tell Luke what will happen at the western gate, and the reader now knows that Luke is waiting for something with feminine characteristics, possibly a woman. This line also mentions that the vines have leaves, implying that crimson denotes their waning stage.

In line 5, the speaker continues to describe what will happen at the western gate: The leaves will whisper about "her," and as they fall, some of them will strike Luke "like flying words." The reader, however, must question whether Luke will actually be "struck" by the leaves, or whether the leaves are being personified or being used as an image or symbol. In line 6, the speaker stops his prophecy and tells Luke to leave. If Luke listens, "she" will call, but if he does not, it is unclear what will happen. The reader might ask the questions, to whom is "she" calling, and from where?

In summarizing the dramatic situation in stanza 1, one can say that the speaker is addressing Luke, but it is not yet possible to determine whether he or she is present or whether Luke is thinking to himself (interior monologue). The time is before twilight; the place is near a wall with a gate. Luke is directed to go to the gate and listen for a female voice to call.

From reading the first line in the second stanza, it is apparent that Luke has posed some kind of question, probably concerned with what will be found at the western gate. The answer given is clearly not a direct answer to whatever question was asked, especially as the directions "east" and "west" are probably symbolic. The reader can expect, however, that the silent persona's response will affect the poem's progress.

Stanza 3 discloses who the speaker is and what his relationship is to Luke. After the mysterious discourse in stanza 2, Luke has probably asked "Who are you?" The equally mysterious reply in stanza 3 raises the issue of whether the voice speaking is a person or a spirit or whether it is Luke's imagination or conscience.

Because the voice says that it comes out of the grave, the reader cannot know who or what it is. It may be a person, a ghost, or only Luke's imagination or conscience. Obviously the answer will affect the dramatic situation.

In line 18, the reader learns that the speaker is on a particular mission: "to quench the kiss," and the reader can assume that when the mission is complete he or she will return to the grave. This information is sudden and shocking, and because of this sharp jolt, the reader tends to believe the speaker and credit him or her with supernatural knowledge.

In stanza 4, it becomes apparent that Luke and the speaker have not been stationary during the course of the poem because the western gate is now visible; the speaker can see the leaves upon the wall (line 26).

The wind is blowing (line 27), creating a sense of urgency, because if all the leaves are blown away they cannot whisper about "her." The speaker gives Luke final instructions, and the poem ends with the speaker again pointing toward the place where Luke will find the female persona.

In summary, one can say that the dramatic situation establishes a set of mysterious circumstances that are not explained or resolved on the dramatic level. Luke has been told to go to the western gate by someone who identifies himself or herself as having come from the grave in order to quench Luke's desire, which seems to be connected with the estranged woman, who is, perhaps, dead. The dramatic situation does not tell whether the commanding voice is an emissary from the woman or from the devil, or is merely Luke's conscience; nor does it suggest that something evil will happen to Luke at the western gate, although other elements in the poem make the reader afraid for him.

The poet, then, is using the dramatic situation to draw the reader into questions which will be answered by other means; at this point, the poem is mysterious, obscure, ambiguous, and deliberately misleading.

STEP II-B: *Point of view*

There are a number of questions that immediately come to mind about the point of view. Is the speaker an evil seducer, or is he or she a friend telling Luke about death? Why is the poem told from his or her point of view?

From a generalized study, readers know that the first-person singular point of view takes the reader deep into the mind of the narrator in order to show what he or she knows or to show a personal reaction to an event.

In "Luke Havergal," the narrator gives the following details about himself and the situation: a sense of direction (lines 1 and 9); the general type and color of the vegetation, but not enough to make a detailed analysis of it (line 2); a pantheistic view of nature (line 4); a feeling of communication with the leaves and "her" (lines 5 and 6); a philosophic view of the universe (stanza 2); the power to "quench the kiss," a sense of mission, and a home—the grave (line 18); special vision (line 20); a sense of destiny (lines 21 and 22); and a sense of time and eternity (lines 27 through 29).

Apparently, the narrator can speak with confidence about the western gate, and can look objectively at Luke to see the kiss on his forehead. Such a vantage point suggests that the speaker might represent some aspect of death. He also knows the "one way to where she is," leaving it reasonable to infer that "she" is dead.

There is another possibility in regard to the role of the speaker. He might be part of Luke himself—the voice of his thoughts, of his unconscious mind—or of part of his past. This role might possibly be combined with that of some sort of spirit of death.

The poem, then, is an internal dialogue in which Luke is attempting to cope with "she," who is probably dead and who might well have been his lover, though neither is certain. He speaks to another persona, which is probably Luke's own spirit which has been deadened by the loss of his lover.

Once it is suggested that Luke is a man who is at the depth of despair, the dramatic situation becomes very important because of the possibility that Luke may be driving himself toward self-destruction.

The dramatic situation, therefore, may not be as it originally seemed; perhaps there is only one person, not two. Luke's psychological condition permits him to look at himself as another person, and this other self is pushing Luke toward the western gate, a place that the reader senses is evil.

If the voice is Luke's, then much of the mystery is clarified. Luke would have known what the western gate looked like, whereas a stranger would have needed supernatural powers to know it; furthermore, Luke had probably heard the leaves whispering before, and in his derangement he could believe that someone would call to him if he would only listen.

Establishing point of view has cleared up most of the inconsistencies in this poem's dramatic situation, but there is still confusion about the grave and the kiss. It is easy to make the grave symbolically consistent with point of view, but the reader should look for other possibilities before settling on this explanation.

In stanzas 1 and 2, there is no problem; the dramatic situation is simple and point of view can be reconciled since there is no evidence to prove that another person is present. If, however, the voice is that of Luke's other self, then why has it come from the grave, and where did the kiss come from? At this point, it is not possible to account for these inconsistencies, but by noting them now, the reader can be on the alert for the answers later. Quite possibly accounting for the inconsistencies will provide the key for the explication.

STEP II-C: *Images and metaphors*

Finding images in poems is usually not a difficult task, although seeing their relation to the theme often is. "Luke Havergal" is imagistically difficult because the images are introduced, then reused as the theme develops.

In stanza 1, the reader is allowed to form his or her own image of the setting and mood at the western gate; most readers will probably imagine some sort of mysterious or supernatural situation related to death or the dead. The colors, the sound of the words, and the particular images (vines, wall, whispering leaves) establish the relationship between the living and the dead as the controlling image of the entire poem.

Within the controlling death-in-life image, the metaphors and conceits are more difficult to handle. Vines clinging crimson on the wall (line 2) and waiting in the twilight for something to come (line 3) are images requiring no particular treatment at this point, but in lines 4 and 5 the reader is forced to contend directly with whispering leaves that are like flying words, and there are several metaphorical possibilities for this image.

First, there is the common image of leaves rustling in a breeze, and in a mysterious or enchanted atmosphere it would be very easy to imagine that they are whispering. Such a whisper, however, would ordinarily require a moderate breeze, as a fierce wind would overpower the rustling sound of leaves; but there is more ambiguity in the image: "The leaves will whisper there for her, and some,/ Like flying words, will strike you as they fall."

Because of the syntactical ambiguity of "some,/ Like flying words, will strike," the reader cannot be sure how close or literal is the similarity or identity of "leaves" and "words." The reader cannot be completely sure whether it is leaves or words or both that will strike Luke, or whether the sight of falling leaves might be forcing him to recall words he has heard in the past. There is a distinct metaphoric connection between leaves and words, however, and these in some way strike Luke, perhaps suggesting that the words are those of an argument (an argument in the past between Luke and "her" before her death) or perhaps meant to suggest random words which somehow recall "her" but do not actually say anything specific.

In stanza 2, the poet forces the reader to acknowledge the light and dark images, but they are as obscure as the falling leaves in stanza 1. The dawn that the reader is asked to visualize (line 9) is clear, but it is immediately contrasted with "the fiery night that's in your eyes"; Luke's smoldering, almost diabolic eyes are imagistically opposed to the dawn.

Line 11 returns to the western gate, or at least to the "west," where twilight is falling. The "western glooms" become imagistic as the twilight falls and depicts Luke's despair. Twilight is not "falling," but dark is "gathering" around him, and glooms not only denotes darkness but also connotes Luke's emotional state.

The paradox in line 12, "The dark will end the dark," beckons the reader to explore it imagistically, but it is not easy to understand how darkness relieves darkness, unless one of the two "darknesses" is symbolic of death or of Luke's gloom. With this beckoning image, the poet has created emphasis on the line and teases with images which may really be symbols or paradoxes. The same thing is true for lines 13 and 14, which tempt the reader to imagine how "God slays Himself" with leaves, and how "hell is more than half of paradise."

The beginning of stanza 3 does not demand an image so much as it serves to tell where the narrator comes from, and to present the narrator's method for quenching the kiss. Line 19, however, presents an image that is as forceful as it is ambiguous. The kiss, which may be the kiss of the estranged woman, or "the kiss of death," or both, flames with a glow, which is also paradoxical. The paradox, however, forms an image which conveys the intensity of Luke's passion.

Stanza 4 returns to the imagery of stanza 1, but now the whispering leaves take on a metaphorical extension. If the leaves are whispering words from the dead, and if the leaves are "her" words, then once the wind tears all the leaves away, there will no longer be any medium for communication between the living and the dead. This adds a sense of urgency for Luke to go to the western gate and do there what must be done.

In summary, the images in "Luke Havergal" do more than set the mood; they also serve an important thematic function because of their ambiguities and paradoxical qualities.

STEP II-D: *Words*

Because the poem is not too old, the reader will find that most of the words have not changed much. It is still important, however, for the reader to look up words as they may have several diverse meanings. Even more important to consider in individual words or phrases, however, is the possibility that they might be symbolic or allusive.

"Luke Havergal" is probably not as symbolic as it at first appears, although poems that use paradox and allusion are often very symbolic. Clearly the western gate is symbolic, but to what degree is questionable. No doubt it represents the last light in Luke's life, and once he passes beyond it he moves into another type of existence. The west and the twilight are points of embarka-

tion; the sun is setting in the west, but even though the sun sets, there will not be a dawn in the east to dispel Luke's dark gloom. Traditionally the dark, which is gathering in the west, is symbolic of death (the west is also traditionally associated with death), and only the dark will end Luke's gloom in life, if anything at all can do it.

There is one important allusion in the poem, which comes in stanza 3; the kiss which the speaker is going to quench may be the "kiss of death," the force that can destroy Luke.

In both concept and language, stanza 3 is reminiscent of the dagger scene and killing of Duncan (act 2, scene 1) in William Shakespeare's *Macbeth* (pr. 1606). Just before the murder, Macbeth has visions of the dagger:

> Art thou not, fatal vision, sensible
> To feeling as to sight? or art thou but
> A dagger of the mind, a false creation,
> Proceeding from the heat-oppressed brain?
> I see thee yet, in form as palpable
> As this which now I draw.
> Thou marshall'st me the way that I was going

And a few lines later (act 2, scene 2) Lady Macbeth says:

> That which hath made them drunk hath made me bold;
> What hath quench'd them hath given me fire.

The reversal in point of view in "Luke Havergal" gives the poem added depth, which is especially enhanced by the comparison with Macbeth. The line, "That blinds you to the way that you must go" is almost a word-for-word equivalent of "Thou marshall'st me the way that I was going," except that in "Luke Havergal" whoever is with Luke is talking, while Macbeth himself is talking to the dagger.

The result of the allusion is that it is almost possible to imagine that it is the dagger that is talking to Luke, and the whole story of Macbeth becomes relevant to the poem because the reader suspects that Luke's end will be similar to Macbeth's.

The words of Lady Macbeth strengthen the allusion's power and suggest a male-female relationship that is leading Luke to his death, especially since, in the resolution of *Macbeth*, Lady Macbeth goes crazy and whispers to the spirits.

If the reader accepts the allusion as a part of the poem, the imagery is enhanced by the vivid descriptions in *Macbeth*. Most critics and writers agree that if a careful reader finds something that fits consistently into a poem, then it is "there" for all readers who see the same thing, whether the poet consciously put it there or not. Robinson undoubtedly read and knew Shakespeare, but it does not matter whether he deliberately alluded to *Macbeth* if the reader can show that it is important to the poem.

There is a basic problem with allusion and symbol that every explicator must resolve for himself: Did the poet intend a symbol or an allusion to be taken in the way that a particular reader has interpreted it? The New Critics answered this question by coining the term "intentional fallacy," meaning that the poet's *intention* is ultimately unimportant when considering the finished poem. It is possible that stanza 3 was not intended to allude to *Macbeth*, and it was simply by accident that Robinson used language similar to Shakespeare's. Perhaps Robinson never read *Macbeth*, or perhaps he read it once and those lines remained in his subconscious. In either case, the reader must decide whether the allusion is important to the meaning of the poem.

STEP II-E: *Meter, rhyme, structure, and tone*

Because "Luke Havergal" is a poem that depends so heavily on all the elements of prosody, it should be scanned carefully. Here is an example of scansion using the second stanza of the poem:

> No, there/ is not/ a dawn/ in eas/tern skies
> To rift/ the fie/ry night/ that's in/ your eyes;
> But there,/ where wes/tern glooms/ are gath/ering,
> The dark/ will end/ the dark,/ if any/thing:
> God slays/ Himself/ with eve/ry leaf/ that flies,
> And hell/ is more/ than half/ of par/adise.
> No, there/ is not/ a dawn/ in east/ern skies—
> In eas/tern skies.

The basic meter of the poem is iambic pentameter, with frequent substitutions, but every line except the last in each stanza contains ten syllables.

The stanza form in "Luke Havergal" is very intri-

cate and delicate. It is only because of the structure that the heavy *a* rhyme (*aabbaaaa*) does not become monotonous; yet it is because of the *a* rhyme that the structure works so well.

The pattern for the first stanza works as follows:

Line	Rhyme	Function
1	a	Sets up ideas and images for the stanza.
2	a	Describes or complements line 1.
3	b	Lines 3, 4, and 5 constitute the central part of the mood and the fears. The return to the a rhyme unifies lines 1-5.
4	b	
5	a	
6	a	Reflects on what has been said in lines 1-5; it serves to make the reader stop, and it adds a mysterious suggestion.
7	a	Continues the deceleration and reflection.
8	a	The repetition and dimeter line stop the stanza completely, and the effect is to prepare for a shift in thought, just as Luke's mind jumps from thought to thought.

Stanza 2 works in a similar manner, except for lines 13 and 14, which tie the stanza together as a couplet. Thus, lines 13 and 14 both unify and reflect, while lines 15 and 16 in the final couplet continue to reflect while slowing down.

Lines	Rhyme	Function
9 and 10	a	Opening couplet.
11 and 12	b	Couplet in lines 11-12 contains the central idea and image.
13 and 14	a	Couplet in 13-14 reflects on that in 11-12, but the autonomy of this third couplet is especially strong. Whereas in stanza 1, only line 5 reflects on the beginning of the stanza to create unity, this entire couplet is now strongly associated with the first, with the effect of nearly equating Luke with God.
15 and 16	a	Final couplet reflects on the first and completes the stanza.

Stanza 3 works in the same manner as stanza 2, while stanza 4 follows the pattern of stanza 1.

Each stanza is autonomous and does not need the others for continuation or progression in plot; each stanza appears to represent a different thought as Luke's mind jumps about.

The overall structure focuses on stanza 3, which is crucial to the theme. Stanzas 1 and 2 clearly present the problem: Luke knows that if he goes he will find "her," and the worst that can happen is that the darkness will remain. With stanza 3, however, there is a break in point of view as the narrator calls attention to himself.

With stanza 4 there is a return to the beginning, reinforced by the repetition of rhyme words; the difference between stanzas 4 and 1 is that the reader has felt the impact of stanza 3; structurally, whatever resolution there is will evolve out of the third stanza, or because of it.

The stanza form of "Luke Havergal" achieves tremendous unity and emphasis; the central image or idea presented in the *b* lines is reinforced in the remainder of the stanza by a tight-knit rhyme structure. There are several types of rhymes being used in the poem, all of which follow the traditional functions of their type. Stanza 1 contains full masculine end rhyme, with a full masculine internal rhyme in line 2 (*There where*). Lines 2 and 3 contain alliteration (*c* in line 2, *t* in line 3) also binding the lines more tightly.

With "go" occurring near the end of stanza 1 and "No" appearing as the first word in stanza 2, this rhyme becomes important in forming associations between lines. Lines 9, 10, 15, 16, and 18 form full masculine end rhyme, with line 14 "paradise" assonating with a full rhyme. Lines 11 and 12 are half falling rhymes; these lines also contain a full internal rhyme ("there," "where") and alliteration (*g* and *w* in line 11). "Dark" in line 12 is an exact internal rhyme. The *l* and *s* in "slays" and "flies" (line 14) create an effect similar to assonance; there is also an *h* alliteration in line 15.

In stanza 3, the plosive consonants *c* and *q* make an alliterative sound in line 18, binding "come" and "quench" together; there is also an *f* alliteration in line 19. All the end rhymes are full masculine in stanza 3 except line 21, which assonates. Stanza 4 contains full masculine end rhyme, with one internal rhyme ("they say") in line 28, one alliteration in line 29, and consonance ("will call") in line 30.

In addition to its function in developing the stanza, rhyme in "Luke Havergal" has important influence on sound, and in associating particular words and lines.

In lines 1 and 2 of "Luke Havergal," there are a number of plosive consonants and long vowels, in addition to the internal rhyme and *c* alliteration. The cadence of these lines is slow, and they reverberate with "cling" and "crimson." The tone of these lines is haunting (which is consistent with the situation), and the rhythm and sound of the poem as a whole suggest an incantation; the speaker's voice is seductive and evil, which is important to the theme, because if Luke goes to the gate he may be persuaded to die, which is what the voice demands.

Through its seductive sound, the poem seems to be having the same effect on the reader that it does on Luke; that is, the reader feels, as Luke does, that there is an urgency in going to the gate before all the leaves are blown away, and that by hearing "her" call, his discomfort will be relieved. The reader, unable to see the evil forces at work in the last stanza, sympathizes with Luke, and thinks that the voice is benevolent.

Whereas sound can be heard and analyzed, tone is a composite of a number of things that the reader can feel only after coming to know the poem. The poet's attitude or tone may be noncommittal or it may be dogmatic (as in allegory); sometimes the tone will affect the theme, while at other times it comes as an aside to the theme.

Poems that attempt to initiate reform frequently have a more readily discernible tone than poems that make observations without judging too harshly, although this is not always true. "Luke Havergal" is, among other things, about how the presence of evil leads toward death, but the poet has not directly included his feelings about that theme. If there is an attitude, it is the poet's acceptance of the inevitability of death and the pain that accompanies it for the living.

Perhaps the poet is angry at how effectively death can seduce life; it is obvious that Robinson wants the poem to haunt and torment the reader, and in doing so make him or her conscious of the hold death has on humanity.

Luke must meet death part way; he must first go to

the gate before he can hear the dead words, which makes him partly responsible for death's hold over him. The tone of "Luke Havergal" is haunting and provocative.

STEP II-F: *Historical context*

Finished in December, 1895, "Luke Havergal" was in Robinson's estimation a Symbolist poem. It is essential, then, that the explicator learn something about the Symbolist movement. If his or her explication is not in accord with the philosophy of the period, the reader must account for the discrepancy.

In a study of other Robinson poems, there are themes parallel to that of "Luke Havergal." One, for example, is that of the alienated self. If Robinson believes in the alienated self, then it is possible that the voice speaking in "Luke Havergal" is Luke's own, but in an alienated state. This view may add credence to an argument that the speaker is Luke's past or subconscious, though it by no means proves it. Although parallelisms may be good support for the explication, the reader must be careful not to misconstrue them.

STEP II-G: *Themes and motifs, or correlating the parts*

Once the poem has been placed in context, the prosodic devices analyzed, and the function of the poetical techniques understood, they should be correlated, and any discrepancies should be studied for possible errors in explication. By this time, every line should be understood, so that stating what the poem is about is merely a matter of explaining the common points of all the area, supporting it with specific items from the poem, secondary sources, other poems, other critics, and history. The reader may use the specific questions given in the outline to help detail the major themes.

BIBLIOGRAPHY

Coleman, Kathleen. *Guide to French Poetry Explication*. New York: G. K. Hall, 1993.

Gioia, Dana, David Mason, and Meg Schoerke, eds. *Twentieth-Century American Poetics: Poets on the Art of Poetry*. Boston: McGraw-Hill, 2003.

Hirsch, Edward. *How to Read a Poem and Fall in Love with Poetry*. New York: Harcourt Brace, 1999.

Kohl, Herbert R. *A Grain of Poetry: How to Read Contemporary Poems and Make Them a Part of Your Life*. New York: HarperFlamingo, 1999.

Lennard, John. *The Poetry Handbook: A Guide to Reading Poetry for Pleasure and Practical Criticism*. 2d ed. New York: Oxford University Press, 2006.

Martínez, Nancy C., and Joseph G. R. Martínez. *Guide to British Poetry Explication*. 4 vols. Boston: G. K. Hall, 1991-1995.

Oliver, Mary. *A Poetry Handbook*. San Diego, Calif.: Harcourt Brace, 1994.

Preminger, Alex, et al., eds. *The New Princeton Encyclopedia of Poetry and Poetics*. 3d rev. ed. Princeton, N.J.: Princeton University Press, 1993.

Ryan, Michael. *A Difficult Grace: On Poets, Poetry, and Writing*. Athens: University of Georgia Press, 2000.

Statman, Mark. *Listener in the Snow: The Practice and Teaching of Poetry*. New York: Teachers & Writers Collaborative, 2000.

Steinman, Lisa M. *Invitation to Poetry: The Pleasures of Studying Poetry and Poetics*. Walden, Mass.: Wiley-Blackwell, 2008.

Strand, Mark, and Eavan Boland, eds. *The Making of a Poem: A Norton Anthology of Poetic Forms*. New York: W. W. Norton, 2000.

Wolosky, Shira. *The Art of Poetry: How to Read a Poem*. New York: Oxford University Press, 2001.

Walton Beacham

LANGUAGE AND LINGUISTICS

Most humans past the infant stage have a spoken language and use it regularly for understanding and speaking, although much of the world's population is still illiterate and cannot read or write. Language is such a natural part of life that people tend to overlook it until they are presented with some special problem: They lose their sight or hearing, have a stroke, or are required to learn a foreign language. Of course, people may also study their own language, but seldom do they stand aside and view language for what it is—a complex human phenomenon with a history reaching back to humankind's beginnings. A study of the development of one language will often reveal intertwinings with other languages. Sometimes such knowledge enables linguists to construct family groups; just as often, the divergences among languages or language families are so great that separate typological variations are established.

True language is characterized by its systematic nature, its arbitrariness of vocabulary and structure, its vocality, and its basis in symbolism. Most linguists believe that language and thought are separate entities. Although language may be necessary to give foundation to thought, it is not, in itself, thinking. Many psychologists, however, contend that language is thought. An examination of language on the basis of these assertions reveals that each language is a purely arbitrary code or set of rules. There is no intrinsic necessity for any word to sound like or mean what it does. Language is essentially speech, and symbolism is somehow the philosophical undergirding of the whole linguistic process. The French author Madame de Staël (1766-1817) once wrote, in describing her native language, that language is even more: "It is not only a means of communicating thoughts, feeling and acts, but an instrument that one loves to play upon, and that stimulates the mental faculties much as music does for some people and strong drink for others."

ORIGIN OF LANGUAGE

How did language originate? First, the evidence for the origin of language is so deeply buried in the past that it is unlikely that people shall ever be able to do more than speculate about the matter. If people had direct knowledge of humankind's immediate ancestors, they should be able to develop some evolutionary theory and be able to say, among other things, how speech production and changes in the brain are related. Some linguists maintain that language ability is innate, but this assertion, true though it may be, rests on the assumption of a monogenetic theory of humanity's origin. Few scholars today are content with the notion that the human race began with Adam and Eve.

According to the Bible, Adam is responsible for human speech. Genesis reports:

> And out of the ground the Lord God formed every beast of the field, and every fowl of the air, and brought them unto Adam to see what he would call them; and whatsoever Adam called every creature, that was the name thereof. And Adam gave names to all cattle, and to the fowl of the air, and to every beast of the field.

If the story of Adam and Eve is taken literally, one might conclude that their language was the original one. Unfortunately, not even the Bible identifies what this language was. Some people have claimed that Hebrew was the first language and that all the other languages of the world are derived from it; Hebrew, however, bears no discernible relationship to any language outside the Hamito-Semitic group. Besides, any so-called original language would have changed so drastically in the intervening millennia before the onset of writing that it would not bear any resemblance to ancient Hebrew. Whatever the "original" language was—and there is every reason to believe that many languages sprang up independently over a very long span of time—it could not sound at all like any language that has been documented.

Many theories of the origin of language have been advanced, but three have been mentioned in textbooks more frequently than others. One, the "bow-wow" or echoic theory, insists that the earliest forms of language were exclusively onomatopoeic—that is, imitative of the sounds of animals and nature, despite the fact that the so-called primitive languages are not largely composed of onomatopoeic words. Furthermore, some measure of conventionalization must take place before echoisms become real "words"; individual young children do not call a dog a "bow-wow" until they hear an older child or adult use the term. Another theory, called the "pooh-pooh" or interjectional theory, maintains that language must have begun with primitive grunts and groans—that is, very loose and disjointed utterances. Many have held that such a theory fits animals better than humans; indeed, this kind of exclamatory speech probably separates humans quite clearly from the animals. Still another theory, dubbed the "ding-dong" theory, claims that language arose as a response to natural stimuli. None of these theories has any strong substantiation. Some linguists have suggested that speech and song may have once been the same. The presence of tones and pitch accent in many older languages lends some plausibility to the idea; it is likely that language, gestures, and song, as forms of communication, were all intertwined at the earliest stages.

Is it a hopeless task to try to discover the origin of language? Linguists have continued to look into the question again, but there is little chance that more than a priori notions can be established. It has been suggested, for example, that prehumans may have gradually developed a kind of grammar by occasionally fitting together unstructured vocal signals in patterns that were repeated and then eventually understood, accepted, and passed on. This process is called compounding, and some forms of it are found in present-day gibbon calls.

THE HISTORY OF LANGUAGE STUDY

In the history of language study, a number of signposts can be erected to mark the path. The simplest outline consists of two major parts: a prescientific and a scientific period. The first can be dispensed with in short order.

The earliest formal grammar of any language is a detailed analysis of classical Sanskrit, written by the Indian scholar Pāṇini in the fourth century B.C.E. He called it the Sutras (instructions), and in it, he codified the rules for the use of proper Sanskrit. It is still an authoritative work. Independently of Pāṇini, the ancient

Greeks established many grammatical concepts that strongly influenced linguistic thinking for hundreds of years. Platonic realism, although by today's standards severely misguided in many respects, offered a number of useful insights into language, among them the basic division of the sentence into subject and predicate, the recognition of word stress, and the twofold classification of sounds into consonants and vowels. In the third century B.C.E., Aristotle defined the various parts of speech. In the next century, Dionysius Thrax produced a grammar that not only improved understanding of the sound system of Greek but also classified even more clearly the basic parts of speech and commented at length on such properties of language as gender, number, case, mood, voice, tense, and person. At no time, though, did the Hindu and Greek scholars break away from a focus on their own language to make a comparison with other languages. This fault was also largely one of the Romans, who merely adapted Greek scholarship to their own needs. If they did any comparing of languages, it was not of the languages in the Roman world, but only of Latin as a "corrupt" descendant of Greek. In sum, the Romans introduced no new concepts; they were, instead, content to synthesize or reorganize their legacy from ancient Greece. Only two grammarians come to mind from the fourth and fifth centuries of the Roman Empire—Priscian and Donatus, whose works served for centuries as basic texts for the teaching of Latin.

The scientific period of language study began with a British Sanskrit scholar, Sir William Jones, who headed a society organized in Calcutta for the exploration of Asia. In 1786, he delivered a paper in which he stated that

> the Sanskrit language . . . [was] more perfect than the Greek, more copious than the Latin, and more exquisitely refined than either; yet [bore] to both of them a stronger affinity . . . than could possibly have been produced by accident; so strong, indeed, that no philologer could examine them all three without believing them to have sprung from some common source, which, perhaps, no longer exists.

He went on to say that Germanic and Celtic probably had the same origin. His revolutionary assertion that Sanskrit and most of the languages of Europe had descended from a single language no longer spoken and never recorded first produced considerable scholarly opposition, but shortly thereafter set the stage for comparative analysis. He insisted that a close examination of the "inner structures" of this family of languages would reveal heretofore unsuspected relationships.

Franz Bopp, a German born in 1791 and a student of Oriental languages, including Sanskrit, was the founder of comparative grammar. In his epochmaking book *Über das Conjugationssystem der Sanskritsprache in Vergleichung mit jenem der griechischen, lateinischen, persischen und germanischen Sprache* (1816), he demonstrated for all time what Jones and Friedrich von Schlegel and other researchers had only surmised. A young Danish contemporary named Rasmus Rask corroborated his results and established that Armenian and Lithuanian belong to the same language group, the Indo-European. The tool to establish these relationships was the "comparative method," one of the greatest achievements of nineteenth century linguistics. In applying this method, linguists searched in the various languages under investigation for cognates—words with similar spelling, similar sound, and similar meaning. They then set up sound correspondences among the cognates, much like looking for the lowest common denominator in a mathematical construction, from which the original linguistic forms could be constructed.

The German linguist Jakob Grimm (one of the Brothers Grimm known for books of fairy tales) took Rask's work one step further and, in a four-volume work published between 1819 and 1822, showed conclusively the systematic correspondences and differences between Sanskrit, Greek, and Latin, on one hand, and the Germanic languages, on the other hand. The formulation of this system of sound changes came to be known as Grimm's law, or the First Sound Shift, and the changes involved can be diagramed as follows:

Proto-Indo-European: *bh dh gh b d g p t k*
Proto-Germanic: *b d g p t k f ϴ h*

Where the Indo-European, as transmitted through Latin or Greek, had a *p* sound (as in *piscis* and *pēd*), the German-based English word has an *f* ("fish" and "foot");

the Latinate *trēs* becomes the English "three." In addition to the changes described above, another important change took place in the Germanic languages. If the *f ϴ h* resulting from the change of *p t k* stood after an unaccented vowel but before another vowel, they became voiced fricatives, later voiced stops, as in the pair *seethe : sodden.* This change also affected *s*, yielding *z*, which later became *r* (Rhotacism) and explains, for example, the alternations in *was : were.* It was described by Karl Verner, a Danish linguist, and is known appropriately as Verner's law. There are one or two other "laws" that explain apparent exceptions to Grimm's law, illustrating the basic regularity of Grimm's formulations. At the very end of the nineteenth century, the neo-Grammarians, led by Karl Brugmann, insisted that all exceptions could be explained—that, in fact, "phonetic laws are natural laws and have no exceptions." Even those studying the natural sciences do not make such a strong assertion, but the war cry of the neo-Grammarians did inspire scholars to search for regularity in language.

The German language itself underwent a profound change beginning probably in the far south of the German-speaking lands sometime during the fifth century, causing a restructuring of the sounds of all of the southern and many of the midland dialects. These became known, for geographical reasons, as High German, while those dialects in the north came to be known as Low German. Six consonants in various positions were affected, but the most consistently shifted sounds were the Indo-European *b*, which in English became *p* and in German *pf*, and the *d* to *t* and *ts*. For example, the Latin *decim* became the English "ten" and the German *zehn.*

In the course of the nineteenth century, all such changes were recognized, and scholars were enabled to identify and diagram the reflex languages of Indo-European into five subgroups known as *satem* languages and four known as *centum* languages. This division is significant both geographically—the *satem* languages are located clearly to the east of where the original home of the Indo-Europeans probably was—and linguistically—the *satem* languages have, among other characteristics, *s* sounds where the *centum* languages have *k* sounds (the word *centum* is pronounced

> ## THE *SATEM* LANGUAGES
>
> | | |
> |---|---|
> | Indo-Iranian | Earliest attested form, Sanskrit; modern languages include Hindi, Bengali, and Persian. |
> | Albanian | Spoken by a small number of Balkan people. |
> | Armenian | Spoken by a small number of people in that country. |
> | Slavic | Divided into East Slavic (Great Russian, the standard language; Little Russian or Ukrainian; White Russian, spoken in the region adjacent to and partly in modern-day Poland); West Slavic (Czech, Slovak, Polish); South Slavic (Slovenian and Serbo-Croatian; Bulgarian). |
> | Baltic | Lithuanian and Lettic, spoken in the Baltic states. |

with an initial hard *c*). The very words *satem* and *centum*, meaning "hundred" in Avestan (an Indo-Iranian language) and Latin, respectively, illustrate the sound divergence.

INDO-EUROPEAN LANGUAGES

The original home of the Indo-Europeans is not known for certain, but it is safe to say that it was in Europe, and probably close to present-day Lithuania. For one thing, the Lithuanians have resided in a single area since the Neolithic Age (2500-2000 B.C.E.) and speak a language of great complexity. Furthermore, Lithuania is situated on the dividing line between *centum* and *satem* languages. One would also assume that the original home was somewhere close to the area where the reflex languages are to be found today and not, for example, in Africa, Australia, or North or South America. For historical and archaeological reasons, scholars have ruled out the British Isles and the peninsulas of southern Europe. Last, there are indications that the Indo-Europeans entered

India from the northwest, for there is no evidence of their early acquaintanceship with the Ganges River, but only with the Indus (hence "Indo-"). Certain common words for weather conditions, geography, and flora and fauna militate in favor of a European homeland.

Scholars have classified the Indo-European languages as a family apart from certain other languages on the basis of two principal features: their common word stock and their inflectional structure. This type of classification, called genetic, is one of three. Another, called geographical, is usually employed initially. For example, if nothing whatsoever was known about American Indian languages, one might divide them into North American and South American, Eastern North American and Western North American, and perhaps some other geographical categories. A third variety of classification, called typological, is possible only when a good deal is

> ## THE *CENTUM* LANGUAGES
>
> | | |
> |---|---|
> | Greek (Hellenic) | Attic, Ionic, and Doric, formerly spoken throughout the eastern areas around the Mediterranean; modern Greek. |
> | Italic | Latin; modern Italian, French, Spanish, Portuguese, Catalan, Sardinian, Romanian, and Rhaeto-Romanic. |
> | Celtic | Modern Welsh, Cornish, Breton, Irish, and Scots Gaelic. |
> | Germanic (Teutonic) | East Germanic (Gothic, now extinct); North Germanic (Danish, Norwegian, Swedish, Icelandic); West Germanic (Low German: English, Dutch, Frisian, Plattdeutsch; High German: standard German). |
> | In addition | Several extinct Indo-European languages, such as Tocharian and the Anatolian languages, especially Hittite. |

known about the structure of a language. The four main types of languages arrived at through such classification are inflectional, meaning that such syntactic distinctions as gender, number, case, tense, and so forth are usually communicated by altering the form of a word, as in English when -*s* added to a noun indicates plurality but, when added to a verb, singularity; agglutinative, meaning that suffixes are piled onto word bases in a definite order and without change in phonetic shape (for example, Turkish *evlerimden*, "house-s-my-from"); isolating, meaning that invariable word forms, mostly monosyllabic, are employed in variable word order (for example, Chinese *wŏ*, meaning, according to its position in the utterance, "I," "me," "to me," or "my"); and incorporating or polysynthetic, meaning that a sentence, with its various syntactic features, may be "incorporated" as a single word (for example, Eskimo /a: wlisa-utiss?ar-siniarpu-na/, "I am looking for something suitable for a fish-line").

OTHER LANGUAGES

Although the Indo-European languages have been studied in more detail than other language families, it is possible to classify and describe many of the remaining language families of the world, the total comprising more than twenty-seven hundred separate languages. In Europe and Asia, relatively few languages are spoken by very large numbers of people; elsewhere many distinct languages are spoken by small communities. In Europe, all languages are Indo-European except for Finnish, Estonian, Hungarian, and Basque. The last-named is something of a mystery; it appears to predate Indo-European by such a long period that it could conceivably be descended from a prehistoric language. The first three belong to the same family, the Finno-Urgic. Sometimes Turkish is added to the group, and the four are called the Ural-Altaic family. All are agglutinative.

The most extensive language family in eastern Asia is the Sino-Tibetan. It consists of two branches, the Tibeto-Burman and Chinese. Mandarin is the language of the northern half of China, although there are three different varieties—northern, southwestern, and southern. In the south, there is a range of mutually unintelligible dialects. All are isolating in structure.

In other parts of Asia are found the Kadai family, consisting of Thai, Laotian, and the Shan languages of Burma, and in southern Asia, the Munda languages and Vietnamese. The latter has a considerable number of speakers.

Japanese and Korean are separate families, even though cultural relationships between the two countries have produced some borrowing over the years. Japanese is essentially agglutinative.

On the continent of Africa, the linguistic family of prime importance is the Hamito-Semitic family. Hebrew, Arabic, and some of the languages of Ethiopia make up the Semitic side. There are four Hamitic languages: Egyptian, Berber, Cushitic, and Chad. All exhibit some inflectional characteristics. In addition to these languages, Hausa, an important trade language, is used throughout the northern part of the continent.

In central and southern Africa, the Niger-Congo language family is dominant. The largest subgroup of this family is Bantu, which includes Swahili in central and eastern Africa, Kikuyu in Kenya, and Zulu in the south. Most appear to be either agglutinative or polysynthetic.

The Malayo-Polynesian languages are spoken as original tongues all the way from Madagascar to the Malay Peninsula, the East Indies, and, across the Pacific, to Hawaii. Many seem to be isolating with traces of earlier inflections.

The Indian languages of the Americas are all polysynthetic. Until recently, these Indian languages were classified geographically. Many of the North American languages have been investigated, and linguists group them into distinct families, such as Algonquian, Athabaskan, Natchez-Muskogean, Uto-Aztecan, Penutian, and Hokan.

MODERN LANGUAGES

In addition to the distinction between prescientific and scientific periods of language study, there are other divisions that can help clarify the various approaches to this vast topic. For example, the entire period from earliest times until the late nineteenth century was largely historical, comparative at best, but scarcely truly scientific in terms of rigor. Beginning with the neo-Grammarians Brugmann and Delbrück, the stage was set for what may be called a period of general or descriptive linguistics. Languages were examined not only diachronically—that is, historically—but also synchronically, where a segment or feature of language was scrutinized without regard to an earlier stage. The most important names associated with this descriptive school are those of N. S. Trubetzkoy and Roman Jakobson. Strongly influenced by the theories of the Swiss linguist Ferdinand de Saussure, they examined each detail of language as a part of a system. In other words, they were ultimately more interested in the system and the way it hung together than in each individual detail. These scholars were members of the European school of linguistic thought that had its origin in Jakobson's Prague circle. Across the Atlantic, their most important counterpart was Leonard Bloomfield, who, in 1933, published his classic linguistics text, *Language*. Like his contemporary, Edward Sapir, Bloomfield began as a comparativist in Germanic linguistics, then studied American Indian languages, and finally became an expert in the general principles of language. Bloomfield's theory of structuralism has been criticized for its resemblance to the psychological theory of behaviorism, which restricts itself to the observable and rejects the concept of mind.

Since the 1930's, there has been a steady procession of American linguists studying and reporting on the sounds and grammatical features of many different languages, in some sense all derivative from the foundation laid by the phonemicists beginning with Saussure and Bloomfield. Kenneth Pike's tagmemics, in part an attempt to present language behavior empirically through a description at each level of grammatical form, evolved directly out of descriptive linguistics. In 1957, Noam Chomsky launched transformational-generative grammar, concerned at first only with syntax, but later also with phonology. Considerable tension has developed between structuralists and transformational-generative grammarians, concerning not only syntactic analysis but also the representation of sounds. For some, stratificational grammar provides a connection, through strata or levels of description, among descriptive, tagmemic, and computational analyses.

THE TECHNICAL SIDE OF LANGUAGE

A language is made up of its sound system, grammar, and vocabulary. The former two may differ considerably from language family to language family, but there is a workable range in the extent and type of sounds and grammatical functions. The inventory of significant sounds in a given language, called phonemes, extends from about twenty to about sixty. English has forty-six, including phonemes of pitch, stress, and juncture. If the grammatical facts of a complicated language can be written out on one or two sheets of paper, the grammar of English can be laid out on the back of an envelope. In short, some languages are simpler phonologically or grammatically than others, but none is so complicated in either respect that every child cannot learn his or her language in about the same time.

The study of the sounds of which speech is made up became scientific in method by the end of the nineteenth century, when Paul Passy founded the International Phonetic Association. Down to the present day, articulatory phonetics has borne a close relationship to physiology in the description of the sounds of speech according to the organs producing them and the position of these organs in relation to surrounding structures.

By the mid-1920's, phoneticians realized that the unit of description of the phonology of a language had to be a concept rather than some physical entity. The term phoneme was chosen; it designates a minimally significant sound unit, an abstraction around which cluster all the phonetic realizations of that generalized sound. Thus, the English phoneme /p/ represents all recognizably similar pronunciations of [p], with more or less or no aspiration depending on position within a word or the speech habits of a given speaker. In other words, it designates a class of sounds distinct from others in the language. It carries no meaning as such, but it serves to distinguish one sound from another and, together with other phonemes, produces morphemic, or meaning, differences. Thus /p/, /i/, and /n/ are separate phonemes, but, taken together, make up a morpheme—the word *pin*—which is distinct, by virtue of a single phoneme, from, say, /bin/, "bin," or /tin/ "tin." Sometimes, morphemes show relations between words, as when -*s* is added to a noun to indicate plurality or possession or to a verb to indicate singularity.

The sound system and grammar of a language are thus closely related. Grammar, at least for Indo-European languages and many others, can be defined as consisting of a morphology and syntax, where, expressed simply, the former refers to the words and their endings and the latter to the order of words. Accompanying the words are, however, other features of language that can alter meaning. It matters, for example, whether the stress occurs on the first or second syllable of the word *pervert* or *permit*. If the stress falls on the first syllable, the word is a noun; if on the second, it is a verb. It matters whether the last few sounds of an utterance convey an upturn or a downturn and trail-off, for a question or a statement may result. It matters also what the pitch level is and whether juncture is present. These features, too, are phonemic.

To function in a language, one must have control of close to 100 percent of the phonology and 75 percent or more of the grammar, but a mere 1 percent of the vocabulary will enable the speaker to function in many situations. For a speaker of a language the size of English, a vocabulary of six thousand words will suffice. Possessing a vocabulary implies an unconscious knowledge of the semantic relationship to the phonology and grammar of the language. One theory of the word regards the word as a compound formed of two components: a physical element, the sequence of sounds of speech; and a semantic element, the amount of meaning expressed by the segment of speech. The first is called the formant, the second the morpheme. The word "cook" /kuk/ is one morpheme expressed by one formant—the formant consisting of one syllable, a sequence of three phonemes. In the plural of "cook," -*s* is a formant that is not even a syllable. In fact, a formant is not even necessarily a phoneme, but can be the use of one form instead of another, as in "her" instead of "she." There is no reason that the same formant, such as -*s*, cannot express more than one morpheme: "cooks" (noun) versus "cook's" versus "cooks" (verb). The same morpheme can also be expressed by more than one formant; there are, for example, many different formants for the plural, such as basis/bases, curriculum/curricula, datum/data, ox/oxen, child/children, man/men, woman/women, cherub/cherubim, monsignore/monsignori.

The distinction in morphology made above between words and their endings needs further amplification. An examination of a stanza from Lewis Carroll's "Jabberwocky" (from *Alice's Adventures in Wonderland*, 1865) illustrates the manner in which the poet uses formants with no evident meaning to the average speaker:

> 'Twas brilling, and the slithy toves
> Did gyre and gimble in the wabe;
> All mimsy were the borogoves,
> And the mome raths outgrabe.

Alice herself remarks that the words fill her head with ideas, but she does not know what they are. There is a rightness about the way the poem sounds because the endings, the structural morphemes, are correctly placed. When the message is of primary importance and the speaker knows the language only imperfectly, the structural morphemes may be incorrect or missing and a string of pure message morphemes may be the result: Her give man bag money.

Message morphemes have their own peculiar properties, limiting their use to certain contexts, regardless of the accuracy of the combined structural morphemes. To illustrate this principle, Chomsky composed the sentence "Colorless green ideas sleep furiously." The subject is "colorless green ideas"; the predicate, "sleep furiously." This sentence has the same structure as any sentence of the shape: adjective/adjective/noun/intransitive verb/adverb. However, there is something semantically troubling. How can one describe something green as colorless? Can ideas be green? How can an intransitive verb that describes such a passive activity be furiously involved in an action?

Chomsky's example was designed to combine structural familiarity with semantic impossibility. It is possible to devise similar sentences that, though semantically improbable, could conceivably be used by an actual speaker. The sentence "Virtue swims home every night" attributes to an abstract noun an action performed by animate beings, and poses other difficulties as well (in what setting can one swim home?), yet such strange semantic violations, given a meaningful context, are the stuff of poetry.

Indeed, semantic change actually occurs with a

measure of frequency in the history of a language. It is usually of two types. Words that are rather specific in meaning sometimes become generalized; for example, Latin *molīna* (gristmill) originally meant "mill" but expanded to cover "sawmill," "steel mill," even "diploma mill." Many words in English of very broad meanings, such as "do," "make," "go," and "things," derive from words of more specific notions. At the same time, the opposite often happens. Words that once were very general in meaning have become specific. Examples include *deer*, which formerly meant merely "animal" (compare German *Tier*), and *hound*, "dog," now a particular kind of dog. Sometimes, words undergo melioration, as in the change in *knight*, meaning originally a "servant," to "king's servant," or pejoration, as in the change in *knave*, meaning "boy" (compare German *Knabe*), to "rascal."

Perhaps the most significant force for change in language is analogy. It is occasioned by mental associations arising because of similarity or contrast of meaning and may affect the meaning or the form of words or even create new words. Most verbs in English are regular and form their preterit and past participles by the addition of *-ed* (or *-t*), as "dream, dreamed, dreamt," and not by vowel change, as in "drink, drank, drunk." New words taken into the language, as well as some of the irregular ones already in use, will usually become regular. It is by no means unusual to hear a child use analogy in forming the past of, say, "teach" or "see" as "teached" and "see'd" instead of "taught" and "saw." Since most English nouns form their plural by the addition of *-s*, it is to be expected that unfamiliar words or words with little-used, learned plural forms will be pluralized in the same way: for example, "memorandums" (or "memos") for *memoranda*, "stadiums" for *stadia*, "gymnasiums" for *gymnasia*, "prima donnas" for *prime donne*, and "formulas" for *formulae*. Sometimes a resemblance in the form of a word may suggest a relationship that causes a further assimilation in form. This process is known as folk etymology and often occurs when an unfamiliar or foreign word or phrase is altered to give it a more meaningful form. There are many examples: "crayfish" comes from Old French *crevisse* (crab), but *-visse* meant nothing and thus was changed to the phonetically similar *-fish*; a hangnail is not a (fin-

ger)nail that hangs, but one that hurts (from Old English *ang*); the second element of "titmouse" has nothing to do with a mouse, but comes from Middle English *mose*, the name for several species of birds.

There are many other processes in language by which changes are brought about. Among them are several of great importance: assimilation, dissimilation, conversion, back formation, blending, and the creation of euphemisms and slang.

Assimilation causes a sound to change in conformance with a neighboring sound, as in the plural of "kit" with [-s] (/kits/), as opposed to the plural of "limb" with [-z] (/limz/), or in the preterit and participial forms of regular verbs: "grazed" [greyzd], but "choked" [čowkt].

Dissimilation is the opposite process, whereby neighboring sounds are made unlike, as in "pilgrim" from Latin *peregrīnus*, where the first *r* dissimilates.

Conversion is the change of one part of speech or form class into another, as the change from noun to verb: The nouns "bridge," "color," and "shoulder" are converted to verbs in "to bridge a gap," "to color a book," and "to shoulder a load."

A back formation occurs when a word is mistakenly assumed to be the base form from which a new word is formed, as in "edit" from "editor," "beg" from "beggar," "peddle" from "pedlar."

Some words are blends: "flash" + "blush" = "flush"; "slight" (slim) + "tender" = "slender"; "twist" + "whirl" = "twirl"; "breakfast" + "lunch" = "brunch."

Euphemisms are words and expressions with new, better-sounding connotations—for example, to "pass away" or "breathe one's last" or "cross the river" for "to die"; "lingerie" or "intimate wear" for "underwear"; "acute indigestion" for "bellyache."

Slang consists of informal, often ephemeral expressions and coinages, such as "turkey" for "stupid person," "blow away" for "to kill," and "kook," meaning "odd or eccentric person," from "cuckoo."

All three constituents of language change over a long period of time—sounds, structure, and vocabulary—but each language or dialect retains its distinctiveness. The most durable and unchanging aspect of language is writing, of which there are two major varieties: picture writing, also called ideographic writing, and alphabetic writing. The former kind of writing began as actual pictures and developed gradually into ideograms linked directly to the objects or concepts and having no connection with the sounds of the language. The latter variety began as symbols for syllables, until each symbol was taken to represent a single spoken sound. Although alphabetic writing is much more widespread and easier to learn and use, ideographic writing has the advantage of maintaining cultural unity among speakers of dialects and languages not mutually intelligible. An alphabetic writing system can, over time, act as a conservative influence on the spoken language as well as provide valuable etymological clues. Ideographic writing can be, and often is, seen as art capable of conveying messages separate from speech. Both systems are vehicles for the transmission of history and literature without which civilization would falter and perish.

THE SOCIAL SIDE OF LANGUAGE

The social side of language is inextricably linked to behavior. It is concerned with the use of language to create attitudes and responses toward language, objects, and people. For example, certain overt behaviors toward language and its users can create unusual political pressures. The insistence by the Québecois on French as the primary, if not sole, language of their province of Canada has led to near secession and to bitter interprovincial feelings. The creation of modern Hebrew has helped to create and sustain the state of Israel. The Irish are striving to make Irish the first language of that part of the British Isles. The Flemish urge full status for their variety of Dutch in the Brussels area. African Americans sometimes advocate clearer recognition of black English. Frisians, Bretons, Basques, Catalans, and Provençals are all insisting on greater acceptance of their mother tongues.

Within a language or dialect, there can be specialized vocabulary and pronunciation not generally understood. The term "dialect" is commonly taken to mean a regional variety of language or one spoken by the undereducated, but, strictly speaking, it is differentiated from language as such, being largely what people actually speak. Some dialects differ so substantially from standard, national tongues that, to all intents and

purposes, they are languages in their own right. The term "vernacular" is similar in that it designates everyday speech as opposed to learned discourse. "Lingo" designates, somewhat contemptuously, any dialect or language not readily comprehended. "Jargon" is specialized or professional language, often of a technical nature; in this context, the term "cant," as in "thieves' cant," is virtually synonymous with "jargon." Closely related to these two terms is the term "argot," referring to the idiom of a closely knit group, as in "criminal argot." Finally, "slang," discussed above, refers to the colorful, innovative, often short-lived popular vocabulary drawn from many levels of language use, both specialized and nonspecialized.

Words, like music, can produce moods. They can raise one's spirits or lower them. They can stir up discontent or soothe human anger. They can inspire and console, ingratiate and manipulate, mislead and ridicule. They can create enough hatred to destroy but also enough trust to overcome obstacles. While a mood may originate in physical well-being or physical discomfort and pain, language can express that mood, intensify it, or deny it. Language can be informative (emotionally neutral), biased (emotionally charged), or propagandistic (informatively neutral).

Language is informative when it states indisputable facts or asks questions dealing with such facts, even though those facts are very broad and general. One can also inform with misstatements, half-truths, or outright lies. It does not matter whether the statement is actually true or false, only that the question can be posed.

Language often reflects bias by distorting facts. Frequently, the substitution of a single derogatory term is sufficient to load the atmosphere. Admittedly, some words are favorably charged for some people, unfavorably for others. Much depends on the context, word and sentence stress, gestures, and former relationship.

Language can be propagandistic when the speaker desires to promote some activity or cause. The load that propaganda carries is directly proportional to the receiver's enthusiasm, bias, or readiness to be deceived. Almost invariably, propaganda terms arise out of the specialized language of religion, art, commerce, education, finance, government, and so forth. Propaganda is a kind of name calling, using words from a stock of esoteric and exclusive terms. Not many people are thoroughly familiar with the exact meanings of words such as "totalitarian," "fascist," "proletarian," and "bourgeois," but they think they know whether these words are good or bad, words of approval or disapproval. The effect is to call forth emotions as strong as those prompted by invectives.

The language of advertising achieves its effectiveness by conveniently combining information, bias, and propaganda. A good advertisement must gain immediate attention, make the reader or listener receptive to the message, ensure its retention, create a desire, and cause the person to buy the product without setting up resistance. Advertising must, moreover, link the product to "pleasant" or "healthy" things. In advertising circles, there is no widespread agreement as to which is more important: the avoidance of all associations that can create resistance or the creation of desire for a particular object. Even if the latter is regarded as the prime objective, it is still important to avoid resistance. The most powerful tools of the advertiser are exaggeration and cliché. The words generally used in ads deal with the basic component and qualities of a product, while the qualifiers are hackneyed and overblown: lather (rich, creamy, full-bodied); toothpaste (fights cavities three ways, ten ways, tastes zesty); cleanser (all-purpose, powerful, one-step); coffee (full of flavor buds, brewed to perfection, marvelous bouquet). The danger of advertising is evident when its pathology carries over into other areas of life. Every culture must be on guard against the effect of advertising on the health of its citizenry and the shaping of its national image. Even foreign policy can be the victim of advertising that stresses youth over maturity, beauty of body over soundness of mind, physical health over mental serenity, or the power of sex appeal over everything else.

In the latter part of the twentieth century, language began to be closely examined by certain groups aiming to rid it of inherent prejudice. Of all of these groups, perhaps feminists have had the greatest effect on the vocabulary, and even the structure, of languages that differentiate along sex lines. A vociferous contingent of women contend that the symbols of perception—words—give both meaning and value to the objects they define and that many of these words are loaded with a male-chauvinist aspect. For example, words with the affix *-man* are being avoided or paired with *-woman* or *-person:* "congressman"/"congresswoman," "chairman"/"chairwoman"/"chairperson." In some instances, gender is eliminated altogether: "humankind" for "mankind," "chair" for "chairman" or "chairwoman." There are many more techniques employed to desexualize English; some even involve tampering with personal pronouns, a much less likely area for success. Nevertheless, any language can cope with any pressing linguistic problem. The impetus for a solution begins with the individual or a small group, but the community as a whole often applies brakes to change that is too rapid or drastic, dramatizing the fact that language exists not for the individual alone but for the community as a whole.

APPLICATIONS

Almost everybody is intimately acquainted with at least one language. Everybody can produce the sounds and sound combinations of his or her language and understand the meanings of the sounds produced by other speakers. Everybody knows which sounds and sound combinations are allowable and which do not fit the language. Sentences that are grammatically or semantically unacceptable or strange are easily recognized. Despite this intuitive or unconscious knowledge of one's language, the average native speaker cannot comment authoritatively on the sound system or the structure of his or her language. Furthermore, there are no books containing the complete language of English or Arabic or Mandarin Chinese in which all possible sentences and sound combinations are listed. Instead, people must rely largely on dictionaries for a list of words and on grammars and linguistic texts for a statement of rules dealing with sounds, morphology, and syntax. To study one's language as an object or phenomenon is to raise one's consciousness of how language functions.

Some people have a professional need to know a lot about a language as opposed to simply being able to use it. Some of the more obvious examples include language teachers, speech therapists, advertising writers, communications engineers, and computer programmers. Others, such as the anthropologist or the historian, who often work with documents, employ their knowledge as an ancillary tool. The missionary may have to learn about some very esoteric language for which there is no grammar book and perhaps even no writing. The psychologist studies language as a part of human behavior. The philosopher is often primarily interested in the "logical" side of language. Students of foreign languages can benefit greatly from linguistic knowledge; they can often learn more efficiently and make helpful comparisons of sounds and structures between their own and the target language.

Translation and interpretation are two activities requiring considerable knowledge about language. Strictly speaking, the terms are not interchangeable; translation refers to the activity of rendering, in writing, one language text into another, whereas interpretation is oral translation. Translation is of two kinds, scientific and literary, and can be accomplished by people or machines. In general, machine translation has been a disappointment because of the grave difficulties involved in programming the many complexities of natural language. Interpretation is also of two kinds: legal and diplomatic. Whereas the legal interpreter requires a precise knowledge of the terminology of the court and must tread a thin line between literal and free interpretation, the diplomatic interpreter has the even more difficult task of adding, or subtracting, as circumstances dictate, allusions, innuendos, insinuations, and implications. Interpretation is accomplished in two ways: simultaneously with the speaker, or consecutively after a given segment of speech.

One of the important questions before linguistics is: Does linguistics aid in the study and appreciation of literature? Many would automatically assume that the answer is an unqualified yes, since the material of which literature is made is language. There are others, however, who find linguistic techniques of analysis too mechanical and lacking in the very feeling that literature tries to communicate. Probably most thoughtful people would agree that linguistics can make a contribution in tandem with more traditional analytical approaches, but that alone it cannot yet, if ever, disclose the intrinsic qualities of great literary works.

By one definition at least, literature consists of texts constructed according to certain phonological, morpho-logical, and syntactic restrictions, where the result is the creation of excellence of form and expression. For poetry in the Western tradition, for example, the restriction most frequently imposed is that of rhythm based on stress or vowel quantity. In other cultures, syntactic and semantic prescriptions can produce the same effect.

For both poetic and prose texts, the discovery and description of the author's style are essential to analysis. In contrast to the methods of traditional literary criticism, linguistics offers the possibility of quantitative stylistic analysis. Computer-aided analysis yields textual statistics based on an examination of various features of phonology and grammar. The results will often place an author within a literary period, confirm his region or dialect, explain the foreign-vocabulary influences, describe syllabication in terms of vowel and consonant count, list euphemisms and metaphors, and delineate sentence structure with regard to subordinating elements, to mention some of the possibilities. All of these applications are based on the taxemes of selection employed by an individual author.

Of all literary endeavors, literary translation seems to stand in the closest possible relationship to linguistics. The translator must perform his task within the framework of an awareness, be it conscious or intuitive, of the phonology, syntax, and morphology of both the source language and the target language. Like the linguist, he should also be acquainted in at least a rudimentary fashion with the society that has produced the text he is attempting to translate. His work involves much more than the mechanical or one-to-one exchange of word for word, phrase for phrase, or even concept for concept. The practice of translation makes possible the scope and breadth of knowledge encompassed in the ideal of liberal arts, and without translation relatively few scholars could claim knowledge and understanding of many of the world's great thinkers and literary artists.

BIBLIOGRAPHY

Akmajian, Adrian, et al. *Linguistics: An Introduction to Language and Communication.* Cambridge, Mass.: MIT Press, 2001. The first part of this work deals with the structural and interpretive parts of language, and the second part is cognitively oriented and includes chapters on pragmatics, psychology of language, language acquisition, and language and the brain.

Beekes, Robert S. P. *Comparative Indo-European Linguistics: An Introduction*. Philadelphia: John Benjamins, 1996. Examines the history of Indo-European languages and explores comparative grammar and linguistics.

Cavalli-Sforza, L. L. *Genes, Peoples, and Languages*. Berkeley: University of California Press, 2001. Cavalli-Sforza was among the first to ask whether the genes of modern populations contain a historical record of the human species. This collection comprises five lectures that serve as a summation of the author's work over several decades, the goal of which has been nothing less than tracking the past hundred thousand years of human evolution.

Chomsky, Noam. *Language and Thought*. Wakefield, R.I.: Moyer Bell, 1998. Presents an analysis of human language and its influence on other disciplines.

Lycan, William G. *Philosophy of Language: A Contemporary Introduction*. 2d ed. New York: Routledge, 2008. Introduces nonspecialists to the main issues and theories in the philosophy of language, focusing specifically on linguistic phenomena.

Pinker, Stephen. *The Language Instinct: How the Mind Creates Language*. New York: HarperPerennial Modern Classics, 2009. Explores how humans learn to talk, how the study of language can provide insight into the way genes interact with experience to create behavior and thought, and how the arbitrary sounds people call language evoke emotion and meaning.

Ruhlen, Merritt. *The Origin of Language: Tracing the Evolution of the Mother Tongue*. New York: John Wiley & Sons, 1996. Provides an accessible examination of nearly 100,000 years of human history and prehistory to uncover the roots of the language from which all modern tongues derive.

Trudgill, Peter. *Sociolinguistics: An Introduction to Language and Society*. 4th ed. New York: Penguin Books, 2007. Examines how speech is deeply influenced by class, gender, and ethnic background and explores the implications of language for social and educational policy.

Vygotsky, Lev S. *Thought and Language*. Edited by Alex Kozulin. Rev. ed. Cambridge, Mass.: MIT Press, 1986. A classic foundational work of cognitive science. Vygotsky analyzes the relationship between words and consciousness, arguing that speech is social in its origins and that only as a child develops does it become internalized verbal thought. Revised edition offers an introductory essay by editor Kozulin that offers new insight into the author's life, intellectual milieu, and research methods.

Yule, George. *The Study of Language*. 4th ed. New York: Cambridge University Press, 2010. Revised edition includes a new chapter on pragmatics and an expanded chapter on semantics; incorporates many changes that reflect developments in language study in the twenty-first century.

Donald D. Hook

GLOSSARY OF POETICAL TERMS

Accentual meter: A base meter in which the occurrence of a syllable marked by a stress determines the basic unit, regardless of the number of unstressed syllables. It is one of four base meters used in English (accentual, accentual-syllabic, syllabic, and quantitative). An example from modern poetry is "Blue Moles" by Sylvia Plath, the first line of which scans: "They're out of the dark's ragbag, these two." Because there are five stressed syllables in this accentually based poem, the reader can expect that many of the other lines will also contain five stresses. See also *Scansion.*

Accentual-syllabic meter: A base meter that measures the pattern of stressed syllables relative to the unstressed ones. It is the most common base meter for English poetry. In the first line of William Shakespeare's sonnet 130, "My mistress' eyes are nothing like the sun," there is a pattern of alternating unstressed with stressed syllables, although there is a substitution of an unstressed syllable for a stressed syllable at the word "like." In the accentual-syllabic system, stressed and unstressed syllables are grouped together into feet.

Allegory: A literary mode in which a second level of meaning—wherein characters, events, and settings represent abstractions—is encoded within the surface narrative. The allegorical mode may dominate the entire work, in which case the encoded message is the work's primary excuse for being, or it may be an element in a work otherwise interesting and meaningful for its surface story alone.

Alliteration: The repetition of consonants at the beginning of syllables; for example, "Large mannered motions of his mythy mind." Alliteration is used when the poet wishes to focus on the details of a sequence of words and to show relationships between words within a line. Because a reader cannot easily skim over an alliterative line, it is conspicuous and demands emphasis.

Allusion: A reference to a historical or literary event whose story or outcome adds dimension to the poem. "Fire and Ice" by Robert Frost, for example, alludes to the biblical account of the flood and the prophecy that the next destruction will come by fire, not water. Without recognizing the allusion and understanding the bib-

lical reference to Noah and the surrounding associations of hate and desire, the reader cannot fully appreciate the poem.

Anacrusis: The addition of an extra unstressed syllable to the beginning or end of a line; the opposite of truncation. For example, anacrusis occurs in the line: "their shoul/ders held the sky/suspended." This line is described as iambic tetrameter with terminal anacrusis. Anacrusis is used to change a rising meter to falling and vice versa to alter the reader's emotional response to the subject.

Anapest: A foot in which two unstressed syllables are associated with one stressed syllable, as in the line, "With the sift/ed, harmon/ious pause." The anapestic foot is one of the three most common in English poetry and is used to create a highly rhythmical, usually emotional, line.

Anaphora: The use of the same word or words to begin successive phrases or lines. Timothy Steele's "Sapphics Against Anger" uses anaphora in the repetition of the phrase "May I."

Approximate rhyme: Assonance and half rhyme (or slant rhyme). Assonance occurs when words with identical vowel sounds but different consonants are associated. "Stars," "arms," and "park" all contain identical *a* (and *ar*) sounds, but because the consonants are different the words are not full rhymes. Half rhyme or slant rhymes contain identical consonants but different vowels, as in "fall" and "well." "Table" and "bauble" constitute half rhymes; "law," "cough," and "fawn" assonate.

Archetype: 1) Primordial image from the collective unconscious of humankind, according to psychologist Carl Jung, who believed that works of art, including poetry, derive much of their power from the unconscious appeal of these images to ancestral memories. 2) A symbol, usually an image, that recurs so frequently in literature that it becomes an element of the literary experience, according to Northrop Frye in his extremely influential *Anatomy of Criticism* (1957).

Assonance: See *Approximate rhyme*

Aubade: A type of poem welcoming or decrying the arrival of the dawn. Often the dawn symbolizes the separation of two lovers. An example is William Empson's "Aubade" (1937).

Ballad: A poem composed of four-line stanzas that alternate rhyme schemes of *abab* or *abcb*. If all four lines contain four feet each (tetrameter), the stanza is called a long ballad; if one or more of the lines contain only three feet (trimeter), it is called a short ballad. Ballad stanzas, which are highly mnemonic, originated with verse adapted to singing. For this reason, the poetic ballad is well suited for presenting stories. Popular ballads are songs or verse that tell tales, usually impersonal, and they usually impart folk wisdom. Supernatural events, courage, and love are frequent themes, but any experience that appeals to people is acceptable material. A famous use of the ballad form is *The Rime of the Ancient Mariner* (1798), by Samuel Taylor Coleridge.

Ballade: A popular and sophisticated French form, commonly (but not necessarily) composed of an eight-line stanza rhyming *ababbcbc*. Early ballades usually contained three stanzas and an envoy, commonly addressed to a nobleman, priest, or the poet's patron, but no consistent syllable count. Another common characteristic of the ballade is a refrain that occurs at the end of each stanza.

Base meter: Also called metrical base. The primary meter employed in poems in English and in most European languages that are not free verse. Based on the number, pattern, or duration of the syllables within a line or stanza, base meters fall into four types: accentual, accentual-syllabic, syllabic, or quantitative. Rhythm in verse occurs because of meter, and the use of meter depends on the type of base into which it is placed.

Blank verse: A type of poem having a base meter of iambic pentameter and with unrhymed lines usually arranged in stichic form (that is, not in stanzas). Most of William Shakespeare's plays are written in blank verse; in poetry it is often used for subject matter that requires much narration or reflection. In both poetry and drama, blank verse elevates emotion and gives a dramatic sense of importance. Although the base meter of blank verse is iambic pentameter, the form is very flexible, and substitution, enjambment, feminine rhyme, and extra syllables can relax the rigidity of the base. The flexi-

bility of blank verse gives the poet an opportunity to use a formal structure without seeming unnecessarily decorous. T. S. Eliot's "Burnt Norton," written in the 1930's, is a modern blank-verse poem.

Cadence: The rhythmic speed or tempo with which a line is read. All language has cadence, but when the cadence of words is forced into some pattern, it becomes meter, thus distinguishing poetry from prose. A prose poem may possess strong cadence, combined with poetic uses of imagery, symbolism, and other poetic devices.

Caesura: A pause or break in a poem, created with or without punctuation marks. The comma, question mark, colon, and dash are the most common signals for pausing, and these are properly termed caesuras; pauses may also be achieved through syntax, lines, meter, rhyme, and the sound of words. The type of punctuation determines the length of the pause. Periods and question marks demand full stops, colons take almost a full stop, semicolons take a long pause, and commas take a short pause. The end of a line usually demands some pause even if there is no punctuation.

Cinquain: Any five-line stanza, including the madsong and the limerick. Cinquains are most often composed of a ballad stanza with an extra line added to the middle.

Classicism: A literary stance or value system consciously based on the example of classical Greek and Roman literature. Although the term is applied to an enormous diversity of artists in many different periods and in many different national literatures, classicism generally denotes a cluster of values including formal discipline, restrained expression, reverence for tradition, and an objective rather than a subjective orientation. As a literary tendency, classicism is often opposed to Romanticism, although many writers combine classical and romantic elements.

Conceit: A type of metaphor that uses a highly intellectualized comparison; an extended, elaborate, or complex metaphor. The term is frequently applied to the work of the Metaphysical poets, notably John Donne.

Connotation: An additional meaning for a word other than its denotative, formal definition. The word "mercenary," for example, simply means a soldier who is paid to fight in an army not of his own region, but connotatively a mercenary is an unprincipled scoundrel who kills for money and pleasure, not for honor and patriotism. Connotation is one of the most important devices for achieving irony, and readers may be fooled into believing a poem has one meaning because they have missed connotations that reverse the poem's apparent theme.

Consonance: Repetition or recurrence of the final consonants of stressed syllables without the correspondence of the preceding vowels. "Chair/star" is an example of consonance, since both words end with *r* preceded by different vowels. Terminal consonance creates half or slant rhyme (see *Approximate rhyme*). Consonance differs from alliteration in that the final consonants are repeated rather than the initial consonants. In the twentieth century, consonance became one of the principal rhyming devices, used to achieve formality without seeming stilted or old-fashioned.

Consonants: All letters except the vowels, *a, e, i, o, u*, and sometimes *y*; one of the most important sound-producing devices in poetry. There are five basic effects that certain consonants will produce: resonance, harshness, plosiveness, exhaustiveness, and liquidity. Resonance, exhaustiveness, and liquidity tend to give words—and consequently the whole line if several of these consonants are used—a soft effect. Plosiveness and harshness, on the other hand, tend to create tension. Resonance is the property of long duration produced by nasals, such as *n* and *m*, and by voiced fricating consonants such as *z, v*, and the voiced *th*, as in "them." Exhaustiveness is created by the voiceless fricating consonants and consonant combinations, such as *h, f*, and the voiceless *th* and *s*. Liquidity results from using the liquids and semivowels *l, r, w*, and *y*, as in the word "silken." Plosiveness occurs when certain consonants create a stoppage of breath before releasing it, especially *b, p, t, d, g, k, ch*, and *j*.

Controlling image/controlling metaphor: Just as a poem may include as structural devices form, theme, action, or dramatic situation, it may also use imagery for structure. When an image runs throughout a poem, giving unity to lesser images or ideas, it is called a controlling image. Usually the poet establishes a single idea and then expands and complicates it; in Edward

Taylor's "Huswifery," for example, the image of the spinning wheel is expanded into images of weaving until the reader begins to see life as a tapestry. Robert Frost's "The Silken Tent" is a fine example of a controlling image and extended metaphor.

Couplet: Any two succeeding lines that rhyme. Because the couplet has been used in so many different ways and because of its long tradition in English poetry, various names and functions have been given to types of couplets. One of the most common is the decasyllabic (ten-syllable) couplet. When there is an end-stop on the second line of a couplet, it is said to be closed; an enjambed couplet is open. An end-stopped decasyllabic couplet is called a heroic couplet, because the form has often been used to sing the praise of heroes. The heroic couplet was widely used by the neoclassical poets of the eighteenth century. Because it is so stately and sometimes pompous, the heroic couplet invites satire, and many poems have been written in "mock-heroic verse," such as Alexander Pope's *The Rape of the Lock* (1712, 1714). Another commonly used couplet is the octasyllabic (eight-syllable) couplet, formed from two lines of iambic tetrameter, as in "L'Allegro" by John Milton: "Come, and trip as we go/ On the light fantastic toe." The light, singsong tone of the octasyllabic couplet also invited satire, and Samuel Butler wrote one of the most famous of all satires, *Hudibras* (1663, 1664, 1678), in this couplet. When a couplet is used to break another rhyme scheme, it generally produces a summing-up effect and has an air of profundity. William Shakespeare found this characteristic particularly useful when he needed to give his newly invented Shakespearean sonnet a final note of authority and purpose.

Dactyl: A foot formed of a stress followed by two unstressed syllables (ˊ ˘ ˘). It is fairly common in isolated words, but when this pattern is included in a line of poetry, it tends to break down and rearrange itself into components of other types of feet. Isolated, the word "meaningless" is a dactyl, but in the line "Políte/ méaning/less wórds," the last syllable becomes attached to the stressed "words" and creates a split foot, forming a trochee and an iamb. Nevertheless, a few dactylic poems do exist. "Áfter the/pángs of a/ désperate/lóver" is a dactyllic line.

Deconstruction: An extremely influential contemporary school of criticism based on the works of the French philosopher Jacques Derrida. Deconstruction treats literary works as unconscious reflections of the reigning myths of Western culture. The primary myth is that there is a meaningful world that language signifies or represents. The deconstructionist critic is most often concerned with showing how a literary text tacitly subverts the very assumptions or myths on which it ostensibly rests.

Denotation: The explicit formal definition of a word, exclusive of its implications and emotional associations (see *Connotation*).

Depressed foot: A foot in which two syllables occur in a pattern in such a way as to be taken as one syllable without actually being an elision. In the line: "To each/ he boul/ders (that have)/fallen/to each," the base meter consists of five iambic feet, but in the third foot, there is an extra syllable that disrupts the meter but does not break it, so that "that have" functions as the second half of the iambic foot.

Diction: The poet's "choice of words," according to John Dryden. In Dryden's time, and for most of the history of English verse, the diction of poetry was elevated, sharply distinct from everyday speech. Since the early twentieth century, however, the diction of poetry has ranged from the banal and the conversational to the highly formal, and from obscenity and slang to technical vocabulary, sometimes in the same poem. The diction of a poem often reveals its persona's values and attitudes.

Dieresis: Caesuras that come after the foot (see *Split foot* for a discussion of caesuras that break feet). They can be used to create long pauses in the line and are often used to prepare the line for enjambment.

Dramatic dialogue: An exchange between two or more personas in a poem or a play. Unlike a dramatic monologue, both characters speak, and in the best dramatic dialogues, their conversation leads to a final resolution in which both characters and the reader come to the same realization at the same time.

Dramatic irony: See *Irony*

Dramatic monologue: An address to a silent person by a narrator; the words of the narrator are greatly influenced by the persona's presence. The principal reason for writing in dramatic monologue form is to control the speech of the major persona through the implied reaction of the silent one. The effect is one of continuing change and often surprise. In Robert Browning's "My Last Duchess," for example, the duke believes that he is in control of the situation, when in fact he has provided the emissary with terrible insights about the way he treated his former duchess. The emissary, who is the silent persona, has asked questions that the duke has answered; in doing so he has given away secrets. Dramatic monologue is somewhat like hearing one side of a telephone conversation in which the reader learns much about both participants.

Duration: The length of the syllables, which is the measure of quantitative meter. Duration can alter the tone and the relative stress of a line and influence meaning as much as the foot can.

Elegy: Usually a long, rhymed, strophic poem whose subject is meditation on death or a lamentable theme. The pastoral elegy uses the natural setting of a pastoral scene to sing of death or love. Within the pastoral setting the simplicity of the characters and the scene lends a peaceful air despite the grief the narrator feels.

Elision: The joining of two vowels into a single vowel (synaeresis) or omitting of a vowel altogether (syncope), usually to maintain a regular base meter. Synaeresis can be seen in the line "Of man's first disobedience, and the fruit," in which the "ie" in "disobedience" is pronounced as a "y" ("ye") so that the word reads dis/o/bed/yence, thereby making a five-syllable word into a four-syllable word. An example of syncope is when "natural" becomes "nat'ral" and "hastening" becomes "hast'ning." Less frequent uses of elision are to change the sound of a word, to spell words as they are pronounced, and to indicate dialect.

Emphasis: The highlighting of or calling attention to a phrase or line or a poem by altering its meter. A number of techniques, such as caesura, relative stress, counterpointing, and substitution can be used.

End rhyme: See *Rhyme*

End-stop: A punctuated pause at the end of a line in a poem. The function of end-stops is to show the relationship between lines and to emphasize particular words or lines. End-stopping in rhymed poems creates more emphasis on the rhyme words, which already carry a great deal of emphasis by virtue of their rhymes. Enjambment is the opposite of end-stopping.

Enjambment: When a line is not end-stopped—that is, when it carries over to the following line—the line is said to be "enjambed," as in John Milton's: "Avenge, O Lord, thy slaughtered saints, whose bones/ Lie scattered on the Alpine mountains cold." Enjambment is used to change the natural emphasis of the line, to strengthen or weaken the effect of rhyme, or to alter meter.

Envoy: Any short poem or stanza addressed to the reader as a beginning or end to a longer work. Specifically, the envoy is the final stanza of a sestina or a ballade in which all the rhyme words are repeated or echoed.

Epic: A long narrative poem that presents the exploits of a central figure of high position.

Extended metaphor: Metaphors added to one another so that they run in a series. Robert Frost's poem "The Silken Tent" uses an extended metaphor; it compares the "she" of the poem to the freedom and bondage of a silken tent. See also *Controlling image/controlling metaphor.*

Eye rhyme: Words that appear to be identical because of their spelling but that sound different. "Bough/ enough/cough" and "ballet/pallet" are examples. Because of changes in pronunciation, many older poems appear to use eye rhymes but do not. For example, "wind" (meaning moving air) once rhymed with "find." Eye rhymes that are intentional and do not result from a change in pronunciation may be used to create a disconcerting effect.

Fabliau: A bawdy medieval verse, such as many found in Geoffrey Chaucer's *The Canterbury Tales* (1387-1400).

Falling rhyme: Rhyme in which the correspondence of sound comes only in the final unstressed syllable, which is preceded by another unstressed syllable. T. S. Eliot rhymes "me-tic-u-lous" with "ri-dic-u-lous" and creates a falling rhyme. See also *Feminine rhyme; Masculine rhyme.*

Falling rhythm: A line in which feet move from stressed to unstressed syllables (trochaic or dactyllic). An example can be seen in this line from "The Naming

of Parts," by Henry Reed: "Glistens/like cor'al in/all of the/neighboring/gardens." Because English and other Germanic-based languages naturally rise, imposing a falling rhythm on a rising base meter creates counterpointing.

Feminine rhyme: A rhyme pattern in which a line's final accented syllable is followed by a single unaccented syllable and the accented syllables rhyme, while the unaccented syllables are phonetically identical, as with "flick-er/snick-er" and "fin-gers/ma-lin-gers." Feminine rhymes are often used for lightness in tone and delicacy in movement.

Feminist criticism: A criticism advocating equal rights for women in a political, economic, social, psychological, personal, and aesthetic sense. On the thematic level, the feminist reader should identify with female characters and their concerns. The object is to provide a critique of phallocentric assumptions and an analysis of patriarchal ideologies inscribed in male-centered and male-dominated literature. On the ideological level, feminist critics see gender, as well as the stereotypes that go along with it, as a cultural construct. They strive to define a particularly feminine content and to extend the canon so that it might include works by lesbians, feminists, women of color, and women writers in general.

First person: The use of linguistic forms that present a poem from the point of view of the speaker. It is particularly useful in short lyrical poems, which tend to be highly subjective, taking the reader deep into the narrator's thoughts. First-person poems normally, though not necessarily, signal the use of the first person through the pronoun "I," allowing the reader direct access to the narrator's thoughts or providing a character who can convey a personal reaction to an event. See also *Third person.*

Foot/feet: Rhythmic unit in which syllables are grouped together; this is the natural speech pattern in English and other Germanic-based languages. In English, the most common of these rhythmic units is composed of one unstressed syllable attached to one stressed syllable (an iamb). When these family groups are forced into a line of poetry, they are called feet in the accentual-syllabic metrical system. In the line "My mis/tress' eyes/are noth/ing like/the sun" there are four iambic feet (◡ˊ) and one pyrrhic foot (◡◡), but in the line "Thére whére/the vines/clíng crím/son ón/the wáll," there are three substitutions for the iamb—in the first, third, and fourth feet. The six basic feet in English poetry are the iamb (◡ˊ), trochee (ˊ◡), anapest (◡◡ˊ), dactyl (ˊ◡◡), spondee (ˊˊ), and pyrrhus (◡◡).

Form: The arrangement of the lines of a poem on the page, its base meter, its rhyme scheme, and occasionally its subject matter. Poems that are arranged into stanzas are called strophic, and because the strophic tradition is so old, a large number of commonly used stanzas have evolved particular uses and characteristics. Poems that run from beginning to end without a break are called stichic. The form of pattern poetry is determined by its visual appearance rather than by lines and stanzas, while the definition of free verse is that it has no discernible form. Some poem types, such as the sestina, sonnet, and ode, are written in particular forms and frequently are restricted to particular subject matter.

Formalism, Russian: A twentieth century Russian school of criticism that employed the conventional devices used in literature to defamiliarize that which habit has made familiar. The most extreme formalists treated literary works as artifacts or constructs divorced from their biographical and social contexts.

Found poetry: Poems created from language that is "found" in print in nonliterary settings. They can use any language that is already constructed, but usually use language that appears on cultural artifacts, such as cereal boxes. The rules for writing a found poem vary, but generally the found language is used intact or altered only slightly.

Free verse: A poem that does not conform to any traditional convention, such as meter, rhyme, or form, and that does not establish any pattern within itself. There is, however, great dispute over whether "free" verse actually exists. T. S. Eliot said that by definition poetry must establish some kind of pattern, and Robert Frost said that "writing free verse is like playing tennis with the net down." However, some would agree with Carl Sandburg, who insisted that "you can play a better game with the net down." Free verse depends more on cadence than on meter.

Ghazal: A poetic form based on a type of Persian poetry. It is composed of couplets, often unrhymed,

that function as individual images or observations but that also interrelate in sometimes subtle ways.

Gnomic verse: Poetry that typically includes many proverbs or maxims.

Haiku: A Japanese form that appeared in the sixteenth century and is still practiced in Japan. A haiku consists of three lines of five, seven, and five syllables each; in Japanese there are other conventions regarding content that are not observed in Western haiku. The traditional haiku took virtually all of its images from nature, using the natural world as a metaphor for the spiritual.

Half rhyme: See *Approximate rhyme*

Heroic couplet: See *Couplet*

Historical criticism: A school of criticism that emphasizes the historical context of literature. Ernst Robert Curtius's *European Literature and the Latin Middle Ages* (1940) is a prominent example of historical criticism.

Hymn stanza: See *Ballad*

Hyperbole: A deliberate overstatement made in order to heighten the reader's awareness. As with irony, hyperbole works because the reader can perceive the difference between the importance of the dramatic situation and the manner in which it is described.

Iamb: A foot consisting of one unstressed and one stressed syllable (◡ˊ). The line "So lóng/as mén/can bréathe/or eyés/can seé" is composed of five iambs. In the line "Acóld/cóming/we hád/of it," a trochaic foot (a trochee) has been substituted for the expected iamb in the second foot, thus emphasizing that this is a "coming" rather than a "going," an important distinction in T. S. Eliot's "The Journey of the Magi."

Iambic pentameter: A very common poetic line consisting of five iambic feet. The following two lines by Thomas Wyatt are in iambic pentameter: "I find no peace and all my war is done,/ I fear and hope, I burn and freeze like ice." See also *Foot/feet*; *iamb*.

Identical rhyme: A rhyme in which the entire final stressed syllables contain exactly the same sounds, such as "break/brake," or "bear" (noun), "bear" (verb), "bare" (adjective), "bare" (verb).

Imagery: The verbal simulation of sensory perception. Like so many critical terms, imagery betrays a visual bias: It suggests that a poetic image is necessarily visual, a picture in words. In fact, however, imagery calls on all five senses, although the visual is predominant in many poets. In its simplest form, an image recreates a physical sensation in a clear, literal manner, as in Robert Lowell's lines, "A sweetish smell of shavings, wax and oil/ blows through the redone bedroom newly aged" ("Marriage"). Imagery becomes more complex when the poet employs metaphor and other figures of speech to re-create experience, as in Seamus Heaney's lines, "Right along the lough shore/ A smoke of flies/ Drifts thick in the sunset" ("At Ardboe Point"), substituting a fresh metaphor ("A smoke of flies") for a trite one (a cloud of flies) to help the reader visualize the scene more clearly.

Interior monologue: A first-person representation of a persona's or character's thoughts or feelings. It differs from a dramatic monologue in that it deals with thoughts rather than spoken words or conversation.

Internal rhyme: See *Rhyme*

Irony: A figure of speech in which the speaker's real meaning is different from (and often exactly opposite to) the apparent meaning. Irony is among the three or four most important concepts in modern literary criticism. Although the term originated in classical Greece and has been in the vocabulary of criticism since that time, only in the nineteenth and twentieth centuries did it assume central importance. In Andrew Marvell's lines, "The Grave's a fine and private place,/ But none I think do there embrace" ("To His Coy Mistress"), the speaker's literal meaning—in praise of the grave—is quite different from his real meaning. This kind of irony is often called verbal irony. Another kind of irony is found in narrative and dramatic poetry. In the *Iliad* (c. 750 B.C.E.; English translation, 1611), for example, the reader is made privy to the counsels of the gods, which greatly affect the course of action in the epic, while the human characters are kept in ignorance. This discrepancy between the knowledge of the reader and that of the character (or characters) is called dramatic irony. Beyond these narrow, well-defined varieties of irony are many wider applications.

Limerick: A comic five-line poem rhyming *aabba* in which the third and fourth lines are shorter (usually five syllables each) than the first, second, and last lines, which are usually eight syllables each. The limerick's

anapestic base makes the verse sound silly; modern limericks are almost invariably associated with bizarre indecency or with ethnic or anticlerical jokes.

Line: A poetical unit characterized by the presence of meter; lines are categorized according to the number of feet (see *Foot/feet*) they contain. A pentameter line, for example, contains five feet. This definition does not apply to a great deal of modern poetry, however, which is written in free verse. Ultimately, then, a line must be defined as a typographical unit on the page that performs various functions in different kinds of poetry.

Lyric poetry: Short poems, adaptable to metrical variation, and usually personal rather than having a cultural function. Lyric poetry developed when music was accompanied by words, and although the lyrics were later separated from the music, the characteristics of lyric poetry have been shaped by the constraints of music. Lyric poetry sings of the self, exploring deeply personal feelings about life.

Mad-song: Verse uttered by someone presumed to have a severe mental illness that manifests in a happy, harmless, inventive way. The typical rhyme scheme of the mad-song is *abccb*, and the unrhymed first line helps to set a tone of oddity and unpredictability, since it controverts the expectation that there will be a rhyme for it. The standard mad-song has short lines.

Marxist criticism: A school of criticism based on the nineteenth century writings of Karl Marx and Friedrich Engels that views literature as a product of ideological forces determined by the dominant class However, many Marxists believe that literature operates according to its own autonomous standards of production and reception: It is both a product of ideology and able to determine ideology. As such, literature may overcome the dominant paradigms of its age and play a revolutionary role in society.

Masculine rhyme: A rhyme pattern in which rhyme exists in the stressed syllables. "Men/then" constitute masculine rhyme, but so do "af-ter-noons/spoons." Masculine rhyme is generally considered more forceful than feminine rhyme, and while it has a variety of uses, it generally gives authority and assurance to the line, especially when the final syllables are of short duration.

Metaphor: A figure of speech in which two strikingly different things are identified with each other, as in "the waves were soldiers moving" (Wallace Stevens). Metaphor is one of a handful of key concepts in modern literary criticism. A metaphor contains a "tenor" and a "vehicle." The tenor is the subject of the metaphor, and the vehicle is the imagery by which the subject is presented. In D. H. Lawrence's lines, "Reach me a gentian, give me a torch/ let me guide myself with the blue, forked torch of this flower" ("Bavarian Gentians"), the tenor is the gentian and the vehicle is the torch. This relatively restricted definition of metaphor by no means covers the usage of the word in modern criticism. Some critics argue that metaphorical perception underlies all figures of speech. Others dispute the distinction between literal and metaphorical description, saying that language is essentially metaphorical. Metaphor has become widely used to identify analogies of all kinds in literature, painting, film, and even music. See also *Simile*.

Meter: The pattern that language takes when it is forced into a line of poetry. All language has rhythm; when that rhythm is organized and regulated in the line so as to affect the meaning and emotional response to the words, then the rhythm has been refined into meter. Because the lines of most poems maintain a similar meter throughout, poems are said to have a base meter. The meter is determined by the number of syllables in a line and by the relationship between them.

Metrical base. See *Base meter*

Metonymy: Using an object that is closely related to an idea stand for the idea itself, such as saying "the crown" to mean the king. Used to emphasize a particular part of the whole or one particular aspect of it. See also *Synecdoche*.

Mnemonic verse: Poetry in which rhythmic patterns aid memorization but are not crucial to meaning. Ancient bards were able to remember long poems partly through the use of stock phrases and other mnemonic devices.

Mock-heroic: See *Couplet*

Modernism: An international movement in the arts that began in the early years of the twentieth century. Although the term is used to describe artists of widely varying persuasions, modernism in general was characterized by its international idiom, by its interest in cultures distant in space or time, by its emphasis on for-mal experimentation, and by its sense of dislocation and radical change.

Multiculturalism: The tendency to recognize the perspectives of works by authors (particularly women and non-European writers) who, until the latter part of the twentieth century, were excluded from the canon of Western art and literature. To promote multiculturalism, publishers and educators have revised textbooks and school curricula to incorporate material by and about women, ethnic and racial minorities, non-Western cultures, gays, and lesbians.

Myth: Anonymous traditional stories dealing with basic human concepts and antinomies. Claude Lévi-Strauss says that myth is that part of language where the "formula *tradutore, traddittore* reaches its lowest truth value. . . . Its substance does not lie in its style, its original music, or its syntax, but in the story which it tells."

Myth criticism: A school of criticism concerned with the basic structural principles of literature. Myth criticism is not to be confused with mythological criticism, which is primarily concerned with finding mythological parallels in the surface action of a narrative.

Narrator: The person who is doing the talking—or observing or thinking—in a poem. Roughly synonymous with persona and speaker. Lyric poetry most often consists of the poet expressing his or her own personal feelings directly. Other poems, however, may involve the poet adopting the point of view of another person entirely. In some poems—notably in a dramatic monologue—it is relatively easy to determine that the narrative is being related by a fictional (or perhaps historical) character, but in others it may be more difficult to identify the "I."

New Criticism: A formalist movement whose members held that literary criticism is a description and evaluation of its object and that the primary concern of the critic is with the work's unity. At their most extreme, these critics treated literary works as artifacts or constructs divorced from their biographical and social contexts.

Occasional verse: Any poem written for a specific occasion, such as a wedding, a birthday, a death, or a public event. Edmund Spenser's *Epithalamion* (1595), which was written for his marriage, and John Milton's "Lycidas," which commemorated the death of his schoolmate Edward King, are examples of occasional verse, as are W. H. Auden's "September 1, 1939" and Frank O'Hara's "The Day Lady Died."

Octave: A poem in eight lines. Octaves may have many different variations of meter, such as ottava rima.

Ode: A lyric poem that treats a unified subject with elevated emotion, usually ending with a satisfactory resolution. There is no set form for the ode, but it must be long enough to build intense emotional response. Often the ode will address itself to some omnipotent source and will take on a spiritual hue. When explicating an ode, readers should look for the relationship between the narrator and some transcendental power to which the narrator must submit to find contentment. Modern poets have used the ode to treat subjects that are not religious in the theological sense but that have become innate beliefs of society.

Ottava rima: An eight-line stanza of iambic pentameter, rhyming *ababab cc*. Probably the most famous English poem written in ottava rima is Lord Byron's *Don Juan* (1819-1824), and because the poem was so successful as a spoof, the form has come to be associated with poetic high jinks. However, the stanza has also been used brilliantly for just the opposite effect, to reflect seriousness and meditation.

Oxymoron: The juxtaposition of two paradoxical words, such as "wise fool" or "devilish angel."

Pantoum: A French form of poetry consisting of four quatrains in which entire lines are repeated in a strict pattern of 1234, 2546, 5768, 7183. Peter Meinke's "Atomic Pantoum" is an example.

Paradox: A statement that contains an inherent contradiction. It may be a statement that at first seems true but is in reality contradictory. It may also be a statement that appears contradictory but is actually true or that contains an element of truth that reconciles the contradiction.

Pentameter: A type of rhythmic pattern in which each line consists of five poetic feet. See also *Accentual-syllabic meter*; *Foot/feet*; *Iamb*; *Iambic pentameter*; *Line*.

Periphrasis: The use of a wordy phrase to describe something that could be described simply in one word.

Persona: See *Narrator*

Phenomenological criticism: A school of criticism that examines literature as an act and focuses less on individual works and genres. The work is not seen as an object, but rather as part of a strand of latent impulses in the work of a single author or an epoch. Proponents include Georges Poulet in Europe and J. Hillis Miller in the United States.

Point of view: The mental position through which readers experience the situation of a poem. As with fiction, poems may be related in the first person, second person (unusual), or third person. (The presence of the words "I" or "we" indicates singular or plural first-person narration.) Point of view may be limited or omniscient. A limited point of view means that the narrator can see only what the poet wants him or her to see, while from an omniscient point of view the narrator can know everything, including the thoughts and motives of others.

Postcolonialism: The literature that emerged in the mid-twentieth century when colonies in Asia, Africa, and the Caribbean began gaining their independence from the European nations that had long controlled them. Postcolonial authors, such as Salman Rushdie, V. S. Naipaul, and Derek Walcott, tend to focus on both the freedom and the conflict inherent in living in a postcolonial state.

Postmodernism: A ubiquitous but elusive term in contemporary criticism that is loosely applied to the various artistic movements that followed the era of so-called high modernism, represented by such giants as writer James Joyce and painter and sculptor Pablo Picasso. In critical discussions of contemporary fiction, postmodernism is frequently applied to the works of writers such as Thomas Pynchon, John Barth, and Donald Barthelme, who exhibit a self-conscious awareness of their modernist predecessors as well as a reflexive treatment of fictional form. Such reflexive treatments can extend to poetry as well.

Prose poem: A poem that looks like prose on the page, with no line breaks. There are no formal characteristics by which a prose poem can be distinguished from a piece of prose. Many prose poems employ rhythmic repetition and other poetic devices not normally found in prose, but others use such devices sparingly if at all. Prose poems range in length from a few lines to three or four pages; most prose poems occupy a page or less.

Psychological criticism: A school of criticism that places a strong emphasis on a causal relation between the writer's psychological state, variously interpreted, and his or her works. A notable example of psychological criticism is Norman Fruman's *Coleridge, the Damaged Archangel* (1971).

Pun: The use of words that have similar pronunciations but entirely different meanings to establish a connection between two meanings or contexts that the reader would not ordinarily make. The result may be a surprise recognition of an unusual or striking connection, or, more often, a humorously accidental connection.

Pyrrhus: A poetic foot consisting of two unstressed syllables, as in the line "Appéar/and dís/appéar/in the/ blue depth/of the sky," in which foot four is a pyrrhus.

Quatrain: Any four-line stanza. Aside from the couplet, it is the most common stanza type. The quatrain's popularity among both sophisticated and unsophisticated readers suggests that there is something inherently pleasing about the form. For many readers, poetry and quatrains are almost synonymous. Balance and antithesis, contrast and comparison not possible in other stanza types are indigenous to the quatrain.

Realism: A literary technique in which the primary convention is to render an illusion of fidelity to external reality. Realism is often identified as the primary method of the novel form: It focuses on surface details, maintains a fidelity to the everyday experiences of middle-class society, and strives for a one-to-one relationship between the fiction and the action imitated. The realist movement in the late nineteenth century coincides with the full development of the novel form.

Regular meter: A line of poetry that contains only one type of foot. Only the dullest of poems maintain a regular meter throughout, however; skillful poets create interest and emphasis through substitution.

Relative stress: The degree to which a syllable in pattern receives more or less emphasis than other syllables in the pattern. Once the dominant stress in the line has been determined, every other syllable can be assigned a stress factor relative to the dominant syllable. The stress factor is created by several aspects of prosody: the position of the syllable in the line, the position of the syllable in its word, the surrounding syllables, the type of vowels and consonants that constitute the syllable, and the syllable's relation to the foot, base meter, and caesura. Because every syllable will have a different stress factor, there could be as many values as there are syllables, although most prosodists scan poems using primary, secondary, and unstressed notations. In the line "I am there like the dead, or the beast," the anapestic base meter will not permit "I" to take a full stress, but it is a more forceful syllable than the unstressed ones, so it is assigned a secondary stress. Relative to "dead" and "beast," it takes less pressure; relative to the articles in the line, it takes much more.

Resolution: Any natural conclusion to a poem, especially to a short lyric poem that establishes some sort of dilemma or conflict that the narrator must solve. Specifically, the resolution is the octave stanza of a Petrarchan sonnet or the couplet of a Shakespearean sonnet in which the first part of the poem presents a situation that must find balance in the resolution.

Rhyme: A correspondence of sound between syllables within a line or between lines whose proximity to each other allows the sounds to be sustained. Rhyme may be classified in a number of ways: according to the sound relationship between rhyming words, the position of the rhyming words in the line, and the number and position of the syllables in the rhyming words. Sound classifications include full rhyme and approximate rhyme. Full rhyme is defined as words that have the same vowel sound, followed by the same consonants in their last stressed syllables, and in which all succeeding syllables are phonetically identical. "Hat/ cat" and "laughter/after" are full rhymes. Categories of approximate rhyme are assonance, slant rhyme, alliteration, eye rhyme, and identical rhyme.

Rhyme classified by its position in the line includes end, internal, and initial rhyme. End rhyme occurs when the last words of lines rhyme. Internal rhyme occurs when two words within the same line or within various lines recall the same sound, as in "Wet, below the snow line, smelling of vegetation" in which "below" and "snow" rhyme. Initial rhyme occurs when the first syllables of two or more lines rhyme. See also *Masculine rhyme*; *Feminine rhyme*.

Rhyme scheme: A pattern of rhyme in a poem, designated by lowercase (and often italicized) letters. The letters stand for the pattern of rhyming sounds of the last word in each line. For example, the following A. E. Housman quatrain has an *abab* rhyme scheme.

> Into my heart an air that kills
> From yon far country blows:
> What are those blue remembered hills,
> What spires, what farms are those?

As another example, the rhyme scheme of the poetic form known as ottava rima is *abababcc*. Traditional stanza forms are categorized by their rhyme scheme and base meter.

Rime royal: A seven-line stanza in English prosody consisting of iambic pentameter lines rhyming *ababbcc*. William Shakespeare's *The Rape of Lucrece* (1594) is written in this form. The only variation permitted is to make the last line hexameter.

Romanticism: A widespread cultural movement in the late eighteenth and early nineteenth centuries, the influence of which is still felt. As a general literary tendency, Romanticism is frequently contrasted with classicism or neoclassicism. Although there were many varieties of Romanticism indigenous to various national literatures, the term generally suggests an assertion of the preeminence of the imagination. Other values associated with various schools of Romanticism include primitivism, an interest in folklore, a reverence for nature, and a fascination with the demoniac and the macabre.

Rondeau: One of three standard French forms assimilated by English prosody; generally contains thirteen lines divided into three groups. A common stanzaic grouping rhymes *aabba, aabR, aabbaR*, where the *a* and *b* lines are tetrameter and the *R* (refrain) lines are dimeter. The rondel, another French form, contains fourteen lines of trimeter with alternating rhyme (*abababa bababab*) and is divided into two stanzas. The rondeau and rondel forms are always light and playful.

Rondel: See *Rondeau*

Rubaiyat stanza: An iambic pentameter quatrain that has a rhyme scheme of *aaba*.

Scansion: The assigning of relative stresses and meter to a line of poetry, usually for the purpose of determining where variations, and thus emphasis, in the base meter occur. Scansion can help explain how a poem generates tension and offer clues as to the key words. E. E. Cummings's "singing each morning out of each night" could be scanned in two ways: (1) singing/each morn/ing out/of each night or (2) sing/ing each/morning/out of/each night. Scansion will not only affect the way the line is read aloud but also influences the meaning of the line.

Secondary stress: See *Relative stress*

Seguidilla: An imagistic or mood poem in Spanish, which, like a haiku, creates emotional recognition or spiritual insight in the reader. Although there is no agreement as to what form the English seguidilla should take, most of the successful ones are either four or seven lines with an alternating rhyme scheme of *ababcbc*. Lines 1, 3, and 6 are trimeter; lines 2, 4, 5, and 7 dimeter.

Semiotics: The science of signs and sign systems in communication. Literary critic Roman Jakobson says that semiotics deals with the principles that underlie the structure of signs, their use in language of all kinds, and the specific nature of various sign systems.

Sestet: A six-line stanza. A Petrarchan or Italian sonnet is composed of an octave followed by a sestet.

Sestina: Six six-line stanzas followed by a three-line envoy. The words ending the lines in the first stanza are repeated in different order at the ends of lines in the following stanzas as well as in the middle and end of each line of the envoy. Elizabeth Bishop's "Sestina" is a good example.

Shakespearean sonnet: See *Sonnet*

Simile: A type of metaphor that signals a comparison by the use of the words "like" or "as." William Shakespeare's line "My mistress' eyes are nothing like the sun" is a simile that establishes a comparison between the woman's eyes and the sun. See also *Metaphor*.

Slant rhyme: See *Approximate rhyme*

Sonnet: A poem consisting of fourteen lines of iambic pentameter with some form of alternating rhyme and a turning point that divides the poem into two parts. The sonnet is the most important and widely used of traditional poem types. The two major sonnet types are the Petrarchan (or Italian) sonnet and the Shakespearean sonnet. The original sonnet form, the Petrarchan (adopted from the poetry of Petrarch), presents a problem or situation in the first eight lines, the octave, then resolves it in the last six, the sestet. The octave is composed of two quatrains (*abbaabba*), the second of which complicates the first and gradually defines and heightens the problem. The sestet then diminishes the problem slowly until a satisfying resolution is achieved.

During the fifteenth century, the Italian sonnet became an integral part of the courtship ritual, and most sonnets during that time consisted of a young man's description of his perfect lover. Because so many unpoetic young men had generated a nation full of bad sonnets by the end of the century, the form became an object of ridicule, and the English sonnet developed as a reaction against all the bad verse being turned out in the Italian tradition. When Shakespeare wrote "My mistress' eyes are nothing like the sun," he was deliberately negating the Petrarchan conceit, rejoicing in the fact that his loved one was much more interesting and unpredictable than nature. Shakespeare also altered the sonnet's formal balance. Instead of an octave, the Shakespearean sonnet has three quatrains of alternating rhyme and is resolved in a final couplet. During the sixteenth century, long stories were told in sonnet form, one sonnet after the next, to produce sonnet sequences. Although most sonnets contain fourteen lines, some contain as few as ten (the curtal sonnet) or as many as seventeen.

Speaker: See *Narrator*

Split foot: The alteration of the natural division of a word as a result of being forced into a metrical base. For example, the words "point/ed," "lad/der," and "stick/ing" have a natural falling rhythm, but in the line "My long/two-point/ed lad/der's stick/ing through/a tree" the syllables are rearranged so as to turn the falling rhythm into a rising meter. The result of splitting feet is to create an uncertainty and delicate imbalance in the line.

Spondee: When two relatively stressed syllables occur together in a foot, the unit is called a spondee or spondaic foot, as in the line "Appear/and dis/appear/in the/blue depth/of the sky."

Sprung rhythm: An unpredictable pattern of stresses in a line, first described near the end of the nineteenth century by Gerard Manley Hopkins, that results from taking accentual meter is to its extreme. According to Hopkins, in sprung rhythm "any two stresses may either follow one another running, or be divided by one, two, or three slack syllables."

Stanza: A certain number of lines meant to be taken as a unit, or that unit. Although a stanza is traditionally considered a unit that contains rhyme and recurs predictably throughout a poem, the term is also sometimes applied to nonrhyming and even irregular units. Poems that are divided into fairly regular and patterned stanzas are called strophic; poems that appear as a single unit, whether rhymed or unrhymed, or that have no predictable stanzas, are called stichic. Both strophic and stichic units represent logical divisions within the poem, and the difference between them lies in the formality and strength of the interwoven unit. Stanza breaks are commonly indicated by a line of space.

Stichic verse: See *Stanza*

Stress: See *Relative stress*

Strophic verse: See *Stanza*

Structuralism: A movement based on the idea of intrinsic, self-sufficient structures that do not require reference to external elements. A structure is a system of transformations that involves the interplay of laws inherent in the system itself. The study of language is the primary model for contemporary structuralism. The structuralist literary critic attempts to define structural principles that operate intertextually throughout the whole of literature as well as principles that operate in genres and in individual works. The most accessible survey of structuralism and literature is Jonathan Culler's *Structuralist Poetics* (1975).

Substitution: The replacement of one type of foot by another within a base meter. One of the most common and effective methods by which the poet can emphasize a foot. For example, in the line "Thy life/a long/dead calm/of fixed/repose," a spondaic foot (´ ´) has been substituted for an iambic foot (˘ ´). Before substitution is possible, the reader's expectations must have been established by a base meter so that a change in those expectations will have an effect. See also *Foot/feet*; *iamb*; *spondee*.

Syllabic meter: The system of meter that measures only the number of syllables per line, without regard to stressed and unstressed syllables.

Symbol: Any sign that a number of people agree stands for something else. Poetic symbols cannot be rigidly defined; a symbol often evokes a cluster of meanings rather than a single specific meaning. For example, the rose, which suggests fragile beauty, gentleness, softness, and sweet aroma, has come to symbolize love, eternal beauty, or virginity. The tide traditionally symbolizes, among other things, time and eternity. Modern poets may use personal symbols; these take on significance in the context of the poem or of a poet's body of work, particularly if they are reinforced throughout. For example, through constant reinforcement, swans in William Butler Yeats's poetry come to mean as much to the reader as they do to the narrator.

Synaeresis: See *Elision*

Synecdoche: The use of a part of an object to stand for the entire object, such as using "heart" to mean a person. Used to emphasize a particular part of the whole or one particular aspect of it. See also *Metonymy*.

Tenor: See *Metaphor*

Tercet: Any form of a rhyming triplet. Examples are *aaa bbb*, as used in Thomas Hardy's "Convergence of the Twain"; *aba cdc*, in which *b* and *d* do not rhyme; *aba bcb*, also known as terza rima.

Terza rima: A three-line stanzaic form in which the middle line of one stanza rhymes with the first line of the following stanza, and whose rhyme scheme is *aba bcb cdc*, and so on. Since the rhyme scheme of one stanza can be completed only by adding the next stanza, terza rima tends to propel itself forward, and as a result of this strong forward motion it is well suited to long narration.

Theme: Recurring elements in a poem that give it meaning; sometimes used interchangeably with motif. A motif is any recurring pattern of images, symbols, ideas, or language, and is usually restricted to the internal workings of the poem. Thus, one might say that there is an animal motif in William Butler Yeats's poem "Sailing to Byzantium." Theme, however, is usually more general and philosophical, so that the theme of "Sailing to Byzantium" might be interpreted as the failure of human attempts to isolate oneself within the world of art.

Third person: The use of linguistic forms that present a poem from the point of view of a narrator, or speaker, who has not been part of the events described and is not probing his or her own relationship to them; rather, the speaker is describing what happened without the use of the word "I" (which would indicate first-person narration). A poet may use a third-person point of view, either limited or omniscient, to establish a distance between the reader and the subject, to give credi-

bility to a large expanse of narration, or to allow the poem to include a number of characters who can be commented on by the narrator.

Tone: The expression of a poet's attitude toward the subject and persona of the poem as well as about himself or herself, society, and the poem's readers. If the ultimate aim of art is to express and control emotions and attitudes, then tone is one of the most important elements of poetry. Tone is created through the denotative and connotative meanings of words and through the sound of language (principally rhyme, consonants, and diction). Adjectives such as "satirical," "compassionate," "empathetic," "ironic," and "sarcastic" are used to describe tone.

Trochee: A foot with one stressed syllable and one unstressed syllable (´˘), as in the line: "Double/double toil and/trouble." Trochaic lines are frequently substituted in an iambic base meter in order to create counterpointing. See also *Foot/feet; iamb*.

Truncation: The omission of the last, unstressed syllable of a falling line, as in the line: "Tyger,/tyger/ burning/bright," where the "ly" has been dropped from bright.

Vehicle: See *Metaphor*

Verse: A generic term for poetry, as in *The Oxford Book of English Verse* (1939); poetry that is humorous or superficial, as in light verse or greeting-card verse; and a stanza or line.

Verse drama: Drama that is written in poetic rather than ordinary language and characterized and delivered by the line. Verse drama flourished during the eighteenth century, when the couplet became a standard literary form.

Verse paragraph: A division created within a stichic poem (see *Stanza*) by logic or syntax, rather than by form. Such divisions are important for determining the movement of a poem and the logical association between ideas.

Villanelle: A French verse form that has been assimilated by English prosody, usually composed of nineteen lines divided into five tercets and a quatrain, rhyming *aba, bba, aba, aba, abaa*. The third line is repeated in the ninth and fifteenth lines. Dylan Thomas's "Do Not Go Gentle into That Good Night" is a modern English example of a villanelle.

BIBLIOGRAPHY

CONTENTS

ABOUT THIS BIBLIOGRAPHY

This bibliography contains three main sections. The first, "General Reference Sources," lists books that treat poetry of all time periods and countries, including American poets. The section "History of American Poetry" includes sources primarily relevant to American poetry written in three different eras. The final section, "Ethnic and Other Groups," is divided into four ethnic groups (with added subdivisions for African American poets), U.S. regional poets, and American women.

GENERAL REFERENCE SOURCES

BIOGRAPHICAL SOURCES

Alfonsi, Ferdinando. *Dictionary of Italian-American Poets*. American University Studies. Series II, Romance Languages and Literature 112. New York: Peter Lang, 1989.

Baughman, Ronald, ed. *American Poets*. Vol. 3 in *Contemporary Authors: Bibliographical Series*. Detroit: Gale Research, 1986.

Bold, Alan. *Longman Dictionary of Poets: The Lives and Works of 1001 Poets in the English Language*. Harlow, Essex: Longman, 1985.

Colby, Vineta, ed. *World Authors, 1975-1980*. Wilson Authors Series. New York: H. W. Wilson, 1985.

_____. *World Authors, 1980-1985*. Wilson Authors Series. New York: H. W. Wilson, 1991.

_____. *World Authors, 1985-1990*. Wilson Authors Series. New York: H. W. Wilson, 1995.

Conte, Joseph, ed. *American Poets Since World War II: Fourth Series*. Dictionary of Literary Biography 165. Detroit: Gale Research, 1996.

_____. *American Poets Since World War II: Fifth Series*. Dictionary of Literary Biography 169. Detroit: Gale Research, 1996.

_____. *American Poets Since World War II: Sixth Series*. Dictionary of Literary Biography 193. Detroit: Gale Research, 1998.

Cyclopedia of World Authors. 4th rev. ed. 5 vols. Pasadena, Calif.: Salem Press, 2003.

Dictionary of Literary Biography. 254 vols. Detroit: Gale Research, 1978-   .

Greiner, Donald J., ed. *American Poets Since World War II*. Dictionary of Literary Biography 5. Detroit: Gale Research, 1980.

Gwynn, R. S., ed. *American Poets Since World War II: Second Series*. Dictionary of Literary Biography 105. Detroit: Gale Research, 1991.

_____. *American Poets Since World War II: Third Series*. Dictionary of Literary Biography 120. Detroit: Gale Research, 1992.

International Who's Who in Poetry and Poets' Encyclopaedia. Cambridge, England: International Biographical Centre, 1993.

Quartermain, Peter, ed. *American Poets, 1880-1945: First Series*. Dictionary of Literary Biography 45. Detroit: Gale Research, 1986.

_____. *American Poets, 1880-1945: Second Series*. Dictionary of Literary Biography 48. Detroit: Gale Research, 1986.

_____. *American Poets, 1880-1945: Third Series*. Dictionary of Literary Biography 54. Detroit: Gale Research, 1987.

Riggs, Thomas, ed. *Contemporary Poets*. Contemporary Writers Series. 7th ed. Detroit: St. James Press, 2001.

Seymour-Smith, Martin, and Andrew C. Kimmens, eds. *World Authors, 1900-1950*. Wilson Authors Series. 4 vols. New York: H. W. Wilson, 1996.

Thompson, Clifford, ed. *World Authors, 1990-1995*. Wilson Authors Series. New York: H. W. Wilson, 1999.

Wakeman, John, ed. *World Authors, 1950-1970*. New York: H. W. Wilson, 1975.

_____. *World Authors, 1970-1975*. Wilson Authors Series. New York: H. W. Wilson, 1991.

Willhardt, Mark, and Alan Michael Parker, eds. *Who's Who in Twentieth Century World Poetry*. New York: Routledge, 2000.

CRITICISM

Alexander, Harriet Semmes, comp. *American and British Poetry: A Guide to the Criticism, 1925-1978*. Manchester, England: Manchester University Press, 1984.

_____. *American and British Poetry: A Guide to the Criticism, 1979-1990*. 2 vols. Athens, Ohio: Swallow Press, 1995.

Annual Bibliography of English Language and Literature. Cambridge, England: Modern Humanities Research Association, 1920-   .

Brooks, Cleanth, and Robert Penn Warren. *Understanding Poetry*. 4th ed. Reprint. Fort Worth, Tex.: Heinle & Heinle, 2003.

Childs, Peter. *The Twentieth Century in Poetry: A Critical Survey*. New York: Routledge, 1999.

Cline, Gloria Stark, and Jeffrey A. Baker. *An Index to Criticism of British and American Poetry*. Metuchen, N.J.: Scarecrow Press, 1973.

Coleman, Arthur. *Epic and Romance Criticism: A Checklist of Interpretations, 1940-1972*. New York: Watermill Publishers, 1973.

Contemporary Literary Criticism. Detroit: Gale Research, 1973-   .

Day, Gary. *Literary Criticism: A New History*. Edinburgh, Scotland: Edinburgh University Press, 2008.

Donow, Herbert S., comp. *The Sonnet in England and America: A Bibliography of Criticism*. Westport, Conn.: Greenwood Press, 1982.

Draper, James P., ed. *World Literature Criticism 1500 to the Present: A Selection of Major Authors from Gale's Literary Criticism Series*. 6 vols. Detroit: Gale Research, 1992.

Guide to American Poetry Explication. Reference Publication in Literature. 2 vols. Boston: G. K. Hall, 1989.

Habib, M. A. R. *A History of Literary Criticism: From Plato to the Present*. Malden, Mass.: Wiley-Blackwell, 2005.

Jason, Philip K., ed. *Masterplots II: Poetry Series, Revised Edition*. 8 vols. Pasadena, Calif.: Salem Press, 2002.

Kuntz, Joseph M., and Nancy C. Martinez. *Poetry Explication: A Checklist of Interpretation Since 1925 of British and American Poems Past and Present*. 3d ed. Boston: Hall, 1980.

Lodge, David, and Nigel Wood. *Modern Criticism and Theory*. 3d ed. New York: Longman, 2008.

Magill, Frank N., ed. *Magill's Bibliography of Literary Criticism*. 4 vols. Englewood Cliffs, N.J.: Salem Press, 1979.

MLA International Bibliography. New York: Modern Language Association of America, 1922-   .

Nineteenth-Century Literature Criticism. Detroit: Gale Research, 1981-   .

Roberts, Neil, ed. *A Companion to Twentieth-Century Poetry*. Malden, Mass.: Blackwell Publishers, 2001.

Twentieth-Century Literary Criticism. Detroit: Gale Research, 1978-   .

Vedder, Polly, ed. *World Literature Criticism Supplement: A Selection of Major Authors from Gale's Literary Criticism Series.* 2 vols. Detroit: Gale Research, 1997.

Walcutt, Charles Child, and J. Edwin Whitesell, eds. *Modern Poetry.* Vol. 1 in *The Explicator Cyclopedia.* Chicago: Quadrangle Books, 1968.

The Year's Work in English Studies. 1921-   .

Young, Robyn V., ed. *Poetry Criticism: Excerpts from Criticism of the Works of the Most Significant and Widely Studied Poets of World Literature.* 29 vols. Detroit: Gale Research, 1991.

DICTIONARIES, HISTORIES, AND HANDBOOKS

Carey, Gary, and Mary Ellen Snodgrass. *A Multicultural Dictionary of Literary Terms.* Jefferson, N.C.: McFarland, 1999.

Deutsch, Babette. *Poetry Handbook: A Dictionary of Terms.* 4th ed. New York: Funk & Wagnalls, 1974.

Draper, Ronald P. *An Introduction to Twentieth-Century Poetry in English.* New York: St. Martin's Press, 1999.

Drury, John. *The Poetry Dictionary.* Cincinnati, Ohio: Story Press, 1995.

Gingerich, Martin E. *Contemporary Poetry in America and England, 1950-1975: A Guide to Information Sources.* American Literature, English Literature, and World Literatures in English: An Information Guide Series 41. Detroit: Gale Research, 1983.

Hamilton, Ian, ed. *The Oxford Companion to Twentieth-Century Poetry in English.* New York: Oxford University Press, 1994.

Kamp, Jim, ed. *Reference Guide to American Literature.* 3d ed. Detroit: St. James Press, 1994.

Kinzie, Mary. *A Poet's Guide to Poetry.* Chicago: University of Chicago Press, 1999.

Lennard, John. *The Poetry Handbook: A Guide to Reading Poetry for Pleasure and Practical Criticism.* New York: Oxford University Press, 1996.

Matterson, Stephen, and Darryl Jones. *Studying Poetry.* New York: Oxford University Press, 2000.

Packard, William. *The Poet's Dictionary: A Handbook of Prosody and Poetic Devices.* New York: Harper & Row, 1989.

Parini, Jay, ed. *The Columbia History of American Poetry.* New York: Columbia University Press, 1993.

Perkins, David. *From the 1890's to the High Modernist Mode.* Vol. 1 in *A History of Modern Poetry.* Cambridge, Mass.: Belknap-Harvard University Press, 1976.

_____. *Modernism and After.* Vol. 2 in *A History of Modern Poetry.* 2 vols. Cambridge, Mass.: Belknap-Harvard University Press, 1987.

Perkins, George, Barbara Perkins, and Phillip Leininger, eds. *Benét's Reader's Encyclopedia of American Literature.* New York: HarperCollins, 1991.

Preminger, Alex, et al., eds. *The New Princeton Encyclopedia of Poetry and Poetics.* 3d rev. ed. Princeton, N.J.: Princeton University Press, 1993.

Shipley, Joseph Twadell, ed. *Dictionary of World Literary Terms, Forms, Technique, Criticism.* Rev. ed. Boston: Writer, 1970.

Shucard, Alan. *American Poetry: The Puritans Through Walt Whitman.* Twayne's Critical History of Poetry Series. Boston: Twayne, 1988.

Waggoner, Hyatt H. *American Poets from the Puritans to the Present.* Rev. ed. Baton Rouge: Louisiana University Press, 1984.

INDEXES OF PRIMARY WORKS

American Poetry Index: An Author, Title, and Subject Guide to Poetry by Americans in Single-Author Collections. Great Neck, N.Y.: Granger, 1983-1988.

Annual Index to Poetry in Periodicals. Great Neck, N.Y.: Poetry Index Press, 1985-1988.

Caskey, Jefferson D., comp. *Index to Poetry in Popular Periodicals, 1955-1959.* Westport, Conn.: Greenwood Press, 1984.

Frankovich, Nicholas, ed. *The Columbia Granger's Index to Poetry in Anthologies.* 11th ed. New York: Columbia University Press, 1997.

_____. *The Columbia Granger's Index to Poetry in Collected and Selected Works.* New York: Columbia University Press, 1997.

Guy, Patricia. *A Women's Poetry Index.* Phoenix, Ariz.: Oryx Press, 1985.

Hazen, Edith P., ed. *Columbia Granger's Index to Po-*

etry. 10th ed. New York: Columbia University Press, 1994.

Hoffman, Herbert H., and Rita Ludwig Hoffman, comps. *International Index to Recorded Poetry*. New York: H. W. Wilson, 1983.

Index of American Periodical Verse. Lanham, Md.: Scarecrow, 1971.

Index to Poetry in Periodicals: American Poetic Renaissance, 1915-1919: An Index of Poets and Poems Published in American Magazines and Newspapers. Great Neck, N.Y.: Granger, 1981.

Index to Poetry in Periodicals, 1920-1924: An Index of Poets and Poems Published in American Magazines and Newspapers. Great Neck, N.Y.: Granger, 1983.

Index to Poetry in Periodicals, 1925-1992: An Index of Poets and Poems Published in American Magazines and Newspapers. Great Neck, N.Y.: Granger, 1984.

Kline, Victoria. *Last Lines: An Index to the Last Lines of Poetry*. 2 vols. Vol. 1, *Last Line Index, Title Index*; Vol. 2, *Author Index, Keyword Index*. New York: Facts On File, 1991.

Marcan, Peter. *Poetry Themes: A Bibliographical Index to Subject Anthologies and Related Criticisms in the English Language, 1875-1975*. Hamden, Conn.: Linnet Books, 1977.

Poem Finder. Great Neck, N.Y.: Roth, 2000.

Poetry Index Annual: A Title, Author, First Line, Keyword, and Subject Index to Poetry in Anthologies. Great Neck, N.Y.: Poetry Index, 1982-   .

POETICS, POETIC FORMS, AND GENRES

Attridge, Derek. *Poetic Rhythm: An Introduction*. New York: Cambridge University Press, 1995.

Brogan, T. V. F. *English Versification, 1570-1980: A Reference Guide with a Global Appendix*. Baltimore: Johns Hopkins University Press, 1981.

_____. *Verseform: A Comparative Bibliography*. Baltimore: Johns Hopkins University Press, 1989.

Fussell, Paul. *Poetic Meter and Poetic Form*. Rev. ed. New York: McGraw-Hill, 1979.

Hollander, John. *Rhyme's Reason*. 3d ed. New Haven, Conn.: Yale University Press, 2001.

Malof, Joseph. *A Manual of English Meters*. Bloomington: Indiana University Press, 1970.

Padgett, Ron, ed. *The Teachers and Writers Handbook of Poetic Forms*. 2d ed. New York: Teachers & Writers Collaborative, 2000.

Pinsky, Robert. *The Sounds of Poetry: A Brief Guide*. New York: Farrar, Straus and Giroux, 1998.

Preminger, Alex, and T. V. F. Brogan, eds. *New Princeton Encyclopedia of Poetry and Poetics*. 3d ed. Princeton, N.J.: Princeton University Press, 1993.

Shapiro, Karl, and Robert Beum. *A Prosody Handbook*. New York: Harper, 1965.

Spiller, Michael R. G. *The Sonnet Sequence: A Study of Its Strategies*. Studies in Literary Themes and Genres 13. New York: Twayne, 1997.

Turco, Lewis. *The New Book of Forms: A Handbook of Poetics*. Hanover, N.H.: University Press of New England, 1986.

Williams, Miller. *Patterns of Poetry: An Encyclopedia of Forms*. Baton Rouge: Louisiana State University Press, 1986.

HISTORY OF AMERICAN POETRY

COLONIAL TO 1800

Lemay, J. A. Leo. *A Calendar of American Poetry in the Colonial Newspapers and Magazines and in the Major English Magazines Through 1765*. Worcester, Mass.: American Antiquarian Society, 1972.

Scheick, William J., and JoElla Doggett. *Seventeenth-*

Century American Poetry: A Reference Guide. Reference Guides in Literature 14. Boston: G. K. Hall, 1977.

Wegelin, Oscar. *Early American Poetry: A Compilation of the Titles of Volumes of Verse and Broadsides by Writers Born or Residing in North Amer-*

ica, North of the Mexican Border, 1650-1820. 2d ed. 2 vols. New York: Smith, 1930.

NINETEENTH CENTURY

Bennett, Paula, Karen L. Kilcup, and Philipp Schweighauser. *Teaching Nineteenth-Century American Poetry*. New York: Modern Language Association of America, 2007.

Haralson, Eric L., ed. *Encyclopedia of American Poetry: The Nineteenth Century*. Chicago: Fitzroy Dearborn, 1998.

Jason, Philip K. *Nineteenth Century American Poetry: An Annotated Bibliography*. Pasadena, Calif.: Salem Press, 1989.

Lee, A. Robert, ed. *Nineteenth-Century American Poetry*. Critical Studies Series. Totowa, N.J.: Barnes & Noble, 1985.

Olson, Steven. *The Prairie in Nineteenth Century American Poetry*. Norman: University of Oklahoma Press, 1995.

Ruppert, James. *Colonial and Nineteenth Century*. Vol. 1 in *Guide to American Poetry Explication*. Boston: G. K. Hall, 1989.

Sorby, Angela. *Schoolroom Poets: Childhood and the Place of American Poetry, 1865-1917*. Durham: University of New Hampshire Press, 2005.

TWENTIETH CENTURY AND CONTEMPORARY

Altieri, Charles. *The Art of Twentieth-Century American Poetry: Modernism and After*. Malden, Mass.: Blackwell, 2006.

Axelrod, Steven Gould, and Camille Roman, eds. *Modernisms, 1900-1950*. Vol. 2 in *The New Anthology of American Poetry*. New Brunswick, N.J.: Rutgers University Press, 2005.

Beach, Christopher. *The Cambridge Introduction to Twentieth-Century American Poetry*. New York: Cambridge University Press, 2003.

Davis, Lloyd, and Robert Irwin. *Contemporary American Poetry: A Checklist*. Metuchen, N.J.: Scarecrow Press, 1975.

Gioia, Dana, David Mason, and Meg Schoerke, eds. *Twentieth-Century American Poetics: Poets on the Art of Poetry*. Boston: McGraw-Hill, 2004.

_____. *Twentieth-Century American Poetry*. Boston: McGraw-Hill, 2003.

Green, Scott E. *Contemporary Science Fiction, Fantasy, and Horror Poetry: A Resource Guide and Biographical Directory*. New York: Greenwood Press, 1989.

Haralson, Eric L., ed. *Encyclopedia of American Poetry: The Twentieth Century*. Chicago: Fitzroy Dearborn, 2001.

Kane, Daniel. *All Poets Welcome: The Lower East Side Poetry Scene in the 1960's*. Berkeley: University of California Press, 2003.

Kirsch, Adam. *The Wounded Surgeon: Confession and Transformation in Six American Poets*. New York: W. W. Norton, 2005.

Leo, John R. *Modern and Contemporary*. Vol. 2 in *Guide to American Poetry Explication*. Boston: G. K. Hall, 1989.

McPheron, William. *The Bibliography of Contemporary American Poetry, 1945-1985: An Annotated Checklist*. Westport, Conn.: Meckler, 1986.

Moramarco, Fred, and William Sullivan. *Containing Multitudes: Poetry in the United States Since 1950*. Critical History of Poetry Series. New York: Twayne, 1998.

Rasula, Jed. *This Compost: Ecological Imperatives in American Poetry*. Athens: University of Georgia Press, 2002.

Shucard, Alan, Fred Moramarco, and William Sullivan. *Modern American Poetry, 1865-1950*. Boston: Twayne, 1989.

Ward, Geoffrey. *Statutes of Liberty: The New York School of Poets*. New York: Palgrave Macmillan, 2001.

ETHNIC AND OTHER GROUPS

AFRICAN AMERICAN POETS
Biographical sources
Harris, Trudier, ed. *Afro-American Writers Before the Harlem Renaissance*. Dictionary of Literary Biography 50. Detroit: Gale Research, 1986.

_____. *Afro-American Writers from the Harlem Renaissance to 1940*. Dictionary of Literary Biography 51. Detroit: Gale Research, 1987.

Harris, Trudier, and Thadious M. Davis, eds. *Afro-American Poets Since 1955*. Dictionary of Literary Biography 41. Detroit: Gale Research, 1985.

Indexes of primary works
Chapman, Dorothy Hilton, comp. *Index to Black Poetry*. Boston, G. K. Hall, 1974.

Frankovich, Nicholas, and David Larzelere, eds. *The Columbia Granger's Index to African-American Poetry*. New York: Columbia University Press, 1999.

Dictionaries, histories, and handbooks
French, William P., et al. *Afro-American Poetry and Drama, 1760-1975: A Guide to Information Sources*. American Literature, English Literature, and World Literatures in English: An Information Guide Series 17. Detroit: Gale Research, 1979.

Major, Clarence, ed. *The Garden Thrives: Twentieth Century African-American Poetry*. New York: HarperPerennial, 1996.

Rampersad, Arnold, and Hilary Herbold, eds. *The Oxford Anthology of African-American Poetry*. New York: Oxford University Press, 2005.

Sherman, Joan R. *Invisible Poets: Afro-Americans of the Nineteenth Century*. 2d ed. Urbana: University of Illinois Press, 1989.

Wagner, Jean, and Kenneth Douglas, trans. *Black Poets of the United States: From Paul Laurence Dunbar to Langston Hughes*. Urbana: University of Illinois Press, 1973.

Women writers
Chapman, Dorothy Hilton, comp. *Index to Poetry by Black American Women*. Bibliographies and Indexes in Afro-American and African Studies 15. New York: Greenwood Press, 1986.

Lee, Valerie, ed. *The Prentice Hall Anthology of African American Women's Literature*. Upper Saddle River, N.J.: Pearson Prentice Hall, 2006.

ASIAN AMERICAN POETS
Chang, Juliana, ed. *Quiet Fire: A Historical Anthology of Asian American Poetry, 1892-1970*. New York: Asian American Writers' Workshop, 1996.

Chang, Victoria, ed. *Asian American Poetry: The Next Generation*. Urbana: University of Illinois Press, 2004.

Cheung, King-Kok, ed. *An Interethnic Companion to Asian American Literature*. New York: Cambridge University Press, 1997.

Cheung, King-Kok, and Stan Yogi. *Asian American Literature: An Annotated Bibliography*. New York: MLA, 1988.

Huang, Guiyou, ed. *Asian American Poets: A Bio-Bibliographical Critical Sourcebook*. Westport, Conn.: Greenwood Press, 2002.

Yu, Timothy. *Race and the Avant-Garde: Experimental and Asian American Poetry Since 1965*. Stanford, Calif.: Stanford University Press, 2009.

Zhou, Xiaojing. *The Ethics and Poetics of Alterity in Asian American Poetry*. Iowa City: University of Iowa Press, 2006.

LATINO POETS
Aragón, Francisco, ed. *The Wind Shifts: New Latino Poetry*. Tucson: University of Arizona Press, 2007.

Bleznick, Donald William. *A Sourcebook for Hispanic Literature and Language: A Selected, Annotated Guide to Spanish, Spanish-American, and United States Hispanic Bibliography, Literature, Linguistics, Journals, and Other Source Materials*. 3d ed. Lanham, Md.: Scarecrow Press, 1995.

Candelaria, Cordelia. *Chicano Poetry: A Critical Introduction*. Westport, Conn.: Greenwood Press, 1986.

Dick, Bruce Allen, ed. *A Poet's Truth: Conversations with Latino/Latina Poets*. Tucson: University of Arizona Press, 2003.

Eger, Ernestina N. *A Bibliography of Criticism of Con-

temporary Chicano Literature. Berkeley: Chicano Library Publications, University of California, 1982.

Kanellos, Nicolás, ed. *Biographical Dictionary of Hispanic Literature in the United States: The Literature of Puerto Ricans, Cuban Americans, and Other Hispanic Writers*. New York: Greenwood Press, 1989.

Lomelí, Francisco A., and Carl R. Shirley, eds. *Chicano Writers: First Series*. Dictionary of Literary Biography 82. Detroit: Gale Research, 1989.

_____. *Chicano Writers: Second Series*. Dictionary of Literary Biography 122. Detroit: Gale Research, 1992.

_____. *Chicano Writers: Third Series*. Dictionary of Literary Biography 209. Detroit: Gale Group, 1999.

Martínez, Julio A., and Francisco A. Lomelí, eds. *Chicano Literature: A Reference Guide*. Westport, Conn.: Greenwood Press, 1985.

NATIVE AMERICAN POETS

Fast, Robin Riley. *The Heart as a Drum: Continuance and Resistance in American Indian Poetry*. Ann Arbor: University of Michigan Press, 1999.

Howard, Helen Addison. *American Indian Poetry*. Twayne's United States Authors Series 334. Boston: Twayne, 1979.

Littlefield, Daniel F., Jr., and James W. Parins. *A Biobibliography of Native American Writers, 1772-1924*. Native American Bibliography Series 2. Metuchen, N.J.: Scarecrow Press, 1981.

_____. *A Biobibliography of Native American Writers, 1772-1924: Supplement*. Native American Bibliography Series 5. Metuchen, N.J.: Scarecrow Press, 1985.

Lundquist, Suzanne Evertsen. *Native American Literatures: An Introduction*. New York: Continuum, 2004.

Porter, Joy, and Kenneth M. Roemer, eds. *The Cambridge Companion to Native American Literature*. New York: Cambridge University Press, 2005.

Rader, Dean, and Janice Gould, eds. *Speak to Me Words: Essays on Contemporary American Indian Poetry*. Tucson: University of Arizona Press, 2003.

Roemer, Kenneth M., ed. *Native American Writers of the United States*. Dictionary of Literary Biography 175. Detroit: Gale Research, 1997.

Ruoff, A. LaVonne Brown. *American Indian Literatures: An Introduction, Bibliographic Review, and Selected Bibliography*. New York: Modern Language Association, 1990.

Wiget, Andrew. *Native American Literature*. Twayne's United States Authors Series 467. Boston: Twayne, 1985.

_____, ed. *Dictionary of Native American Literature*. Garland Reference Library of the Humanities 1815. New York: Garland, 1994.

Wilson, Norma. *The Nature of Native American Poetry*. Albuquerque: University of New Mexico Press, 2000.

REGIONAL POETS

Bain, Robert, and Joseph M. Flora, eds. *Contemporary Poets, Dramatists, Essayists, and Novelists of the South: A Bio-bibliographical Sourcebook*. Westport Conn.: Greenwood Press, 1994.

Jantz, Harold S. *The First Century of New England Verse*. Worcester, Mass.: American Antiquarian Society, 1944.

WOMEN WRITERS

Davidson, Phebe, ed. *Conversations with the World: American Women Poets and Their Work*. Pasadena, Calif.: Trilogy Books, 1998.

Davis, Gwenn, and Beverly A. Joyce, comps. *Poetry by Women to 1900: A Bibliography of American and British Writers*. Toronto: University of Toronto Press, 1991.

Drake, William. *The First Wave: Women Poets in America, 1915-1945*. New York: Macmillan, 1987.

Gray, Janet, ed. *She Wields a Pen: American Women Poets of the Nineteenth Century*. Iowa City: University of Iowa Press, 1997.

Mark, Alison, and Deryn Rees-Jones. *Contemporary Women's Poetry: Reading, Writing, Practice*. New York: St. Martin's Press, 2000.

Reardon, Joan, and Kristine A. Thorsen. *Poetry by American Women, 1900-1975: A Bibliography*. Metuchen, N.J.: Scarecrow Press, 1979.

_____. *Poetry by American Women, 1975-1989: A Bibliography*. Metuchen, N.J.: Scarecrow Press, 1990.

Maura Ives; updated by Tracy Irons-Georges

GUIDE TO ONLINE RESOURCES

The following sites were visited by the editors of Salem Press in 2010. Because URLs frequently change, the accuracy of these addresses cannot be guaranteed; however, long-standing sites, such as those of colleges and universities, national organizations, and government agencies, generally maintain links when their sites are moved.

Academy of American Poets

http://www.poets.org

The mission of the Academy of American Poets is to "support American poets at all stages of their careers and to foster the appreciation of contemporary poetry." The academy's comprehensive Web site features information on poetic schools and movements; a Poetic Forms Database; an Online Poetry Classroom, with educator and teaching resources; an index of poets and poems; essays and interviews; general Web resources; links for further study; and more.

The Cambridge History of English and American Literature

http://www.bartleby.com/cambridge

This site provides an exhaustive examination of the development of all forms of literature in Great Britain and the United States. The multivolume set on which this site is based was published in 1907-1921 but remains a relevant, classic work. It offers "a wide selection of writing on orators, humorists, poets, newspaper columnists, religious leaders, economists, Native Americans, song writers, and even non-English writing, such as Yiddish and Creole."

A Celebration of Women Writers

http://digital.library.upenn.edu/women

This site is an extensive compendium on the contributions of women writers throughout history. The "Local Editions by Authors" and "Local Editions by Category" pages include access to electronic texts of the works of numerous writers. Users can also access biographical and bibliographical information by browsing lists arranged by writers' names, countries of origin, ethnicities, and the centuries in which they lived.

Internet Public Library: Native American Authors

http://www.ipl.org/div/natam

The Internet Public Library, a Web-based collection of resource materials, includes this informational index to writers of Native American heritage. An alphabetical list of authors features links to biographies, lists of works, electronic texts, tribal Web sites, and other online resources. The majority of the writers covered are contemporary Indian authors, but some historical authors also are featured. Users also can retrieve information by browsing lists of titles and tribes. In addition, the site contains a bibliography of print and online materials about Native American literature.

Literary Resources on the Net

http://andromeda.rutgers.edu/~jlynch/Lit

Jack Lynch of Rutgers University maintains this extensive collection of links to Web sites that are useful to researchers, including numerous sites about American and English literature. This collection is a good place to begin online research about poetry, as it links to other sites with broad ranges of literary topics. The site is organized chronologically, with separate pages about the Middle Ages, the Renaissance, the eighteenth century, the Romantic and Victorian eras, and twentieth century British and Irish literature. It also has separate pages providing links to Web sites about American literature and to women's literature and feminism.

LiteraryHistory.com

http://www.literaryhistory.com

This site is an excellent source of academic, scholarly, and critical literature about eighteenth, nineteenth, and twentieth century American and English writers. It provides numerous pages about specific eras and genres, including individual pages for eighteenth, nineteenth, and twentieth century literature and for African American and postcolonial literatures. These pages contain alphabetical lists of authors that link to articles, reviews, overviews, excerpts of works, teaching guides, podcasts, and other materials.

LitWeb

http://litweb.net

LitWeb provides biographies of hundreds of world authors throughout history that can be accessed through an alphabetical listing. The pages about each writer contain a list of his or her works, suggestions for further reading, and illustrations. The site also offers information about past and present winners of major literary prizes.

The Modern Word: Authors of the Libyrinth

http://www.themodernword.com/authors.html

The Modern Word site, although somewhat haphazard in its organization, provides a great deal of critical information about writers. The "Authors of the Libyrinth" page is very useful, linking author names to essays about them and other resources. The section of the page headed "The Scriptorium" presents "an index of pages featuring writers who have pushed the edges of their medium, combining literary talent with a sense of experimentation to produce some remarkable works of modern literature."

Outline of American Literature

http://www.america.gov/publications/books/outline-of-american-literature.html

This page of the America.gov site provides access to an electronic version of the ten-chapter volume *Outline of American Literature*, a historical overview of poetry and prose from colonial times to the present published by the Bureau of International Information Programs of the U.S. Department of State.

Poetry Foundation

http://www.poetryfoundation.org

The Poetry Foundation, publisher of *Poetry* magazine, is an independent literary organization. Its Web site offers links to essays; news; events; online poetry resources, such as blogs, organizations, publications, and references and research; a glossary of literary terms; and a Learning Lab that includes poem guides and essays on poetics.

Poetry in Translation

http://poetryintranslation.com

This independent resource provides modern translations of classic texts by famous poets and also provides original poetry and critical works. Visitors can choose from several languages, including English, Spanish, Chinese, Russian, Italian, and Greek. Original text is available as well. Also includes links to further literary resources.

Poetry International Web

http://international.poetryinternationalweb.org

Poetry International Web features information on poets from countries such as Indonesia, Zimbabwe, Iceland, India, Slovenia, Morocco, Albania, Afghanistan, Russia, and Brazil. The site offers news, essays, interviews and discussion, and hundreds of poems, both in their original languages and in English translation.

Poet's Corner

http://theotherpages.org/poems

The Poet's Corner, one of the oldest text resources on the Web, provides access to about seven thousand works of poetry by several hundred different poets from around the world. Indexes are arranged and searchable by title, name of poet, or subject. The site also offers its own resources, including Faces of the Poets—a gallery of portraits—and Lives of the Poets—a growing collection of biographies.

Representative Poetry Online

http://rpo.library.utoronto.ca

This award-winning resource site, maintained by Ian Lancashire of the Department of English at the University of Toronto in Canada, has several thousand English-language poems by hundreds of poets. The collection is searchable by poet's name, title of work, first line of a poem, and keyword. The site also includes a time line, a glossary, essays, an extensive bibliography, and countless links organized by country and by subject.

Voice of the Shuttle

http://vos.ucsb.edu

One of the most complete and authoritative places for online information about literature, Voice of the Shuttle is maintained by professors and students in the English Department at the University of California, Santa Barbara. The site provides countless links to electronic books, academic journals, literary association Web sites, sites created by university professors, and many other resources.

Voices from the Gaps

http://voices.cla.umn.edu/

Voices from the Gaps is a site of the English Department at the University of Minnesota, dedicated to providing resources on the study of women artists of color, including writers. The site features a comprehensive index searchable by name, and it provides biographical information on each writer or artist and other resources for further study.

ELECTRONIC DATABASES

Electronic databases usually do not have their own URLs. Instead, public, college, and university libraries subscribe to these databases, provide links to them on their Web sites, and make them available to library card holders or other specified patrons. Readers can visit library Web sites or ask reference librarians to check on availability.

Bloom's Literary Reference Online

Facts On File publishes this database of thousands of articles by renowned scholar Harold Bloom and other literary critics, examining the lives and works of great writers worldwide. The database also includes information on more than forty-two thousand literary characters, literary topics, themes, movements, and genres, plus video segments about literature. Users can retrieve information by browsing writers' names, titles of works, time periods, genres, or writers' nationalities.

Literary Reference Center

EBSCO's Literary Reference Center (LRC) is a comprehensive full-text database designed primarily to help high school and undergraduate students in English and the humanities with homework and research assignments about literature. The database contains massive amounts of information from reference works, books, literary journals, and other materials, including more than 31,000 plot summaries, synopses, and overviews of literary works; almost 100,000 essays and articles of literary criticism; about 140,000 author biographies; more than 605,000 book reviews; and more than 5,200 author interviews. It also contains the entire contents of Salem Press's MagillOnLiterature Plus. Users can retrieve information by browsing a list of authors' names or titles of literary works; they can also use an advanced search engine to access information by numerous categories, including author name, gender, cultural identity, national identity, and the years in which he or she lived, or by literary title, character, locale, genre, and publication date. The Literary Reference Center also features a literary-historical time line, an encyclopedia of literature, and a glossary of literary terms.

Literary Resource Center

Published by Gale, this comprehensive literary database contains information on the lives and works of more than 130,000 authors in all genres, in all time periods, and throughout the world. In addition, the database offers more than 70,000 full-text critical essays and reviews from some of Gale's reference publications, including *Contemporary Literary Criticism, Literature Criticism from 1400-1800, Nineteenth-Century Literature Criticism*, and *Twentieth-Century Literary Criticism*; more than 7,000 overviews of frequently studied works; more than 650,000 full-text articles, critical essays, and reviews from about three hundred scholarly journals and literary magazines; more than 4,500 interviews; and about 500 links to selected Web sites. Users can retrieve information by browsing author name, ethnicity, nationality, years of birth and death; titles of literary works; genres; selected literary movements or time periods; keywords; and themes of literary works. Literary Resource Center also features a literary-historical time line and an encyclopedia of literature.

MagillOnLiterature Plus

MagillOnLiterature Plus is a comprehensive, integrated literature database produced by Salem Press and available on the EBSCOhost platform. The database contains the full text of essays in Salem's many literature-related reference works, including *Masterplots*, *Cyclopedia of World Authors*, *Cyclopedia of Literary Characters*, *Cyclopedia of Literary Places*, *Critical Survey of Poetry*, *Critical Survey of Long Fiction*, *Critical Survey of Short Fiction*, *World Philosophers and Their Works*, *Magill's Literary Annual*, and *Magill's Book Reviews*. Among its contents are articles on more than 35,000 literary works and more than 8,500 poets, writers, dramatists, essayists, and philosophers; more than 1,000 images; and a glossary of more than 1,300 literary terms. The biographical essays include lists of authors' works and secondary bibliographies, and hundreds of overview essays examine and discuss literary genres, time periods, and national literatures.

Rebecca Kuzins; updated by Desiree Dreeuws

TIME LINE

1650	Anne Bradstreet's *The Tenth Muse Lately Sprung Up in America: Or, Several Poems Compiled with Great Variety of Wit and Learning, Full of Delight* is published. Bradstreet is one of America's foremost colonial poets and the first female poet to be published in America.
June 24, 1729	Edward Taylor, an English-born minister and one of the premier American colonial poets, dies in Westfield, Massachusetts.
1773	Phillis Wheatley's *Poems on Various Subjects, Religious and Moral* is published. Wheatley is America's first black poet and the second female poet to be published in America, after Anne Bradstreet.
December 17, 1807	John Greenleaf Whittier is born in Haverhill, Massachusetts. He and several other Americans—Henry Wadsworth Longfellow, James Russell Lowell, Oliver Wendell Holmes, and William Cullen Bryant—would later be known as the Fireside Poets because nineteenth century Americans often gathered around the fireside to hear a family member read these writers' works.
December 10, 1830	Emily Dickinson is born in Amherst, Massachusetts. Although she gained little recognition for her work during her lifetime, Dickinson would later be considered one of America's greatest lyric poets.
October 7, 1849	Edgar Allan Poe dies in Baltimore, Maryland, at the age of forty. Poe's poetry would influence many British poets and writers. He also wrote literary criticism in which he maintained that critics should protect readers from bad poetry and encourage poets to live up to their potential.
1855	Henry Wadsworth Longfellow, the most popular English-language poet of the nineteenth century, publishes *The Song of Hiawatha*.
1855	The first edition of Walt Whitman's *Leaves of Grass* is published. Whitman radically alters conventional poetry by using free verse and ordinary diction.
1908	*A Lume Spento*, the first volume of poetry by Ezra Pound, is published. In the first two decades of the twentieth century, Pound and T. S. Eliot will create the idiom that will characterize modern American and English poetry.
1912	Harriet Monroe founds *Poetry* magazine, which will continue to be issued into the twenty-first century. The magazine will publish works by many of the world's leading poets, including Ezra Pound, T. S. Eliot, Marianne Moore, Carl Sandburg, and Rabindranath Tagore, and will discover such poets as Gwendolyn Brooks, John Ashbery, and James Merrill.
1918	Sara Teasdale receives the Pulitzer Prize in Poetry for *Love Songs*.
1919-1935	The Harlem Renaissance produces some of the finest African-American literature, music, and art of the twentieth century. Poets associated with this movement include Langston Hughes, Countée Cullen, and Claude McKay.
1930	*The Bridge*, by Hart Crane, is published. In this lengthy poem, Crane seeks to provide a synthesis of the American identity.
1930	Conrad Aiken receives the Pulitzer Prize in Poetry for *Selected Poems*.
1941	Robert Frost receives the Frost Medal from the Poetry Society of America for distinguished lifetime service to American poetry.

1945-1946	Louise Bogan serves as America's poet laureate.
1947-1948	Robert Lowell serves as America's poet laureate.
1950	E. E. Cummings receives the Academy of American Poets Fellowship.
1950	Wallace Stevens receives the Bollingen Prize in Poetry.
1952	Frank O'Hara's first collection, *A City Winter, and Other Poems*, is published. O'Hara, Kenneth Koch, James Schuyler, and John Ashbery were the central members of the New York School of poets, an influential group of writers during the late 1950's.
1953	Archibald MacLeish and William Carlos Williams receive the Bollingen Prize in Poetry.
1956	"Howl," by Allen Ginsberg, is published. This poem is the best-known work by one of the Beat writers, a group whose other members include poets Kenneth Rexroth, Lawrence Ferlinghetti, Michael McClure, Gregory Corso, and Philip Whalen.
1956	Elizabeth Bishop receives the Pulitzer Prize in Poetry for *Poems: North and South*.
1959	Gary Snyder publishes his first collection, *Riprap*. Snyder's environmentally conscious poetry will later make him a member of the Green movement, a group of writers who advocate the need to repair and sustain the damaged environment.
1960	*The Colossus, and Other Poems*, Sylvia Plath's first poetry collection, is published.
1960	Donald Allen's anthology *The New American Poetry: 1945-1960*, is published. This collection contains the work of several poets associated with the Black Mountain School, including Charles Olson, Robert Creeley, Robert Duncan, Edward Dorn, Denise Levertov, Paul Blackburn, Joel Oppenheimer, and Hilda Morley.
1960	Delmore Schwartz receives the Bollingen Prize in Poetry.
1961	X. J. Kennedy receives the Lamont Poetry Selection (now the James Laughlin Award) for *Nude Descending a Staircase*.
1961	Randall Jarrell receives the National Book Award in Poetry for *The Woman at the Washington Zoo*.
1965	Marianne Moore is awarded the Academy of American Poets Fellowship.
1965	Henri Coulette receives the Lamont Poetry Selection (now the James Laughlin Award) for *The War of the Secret Agents*.
1965	Theodore Roethke receives the National Book Award in Poetry for *The Far Field*.
1967	Anne Sexton is awarded the Pulitzer Prize in Poetry for *Live or Die*.
1968	Nikki Giovanni's first book of poetry, *Black Feeling, Black Talk*, is published to critical acclaim, with some praising her as the "Princess of Black Poetry."
1969	John Berryman receives the National Book Award in Poetry for *His Toy, His Dream, His Rest*.
1974-1976	Stanley Kunitz serves as America's poet laureate. He will hold this position again in 2000-2001.
1978	Josephine Miles receives the Academy of American Poets Fellowship.
1978	Howard Nemerov is awarded the Pulitzer Prize in Poetry for *Collected Poems*.
1979	W. S. Merwin is awarded the Bollingen Prize in Poetry.
1981	Carolyn Forché receives the Lamont Poetry Selection (now the James Laughlin Award) for *The Country Between Us*.
1985-1986	Gwendolyn Brooks serves as America's poet laureate.

1987	Joseph Brodsky, a Soviet writer exiled in the United States, receives the Nobel Prize in Literature. Brodsky wrote his poetry in Russian, and it was translated into many languages, with the English translations earning him high regard in the West.
1987	Philip Levine receives the Ruth Lilly Poetry Prize, awarded by the Poetry Foundation in recognition of lifetime achievement im English-language poetry.
1991	Donald Hall receives the Frost Medal from the Poetry Society of America for distinguished lifetime service to American poetry.
1992	Mary Oliver receives the National Book Award in Poetry for *New and Selected Poems*.
1993	Thom Gunn receives the Lenore Marshall Poetry Prize from the Academy of American Poets for *The Man with Night Sweats*.
January 20, 1993	Maya Angelou reads her poem "On the Pulse of Morning" during the inauguration of President Bill Clinton.
1994	Irish poet Eavan Boland and American poets Linda Hogan and Jack Gilbert are among the five recipients of the Lannan Literary Award for Poetry.
1994	Brigit Pegeen Kelley receives the Lamont Poetry Selection (now the James Laughlin Award) for *Song*.
1995	Denise Levertov receives the Academy of American Poets Fellowship.
1997-2000	Robert Pinsky serves as America's poet laureate.
1999	Maxine Kumin receives the Ruth Lilly Poetry Prize, awarded by the Poetry Foundation in recognition of lifetime achievement in English-language poetry.
2001	Louise Glück receives the Bollingen Prize in Poetry.
2001	Sonia Sanchez receives the Frost Medal from the Poetry Society of America for distinguished lifetime service to American poetry.
2002	Sharon Olds receives the Academy of American Poets Fellowship.
2003	Li-Young Lee receives the Academy of American Poets Fellowship.
2003	Eamon Grennan receives the Lenore Marshall Poetry Prize from the Academy of American Poets for *Still Life with Waterfall*.
2007	Robert Haas receives the National Book Award in Poetry for *Time and Materials*.
2007-2008	Charles Simic is America's poet laureate.
2009	Harryette Mullen receives the Academy of American Poets Fellowship.
2009	Allen Grossman receives the Bollingen Prize in Poetry.
2009	Linda Gregg receives the Lenore Marshall Poetry Prize from the Academy of American Poets for *All of It Singing: New and Selected Poems*.
January 20, 2009	Elizabeth Alexander reads her poem "Praise Song for the Day" at the inauguration of President Barack Obama.
July 1, 2010	The Library of Congress announces that W. S. Merwin will replace Kay Ryan as the seventeenth poet laureate of the United States. Merwin is the recipient of two Pulitzer Prizes, the National Book Award, and the Bollingen Prize in Poetry.

Rebecca Kuzins

Major Awards

Academy of American Poets Fellowship

The Academy of American Poets awards American poets with fellowships for distinguished poetic achievement. No awards were given between 1938 and 1945, or in 1949 and 1951.

1937: Edwin Markham
1946: Edgar Lee Masters
1947: Ridgely Torrence
1948: Percy MacKaye
1950: E. E. Cummings
1952: Padraic Colum
1953: Robert Frost
1954: Louise Townsend Nicholl and Oliver St. John Gogarty
1955: Rolfe Humphries
1956: William Carlos Williams
1957: Conrad Aiken
1958: Robinson Jeffers
1959: Louise Bogan
1960: Jesse Stuart
1961: Horace Gregory
1962: John Crowe Ransom
1963: Ezra Pound and Allen Tate
1964: Elizabeth Bishop
1965: Marianne Moore
1966: Archibald MacLeish and John Berryman
1967: Mark Van Doren
1968: Stanley Kunitz
1969: Richard Eberhart
1970: Howard Nemerov
1971: James Wright
1972: W. D. Snodgrass
1973: W. S. Merwin
1974: Léonie Adams
1975: Robert Hayden
1976: J. V. Cunningham
1977: Louis Coxe

1978: Josephine Miles
1979: May Swenson and Mark Strand
1980: Mona Van Duyn
1981: Richard Hugo
1982: John Frederick Nims and John Ashbery
1983: James Schuyler and Philip Booth
1984: Richmond Lattimore and Robert Francis
1985: Amy Clampitt and Maxine Kumin
1986: Irving Feldman and Howard Moss
1987: Josephine Jacobsen and Alfred Corn
1988: Donald Justice
1989: Richard Howard
1990: William Meredith
1991: J. D. McClatchy
1992: Adrienne Rich
1993: Gerald Stern
1994: David Ferry
1995: Denise Levertov
1996: Jay Wright
1997: John Haines
1998: Charles Simic
1999: Gwendolyn Brooks
2000: Lyn Hejinian
2001: Ellen Bryant Voigt
2002: Sharon Olds
2003: Li-Young Lee
2004: Jane Hirschfield
2005: Claudia Rankine
2006: Carl Phillips
2007: James McMichael
2008: Brigit Pegeen Kelly
2009: Harryette Mullen

BOLLINGEN PRIZE IN POETRY

Administered by Yale University Library, this award is given to an American poet. Awarded every two years since 1963.

1949: Ezra Pound
1950: Wallace Stevens
1951: John Crowe Ransom
1952: Marianne Moore
1953: Archibald MacLeish and William Carlos Williams
1954: W. H. Auden
1955: Léonie Adams and Louise Bogan
1956: Conrad Aiken
1957: Allen Tate
1958: E. E. Cummings
1959: Theodore Roethke
1960: Delmore Schwartz
1961: Yvor Winters
1962: John Hall Wheelock and Richard Eberhart
1963: Robert Frost
1965: Horace Gregory
1967: Robert Penn Warren
1969: John Berryman and Karl Shapiro
1971: Richard Wilbur and Mona Van Duyn

1973: James Merrill
1975: A. R. Ammons
1977: David Ignatow
1979: W. S. Merwin
1981: Howard Nemerov and May Swenson
1983: Anthony Hecht and John Hollander
1985: John Ashbery and Fred Chappell
1987: Stanley Kunitz
1989: Edgar Bowers
1991: Laura Riding Jackson and Donald Justice
1993: Mark Strand
1995: Kenneth Koch
1997: Gary Snyder
1999: Robert Creeley
2001: Louise Glück
2003: Adrienne Rich
2005: Jay Wright
2007: Frank Bidart
2009: Allen Grossman

FROST MEDAL

Awarded by the Poetry Society of America to a poet for distinguished lifetime service to American poetry. Awarded annually since 1984.

1930: Jessie Rittenhouse
1941: Robert Frost
1942: Edgar Lee Masters
1943: Edna St. Vincent Millay
1947: Gustav Davidson
1951: Wallace Stevens
1952: Carl Sandburg
1955: Leonora Speyer
1967: Marianne Moore
1971: Melville Cane
1974: John Hall Wheelock
1976: A. M. Sullivan
1984: Jack Stadler
1985: Robert Penn Warren

1986: Allen Ginsberg and Richard Eberhart
1987: Robert Creeley and Sterling Brown
1988: Carolyn Kizer
1989: Gwendolyn Brooks
1990: Denise Levertov and James Laughlin
1991: Donald Hall
1992: Adrienne Rich and David Ignatow
1993: William Stafford
1994: A. R. Ammons
1995: John Ashbery
1996: Richard Wilbur
1997: Josephine Jacobsen
1998: Stanley Kunitz
1999: Barbara Guest

2000: Anthony Hecht
2001: Sonia Sanchez
2002: Galway Kinnell
2003: Lawrence Ferlinghetti
2004: Richard Howard
2005: Marie Ponsot

2006: Maxine Kumin
2007: John Hollander
2008: Michael S. Harper
2009: X. J. Kennedy
2010: Lucille Clifton

GRIFFIN POETRY PRIZE

The Griffin Poetry Prize is given by Canada each year, beginning in 2001, to collections by one living Canadian poet and one living international poet writing in the English language. Lifetime Recognition Awards to poets from all countries and languages were added in 2006.

2001: Anne Carson—*Men in the Off Hours* (Canada); Nikolai Popov and Heather McHugh, translation of *Glottal Stop: 101 Poems by Paul Celan* (international)
2002: Christian Bök—*Eunoia* (Canada); Alice Notley—*Disobedience* (international)
2003: Margaret Avison—*Concrete and Wild Carrot* (Canada); Paul Muldoon—*Moy Sand and Gravel* (international)
2004: Anne Simpson—*Loop* (Canada); August Kleinzahler—*The Strange Hours Travelers Keep* (international)
2005: Roo Borson—*Short Journey Upriver Toward Oishida* (Canada); Charles Simic—*Selected Poems, 1963-2003* (international)
2006: Sylvia Legris—*Nerve Squall* (Canada); Kamau Brathwaite—*Born to Slow Horses*

(international); Lifetime Recognition Award, Robin Blaser
2007: Don McKay—*Strike/Slip* (Canada); Charles Wright—*Scar Tissue* (international); Lifetime Recognition Award, Tomas Tranströmer
2008: Robin Blaser—*The Holy Forest: Collected Poems of Robin Blaser* (Canada); John Ashbery—*Notes from the Air: Selected Later Poems* (international); Lifetime Recognition Award, Ko Un
2009: A. F. Moritz—*The Sentinel* (Canada); C. D. Wright—*Rising, Falling, Hovering* (international); Lifetime Recognition Award, Hans Magnus Enzensberger
2010: Karen Solie—*Pigeon* (Canada); Eilean Ni Chuilleanain—*The Sun-fish* (international); Lifetime Recognition Award, Adrienne Rich

LANNAN LITERARY AWARD FOR POETRY

The Lannan Literary Awards are a series of awards and literary fellowships given out in various fields by the Lannan Foundation. Established in 1989, the awards "honor both established and emerging writers whose work is of exceptional quality."

1989: Cid Corman, George Evans, Peter Levitt
1990: Derek Mahon, Seamus Heaney
1991: William Bronk, Chrystos, Pattiann Rogers, Herbert Morris
1992: A. R. Ammons, Thomas Centolella, Killarney Clary, Suzanne Gardinier, Susan Mitchell, Luis J. Rodriguez
1993: Cyrus Cassells, Denise Levertov, Benjamin Alire Saenz

1994: Simon Armitage, Eavan Boland, Linda Hogan, Jack Gilbert, Richard Kenney
1995: Hayden Carruth, Carol Ann Duffy, Arthur Sze, Li-Young Lee
1996: Anne Carson, Lucille Clifton, William Trevor, Donald Justice
1997: Ken Smith
1998: Frank Bidart, Jon Davis, Mary Oliver
1999: Dennis O'Driscoll, C. D. Wright, Louise Glück

2000: Herbert Morris, Jay Wright
2001: no award
2002: Alan Dugan, Peter Dale Scott
2003: no award
2004: Peter Reading

2005: Pattiann Rogers
2006: Bruce Weigl
2007: no award
2008: August Kleinzahler
2009: no award

JAMES LAUGHLIN AWARD

The Academy of American Poets gives this annual award to a poet for the publication of an outstanding second poetry collection. Originally known as the Lamont Poetry Selection, the name was changed in 1995 to honor poet and publisher James Laughlin.

1954: Constance Carrier—*The Middle Voice*
1955: Donald Hall—*Exiles and Marriages*
1956: Philip Booth—*Letter from a Distant Land*
1957: Daniel Berrigan, S. J.—*Time Without Number*
1958: Ned O'Gorman—*The Night of the Hammer*
1959: Donald Justice—*The Summer Anniversaries*
1960: Robert Mezey—*The Lovemaker*
1961: X. J. Kennedy—*Nude Descending a Staircase*
1962: Edward Field—*Stand Up, Friend, with Me*
1963: no award
1964: Adrien Stoutenberg—*Heroes, Advise Us*
1965: Henri Coulette—*The War of the Secret Agents*
1966: Kenneth O. Hanson—*The Distance Anywhere*
1967: James Scully—*The Marches*
1968: Jane Cooper—*The Weather of Six Mornings*
1969: Marvin Bell—*A Probable Volume of Dreams*
1970: William Harmon—*Treasury Holiday*
1971: Stephen Dobyns—*Concurring Beasts*
1972: Peter Everwine—*Collecting the Animals*
1973: Marilyn Hacker—*Presentation Piece*
1974: John Balaban—*After Our War*
1975: Lisel Mueller—*The Private Life*
1976: Larry Levis—*The Afterlife*
1977: Gerald Stern—*Lucky Life*
1978: Ai—*Killing Floor*
1979: Frederick Seidel—*Sunrise*
1980: Michael Van Walleghen—*More Trouble with the Obvious*
1981: Carolyn Forché—*The Country Between Us*
1982: Margaret Gibson—*Long Walks in the Afternoon*
1983: Sharon Olds—*The Dead and the Living*

1984: Philip Schultz—*Deep Within the Ravine*
1985: Cornelius Eady—*Victims of the Latest Dance Craze*
1986: Jane Shore—*The Minute Hand*
1987: Garrett Kaoru Hongo—*The River of Heaven*
1988: Mary Jo Salter—*Unfinished Painting*
1989: Minnie Bruce Pratt—*Crime Against Nature*
1990: Li-Young Lee—*The City in Which I Love You*
1991: Susan Wood—*Campo Santo*
1992: Kathryn Stripling Byer—*Wildwood Flower*
1993: Rosanna Warren—*Stained Glass*
1994: Brigit Pegeen Kelly—*Song*
1995: Ralph Angel—*Neither World*
1996: David Rivard—*Wise Poison*
1997: Tony Hoagland—*Donkey Gospel*
1998: Sandra Alcosser—*Except by Nature*
1999: Tory Dent—*HIV, Mon Amour*
2000: Liz Waldner—*A Point Is That Which Has No Point*
2001: Peter Johnson—*Miracles and Mortifications*
2002: Karen Volkman—*Spar*
2003: Vijay Seshadri—*The Long Meadow*
2004: Jeff Clark—*Music and Suicide*
2005: Barbara Jane Reyes—*Poeta en San Francisco*
2006: Tracy K. Smith—*Duende*
2007: Brenda Shaughnessy—*Human Dark with Sugar*
2008: Rusty Morrison—*the true keeps calm biding its story*
2009: Jennifer K. Sweeney—*How to Live on Bread and Music*

RUTH LILLY POETRY PRIZE

This annual prize, awarded by the Poetry Foundation, recognizes lifetime achievement in English-language poetry.

1986: Adrienne Rich
1987: Philip Levine
1988: Anthony Hecht
1989: Mona Van Duyn
1990: Hayden Carruth
1991: David Wagoner
1992: John Ashbery
1993: Charles Wright
1994: Donald Hall
1995: A. R. Ammons
1996: Gerald Stern
1997: William Matthews
1998: W. S. Merwin

1999: Maxine Kumin
2000: Carl Dennis
2001: Yusef Komunyakaa
2002: Lisel Mueller
2003: Linda Pastan
2004: Kay Ryan
2005: C. K. Williams
2006: Richard Wilbur
2007: Lucille Clifton
2008: Gary Snyder
2009: Fanny Howe
2010: Eleanor Ross Taylor

LENORE MARSHALL POETRY PRIZE

Awarded by the Academy of American Poets annually to a poet for the publication in the United States of an outstanding poetry collection.

1975: Cid Corman—*O/I*
1976: Denise Levertov—*The Freeing of the Dust*
1977: Philip Levine—*The Names of the Lost*
1978: Allen Tate—*Collected Poems, 1919-1976*
1979: Hayden Carruth—*Brothers, I Loved You All*
1980: Stanley Kunitz—*The Poems of Stanley Kunitz, 1928-1978*
1981: Sterling A. Brown—*The Collected Poems of Sterling A. Brown*
1982: John Logan—*The Bridge of Chance: Poems, 1974-1980*
1983: George Starbuck—*The Argot Merchant Disaster*
1984: Josephine Miles—*Collected Poems, 1930-1983*
1985: John Ashbery—*A Wave*
1986: Howard Moss—*New Selected Poems*
1987: Donald Hall—*The Happy Man*
1988: Josephine Jacobsen—*The Sisters: New and Selected Poems*
1989: Thomas McGrath—*Selected Poems, 1938-1988*
1990: Michael Ryan—*God Hunger*
1991: John Haines—*New Poems, 1980-1988*
1992: Adrienne Rich—*An Atlas of the Difficult World*

1993: Thom Gunn—*The Man with Night Sweats*
1994: W. S. Merwin—*Travels*
1995: Marilyn Hacker—*Winter Numbers*
1996: Charles Wright—*Chickamauga*
1997: Robert Pinsky—*The Figured Wheel: New and Collected Poems, 1966-1996*
1998: Mark Jarman—*Questions for Ecclesiastes*
1999: Wanda Coleman—*Bathwater Wine*
2000: David Ferry—*Of No Country I Know: New and Selected Poems and Translations*
2001: Fanny Howe—*Selected Poems*
2002: Madeline DeFrees—*Blue Dusk*
2003: Eamon Grennan—*Still Life with Waterfall*
2004: Donald Revell—*My Mojave*
2005: Anne Winters—*The Displaced of Capital*
2006: Eleanor Lerman—*Our Post-Soviet History Unfolds*
2007: Alice Notley—*Grave of Light: New and Selected Poems, 1970-2005*
2008: Henri Cole—*Blackbird and Wolf*
2009: Linda Gregg—*All of It Singing: New and Selected Poems*

NATIONAL BOOK AWARD IN POETRY

Awarded by the National Book Foundation to an American poet for the publication of the best book of poetry during the year. Not awarded from 1984 to 1990.

1950: William Carlos Williams—*Paterson: Book III and Selected Poems*

1951: Wallace Stevens—*The Auroras of Autumn*

1952: Marianne Moore—*Collected Poems*

1953: Archibald MacLeish—*Collected Poems, 1917-1952*

1954: Conrad Aiken—*Collected Poems*

1955: Wallace Stevens—*The Collected Poems of Wallace Stevens*

1956: W. H. Auden—*The Shield of Achilles*

1957: Richard Wilbur—*Things of the World*

1958: Robert Penn Warren—*Promises: Poems, 1954-1956*

1959: Theodore Roethke—*Words for the Wind*

1960: Robert Lowell—*Life Studies*

1961: Randall Jarrell—*The Woman at the Washington Zoo*

1962: Alan Dugan—*Poems*

1963: William Stafford—*Traveling Through the Dark*

1964: John Crowe Ransom—*Selected Poems*

1965: Theodore Roethke—*The Far Field*

1966: James Dickey—*Buckdancer's Choice: Poems*

1967: James Merrill—*Nights and Days*

1968: Robert Bly—*The Light Around the Body*

1969: John Berryman—*His Toy, His Dream, His Rest*

1970: Elizabeth Bishop—*The Complete Poems*

1971: Mona Van Duyn—*To See, to Take*

1972: Frank O'Hara—*The Collected Poems of Frank O'Hara* and Howard Moss—*Selected Poems*

1973: A. R. Ammons—*Collected Poems, 1951-1971*

1974: Allen Ginsberg—*The Fall of America: Poems of These States* and Adrienne Rich—*Diving into the Wreck: Poems, 1971-1972*

1975: Marilyn Hacker—*Presentation Piece*

1976: John Ashbery—*Self-Portrait in a Convex Mirror*

1977: Richard Eberhart—*Collected Poems, 1930-1976*

1978: Howard Nemerov—*The Collected Poems of Howard Nemerov*

1979: James Merrill—*Mirabell: Book of Numbers*

1980: Philip Levine—*Ashes*

1981: Lisel Mueller—*The Need to Hold Still*

1982: William Bronk—*Life Supports: New and Collected Poems*

1983: Galway Kinnell—*Selected Poems* and Charles Wright—*Country Music: Selected Early Poems*

1991: Philip Levine—*What Work Is*

1992: Mary Oliver—*New and Selected Poems*

1993: A. R. Ammons—*Garbage*

1994: James Tate—*A Worshipful Company of Fletchers*

1995: Stanley Kunitz—*Passing Through: The Later Poems*

1996: Hayden Carruth—*Scrambled Eggs and Whiskey: Poems, 1991-1995*

1997: William Meredith—*Effort at Speech: New and Selected Poems*

1998: Gerald Stern—*This Time: New and Selected Poems*

1999: Ai—*Vice: New and Selected Poems*

2000: Lucille Clifton—*Blessing the Boats: New and Selected Poems, 1988-2000*

2001: Alan Dugan—*Poems Seven: New and Complete Poetry*

2002: Ruth Stone—*In the Next Galaxy*

2003: C. K. Williams—*The Singing*

2004: Jean Valentine—*Door in the Mountain: New and Collected Poems, 1965-2003*

2005: W. S. Merwin—*Migration: New and Selected Poems*

2006: Nathaniel Mackey—*Splay Anthem*

2007: Robert Hass—*Time and Materials*

2008: Mark Doty—*Fire to Fire: New and Collected Poems*

2009: Keith Waldrop—*Transcendental Studies: A Trilogy*

NOBEL PRIZE IN LITERATURE

Awarded annually since 1901, this prize is given to an author for his or her entire body of literary work. The list below includes only the poets who have been so honored.

1901: Sully Prudhomme
1906: Giosuè Carducci
1907: Rudyard Kipling
1913: Rabindranath Tagore
1923: William Butler Yeats
1945: Gabriela Mistral
1946: Hermann Hesse
1948: T. S. Eliot
1956: Juan Ramón Jiménez
1958: Boris Pasternak
1959: Salvatore Quasimodo
1960: Saint-John Perse
1963: George Seferis
1966: Nelly Sachs
1969: Samuel Beckett

1971: Pablo Neruda
1974: Harry Martinson
1975: Eugenio Montale
1977: Vicente Aleixandre
1979: Odysseus Elytis
1980: Czesław Miłosz
1984: Jaroslav Seifert
1986: Wole Soyinka
1987: Joseph Brodsky
1990: Octavio Paz
1992: Derek Walcott
1995: Seamus Heaney
1996: Wisława Szymborska
2005: Harold Pinter
2009: Herta Müller

PEN/VOELCKER AWARD FOR POETRY

The PEN/Voelcker Award for Poetry is given biennially to an American poet whose distinguished body of work represents a notable and accomplished presence in U.S. literature.

1994: Martín Espada
1996: Franz Wright
1998: C. K. Williams
2000: Heather McHugh

2002: Frederick Seidel
2004: Robert Pinsky
2006: Linda Gregg
2008: Kimiko Hahn

POET LAUREATE CONSULTANT IN POETRY

An appointment is given through the Library of Congress to a poet who then serves as the United States' official poet, or poet laureate.

1937-1941: Joseph Auslander
1943-1944: Allen Tate
1944-1945: Robert Penn Warren
1945-1946: Louise Bogan
1946-1947: Karl Shapiro
1947-1948: Robert Lowell
1948-1949: Léonie Adams
1949-1950: Elizabeth Bishop

1950-1952: Conrad Aiken
1952: William Carlos Williams (did not serve)
1956-1958: Randall Jarrell
1958-1959: Robert Frost
1959-1961: Richard Eberhart
1961-1963: Louis Untermeyer
1963-1964: Howard Nemerov
1964-1965: Reed Whittemore

1965-1966: Stephen Spender
1966-1968: James Dickey
1968-1970: William Jay Smith
1970-1971: William Stafford
1971-1973: Josephine Jacobsen
1973-1974: Daniel Hoffman
1974-1976: Stanley Kunitz
1976-1978: Robert Hayden
1978-1980: William Meredith
1981-1982: Maxine Kumin
1982-1984: Anthony Hecht
1984-1985: Robert Fitzgerald (limited by health) and
    Reed Whittemore (interim consultant)
1985-1986: Gwendolyn Brooks
1986-1987: Robert Penn Warren (first poet to be
    designated Poet Laureate Consultant in Poetry)
1987-1988: Richard Wilbur
1988-1990: Howard Nemerov

1990-1991: Mark Strand
1991-1992: Joseph Brodsky
1992-1993: Mona Van Duyn
1993-1995: Rita Dove
1995-1997: Robert Hass
1997-2000: Robert Pinsky
1999-2000: Rita Dove, Louise Glück, and W. S.
    Merwin (special consultants for Library of
    Congress bicentennial)
2000-2001: Stanley Kunitz
2001-2003: Billy Collins
2003-2004: Louise Glück
2004-2006: Ted Kooser
2006-2007: Donald Hall
2007-2008: Charles Simic
2008-2010: Kay Ryan
2010-   : W. S. Merwin

PULITZER PRIZE IN POETRY

Awarded by Columbia University's Graduate School of Journalism to honor an American poet who has published a distinguished collection of poetry.

1918: Sara Teasdale—*Love Songs*
1919: Margaret Widdemer—*Old Road to Paradise* and
    Carl Sandburg—*Cornhuskers*
1920: no award
1921: no award
1922: Edwin Arlington Robinson—*Collected Poems*
1923: Edna St. Vincent Millay—*The Ballad of the
    Harp-Weaver*
1924: Robert Frost—*New Hampshire: A Poem with
    Notes and Grace Notes*
1925: Edwin Arlington Robinson—*The Man Who Died
    Twice*
1926: Amy Lowell—*What's O'Clock*
1927: Leonora Speyer—*Fiddler's Farewell*
1928: Edwin Arlington Robinson—*Tristram*
1929: Stephen Vincent Benét—*John Brown's Body*
1930: Conrad Aiken—*Selected Poems*
1931: Robert Frost—*Collected Poems*
1932: George Dillon—*The Flowering Stone*
1933: Archibald MacLeish—*Conquistador*
1934: Robert Hillyer—*Collected Verse*

1935: Audrey Wurdemann—*Bright Ambush*
1936: Robert P. Tristram Coffin—*Strange Holiness*
1937: Robert Frost—*A Further Range*
1938: Marya Zaturenska—*Cold Morning Sky*
1939: John Gould Fletcher—*Selected Poems*
1940: Mark Van Doren—*Selected Poems*
1941: Leonard Bacon—*Sunderland Capture*
1942: William Rose Benet—*The Dust Which Is God*
1943: Robert Frost—*A Witness Tree*
1944: Stephen Vincent Benét—*Western Star*
1945: Karl Shapiro—*V-Letter and Other Poems*
1946: no award
1947: Robert Lowell—*Lord Weary's Castle*
1948: W. H. Auden—*The Age of Anxiety*
1949: Peter Viereck—*Terror and Decorum*
1950: Gwendolyn Brooks—*Annie Allen*
1951: Carl Sandburg—*Complete Poems*
1952: Marianne Moore—*Collected Poems*
1953: Archibald MacLeish—*Collected Poems, 1917-
    1952*
1954: Theodore Roethke—*The Waking*

1955: Wallace Stevens—*Collected Poems*

1956: Elizabeth Bishop—*Poems: North and South*

1957: Richard Wilbur—*Things of This World*

1958: Robert Penn Warren—*Promises: Poems, 1954-1956*

1959: Stanley Kunitz—*Selected Poems, 1928-1958*

1960: W. D. Snodgrass—*Heart's Needle*

1961: Phyllis McGinley—*Times Three: Selected Verse from Three Decades*

1962: Alan Dugan—*Poems*

1963: William Carlos Williams—*Pictures from Breughel*

1964: Louis Simpson—*At the End of the Open Road*

1965: John Berryman—*Seventy-seven Dream Songs*

1966: Richard Eberhart—*Selected Poems*

1967: Anne Sexton—*Live or Die*

1968: Anthony Hecht—*The Hard Hours*

1969: George Oppen—*Of Being Numerous*

1970: Richard Howard—*Untitled Subjects*

1971: W. S. Merwin—*The Carrier of Ladders*

1972: James Wright—*Collected Poems*

1973: Maxine Kumin—*Up Country*

1974: Robert Lowell—*The Dolphin*

1975: Gary Snyder—*Turtle Island*

1976: John Ashbery—*Self-Portrait in a Convex Mirror*

1977: James Merrill—*Divine Comedies*

1978: Howard Nemerov—*Collected Poems*

1979: Robert Penn Warren—*Now and Then*

1980: Donald Justice—*Selected Poems*

1981: James Schuyler—*The Morning of the Poem*

1982: Sylvia Plath—*The Collected Poems*

1983: Galway Kinnell—*Selected Poems*

1984: Mary Oliver—*American Primitive*

1985: Carolyn Kizer—*Yin*

1986: Henry Taylor—*The Flying Change*

1987: Rita Dove—*Thomas and Beulah*

1988: William Meredith—*Partial Accounts: New and Selected Poems*

1989: Richard Wilbur—*New and Collected Poems*

1990: Charles Simic—*The World Doesn't End*

1991: Mona Van Duyn—*Near Changes*

1992: James Tate—*Selected Poems*

1993: Louise Glück—*The Wild Iris*

1994: Yusef Komunyakaa—*Neon Vernacular: New and Selected Poems*

1995: Philip Levine—*The Simple Truth*

1996: Jorie Graham—*The Dream of the Unified Field*

1997: Lisel Mueller—*Alive Together: New and Selected Poems*

1998: Charles Wright—*Black Zodiac*

1999: Mark Strand—*Blizzard of One*

2000: C. K. Williams—*Repair*

2001: Stephen Dunn—*Different Hours*

2002: Carl Dennis—*Practical Gods*

2003: Paul Muldoon—*Moy Sand and Gravel*

2004: Franz Wright—*Walking to Martha's Vineyard*

2005: Ted Kooser—*Delights and Shadows*

2006: Claudia Emerson—*Late Wife*

2007: Natasha Trethewey—*Native Guard*

2008: Robert Hass—*Time and Materials*

2009: W. S. Merwin—*The Shadow of Sirius*

2010: Rae Armantrout—*Versed*

SHELLEY MEMORIAL AWARD

Awarded by the Poetry Society of America to an American poet on the basis of genius and need.

1929: Conrad Aiken

1930: Lizette Woodworth Reese

1931: Archibald MacLeish

1932: no award

1933: Lola Ridge and Frances Frost

1934: Lola Ridge and Marya Zaturenska

1935: Josephine Miles

1936: Charlotte Wilder and Ben Belitt

1937: Lincoln Fitzell

1938: Robert Francis and Harry Brown

1939: Herbert Bruncken and Winfield T. Scott

1940: Marianne Moore

1941: Ridgely Torrence

1942: Robert Penn Warren

1943: Edgar Lee Masters

1944: E. E. Cummings

1945: Karl Shapiro

1946: Rolfe Humphries

1947: Janet Lewis
1948: John Berryman
1949: Louis Kent
1950: Jeremy Ingalls
1951: Richard Eberhart
1952: Elizabeth Bishop
1953: Kenneth Patchen
1954: Leonie Adams
1955: Robert Fitzgerald
1956: George Abbe
1957: Kenneth Rexroth
1958: Rose Garcia Villa
1959: Delmore Schwartz
1960: Robinson Jeffers
1961: Theodore Roethke
1962: Eric Barker
1963: William Stafford
1964: Ruth Stone
1965: David Ignatow
1966: Anne Sexton
1967: May Swenson
1968: Anne Stanford
1969: X. J. Kennedy and Mary Oliver
1970: Adrienne Rich and Louise Townsend Nicholl
1971: Galway Kinnell
1972: John Ashbery and Richard Wilbur
1973: W. S. Merwin
1974: Edward Field
1975: Gwendolyn Brooks
1976: Muriel Rukeyser
1977: Jane Cooper and William Everson
1978: Hayden Carruth

1979: Julia Randall
1980: Robert Creeley
1981: Alan Dugan
1982: Jon Anderson and Leo Connellan
1983: Denise Levertov and Robert Duncan
1984: Etheridge Knight
1986: Gary Snyder
1987: Mona Van Duyn
1988: Dennis Schmitz
1989: no award
1990: Thomas McGrath and Theodore Weiss
1991: Shirley Kaufman
1992: Lucille Clifton
1993: Josephine Jacobsen
1994: Kenneth Koch and Cathy Song
1995: Stanley Kunitz
1996: Robert Pinsky and Anne Waldman
1997: Frank Bidart
1998: Eleanor Ross Taylor
1999: Tom Sleigh
2000: Jean Valentine
2001: Alice Notley and Michael Palmer
2002: Angela Jackson and Marie Ponsot
2003: James McMichael
2004: Yusef Komunyakaa
2005: Lyn Hejinian
2006: George Stanley
2007: Kimiko Hahn
2008: Ed Roberson
2009: Ron Padgett and Gary Young
2010: Kenneth Irby and Eileen Myles

WALLACE STEVENS AWARD

Awarded by the Academy of American Poets to a poet for outstanding and proven mastery of the art of poetry.

1994: W. S. Merwin
1995: James Tate
1996: Adrienne Rich
1997: Anthony Hecht
1998: A. R. Ammons
1999: Jackson MacLow
2000: Frank Bidart
2001: John Ashbery

2002: Ruth Stone
2003: Richard Wilbur
2004: Mark Strand
2005: Gerald Stern
2006: Michael Palmer
2007: Charles Simic
2008: Louise Glück
2009: Jean Valentine

KINGSLEY TUFTS POETRY AWARD

Claremont Graduate University presents the annual Kingsley Tufts Poetry Award for a single collection of a poet's work.

1993: Susan Mitchell—*Rapture*

1994: Yusef Komunyakaa—*Neon Vernacular*

1995: Thomas Lux—*Split Horizon*

1996: Deborah Digges—*Rough Music*

1997: Campbell McGrath—*Spring Comes to Chicago*

1998: John Koethe—*Falling Water*

1999: B. H. Fairchild—*The Art of the Lathe*

2000: Robert Wrigley—*Reign of Snakes*

2001: Alan Shapiro—*The Dead Alive and Busy*

2002: Carl Phillips—*The Tether*

2003: Linda Gregerson—*Waterborne*

2004: Henri Cole—*Middle Earth*

2005: Michael Ryan—*New and Selected Poems*

2006: Lucia Perillo—*Luck Is Luck*

2007: Rodney Jones—*Salvation Blues*

2008: Tom Sleigh—*Space Walk*

2009: Matthea Harvey—*Modern Life*

2010: D. A. Powell—*Chronic*

WALT WHITMAN AWARD

Awarded by the Academy of American Poets to a poet for the publication of a distinguished first collection of poetry.

1975: Reg Saner—*Climbing into the Roots*

1976: Laura Gilpin—*The Hocus-Pocus of the Universe*

1977: Lauren Shakely—*Guilty Bystander*

1978: Karen Snow—*Wonders*

1979: David Bottoms—*Shooting Rats at the Bibb County Dump*

1980: Jared Carter—*Work, for the Night Is Coming*

1981: Alberto Ríos—*Whispering to Fool the Wind*

1982: Anthony Petrosky—*Jurgis Petraskas*

1983: Christopher Gilbert—*Across the Mutual Landscape*

1984: Eric Pankey—*For the New Year*

1985: Christianne Balk—*Bindweed*

1986: Chris Llewellyn—*Fragments from the Fire*

1987: Judith Baumel—*The Weight of Numbers*

1988: April Bernard—*Blackbird Bye Bye*

1989: Martha Hollander—*The Game of Statues*

1990: Elaine Terranova—*The Cult of the Right Hand*

1991: Greg Glazner—*From the Iron Chair*

1992: Stephen Yenser—*The Fire in All Things*

1993: Alison Hawthorne Deming—*Science and Other Poems*

1994: Jan Richman—*Because the Brain Can Be Talked into Anything*

1995: Nicole Cooley—*Resurrection*

1996: Joshua Clover—*Madonna anno domini*

1997: Barbara Ras—*Bite Every Sorrow*

1998: Jan Heller Levi—*Once I Gazed at You in Wonder*

1999: Judy Jordan—*Carolina Ghost Woods*

2000: Ben Doyle—*Radio, Radio*

2001: John Canaday—*The Invisible World*

2002: Sue Kwock Kim—*Notes from the Divided Country*

2003: Tony Tost—*Invisible Bride*

2004: Geri Doran—*Resin*

2005: Mary Rose O'Reilley—*Half Wild*

2006: Anne Pierson Wiese—*Floating City*

2007: Sally Van Doren—*Sex at Noon Taxes*

2008: Jonathan Thirkield—*The Walker's Corridor*

2009: J. Michael Martinez—*Heredities*

2010: Carl Adamshick—*Curses and Wishes*

YALE SERIES OF YOUNGER POETS

This annual event of Yale University Press aims to publish the first collection of a promising American poet. Founded in 1919, it is the oldest annual literary award in the United States. Judges have included Stephen Vincent Benét (1933-1942), Archibald MacLeish (1944-1946), W. H. Auden (1947-1959), Stanley Kunitz (1969-1977), W. S. Merwin (1998-2003), Louise Glück (2003-2010), and Carl Phillips (2011-   ). Years reflect publication dates.

1919: John Chipman—*Farrar Forgotten Shrines*

1919: Howard Buck—*The Tempering*

1920: Darl MacLeod Boyle—*Where Lilith Dances*

1920: Thomas Caldecot Chubb—*The White God, and Other Poems*

1920: David Osborne Hamilton—*Four Gardens*

1920: Alfred Raymond Bellinger—*Spires and Poplars*

1921: Hervey Allen—*Wampum and Old Gold*

1921: Viola C. White—*Horizons*

1921: Oscar Williams—*Golden Darkness*

1921: Theodore H. Banks, Jr.—*Wild Geese*

1922: Bernard Raymund—*Hidden Waters*

1922: Medora C. Addison—*Dreams and a Sword*

1922: Paul Tanaquil—*Attitudes*

1922: Harold Vinal—*White April*

1923: Marion M. Boyd—*Silver Wands*

1923: Amos Niven Wilder—*Battle-Retrospect*

1923: Beatrice E. Harmon—*Mosaics*

1923: Dean B. Lyman, Jr.—*The Last Lutanist*

1924: Elizabeth Jessup—*Blake Up and Down*

1925: Dorothy E. Reid—*Coach into Pumpkin*

1926: Eleanor Slater—*Quest*

1926: Thomas Hornsby Ferril—*High Passage*

1927: Lindley Williams Hubbell—*Dark Pavilion*

1928: Ted Olson—*A Stranger and Afraid*

1928: Francis Claiborne Mason—*This Unchanging Mask*

1928: Mildred Bowers—*Twist o' Smoke*

1929: Frances M. Frost—*Hemlock Wall*

1929: Henri Faust—*Half-Light and Overture*

1930: Louise Owen—*Virtuosa*

1931: Dorothy Belle Flanagan—*Dark Certainty*

1932: Paul Engle—*Worn Earth*

1933: Shirley Barker—*The Dark Hills Under*

1934: James Agee—*Permit Me Voyage*

1935: Muriel Rukeyser—*Theory of Flight*

1936: Edward Weismiller—*The Deer Come Down*

1937: Margaret Haley—*The Gardener Mind*

1938: Joy Davidman—*Letter to a Comrade*

1939: Reuel Denney—*The Connecticut River, and Other Poems*

1940: Norman Rosten—*Return Again, Traveler*

1941: Jeremy Ingalls—*The Metaphysical Sword*

1942: Margaret Walker—*For My People*

1944: William Meredith—*Love Letters from an Impossible Land*

1945: Charles E. Butler—*Cut Is the Branch*

1946: Eve Merriam—*Family Circle*

1947: Joan Murray—*Poems*

1948: Robert Horan—*A Beginning*

1949: Rosalie Moore—*The Grasshopper's Man, and Other Poems*

1951: Adrienne Rich—*A Change of World*

1952: W. S. Merwin—*A Mask for Janus*

1953: Edgar Bogardus—*Various Jangling Keys*

1954: Daniel Hoffman—*An Armada of Thirty Whales*

1956: John Ashbery—*Some Trees*

1957: James Wright—*The Green Wall*

1958: John Hollander—*A Crackling of Thorns*

1959: William Dickey—*Of the Festivity*

1960: George Starbuck—*Bone Thoughts*

1961: Alan Dugan—*Poems*

1962: Jack Gilbert—*Views of Jeopardy*

1963: Sandra Hochman—*Manhattan Pastures*

1964: Peter Davison—*The Breaking of the Day*

1965: Jean Valentine—*Dream Barker*

1967: James Tate—*The Lost Pilot*

1968: Helen Chasin—*Coming Close, and Other Poems*

1969: Judith Johnson—*Sherwin Uranium Poems*

1970: Hugh Seidman—*Collecting Evidence*

1971: Peter Klappert—*Lugging Vegetables to Nantucket*

1972: Michael Casey—*Obscenities*

1973: Robert Hass—*Field Guide*

1974: Michael Ryan—*Threats Instead of Trees*

1975: Maura Stanton—*Snow on Snow*

1976: Carolyn Forché—*Gathering the Tribes*

1977: Olga Broumas—*Beginning with O*

1978: Bin Ramke—*The Difference Between Night and Day*

1979: Leslie Ullman—*Natural Histories*

1980: William Virgil Davis—*One Way to Reconstruct the Scene*

1981: John Bensko—*Green Soldiers*

1982: David Wojahn—*Icehouse Lights*

1983: Cathy Song—*Picture Bride*

1984: Richard Kenney—*The Evolution of the Flightless Bird*

1985: Pamela Alexander—*Navigable Waterways*

1986: George Bradley—*Terms to Be Met*

1987: Julie Agoos—*Above the Land*

1988: Brigit Pegeen Kelly—*To the Place of Trumpets*

1989: Thomas Bolt—*Out of the Woods*

1990: Daniel Hall—*Hermit with Landscape*

1991: Christiane Jacox Kyle—*Bears Dancing in the Northern Air*

1992: Nicholas Samaras—*Hands of the Saddlemaker*

1993: Jody Gladding—*Stone Crop*

1994: Valerie Wohlfeld—*Thinking the World Visible*

1995: Tony Crunk—*Living in the Resurrection*

1996: Ellen Hinsey—*Cities of Memory*

1997: Talvikki Ansel—*My Shining Archipelago*

1999: Craig Arnold—*Shells*

2000: Davis McCombs—*Ultima Thule*

2001: Maurice Manning—*Laurence Booth's Book of Visions*

2002: Sean Singer—*Discography*

2003: Loren Goodman—*Famous Americans*

2004: Peter Streckfus—*The Cuckoo*

2005: Richard Siken—*Crush*

2006: Jay Hopler—*Green Squall*

2007: Jessica Fisher—*Frail-Craft*

2008: Fady Joudah—*The Earth in the Attic*

2009: Arda Collins—*It Is Daylight*

2010: Ken Chen—*Juvenilia*

2011: Katherine Larson—*Radial Symmetry*

CHRONOLOGICAL LIST OF POETS

This chronology of the poets covered in these volumes serves as a time line for students interested in the development of American poetry from colonial days to modern times. The arrangement is chronological on the basis of birth years, and the proximity of writers provides students with some insights into potential influences and contemporaneous developments.

BORN UP TO 1700
Bradstreet, Anne (1612?)
Taylor, Edward (c. 1645)

BORN 1701-1800
Freneau, Philip (January 2, 1752)
Wheatley, Phillis (1753?)
Bryant, William Cullen (November 3, 1794)
Horton, George Moses (c. 1797)

BORN 1801-1850
Emerson, Ralph Waldo (May 25, 1803)
Longfellow, Henry Wadsworth (February 27, 1807)
Whittier, John Greenleaf (December 17, 1807)
Poe, Edgar Allan (January 19, 1809)
Holmes, Oliver Wendell (August 29, 1809)
Very, Jones (August 28, 1813)
Thoreau, Henry David (July 12, 1817)
Lowell, James Russell (February 22, 1819)
Whitman, Walt (May 31, 1819)
Melville, Herman (August 1, 1819)
Tuckerman, Frederick Goddard (February 4, 1821)
Dickinson, Emily (December 10, 1830)
Lanier, Sidney (February 3, 1842)
Riley, James Whitcomb (October 7, 1849)

BORN 1851-1880
Markham, Edwin (April 23, 1852)
Reese, Lizette Woodworth (January 9, 1856)
Masters, Edgar Lee (August 23, 1868)
Robinson, Edwin Arlington (December 22, 1869)
Johnson, James Weldon (June 17, 1871)
Crane, Stephen (November 1, 1871)
Dunbar, Paul Laurence (June 27, 1872)
Stein, Gertrude (February 3, 1874)
Lowell, Amy (February 9, 1874)

Frost, Robert (March 26, 1874)
Sandburg, Carl (January 6, 1878)
Stevens, Wallace (October 2, 1879)
Lindsay, Vachel (November 10, 1879)

BORN 1881-1890
Neihardt, John G. (January 8, 1881)
Bynner, Witter (August 10, 1881)
Guest, Edgar A. (August 20, 1881)
Loy, Mina (December 27, 1882)
Gibran, Kahlil (January 6, 1883)
Williams, William Carlos (September 17, 1883)
Teasdale, Sara (August 8, 1884)
Wylie, Elinor (September 17, 1885)
Untermeyer, Louis (October 1, 1885)
Pound, Ezra (October 30, 1885)
Benét, William Rose (February 2, 1886)
Wheelock, John Hall (September 9, 1886)
H. D. (Hilda Doolittle) (September 10, 1886)
Jeffers, Robinson (January 10, 1887)
Moore, Marianne (November 15, 1887)
Ransom, John Crowe (April 30, 1888)
Seeger, Alan (June 22, 1888)
Aiken, Conrad (August 5, 1889)
McKay, Claude (September 15, 1889)

BORN 1891-1900
Millay, Edna St. Vincent (February 22, 1892)
MacLeish, Archibald (May 7, 1892)
Bishop, John Peale (May 21, 1892)
Parker, Dorothy (August 22, 1893)
Van Doren, Mark (June 13, 1894)
Reznikoff, Charles (August 31, 1894)
Cummings, E. E. (October 14, 1894)
Toomer, Jean (December 26, 1894)
Hillyer, Robert (June 3, 1895)

Bogan, Louise (August 11, 1897)
Wheelwright, John (September 9, 1897)
Tolson, Melvin B. (February 6, 1898)
Gregory, Horace (April 10, 1898)
Benét, Stephen Vincent (July 22, 1898)
Cowley, Malcolm (August 24, 1898)
Crane, Hart (July 21, 1899)
Lewis, Janet (August 17, 1899)
Tate, Allen (November 19, 1899)
Adams, Léonie (December 9, 1899)
Winters, Yvor (October 17, 1900)

BORN 1901-1910
Riding, Laura (January 16, 1901)
Brown, Sterling A. (May 1, 1901)
Ausländer, Rose (May 11, 1901)
Hughes, Langston (February 1, 1902)
Fearing, Kenneth (July 28, 1902)
Nash, Ogden (August 19, 1902)
Bontemps, Arna (October 13, 1902)
Niedecker, Lorine (May 12, 1903)
Cullen, Countée (May 30, 1903)
Rakosi, Carl (November 6, 1903)
Zukofsky, Louis (January 23, 1904)
Eberhart, Richard (April 5, 1904)
McGinley, Phyllis (March 21, 1905)
Warren, Robert Penn (April 24, 1905)
Kunitz, Stanley (July 29, 1905)
Rexroth, Kenneth (December 22, 1905)
Still, James (July 16, 1906)
Kirstein, Lincoln (May 4, 1907)
Oppen, George (April 24, 1908)
Roethke, Theodore (May 25, 1908)
Jacobsen, Josephine (August 19, 1908)
Rolfe, Edwin (September 7, 1909)
Barnard, Mary (December 6, 1909)
Scott, Winfield Townley (April 30, 1910)
Olson, Charles (December 27, 1910)

BORN 1911-1920
Bishop, Elizabeth (February 8, 1911)
Belitt, Ben (May 2, 1911)
Miles, Josephine (June 11, 1911)
Porter, Anne (November 6, 1911)
Cunningham, J. V. (August 23, 1911)

Patchen, Kenneth (December 13, 1911)
Sarton, May (May 3, 1912)
Everson, William (September 10, 1912)
Hayden, Robert (August 4, 1913)
Shapiro, Karl (November 10, 1913)
Nims, John Frederick (November 20, 1913)
Schwartz, Delmore (December 8, 1913)
Rukeyser, Muriel (December 15, 1913)
Randall, Dudley (January 14, 1914)
Stafford, William (January 17, 1914)
Ignatow, David (February 7, 1914)
Kees, Weldon (February 24, 1914)
Howes, Barbara (May 1, 1914)
Jarrell, Randall (May 6, 1914)
Villa, José García (August 5, 1914)
Berryman, John (October 25, 1914)
Dodson, Owen (November 28, 1914)
Merton, Thomas (January 31, 1915)
Walker, Margaret (July 7, 1915)
Gardner, Isabella (September 7, 1915)
Ciardi, John (June 24, 1916)
Viereck, Peter (August 5, 1916)
McGrath, Thomas (November 20, 1916)
Lowell, Robert (March 1, 1917)
Brooks, Gwendolyn (June 7, 1917)
Bronk, William (February 17, 1918)
Coxe, Louis (April 15, 1918)
Smith, William Jay (April 22, 1918)
Duncan, Robert (January 7, 1919)
Meredith, William (January 9, 1919)
Ferlinghetti, Lawrence (March 24, 1919)
Swenson, May (May 28, 1919)
Whittemore, Reed (September 11, 1919)
Nemerov, Howard (March 1, 1920)
Clampitt, Amy (June 15, 1920)
Bukowski, Charles (August 16, 1920)
Guest, Barbara (September 6, 1920)

BORN 1921-1925
Ponsot, Marie (1921)
Wilbur, Richard (March 1, 1921)
Berrigan, Daniel (May 9, 1921)
Van Duyn, Mona (May 9, 1921)
Emanuel, James A. (June 15, 1921)
Carruth, Hayden (August 3, 1921)

Moss, Howard (January 22, 1922)
Paley, Grace (December 11, 1922)
Hecht, Anthony (January 16, 1923)
Logan, John (January 23, 1923)
Dickey, James (February 2, 1923)
Dugan, Alan (February 12, 1923)
Simpson, Louis (March 27, 1923)
Hoffman, Daniel (April 3, 1923)
Yamada, Mitsuye (July 5, 1923)
Evans, Mari (July 16, 1923)
Whalen, Philip (October 20, 1923)
Levertov, Denise (October 24, 1923)
Schuyler, James (November 9, 1923)
Hugo, Richard (December 21, 1923)
Mueller, Lisel (February 8, 1924)
Bowers, Edgar (March 2, 1924)
Stryk, Lucien (April 7, 1924)
Field, Edward (June 7, 1924)
Corman, Cid (June 29, 1924)
Haines, John Meade (June 29, 1924)
Miller, Vassar (July 19, 1924)
Spicer, Jack (January 30, 1925)
Gilbert, Jack (February 17, 1925)
Stern, Gerald (February 22, 1925)
Koch, Kenneth (February 27, 1925)
Kaufman, Bob (April 18, 1925)
Kumin, Maxine (June 6, 1925)
Justice, Donald (August 12, 1925)
Menashe, Samuel (September 16, 1925)
Booth, Philip (October 8, 1925)
Kizer, Carolyn (December 10, 1925)

BORN 1926-1930
Snodgrass, W. D. (January 5, 1926)
Ammons, A. R. (February 18, 1926)
Merrill, James (March 3, 1926)
Creeley, Robert (May 21, 1926)
Ginsberg, Allen (June 3, 1926)
Wagoner, David (June 5, 1926)
O'Hara, Frank (June 27, 1926)
Blackburn, Paul (November 24, 1926)
Bly, Robert (December 23, 1926)
Kinnell, Galway (February 1, 1927)
Ashbery, John (July 28, 1927)
Merwin, W. S. (September 30, 1927)

Coulette, Henri (November 11, 1927)
Wright, James (December 13, 1927)
Sissman, L. E. (January 1, 1928)
Levine, Philip (January 10, 1928)
Macdonald, Cynthia (February 2, 1928)
Angelou, Maya (April 4, 1928)
Davison, Peter (June 27, 1928)
Hall, Donald (September 20, 1928)
Feldman, Irving (September 22, 1928)
Sexton, Anne (November 9, 1928)
Cassity, Turner (January 12, 1929)
Dorn, Edward (April 2, 1929)
Sorrentino, Gilbert (April 27, 1929)
Rich, Adrienne (May 16, 1929)
Dana, Robert (June 2, 1929)
Garrett, George (June 11, 1929)
Kennedy, X. J. (August 21, 1929)
Howard, Richard (October 13, 1929)
Hollander, John (October 28, 1929)
Oppenheimer, Joel (February 18, 1930)
Corso, Gregory (March 26, 1930)
Williams, Miller (April 8, 1930)
Snyder, Gary (May 8, 1930)
Brathwaite, Edward Kamau (May 11, 1930)
Silverstein, Shel (September 25, 1930 or 1932)

BORN 1931-1935
Knight, Etheridge (April 19, 1931)
Updike, John (March 18, 1932)
Pastan, Linda (May 27, 1932)
McClure, Michael (October 20, 1932)
Plath, Sylvia (October 27, 1932)
Meinke, Peter (December 29, 1932)
Price, Reynolds (February 1, 1933)
Lorde, Audre (February 18, 1934)
Flint, Roland (February 27, 1934)
Momaday, N. Scott (February 27, 1934)
Strand, Mark (April 11, 1934)
Hollo, Anselm (April 12, 1934)
Valentine, Jean (April 27, 1934)
McDonald, Walt (July 18, 1934)
Berry, Wendell (August 5, 1934)
Di Prima, Diane (August 6, 1934)
Sanchez, Sonia (September 9, 1934)
Zimmer, Paul (September 18, 1934)

Baraka, Amiri (October 7, 1934)
Berrigan, Ted (November 15, 1934)
Brautigan, Richard (January 30, 1935)
Slavitt, David (March 23, 1935)
Wright, Jay (May 25, 1935)
Applewhite, James (August 8, 1935)
Wright, Charles (August 25, 1935)
Oliver, Mary (September 10, 1935)
Kelly, Robert (September 24, 1935)
Johnson, Ronald (November 25, 1935)
Rivera, Tomás (December 22, 1935)

BORN 1936-1940

Piercy, Marge (March 31, 1936)
Chappell, Fred (May 28, 1936)
Clifton, Lucille (June 27, 1936)
Jordan, June (July 9, 1936)
Williams, C. K. (November 4, 1936)
Howe, Susan (June 10, 1937)
Bell, Marvin (August 3, 1937)
Wakoski, Diane (August 3, 1937)
Ostriker, Alicia Suskin (November 11, 1937)
Harrison, Jim (December 11, 1937)
Reed, Ishmael (February 22, 1938)
Harper, Michael S. (March 18, 1938)
Simic, Charles (May 9, 1938)
Carver, Raymond (May 25, 1938)
Oates, Joyce Carol (June 16, 1938)
Galvin, Brendan (October 20, 1938)
Kooser, Ted (April 25, 1939)
Dacey, Philip (May 9, 1939)
Young, Al (May 31, 1939)
Plumly, Stanley (May 23, 1939)
Bidart, Frank (May 27, 1939)
Dunn, Stephen (June 24, 1939)
McMichael, James (July 19, 1939)
Dennis, Carl (September 17, 1939)
Allen, Paula Gunn (October 24, 1939)
Mitsui, James Masao (February 4, 1940)
Rogers, Pattiann (March 23, 1940)
Pinsky, Robert (October 20, 1940)
Heyen, William (November 1, 1940)
Welch, James (November 18, 1940)
Rodgers, Carolyn M. (December 14, 1940)

BORN 1941-1945

Hass, Robert (March 1, 1941)
Glancy, Diane (March 18, 1941)
Collins, Billy (March 22, 1941)
Derricotte, Toi (April 12, 1941)
Hejinian, Lyn (May 17, 1941)
Ortiz, Simon (May 27, 1941)
Grennan, Eamon (November 13, 1941)
Mora, Pat (January 19, 1942)
Madhubuti, Haki R. (February 23, 1942)
Taylor, Henry (June 21, 1942)
Gregg, Linda (September 9, 1942)
Fairchild, B. H. (October 17, 1942)
Matthews, William (November 11, 1942)
Olds, Sharon (November 19, 1942)
Hacker, Marilyn (November 27, 1942)
Smith, Dave (December 19, 1942)
Glück, Louise (April 22, 1943)
Voigt, Ellen Bryant (May 9, 1943)
Glenn, Mel (May 10, 1943)
Giovanni, Nikki (June 7, 1943)
Gallagher, Tess (July 21, 1943)
McPherson, Sandra (August 2, 1943)
Corn, Alfred (August 14, 1943)
Balaban, John (December 2, 1943)
Tate, James (December 8, 1943)
Shomer, Enid (February 2, 1944)
Walker, Alice (February 9, 1944)
Gibson, Margaret (February 17, 1944)
Lifshin, Lyn (July 12, 1944)
Williams, Sherley Anne (August 25, 1944)
Kirby, David (November 29, 1944)
Wallace, Ronald (February 18, 1945)
Waldman, Anne (April 2, 1945)
Dubie, Norman (April 10, 1945)
Notley, Alice (November 8, 1945)
Muske, Carol (December 17, 1945)

BORN 1946-1950

Hampl, Patricia (March 12, 1946)
Levis, Larry (September 30, 1946)
Bang, Mary Jo (October 22, 1946)
Lum, Wing Tek (November 11, 1946)
Codrescu, Andrei (December 20, 1946)
Orr, Gregory (February 3, 1947)

Shore, Jane (March 10, 1947)
Komunyakaa, Yusef (April 29, 1947)
Kenyon, Jane (May 23, 1947)
Peacock, Molly (June 30, 1947)
Hogan, Linda (July 16, 1947)
Scalapino, Leslie (July 25, 1947)
Norris, Kathleen (July 27, 1947)
Ai (October 21, 1947)
Mackey, Nathaniel (October 25, 1947)
Steele, Timothy (January 22, 1948)
Goldbarth, Albert (January 31, 1948)
Wormser, Baron (February 4, 1948)
Silko, Leslie Marmon (March 5, 1948)
McHugh, Heather (August 20, 1948)
Santos, Sherod (September 9, 1948)
Anderson, Maggie (September 23, 1948)
Ehrhart, W. D. (September 30, 1948)
Ackerman, Diane (October 7, 1948)
Wright, C. D. (January 6, 1949)
Weigl, Bruce (January 27, 1949)
Ali, Agha Shahid (February 4, 1949)
Cruz, Victor Hernández (February 6, 1949)
St. John, David (July 24, 1949)
Bottoms, David (September 11, 1949)
Hirsch, Edward (January 20, 1950)
Alvarez, Julia (March 27, 1950)
Bernstein, Charles (April 4, 1950)
Forché, Carolyn (April 28, 1950)
Gregerson, Linda (August 5, 1950)
Twichell, Chase (August 20, 1950)
Gioia, Dana (December 24, 1950)

BORN 1951-1960
Kelly, Brigit Pegeen (April 21, 1951)
Hudgins, Andrew (April 22, 1951)
Graham, Jorie (May 9, 1951)
Harjo, Joy (May 9, 1951)
Hongo, Garrett Kaoru (May 30, 1951)
Baca, Jimmy Santiago (January 2, 1952)
Fulton, Alice (January 25, 1952)
Shapiro, Alan (February 18, 1952)
Ortiz Cofer, Judith (February 24, 1952)
Nye, Naomi Shihab (March 12, 1952)

Soto, Gary (April 12, 1952)
Jarman, Mark (June 5, 1952)
Mura, David (June 17, 1952)
Dove, Rita (August 28, 1952)
Ríos, Alberto (September 18, 1952)
Hirshfield, Jane (February 24, 1953)
Leithauser, Brad (February 27, 1953)
Wright, Franz (March 18, 1953)
Collier, Michael (May 25, 1953)
Mullen, Harryette (July 1, 1953)
Doty, Mark (August 10, 1953)
Wojahn, David (August 22, 1953)
Schnackenberg, Gjertrud (August 27, 1953)
Eady, Cornelius (January 7, 1954)
Moss, Thylias (February 27, 1954)
Erdrich, Louise (June 7, 1954)
Cervantes, Lorna Dee (August 6, 1954)
Cisneros, Sandra (December 20, 1954)
Baker, David (December 27, 1954)
Hunt, Erica (1955)
Swensen, Cole (1955)
Chin, Marilyn (January 14, 1955)
Karr, Mary (January 16, 1955)
Hahn, Kimiko (July 5, 1955)
Young, Dean (July 18, 1955)
Song, Cathy (August 20, 1955)
Cole, Henri (1956)
Gerstler, Amy (October 24, 1956)
Emerson, Claudia (January 13, 1957)
Espada, Martín (August 7, 1957)
Lee, Li-Young (August 19, 1957)
Lindsay, Sarah (December 31, 1958)
Phillips, Carl (July 23, 1959)

BORN 1961 AND LATER
Kasischke, Laura (1961)
Beatty, Paul (1962)
Alexander, Elizabeth (May 30, 1962)
Kasdorf, Julia (December 6, 1962)
Rankine, Claudia (1963)
Trethewey, Natasha (April 26, 1966)
Alexie, Sherman (October 7, 1966)
Fennelly, Beth Ann (May 22, 1971)

INDEXES

CATEGORIZED INDEX OF POETS

The Categorized Index of Poets covers three primary subject areas: Culture/Group Identities, Historical Periods/Literary Movements, and Poetic Forms and Themes.

Cultural/Group Identities

Historical Periods/Literary Movements

Poetic Forms and Themes

AESTHETIC POETS

Emerson, Ralph Waldo, 544

Poe, Edgar Allan, 1561

AFRICAN AMERICAN CULTURE. *See also* BLACK ARTS MOVEMENT; HARLEM RENAISSANCE; JAZZ POETS

Ai, 8

Alexander, Elizabeth, 17

Angelou, Maya, 46

Baraka, Amiri, 89

Beatty, Paul, 107

Bontemps, Arna, 205

Brathwaite, Edward Kamau, 228

Brooks, Gwendolyn, 247

Brown, Sterling A., 254

Clifton, Lucille, 326

Cruz, Victor Hernández, 400

Cullen, Countée, 404

Derricotte, Toi, 444

Dodson, Owen, 471

Dove, Rita, 486

Dunbar, Paul Laurence, 502

Eady, Cornelius, 521

Emanuel, James A., 538

Evans, Mari, 563

Giovanni, Nikki, 692

Harper, Michael S., 794

Hayden, Robert, 820

Horton, George Moses, 905

Hughes, Langston, 927

Hunt, Erica, 938

Johnson, James Weldon, 972

Jordan, June, 981

Kaufman, Bob, 1002

Knight, Etheridge, 1053

Komunyakaa, Yusef, 1064

Lorde, Audre, 1166

McKay, Claude, 1234

Mackey, Nathaniel, 1241

Madhubuti, Haki R., 1265

Moss, Thylias, 1380

Mullen, Harryette, 1387

Phillips, Carl, 1529

Randall, Dudley, 1595

Rankine, Claudia, 1602

Reed, Ishmael, 1612

Rodgers, Carolyn M., 1668

Sanchez, Sonia, 1698

Tolson, Melvin B., 1984

Toomer, Jean, 1988

Trethewey, Natasha, 1995

Walker, Alice, 2080

Walker, Margaret, 2086

Wheatley, Phillis, 2114

Williams, Sherley Anne, 2172

Wright, Jay, 2231

Young, Al, 2248

AGRARIAN POETS. *See* SOUTHERN AGRARIANS

AMERICAN COLONIAL POETS

Bradstreet, Anne, 223

Freneau, Philip, 618

Taylor, Edward, 1959

Wheatley, Phillis, 2114

AMERICAN EARLY NATIONAL POETS

Bryant, William Cullen, 259

Dickinson, Emily, 455

Emerson, Ralph Waldo, 544

Freneau, Philip, 618

Holmes, Oliver Wendell, 893

Horton, George Moses, 905

Lanier, Sidney, 1095

Longfellow, Henry Wadsworth, 1157

Lowell, James Russell, 1180

Melville, Herman, 1294

Poe, Edgar Allan, 1561

Riley, James Whitcomb, 1645

Thoreau, Henry David, 1977

Tuckerman, Frederick Goddard, 1998

Very, Jones, 2039

Whitman, Walt, 2130

Whittier, John Greenleaf, 2144

NATIVE AMERICAN CULTURE

NATIVE AMERICAN RENAISSANCE

NATURALISM, AMERICAN

NATURE POETRY. *See also* ECOPOETRY

PROJECTIVIST SCHOOL. *See* **BLACK MOUNTAIN POETS**

PROSE POETRY

YOUNG ADULT POETRY. *See* **CHILDREN'S/YOUNG ADULT POETRY**

Critical Survey of Poetry Series: Master List of Contents

The Critical Survey of Poetry, Fourth Edition, *profiles more than eight hundred poets in four subsets:* American Poets*; British, Irish, and Commonwealth Poets; European Poets; and* World Poets. *Although some individuals could have been included in more than one subset, each poet appears in only one subset. A fifth subset,* Topical Essays, *includes more than seventy overviews covering geographical areas, historical periods, movements, and critical approaches.*

AMERICAN POETS

BRITISH, IRISH, AND COMMONWEALTH POETS

EUROPEAN POETS

WORLD POETS

TOPICAL ESSAYS

CUMULATIVE INDEXES

SUBJECT INDEX

All personages whose names appear in **boldface type** in this index are the subject of articles in *Critical Survey of Poetry, Fourth Edition.*